Study Smarter with LearningCurve!

What is LearningCurve?

LearningCurve is a cutting-edge study tool designed to increase your understanding and memory of the core concepts in every chapter. Based on insights from the latest learning and memory research, the LearningCurve system pairs multiple-choice and fill-in-the-blank questions with instantaneous feedback and a rich array of study tools including videos, animations, and lab simulations.

The LearningCurve system is adaptive, so the quiz you take is customized to your level of understanding. The more questions you answer correctly, the more challenging questions become. Best of all, the e-book of *Psychology,* Canadian Fifth Edition, is fully integrated, so you can easily review the text as you study and answer questions. LearningCurve is a smart and fun way to study each chapter.

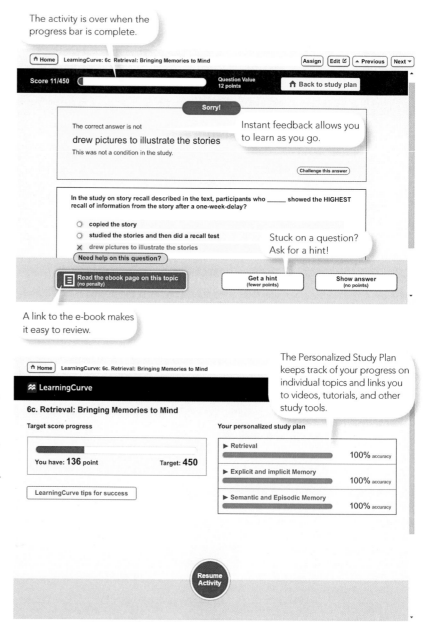

LaunchPad for *Psychology*, Canadian Fifth Edition

Available May 2020 at launchpadworks.com

Each chapter in LaunchPad for *Psychology*, Canadian Fifth Edition, features a collection of activities carefully chosen to help master the major concepts. The site serves students as a comprehensive online study guide, available any time, with opportunities for self-quizzing with instant feedback, exam preparation, and further explorations of topics from the textbook. For instructors, all units and activities can be instantly assigned and students' results and analytics are collected in the Gradebook.

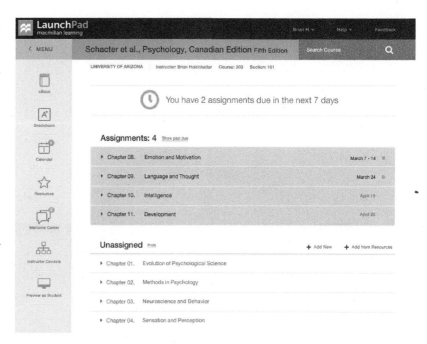

For Students

- Full e-book of *Psychology*, Canadian Fifth Edition
- LearningCurve Quizzing
- Student Video Activities
- Data Visualization Activities
- Concept Practice Activities
- PsychSim 6.0 by Thomas Ludwig and John Krantz

For Instructors

- Gradebook
- Presentation Slides
- iClicker Questions
- Chapter Figures and Photos
- Correlation of *Psychology*, Canadian Fifth Edition, to APA Learning Goals
- Correlation of *Psychology*, Canadian Fifth Edition, to MCAT Topics

PSYCHOLOGY

CANADIAN FIFTH EDITION

DANIEL L. SCHACTER

Harvard University

DANIEL T. GILBERT

Harvard University

MATTHEW K. NOCK

Harvard University

INGRID JOHNSRUDE

University of Western Ontario

DANIEL M. WEGNER

Harvard University

worth publishers
Macmillan Learning

New York

Senior Vice President, Content Strategy: Charles Linsmeier
Program Director: Shani Fisher
Executive Program Manager: Daniel DeBonis
Development Editors: Valerie Raymond, Katie Pachnos
Editorial Assistant: Nicholas Rizzuti
Executive Marketing Manager: Katherine Nurre
Marketing Assistant: Chelsea Simens
Director of Media Editorial and Assessment: Noel Hohnstine
Media Editor: Stefani Wallace
Lead Media Project Manager: Joseph Tomasso
Director, Content Management Enhancement: Tracey Kuehn
Senior Managing Editor: Lisa Kinne
Senior Content Project Manager: Vivien Weiss
Project Managers: Jana Lewis, Vanavan Jayaraman, Lumina Datamatics, Inc.
Senior Workflow Project Supervisor: Susan Wein
Design Services Manager: Natasha Wolfe
Design Manager and Cover Designer: John Callahan
Interior Designer: Patrice Sheridan
Executive Permissions Editor: Robin Fadool
Photo Editor: Jennifer Atkins
Art Manager: Matthew McAdams
Illustrations: Eli Ensor, Matthew McAdams
Composition: Lumina Datamatics, Inc.
Printing and Binding: King Printing Co., Inc.
Cover Photograph: RJ Muna

Library of Congress Control Number: 2019953277

ISBN-13: 978-1-319-19079-8
ISBN-10: 1-319-19079-0

Printed in the United States of America

1 2 3 4 5 6   24 23 22 21 20

Worth Publishers
One New York Plaza
Suite 4600
New York, NY 10004-1562
www.macmillanlearning.com

Dedication

*We dedicate this edition to **Dan Wegner**—co-author, colleague, and friend. His brilliant ideas and beautiful words remain in our pages, and in our hearts. Ad perpetuam rei memoriam.*

ABOUT THE AUTHORS

Daniel Schacter is William R. Kenan, Jr. Professor of Psychology at Harvard University. Dan received his BA degree from the University of North Carolina at Chapel Hill. He subsequently developed a keen interest in amnesic disorders associated with various kinds of brain damage. He continued his research and education at the University of Toronto, where he received his PhD in 1981. He taught on the faculty at Toronto for the next six years before joining the psychology department at the University of Arizona in 1987. In 1991, he joined the faculty at Harvard University. His research explores the relationship between conscious and unconscious forms of memory, the nature of distortions and errors in remembering, and the ways in which we use memory to imagine future events. Many of his studies are summarized in his 1996 book, *Searching for Memory: The Brain, the Mind, and the Past,* and his 2001 book, *The Seven Sins of Memory: How the Mind Forgets and Remembers,* both winners of the American Psychological Association's William James Book Award. He has also received awards for his teaching and research, including the Harvard-Radcliffe Phi Beta Kappa Teaching Prize, the Distinguished Scientific Contributions Award from the American Psychological Association, and the William James Fellow Award from the Association for Psychological Science for "a lifetime of significant intellectual contributions to the basic science of psychology." In 2013, he was elected to the National Academy of Sciences.

Daniel Gilbert is the Edgar Pierce Professor of Psychology at Harvard University. Dan received his BA from the University of Colorado at Denver in 1981 and his PhD from Princeton University in 1985. He taught at the University of Texas at Austin, and in 1996 joined the faculty of Harvard University. He has received the Distinguished Scientific Award for an Early Career Contribution to Psychology from the American Psychological Association; the Diener Award for "outstanding contributions to social psychology" from the Foundation for Personality and Social Psychology; the Campbell Award for "distinguished scholarly achievement and sustained excellence in research in social psychology" from the Society for Personality and Social Psychology; and the William James Fellow Award for "a lifetime of significant intellectual contributions to the basic science of psychology" from the Association for Psychological Science. He teaches Introductory Psychology and has won teaching awards that include the Phi Beta Kappa Teaching Prize and the Harvard College Professorship. His research focuses on how and how well people think about their emotional reactions to future events. He is the author of the best seller *Stumbling on Happiness,* which won the Royal Society's General Prize for best popular science book of the year, and the cowriter and host of the PBS television series *This Emotional Life.*

Matthew Nock is the Edgar Pierce Professor of Psychology at Harvard University. Matt received his BA from Boston University in 1995 and his PhD from Yale University in 2003. He completed his clinical internship at Bellevue Hospital and the New York University Child Study Center, and then joined the faculty of Harvard University in 2003. While an undergraduate, he became interested in understanding why people do things to intentionally harm themselves, and he has been conducting research to answer that question ever since. His research is multidisciplinary and uses a wide range of methodological approaches (e.g., epidemiologic surveys, laboratory-based experiments, and clinic-based studies) to understand how these behaviours develop, how to predict them, and how to prevent their occurrence. He has received many teaching awards at Harvard, as well as four Early Career awards recognizing his research. In 2011 he was named a MacArthur Fellow.

Ingrid Johnsrude is Professor and Western Research Chair in Cognitive Neuroscience at the University of Western Ontario, and director of Western's Brain and Mind Institute. Ingrid received her BS from Queen's University (1989), and her PhD from McGill University (1997), where she was supervised by the pioneering neuropsychologist Brenda Milner. After earning her doctorate, she spent time in the United Kingdom as a postdoctoral fellow at University College London and then as an Investigator Scientist in Cambridge, before returning to Queen's in 2004, and then moving to Western in 2014. During her time in England, she contributed to a paper showing that taxi drivers in London with extensive navigation experience have larger hippocampi than the general population, revealing one of the ways that experience can alter the structure of the human brain. This finding, notable for both the content of the study and the pioneering methods used, is a common example in introductory psychology texts. Ingrid's principal area of investigation is the neural basis of understanding speech and language. Her investigations span multiple levels—from understanding the brain structures involved in hearing and speech comprehension to observing the ways listeners deal with challenges such as background noise.

Daniel Wegner was the John Lindsley Professor of Psychology in Memory of William James at Harvard University. He received his BS in 1970 and his PhD in 1974, both from Michigan State University. He began his teaching career at Trinity University in San Antonio, Texas, before joining the faculties at the University of Virginia in 1990 and then Harvard University in 2000. He received the Distinguished Scientific Contributions Award from the American Psychological Association, the William James Fellow Award for "a lifetime of significant intellectual contributions to the basic science of psychology" from the Association for Psychological Science, and the Distinguished Scientist Award from the Society of Experimental Social Psychology. His research focused on thought suppression and mental control, transactive memory in relationships and groups, and the experience of conscious will. His work on thought suppression and consciousness served as the basis of two popular books, *White Bears and Other Unwanted Thoughts* and the *Illusion of Conscious Will*, both of which were named *Choice* Outstanding Academic Books. He was a dedicated mentor, a popular teacher, and a cherished colleague and friend. Dan was diagnosed with ALS and died in 2013.

BRIEF CONTENTS

CONTENTS

STORIEDEYE/ALAMY

BRUCE ROLFF/ALAMY

© SPL/SCIENCE SOURCE

PURESTOCK/GETTY IMAGES

4 Sensation and Perception   123

WESTEND61/GETTY IMAGES

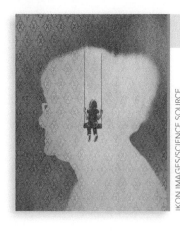

MARILYN NIEVES/GETTY IMAGES

ECHO/GETTY IMAGES

MURIEL DE SEZE/GETTY IMAGES

9 Language and Thought   351

CHRISTOPHER WILSON

JOHN LUND/GETTY IMAGES

PEOPLEIMAGES/E+/GETTY IMAGES

DAVID GILLIVER/BARCROFT MEDIA

FOTOSEARCH/AGE FOTOSTOCK

14 Stress and Health   547

TREVOR WILLIAMS/GETTY IMAGES

LÍVIA FERNANDES-BRAZIL/MOMENT SELECT/ GETTY IMAGES

A NOTE TO STUDENTS

Dear Student,

The world is full of mysteries—from stars to fossils, from quarks to cells. But for us, the greatest mystery has always been other people, and that's what drew each of us into our first psychology course in university. What we remember about those courses is that we were blown away by the ideas we encountered and by the lectures we heard, but what we don't remember are the textbooks. That's probably because they were little more than jargon-filled encyclopedias of names and dates that we eagerly sold to some other unsuspecting sucker the moment we finished our final exams.

After we became psychology professors, we started to wonder why textbooks had to be like that. We decided they didn't, so in 2008 we wrote the textbook that we wished we'd been given when we were students. The reaction to it was nothing short of astounding. We'd never written a textbook before, so we had no idea what to expect, but never in our wildest dreams did we imagine that we would end up winning *the Pulitzer Prize!*

Which was good, because we didn't. But what actually happened was even better: We started getting e-mails from students all over North America who told us (with seeming surprise) that they actually *liked* reading our textbook. They liked the content, of course, because psychology is an inherently fascinating subject, but they liked some other things too. First, they liked the fact that our textbook didn't *sound* like a textbook. It wasn't written in the stodgy dad-voice of that guy who seems to be the narrator in every high school biology film ever made ("Behold the sea otter, nature's furry little scavenger"). Rather, it was written in *our* voices—the same voices we use when we talk to our students, our friends, and our pets, which is why Chapter 12 was originally titled "Stop Chewing My Shoes." Students also liked the fact that we told the *story* of psychology—that we integrated topics rather than just listing them, that we illustrated ideas rather than just describing them, and that we made fun of ourselves and anyone else who didn't run away fast enough. That kind of feedback is what's kept us going for five editions.

Of course, a textbook has to do more than just tell an interesting and entertaining story. It also has to *help you learn*. That's why in addition to all the stuff that novels, cookbooks, and owner's manuals have—words and sentences, graphs and diagrams—textbooks also have features that are meant to help you understand and remember the material you're reading. Designing these features requires a keen understanding of how human beings learn, and, as luck would have it, that's one of the subjects on which psychologists happen to be experts. The features in our textbook all make use of basic principles of psychology. To introduce you to those features, we'll start by giving you six tips for reading our textbook, and then, after you've read those tips, we'll explain how our textbook's features will help you implement them.

Six Tips for Reading This Textbook

Reading just happens. You look at a printed page and your eyes instantly start to glide across it, turning black squiggles into words and sentences without any help from you. Unlike reading, understanding and remembering don't just happen, which is why you can read a sentence, look up, and 10 seconds later have no freaking idea what you just read. (If that's happening now, please start this section over.)

Research shows that the best way to turn *reading* into *understanding and remembering* is to not just let reading happen but, rather, to take an active role in reading. Here are five ways to do that.

- **Rehearse.** No, we don't mean dress up and recite Shakespeare. In psychology, rehearsal simply means repeating information to yourself, and if you do it right, it turns out to be a remarkably useful way to memorize facts. For example, suppose you wanted to remember the name of the person who built the first psychology laboratory (which you will probably want to do when you read Chapter 1). First you might say something like "Wilhelm Wundt built the first psychology laboratory" a few times to yourself, wait a few seconds, then say it a few times again, wait even longer, then say it again, then . . . well, you get the idea. By increasing the interval between rehearsals you will be making it a little bit harder to remember the fact each time—kind of like doing bench presses and adding increasing amounts of weight with each set of repetitions—and research shows that this is an effective way to commit information to memory.

- **Interpret.** Rehearsal is good for memorizing facts, but if you want to learn psychology, you're going to need to understand *ideas*. Research shows that one of the best ways to understand and remember ideas is to stop reading for a moment and *interpret* them—that is, to think about what they mean and how they relate to you. For example, suppose you wanted to learn the basic ideas behind behaviourism (which you will indeed want to do when you read Chapter 7). You will be tempted to read what we've written about behaviourism and move on, but you'd be better off pausing and asking yourself a question such as "How would a behaviourist explain my choice of major?" To answer this question, you will not only need to recall what you read about behaviourism, but you will also need to relate it to other things that you already know (e.g., that you struggled to decide whether you should major in psychology or in something your parents incorrectly told you was more important). It turns out that it is much easier to remember new information when you relate it to something with which you are already familiar.

- **Organize.** If someone asked you to memorize the words "Greet, Ask, Beg, Sign, Fold, Insert, Lick," in that order, you might find it difficult—unless you noticed that these are the steps involved in composing a letter that asks for money and then mailing it to your parents. Organizing information in a meaningful way is one of the best methods for learning and remembering it, which is why after reading each chapter, you should try telling yourself its story. This doesn't just mean rehearsing the facts or interpreting the various ideas, but rather, it means linking them together and asking how one leads to the other.

- **Test.** You may be tempted to use a yellow highlighter as you read, and then to study by re-reading the material you highlighted. This is a mistake (especially if you have an electronic copy of the textbook) because as you re-read the highlighted material it will start to seem more and more familiar to you, and you will mistakenly assume that because the material is familiar, you know it pretty well. But the fact is that you only "know it" when you're reading it! A much better way to learn is to *test yourself* on the material while you are *not* looking at the textbook. Better yet, study with someone else and test each other.

- **Space.** *When* should you do all this stuff? The wrong answer is "The night before the exam." Research shows that you are much more likely to remember what you learn if you read a bit of the textbook every day and do these exercises while you're reading. Cramming the night before an exam is not only a painful experience (as you might have guessed from the word *cramming*), it is also one of the very worst things you can do if you want to learn, remember what you've learned, and do well on an exam. Reading the textbook the night before is only slightly better than not reading it at all.

- **Sleep.** You already know that it's a good idea to get plenty of sleep the night before an exam. But as you will discover in Chapter 6, it is equally important to get plenty of sleep on the days that you do the study exercises we've just described. When you sleep, your brain rehearses information you encountered during the day, sifting through it, finding patterns in it, and storing it efficiently. Letting your brain "sleep on it" is nearly as important as having your brain "read it" in the first place.

Features That Help You Implement These Tips

So yes, those are six excellent pieces of advice. But how in the world are you supposed to remember them—or remember to use them? Don't worry. We've got your back. Our textbook contains a variety of features that we specifically designed to help you implement these and other research-based learning strategies. In fact, we even wrote one really boring chapter just to help you sleep! (Kidding.)

For example, you'll notice that every chapter is divided into a few major sections, and at the beginning of each major section are a set of **Learning Outcomes** that allow you to "be on the lookout" for key concepts as you are reading. This will help you organize the material in your mind—kind of like how knowing beforehand that Romeo and Juliet are star-crossed lovers can help you make sense of the play when you are watching it. Just as the Learning Outcomes tell you what to look for before you read, the **Build to the Outcomes** questions (which you'll find at the end of each major section) help you decide whether you found what you were looking for. These questions will help you determine whether your reading has produced the level of understanding you should desire—and that your instructor will require! If not, then you can re-read the section, or find the information you missed in the **Chapter Review** that appears at the end of each chapter.

We've also built features to help you interpret the material you're reading. For instance, at the end of each chapter, you will find a series of **Changing Minds** scenarios that describe everyday situations in which misconceptions about human behaviour arise, and that then ask you to use the chapter's material to correct them. The **Data Visualization Activities** that are available in LaunchPad invite you to engage with the material by answering questions the way psychologists do—namely, by looking at data! Each activity presents an interactive graph that displays real data from a published study, followed by questions that allow you to test your understanding of the study as well as your ability to reason about the data. The **LearningCurve** adaptive quizzing system will also allow you to test yourself—and it will design quizzes just for you.

A Box of Words

You may have noticed that when people tell stories ("When I was in Rome this summer, I saw the Trevi Fountain, the Sistine Chapel, and the Colosseum"), they occasionally pause to tell you some related thing that they found especially interesting ("Did you know that in the 16th century, the Pope tried to turn the Colosseum into a wool factory?"). Then when they're done, they pick up their story again. Well, every chapter in our textbook also tells a story, and once in a while we pause that story to tell you some related thing that we found especially interesting—not about Italian wool factories, but about psychology. The way you'll know we're pausing is that you will bump into a box of words. These boxes come in four flavours, and we've given each a name.

- One box is called **A World of Difference.** People differ in countless ways—by culture, gender, race, religion, age, wealth, sexual orientation, and a whole host of other differences. These sources of diversity influence just about everything people think, feel, and do, so in every chapter we pause our story to highlight one or more of them.

- A second box is called **Other Voices.** Long before psychologists appeared on earth, poets, pundits, playwrights, and philosophers were having insights into human nature. So we decided to invite some of them to share their insights with you. In every chapter, you will find a short essay by someone who thinks deeply, writes beautifully, and, most importantly, isn't us.

- A third box is called **The Real World.** From rats in mazes to humans in brain scanners, a textbook can sometimes seem like a report from places that aren't much like the place you live. That's why in every chapter we have included a box that shows how the material you are reading can be applied to the stuff of everyday life—from dating to studying to going on a job interview.

- Finally, in every chapter you will bump into a box called **Hot Science.** When we wrote the last edition, Donald Trump was a real estate developer and no one had ever heard the phrase "me too," which is to say that things change fast. That's why in every chapter, we take a moment to share with you a brand-new scientific finding that has changed the way we think—and that might change the way you think as well.

Those are the features and those are the boxes and that's probably enough for one preface. We could drone on because, after all, we *are* professors, but we trust you get the point: We love the science of psychology and we've written a book that we hope makes you fall in love with it as well. Whether or not that happens, we're eager to hear what you think about our new edition. Feel free to reach out to us at **PsychCanada@ macmillan.com.**

A NOTE TO INSTRUCTORS

Dear Instructor,

Why do we do this to ourselves? You've spent days and days browsing textbooks when you could have been baking cookies, reading poetry, or binge-watching *Stranger Things*. We've spent years and years reading papers, writing chapters, and finding photographs when we could have been listening to music, visiting museums, or binge-watching *Stranger Things*. Why have we all chosen to get lost in Textbookland when there are so many supernatural events to stream?

For the love of science. You and we may be different ages, genders, races, and religions; we may come from different places or speak different first languages; but much greater than our differences is our common bond, and that is our shared and unshakeable belief that science provides the best tools for understanding the mysteries of human behaviour. Somewhere along the way, we all stumbled on a field called psychology and got stuck there because we fell in love with a simple idea—the idea that the methods scientists use to figure out what causes cancer or to understand how butterflies migrate can also be used to answer age-old questions about the hearts and minds of our kind. Honestly, anyone who stumbles on that idea and isn't excited by it has to be a creature from the Upside Down.

Is our textbook right for you? We don't know. But we do know that when you choose a textbook you are entrusting part of your students' education to someone else, and that trust needs to be earned. We've tried to do that by writing a textbook that has a single overarching goal: To make your students fall in love with this amazing young science for just the reasons that you did and we did. Whatever they do with that passion—whether they become psychologists, better parents, smarter consumers, or more informed citizens—our job is to ignite it by spreading the good news about our science. That's what we try to do on every one of the pages that follow, and you will decide if we've succeeded.

Okay, give us a minute to dry our eyes. There, that's better. Now let's get into some of the nutsy-boltsy stuff you'll want to know about our textbook, and about our fifth edition in particular.

Ch-ch-ch-ch-changes!

The words *new* and *improved* sell a lot of mobile phones and coffee makers, and they probably sell a lot of textbooks too. But we won't use them. After all, this is the fifth edition of our textbook, and if everything in it were new and improved, then everything in the previous editions would have to be obsolete or in desperate need of repair. That's simply not the case. We've spent more than a decade working on this textbook, and we've learned a lot—not just from writing and re-writing it, but also from the many instructors and students across the country who have taken the time to tell us what they liked, what they didn't like, and how we could turn the latter into the former.

We've listened, and the reason our fifth edition is the best one ever is that rather than *changing* everything just so we could point to some new bells and whistles, we put most of our energies into *perfecting* the things that were already working well. Instructors told us that our pedagogical tools were strong, so we sharpened them rather than replacing them. They told us that our coverage was right on target, so we steadied our aim rather than aiming elsewhere. And they told us that their students enjoyed our casual and sometimes irreverent narrative voice, so we updated our jokes rather than admitting to ourselves that they were really, really bad. If the fifth edition looks familiar to you, that's because with each edition we've learned to make more babies and less bathwater.

With that said, the fifth edition is by no means the fourth with a new cover. You will see several significant changes right off the bat. For instance, we pretty much burned down Chapter 1 (Psychology: The Evolution of a Science) for the insurance money and rebuilt it from scratch. We think the new version provides a clearer and more engaging exploration of psychology's rich history. We've also done major renovations of Chapter 4 (Sensation and Perception), Chapter 8 (Emotion and Motivation), and Chapter 9 (Language and Thought), and added extended coverage to other chapters—for instance, further explanation of action potentials in Chapter 3 (Neuroscience and Behaviour) and the new section on replication in Chapter 2 (Methods). Most importantly, we sneaked a photo of Pete Townshend onto page 461 so that the young people in your class will know who The Who were. Some things are just too important to leave to chance. You'll find a complete list of changes at macmillanlearning.com.

About the Canadian Fifth Edition

Writing a Canadian edition of an American psychology textbook is not simply a matter of putting a lot of extra *u*'s in words like *color* and *behavior*. Although the principles of psychology are universal, behaviour depends on demographics, history, geography, and culture. The United States may be culturally familiar to Canadians, but Canadian students deserve a book that reflects their own experience. Cultural references need to be relatable, and information about incidence and prevalence should be appropriate for the society in which our students live. Canada is a multicultural and outward-looking place, and a Canadian book should reflect that also. Finally, Canadian scientists have made foundational discoveries in psychology, and these should be highlighted so they can inspire the Canadian scientists of tomorrow who are reading this book.

This new edition retains the highly engaging examples and international perspective of the Fourth Canadian Edition while incorporating the new research and features of the American Fifth Edition. Wherever possible, U.S. statistics were replaced with ones from Statistics Canada, and Canadian or international examples or topics were substituted for those that had a specifically American focus and context.

In the Canadian edition, we have aimed to maintain the benefits of the parent text and its narrative while appealing to Canadian students. Psychology is an international endeavour, and research foundational to the field has been conducted in many countries outside the United States. Consequently, we did not "Canadianize" the textbook as much as make it less America-centric. To highlight the international dimension, we have indicated the nationality of non-American scientists responsible for particularly important discoveries. When these happened in Canada, we also indicate the university. We have also tried to highlight the remarkable scientific discoveries made by pioneering Canadian scientists such as Albert Bandura, Donald Hebb, Ronald Melzack, Brenda Milner, Wilder Penfield, and others.

To illustrate how we have incorporated a Canadian perspective, we highlight some of the specific information included in each of the chapters:

- Chapter 1: The Evolution of Psychological Science: We discuss the development of cognitive neuroscience in Canada, highlighting Canadian pioneers such as Hebb, Milner, and Penfield. Besides the American Psychological Association, we include descriptions of other Canadian psychological organizations, such as the Canadian Psychological Association, the Canadian Society for Brain, Behaviour and Cognitive Science, and the Canadian Association of Neuroscience, and indicate career paths for psychologists in Canada.

- Chapter 2: Methods in Psychology: We use examples of statistical data in our explanations that would appeal beyond the United States, and we present the ethical guidelines that all Canadian psychologists are to follow, whether in conducting research or dealing with clients using the wording of the Tri-Agency TCPS 2 (Government of Canada, 2017), the Canadian Psychological Association Code of Ethics, and the Canadian Council on Animal Care.

- Chapter 3: Neuroscience and Behaviour: We start with stories of Canadian athletes to illustrate the issue of sports-related head trauma and chronic traumatic encephalopathy. We highlight the contributions of Montreal neurosurgeon Wilder Penfield in mapping the somatosensory and motor cortex and McGill researcher Michael Meaney's work demonstrating that maternal caretaking behaviour has a profound influence on the stress response in offspring.

- Chapter 4: Sensation and Perception: This chapter was extensively edited for this new edition by the Canadian author and perceptual psychologist Ingrid Johnsrude. This rewrite is international in scope, with the foundational work of Goodale (University of Western Ontario) related to perception and action and the complementary specializations of the dorsal and ventral pathways highlighted.

- Chapter 5: Consciousness: We have added a section on Disorders of Consciousness (e.g., coma, vegetative state, minimally conscious state, and locked-in syndrome), and highlight a case study by Adrian Owen (University of Western Ontario) and his team, who used fMRI technology to determine that a patient who was thought to be in a persistent vegetative state actually possessed consciousness and intentionality, but was locked in by his injury. We've revised the section on the opioid epidemic in the United States to place it in a Canadian context. We also replace American statistics on drug and alcohol use and abuse with Canadian ones, and replace the Other Voices piece, on why pot should be legalized in the United States, with an editorial from *The New York Times* on how Canadian legalization of pot might benefit research.

- Chapter 6: Memory: We cover the foundational research on the levels-of-processing account (Fergus Craik and Endel Tulving, University of Toronto) which has been so influential in our understanding of how humans encode information. We also discuss Brenda Milner's discovery, through her early work with Henry Molaison (H.M.), of the role of the hippocampus in long-term memory, and Hebb's idea, crystallized as "cells that fire together, wire together," that is the neural basis of long-term memory. We also replace specific American examples in the section on "Seven Sins of Memory" with ones to which Canadian students can relate more easily.

- Chapter 7: Learning: We discuss some of McMaster University researcher Shepard Siegel's work on classical conditioning and how it can be used to explain how drug overdoses occur with experienced drug abusers. We also describe the discovery of brain stimulation reward in rats by Peter Milner & James Olds (McGill University) that first demonstrated brain "pleasure centres," as well as Bandura's work on observational learning.

- Chapter 8: Emotion and Motivation: We use a Canadian geographic example to present multidimensional scaling and discuss obesity in a Canadian context. The Hot Science box highlights a study of eating behaviour conducted at the Montreal Neurological Institute by Alain Dagher and his team. We've replaced the Other Voices piece, on American political outrage on social media, with a piece from *The New York Times* by Frans de Waal on emotions in dogs.

- Chapter 9: Language and Thought: We discuss the future of bilingualism in Canada, and the remarkable finding made by McGill researchers Laura Petitto and Paula Marentette (1991) that deaf babies "babble" with their hands, and the finding by South African-Canadian psychologist Denise Klein, that a child's first language leaves lasting traces in the brain. We also highlight Gordon Pennycook, University of Regina, who co-authored the Other Voices piece in the chapter.

- Chapter 10: Intelligence: We re-situate the historical material on eugenics in an international and Canadian context. We replaced The Real World piece on intelligence testing and the effect of racism on admission to gifted and talented programs in U.S. schools with a piece later in the chapter on a U.K. study demonstrating the surprising plasticity of the brain in adolescence when it comes to cognitive ability.

- Chapter 11: Development: We highlight Canadian statistics on prenatal factors and health care. We replace the Other Voices piece on active shooter drills with a piece by Cindy Blackstock, executive director of the First Nations Child and Family Caring Society of Canada, on how social welfare policies in Canada damage the development of Indigenous youth, contributing to intergenerational trauma in this group. In light of the greater use of daycare facilities in Canada compared to the United States, we include a short discussion of research on the effects of high-quality daycare on attachment. We describe work by Canadian researcher Tomáš Paus (University of Toronto) showing how areas of the brain develop with age. We replace the discussion of sex education in American schools, and of American teen behaviour, with statistics on Canadian teen sexual and other behaviour. We highlight the work of Queen's University psychologist Meredith Chivers on the effects of sexual orientation on arousal, and include "two spirit," a term used by some Indigenous people to describe their sexual, gender, and/or spiritual identity, in The Real World piece on gender and sexual orientation. Finally, the exclusive emphasis on marriage in the section on adult committed relationships has been altered to be more inclusive, since many couples (particularly in Quebec) in long-term committed relationships do not get married. The much higher rates of stay-at-home fathers in Canada in recent years has also been highlighted.

- Chapter 12: Personality: We use relatable examples in the figure on page 468, "How would you describe each of these personalities?," specifically replacing the picture of U.S. Chief Justice Ruth Bader Ginsburg with a picture of Justin Trudeau, and we use a picture of Tessa Virtue and Scott Moir from the 2018 Winter Olympics instead of Shaun White of the United States to make a point about self-esteem. Finally, we change the example of implicit egotism, the idea that people's preferences are influenced by their name, to a story about Henry Head and Lord Walter Russell Brain, two British neurologists who were both editors of the journal *Brain*.

- Chapter 13: Social Psychology: Figure 13.1, showing the relationship between heat and aggression in Philadelphia, was remade using available data from Toronto, and American violent crime statistics were replaced with Canadian ones. Figure 13.5 on altruism in American states was replaced with a figure showing organ donation rates by province, and highlights the Vancouver Capilano Bridge experiment in which University of British Columbia researchers Dutton and Aron demonstrated that physiological arousal accompanying fear can be mistaken for attraction. The section on Love and Marriage has been revised to discuss long-term committed relationships generally, not just marriages, and the section on stereotyping and unconscious bias is put in a Canadian context (i.e., Figure 13.10 has been replaced with Canadian data, and the discussion of implicit bias has been widened beyond a consideration of black and white Americans). We now include a discussion of how implicit bias in Canada has created systemic barriers for Indigenous people, and we use the TV reality show *The Voice (La Voix)* as an example of bias-free auditions (instead of a female violinist in Pittsburgh). Finally, we've changed a football example of Green Bay Packers fans wearing cheese hats to Saskatchewan Roughriders fans wearing watermelon helmets (no detail too small!).

- Chapter 14: Stress and Health: We discuss how racism and discrimination against Indigenous people in Canada leads to increased stress and poorer health (A World of Difference); highlight the work of Hans Selye (Université de Montréal) in developing the General Adaptation Syndrome; and internationalize the pictures on page 554, so that they no longer exclusively show American presidents, but other world leaders as well. We use the van attack on Yonge Street in Toronto (April 23, 2018) as an example of a stressful life event and coping, and include Canadian statistics on religious belief, lifestyle factors in health and wellness, and the health of immigrant groups in Canada.

- Chapter 15: Psychological Disorders: We include incidence and prevalence statistics for psychological disorders in Canada instead of the United States. As an illustration of how complex the causes of mental disorders can be, and how difficult it can be to trace causes, we discuss the example of intergenerational trauma in Indigenous groups (as a result of systematic discrimination, including residential schools), which can have persistent effects even two generations later. We also discuss the large demographic and geographic differences in suicide rates across the country (and links between intergenerational trauma and suicide rates).

- Chapter 16: Treatment of Psychological Disorders: We discuss the cost of mental disorders to the Canadian economy and the statistics around provision, access, and use of mental-health services by different demographic groups in Canada. The Real World box on Types of Psychotherapists describes how practitioners are trained and what types of therapy orientations are prevalent in Canada. We also re-situate discussions of antidepressant use based on OECD data. Finally, we present the Canadian Code of Ethics for treating vulnerable individuals with mental disorders.

But Wait . . . There's More!

Our primary job as textbook authors is to give your students a solid overview of the vast literature in psychological science so that you can spend your class time focusing on the things you really want to tell them, or ask them, or do with them, rather than trying to cover all that territory yourself. Maybe that's all you wanted us to do, in which case . . . um, you're welcome.

But if you think textbook authors can do more than that, well then, we happen to agree with you. That's why we (and *we* of course means "a team of dedicated people whose hard work we will now try to take credit for") have developed a variety of resources to make your job easier and your teaching more effective. Here are just a few of them:

- **LaunchPad** is the name of Macmillan Learning's online platform, which combines the full e-book version of our textbook with a whole bunch of interesting activities, award-winning media, and state-of-the-art assessment tools. For students, LaunchPad is the ultimate online study guide; for you, it is a place where class documents can be posted, assignments given, quizzes graded, and progress measured. Best of all, LaunchPad integrates seamlessly with all the major learning management systems used by universities these days, including Blackboard, Brightspace by D2L, Canvas, and Moodle.

- One of the features of LaunchPad that we personally like best is the **LearningCurve** adaptive quizzing system. This system measures a student's performance and then chooses quiz questions based on how well they are doing, which means that every student in your class can take a quiz that has been custom-designed for them. What's more, LearningCurve gives students instant feedback about their performance, while providing you with a report on the progress of individual students and on your class as a whole. You really have to see how beautiful the platform is and how easily it works. Go to launchpadworks.com and take it for a test drive.

- Students hate taking exams. What they don't realize is that we hate making them even more! That's why our book comes with a **Test Bank** (revised by a team overseen by Ingrid Johnsrude of the University of Western Ontario) that includes more than 250 multiple-choice, true/false, and essay questions for every chapter. You may have designed your class around the APA's outcomes for introductory psychology students, and, if so, you'll be happy to know that we link the test bank questions to these outcomes, making it easy for you to see which goals are being achieved.

- Can we help you make some **lecture slides**? We hope so, because our book comes with a fully updated set. Can we suggest some **lecture topics and class activities**? We hope so, because our book also comes with a downloadable **Instructor's Resource Manual** (created by Jeffrey B. Henriques of the University of Wisconsin, Madison), which contains plenty of them. Can we get you a cup of coffee? Just checking to see if you were still with us.

- Our textbook gives you access to a large number of **supplements** that your students may find useful, depending on how you've chosen to focus your teaching. For instance, if you focus a lot on critical thinking skills, then you might want to supplement our coverage of that topic in Chapter 2 by having your students read *The Critical Thinking Companion for Introductory Psychology* or *The Worth Expert Guide to Scientific Literacy*. Or maybe you and your students care a lot about the application of psychology in the real world, in which case you might want to supplement our textbook by having them read *Psychology and the Real World* or *The Psychology Major's Companion*. And if none of these or our many other titles quite do the trick, you can use **Macmillan's Custom Publishing Program** to produce a supplement that is specifically tailored to the material you want to emphasize. Pretty much the only supplement we can't provide is one that will give you energy to spare and mental capacity to burn. But maybe soon.

- Is there a doctor in the house? Some of your students may be preparing to take the **MCAT,** and if so, we've got them covered. We prepared a special resource that connects the contents of our textbook to the specific topics that are covered on the MCAT exam. Furthermore, our test bank includes a special set of questions for each chapter that test quantitative reasoning ability in the style of the MCAT.

These are just a few of the resources that help make our textbook more than the sum of its chapters. Rather than chopping down trees to tell you about the rest of them, we've put the details online at macmillanlearning.com.

ACKNOWLEDGEMENTS

Despite what you might guess by looking at our pictures, we all found people who were willing to marry us after some special pleading. We are grateful to Susan McGlynn, Marilynn Oliphant, Keesha Nock, and Mark Wolforth, who never complained about those long nights and weekends when we were writing this textbook rather than hanging out with them. Um . . . you did miss us, didn't you?

Although ours are the only names on the cover, writing a textbook is a team sport, and we've been fortunate to have a terrific group of professionals supporting us. They have helped us more than we can say, and more than they probably realize:

Rebecca Addington
University of Wisconsin–Madison

George Alder
Simon Fraser University

Christine Bartholomew
Kent State University

Dave Baskind
Delta College

Elizabeth A. Becker
St. Joseph's University

Joan Bihun
University of Colorado Denver

Dawn Brinkley
University of Texas–Dallas

Jennifer L. Butler
Case Western Reserve University

Marci Campbell
Salt Lake Community College

Diana L. Ciesko
Valencia College

Emily Cohen-Shikora
Washington University–St. Louis

Rebecca DesRoches
Regis College

Chris De La Ronde
Austin Community College

Michael Disch
St. Edwards University

Kimberly Duff
Cerritos College

April K. Dye
Carson-Newman University

John E. Edlund
Rochester Institute of Technology

Kim Ernst
Loyola University New Orleans

Lauren Ethridge
University of Oklahoma

Celeste Favela
El Paso Community College

Mark Ferguson
University of Wisconsin–Stevens Point

Sara Finley
Pacific Lutheran University

Jocelyn R. Folk
Kent State University

Ken Fowler
Memorial University of Newfoundland

Jim Fryer
SUNY Pottsdam

Sophie A. George
Dixie State University

Afshin Gharib
Dominican University of California

Jerry Green
Tarrant County College

Maria E. Guarneri-White
Pacific Lutheran University

Jane S. Halonen
University of West Florida

Edward Hansen
Florida State University

Shani N. Harris
Spelman College

Erin Henshaw
Denison University

L. E. Holliman
Georgia State University at Perimeter–Clarkston Campus

Keith Holyoak
University of California Los Angeles

Kathleen Hughes
University of Calgary

George-Harold Jennings
Drew University

Janna Kline
Rutgers University

Michael M. Knepp
University of Mount Union

Karen Kwan
Salt Lake Community College

Christopher B. Mayhorn
North Carolina State University

Michael Jason McCoy
Cape Fear Community College

Wendy Mendes
University of California San Francisco

Dennis K. Miller
University of Missouri–Columbia

Rikki L. A. Miller
University of Southern Maine

Erin M. Myers
Western Carolina University

Khu Nguyen
Washington University in St. Louis

Bradley M. Okdie
Ohio State University–Newark

Caroline Olko
Nassau Community College

Natasha Otto
Morgan State University

Doug A. Peterson
University of South Dakota

Jessica Petok
St. Olaf College

Catherine Phillips
Northwest Vista College

Gary Popoli
Stevenson University

Mixalis Poulakis
University of Indianapolis

Danielle Quigley
Douglas College

G. A. Radvansky
University of Notre Dame

Marjorie Rhodes
New York University

Kiefer Rich
San Diego City College

Blake Riek
Calvin College

Gwendolyn Scott-Jones
Delaware State University

Keith M. Shafritz
Hofstra University

Shubam Sharma
University of Florida

Michelle Shiota
Arizona State University

Denise Simanic
Humbler College

Hiroko Sotozaki
Western Illinois University

Jonathan N. Sparks
Vance-Granville Community College

Peter Sparks
Oregon State University–Cascades

Helen T. Sullivan
Rider University

Donald Tellinghuisen
Calvin College

David G. Thomas
Oklahoma State University

Travis Tubré
University of Wisconsin–River Falls

Lora Vasiliauskas
Virginia Western Community College

Nicole Vittoz
Douglas College

Constance Walsh
Fullerton College

Megan Kozak Williams
Linfield College

James Thomas Wright
Forsyth Technical Community College

Dasa Zeithamova
University of Oregon

We'd also like to thank Chad Galuska and Jeff Henriques, who wrote the supplemental materials that support our textbook's educational mission. The insight and experience they brought to this task was extraordinary, and it shows.

As always, we are deeply grateful to our good friends at Worth Publishers, with whom we have happily worked for so many years. They include:

- Senior vice president Chuck Linsmeier, who has been providing much-needed wisdom, encouragement, and gin since our very first day.

- Our executive program manager, Dan DeBonis, who has managed our project with panache while keeping the trains, planes, automobiles, submarines, and pachyderms all running on time.

- Our brilliant, talented, and preternaturally cheerful senior development editor, Valerie Raymond, without whom we would all jump off a tall building (just behind Dan DeBonis who might need a push), along with Katie Pachnos, development editor for the Canadian edition.

- Our project managers Jana Lewis and Vanavan Jayaraman, our senior content project manager Vivien Weiss, our senior workflow project supervisor Susan Wein, and our editorial assistant Nick Rizzuti, all of whom seem to know some magic spell that turns a bunch of disorganized text files into a set of beautiful pages.

- Our senior design manager Natasha Wolfe, our design manager John Callahan, our art manager Matt McAdams, our photo manager Robin Fadool, and our photo researcher Jennifer Atkins, who worked together to make our textbook as delightful to look at as it is to read.

- Our media editor Stefani Wallace, who expertly guided the development and creation of our superb supplements package.

- Our executive marketing manager Kate Nurre and marketing assistant Chelsea Simens, who have always been and continue to be tireless public advocates for our vision.

- Our editorial assistants, Molly Evans and Franchesca Ramirez, who provided capable assistance even when we didn't know we needed it.

What would we have done without all of you? Gracias, arigato, danke, merci, xie xie, and a way big thanks!

Daniel L. Schacter
Cambridge, 2020

Daniel T. Gilbert
Cambridge, 2020

Matthew K. Nock
Cambridge, 2020

Ingrid Johnsrude
London, Ontario, 2020

The Evolution of Psychological Science

A LOT WAS HAPPENING IN 1860. In the British colony of the United Canadas, the cornerstone of the Canadian Parliament buildings was laid in Ottawa, and the Cariboo gold rush was about to begin in British Columbia. In the United States, Abraham Lincoln became President, the Pony Express began delivering mail across the country, and a woman named Anne Kellogg had just given birth to a child who would grow up to invent the cornflake. On the U.S. East Coast, an 18-year-old named William James (1842–1910) started worrying about what to do with the rest of his life. He loved to paint and draw, but realized that he wasn't talented enough to become a serious artist. At his father's urging, he decided to go to school to study chemistry, but he soon found that chemistry didn't interest him. He switched to physiology and then to medicine, only to find that those subjects didn't interest him either. So William took a leave of absence from school and joined a scientific expedition to the Amazon, hoping to discover his true passion, but all he discovered was that he passionately hated leeches. He returned to school, but soon became so depressed that he was required to take another leave of absence.

William James (*left*) started out as a restless student who didn't know what he wanted to do with his life. Forty years later (*right*), he had become one of the founders of the new discipline of psychology. Throughout his illustrious career, James remained a devoted and beloved teacher who was "so vivacious and humorous that one day a student interrupted and asked him to be serious for a moment" (Hunt, 2007, p. 169).

This time, instead of heading south to the Amazon, he headed east to what is now Germany, which, at that time, was a leading centre for scientific enquiry, especially in the field of physiology. As he talked and listened, he learned about a new science called **psychology** (from a combination of the Greek *psyche* [soul] and *logos* [to study]). He saw that this developing field was taking a modern, scientific approach to age-old questions about human nature—questions that had become painfully familiar to him during his personal search for meaning, but to which only poets and philosophers had ever before offered answers. Excited about the new discipline, James returned to America and quickly finished his medical degree. But he never practiced medicine and never intended to. Rather, he became a professor at Harvard University and devoted the rest of his life to philosophy and psychology. His landmark book *The Principles of Psychology* is still widely read and remains one of the most influential books ever written on the subject (James, 1890).

"This is no science," James said of psychology in 1892, "it is only the hope of a science." And at that time, he was right. But now, more than a century later, psychology's hope has been realized, and the book you hold in your hand is that realization (see Other Voices: Is Psychology a Science?). How did it happen? How did we get here from there? How did the psychology taught in William James's classroom become the psychology taught in yours? This chapter tells that story. We'll start at the beginning and examine psychology's intellectual roots in philosophy. Next, we'll explore some early attempts to develop a science of the mind by some of the very people whom James met when he travelled to Germany in the late 1800s. Then we'll see how the 1900s gave rise to two utterly incompatible approaches to psychology—one that viewed the mind as an infinitely complex mystery, and one that viewed the mind as an irrelevant fiction. Next we'll see how one of these approaches came to dominate experimental psychology in the 20th century, and how that dominance was ended by the invention of a machine. Finally, we'll take a look at psychology as a profession, and see who these people who call themselves psychologists really are, and how they got to be that way.

Psychology's Philosophical Roots

Learning Outcomes

- Explain the distinction between dualism and materialism.
- Explain the distinction between realism and idealism.
- Explain the distinction between empiricism and nativism.

psychology The scientific study of mind and behaviour.

Psychology is *the scientific study of mind and behaviour.* The word *mind* refers to a set of private events that happen inside a person—the thoughts and feelings that we experience at every moment but that no one else can see—and the word *behaviour* refers to a set of public events—the things we say and do that can potentially be observed by others. Both human minds and human behaviours have been around for quite a while, and psychologists were not the first to try to make sense of them. That distinction belongs to philosophers, who have been thinking deeply about these topics for several thousand years. Although their ideas could fill several volumes (and if you study philosophy, you'll find that they fill many more than that), three of these ideas are especially important to understanding modern psychology.

Dualism and Materialism

Our bodies are physical objects that can be seen, smelled, and touched. Our minds are not. The word *mind* refers to a set of subjective events—perceptions and memories, thoughts and feelings—that have no actual physical presence. You can't hear an emotion or taste a belief. The philosopher René Descartes (1596–1650) thought the "stuff in here" and the "stuff out there" were so different that they must be made of different substances. The body, he argued, is made of a material substance, the mind is made of an immaterial substance, and every person is therefore a physical container of a nonphysical thing—or what the philosopher Gilbert Ryle (1949) called the "ghost in the machine." Descartes embraced **philosophical dualism,** which is *the view that mind and body are fundamentally different things.*

But if the mind and the body are fundamentally different things, then how do they interact? How does the immaterial mind tell the material body to put its best foot forward? And when the material body steps on a rusty nail, why does the immaterial mind say ouch? Descartes came up with some answers to these questions that satisfied no one, including himself, but they especially dissatisfied philosophers like Thomas Hobbes (1588–1679), who argued that the mind and body aren't fundamentally different things at all. Rather, the mind *is* what the brain *does.* From Hobbes's perspective, looking for a place in the brain where the mind meets the body is like looking for the place on your phone where the picture meets the screen. The picture *is* what the screen *does,* and they don't "meet" in some third place. The brain is a physical object whose activity is known as "the mind," and therefore all mental phenomena—every thought and feeling, every sight and sound—is the result of some physical activity in the physical brain. **Philosophical materialism** is *the view that all mental phenomena are reducible to physical phenomena.*

philosophical dualism The view that mind and body are fundamentally different things.

philosophical materialism The view that all mental phenomena are reducible to physical phenomena.

René Descartes (*left*) was a dualist who believed that the mind was an "incorporeal" or nonphysical substance. "It is certain that this I—that is to say, my soul by which I am what I am—is entirely and absolutely distinct from my body, and can exist without it," he wrote. But Thomas Hobbes (*right*) was a materialist who thought the term "incorporeal substance" was a nonsensical contradiction. "Substance and body signify the same thing," he wrote, "and therefore *substance incorporeal* are words which, when they are joined together, destroy one another."

So which philosopher was right? The debate between dualism and materialism cannot be settled by facts. Many human beings today believe that there is something other than the physical universe and that the body is a material container of an immaterial spirit, and there isn't any objective evidence that requires them to change their minds. This is an issue about which people pretty much just have to make up their own minds and choose their own sides, and most of the world's religions—from Christianity and Judaism to Hinduism and Islam—have chosen to side with the dualists and embrace the notion of a nonphysical soul. Most psychologists have gone the other way and have chosen to embrace materialism (Ecklund, Scheitle, & Pennsylvania, 2007). As you will see throughout this book, psychologists typically believe that all mental phenomena—from attention and memory to belief and emotion—are ultimately explainable in terms of the physical processes that produce them. The mind is what the brain does—nothing less and certainly nothing more. We are remarkably complex machines whose operations somehow give rise to consciousness, and one of psychology's jobs is to figure out what that "somehow" is.

Realism and Idealism

You probably have the sense that this thing called "you" is somewhere inside your skull—not your foot or your knee—and that right now it is looking out through your eyes and reading the words on this page. It *feels* as though our eyes are some sort of camera, and that "you" are "in here" seeing pictures of the things "out there." The philosopher John Locke (1632–1704) referred to this theory as **philosophical realism,** which is the view that *perceptions of the physical world are produced entirely by information from the sensory organs.* According to the realist account, light is right now bouncing off the page and hitting your eye, and your brain is using that information *and only that information* to produce your perception of the book in front of you. And because your eye is like a camera, the pictures it produces are generally accurate depictions of the world.

This theory is simple, but philosophers such as Immanuel Kant (1724–1804) thought that simplicity was its major flaw. Kant suggested that our perceptions of the world are less like photographs and more like paintings. **Philosophical idealism** is the view that *perceptions of the physical world are the brain's interpretation of information from the sensory organs.* According to the idealist account, light is bouncing off the page and hitting your eye, and your brain is using that information—*plus all the other information it has about the world*—to produce your perception of the book. Before you ever looked at this book, you already knew many things about books in general—what they are made of, how large they are, that the cover is heavier than the pages—and your brain is right now using everything it knows about books to *interpret* the information it is receiving from your eyes. It is painting a picture of what it *believes* is out there, and although you think you are "seeing" a book, you are really just seeing that picture.

So which philosopher was right? Modern psychology has come down strongly on the side of idealism. As you will see in many of the upcoming chapters, our perception of the world is an *inference*—our brain's best guess about what's likely to be out there. Because our brains are such good guessers and such fast guessers, we typically don't realize they are guessing at all. We feel like our eyes are cameras taking photos, but that's only because the artist between our ears can produce realistic paintings at lightning speed.

In his 1781 masterpiece *The Critique of Pure Reason*, Immanuel Kant argued that the mind comes hardwired with certain kinds of knowledge and that it uses this knowledge to create our perceptions of the world. "Perceptions without conceptions are blind," he wrote, meaning that without prior knowledge or "conceptions" of the world, we could not see or "have perceptions" of it.

philosophical realism The view that perceptions of the physical world are produced entirely by information from the sensory organs.

philosophical idealism The view that perceptions of the physical world are the brain's interpretation of information from the sensory organs.

GL ARCHIVE/ALAMY

Empiricism and Nativism

Here are some other things you know about books: You know that four books are more than two, that a book can't pass through a wall, that pushing a book off the table will cause it to fall, and that when it falls it will go down and not up. How do you know all this stuff? **Philosophical empiricism** is *the view that all knowledge is acquired through experience.* Philosophers such as Locke believed that a newborn baby is a *tabula rasa,* or "blank slate" upon which experience writes its story. As Locke wrote in his 1690 *Essay on Human Understanding:*

> If we will attentively consider new-born children, we shall have little reason to think that they bring many ideas into the world with them. . . . One may perceive how, by degrees, afterwards, ideas come into their minds; and that they get no more, nor other, than what experience, and the observation of things that come in their way, furnish them with; which might be enough to satisfy us that they are not original characters stamped on the mind.

In other words, you know about books—and about teacups and tea kettles and tee-shirts and tee-balls and a huge number of other objects—because you've seen them, or interacted with them, or seen someone else interact with them.

Kant thought Locke was wrong about this, too. **Philosophical nativism** is *the view that some knowledge is innate rather than acquired.* Kant argued that human beings must be born with some basic knowledge of the world that allows them to acquire additional knowledge of the world. After all, how could you learn that pushing a book off a table *causes* it to fall if you didn't already know what causation was? The fact that you can acquire knowledge about what books do when pushed suggests that your mind came with at least a few bits of knowledge already programmed into it. For Kant, those few pre-programmed bits of knowledge were concepts such as space, time, causality, and number. You can't learn these concepts, he argued, and yet you have to have them in order to learn anything else. So they must come factory-installed.

Which philosopher was right? Most modern psychologists embrace some version of nativism. It is all too obvious that much of what we know is acquired through experience, and no one thinks otherwise. But research suggests that at least *some* of what we know is indeed hardwired into our brains, just as Kant thought. As you'll see in the Development chapter, even newborn infants seem to have some basic knowledge of the laws of physics and mathematics. The tabula is not rasa, the slate is not blank, which leads to some interesting questions: What exactly is written on the slate at birth? How and when in our evolutionary history did it get there? Can experience erase the slate as well as write on it? Psychologists refer to these types of questions as "nature-versus-nurture" questions, and as you will see in some of the upcoming chapters, they have devised clever techniques for answering them.

John Locke was a British philosopher, physician, and political theorist whose writings about the separation of church and state, religious freedom, and liberty strongly influenced America's founding fathers, such as Thomas Jefferson, who incorporated Locke's phrase "the pursuit of happiness" into the Declaration of Independence.

philosophical empiricism The view that all knowledge is acquired through experience.

philosophical nativism The view that some knowledge is innate rather than acquired.

Build to the Outcomes

1. How does materialism differ from dualism, and which do modern psychologists favour?
2. How does realism differ from idealism, and which do modern psychologists favour?
3. How does empiricism differ from nativism, and which do modern psychologists favour?

The Late 1800s: Towards a Science of the Mind

The psychologist Hermann Ebbinghaus (1908) once remarked that "psychology has a long past but a short history." Indeed, psychology's philosophical roots go back thousands of years, but its history as an independent science began a mere 150 or so years ago, when a few German scientists began to wonder whether the methods of the physical and natural sciences might be used to study the human mind.

Structuralism: What Is the Mind Like?

During his visit to Berlin in 1867, William James sent a letter to a friend:

> It seems to me that perhaps the time has come for psychology to begin to be a science. . . . I am going on to study what is already known and perhaps may be able to do some work at it. Helmholtz and a man called Wundt at Heidelberg are working at it, and I hope I live through this winter to go to them in the summer.

Who were the people James was talking about? Hermann von Helmholtz (1821–1894) was a brilliant experimenter and scientist with a background in both physiology and physics. He is best known in psychology for major contributions to our understanding of vision and hearing, but he also would ask people to close their eyes and respond as quickly as possible when he touched different parts of their legs. That's not as creepy as it sounds. Helmholtz recorded each person's **reaction time,** or *the amount of time between the onset of a stimulus and a person's response to that stimulus,* and discovered that people generally took longer to respond when he touched their toes than when he touched their thighs. Why? When something touches your body, your nerves transmit a signal from the point of contact to your brain, and when that signal arrives at your brain, you "feel" the touch. Because your thighs are closer to your brain than your toes are, the signal from your thigh has a shorter distance to travel. By carefully measuring how long it took people to feel a thigh touch and a toe touch and then comparing the two measurements, Helmholtz was able to do something remarkable: He calculated the speed at which nerves transmit information!

But if Helmholtz's experiments set the stage for the birth of psychology, it was his research assistant, Wilhelm Wundt (1832–1920), who rented the theatre. Wundt (pronounced "Voohnt") taught the first course in scientific or "experimental" psychology at the University of Heidelberg in Germany in 1867, published the first psychology textbook in 1874, and opened the world's first psychology laboratory at the University of Leipzig in 1879. Wundt believed that the primary goal of psychology should be to understand "the facts of consciousness, its combinations and relations, so that it may ultimately discover the laws which govern these relations and combinations" (Wundt, 1912/1973, p. 1). Natural scientists had had great success in understanding the physical world by breaking it down into its basic elements, such as cells and molecules and atoms, and Wundt decided to take the same approach to understanding the mind. His approach later came to be known as **structuralism,** which was *an approach to psychology that attempted to isolate and analyze the mind's basic elements.*

How could these elements be discovered? Wundt's student, Edward Titchener (1867–1927) pioneered a technique he called "systematic self-observation" but that everyone since has called **introspection,** which is *the analysis of subjective experience by trained observers.* Titchener trained his research assistants to report on the contents of their moment-to-moment experience, teaching them to report their "raw experience" rather than their interpretation of it. He presented his trained observers with a wide variety of stimuli, from patches of colour to musical tones, and then asked them

reaction time The amount of time between the onset of a stimulus and a person's response to that stimulus.

structuralism An approach to psychology that attempted to isolate and analyze the mind's basic elements.

introspection The analysis of subjective experience by trained observers.

WONTORRA, M., MEISCHNER-METGE, A., & SCHRÖIGER, E. (EDS.). (2004). WILHELM WUNDT (1832–1920) AND THE ADVENT OF EXPERIMENTAL PSYCHOLOGY. (CD [ISBN 3-00-013477-8.] ED.

Wilhelm Wundt (standing in the *middle*) taught the world's first psychology course and published the world's first psychology textbook, *Principles of Physiological Psychology*. (The word *physiological* simply meant "experimental" back then.) He also opened the world's first psychology laboratory at the University of Leipzig. He was the advisor to a remarkable 184 PhD students, many of whom went on to become well-known psychologists, which is why a large percentage of modern psychologists can trace their intellectual lineage back to him. It is fair to say that modern psychology just Wundt be the same without him.

to describe what was happening in their minds. The observer might describe the hue and luminance of the colour, the feelings he had when he heard the tone, and so on. Titchener believed that by carefully analyzing the reports from many trained observers who had been exposed to many stimuli, he would eventually discover the basic building blocks of subjective experience. This method led to some successes. For example, Wundt himself used it to identify three basic dimensions of sensation—pleasure/pain, strain/relaxation, and excitation/quiescence—and these three dimensions have, in fact, been shown to underlie the words people use to describe subjective experiences in many languages (Osgood, Suci, & Tannenbaum, 1967).

But structuralism didn't last long as the only way to explore psychology, and you can probably guess why. Natural scientists had indeed been (and continue to be) successful in understanding the natural world by breaking it into small parts, but that approach is successful only when it is clear what those parts are. When two biologists looked at blood under a microscope, they saw the same blood cells. This wasn't true of everyone who looked at the colour green or heard C# played on a piano. The problem with Titchener's introspection was that each person's inner experience was an inherently private event—a 3-D movie with an audience of one. As such, there was simply no way to tell if a person's description of her experience was accurate, and no way to tell if her experience was the same as or different from someone else's. So one of structuralism's problems was the method that some of its influential followers used. But an even bigger problem was its competition, because while the structuralists were busy introspecting, a young upstart was taking a very different approach to the study of the mind.

Functionalism: What Is the Mind For?

During William James's time in Heidelberg, Wundt sold him on psychology, but not on structuralism. James felt that subjective experience was less like a molecule made of atoms and more like a river—a "stream of consciousness" as he called it—and that trying to isolate its basic elements was a losing proposition. "The attempt at introspective analysis in these cases is in fact like seizing a spinning top to catch its motion, or trying

On the Origin of Species (1859) by Charles Darwin (*left*) is one of the most important scientific books ever written, and it had a big impact on William James and the birth of functionalism. Darwin developed his theory in the 1830s but did not write about it. A naturalist named Alfred Russel Wallace (1823–1913, *right*) developed the same theory at the same time and in 1855 sent Darwin a paper describing it. The two men decided to announce the theory jointly at a meeting of the Linnean Society in 1858. The next year, Darwin published a book describing the theory, and the world pretty much forgot about good old Wallace.

to turn up the gas quickly enough to see how the darkness looks," he wrote. James thought psychologists should worry less about what mental life was *like*, and more about what it was *for*. Together with psychologists such as John Dewey (1859–1952) and James Angell (1869–1949), James developed a new approach to psychology called **functionalism,** which was *an approach to psychology that emphasized the adaptive significance of mental processes*. What does "adaptive significance" mean?

As one historian wrote, functionalism "inherited its physical body from German experimentalism, but it got its mind from Darwin" (Boring, 1929). Charles Darwin (1809–1882) was a naturalist who had recently published a book entitled *On the Origin of Species by Means of Natural Selection* (1859). In it, Darwin had proposed the principle of **natural selection,** which refers to *the process by which the specific attributes that promote an organism's survival and reproduction become more prevalent in the population over time*. How does natural selection work? Animals pass their physical attributes to their offspring, and those attributes that are most "adaptive"— that is, those that promote the offspring's survival and reproduction—are more likely to be passed along from one generation to the next. Over time, these adaptive attributes become increasingly prevalent in the population simply because "the population" refers to those animals that have managed to survive and reproduce.

Darwin's reasoning was brilliantly circular. Humans have fingers instead of flippers because at some point in the distant past, those of our ancestors who developed fingers were better able to survive and reproduce than those who did not, and they passed their flipperless fingeredness on to us. That's the principle of natural selection at work, shaping the human body. James reasoned that if our physical characteristics had evolved because they were adaptive, then the same should be true of our psychological characteristics. In other words, natural selection should also have shaped the mind. "Consciousness," James wrote in 1892, "has in all probability been evolved, like all other functions, for a use—it is to the highest degree improbable a priori that it should have no use." The mind serves a function and according to James, the task for psychologists was to figure out what that function was.

functionalism An approach to psychology that emphasized the adaptive significance of mental processes.

natural selection The process by which the specific attributes that promote an organism's survival and reproduction become more prevalent in the population over time.

Build to the Outcomes

1. How did Helmholtz calculate the speed at which nerves transmit impulses?

2. What is introspection and how did Titchener use it?

3. What is structuralism?

4. What is natural selection and how did it influence the rise of functionalism?

Other Voices | Is Psychology a Science?

Nobody can deny that you are taking a course in psychology, but are you taking a course in science? We think so, but not everyone agrees. Some critics say that psychology isn't really a science, but we think those critics should have a little chat with Timothy Wilson, a psychology professor at the University of Virginia. Here's what he has to say on the subject:

Once, during a meeting at my university, a biologist mentioned that he was the only faculty member present from a science department. When I corrected him, noting that I was from the Department of Psychology, he waved his hand dismissively, as if I were a Little Leaguer telling a member of the New York Yankees that I too played baseball.

There has long been snobbery in the sciences, with the "hard" ones (physics, chemistry, biology) considering themselves to be more legitimate than the "soft" ones (psychology, sociology). It is thus no surprise that many members of the general public feel the same way. But of late, skepticism about the rigors of social science has reached absurd heights.

The U.S. House of Representatives recently voted to eliminate funding for political science research through the National Science Foundation. In the wake of that action, an opinion writer for the Washington Post suggested that the House didn't go far enough. The NSF should not fund any research in the social sciences, wrote Charles Lane, because "unlike hypotheses in the hard sciences, hypotheses about society usually can't be proven or disproven by experimentation."

Lane's comments echoed ones by Gary Gutting in the Opinionator blog of the *New York Times*. "While the physical sciences produce many detailed and precise predictions," wrote Gutting, "the social sciences do not. The reason is that such predictions almost always require randomized controlled experiments, which are seldom possible when people are involved."

This is news to me and the many other social scientists who have spent their careers doing carefully controlled experiments on human behavior, inside and outside the laboratory. What makes the criticism so galling is that those who voice it, or members of their families, have undoubtedly benefited from research in the disciplines they dismiss.

Most of us know someone who has suffered from depression and sought psychotherapy. He or she probably benefited from therapies, such as cognitive behavioral therapy, that have been shown to work in randomized clinical trials.

Problems such as child abuse and teenage pregnancy take a huge toll on society. Interventions developed by research psychologists, tested with the experimental method, have been found to lower the incidence of child abuse and reduce the rate of teenage pregnancies.

Ever hear of stereotype threat? It is the double jeopardy that people face when they are at risk of confirming a negative stereotype of their group. When African American students take a difficult test, for example, they are concerned not only about how well they will do but also about the possibility that performing poorly will reflect badly on their entire group. This added worry has been shown time and again, in carefully controlled experiments, to lower academic performance. But fortunately, experiments have also showed promising ways to reduce this threat. One intervention, for example, conducted in a middle school, reduced the achievement gap by 40%.

If you know someone who was unlucky enough to be arrested for a crime he didn't commit, he may have benefited from social psychological experiments that have resulted in fairer lineups and interrogations, making it less likely that innocent people are convicted.

An often-overlooked advantage of the experimental method is that it can demonstrate what doesn't work. Consider three popular programs that research psychologists have debunked: Critical Incident Stress Debriefing, used to prevent post-traumatic stress disorders in first responders and others who have witnessed horrific events; the D.A.R.E. anti-drug program, used in many schools throughout America; and Scared Straight programs designed to prevent at-risk teens from engaging in criminal behavior.

Timothy D. Wilson is a professor of psychology at the University of Virginia and the author of several popular books, including *Redirect: The Surprising New Science of Psychological Change* (2011).

All three of these programs have been shown, with well-designed experimental studies, to be ineffective or, in some cases, to make matters worse. And as a result, the programs have become less popular or have changed their methods. By discovering what doesn't work, social scientists have saved the public billions of dollars.

To be fair to the critics, social scientists have not always taken advantage of the experimental method as much as they could. Too often, for example, educational programs have been implemented widely without being adequately tested. But increasingly, educational researchers are employing better methodologies. For example, in a recent study, researchers randomly assigned teachers to a program called My Teaching Partner, which is designed to improve teaching skills, or to a control group. Students taught by the teachers who participated in the program did significantly better on achievement tests than did students taught by teachers in the control group.

Are the social sciences perfect? Of course not. Human behavior is complex, and it is not possible to conduct experiments to test all aspects of what people do or why. There are entire disciplines devoted to the experimental study of human behavior, however, in tightly controlled, ethically acceptable ways. Many people benefit from the results, including those who, in their ignorance, believe that science is limited to the study of molecules.

Wilson says that psychology is a science and we agree. But it isn't the same kind of science that, say, physics is, and that's okay. A penguin isn't the same kind of bird that an ostrich is, and yet, it *is* a bird. What makes psychology unique is that it is an especially young science that has taken upon itself the extraordinarily difficult task of understanding the most complex object in the known universe: the human mind. As you'll see in this chapter, it hasn't always been clear how best to do that; and as a result, psychology has had more than its share of revolutions and counter-revolutions, lurching from one approach to another as it has tried to find the right questions to ask and the best ways to answer them. But so what? Trial and error is how rats learn, so why not psychologists? We hope to convince you in this chapter and all the others that psychology has learned a whole lot since the days of William James. Let's see how we do.

The Early 1900s: Psychoanalysis and Behaviourism

Learning Outcomes

- Outline the basic ideas behind Freud's psychoanalytic theory.
- Define the basic idea behind behaviourism.
- Give an example of the principle of reinforcement.

Structuralism and functionalism were important ideas—to the hundred or so people who knew anything about them. While 19th-century academics debated the best way to study the mind, the rest of the world paid approximately no attention. But all that would change in the next century, when a restless neurologist from Vienna and a failed writer from the U.S. state of Pennsylvania would pull psychology in opposite directions and, in the process, take their places on the public stage and eventually become two of the most influential thinkers of all time.

Psychoanalysis: The Mind Does Not Know Itself

While experimental psychologists were trying to understand the mind, physicians were trying to heal it. The French physicians Jean-Martin Charcot (1825–1893) and Pierre Janet (1859–1947) became interested in patients who had an odd collection of symptoms—some were blind, some were paralyzed, and some were unable to remember their identities—but who had no obvious physical illness or injury. What's more, when these patients were hypnotized, their symptoms disappeared, and when the patients emerged from their hypnotic trances, their symptoms returned. Charcot and Janet referred to their patients' condition as **hysteria,** which is *a loss of function that has no obvious physical origin.* What could possibly explain it?

Enter Sigmund Freud (1856–1939), a handsome young Viennese physician in his late 20s who began his career studying the effects of cocaine and the sexual anatomy of eels (though not at the same time). In 1885, Freud went to Paris on a fellowship to study with Charcot, and when he returned to Vienna he began treating patients with hysteria and other "nervous disorders." Freud suspected that many of these patients had suffered a childhood experience so painful that they couldn't allow themselves to remember it. These memories, he reasoned, had been hidden from consciousness and relegated to a place Freud called the **unconscious,** which is *the part of the mind that contains information of which people are not aware.* Freud felt confident that these exiled or "repressed" memories were the source of his patients' hysterical symptoms, and he spent the next several years developing an elaborate theory of the mind known as **psychoanalytic theory,** which is *a general theory that emphasizes the influence of the unconscious on feelings, thoughts, and behaviours.*

Freud's theory was complex, and you'll learn more about it in the Consciousness, Personality, Disorders, and Treatment chapters. But in brief, Freud saw the mind as a set of processes that were largely hidden from our view, and he regarded the conscious thoughts and feelings that the structuralists had worked so hard to identify as little more than flotsam and jetsam, bobbing on the surface of a vast and mysterious ocean. To understand the ocean, Freud suggested, you can't just skim the surface. You have to learn to dive—and when you do, you should expect to encounter some frightening things. For Freud, those frightening things were the person's anxieties and impulses—the fear of death, the desire to kill, forbidden sexual urges, and so on—all of which were lurking beneath the waves.

Freud believed that the only way to confront these denizens of the deep was through **psychoanalysis,** which is *a therapy that aims to give people insight into the contents of their unconscious minds.* A therapeutic session with Sigmund Freud began with the patient lying on a couch and Freud sitting just behind her (probably smoking a cigar). He might ask the patient to describe her dreams or to "free associate" by talking about anything she wished or by responding quickly to a word ("What pops

hysteria A loss of function that has no obvious physical origin.

unconscious The part of the mind that contains information of which people are not aware.

psychoanalytic theory A general theory that emphasizes the influence of the unconscious on feelings, thoughts, and behaviours.

psychoanalysis A therapy that aims to give people insight into the contents of their unconscious minds.

Sigmund Freud's first major book, *The Interpretation of Dreams*, sold only 600 copies in the first eight years. In a letter to a friend, Freud wrote, "Do you suppose that someday a marble tablet will be placed on the house, inscribed with these words: 'In this house on July 24, 1895, the secret of dreams was revealed to Dr. Sigm. Freud'? At the moment I see little prospect of it." But Freud was wrong, and today the site of that house bears a memorial plaque with precisely that inscription.

into your head when I say 'mother?'"). Freud believed that his patients' dreams and free associations offered a glimpse into the contents of their unconscious minds, and that if he could see what was there, he could heal them.

Freud's theories had little impact on some people and an astonishing impact on others. The people on whom they had little impact were the experimental psychologists. William James, for instance, admired some of Freud's insights but thought most of his theorizing was nonsense. "I strongly suspect Freud, with his dream theory, of being a regular hallucine," he wrote in a letter to a friend in 1909. "Hallucine" is an old-fashioned word for "lunatic," so this was not meant as a compliment. Most experimental psychologists shared James's assessment and paid scant attention to Freud's ideas. On the other hand, clinicians paid a lot of attention, and within a decade, Freud's psychoanalytic movement had attracted a virtual army of disciples, including people like Carl Jung (1875–1961) and Alfred Adler (1870–1937). Indeed, Freud's thinking may not have influenced experimental psychology, but it influenced just about everything else in the 20th century—from history and philosophy to literature, art, and popular culture.

Behaviourism: The Mind Does Not Matter

James had a somewhat dim view of Freud, but as the 20th century got rolling, another, much younger psychologist took an even dimmer view of Freud—and of James, Wundt, Titchner, and everyone else who had ever talked about the "science of the mind." That young psychologist had been born in the tiny town of Traveler's Rest, South Carolina, and went on to the University of Chicago to study the behaviour of rats. When his interest changed to the behaviour of people, his changing interest changed the world.

Pavlov and Watson

To John Broadus Watson (1878–1958), everything worth knowing about a rat—how it feeds and mates, how it builds its nest and rears its young—could be known just by watching it, and he wondered why human beings couldn't be known the same way. Why should the study of human behaviour require a bunch of idle speculation about the human mind? Mental life was idiosyncratic, undefinable, and unmeasurable, and Watson felt that if psychology wanted to become a real science, it should

behaviourism An approach to psychology that restricts scientific inquiry to observable behaviour.

These historic photos show Ivan Pavlov and one of his dogs, Baika. Both became quite famous: Pavlov won the Nobel Prize in 1904 for his research on digestion, and Baika was immortalized in the 1971 song "Bitch," by the Rolling Stones ("Yeah when you call my name, I salivate like a Pavlov dog"). There is some debate about who earned the higher honour.

limit itself to studying the things people *do* rather than the things they claim to think and feel. Watson called this idea **behaviourism,** which is *an approach to psychology that restricts scientific inquiry to observable behaviour.*

What might a purely "behaviourist" psychology look like? Watson was impressed by the work of the Russian physiologist Ivan Pavlov (1849–1936), about whom you will hear more in the Learning chapter. Pavlov studied digestion in dogs, and he knew that dogs naturally start salivating when they are presented with food. But one day Pavlov noticed something curious: The dogs in his laboratory had started salivating *before* their food arrived—in fact, they seemed to start salivating when they heard the footsteps of the research assistant who was coming down the hall to feed them! Pavlov suspected that his dogs had come to associate the feeder's footsteps with the arrival of food and that the dogs were responding to the footsteps as though they were food. He devised an experiment to test this hypothesis. First, he sounded a tone every time he fed his dogs. Then, after a few days, he sounded the tone without feeding the dogs. What happened? The dogs salivated when they heard the tone. Pavlov called the tone a *stimulus* and the salivation a *response.*

When Watson read about this research, he quickly realized that these two concepts—stimulus and response—could be the building blocks of a new behaviourist approach. Psychology, Watson argued, should be the scientific study of the relationship between stimuli and responses—nothing less, and certainly nothing more. In his 1919 book, *Psychology from the Standpoint of a Behaviorist,* he wrote: "The goal of psychological study is the ascertaining of such data and laws that, given the stimulus, psychology can predict what the response will be; or, on the other hand, given the response, it can specify the nature of the effective stimulus." He proudly noted that in *his* book "the reader will find no discussion of consciousness and no reference to such terms as sensation, perception, attention, will, image and the like" because "I frankly do not know what they mean, nor do I believe that anyone else can use them consistently."

Watson's arguments were not just persuasive—they were *wildly* persuasive. As one historian wrote, "Some conservatives were [structuralists], some radicals were functionalists, more psychologists were agnostics. Then Watson touched a match to the mass, there was an explosion, and only behaviourism was left" (Boring, 1929). By the 1930s, experimental psychology *was* behaviourism, and structuralism and functionalism had become little more than historical curiosities. But if Watson had convinced psychologists that behaviourism was the one and only proper way to study human behaviour, it would take a skinny kid from Pennsylvania to convince the rest of the world of the same thing.

John B. Watson was the founder of behaviourism, which revolutionized American psychology in the early 20th century. Watson was married, and his academic career was cut short when a scandalous love affair led Johns Hopkins University to dismiss him in 1920. He took a job in advertising, where he spent the remainder of his life working on campaigns for products such as Maxwell House coffee, Johnson & Johnson baby powder, and Pebeco toothpaste.

B.F. SKINNER FOUNDATION

BERNARD HOFFMAN/THE LIFE PICTURE COLLECTION/GETTY IMAGES

B. F. Skinner's books and ideas were influential but often mischaracterized. For instance, when his second child was born, Skinner designed a device called an "air crib" (*right*), which was simply a climate controlled chamber meant to help infants sleep. But when the *Ladies' Home Journal* ran a story entitled "Baby in a Box," outraged readers assumed that Skinner was experimenting on his children at home the way he experimented on rats in his lab and called him "a monster." Skinner died in 1990 at the age of 86, and though psychology had long since renounced its allegiance to behaviourism, he remained a staunch defender. "The appeal to cognitive states and processes is a diversion which could well be responsible for much of our failure to solve our problems. We need to change our behaviour and we can do so only by changing our physical and social environments. We choose the wrong path at the very start when we suppose that our goal is to change the 'minds and hearts of men and women' rather than the world in which they live" (Skinner, 1977).

Skinner

Burrhus Frederick Skinner (1904–1990) grew up in the United States in the state of Pennsylvania and graduated from Hamilton College in 1926 with the intention of becoming a writer. Like many young people with that particular aspiration, he took a job at a bookstore in New York City. After a year or so, the writing wasn't going so well, and one day while browsing the shelves he came across books by Pavlov and by Watson. He was captivated. He abandoned his nascent writing career and, in 1928, enrolled as a graduate student in the psychology department at Harvard University—the same department from which William James had retired 20 years earlier.

Skinner greatly admired the work of Pavlov and Watson, but as he studied them, he started to suspect that their simple stimulus–response psychology was missing something important. Pavlov's dogs lived in a laboratory where they sat around and waited to be fed; but in the real world, animals had to *act* on their environments to find food. How did they learn to do that? Skinner sought to answer this question by building two devices. The first was a cage for laboratory animals that the world would soon come to call a "Skinner Box." The cage had a lever which, when pressed by a hungry rat, delivered food through a tube. The second device was a "cumulative recorder," which recorded the frequency of the rat's lever-presses in real time. These inventions don't sound like much today, but in 1930 they were serious technology. Moreover, they allowed Skinner to discover something remarkable.

Skinner observed that when he put a rat in one of his special cages, it would typically wander around for a while, sniffing and exploring, until it accidentally bumped the lever, causing a food pellet to appear as if by magic. After this happy accident had happened a few times, the rat would suddenly start *pressing* the lever—tentatively at first, then more quickly and more often, until it basically looked like the conga player in a hot Latin jazz band. Unlike Pavlov's dogs, which had learned to monitor their environments and anticipate food, Skinner's rats had learned to *operate* on their environments to *produce* food. When the rat's behaviour produced food (which Skinner called a "reinforcement"), the rat would repeat the behaviour; and when it didn't, the rat wouldn't. Animals do what they are rewarded for doing, Skinner concluded, and he called this the **principle of reinforcement,** which is *a principle stating that any behaviour that is rewarded will be repeated and any behaviour that isn't won't.*

Skinner argued that this simple principle could explain how rats learn to find food, but that it could also explain the most complex human behaviours, and he

principle of reinforcement
A principle stating that any behaviour that is rewarded will be repeated and any behaviour that isn't rewarded won't be repeated.

made it the centrepiece of his theorizing. In a relatively short time, Skinner's theories about the effects of reward came to dominate psychology. Indeed, by the 1940s, the majority of experimental psychologists had been converted to Skinner's "radical behaviourism" and were busy studying how an animal's behaviour was shaped by the consequences it produced. Structuralism, functionalism, and every other -ism that mentioned the human mind had quietly disappeared, and "behaviourism was viewed as the one right way to do psychological science" (Baars, 1986, p. 32).

Like Freud, Skinner's influence went far beyond the ivy-covered walls of the academy. His theories spread across the globe and became the foundation of classroom education, government programs, psychological therapies, and even child-rearing practices. He extended his influence by writing two controversial best-sellers—*Walden II* (1948) and *Beyond Freedom and Dignity* (1971)—in which he laid out his vision for a utopian society in which all human behaviour was controlled by the judicious application of the principle of reinforcement. In these books, Skinner claimed that free will was an illusion, and that the world could solve its most pressing social problems if only it would realize that behaviour is nothing more than the sum of its consequences, that people do what they are reinforced for doing, and that their sense of "choosing" and "deciding" is a dangerous fiction. "In the behaviouristic view," wrote Skinner (1974), "man can now control his destiny because he knows what must be done and how to do it."

As you might expect, Skinner's critics were many and fierce. *Time* magazine featured him on its cover beneath the words "B. F. Skinner Says: We Can't Afford Freedom." One reviewer called his 1971 book "fascism without tears," and another called it "a corpse patched with nuts, bolts and screws from the junkyard of philosophy." Even the normally nonpartisan *TV Guide* got into the act, warning that Skinner was advocating "the taming of mankind through a system of dog obedience schools for all." These attacks were predictable but mistaken. Skinner did not want to turn classrooms into obedience schools or strip citizens of their civil rights. Rather, he simply believed that a scientific understanding of the principles that govern behaviour could be used to improve social welfare and that behaviourists knew what those principles were.

Build to the Outcomes

1. Why did Freud have so little influence on experimental psychology? Where *did* he have influence?

2. What was the key idea behind Watson's behaviourism?
3. How did Skinner's contributions differ from Pavlov's?

The Early 1900s: Resistance to Behaviourism

Learning Outcomes

- Explain why several European psychologists resisted behaviourism.
- Explain why American social psychologists resisted behaviourism.

For the first few decades of the 20th century, behaviourism was king; but not all its subjects were loyal. In fact, several pockets of resistance could be found throughout the kingdom—groups of psychologists who refused to swear allegiance to the crown and whose work would soon foment a counter-revolution. Who were these dissidents?

Gestalt Psychology and Developmental Psychology

Many of them were in Europe. The German psychologist Max Wertheimer (1880–1943) was interested in how people perceive motion, and in one of his experiments, participants were shown two lights that flashed quickly on a screen, one after the other. When the time between the flashes was relatively long, the participant would correctly report that the two lights were flashing in sequence; but when the time between

If you look up at a "news ticker," the words in the headlines seem to be scrolling by, moving from right to left. But they aren't really moving. Rather, contiguous lights are going on and off in rapid succession. This is the phenomenon that the Gestalt psychologist, Max Wertheimer, was studying in Germany in 1912. Wertheimer was Jewish, and in 1933 he and his family fled Europe, emigrating to New York City, where he taught at the New School for Social Research until his death in 1943.

flashes was reduced to about 1/5th of a second, participants reported that a single light was moving back and forth (Fancher, 1979; Sarris, 1989). Wertheimer argued that this "illusory motion" occurs because the mind has theories about how the world works (e.g., "when an object is in one location and then instantly appears in a contiguous location, it probably moved") and it uses these theories to make sense of incoming sensory data. (You've already encountered this idea under the name "philosophical idealism.") In both conditions of Wertheimer's experiment, participants had been shown exactly the same physical stimuli, but they had *seen* different things. Physical stimuli, Wertheimer concluded, are part of the perceptual experience, but the whole is more than the sum of its parts. The German word for "whole" is *gestalt,* and Wertheimer and his colleagues called their approach **Gestalt psychology,** which is *an approach to psychology that emphasized the way in which the mind creates perceptual experience.*

While German psychologists were studying why people sometimes see things that aren't really there, the British psychologist Sir Frederic Bartlett (1886–1969) was studying why people sometimes remember things that didn't really happen. Bartlett asked participants to read stories and then try to remember what they had read after varying amounts of time had passed—from 15 minutes to several years. When Bartlett analyzed their errors, he found that participants often remembered what they had *expected* to read rather than what they actually read, and that this tendency became more pronounced with the passage of time. For example, some of his participants read a story called "War of the Ghosts," which described a group of Native American men hunting seals—an exotic activity that was unfamiliar to most of Bartlett's British participants in 1932. When asked to recount the story later, many of these participants mistakenly said that the men had been fishing—an activity that most of these participants would have *expected* men to do. Bartlett argued that memory is not a simple recording device, but rather, that our minds use their theories of how the world usually works ("Most men fish") to construct our memories of past experience (see The Real World: Beneath the Ocean of Memory).

While German and British psychologists were trying to understand the minds of adults, Swiss psychologist Jean Piaget (1896–1980) was trying to understand the minds of children, which he often did by examining the mistakes they made. For example, in one study, Piaget showed 3-year-olds two equally large mounds of clay and then broke one mound into little pieces. When the children were asked which mound now had "more clay," they typically said that the unbroken one did. By the age of 6 or 7, children no longer made this mistake. Piaget concluded that the mind has theories about how the world works ("Breaking a material object into pieces doesn't change the amount of material in it") and that, because small children have not yet learned these theories, they see the world in

Frederic Bartlett was one of the early-20th-century European psychologists who defied the edicts of behaviourism to study "mentalistic" phenomena such as memory.

Gestalt psychology An approach to psychology that emphasized the way in which the mind creates perceptual experience.

The Real World | Beneath the Ocean of Memory

Sir Frederic Bartlett was interested in how memory worked in "the real world," and despite the ascendance of behaviourism, he spent his life studying it. During World War II, he established the Applied Psychology Unit at the Cambridge Laboratory of Industrial Research in order to help the British military in its efforts to defeat Hitler. So it was more than fitting that nearly a half century after his death, Bartlett's pioneering studies of human memory helped solve a naval mystery.

During World War II, the Australian warship *Sydney* (shown in the photo) battled the German warship Kormoran, and both ships sank in the Indian Ocean. There were just a few survivors, and when they were interrogated months later, each had a different memory of the precise spot where the two ships went down. Despite numerous attempts to locate the ships, the wreckage remained lost at the bottom of the sea.

Then, in 1998, psychologists John Dunn and Kim Kirsner decided to see if they could use Bartlett's research to estimate how the survivors' memories might

have become distorted over time (Dunn & Kirsner, 2011). "What we found was that there was a correspondence—that our data looked like the kind of data that Bartlett had generated in his study," said Dunn (Spiegel, 2011). By combining the survivors' testimony with Bartlett's ideas about memory distortion, the psychologists were able to make a prediction about where the ships might actually be.

"I never really thought that I would ever find out whether it would be right or wrong," said Dunn. But he did find out, because in 2008, a team of shipwreck-hunters found the ships on the ocean floor—right about where the two psychologists had predicted they would be. Despite what his behaviourist colleagues had claimed, Sir Frederic Bartlett's mentalistic research was "real science" after all.

Jean Piaget (*left*) published his first scientific paper at the age of 10. It was about molluscs. A few years later, his interests shifted to people, especially to how they learn to think. Piaget believed the best way to understand children's minds was to ask them questions—a technique that behaviourists considered worse than useless. In 1933, Piaget met a 20-year-old student named Bärbel Inhelder (*right*) and suggested that she drop a sugar cube in a glass of water and ask children to describe what happened. She did, and the experiment led to her first scientific publication. Inhelder went on to earn a PhD and collaborated with Piaget for nearly 50 years. In one of their studies (Piaget & Inhelder, 1974), they showed that young children mistakenly believe that when an object changes shape, it also changes mass—that a ball of clay becomes "more clay" when it is flattened into a log (*middle*). Although the world rightfully remembers the brilliance of Piaget's work, it often forgets that the work—and the brilliance—was also Inhelder's.

a fundamentally different way than adults do. Along with psychologists such as Lev Vygotsky (1896–1934), Piaget helped create an area of experimental psychology called **developmental psychology,** which is *the study of the ways in which psychological phenomena change over the life span.*

In short, while many early 20th-century psychologists (particularly those in the United States) were flying the behaviourist flag, a small number of European psychologists were quietly doing the very thing that behaviourism forbade: studying people's perceptions, memories, and judgements in order to understand the nature of an unobservable entity called the mind.

Social Psychology

Not all the dissidents were in Europe. Some had already come to America. Like many Jews, Kurt Lewin (1890–1947) had fled Europe in the early 1930s when Hitler came to power. He had studied with the Gestalt psychologists and had inherited their interest in mental phenomena, but he was less interested in how people treated moving lights and more interested in how they treated each other. So after taking a job as a professor at MIT, Lewin started the Institute for Group Dynamics and began studying topics such as leadership, communication, attitude change, and racial prejudice. At the heart of his many different research projects was a single, simple idea: Behaviour is not a function of the environment, but of the person's *subjective construal* of the environment. Responses do not depend on stimuli, as the behaviourists claimed; rather, they depend on how people *think* about those stimuli.

Lewin's research and theorizing gave birth to a new area of experimental psychology called **social psychology,** which is *the study of the causes and consequences of sociality.* Although behaviourism was ascendant, Lewin and the other social psychologists pretty much ignored it as they sought to understand how people see the social world. For example, Solomon Asch (1907–1996) told a group of participants about a man who was envious, stubborn, critical, impulsive, industrious, and intelligent—a string of adjectives that went from bad to good. He told another group about a man who was intelligent, industrious, impulsive, critical, stubborn, and envious—exactly the same list of adjectives but in the opposite order. Asch discovered that the participants who heard the man's good traits first liked him more. Asch argued that this "primacy effect" occurred because the early words in each list created a theory ("*Intelligent* and *industrious*—wow, this is a really great guy") that the mind then used to interpret the later words in that list ("*Stubborn* probably means that he sticks to his principles"). Asch's studies led to an avalanche of research on how people draw inferences about others.

developmental psychology The study of the ways in which psychological phenomena change over the life span.

social psychology The study of the causes and consequences of sociality.

Kurt Lewin (*left*) fled Germany the year that Hitler came to power, and he became deeply interested in the psychological differences between autocracy (in which one person has power over all others) and democracy (in which all people share power). In a series of studies, he and his colleagues (Lewin, Lippitt, & White, 1939) assigned 10-year-old boys to work together in autocratic groups on some days and in democratic groups on other days. He observed that "the change from autocracy to democracy seemed to take somewhat more time than from democracy to autocracy" and concluded that this was because "Autocracy is imposed upon the individual. Democracy he has to learn." (Lewin, 1948).

Solomon Asch was one of many social psychologists who were influenced by Gestalt psychology and who resisted the edicts of behaviourism by studying how people think about each other. His early studies of the "primacy effect" showed that early information about a person changes the interpretation of later information, which is why first impressions matter so much. If you saw the photo in the *middle* before the photo on the *right*, you'd form one impression of the man ("He's a fairly straight-ahead guy who likes to party on weekends"); but if you saw the photos in the opposite order, you'd probably form a very different impression ("He's a total hipster who covers his ink for his day job").

Other social psychologists studied similarly "mentalistic" phenomena. Carl Hovland (1912–1961) and Irving Janis (1918–1990) studied how people persuade each other to change their beliefs; Gordon Allport (1897–1967) studied how people form stereotypes; Muzafer Sherif (1906–1988) studied how people create identities based on their social groups; Fritz Heider (1896–1988) studied how people infer each other's intentions; and the list goes on. Beliefs, stereotypes, identities, intentions—concepts like these had been banished from behaviourism but were the heart and soul of social psychology. Understanding the richness and complexity of social life in terms of lever-pressing never struck most social psychologists as a realistic possibility, so they banded together, created their own scientific journals and academic societies, and went their separate way. "The power, the honors, the authority, the textbooks, the money, everything in psychology was owned by the behaviouristic school," psychologist George Miller later remembered (Baars, 1986, p. 203). "Those who didn't give a damn, in clinical or social psychology, went off and did their own thing" What the social psychologists didn't know at the time was that their thing would soon be everybody's thing because the behaviourist kingdom was about to be attacked, invaded, and conquered.

Build to the Outcomes

1. What was similar about Wertheimer's and Bartlett's findings?

2. In what way was Piaget's work incompatible with behaviourism?

3. What basic idea underlay Kurt Lewin's work and why did social psychologists reject behaviourism?

The Late 1900s: The Cognitive Revolution

Learning Outcomes

- Summarize Chomsky's critique of Skinner.

- Explain what cognitive psychology is and how it emerged.

- Explain what evolutionary psychology is and why it emerged.

As the 20th century transitioned from its first to second half, Skinner (1957) published a book called *Verbal Behavior*, in which he offered a behaviourist account of how children learn language. The linguist, Noam Chomsky, decided that there had been enough passive resistance to behaviourism over the last 40 years and that it was time to mount a full-scale attack. In 1959, he published a devastating 33-page critique of Skinner's book, arguing that behaviourist principles could *never* explain some of the most obvious features of language-learning.

For example, children create novel sentences that they have never heard before. How do they produce them? The obvious answer is that they use grammar—a

2 mm

In 1959, the linguist Noam Chomsky (b. 1928) published a critique of Skinner's theory of verbal behaviour that heralded the decline of behaviourism. Chomsky went on to become an outspoken political activist and social critic. Perhaps because his critiques were so stinging, in 2013, a zoologist named a newly discovered species of bee after him. Unlike its namesake, *Megachile chomskyi* is found only in Texas and has an unusually long tongue.

complex set of rules that tells them which of an infinitely large number of possible sentences are permissible ("The girl ran after the ball") and which are not ("The girl after the ball ran"). So how do they learn these rules? Using formal mathematical logic, Chomsky showed that a purely behaviourist account of learning could never explain how children learn grammar. It wasn't just that the behaviourist account *didn't* work; Chomsky showed that it *couldn't* work—not today, not tomorrow, not ever. Chomsky (1959) suggested that it was time to toss behaviourism into the dustbin of history: "If the study of language is limited in these ways," he wrote, "it seems inevitable that major aspects of verbal behaviour will remain a mystery."

The world was listening. But "Out with the old!" is a successful rallying cry only when followed by "In with the new!" and there was indeed something new happening in the 1960s that would spark a flame and push behaviourism to psychology's back burner. It wasn't a new philosophy, scientific discovery, or social movement. It was a mindless, soulless machine.

Cognitive Psychology

ENIAC, the first general-purpose electronic digital computer, was built in 1945. It weighed 30 tonnes, was the size of a small house, cost the equivalent of $7,300,000 (CAD), and didn't do anything that an ordinary person could possibly care about, which meant that it was of interest mainly to a handful of engineers, the U.S. Army, and a few random geeks. But by the 1960s, computers were becoming smaller and more widely available, and a small group of scientists and mathematicians were starting to wonder whether they could ever be made to think. Norbert Wiener (1894–1964) was busy inventing cybernetics, Marvin Minsky (1927–2016) and John McCarthy (1927–2011) were busy inventing artificial intelligence, and Allen Newell (1927–1992) and Herb Simon (1916–2001) were busy teaching computers to play chess. Those early computers performed remarkable calculations at lightning speed, but for psychologists, they did something much more important: They gave them permission once again to talk about the mind. How did they do that?

A computer's observable behaviour is as simple as a rat's. Present the computer with a stimulus ("$2 + 2 = ?$") and it will produce a response ("4"). But unlike a rat, the *way* the computer produces its response is neither hidden nor mysterious. It produces its response by processing information—that is, by encoded information, storing it in memory, retrieving it on demand, and combining it in lawful ways. Computers contain circuits, not ghosts, and those circuits allow computers to do things that from the outside look a whole lot like *learning, reasoning, remembering*—and maybe even *thinking*. If those words could legitimately be used

In this 1946 photo, Marlyn Wescoff (*left*) and Ruth Lichterman (*right*) are programming ENIAC, the world's first digital computer. This revolutionary device did many things, but one of the most important is that it gave psychologists a scientifically respectable way to talk about mental processes.

By the 1960s, computers were getting smaller and cheaper, and they were inspiring psychologists such as Jerome Bruner (*left*) and George Miller (right) to develop a cognitive approach to psychology. "The mind had never disappeared from social or clinical psychology. It was only experimentalists in the United States who really believed that behaviourism would work," Miller (2003, p. 142) later recalled.

to describe the physical information-processing operations that happen inside a machine, why couldn't they also be used to describe the physical information-processing operations that happen inside a brain? If the brain is hardware, then the mind is software—and there is nothing spooky or unmeasurable about the way a software program works.

With the digital computer as their liberator, existence proof, and guiding metaphor, psychologists of the 1950s and 1960s suddenly felt emboldened to study topics that everyone but the dissidents had ignored for decades. Donald Broadbent (1926–1993) began studying how people shift their attention from one stimulus to another; George Miller (1920–2012) began studying how people expand their capacity to process information by combining it into chunks; Jerome Bruner (1915–2016) began studying how a person's desires can shape their perceptions of physical objects; George Sperling (b. 1934) began studying the nature of brief visual memory; and the list went on. This dramatic shift in psychology's orientation came to be known—for better or for worse—as "the cognitive revolution." In 1967, Ulric Neisser (1928–2012) summarized this new way of thinking in a book titled *Cognitive Psychology*, and in so doing, christened a new field. **Cognitive psychology** is *the study of human information-processing*, and for more than 50 years it has been producing deep insights into the nature of the human mind—many of which you will learn about in the chapters to come.

Evolutionary Psychology

Behaviourism set the mind aside and cognitive psychology brought it back. But behaviourism also set something else aside: the past. Behaviourists viewed individuals as blank slates who came into the world with nothing but a readiness to be shaped by their environments. As John Watson (1930, p. 89) wrote:

> Give me a dozen healthy infants, well-formed, and my own specified world to bring them up in and I'll guarantee to take any one at random and train him to become any type of specialist I might select—doctor, lawyer, artist, merchant-chief and, yes, even beggar-man and thief, regardless of his talents, penchants, tendencies, abilities, vocations, and race of his ancestors.

Watson's view was egalitarian, optimistic, and quintessentially American. But it was also wrong. In the 1960s, the psychologist John Garcia (1917–2012) was studying how rats react to radiation sickness. He noticed that his rats instantly learned to associate their nausea with the taste of the food they ate just before

cognitive psychology The study of human information-processing.

John Garcia's (*left*) experiments showed that the ease with which associations are learned can be influenced by an organism's evolutionary history, and E. O. Wilson's (right) research suggested that a great deal of human behaviour might be similarly influenced.

getting sick, and they instantly developed an aversion to that food. On the other hand, no matter how much training they received, his rats could not learn to associate their nausea with a flashing light or the sound of a buzzer. That just didn't make sense. Pavlov had shown that when two stimuli are paired (e.g., a researcher's footsteps and the appearance of food), animals will learn to associate one with the other—and it wasn't supposed to matter whether those stimuli were foods, footsteps, lights, or buzzers. It wasn't *supposed* to matter, but it *did*. What could that mean?

Garcia thought it meant that every organism is evolved to respond to particular stimuli in particular ways—that animals come into the world "biologically prepared" to learn some associations more easily than others. In the real world of forests and sewers, a rat's nausea is *usually* caused by eating spoiled food, and although Garcia's rats had been born in a laboratory and had never eaten spoiled food, their ancestors had. Millions of years of evolution had designed the rat brain so that it would quickly learn to associate an episode of nausea with the taste of food, and that's why rats learned *this* association so much more quickly and easily than they learned others. Rats, it turned out, were not blank slates—so why should psychologists think of people that way?

The biologist E. O. Wilson (b. 1929) was an admirer of Garcia's experiments, and in 1975 he published a book entitled *Sociobiology: The New Synthesis,* in which he brought together research from many areas of science to support his claim that social behaviour had been shaped by natural selection. Although the book primarily discussed the social behaviour of rats, birds, and ants (Wilson's specialty), its brief, final chapter speculated about the evolutionary origins of human behaviour, and that speculation had two consequences. First, it led to a groundswell of protest and criticism by those who felt that Wilson was offering a "biological justification" for sexism and racism, which he clearly was not. Second, it led to a wave of interest from psychologists, who argued that the best way to understand the mind was to understand the specific problems it had been "designed" by evolution to solve. Why did people save their children even when it cost them their own lives? Why did men experience more sexual jealousy than women? Why were people all over the world afraid of snakes and spiders, even if they'd never seen one? Questions like these seemed difficult to answer unless one considered how the hunter-gatherers from whom modern humans descended had coped with the challenges of survival and reproduction.

And so psychologists created a new area of experimental psychology called **evolutionary psychology,** which is *the study of the ways in which the human mind has been shaped by natural selection.* Donald Symons (b. 1942) began studying gender differences in sexual promiscuity; Leda Cosmides (b. 1957) and John Tooby (b. 1952) began studying how people detect cheaters in a social exchange; David Buss (b. 1953) began to study how people select their ideal mate; and the list went on. Evolutionary psychology "is not a specific subfield of psychology, such as the study of vision, reasoning, or social behaviour. It is a way of thinking about psychology that can be applied to any topic within it" (Cosmides & Tooby, 2000, p. 115), and, as you will see in the upcoming chapters, modern psychologists now apply evolutionary thinking to a wide array of topics.

After the Revolution

evolutionary psychology The study of the ways in which the human mind has been shaped by natural selection.

Behaviourism has been a valuable approach that has led to many important discoveries about human behaviour, but it ignored the mind and it ignored the past—both of which are just too important to stay ignored for long. Although many modern psychologists still study how rats learn and how reinforcement shapes behaviour, few are behaviourists who regard humans as blank slates or who believe that mental processes are unmeasurable fictions. In the aftermath of the cognitive revolution, most modern psychologists are concerned with some aspect of mental life, and most agree that mental life is influenced by its evolutionary origins. Ironically, the emergence of cognitive and evolutionary psychology has in some ways brought psychology full circle. Like the structuralists, cognitive psychologists now ask what the mind is like; and like the functionalists, evolutionary psychologists now ask what the mind is for. Apparently, some questions are just too interesting to go gently into that good night.

Build to the Outcomes

1. What was wrong with Skinner's explanation of how children learn language?
2. How did the advent of the computer allow psychologists to talk about the mind?

3. What kind of evidence suggested that behaviourism was wrong to ignore the organism's evolutionary history?

The Early 2000s: New Frontiers

Learning Outcomes

- Define neuroscience and explain how modern psychologists study the brain.
- Define cultural psychology and explain why it matters.

The cognitive revolution fundamentally changed psychology at the close of the 20th century. But science doesn't stand still. In the 20 years since the present century began, psychology has continued to evolve, and several new and exciting areas have emerged. We'll discuss two of them—one that has psychologists looking "down a level" to biology as they search for the neural substrates of mental life, and another that has psychologists looking "up a level" to sociology and anthropology as they seek to understand its cultural origins.

Neuroscience

The mind is what the brain does. But until recently, knowledge of the brain was based primarily on studies of brains that had been damaged. For instance, in 1861, the French physician Paul Broca (1824–1880) performed an autopsy on a man who had

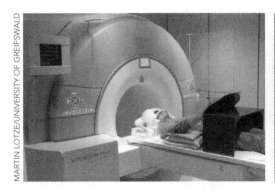

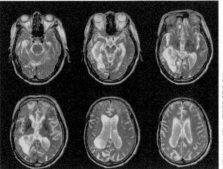

Technologies such as fMRI allow cognitive neuroscientists to determine which areas of the brain are most and least active when people perform various mental tasks, such as reading, writing, thinking, or remembering. The machine (*left*) produces what are commonly called "brain scans" (*right*).

been able to understand words but not produce them; he found damage in a small region on the left side of that man's brain. Broca concluded that the ability to speak somehow depended on this particular region—and the fact that this region is today called Broca's area tells you that he was right. Psychologists learned from brains that were damaged by nature, but they also learned from brains that they damaged themselves. In the 1930s, for instance, the psychologist Karl Lashley (1890–1958) taught rats to run a maze and then surgically damaged different parts of the rats' cerebral cortices and measured changes in their performance. To his surprise, he found that while brain damage impaired performance, it didn't really matter *where* on the cortex the damage was inflicted, which led Lashley to conclude that learning is *not* "localized" or tied to a specific brain area in the same way that language seemed to be.

Of course, damaged brains can only teach us so much. Imagine how hard it would be to figure out how an engine works if all you could do was smash different parts with a hammer and then measure how well the car drove. Fortunately, the last few decades have seen the invention of new technologies that allow psychologists to observe the undamaged brain in action. For example, functional magnetic resonance imaging (fMRI) is a technology that produces the "brain scans" you often hear about in the news. Despite their name, these scans are not photos of the brain; they are maps showing the amount of blood that was flowing in different parts of a person's brain at a particular moment in time. Because neural activity requires oxygen, and because blood supplies it, these scans can tell us which areas of a brain were processing the most information at any particular time, and this has taught us things we could never have learned by merely examining damaged brains.

For instance, Broca would not have been surprised to learn that people using their hands to speak American Sign Language (ASL) show increased neural activity in the same region of the left hemisphere that he identified in 1861. But he might have been surprised by research that has used fMRI to show that this left-hemisphere activity occurs only in the brains of speakers who became deaf in adulthood. Speakers who were *born* deaf show increased neural activity in both the left and right hemispheres, suggesting that they are speaking ASL in a very different way (Newman et al., 2002). The advent of the fMRI and other technologies that you'll learn about in the Neuroscience and Behaviour chapter has given birth to two new areas of psychology: **cognitive neuroscience,** which is *the study of the relationship between the brain and the mind (especially in humans)*, and **behavioural neuroscience,** which is *the study of the relationship between the brain and behaviour (especially in non-human animals)*.

Montreal: A Birthplace of Cognitive Neuroscience

The 1940s and 1950s were great decades for the Montreal Canadiens hockey team. Maurice "Rocket" Richard joined the team in 1942, and played with the Canadiens for 18 seasons—the Canadiens made it to the Stanley Cup Finals 12 times in those

Donald Olding Hebb (1904–1985) was a Canadian psychologist whose work has had a profound impact on cognitive neuroscience. He studied how brain cells (neurons) contribute to psychological processes. Hebb suggested, in a nutshell, that "neurons that fire together, wire together." This famous rule is now widely considered to describe one of the most important cellular mechanisms of learning and memory. Although Hebb made the suggestion in 1949, the biological techniques required to observe it did not become available until the late 1960s.

cognitive neuroscience The study of the relationship between the brain and the mind (especially in humans).

behavioural neuroscience The study of the relationship between the brain and behaviour (especially in non-human animals).

During his life, Wilder Graves Penfield (1891–1976) was called "the greatest living Canadian." He was a neurosurgeon who pioneered the surgical treatment of epilepsy by carefully removing in each patient the specific part of his or her brain causing seizures. In the process, he was able to create the first detailed functional maps of the human brain—locating the regions responsible for feeling touch on different parts of the body, for moving different parts of the body, and for understanding and producing language. He relied on Hebb and Milner to evaluate the psychological effects of the surgeries that he conducted.

Brenda Milner (1918–) is a Canadian psychologist best known for her discovery of the critical importance of a specific part of the brain, the hippocampus, to memory. She studied patients with removals of different parts of the brain (usually to relieve seizure disorders), in order to understand how the different regions contribute to human cognition and behaviour.

years, and won the Cup 8 times. Roch Carrier's iconic story "The Hockey Sweater" pivots on the legend of the Rocket, and vividly describes the passion that Canadians, especially kids, felt for the game.

Just a few kilometres from the Montreal Forum where the Rocket and the Canadiens were making hockey history, a trio of scientists were working together to take the first steps in a new field of inquiry that would come to be known as cognitive neuroscience. They were Donald Hebb, Wilder Penfield, and Brenda Milner.

One of the first graduate students in the new Department of Psychology (founded in 1922) at McGill University was Donald Olding Hebb (1904–1985) from Nova Scotia. Hebb was working as a school principal in a troubled Montreal suburb, and pursuing a master's thesis at McGill part-time. He fell in love with physiological psychology (as cognitive neuroscience was then called) and applied to a PhD program in the United States overseen by Karl Lashley, whom you met earlier in this chapter. After obtaining his PhD (he studied the effects of being reared in darkness on the development of vision in rats), he applied for a job in Montreal working with Penfield, then one of the most famous neurosurgeons in the world. Hebb wanted to study the effects on psychological processes of the very specific brain removals that Penfield was producing. Hebb moved back to Montreal in 1937.

Wilder Penfield (1891–1976) founded the Montreal Neurological Institute in the 1920s, and pioneered the surgical removal of brain tissue to relieve seizure disorders—his approach became known as "the Montreal procedure." By stimulating the brain of awake patients during surgery, Penfield discovered how different parts of the brain support different mental functions and behaviours. You'll learn more about Penfield's work in the Neuroscience and Behaviour chapter.

By 1948, Hebb was chair of the Department of Psychology at McGill, and in 1949 he published his landmark book *The Organization of Behaviour*, in which he lays out his theory of the neural basis of learning. As you will learn in the Memory chapter, this theory was extraordinarily prescient, and Hebb's ideas are now the basis of our understanding of how the physical structure of the brain changes with experience.

Brenda Milner (1918–), a Cambridge-trained psychologist, came to Canada as a bride in 1944. Her husband was an engineer who had been invited to help develop Canada's first nuclear reactors. Milner enrolled as a PhD student with Hebb and worked with Penfield's patients, studying how the removals of specific parts of the brain affected perception and memory. Over her long career, she has made several fundamental contributions to our understanding of how human thinking and behaviour depend on different parts of the brain. She is probably best known for the discovery of the brain basis of long-term memory—a topic that you will learn more about in the Memory chapter.

Cultural Psychology

Although we're all more alike than we are different, human beings vary dramatically in social practices, customs, and ways of living. *Culture* refers to the values, traditions, and beliefs that are shared by a particular group of people, and although we usually think of culture in terms of nationality and ethnicity, it can also be defined by age (e.g., youth culture), sexual orientation (e.g., gay culture), religion (e.g., Jewish culture), occupation (academic culture), and many of the other dimensions on which people differ (see A World of Difference: To Have or Have Not).

A World of Difference | **To Have or Have Not**

When we think about "other cultures," most of us imagine faraway lands filled with people eating exotic foods, wearing unfamiliar clothes, and speaking languages we can't understand. But you don't have to board an airplane to visit a culture much different from your own, because in just about every place on earth, there are two distinctly different cultures living side by side: those who have more—more money, more education, more prestige—and those who have less (Kraus, Piff, & Keltner, 2011). In even the most egalitarian societies, people can be divided into higher and lower social classes, and as it turns out, social class is a powerful determinant of human behaviour.

Consider an example. Because upper-class people have ample material resources, they don't need to depend much on others. When problems arise, upper-class people rely on their bank accounts, whereas lower-class people rely on family, friends, and neighbours with whom they must maintain good relationships. In a way, one of the luxuries that upper-class people enjoy is the luxury of not worrying too much about what others feel or think. Does having that luxury influence their behaviour?

Indeed it does. In laboratory studies, upper-class people often prove to be less generous, less charitable, less trusting, and less helpful towards others (Piff et al., 2010), as well as more likely to lie and cheat for personal gain (Gino & Pierce, 2009; Piff et al., 2012). This "me first" orientation is easy to see outside of the laboratory, too. For example, in one

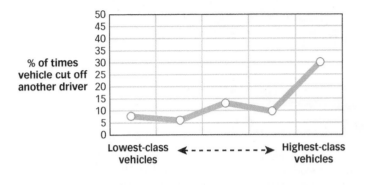

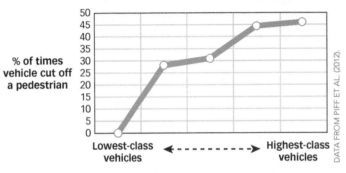

DATA FROM PIFF ET AL. (2012).

study, researchers stood near the intersection of two busy streets and recorded the make, model, and year of the cars that approached. They then watched to see whether the drivers cut off other cars and pedestrians in the intersection. As the two graphs show, the drivers of new, expensive cars were considerably more likely to zip through intersections without regard for others. Is this because being upper-class makes people selfish? Or is it because being selfish makes people upper-class? Some studies suggest that the first explanation is the right one. For instance, when participants in experiments are randomly assigned to *think* of themselves as

upper-class—for instance, when they are asked to compare their incomes to those who have less—they also behave more selfishly (Piff et al., 2012).

Social class matters. So do gender, race, religion, age, and most of the other dimensions on which human beings differ. Psychological science often produces conclusions about "people on average," but it is important to keep in mind that while averages are useful for understanding and predicting behaviour, people actually come in nearly infinite varieties, and the things that distinguish them are often as interesting as the things they have in common.

Scholars have been interested in cultural differences since at least the days of the ancient Greeks, but modern *anthropology* (the study of human societies and cultures) really got its start in the 19th century, when scholars such as Franz Boaz (1858–1942) and James Frazer (1854–1941) began to develop detailed theories to explain the psychological differences they observed among the people of different nations. Some early psychologists such as Wundt recognized the importance of these anthropological insights for psychology, but most 19th-century psychologists were content to ignore them and to assume that what they were studying was universal,

Culture can influence how and what we see. Participants in a study were shown this scene and then another version of this scene in which something was changed. American participants were more likely to spot changes to the red car, but Japanese participants were more likely to spot changes to the buildings.   CULTURE AND POINT OF VIEW, RICHARD E. NISBETT, TAKAHIKO MASUDA, PROCEEDINGS OF THE NATIONAL ACADEMY OF SCIENCES SEP 2003, 100 (19) 11163–11170. © 2003 NATIONAL ACADEMY OF SCIENCES, U.S.A

or that exceptions to the rule didn't really matter. With the rise of behaviourism in the 20th century, culture became a topic of great interest to the social psychologists (e.g., the *Handbook of Social Psychology* has contained chapters on culture ever since 1935), but the rest of psychology ignored it. After all, how important could culture be if rats didn't have any?

All of that has now changed. **Cultural psychology** is *the study of how culture influences mental life,* and in the last few decades, research has shown that those influences can be quite profound. For example, in one study, American and Japanese participants were shown two drawings that differed in a few small details and were then asked to spot the differences. The Americans detected more differences in the foreground objects, whereas the Japanese detected more differences in the background objects (Masuda & Nisbett, 2001). Why? Because while Americans live in an independent and individualistic society, the Japanese live in an interdependent society with many role prescriptions that require them to attend to relationships and context, and this cultural difference appears to influence the kinds of visual information to which they naturally attend. Whereas Westerners tend to process visual information "analytically" by attending to objects in the foreground, Easterners tend to process visual information "holistically" by attending to the background. Because culture can influence just about everything psychologists study, you'll learn about work in cultural psychology in every one of the upcoming chapters.

Build to the Outcomes

1. What kinds of things can be learned from brain scans?
2. What is the difference between behavioural neuroscience and cognitive neuroscience?
3. Give an example of a way in which culture shapes perception.

Becoming a Psychologist

Learning Outcomes

- Describe the diversity of psychology.
- Outline the different kinds of training psychologists may receive.
- Identify the careers available to psychologists.

If you tell someone you're a psychologist, they typically (a) run away or (b) ask if you are analyzing them, and then run away. Although most ordinary people don't know exactly what psychology is, they have a sneaking suspicion that psychologists can look directly into their minds and read their thoughts, especially the sexual ones. In fact, psychologists can't do this, but they can do other things that are much more useful, such as helping people, doing research, and making lists with three examples. Now that you know where psychology came from, and how it got from there to here, we'll close this chapter by looking at modern psychology as a profession.

Who Becomes a Psychologist?

In July of 1892, William James and six other American psychologists decided to form an organization that represented psychology as a profession, and so the American Psychological Association (APA) was born. James and his buddies would not have guessed that today their little club would boast more than 75,000 members—or that in 1988, a second professional organization would form, and that this Association for Psychological Science (APS) would soon expand to 30,000 members. James and his friends would never have guessed how massive their profession would soon become.

cultural psychology The study of how culture influences mental life.

Although many Canadians belong to the APA and/or the APS, Canada also has the Canadian Psychological Association (CPA; like the APA) and the Canadian Society for Brain, Behaviour and Cognitive Science (CSBBCS) for psychologists oriented towards scientific research. Finally, the Canadian Association for Neuroscience–Association Canadienne des Neurosciences (CAN-ACN) is a rapidly growing society of neuroscientists, including many psychologists.

There were no women at APA's founding meeting in 1892, and neither were there any people of colour. But that also changed quickly. Today, about half of all APA and CPA members are women, and the percentage of non-White members continues to grow. In addition, about 70% of the people receiving PhDs in psychology are women (National Science Foundation, 2018), and the number of racial minorities receiving PhDs in psychology continues to rise. Clearly, North American psychology is increasingly reflecting the diversity of society.

How Do People Become Psychologists?

University students who major in psychology usually come away with a bachelor's degree. They can call themselves educated, they can call themselves graduated, and if they really want to, they can call themselves bachelors. But they can't call themselves psychologists. To be called a psychologist requires earning an additional advanced degree. One of the most common of these is the PhD in Psychology. The abbreviation stands for "Doctor of Philosophy" (which actually has nothing to do with philosophy and a lot to do with the history of 19th-century German universities—don't ask).

DATA VISUALIZATION

Psychology: Understanding How to Read and Use (or Misuse!) Data Go to launchpadworks.com.

To earn a PhD, students must attend graduate school, where they take classes and learn to do original research by collaborating with professors. Although William James was able to master the entire field of psychology in just a few years because the body of knowledge was so small, graduate students today typically concentrate their training in a specific area of psychology (e.g., social, cognitive, developmental, or clinical). They spend an average of six years in graduate school before attaining their PhDs (National Science Foundation, 2018), and afterward many go on for more training in a laboratory or a hospital.

All that training is nice, but at some point, parents, spouses, and accountants make graduate students get jobs. For some of those who attain a PhD in psychology, that job is a professorship at a university, where they usually do some combination of teaching and scientific research. You are probably taking a class from one of those people right now, and may we take just a moment to say that he or she has excellent taste in textbooks? But many people who receive a PhD in psychology do not become professors, and instead work primarily as clinical psychologists, assessing or treating people with cognitive or psychological problems. They work in hospitals, schools, clinics, correctional facilities, employee assistance programs, and private offices. Some clinical psychologists have academic positions in universities and are active in both research and clinical practice.

Clinical psychologists often work in partnership with other mental health professionals, such as psychiatrists (who have earned an MD or a Medical Doctor degree) and counselors (who may have earned one of many master's-level degrees). There are many other advanced degrees that allow people to call themselves psychologists and provide therapy, such as the PsyD (Doctor of Psychology) and the MEd (Master of Education). Why does a practice need so many different kinds of people? First, different degrees come with different privileges: People with an MD can prescribe medications, but people with a PhD cannot. Second, most

Figure 1.1

The Major Subfields of Psychology
Psychologists are drawn to many different subfields in psychology. Here are the percentages of people receiving PhDs in various subfields. Clinical psychology makes up over half of the doctorates awarded in psychology.
DATA FROM GRADUATE STUDY IN PSYCHOLOGY, 2016 EDITION. PREPARED BY APA OFFICE OF GRADUATE AND POSTGRADUATE EDUCATION AND TRAINING..

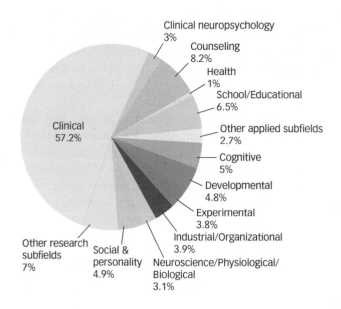

Clinical neuropsychology 3%
Counseling 8.2%
Health 1%
School/Educational 6.5%
Other applied subfields 2.7%
Cognitive 5%
Developmental 4.8%
Experimental 3.8%
Industrial/Organizational 3.9%
Neuroscience/Physiological/Biological 3.1%
Social & personality 4.9%
Other research subfields 7%
Clinical 57.2%

clinical psychologists specialize in treating specific problems such as depression, anxiety, eating disorders, and so on, and they may even specialize in treating specific populations, such as children, older adults, or particular ethnic groups (see **FIGURE 1.1**). It takes a village to look after people's mental health.

So some psychologists become professors, and others become clinical psychologists. Does that account for all of them? Not by a long shot. Psychologists are employed in a wide variety of other settings. For example, *school psychologists* offer guidance to students, parents, and teachers; *industrial/organizational psychologists* help businesses and organizations hire employees and maximize the employees' performances; *sports psychologists* help athletes train and compete; *forensic psychologists* assist attorneys and courts in dealing with crime; *consumer psychologists* help companies develop and market new products; and the list goes on. Indeed, it is difficult to think of any major institution or enterprise that doesn't employ psychologists in some capacity—and that includes municipal police departments and Canada's Olympic women's curling team. The fact is that modern psychologists are a diverse set of women and men who teach, do research, help people in distress, and aid the missions of public and private institutions. If you like what you learn in the upcoming chapters, you might even to decide to become one of them—if only so you can make people run away.

A person earning a PhD in psychology can go on to a wide range of fields, such as these three individuals did (from *left* to *right*): Lynne Madden is a clinical psychologist who works with both individuals and groups. Gloria Balague applies her training as a clinical psychologist to her work with athletes. Lynne Owens Mock directs a community mental health centre .

Build to the Outcomes

1. How has the makeup of psychology changed over the past 150 years?

2. What do most people who earn a PhD in psychology do with that degree?

3. What are some of the careers that psychologists might pursue?

Chapter Review

Psychology's Philosophical Roots

- Psychology is the scientific study of mind and behaviour, and it has deep philosophical roots.

- Some philosophers have embraced philosophical dualism, which is the view that mind and body are fundamentally different things, whereas others have embraced philosophical materialism, which is the view that all mental phenomena are reducible to physical phenomena. Most modern psychologists are philosophical materialists.

- Some philosophers have embraced philosophical realism, which is the view that perceptions of the physical world are produced entirely by information from the sensory organs, whereas others have embraced philosophical idealism, which is the view that perceptions of the physical world are the brain's interpretation of information from the sensory organs. Most modern psychologists are philosophical idealists.

- Some philosophers have embraced philosophical empiricism, which is the view that all knowledge is acquired through experience, whereas others have embraced philosophical nativism, which is the view that some knowledge is innate rather than acquired. Most modern psychologists are philosophical nativists.

The Late 1800s: Towards a Science of the Mind

- In the late 19th century, many European psychologists embraced structuralism, which was an approach to psychology that attempted to isolate and analyze the mind's basic elements.

- Introspection proved to be an unreliable method, however, and structuralism soon gave way to functionalism, which was an approach to psychology that was influenced by Darwin's theory of natural selection, emphasizing the adaptive significance of mental processes.

The Early 1900s: Psychoanalysis and Behaviourism

- In the early 20th century, Sigmund Freud developed psychoanalytic theory, which emphasized the influence of the unconscious on feelings, thoughts, and behaviours. He devised a therapy called psychoanalysis that he believed could help people gain insight into the contents of their unconscious minds.

- Freud had little impact on experimental psychology, but a tremendous impact on the treatment of psychological disorders and on the intellectual climate of the Western world.

- John Watson admired Ivan Pavlov's research on dogs, and he developed behaviourism, which was an approach to psychology that restricted scientific inquiry to observable behaviour. Behaviourism soon came to dominate experimental psychology in North America.

- B. F. Skinner took a behaviourist approach to understanding how organisms learn to operate on their environments, and he developed the principle of reinforcement. He believed this principle could explain complex human behaviour, including how people learn language.

The Early 1900s: Resistance to Behaviourism

- In the first half of the 20th century, behaviourism reigned, but some psychologists resisted it and continued to do research on mentalistic phenomena such as perception, memory, and judgement.

- At the same time, social psychologists also resisted behaviourism and continued to do research on mentalistic phenomena such as beliefs, attitudes, stereotypes, identity, and intention.

The Late 1900s: The Cognitive Revolution

- In the 1950s and 1960s, Noam Chomsky's critique of Skinner's theory of language, as well as the advent of the digital computer, helped ignite the "cognitive revolution." The emergence of cognitive psychology allowed psychologists to use the language of information processing to once again study mentalistic phenomena.

- In the 1970s and 1980s, psychologists began to incorporate theories from evolutionary biology into their work, which led to the emergence of evolutionary psychology.

The Early 2000s: New Frontiers

- In the 21st century, several new areas of psychology have emerged. Cognitive neuroscientists study the relationship between psychological processes and neural activity, behavioural neuroscientists study the relationship between behaviour and neural activity, and cultural psychologists study the ways in which culture influences mental life.

Becoming a Psychologist

- Psychology is a diverse science. In North America, women earn more than half of all PhDs in psychology.

- To become a psychologist, one must attain an advanced degree. Many psychologists become clinicians, but some become professors; and many are employed in government, industry, and a variety of other enterprises and institutions.

Key Concept Quiz

1. The philosophical idea that all mental processes in the mind are reducible to physical processes in the brain is known as
   a. philosophical materialism.
   b. philosophical nativism.
   c. philosophical empiricism.
   d. philosophical realism.

2. The idea that complex mental phenomena like conscious awareness can be understood by breaking them down into elemental parts and studying these is called
   a. idealism.
   b. structuralism.
   c. behaviourism.
   d. Gestalt psychology.

3. Which of these people most influenced functionalism?
   a. Skinner
   b. Freud
   c. Darwin
   d. Pavlov

4. Psychoanalysis is meant to help people
   a. isolate the basic elements of conscious experience.
   b. respond to stimuli.
   c. obtain reinforcements.
   d. attain insight into their unconscious minds.

5. John Watson thought behaviourism
   a. was the right way to study animals but the wrong way to study people.
   b. should consider the evolutionary history of the organism.
   c. would make psychology an objective science.
   d. could provide glimpses into a person's unconscious mind.

6. B. F. Skinner's principle of reinforcement explains
   a. the emergence of cultural psychology.
   b. why lights can appear to be moving even when they really aren't.
   c. why structuralism failed.
   d. how behaviour is shaped by its consequences.

7. The American psychologists who resisted behaviourism in the early 1900s were
   a. social psychologists.
   b. neuroscientists.
   c. evolutionary psychologists.
   d. philosophical dualists.

8. The cognitive revolution was made possible by
   a. Chomsky's critique of Pavlov.
   b. the advent of the digital computer.
   c. the invention of fMRI.
   d. the invention of the Skinner box.

9. John Garcia's experiments showing that rats quickly learn to associate nausea with the taste of food
   a. were important to establishing behaviourism in America.
   b. led to his dismissal from his university.
   c. helped bring about evolutionary psychology.
   d. helped bring about cultural psychology.

10. Two new areas of psychology that have emerged in the 21st century are
    a. behavioural neuroscience and cultural psychology.
    b. cognitive neuroscience and evolutionary psychology.
    c. Gestalt psychology and developmental psychology.
    d. social psychology and cultural psychology.

 **LearningCurve**
macmillan learning

Don't stop now! Quizzing yourself is a powerful study tool. Go to LaunchPad to access the LearningCurve adaptive quizzing system and your own personalized learning plan. Visit launchpadworks.com.

Key Terms

psychology (p. 2)

philosophical dualism (p. 3)

philosophical materialism (p. 3)

philosophical realism (p. 4)

philosophical idealism (p. 4)

philosophical empiricism (p. 5)

philosophical nativism (p. 5)

reaction time (p. 6)

structuralism (p. 6)

introspection (p. 6)

functionalism (p. 8)

natural selection (p. 8)

hysteria (p. 10)

unconscious (p. 10)

psychoanalytic theory (p. 10)

psychoanalysis (p. 10)

behaviourism (p. 12)

principle of reinforcement (p. 13)

gestalt psychology (p. 15)

developmental psychology (p. 17)

social psychology (p. 17)

cognitive psychology (p. 20)

evolutionary psychology (p. 22)

cognitive neuroscience (p. 23)

behavioural neuroscience (p. 23)

cultural psychology (p. 26)

Changing Minds

1. While scrolling through your newsfeed, you come across a story describing some research that shows that when people feel love, particular regions of their brains "light up." You scroll down and see that someone has commented: "This is crazy. Love is more than brain chemistry. It's about the heart!" Given what you know about materialism, dualism, and fMRI, how would you respond?

2. May 6 is Sigmund Freud's birthday. Someone will surely notice this and describe him on social media as "the father of modern psychology." How accurate is that title? Who else might deserve it more?

3. One of your friends is a chemistry major. She sees your psychology textbook on your desk and starts flipping through it. "Psychology is just so stupid," she says. "I mean, how can it claim to be a science when it studies things no one can see, like thoughts and memories and emotions? Why don't they just stick to studying what they can actually measure?" Given what you know about the history of psychology, what would you tell your friend?

4. High school students are touring your campus today—and you get to meet them. Yippie! One of them tells you he's considering a major in psychology. "I figure I can get my degree in four years and then start doing therapy." Given what you've learned about careers in psychology, what should you tell him?

Answers to Key Concept Quiz

1. a; 2. b; 3. c; 4. d; 5. c; 6. d; 7. a; 8. b; 9. c; 10. a.

LaunchPad features the full e-book of *Psychology*, the LearningCurve adaptive quizzing system, videos, and a variety of activities to boost your learning. Visit LaunchPad at launchpadworks.com.

Methods in Psychology

WHEN LOUISE HAY DIED IN 2017, her net worth was estimated at around $50 million. Her most popular book, *You Can Heal Your Life*, had sold over 35 million copies. In it, she explained that everything that happens to people—including diseases, accidents, and other misfortunes—is a result of the thoughts they choose to think. She claimed that she had been diagnosed with incurable cancer but had cured herself by changing the way she thought, and she amassed a fortune by promising people that they could learn to do the same thing if only they attended one of her seminars or bought a few of her videos or books. In a 2010 television interview with one of the authors of this textbook, Hay was asked why she believed her techniques were actually effective.

> **Gilbert:** How do you know what you're saying is right?
> **Hay:** Oh, my inner ding.
> **Gilbert:** Ding?
> **Hay:** My inner ding. It speaks to me. It feels right or it doesn't feel right. Happiness is choosing thoughts that make you feel good. It's really very simple.
> **Gilbert:** But I hear you saying that even if there were no proof for what you believed, or even if there were scientific evidence against it, it wouldn't change?
> **Hay:** Well, I don't believe in scientific evidence, I really don't. Science is fairly new. It hasn't been around that long. We think it's such a big deal, but it's, you know, it's just a way of looking at life.

Louise Hay said that she didn't "believe in scientific evidence"—but what could that possibly mean? After all, if her techniques really did cure cancer, then cancer victims who practice her techniques should on average live longer than those who don't. That isn't "a way of looking at life." It's just plain old common sense—exactly the kind of common sense that lies at the heart of science. Science tells us that there is one and only one way to know for sure whether claims like Louise Hay's are true, and that's to

Louise Hay claimed that people can cure cancer with their minds. How can we tell whether her claim is right or wrong?

gather evidence. Sorry, but inner dings don't count. If we really want to know what's true about the world, then we actually have to go there and take a look around.

But what exactly should we be looking for? Should we show up at a "Hay House" seminar and ask people in the audience whether they think they've been healed by her techniques? Should we examine the medical records of people who have and haven't bought one of her books? Should we invite people to sign up for a class that teaches her techniques and then wait to see how many of them get cancer over the next few years? All of these may strike you as fairly reasonable ways to test Louise Hay's claim, but in fact, every one of them has important shortcomings that would make it impossible to draw conclusions from the results. It turns out that there are a few very good ways to test claims about the world and a whole lot of bad ways, and the main point of this chapter is to teach you the difference between them. Scientists have developed powerful tools for determining when a claim is right and when it is wrong, and these tools are what makes science so different from all other ways of knowing. As the British philosopher Bertrand Russell (1945, p. 527) wrote, "It is not what the man of science believes that distinguishes him, but how and why he believes it." That goes for women of science too.

WE'LL START BY EXAMINING THE GENERAL PRINCIPLES THAT GUIDE scientific research and distinguish it from other human enterprises. Next, we'll see how the methods of psychology allow us to answer two basic questions: What do people do, and why? Psychologists answer the first question by measuring stuff, and they answer the second question by looking for relationships between the stuff they measure. We'll see that scientific evidence allows us to draw certain kinds of conclusions but not others, and that thinking critically about scientific evidence doesn't come naturally to most people. Finally, we'll consider some of the unique ethical questions that confront scientists who study human beings and other animals.

Empiricism: How to Know Stuff

Learning Outcomes

- Explain why direct observation is essential to an accurate understanding of nature.

- Outline the process of the scientific method.

- Identify the challenges to studying human behaviour.

empiricism The belief that accurate knowledge can be acquired through observation.

When ancient Greeks sprained their ankles, caught the flu, or accidentally set their beards on fire, they had to choose between two kinds of doctors. The dogmatists (from *dogmatikos*, meaning "belief") thought the best way to understand illness was to develop theories of the body's functions, and the empiricists (from *empeirikos*, meaning "experience") thought the best way was to watch sick people and see what happened. The rivalry between these two schools of medicine didn't last long because the people who went to see dogmatists tended to die a lot, which was bad for business. That's why today we use the word *dogmatism* to describe people's tendency to cling to their beliefs and assumptions and we use the word **empiricism** to describe *the belief that accurate knowledge can be acquired through observation*. The fact that we can answer questions about the natural world by observing probably seems obvious to you, but this obvious fact has only recently gained wide acceptance. For most of human history, people trusted authority to provide answers to life's important questions, and it is only in the last millennium (and especially in the past three centuries) that people have begun to trust their eyes and ears more than their elders.

The Scientific Method

Empiricism is the backbone of the **scientific method,** which is *a procedure for using empirical evidence to establish facts.* Essentially, the scientific method suggests that when we have an idea about how something in the world works—about how bats navigate, or where the moon came from, or why people can't forget traumatic events—we must go out into the world, make observations, and then use those observations to determine whether our idea is true. Scientists generally refer to these "ideas about how something works" as **theories,** which are *hypothetical explanations of natural phenomena.* So, for instance, we might theorize that bats navigate by making sounds and then listening for the echo, or that the moon was formed when a small planet collided with the earth, or that the brain responds to traumatic events by producing chemicals that facilitate memory. Each of these theories is an explanation of how something in the natural world works and why it works that way.

How do we decide if a theory is right? A good theory makes specific predictions about what we should observe in the world if the theory is true. For example, if bats really do navigate by making sounds and then listening for echoes, then deaf bats should not be able to navigate very well. That "should" statement is technically known as a **hypothesis,** which is *a falsifiable prediction made by a theory.* The word *falsifiable* is a critical part of that definition. Some theories, such as "Things happen the way they do because that's how God wants it," do not tell us what we should observe if the theory is true; therefore, no amount of observation can ever falsify them. That doesn't mean the theory is wrong. It just means that we can't use the scientific method to evaluate its veracity.

So, good theories give rise to hypotheses that can be falsified, and when that happens the theory is proved wrong. But how can we prove it *right*? Alas, although a theory can be proved wrong, it can *never* be proved right. For example, imagine that you decided to test the theory that bats navigate by using sound. The theory gives rise to a hypothesis: Deaf bats should not be able to navigate. Now, if you observed a deaf bat navigating perfectly well, your observation would be clearly inconsistent with the predictions of your theory, which must therefore be wrong. On the other hand, if you observed deaf bats navigating badly, then your observation would be perfectly consistent with the predictions of your theory—but it would not prove your theory right. Why? Because even if you didn't see a deaf bat navigating perfectly well today, it is always possible that you will see one tomorrow, or the day after that, or maybe 30 years from now. You did not observe every bat that has ever been and will ever be, so even if today's observation didn't prove your theory wrong, there is always a chance that some future observation will. The point here is that observations that are consistent with a theory can increase our confidence that the theory is right, but they can never make us absolutely sure it is right. So the next time you see a headline that says "Scientists prove theory *X*," you are hereby authorized to roll your eyes. And make a noise like a bat.

The scientific method tells us that the only way to learn the truth about the world is to develop a theory, derive a falsifiable hypothesis from it, and then test that hypothesis by observing the world—or, in fancier language, gathering empirical evidence. You now know all about theories and hypotheses, so let's see what this "evidence gathering" stuff actually entails.

The Art of Looking

For centuries, people argued about whether all four of a horse's feet ever leave the ground at the same time. They would all go out and watch the same horse

The astronomer Galileo Galilei (1564–1642) was excommunicated and sentenced to prison for sticking to his empirical observations of the solar system rather than accepting the teachings of the Church. In 1597 he wrote to his friend and fellow astronomer Johannes Kepler (1571–1630), "What would you say of the learned here, who, replete with the pertinacity of the asp, have steadfastly refused to cast a glance through the telescope? What shall we make of this? Shall we laugh, or shall we cry?" As he later learned, the answer was cry.

Classical thinkers such as Euclid and Ptolemy believed that our eyes work by emitting rays that go out and "touch" the objects we see. But the Persian genius, Ibn al-Haytham (Alhazen) (965–1039), argued that if this theory was right, then when we open our eyes it should take longer to see something far away than something nearby. And guess what? It doesn't. The classical theory of vision gave rise to a hypothesis, that hypothesis was disconfirmed by observation, and an ancient theory vanished in the blink of an eye.

scientific method A procedure for using empirical evidence to establish facts.

theory A hypothetical explanation of a natural phenomenon.

hypothesis A falsifiable prediction made by a theory.

If anyone ever tells you that horses keep one foot on the ground at all times, just say nay, and then trot out Frames 2 and 3 of this historic series of photos by Eadweard Muybridge (1830–1904).

People are highly reactive—that is, they behave differently when they know they are being observed. For example, if actress Mila Kunis had realized that a photographer was lurking nearby, she might have found a more discreet way to express her opinion of passion fruit tea.

empirical method A set of rules and techniques for observation.

run, and then some would swear that all four feet left the ground at the same time, some would swear that they didn't, and some would just swear. Then, in 1877, a man named Eadweard Muybridge invented a technique for taking photographs in rapid succession. His photos showed that when horses gallop . . . why yes, they really do go airborne! And that was that. Never again did a group of friends get to engage in a flying-horse debate because Muybridge's pictures had settled the matter forever.

But why did it take so long? Human beings had been watching horses gallop for centuries, so why were some of them sure that horses left the ground completely while others were equally sure they didn't? Because as wonderful as human eyes may be, there are many things they see inaccurately, and many things they don't see at all. From where you are sitting right now, the earth looks perfectly flat when it is in fact imperfectly round. From where you are sitting right now, you can't see a microbe, or ultraviolet light, or the 14 moons of Neptune, but all of them are real and all of them are there. As Muybridge knew, empiricism is the right approach, but to do it properly requires more than a set of eyes. It requires an **empirical method,** which is *a set of rules and techniques for observation.*

In many sciences, the word *method* refers to technologies that enhance the powers of the senses. Biologists use microscopes and astronomers use telescopes because the things they want to observe are invisible to the naked eye. Human behaviour, on the other hand, is easy to see, so you might expect psychology's methods to be relatively simple. But they aren't simple, and that's because human beings have three qualities that make them more difficult to study than either cells or stars. First, people are highly *complex*. Although scientists can describe the birth of a star or the death of a cell in exquisite detail, they can barely begin to say how the 100 billion interconnected neurons that constitute the human brain give rise to the thoughts, feelings, and actions that are psychology's core concerns. Second, people are highly *variable*. One ribosome may be a lot like another, but no two people ever do, say, think, or feel exactly the same thing under exactly the same circumstances. Third, people are highly *reactive*. A cesium atom oscillates at the same rate regardless of who might be watching, but people tend to think, feel, and act differently when they are, or are not, being observed.

The fact that human beings are highly complex, variable, and reactive presents a challenge to the scientific study of their behaviour. Psychologists have met this challenge by developing two kinds of methods: *methods of observation*, which allow them to determine what people do, and *methods of explanation*, which allow them to determine why people do it. We'll examine each of these methods in the sections that follow.

Build to the Outcomes

1. What is the scientific method?
2. What is the difference between a theory and a hypothesis?
3. Why can theories be proven wrong but not right?
4. What makes human behaviour especially difficult to study scientifically?

A World of Difference | Are Heroes and Sheroes Divided by Zeroes?

Galileo, Newton, Mendel, Darwin, Faraday, Einstein, Turing, Tesla, Skinner—what do all these people have in common? First, they were all brilliant scientists. And second, they were all men. The history of science is pretty much the history of smart men having big ideas and making big discoveries. So where are all the women? There are two answers to this question. The first is that, until quite recently, educational and employment opportunities for women were limited. For most of history, women were either subtly discouraged or actively prohibited from studying science—and you really can't win the Nobel Prize in Physics if they won't let you take algebra. In 1914, the sociologist Leta Hollingworth cheekily noted that "women bear and rear the children, and this has had as an inevitable sequel the occupation of housekeeping, a field where eminence is not possible." Women, it seems, have been right where society put them: in the kitchen.

The second answer is that men and women may have different interests and talents, and the interests and talents that men have may be the ones people need to become great scientists. Is there any truth to this suggestion? A few years ago, a group of male and female scientists got together, surveyed all the scientific evidence on this topic, and drew a striking conclusion: Yes, they concluded, the evidence does show that men and women differ with regard to certain interests and talents (Halpern et al., 2007). First, men are often more interested in the topics that scientists study. Second, men and women differ in scientifically relevant abilities: Specifically, men are more *variable* than women on most measures of quantitative ability (the ability to use numbers) and visuo-spatial ability (the ability to use images), both of which are important to success in many sciences.

Being more variable doesn't mean being better, however. It means that although men and women have the same average amount of talent on these dimensions, there are more men at both the very lowest and very highest ends of the spectrum. If great scientists tend to come from the highest end of the spectrum, then men will naturally be overrepresented among great scientists. In fact, recent data show that while men are overrepresented in scientific fields that are "math intensive"—such as geoscience, engineering, economics, mathematics, computer science, and the physical sciences—they are not overrepresented in scientific fields that place less emphasis on math, such as biology, psychology, and sociology (Ceci et al., 2014). Indeed, while women earn fewer than 20% percent of the degrees in computer science and engineering, they earn the *majority* of degrees in the life and social sciences. With regard to having different interests, it is worth noting that the largest gender gaps in the "hard sciences" emerge in the nations with the *highest* gender equality, suggesting that when women have a choice, they tend not to choose those fields (Stoet & Geary, 2018).

So yes, men are more interested in certain topics and are more variable on certain dimensions. Why? Is it because there is some innate difference in the structure or function of the male and female brains, or is it because men are encouraged to develop their interests and hone their quantitative skills by parents who buy them video games instead of dolls, and by teachers who encourage them to join the math team rather than the debate team? Once again, an expert review of the evidence concludes that "sex differences in spatial and mathematical reasoning need not stem from biological bases, that the gap between average female and male math ability is narrowing (suggesting strong environmental influences), and that sex differences in math ability at the right tail [which is the "high" end of the ability spectrum] show variation over time and across nationalities, ethnicities, and other factors, indicating that the ratio of males to females at the right tail can and does change" (Ceci et al., 2014, p. 75). In other words, men may be more interested in certain scientific topics and may be more likely to be unusually talented (or untalented!) when it comes to math, but there is *no compelling evidence to suggest that these differences are innate.*

We agree with the experts who concluded that "there are no single or simple answers to the complex questions about sex differences in science and mathematics" (Halpern et al., 2007, p. 75). But we feel confident that someday a brilliant young psychological scientist will discover the true answers to these complex questions. We hope to be here when she does.

In 1834, William Whewell coined the word "scientist" to describe a remarkable astronomer, physicist, and chemist named Mary Somerville. Few people remember that the world's first scientist was a woman.

HISTORIA/SHUTTERSTOCK

Methods of Observation: Finding Out What People Do

When you observe an apple, your brain uses the pattern of light that enters your eyes to make inferences about the apple's colour, shape, and size. That kind of observation is good enough for buying fruit, but not for doing science. Why? First, everyday observations are often *inconsistent*: The same apple can appear red in the daylight and crimson at night, or spherical to one person and elliptical to another. Second, everyday observations are often *incomplete,* which is to say that they simply can't provide a lot of the information we might want. No matter how long and hard you stared at an apple, you would never be able to determine its melting point or pectin content. Luckily, scientists have devised techniques that allow them to overcome these limitations. In the sections that follow, we'll first see how psychologists measure the things that everyday observation misses (Measurement), and then we'll see what psychologists do with their measurements once they've made them (Description).

Measurement

We live in a world of clocks and calendars, scales and yardsticks, odometers and thermometers. Measurement is not just a part of modern science, it is a part of modern life. But regardless of what we want to measure—the intensity of an earthquake, the size of an elephant, or the attitude of a registered voter—we must always do two things. First, we must *define* the property we want to measure, and second, we must find a way to *detect* it (**FIGURE 2.1**). For example, to measure a person's level of happiness, we would start by generating an **operational definition,** which is *a description of a property in measurable terms.* So, for example, we might operationally define happiness as "a person's self-assessment" or "the amount of dopamine in a person's brain" or "the number of times a person smiles in an hour." Once we had this definition in hand, we would need to find a detector—that is, some sort of instrument or device that can detect the property as we just defined it—such as a rating scale (to detect a person's self-assessment), a carbon electrode (to detect dopamine in the brain), or an electromyograph (to detect a smile).

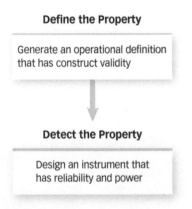

Define the Property

Generate an operational definition that has construct validity

Detect the Property

Design an instrument that has reliability and power

Figure 2.1
Measurement There are two steps in the measurement of a property.

operational definition A description of a property in measurable terms.

construct validity The extent to which the thing being measured adequately characterizes the property.

power A detector's ability to detect the presence of differences or changes in the magnitude of a property.

reliability A detector's ability to detect the absence of differences or changes in the magnitude of a property.

What makes a good operational definition? **Construct validity** is *the extent to which a videocamera aimed at a face adequately characterizes the property.* For example, most of us would consider the frequency with which a person smiles to be a reasonable way to operationally define the property called "happiness" because we all know from our own experience that happy people tend to smile more than unhappy people do. Do they also eat more or talk more or spend more money? Well, maybe. But then again, maybe not. And that's why most psychologists would consider "smiles per hour" to be a reasonable way to operationally define happiness, but they would not feel the same way about "number of chocolates eaten" or "number of words spoken" or "number of dollars spent." To a large extent, construct validity is in the eye of the beholder, and an operational definition is said to have construct validity when most beholders agree that it adequately characterizes a property.

What makes a good detector? The two key features of a good detector are **power,** which refers to *a detector's ability to detect the presence of differences or changes in the magnitude of a property,* and **reliability,** which refers to *a detector's ability to detect the absence of differences or changes in the magnitude of a property.* If a person smiles a bit more often on Tuesday than on Wednesday, a powerful smile-detector will detect different amounts of smiling on those two days. If a person smiles exactly as much on Wednesday as she did on Tuesday, then a reliable smile-detector will detect identical amounts of smiling on those two days. A good detector detects differences or changes in the magnitude of a property when they do exist (power), but not when they don't (reliability).

Power and Reliability at the Olympics
Usain Bolt ran the 100-meter race in 9.58 seconds, and Yohan Blake ran it in 9.75 seconds. If judges did not have powerful speed-detectors, they might have mistakenly concluded that the two men were tied. Timing is also an important measurement in ice dancing, but competitors are measured on other qualities related to athleticism and artistry as well. Champion ice dancers Tessa Virtue and Scott Moir clearly measure up.

Demand Characteristics: Doing What Is Expected

Once we have an operational definition that has construct validity, and a detector that is both powerful and reliable, are we *finally* ready to measure some behaviour? Yes—as long as we want to measure the behaviour of a worm, a thunderstorm, a stock market, or anything else that doesn't care about being observed. But if we want to measure the behaviour of a human being, then we still have some work to do because when human beings know they are being observed, they will often try to behave as they think the observer wants or expects them to. **Demand characteristics** are *those aspects of an observational setting that cause people to behave as they think someone else wants or expects.* If a friend asked, "Do you think I'm smart?" you would probably say yes whether you meant it or not. You know what your friend is hoping to hear and so you dutifully supply it. Similarly, if a researcher asked, "Do you think it is wrong to cheat on exams?" then you would probably say yes as well, if only because you know that's the response the researcher expects of you. A study that asked such a question would be said to have demand characteristics because the question "demands" or requires participants to give a response that may or may not reflect his or her true feelings. How can we avoid demand characteristics?

Naturalistic Observation One way that psychologists avoid demand characteristics is by observing people without their knowledge. **Naturalistic observation** is *a technique for gathering scientific information by unobtrusively observing people in their natural environments.* Naturalistic observation has shown that the biggest groups leave the smallest tips in restaurants (Freeman et al., 1975), that golfers are most likely to cheat when they play several opponents at once (Erffmeyer, 1984), that men usually don't approach the most beautiful woman at a club (Glenwick, Jason, & Elman, 1978), and that Olympic athletes smile more when they win the bronze medal than the silver medal (Medvec, Madey, & Gilovich, 1995). Each of these conclusions is the result of measurements made by psychologists who observed people who didn't know they were being observed by psychologists. It seems unlikely that the psychologists could have made the same observations if the diners, golfers, clubbers, and athletes had realized that they were being observed.

demand characteristics Those aspects of an observational setting that cause people to behave as they think someone else wants or expects them to.

naturalistic observation A technique for gathering scientific information by unobtrusively observing people in their natural environments.

Countries that have a faster pace of life tend to have higher rates of heart disease. How do researchers measure the "pace of life"? They make naturalistic observations—in this case, by measuring the average walking speed of pedestrians in different cities. By the way, the fastest pedestrians are the Irish (*left*) and the slowest are the Romanians (*right*) (Levine & Norenzayan, 1999).

Unfortunately, naturalistic observation isn't always practical. First, some events just don't occur naturally. If we wanted to know whether people who have undergone sensory deprivation perform poorly on fine-motor tasks, we would have to stand on the street corner for a very long time before we just so happened to spot a bunch of blindfolded people with earplugs trying to text with one hand. Second, some events can only be observed through direct interaction, such as by conducting an interview or by hooking someone up to a heart rate monitor. If we wanted to know how often people worried about dying, how accurately they remember their high school graduations, or how much electrical activity their brains produce when they feel jealous, then hiding in the bushes and watching them with binoculars just won't do. What can we do instead?

Privacy and Control When naturalistic observation isn't possible, psychologists have a number of other techniques for avoiding demand characteristics. For instance, people are less likely to be influenced by demand characteristics when they can't be identified as the authors of their actions, and psychologists often take advantage of this fact by allowing people to respond privately (e.g., by having them complete questionnaires when they are alone) and/or anonymously (e.g., by not collecting personal information, such as people's names or addresses). In addition, psychologists may avoid demand characteristics by measuring behaviours that are not under a person's voluntary control. If a psychologist asked whether you were interested in stupid celebrity gossip, you might lie and say no. Because you can control what you say, that measure is susceptible to demand. But if the psychologist instead gauged your interest in stupid celebrity gossip by measuring the dilation of your pupils as you paged through the latest issue of *People* magazine, there would be no way for you to hide the fact that you are deeply interested in the details of Kim and Kanye's latest pregnancy. C'mon. You know you are.

Unawareness One of the best ways to avoid demand characteristics is to make sure that the people who are being observed are unaware of the true purpose of the observation. People can't try to behave how they should behave if they don't *know* how they should behave. For example, if you didn't know that a psychologist was studying the effects of classical music on mood, you wouldn't feel obligated to smile when Bach's *Concerto #1 in F Major* started playing in the background. That's why psychologists typically don't reveal the true purpose of an observation to the people being observed until the study is over. And it's also why psychologists sometimes mislead people by telling them that they are studying one thing when they are really studying another, or by giving people pointless tasks or asking pointless questions simply so that people can't easily guess the study's true purpose. (We will discuss the ethical implications of misleading people later in this chapter.)

Observer Bias: Seeing What Is Expected

More than half a century ago, students in a psychology class were asked to measure the speed with which a rat learned to navigate a maze (Rosenthal & Fode, 1963). Some students were told that their rat had been specially bred to be a slow learner while others were told that their rat had been specially bred to be a fast learner. The truth was that the rats were all exactly the same breed. Nonetheless, students who *thought* they were measuring the speed of a slow learner reported that their rats took 3.47 minutes to navigate the maze, whereas students who *thought* they were measuring the speed of a fast learner reported that their rats took 2.35 minutes to navigate the maze. In other words, the measurements revealed precisely what the students expected, even though those expectations had no basis in reality, and the students did not realize that their measurements were being affected by anything other than the rat's speed.

There are two reasons why this happened. First, *expectations can influence observations*. Just think about all the decisions the students had to make when they were measuring the speed of their rat. If a rat puts one leg over the finish line, does that count as finishing, or does it have to have all four legs over the line? If a rat falls asleep, should the stopwatch keep running or should it be stopped until the rat wakes up?

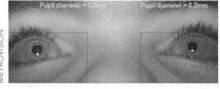

One way to avoid demand characteristics is to measure behaviours that people are unable or unlikely to control. For example, our pupils contract when we are bored (top photo) and dilate when we are interested (bottom photo), which makes pupillary dilation a useful measure of a person's level of engagement in a task.

If a rat runs the maze in 18.5 seconds, should that number be rounded up to 19 or down to 18 before it is recorded? How students answered questions like these may have depended on whether they thought their rats were fast or slow learners. "Micky is a fast learner, so let's just call it 18" or "Topo sure is a slow learner. When will he ever drag his last leg over the finish line?" Second, *expectations can influence reality.* Students who expected their rats to be fast learners unwittingly did things that might have helped that learning along. For instance, students handled their rats more often and more gently when they thought they were fast learners, and the rats may well have responded to this superior treatment by turning in a superior performance. The students probably tried their best to be fair and objective, but their expectations nonetheless seem to have influenced both their rat's behaviour and their observations of it.

This problem is so significant that psychologists have given it a name: **Observer bias** is *the tendency for observers' expectations to influence both what they believe they observed and what they actually observed.* To avoid observer bias, psychologists use a number of techniques, the most common of which is called the **double-blind study,** which is *a study in which neither the researcher nor the participant knows how the participants are expected to behave.* For example, if we wanted to know whether people smile more when listening to classical music than to hip-hop, we might give participants a task to do while one of these two kinds of music played in the background, and have a research assistant watch them and record how often they smiled. We would take steps to ensure that our participants did not know what we were studying so that they would not feel obliged to behave as we expected them to; but we would also take steps to ensure that the research assistants did not know how the participants were expected to behave, perhaps by having the research assistants wear noise-cancelling headphones so that they wouldn't know which kind of music was playing as they recorded the participants' rate of smiling. If the research assistants don't *have* expectations, then their expectations cannot influence either their observations or their participants' behaviour. That's why psychologists typically make sure that the people who are making the observations in a study are as "blind" to the hypothesis as are the people who are being observed.

ABEL ALONSO/EPA/SHUTTERSTOCK

Robert Parker is one of the world's foremost wine critics. His ratings indicate how good a wine tastes—but can they also *influence* how good a wine tastes? Researchers gave participants a glass of wine and told some of them that Parker had awarded that wine 92 out of 100 points; others were told that he had awarded it only 72 points (Siegrist & Cousin, 2009). Sure enough, participants who thought the wine was highly rated thought the wine tasted much better and were willing to pay about 50% more for a bottle.

Description

You now know how to measure. That is, you know how to generate an operational definition of a property that has construct validity, how to find a reliable and powerful detector of that property, and how to use that detector while avoiding demand characteristics and observer bias. So who are you going to measure? Psychologists rarely measure the properties of an entire **population,** which is *a complete collection of people*—such as the population of human beings (about 7 billion), the population of Canadians (about 37 million), or the population of people with Down syndrome in the United States (about 1 million). Rather, they tend to measure the properties of a **sample,** which is *a partial collection of people or animals or things drawn from a population*. We'll talk later about how psychologists typically get their samples, but for now, just imagine you have taken a sample and measured its properties.

Congratulations! You are now the proud owner of some *data*. Your data probably take the form of a big spreadsheet filled with numbers that represent things like the frequency with which 211 people smiled in an hour, or the amount of time it took 37 rats to run a maze. And if you are like most researchers, you will look at your data and feel precisely as ignorant as you were before you started, because for most researchers, a big spreadsheet full of numbers just isn't very informative. But that's okay, because psychologists have two techniques for making sense out of big spreadsheets full of numbers: graphic representations and descriptive statistics. Let's have a look at each of these.

Graphic Representations: Picturing the Data

Ever wonder why a map is so much better than a list of step-by-step directions? Most people find it easier to understand facts when those facts are represented visually rather

observer bias The tendency for observers' expectations to influence both what they believe they observed and what they actually observed.

double-blind study A study in which neither the researcher nor the participant knows how the participants are expected to behave.

population A complete collection of people.

sample A partial collection of people or animals or things drawn from a population.

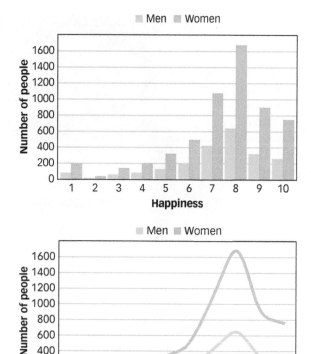

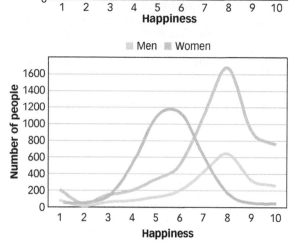

Figure 2.2

Frequency Distributions The graph in the top panel uses bars to show the number of male residents (shown in green) and female residents (shown in orange) of Somerville, MA, USA, who rated their happiness at each value on a 10-point scale. The graph in the middle panel shows the same data using smoothed lines. The graph in the bottom panel shows how these real data compare to a hypothetical normal distribution (shown in purple).

frequency distribution A graphic representation showing the number of times that the measurement of a property takes on each of its possible values.

than by numbers or words. That's why scientists typically make sense of their data by creating pictures or *graphic representations*. The most common kind of graphic representation is called a **frequency distribution,** which is *a graphic representation showing the number of times in which the measurement of a property takes on each of its possible values.*

The frequency distribution in the top panel of **FIGURE 2.2** shows the results of a city-wide census in which residents of Somerville, Massachusetts, USA, were asked to report their current level of happiness by using a rating scale that ranged from 1 (very unhappy) to 10 (very happy). The property being measured was happiness, the operational definition of happiness was a scale rating, and all the possible values of that rating (1 through 10) are shown on the horizontal axis. The vertical axis shows the number of men and women who responded to the census and used each of these values to rate their happiness. (People who identified as something other than male or female are not shown in this graph.) So, for example, the graph shows that 1,677 women and 646 men rated their happiness as 8 on a 10-point scale. The middle panel shows exactly the same data, but it uses smooth lines rather than bars, which is an equally common way to display a frequency distribution.

In a single glance, these graphs reveal things about the sample that a page full of numbers does not. For instance, when you look at the shape of the distributions, you instantly know that the people in this sample tend to be fairly happy. Your eyes also tell you that far fewer men than women responded to the census, but that the general shapes of the two distributions are roughly the same, which suggests that the men in this sample are generally about as happy as the women. You can see other things too—for instance, that 8 is the most popular rating for both men and women, and that both genders are about 3 times as likely to rate their happiness as 10 than to rate it as 1. All of that information from a simple drawing!

The distributions in the middle panel are *negatively skewed* (which means that they lean to the right) rather than *positively skewed* (which means that they lean to the left) because very few people use numbers that are below the midpoint of the scale to rate their happiness. Although a frequency distribution can have just about any shape, a special shape is shown in purple in the bottom panel of Figure 2.2. As you can see, this distribution has a peak exactly in the middle and then trails off in the same way at both ends. This distribution is unskewed or *symmetrical*, which is to say that the left half is a mirror image of the right half. Although frequency distributions showing data from the real world are rarely as symmetrical as the purple one is, they are often fairly close, especially when the amount of data used to construct them is quite large. That's why the distribution shown in purple is called the **normal distribution,** which is *a mathematically defined distribution in which the frequency of measurements is highest in the middle and decreases symmetrically in both directions.* The normal distribution is often called a *bell curve,* but if you'd like to be single for the rest of your life you can refer to it in public as a *Gaussian distribution.*

Descriptive Statistics: Summarizing the Data

A frequency distribution depicts every measurement in a sample and thus provides a full and complete picture of that sample. But sometimes a full and complete picture is more than we want to know. When we ask a friend how she's been doing, we don't really want her to show us a frequency distribution of her happiness ratings on each day of the previous 6 months. Rather, we want her to provide a brief summary statement that captures the essential information from that graph—for example, "I've been doing pretty well," or maybe "I've been having a few ups and downs." In psychology, brief summary statements that capture the essential information from a frequency distribution are called *descriptive statistics*.

The two most common kinds of descriptive statistics are those that describe the *central tendency* of a frequency distribution, and those that describe the *variability* in a frequency distribution. What do these terms mean? Descriptions of central tendency are statements about the value of the measurements that *tend* to lie near the *centre* or midpoint of the frequency distribution. When a friend says that she's been "doing pretty well," she is describing the central tendency (or approximate location of the midpoint) of the frequency distribution of her happiness ratings over time (see **FIGURE 2.3**). Descriptions of variability, on the other hand, are statements about the extent to which the measurements in a frequency distribution differ from each other. When your friend says that she has been "having some ups and downs," she is describing the variability among her happiness ratings. Let's dig a little deeper into each of these concepts.

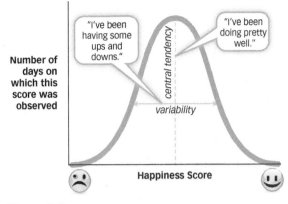

Figure 2.3

Two Kinds of Descriptive Statistics The most common descriptive statistics describe a frequency distribution's central tendency (where do most of the measurements lie?) and variability (how much do the measurements differ from one another?).

Central Tendency: Where Is The Middle Of The Distribution?

The three most common descriptions of central tendency are: the **mode** (*the value of the most frequently observed measurement*); the **mean** (*the average value of all the measurements*); and the **median** (*the value that is in the middle, i.e., greater than or equal to half the measurements and less than or equal to half the measurements*). **FIGURE 2.4** shows how each of these descriptive statistics is calculated.

Why do we need three different measures of central tendency? When a distribution is normal, we don't, because these three measures all have exactly the same value. But when a distribution is skewed, the mean gets dragged towards the end of the long tail, the median follows it but doesn't get as far, and the mode stays put at the hump (see **FIGURE 2.5**). When these three measures have different values, then calculating just one of them can provide a misleading picture of the data. For instance, in 2015 the mean annual income of the roughly 961,000 households in Vancouver, BC, was about $96,400. But that sample includes a few unusual households—9 of the 100 wealthiest Canadians (all worth more than $1 billion) live in Vancouver, and 15% of households there earn more than $150,000 per year.

Vancouver is home to a few hundred ridiculously rich people, so considering the mean alone might lead you to overestimate the affluence of the typical Vancouverite. But if, in addition to the mean, you also calculated the median, you'd find it has the considerably lower value of $72,700. Each measure can potentially be misleading in isolation, but when considered together they paint a much more accurate picture of Vancouver as a middle-class city with some wealthy residents. You should be very suspicious whenever you hear some new fact about the "average person" but don't hear anything about the median, the mode, or the shape of the frequency distribution.

normal distribution A mathematically defined distribution in which the frequency of measurements is highest in the middle and decreases symmetrically in both directions.

mode The value of the most frequently observed measurement.

mean The average value of all the measurements.

median The value that is greater than or equal to half the measurements and less than or equal to half the measurements.

Variability: How Wide Is The Distribution?

Descriptions of central tendency are statements about where the measurements in a frequency distribution tend to lie relative to the values on the vertical axis. Descriptions of variability, on the other hand,

Figure 2.4

Calculating Descriptive Statistics This frequency distribution shows the data from 20 individuals who rated their happiness on a 10-point scale. Descriptive statistics include measures of central tendency (such as the mean, median, and mode) and measures of variability (such as the range and the standard deviation).

- Mode = 5 because there are four 5's, and fewer of every other value.

- Mean = 5.95 because (1+2+3+4+4+5+5+5+5+6+6+7+7+7+8+8+8+9+9+10) / 20 = 5.95

- Median = 6 because 11 of the values are ≥ 6 and 11 of the values are ≤ 6.

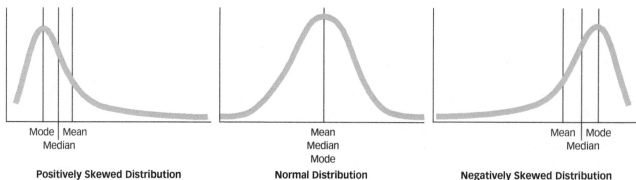

Mode | Mean
Median

Positively Skewed Distribution

Mean
Median
Mode

Normal Distribution

Mean | Mode
Median

Negatively Skewed Distribution

Figure 2.5
Differently Shaped Distributions
When a frequency distribution is normal, the mean, median, and mode all have the same value, but when it is positively or negatively skewed, these three measures of central tendency have quite different values.

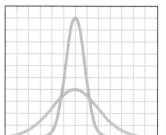

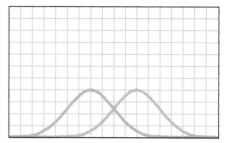

Figure 2.6
Distributions Can Differ in Terms of Variability or Central Tendency The panel on the left shows two distributions with the same central tendency but different amounts of variability. The panel on the right shows two distributions with the same amount of variability but different central tendencies.

are statements about where the measurements in a frequency distribution tend to lie relative to each other. Descriptions of variability tell us how much the measurements differ from each other, or roughly how *wide* the distribution is. Variability is important: knowing that the mean temperature in Winnipeg is 2.6°C and that the median temperature is 4.4°C tells you nothing about how hot it gets in the summer and how cold in the winter. To know about that is to know about the variability in temperature.

The simplest measure of variability is the **range**, which is *the value of the largest measurement in a frequency distribution minus the value of the smallest measurement*. When the range is small, the distribution has less variability than when the range is large. The range is easy to compute, but like the mean it can be dramatically influenced by a few extreme measurements. If someone told you that the temperature in San Diego, California, ranged from −4°C to 44°C, you might get the mistaken impression that San Diego has a remarkably varied climate when, in fact, it has a remarkably stable climate, rarely getting warmer than 25°C or colder than 10°C. The temperature in San Diego did hit −4°C to 44°C, but just once in the last 100 years.

Other measures of variability aren't as easily distorted by extreme values, but they are a little trickier to compute. One such measure is the **standard deviation**, which is a statistic that describes *how each of the measurements in a frequency distribution differs from the mean*. (Technically, it is the square root of the averaged squared difference between each measurement and the mean, and if you say that three times backwards you will enter a hypnotic trance that requires medical attention.) In other words, the standard deviation is an estimate of how far, on average, the various measurements are from the centre of the distribution. The standard deviation of average monthly temperatures over the year in Winnipeg is about 13°C, while in San Diego it is much smaller: about 3°C. It is worth noting that variability and central tendency are independent features of a frequency distribution. As **FIGURE 2.6** shows, two frequency distributions can have the same central tendencies but different amounts of variability, just as they can have the same amounts of variability but different central tendencies.

Build to the Outcomes

1. What are the essential features of an operational definition?
2. What two properties must a good detector have?
3. What techniques do psychologists use to avoid demand characteristics and observer bias?
4. What is the difference between a population and a sample?
5. What is a frequency distribution, and what makes the normal distribution special?
6. What is the difference between measures of central tendency and measures of variability?
7. Why can a single descriptive statistic (mode, mean, or median) sometimes be misleading?

Methods of Explanation: Figuring Out Why People Do What They Do

In 1639, a pastor named John Clarke suggested that "Early to bed and early to rise, makes a man healthy, wealthy, and wise." People have been repeating this little rhyme ever since, but is there any truth to it? The methods you've learned about so far would allow you to measure the health, wealth, and wisdom of a sample of people, as well as draw some pictures and make some summary statements about the measurements you made. That's nice, but it isn't what you want to know. You want to know if all that health and happiness and wisdom that some people seem to have was *caused* by getting in and out of bed early. Is there any way to use your new measurement skills to answer questions like this one?

Indeed there is, and that's what this part of the chapter is all about. In the first section (Correlation), we'll examine a technique that can tell us whether two properties—such as wisdom and bedtime—are in fact related. In the second section (Causation), we'll examine a technique that can tell us whether one of these properties (e.g., bedtime) actually *causes* the other (e.g., wisdom). And in the third and final section (Drawing Conclusions), we'll examine the kinds of conclusions these two techniques do and do not allow us to draw.

Correlation

Speaking of early to bed and early to rise, how much sleep did you get last night? Okay, now how many countries can you name in one minute without asking Alexa, Siri, or Google? If you were to ask a dozen university students those two questions, you'd probably find that the students who had gotten a solid eight hours could recall more countries' names, on average, than students who had pulled an all-nighter. If you kept careful track of their responses (yes, that means writing them down), you would probably find that you had a series of measurements much like the ones shown in **TABLE 2.1**. And from those measurements you would probably conclude that sleep deprivation causes poor memory.

But wait a minute. Those measurements simply tell you *how much* sleeping and remembering the people in your sample did. So what led you to conclude that there was a *causal relationship* between sleeping and remembering?

Synchronized Patterns of Variation

When you asked a dozen university students how much they slept the night before and then asked them to name as many countries as possible in one minute, you may not have realized that you were doing three important things:

- First, you were measuring a pair of **variables,** which are *properties that can take on different values.* When you took your first algebra course you were probably horrified to learn that everything you'd been taught in grade school about the distinction between letters and numbers was a lie, that mathematical equations could contain Xs and Ys as well as 7s and 4s, and that the letters were called *variables* because they could have different values under different circumstances. Same idea here. When you asked about sleep, you were measuring a variable whose value could vary from 0 to 24, and when you asked about names of countries, you were measuring a second variable whose value could vary from 0 to 60 or so.[1]

---

[1] Although there are about 195 countries in the world, anyone would be hard pressed to name more than 1 per second.

Learning Outcomes

- Explain what you can and cannot conclude from correlational research.

- Outline the essential ingredients of an experiment and explain how experiments solve the third-variable problem.

- Distinguish the kinds of conclusions that can and cannot be drawn from experimental evidence.

- Define both Type I and Type II errors in the context of psychological research.

- Explain why psychologists should worry if the replication rate is too low or too high.

range The value of the largest measurement in a frequency distribution minus the value of the smallest measurement.

standard deviation A statistic that describes how each of the measurements in a frequency distribution differs from the mean.

variable A property that can take on different values.

TABLE 2.1

HYPOTHETICAL DATA SHOWING THE RELATIONSHIP BETWEEN SLEEP AND MEMORY

Participant	Hours of Sleep	No. of Countries Named in One Minute
A	0	11
B	0	17
C	2.7	16
D	3.1	21
E	4.4	17
F	5.5	16
G	7.6	31
H	7.9	41
I	8	40
J	8.1	35
K	8.6	38
L	9	43

- Second, you did this again. And then again. And then again. That is, you made a *series* of measurements (across a sample of people) rather than just one.

- Third and last, you looked at the measurements you made and tried to discern a pattern. If you look at the second column of Table 2.1, you will see that as you move your eyes from top to bottom, the numbers vary from small to large. We could say that this column of numbers has a particular *pattern of variation.* Now, if you compare the third column with the second, you will notice the numbers there have a similar (though not identical) pattern of variation. With just a few exceptions, they also tend to vary from small to large as you move your eyes from top to bottom. The patterns of variation in these two columns are somewhat synchronized, and this synchrony is known as a **correlation,** which occurs when *variations in the value of one variable are synchronized with variations in the value of the other.* When patterns of variation are synchronized, two variables are said to be correlated—or "co-related."

Now here's why this matters: When two variables are correlated, you can use your knowledge of the value of one variable to predict the value of the other variable *without having to measure it!* For example, imagine that after you collected your sleep and memory data, you ran into a friend who lamented that she'd only gotten two hours of sleep the previous night. Without even asking her, you already have a fairly good idea of how many countries she could name in one minute—somewhere in the 15 to 25 range, right? And if you ran into another friend, asked him to do the country-naming task, and found that he named 40, you would have a pretty good idea of how many hours he'd slept the night before—somewhere in the 7 to 9 range, right?

Correlations allow us to make educated guesses about measurements without having to do the hard work of measuring. If you know that a man is more than 2 metres tall, you can guess that he probably weighs more than 92 kilograms because height and weight are correlated. If you know that a woman earns $1 million per year, you can guess that she probably went to university because income and education are correlated. As you can see, correlations are knowledge—and knowledge is power! But how much power?

If you predict that a rich woman went to university, that a tall man is heavy, or that a sleep-deprived person won't be able to name many presidents, you will be right far more often than you'll be wrong. But you won't be right every time. Queen Elizabeth did not attend university, but she is worth something over $88 billion; and Toronto Raptors basketball player Chris Boucher is 2.1 metres tall but weighs only 91 kilograms. The point is that correlations do allow us to make predictions, but those predictions are not always accurate.

Measuring the Direction and Strength of a Correlation

Statisticians have developed a way to estimate just how accurate predictions are likely to be by measuring the *direction* and *strength* of the correlation on which the predictions are based. Direction is easy to measure because the direction of a correlation is either positive or negative. A positive correlation exists when two variables have a "more-is-more" relationship. So, for example, consider pastor John Clarke's suggestion that the properties "healthy, wealthy, and wise" tend to be bundled together such that people who have a lot of one also have a lot of the others. When we say that *more health* is associated with *more wealth*, we are describing a positive correlation. Conversely, a negative correlation exists when two variables have a "more-is-less" relationship. When we say that *more health* is associated with *less poverty,* we are describing a negative correlation. More wealth and less poverty are, of course, two ways of saying the same thing, and any relationship can be described either positively or negatively. Scientists tend to use whichever description makes the most sense given the particular variables they are studying.

correlation The relationship that results when variations in the value of one variable are synchronized with variations in the value of the other.

The direction of a correlation is easy to measure, but the strength is a little more complicated. The **correlation coefficient** is *a mathematical measure of both the direction and strength of a correlation,* and it is symbolized by the letter *r.* The first thing to know about it is that like most measures, *r* has a *limited range.* What does that mean? Well, if you measure the number of hours of sunshine you experience tomorrow, the value of your measurement will definitely be somewhere in the range of 0 to 24. It cannot possibly be −7 or 329, which is to say that any numbers outside the limited range of 0 to 24 are meaningless. Similarly, the value of *r* can range from −1 to 1, and numbers outside that range are meaningless.

So what do the numbers *inside* that range mean? Let's start by saying what the two most extreme numbers (1 and −1) and the middle number (0) mean.

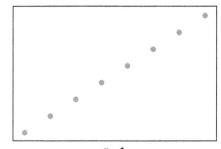

r = 1
Perfectly Positive Correlation

- If every time the value of a variable increases by a certain amount, the value of a second variable also increases by a certain amount, then the variables have a *perfect positive correlation* and *r* = 1 (see the top graph in **FIGURE 2.7**). For example, if every *x*-unit increase in health were associated with a *y*-unit increase in wealth, then the correlation between these two variables would be perfectly positive. In this case, if you know exactly how healthy a person is, you can predict down to the penny how educated he or she is.

- If every time the value of a variable increases by a certain amount the value of a second variable decreases by a certain amount, then the variables have a *perfect negative correlation* and *r* = −1 (see the middle graph in Figure 2.7). For example, if every *x*-unit increase in education were associated with a *y*-unit decrease in wealth, then the correlation between these two variables would be perfectly negative. In this case, too, if you know exactly how healthy a person is, you can predict down to the penny how educated he or she is.

r = −1
Perfectly Negative Correlation

- If every time the value of a variable increases by a certain amount the value of a second variable neither increases nor decreases systematically, then the variables have *no correlation* and *r* = 0 (see the bottom graph in Figure 2.7). For example, if an *x*-unit increase in health were sometimes associated with an increase in wealth, sometimes associated with a decrease in poverty, and sometimes associated with no change in wealth at all, then there would be no correlation between the two variables. In this case, knowing how healthy a person is would not allow you to predict anything about his or her wealth.

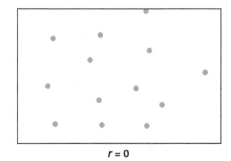

r = 0
No Correlation

Figure 2.7
Graphing Correlations This is what three different kinds of correlations look like when graphed.

Correlations of 1 and −1 are extremely common—in textbooks. They are almost unheard of in the real world. Yes, in the real world, health and wealth *do* have a positive correlation—that is, people who have more of one tend to have more of the other—but they have an *imperfect* positive correlation. A person with an extra unit of health probably also has some extra wealth, but that extra unit of health doesn't tell us *exactly* how much extra wealth that person has. Statements like "increases in health are associated with increases in wealth" do not mean that when the health of a group of people increases by 1 unit, every single individual in that group also experiences a 1-unit increase in wealth. Rather, we mean that for most of the people in the group, wealth increases a bit; for many it increases a lot, for a few it doesn't increase at all, and for some it may actually decrease.

There are always exceptions to the rule, which means that the value of *r* will lie somewhere between 0 and 1—and the number and size of the exceptions indicate where in that range it will lie. If there are just a few exceptions to the rule, then *r* will be closer to 1 than to 0, and predictions about someone's wealth based solely on knowledge of his or her health will be fairly accurate. But as the number of exceptions increases, then the value of *r* will begin to move towards 0 and such predictions will become less and less accurate, until finally, when *r* hits 0, they will become completely useless and you might as well just guess.

correlation coefficient (r) A mathematical measure of both the direction and strength of a correlation, which is symbolized by the letter *r.*

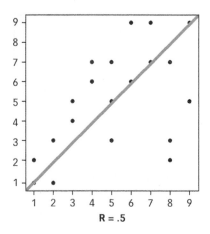

R = .5

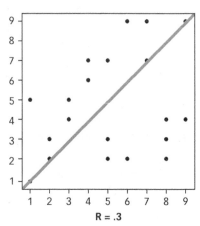

R = .3

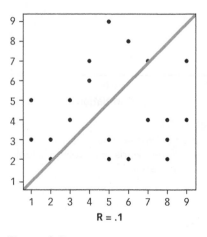

R = .1

Figure 2.8
Positive Correlations of Different Strengths The diagonal lines on each of these three graphs shows "the rule." When the exceptions to the rule are few and small, then the positive correlation is strong, and r moves towards 1. But when the exceptions are many and large, the positive correlation is weak, and r moves towards 0.

natural correlation A correlation observed in the world around us.

FIGURE 2.8 illustrates three cases in which two variables are positively correlated but have different numbers of exceptions. In each graph, the diagonal line shows the data you would expect to see if the two variables were perfectly positively correlated. In a sense, the diagonal line represents "the rule" that "when one variable increases by 1 unit, then the other variable increases by 1 unit," therefore every dot that is not on the diagonal line is "an exception to the rule." The farther a dot is from the line, the greater an exception it is. As you can see, the size and number of the many "exceptions to the rule" change the value of r quite dramatically. The two variables shown in the graph at the top of Figure 2.8 have a strong correlation of r = .5, the two variables shown in the graph in the middle have a moderate correlation of r = .3, and the two variables shown in the graph at the bottom have a weak correlation of r = .1. The only difference between the graphs of the strong and weak correlations is that the latter has more data points that are farther from the line.

A few pages ago, you thought r was just another Sesame Street letter of the day. Now you know that r is a measure of both the *direction* and *strength* of the relationship between two variables. The sign of r (plus or minus) tells you the direction of the relationship (positive or negative), and the absolute value of r (between 0 and 1) tells you about the number and size of the exceptions to the rule—hence, about how accurate you are likely to be when using knowledge of one variable to make predictions about the other. Big Bird would be so proud.

Causation

The mathematics of correlation may have been new to you, but the concept surely was not. You've been noticing correlations all your life—between height and weight, between sleep and memory, between age and musical preference, and so on. **Natural correlations** are *the correlations we observe in the world around us*; and although the mere observation of a synchronized pattern of variation tells us that two variables have a relationship, it cannot tell us *why* the relationship exists. For example, many studies (Anderson & Bushman, 2002; C. A. Anderson et al., 2003, 2017; Huesmann et al., 2003) have observed a positive correlation between the aggressiveness of a child's behaviour and the amount of violence to which that child is exposed through media such as television, movies, and video games. The more violence children see, the more aggressively they tend to behave. These two variables clearly have a relationship, but what kind of relationship do they have? In other words, *why* are they correlated?

The Third-Variable Problem: Correlation Is Not Causation

One possibility is that exposure to media violence (let's call it variable X) causes aggressiveness (let's call it variable Y). For instance, media violence may teach children that aggression is an acceptable way to vent anger or solve problems. We'll denote this possible relationship as X → Y, which simply means X *causes* Y. A second possibility is that Y → X, which is to say that aggressiveness causes exposure to media violence. For example, children who are naturally aggressive may be especially inclined to play violent video games and watch violent movies. When you first heard that exposure to media violence and aggressiveness were positively correlated, you probably thought of these two possibilities yourself.

But there is an additional possibility you might not have considered. It is possible that another variable—a heretofore unnamed "third variable" that we will call variable Z—causes children to behave aggressively *and also* causes children to be exposed to media violence (see **FIGURE 2.9**). For instance, it might be that a lack of adult supervision (Z) allows children to get away with playing violent video games that adults would normally prohibit (Z → X), and it may also be that a lack of adult supervision allows children to get away with bullying others simply because no adult is around to stop them ($Z \rightarrow Y$). If so, then X and Y may be correlated only because $Z \rightarrow X$ & Y, which is to say that being exposed to media violence and behaving aggressively may be two independent effects of the lack of adult supervision and may not be causally related to each other at all.

How can we tell if X and Y are being caused by this third variable Z—or perhaps by some other third variable? We can't. The **third-variable problem** refers to the fact that *the natural correlation between two variables cannot be taken as evidence of a causal relationship between them because a third variable might be causing them both.* What this means is that if we want to know about the causal relationship between two variables, then observing a natural correlation between them can never tell us what we want to know. Luckily, another technique can.

Experimentation: Establishing Causation

Experimentation is *a technique for establishing the causal relationship between variables.* The logic underlying experimentation is simple: There are three possible causes of any correlation, so if we can eliminate two of them, then the one that remains must be the real one. If we know that X did not cause Y, and if we know that Z did not cause X and Y, then we know that Y must have caused X. The logic is simple, but exactly *how* do experiments eliminate two of the three possible causes? They do this by using a pair of techniques called *manipulation* and *random assignment.* Let's explore each of them in turn.

Manipulation: Making Different Conditions

Imagine that one evening you are working on your laptop, when you notice that your internet connection has suddenly slowed to a crawl. Your roommate is upstairs playing with his new Xbox, which you suspect could be sucking up bandwidth, which is making your internet slow. How would you test your suspicion? You now know that simply observing a natural correlation won't be of much help because even if you experienced slow internet every time your roommate used his Xbox and the internet ran fast every time he didn't, you still couldn't conclude that the Xbox was *causing* the slowdown because of the third-variable problem. For instance, it is possible that your roommate only uses his Xbox in the evenings, which happens to be the time when a whole lot of other people in your neighbourhood are home watching Netflix, playing video games, downloading music, and otherwise sucking up bandwidth. "Evening" may be a third variable that causes your roommate to fire up the Xbox and that also causes your internet to slow down.

So how can you tell whether your slowdown is actually being caused by the Xbox? Rather than observing the natural correlation between your roommate's Xbox usage and your internet speed, you could go upstairs when your roommate isn't home and turn his Xbox on and off while observing the upload and download speeds. If your internet speeds were slower every time you turned the Xbox on and then were faster every time you turned the Xbox off, you would know that the Xbox was in fact the cause of the slowdown. What you just did is called **manipulation,** which is *a technique for determining the causal power of a variable by actively changing its value.* Rather than measuring two variables, as we do when we observe correlations, experiments require that we *manipulate* one variable—that is, actively change its value—and then measure the other. Changing the value of the Xbox from on to off is an example of manipulation.

The same technique could be used to determine whether exposure to media violence causes aggressiveness. For instance, we could invite some children to our laboratory and give them one of two experiences: Half could be given a violent video game to play, and the other half could be given a nonviolent video game to play. These two experiences are called the *conditions* of our study, and we could refer to them as "the violent exposure condition" and "the nonviolent exposure condition."

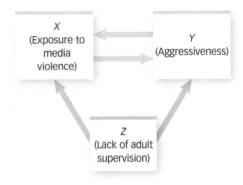

Figure 2.9
Causes of Correlation Three possible reasons X and Y are correlated: $X \rightarrow Y$, $Y \rightarrow X$, or $Z \rightarrow X$ & Y.

In 1949, American physician Dr. Benjamin Sandler noticed a correlation between the incidence of polio and the consumption of ice cream. He concluded that sugar made children susceptible to the disease. Public health officials were so convinced by his findings that they issued public warnings. But as it turned out, the correlation was caused by a third variable: Warm weather had caused an increase in the incidence of polio (because viruses become more active in the summer) and an increase in the consumption of ice cream (because children become more active in the summer).

third-variable problem The fact that the natural correlation between two variables cannot be taken as evidence of a causal relationship between them because a third variable might be causing them both.

experimentation A technique for establishing the causal relatiosnship between variables.

manipulation A technique for determining the causal power of a variable by actively changing its value.

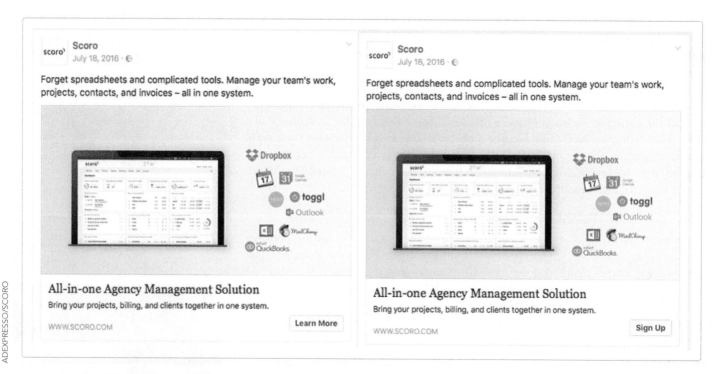

Can you see the difference between these two ads? Don't worry. It's subtle. The one and only difference is that the ad on the left has a "Learn More" button and the ad on the right has a "Sign Up" button. By manipulating the label on the button, the advertiser was able to determine whether a label can cause people to click. And it can! The "Learn More" label led 15% more Facebook users to click (Karlson, 2016).

At the end of an hour of game playing, we could measure the children's aggressiveness, perhaps by observing whether they push to get to the front of a line or by asking whether they think it's okay for someone to kick a growling dog. Then we could compare the measurements of aggressiveness in one condition with the measurements of aggressiveness in the other condition.

When we compare these measurements across conditions, we are essentially asking whether the value of aggressiveness went from low to high when exposure to media violence went from low to high. If you think about it, we would essentially be computing the correlation between the variable we manipulated (exposure) and the variable we measured (aggressiveness). Now here is the cool part: Because we *manipulated* exposure rather than just *measuring* it, we could instantly eliminate two of the possible causes of the correlation we had just observed. Specifically, we'd know for sure that aggressiveness did not cause exposure to media violence, and we'd know that lack of adult supervision did not cause exposure to media violence—and we'd know these two things because we know what *did* cause exposure to media violence: We did! And that would leave just one possibility: Exposure to media violence must have caused aggressiveness, which is what we wanted to know in the first place.

Experimentation is a technique that allows us to establish the causal relationship between variables by taking three simple steps:

1. *Manipulate*: The first step in an experiment is to manipulate a variable. *The variable that is manipulated in an experiment* is called the **independent variable** because its value is determined entirely by the experimenter and therefore does not depend on—or is "independent of"—the participants. A manipulation creates at least two conditions: in our example, a violent exposure condition and a nonviolent exposure condition.

2. *Measure*: The second step in an experiment is to measure a variable. *The variable that is measured in an experiment* is called the **dependent variable** because its value does "depend on" the participants.

independent variable The variable that is manipulated in an experiment.

dependent variable The variable that is measured in an experiment.

3. *Compare*: The third step in an experiment is to compare the value of the variable in one condition with the value of the variable in the other. If the values differ on average, then we know that changes to the value of the independent variable *caused* changes to the value of the dependent variable. **FIGURE 2.10** shows exactly how manipulation works (and the Hot Science box on p. 52 shows how nature occasionally does experiments by creating manipulations of her own).

Random Assignment: Making Sure Conditions Differ in Just One Way

Manipulation is an essential ingredient in experimentation. But what kind of recipe has just one ingredient? In fact, experimentation has a second and equally important ingredient, and to understand what it is and what it does, let's return to the study we just designed in which children were given violent or nonviolent video games to play and then their aggressiveness was measured an hour later. When the children show up at our laboratory to participate in our study, how should we decide which child will play which game?

One possibility is that we could be polite for a change and ask each child which kind of game he or she would prefer to play. So imagine we did that and that half the children choose to play a violent game and the other half choose to play a nonviolent game. We let them play their preferred game for an hour, then measure their aggressiveness and discover that the children who played the violent game were in fact more aggressive than those who played the nonviolent game. Could we now conclude that playing violent video games caused aggressiveness? No! But why not? After all, we manipulated exposure to media violence, switching it on and off as though it were an Xbox, and then we measured aggressiveness and found that it went on and off too. We manipulated, we measured, and we compared—we did all three of the three steps. So where did we go wrong?

We went wrong by letting the children *select* which video game to play—because children who *select* violent video games probably differ in many ways from children who don't. They may be older or meaner. They may be younger or sweeter. They may have different brain chemistry, different home environments, different genes, different talents, different numbers of siblings, or different levels of adult supervision. The list of possible differences is endless. The whole point of doing the experiment was to create two conditions whose participants differed from each other in *one and only one way*, namely, in terms of how much media violence they were exposed to in our laboratory. By letting the children decide for themselves which condition of the experiment they would experience, we ended up with two conditions whose participants may have differed in many ways—and every one of those differences is a third variable that could potentially have caused the differences in aggressiveness that we observed when comparing across conditions. Apparently, it just doesn't pay to be polite. **Self-selection** is *a problem that occurs when anything about a participant determines the participant's condition;* and as you can see, it is a problem that leaves us with the same conundrum that led us to do an experiment in the first place.

So how should we determine which video game each child will play? We should flip a coin. **Random assignment** is a *procedure that assigns participants to a condition by chance.* Just think about what would happen if we used a coin flip to randomly assign each child to play either a violent or nonviolent video game. As **FIGURE 2.11** shows, the first thing that would happen is that roughly half the children would be assigned to play violent video games and roughly half would be assigned to play nonviolent video games. Coins land heads up about as often as they land tails up, so if we use a coin to randomly assign children to one of two conditions, then the two conditions should have roughly equal numbers of children.

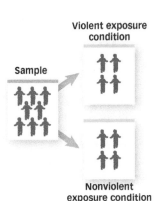

	Exposed to media violence?	Aggression
Violent exposure condition	Yes	High
	Yes	High
	Yes	High
	Yes	High

	Exposed to media violence?	Aggression
Nonviolent exposure condition	No	Low
	No	Low
	No	Low
	No	Low

Figure 2.10
The Three Steps of Experimentation
Manipulate the independent variable, measure the dependent variable, then compare the values across conditions. Notice that "comparing the values" just means "looking for a synchronized pattern of variation between two variables," which is why the table to the far right in this figure looks so much like Table 2.1.

NICOSAN / ALAMY

There is no evidence that Louise Hay's techniques can cure cancer. But even if cancer victims who bought her books did show a higher rate of remission than those who didn't, there would still be no evidence because buyers are self-selected and thus may differ from nonbuyers in countless ways.

self-selection A problem that occurs when anything about a participant determines the participant's condition.

random assignment A procedure that assigns participants to a condition by chance.

Hot Science | Hate Posts and Hate Crimes: Not Just a Correlation

In 2004, a university student named Mark Zuckerberg built a website called "The Facebook" so that he and his fellow students could learn about each other online. He had no idea that in just 10 years, his company would be one of the most powerful and profitable in human history, and that he would be one of the richest people on earth. Facebook has been very good for its inventor, but has it been very good for the rest of us? It lets us post videos of our pets, share stories of our vacations, and find out what people we barely know had for lunch—and who could possibly argue with the goodness of that? But has it also become a platform in which people's worst impulses are brought together, amplified, and then unleashed upon the world? Do Facebook posts lead people to do terrible things in the real world, such as commit arson, or assault, or even murder?

Karsten Müller and Carlo Schwarz (2018) worried that the answer might be yes. So they conducted a study in Germany, where a right-wing anti-immigrant party (the Alternative für Deutschland, or AfD) had recently developed a significant presence on Facebook. The study involved nothing more than measuring the correlation between two variables: the number of anti-refugee Facebook posts that appeared on the AfD website each week and the number of violent crimes against refugees that occurred each week. The accompanying figure shows what they found. As you can see, the two variables were indeed positively correlated: The more "hate posts" that appeared on AfD's Facebook page at any moment in time, the more "hate crimes" happened on German streets.

But wait a minute. What about the third-variable problem? Hate posts and

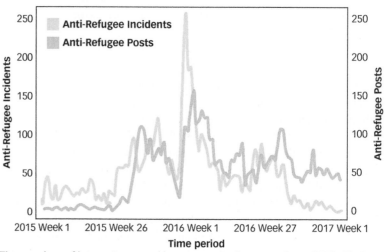

The number of hate crimes and hate posts in Germany from 2015–2017.

hate crimes may well be correlated, but that doesn't mean the former *caused* the latter. Maybe the hate crimes caused the hate posts, or maybe some third variable—such as a change in the weather or the parliament or the stock market—caused them both. Drawing conclusions about the causal relationship between two variables requires that one of those variables be *manipulated,* right?

Yes, it does, but luckily for the researchers, nature did just that. Internet service in Germany is not as reliable as it is in Canada, and German Facebook users experience frequent interruptions that can knock everyone offline for hours or even days at a time. So what happens when Internet access is randomly turned on and off and then on again? When the researchers analyzed the historical data on service interruptions, they discovered that when Facebook went down, hate crimes went down too; and when Facebook came back up again, so did hate crimes.

Because service interruptions are basically random events, they serve as a manipulation of one variable (the number of hate posts) whose impact on the other variable (the number of hate crimes) can then be measured. When the researchers did that, the impact was clear. As the researchers themselves concluded, "Social media has not only become a fertile soil for the spread of hateful ideas but also motivates real-life action" (Müller & Schwarz, 2018, p. 40).

Psychologists are often faced with a tough choice: They can either (a) observe a correlation in the real world but be unsure about causation, or (b) firmly establish causation in the laboratory but be unsure about whether it generalizes to the real world. But every once in a while, nature resolves this dilemma by randomly manipulating a variable in the real world. When that happens, clever researchers may take advantage of the situation and use it to answer pressing social questions—and to produce some very hot science.

Second—and *much* more important—we could expect the two conditions to have roughly equal numbers of mean children and sweet children, of older children and younger children, of children who have a lot of adult supervision at home and children who have little, and so on. In other words, we could expect the two conditions to have roughly equal numbers of children who are anything-you-can-ever-name-and-everything-you-can't! Because the children in the two conditions will be the same *on average* in terms of meanness, age, adult supervision, and every other variable in the known universe *except the variable we manipulated,* we could be sure that the variable we manipulated was the cause of the differences in the variable we measured. Because exposure to media violence would be the *only* difference between the two conditions when we started the experiment, it *must* be the cause of any differences in aggressiveness we observed at the end of the experiment.

Statistical Testing: Making Sure Conditions Don't Differ by Chance

Random assignment is a powerful tool. Unfortunately, like a lot of tools, it doesn't work every time you use it. If we randomly assigned children to two conditions, we could expect the two conditions to have roughly equal numbers of mean children, young children, supervised children, and so on. But the key word in that sentence is *roughly.* When you flip a coin 100 times, you expect it to come up heads *roughly* 50 of those times. But every once in a very, very long while, it will come up heads 60 times, or 70 times, or even 100 times, by sheer chance alone (see The Real World: The Surprisingly High Likelihood of Unlikely Coincidences). This will not happen often, of course, but if you execute 100 coin flips enough times, it will eventually happen.[2]

Because random assignment is achieved by using a randomizing device such as a coin, every once in a long while the coin will assign more unsupervised kids to play violent video games and more supervised kids to play nonviolent video games by sheer chance alone. When this happens, scientists say that "random assignment has failed" (though they should actually say that the coin has failed to produce random assignment). When random assignment fails, we are right back where we started when we politely allowed the children to self-select their conditions, and as you will recall, that is not a very good place to be right back to.

How can we know whether random assignment has failed? Unfortunately, we can never know for sure. But what we *can* do is calculate the *odds* that random assignment has failed each time we conduct an experiment. It's not important for you to know how to do this calculation, but it is important for you to understand how psychologists interpret its results. Psychologists perform this calculation every time they do an experiment, and they generally do not accept the results of their experiments unless the calculation suggests that there is less than a 5% chance that those results would have occurred if random assignment had failed. Such results are said to be *statistically significant,* and psychologists typically indicate this by writing "$p < .05$," which simply means that the probability (p) that the result would have been observed if random assignment had failed is less than 5% ($<.05$). Psychologists have several other ways to calculate the odds that random assignment has failed, but this calculation is the most common.

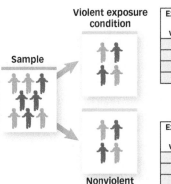

Violent exposure condition			
	Exposed to media violence?	Adult supervision?	Aggression
	Yes	Yes	High
	Yes	No	High
	Yes	Yes	High
	Yes	No	High

Nonviolent exposure condition			
	Exposed to media violence?	Adult supervision?	Aggression
	No	Yes	Low
	No	No	Low
	No	Yes	Low
	No	No	Low

Figure 2.11
Random Assignment Random assignment ensures that participants in the two conditions are, on average, equal in terms of all possible third variables.

Do strawberries taste better when dipped in chocolate? If you dip the big juicy ones and don't dip the small dry ones, then you won't know if the chocolate is what made the difference. But if you randomly assign some to be dipped and others not to be dipped, and if the dipped ones taste better on average, then you will have demonstrated scientifically what every 3-year-old already knows.

Drawing Conclusions

If we applied all the techniques discussed so far, we could design an experiment that had a very good chance of establishing the causal relationship between two variables. That experiment would be said to have **internal validity,** which is *an*

---

[2] How long is "eventually"? Odds are that you would have to execute the 100 coin flips 12,680,000,000,000,000,000,000,000,000,000 times in order for the coin to come up heads every time by chance alone. Assuming you could flip one coin per second, this would take you about 4^{25} years, which is considerably longer than the universe has existed. In other words, don't try this at home.

internal validity An attribute of an experiment that allows it to establish causal relationships.

The Real World | The Surprisingly High Likelihood of Unlikely Coincidences

A recent survey found that more than half of university graduates believe in extrasensory perception, or ESP, and it is easy to understand why. Just consider the case of the Truly Amazing Coincidence. One night you dream that a panda is piloting an airplane over the Indian Ocean, and the next day you tell a friend, who says, "Wow, I had exactly the same dream!" One morning you wake up humming an old Katy Perry tune (probably "Part of Me"), and an hour later you hear it playing in the mall. You and your roommate are sitting around watching television when suddenly you turn to each other and say in perfect unison, "Wanna pizza?" Coincidences like these might make anyone believe in strange and spooky supernatural weirdness.

Well, not anyone. While the Nobel laureate Luis Alvarez was reading the newspaper one day, a particular story got him thinking about an old university friend whom he hadn't seen in years. A few minutes later, he turned the page and was shocked to see the very same friend's obituary. But before concluding that he had suddenly developed an acute case of ESP, Alvarez decided to use probability theory to determine just how amazing this coincidence really was. He estimated the number of friends an average person has, estimated how often an average person thinks about each of those friends, did a few simple calculations, and determined the probability that someone would think about a friend

5 minutes before learning about that friend's death. The odds were astonishing. In a country the size of the United States, Alvarez calculated that this coincidence should happen to 10 people every day (Alvarez, 1965). A fellow Nobel laureate put the number closer to 80 people a day (Charpak & Broch, 2004)!

"In ten years there are five million minutes," says the statistics professor Irving Jack. "That means each person has plenty of opportunity to have some remarkable coincidences in his life" (Neimark, 2004). If 37 million Canadians dream for about 2 hours every night, that's 74 million hours of dreaming, so it isn't really surprising that two people might have the same dream, or that someone would dream about something that actually happened the next day. As the mathematics professor John Paulos noted, "In reality, the most astonishingly incredible coincidence imaginable would be the complete absence of all coincidence" (Neimark, 2004).

If all of this seems surprising to you, then you are not alone. Research shows that people routinely underestimate the likelihood of coincidences happening by chance (Diaconis & Mosteller, 1989; Falk & McGregor,

"Idaho! What a coincidence—I'm from Idaho."

1983; Hintzman, Asher, & Stern, 1978). If you want to profit from this fact, just assemble a group of 24 or more people and offer to bet anyone $1 that at least two of the people in the group share a birthday. The odds are in your favour, and the bigger the group, the better those odds are. In fact, in a group of 35 people, the odds are a remarkable 85%. When everyone starts handing you their loonies and asking how in the world you knew that two of the people in your group shared a birthday, you can honestly tell them it was ESP—also known as Especially Straightforward Probability.

attribute of an experiment that allows it to establish causal relationships. When we say that an experiment is internally valid, we mean that everything *inside* the experiment is working exactly as it should in order for us to use its results to draw conclusions about the causal relationship between the independent and dependent variables. But exactly *what* conclusions are we entitled to draw? If our imaginary experiment revealed a difference between the aggressiveness of children who were exposed to high or low levels of media violence, could we conclude that media violence causes aggressiveness?

Actually, no. The conclusion we'd be entitled to draw would have to be much more restricted than that. What we *could* conclude is this: "It is likely that media violence as we defined that variable caused aggressiveness as we defined that variable in the people we studied." That sentence is obnoxiously long and sounds a little too much like a legal disclaimer because it contains these phrases: *as we defined that variable,* and *in the people we studied,* and *it is likely that.* Each phrase describes an important restriction on the conclusions we can draw from this or any other experimental result. Let's consider them in turn, as well as the kinds of restrictions they place on our conclusions.

The Representativeness Restriction: "As We Defined That Variable . . ."

The results of an experiment naturally depend on how the independent and dependent variables are operationally defined. For instance, we are more likely to find that exposure to media violence causes aggressiveness if we operationally define exposure as "watching 2 hours of gory axe murders" rather than "watching 10 minutes of football," or if we define aggressiveness as "interrupting another person who is talking" rather than "beating someone with a tire iron." The way we operationally define variables can have a profound influence on what we find, so which of these ways of operationally defining them is the *right* way?

One common answer is that we should operationally define variables in an experiment as they are defined in the real world. **External validity** is *an attribute of an experiment in which variables have been operationally defined in a normal, typical, or realistic way.* It seems pretty clear that the kind of aggressive behaviour that concerns teachers and parents lies somewhere between an interruption and an assault, and that the kind of media violence to which children are typically exposed lies somewhere between sports and torture. If the goal of an experiment is to determine whether the kinds of media violence to which children are typically exposed causes the kinds of aggressiveness with which societies are typically concerned, then external validity is important. When variables are defined in an experiment as they typically are in the real world, we say that the variables are *representative* of the real world.

External validity sounds like such a good idea that you may be surprised to learn that most psychology experiments are externally *in*valid—and that most psychologists don't consider this a problem (Mook, 1983). To understand why, consider a simple example from physics. Physicists have a theory: *Heat is the result of the rapid motion of molecules.* This theory gives rise to a hypothesis: *When the molecules that constitute an object are slowed, the object should become cooler.* Imagine that a physicist tested this hypothesis by performing a laboratory experiment in which she used a laser to slow the motion of the molecules in a steel ball, measured the temperature of the ball before and after, and found that the temperature of the ball decreased by a large amount when its molecules were slowed. Are you worried about external invalidity? Are you thinking, "How can this experiment teach us anything about the real world when in the real world no one uses lasers to slow the movement of the molecules in steel balls?"

Probably not, and that's because you intuitively understand that the physicist's theory led to a clear hypothesis about *what would happen in the laboratory,* and that the events the physicist manipulated and measured in the laboratory therefore tested the hypothesis quite nicely. Similarly, a well-thought-out theory about the causal relationship between exposure to media violence and aggressiveness should lead to hypotheses about how children *in a laboratory* will behave after playing a violent video game, and thus their behaviour tests that hypothesis quite nicely. If children who play *Call of Duty* in a laboratory are more likely to shove each other than are children who play *Minecraft* in creative mode, then any theory claiming that media violence cannot influence aggressiveness has just been proved wrong.

In short, theories allow us to generate hypotheses about what can, must, or will happen under particular circumstances; and experiments are usually meant to create some of those circumstances, and test the hypotheses, and thereby provide evidence for or against the theories that generated them (see also Hot Science: Hate Posts and Hate

Does piercing make a person more or less attractive? The answer, of course, depends entirely on your operational definition of piercing.

external validity An attribute of an experiment in which variables have been defined in a normal, typical, or realistic way.

RICK FINDLER - PA IMAGES/GETTY IMAGES

Alma Deutscher wrote the opera *Cinderella* for an ensemble of 20 musicians. It premiered at the State Opera in Vienna when Alma was 11, and received a standing ovation and critical acclaim. It was recorded for commercial release by Sony Classical the following year. Alma's works have been performed in Europe, Israel, and the United States.

case method A procedure for gathering scientific information by studying a single individual.

random sampling A technique for choosing participants that ensures that every member of a population has an equal chance of being included in the sample.

Crimes: Not Just a Correlation). Experiments are not usually meant to be miniature versions of everyday life, and as such, external invalidity is not usually a problem.

The Generalizability Restriction: "In the People We Studied . . ."

You already know that psychologists rarely measure an entire population, but instead measure a sample from that population. How big should that sample be? The size of a population is signified by the uppercase letter N, the size of a sample is signified by the lowercase letter n, and therefore $0 < n < N$. However, in most studies, n is a whole lot closer to 0 than it is to N, and indeed, in some cases $n = 1$.

For example, some individuals are so remarkable that they deserve close study, and the psychologists who study them are using the **case method,** which is *a procedure for gathering scientific information by studying a single individual.* We can learn a lot about, say, memory by studying someone such as Rajveer Meena, who memorized the first 70,000 digits of pi; about consciousness by studying someone such as Henry Molaison, whose ability to look backwards and forwards in time was impaired by brain surgery; about intelligence and creativity by studying someone such as Alma Deutscher, a 14-year-old composer, pianist, and violinist. She wrote her first piano sonata at the age of 6, a violin concerto at age 9, and her first full-length opera, *Cinderella,* when she was 10. Such people are not only interesting in their own right, but their remarkable abilities can also provide important insights into how the rest of us work.

With that said, the vast majority of studies you will read about in this textbook use samples of 10, 100, 1,000, or even many thousands of people. Psychologists typically use the largest samples they can get because the larger the sample, the more confidence they can have in their findings. Why? Well, if a coin came up heads 7 out of 10 times, you might *suspect* it was an unfair coin—that is, that the coin was slightly heavier on the tail than the head. But you would not be highly confident in that conclusion because it was based on a small sample of coin flips. If the same coin came up heads 700 out of 1,000 times, however, you would be extremely confident that it was an unfair coin. Because large samples allow us to be more confident in our results, in an ideal world, n would be very close to N itself. Alas, psychologists in the real world have limited time, limited research funds, and limited access to participants, so they have to settle for the largest n that circumstances allow.

So how do psychologists determine which people they will include in their sample and which people they won't? One method is by **random sampling,** which is *a technique for selecting participants that ensures that every member of a population has an equal chance of being included in the sample.* (Note to self: Do not confuse random sampling with random assignment. The only thing they have in common is the word *random.*) When we randomly sample participants from a population, the sample is said to be *representative* of the population. This allows us to *generalize* from the sample to the population—that is, to conclude that what we observed in our sample would also have been observed if we had measured the entire population.

You probably already have solid intuitions about the value of random sampling. For example, if you stopped at a roadside farm stand to buy a bag of cherries and the farmer offered to let you taste a few that she had carefully selected from the bag, you'd be reluctant to generalize from that sample to the population of cherries in the bag because you'd know that the cherries you were offered had been . . . well, cherry-picked. But on the other hand, if the farmer invited you to close your eyes and pull a few cherries from the bag at random, you'd probably consider those cherries to be a representative sample and you would naturally generalize from that sample ("The cherries I tasted were quite sweet") to the population ("I bet the other cherries in the bag are sweet too").

Like external validity, random sampling sounds like an obviously good idea, so you may be surprised once again to find that most psychological studies involve *nonrandom* samples. Indeed, virtually every participant in every psychology experiment you will ever read about was a volunteer, and a large share were university students who were significantly younger, smarter, healthier, and wealthier than the average Earthling. About 96% of the people whom psychologists study come from countries that have just 12% of the world's population, and 70% come from the United States alone (Henrich, Heine, & Norenzayan, 2010). Why do psychologists sample people nonrandomly?

Because they have to. Even if there were a list of all the world's human inhabitants from which we could randomly sample our research participants (there isn't), how would we locate the 5-year-old Bedouin girl whose family roams the desert so that we could measure the electrical activity in her brain while she watched cartoons? How would we convince an illiterate farmer in South Sudan to complete a lengthy questionnaire about his political beliefs? How could we sample the Ayoreo-Totobiegosode tribe of Paraguay, which has never had any contact with the outside world? Most psychology experiments are conducted by professors and graduate students at universities in the Western Hemisphere, and as much as they might *like* to randomly sample the population of our planet, the fact is that they are pretty much stuck studying the local folks who volunteer for their studies.

Is this a fatal flaw in psychological science? No, and there are two reasons why. First, *sometimes the representativeness of a sample doesn't matter*. If one pig flew over the CN Tower just one time, it would instantly disprove the Standard Theory of Porcine Locomotion, and it really wouldn't matter if other pigs could do the same trick. Similarly, if playing *Call of Duty* for an hour caused a group of 5th graders from a public school in Edmonton, to start shoving other kids in the laboratory, then even if the game did not have a similar effect on 9th graders from a private school in Montreal, we would still know that media violence *can* influence aggressiveness—which means that any theory that says it can't is just plain wrong. Sometimes psychologists aren't concerned with whether *everyone* does something; they just want to know if *anyone* does it.

The second reason why nonrandom sampling is not a fatal flaw is that *sometimes the representativeness of the sample is a reasonable starting assumption*. Instead of asking, "Do I have a compelling reason to believe that my sample is representative of the population?" we could just as well ask, "Do I have a compelling reason to believe that my sample is *not* representative of the population?" For example, few of us would be willing to take a new medicine if a nonrandom sample of participants took it and died. Indeed, we would probably refuse to take the medicine even if those participants were mice! Although these nonrandomly sampled participants would be different from us in many ways (for example, tails and whiskers), most of us would assume that anything that kills them has some reasonable chance of killing us. Similarly, if a psychology experiment demonstrated that a sample of Canadian children behaved aggressively after playing violent video games, we might ask whether there is a compelling reason to suspect that Ecuadorian university students or middle-aged Australians would respond any differently. If the answer is yes, then we can conduct experiments to test that possibility.

The bottom line is that learning about *some people* does not necessarily tell us about *all people,* but it can still tell us a lot—and it certainly tells us more than learning about *no people* at all, which is often the only other choice.

It can be a mistake to generalize from a nonrandom sample. In the American presidential election of 1948, pollsters mistakenly predicted that the Republican candidate, Thomas Dewey, would beat the Democratic Party candidate, Harry Truman. Why? Because polling was done by telephone, and Dewey Republicans were more likely to have telephones than were Truman Democrats.

If this mouse keeled over and died immediately after sampling this wine, would you be willing to take a few sips? Why not? You're not a mouse, are you?

Headlines suggest that the results of most psychology studies can't be replicated. Should you believe those headlines?

replication An experiment that uses the same procedures as a previous experiment but with a new sample from the same population.

The Reliability Restriction: "It Is Likely That . . ."

A **replication** is *an experiment that uses the same procedures as a previous experiment but with a new sample from the same population.* In the last few years, many major media outlets have reported that when psychologists replicate the experiments of other psychologists, they *usually* fail to replicate their results, which suggests that the initial result was some sort of fluke. Could that be right? Are the headlines true?

Estimating Psychology's Replication Rate If a researcher finds that children who were randomly assigned to play violent video games are more aggressive than those who were randomly assigned to play nonviolent video games, we would expect that other researchers who use the same video games and the same measures of aggressiveness under the same conditions should get the same result. We might not expect this to happen every single time, but we would expect it to happen most of the time—and if it happened a whole lot less than most of the time, we would have good reason to suspect that the original finding was a fluke. You already know that psychologists publish their results only when the odds that random assignment failed are less than 5%, but that means that 5% of the time, the original result was indeed a fluke and therefore we would not expect it to be replicated. We can live with that. But what if these flukes happen way more than 5% of the time? What if they happen the *majority* of the time, just as the headlines suggest?

In the last few years, teams of psychologists have tried to estimate the proportion of flukes in the scientific literature by selecting a sample of published studies and then attempting to replicate them. Some teams have found the replication rate in their samples to be frighteningly low (Open Science Collaboration [OSC] et al., 2015) while others have found it to be reasonably high (Klein et al., 2014). But do any of these findings tell us the actual replication rate of studies in psychology? Probably not (Gilbert et al., 2016). First, the teams who did these replications did not randomly sample the population of published studies in psychology. Rather, they chose studies of particular kinds (e.g., those that are easy for anyone to do rather than those that require a lot of time, money, or expertise) from particular areas of psychology (e.g., almost always from social, and almost never from neuroscience, developmental, or clinical). Because the studies they chose are not representative of psychology as a whole, their results may tell us something about the replicability of the specific studies in the samples, but they are unlikely to tell us much about the replication rate of the entire discipline.

Second, the teams did not always use the same methods that were used in the original studies—sometimes because details of the original methods were not known, and sometimes because the teams made mistakes. This means that some of their studies were not really replications at all; and yet, the results of these studies are typically included when journalists report that there is a "replication crisis" in psychology. Indeed, when the National Academies of Sciences, Engineering, and Medicine recently considered all the evidence, they concluded that contrary to what you may read in the news, "it is not helpful, or justified, to refer to psychology as in a state of 'crisis'" (National Academies of Sciences, Engineering, and Medicine, 2019, p. 124). The bottom line is that, no one knows the actual replication rate of experiments in psychology.

Type I And Type II Errors If we can't answer the question about the real replication rate, then maybe we can answer an easier one: What is the *ideal* replication rate? What percentage of the results published in scientific journals do we *wish* would replicate perfectly? You are probably tempted to say 100%, but that answer is wrong. To understand why that answer is wrong requires understanding the two errors researchers can make when they draw conclusions from evidence.

A **Type I error** occurs *when researchers conclude that there is a relationship between two variables when in fact there is not.* If a psychologist concluded that playing violent video games had increased aggressiveness in a sample of children when in fact it hadn't, that conclusion would be a Type I error, also known as a *false positive.* A **Type II error** occurs *when researchers conclude that there is not a relationship between two variables when in fact there is.* If a psychologist concluded that playing violent video games had not increased aggressiveness in a sample of children when in fact it had, that conclusion would be a Type II error, also known as a *false negative.* You can think of these mistaken conclusions as *flukes* and *flunks:* A fluke happens when we detect something that isn't really there, and a flunk happens when we fail to detect something that is.

Now, the annoying thing about flukes and flunks is that anything you do to reduce the likelihood of one will increase the likelihood of the other. Why? Well, just consider a home security system that sounds an alarm whenever the motion detector is triggered. If you set the sensitivity of the motion detector to *high,* the alarm will always ring when a burglar opens a window, but sometimes it will ring when a houseplant drops a leaf. You will always detect a burglar when he is really there, but sometimes you'll also detect him when he's not. On the other hand, if you set the detector's sensitivity to *low,* the alarm will never mistakenly ring for a houseplant, but sometimes it will fail to ring when a burglar opens a window. You will never detect a burglar when he isn't really there, but sometimes you'll fail to detect him when he is. See the problem? If you want to catch every single burglar, then you'll just have to put up with a few false alarms, and if you want to eliminate every single false alarm then you'll just have to put up with a few uncaught burglars. When an alarm rings even though there is no burglar, the alarm is making a Type I error; and when an alarm fails to ring when there is a burglar, the alarm is making a Type II error. So when setting the sensitivity of your motion detector, you just have to decide which of these errors worries you the most.

Psychologists worry too—not about burglars and houseplants, but about flukes and flunks. They don't want to draw false conclusions from their results, but they also don't want to miss the chance to draw true ones. If psychologists designed their experiments to avoid all Type II errors, they would rarely miss discovering a real and important fact about human behaviour, but a sizeable chunk of those "facts" would turn out to be flukes and the replication rate would be very low. On the other hand, if psychologists designed their experiments to avoid all Type I errors, they would never be fooled by flukes and the replication rate would be very high, but a lot of their studies would be flunks that failed to discover real and important facts about human behaviour.

Neither of these are happy outcomes, so psychologists do exactly what you would do if you were setting up a home security system: They try to strike a balance between the two mistakes they are in danger of making by minimizing the risk of whichever mistake seems worse in a particular situation, and accepting an elevated risk of its opposite (Finkel, Eastwick, & Reis, 2017). The National Academies of Sciences, Engineering, and Medicine noted that "even if there were a definitive estimate of replicability in psychology, no one knows the expected level of non-replicability in a healthy science" (2019, p. 124). In other words, we do not know what the replication rate should be, but we do know that if it were 100%, psychologists would be failing to make important discoveries.

Replication serves an important function in psychology, as it does in every science. And it reminds us that even the best experimental evidence does not allow us to conclude that two variables *are* causally related; rather, it allows us to conclude that two variables *are likely to be* causally related. The more easily and more often that evidence is reproduced, the more confident we can be in the causal relationship between the variables. We can never be completely confident in any result, of course, but replications can move us ever closer to certainty.

Type I error An error that occurs when researchers conclude that there is a causal relationship between two variables when in fact there is not.

Type II error An error that occurs when researchers conclude that there is not a causal relationship between two variables when in fact there is.

Build to the Outcomes

1. What is a natural correlation and how can it be measured?
2. What does it mean for a correlation to be positive or negative, strong or weak?
3. What is the correlation coefficient and what do its values mean?
4. What is the third-variable problem?
5. How do manipulation and random assignment solve the third-variable problem?
6. Why is self-selection a problem?
7. What is the difference between a dependent variable and an independent variable?
8. What is the difference between internal validity and external validity?
9. What can be learned from nonrandom samples?
10. What are Type I and Type II errors?

Thinking Critically About Evidence

Learning Outcomes

*   Identify the psychological tendencies that make critical thinking so difficult.

*   Describe the two steps people can take to help them think critically.

Sir Francis Bacon (1561–1626) devised the scientific method, but underestimated its occupational hazards. While conducting experiments to determine the effect of low temperatures on the preservation of meat, he caught pneumonia and died.

In 1620, Sir Francis Bacon published a book called *Novum Organum,* in which he described a new method for discovering facts about the natural world. What was once called the "Baconian method" is now widely known as the *scientific method,* and that method has allowed human beings to learn more about themselves and the world in the last four centuries than in all the previous centuries combined.

As you've seen in this chapter, the scientific method produces empirical evidence. But empirical evidence is useful only if we know how to think about it—and the fact is that most of us don't. Using evidence requires *critical thinking,* which involves asking ourselves tough questions about whether we have interpreted the evidence in an unbiased way, and about whether the evidence tells not just the truth, but the *whole* truth. Research suggests that most of us have trouble doing these two things and that educational programs designed to teach or improve our critical thinking skills are not particularly effective (Willingham, 2007). Why do we have so much trouble thinking critically?

Consider the armadillo. Some animals freeze when threatened; others duck, run, or growl. Armadillos jump. This natural tendency served armadillos quite well for millennia because for millennia the most common threat to an armadillo's well-being was a rattlesnake. Alas, this natural tendency serves armadillos rather poorly today, because when they wander onto a Texas highway and are threatened by a speeding car, they jump up and hit the bumper. No armadillo makes this mistake twice. Human beings also have natural tendencies that once served them well but no longer do. Our natural and intuitive ways of thinking about evidence, for example, worked just fine when we were hunter-gatherers living in small groups on the African savannah. But today, most of us live in large, complex societies, and our natural ways of thinking about the world don't serve us so well. Sir Francis Bacon understood this. In the very same book in which he developed the scientific method, he argued that two natural human tendencies—the tendency to see what we expect or want to see, and the tendency to ignore what we can't see—are the enemies of critical thinking. Let's examine each of these tendencies and see how they thwart critical thinking.

We See What We Expect and Want to See

When two people are presented with the same evidence, they often draw different conclusions, and Sir Francis Bacon knew why: "The human understanding, once it has adopted opinions . . . draws everything else to support and agree with them . . . [and therefore our] first conclusion colours and brings into conformity with itself all that come after." In other words, our preexisting beliefs colour our view of new evidence, causing us to see what we expect to see. As such, evidence often seems to confirm what we believed all along.

This tendency has been widely documented in psychological science. For instance, participants in one study (Darley & Gross, 1983) learned about a little girl named Hannah. One group of participants was told that Hannah came from an affluent family, while the other group was told that Hannah came from a poor family. All participants were then shown some evidence about Hannah's academic abilities (specifically, they watched a video of Hannah taking a reading test) and were then asked to rate Hannah. Although the video was exactly the same for all participants, those who believed that Hannah's family was affluent rated her performance more positively than did those who believed that her family was poor. What's more, both groups of participants defended their conclusions by citing evidence from the video! Experiments like this one suggest that when we consider evidence, what we see depends on what we *expected* to see.

Our beliefs aren't the only things that colour our views of evidence. They are also coloured by our preferences and prejudices, our ambitions and aversions, our hopes and needs and wants and dreams. As Bacon noted, "The human understanding is not a dry light, but is infused by desire and emotion which give rise to wishful science. For man prefers to believe what he wants to be true." Research suggests that Bacon was right about this, too. For example, participants in one study (Lord, Ross, & Lepper, 1979) were shown some scientific evidence about the effectiveness of the death penalty. Some of the evidence suggested that the death penalty deterred crime, whereas some suggested it did not. What did participants make of this mixed bag of evidence? Participants who originally supported the death penalty became even *more* supportive, and participants who originally opposed the death penalty became even *more* opposed. In other words, when presented with exactly the same evidence, participants saw what they *wanted* to see and ended up feeling even more sure about their initial views. Subsequent research has shown that the same pattern emerges when professional scientists are asked to rate the quality of scientific studies that either confirm or disconfirm what they want to believe (Koehler, 1993).

Exactly how do beliefs and desires shape our view of the evidence? One way is that we tend to hold different kinds of evidence to different standards (McPhetres & Zuckerman, 2017). When evidence confirms what we believe or want to believe, we ask ourselves, "*Can* I believe this evidence?" But when evidence disconfirms what we believe or want to believe, we ask ourselves, "*Must* I believe this evidence?" (Gilovich, 1991). The problem is that *can* is a low standard and *must* is a high one: You *can* believe almost anything, but you *must* believe almost nothing. For instance, *can* you believe that people with university degrees are happier than people without them? Of course. Plenty of surveys show that just such a relationship exists, and a reasonable person who studied the evidence could easily defend this conclusion. Now, *must* you believe it? Well, no. After all, those surveys didn't measure every single person on earth, did they? And if the survey questions had been asked differently, they might well have produced different answers, right? A reasonable person who studied the evidence could easily conclude that the relationship between education and happiness is not yet clear enough to warrant such a strong conclusion.

A second way in which our beliefs and desires shape our view of the evidence is by influencing *which* evidence we consider in the first place. Most people surround themselves with others who believe the same things they believe and want the same things they want, which means that our friends and families are much more likely to validate our beliefs and desires than to challenge them. Studies also show that when given the opportunity to search for evidence, people preferentially search for evidence that confirms their beliefs and fulfills their desires (Hart et al., 2009). What's more, when people find evidence that confirms their beliefs and fulfills their desires, they tend to stop looking; yet when they find evidence that does the opposite, they keep searching for more evidence (Kunda, 1990).

What all of these studies have in common is that they suggest that most evidence leaves room for interpretation, and that's the room in which our beliefs and desires love to hang out. Because it is so easy to see what we expect to see, or to see what we want to see, the first rule of critical thinking is this: *Doubt your own conclusions.* One

The first rule of critical thinking is to doubt your own conclusions—but that's hard to do when everyone tells you you're right! Recent research shows that Facebook users create "echo chambers" by sharing stories and links mainly with friends who already share their points of view (Del Vicario et al., 2016).

of the best ways to find the truth about the world is to seek out people who don't see the world your way and then listen carefully to what they have to say. Most of us find this painful but the outcome is often worth the pain. Scientists go out of their way to expose themselves to criticism by sending their papers to the colleagues who are most likely to disagree with them or by presenting their findings to audiences full of critics, and they do this largely so that they can achieve a more balanced view of their own conclusions (as well as their self-worth). If you want to be happy, take your friend to lunch; but if you want to be right, take your enemy.

We Don't Consider What We Don't See

In another part of his remarkable book, Francis Bacon recounted an old story about a man who visited a Roman temple. The priest showed the man a portrait of several sailors who had taken religious vows and then miraculously survived a shipwreck, and suggested that this was clear evidence of the power of the gods. The visitor paused a moment and then asked precisely the right question: "But where are the pictures of those who perished after taking their vows?" According to Bacon, most of us never think to ask this kind of question. We consider the evidence we can see and forget about the evidence we can't. Bacon claimed that "little or no attention is paid to things invisible" and argued that this natural tendency was "the greatest impediment and aberration of the human understanding."

Bacon was right when he claimed that people rarely pay attention to what is missing (Kardes & Sanbonmatsu, 2003). For example, participants in one study (Newman, Wolff, & Hearst, 1980) played a game in which they were shown a set of trigrams, which are three-letter combinations such as *SXY, GTR, BCG,* and *EVX*. On each trial, the experimenter pointed to one of the trigrams in the set and told the participants that *this* trigram was the special one. The participants' job was to figure out what made the special trigram so special. How many trials did it take before participants figured it out? It depended on the trigram's special feature. For half the participants, the special trigram was always the one that contained the letter *T*, and participants in this condition needed to see about 34 sets of trigrams before they figured out that the presence of *T* was what made the trigram special. But for the other half of the participants, the special trigram was always the one that *lacked* the letter *T*. How many trials did it take before participants figured it out? They *never* figured it out—never. It is much easier to think about what *is* there than what *isn't*.

The tendency to ignore missing evidence can lead to erroneous conclusions (Wainer & Zwerling, 2006). For instance, some universities in Canada have reputations as party schools. **FIGURE 2.12a** shows the number of hours per week that students at different Canadian universities said they spend partying. You might look at this graph and think, "Wow, Queen's University must be a pretty slack school—students there spend a lot of time having fun."

That's a reasonable hypothesis based on the evidence, but it's *not* quite correct—because of evidence not shown in Figure 2.12a. How many hours per week do students spend hitting the books? You might have assumed that the more time students spend partying, the less time they spend studying (in other words, that these two variables are negatively correlated), but this is not the case. Figure 2.12b shows the relationship between hours spent partying and hours spent studying at different schools. There is *no* correlation between these two variables. Queen's students do spend a lot of time partying, but they are also near the top in terms of reported hours spent studying per week. These students play hard—and work harder!

Ever since I began using your product, I haven't had a single unwanted thought about white bears. Thank you so much for this amazing discovery. It has really changed my life!

Mr. Ferb Kushman
Lansing, MI

DANIEL GILBERT

The second rule of critical thinking is to consider what you don't see. Businesses often provide testimonials from satisfied customers—but where are all the dissatisfied customers, and what might they have to say?

DATA VISUALIZATION

Does SAT Performance Correlate with Family Income and Education Level? Go to launchpadworks.com.

Someone who is shown the evidence in the red map and who forgets to ask about the missing evidence in the green map would draw the wrong conclusion about the relationship between partying and dedication to academic pursuits. And yet, forgetting to ask for missing evidence is something that happens all the

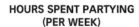

**HOURS SPENT PARTYING
(PER WEEK)**

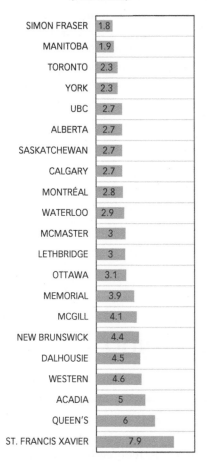

SIMON FRASER	1.8
MANITOBA	1.9
TORONTO	2.3
YORK	2.3
UBC	2.7
ALBERTA	2.7
SASKATCHEWAN	2.7
CALGARY	2.7
MONTRÉAL	2.8
WATERLOO	2.9
MCMASTER	3
LETHBRIDGE	3
OTTAWA	3.1
MEMORIAL	3.9
MCGILL	4.1
NEW BRUNSWICK	4.4
DALHOUSIE	4.5
WESTERN	4.6
ACADIA	5
QUEEN'S	6
ST. FRANCIS XAVIER	7.9

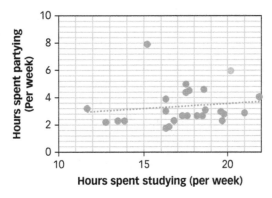

Figure 2.12

Hours Spent Partying or Studying at Some Canadian Universities The bar graph at left shows the hours per week that students at various Canadian universities reported they spend partying. Queen's, with the second most hours, must be full of slackers, right? Wrong. The scatterplot above compares hours spent partying and studying at Canadian universities—and there is no relationship between the two variables. Queen's is shown in orange. Ignoring the missing data (about study habits) would lead to the wrong conclusion about the academic rigour of one of Canada's oldest universities. DATA FROM BROWN (2017).

time. Much of World War II was fought in the air, and the question of how best to armour planes to protect them from enemy fire was something that people worried about. Too much armour, and the plane was too heavy to fly properly. Too little armour—and bye-bye airplane. The Allied military collected data on airplanes that had returned from engagements. There were regularly more bullet holes in the fuselage than in the engines. Officers reasoned that it would be most efficient to concentrate armour where the need was greatest: clearly around the fuselage, right? The officers consulted Alexander Wald, a refugee mathematician from eastern Europe. He did not agree. Dr. Wald instead wondered about the *missing* holes—the ones that should have been in the engines, but weren't. He guessed pretty quickly where those holes were—on the engines of the planes that did *not* return. Those planes probably crashed because of the damage. Based on Dr. Wald's reasoning, the armour was concentrated on the engines, not the fuselage. If the first rule of critical thinking is to doubt what you *do* see, then the second rule is to consider what you *don't* see.

The Skeptical Stance

Science is a human enterprise and humans make mistakes: They see what they expect to see, they see what they want to see, and they often fail to consider what they can't see at all. What makes science different from most other human enterprises is that scientists actively seek to discover and remedy their mistakes. Scientists are constantly striving to make their observations more accurate and their reasoning more rigorous, and they invite anyone and everyone to examine their evidence and challenge their conclusions. As a result, science is the ultimate democracy in which the lowliest nobody can triumph over the most celebrated somebody. When an unknown Swiss patent clerk with a vivid imagination challenged the greatest physicists of his day, he didn't have a famous father, a fancy degree, powerful friends, or a fat wallet. Albert Einstein won the scientific debate for one reason and one reason alone: He was right.

So think of the remaining chapters in this textbook as a report from the field—a description of the work that psychological scientists have done so far as they stumble towards knowledge. These chapters tell the story of the men and women who have put their faith in Francis Bacon's method and used it to pry loose small pieces of the truth about who we are, how we think, feel, and behave, and what we are all doing here together on the third rock from the sun. Some of their reports will turn out to be flukes, others will turn out to be flunks, but every one of them is somebody's best guess about the way people work. Read these reports with interest but think critically about their claims—and for that matter, about everything else.

Build to the Outcomes

1. According to Francis Bacon, what are the two enemies of critical thinking?

2. What does it mean to say, "If you want to be happy, take your friend to lunch; if you want to be right, take your enemy?"

3. What makes science different from most other human enterprises?

The Ethics of Science: Doing What's Right

Learning Outcomes

- Identify the three basic principles that ethical research must follow.

- Summarize the ways in which psychologists ensure that their research respects people.

- Explain the ways in which psychologists ensure that their research respects truth.

Somewhere along the way, someone probably told you that it isn't nice to treat people like objects. And yet, psychologists may appear to be doing just that when they create experimental situations that cause people to feel fearful or sad, to do things that are embarrassing or immoral, and to learn things about themselves and others that they might not really want to know. Don't be fooled by appearances. The fact is that psychologists go to great lengths to protect the well-being of their research participants, and they are bound by a code of ethics that is as detailed and demanding as the professional codes that bind physicians, lawyers, and accountants. That code requires psychologists to show respect for people, for animals, and for the truth. Let's examine each of these obligations in turn.

Respecting People

During World War II, Nazi doctors performed barbaric experiments on human subjects, such as removing organs without anaesthesia or submerging people in ice water just to see how long it would take them to die. After the war ended, the international community developed the Nuremberg Code of 1947 and then the Declaration of Helsinki in 1964, which spelled out rules for the ethical treatment of the people who participate in experiments. Unfortunately, not everyone obeyed the rules. For example, from 1932 until 1972, the U.S. Public Health Service conducted the infamous Tuskegee experiment, in which 399 African American men with syphilis were denied treatment so that researchers could observe the progression of the disease. As one journalist noted, the government "used human beings as laboratory animals in a long and inefficient study of how long it takes syphilis to kill someone" (Jones, 1993, p. 10).

Over time, the basic tenets of the Declaration of Helsinki have become increasingly enshrined in national legislation and regulations. In Canada, all research involving human persons or tissue is covered by the Tri-Council Policy Statement (TCPS): Ethical Conduct for Research Involving Humans. The "tri-council" refers to the three federal research funding agencies: the Canadian Institutes of Health Research (CIHR), the National Sciences and Engineering Research Council (NSERC), and the Social Sciences and Humanities Research Council (SSHRC), which cover health-related, basic science, and social science-related research, respectively. (See Other Voices: Can We Afford Science? on page 67 for more on the federal funding of psychological science). The TCPS describes the core principles, based on respect for human dignity, that all research involving human participants must follow. First, research should show *respect for persons* and their right to make decisions for and about themselves without undue influence or coercion. Second, research should *show concern for welfare,* which means that it should attempt to maximize benefits and reduce risks to the participant. Third, research should be *just,* which means that it should distribute benefits and risks equally to participants without prejudice towards particular individuals or groups.

The specific ethical code that psychologists follow incorporates these basic principles and expands them. (You can find the American Psychological Association's *Ethical Principles of Psychologists and Code of Conduct* [2017] at http://www.apa.org/ethics/code; the Canadian Psychological Association's *Canadian Code of Ethics for Psychologists* is very similar.) Here are a few of the most important rules that govern the conduct of psychological research:

Why is the man at this bar so upset? He just saw some guy slip a drug into a woman's drink and he is alerting the bartender. What he doesn't know is that all the people at the bar are actors and that he is being filmed for the television show *What Would You Do?* The man behaved ethically, but what about the producers of the show? Was it ethical for them to put the man in such a stressful situation without his consent?

- *Informed consent:* Participants may not take part in a psychological study unless they have given **informed consent,** which is *a verbal agreement to participate in a study made by an adult who has been informed of all the risks that participation may entail.* This doesn't mean that the person must know everything about the study (e.g., the hypothesis), but it does mean that the person must know about anything that might potentially be harmful or painful. If people cannot give informed consent (e.g., because they are minors or are mentally incapable), then informed consent must be obtained from their legal guardians. And even after people give informed consent, they always have the right to withdraw from the study at any time without penalty.

- *Freedom from coercion:* Psychologists may not coerce participation. Coercion not only means physical and psychological coercion but monetary coercion as well. It is unethical to offer people large amounts of money to do something that they might otherwise decline to do. University students may be invited to participate in studies as part of their training in psychology, but they are ordinarily offered the option of learning the same things by other means.

- *Protection from harm:* Psychologists must take every possible precaution to protect their research participants from physical or psychological harm. If there are two equally effective ways to study something, the psychologist must use the safer method. If no safe method is available, the psychologist may not perform the study.

- *Risk–benefit analysis:* Although participants may be asked to accept small risks, such as a minor shock or a small embarrassment, they may not even be *asked* to accept large risks, such as severe pain, psychological trauma, or any risk that is greater than the risks they would ordinarily take in their everyday lives. Furthermore, even when participants are asked to take small risks, the psychologist must first demonstrate that these risks are outweighed by the social benefits of the new knowledge that might be gained from the study.

- *Deception:* Psychologists may use deception only when it is justified by the study's scientific, educational, or applied value and when alternative procedures are not feasible. They may never deceive participants about any aspect of a study that could cause them physical or psychological harm or pain.

- *Debriefing:* If a participant is deceived in any way before or during a study, the psychologist must provide a **debriefing,** which is *a verbal description of the true nature and purpose of a study.* If the participant was changed in any way (e.g., made to feel sad), the psychologist must attempt to undo that change (e.g., ask the person to do a task that will make him or her happy) and restore the participant to the state he or she was in before the study.

informed consent A verbal agreement to participate in a study made by an adult who has been informed of all the risks that participation may entail.

debriefing A verbal description of the true nature and purpose of a study.

- *Confidentiality*: Psychologists are obligated to keep private and personal information obtained during a study confidential.

These are just some of the rules that psychologists must follow. But how are those rules enforced? Almost all psychology studies are performed by psychologists who work at universities. These institutions have research ethics boards (REBs) that are composed of researchers, university staff, and laypeople from the community (e.g., business leaders or members of the clergy). A psychologist may conduct a study only after the REB has reviewed and approved it.

As you can imagine, the code of ethics and the procedure for approval are so strict that many studies simply cannot be performed anywhere, by anyone, at any time. For example, psychologists would love to know how growing up without exposure to language affects a person's subsequent ability to speak and think, but they cannot ethically manipulate that variable in an experiment. They can only study the natural correlations between language exposure and speaking ability, and so may never be able to firmly establish the causal relationships between these variables. Indeed, there are many questions that psychologists will never be able to answer definitively because doing so would require unethical experiments that violate basic human rights.

Respecting Animals

Not all research participants have human rights because not all research participants are human. Some are macaque monkeys, rats, pigeons, or other nonhuman animals. The Canadian Council on Animal Care (CCAC) is the national organization responsible for establishing standards for the ethical use and care of animals in research. It describes the special rights of these nonhuman participants and provides guidelines that all research must follow. The Three Rs tenet (Replacement, Reduction, and Refinement) guides the ethical use of animals in science, ensuring appropriate consideration of the animals' welfare, including comfort, health, and humane treatment.

Replacement means that researchers have to prove there is no alternative to using animals in research and that the use of animals is justified by the scientific or clinical value of the study. *Reduction* means that researchers must use the smallest number of animals possible to achieve the research. *Refinement* means that procedures must be modified to minimize the discomfort, infection, illness, and pain of animals. This requires that animals be treated humanely, with comfortable housing and the ability to satisfy their basic instincts (e.g., mice have to make nests), as well as the appropriate administration of painkillers.

That's good—but is it good enough? Some people don't think so. For example, philosopher Peter Singer (1975) has argued that all creatures capable of feeling pain have the same fundamental rights, and that treating nonhumans differently from humans is a form of speciesism that is every bit as abhorrent as racism or sexism. Singer's philosophy has inspired groups such as People for the Ethical Treatment of Animals to call for an end to all research involving nonhuman animals. Unfortunately, it has also inspired some groups to attack psychologists who legally conduct such research. As two researchers (Ringach & Jentsch, 2009, p. 11417) reported:

> We have seen our cars and homes firebombed or flooded, and we have received letters packed with poisoned razors and death threats via e-mail and voicemail. Our families and neighbors have been terrorized by angry mobs of masked protesters who throw rocks, break windows, and chant that "you should stop or be stopped" and that they "know where you sleep at night." Some of the attacks have been cataloged as attempted murder. Adding insult to injury, misguided animal-rights militants openly incite others to violence on the Internet, brag about the resulting crimes, and go as far as to call plots for our assassination "morally justifiable."

Where do most people stand on this issue? A 2013 Nanos poll conducted on behalf of the CCAC revealed that most Canadians (at least 57–64%) support the use of animals in research (Nanos Research, 2013). Indeed, most Americans eat meat, wear

Some people consider it unethical to use animals for clothing or research. Others see an important distinction between these two purposes.

PAUL MCERLANE/REUTERS/NEWSCOM

Other Voices | **Can We Afford Science?**

Who pays for all the research described in textbooks like this one? The answer is you. By and large, scientific research is funded by government agencies, such as the Social Sciences and Humanities Research Council (SSHRC), the Canadian Institutes of Heath Research (CIHR), and the Natural Sciences and Engineering Research Council (NSERC), which give scientists grants (also known as money) to do particular research projects that the scientists have proposed. Of course, this money could be spent on other things, such as feeding the poor, housing the homeless, caring for the ill and elderly, and so on. Does it make sense to spend taxpayer dollars on psychological science when some of our fellow citizens are cold and hungry?

The legal scholar Cass Sunstein argues that research in the behavioural sciences in the United States, at least, is not an expenditure—it is an investment that pays for itself, and more. Dr Sunstein is an American but his view applies to Canada as well. Here's some of what he has to say:

> When government programs fail, it is often because public officials are clueless about how human beings think and act. Federal, state and local governments make it far too hard for small businesses, developers, farmers, veterans and poor people to get permits, licenses, training and economic assistance. It's one thing to make financial aid available to students, so they can attend college. It's another thing to design forms that students can actually fill out.
>
> Building on impressive new findings from the White House's Social and Behavioral Sciences Team, Mr. Obama ordered his government to use behavioral insights to simplify forms, cut wait times, eliminate administrative hurdles and reduce regulatory burdens. A new report from the team, which has been up and running for more than a year, shows that small reforms can make a big difference.
>
> For example, the team helped to design a new email campaign to increase savings by service members, which nearly doubled enrollment in federal savings plans. It found that simple text messages to lower-income students, reminding them to complete required pre-matriculation tasks, increased college enrollment among those students by 5.7 percentage points. An outreach letter to farmers, designed to promote awareness of a loan program, produced a 22 percent increase in the proportion of farmers who ultimately obtained loans. A new signature box on an online form, requiring vendors to confirm the accuracy of self-reported sales, produced an additional $1.59 million in fees collected by the government in just one quarter, apparently because the box increased honest reporting.
>
> Notwithstanding the success stories, official use of behavioral science raises two legitimate concerns. The first is practical: How much good can it do? Improvements might be a matter of just a few percentage points—and perhaps a distraction from ambitious fiscal or regulatory reforms that could make a much bigger difference. It's a fair point, but incremental improvements should not be disparaged, especially if they help hundreds of thousands of people. And if the goal is to produce large-scale

> change, behaviorally informed approaches might accomplish more than we expect. For example, behavioral scientists have found that the default rule, establishing what happens if people do nothing, has surprisingly big effects. If employers automatically enroll new employees in savings programs, they can produce significant increases in participation—in one study, an increase of more than 30 percentage points. And more controversially, if utility companies automatically enrolled people in green energy, there would inevitably be reductions in greenhouse gas emissions, even with the right to opt out.
>
> These examples raise a second concern, about ethics: What about the risk of manipulation? Should the national government really be conducting psychological experiments on the American people? It is true that behavioral science can be misused. A graphic warning, designed to produce fear, might discourage people from purchasing products that create little harm. People might be automatically enrolled in programs that do them no good. The best safeguard against manipulation is accountability. Official uses of behavioral science should never be hidden, and they should always be undertaken within the limits of law and for legitimate ends, such as promoting retirement security, lowering barriers to college, increasing employment and saving taxpayers money. If the law requires people to obtain licenses or permits, to pay taxes, or to apply for benefits or training, the government must select some method of communication. Public officials need to experiment if they want to know the effects of different methods.
>
> Behavioral research shows that efforts at simplification, or slight variations in wording, can make all the difference. Since 2010, Britain has had its own Behavioral Insights Team, which experimented with a brief addition to a letter to late-paying taxpayers: "The great majority of people in your local area pay their tax on time." The change, which is being introduced nationally, produced a 15 percent increase in on-time payments and is projected to bring in millions of dollars worth of revenue. When government programs aren't working, those on the left tend to support more funding, while those on the right want to scrap them altogether. It is better to ask whether the problem is complexity and poor design. We can solve those problems—sometimes without spending a penny.

What do you think? Is Sunstein right? Is psychological science a wise use of public funds? Or is it a luxury that we simply can't afford?

Cass R. Sunstein is a law professor at Harvard University and was the administrator of the White House Office of Information and Regulatory Affairs under American President Barack Obama.

leather, and support the rights of hunters, which is to say that most Canadians see a sharp distinction between animal and human rights. Science is not in the business of resolving moral controversies, and every individual must draw his or her own conclusions about this issue. But whatever position you take, it is important to note that only a small percentage of the people who champion animal rights engage in abusive or illegal behaviour. It is also important to note that only a small percentage of psychological studies involve animals, and that only a small percentage of those studies cause animals pain or harm. Psychologists mainly study people, and when they do study animals, they mainly study their behaviour.

Respecting Truth

Research ethics boards (REBs) ensure that data are collected ethically. But once the data are collected, who ensures that they are ethically analyzed and reported? No one. Psychology, like all sciences, works on the honour system. No authority is charged with monitoring what psychologists do with the data they've collected, and no authority is charged with checking to see if the claims they make are true. You may find that a bit odd. After all, we don't use the honour system in stores ("Take the microwave home and pay us next time you're in the neighbourhood"), banks ("I don't need to look up your account, just tell me how much money you want to withdraw"), or courtrooms ("If you say you're innocent, well then, that's good enough for me"), so why would we expect it to work in science? Are scientists more honest than everyone else?

Definitely! Okay, we just lied. But the honour system doesn't depend on scientists being especially honest; it depends on the fact that science is a community enterprise. When scientists claim to have discovered something important, other scientists don't just applaud: They start studying it too. When the physicist Jan Hendrik Schön announced in 2001 that he had produced a molecular-scale transistor, other physicists were deeply impressed—that is, until they tried to replicate his work and discovered that Schön had fabricated his data (Agin, 2007). Schön lost his job and his PhD, but the important point is that such frauds can't last long because one scientist's conclusion is the next scientist's research question.

This doesn't mean that all frauds are uncovered swiftly, however. The psychologist Diederik Stapel lied, cheated, and made up his data for decades before people became suspicious enough to investigate (Levelt Committee, Noort Committee, Drenth Committee, 2012), and that's mainly because the discoveries he claimed to have made were not particularly important to begin with. Not all frauds are uncovered, but all of the *important* ones are. The psychologist who fraudulently claims to have shown that chimps are smarter than goldfish may never get caught because no one is likely to follow up on such an obvious finding, but the psychologist who fraudulently claims to have shown the opposite will soon have a lot of explaining to do.

What exactly are psychologists on their honour to do? At least three things. First, when writing reports of their studies and publishing them in scientific journals, psychologists are obligated to report truthfully on what they did and what they found. They can't fabricate results (e.g., by claiming to have performed studies that they never really performed) or fudge results (e.g., by changing records of data that were actually collected), and they can't mislead by omission (e.g., by reporting only the results that confirm their hypothesis and saying nothing about the results that don't). Second, psychologists are obligated to share credit fairly by including as co-authors of their reports the other people who contributed to the work, as well as by mentioning in their reports the other scientists who have done related work. And third, psychologists are obligated to share their data. The American Psychological Association's code of conduct states that ethical psychologists "do not withhold the data on which their conclusions are based from other competent professionals who seek to verify the substantive claims through reanalysis." Most scientific frauds have been uncovered by fellow scientists who became suspicious when they looked closely at the fraudster's data. The fact that anyone can check up on anyone else is part of why the honour system works as well as it does.

Build to the Outcomes

1. What is a research ethics board (REB)?
2. What is informed consent?
3. What is debriefing?
4. What steps must psychologists take to protect nonhuman subjects?
5. What three things must psychologists do when they report the results of their research?
6. How does science uncover fraud?

Chapter Review

Empiricism: How to Know Stuff

- Empiricism is the belief that the best way to understand the world is to observe it firsthand. It is only in the past few centuries that people have begun to systematically collect and evaluate evidence to test the accuracy of their beliefs about the world.

- Observation doesn't just mean "looking." It requires a method. The scientific method involves (a) developing a theory that gives rise to a falsifiable hypothesis; and then (b) making observations that serve to test that hypothesis. Although these tests may prove that a theory is false, they can never prove that it is true.

- The methods of psychology are special because human beings are more complex, variable, and reactive than almost anything else that scientists study.

Methods of Observation: Finding Out What People Do

- Measurement involves (a) defining a property in measurable terms and then (b) using a device that can detect that property. A good definition has construct validity (the concrete condition being measured adequately characterizes the property), and a good detector has both power (it can tell when properties are different) and reliability (it can tell when properties are the same).

- When people know they are being observed, they may behave as they think they should. Demand characteristics are aspects of an observational setting that cause people to behave as they think someone else wants or expects them to. Psychologists try to reduce or eliminate demand characteristics by observing participants in their natural habitats or by hiding their expectations from the participant. Observer bias is the tendency for observers' expectations to influence both what they believe they observed and what actually happened. Psychologists try to avoid observer bias by conducting double-blind studies.

- Psychologists usually measure samples rather than entire populations. They often describe their measurements with a graphic representation called a frequency distribution, which often has a special shape known as the normal distribution. They also describe their measurements with descriptive statistics; the most common are descriptions of central tendency (such as the mean, median, and mode) and descriptions of variability (such as the range and the standard deviation).

Methods of Explanation: Figuring Out Why People Do What They Do

- To determine whether two variables are causally related, we must first determine whether they are related at all. This can be done by measuring each variable many times and then comparing the patterns of variation within each series of measurements. If the patterns are synchronized, then the variables are correlated. Correlations allow us to predict the value of one variable from knowledge of the value of the other. The direction and strength of a correlation are measured by the correlation coefficient (r).

- Even when we observe a correlation between two variables, we can't conclude that they are causally related because a "third variable" could be causing them both. Experiments solve this third-variable problem by manipulating an independent variable, randomly assigning participants to the conditions that this manipulation creates, and then measuring a dependent variable. These measurements are then compared across conditions. If calculations show that the results would only happen 5% of the time if random assignment had failed, then the differences in the measurements across conditions are assumed to have been caused by the manipulation.

- An internally valid experiment establishes the likelihood of a causal relationship between variables as they were defined and among the participants who were studied. When an experiment mimics the real world, it is externally valid. But most psychology experiments are not attempts to mimic the real world; rather, they test hypotheses derived from theories.

- Random sampling allows researchers to generalize from their samples to the populations from which the samples were drawn, but most psychology studies cannot use random sampling and therefore there are restrictions on the conclusions that can be drawn from them. One restriction is that we can never be absolutely sure that a result is not a fluke, yet replications do help to increase our confidence.

- Replication is an attempt to reproduce a result by using the same procedures and sampling from the same population as the original study. Although no one knows the real replication rate in psychological science, the fact that researchers must balance the risk of Type I and Type II errors means that we would not expect the rate to be—or want it to be—100%.

Thinking Critically About Evidence

- Thinking critically about evidence is difficult because people have a natural tendency to see what they expect to see, to see what they want to see, and to consider what they see but not what they don't see.

- Critical thinkers consider evidence that disconfirms their own opinions. They also consider the evidence that is absent, not just the evidence that is present.

- What makes science different from most other human enterprises is that science actively seeks to discover and remedy its own biases and errors.

The Ethics of Science: Doing What's Right

- Research ethics boards ensure that the rights of human beings who participate in scientific research are based on the principles of respect for persons, concern for welfare, and justice.

- Psychologists are obligated to uphold these principles by getting informed consent from participants, not coercing their participation, protecting participants from harm, weighing benefits against risks, avoiding deception, and keeping information confidential.

- Psychologists are obligated to respect the rights of animals and to treat them humanely. Most people are in favour of using animals in scientific research.

- Psychologists are obligated to tell the truth about their studies, to share credit appropriately, and to grant others access to their data.

Key Concept Quiz

1. The belief that accurate knowledge can be acquired through observation is the definition of
   a. critical thinking.
   b. dogmatism.
   c. empiricism.
   d. correlation.

2. Which of the following is the best definition of a hypothesis?
   a. empirical evidence
   b. a scientific investigation
   c. a falsifiable prediction
   d. a theoretical idea

3. If a detector is used to measure the same property twice but produces different measurements, then it lacks
   a. validity.
   b. reliability.
   c. power.
   d. concreteness.

4. Aspects of an observational setting that cause people to behave as they think someone wants or expects them to are called
   a. observer biases.
   b. Type I errors.
   c. Type II errors.
   d. demand characteristics.

5. Which of the following describes the average value of all the measurements in a particular distribution?
   a. mean
   b. median
   c. mode
   d. range

6. What does the sign of r (the correlation coefficient) show?
   a. the strength of a correlation
   b. the direction of a correlation
   c. the likelihood that random assignment failed
   d. the degree of replicability

7. When two variables are correlated, what keeps us from concluding that one is the cause and the other is the effect?
   a. the third-variable problem
   b. observer bias
   c. the strength of the manipulation
   d. the failure of random assignment

8. A researcher administers a questionnaire concerning attitudes towards tax increases to people of all genders and ages who live all across Canada. The dependent variable in the study is the _____ of the participants.
   a. age
   b. gender
   c. attitude
   d. geographic location

9. An experiment that defines variables as they are defined in the real world is
   a. externally valid.
   b. internally valid.
   c. operationally defined.
   d. statistically significant.

10. When people find evidence that confirms their beliefs, they often
    a. stop looking.
    b. seek more evidence.
    c. refuse to believe it.
    d. take their enemies to lunch.

LearningCurve
macmillan learning

Don't stop now! Quizzing yourself is a powerful study tool. Go to LaunchPad to access the LearningCurve adaptive quizzing system and your own personalized learning plan. Visit launchpadworks.com.

Key Terms

empiricism (p. 34)

scientific method (p. 35)

theories (p. 35)

hypothesis (p. 35)

empirical method (p. 36)

operational definition (p. 38)

construct validity (p. 38)

power (p. 38)

reliability (p. 38)

demand characteristics (p. 39)

naturalistic observation (p. 39)

observer bias (p. 41)

double-blind study (p. 41)

population (p. 41)

sample (p. 41)

frequency distribution (p. 42)

normal distribution (p. 42)

mode (p. 43)

mean (p. 43)

median (p. 43)

range (p. 44)

standard deviation (p. 44)

variable (p. 45)

correlation (p. 46)

correlation coefficient (r) (p. 47)

natural correlation (p. 48)

third-variable problem (p. 49)

experimentation (p. 49)

manipulation (p. 49)

independent variable (p. 50)

dependent variable (p. 50)

self-selection (p. 51)

random assignment (p. 51)

internal validity (p. 53)

external validity (p. 55)

case method (p. 56)

random sampling (p. 56)

replication (p. 58)

Type I error (p. 59)

Type II error (p. 59)

informed consent (p. 65)

debriefing (p. 65)

Changing Minds

1. A research study shows that getting a good night's sleep increases people's performance on almost any kind of task. You tell a classmate about this study and she shrugs. "Who didn't already know that? If you ask me, psychology is just common sense. Why conduct experiments to show what everyone already knows?" How would you explain the value of studying something that seems like "common sense"?

2. Your friend texts you a link to a study showing that Europeans who work longer hours are less happy than those who work shorter hours, but that in the United States and Canada it's the other way around. The text reads "Cool experiment!" so you reply "Study—not experiment," either because you are very wise or because you don't know much about friendship. Why aren't all research studies experiments? What can't you learn from this study that you *could* learn from an experiment?

3. After the first exam, your professor says she's noticed a positive correlation between the location of students' seats and their exam scores: "The closer students sit to the front of the room, the higher their scores on the exam," she announces. After class, your friend suggests that the two of you should sit up front for the rest of the semester to improve your grades. Having read about correlation and causation, should you be skeptical? What are some possible reasons for the correlation between seating position and good grades? Could you design an experiment to test whether sitting up front actually causes good grades?

4. A classmate in your criminal justice course suggests that mental illness is a major cause of violent crimes in North America. As evidence, he mentions a highly publicized murder trial in which the convicted suspect was diagnosed with schizophrenia. What scientific evidence would he need to support this claim?

5. You ask your friend if she wants to go to the gym with you. "No," she says, "I never exercise." You tell her that regular exercise has all kinds of health benefits, including greatly reducing the risk of heart disease. "I don't believe that," she replies. "I had an uncle who got up at 6 a.m. every day of his life to go jogging, and he still died of a heart attack at age 53." What would you tell your friend? Does her uncle's case prove that exercise really doesn't protect against heart disease after all?

Answers to Key Concept Quiz

1. c; 2. c; 3. b; 4. d; 5. a; 6. b; 7. a; 8. c; 9. a; 10. a

LaunchPad features the full e-Book of *Psychology*, the LearningCurve adaptive quizzing system, videos, and a variety of activities to boost your learning. Visit LaunchPad at launchpadworks.com.

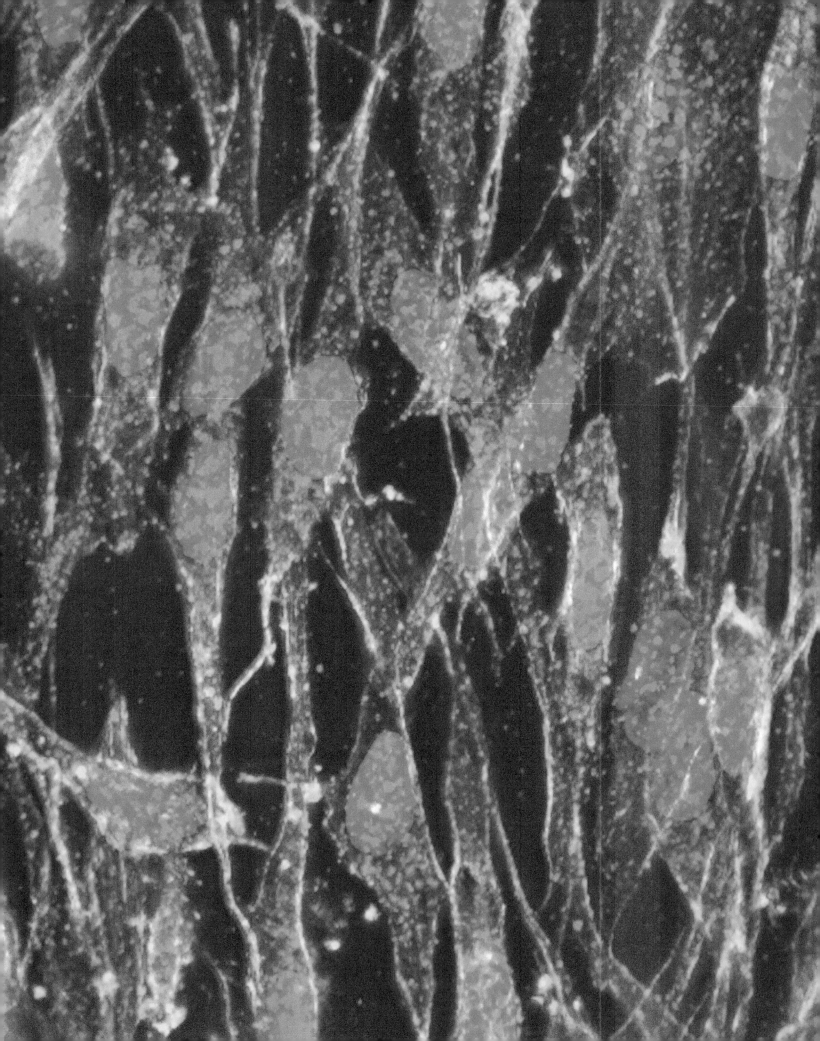

Neuroscience and Behaviour

3

IN THE SUMMER OF 2011, THREE National Hockey League (NHL) players died within a few months of each other. Wade Belak, the oldest of the three, was born in Saskatoon in 1976. He was drafted into the NHL when he was 17 and played for six teams over his career, including the Quebec Nordiques and the Toronto Maple Leafs. He died accidentally (the police treated it as a suicide) in a Toronto apartment, leaving behind a wife and two young daughters. He was 35. Derek Boogaard, another native of Saskatchewan and the son of a Mountie, played for the Minnesota Wild and the New York Rangers. He was 28 years old when he died of a drug overdose, having mixed powerful painkillers and alcohol on a night out with friends. Rick Rypien, from Blairmore, Alberta, was the youngest of the three. He spent some time with the Regina major junior team and then with a minor professional team in Manitoba. When he was 22, he joined the Vancouver Canucks and played six seasons with them. He took his own life in his home in Crowsnest Pass, Alberta—he was 27.

What did these three young men have in common, besides their passion for hockey and their tragic, early deaths? They were all "enforcers," players who are expected to use aggressive methods, such as fighting and checking, to respond to violence against their team members, especially star players and goalies. They had all suffered blows to the head and concussions in their hockey careers. Both Rypien and Belak suffered from clinical depression and Boogaard battled an addiction to painkillers, as well as depression.

Postmortem analysis of Boogaard's brain revealed the presence of a condition known as chronic traumatic encephalopathy (CTE), a form of progressive brain damage that has been linked to repeated concussions (McKee et al., 2009). Although their brains were not examined, CTE is strongly suspected to have played a role in the deaths of Belak and Rypien as well, and is a confirmed diagnosis in many other deceased professional hockey players, particularly enforcers. CTE has been confirmed in the brains of at least 34 professional football players, and it has also been observed after repeated head injuries in boxing, wrestling, and rugby (Costanza et al., 2011; Daneshvar et al., 2011; Lakhan & Kirchgessner, 2012; McKee et al., 2009).

Derek Boogard, a professional hockey player for the New York Rangers, died of a drug overdose in 2011, when he was 28. After his death, his brain was observed to be reduced in size, with fluid-filled spaces where brain tissue should have been. This is characteristic of chronic traumatic encephalopathy (CTE), a progressive degenerative disease that is seen in individuals who have received repeated blows to the head.

In December 2015, attention to CTE was further heightened by the release of the movie *Concussion*, which focuses on the story of Bennet Omalu (played by Will Smith), the pathologist who first uncovered evidence for CTE in the brain of an NFL player. Although statements by the Omalu character in the movie imply that CTE has caused the decline and death of former National Football League (NFL) players, others have claimed that the science linking CTE and bad outcomes after football is inconclusive and even flawed (Barr & Karantzoulis, 2019; Hoge, 2018). In fact, we don't know whether playing football and hockey causes CTE, or whether CTE causes such extreme outcomes as suicide. Indeed, former NFL players are at lower risk for suicide than men in the general population (Iverson, 2015), and scientists are actively debating the nature and consequences of CTE (Castellani, Perry, & Iverson, 2015). However, we do know that CTE is associated with an array of cognitive and emotional deficits in afflicted individuals, including inability to concentrate, memory loss, irritability, and depression, usually beginning within a decade after repeated concussions and worsening with time (McKee et al., 2009; Montenigro et al., 2015). Fortunately, there is growing awareness of CTE and its associated symptoms, which is leading professional sports organizations, as well as universities, schools, and others involved in youth sports, to take steps to address the problem.

The symptoms of CTE are reminders that our psychological, emotional, and social well-being depend critically on the health and integrity of the brain. They also highlight that understanding neuroscience isn't just an academic exercise confined to scientific laboratories: The more we know about the brain, and the more people who know it, the better our chances of finding solutions to problems such as CTE.

IN THIS CHAPTER, WE'LL CONSIDER HOW THE BRAIN WORKS, what happens when it doesn't, and how both states of affairs determine behaviour. First, we'll introduce the basic unit of information processing in the brain, the neuron. The electrical and chemical activities of neurons are the starting point of all behaviour, thought, and emotion. Next, we'll consider the anatomy of the central nervous system, focusing especially on the brain, including its overall organization, the key structures that perform its different functions, and its evolutionary development. We then examine the interplay between genetics and the environment, as well as the role they play in directing behaviour. Finally, we'll discuss methods that allow us to study the brain and clarify our understanding of how it works. These include methods that examine the damaged brain and methods for scanning the living and healthy brain.

DATA VISUALIZATION

Which Sports Have the Highest Rates of Concussion? Go to launchpadworks.com.

Neurons: The Origin of Behaviour

Learning Outcomes

- Explain the function of neurons.
- Outline the components of the neuron.
- Differentiate the three major types of neurons by their function.

An estimated 1 billion people watch the final game of World Cup soccer every four years. That's a whole lot of people, but to put it in perspective, it's only a little over 14% of the estimated 7 billion people currently living on earth. A more impressive number might be the 30 billion viewers who tune in to watch any of the World Cup action over the course of the tournament. But a really, really big number is inside your skull right now, helping you make sense of these big numbers you're reading about. Scientists estimate that there are as many as *86 billion* nerve cells (von Bartheld, Bahney, & Herculano-Houzel, 2016) in your brain that perform a variety of tasks to allow you to function as a human being.

Humans have thoughts, feelings, and behaviours that are often accompanied by visible signals. Consider how you might feel on your way to meet a good friend. An observer might see a smile on your face or notice how fast you are walking; internally, you might mentally rehearse what you'll say to your friend and feel a surge of happiness as you get closer. All those visible and experiential signs are coordinated by the activity of your brain cells. The anticipation you have, the happiness you feel, and the speed of your feet are the result of information processing in your brain. In a way, all of your thoughts, feelings, and behaviours spring from cells in the brain that take in information and produce some kind of output trillions of times a day. These cells are **neurons,** *cells in the nervous system that communicate with each other to perform information-processing tasks.*

Components of the Neuron

During the 1800s, scientists began to turn their attention from studying the mechanics of limbs, lungs, and livers to studying the harder-to-observe workings of the brain. Philosophers wrote poetically about an "enchanted loom" that mysteriously wove a tapestry of behaviour, and many scientists confirmed that metaphor (Corsi, 1991). To those scientists, the brain looked as though it were composed of a continuously connected lattice of fine threads, leading them to conclude that it was one big woven web of material. However, in the late 1880s, the Spanish physician Santiago Ramón y Cajal (1852–1934) learned about a new technique for staining neurons in the brain (DeFelipe & Jones, 1988). The stain highlighted the appearance of entire cells, revealing that they came in different shapes and sizes (see **FIGURE 3.1**).

Ramón y Cajal discovered that neurons are complex structures composed of three basic parts: the cell body, the dendrites, and the axon (see **FIGURE 3.2**). Like cells in all organs of the body, neurons have a **cell body** (also called the *soma*), the largest *component of the neuron that coordinates the information-processing tasks and keeps the cell alive.* Functions such as protein synthesis, energy production, and metabolism take place here. The cell body contains a *nucleus,* which houses chromosomes that contain your DNA, or the genetic blueprint of who you are. The cell body is enclosed by a porous cell membrane that allows some molecules to flow into and out of the cell.

Unlike other cells in the body, neurons have two types of specialized extensions of the cell membrane that allow them to communicate: dendrites and axons. **Dendrites** *receive information from other neurons and relay it to the cell body.* The term *dendrite* comes from the Greek word for "tree"; indeed, most neurons have many dendrites that look like tree branches. The **axon** *carries information to other neurons, muscles, or glands.* Axons can be very long, even stretching up to a metre from the base of the spinal cord down to the big toe.

In many neurons, the axon is covered by a **myelin sheath,** *an insulating layer of fatty material.* The myelin sheath is composed of **glial cells** (named for the Greek word for "glue"), which are *support cells found in the nervous system.* Recent estimates suggest there are fewer glial cells in the brain than neurons; nevertheless, they serve a variety of roles critical to the function of the nervous system (von Bartheld et al., 2016). Some glial cells digest parts of dead neurons, others provide physical and nutritional support for neurons, and others form myelin that insulates the axon and allows it to carry information more efficiently. In fact, *demyelinating diseases,* such as multiple sclerosis, cause the myelin sheath to deteriorate, slowing communication from one neuron to another (Schwartz & Westbrook, 2000). This slowdown leads to a variety of problems, including loss of feeling in the limbs, partial blindness, and difficulties in coordinated movement and cognition (Butler, Corboy, & Filley, 2009).

Ramón y Cajal also observed that the dendrites and axons of neurons do not actually touch each other. There's a small gap between the axon of one neuron and the dendrites or cell body of another. This gap is part of the **synapse,** *the junction or region between the axon of one neuron and the dendrites or cell body of another* (see Figure 3.2). Many of the billions of neurons in your brain have a few thousand synaptic junctions,

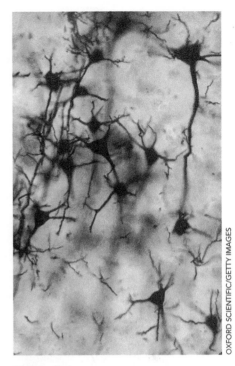

OXFORD SCIENTIFIC/GETTY IMAGES

Figure 3.1
Golgi-Stained Neurons Santiago Ramón y Cajal used a Golgi stain (like the one shown here) to highlight the appearance of neurons. He was the first to see that each neuron is composed of a body with many threads extending outward towards other neurons. In a surprising finding, he also saw that the threads of each neuron do not actually touch other neurons.

neurons Cells in the nervous system that communicate with one another to perform information-processing tasks.

cell body (soma) The part of a neuron that coordinates information-processing tasks and keeps the cell alive.

dendrite The part of a neuron that receives information from other neurons and relays it to the cell body.

axon The part of a neuron that carries information to other neurons, muscles, or glands.

myelin sheath An insulating layer of fatty material.

glial cells Support cells found in the nervous system.

synapse The junction or region between the axon of one neuron and the dendrites or cell body of another.

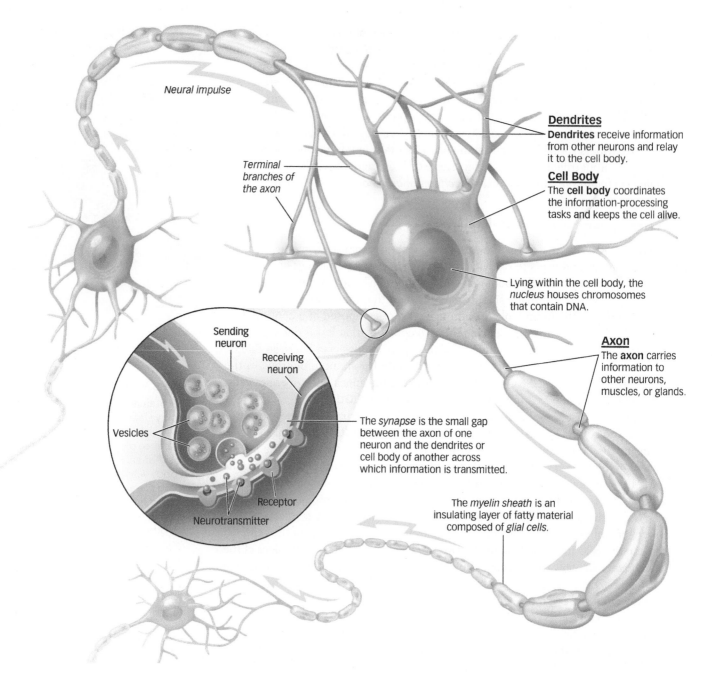

Neural impulse

Terminal branches of the axon

Dendrites
Dendrites receive information from other neurons and relay it to the cell body.

Cell Body
The **cell body** coordinates the information-processing tasks and keeps the cell alive.

Lying within the cell body, the *nucleus* houses chromosomes that contain DNA.

Axon
The **axon** carries information to other neurons, muscles, or glands.

Sending neuron

Receiving neuron

Vesicles

The *synapse* is the small gap between the axon of one neuron and the dendrites or cell body of another across which information is transmitted.

Receptor

Neurotransmitter

The *myelin sheath* is an insulating layer of fatty material composed of *glial cells*.

Figure 3.2

Components of a Neuron
A neuron is made up of three parts: a cell body, dendrites, and an axon. Notice that neurons do not actually touch one another: There is a small synaptic space between them across which information is transmitted.

sensory neurons Neurons that receive information from the external world and convey this information to the brain via the spinal cord.

so it should come as no shock that adults have trillions of synapses. As you'll read shortly, the transmission of information across the synapse is fundamental to communication between neurons, a process that allows us to think, feel, and behave.

Neurons Specialized by Function

There are three major types of neurons, each performing a distinct function: sensory neurons, motor neurons, and interneurons.

- **Sensory neurons** *receive information from the external world and convey this information to the brain via the spinal cord.* They have specialized endings on

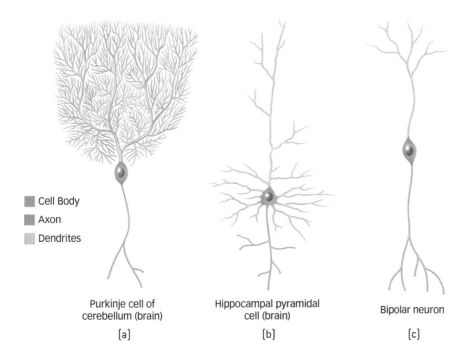

Cell Body

Axon

Dendrites

Purkinje cell of cerebellum (brain)

(a)

Hippocampal pyramidal cell (brain)

(b)

Bipolar neuron

(c)

Figure 3.3
Neurons Specialized by Location
Neurons have a cell body, an axon, and at least one dendrite. The size and shape of neurons vary considerably, however. The Purkinje cell has an elaborate treelike assemblage of dendrites (a). Pyramidal cells have a triangular cell body and a single, long dendrite with many smaller dendrites (b). Bipolar cells have only one dendrite and a single axon (c).

their dendrites that receive signals for light, sound, touch, taste, and smell. For example, sensory neurons' endings in our eyes are sensitive to light.

- **Motor neurons** *carry signals from the spinal cord to the muscles to produce movement.* These neurons often have long axons that reach to muscles at our extremities.
- **Interneurons** *connect sensory neurons, motor neurons, or other interneurons.* Most of the nervous system is composed of the interneurons. Some carry information from sensory neurons into the nervous system, others carry information from the nervous system to motor neurons, and still others perform a variety of information-processing functions within the nervous system. Interneurons work together in small circuits to perform simple tasks, such as identifying the location of a sensory signal, and much more complicated ones, such as recognizing a familiar face.

Neurons Specialized by Location

Besides specialization for sensory, motor, or connective functions, neurons are also somewhat specialized, depending on their location (see **FIGURE 3.3**). For example, *Purkinje cells* are a type of interneuron that carries information from the cerebellum to the rest of the brain and the spinal cord. These neurons have dense, elaborate dendrites that resemble bushes. *Pyramidal cells,* found in the cerebral cortex, have a triangular cell body and a single, long dendrite among many smaller dendrites. *Bipolar cells,* a type of sensory neuron found in the retinas of the eye, have a single axon and a single dendrite. The brain processes different types of information, so a substantial amount of specialization at the cellular level has evolved to handle these tasks.

motor neurons Neurons that carry signals from the spinal cord to the muscles to produce movement.

interneurons Neurons that connect sensory neurons, motor neurons, or other interneurons.

Build to the Outcomes

1. What do neurons do?
2. What are the three primary components of the neuron?
3. Do neurons actually touch when they communicate? Explain your answer.
4. What is the function of the myelin sheath?
5. What critical functions do the glial cells play?
6. How do the three types of neurons work together to transmit information?

The Electrochemical Actions of Neurons: Information Processing

Our thoughts, feelings, and actions depend on neural communication, but how does it happen? Neurons are electronically excitable cells and communication of information happens in the form of electrical signals within neurons and chemical signals between them. This occurs in two stages:

- *Conduction* is the movement of an electric signal within neurons, from the dendrites to the cell body, then throughout the axon.
- *Transmission* is the movement of a signal from one neuron to another as a result of chemical signalling across the synapse.

Together, these stages are what scientists generally refer to as the *electrochemical action* of neurons.

Electric Signalling: Conducting Information Within a Neuron

The neuron's cell membrane has small pores that act as channels to allow small electrically charged molecules, called *ions*, to flow in and out of the cell. It is this flow of ions across the neuron's cell membrane that creates the conduction of an electric signal within the neuron. How does it happen?

The Resting Potential: The Origin of the Neuron's Electrical Properties

resting potential The difference in electric charge between the inside and outside of a neuron's cell membrane.

AGE FOTOSTOCK/GETTY IMAGES

The British biologists Alan Hodgkin and Andrew Huxley discovered the resting potential in the summer of 1939 while studying marine invertebrates—sea creatures that lack a spine, such as clams, squid, and lobsters (Stevens, 1971). Hodgkin and Huxley worked with the squid giant axon because it is 100 times larger than the biggest axon in humans. They inserted a thin wire into the squid axon so that it touched the jellylike fluid inside. Then they placed another wire just outside the axon in the watery fluid that surrounds it. They found a substantial difference between the electric charges inside and outside the axon, which they called the resting potential.

Neurons have a natural electric charge called the **resting potential,** *the difference in electric charge between the inside and outside of a neuron's cell membrane* (Kandel, 2000). When first discovered by biologists in the 1930s, the resting potential was measured at about −70 millivolts. This is a much smaller charge than a typical battery has; for example, a 9-volt battery has 9,000 millivolts.

The resting potential is caused by the difference in concentrations of ions inside and outside the neuron's cell membrane (see **FIGURE 3.4a**). Ions can carry a positive (+) or a negative (−) charge. In the resting state, there is a high concentration of positively charged potassium ions (K^+), as well as larger, negatively charged protein ions (A^-), *inside* the neuron's cell membrane compared to outside it. By contrast, there is a high concentration of positively charged sodium ions (Na^+) and negatively charged chloride ions (Cl^-) *outside* the neuron's cell membrane. Because the A^- ions are larger and carry a much stronger charge than the other ions, during the resting potential, the inside of the cell membrane is negatively charged at −70 millivolts relative to the outside.

Normally, ions from the area of higher concentration move to the area of lower concentration until the concentrations are equal—or in equilibrium—but special channels in the cell membrane restrict the movement of the ions in and out of the cell. An active chemical "pump" in the cell membrane helps maintain the high concentration of K^+ ions inside by pushing Na^+ ions out of the cell and pulling K^+ ions into the cell. This pump and other structures in the cell membrane ensure that during the resting potential, excess K^+ ions are built up inside the cell, ready to rush out to create equilibrium with the low concentration of K^+ ions outside the cell. Similarly, excess Na^+ ions outside the cell are ready to rush in to create equilibrium with the low concentration of Na^+ ions within the cell. Channels specific to K^+ and Na^+ ions in the membrane are voltage-gated, so they open or close in response to changes in the voltage across the membrane. During the resting potential, these channels are closed, which allows the electrical charge inside the neuron to build up to −70 millivolts relative to the outside. Like a dam holding back a river until the floodgates open, these channels in the cell membrane hold back the ions, building potential energy that can be released in a fraction of a second.

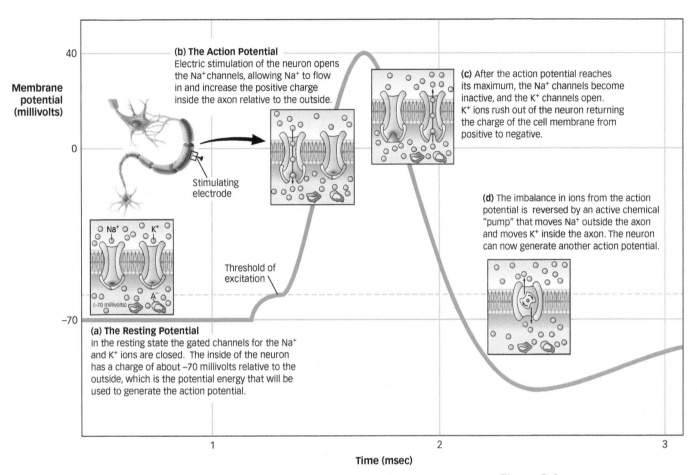

Membrane potential (millivolts)

40

0

−70

(b) The Action Potential
Electric stimulation of the neuron opens the Na⁺ channels, allowing Na⁺ to flow in and increase the positive charge inside the axon relative to the outside.

(c) After the action potential reaches its maximum, the Na⁺ channels become inactive, and the K⁺ channels open. K⁺ ions rush out of the neuron returning the charge of the cell membrane from positive to negative.

(d) The imbalance in ions from the action potential is reversed by an active chemical "pump" that moves Na⁺ outside the axon and moves K⁺ inside the axon. The neuron can now generate another action potential.

Stimulating electrode

Threshold of excitation

Na⁺   K⁺

(−70 millivolts)   A⁻

(a) The Resting Potential
In the resting state the gated channels for the Na⁺ and K⁺ ions are closed. The inside of the neuron has a charge of about −70 millivolts relative to the outside, which is the potential energy that will be used to generate the action potential.

1   2   3

Time (msec)

The Action Potential: Sending Signals Across the Neuron

The biologists working with the squid giant axon noticed something strange. When they stimulated the axon with an electric shock, it set off a much larger electrical impulse, a spike in voltage that travelled down the axon in a wave without losing any intensity along the way (Häusser, 2000; Hodgkin & Huxley, 1939). This electric impulse is called an **action potential,** *an electric signal that is conducted along the length of a neuron's axon to a synapse.*

The action potential occurred only when the electric shock reached a certain level, or *threshold.* When the shock was below this threshold, the researchers recorded only tiny signals that dissipated rapidly, leaving the rest of the axon unaffected. But when the shock reached the threshold, the action potential fired down the axon. Oddly, increases in the electric shock above the threshold did *not* increase the strength of the action potential. The action potential is *all or none*: Electric stimulation below the threshold fails to produce an action potential, whereas electric stimulation at or above the threshold always produces the action potential and always at the same magnitude.

The biologists working with the squid giant axon observed another surprising property of the action potential: They measured it at a charge of about +40 millivolts, which is well above zero. This suggests that the mechanism driving the action potential could not simply be the loss of the −70 millivolt resting potential because that only would have brought the charge back to zero. So why does the action potential surge to a value above zero?

Membrane Channels Change to Allow in Positively Charged Ions

The action potential occurs due to changes in the axon's membrane channels. Remember, during the resting potential, the voltage-gated channels for the Na⁺ ions are closed. However, when the voltage across the cell body membrane reaches the threshold value, the sodium-specific channels on the nearby axon open up like the floodgate of a dam, and the Na⁺ ions rush into the cell instantaneously (see Figure 3.4b). The surge to +40

Figure 3.4
The Resting and Action Potentials
Neurons have a natural electric charge called a resting potential. Electric stimulation causes an action potential.

action potential An electric signal that is conducted along a neuron's axon to a synapse.

GUELPHITE/ISTOCK/GETTY IMAGES

Like the flow of electricity when you turn on a light, the action potential is all or none. It doesn't matter if you gently nudge the switch or force it on with all your strength. Either the switch is turned on or the room remains dark. Similarly, either the electrical stimulation in the neuron reaches the threshold to fire an action potential, or it remains at the resting potential.

millivolts is the direct result of the Na⁺ ions flooding into the cell, changing the total charge inside the axon from negative to positive in less than one millisecond.

At this point, two events restore the negative charge of the resting potential. First, the Na⁺ channels inactivate themselves for several milliseconds, stopping the flow of Na⁺ ions. During this inactivation time, the section of the axon is said to be in a **refractory period,** *the time following an action potential during which a new action potential cannot be initiated.* The refractory period limits the number of times per second a neuron can fire and keeps the action potential from travelling back towards the cell body. In the second event, channels specific to the K⁺ ions open, allowing the excess K⁺ ions inside the cell to escape (see Figure 3.4c). The rapid exit of the positively charged K⁺ ions returns the electrical charge of the membrane to a negative state, after which the K⁺ channels close. Ion pumps continue to push Na⁺ ions out of the cell and bring in additional K⁺ ions. Along with other special channels, they return the concentrations of ions to the resting potential (see Figure 3.4d). The entire process is so fast that some neurons fire more than 100 times in a single second.

The Action Potential Moves Across the Neuron in a Domino Effect

So far, we've described how the action potential occurs at one point in the neuron. But how does it move down the axon? And why doesn't the intensity of the action potential decrease as it travels farther? It's a domino effect. Once the first voltage-gated channels open and Na⁺ ions rush into the cell, the ions spread and increase the electrical charge down the inside of the axon. When the voltage around adjacent voltage-gated channels reaches the threshold, those channels open and let in more Na⁺ ions that spread even farther. Just as one domino knocks over another, the influx of Na⁺ ions triggers nearby channels to open, and the process repeats down the entire axon. And just as each falling domino releases the same amount of energy, each open channel lets in just enough Na⁺ ions to cause a spike to +40 millivolts. This simple mechanism ensures that the action potential travels the full length of the axon and that it achieves its full intensity at each step, regardless of the distance travelled.

In many neurons, the conduction of the action potential is greatly increased by the presence of a myelin sheath around the axon. Myelin doesn't cover the entire axon; rather, it clumps around the axon with little break points between clumps, looking kind of like sausage links. These breakpoints are called the *nodes of Ranvier,* after the French pathologist Louis-Antoine Ranvier, who discovered them (see **FIGURE 3.5**). Because the myelin prevents electric current from leaking out of the axon, the current seems to "jump" quickly from node to node where it slows down (Poliak & Peles, 2003). This process is called *salitory conduction,* and it helps speed the flow of information down the axon.

Chemical Signalling: Transmission Between Neurons

When the action potential reaches the end of an axon, you might think that it stops there. After all, the synaptic space between neurons means that the axon of one neuron and the neighbouring neuron's dendrites do not actually touch one another.

refractory period The time following an action potential during which a new action potential cannot be initiated.

Figure 3.5

Myelin and Nodes of Ranvier Myelin is formed by a type of glial cell. It wraps around a neuron's axon to speed the movement of the action potential along the length of the axon. Breaks in the myelin sheath are called the nodes of Ranvier. The electric impulse jumps from node to node, thereby speeding the conduction of information down the axon.

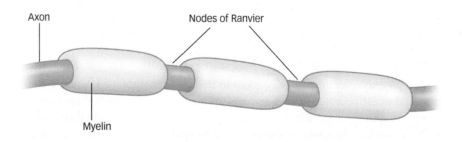

However, the electric action potential takes a form that crosses the synaptic gap by relying on a bit of chemistry.

Although a neuron has only one axon, the axon may end in hundreds or even thousands of branches that reach out to other neurons and organs. Axons usually end in **terminal buttons,** *knoblike structures at the end of an axon.* Each terminal button is filled with tiny *vesicles* or bags that contain **neurotransmitters,** *chemicals that transmit information across the synapse to a receiving neuron's dendrites.* The dendrites of the receiving neuron contain **receptors,** *parts of the cell membrane that receive neurotransmitters and either initiate or prevent a new electric signal.*

The action potential in the sending neuron, or *presynaptic neuron*, travels down the length of the axon to the terminal buttons, where it stimulates the release of neurotransmitters from vesicles into the synapses. The neurotransmitters quickly float across the synapse and bind to receptor sites on the nearby dendrite of the receiving neuron, or *postsynaptic neuron*. The sending and receiving of chemical neurotransmitters is called *synaptic transmission* (see **FIGURE 3.6**), and it ultimately underlies your thoughts, emotions, and behaviour. When the postsynaptic neuron receives a neurotransmitter, it may activate nearby ion channels, which can either raise or lower the voltage across the membrane. Depending on the combination and timing of the neurotransmitters acting on the neuron, the voltage inside the cell body membrane may reach the threshold and trigger a new action potential. In this way, the neurotransmitters' chemical messages create an electrical signal, and the electrochemical process of neuronal communication continues.

Now that you understand the basic process of how information moves from one neuron to another, let's refine things a bit. If a given neuron makes a few thousand synaptic connections with other neurons, what tells the dendrites which of the neurotransmitters flooding into the synapse to receive? First, neurons tend to form pathways in the brain that are characterized by specific types of neurotransmitters; one neurotransmitter might be prevalent in one part of the brain, whereas a different neurotransmitter might be prevalent in a different part of the brain.

Second, neurotransmitters and receptor sites act like a lock-and-key system. Just as a particular key will fit only in a particular lock, so too will only some neurotransmitters bind to specific receptor sites on a dendrite. The molecular structure of the neurotransmitter must fit the molecular structure of the receptor site.

Another question is what happens to the neurotransmitters left in the synapse after the chemical message is relayed to the postsynaptic neuron? Something must make neurotransmitters stop acting on neurons; otherwise, there would be no end to the signals that they send. Neurotransmitters leave the synapse through three processes (see Figure 3.6). First, *reuptake* occurs when neurotransmitters are absorbed by the terminal buttons of the presynaptic neuron's axon or by neighbouring glial cells. Second, neurotransmitters can be destroyed by enzymes in the synapse in a process called *enzyme deactivation,* in which specific enzymes break down specific neurotransmitters. Third, *diffusion* occurs when neurotransmitters drift out of the synapse and can no longer reach receptors.

 Neurotransmitters can also bind to receptor sites on the presynaptic neuron called *autoreceptors.* Autoreceptors detect how much of a neurotransmitter has been released into a synapse and may stop the release of more.

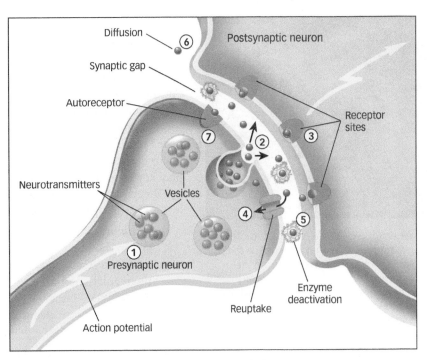

Figure 3.6
Synaptic Transmission (1) The action potential travels down the axon and (2) stimulates the release of neurotransmitters from vesicles. (3) The neurotransmitters are released into the synapse, where they float to bind with receptor sites on a dendrite of a postsynaptic neuron, initiating a new action potential. The neurotransmitters are cleared out of the synapse by (4) reuptake into the sending neuron, (5) being broken down by enzymes in the synapse, or (6) diffusion away from the synapse. (7) Neurotransmitters bind to autoreceptors on the sending neuron, stopping the release of more neurotransmitters.

terminal buttons Knoblike structures that branch out from an axon.

neurotransmitters Chemicals that transmit information across the synapse to a receiving neuron's dendrites.

receptors Parts of the cell membrane that receive the neurotransmitter and initiate or prevent a new electric signal.

When long-distance runners complete a marathon, they may experience the subjective highs that result from the release of endorphins — chemical messengers acting in emotion and pain centres that elevate mood and dull the experience of pain.

Types and Functions of Neurotransmitters

Given the important role of neurotransmitters, you might wonder how many types of neurotransmitters are floating across synapses in your brain right now. Today, we know that more than 100 chemicals play a role in transmitting information throughout the brain and body and differentially affect thought, feeling, and behaviour. Simple actions such as waving hello, enjoying a bite of ice cream, or falling asleep involve the combined action of many different types of neurotransmitters flowing across synapses in different parts of the nervous system. Researchers have identified a few major classes of neurotransmitters that are most common in the nervous system and play key roles in certain fundamental behaviours. We'll summarize those here, and you'll encounter some of these neurotransmitters again in later chapters.

- **Acetylcholine (ACh)** is *a neurotransmitter involved in a number of functions, including voluntary motor control.* Acetylcholine is found in neurons of the brain and in the synapses where axons connect to muscles and body organs, such as the heart. Acetylcholine activates muscle movements, and it also contributes to the regulation of attention, learning, sleeping, dreaming, and memory (Gais & Born, 2004; Hasselmo, 2006; Wrenn et al., 2006). Alzheimer's disease, a medical condition involving severe memory impairments (Salmon & Bondi, 2009), is associated with the deterioration of ACh-producing neurons.

- **Dopamine** is *a neurotransmitter that regulates motor behaviour, motivation, pleasure, and emotional arousal.* Because of its role in basic motivated behaviours, such as seeking pleasure or associating actions with rewards, dopamine plays a role in drug addiction (Baler & Volkow, 2006). High levels of dopamine in some brain pathways are linked to schizophrenia (Winterer & Weinberger, 2004), whereas low levels in other areas are linked to Parkinson's disease.

- **Glutamate** is the *major excitatory neurotransmitter in the brain,* meaning that it enhances the transmission of information between neurons. **GABA (gamma-aminobutyric acid),** in contrast, is *the primary inhibitory neurotransmitter in the brain,* meaning that it tends to prevent the firing of neurons. Too much glutamate, or too little GABA, can cause neurons to become overactive, causing seizures.

- Two related neurotransmitters influence mood and arousal: norepinephrine and serotonin. **Norepinephrine** is *involved in states of vigilance, or a heightened awareness of dangers in the environment* (Ressler & Nemeroff, 1999). **Serotonin** is *involved in the regulation of sleep and wakefulness, eating, and aggressive behaviour* (Dayan & Huys, 2009; Kroeze & Roth, 1998). Because both neurotransmitters affect mood and arousal, low levels of each have been implicated in mood disorders (Tamminga et al., 2002).

- **Endorphins** *are chemicals that act within the pain pathways and emotion centres of the brain* (Keefe et al., 2001). The term *endorphin* is a contraction of *endogenous morphine,* which is a pretty apt description. Morphine is a drug that has an intensely pleasurable and pain-relieving effect; an endorphin is an internally produced substance that has similar but less intense properties, such as dulling the experience of pain and elevating moods. The "runner's high" experienced by many athletes as they push their bodies to painful limits of endurance can be explained by the release of endorphins in the brain (Boecker et al., 2008).

Each of these neurotransmitters affects thought, feeling, and behaviour in different ways, so normal functioning involves a delicate balance of each. Even a slight imbalance—too much of one neurotransmitter or not enough of another—can dramatically affect behaviour. These imbalances can occur naturally: Sometimes the brain doesn't produce enough serotonin, for example, which contributes to depressed or anxious moods. Other times a person may actively seek to cause imbalances. People who smoke, drink alcohol, or take drugs (legal or not) are altering the balance of neurotransmitters in their brains. The drug LSD, for example, is structurally similar to serotonin,

acetylcholine (ACh) A neurotransmitter involved in a number of functions, including voluntary motor control.

dopamine A neurotransmitter that regulates motor behaviour, motivation, pleasure, and emotional arousal.

glutamate The major excitatory neurotransmitter in the brain.

GABA (gamma-aminobutyric acid) The primary inhibitory neurotransmitter in the brain.

norepinephrine A neurotransmitter that is particularly involved in states of vigilance or heightened awareness of dangers in the environment.

serotonin A neurotransmitter that is involved in the regulation of sleep and wakefulness, eating, and aggressive behaviour.

endorphins Chemicals that act within the pain pathways and emotion centres of the brain.

Agonists increase the action of a neurotransmitter

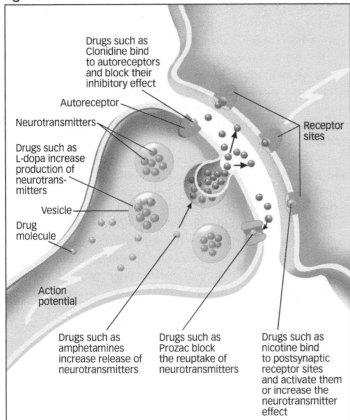

Drugs such as Clonidine bind to autoreceptors and block their inhibitory effect

Autoreceptor

Neurotransmitters

Drugs such as L-dopa increase production of neurotransmitters

Vesicle

Drug molecule

Receptor sites

Action potential

Drugs such as amphetamines increase release of neurotransmitters

Drugs such as Prozac block the reuptake of neurotransmitters

Drugs such as nicotine bind to postsynaptic receptor sites and activate them or increase the neurotransmitter effect

Antagonists block the function of a neurotransmitter

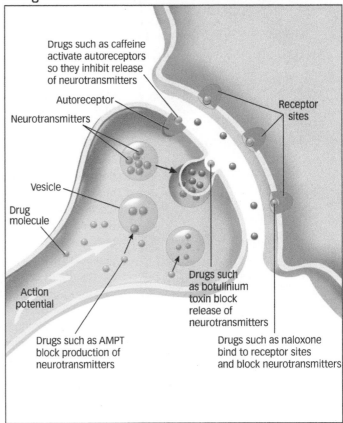

Drugs such as caffeine activate autoreceptors so they inhibit release of neurotransmitters

Autoreceptor

Neurotransmitters

Vesicle

Drug molecule

Receptor sites

Action potential

Drugs such as AMPT block production of neurotransmitters

Drugs such as botulinium toxin block release of neurotransmitters

Drugs such as naloxone bind to receptor sites and block neurotransmitters

Figure 3.7

The Actions of Agonist and Antagonist Drugs Agonist and antagonist drugs can enhance or interfere with synaptic transmission at every point in the process: in the production of neurotransmitters, in the release of neurotransmitters, at the autoreceptors, in reuptake, in the postsynaptic receptors, and in the synapse itself.

so it binds easily with serotonin receptors in the brain, producing similar effects. In the next section, we'll look at how some drugs are able to "trick" receptor sites in just this way.

How Drugs Mimic Neurotransmitters

Many drugs that affect the nervous system operate by increasing, interfering with, or mimicking the manufacture or function of neurotransmitters (Cooper, Bloom, & Roth, 2003; Sarter, 2006). **Agonists** are *drugs that increase the action of a neurotransmitter.* **Antagonists** are *drugs that diminish the function of a neurotransmitter.* Some drugs alter a step in the production or release of the neurotransmitter, whereas others have a chemical structure so similar to a neurotransmitter that the drug is able to bind to that neuron's receptor. If, by binding to a receptor, a drug activates the neurotransmitter, it is an agonist; if it prevents the neurotransmitter from acting or lessens its effect, it is an antagonist (see **FIGURE 3.7**).

For example, the drug L-dopa is used to treat Parkinson's disease, a movement disorder characterized by tremors and difficulty initiating movement. The Canadian actor Michael J. Fox, who was diagnosed with Parkinson's disease in 1991 and takes L-dopa, described in his memoir the simple act of trying to brush his teeth:

Grasping the toothpaste is nothing compared to the effort it takes to coordinate the two-handed task of wrangling the toothbrush and strangling out a line of paste onto the bristles. By now, my right hand has started up again, rotating at the wrist in a circular motion, perfect for what I'm about to do. My left hand guides my right hand up to my mouth, and once the back of the Oral-B touches the inside of my upper lip, I let go. It's like releasing the tension on a slingshot and compares favorably to the most powerful state-of-the-art electric toothbrush on the market. With no off switch, stopping means seizing my right wrist with my left hand, forcing it down to the sink basin, and shaking the brush loose as though disarming a knife-wielding attacker. (Fox, 2009, pp. 2–3)

agonists Drugs that increase the action of a neurotransmitter.

antagonists Drugs that block the function of a neurotransmitter.

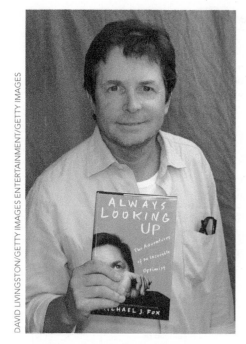

Michael J. Fox vividly described his struggles with Parkinson's disease in his 2009 memoir. Fox's visibility has increased public awareness of the disease and spurred greater efforts towards finding a cure.

Parkinson's disease is caused by the loss of neurons that make the neurotransmitter dopamine by modifying L-dopa produced naturally in the body. Ingesting L-dopa as a drug elevates its concentration in the brain and spurs the surviving neurons to produce more dopamine. In other words, L-dopa acts as an agonist for dopamine by increasing its production. The use of L-dopa has been reasonably successful in the alleviation of Parkinson's disease symptoms (Muenter & Tyce, 1971; Schapira et al., 2009). However, its effectiveness typically decreases when used over a long period of time, so many longtime users experience some symptoms of the disease.

Many other drugs, including street drugs, alter the actions of neurotransmitters. Let's look at a few more examples.

Amphetamine is a popular drug that stimulates the release of norepinephrine and dopamine and also blocks their reuptake. This combination creates an excess of neurotransmitters that flood the synapse, activating their receptors over and over. *Cocaine* is another drug that acts by preventing the reuptake of neurotransmitters. Both of these drugs therefore are agonists, although their psychological effects differ because of where and how each acts on the brain. Norepinephrine and dopamine play a critical role in mood control, such that an increase in either neurotransmitter results in euphoria, wakefulness, and a burst of energy. However, norepinephrine also increases heart rate. An overdose of amphetamine or cocaine can cause the heart to contract so rapidly that heartbeats do not last long enough to pump blood effectively, leading to fainting and sometimes death.

Opioids are a class of chemically similar drugs either derived naturally from the opium poppy (such as morphine and heroin) or made synthetically (such as oxycodone, hydrocodone, and fentanyl). Most opioids work in part by acting as agonists for endorphins, which creates powerful feelings of calm and euphoria. Opioids have been widely prescribed for pain relief because they are also highly effective antagonists that decrease the release of neurotransmitters involved in the perception of pain. At the same time, opioids also diminish the brain stem's sensitivity to rising levels of carbon dioxide in the blood, which depresses breathing. In the case of overdose, this can lead to asphyxiation and death.

These properties, as well as the availability of opioids both as pharmaceuticals and street drugs, have raised opioid addiction to the level of a public health emergency in the United States. In 2017, the Centers for Disease Control estimated that 115 people in the United States die from an opioid overdose every day. One widespread response is to equip first responders with the drug naloxone, the active ingredient in the nasal spray Narcan. Technically, naloxone is also an opioid but one that acts as an antagonist: It binds with opioid receptors, blocking agonists like heroin and preventing their effects on neurons.

Prozac, a drug commonly used to treat depression, is another example of a neurotransmitter agonist. Prozac blocks the reuptake of the neurotransmitter *serotonin*, making it part of a category of drugs called *selective serotonin reuptake inhibitors,* or *SSRIs* (Wong, Bymaster, & Engleman, 1995). People suffering from clinical depression typically have reduced levels of serotonin in their brains. By blocking reuptake, more of the neurotransmitter remains in the synapse longer and produces greater activation of serotonin receptors. Serotonin elevates mood, which can help relieve depression (Mann, 2005).

An antagonist with important medical implications is a drug called *propranalol*, one of a class of drugs called *beta blockers*. These drugs obstruct receptor sites in the heart for norepinephrine, a neurotransmitter that increases one's heartbeat. Because norepinephrine cannot bind to these receptors, the heart rate slows down, which is helpful for disorders in which the heart beats too fast or irregularly. Beta blockers are also prescribed to reduce the agitation, racing heart, and nervousness associated with stage fright (Mills & Dimsdale, 1991) (for additional discussion of antianxiety and antidepression drug treatments, see the Treatment of Psychological Disorders chapter).

Build to the Outcomes

1. What difference between the inside and outside of the neuron's cell membrane creates the resting potential?

2. How does the neuron's membrane change over the course of an action potential?

3. What is the importance of the "pump" in the last stage of the action potential?

4. What is the role of neurotransmitters in neural communication?

5. Choose two neurotransmitters and compare and contrast their functions.

6. Is L-dopa an agonist for dopamine or an antagonist? Explain your answer.

The Organization of the Nervous System

We've seen how individual neurons communicate with each other. What's the bigger picture? Neurons work by forming circuits and pathways in the brain, which in turn influence circuits and pathways in other areas of the body. Without this kind of organization and delegation, neurons would be churning away with little purpose. Neurons are the building blocks that form *nerves,* or bundles of axons and the glial cells that support them. The **nervous system** is *an interacting network of neurons that conveys electrochemical information throughout the body.* In this section, we'll look at the major divisions and components of the nervous system.

Divisions of the Nervous System

There are two major divisions of the nervous system: the central nervous system and the peripheral nervous system (see **FIGURE 3.8**). The **central nervous system (CNS)** is *composed of the brain and spinal cord.* It receives sensory information from the external world, processes and coordinates this information, and sends commands to the skeletal and muscular systems for action. At the top of the CNS rests the brain, which contains structures that support the most complex perceptual, motor, emotional, and cognitive functions of the nervous system. The spinal cord branches down from the brain; nerves that process sensory information and relay commands to the body connect to the spinal cord.

The **peripheral nervous system (PNS)** *connects the central nervous system to the body's organs and muscles.* The peripheral nervous system is itself composed of two major subdivisions, the somatic nervous system and the autonomic nervous system. The **somatic nervous system** is *a set of nerves that conveys information between voluntary muscles and the central nervous system.* Humans have conscious control over this system and use it to perceive, think, and coordinate their behaviours. For example, reaching for your morning cup of coffee involves the elegantly orchestrated activities of the somatic nervous system: Information from the receptors in your eyes travels to your brain, registering that a cup is on the table; signals from your brain travel to the muscles in your arm and hand; feedback from those muscles tells your brain that the cup has been grasped, and so on.

In contrast, the **autonomic nervous system (ANS)** is *a set of nerves that carries involuntary and automatic commands that control blood vessels, body organs, and glands.* As suggested by its name, this system works on its own to regulate bodily systems, largely outside of conscious control. The ANS has two major subdivisions,

Learning Outcomes

- Differentiate the functions of the central and peripheral nervous systems.

- Understand the nature of the reflex arc.

- Demonstrate the hierarchical structure of the central nervous system.

nervous system An interacting network of neurons that conveys electrochemical information throughout the body.

central nervous system (CNS) The part of the nervous system that is composed of the brain and spinal cord.

peripheral nervous system (PNS) The part of the nervous system that connects the central nervous system to the body's organs and muscles.

somatic nervous system A set of nerves that conveys information between voluntary muscles and the central nervous system.

autonomic nervous system (ANS) A set of nerves that carries involuntary and automatic commands that control blood vessels, body organs, and glands.

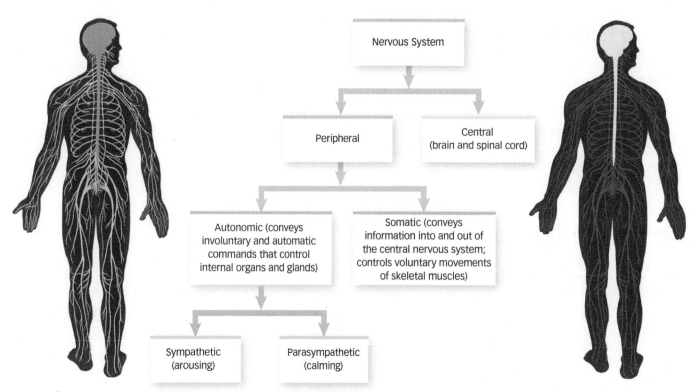

Figure 3.8
The Human Nervous System The nervous system is organized into the peripheral and central nervous systems. The peripheral nervous system is further divided into the autonomic and somatic nervous systems.

sympathetic nervous system
A set of nerves that prepares the body for action in challenging or threatening situations.

parasympathetic nervous system A set of nerves that helps the body return to a normal resting state.

the sympathetic nervous system and the parasympathetic nervous system. Each exerts a different type of control on the body. The **sympathetic nervous system** is *a set of nerves that prepares the body for action in challenging or threatening situations* (see **FIGURE 3.9**). For example, imagine that you are walking alone late at night and are frightened by footsteps behind you in a dark alley. Your sympathetic nervous system kicks into action at this point: It dilates your pupils to let in more light, increases your heart rate and respiration to pump more oxygen to your muscles, diverts blood flow to your brain and muscles, and activates sweat glands to cool your body. To conserve energy, the sympathetic nervous system inhibits salivation and bowel movements, suppresses the body's immune responses, and suppresses responses to pain and injury. The sum total of these fast, automatic responses is that they increase the likelihood that you can escape.

The **parasympathetic nervous system** *helps the body return to a normal resting state*. When you're far away from your would-be attacker, your body doesn't need to remain on red alert. Now the parasympathetic nervous system kicks in to reverse the effects of the sympathetic nervous system and return your body to its normal state. The parasympathetic nervous system generally mirrors the connections of the sympathetic nervous system. For instance, the parasympathetic nervous system constricts your pupils, slows your heart rate and respiration, diverts blood flow to your digestive system, and decreases activity in your sweat glands.

As you might imagine, the sympathetic and parasympathetic nervous systems coordinate to control many bodily functions. One example is sexual behaviour. In men, the parasympathetic nervous system engorges the blood vessels of the penis to produce an erection, but the sympathetic nervous system is responsible for ejaculation. In women, the parasympathetic nervous system produces vaginal lubrication, but the sympathetic nervous system underlies orgasm. In both men and women, a successful sexual experience depends on a delicate balance of these two systems; in

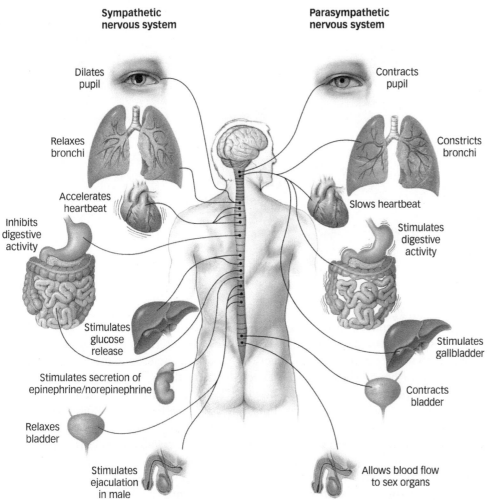

Sympathetic nervous system

- Dilates pupil
- Relaxes bronchi
- Accelerates heartbeat
- Inhibits digestive activity
- Stimulates glucose release
- Stimulates secretion of epinephrine/norepinephrine
- Relaxes bladder
- Stimulates ejaculation in male

Parasympathetic nervous system

- Contracts pupil
- Constricts bronchi
- Slows heartbeat
- Stimulates digestive activity
- Stimulates gallbladder
- Contracts bladder
- Allows blood flow to sex organs

Figure 3.9
Sympathetic and Parasympathetic Systems The autonomic nervous system is composed of two subsystems that complement each other. Activation of the sympathetic system serves several aspects of arousal, whereas the parasympathetic nervous system returns the body to its normal resting state.

fact, anxiety about sexual performance can disrupt this balance. For instance, sympathetic nervous system activation caused by anxiety can lead to premature ejaculation in males and lack of lubrication in females.

Components of the Central Nervous System

Compared with the many divisions of the peripheral nervous system, the central nervous system may seem simple. After all, it has only two elements: the brain and the spinal cord. But those two elements are ultimately responsible for most of what we do as humans.

The spinal cord often seems like the brain's poor relation: The brain gets all the glory, and the spinal cord just hangs around, doing relatively simple tasks. Those tasks, however, are pretty important: They keep you breathing, respond to pain, and move your muscles, allowing you to walk. What's more, without the spinal cord, the brain would not be able to put any of its higher processing into action.

Do you need your brain to tell you to pull your hand away from a hot stove? For some very basic behaviours such as this, the spinal cord doesn't need input from the brain at all. Connections between the sensory inputs and motor neurons in the spinal cord mediate **spinal reflexes,** *simple pathways in the nervous system that rapidly generate muscle contractions.* If you touch a hot stove, the sensory neurons that

spinal reflexes Simple pathways in the nervous system that rapidly generate muscle contractions.

reflex arc A neural pathway that controls reflex actions.

Figure 3.10

The Pain Withdrawal Reflex Many actions of the central nervous system don't require the brain's input. For example, withdrawing from pain is a reflexive activity controlled by the spinal cord. Painful sensations (such as the heat of fire) travel directly to the spinal cord via sensory neurons, which then issue an immediate command to motor neurons to retract the hand.

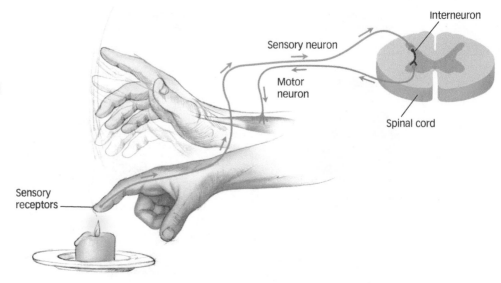

Figure 3.11

Regions of the Spinal Cord The spinal cord is divided into four main sections; each controls different parts of the body. Damage higher on the spinal cord usually means greater impairment.

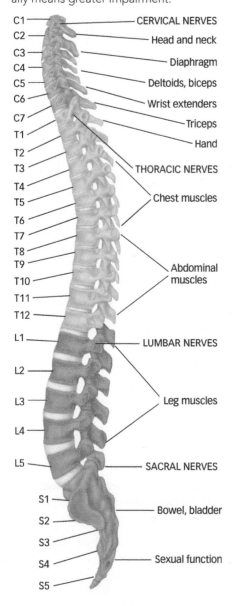

register pain send inputs directly into the spinal cord (see **FIGURE 3.10**). Through just a few synaptic connections within the spinal cord, interneurons relay these sensory inputs to motor neurons that connect to your arm muscles and direct you to quickly retract your hand. These spinal reflexes illustrate the operation of a **reflex arc,** *a neural pathway that controls reflex actions.* Reflex arcs can include sensory neurons, interneurons, and motor neurons, but some simple reflex arcs are comprised of only sensory and motor neurons.

Beyond reflexes, more elaborate tasks require the collaboration of the spinal cord and the brain. The peripheral nervous system sends messages from sensory neurons through the spinal cord into the brain. The brain sends commands for voluntary movement through the spinal cord to motor neurons, whose axons project out to skeletal muscles. Damage to the spinal cord severs the connection from the brain to the sensory and motor neurons that are essential to sensory perception and movement. The location of the spinal injury often determines the extent of the abilities that are lost. As you can see in **FIGURE 3.11**, different regions of the spinal cord control different systems of the body. Individuals with damage at a particular level of the spinal cord lose sensations of touch and pain in body parts below the level of the injury, as well as a loss of motor control of the muscles in the same areas. A spinal injury higher up the cord usually predicts a much poorer prognosis, such as quadriplegia (loss of sensation and motor control over all limbs), breathing through a respirator, and lifelong immobility.

The late actor Christopher Reeve, who starred as Superman in four *Superman* movies, damaged his spinal cord in a horseback riding accident in 1995, resulting in loss of sensation and motor control in all of his body parts below the neck. Despite great efforts over several years, Reeve made only modest gains in his motor control and sensation, highlighting the extent to which we depend on communication from the brain through the spinal cord to the body, and showing how difficult it is to compensate for the loss of these connections (Edgerton et al., 2004). Unfortunately, Christopher Reeve died at age 52 in 2004 from complications due to his paralysis. On a brighter note, researchers are making progress in understanding the nature of spinal cord injuries and how to treat them by focusing on how the brain changes in response to injury (Blesch & Tuszynski, 2009; Dunlop, 2008), a process that is closely related to the concept of brain plasticity that we will examine later in this chapter. Progress in constructing brain–machine interfaces could also improve the lives of people who have suffered paralysis from spinal cord injuries (see The Real World: The Power of Thought: Brain–Machine Interfaces).

The Real World | The Power of Thought: Brain–Machine Interfaces

In the wildly popular James Cameron movie *Avatar*, the paraplegic marine Jake Sully's brain is able to control, via computer, the actions of an avatar body. Though this scenario is seemingly far-fetched, scientists recently have been taking steps to bring this type of science-fiction fantasy closer to reality.

Experiments with monkeys conducted a little over a decade ago provided initial evidence that the brain can control mechanical devices through thoughts alone (Carmena et al., 2003). The researchers implanted multiple wires into the monkeys' motor cortices and trained them to obtain a juice reward by moving a joystick that controlled a cursor on a computer screen. Using the activity patterns of many neurons, they created a computer model of the neural activity that corresponded to different directions of joystick movements. Then they disconnected the joystick from the computer and instead connected directly to the computer the signals that their model extracted from the monkey's motor cortex activity. With just a few days of practice, the monkeys learned to adjust their motor cortex activity patterns to hit the targets successfully. In effect, the monkeys were controlling the cursor with their thoughts.

These findings raised the possibility that cortical recordings and state-of-the-art computer programs could be developed into a kind of neuroprosthesis to help people with brain or spinal injuries that have left them paralyzed. Important recent evidence supports this idea. For example, Hochberg et al. (2012) studied a 58-year-old woman and a 66-year-old man who had suffered strokes to the brainstem that produced tetraplegia: paralysis resulting in the loss of use of all limbs. They examined whether the patients could use a brain–machine interface to control a robotic arm for performing reaching and grasping movements. In order to guide movement, the researchers sent the robotic arm signals that were decoded by a computer program from a small population of neurons in each individual's motor cortex, similar to the earlier experiments with monkeys. The participants' task was to reach for and grasp purple spheres that were elevated above a table. Both participants were able to perform the task with relatively high levels of accuracy and speed, though they were not as accurate or as fast as able-bodied participants. Using signals decoded from her motor cortex, the female patient was even able to use the robotic arm to drink her coffee (see photo)!

These results are exciting, and researchers continue to develop new ways to improve brain–machine interfaces. One study used a computer program that decodes brain signals that convey cognitive information about whether an individual judges that the action being carried out by a robotic arm attempting to touch a target (a square of a particular colour) is correct or erroneous (Iturrate et al., 2015). The researchers recorded EEG activity from the scalp in healthy young volunteers as they attempted to control the robotic arm, extracting specific signals that arise when people are aware that they have made a correct response or an error. The researchers found that after a relatively brief training period of about 25 minutes, participants were successful in guiding the robot arm to specific targets on the basis of the brain activity associated with evaluating actions as correct or erroneous.

These findings are important because the same kinds of evaluation or monitoring signals used here could potentially be applied to a wide variety of situations. Recent studies have increasingly focused on decoding an individual's goal and intentions based on signals in the frontal lobe, which plays a key role in high-level cognitive functions such as planning (see page 98); the ability to do so could prove to be extremely useful in cognitive rehabilitation (Min, Chavarriaga, & Millán, 2017).

Although these studies do not quite take us all the way to the world envisioned in *Avatar*, they provide clear evidence that what we once thought of as pure science fiction is well on its way to becoming science fact.

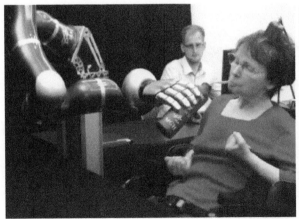

REACH AND GRASP BY PEOPLE WITH TETRAPLEGIA USING A NEURALLY CONTROLLED ROBOTIC ARM. HOCHBERG, ET AL. NATURE 485, 372–375 (17 MAY 2012) ©2012 MACMILLAN PUBLISHERS LIMITED

A participant drinking from a bottle using the robotic arm.

Build to the Outcomes

1. What is the neuron's role in the body's nervous system?

2. What are the components of the central nervous system?

3. What are the two divisions of the peripheral nervous system?

4. What triggers the increase in your heart rate when you feel threatened?

5. What important functions does the spinal cord perform on its own?

Structure of the Brain

Learning Outcomes

- Differentiate the functions of the major divisions of the brain.

- Explain the functions of the cerebral cortex according to organization across hemispheres, within hemispheres, and within specific lobes.

- Identify the causes and consequences of brain plasticity.

- Explain the progression of the human brain's evolution.

The human brain, weighing in at about 1,300–1,400 grams, is really not much to look at. You already know that its neurons and glial cells are busy humming away, giving you potentially brilliant ideas, consciousness, and feelings. But which neurons in which parts of the brain control which functions?

To answer that question, neuroscientists had to find a way of describing the brain that allows researchers to communicate with one another. It can be helpful to talk about areas of the brain from "bottom to top," noting how the different regions are specialized for different kinds of tasks. In general, simpler functions are performed at the "lower" levels of the brain, whereas more complex functions are performed at successively "higher" levels (see **FIGURE 3.12a**). Or, as you'll see shortly, the brain can also be approached in a "side-by-side" fashion: Although the two sides of the brain are largely mirror symmetric, there are exceptions, and one half of the brain specializes in some tasks that the other half doesn't. Although these divisions make it easier to understand areas of the brain and their functions, keep in mind that none of these structures or areas in the brain can act alone. Individual regions within the brain are organized into larger scale *networks*, which consist of interacting and interdependent regions that work together to support complex psychological functions (Avena-Koenigsberger, Misic, & Sporns, 2018; Sporns & Betzel, 2016). Individual regions make specific contributions to these networks that reflect their specialized nature, but they operate as part of an interdependent unit (for an example, see page 115).

Let's look first at the divisions of the brain, and the responsibilities of each part, moving from the bottom to the top. Using this view, we can divide the brain into three parts: the hindbrain, the midbrain, and the forebrain (see Figure 3.12a).

Figure 3.12
Structure of the Brain

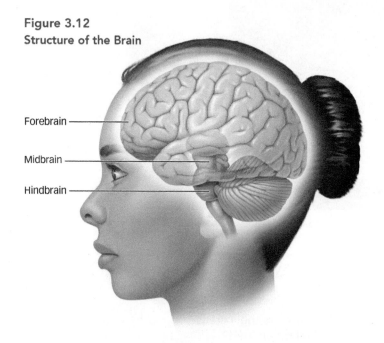

Forebrain

Midbrain

Hindbrain

(a)
The Major Divisions of the Brain
The brain can be organized into three parts, moving from the bottom to the top, from simpler functions to the more complex: the hindbrain, the midbrain, and the forebrain.

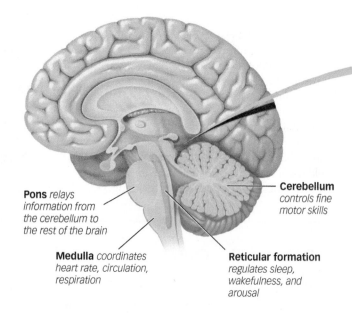

Pons *relays information from the cerebellum to the rest of the brain*

Medulla *coordinates heart rate, circulation, respiration*

Cerebellum *controls fine motor skills*

Reticular formation *regulates sleep, wakefulness, and arousal*

(b)
The Hindbrain
The hindbrain coordinates information coming into and out of the spinal cord and controls the basic functions of life.

The Hindbrain

If you follow the spinal cord from your tailbone to where it enters your skull, you'll find it difficult to determine where your spinal cord ends and your brain begins. That's because the spinal cord is continuous with the **hindbrain,** *an area of the brain that coordinates information coming into and out of the spinal cord.* The hindbrain looks like a stalk on which the rest of the brain sits, and it controls the most basic functions of life: respiration, alertness, and motor skills. The structures that make up the hindbrain include the medulla, the reticular formation, the cerebellum, and the pons (see Figure 3.12b).

The **medulla** is *an extension of the spinal cord into the skull that coordinates heart rate, circulation, and respiration.* Beginning inside the medulla and extending upward is a small cluster of neurons called the **reticular formation,** which *regulates sleep, wakefulness, and levels of arousal.* In one early experiment, researchers stimulated the reticular formation of a sleeping cat. This caused the animal to awaken almost instantaneously and remain alert. Conversely, severing the connections between the reticular formation and the rest of the brain caused the animal to lapse into an irreversible coma (Moruzzi & Magoun, 1949). The reticular formation maintains the same delicate balance between alertness and unconsciousness in humans. In fact, many general anaesthetics work by reducing activity in the reticular formation, rendering the patient unconscious.

Behind the medulla is the **cerebellum,** *a large structure of the hindbrain that controls fine motor skills.* (*Cerebellum* is Latin for "little brain," and this structure does look like a small replica of the brain.) The cerebellum orchestrates the proper sequence of movements when we ride a bike, play the piano, or maintain balance while walking and running. It contributes to the fine-tuning of behaviour: smoothing our actions to allow their graceful execution rather than initiating the actions (Smetacek, 2002). The initiation of behaviour involves other areas of the brain; as you'll recall, different brain systems interact and are interdependent with each other. Recent research, capitalizing on advances in brain imaging, reveals that the cerebellum is involved in a much broader range of cognitive, social, and emotional functions beyond motor control (e.g., see Diedrichsen et al., 2019). Perhaps the cerebellum is

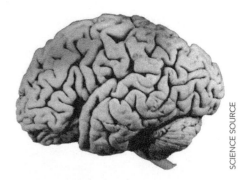

The human brain weighs only 1,300–1,400 grams and isn't much to look at, but its accomplishments are staggering.

hindbrain The area of the brain that coordinates information coming into and out of the spinal cord.

medulla An extension of the spinal cord into the skull that coordinates heart rate, circulation, and respiration.

reticular formation A brain structure that regulates sleep, wakefulness, and levels of arousal.

cerebellum A large structure of the hindbrain that controls fine motor skills.

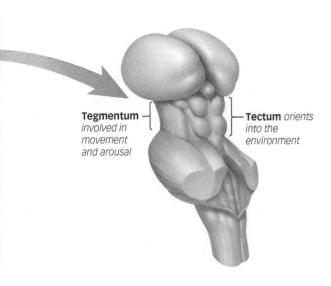

Tegmentum *involved in movement and arousal*

Tectum *orients into the environment*

(c)
The Midbrain
The midbrain is important for orientation and movement.

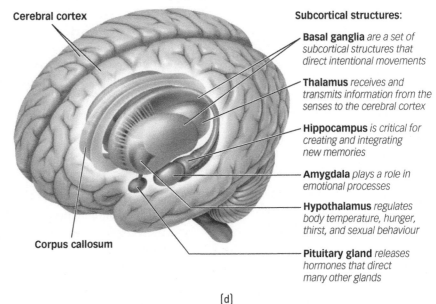

Cerebral cortex

Corpus callosum

Subcortical structures:

Basal ganglia *are a set of subcortical structures that direct intentional movements*

Thalamus *receives and transmits information from the senses to the cerebral cortex*

Hippocampus *is critical for creating and integrating new memories*

Amygdala *plays a role in emotional processes*

Hypothalamus *regulates body temperature, hunger, thirst, and sexual behaviour*

Pituitary gland *releases hormones that direct many other glands*

(d)
The Forebrain
The forebrain is the highest level of the brain and is critical for complex cognitive, emotional, sensory, and motor functions. The forebrain is divided into two parts: the cerebral cortex and the underlying subcortical structures. The cerebral cortex, the outermost layer of the brain, is divided into two hemispheres, connected by the corpus callosum (see Figure 3.15).

The high-wire artist Freddy Nock relied on his cerebellum to coordinate the movements necessary to walk on the rope of the Corvatsch cable car from more than 3050 metres over sea level down to the base station in Silvaplana, Switzerland.

a timing device that serves to coordinate the brain processes required for any complex cognition or behaviour (Bareš et al., 2019; Braitenberg, 1961). Cerebellum function is an area of active investigation.

The last major area of the hindbrain is the **pons**, *a structure that relays information from the cerebellum to the rest of the brain.* (*Pons* means "bridge" in Latin.) Although the detailed functions of the pons remain poorly understood, it essentially acts as a relay station or bridge between the cerebellum and other structures in the brain.

The Midbrain

Sitting on top of the hindbrain is the *midbrain,* which is relatively small in humans. As you can see in Figure 3.12c, the midbrain contains two main structures: the tectum and the tegmentum. The **tectum** *orients an organism in the environment.* The tectum receives stimulus input from the eyes, ears, and skin and moves the organism in a coordinated way towards the stimulus. For example, when you're studying in a quiet room and you hear a *click* behind and to the right of you, your body will swivel and orient to the direction of the sound; this is your tectum in action.

The **tegmentum** is *involved in movement and arousal*; it also helps to orient an organism towards sensory stimuli. The midbrain may be relatively small, but it is a central location of neurotransmitters involved in arousal, mood, and motivation and the brain structures that rely on them (White, 1996). You could survive if you had only a hindbrain and a midbrain. The structures in the hindbrain would take care of all the bodily functions necessary to sustain life, and the structures in the midbrain would orient you towards or away from pleasurable or threatening stimuli in the environment. But this wouldn't be much of a life. To understand where the abilities that make us fully human come from, we need to consider the last division of the brain.

The Forebrain

When you appreciate the beauty of a poem, detect the sarcasm in a friend's remark, plan to go skiing next winter, or notice the faint glimmer of sadness on a loved one's face, you are enlisting the forebrain. The *forebrain* is the highest level of the brain—literally and figuratively—and controls complex cognitive, emotional, sensory, and motor functions. The forebrain itself is divided into two main sections: the cerebral cortex and the subcortical structures.

The **cerebral cortex** is *the outermost layer of the brain, visible to the naked eye, and divided into two hemispheres.* The **subcortical structures** are *areas of the forebrain housed under the cerebral cortex near the centre of the brain* (see Figure 3.12d). We'll have much more to say about the two hemispheres of the cerebral cortex and the functions they serve in the next section, with the highest level of the brain fittingly saved for last. First, we'll examine the subcortical structures.

Subcortical Structures

The subcortical (beneath the cortex) structures are nestled deep inside the brain, where they are quite protected. If you imagine sticking an index finger in each of your ears and pushing inward until they touch, that's about where you'd find the *thalamus,* three components of the limbic system (the *hypothalamus*, the *hippocampus*, and the *amygdala*), the basal ganglia, and the pituitary gland, which is part of the endocrine system (see Figure 3.12d). Each of these subcortical structures plays an important role in relaying information throughout the brain, as well as in performing specific tasks that allow us to think, feel, and behave as humans. Here we'll give you

pons A brain structure that relays information from the cerebellum to the rest of the brain.

tectum A part of the midbrain that orients an organism in the environment.

tegmentum A part of the midbrain that is involved in movement and arousal.

cerebral cortex The outermost layer of the brain, visible to the naked eye and divided into two hemispheres.

subcortical structures Areas of the forebrain housed under the cerebral cortex near the very centre of the brain.

a brief introduction to each, and you'll read more about many of these structures in later chapters.

Thalamus and Hypothalamus The thalamus and hypothalamus, located in the centre of the brain, interact closely with several other brain structures. They relay signals to and from these structures and also help to regulate them.

The **thalamus** *relays and filters information from the senses and transmits the information to the cerebral cortex.* The thalamus receives inputs from all the major senses except smell, which has direct connections to the cerebral cortex. The thalamus acts as a kind of computer server in a networked system, taking in multiple inputs and relaying them to a variety of locations (Guillery & Sherman, 2002). However, unlike the mechanical operations of a computer ("send input A to location B"), the thalamus actively filters sensory information, giving more weight to some inputs and less weight to others. The thalamus also closes the pathways of incoming sensations during sleep, providing a valuable function in *not* allowing information to pass to the rest of the brain.

The **hypothalamus,** located below the thalamus (*hypo-* is Greek for "under"), *regulates body temperature, hunger, thirst, and sexual behaviour.* Although the hypothalamus is a tiny area of the brain, clusters of neurons in the hypothalamus oversee a wide range of basic behaviours, keeping body temperature, blood sugar levels, and metabolism within an optimal range for normal human functioning. Lesions to some areas of the hypothalamus result in overeating, whereas lesions to other areas leave an animal with no desire for food at all, highlighting that the hypothalamus plays a key role in regulating food intake (Berthoud & Morrison, 2008). Also, when you think about sex, messages from your cerebral cortex are sent to the hypothalamus to trigger the release of hormones. Finally, electric stimulation of some areas of the hypothalamus in cats can produce hissing and biting, whereas stimulation of other areas in the hypothalamus can produce what appears to be intense pleasure for an animal (Siegel et al., 1999).

The researchers James Olds and Peter Milner, working at McGill University, found that a small electric current delivered to a certain region of a rat's hypothalamus was extremely rewarding for the animal (Olds & Milner, 1954). In fact, when allowed to press a bar attached to the electrode to initiate their own stimulation, rats would do so several thousand times an hour, often to the point of exhaustion!

The Limbic System The hypothalamus is also part of the limbic system, a group of forebrain structures that includes the hypothalamus, the hippocampus, and the amygdala, which are involved in motivation, emotion, learning, and memory (Maclean, 1970; Papez, 1937). The limbic system is where the subcortical structures meet the cerebral cortex.

The **hippocampus** (from Latin for "sea horse," due to its shape) is *critical for creating new memories and integrating them into a network of knowledge so that they can be stored indefinitely in other parts of the cerebral cortex.* Individuals with damage to the hippocampus can acquire new information and keep it in awareness for a few seconds, but as soon as they are distracted, they forget the information and the experience that produced it (Scoville & Milner, 1957; Squire, 2009). This kind of disruption is limited to everyday memory for facts and events that we can bring to consciousness; memory of learned habitual routines or emotional reactions remains intact (Squire, Knowlton, & Musen, 1993). For example, people with damage to the hippocampus can remember how to drive and talk, but they cannot recall where they have recently driven or a conversation they have just had (see A World of Difference: Alzheimer's Disease and the Hippocampus: Sex Differences). You will read more about the hippocampus and its role in creating, storing, and combining memories in the Memory chapter.

The thalamus receives inputs from all the major senses except smell. You can thank your thalamus when you see the red apple, feel its smoothness in your hand, hear the crunch as you bite into it, and taste its sweetness.

thalamus A subcortical structure that relays and filters information from the senses and transmits the information to the cerebral cortex.

hypothalamus A subcortical structure that regulates body temperature, hunger, thirst, and sexual behaviour.

hippocampus A structure critical for creating new memories and integrating them into a network of knowledge so that they can be stored indefinitely in other parts of the cerebral cortex.

A World of Difference | Alzheimer's Disease and the Hippocampus: Sex Differences

Alzheimer's disease (AD) is a devastating progressive brain disorder that gradually impairs and ultimately wipes out memory and other cognitive functions. Among older adults, it is a leading cause of death, and it is estimated to affect more than half a million Canadians (Public Health Agency of Canada, 2018). AD has a massive and growing impact on people and societies across the globe, with 90 million cases expected worldwide by 2050 (Prince et al., 2015).

But AD does not affect men and women equally. A recent report by a large group of leading experts concluded that AD is more prevalent among women than men in many regions of the world (Mazure & Swendsen, 2016; Winblad et al., 2016). Although scientists are just beginning to unravel the reasons why this is so, recent evidence indicates that the hippocampus, a brain region critical for learning and memory, shows potentially important sex differences.

Using measurements from a technique called magnetic resonance imaging (MRI), which you will learn more about later in this chapter, one study analyzed the volume of the hippocampus in 43 patients who had been diagnosed with probable AD and in 23 cognitively normal older adults (Ardekani, Convit, & Bachman, 2016). Importantly, hippocampal volume was measured several times in each individual during the course of a year, allowing researchers to assess possible changes that occurred during this time. Overall, hippocampal volume was reduced in the AD group compared to the controls, and the measurements also showed a larger volume decline over the year in the AD patients. However, the magnitude of the volume decline among the AD patients was significantly larger in women: hippocampal atrophy progressed about 1.5 times faster in women than in men during the year. A more recent study found that changes in hippocampal volume over time in individuals who were cognitively normal when assessed initially are more predictive of an eventual diagnosis of probable AD in women than in men (Burke et al., 2019).

These findings are important clinically because they suggest that measurements of hippocampal volume might be a particularly reliable early indication of the onset of AD in women. Changes in hippocampal volume are not the only sex difference related to AD. Compared with men, women exhibit greater rates of brain atrophy in several other regions (Hua et al., 2010) and faster cognitive decline (Ferretti et al., 2018). Researchers and clinicians are increasingly coming to realize that these sex differences likely have important implications for diagnosis and treatment, which should ultimately help scientists craft sex-specific approaches to both diagnosis and treatment of AD (Ferretti et al., 2018; Fisher, Bennett, & Dong, 2018). Given the worldwide impact of AD, it is difficult to imagine a more important arena for the investigation of sex differences.

A scary movie is designed to stimulate your amygdala, but only a little.

amygdala A part of the limbic system, located at the tip of each horn of the hippocampus, that plays a central role in many emotional processes, particularly the formation of emotional memories.

The **amygdala** (from Latin for "almond," also due to its shape), *located at the tip of each horn of the hippocampus, plays a central role in many emotional processes, particularly the formation of emotional memories* (Aggleton, 1992). The amygdala attaches significance to previously neutral events that are associated with fear, punishment, or reward (LeDoux, 1992). For example, think of the last time something scary or unpleasant happened to you: A car came barrelling towards you as you started walking into an intersection, or a ferocious dog leaped out of an alley as you passed by. Those stimuli—a car or a dog—are fairly neutral; you don't have a panic attack every time you walk by a used car lot. The emotional significance attached to events involving those stimuli is the work of the amygdala (McGaugh, 2006, 2015). When we are in emotionally arousing situations, the amygdala stimulates the hippocampus to remember many details surrounding the situation (Kensinger & Schacter, 2005).

For instance, people who lived through the terrorist attacks of September 11, 2001, remember vivid details about where they were, what they were doing, and how they felt when they heard the news, even years later (Hirst et al., 2009, 2015). In particular, the amygdala seems to be especially involved in encoding events as *fearful* (Adolphs et al., 1995; Sigurdsson et al., 2007). We'll have more to say about the amygdala in the Emotion and Motivation chapter. For now, keep in mind that a group of neurons the size of a lima bean buried deep in your brain help you to laugh, weep, or shriek in fright when the circumstances call for it.

The Basal Ganglia There are several other structures in the subcortical area, but we'll consider just one more. The **basal ganglia** is not one structure but *a set of subcortical structures that directs intentional movements*. Located near the thalamus and hypothalamus, the basal ganglia receive input from the cerebral cortex and send outputs to the motor centres in the brain stem (Nelson & Kreitzer, 2015). One part of the basal ganglia, the *striatum*, has an important role in the control of posture and movement. As we saw in the excerpt from Michael J. Fox's book, people who suffer from Parkinson's disease typically show symptoms of uncontrollable shaking and sudden jerks of the limbs and are unable to initiate a sequence of movements to achieve a specific goal. This happens because Parkinson's disease damages parts of the midbrain that normally supply the striatum with dopamine (Dauer & Przedborski, 2003). The undersupply of dopamine impairs the function of the striatum, which in turn leads to the visible tremors of Parkinson's.

So what's the problem in Parkinson's: the jerky movements, the ineffectiveness of the striatum in directing behaviour, or the underproduction of dopamine at the neuronal level? The answer is all of the above (Weiner, Shulman, & Lang, 2013). This disease clearly illustrates two themes of the brain and behaviour. First, actions at the microscopic level of neurons in the brain can produce substantial effects at the level of observable behaviour. Second, the structures in the hindbrain, midbrain, and forebrain don't function in isolation; they are interdependent, and damage in one area affects other areas in turn.

The Endocrine System

The **endocrine system** is *a network of glands that produce and secrete into the bloodstream chemical messages known as hormones, which influence a wide variety of basic functions, including metabolism, growth, and sexual development*. The endocrine system is distinct from the nervous system but works closely with it, especially the limbic system, to regulate thoughts, emotions, and behaviours. Some of the main glands in the endocrine system include the thyroid, which regulates bodily functions such as body temperature and heart rate; the adrenals, which regulate stress responses; the pancreas, which controls digestion; and the pineal, which secretes melatonin, influencing the sleep/wake cycle. The overall functioning of the endocrine system is orchestrated by the **pituitary gland,** *the "master gland" of the body's hormone-producing system, which releases hormones that direct the functions of many other glands in the body* (see **FIGURE 3.13**).

The hypothalamus sends hormonal signals to the pituitary gland, which in turn sends hormonal signals to other glands to control stress, digestive activities, and reproductive processes. For example, when a baby suckles its mother's breast, sensory neurons in her breast send signals to her hypothalamus, which then signals her pituitary gland to release a hormone called *oxytocin* into the bloodstream (McNeilly et al., 1983). Oxytocin, in turn, stimulates the release of milk from reservoirs in the breast. The pituitary gland is also involved in the response to stress. When we sense a threat, sensory neurons send signals to the hypothalamus, which stimulates the release of adrenocorticotropic hormone (ACTH) from the pituitary gland. ACTH, in turn, stimulates the adrenal glands to release hormones that activate the sympathetic nervous system (Selye & Fortier, 1950). As you read earlier in this chapter, the sympathetic nervous system prepares the body either to meet the threat head on or to flee from the situation.

The endocrine system also plays a key role in sexual behaviour and reproduction. The sexual reproductive glands are the ovaries in females, which make the hormone *estrogen*, and the testes in males, which make the hormone *testosterone* (see Figure 3.13). However, testosterone is not exclusive to males, and estrogen is not exclusive to females: the ovaries generate small amounts of testosterone, and the testes generate small amounts of estrogen (Davis & Wahlin-Jacobsen, 2015; Wibowo &

basal ganglia A set of subcortical structures that directs intentional movements.

endocrine system A network of glands that produce and secrete into the bloodstream chemical messages known as hormones, which influence a wide variety of basic functions, including metabolism, growth, and sexual development.

pituitary gland The "master gland" of the body's hormone-producing system, which releases hormones that direct the functions of many other glands in the body.

Figure 3.13
Major Glands Of the Endocrine System The endocrine system is a network of glands that works with the nervous system and impacts many basic functions by releasing hormones into the bloodstream.

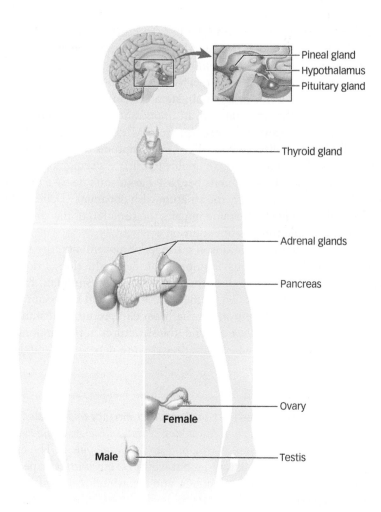

- Pineal gland
- Hypothalamus
- Pituitary gland
- Thyroid gland
- Adrenal glands
- Pancreas
- Ovary
- Testis

Female

Male

DONNA RANIERI

Crumpling a newspaper allows the same amount of surface area to fit into a much smaller space, just as the wrinkles (sulci) and folds (gyri) in the cortex allow a great deal of brain power to fit inside the human skull.

Wassersug, 2014). Although it is widely believed that fluctuations in sexual desire are closely linked to fluctuations in sex hormones, recent research has failed to reveal a strong link between testosterone levels and sexual desire in men or women (Roney & Simmons, 2013; van Anders, 2012), whereas there is evidence for a link between estrogen levels and sexual desire in women (Gangestad & Haselton, 2015; Roney & Simmons, 2013).

The Cerebral Cortex

Our tour of the brain has taken us from the very small (neurons) to the somewhat bigger (major divisions of the brain) to the very large: the cerebral cortex. The cortex is the highest level of the brain, and it is responsible for the most complex aspects of perception, emotion, movement, and thought (Fuster, 2003). It sits over the rest of the brain, like a mushroom cap shielding the underside and stem, and it is the wrinkled surface you see when looking at the brain with the naked eye.

The smooth surfaces of the cortex—the raised part—are called *gyri* (*gyrus* if you're talking about just one), and the indentations or fissures are called *sulci* (*sulcus* when singular). The sulci and gyri are a triumph of evolution. The cerebral cortex occupies roughly the area of a newspaper page, so fitting that much cortex into a human skull is a tough task. But if you crumple a sheet of newspaper, you'll see that the same surface area now fits compactly into a much smaller space. The cortex, with its wrinkles and folds, holds a lot of brainpower in a relatively small package that fits comfortably inside the human skull (see **FIGURE 3.14**). The functions of the cerebral cortex can be understood at three levels: the separation of the cortex into two hemispheres, the functions of each hemisphere, and the role of specific cortical areas.

Organization Across Hemispheres   The first level of organization divides the cortex into the left and right hemispheres. The two hemispheres are more or less symmetrical in their appearance and, to some extent, in their functions. However, each hemisphere controls the functions of the opposite side of the body. This is called *contralateral control*, meaning that your right cerebral hemisphere perceives stimuli from and controls movements on the left side of your body, whereas your left cerebral hemisphere perceives stimuli from and controls movement on the right side of your body.

The cerebral hemispheres are connected to each other by *commissures*, bundles of axons that make possible communication between parallel areas of the cortex in each half. The largest of these commissures is the **corpus callosum,** which *connects large areas of the cerebral cortex on each side of the brain and supports communication of information across the hemispheres* (see **FIGURE 3.15**). This means that information received in the right hemisphere, for example, can pass across the corpus callosum and be registered, virtually instantaneously, in the left hemisphere.

Organization Within Hemispheres   The second level of organization in the cerebral cortex distinguishes the functions of the different regions within each hemisphere of the brain. Each hemisphere of the cerebral cortex is divided into four areas, or *lobes*: From back to front, these are the occipital lobe, the parietal lobe, the temporal lobe, and the frontal lobe, as shown in Figure 3.14. We'll examine the functions of these lobes in more detail in later chapters, noting how scientists have used a variety of techniques to understand the operations of the brain. For now, here's a brief overview of the main functions of each lobe.

The **occipital lobe,** located at the back of the cerebral cortex, *processes visual information*. Sensory receptors in the eyes send information to the thalamus, which in turn sends information to the primary areas of the occipital lobe, where simple features of the stimulus are extracted, such as the location and orientation of an object's edges (see the Sensation and Perception chapter for more details). These features are then processed into a more complex "map" of the stimulus onto the occipital cortex, leading to comprehension of what's being seen. As you might imagine, damage to the primary visual areas of the occipital lobe can leave a person with partial or complete blindness. Information still enters the eyes, which work just fine. But without the ability to process and make sense of the information at the level of the cerebral cortex, the information is as good as lost (Zeki, 2001).

The **parietal lobe,** located in front of the occipital lobe, carries out functions that include *processing information about touch*. The parietal lobe contains the *somatosensory cortex,* a strip of brain tissue running from the top of the brain down to the sides (see **FIGURE 3.16**). Within each hemisphere, the somatosensory cortex represents the skin areas on the contralateral surface of the body. Each part of the somatosensory cortex maps onto a particular part of the body. If a body area is more sensitive, a larger part of the somatosensory cortex is devoted to it. For example, the part of the somatosensory cortex that corresponds to the lips and tongue is larger than the area corresponding to the feet. The somatosensory cortex can be illustrated as a distorted figure, called a *homunculus* ("little man"), in which the body parts are rendered according to how much of the somatosensory cortex is devoted to them (Penfield & Rasmussen, 1950). This map of the body in the brain was developed by Montreal neurosurgeon Wilder Penfield by stimulating the brains of his awake patients during surgery and recording where the patient reported feeling a sensation. Directly in front of the somatosensory cortex, in the frontal lobe, is a parallel strip of brain tissue called the *motor cortex.*

As in the somatosensory cortex, different parts of the motor cortex correspond to different body parts. The motor cortex initiates voluntary movements and sends

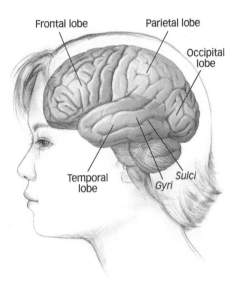

Figure 3.14
Cerebral Cortex and Lobes   The four major lobes of the cerebral cortex are the occipital lobe, the parietal lobe, the temporal lobe, and the frontal lobe. The smooth surfaces of the cortex are called gyri, and the indentations are called sulci.

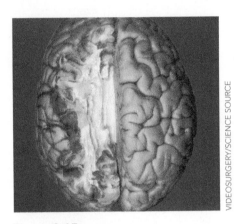

VIDEOSURGERY/SCIENCE SOURCE

Figure 3.15
Cerebral Hemispheres   The corpus callosum connects the two hemispheres of the brain and supports communication between them.

corpus callosum   A thick band of nerve fibres that connects large areas of the cerebral cortex on each side of the brain and supports communication of information across the hemispheres.

occipital lobe   A region of the cerebral cortex that processes visual information.

parietal lobe   A region of the cerebral cortex whose functions include processing information about touch.

Figure 3.16
Somatosensory and Motor Cortices The motor cortex, a strip of brain tissue in the frontal lobe, represents and controls different skin and body areas on the contralateral side of the body. Directly behind the motor cortex, in the parietal lobe, lies the somatosensory cortex. Like the motor cortex, the somatosensory cortex represents skin areas of particular parts on the contralateral side of the body.

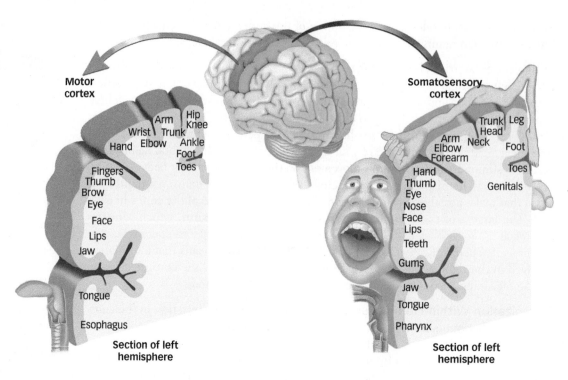

messages to the basal ganglia, cerebellum, and spinal cord. The motor and somatosensory cortices, then, are akin to sending and receiving areas of the cerebral cortex, taking in information and sending out commands, as the case might be.

The **temporal lobe,** located on the lower side of each hemisphere, is *responsible for hearing and language.* The *primary auditory cortex* in the temporal lobe is analogous to the somatosensory cortex in the parietal lobe and the primary visual areas of the occipital lobe: It receives sensory information from the ears based on the frequencies of sounds. Secondary areas of the temporal lobe then process the information into meaningful units, such as speech and words. The temporal lobe also houses areas that interpret the meaning of visual stimuli and help us recognize common objects in the environment (Martin, 2007).

The **frontal lobe,** which sits behind the forehead, has *specialized areas for movement, abstract thinking, planning, memory, and judgement.* As you just read, it contains the motor cortex, which coordinates movements of muscle groups throughout the body. Other areas in the frontal lobe coordinate thought processes that help us manipulate information and retrieve memories, which we can use to plan our behaviours and interact socially with others. In short, the frontal cortex allows us to do the kind of thinking, imagining, planning, and anticipating that sets humans apart from most other species (Schoenemann, Sheenan, & Glotzer, 2005; Stuss & Benson, 1986; Suddendorf & Corballis, 2007).

Organization Within Specific Lobes The third level of organization in the cerebral cortex involves the representation of information within specific lobes in the cortex. A hierarchy of processing stages from primary areas handles fine details of information all the way up to **association areas,** which are *composed of neurons that help provide sense and meaning to information registered in the cortex.* For example, neurons in the primary visual cortex are highly specialized: Some detect features of the environment that are in a horizontal orientation, others detect movement, and still others process information about human versus nonhuman forms. Association areas interpret the information extracted by these primary areas (shape, motion, etc.) to make sense of what's being perceived; in this case, perhaps a large cat leaping towards your face (Martin, 2007).

temporal lobe A region of the cerebral cortex responsible for hearing and language.

frontal lobe The region of the cerebral cortex that has specialized areas for movement, abstract thinking, planning, memory, and judgement.

association areas Areas in the cerebral cortex composed of neurons that help provide sense and meaning to information registered in the cortex.

Similarly, neurons in the primary auditory cortex register sound frequencies, but it's the association areas of the temporal lobe that allow you to turn those noises into the meaning of your friend screaming, "Look out for the cat!" Association areas, then, help stitch together the threads of information in the various parts of the cortex to produce a meaningful understanding of what's being registered in the brain.

A striking example of this property of association areas comes from the discovery of the mirror-neuron system. **Mirror neurons** are *active when an animal performs a behaviour, such as reaching for or manipulating an object, and are also activated when another animal observes that animal performing the same behaviour.* Mirror neurons are found in the frontal lobe (near the motor cortex) and in the parietal lobe (Rizzolatti & Craighero, 2004; Rizzolatti & Sinigaglia, 2010). They have been identified in birds, monkeys, and humans, and their name reflects the function they serve. Neuroimaging studies with humans have shown that mirror neurons are active when people watch someone perform a behaviour, such as grasping in midair. But they are more highly activated when that behaviour has some purpose or context, such as grasping a cup to take a drink (Iacoboni et al., 2005), and they seem to be related to recognizing the goal someone has in carrying out an action and the outcome of the action, rather than to the particular movements a person makes while performing that action (Hamilton & Grafton, 2006, 2008; Iacoboni, 2009; Rizzolatti & Sinigaglia, 2010).

There is controversy about how to interpret the activity of mirror neurons, particularly in humans (Hickok, 2009, 2014), and about whether, as claimed by some researchers, impairments to the mirror-neuron system contribute to difficulties with understanding the minds of other people, as occurs in autism spectrum disorder (Hamilton, 2013; see the chapter on Psychological Disorders). Nonetheless, the existence of mirror neurons is supported by experimental evidence (Rizzolatti & Rozzi, 2018). In the Learning chapter we'll find out more about the role of mirror neurons in learning.

Finally, neurons in the association areas are usually less specialized and more flexible than neurons in the primary areas. Thus, they can be shaped by learning and experience to do their job more effectively. This kind of shaping of neurons by environmental forces allows the brain flexibility, or plasticity, our next topic.

When one animal observes another engaging in a particular behaviour, some of the same neurons become active in the observer's brain as in the brain of the animal exhibiting the behaviour. These mirror neurons seem to play an important role in social behaviour.

Brain Plasticity

The cerebral cortex may seem to be a fixed structure, one big sheet of neurons designed to help us make sense of our external world. Remarkably, however, sensory cortices are not fixed. They can adapt to changes in sensory inputs, a quality that researchers call *plasticity* (i.e., the ability to be moulded). As an example, if you lose your middle finger in an accident, the part of the somatosensory area that represents that finger is initially unresponsive (Kaas, 1991). After all, there's no longer any sensory input going from that location to that part of the brain. You might expect the left middle-finger neurons of the somatosensory cortex to wither away. However, over time, that area in the somatosensory cortex becomes responsive to stimulation of the fingers *adjacent* to the missing finger. The brain is plastic: Functions that were assigned to certain areas of the brain may be capable of being reassigned to other areas of the brain to accommodate changing input from the environment (Feldman, 2009). This suggests that sensory inputs "compete" for representation in each cortical area.

New Mapping

A striking example comes from amputees who continue to experience sensations where the missing limb would be, a phenomenon called *phantom limb syndrome.* Patients can feel their missing limbs moving, even in coordinated gestures such as shaking hands. Some even report feeling pain in their phantom limbs (Kuffler, 2018; Ramachandran & Brang, 2015). Why does this happen?

mirror neurons Neurons that are active when an animal performs a behaviour (e.g., reaching for or manipulating an object), as well as when another animal observes that animal performing the same behaviour.

To find out, researchers stimulated the skin surface in various regions around the face, torso, and arms while monitoring brain activity in amputees and nonamputee volunteers (Ramachandran & Blakeslee, 1998; Ramachandran, Brang, & McGeoch, 2010; Ramachandran, Rodgers-Ramachandran, & Stewart, 1992). Brain-imaging techniques displayed the somatosensory cortical areas that were activated when the skin was stimulated, enabling the researchers to map how touch is represented in the somatosensory cortex for different areas of the body. For instance, when the face was touched, the researchers could determine which areas in the somatosensory cortex were most active; when the torso was stimulated, they could see which areas responded, and so on.

Brain scans of the amputees revealed that stimulating areas of the face and upper arm activated an area in the somatosensory cortex that previously would have been activated by a now-missing hand (**FIGURE 3.17**). The face and arm were represented in the somatosensory cortex in an area adjacent to where the person's hand—now amputated—would have been represented. Stimulating the face or arm produced phantom limb sensations in the amputees; they reported "feeling" a sensation in their missing limbs.

Brain plasticity can explain these results (Pascual-Leone et al., 2005). The cortical representations for the face and the upper arm normally lie on either side of the representation for the hand (see Figure 3.16). The somatosensory areas for the face and upper arm were larger in amputees and had taken over the part of the cortex normally representing the hand. Indeed, the new face and arm representations were now contiguous with each other, filling in the space occupied by the hand representation. Some of these new mappings were quite concise. For example, in some amputees, when specific areas of the facial skin were activated, the patient reported sensations in just one finger of the phantom hand (Figure 3.17)!

The Influence of Practice

Plasticity doesn't occur only to compensate for missing digits or limbs, however. An extraordinary amount of stimulation of one finger can result in that finger's "taking over" the representation of the part of the cortex that usually represents other, adjacent fingers (Merzenich et al., 1990). Based on this work, it is likely that concert pianists have highly developed cortical areas for finger control: The continued input from the fingers commands a larger area of representation in the somatosensory

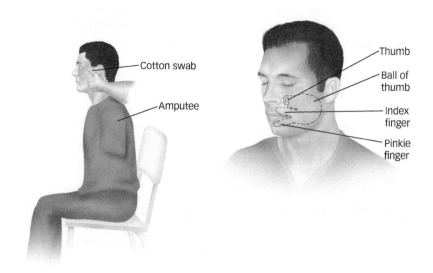

Figure 3.17

Mapping Sensations in Phantom Limbs Researchers lightly touch an amputee's face with a cotton swab, eliciting sensations in the "missing" hand. Touching different parts of the cheek can even result in sensations in particular fingers or the thumb of the missing hand.

cortices in the brain. Consistent with this idea, research indicates greater plasticity within the motor cortex of professional musicians compared with nonmusicians, perhaps reflecting an increase in the number of motor synapses as a result of extended practice (Rosenkranz, Williamon, & Rothwell, 2007). Similar findings have been obtained with quilters (who have highly developed areas for the thumb and forefinger, which are critical to their profession) and taxi drivers (who have overdeveloped brain areas in the hippocampus that are used during spatial navigation) (Maguire et al., 2000).

The Influence of Exercise

Plasticity is also related to a question you might not expect to find in a psychology textbook: How much have you been exercising lately? Although we expect that you are spending countless happy hours reading this textbook, we also hope that you've been finding enough time for physical exercise. A large number of studies in rats and other nonhuman animals indicate that physical exercise can increase the number of synapses and even promote the development of new neurons in the hippocampus (Hillman, Erickson, & Kramer, 2008; van Praag, 2009). Recent studies with people have begun to document beneficial effects of cardiovascular exercise on aspects of brain function and cognitive performance (Colcombe et al., 2004, 2006; Prakash et al., 2015).

Although these effects tend to be seen most clearly in older adults (okay, so it's time for your textbook authors to get on a treadmill), benefits have also been documented throughout the life span (Hertig & Nagel, 2012; Hillman et al., 2008). Some evidence indicates that even a single session of moderate-to-intensive exercise can boost aspects of memory and motor skills (Roig et al., 2012; Statton et al., 2015). In fact, some researchers believe that this kind of activity-dependent brain plasticity is relevant to treating spinal cord injuries (which, as we have seen, have a devastating impact on people's lives) because understanding how to maximize plasticity through exercise and training may help to guide rehabilitation efforts (Dunlop, 2008). It should be clear by now that the plasticity of the brain is not just an interesting theoretical idea; it has potentially important applications to everyday life (Bryck & Fisher, 2012).

Keith Jarrett is a virtuoso who has been playing piano for more than 60 years. Compared with those of a novice, the brain regions that control Jarrett's fingers are relatively less active when he plays.

The Adaptive Brain: Understanding Its Evolution

Far from being a single, elegant machine, the human brain is instead a system comprising many distinct components that have been added at different times over the course of evolution. The human species has retained what worked best in earlier versions of the brain, then added bits and pieces to get us to our present state through evolution.

The central nervous system evolved from the very basic ones found in simple animals to the elaborate nervous system in humans today. Even the simplest animals have sensory neurons and motor neurons for responding to the environment (Shepherd, 1988). For example, single-celled protozoa have molecules in their cell membrane that are sensitive to food in the water. The first neurons appeared in invertebrates, such as jellyfish; the sensory neurons in the jellyfish's tentacles can feel the touch of a potentially dangerous predator, which prompts the jellyfish to swim to safety. If you're a jellyfish, this simple neural system is sufficient to keep you alive. The first central nervous system worthy of the name, though, appeared in flatworms. The flatworm has a primitive kind of brain that includes sensory neurons for vision and taste, as well as motor neurons that control feeding behaviour. Emerging from the brain is a pair of tracts that form a spinal cord.

Flatworms don't have much of a brain, but then again, they don't need much of a brain. The rudimentary brain areas found in simple invertebrates eventually evolved into the complex brain structures found in humans.

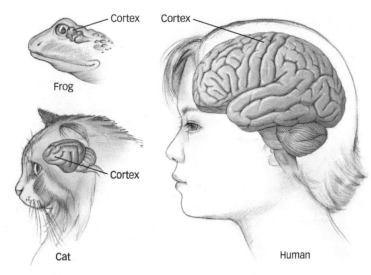

Figure 3.18
Development of the Forebrain
Reptiles and birds have almost no cerebral cortex. Mammals such as rats and cats do have a cerebral cortex, but their frontal lobes are proportionately much smaller than the frontal lobes of humans and other primates. How might this explain the fact that only humans have developed complex language, computer technology, and calculus?

A Division Forms: Vertebrates and Invertebrates

During the course of evolution, a major split in the organization of the nervous system occurred between invertebrate animals (those without a spinal column) and vertebrate animals (those with a spinal column). In all vertebrates, the central nervous system is organized into a hierarchy: The lower levels of the brain and spinal cord execute simpler functions, while the higher levels of the nervous system perform more complex functions. As you saw earlier, in humans, reflexes are accomplished in the spinal cord. At the next level, the midbrain executes the more complex task of orienting towards an important stimulus in the environment. Finally, an even more complex task, such as imagining what your life will be like 20 years from now, is performed in the forebrain (Addis, Wong, & Schacter, 2007; Schacter et al., 2012; Szpunar, Watson, & McDermott, 2007).

The forebrain undergoes further evolutionary advances in vertebrates. In lower vertebrate species such as amphibians (frogs and newts), the forebrain consists only of small clusters of neurons at the end of the neural tube. In higher vertebrates, including reptiles, birds, and mammals, the forebrain is much larger, and it evolves in two different patterns. Reptiles and birds have almost no cerebral cortex. By contrast, mammals have a highly developed cerebral cortex consisting of multiple areas that serve a broad range of higher mental functions. This forebrain development has reached its peak—so far—in humans (**FIGURE 3.18**).

The human brain, then, is not so much one remarkable thing; rather, it is a succession of extensions from a quite serviceable foundation. The forebrain of a bullfrog is about as differentiated as it needs to be to survive in a frog's world. The human forebrain, however, shows substantial refinement, which allows for some remarkable, uniquely human abilities: self-awareness, sophisticated language use, abstract reasoning, and imagining, among others.

Build to the Outcomes

1. Which part of the brain controls the basic functions of life, such as respiration?
2. Which part of the brain helps with orientation to the environment?
3. How is the thalamus like a computer?
4. Which area of the brain is associated with emotional memories?
5. Why is Parkinson's disease a good example of the interrelationship between the brain and behaviour?
6. What is the main function of the pituitary gland?
7. Why is the part of the somatosensory cortex relating to the lips bigger than the area corresponding to the feet?
8. What types of thinking occur in the frontal lobe?
9. Give examples of research that proves that the brain is able to change because of a person's life experience.
10. What is the structural difference between the brain of a reptile or bird, and the brain of a mammal?

Genes, Epigenetics, and the Environment

Is it genetics (nature) or the environment (nurture) that reigns supreme in directing a person's behaviour? The emerging picture from current research is that both nature *and* nurture play a role in directing behaviour, and the focus has shifted to examining the interaction of the two rather than the absolute contributions of either alone (Gottesman & Hanson, 2005; Rutter & Silberg, 2002; Zhang & Meaney, 2010).

What Are Genes?

A **gene** is *the major unit of hereditary transmission*. Over time, the term *gene* has been used to refer to two distinct but related concepts. The initial, relatively abstract concept of a gene referred to units of inheritance that specify traits such as eye colour. More recently, genes have been defined as sections on a strand of DNA (deoxyribonucleic acid) that code for the protein molecules that affect traits. Genes are organized into large threads called **chromosomes,** *strands of DNA wound around each other in a double-helix configuration* (see **FIGURE 3.19a**). The DNA in our chromosomes produces protein molecules through the action of a molecule known as messenger RNA (ribonucleic acid; mRNA), which communicates a copy of the DNA code to cells that produce proteins. Chromosomes come in pairs, and humans have 23 pairs each. These pairs of chromosomes are similar but not identical: You inherit one of each pair from your father and one from your mother. There's a twist, however: The selection of *which* of each pair is given to you is random.

Perhaps the most striking example of this random distribution is the determination of sex. In mammals, the chromosomes that determine sex are the X and Y chromosomes; females have two X chromosomes, whereas males have one X and one Y chromosome. You inherited an X chromosome from your mother because she has only X chromosomes to give. Your biological sex, therefore, was determined by whether you received an additional X chromosome or a Y chromosome from your father.

Learning Outcomes

- Outline the structure of a gene.
- Differentiate between monozygotic and dizygotic twins.
- Explain how epigenetic influences work.
- Give examples of the influence of genetics and the environment to human behaviour.

gene The major unit of hereditary transmission.

chromosomes Strands of DNA wound around each other in a double-helix configuration.

Figure 3.19

Genes and Epigenetics (a) Genes, Chromosomes, and Their Recombination. The cell nucleus houses chromosomes, which are made up of double-helix strands of DNA. Every cell in our bodies has 23 pairs of chromosomes. Genes are segments on the strand of DNA. **(b) Epigenetics.** Studies suggest that DNA methylation and histone modification play a key role in the long-lasting effects of early life experiences for both rodents and humans.

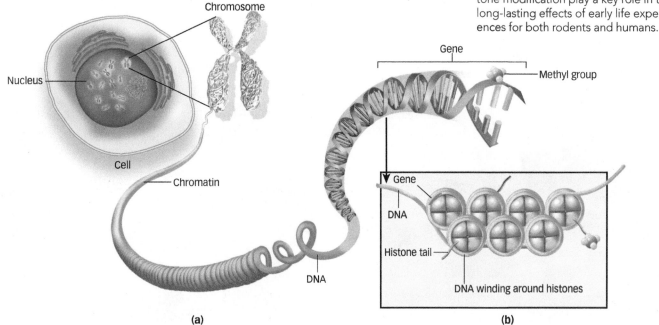

(a)

(b)

"The title of my science project is 'My Little Brother: Nature or Nurture.'"

As a species, we share about 99% of the same DNA (and almost as much with other apes), but a portion of DNA varies across individuals. Children share more of this variable portion of DNA with their parents than with more distant relatives or with nonrelatives: They share half their genes with each parent, a quarter of their genes with their grandparents, an eighth of their genes with cousins, and so on. The probability of sharing genes is called *degree of relatedness*. The most genetically related people are *monozygotic twins* (also called *identical twins*), who develop from the splitting of a single fertilized egg and therefore share 100% of their genes. *Dizygotic twins (fraternal twins)* develop from two separate fertilized eggs and share 50% of their genes, the same as any two siblings born separately.

Many researchers have tried to determine the relative influence of genetics on behaviour. One way to do this is to compare a trait shown by monozygotic twins with that same trait among dizygotic twins. This type of research usually enlists twins who were raised in the same household, so that the impact of their environment (their socioeconomic status, access to education, parental child-rearing practices, environmental stressors) remains relatively constant. Finding that monozygotic twins have a higher presence of a specific trait suggests a genetic influence (Boomsma, Busjahn, & Peltonen, 2002).

For example, the likelihood that the dizygotic twin of a person who has schizophrenia (a mental disorder we'll discuss in greater detail in the Psychological Disorders chapter) will *also* develop schizophrenia is 27%. However, this statistic rises to 50% for monozygotic twins. This observation suggests a substantial genetic influence on the likelihood of developing schizophrenia. Monozygotic twins share 100% of their genes, and if one assumes environmental influences are relatively consistent for both members of the twin pair, the 50% likelihood can be traced to genetic factors. That sounds scarily high—until you realize that the remaining 50% probability must be due to environmental influences. In short, genetics can contribute to the development, likelihood, or onset of a variety of traits. But a more complete picture of genetic influences on behaviour must always take the environmental context into consideration. Genes express themselves within an environment, not in isolation.

Monozygotic twins (*left*) share 100% of their genes in common, whereas dizygotic twins (*right*) share 50% of their genes, the same as other siblings. Studies of monozygotic and dizygotic twins help researchers estimate the relative contributions of genes and environmental influences on behaviour.

A Role for Epigenetics

The idea that genes are expressed within an environment is central to an important and rapidly growing area of research known as **epigenetics:** *the study of environmental influences that determine whether or not genes are expressed, or the degree to which they are expressed, without altering the basic DNA sequences that constitute the genes themselves.* To understand how epigenetic influences work, it is useful to think about DNA as analogous to a script for a play or a movie. The biologist Nessa Carey (2012) offers the example of Shakespeare's *Romeo and Juliet,* which was made into a movie back in 1936 starring the classic actors Leslie Howard and Norma Shearer, and in 1996 starring Leonardo DiCaprio and Claire Danes. Shakespeare's tragedy formed the basis of both screenplays, but the directors of the two films used Shakespeare's material in different ways, and the actors in the two films gave different performances. Thus, the final products departed from Shakespeare's play and were different from one another, even though Shakespeare's original play still exists. Something similar happens with epigenetics: depending on the environment, a gene can be expressed or not expressed without altering the underlying DNA code.

The environment can influence gene expression through **epigenetic marks,** *chemical modifications to DNA that can turn genes on or off.* You can think of epigenetic marks as analogous to notes that the movie directors made on Shakespeare's play that determined how the play was used in a particular film. There are two widely studied epigenetic marks:

- **DNA methylation** involves *adding a methyl group to DNA.* There are special enzymes, referred to as *epigenetic writers,* whose role is to add methyl groups to DNA. Although adding a methyl group doesn't alter the basic DNA sequence, it switches off the methylated gene (see Figure 3.19b). This process is roughly analogous to Claire Danes's director making notes that instruct her to ignore a certain portion of the Shakespeare play. That portion of the play—like the switched-off gene—is still there, but its contents are not expressed.

- **Histone modification** involves *adding chemical modifications to proteins called histones that are involved in packaging DNA.* We tend to visualize DNA as the free-floating double helix shown in Figure 3.19a, but DNA is actually tightly wrapped around groups of histone proteins, as shown in Figure 3.19b. However, whereas DNA methylation switches genes off, histone modification can either switch genes off or turn them on. But just like DNA methylation, histone modifications influence gene expression without altering the underlying DNA sequence (Carey, 2012).

The Relevance of Epigenetics to the Brain

So far, you have learned a lot of strange new terms and may have wondered whether Claire Danes's performance in *Romeo and Juliet* prepared her to play Carrie in *Homeland.* But what is the relevance of epigenetics to the brain and to psychology? In the past decade or so, it has turned out to be more relevant than anyone suspected. Experiments with rats and mice have shown that epigenetic marks left by DNA methylation and histone modification play a role in learning and memory (Bredy et al., 2007; Day & Sweatt, 2011; Levenson & Sweatt, 2005). Several studies have linked epigenetic changes with responses to stress (Zhang & Meaney, 2010), including recent research with humans. For example, studies of nurses working in high-stress versus low-stress environments found differences between the two groups in DNA methylation (Alasaari et al., 2012). Subjective levels of stress in a sample of 92 Canadian adults, as well as physiological signs of stress, were correlated with levels of DNA methylation (Lam et al., 2012).

epigenetics The study of environmental influences that determine whether or not genes are expressed, or the degree to which they are expressed, without altering the basic DNA sequences that constitute the genes themselves.

epigenetic marks Chemical modifications to DNA that can turn genes on or off.

DNA methylation Adding a methyl group to DNA.

histone modification Adding chemical modifications to proteins called histones that are involved in packaging DNA.

Epigenetics and Early Life Experiences

DNA methylation and histone modifications also play a key role in the long-lasting effects of early experiences for both rats and humans. Key early work from the laboratory of McGill researcher Michael Meaney and his colleagues (Francis et al., 1999; Liu et al., 1997) built on the finding that there are notable differences in the mothering styles of rats: Some mothers spend a lot of time licking and grooming their young pups (high LG mothers), which rat pups greatly enjoy, whereas others spend little time doing so (low LG mothers). The researchers found that pups of high LG mothers are much less fearful as adults when placed in stressful situations than are the adult pups of low LG mothers. Perhaps this simply reflects the effects of a genetic profile shared by the mother and her pups? Not so: The same effects were obtained when the offspring of high LG mothers are raised by low LG mothers, and vice versa.

These effects were accompanied by physiological changes. When placed in fear-inducing situations, adult rats raised by the high LG mothers showed lower levels of several stress-related hormones than did adult rats that had been raised by low LG mothers. There was also increased evidence of hippocampal serotonin in the adult pups of high LG mothers; as you learned earlier in this chapter, increased levels of serotonin are associated with elevated mood. In other words, the high LG pups grow up to become "chilled out" adults. But exactly how did these effects persist from infancy to adulthood? This is where epigenetics comes in. The increased serotonin response produced by high LG mothers triggers a decrease in DNA methylation of the glucocorticoid receptor gene (see the Stress and Health chapter for a discussion of glucocorticoids and stress), which leads to greater expression of the gene and a corresponding ability to respond more calmly to stress (Weaver et al., 2004).

The rats raised by low LG mothers showed relatively increased DNA methylation of the glucocorticoid receptor gene, which leads to reduced expression of the gene and a corresponding inability to respond calmly to stress. Because DNA methylation can be very stable over time, these studies with rats provided the foundation for more recent studies with humans. The human equivalent of high LG is probably loving and attentive parenting, and the equivalent of low LG is probably childhood neglect and abuse. Indeed, studies show a role for epigenetics in the persisting effects of childhood abuse in adult men (McGowan et al., 2009). Related studies suggest that the effects of early experience are not restricted to a single gene, but occur more broadly (McGowan et al., 2011; Suderman et al., 2012). These results have led both clinicians and researchers to increasingly recognize the importance of epigenetics for various psychological disorders in which early life stress is a risk factor, including depression, schizophrenia, and posttraumatic stress disorder (Kundakovic et al., 2015; Provencal & Binder, 2015). Although we are far from fully understanding the complex relationship between epigenetic changes and psychological phenomena, scientists are increasingly recognizing the relevance of epigenetics for psychology (Jones, Moore, & Kobor, 2018; Sweatt, 2019; Zhang & Meaney, 2010).

The Role of Environmental Factors

Genes set the range of possibilities that can be observed in a population, but the characteristics of any individual within that range are determined by environmental factors and experience. The genetic capabilities that another species might enjoy, such as being able to breathe underwater, are outside the range of *your* possibilities, no matter how much you might desire them.

With these parameters in mind, behavioural geneticists use calculations based on relatedness to compute the heritability of behaviours (Plomin et al., 2001). **Heritability** is *a measure of the variability of behavioural traits among individuals*

Rodent pups raised by mothers who spend a lot of time licking and grooming them are less fearful as adults in stressful situations.

JUNIORS BILDARCHIV GMBH/R211/ALAMY

heritability A measure of the variability of behavioural traits among individuals that can be accounted for by genetic factors.

that can be accounted for by genetic factors. Heritability is calculated as a proportion, and its numerical value (index) ranges from 0 to 1.00. A heritability of 0 means that genes do not contribute to individual differences in the behavioural trait; a heritability of 1.00 means that genes are the *only* reason for the individual differences. As you might guess, scores of 0 or 1.00 occur so infrequently that they are theoretical limits rather than realistic values; almost nothing in human behaviour is completely due to the environment or owed *completely* to genetic inheritance. Scores between 0 and 1.00, then, indicate that individual differences are caused by varying *degrees* of genetic and environmental contributions—a little stronger influence of genetics here, a little stronger influence of the environment there—but each always within the context of the other (Moffitt, 2005; Zhang & Meaney, 2010).

For human behaviour, almost all estimates of heritability are in the moderate range, between .30 and .60. For example, a heritability index of .50 for intelligence indicates that half of the variability in intelligence test scores is attributable to genetic influences and the remaining half is due to environmental influences. Smart parents often (but not always) produce smart children; genetics certainly plays a role. But smart and not-so-smart children attend good or not-so-good schools, practice their piano lessons with more or less regularity, study or don't study as hard as they might, have good and not-so-good teachers and role models, and so on. Genetics is only half the story in intelligence. Environmental influences also play a significant role in predicting the basis of intelligence (see the Intelligence chapter).

Heritability has proven to be a theoretically useful and statistically sound concept in helping scientists understand the relative genetic and environmental influences on behaviour. However, there are four important points about heritability to bear in mind.

- *Heritability is an abstract concept*: It tells us nothing about the *specific* genes that contribute to a trait.
- *Heritability is a population concept*: It tells us nothing about an individual. Heritability provides guidance for understanding differences across individuals in a population rather than abilities within an individual.
- *Heritability is dependent on the environment*: Just as behaviour occurs within certain contexts, so do genetic influences. For example, intelligence isn't an unchanging quality: People are intelligent within a particular learning context, a social setting, a family environment, a socioeconomic class, and so on. Heritability, therefore, is meaningful only for the environmental conditions in which it was computed, and heritability estimates may change dramatically under other environmental conditions.
- *Heritability is not fate*: It tells us nothing about the degree to which interventions can change a behavioural trait. Heritability is useful for identifying behavioural traits that are influenced by genes, but it is not useful for determining how individuals will respond to particular environmental conditions or treatments.

Build to the Outcomes

1. What are the two ways that "genes" can be defined?

2. Why do dizygotic twins share 50% of their genes, just as do siblings born separately?

3. Are abilities, such as intelligence and memory, inherited through our genes?

4. What do epigenetic studies suggest about how early life experiences may influence whether genes are expressed?

Investigating the Brain

Learning Outcome

- Identify the three main ways that researchers study the human brain.

- Compare and contrast advantages and disadvantages of techniques used to study the brain in action.

So far, you've read a great deal about the nervous system: how it's organized, how it works, what its components are, and what those components do. But one question remains largely unanswered: *How* do we know all of this? Anatomists can dissect a human brain and identify its structures, but they cannot determine which structures play a role in producing which behaviours by dissecting a nonliving brain.

Scientists use a variety of methods to understand how the brain affects behaviour. Let's consider three of the main ones: studying people with brain damage; studying the brain's electrical activity; and using brain imaging to study brain structure and watch the brain in action. Let's examine each of these ways of investigating the brain.

Studying the Damaged Brain

To better understand the normal operation of a process, it is instructive to identify what happens when that process fails. Much research in neuroscience seeks to link the loss of specific perceptual, motor, emotional, or cognitive functions with specific areas of brain damage (Andrewes, 2001; Kolb & Whishaw, 2015). By studying behaviour and cognition in people with known patterns of brain damage, neuroscientists can theorize about the functions those brain areas normally perform.

The modern history of neuroscience can be dated to the work of Paul Broca (1824–1880) (see The Evolution of Psychological Science chapter). In 1861, Broca described a patient who had lost the capacity to produce spoken language (but not the ability to understand language) due to damage in a small area in the left frontal lobe. In 1874, Carl Wernicke (1848–1905) described a patient with an impairment in language comprehension (but not the ability to produce speech) associated with damage to an area in the upper-left temporal lobe. These areas were named, respectively, *Broca's area* and *Wernicke's area* (see Figure 9.3 in the Language and Thought chapter), and they provided the earliest evidence that the brain locations for speech production and speech comprehension are separate and that for most people, the left hemisphere is critical to producing and understanding language (Young, 1990).

The Emotional Functions of the Frontal Lobes

As you've already seen, the human frontal lobes are a remarkable evolutionary achievement. However, psychology's first glimpse at some functions of the frontal lobes came from a rather unremarkable fellow. He was so unremarkable, in fact, that a single event in his life defined his place in the annals of psychology's history (Macmillan, 2000). Phineas Gage was a muscular 25-year-old railroad worker. On September 13, 1848, in Cavendish, Vermont, he was packing an explosive charge into a crevice in a rock when

the powder exploded, driving a 3-foot, 13-pound iron rod through his head at high speed (Harlow, 1868). As **FIGURE 3.20** shows, the rod entered through his lower left jaw and exited through the middle top of his head. Incredibly, Gage lived to tell the tale. But his personality underwent a significant change.

Before the accident, Gage had been mild-mannered, quiet, conscientious, and a hard worker. After the accident, however, Harlow (1868) reported that he became irritable, irresponsible, indecisive, and given to profanity. The sad change in Gage's personality and emotional life nonetheless provided an unexpected benefit to psychology. His case study was the first to allow researchers to investigate the hypothesis that

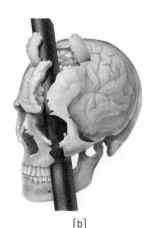

Figure 3.20

Phineas Gage (a) Phineas Gage's traumatic accident allowed researchers to investigate the functions of the frontal lobe and its connections with emotion centres in the subcortical structures. (b) The likely path of the metal rod through Gage's skull is reconstructed here.

(a)   (b)

the frontal lobe is involved in emotion regulation, planning, and decision making. Furthermore, because the connections between the frontal lobe and the subcortical structures of the limbic system were affected, scientists were able to better understand how the amygdala, hippocampus, and related brain structures interacted with the cerebral cortex (Damasio, 2005).

The Distinct Roles of the Left and Right Hemispheres

You'll recall that the cerebral cortex is divided into two hemispheres, although typically the two hemispheres act as one integrated unit. Sometimes, however, disorders can threaten the ability of the brain to function, and the only way to stop them is with radical methods. This is sometimes the case for people who suffer from severe, intractable epilepsy. Seizures that begin in one hemisphere cross the corpus callosum (the thick band of nerve fibres that allows the two hemispheres to communicate) to the opposite hemisphere and start a feedback loop that results in a kind of firestorm in the brain. To alleviate the severity of the seizures, surgeons can sever the corpus callosum in an operation called a *split-brain procedure*. The result is that a seizure that starts in one hemisphere is isolated in that hemisphere because there is no longer a connection to the other side. This procedure helps people with epilepsy but also produces some unusual, if not unpredictable, behaviours.

The Nobel laureate Roger Sperry (1913–1994) was intrigued by the observation that the everyday behaviour of people who had their corpus collosum severed did not seem to be affected by the operation. Did this mean that the corpus callosum played no role at all in behaviour? Sperry thought this conclusion was premature, reasoning that casual observations of everyday behaviours could easily fail to detect impairments that might be picked up by sensitive tests. To evaluate this idea experimentally, Sperry and his colleagues first showed that when the corpus callosum was severed in cats, learning was not transferred from one hemisphere to the other (Sperry, 1964). Later, Sperry designed several experiments that investigated the behaviours of people with split brains and in the process revealed a great deal about the independent functions of the left and right hemispheres (Sperry, 1964).

Normally, any information that initially enters the left hemisphere is also registered in the right hemisphere and vice versa: The information comes in and travels across the corpus callosum, and both hemispheres understand what's going on (see **FIGURE 3.21**). But in a person with a split brain, information entering one hemisphere stays there. Without an intact corpus callosum, there's no way for that information to reach the other hemisphere. Sperry and his colleagues used this understanding in a series of experiments. For example, they asked a person with a split brain to look at a spot in the centre of a screen and then projected a stimulus either on the left side of the screen (the left visual field) or the right side of the screen (the right visual field), isolating the stimulus to the opposite hemisphere (see Figure 4.10 in the Sensation and Perception chapter for more details about how information from one visual field enters the opposite hemisphere).

The hemispheres themselves are specialized for different kinds of tasks. You've just learned about Broca's and Wernicke's areas, which revealed that language processing is largely a left-hemisphere activity. So, imagine that some information came into the left hemisphere of a person with a split brain, and she was asked to describe verbally what it was. No problem: The left hemisphere has the information, it's the "speaking" hemisphere, and so she should have no difficulty verbally describing what she saw. But suppose she was asked to reach behind the screen with her left hand and pick up the object she just saw. Remember that the hemispheres exert contralateral control over the body, meaning that the left hand is controlled by the right hemisphere. Yet this person's right hemisphere has no clue

Roger Wolcott Sperry (1913–1994) received the Nobel Prize in Physiology in 1981 for his pioneering work investigating the independent functions of the cerebral hemispheres.

KEYSTONE/GETTY IMAGES

Figure 3.21

Split-Brain Experiment When a person with a split brain is presented with the picture of a ring on the right and a picture of a key on the left side of a screen, she can verbalize "ring" but not "key" because the left hemisphere "sees" the ring and language is usually located in the left hemisphere. She would be able to choose a key with her left hand from a set of objects behind a screen. She would not, however, be able to pick out a ring with her left hand because what the left hemisphere "sees" is not communicated to the left side of her body.

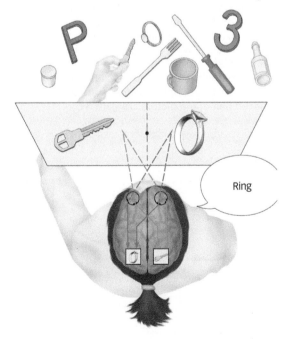

Ring

what the object was because that information was received in the left hemisphere and was unable to travel to the right hemisphere! So even though she saw the object and could verbally describe it, she would be unable to use the right hemisphere to perform other tasks regarding that object, such as correctly selecting it from a group with her left hand (see Figure 3.21).

Of course, information presented to the right hemisphere would produce complementary deficits. In this case, she might be presented with a familiar object in her left hand (e.g., a key), be able to demonstrate that she knew what it was (by twisting and turning the key in midair), yet be unable to verbally describe what she was holding. In this case, the information in the right hemisphere is unable to travel to the left hemisphere, which controls the production of speech.

Furthermore, suppose a person with a split brain was briefly flashed the unusual face in **FIGURE 3.22** while their eyes were staring straight ahead. This is called a *chimeric face,* assembled from half-face components of the full faces also shown in the figure. When asked to indicate which face was presented, her answer would depend on how she was asked to respond (Levy, Trevarthen, & Sperry, 1972). If she was asked to name who she saw, her response would depend on the left, language-dominant, hemisphere; she would report that she saw whoever's half-face had been presented on the right (Leonardo DiCaprio in Figure 3.22). In contrast, if she was shown both faces and allowed to move her eyes around, and asked to point with her left hand (controlled by the right hemisphere), she would indicate the picture of Brad Pitt, because Brad's half-face had been flashed to only the right hemisphere.

Figure 3.22

Chimeric Faces and the Split Brain
(a) When a person with a split brain is given a very brief exposure to a chimeric face of Brad Pitt and Leonardo DiCaprio that restricts the information from each side to a single hemisphere, her left hemisphere is aware only of Leonardo DiCaprio, while her right hemisphere sees only Brad Pitt. (b) When asked whom she just saw, she answers, "Leonardo DiCaprio," because speech is controlled by the left hemisphere (in most people). (c) When shown each of the full faces in free viewing and asked to point with her left hand to the face she just saw, she points to Brad Pitt, because her right hemisphere only became aware of the left half of the picture. BRAD PITT PHOTO: ALEX BRANDON/AP IMAGES; LEONARDO DICAPRIO PHOTO: FREDERICK M. BROWN/GETTY IMAGES

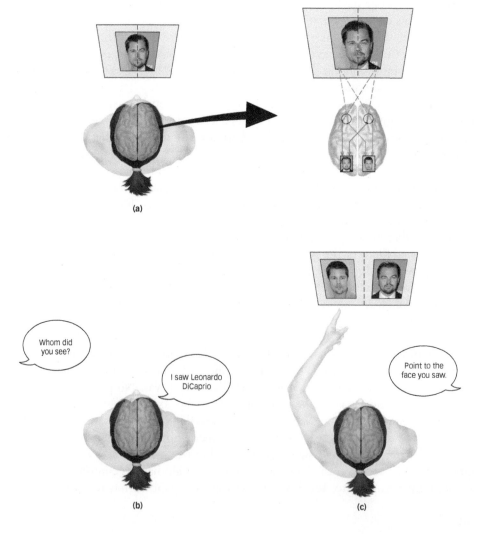

These split-brain studies reveal that the two hemispheres perform different functions and can work together seamlessly as long as the corpus callosum is intact. Without a way to transmit information from one hemisphere to the other, information remains in the hemisphere it initially entered, and we become acutely aware of the different functions of each hemisphere. Of course, a person with a split brain can adapt to this by simply moving her eyes a little so that the same information independently enters both hemispheres. Split-brain studies have continued over the past few decades and continue to play an important role in shaping our understanding of how the brain works (Gazzaniga, 2006).

Studying the Brain's Electrical Activity

A second approach to studying the link between brain structures and behaviour involves recording the pattern of electrical activity of neurons. An **electroencephalograph (EEG)** is *a device used to record electrical activity in the brain*. Typically, electrodes are placed on the outside of the head, and even though the source of electrical activity in synapses and action potentials is far removed from these wires, the EEG can amplify the electric signals several thousand times. This provides a visual record of the underlying electrical activity, as shown in **FIGURE 3.23.**

Using this technique, researchers can determine the amount of brain activity during different experiences and states of consciousness. For example, as you'll read in the Consciousness chapter, the brain shows distinctive patterns of electrical activity when awake versus asleep; in fact, different brain-wave patterns are even associated with different stages of sleep. EEG recordings allow researchers to make these fundamental discoveries about the nature of sleep and wakefulness (Dement, 1978). The EEG can also be used to examine the brain's electrical activity when awake individuals engage in a variety of psychological functions, such as perceiving, learning, and remembering. Because the EEG is noninvasive and relatively inexpensive, it is also widely used in research, medicine, and industry to understand brain processes involved in social interactions, sleep problems, and other everyday activities.

A different approach to recording electrical activity resulted in a more refined understanding of the brain's division of responsibilities, even at a cellular level. The Nobel laureates David Hubel and Torsten Wiesel used a technique in which they inserted electrodes into the occipital lobes of anaesthetized cats and observed the patterns of action potentials of individual neurons (Hubel, 1988). Hubel and Wiesel amplified the action potential signals through a loudspeaker so that they could hear the signals as clicks, as well as see them on an oscilloscope. While flashing lights in front of the animal's eye, Hubel and Wiesel recorded the resulting activity of neurons in the occipital cortex. They discovered that neurons in the primary visual cortex are activated whenever a contrast between light and dark occurs in part of the visual field, seen particularly well when the visual stimulus was a thick line of light against a dark background. They then found that each neuron responded vigorously only when presented with a contrasting edge at a particular orientation. Since then, many studies have shown that neurons in the primary visual cortex respond to particular features of visual stimuli, such as contrast, shape, and colour (Zeki, 1993).

These neurons in the visual cortex are known as *feature detectors* because they selectively respond to certain aspects of a visual image. For example, some neurons fire only when detecting a vertical line in the middle of the visual field, other neurons fire when a line at a 45° angle is perceived, and still others in response to wider lines, horizontal lines, lines in the periphery of the visual field, and so on (Livingstone & Hubel, 1988). The discovery of this specialized function for neurons was a huge leap forwards in our understanding of how the visual cortex works. Feature detectors identify basic dimensions of a stimulus ("slanted line . . . other slanted line . . . horizontal line"); those dimensions are then combined during a later stage of visual processing to allow recognition and perception of a stimulus ("Oh, it's a letter *A*").

Figure 3.23
Does the EEG Read Minds? The electroencephalograph (EEG) records electrical activity in the brain but cannot discern the content of your thoughts. Many states of consciousness, such as wakefulness and stages of sleep, are characterized by particular types of brain waves. This allows researchers to measure variables like a person's level of attention over time. Medically, the EEG can reveal abnormal patterns of activity associated with brain injuries and disorders.

electroencephalograph (EEG) A device used to record electrical activity in the brain.

David Hubel (*left*, b. 1926) and Torsten Wiesel (*right*, b. 1924) received the Nobel Prize in Physiology in 1981 for their work on mapping the visual cortex.

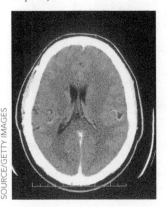

Other studies have identified a variety of features that are detected by sensory neurons. For instance, some visual processing neurons in the temporal lobe are activated only when detecting faces (Kanwisher, 2000; Perrett, Rolls, & Caan, 1982). Neurons in this area are specialized for processing faces; damage to this area results in an inability to perceive faces. These complementary observations (showing that the type of function that is lost or altered when a brain area is damaged corresponds to the kind of information processed by neurons in that cortical area) provide the most compelling evidence linking the brain to behaviour.

Using Brain Imaging to Study Structure and to Watch the Brain in Action

The third major way that neuroscientists can peer into the workings of the human brain has only become possible within the past several decades. EEG readouts give an overall picture of a person's level of consciousness, and single-cell recordings shed light on the actions of particular clumps of neurons. The ideal of neuroscience, however, has been to gain the ability to see the brain in operation during behaviour. This goal has been steadily achieved thanks to a wide range of *neuroimaging techniques* that use advanced technology to create images of the living, healthy brain (Posner & Raichle, 1994; Raichle & Mintun, 2006). *Structural brain imaging* provides information about the basic structure of the brain and allows clinicians or researchers to see abnormalities in brain structure. *Functional brain imaging,* in contrast, provides information about the activity of the brain while people perform various kinds of cognitive or motor tasks.

Structural Brain Imaging

One of the first neuroimaging techniques developed was the *computerized axial tomography (CT) scan,* in which a scanner rotates a device around a person's head and takes a series of X-ray photographs from different angles. Computer programs then combine these images to provide views from any angle. CT scans show different densities of tissue in the brain. For example, the higher-density skull looks white on a CT scan, the cortex shows up as grey, and the least dense fissures and ventricles in the brain look dark (see **FIGURE 3.24**). CT scans are used to locate lesions or tumours, which typically appear darker because they are less dense than the cortex.

Magnetic resonance imaging (MRI) uses a strong magnetic field to line up the nuclei of specific molecules in the brain tissue. Brief but powerful pulses of radio waves cause the nuclei to rotate out of alignment. When a pulse ends, the nuclei snap back in line with the magnetic field and give off a small amount of energy in the process. Different molecules have unique energy signatures when they snap back in line with the magnetic field, so these signatures can be used to reveal brain structures with different molecular compositions. MRI produces pictures of soft tissue at a better resolution than a CT scan, as you can see in Figure 3.24. These techniques give psychologists a clearer picture of the structure and volume of the brain (see Hot Science: Big Brain, Smart Brain?) and can help localize brain damage (as when someone suffers a stroke), but they reveal nothing about the functions of the brain.

Diffusion tensor imaging (DTI) is a type of MRI, developed relatively recently, that is used to visualize white matter pathways, which are fibre bundles that connect both nearby and distant brain regions to each other. DTI measures the rate and direction of diffusion or movement of water molecules, which reveal where a white matter pathway goes. Scientists can use measures based on the rate and direction of diffusion to assess the integrity of a white matter pathway, which is very

Figure 3.24

Structural Imaging Techniques (CT and MRI) CT (*left*) and MRI (*right*) scans are used to provide information about the structure of the brain and can help to spot tumours and other kinds of damage. Each scan shown here provides a snapshot of a single slice in the brain. Note that the MRI scan provides a clearer, higher-resolution image than the CT scan. (See the text for further discussion of how these images are constructed and what they depict.)

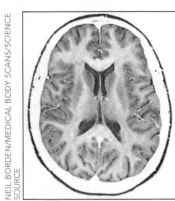

Hot Science ▸ **Big Brain, Smart Brain?**

Is a bigger brain a smarter brain? This seemingly straightforward question has fascinated psychologists, neuroscientists, and philosophers for centuries. For example, the British psychologist Sir Francis Galton noted that measurements of head volume in University of Cambridge students who obtained high honours revealed that these students "had considerably larger brains than others at the age of nineteen" (Galton, 1869, p. 156). Does that mean you should grab a tape measure to try to predict how you and your friends will do on an upcoming exam? Not so fast. A century later, a literature review uncovered deficiencies in previous studies that had claimed to find a positive correlation between brain volume and intelligence; the review also highlighted more recent evidence that failed to establish any such relationship (Stott, 1983).

These discrepancies are perhaps not surprising, because early studies used indirect and inadequate methods, such as attempting to estimate brain volume by measuring head circumference. However, the advent of modern brain-imaging techniques such as MRI has made it possible to obtain direct and precise measurements of brain volume. Indeed, studies using MRI have typically reported a positive correlation between overall brain volume and various measures of intelligence (Gignac & Bates, 2017; Pietschnig et al., 2015). But there is still debate about the strength of that correlation. As you learned in the Methods in Psychology chapter, a positive correlation

can fall anywhere from very weak (near 0) to very strong (near +1.00); we would think differently about the relation between brain volume and intelligence depending on whether the actual correlation between them is +.05, +.25, or +.75. Also, as you learned in the Methods chapter, interpreting correlations can be difficult because of the third-variable problem—that is, a relationship between two variables may be caused by an unmeasured third variable. Some or all of the correlation between brain volume and intelligence could be due to third variables such as age, socioeconomic status, height, or sex.

A recent large-scale study by Nave and colleagues (2019) has taken a large step forwards in attempting to resolve these issues. The researchers used a valuable new resource known as the UK Biobank (UKB), a massive database of health-related information from volunteer participants being built in the United Kingdom (Miller et al., 2016). UKB has already acquired genetic data from nearly 500,000 adults and, as of April 2018, had acquired structural MRI scans from about 15,000 adults. Nave et al. (2019) analyzed MRI-measured brain volume in 13,608 UKB participants and related it to several cognitive measures that were obtained from those same participants. This sample dwarfs all other previous studies on this topic: In fact, it is 70% larger than the sample size from all previous studies combined! This is important, because with such a large sample, the data obtained are

likely to be very stable, and if there is a correlation between brain volume and cognitive measures, the researchers should be able to detect it. A large sample size also helps the researchers to control statistically for the possible influence of variables such as age, socioeconomic status, height, and sex.

The most important of the cognitive measures analyzed by Nave et al. (2019) focused on the ability to solve novel problems that demand logic and reasoning ability, which is known as *fluid intelligence* (discussed in more detail in the Intelligence chapter). After controlling for other variables, Nave et al. (2019) found a significant correlation of +.19 between brain volume and fluid intelligence. This finding is important because it clearly establishes a relationship between brain volume and intelligence that cannot be explained by age, socioeconomic status, height, or sex. However, the correlation is not strong, and suggests that brain volume accounts for only a small portion of the variation in fluid intelligence across the sample. Moreover, because the data are correlational, we still don't know whether larger overall brain volume causes increases in intelligence or vice versa—it is conceivable that people with higher levels of intelligence use their brain in a way that produces increased volume. Although these results provide a solid basis for evaluating the extent to which a bigger brain is a smarter brain, you should still leave your tape measure in the drawer next time you try to predict your academic success or anyone else's.

useful in cases of neurological and psychological disorders (Thomason & Thompson, 2011).

Because DTI provides information about pathways that connect brain areas to one another, it is a critical tool in mapping the connectivity of the human brain and it plays a central role in an ambitious undertaking known as the Human Connectome Project. This is a collaborative effort funded by the American National Institutes of Health that began in 2009 and involves several groups of researchers in the United States and a group in the United Kingdom. The main goal of the project is to provide a complete map of the connectivity of neural pathways in the brain: the human connectome (Toga et al., 2012). A unique and exciting feature of the Human Connectome Project is that the researchers have made available some of the results at their website (www.humanconnectomeproject.org), which includes fascinating colourful images of some of the connection pathways they have discovered.

DTI allows researchers to visualize white matter pathways in the brain, the fibre bundles that play an important role by connecting brain regions to one another.

Functional Brain Imaging

Functional brain-imaging techniques show researchers much more than just the structure of the brain—they allow us to watch the brain in action. These techniques rely on the fact that activated brain areas demand more energy, which is supplied by increased blood flow; and functional-imaging techniques can detect such changes in blood flow. For instance, in *positron emission tomography (PET)*, a harmless radioactive substance is injected into a person's bloodstream. The brain is then scanned by radiation detectors as the person performs perceptual or cognitive tasks, such as reading or speaking. Areas of the brain that are activated during these tasks demand more energy and greater blood flow, resulting in a higher amount of radioactivity in that region. The radiation detectors record the level of radioactivity in each region, producing a computerized image of the activated areas (see **FIGURE 3.25**). Note that PET scans differ from CT scans and MRIs in that the image produced shows activity in the brain while the person performs certain tasks. So, for example, a PET scan of a person speaking would show activation in Broca's area in the left frontal lobe.

For psychologists today, the most widely used functional brain-imaging technique is *functional magnetic resonance imaging (fMRI)*, which detects the difference between oxygenated hemoglobin and deoxygenated hemoglobin when exposed to magnetic pulses. Hemoglobin is the molecule in the blood that carries oxygen to our tissues, including the brain. When active neurons demand more energy and blood flow, oxygenated hemoglobin concentrates in the active areas; fMRI detects the oxygenated hemoglobin and provides a picture of the level of activation in each brain area (see Figure 3.25). Just as MRI was a major advance over CT scans, *functional* MRI is a similar leap in our ability to record the brain's activity during behaviour.

Both fMRI and PET enable researchers to localize changes in the brain very accurately. However, fMRI has a couple of advantages over PET. First, fMRI does not require any exposure to a radioactive substance. Second, fMRI can localize changes in brain activity across briefer periods than PET, which makes it more useful for analyzing psychological processes that occur extremely quickly, such as reading a word or recognizing a face. With PET, researchers often have to use experimental designs that differ from those they would use in the psychology laboratory in order to adapt to the limitations of PET technology. With fMRI, researchers can design experiments that more closely resemble the ones they carry out in the psychology laboratory.

Functional MRI can also be used to explore the relationship of brain regions with each other, using a recently developed technique referred to as *resting state functional connectivity*. As implied by the name, this technique does not require participants to perform a task; they simply rest quietly while fMRI measurements are made. Functional connectivity measures the extent to which spontaneous activity in different brain regions is correlated over time; brain regions whose activity is

Figure 3.25

Functional Imaging Techniques (PET and FMRI) PET and fMRI scans provide information about the function of the brain by revealing which brain areas become more or less active in different conditions. The PET scan (directly below) shows areas in the left hemisphere (Broca's area, *left*; lower parietal–upper temporal area, *right*) that become active when people hold in mind a string of letters for a few seconds. The yellow areas in the fMRI scans (all views to the right) indicate activity in the auditory cortex of a person listening to music.

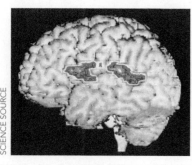

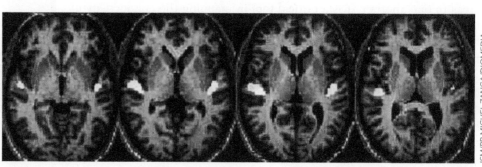

highly correlated are thought to be functionally connected with each other (Lee, Smyser, & Shimony, 2013).

Functional connectivity measures have been used extensively in recent years to identify brain *networks*, which, as you learned earlier in the chapter, are sets of brain regions that are closely connected to each other (Yeo et al., 2011). For example, functional connectivity helped to identify the *default network* (Gusnard & Raichle, 2001; Raichle, 2015), a group of interconnected regions in the frontal, temporal, and parietal lobes that is involved in internally focused cognitive activities, such as remembering past events, imagining future events, daydreaming, and mind wandering (Andrews-Hanna, 2012; Buckner, Andrews-Hanna, & Schacter, 2008) (see the chapters on Memory and Consciousness).

Functional connectivity, along with DTI (which measures structural connectivity), is used in studies conducted by the Human Connectome Project and will contribute important information to the map of the human connectome. It also has potentially important applications because researchers believe that advances in understanding brain connectivity can enhance our ability to predict and characterize the clinical course of brain disorders, such as Alzheimer's disease (Fornito, Zalesky, & Breakspear, 2015).

Caution Is Needed Before Jumping to Conclusions Although the insights being obtained from fMRI are exciting, it is important that we don't get too carried away with them, as sometimes happens in media depictions of fMRI results (Marcus, 2012; Poldrack, 2018). Consider as an example the topic of memory accuracy and distortion. Using experimental paradigms that you'll learn about in the chapter on Memory, fMRI studies have shown that activity in some parts of the brain is greater during the retrieval of accurate rather than inaccurate memories (Schacter & Loftus, 2013). Does that mean we are ready to use fMRI in the courtroom to determine whether a witness is recounting an accurate memory or an inaccurate memory?

Schacter and Loftus argued that the answer to this question is an emphatic no. For instance, we don't yet know whether the results of laboratory fMRI studies of memory, which typically use simple materials like words or pictures, generalize to the kinds of complex everyday events that are relevant in the courtroom. Furthermore, evidence that fMRI can distinguish accurate from inaccurate memories comes from studies in which brain activity is averaged across a *group* of participants. But in the courtroom, we need to determine whether an *individual* is remembering accurately or not, and there is little evidence yet that fMRI can do so. More generally, it is important to think carefully about how fMRI evidence is obtained before we leap to conclusions about how that evidence can be used in everyday life (Poldrack, 2018).

Transcranial Magnetic Stimulation

We noted earlier that researchers have learned a lot about the brain by studying the behaviour of people with brain injuries. Scientists have discovered a way to mimic brain damage with a benign technique called *transcranial magnetic stimulation* (*TMS*) (Barker, Jalinous, & Freeston, 1985; Hallett, 2000). If you've ever held a magnet under a piece of paper and used it to drag a pin across the paper's surface, you know that magnetic fields can pass through insulating material. The human skull is no exception. TMS delivers a magnetic pulse that passes through the skull and deactivates neurons in the cerebral cortex for a short period. Researchers can direct TMS pulses to particular brain regions (essentially turning them off) and then measure temporary changes in the way a person moves, sees, thinks, remembers, speaks, or feels. By manipulating the state of the brain, scientists can perform experiments that establish causal relationships.

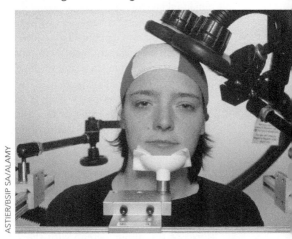

Transcranial magnetic stimulation (TMS) activates and deactivates regions of the brain with a magnetic pulse, temporarily mimicking brain damage.

ASTIER/BSIP SA/ALAMY

Other Voices | Neuromyths

You've no doubt heard the phrase "We only use 10% of our brains," and perhaps you've wondered whether there is anything to it. Chabris and Simons (2012) discussed this and other statements about the brain that they believe to be merely myths, based in part on a contemporaneous study by Dekker et al. (2012).

Pop quiz: Which of these statements is false?

1. We use only 10% of our brain.
2. Environments rich in stimuli improve the brains of pre-school children.
3. Individuals learn better when they receive information in their preferred learning style, whether auditory, visual, or kinesthetic.

If you picked the first one, congratulations. The idea that we use only 10% of our brain is patently false. Yet it so permeates popular culture that, among psychologists and neuroscientists, it is known as the "10% myth." Contrary to popular belief, the entire brain is put to use—unused neurons die and unused circuits atrophy. Reports of neuroimaging research might perpetuate the myth by showing only a small number of areas "lighting up" in a brain scan, but those are just areas that have more than a base line level of activity; the dark regions aren't dormant or unused.

Did you agree with the other two statements? If so, you fell into our trap. All three statements are false—or at least not substantiated by scientific evidence. Unfortunately, if you got any of them wrong, you're hardly alone.

These "neuromyths," along with others, were presented to 242 primary and secondary school teachers in the Netherlands and the United Kingdom as part of a study by Sanne Dekker and colleagues at VU University Amsterdam and Bristol University, and just published in the journal *Frontiers in Psychology*. They found that 47% of the teachers believed the 10% myth. Even more, 76%, believed that enriching children's environments will strengthen their brains.

This belief might have emerged from evidence that rats raised in cages with amenities like exercise wheels, tunnels, and other rats showed better cognitive abilities and improvements in brain structure compared with rats that grew up isolated in bare cages. But such experiments show only that a truly impoverished and unnatural environment leads to poorer developmental outcomes than a more natural environment with opportunities to play and interact. It follows that growing up locked in a closet or otherwise cut off from human contact will impair a child's brain development. It does not follow that "enriching" a child's environment beyond what is already typical (e.g., by constant exposure to "Baby Einstein"-type videos) will boost cognitive development.

The myth about learning styles was the most popular: 94% of the teachers believed that students perform better when lessons are delivered in their preferred learning style. Indeed, students do have preferences about how they learn; the problem is that these preferences have little to do with how effectively they learn. . . .

Our own surveys of the U.S. population have found even more widespread belief in myths about the brain. About two-thirds of the public agreed with the 10% myth. Many also believed that memory works like a video recording or that they can tell when someone is staring at the back of their head.

Christopher Chabris (*left*) is an associate professor of psychology at Union College. Daniel Simons (*right*) is a professor of psychology at the University of Illinois. Chabris and Simons coauthored *The Invisible Gorilla: And Other Ways Our Intuitions Deceive Us* (2010).

Ironically, in the Dekker group's study, the teachers who knew the most about neuroscience also believed in the most myths. Apparently, teachers who are (admirably) enthusiastic about expanding their knowledge of the mind and brain have trouble separating fact from fiction as they learn. Neuromyths have so much intuitive appeal, and they spread so rapidly in fields like business and self-help, that eradicating them from popular consciousness might be a Sisyphean task. But reducing their influence in the classroom would be a good start.

If for some perverse reason you wanted to annoy the instructor of your psychology course, you probably could do no better than to claim that "we use only 10% of our brains." Even though, as pointed out by Chabris and Simons (2012), a surprisingly high proportion of elementary and secondary schoolteachers in the Netherlands and the United Kingdom subscribe to this myth, we don't know any psychologists teaching courses like the one you are taking who would endorse it, and we hope that there aren't any. How did the myth get started? Nobody really knows. Some think it may have arisen from a quotation by the great psychologist William James ("We are making use of only a small part of our possible mental and physical resources") or that it possibly owes to Albert Einstein's attempt to make sense of his own massive intellect (Boyd, 2008).

The key point for our purposes is that when you hear such bold claims from, say, a friend who heard it from somebody else, it's time for you to put into action the kinds of critical thinking skills that we focus on in this text and start asking questions: What's the evidence for the claim? Is there a specific study or studies that your friend can name to provide evidence in support of the claim? Are any such studies published in peer-reviewed scientific journals? What kind of sample was used in the study? Is it large enough to support a clear conclusion? Has the finding been replicated? Tall tales such as the 10% myth don't stand much chance of surviving for long if claims for their existence are met head on with critical thinking.

For example, as mentioned earlier, fMRI studies have linked the default network with remembering past experiences and imagining future experiences. But these observations don't tell us whether particular regions in the default network play a *causal* role in remembering or imagining. In recent studies, researchers used TMS to interfere with the operation of a particular region in the default network, the angular gyrus in the parietal lobe, just before people performed memory and imagination tasks (Bonnici et al., 2018; Thakral, Madore, & Schacter, 2017). TMS reduced the number of details that people remembered from past experiences and imagined in future experiences, thereby establishing that this part of the default network does play a causal role in remembering and imagining.

Scientists have also begun to combine TMS with fMRI, allowing them to localize precisely where in the brain TMS is having its effect (Parkin, Ekhtiari, & Walsh, 2015). Studies suggest that TMS has no harmful side effects (Anand & Hotson, 2002; Pascual-Leone et al., 1993), and this new tool has changed the study of how our brains create our thoughts, feelings, and actions. Hopefully, the picture of human brain activity that emerges from these new methods can help to dispel common myths about the brain that remain popular even today (see Other Voices: Neuromyths).

Perhaps the most important takeaway from our review of methods for studying the brain is that each method provides psychologists with a specific type of tool for exploring how various aspects of brain structure or function are related to psychological constructs. Each method has strengths and weaknesses, so an important task for researchers is to decide which of the available tools is the most appropriate for their particular scientific question. Making that decision requires both an understanding of the possibilities and limitations of each tool, as well as framing a scientific question clearly enough to make an informed choice among the available tools.

Build to the Outcomes

1. How have brain disorders been central to the study of specific areas of the brain?
2. What role does the corpus callosum play in behaviour?
3. How does the EEG record electrical activity in the brain?
4. Compare what can be learned from structural brain imaging with results from functional brain imaging.
5. What does an fMRI track in an active brain?
6. Why should we avoid jumping to conclusions based on fMRI results?

Chapter Review

Neurons: The Origin of Behaviour

- Neurons are the building blocks of the nervous system: They process information received from the outside world, communicate with each other, and send messages to the body's muscles and organs.
- Neurons are composed of three major parts: the cell body, dendrites, and the axon. The cell body contains the nucleus, which houses the organism's genetic material. Dendrites receive sensory signals from other neurons and transmit this information to the cell body. Each axon carries signals from the cell body to other neurons or to muscles and organs in the body.

- Neurons don't actually touch. They are separated by a small gap, which is part of the synapse across which signals are transmitted from one neuron to another.
- Glial cells provide support for neurons, usually in the form of the myelin sheath, which coats the axon to facilitate the transmission of information. In demyelinating diseases, the myelin sheath deteriorates.
- Neurons are differentiated according to the functions they perform. The three major types of neurons include sensory neurons (e.g., bipolar neurons), motor neurons, and interneurons (e.g., Purkinje cells).

The Electrochemical Actions of Neurons: Information Processing

- The neuron's resting potential is due to differences in the potassium (K^+) concentrations inside and outside the cell membrane, resulting from open channels that allow K^+ to flow outside the membrane while closed channels prevent sodium ions (Na^+) and other ions from flowing into the neuron. The conduction of an electric signal within a neuron happens when the resting potential is reversed by an electric impulse called an action potential.

- If electric signals reach a threshold, this initiates an action potential, an all-or-none signal that moves down the entire length of the axon. The action potential occurs when K^+ channels in the axon membrane close and Na^+ channels open, allowing the Na^+ ions to flow inside the axon.

- After the action potential has reached its maximum, a chemical pump reverses the imbalance in ions, returning the neuron to its resting potential. For a brief refractory period, the action potential cannot be reinitiated. Once it is initiated, the action potential spreads down the axon, jumping across the nodes of Ranvier to the synapse.

- Communication between neurons takes place through synaptic transmission, where an action potential triggers release of neurotransmitters from the terminal buttons of the sending neuron's axon, which travel across the synapse to bind with receptors in the receiving neuron's dendrite. Neurotransmitters bind to dendrites on specific receptor sites; they leave the synapse through reuptake, through enzyme deactivation, and by binding to autoreceptors.

- Some of the major neurotransmitters are acetylcholine (ACh), dopamine, glutamate, GABA, norepinephrine, serotonin, and endorphins.

- Drugs can affect behaviour by acting as agonists—that is, by facilitating or increasing the actions of neurotransmitters—or as antagonists, by blocking the action of neurotransmitters. Recreational drug use can have an effect on brain function.

The Organization of the Nervous System

- Neurons make up nerves, which in turn form the human nervous system.

- The nervous system is divided into the peripheral and the central nervous systems. The central nervous system is composed of the spinal cord and the brain.

- The peripheral nervous system connects the central nervous system with the rest of the body and is itself divided into the somatic nervous system and the autonomic nervous system. The somatic nervous system, which conveys information into and out of the central nervous system, controls voluntary muscles, whereas the autonomic nervous system automatically controls the body's organs.

- The autonomic nervous system is further divided into the sympathetic and parasympathetic nervous systems, which complement each other in their effects on the body. The sympathetic nervous system prepares the body for action in threatening situations, and the parasympathetic nervous system returns the body to its normal state.

- The spinal cord can control some basic behaviours such as spinal reflexes without input from the brain.

Structure of the Brain

- The brain can be divided into the hindbrain, midbrain, and forebrain.

- The hindbrain generally coordinates information coming into and out of the spinal cord with structures such as the medulla, the reticular formation, the cerebellum, and the pons. These structures respectively coordinate breathing and heart rate, regulate sleep and arousal levels, coordinate fine motor skills, and communicate this information to the cortex.

- The structures of the midbrain, the tectum and tegmentum, generally coordinate functions such as orientation to the environment and movement and arousal towards sensory stimuli.

- The forebrain generally coordinates higher-level functions, such as perceiving, feeling, and thinking. The forebrain houses subcortical structures, such as the thalamus, hypothalamus, limbic system (including the hippocampus and amygdala), and basal ganglia; all these structures perform a variety of functions related to motivation and emotion.

- The endocrine system works closely with the nervous system to regulate thoughts, emotions, and behaviours through the release of hormones. The pituitary gland orchestrates the functioning of the endocrine system by releasing hormones that direct the functions of other glands.

- Also in the forebrain, the cerebral cortex, composed of two hemispheres with four lobes each (occipital, parietal, temporal, and frontal), performs tasks that help make us fully human: thinking, planning, judging, perceiving, and behaving purposefully and voluntarily.

- Neurons in the brain can be shaped by experience and by the environment, making the human brain amazingly plastic.

- Nervous systems evolved from simple collections of sensory and motor neurons in simple animals (e.g., flatworms) to the elaborate centralized nervous systems found in mammals. The evolution of the human nervous system can be thought of as a process of refining, elaborating, and expanding structures present in other species. Reptiles and birds have almost no cerebral cortex. By contrast, mammals have a highly developed cerebral cortex. The human brain appears to have evolved more quickly than those of other species, to become adapted to a more complex environment.

Genes, Epigenetics, and the Environment

- The gene, or the unit of hereditary transmission, is built from strands of DNA in a double-helix formation that is organized into chromosomes. Humans have 23 pairs of chromosomes, half of which come from each parent. A child shares 50% of his or her genes with each parent.

- Monozygotic twins share 100% of their genes, whereas dizygotic twins share 50%, the same as any other siblings. Because of their genetic relatedness, twins are often participants in genetic research.

- Epigenetics refers to the study of environmental influences that determine whether or not genes are expressed, without altering the basic DNA sequences that constitute the genes themselves. Epigenetic marks such as DNA methylation and histone modification influence whether specific genes are switched on or off. Epigenetic influences have been shown to play a critical role in the persisting effects of early experiences in rats and humans.

- The study of genetics indicates that both genes and the environment work together to influence behaviour. Genes set the range of variation in populations within a given environment, but they do not predict individual characteristics; experience and other environmental factors play a crucial role as well.

Investigating the Brain

- There are three major approaches to studying the link between the brain and behaviour, outlined as follows.

- One approach is to observe how perceptual, motor, intellectual, and emotional capacities are affected after brain damage. By carefully relating specific psychological and behavioural disruptions to damage in particular areas of the brain, researchers can better understand how the brain area normally plays a role in producing those behaviours.

- A second approach is to examine global electrical activity in the brain and the activity patterns of single neurons. The patterns of electrical activity in large brain areas can be examined from outside the skull using the electroencephalograph (EEG). Single-cell recordings taken from specific neurons can be linked to specific perceptual or behavioural events, suggesting that those neurons represent particular kinds of stimuli or control particular aspects of behaviour.

- The third approach is to use brain imaging to scan the brain as people perform different perceptual or intellectual tasks. Correlating energy consumption in particular brain areas with specific cognitive and behavioural events suggests that those brain areas are involved in specific types of perceptual, motor, cognitive, or emotional processing.

Key Concept Quiz

1. Signals are transmitted from one neuron to another
   a. across a synapse.
   b. through a glial cell.
   c. by the myelin sheath.
   d. in the cell body.

2. Which type of neuron receives information from the external world and conveys this information to the brain via the spinal cord?
   a. sensory neuron
   b. motor neuron
   c. interneuron
   d. axon

3. An electric signal that is conducted along the length of a neuron's axon to the synapse is called
   a. a resting potential.
   b. an action potential.
   c. a node of Ranvier.
   d. an ion.

4. The chemicals that transmit information across the synapse to a receiving neuron's dendrites are called
   a. vesicles.
   b. terminal buttons.
   c. postsynaptic neurons.
   d. neurotransmitters.

5. The _____ automatically controls the organs of the body.
   a. autonomic nervous system
   b. parasympathetic nervous system
   c. sympathetic nervous system
   d. somatic nervous system

6. Which part of the hindbrain coordinates fine motor skills?
   a. the medulla
   b. the cerebellum
   c. the pons
   d. the tegmentum

7. What part of the brain is involved in movement and arousal?
   a. the hindbrain
   b. the midbrain
   c. the forebrain
   d. the reticular formation

8. The _____ regulates body temperature, hunger, thirst, and sexual behaviour.
   a. cerebral cortex
   b. pituitary gland
   c. hypothalamus
   d. hippocampus

9. What explains the apparent beneficial effects of cardiovascular exercise on aspects of brain function and cognitive performance?
   a. the different sizes of the somatosensory cortices
   b. the position of the cerebral cortex
   c. specialization of association areas
   d. neuron plasticity

10. Genes set the _____ in populations within a given environment.
   a. individual characteristics
   b. range of variation
   c. environmental possibilities
   d. behavioural standards

 **LearningCurve** macmillan learning   Don't stop now! Quizzing yourself is a powerful study tool. Go to LaunchPad to access the LearningCurve adaptive quizzing system and your own personalized learning plan. Visit launchpadworks.com.

Key Terms

neurons (p. 75)
cell body (soma) (p. 75)
dendrite (p. 75)
axon (p. 75)
myelin sheath (p. 75)
glial cells (p. 75)
synapse (p. 75)
sensory neurons (p. 76)
motor neurons (p. 77)
interneurons (p. 77)
resting potential (p. 78)
action potential (p. 79)
refractory period (p. 80)
terminal buttons (p. 81)
neurotransmitters (p. 81)
receptors (p. 81)
acetylcholine (ACh) (p. 82)
dopamine (p. 82)

glutamate (p. 82)
GABA (gamma-aminobutyric acid) (p. 82)
norepinephrine (p. 82)
serotonin (p. 82)
endorphins (p. 82)
agonists (p. 83)
antagonists (p. 83)
nervous system (p. 85)
central nervous system (CNS) (p. 85)
peripheral nervous system (PNS) (p. 85)
somatic nervous system (p. 85)
autonomic nervous system (ANS) (p. 85)
sympathetic nervous system (p. 86)

parasympathetic nervous system (p. 86)
spinal reflexes (p. 87)
reflex arc (p. 88)
hindbrain (p. 91)
medulla (p. 91)
reticular formation (p. 91)
cerebellum (p. 91)
pons (p. 92)
tectum (p. 92)
tegmentum (p. 92)
cerebral cortex (p. 92)
subcortical structures (p. 92)
thalamus (p. 93)
hypothalamus (p. 93)
hippocampus (p. 93)
amygdala (p. 94)
basal ganglia (p. 95)

endocrine system (p. 95)
pituitary gland (p. 95)
corpus callosum (p. 97)
occipital lobe (p. 97)
parietal lobe (p. 97)
temporal lobe (p. 98)
frontal lobe (p. 98)
association areas (p. 98)
mirror neurons (p. 99)
gene (p. 103)
chromosomes (p. 103)
epigenetics (p. 105)
epigenetic marks (p. 105)
DNA methylation (p. 105)
histone modification (p. 105)
heritability (p. 106)
electroencephalograph (EEG) (p. 111)

Changing Minds

1. While watching late-night TV, you come across an infomercial for all-natural BrainGro. "It's a well-known fact that most people use only 10% of their brain," the spokesman promises, "but with BrainGro you can increase that number from 10% to 99%!" Why should you be skeptical of the claim that we use only 10% of our brains? What would happen if a drug actually increased neuronal activity tenfold?

2. Your friend has been feeling depressed and has gone to a psychiatrist for help. "He prescribed a medication that's supposed to increase serotonin in my brain. But my feelings depend on me, not on a bunch of chemicals in my head," she said. What examples could you give your friend to convince her that hormones and neurotransmitters really do influence our cognition, mood, and behaviour?

3. A classmate has read the section in this chapter about the evolution of the central nervous system. "Evolution is just a theory," he says. "Not everyone believes in it. And even if it's true that we're all descended from monkeys, that doesn't have anything to do with the psychology of humans alive today." What is your friend misunderstanding about evolution? How would you explain to him the relevance of evolution to modern psychology?

4. A news program reports on a study (Hölzel et al., 2011) in which people who practiced meditation for about 30 minutes a day for 8 weeks showed changes in their brains, including increases in the size of the hippocampus and the amygdala. You tell a friend, who's skeptical. "The brain doesn't change like that. Basically, the brain you're born with is the brain you're stuck with for the rest of your life," your friend says. Why is her statement wrong? What are several specific ways in which the brain does change over time?

5. A friend of yours announces that he's figured out why he's bad at math. "I read it in a book," he says. "Left-brained people are analytical and logical, but right-brained people are creative and artistic. I'm an art major, so I must be right-brained, and that's why I'm not good at math." Why is your friend's view too simplistic?

Answers to Key Concept Quiz

1. a; 2. a; 3. b; 4. d; 5. a; 6. b; 7. b; 8. c; 9. d; 10. b.

LaunchPad features the full e-Book of *Psychology*, the LearningCurve adaptive quizzing system, videos, and a variety of activities to boost your learning. Visit LaunchPad at launchpadworks.com.

Sensation and Perception

DANIEL KISH IS A MIDDLE-AGED CALIFORNIAN with Master's degrees in psychology and education. Growing up, he wanted to be either a pilot or Batman. He enjoys making music, solo hiking, and mountain biking. He founded and now leads a nonprofit organization and spends much of his time working with and teaching children. Daniel is also totally blind.

When Daniel was a year old, he had to have both eyes removed because of cancer. He "sees" using a form of echolocation, or sonar, rather like that used by bats and dolphins. He clicks his tongue quietly against the roof of his mouth (once every few seconds) as he moves around the world. The clicks are reflected off physical surfaces—trees, walls, fences, lampposts— and Daniel uses the echoes of these clicks to create a mental image of his environment. The echoes inform Daniel about the location of objects, their size and shape, and even what they are made of. The images that are created using this "flash sonar" technique are not as precise as vision would be, but they are informative about the space around him. Daniel says, "You do get a continuous sort of vision, the way you might if you used flashes to light up a darkened scene. It comes into clarity and focus with every flash, a kind of three-dimensional fuzzy geometry. . . . You have a depth of structure, and you have position and dimension. You also have a pretty strong sense of density and texture that are sort of like the color, if you will, of flash sonar" (Hurst, 2017). The visual analogies are apt: recent brain-imaging studies demonstrate that blind users of flash sonar, including Daniel, activate the "visual" parts of their brain, in the occipital lobe, when they are actively echolocating (Thaler, Arnott, & Goodale, 2011).

Daniel taught himself flash sonar as a child so that he could be active and independent. He now teaches blind people of all ages to use echolocation through his nonprofit World Access for the Blind. Daniel, and other blind people who use echolocation, teach us all that, with enough practice, we can all change our brains to do amazing things, even "see" like bats, even if we can't all be Batman.

Daniel Kish, who has been totally blind since birth, enjoys solo trips in the mountains of his native California.

IN THIS CHAPTER, WE'LL EXPLORE THE NATURE of sensation and perception. These experiences are basic to survival and reproduction; we wouldn't last long without the ability to accurately make sense of the world around us. Indeed, research on sensation and perception is the basis for much of psychology, a pathway towards understanding more complex cognition and behaviour such as memory, emotion, motivation, or decision making. Yet sensation and perception also sometimes reveal illusions that you might see at a science fair or in a novelty shop—reminders that the act of perceiving the world is not so simple or straightforward as it might seem.

We'll look at how physical energy in the world around us is encoded by our senses, converted into electrical activity that is sent to the brain, then enters our conscious awareness. We'll devote a fair amount of space to understanding how the visual system works. Then we'll discuss how we perceive sounds such as words or music or noise, followed by the body senses, emphasizing touch, pain, and balance. We'll end with the chemical senses of smell and taste, which together allow you to savour the foods you eat. But before doing any of that, we will first distinguish between sensation and perception, to illustrate how perception depends on knowledge and experience as well as on sensory information.

Sensation and Perception Are Distinct Activities

Learning Outcomes

- Distinguish between sensation and perception.

- Explain what transduction is.

- Give examples of how sensation and perception are measured.

Imagine the taste of chocolate. Imagine the feeling of stroking a purring kitten. Imagine your favourite song. In all cases, you are remembering *perceptions* that originated, in part, as sensory information (*sensations*) in your mouth, on your skin, and in your ears. Sensation and perception may appear to us to be one seamless event, but sensation precedes, and is transformed by, perception.

- **Sensation** is *simple stimulation of a sense organ*. It is the basic registration of light, sound, pressure, odour, or taste as parts of your body interact with the physical world.

- **Perception** occurs in your brain as sensation is registered there: It is *the organization, identification, and interpretation of a sensation in order to form a mental representation*.

For example, your eyes are coursing across these sentences right now. The sensory receptors in your eyeballs are registering different patterns of light reflecting off the page. Your brain, however, is integrating and processing that light information into the meaningful perception of words, such as *meaningful, perception,* and *words*. Your eyes—the sensory organs—aren't really seeing words; they're simply encoding different lines and curves on a page. Your brain—the perceptual organ—is transforming those lines and curves into a coherent mental representation of words and concepts.

Consciously, it may *seem* as if you're reading words directly, but reading is a learned skill. You may remember how slow and confusing reading was when you first started. After years of practice, it now may feel automatic. But without that learning, the sensory information—the lines and curves on the page—would be meaningless. Particular kinds of damage to the visual processing centres in the brain can interfere with reading and with the interpretation of information coming from the eyes. In this case, the senses are intact, but perceptual ability is compromised.

sensation Simple stimulation of a sense organ.

perception The organization, identification, and interpretation of a sensation in order to form a mental representation.

Sensory Energy and Transduction

How do sensory receptors communicate with the brain? It all depends on the process of **transduction**, which occurs *when sense receptors convert physical signals from the environment into neural signals that are sent to the central nervous system.* In vision, light reflected from surfaces provides the eyes with information about the shape, colour, and position of objects. In hearing, vibrations (e.g., from vocal cords or a guitar string) cause changes in air pressure that propagate through space to a listener's ears. In touch, the pressure of a surface against the skin signals its shape, texture, and temperature. In taste and smell, molecules dispersed in the air or dissolved in saliva reveal the identity of substances that we may or may not want to eat. In each case, physical energy from the world is converted to electrical signals, which are interpreted by your brain to construct what you perceive as the world "out there."

Each type of sensory receptor is uniquely sensitive to a particular type of energy. The eye is sensitive to light (but not to sound); the skin to mechanical pressure (but not to visible light). The eye is sensitive to mechanical pressure, too, but only a little bit. If you close your eye and push on your eyelid with your finger, you might see sparkly dots. This mechanical pressure is registered by the receptors in your eye as light, not touch. Think about what that means: You *perceived* light when sensory receptors in the eye were stimulated, even though the stimulus *was not light.* The physical energy of your finger was transduced into electrical signals that were carried along axons, crossed synapses, and were interpreted by your brain as light. Although perception "feels" direct and immediate, it is not. We'll discuss in more detail how transduction works in different sensory domains including vision, hearing, touch, taste, and smell, in separate sections later in this chapter.

The Illusion of Perception

Bats, rats, and mice communicate with each other using high sound frequencies that humans cannot hear; bees and butterflies find food by seeing "colours" we cannot see. Some animals navigate by sensing the earth's magnetic field. We cannot sense even strong magnetic fields, like those in magnetic resonance imaging (MRI) systems, even though they can be very dangerous.

Your mother is probably grateful that your head wasn't any bigger when you were born. Humans have evolved so that, at birth, all bits of them can fit through a woman's pelvis. That limits maximum head size, which in turn limits the number of neurons your brain can have and, therefore, its capacity for processing sensory information. The senses act like gates. They allow a limited amount of information in and do not admit other information. The illusion of perception is that we perceive a rich, detailed, and complete world around us, despite the sensory signals that we detect being a small subset of what is "out there."

Sensory Adaptation

When you walk into a bakery, the aroma of freshly baked bread overwhelms you, but after a few minutes the smell fades. If you dive into cold water, the temperature is shocking at first, but after a few minutes you get used to it. When you wake up in the middle of the night for a drink of water, the bathroom light blinds you, but after a few minutes you no longer squint. These are all examples of **sensory adaptation**, whereby *sensitivity to prolonged stimulation tends to decline over time as an organism adapts to current (unchanging) conditions.*

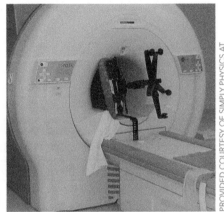

When someone accidentally rolled an office chair into a room containing an MRI system, it flew across the room to the magnet and got stuck as soon as it entered the strong field of the magnet. People can't sense this strong magnetic field, which is why accidents like this happen. Why do you think that we've evolved in such a way that we are not able to detect all the information there is "out there"? Surely, more information would be better than less and would confer a survival advantage, don't you think?

transduction The process whereby sense receptors convert physical signals from the environment into neural signals that are sent to the central nervous system.

sensory adaptation The process whereby sensitivity to prolonged stimulation tends to decline over time as an organism adapts to current (unchanging) conditions.

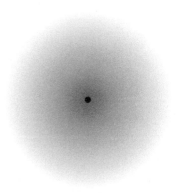

Stare at the central black dot in the image above. After several seconds, the grey cloud around the dot will disappear—this phenomenon, called Troxler fading (see Simons et al., 2006), is another example of adaptation.

Sensory adaptation is a useful process. Imagine what your sensory and perceptual world would be like without it. When you put on your jeans in the morning, the feeling of rough cloth against your bare skin would be as noticeable hours later as it was in the first few minutes. If you had to be constantly aware of how your tongue feels while it is resting in your mouth, you'd be driven to distraction.

Our sensory systems respond more strongly to changes in stimulation than to constant stimulation. A change in stimulation often signals a need for action—that is, if you are walking across a street and suddenly hear squealing brakes, you move! A sensory signal that doesn't change usually doesn't require any action, and your body discards such signals. This is another way that our bodies only perceive a subset of what is "out there."

Psychophysics

When shopping around for a new computer, you consider different models in terms of their performance: What is the resolution of the screen? What is the processing speed? How much data can it store? How long does its battery last? These characteristics can be measured. You already own a human body: you might be interested in the performance of your sensory systems. How sensitive are they? How fast can information be registered? How quickly does adaptation happen? These are all questions that can be answered using **psychophysics**, *methods that systematically relate the physical characteristics of a stimulus to an observer's perception.* In a simple psychophysics experiment, researchers might ask people to decide whether or not they see a faint spot of light, for example. The intensity of the light is changed systematically, and the responses of the observer (yes or no) are recorded as a function of intensity.

Measuring Thresholds

The simplest quantitative measurement in psychophysics is the **absolute threshold**, *the minimal intensity needed to just barely detect a stimulus in 50% of the trials.* A *threshold* is a boundary. Just as the doorway that separates the inside from the outside of a house is a threshold, so is the boundary between two psychological states (awareness and unawareness, or perceiving and not perceiving, in this case). **TABLE 4.1** lists the approximate absolute thresholds for each of the five senses.

To measure the absolute threshold for detecting a sound, for example, an observer wears headphones linked to a computer. The experimenter repeatedly presents a tone using the computer to vary its intensity and records how often the observer reports hearing the tone at each intensity level. The outcome of such an experiment is graphed in **FIGURE 4.1**. Notice from the shape of the curve that the transition from *not hearing* to *hearing* is gradual rather than abrupt.

If we repeat this experiment for many different tones, we can observe and record the thresholds for tones ranging from very low to very high pitch. It turns out that people tend to be most sensitive to the range of tones corresponding to the human voice. If the tone is low enough, such as the lowest note on a pipe organ, most humans cannot hear it at all; we can only feel it.

TABLE 4.1

APPROXIMATE SENSORY THRESHOLDS

Sense	Absolute Threshold	
Vision	A candle flame 48 kilometres away on a clear, dark night	
Hearing	A clock's tick 6 metres away when all is quiet	
Touch	A fly's wing falling on the cheek from 1 centimetre away	
Smell	A single drop of perfume diffused through an area equivalent to the volume of six rooms	
Taste	A teaspoon of sugar dissolved in 7.5 litres of water	

Research from Galanter (1962).

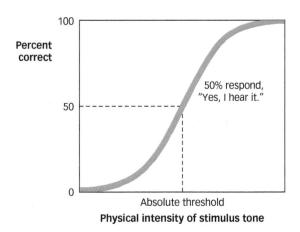

Figure 4.1
Absolute Threshold Absolute threshold is graphed here as the point at which the increasing intensity of the stimulus enables an observer to detect it on 50% of the trials. As its intensity gradually increases, we detect the stimulus more frequently.

If the tone is high enough, we also cannot hear it, but dogs and many other animals can.

The absolute threshold is useful for assessing **sensitivity**, *how responsive we are to faint stimuli;* but sometimes we also want to know about **acuity**, *how well we can distinguish two very similar stimuli,* such as two tones that differ slightly in loudness or two lights that differ slightly in brightness. The **just noticeable difference (JND)** is *the minimal change in a stimulus (e.g., in its loudness or brightness) that can just barely be detected.*

The JND is not a fixed quantity; it depends on the particular sense being measured, as well as on the intensity of the original stimulus. Consider measuring the JND for the brightness of a light. An observer in a dark room is shown a light of fixed intensity, called the *standard* (S), next to a comparison light that is slightly brighter or dimmer than the standard. When S is very dim, observers can perceive even a very small difference in brightness between the two lights: The JND is small. But if S is bright, a much larger increment is needed to detect the difference: The JND is larger.

It turns out that for any sensory domain, the ratio between the JND and the standard stimulus is a constant value except when the standard takes extreme values (e.g, is hard to perceive, or is overwhelming). This relationship was first noticed in 1834 by the German physiologist Ernst Weber (Watson, 1978). Gustav Fechner, who developed the field of psychophysics and the methods we still use today, applied Weber's insight directly to psychophysics (Fechner, 1860/1966). He described a formal relationship called **Weber's law**, which states that *for every sense domain, the change in a stimulus that is just noticeable is a constant ratio of the standard stimulus, over a range of standard intensities.* As an example, if you picked up a 30-gram envelope, then a 60-gram envelope, you'd probably notice the difference between them. But if you picked up a 2-kilogram package, then a 2.05-kilogram package, you'd probably detect no difference at all between them.

Signal Detection

The transition from *not sensing* to *sensing* is gradual (see Figure 4.1). This is because our nervous systems are noisy. Other sights, sounds, and smells in the world at large compete for attention; you rarely have the luxury of attending to just one stimulus apart from everything else. Furthermore, some sensory neurons have "itchy trigger fingers"—they fire action potentials sporadically, for no reason at all. All this internal

psychophysics Methods that systematically relate the physical characteristics of a stimulus to an observer's perception.

absolute threshold The minimal intensity needed to just barely detect a stimulus in 50% of trials.

sensitivity How responsive we are to faint stimuli.

acuity How well we can distinguish two very similar stimuli.

just noticeable difference (JND) The minimal change in a stimulus (e.g., its loudness or brightness) that can just barely be detected.

Weber's law For every sense domain, the change in a stimulus that is just noticeable is a constant ratio of the standard stimulus, over a range of standard intensities.

"noise" changes from moment to moment and can make our accurate perception of a faint sensory stimulus somewhat haphazard. Moreover, knowledge and expectations, your mood, and your goals and motivations interact with what you are seeing, hearing, and smelling at any given time to influence perception. You might not perceive everything that you sense, and you might even perceive things that you haven't sensed. Have you ever been expecting a text (from a crush, or a notification of a job interview) and thought that your phone had just buzzed, but when you checked your phone, there was nothing?

Signal detection theory (SDT) is a way of analyzing data from psychophysics experiments that measures an individual's *perceptual sensitivity* (how effectively the perceptual system represents sensory events) while also taking noise, expectations, motivations, and goals into account. When sensory stimuli are very clear (e.g., a car alarm, or a flash of light), the sensory evidence is very strong, and noise, which is at a much lower intensity, doesn't matter. However, sensory stimuli are often faint, or ambiguous, and in such cases noise and other factors can strongly affect perception.

According to signal detection theory, whether or not you perceive a stimulus (vibrating phone) depends on two independent factors: the *strength of the sensory evidence for that stimulus* and the amount of evidence necessary for your perceptual system to "decide" that the stimulus is present, known as the *decision criterion* (Green & Swets, 1966; Macmillan & Creelman, 2005). If the sensory evidence exceeds the criterion, the observer perceives the stimulus whether or not the stimulus was present. If it falls short of the criterion, the observer does not perceive the stimulus. The criterion depends on many factors, such as your expectations and the relative "badness" of different kinds of error; sometimes missing a call is better than checking your phone by mistake (when you're in the shower and it's cold out there!), but sometimes missing a call is worse.

When sensory evidence is faint, there are two ways to be right, and two ways to be wrong. As an example, a radiologist may have to decide whether a mammogram shows that a woman has breast cancer. The radiologist knows that certain features, such as a mass of a particular size and shape, are associated with the presence of cancer. But noncancerous features can have a very similar appearance to cancerous ones. If the radiologist correctly detects cancer on a scan, the outcome is a *hit*. If she doesn't detect it, the result is a *miss*. If the radiologist reports a scan from a healthy woman as clear, this is a *correct rejection*. If she erroneously detects signs of cancer, a *false alarm* has occurred.

When the evidence is faint, mistakes (i.e., misses and false alarms) will always occur. The decision criterion determines whether the person makes more misses or more false alarms. The radiologist may adopt a *liberal criterion* (not much sensory evidence required) and identify cancer whenever there is the slightest doubt; this decision strategy would minimize the possibility of missing a true cancer, but it would also lead to many unnecessary biopsies. A more *conservative criterion* (stronger sensory evidence required) will cut down on unnecessary biopsies, but it will increase the number of treatable cancers that go undiagnosed. Signal detection theory, then, measures perceptual sensitivity separately from the observer's decision-making strategy, which is often based on expectations, or on the costs and benefits of different kinds of error. For an example of a common everyday task that can interfere with signal detection, see The Real World: Multitasking.

For an example of a common everyday task that can interfere with signal detection, see The Real World: Multitasking on page 129. For an example of when perception may reflect expectations rather than reality, see Other Voices: Hallucinations and the Visual System on page 150.

signal detection theory A way of analyzing data from psychophysics experiments that measures an individual's perceptual sensitivity while also taking noise, expectations, motivations, and goals into account.

The Real World | Multitasking

By one estimate, using a cell phone while driving makes having an accident four times more likely (McEvoy et al., 2005). In response to highway safety experts' concerns, and statistics such as this, provincial legislative assemblies are passing laws that restrict, and sometimes ban, using mobile phones while driving. You might think that's a fine idea . . . for everyone else on the road. But surely *you* can manage to punch in a number on a phone, carry on a conversation, or maybe even text while simultaneously driving in a safe and courteous manner. Right? In a word, *wrong*.

The issue here is *selective attention*, or perceiving only what's currently relevant to you. Perception is an active, moment-to-moment exploration for relevant or interesting information, not a passive receptacle for whatever happens to come along. Talking on a cell phone while driving demands that you juggle two independent sources of sensory input—vision and hearing—at the same time. This is problematic, because research has found that when attention is directed to hearing, activity in visual areas decreases (Shomstein & Yantis, 2004).

This kind of *multitasking* creates problems when you need to react suddenly while driving. Researchers have tested experienced drivers in a highly realistic driving simulator, measuring their response times to brake lights and stop signs while they listened to the radio or carried on phone conversations about a political issue, among other tasks (Strayer, Drews, & Johnston, 2003). These experienced drivers reacted significantly more slowly during phone conversa-

tions than during the other tasks. This is because a phone conversation requires memory retrieval, deliberation, and planning what to say and often carries an emotional stake in the conversation topic. Tasks such as listening to the radio require far less attention.

The tested drivers became so engaged in their conversations that their minds no longer seemed to be in the car. Their slower braking response translated into an increased stopping distance that, depending on the driver's speed, would have resulted in a rear-end collision. Whether the phone was handheld or hands free made little difference, and similar results have been obtained in field studies of actual driving (Horrey & Wickens, 2006). This suggests that laws requiring drivers to use hands-free phones may have little effect on reducing accidents. Even after drivers had extensive practice at driving while using a hands-free cell phone in a simulator, the disruptive effects of cell phone use were still observed (Cooper & Strayer, 2008).

The situation is even worse when text messaging is involved: Compared with a no-texting control condition, when either sending or receiving a text message in the simulator, drivers spent dramatically less time looking at the road, had a much harder time staying in their lane, missed numerous lane changes, and had greater difficulty maintaining an appropriate distance behind the car ahead of them (Hosking, Young, & Regan, 2009). Another review concluded that the impairing effect of texting while driving is comparable with that of alcohol

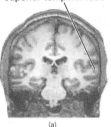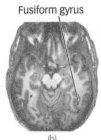

Superior temporal lobe   Fusiform gyrus

(a)   (b)

SHOMSTEIN AND YANTIS, 2004, CONTROL OF ATTENTION SHIFTS BETWEEN VISION AND AUDITION IN HUMAN CORTEX, THE JOURNAL OF NEUROSCIENCE, 24 NOVEMBER 2004, 24(47): 10702–10706; DOI:10.1523/JNEUROSCI.2939-04.2004.

Shifting attention participants received fMRI scans as they performed tasks that required them to shift their attention between visual and auditory information. (a) When participants focused on auditory information, a region in the superior (upper) temporal lobe involved in auditory processing showed increased activity (yellow/orange). (b) In striking contrast, a visual region, the fusiform gyrus, showed decreased activity when participants focused on auditory information (blue).

consumption and greater than that of smoking marijuana (Pascual-Ferrá, Liu, & Beatty, 2012).

In an interesting finding, people who report that they multitask frequently in everyday life have difficulty in laboratory tasks that require focusing attention in the face of distractions, compared with individuals who do not multitask much in daily life (Ophir, Nass, & Wagner, 2009). Frequent multitasking in academic settings (via texting or Facebook use) can have a negative impact on learning (Chen & Yan, 2015; Judd, 2014). So how well do we multitask in a few thousand kilograms of metal hurtling down the highway? Unless you have two heads with one brain each—one to talk and one to concentrate on driving—you would do well to keep your eyes on the road and not on the phone.

Build to the Outcomes

1. Differentiate between sensation and perception using, as an example, a person with healthy eyes, yet who, after brain damage, can no longer make sense of what she reads.

2. What are the benefits of sensory adaptation?

3. By what process do sensory inputs, such as light and sound waves, become messages sent to the brain?

4. Why isn't it enough for a psychophysicist to measure only the physical energy of a stimulus?

5. What is an absolute threshold?

6. What is the importance of a ratio to the measurement of a just noticeable difference?

7. Signal detection theory allows us to distinguish what two factors that work together to determine perception?

Visual Pathways: Connections Between the Eye and the Brain

Learning Outcomes

- Discuss how the physical properties of light relate to the psychological dimensions of brightness, colour, and saturation.

- Describe how the eye converts light waves into neural impulses.

- Discuss how we perceive colour.

- Describe what happens once the neural impulses reach the brain.

- Describe the functions of the dorsal and ventral visual streams.

You might be proud of your 20/20 vision, even if it is corrected by glasses or contact lenses. The term *20/20* refers to a measurement associated with a Snellen chart, named after Hermann Snellen (1834–1908), the Dutch ophthalmologist who developed it as a means of assessing **visual acuity**, *the ability to see fine detail:* It is the smallest line of letters that a typical person can read from a distance of 20 feet (6 metres). But if you dropped into the Birds of Prey Ophthalmologic Office, your visual pride would wither. Hawks, eagles, owls, and other raptors have much greater visual acuity than humans—in many cases, about 8 times greater, or the equivalent of 20/2 vision (meaning that what the normal human can just see from 2 feet [0.6 metres] away can be seen by these birds at a distance of 20 feet [6 metres] away). Your sophisticated visual system has evolved to transduce visual energy in the world into neural signals in the brain. Humans have sensory receptors in their eyes that respond to wavelengths of light energy. When we look at people, places, and things, patterns of light and colour give us information about where one surface stops and another begins. The array of light reflected from those surfaces preserves their shapes and enables us to form a mental representation of a scene (Rodieck, 1998; Snowdon, Thompson, & Troscianko, 2012). Understanding vision, then, starts with understanding light.

Sensing Light

Visible light is simply that portion of the electromagnetic spectrum that we can see, and it is an extremely small slice (see **FIGURE 4.2**). You can think of light as waves of energy. Like ocean waves, light waves vary in height and in the distance between their peaks, or *wavelengths*. Light waves vary on three physical dimensions. Changes in these physical dimensions produce systematic changes in perception (psychological dimensions) (see **TABLE 4.2**). Length and amplitude are properties of the light waves themselves. The *length* of a light wave determines its hue, or what humans perceive as colour. The intensity, or *amplitude,* of a light wave—how high the peaks are—determines what we perceive as the brightness of light.

Purity is a third dimension that refers to the degree to which a light source is emitting just one wavelength, or a mixture of wavelengths. It also influences how colour is perceived. Some synthetic light sources (such as lasers) produce light that is *pure*, consisting of just one wavelength. These lights have high *saturation*, meaning that they are perceived by humans as having very rich colours. Most light sources (such as the sun, fire, luminescent algae, incandescent light bulbs) are composed of many different wavelengths of light at the same time: the colour that is perceived depends on the relative amounts of different wavelengths in the (impure) mixture.

visual acuity The ability to see fine detail.

Figure 4.2
Electromagnetic Spectrum The sliver of light waves visible to humans as a rainbow of colours from violet-blue to red is bounded on the short end by ultraviolet rays, which honeybees can see, and on the long end by infrared waves, on which night-vision equipment operates. Someone wearing night-vision goggles, for example, can detect another person's body heat in complete darkness. Light waves are tiny, but the scale along the bottom of this chart offers a glimpse of their varying lengths, measured in nanometres (nm)—1 nm = 1 billionth of a metre.

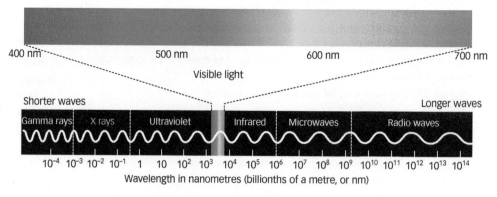

TABLE 4.2

PROPERTIES OF LIGHT WAVES

Physical Dimension	Psychological Dimension
Length	Hue or what we perceive as colour
Amplitude	Brightness
Purity (saturated — desaturated)	Saturation or richness of colour

The full-colour image on the top is what you'd see if your rods and cones are fully at work. The greyscale image on the bottom is what you'd see if only your rods are functioning.

The Eye Detects and Focuses Light

Eyes have evolved as specialized organs to detect light. **FIGURE 4.3a** shows the human eye in cross-section. Light that reaches the eyes passes first through a clear, smooth outer tissue called the *cornea*, which bends the light wave and sends it through the *pupil*, a hole in the coloured part of the eye. This coloured part is the *iris*, which is a translucent, doughnut-shaped muscle that controls the size of the pupil and hence the amount of light that can enter the eye.

Immediately behind the iris, muscles inside the eye control the shape of the *lens* to bend the light again and focus it onto the **retina**, *a layer of light-sensitive tissue lining the back of the eyeball*. The muscles change the shape of the lens to focus objects at different distances, making the lens flatter for objects that are far away or rounder for nearby objects. This change is called **accommodation**, *the process by which the eye maintains a clear image on the retina*. Figure 4.3b shows how accommodation works.

If your eyeballs are a little too long or a little too short, the lens will not focus images properly on the retina. If the eyeball is too long, images are focused in front of the retina, leading to nearsightedness (*myopia*). If the eyeball is too short, images are focused behind the retina, and the result is farsightedness (*hyperopia*). Eyeglasses, contact lenses, and surgical procedures can correct either condition. Eyeglasses and contact lenses both provide an additional lens to help focus light more appropriately, and procedures such as LASIK physically reshape the eye's existing lens.

Light Is Converted into Neural Impulses in the Retina

How does light become a meaningful image? The retina is the interface between the world of light outside the body and the world of vision inside the central nervous system. Two types of *photoreceptor cells* in the retina contain light-sensitive proteins that absorb light and transduce it into electrical signals. **Cones** *detect colour, operate under normal daylight conditions, and allow us to focus on fine detail*. **Rods** *become active only under low-light conditions, for night vision* (see Figure 4.3c).

Rods are much more sensitive photoreceptors than cones, but they provide no information about colour and sense only shades of grey. Think about this the next time you wake up in the middle of the night and make your way to the bathroom for a drink of water. Using only the moonlight from the window to light your way, do you see the room in colour or in shades of grey? Rods and cones differ in several other

retina A layer of light-sensitive tissue lining the back of the eyeball.

accommodation The process whereby the eye maintains a clear image on the retina.

cones Photoreceptors that detect colour, operate under normal daylight conditions, and allow us to focus on fine detail.

rods Photoreceptors that become active under low-light conditions for night vision.

MIKE SONNENBERG/ISTOCKPHOTO/GETTY IMAGES

a. The Eye Captures Light Waves Reflected From an Object's Surface

Light reflected from an object's surface enters the eyes via the transparent **cornea**, bending to pass through the **pupil** at the centre of the coloured **iris**.

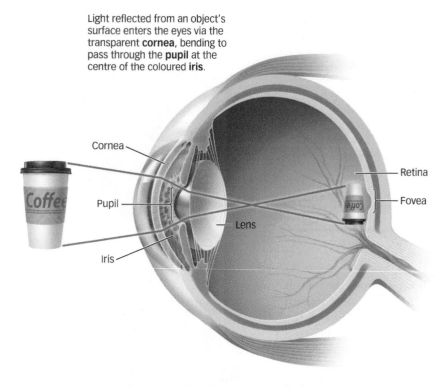

Cornea
Pupil
Iris
Lens
Retina
Fovea

Behind the iris, the thickness and shape of the **lens** adjust to focus light on the **retina**, where the image appears upside down and backwards. Vision is clearest at the **fovea**.

Figure 4.3
The Eye Transduces Light Waves Into Neural Activity

b. Muscles Change the Shape of the Lens to Focus Objects at Different Distances, a Process Called Accommodation

People with **normal vision** focus the image on the retina at the back of the eye, both for near and far objects.

Nearsighted people see clearly what's nearby, but distant objects are blurry because light from them is focused in front of the retina.

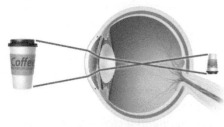

For **farsighted** people, distant objects are clear, but those nearby are blurry because their point of focus falls beyond the surface of the retina.

---

fovea An area of the retina where vision is clearest and there are no rods at all.

ways as well, most notably in their numbers. About 120 million rods are distributed more or less evenly around each retina except at the very centre, known as the **fovea**, *an area of the retina where vision is clearest and there are no rods at all.* The absence of rods in the fovea decreases the sharpness of vision in reduced light, but the benefit is enhanced sensitivity to faint light in the rest of the retina outside the fovea (the *periphery*). For example, when amateur astronomers view dim stars through their telescopes at night, they know to look a little off to the side of the target so that the image will fall not on the rod-free fovea but on some other part of the retina that contains many highly sensitive rods.

Cones are far less numerous than rods. Each retina contains only about 6 million cones, which are densely packed in the fovea and much more sparsely distributed over the rest of the retina, as you can see in Figure 4.3c. This distribution of cones directly affects visual acuity. Light reflected off of objects that you look at directly falls on your fovea. The high density of cones in the fovea means that these objects are seen in great detail, rather like images produced by a state-of-the-art smartphone camera. Objects outside of your direct focus—in other words, objects in your *peripheral vision*—aren't so clear. The light reflecting from those peripheral objects falls

c. The Retina Is the Interface Between the Eye and the Brain

The surface of the retina is composed of photoreceptor cells, the rods and cones, beneath a layer of transparent neurons, the bipolar and retinal ganglion cells (RGCs), connected in sequence. The axon of a retinal ganglion cell joins with all other RGC axons to form the **optic nerve**. The optic nerve creates the blind spot on the retina.

The **fovea**, the area of greatest visual acuity, is where most colour-sensitive cones are concentrated, allowing us to see fine detail as well as colour. Rods, the predominant photoreceptors activated in low-light conditions, are distributed everywhere else on the retina.

d. The Optic Nerve Carries the Neural Energy Into the Brain

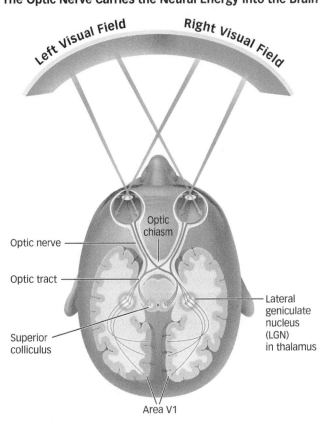

Objects in the right visual field stimulate the left half of each retina, and objects in the left visual field stimulate the right half of each retina. Just before the optic nerves enter the brain about half the nerve fibers from each eye cross. The left half of each optic nerve (representing the right visual field) runs through the brain's left hemisphere via the thalamus, and the right half of each optic nerve (representing the left visual field) travels this route through the right hemisphere. So, information from the right visual field ends up in the left hemisphere and information from the left visual field ends up in the right hemisphere.

outside the fovea where the cell density is lower, resulting in a fuzzier, grainier image, more like a low-end smartphone camera.

The retina consists of several layers of cells. As seen in Figure 4.3c, the photoreceptor cells (rods and cones) form the innermost layer, beneath a layer of transparent neurons called the bipolar and retinal ganglion cells. The *bipolar cells* collect

The image on the left was taken at a higher resolution than the image on the right. The difference in quality is analogous to light falling on the fovea, rather than on the periphery of the retina.

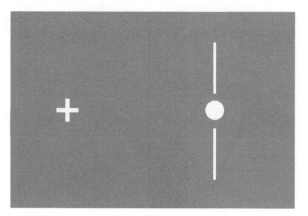

Figure 4.4

Blind Spot Demonstration To find the blind spot in your right eye, close your left eye and stare at the cross with your right eye. Observe this page 6 to 12 inches (15 to 30 centimetres) away from your eyes and move it slowly towards and away from you until the dot disappears. When that happens, the dot is in your blind spot and so is not visible. At this point the vertical lines may appear as one continuous line, because your visual perceptual system *fills in* the area occupied by the missing dot! To test your left eye's blind spot, turn the page upside down and repeat the experiment with your right eye closed.

electrical signals from the rods and cones and transmit them to the outermost layer of the retina, where neurons called *retinal ganglion cells (RGCs)* organize the signals and send them to the brain.

The bundled RGC axons—about 1.5 million per eye—form the *optic nerve,* which leaves the eye through a hole in the retina. Because it contains neither rods nor cones and therefore has no mechanism for sensing light, this hole in the retina creates a **blind spot**, *a location in the visual field that produces no sensation on the retina.* The area of the blind spot makes quite a big hole in the visual field. Imagine looking at a full moon high in the night sky. Now imagine another 11 moons lined up right beside it; if all 12 moons fell on your blind spot, you would not see them (Anstis, 2010). Why don't we notice these big holes in the world we see? Our perceptual system automatically "fills in," using knowledge of the colour or texture around the blind spot, rather like the "paint bucket" in a graphics program might do. Try the demonstration in **FIGURE 4.4** to find the blind spot in your own eyes.

The Optic Nerve Carries Neural Impulses to the Brain

Streams of action potentials (neural impulses) containing information encoded by the retina travel to the brain along the optic nerve. Half of the axons in the optic nerve that leave each eye come from retinal ganglion cells (RGCs) that code information in the right visual field, whereas the other half code information in the left visual field. The right visual field information is relayed to the left hemisphere of the brain, while the left visual field information is relayed to the right hemisphere (see Figure 4.3d). Information first goes to the *lateral geniculate nucleus (LGN),* located in the thalamus of each hemisphere. As you will recall from the Neuroscience and Behaviour chapter, the thalamus receives inputs from all of the senses except smell. From the LGN, the visual signals travel to the back of the brain, to a location called **area V1** (pronounced "vee-one"), the *part of the occipital lobe that contains the primary visual cortex.*

Perceiving Colour

Around 1670, Sir Isaac Newton pointed out that colour is not something "in" light waves. In fact, the perception of colour is created by our brain (see Figure 4.2). If we see pure light (i.e., only one wavelength at a time), we perceive the shortest visible ones as deep purple. As wavelengths become longer, the colours we perceive change gradually and continuously to blue, then green, yellow, orange, and, with the longest visible wavelengths, red. This rainbow of hues and accompanying wavelengths is called the *visible spectrum,* illustrated in Figure 4.2 and **FIGURE 4.5**. The perception of colour from mixtures of wavelengths (as emitted by most light sources) depends on the relative amounts of different wavelengths in the mixture. For example, light is seen as white in colour if it contains about the same amounts of many different wavelengths across the visible spectrum, as shown in **FIGURE 4.6**. Notice that in the centre of the figure, where the red, green, and blue lights overlap, the surface looks white. This is because the surface is reflecting a broad range of visible wavelengths of light, from long (red) through medium (green) to short (blue).

You'll recall that all rods are ideal for low-light vision but cannot distinguish colours. Why? Think of a garden water tap, and compare it to the mixer tap you might have in a kitchen or bathroom (Snowdon et al., 2012). The garden tap only moves one way—that is, it allows you to control the flow of water, but you cannot control the temperature. With a mixer tap, you can go up and down, and side to side—you can control both flow and temperature. With only one type of photopigment,

blind spot A location in the visual field that produces no sensation on the retina.

area V1 The part of the occipital lobe that contains the primary visual cortex.

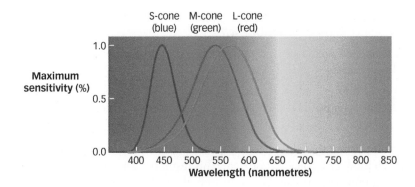

Figure 4.5
Seeing in Colour We perceive a spectrum of colour because objects selectively absorb some wavelengths of light and reflect others. Colour perception corresponds to the relative activity of the three types of cones. The sensitivity of the three types of cones is shown by the three coloured lines. Each type is most sensitive to a range of wavelengths in the visible spectrum—short (bluish light), medium (greenish light), or long (reddish light). DATA FROM STOCKMAN & SHARPE, 2000.

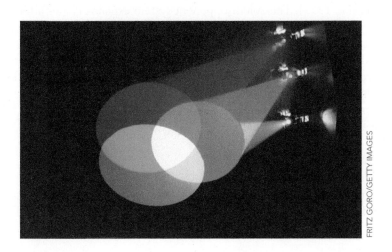

FRITZ GORO/GETTY IMAGES

Figure 4.6
Colour Mixing The millions of shades of colour that humans can perceive are products of the mixture of wavelengths that sources emit or that objects reflect. Coloured spotlights work by causing the surface to reflect light of a particular wavelength, which stimulates the red, blue, or green photopigments in the cones. When all visible wavelengths are present, we see white.

the rod receptor is like the garden tap. Rods can signal only the brightness, not the colour, of the dim light to which they are sensitive. Cones, by contrast, come in three types; one type is especially sensitive to long wavelengths (L-cones), one to medium wavelengths (M-cones), and one to short wavelengths (S-cones). When light (direct from a source, or reflected off an object) hits a region of the retina, the L-, M-, and S-cones in that region are each excited to the degree that the light contains the wavelengths to which they are sensitive, as shown in Figure 4.5. Just as a mixer tap with two channels (up–down, and left–right) allows control of both flow and temperature, three cone types allow the brain to interpret brightness, signalled by the total amount of activity across all three cone types; and colour, signalled by the relative levels of activity between pairs of cone types.

You can think of the three types of cones in the retina (L-, M-, and S-cones) as three channels of information. The relative amount of activity in each channel provides a unique code for each colour you see. Genetic disorders in which one of the cone types is missing—and, in some very rare cases, two or all three cone types—cause a *colour vision deficiency.* Such disorders are sex linked, affecting men much more often than women.

Colour vision deficiency is often referred to as *colour blindness,* but in fact, people who lack only one type of cone can still distinguish many colours, just not as many as someone who has the full complement of three cone types. You can create a kind of temporary colour deficiency by exploiting the idea of sensory adaptation. Just like the rest of your body, cones need an occasional break, too. Staring too long at one colour fatigues the cones that respond to that colour, producing a form of sensory

Figure 4.7
Colour Afterimage Demonstration
Follow the accompanying instructions
in the text, and sensory adaptation will
do the rest. When the afterimage fades,
you can get back to reading the chapter.

adaptation that results in a *colour afterimage*. To demonstrate this effect for yourself, follow these instructions for **FIGURE 4.7**:

- Stare at the small cross between the two colour patches for about 1 minute. Try to keep your eyes as still as possible.
- After a minute, look at the lower cross. You should see a vivid colour aftereffect that lasts for a few seconds. Pay particular attention to the colours in the afterimage.

Were you puzzled that the pinky red patch produces a greenish afterimage and the yellow patch produces a blue afterimage? This result reveals something important about colour perception. The explanation stems from the **colour-opponent system**, in which *pairs of cone types (channels) work in opposition:* the L-cone channel against the M-cone channel (as in Figure 4.7) and the S-cone channel against the M-cone channel (Hurvich & Jameson, 1957). The colour-opponent system explains colour aftereffects. For example, you see "green" when your M-cones are more active than your L-cones, and "red" when your L-cones are more active than your M-cones. If you stare at a red patch, the cones that are firing most strongly (the L-cones) become fatigued over time (recall sensory adaptation). Now, when you stare at a white or grey patch, which reflects all the wavelengths equally and should make L-, M-, and S-cones equally active, the fatigued L-cones respond relatively weakly compared to the M-cones. Since the M-cones are more active than the L-cones, you perceive the patch as tinted green.

The Visual Brain

The optic nerve carries the neural impulses to area V1 in the brain (Figure 4.3d). Here, the information is systematically mapped into a representation of the visual scene.

Neural Systems for Perceiving Shape

One of the most important functions of vision involves perceiving the shapes of objects; our day-to-day lives would be a mess if we couldn't distinguish individual shapes. Imagine not being able to differentiate reliably between a warm glazed doughnut and a straight stalk of celery and you'll get the idea. Perceiving shape depends on the location and orientation of an object's edges. It is not surprising, then, that area V1 (see Figure 4.3d) is sensitive to edge orientation. As you also read in the Neuroscience and Behaviour chapter, neurons in the primary visual cortex (V1) selectively respond to bars and edges in specific orientations in space (Hubel & Wiesel, 1962, 1998). The **visual receptive field**, meaning *the region of the visual field to which each neuron responds,* is also very small for neurons in V1. In effect, area V1 contains populations of neurons, each "tuned" to respond to edges oriented a particular way, in a particular location in space. This means that some neurons fire when we perceive a vertical edge (like the side of a door or window) in a particular location in space, other neurons fire when we perceive a horizontal edge (like the top of a door or window) in that location, still other neurons fire when we perceive edges at a diagonal orientation of 45°, and so on (see **FIGURE 4.8**). Those orientations at other locations in space activate other neurons. All of these edge detectors work together to allow you to distinguish between a doughnut and a celery stalk.

Pathways for What, Where, and How

From area V1, visual information spreads out and is processed through 32 or more (!) distinct brain areas (Felleman & van Essen, 1991). Neurons in V1 and its neighbouring brain regions respond to only a small region of the visual field (i.e., have small *receptive fields*) and are tuned to relatively simple features, like edges. As signals are processed and transformed in progressively later areas farther away from V1,

colour-opponent system Theory
stating that pairs of cone types
(channels) work in opposition.

visual receptive field The region
of the visual field to which each neuron
responds.

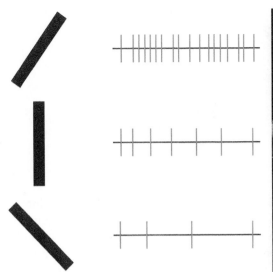

FRITZ GORO/THE LIFE PICTURE COLLECTION/GETTY IMAGES

Figure 4.8

Single-Neuron Feature Detectors Area V1 contains neurons that respond to specific orientations of edges. Here, a single neuron's responses (action potentials shown as pink lines) are recorded (*left*) as a monkey views bars at different orientations (*right*). This neuron fires action potentials at a high rate when the bar is pointing to the right at 45°, less often when it is vertical, and hardly at all when it is pointing to the left at 45°.

receptive fields become larger, and the features to which neurons respond become more complex. The many visual processing areas can be simplified into two functionally distinct pathways, or *visual streams* (see **FIGURE 4.9**):

- The *ventral* (lower) *stream* travels across the occipital lobe into the lower levels of the temporal lobes and includes brain areas that represent an object's shape and identity. Because this stream represents *what* an object is, it is often called the "what" pathway (Kravitz et al., 2013; Ungerleider & Mishkin, 1982).

- The *dorsal* (upper) *stream* travels up from the occipital lobe to the parietal lobes (including some of the middle and upper levels of the temporal lobes) and includes brain areas that identify where an object is and how it is moving (Kravitz et al., 2011). Because the dorsal stream allows us to perceive spatial relations, researchers originally dubbed it the "where" pathway (Ungerleider & Mishkin, 1982). Neuroscientists later argued that because the dorsal stream is crucial for guiding actions, such as aiming, reaching, or tracking with the eyes, the "where" pathway is more appropriately called a "perception for action" pathway (Milner & Goodale, 1995).

How do we know there are two pathways? The most dramatic evidence comes from studying the people with brain injuries within either of the two pathways.

For example, a woman known as DF suffered permanent damage to a large region of the lateral occipital cortex, an area in the ventral stream (Goodale et al., 1991). Her ability to identify objects by sight was greatly impaired, although her ability to identify them by touch was normal. This suggests that her *visual representation* of objects, but not her *memory* for objects, was damaged. DF could still accurately *guide* her actions by sight to an object, even though she could not say what the object was, as demonstrated in **FIGURE 4.10**. When DF's brain was scanned using fMRI, researchers found that regions within the dorsal stream exhibited normal activity during guided movement (James et al., 2003).

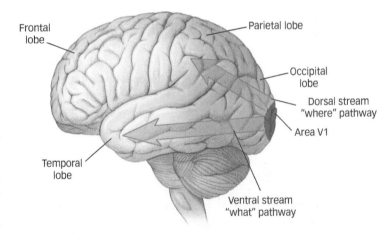

Figure 4.9

Visual Streams One pathway courses from the occipital visual regions into the lower temporal lobe. This ventral pathway enables us to identify what we see. Another pathway travels from the occipital lobe through the upper regions of the temporal lobe into the parietal regions. This dorsal pathway allows us to locate objects, to track their movements, and to act on them.

Figure 4.10

Testing Visual Form Agnosia (*left*) When researchers asked DF to look at the slot in the testing apparatus at various angles, and then turn a handheld card until its orientation matched, she was unable to comply. (*right*) However, when asked to actually insert the card into the slot at various angles, DF accomplished the task almost perfectly.

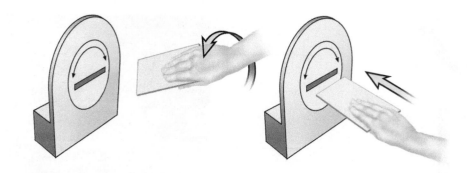

Other people with brain damage to the parietal lobe, a section of the dorsal stream, have difficulty using vision to guide reaching and grasping (Perenin & Vighetto, 1988). However, they can still identify objects they see because their ventral streams are intact. We can conclude from these two patterns of impairment that the ventral and dorsal visual streams are functionally distinct. One stream may be damaged, whereas the other remains intact, but the two streams must still work together during visual perception in order to integrate perception for identification (ventral) and perception for action (dorsal).

When perceiving an object, say, a coffee cup, we are simultaneously aware of what it is, where it is located, and how to reach for it to pick it up. These are not features that are separated in our conscious awareness, despite being represented by different parts of the brain. This is an instance of what researchers call the **binding problem**, which is *how the brain links features together so that we see unified objects in our visual world rather than free-floating or miscombined features* (Treisman, 1998, 2006). How do we perceive the world as an integrated, seamless whole, when different features are processed and represented in different, specialized, parts of the brain? This binding problem pertains to all sensory domains, but it has been studied most in the context of the visual system.

A concept of "binding neurons" in the visual system has been recently proposed, which may provide a solution to the problem (Eguchi et al., 2018). These are neurons that receive coincident (simultaneous) input from other neurons involved in representing different features of an object. They participate in a larger array of neurons that signal a whole object by engaging in an intricate and repeatable dance of action potentials. Solving the binding problem is essential to understanding how our brains make sense of complex visual scenes, and this is an area of active research.

binding problem How the brain links features together so that we see unified objects in our visual world rather than free-floating or miscombined features.

Build to the Outcomes

1. What are the physical and psychological properties of light waves?

2. What is the importance of the process of accommodation in the eye?

3. What is the function of the photoreceptor cells (rods and cones)?

4. What is the function of retinal ganglion cells? What is the relationship between the right and left eyes and between the right and left visual fields?

5. How does colour perception depend on relative activity, generated by light of different wavelengths, in the three cone "channels"?

6. What happens when the cones in your eyes become fatigued?

7. What happens in the brain when an object's shape is perceived? What are the main jobs of the ventral and dorsal streams?

Visual Perception: Recognizing What We See

Our journey into the visual system has already revealed how it accomplishes some pretty astonishing feats. But the system needs to do much more in order for us to be able to interact effectively with our visual world. Let's now consider in more detail how the system links together individual visual features into whole objects, allows us to recognize what those objects are, organizes objects into visual scenes, and detects motion and change in those scenes.

Binding Individual Features into a Whole

Specialized feature detectors in different parts of the visual system analyze each of the multiple features of a visible object: orientation, colour, size, shape, and so forth. **Parallel processing** is *the brain's capacity to perform many activities at the same time.* Ultimately, though, parallel processing of these different features must somehow be integrated into a single, unified perception of an object (Nassi & Callaway, 2009). We have already discussed how different features of one object might be bound together in perception. But usually we see multiple objects at the same time—what allows us to perceive so easily and correctly that the young man in the photo is wearing a grey shirt and the young woman is wearing a red shirt? Why don't we see free-floating patches of grey and red, or even incorrect combinations, such as the young man wearing a red shirt and the young woman wearing a grey shirt? This is another aspect of the binding problem.

Illusory Conjunctions: Perceptual Mistakes

In everyday life, we correctly combine features into unified objects so automatically and effortlessly that it may be difficult to appreciate that binding is ever a problem at all. However, researchers have discovered errors in binding that reveal important clues about how the process works. One such error is known as an **illusory conjunction**, *a perceptual mistake whereby the brain incorrectly combines features from multiple objects.* In a pioneering study of illusory conjunctions, Anne Treisman and Hilary Schmidt (1982) briefly showed study participants visual displays in which black digits flanked coloured letters, then instructed them first to report the black digits and second to describe the coloured letters. Participants frequently reported illusory conjunctions, claiming to have seen, for example, a blue *A* or a red *X* instead of the red *A* and the blue *X* that had actually been shown (see **FIGURE 4.11a, b**).

These illusory conjunctions were not just the result of guessing; they occurred more frequently than other kinds of errors, such as reporting a letter or colour that was not present in the display (see Figure 4.11c). The illusory conjunctions looked real to the participants, who were just as confident about seeing them as they were about the actual coloured letters they perceived correctly.

Why do illusory conjunctions occur? Treisman and her colleagues have tried to explain them by proposing a **feature-integration theory** (Treisman, 1998, 2006; Treisman & Gelade, 1980; Treisman & Schmidt, 1982), which holds that *focused attention is not required to detect the individual features that make up a stimulus (e.g., the colour, shape, size, and location of letters), but it is required to bind those individual features together.* From this perspective, **attention**, which is *the active and conscious processing of particular information,* provides the "glue" necessary to bind features together. Illusory conjunctions occur when it is difficult for participants to

We correctly combine features into unified objects. Thus, for example, we see that the young man is wearing a grey shirt and the young woman is wearing a red shirt.

Learning Outcomes

- List the factors that allow us to recognize objects by sight.

- Describe the visual cues essential for depth perception.

- Discuss how we perceive motion and change.

parallel processing The brain's capacity to perform multiple activities at the same time.

illusory conjunction A perceptual mistake whereby the brain incorrectly combines features from multiple objects.

feature-integration theory The idea that focused attention is not required to detect the individual features that make up a stimulus (e.g., the colour, shape, size, and location of letters), but it is required to bind those individual features together.

attention The active and conscious processing of particular information.

Presented

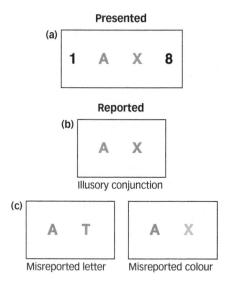

Figure 4.11

Illusory Conjunctions Illusory conjunctions occur when features such as colour and shape are combined incorrectly. For example, when participants are shown a red *A* and a blue *X*, they sometimes report seeing a blue *A* and a red *X*. Other kinds of errors, such as a misreported letter (e.g., reporting *T* when no *T* was presented) or misreported colour (reporting green when no green was presented) occur rarely, indicating that illusory conjunctions are not the result of guessing (based on Robertson, 2003).

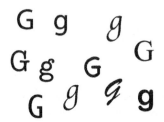

With only a quick glance, you recognize all these letters as *G*, but their varying sizes, shapes, angles, and orientations ought to make this recognition task difficult. What is it about the process of object recognition that allows us to perform this task effortlessly?

pay full attention to the features that need to be glued together. For example, in the experiments we just considered, participants were required to process the digits that flanked the coloured letters, thereby reducing attention to the letters and allowing illusory conjunctions to occur. When experimental conditions are changed so that participants can pay full attention to the coloured letters, and they are able to correctly bind those features together, illusory conjunctions disappear (Treisman, 1998; Treisman & Schmidt, 1982).

Recognizing Objects by Sight

Take a quick look at the letters "G" in the accompanying illustration (below left). Even though they're quite different from each other, you probably effortlessly recognized all of them as examples of the letter *G*. Now consider the same kind of demonstration but using your best friend's face. Suppose one day your friend gets a dramatic new haircut—or adds glasses, hair dye, or a nose ring. Even though your friend now looks strikingly different, you still recognize that person with ease. Just like the variability in *G*s, you somehow are able to extract the underlying features of the face that allow you to accurately identify your friend.

This thought exercise may seem trivial, but it's no small perceptual feat. Machines still have difficulty recognizing objects from different points of view, or recognizing different instances of a thing (like your friend with different haircuts) as the thing itself. The field of *machine learning,* which involves computers learning from very large data sets (e.g., many different instances of your friend's face) to identify patterns (what makes your friend unique, despite variations in dress, hair, and accessories), is developing rapidly, but such systems still fail in unexpected ways (Goodfellow, Bengio, & Courville, 2016). How do we humans recognize patterns, extracting the essential information that makes a *G* a *G* so accurately and effortlessly?

It is not entirely clear how feature detectors help the visual system get from a spatial array of light hitting the eye to the accurate perception of an object, such as your friend's face, in different views and lighting conditions, at different times. In a classic study using fMRI to examine visual processing in healthy young adults, researchers found a subregion in the temporal lobe that responds more strongly to faces than to just about any other object category, whereas a nearby area responds most strongly to buildings and landscapes (Kanwisher, McDermott, & Chun, 1997). Much research since is compatible with the idea that different regions of the ventral stream respond preferentially to different kinds of objects, such as faces, bodies, scenes, and tools (Kanwisher, 2010; Hutchison et al., 2014). Although the findings are not in doubt, researchers disagree about what they mean. Many researchers argue for a *modular view,* suggesting that specialized brain areas, or modules, detect and represent faces or houses, body parts, and even other objects (Kanwisher, 2010)—perhaps because different objects differ in their visual properties, such as their shape, or real-world size (Kornblith & Tsao, 2017; Julian, Ryan, & Epstein, 2017).

Another perspective on this issue is provided by studies that examine how single neurons in the human brain respond to objects and faces (Quiroga, 2016; Suthana & Fried, 2012). For example, in a study by Quiroga et al. (2005), electrodes were placed in the temporal lobes of people suffering from epilepsy to help identify the source of their seizures and so improve treatment. While the electrodes were in place, patients were also shown photographs of faces and objects as the researchers recorded their neural responses. The researchers found that neurons in the temporal lobe respond to specific objects viewed from multiple angles, as well as to people wearing different clothing and facial expressions, and photographed from various angles. In some cases, the neurons also responded to the words for these same objects. For example, a neuron that responded to photographs of the Sydney Opera House also responded when the words *Sydney Opera* were displayed, but not when the words *Eiffel Tower* were displayed.

Recently, researchers have been exploring the importance of *conceptual knowledge* in recognizing objects—the rich store of facts and other meaningful knowledge we have about a familiar object (Clarke & Tyler, 2015; Schwartz & Yovel, 2016). According to this view, when we perceive an object, we don't merely recognize what it looks like, but we understand what it *is*—its characteristics and significance to our behaviour. There wouldn't be much use in recognizing that the thing approaching you as you cross the street is a car, not a canary, if you don't also know that cars are made of unyielding metal, travel fast, and probably cause some damage if they hit you—so you should get out of the way! An object's visual properties are analyzed in the ventral visual stream, which leads to activation of conceptual knowledge at higher levels of the ventral stream, closer to the front of the brain.

Perceptual Constancy and Contrast

The previous section provided examples of the principle of **perceptual constancy**, the idea that *even as aspects of sensory signals change, perception remains constant*. Sometimes we may recognize our friend (constancy) and still notice changes in hair colour or style, or the addition of facial jewelry, but often constancy acts such that we don't even notice that the object has changed. When I pick up my coffee cup, then put it down with the handle pointing in a slightly different direction, and later go to pick it up again, I don't notice that it looks slightly different than it did the last time I reached for it. Similarly, if I see my friend outside in bright sunlight, and then illuminated under blacklight in a dark club, she looks pretty much the same to me despite the light reflecting off my friend's face (and thus the signals from my retinas to my brain) being very different in the two situations. Perceptual constancy is the result of your perceptual system organizing the sensory information into meaningful objects, then supplementing that with information about novel features or stripping away potentially distracting, unnecessary, sensory data entirely.

In other situations, our perceptual system exhibits **perceptual contrast**, the idea that *although the sensory information from two things may be very similar, we perceive the objects as different*. As with perceptual constancy, perceptual contrast is the result of your perceptual system organizing sensory information into meaningful objects, then stripping away potentially distracting, or even misleading, sensory data, so that you can more accurately perceive what the real object is. (See A World of Difference: The Dress, for an example of perceptual contrast.)

Principles of Perceptual Organization

Researchers in the Gestalt psychology movement, whom you read about in The Evolution of Psychological Science chapter, were the first to recognize that we tend to perceive not just collections of separate features but whole objects, organized in meaningful ways. We perceptually *group* features that belong together into one object, while we *segregate* features that belong to different objects. The *process of grouping and segregating features to create whole objects organized in meaningful ways* is called **perceptual organization**. There are usually multiple ways of perceptually organizing a complex scene, but our perceptual system automatically delivers to us the interpretation that is the simplest and most meaningful, consistent with our experience and expectations.

Our visual systems allow us to identify people as the same individuals even when they change such features as hairstyle and skin colour. Despite the extreme changes in these two photos, you can probably tell that they both portray Emma Stone.

perceptual constancy A perceptual principle stating that even as aspects of sensory signals change, perception remains consistent.

perceptual contrast The phenomenon that occurs when the sensory information from two things may be very similar but we perceive the objects as different.

perceptual organization The process of grouping and segregating features to create whole objects organized in meaningful ways.

A World of Difference | **The Dress**

On February 25, 2015, a Tumblr user posted a picture of a dress—not an action that you would expect to produce a firestorm on social media. But that is exactly what happened. The user explained that her friends were divided on the colour of the dress—some saw it as white and gold, others as blue and black. Who was right? Over the next two days, the post attracted over 400,000 notes on Tumblr. Millions responded to a BuzzFeed poll that asked about people's perceptions of the dress: More people claimed that it was white and gold than blue and black. Friends and families across the globe nearly came to blows over the colour of the dress, as people typically insisted that their perception was the correct one and failed to believe that others could see it so differently. In photos of the dress under different lighting conditions posted by the online retailer that sold it, the dress was unambiguously blue and black, as confirmed by the dress's name: Royal-Blue Lace Detail Bodycon Dress.

Vision scientists have begun to grapple with the mystery of the dress, and though we don't yet fully understand why people see its colour so differently, we do have some clues and hypotheses. Consider a study by Lafer-Sousa, Hermann, and Conway (2015). They showed 1,401 people (some in the laboratory, most over the Internet) a smaller version of the photo of the dress posted at Tumblr and asked them to complete the sentence "This is a _____ and _____ dress." The researchers found that 57% called the dress blue/black, 30% called it white/gold, and the remaining participants provided other colour combinations. People who had seen the dress before were somewhat more likely to call it white/gold than those who had not, indicating a role for prior experience in shaping colour perception.

When the researchers increased the size of the image, more people saw the dress as white/gold (perhaps explaining why most people saw it as white/gold on Tumblr, where a larger version was

What colours do you see in the dress? Researchers found that the perception of the dress as white and gold increased as the age of viewers increased.

posted). Surprisingly, there was a significant correlation between age and colour perception: Older people were more likely to see the dress as white/gold than were younger people. And women were more likely to see it as white/gold than were men.

Lafer-Sousa and colleagues (2015), as well as other researchers, suggest that perception of the dress's colour is heavily influenced by how people perceive the lighting of the room where the photo was taken (Lafer-Sousa & Conway, 2017; Gegenfurter, Bloj, & Toscani, 2015; Winkler et al., 2015; Uchikawa, Morimoto, & Matsumoto, 2017); the lighting is highly ambiguous and thus subject to different interpretations. Daylight consists of both "cool" (perceived as blue) short wavelength components and "warm" (perceived as yellowish) medium wavelengths. If you perceive the lighting in the room as "cool" and "bluish," then your visual system assigns the medium wavelengths to the dress, which you then see as white/gold. But if you perceive the room lighting as "warm" and "yellowish," your visual system attributes the short wavelengths to the dress and you see it as blue/black (Uchikawa et al., 2017).

Still, this just changes the ultimate question regarding individual differences to a question about why some people see the lighting of the room as "cool," while others see it as "warm." This may have to do with our lived experience of

lighting conditions—we may perceive the dress in the photograph as being lit by the conditions we're most used to. Lafer-Sousa et al. suggest that people who get up early ("larks") and therefore experience more natural sunlight, which contains a large number of short wavelengths, may be more likely to perceive lighting as "cool" and thus perceive the dress as white/gold. On the other hand, "night owls," who spend more time in artificial illumination, which generally has more medium wavelengths and fewer short wavelengths, may be more likely to perceive lighting as "warm" and thus perceive the dress as blue/black. In a finding consistent with this idea, Lafer-Sousa et al. cited evidence that older adults and women are more likely to be "larks," which would fit with their greater tendency to see the dress as white/gold, but more evidence is needed to evaluate this hypothesis.

Though still not fully understood, "the dress" highlights an important lesson in perceptual contrast. The same stimulus can be seen as very different colours, depending on how we interpret the light hitting it. The colours we perceive are not simply inherent properties of an object; they instead represent our visual system's best guess about colour on the basis of complex patterns of incoming sensory data as well as our past experiences.

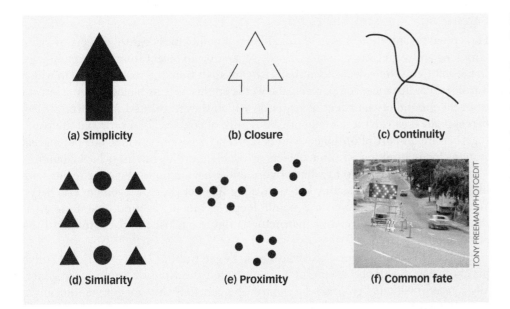

Figure 4.12
Perceptual Grouping Rules
Principles first identified by Gestalt psychologists and now supported by a wealth of experimental evidence demonstrate that the brain is predisposed to impose order on incoming sensations in particular ways. This is probably largely due to experience gathered while moving around and interacting with the world, although some principles may be hardwired from birth.

The Gestalt *perceptual grouping rules* govern how humans are likely to perceptually organize things, even though the information could, in theory, be organized in some other way (Koffka, 1935). Here's a sampling:

- *Simplicity:* When confronted with two or more possible interpretations of an object's shape, the visual system tends to select the simplest or most likely interpretation. In **FIGURE 4.12a**, we perceive the complex shape as an arrow.

- *Closure:* We tend to fill in missing elements of a visual scene, allowing us to perceive edges that are separated by an interruption (e.g., a gap) as belonging to complete objects. In Figure 4.12b, we see an arrow despite the gaps.

- *Continuity:* Edges or contours that have the same orientation have what the Gestalt psychologists called *good continuation,* and we tend to group them together perceptually. In Figure 4.12c, we perceive two crossing lines instead of two V shapes.

- *Similarity:* Regions that are similar in colour, lightness, shape, or texture are perceived as belonging to the same object. In Figure 4.12d, we perceive three columns—a column of circles flanked by two columns of triangles.

- *Proximity:* Objects that are close together tend to be grouped together. In Figure 4.12e, we perceive three groups or "clumps" of 5 or 6 dots each, not just 16 dots.

- *Common fate:* Elements of a visual image that move together are perceived as parts of a single moving object. In Figure 4.12f, the series of flashing lights in the road sign are perceived as a moving arrowhead.

As an example, in the image shown in **FIGURE 4.13**, we may see a mess of meaningless shapes above, but below, the principle of simplicity means we see two kinds of shapes (airplane and the letter *B*) instead. The principle of closure is at work when we see the *B*s as whole, behind the airplane. That we see the contour of the whole airplane, instead of just a bunch of black lines, reflects the principles of continuity and similarity. Finally, the principle of proximity enables us to group the right features of each *B* together—we aren't tempted to "see" a *B* except where the component bits are close together.

Figure 4.13
Gestalt Principles At Work! Above, you may see a meaningless collection of grey and white shapes. The same shapes below (but where the white has been turned to black) give a very different impression. You probably perceptually organize them as an outline of an airplane, superimposed on a bunch of *B*s. You have a lot of experience with *B*s, and with the shapes of aircraft, and with what things look like when other things are in front of them. Your perceptual system uses the sensory information in this image, and your knowledge, to organize it (probably effortlessly and automatically) into this novel scene.

Figure 4.14

Ambiguous Edges Here's how Rubin's classic reversible figure–ground illusion works: Fix your eyes on the centre of the image. Your perception will alternate between a vase and facing silhouettes, even as the sensory stimulation remains constant.

Separating Figure from Ground

Perceptual organization is a powerful aid to our ability to recognize objects by sight. Grouping and segregation involve visually separating an object from its surroundings. In Gestalt terms, this means identifying a *figure* apart from the (back)*ground* in which it resides. For instance, you perceive the words on this page as figural: They stand out from the ground of the sheet of paper on which they're printed. You certainly can perceptually organize these elements differently, of course: The words *and* the paper together are all part of an object you perceive as *a page*. Typically, our perceptual systems focus attention on some objects, while disregarding others as background.

Size provides one clue to what's figure and what's ground: Smaller regions are likely to be figures, such as tiny letters on a big sheet of paper. Movement also helps: Your instructor is (we hope) a dynamic lecturer, moving around in a static environment, so you perceive your instructor as figure against the background of the classroom.

Figure and ground can also swap roles. Edgar Rubin (1886–1951), a Danish psychologist, developed a famous illusion called the *Rubin vase* or, more generally, a *reversible figure–ground relationship*. You can view this "face–vase" illusion in **FIGURE 4.14** in two ways: either as a vase on a black background or as a pair of silhouettes facing each other. Your visual system settles on one or the other interpretation and fluctuates between them every few seconds. This happens because the edge that separates figure and ground equally defines the contours of the vase and the contours of the faces. Evidence from fMRI brain-imaging studies shows, quite nicely, that when people are seeing the Rubin image as faces, there is greater activity in the face-selective region of the temporal lobe discussed earlier than when they are seeing it as a vase (Hasson et al., 2001).

Perceiving Depth and Size

Objects in the world (e.g., tables) generally have three dimensions—length, width, and depth—but the retinal image contains only two dimensions, length and width. How does the brain process a flat, 2-D retinal image so that we perceive the depth of an object and how far away it is? How can we tell whether something is a large object far away, or a small object that is much closer? The answer is that we have to make an educated guess. A guess because we have no way to sense visual depth (or real image size) directly; educated because we've all been alive for many years, moving around in a 3-dimensional world, which has taught us that various visual cues indicate depth and distance. Some of these can be picked up with just one eye (monocular cues) and some rely on a comparison of the images in the two eyes (binocular cues).

Monocular Depth Cues

monocular depth cues Aspects of a scene that yield information about depth when viewed with only one eye.

Monocular depth cues are *aspects of a scene that yield information about depth when viewed with only one eye.* There are many different cues that work this way, and they have been exploited by visual artists for centuries. For instance, even when you have one eye closed, the retinal image of an object you've focused on grows smaller as that object moves farther away and larger as it moves closer. Our brains routinely use these differences in retinal image size, or *relative size,* to perceive distance; this really only works if the typical size of an object is familiar, so this cue is also called "familiar size." Most adults, for example, fall within a narrow range of heights (perhaps 5–6 feet [or 1.5–1.8 metres] tall), so retinal image size alone is usually a reliable cue to how far away they are. Our perceptual system automatically corrects for size differences and attributes them to differences in distance. **FIGURE 4.15** demonstrates the strength of this perceptual correction for familiar size.

THE PHOTO WORKS

THE PHOTO WORKS

Figure 4.15
Familiar Size When you view images of things that have a familiar size, such as the people in the left-hand photo, your perceptual system automatically interprets the smaller object as the same size as the nearer one, but farther away. With a little image manipulation, you can see in the right-hand photo that the relative size difference projected on your retinas is far greater than you perceive. The image of the person in the blue vest is exactly the same size in both photos. This is an example of perceptual constancy—we perceive all people to be about the same size, even though the size on the retina is very different.

In addition to familiar size, there are several more monocular depth cues, such as:

- *Linear perspective,* which describes the phenomenon that parallel lines seem to converge as they recede into the distance (see **FIGURE 4.16a**).
- *Texture gradient,* which describes how textures such as parched ground look more detailed close up but more uniform and smooth when farther away (see Figure 4.16b).

DC PRODUCTIONS/EXACTOSTOCK-1598/ SUPERSTOCK

(a)

AGE FOTOSTOCK/SUPERSTOCK

(b)

NP-E07/ISTOCK/GETTY IMAGES PLUS

(c)

ROB BLAKERS/LONELY PLANET IMAGES/GETTY IMAGES

(d)

Figure 4.16
Pictorial Depth Cues Visual artists rely on a variety of monocular cues to make their work come to life. You can rely on cues in an image such as linear perspective (a), texture gradient (b), interposition (c), and relative height (d) to infer distance, depth, and position, even with only one eye.

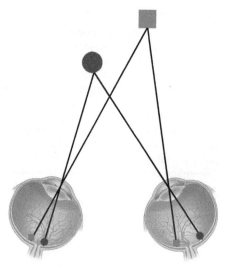

Figure 4.17

Binocular Disparity We see the world in three dimensions because our eyes are a distance apart, so the image of an object falls on a slightly different place on the retina of each eye. In this two-object scene, the images of the square and the circle fall on different points of the retina in each eye. The disparity in the positions of the circle's retinal images is greater than the square's disparity, so the circle is perceived as closer.

Can you see that, by constructing the wagon as a trapezoid similar to an Ames room, Frodo the hobbit (*left*) appears to be much smaller than Gandalf the wizard (*right*) in this scene from *The Fellowship of the Ring* (Warner Brothers)?

binocular disparity The difference in the retinal images of the two eyes that provides information about depth.

- *Interposition*, which occurs when one object partly blocks another (see Figure 4.16c). You can infer that the blocking object (bowl of cherries) is closer than the blocked object (basket of apples). However, interposition by itself cannot provide information about how far apart the two objects are.

- *Relative height in the image* depends on your field of vision (see Figure 4.16d). Objects that are closer to you tend to be lower in a visual scene (or in your visual field of view), whereas faraway objects are higher up in your field of view.

Binocular Depth Cues

We can also use **binocular disparity**, *the difference in the retinal images of the two eyes,* to provide information about depth. Because our eyes are slightly separated, each registers a slightly different view of the world. Your brain computes the difference (disparity) between the two retinal images and uses this to perceive how far away objects are, as shown in **FIGURE 4.17**. If the images fall in very similar places on the two retinas, demonstrating little disparity, the object is perceived as farther away; if the images are more disparate in their retinal location, the object is perceived as closer.

Binocular disparity as a cue to depth perception was first discussed by Sir Charles Wheatstone in 1838. Wheatstone went on to invent the stereoscope, essentially a holder for a pair of photographs or drawings taken from two horizontally displaced locations. (Wheatstone did not lack for original ideas; he also invented the accordion and an early telegraph and coined the term *microphone*.) When viewed, one by each eye, the pairs of images evoked a vivid sense of depth. 3-D movies are based on this same idea.

Illusions of Depth and Size

The ambiguous relation between size and distance has been used to create elaborate illusions that depend on fooling the visual system about how far away objects are. All these illusions depend on the same principle: When you view two objects that project the same retinal image size, the object you perceive as farther away will be perceived as larger. Such illusions are typically constructed to be viewed from just one vantage point—for this reason, they are called *forced perspective illusions*. A famous example is the Ames room, a room that is trapezoidal in shape rather than square: Only two sides are parallel (see **FIGURE 4.18a**). A person standing in one corner of an Ames room is physically twice as far away from the viewer as a person standing in the other corner. But when viewed with one eye through the small peephole placed in one wall, the Ames room looks square because the shapes of the windows and the flooring tiles are carefully crafted to *look* square from the viewing port (Ittelson, 1952).

The perceptual system interprets the far wall as perpendicular to the line of sight, such that people standing at different positions along that wall appear to be at the same distance. The viewer interprets the retinal image size so that the person standing in the right corner appears to be much larger than a person standing in the left corner (see Figure 4.18b). Forced perspective is also commonly used in filmmaking, to make objects or people in the same frame appear to be of different sizes. For example, the actors in the *Lord of the Rings* movies are not very different in size in real life, but you perceive the hobbits as much smaller than the humans, wizards, and elves.

Perceiving Motion and Change

You should now have a good sense of how we see what and where objects are, a process made substantially easier when the objects stay in one place. But real life, of course, is full of moving targets. Objects change position over time: Birds fly, horses gallop; rain and snow fall; trees bend in the wind. Understanding how we

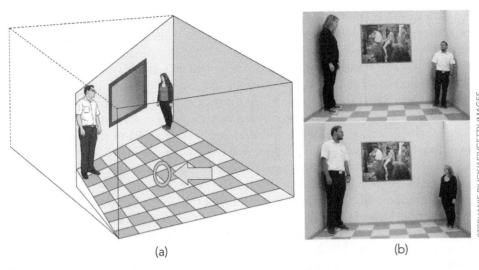

(a)

(b)

Figure 4.18

The Amazing Ames Room (a) A diagram showing the actual proportions of the Ames room reveals its secrets. The sides of the room form a trapezoid with parallel sides but a back wall that's way off square. The uneven floor makes the room's height shorter in the far back corner than in the nearer corner. Add misleading cues such as specially designed windows and flooring and position the room's occupants in each corner, and you're ready to lure an unsuspecting observer. (b) Looking into the Ames room through the viewing port (see yellow arrow in part a) with only one eye, the observer infers a normal size–distance relationship—that both people are the same distance away. And so the image sizes they project on the retina lead the viewer to conclude that one person is very small and the other is very large.

perceive motion and why we sometimes fail to perceive change can bring us closer to appreciating how visual perception works in everyday life.

Motion Perception

To sense motion, the visual system must encode information about both space and time. The simplest case to consider is an observer who is not moving, looking at an object that is.

As an object moves across a stationary observer's visual field, it first stimulates one location on the retina, then soon after stimulates another location on the retina. Neural circuits in the brain can detect this change in position over time and respond to specific speeds and directions of motion (Emerson, Bergen, & Adelson, 1992). A region near the back of the temporal lobe, referred to as *MT* (part of the dorsal stream we discussed earlier), is specialized for the perception of visual motion (Born & Bradley, 2005; Newsome & Paré, 1988), and brain damage in this area causes a deficit in normal motion perception (Zihl, von Cramon, & Mai, 1983).

Of course, in the real world, rarely are you a stationary observer: as you move around, your head and eyes move all the time. The motion-perception system must take into account the position and movement of your eyes, and ultimately of your head and body, in order to perceive the motions of objects correctly and allow you to approach or avoid them. The brain accomplishes this by monitoring your eye and head movements and "subtracting" them from the motion in the retinal image.

Motion perception, like colour perception, operates in part through opponent processes and is subject to sensory adaptation. A motion aftereffect called the *waterfall illusion* is analogous to colour aftereffects. If you stare at the downward rush of a waterfall for several seconds, you'll experience an upward motion aftereffect when you then look at stationary objects near the waterfall, such as trees or rocks. What's going on here?

FABIOFILZI/GETTY IMAGES

Colour perception and motion perception both rely on opponent processing, which is why we fall prey to colour aftereffects and the waterfall illusion, which also depends on neural adaptation.

apparent motion The perception of movement as a result of signals appearing in rapid succession in different locations.

spatial acuity The ability to distinguish two features that are very close together in space.

temporal acuity The ability to distinguish two features that are very close together in time.

multisensory Events that stimulate multiple senses at the same time.

ventriloquist illusion The fact that you depend on your visual system for reliable information about spatial location.

change blindness Failure to detect changes to the visual details of a scene.

This process is similar to seeing green after staring at a patch of red. Just like your perception of colour depends on the relative activity in opposing sets of cones, perception of motion depends on relative activity in opposing sets of motion detector cells. If there is no motion, activity in the two sets of cells is equal. If one set of motion detector cells is fatigued through adaptation to motion in one direction, then, when motion ceases, there is relatively greater firing in the opposing, less fatigued, set of cells, which is interpreted by your perceptual system as motion in the opposite direction. Evidence from research using fMRI to study brain activity indicates that when people experience the waterfall illusion while viewing a stationary stimulus, there is increased activity in region MT, which plays a key role in motion perception (Tootell et al., 1995).

The movement of objects in the world is not the only event that can evoke the perception of motion. The successively flashing lights of a Las Vegas casino sign can evoke a strong sense of motion because people perceive a series of flashing lights as a whole, moving object (see Figure 4.12f). This *perception of movement as a result of alternating signals appearing in rapid succession in different locations* is called **apparent motion**.

Sensory Superpowers

Filmmaking and animation depend on apparent motion. Motion pictures flash 24 still frames per second (fps). A slower rate would produce a much choppier sense of motion; a faster rate would be a waste of resources because we would not perceive the motion as any smoother than it appears at 24 fps. As you will learn in the next section, our auditory system is much more sensitive to rapid changes than our visual system. Although we cannot see the difference between 24 and 50 frames in a second we can very easily hear the difference between 24 and 50 clicks in a second. Every sensory domain has its superpower. Your visual system has amazing **spatial acuity**, or *ability to distinguish two features that are very close together in space,* while your auditory system rocks at **temporal acuity**, the *ability to distinguish two features that are very close together in time.*

In our everyday life, we capitalize on these strengths. Many events in the world are **multisensory**, *stimulating multiple senses at the same time.* We take sensory information into account according to how good it is. For example, when you watch a movie with surround sound, you attribute voices to characters on the screen: you hear them coming from what you can see, even though you know they are coming from speakers elsewhere. This is called the **ventriloquist illusion.** You depend on your visual system for reliable information about spatial location; when you see a moving mouth, simultaneously with hearing speech, you perceive the speech as coming from that mouth. We "believe" our visual system over our auditory system when it comes to determining the spatial location of an event.

Change Blindness and Inattentional Blindness

The visual world is very rich—so rich, in fact, that our perceptual system cannot take it all in, although intuitively we may feel that at any moment we have full awareness of what is around us. However, our comfortable intuitions have been challenged by experimental demonstrations of **change blindness**, which occurs *when people fail to detect changes to the visual details of a scene* (Rensink, 2002; Simons & Rensink, 2005). Change blindness occurs even when major details of a scene are changed—changes that we incorrectly believe we couldn't possibly miss (Beek, Levin, & Angelone, 2007).

In a study that dramatically illustrates this idea, an experimenter asked a person on a university campus for directions (Simons & Levin, 1998). While they were talking, two men walked between them, holding a door that hid a second experimenter (see **FIGURE 4.19**).

(a)   (b)   (c)

Figure 4.19

Change Blindness The white-haired man was giving directions to one experimenter (a), who disappeared behind the moving door (b), only to be replaced by another experimenter (c). Like many other people, the man failed to detect a seemingly obvious change.

Behind the door, the two experimenters traded places, so that when the men carrying the door moved on, a different person was asking for directions than the one who had been there just a second or two earlier. Remarkably, only 7 of 15 participants noticed this change.

Although it is surprising that people can be blind to such dramatic changes, these findings once again illustrate the illusion of perception—we think we are aware of much more of what is "out in the world" than we really are. They also illustrate the importance of focused attention for visual perception (see the discussion of feature-integration theory on page 139). Just as focused attention is critical for binding together the features of objects, it is also necessary for detecting changes to objects and scenes (Rensink, 2002; Simons & Rensink, 2005). Change blindness is most likely to occur when people fail to focus attention on the object that undergoes a change (Rensink, O'Regan, & Clark, 1997).

The role of focused attention in conscious visual experience is also dramatically illustrated by the closely related phenomenon of **inattentional blindness**, *a failure to perceive objects that are not the focus of attention* (Simons & Chabris, 1999). We've already seen that the use of cell phones is a bad idea when driving (see The Real World: Multitasking, page 129). Ira Hyman and colleagues (2010) asked whether cell-phone use results in inattentional blindness in other situations. They recruited a clown to ride a unicycle in the middle of a large courtyard on a university campus in the state of Washington. On a pleasant afternoon, the researchers asked 151 students who had just walked through the square whether they saw the clown. Seventy-five percent of the students who were using cell phones failed to notice the clown, compared with less than 50% who were not using cell phones.

In a follow-up study, walkers using cell phones were less aware than others of obstacles in their path and even failed to notice a tree with money hanging from it (Hyman, Sarb, and Wise-Swanson, 2014)! Using cell phones draws on focused attention, resulting in inattentional blindness and emphasizing again that our conscious experience of our visual environment is restricted to those features or objects selected by focused attention. In some extreme cases, conscious visual experience may reflect what we expect to see rather than what exists in the external world (see Other Voices: Hallucinations and the Visual System).

University students who were using their cell phones while walking through campus failed to notice the unicycling clown more frequently than did students who were not using their cell phones. REPUBLISHED WITH PERMISSION OF JOHN WILEY & SONS, INC. FROM DID YOU SEE THE UNICYCLING CLOWN? INATTENTIONAL BLINDNESS WHILE WALKING AND TALKING ON A CELL PHONE, HYMAN ET AL., APPLIED COGNITIVE PSYCHOLOGY, 24(5), 2009; PERMISSION CONVEYED THROUGH COPYRIGHT CLEARANCE CENTER.

inattentional blindness A failure to perceive objects that are not the focus of attention.

Other Voices | Hallucinations and the Visual System

We rely on our perceptual systems to provide reliable information about the world around us. Yet we've already seen that perception is susceptible to various kinds of illusions. Even more striking, our perceptual systems are capable of creating hallucinations: perceptions of sights, sounds, or other sensory experiences that don't exist in the world outside us. As discussed by the perceptual psychologist V. S. Ramachandran in an interview with the *New York Times,* as reported in an article written by Susan Kruglinski, vivid visual hallucinations can occur in low-vision or even blind individuals with severe damage to their retinas, the tissue at the back of each eye that transduces light into electrical signals sent to the brain.

One day a few years ago, Doris Stowens saw the monsters from Maurice Sendak's "Where the Wild Things Are" stomping into her bedroom. Then the creatures morphed into traditional Thai dancers with long brass fingernails, whose furious dance took them from the floor to the walls to the ceiling.

Although shocked to witness such a spectacle, Ms. Stowens, 85, was aware that she was having hallucinations, and she was certain that they had something to do with the fact that she suffered from the eye disease macular degeneration.

"I knew instantly that something was going on between my brain and my eyes," she said.

Ms. Stowens says that ever since she developed partial vision loss, she has been seeing pink walls and early American quilts floating through the blind spots in her eyes several times each week.

In fact, Ms. Stowens's hallucinations are a result of Charles Bonnet syndrome, a strange but relatively common disorder found in people who have vision problems. Because the overwhelming majority of people with vision problems are more than 70 years old, the syndrome, named after its 18th-century Swiss discoverer, is mostly found among the elderly. And because older people are more susceptible to cognitive deterioration, which can include hallucinations or delusions, Charles Bonnet (pronounced bon-NAY) is easily misdiagnosed as mental illness.

Many patients who have it never consult a doctor, out of fear that they will be labeled mentally ill.

"It is not a rare disorder," said Dr. V. S. Ramachandran, a neurologist at the University of California at San Diego, who has written about the syndrome. "It's quite common. It's just that people don't want to talk about it when they have it."

Researchers estimate that 10 to 15 percent of people whose eyesight is worse than 20/60 develop the disorder. Any eye disease that causes blind spots or low vision can be the source, including cataracts, glaucoma, diabetic retinopathy and, most commonly, macular degeneration. The hallucinations can vary from simple patches of color or patterns to lifelike images of people or landscapes to phantasms straight out of dreams. The hallucinations are usually brief and nonthreatening, and people who have the syndrome usually understand that what they are seeing is not real.

In some ways, researchers say, the hallucinations that define the syndrome are similar to the phenomenon of phantom limbs, where patients still vividly feel limbs that have been amputated, or phantom hearing, where a person hears music or other sounds while going deaf. In all three cases, the perceptions are caused by a loss of the sensory information that normally flows unceasingly into the brain.

In the case of sight, the primary visual cortex is responsible for taking in information, and also for forming remembered or imagined images. This dual function, Dr. Ramachandran and other experts say, suggests that normal vision is in fact a fusion of incoming sensory information with internally generated sensory input, the brain filling in the visual field with what it is used to seeing or expects to see. If you expect the person sitting next to you to be wearing a blue shirt, for example, you might, in a quick sideways glance, mistakenly perceive a red shirt as blue. A more direct gaze allows for more external information to correct the misperception.

"In a sense, we are all hallucinating all the time," Dr. Ramachandran said. "What we call normal vision is our selecting the hallucination that best fits reality."

With extensive vision loss, less external information is available to adjust and guide the brain's tendency to fill in sensory gaps. The results may be Thai dancers or monsters from a children's book.

Charles Bonnet syndrome was first described over 250 years ago by Bonnet, a Swiss scientist whose own blind grandfather experienced hallucinations like those reported by Ms. Stowens. However, neurologists and others have only recently begun to study the syndrome. Can you make some sense of this syndrome, applying what you have learned about the visual system? How can someone who sees poorly or who cannot see at all have intense visual experiences? What brain processes could be responsible for these kinds of visual hallucinations?

Some clues come from neuroimaging studies of people who experience visual hallucinations. These studies have shown that specific types of hallucinations are accompanied by activity in parts of the brain responsible for the particular content of the hallucinations (Allen et al., 2008). For example, facial hallucinations are accompanied by activity in a part of the temporal lobe known to be involved in face processing. Our understanding of the visual system beyond the retina can provide some insight into how and why blind individuals experience visual hallucinations.

Build to the Outcomes

1. How does the study of illusory conjunctions help us understand the role of attention in feature binding?
2. How do we recognize our friends, even when they're hidden behind sunglasses?
3. What are the Gestalt rules of perceptual organization?
4. What does the face–vase illusion tell us about perceptual organization?
5. What are perceptual constancy and perceptual contrast?
6. How do monocular depth cues help us with depth perception?
7. What role does binocular disparity have in perceiving depth?
8. How can flashing lights on a casino sign give the impression of movement?
9. How can a failure of focused attention explain change blindness?

Hearing: More Than Meets the Ear

Ray Charles (1930–2004) was a pioneering American soul-music singer and songwriter who went blind at the age of 6. He said: "I look at blindness like an inconvenience. I can do 98 percent of everything I want to do in my life . . . .[but] it would be a real [expletive deleted] if I ever lost my hearing" (Sager, 2007). It is understandable that a musician would feel this way, but you don't have to be a blind musician to appreciate what hearing adds to your life. Just close your eyes for a few minutes and notice what sounds you hear. Unlike vision, hearing works in the dark, through walls, and around corners. We are social animals, who typically rely on sound as our primary means of communicating with each other.

The sense of hearing depends on *sound waves,* changes in air pressure unfolding over time. Plenty of things produce sound waves: the impact of two hands clapping, the vibration of vocal cords during a stirring speech, the resonance of a bass guitar string during a thrash metal concert. Just as vision is about the perception of meaningful visual objects, hearing involves transforming changes in air pressure into meaningful sound objects (or sources).

Learning Outcomes

- Describe the physical properties of sound waves.
- Describe how the ear converts sound waves into neural impulses.
- Explain how pitch, timbre, and loudness of a sound relate to its physical properties.
- Compare the main causes of hearing loss.

Sensing Sound

Striking a tuning fork produces a *pure tone,* a simple sound wave that consists of regularly alternating regions of higher and lower air pressure, radiating outward in all directions from the source. If your ear is in the path of this spreading sound, the alternating pressure wave causes your ear drum to vibrate in time with the wave, hundreds or even thousands of times per second. Just as there are three physical dimensions of light waves that influence visual perception, so, too, are there three physical dimensions of a sound wave that correspond to dimensions of auditory perception: frequency, amplitude, and complexity (see **TABLE 4.3**).

- The *frequency* (or *repetition rate*) of the sound wave depends on how often the peak in air pressure passes the ear or a microphone, measured in cycles per second, or hertz (Hz). The repetition rate of a sound wave is perceived as the **pitch**, *how high or low a sound is, as ordered on a musical scale.*
- The *amplitude* of a sound wave refers to its intensity, relative to the threshold for human hearing (which is set at zero decibels, or dB). Amplitude is perceived as **loudness**. To give you an idea of the relation between the physical property

pitch How high or low a sound is.

loudness A sound's intensity.

TABLE 4.3

PROPERTIES OF SOUND WAVES

Frequency (repetition rate) Corresponds to our perception of pitch.	Low frequency (low-pitched sound)	High frequency (high-pitched sound)
Amplitude Corresponds to our perception of loudness.	High amplitude (loud sound)	Low amplitude (soft sound)
Complexity Corresponds to our perception of timbre.	Simple (pure tone)	Complex (mix of frequencies)

of intensity (measured in dB) and your subjective impression of loudness, the rustling of leaves in a soft breeze is about 20 dB, normal conversation is about 60 dB, a busy restaurant is about 85 dB, and a Slayer concert is about 130 dB. That's loud enough to cause permanent damage to the auditory system and is well above the pain threshold; in fact, sounds above 85 dB can cause hearing damage, depending on the length of exposure.

- The *complexity* of sound waves, or the mixture of frequencies, influences perception of **timbre**, *the quality of sound that allows you to distinguish two sources with the same pitch and loudness.* Timbre (pronounced "TAM-ber") allows you to tell the difference between a piano and a guitar both playing the same melody in the same key, at the same loudness. Very few sources (other than tuning forks and artificial tone generators) emit pure tones, consisting of just one frequency. Nearly all everyday sounds consist of a broad range of frequencies present at the same time. Timbre (whether it's a piano, guitar, or human voice) is determined, in part, by the relative amounts of the different frequencies in the sound mixture, rather like how colour depends on the relative amounts of different wavelengths in an impure light.

The auditory world is a busy place. Imagine being in a coffee shop, conversing with a friend. In addition to your friend's voice and your own, you hear music in the background; the voices and laughter of strangers conversing at adjacent tables; as well as the clatter of dishes, the hiss of the espresso machine, and the rumble of traffic outside. The different sounds combine in the air to create very complex sound waves in your two ears.

Most sound sources that you encounter in real life are a mixture of many different frequencies, and different sources may have frequencies in common. These mix together into a complex wave that produces an intricate pattern of vibration in the eardrum. Somehow, we perceive auditory scenes not as incoherent jumbles, but as discrete, recognizable sound sources—such as voices, espresso machines, and traffic—in different auditory locations. How does your brain reconstruct the original sounds such that you can hear and understand your friend over all the other sounds? This is the central problem of auditory perception; to answer it, we need to understand how the auditory system converts sound waves into neural signals.

MACIEJ DAKOWICZ/ALAMY

The process of auditory perception is very different from visual perception. This is not surprising: light is a form of electromagnetic radiation, whereas sound is a physical change in air pressure over time. Different forms of energy require different processes of transduction.

timbre The quality of sound that allows you to distinguish two sources with the same pitch and loudness.

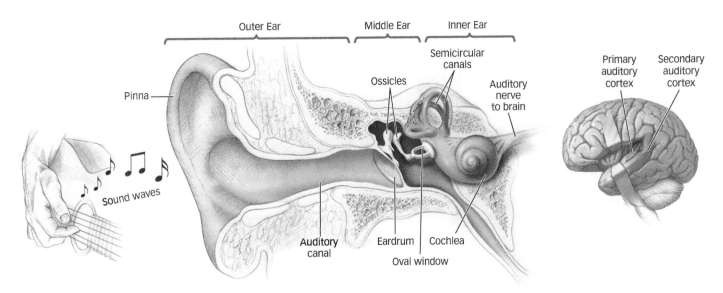

Figure 4.20

Anatomy of the Human Ear The pinna funnels sound waves into the auditory canal, causing the eardrum to vibrate in time with the sound wave. In the middle ear, the ossicles pick up the eardrum vibrations, amplify them, and pass them along, causing vibration of the oval window, and therefore of the fluid-filled cochlea in the inner ear. Here, fluid carries the wave energy to the auditory receptors (inner hair cells) that transduce it into electrical activity, exciting the neurons that form the auditory nerve, leading to the brain.

The Outer Ear Funnels Sound Waves to the Middle Ear

The human ear is divided into three distinct parts, as shown **FIGURE 4.20**. The *outer ear* collects sound waves and funnels them towards the *middle ear*, which transmits the vibrations to the *inner ear*, embedded in the skull, where they are transduced into neural impulses.

The outer ear consists of the visible part on the outside of the head (called the *pinna*); the auditory canal; and the eardrum, an airtight flap of skin that vibrates in response to sound waves gathered by the pinna and channelled into the canal. The middle ear, a tiny, air-filled chamber behind the eardrum, contains the three smallest bones in the body, called *ossicles*. Named for their appearance as hammer, anvil, and stirrup, the ossicles fit together into a lever that mechanically transmits and amplifies vibrations from the eardrum to the inner ear. Amplification is required because the ossicles push against the oval window, which is a membrane that separates the middle ear from the cochlea of the inner ear. The ossicles take the airborne pressure wave at the eardrum and transfer it into a pressure wave in fluid. Fluid requires more energy to vibrate; if you've ever been poolside, trying to talk to someone who is underwater, you know you have to really shout in order for the pressure wave of your voice to carry under the water.

Sound Is Converted into Neural Impulses in the Inner Ear

The inner ear contains the spiral-shaped **cochlea** (Latin for "snail"), *a fluid-filled tube containing cells that transduce sound vibrations into neural impulses.* The cochlea is divided along its length by the **basilar membrane**, *a structure in the inner ear that moves up and down in time with vibrations relayed from the ossicles, transmitted through the oval window* (see **FIGURE 4.21**). Sound causes the basilar membrane to move up and down in a **travelling wave** (see Figure 4.21) (Békésy, 1960). The frequency of the stimulating sound determines where on the basilar membrane the up-and-down motion is highest. When the frequency is low, the wide, floppy tip (*apex*) of the basilar membrane moves the most; when the frequency is high, the narrow, stiff end closest to the oval window (*base*) moves the most.

When the basilar membrane moves up and down, the cochlear fluid moves back and forth. This stimulates thousands of **inner hair cells**, which are *specialized auditory receptor neurons embedded in the basilar membrane.* The hair cells have long hairs sticking out their tops that bend back and forth in the cochlear fluid, like seaweed in a current. This back-and-forth bending generates rhythmic action potentials in the

cochlea A fluid-filled tube that contains cells that transduce sound vibrations into neural impulses.

basilar membrane A structure in the inner ear that moves up and down in time with vibrations relayed from the ossicles, transmitted through the oval window.

travelling wave The up-and-down movement that sound causes in the basilar membrane.

inner hair cells Specialized auditory receptor neurons embedded in the basilar membrane.

Figure 4.21
Auditory Transduction Inside the cochlea (shown here as though the coiled part was uncoiled—note that this never actually happens!), the basilar membrane undulates in response to wave energy in the cochlear fluid. Different locations along the membrane are sensitive to different frequency components, from low frequencies at the apex of the cochlea to high frequencies at the base, and the movement of the basilar membrane causes the hairs of the hair cells at those locations to bend. This bending generates action potentials in the attached auditory nerve axons, which together form the auditory nerve that emerges from the cochlea.

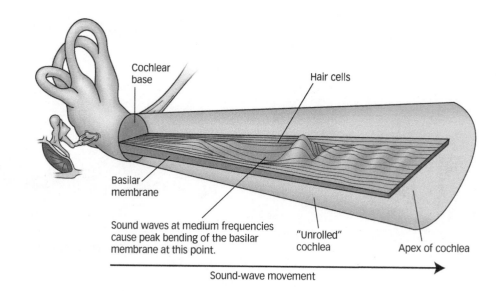

Cochlear base

Hair cells

Basilar membrane

Sound waves at medium frequencies cause peak bending of the basilar membrane at this point.

"Unrolled" cochlea

Apex of cochlea

Sound-wave movement

auditory nerve axons that travel to the brain, and these action potentials are precisely timed with the pressure peaks of the original sound wave. The auditory nerve axons that fire the most are those connected to hair cells in the area of the basilar membrane that moves the most.

The Auditory Nerve Carries the Neural Impulses to the Brain

From the inner ear, action potentials in the auditory nerve travel to several regions of the brainstem in turn, and then to the thalamus and ultimately to an area of the cerebral cortex called **area A1**, *the primary auditory cortex in the temporal lobe* (see **FIGURE 4.22**). There is some evidence that the auditory cortex is composed of two distinct streams, roughly analogous to the dorsal and ventral streams of the visual system. Spatial ("where") auditory features, which allow you to locate the source of a sound in space, are handled by areas towards the back of the temporal lobe and in regions that may overlap with the visual dorsal stream. Features that allow you to

area A1 The primary auditory cortex in the temporal lobe.

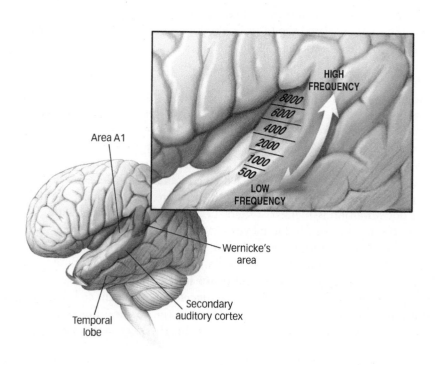

HIGH FREQUENCY

8000
6000
4000
2000
1000
500

LOW FREQUENCY

Area A1

Wernicke's area

Secondary auditory cortex

Temporal lobe

Figure 4.22
Primary Auditory Cortex Area A1 is folded into the temporal lobe beneath the lateral fissure in each hemisphere. The area A1 cortex has a topographic organization (*inset*), with lower frequencies mapping towards the front of the brain and higher frequencies towards the back, mirroring the organization of the basilar membrane along the cochlea (see Figure 4.21).

identify the sound (what it is) are handled by areas in the lower (ventral) part of the temporal lobe, and this pathway may overlap with the ventral visual pathway.

Perceiving Sound Sources

Just as visual objects can be identified based on their shape and size, their colour and location, sound sources—like voices, or clapping hands, or a guitar—have particular perceptual attributes that allow you to identify them. These include loudness, pitch, timbre, and location.

Perceiving Pitch, Loudness, Timbre, and Location

Your brain uses patterns of action potentials in the auditory nerve to perceive sounds in terms of their loudness, pitch, timbre, and location. How does it accomplish this?

- The perceptual attribute of loudness is signalled by the total amount of activity in hair cells, rather like how brightness of light is signalled by the total amount of activity in photoreceptors.

- How we perceive pitch (of, for example, musical notes or voices) has been studied extensively, and it seems to depend on two aspects of auditory nerve activity (Plack, 2018a). First, you learned that different frequencies stimulate neural signals at specific places along the basilar membrane. This provides a **place code**, whereby *the brain uses information about the relative activity of hair cells (e.g., which ones are more active and which are less active) across the whole basilar membrane to help determine the pitch you hear.* Second, you learned that the hair cell hairs move in time with the incoming sound wave, so auditory nerve axons fire synchronously with the sound-wave peaks, which happen regularly at the sound's repetition rate. This provides a **temporal code**, whereby *the brain uses the timing of the action potentials in the auditory nerve to help determine the pitch you hear.*

- Timbre depends, in part, on the relative amounts of different frequency components in a sound and thus, like pitch, depends on the relative activity of hair cells across the whole basilar membrane.

- How we determine the location of a sound has also been studied extensively (Plack, 2018b). Rather like depth in vision, location is not coded in the sensory information directly; we have to work it out using different cues. As in vision, there are monaural (one ear) and binaural (two ear) cues to location. First, your pinnas aren't simply handy places to hook your sunglasses. Their intricate folds alter sound, emphasizing some frequency components over others, depending on where the sound is coming from. You have learned to interpret these changes as indicating a sound's location. Second, the speed of sound is much slower than the speed of light. Sounds arrive a little sooner at the ear nearer to the source than at the far ear. This time-difference is effective for indicating the location of lower frequency components of a sound even when it is as brief as a few microseconds, which occurs when the sound source is nearly straight ahead (i.e., is only a little off to one side). Third, the higher-frequency components of a sound are more intense in the ear closer to the sound than in the farther ear, because the listener's head blocks higher frequencies. The further a sound is off to the side, the greater the between-ear difference in level of these high frequency components.

  Sometimes you may find yourself turning your head from side to side to localize a sound. By doing this, you are changing the relative intensity and timing of sound waves arriving in your ears and collecting better information about the likely source of the sound. Turning your head also allows you to use your eyes to locate the source of the sound—and, as you learned earlier in this chapter, your visual system is much better at pinpointing the location of things than your auditory system is.

place code The process by which the brain uses information about the relative activity of hair cells (e.g. which ones are more active and which are less active) across the whole basilar membrane to help determine the pitch you hear.

temporal code The process whereby the brain uses the timing of the action potentials on the auditory nerve to help determine the pitch you hear.

Organizing Sound Features into Sources

In hearing, your auditory system first analyzes a complex sound wave (like that resulting from the mixture of different coffee shop sounds) into its component frequencies, which activate different regions of the basilar membrane and auditory nerve. Then the brain has to figure out which frequency components belong together in a single source (perceptual grouping) and which frequency components belong to different sources (perceptual segregation). Just as in vision, our perceptual system organizes and automatically delivers to us the interpretation that is the simplest and most meaningful, consistent with expectations based on experience.

The Gestalt rules you learned about earlier in this chapter also apply to sound. For example, sounds that are *similar* in the physical properties of frequency or intensity, or that are similar in the perceptual attributes of loudness, pitch, timbre, or location are grouped together into one source, as are sounds that occur close together in time (proximity). Furthermore, sounds that start together and stop together (like the different frequencies emitted simultaneously by a musical instrument, or a voice) are perceived as coming from the same source.

Hearing Loss

In broad terms, hearing loss has two main causes. *Conductive hearing loss* arises because the eardrum or ossicles are damaged to the point that they cannot conduct sound waves effectively to the cochlea. The cochlea itself, however, is normal, making this a kind of "mechanical problem" with the moving parts of the ear: the hammer, anvil, stirrup, or eardrum. In many cases, medication or surgery can correct the problem. Sound amplification from a hearing aid also can improve hearing through conduction via the bones around the ear directly to the cochlea.

Sensorineural hearing loss is caused by damage to the cochlea, the hair cells, or the auditory nerve, and it happens to almost all of us as we age. It has two main effects: sensitivity decreases so sounds have to be more intense to be heard; and acuity decreases so sounds smear together on the basilar membrane, making voices harder to understand, especially if other sounds are present. Sensorineural hearing loss has many causes, including genetic disorders, premature birth, infections, medications, accumulated damage from sound exposure (particularly intense sounds), and aging (these last two causes are hard to tease apart since older people have been exposed to sound for longer). Hearing aids amplify sounds, helping with decreased sensitivity, but, unlike glasses, which can fix blurry vision, hearing aids cannot fix the acuity problem.

When hearing loss is severe, a *cochlear implant* may restore some hearing. A cochlear implant is an electronic device that replaces the function of the hair cells (Waltzman, 2006). The external parts of the device include a microphone and a processor (about the size of a USB key), worn behind the ear, and a small, flat, external transmitter that sits on the scalp behind the ear. The implanted parts include a receiver just inside the skull and a thin wire containing electrodes inserted into the cochlea to stimulate the auditory nerve. Sound picked up by the microphone is transformed into electric signals by the processor, which is essentially a small computer. The signal is transmitted to the implanted receiver, which activates the electrodes in the cochlea. Cochlear implants are now in routine use and can improve hearing to the point that the wearer can understand speech, although background sound still poses a real challenge. (See Hot Science: Big Technology in Little Ears for how cochlear implants are allowing babies to learn the language of their parents and caregivers.)

Hot Science ⦁ Big Technology in Little Ears

More than 90% of infants who are born deaf are born to hearing parents, who communicate using spoken language, which their babies can't hear. Such children are vulnerable to language disorders, because communication with parents and other caregivers in the first few years is crucial if language is to develop normally, as you'll learn in the Development chapter. Some of these parents compensate by learning a signed language, such as American Sign Language, so they can teach it to, and use it with, their baby. If you have ever attempted to learn a second language, you know how difficult it can be—now imagine trying to learn a second language while also caring for a new baby! This requires an extraordinary commitment of time and resources that is sometimes not practical or even possible. Furthermore, even if parents and child successfully learn to use a sign language together, what about that child's relationships with grandparents, family friends, and others in their hearing community?

Giving a baby cochlear implants allows parents and others to interact with the child using their native spoken language, enabling language development. Newborn hearing screening programs now mean that deafness can be identified at birth, and babies are routinely implanted around their first birthday, and sometimes even earlier. This is a serious decision for parents to make; although it enables hearing, cochlear implantation does have risks, such as a higher chance of the child

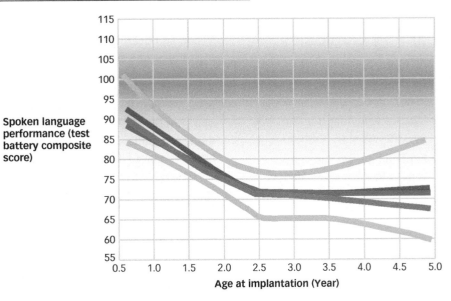

contracting a serious infection such as meningitis. So, it might make sense to wait as long as possible, perhaps until the child is 4 or 5 or even older, before giving the child an implant. Are there any disadvantages to language development, if a family waits to have their child implanted?

Researchers tested 160 children implanted between the ages of 6 months and 5 years of age, to examine the link between spoken language ability, assessed using a battery of tests and age at which the implant was received (Tobey et al., 2013). The results are shown in the figure. The performance of normally hearing children, adjusted for age, is given by the grey-shaded rectangle (average of 100, with two-thirds of children falling between scores of 85

and 115). Whether the kids were tested at 4, 5, and 6 years after implantation didn't really affect the data: the blue (4 years), maroon (5 years), and green (6 years) lines, showing average performance at these test time points, are all pretty similar to each other. What mattered was age at implantation. The orange lines are the upper and lower bounds of performance for 95% of the kids implanted at each age. The children implanted at the youngest ages (starting from the left side of figure) show average performance in the normal range (grey, shaded rectangle), whereas those implanted at older ages, over 1½ years or so, do not. This suggests that there are disadvantages to waiting to have a child implanted at an older age.

Build to the Outcomes

1. What are the three properties of sound waves?
2. Why does one note sound so different on a piano and on a guitar?
3. What are the roles of the outer, middle, and inner parts of the ear in hearing?
4. How do hair cells in the ear enable us to hear?
5. How does the frequency of a sound wave relate to what we hear?
6. How do we determine the location of a sound?
7. In which types of hearing loss does sound amplification help?
8. What causes sensorineural hearing loss?

The Body Senses: More Than Skin Deep

Learning Outcomes

- Describe how touch receptors transmit messages to the brain.

- Discuss why pain is a psychological perception.

- Explain how we use various senses to keep our balance.

Vision and hearing provide information about the world at a distance. By responding to light and sound energy in the environment, these "distance" senses allow us to identify and locate the objects and people around us. In comparison, the body senses, also called *somatosenses* (*soma* from the Greek for "body"), are up close and personal. **Haptic perception** is the *active exploration of the environment by touching and grasping objects with our hands.* We use sensory receptors in our muscles, tendons, and joints as well as a variety of receptors in our skin to get a feel for the world around us (see **FIGURE 4.23**).

Sensing Touch

Touch begins with the transduction of skin sensations into neural signals. Receptors located under the skin's surface enable us to sense pain, pressure, texture, pattern, or vibration against the skin (see Figure 4.23). Each receptor is sensitive to a small patch of skin, its **tactile receptive field**. These specialized cells work together to provide a rich tactile (from Latin, "to touch") experience when you explore an object by feeling it or attempting to grasp it. In addition, *thermoreceptors,* nerve fibres that sense cold and warmth, respond when your skin temperature changes. All these sensations blend seamlessly together in perception, of course, but detailed physiological studies have successfully isolated the parts of the touch system (Hollins, 2010; Johnson, 2002).

There are three important principles regarding the neural representation of the body's surface. First, the left half of the body is represented in the right half of the brain and vice versa. Second, refer back to Figure 3.16 in the Neuroscience and Behaviour chapter; you'll recall that different locations on the body send sensory signals to different locations in the somatosensory cortex in the parietal lobe. Just as more of the visual brain is devoted to foveal vision, where acuity is greatest, more of the tactile brain is devoted to parts of the skin surface where sensitivity to fine spatial detail (acuity) is greatest. Regions such as the fingertips and lips have high acuity,

haptic perception The active exploration of the environment by touching and grasping objects with our hands.

tactile receptive field A small patch of skin that relates information about pain, pressure, texture, pattern, or vibration to a receptor.

Figure 4.23

Touch Receptors Specialized sensory neurons form distinct groups of haptic receptors that detect pressure, temperature, and vibrations against the skin. Each touch receptor responds to stimulation within its receptive field, and the long axons enter the brain via the spinal or cranial nerves. Pain receptors populate all body tissues that feel pain; they are distributed around bones and within muscles and internal organs, as well as under the skin surface. Sensory signals on the body travel to the somatosensory cortex.

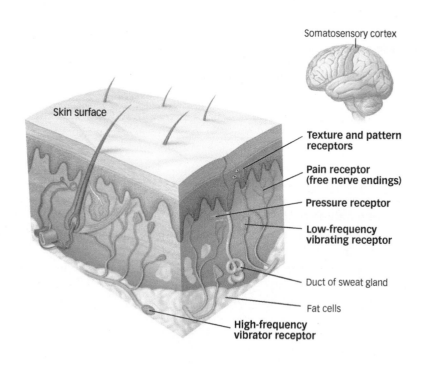

Somatosensory cortex

Skin surface

Texture and pattern receptors

Pain receptor (free nerve endings)

Pressure receptor

Low-frequency vibrating receptor

Duct of sweat gland

Fat cells

High-frequency vibrator receptor

whereas acuity is lower in areas such as the calf. You can test this yourself: if you put two chopsticks together so that their tips are about a centimetre apart, and gently press them into the skin of your fingertip, you should be able to tell that there are two tips, not one. If you do the same on your calf, how far apart do the tips have to be before you can tell them apart? Third, there is mounting evidence for a distinction between "what" and "where" pathways in touch, analogous to similar distinctions we've already considered for vision and hearing. The "what" system for touch provides information about the properties of surfaces and objects; the "where" system provides information about the location in external space that is being touched or a location on the body that is being stimulated (Lederman & Klatzky, 2009).

Sensing Pain

Does the possibility of a life free from pain seem appealing? Although pain is arguably the least pleasant of sensations, this aspect of touch is among the most important for survival: Pain indicates damage or potential damage to the body. Without the ability to feel pain, we might ignore infections, broken bones, or serious burns. Congenital insensitivity to pain, a rare inherited disorder that specifically impairs pain perception, is more of a curse than a blessing: Children who experience this disorder often accidentally mutilate themselves (e.g., biting into their tongues or gouging their skin while scratching) and are at increased risk of dying in childhood (Nagasako, Oaklander, & Dworkin, 2003).

Tissue damage is transduced by the free nerve endings shown in Figure 4.23 that sense painful stimuli. In addition, researchers have distinguished between fast-acting *A-delta fibres,* which are axons that transmit initial sharp pain, and slower *C fibres,* which are axons that transmit the longer-lasting, duller persistent pain. If you were running barefoot outside and stubbed your toe against a rock, you would first feel a sudden stinging pain transmitted by A-delta fibres that would die down quickly, only to be replaced by the throbbing but longer-lasting pain carried by C fibres.

Perceiving Pain

As you'll remember from the chapter on Neuroscience and Behaviour, the pain-withdrawal reflex is coordinated by the spinal cord. No brainpower is required when you touch a hot stove; you retract your hand almost instantaneously. But neural signals for pain—such as wrenching your elbow as you brace yourself to keep from falling—travel to two distinct areas in the brain and evoke two distinct psychological experiences (see **FIGURE 4.24**) (Treede et al., 1999). One pain pathway sends signals to the somatosensory cortex, identifying where the pain is occurring and what sort of pain it is (sharp, burning, or dull). The second pain pathway sends signals to the motivational and emotional centres of the brain, such as the hypothalamus and amygdala, as well as to the frontal lobe. This is the aspect of pain that is unpleasant and motivates us to escape from, or relieve, the pain.

Interestingly, fMRI has demonstrated that some of the brain areas that respond to our own physical pain, particularly in the frontal lobe, also respond when we witness others experiencing pain and feel concern for them (Lamm et al., 2011). Precisely what common features of experiencing pain and witnessing pain result in this overlap (Zaki et al., 2016), and whether or not the overlap extends to perceiving the *social pain* (such as embarrassment or social exclusion) of others, are areas of active research (Bruneau, Jacoby, & Saxe, 2015).

Pain typically feels as though it comes from the site of the tissue damage that caused it. If you burn your finger, you will perceive the pain as originating there. But we have pain receptors in many areas besides the skin, such as around bones and within muscles and internal organs as well. When pain originates internally,

A rather unimposing geodesic dome sits on the floor of the Exploratorium, a world-renowned science museum in San Francisco. Called the Tactile Dome, it was created in 1971 by August Coppola (brother of the director Francis Ford Coppola and father of the actor Nicolas Cage) and Carl Day, who wanted to create an environment in which only haptic perception could be used. The inside of the dome is pitch black; visitors must crawl, wiggle, slide, and otherwise navigate the unfamiliar terrain using only their sense of touch. How would you feel being in that environment for an hour or so?

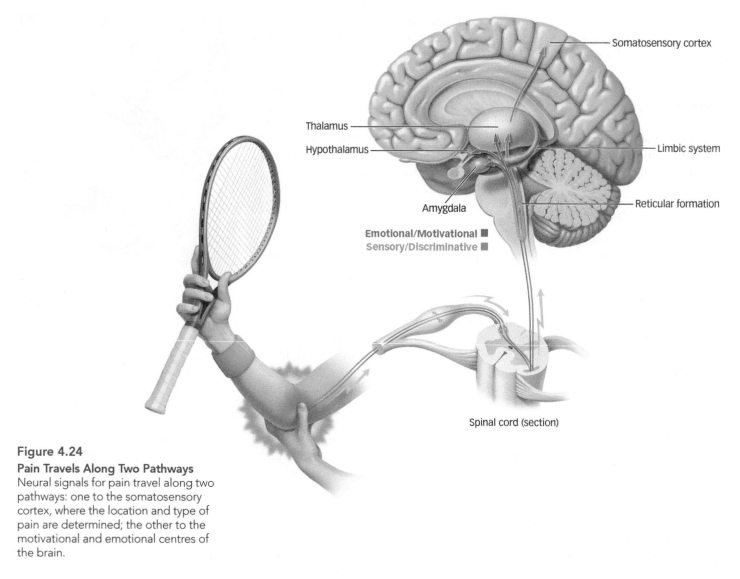

Somatosensory cortex

Thalamus

Hypothalamus

Amygdala

Limbic system

Reticular formation

Emotional/Motivational ■
Sensory/Discriminative ■

Spinal cord (section)

Figure 4.24

Pain Travels Along Two Pathways
Neural signals for pain travel along two
pathways: one to the somatosensory
cortex, where the location and type of
pain are determined; the other to the
motivational and emotional centres of
the brain.

referred pain Feeling of pain on the
surface of the body, but due to internal
damage; occurs because sensory
information from internal and external
areas converges on the same nerve cells
in the spinal cord.

gate-control theory A theory of
pain perception based on the idea that
signals arriving from pain receptors in
the body can be stopped, or *gated*,
by interneurons in the spinal cord via
feedback from the skin or from the
brain.

in a body organ, for instance, we can feel it on the surface of the body. This kind
of **referred pain** occurs when *sensory information from internal and external areas
converges on the same nerve cells in the spinal cord.* One common example is a heart
attack: Victims often feel pain radiating from the left arm rather than from inside
the chest.

Pain intensity cannot always be predicted solely from the extent of the injury that
causes the pain (Keefe, Abernathy, & Campbell, 2005). For instance, *turf toe* sounds
like the mildest of ailments; it is pain at the base of the big toe as a result of bending
or pushing off repeatedly, as a runner or football player might do during a sporting
event. This small-sounding injury in a small area of the body can nonetheless sideline
an athlete for a month with considerable pain. On the other hand, you've probably
heard a story or two about someone treading bone-chilling water for hours on end, or
dragging their shattered legs a mile down a country road to seek help after a tractor
accident, or performing some other incredible feat despite searing pain and extensive
tissue damage. Pain type and pain intensity show a less-than-perfect correlation, a
fact that intrigues researchers.

One influential account of pain perception is known as the **gate-control theory**,
which holds that *signals arriving from pain receptors in the body can be stopped, or
gated, by interneurons in the spinal cord via feedback from the skin or from the brain*
(Melzack & Wall, 1965). Pain can be gated by the skin receptors, for example, by

rubbing the affected area. Rubbing your stubbed toe activates neurons that "close the gate" to stop pain signals from travelling to the brain. Pain can also be gated from the brain, which can modulate the activity of pain-transmission neurons.

The brain's feedback to the spinal cord comes from a region in the midbrain called the *periaqueductal grey* (PAG). Under extreme conditions, such as high stress, naturally occurring endorphins can activate the PAG to send inhibitory signals to neurons in the spinal cord that then suppress pain signals to the brain, thereby modulating the experience of pain. The PAG also responds to the action of opiate drugs, such as morphine.

A different kind of feedback signal from the brain can *increase* the sensation of pain. This system is activated by events such as infection and learned danger signals. When we are quite ill, what we otherwise might experience as mild discomfort can feel quite painful. This pain facilitation signal presumably evolved to motivate people who are ill to rest and avoid strenuous activity, allowing their energy to be devoted to healing.

Although some details of the gate-control theory of pain have been challenged, a key concept underlying the theory—that perception is a two-way street—has broad implications. The senses feed information such as pain sensations to the brain, which processes these sensory data into perceptions, as you have learned in this chapter. Perceptual psychologists call control of perception by senses *bottom-up control*. But, as you have also learned, perceptions are not just shaped by sense data—they are affected by your knowledge, by your expectations, and by other factors such as your mood and motivational state. Visual illusions and the Gestalt principles of closure (filling in what isn't really there) provide some examples. This kind of *top-down control* also explains how the brain influences the experience of touch and pain (Kucyi & Davis, 2015; Wager & Atlas, 2013).

Body Position, Movement, and Balance

Shut your eyes and notice the position of your legs and feet, and arms and hands. Can you feel where they are in space? This is a sense that isn't often talked about—**proprioception** is *your sense of body position*. After all, you need some way to sense your position in physical space other than moving your eyes constantly to see the location of your limbs. Your perception of the position (and movement) of your torso, limbs, hands, and feet in space depend on stimulation of receptors in the muscles, tendons, and joints of your body, whereas information about which way is up and about head movement (to serve your balance) originates in the inner ear.

Sensory receptors provide the information we need to perceive the position and movement of our limbs, head, and body. These receptors also provide feedback about whether we are performing a desired movement correctly and how resistance from held objects may be influencing the movement. For example, when you swing a baseball bat, the weight of the bat affects how your muscles move your arm, as well as the sensation when the bat hits the ball. You can use muscle, joint, and tendon feedback about how your arms actually moved to improve performance through learning.

Maintaining balance depends primarily on the **vestibular system**, *the three fluid-filled semicircular canals and adjacent organs located next to the cochlea in each inner ear* (see Figure 4.20). The semicircular canals are arranged in three perpendicular orientations and studded with hair cells that detect movement of the fluid when the head moves or accelerates. The bending of the hairs of these cells generates activity in the vestibular nerve that is then conveyed to the brain. This detected motion enables us to maintain our balance (Lackner & DiZio, 2005).

Vision also helps us keep our balance. If you see that you are swaying relative to a vertical orientation, such as the walls of a room, you adjust your posture to keep from falling over. Psychologists have experimented with this visual aspect of balance by placing people in rooms where the floor is stationary but the walls sway forwards

RICK RYCROFT/AP IMAGES

Hitting a ball with a bat or racquet provides feedback about where your arms and body are in space, as well as how the resistance of these objects affects your movement and balance. Successful athletes, such as Serena Williams, have particularly well-developed body senses.

proprioception Your sense of bodily position.

vestibular system The three fluid-filled semicircular canals and adjacent organs located next to the cochlea in the inner ear.

and backwards (Bertenthal, Rose, & Bai, 1997; Lee & Aronson, 1974). If the room sways enough, people—particularly small children—will topple over as they try to compensate for what their visual system is telling them. When a mismatch between the information provided by visual cues and vestibular feedback occurs, motion sickness can result. Remember this the next time you try reading in the back seat of a moving car!

Build to the Outcomes

1. What is the difference between vision and hearing, and the somatosenses?
2. What types of physical energy stimulate touch receptors?
3. Why might discriminating spatial detail be important for fingertips and lips?
4. What is the role of the various parts of the skin in touch and pain?
5. Why does rubbing an injured area sometimes help alleviate pain?
6. What is the vestibular system?
7. Why is it so hard to stand on one foot with your eyes closed?

The Chemical Senses: Adding Flavour

Learning Outcomes

- Describe how odourant molecules are converted into neural impulses.
- Explain the importance of smell in personal and social experiences.
- Describe how taste sensations are converted into neural impulses by the tongue.
- Explain what senses contribute to the perception of flavour.

Vision and hearing begin with physical energy in the world—light and sound waves—and touch is activated by physical energy in or on the body surface. The last set of senses we'll consider rely on chemicals that enter our mouths (the sense of taste, or gustation) or float into our noses (the sense of smell, or olfaction). Some have called smell "taste at a distance," and taste and smell have a common, impossibly ancient, evolutionary basis that allowed our distant ancestors, the earliest cells, to sense beneficial and dangerous chemicals in the seawater around them. Smell and taste combine to produce the perceptual experience we call *flavour.*

Sense of Smell

Olfaction is the least understood sense, and one of the most fascinating. Recall from the Neuroscience and Behaviour chapter that whereas the other senses connect first to the thalamus, olfactory information enters the frontal lobe, amygdala, hippocampus, and other forebrain structures almost directly. This anatomy indicates that smell has a close relationship with areas involved in emotional and social behaviour, as well as memory. Smell can signal whether a creature is unfriendly or friendly (or is a potential mate); whether a substance is probably delicious or is more likely to be toxic and dangerous; and it has an uncanny ability to remind us of long-ago places and people. Helen Keller, a blind and deaf writer (1880–1968), said: "Smell is a potent wizard that transports you across thousands of miles and all the years you have lived. The odors of fruits waft me to my southern home, to my childhood frolics in the peach orchard. Other odors, instantaneous and fleeting, cause my heart to dilate joyously or contract with remembered grief" (Keller, 1908, p. 75).

Countless substances release odours into the air. Like natural lights and sounds are mixtures of wavelengths and frequencies, most natural odours (such as baking bread, coffee, and farts) are actually mixtures of different *odourant molecules.* Odourants are chemicals such as hydrogen sulfide (which on its own smells like rotten eggs), benzaldehyde (which smells like almonds), and vanillin (which gives vanilla its distinctive smell). Odourant molecules make their way into our noses, drifting in on the air we breathe. Situated along the top of the nasal cavity, shown in **FIGURE 4.25,**

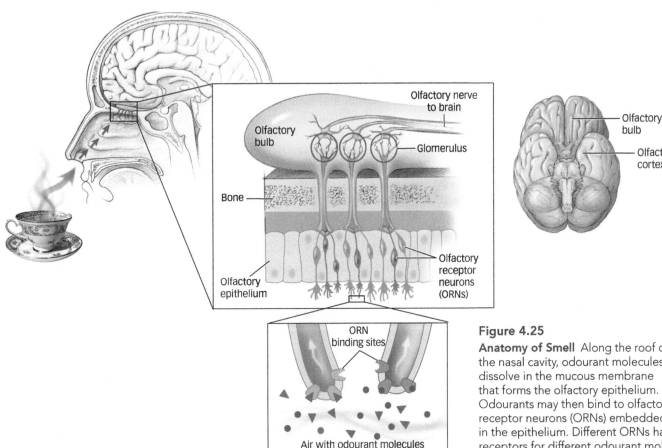

Figure 4.25

Anatomy of Smell Along the roof of the nasal cavity, odourant molecules dissolve in the mucous membrane that forms the olfactory epithelium. Odourants may then bind to olfactory receptor neurons (ORNs) embedded in the epithelium. Different ORNs have receptors for different odourant molecules. Once activated, ORNs relay action potentials to the olfactory bulb, located just beneath the frontal lobes. The output from the olfactory bulb is to axons that form the olfactory nerve, which projects directly into the brain.

is a mucous membrane called the *olfactory epithelium,* which contains about 10 million **olfactory receptor neurons (ORNs)**, *receptor cells that transduce odourant molecules into neural impulses* (Dalton, 2003). Each ORN has receptors that bind to some odourants but not to others, as if the receptor is a lock and the odourant is the key (see Figure 4.25). Groups of ORNs sensitive to the same odourant send their axons from the olfactory epithelium into the **olfactory bulb**, *a brain structure located above the nasal cavity beneath the frontal lobes.* Humans possess about 350 different ORN types that permit us to discriminate up to one trillion (!) odours through the unique patterns of neural activity each odour evokes (Bushdid et al., 2014). This setup is similar to our ability to see a vast range of colours through only a small number of retinal receptor cell types or to feel a range of skin sensations through only a handful of touch-receptor cell types.

Dogs and mice have up to 900 different ORN types, and up to 100 times as many ORNs; they have a correspondingly sharpened *olfactory sensitivity* (ability to detect odours) and *olfactory acuity* (ability to discriminate among odours). Nevertheless, humans are sensitive to the smells of some substances in extremely small concentrations. For example, we can sense mercaptan, a chemical compound that is added to natural gas to help detect gas leaks, at a concentration of just 0.0003 part per million. By contrast, acetone (nail polish remover), something most people regard as pungent, can be detected only if its concentration is 15 parts per million or greater.

Perceiving Smell

Just as the output of the final stage of retinal processing is retinal ganglion cell axons that form the optic nerve, the output of the final stage of olfactory bulb processing is in the axons that form the olfactory nerve. The olfactory bulb sends outputs to

olfactory receptor neurons (ORNs) Receptor cells that transduce odourant molecules into neural impulses.

olfactory bulb A brain structure located above the nasal cavity beneath the frontal lobes.

various centres in the brain, including the parts that are responsible for controlling basic drives, emotions, and memories. The relationship between smell and emotion explains why smells can have immediate, strongly positive or negative effects on us. Fortunately, sensory adaptation is at work when it comes to smell, just as it is with the other senses. Whether the associations are good or bad, after just a few minutes the smell fades. Smell adaptation makes sense: It allows us to detect new odours that may require us to act, but after that initial evaluation has occurred, it may be best to reduce our sensitivity to allow us to detect other smells.

Our experience of smell is determined not only by bottom-up influences, such as odourant molecules binding to sites on ORNs, but also by top-down influences, such as our previous experiences with an odour (Gottfried, 2008; Rolls, 2015). Consistent with this idea, people rate the identical odour as more pleasant when it is paired with an appealing verbal label such as *cheddar cheese* rather than an unappealing one such as *body odour* (de Araujo et al., 2005; Herz & von Clef, 2001).

Smell may also play a role in social behaviour. Other animals can detect odours from **pheromones**, *biochemical odourants emitted by other members of an animal's species that can affect its behaviour or physiology*. Pheromones play an important role in reproductive and social behaviour in insects and in several mammalian species, including mice, dogs, and primates (Brennan & Zufall, 2006). What about humans?

Since humans are mammals, it is possible, perhaps even probable, that we, like other mammals, both secrete and sense pheromones. However, evidence for human pheromones from well-conducted and replicable experiments is scant (Wyatt, 2015). Studies have tended to use small sample sizes (which raises the risk of a result that isn't true) and they have not been successfully replicated. In order to prove the existence of human pheromones, we would first want to observe a behavioural or physiological response that could be attributed to an airborne chemical, then identify and synthesize the active molecule, and ultimately confirm that humans have a specialized cell receptor and transduction mechanism for that chemical (Wyatt, 2015). Tristan Wyatt, a zoologist at Oxford University, points out, "we become smellier in puberty, apart from other changes in sexual development (the growth of more visible secondary sexual characteristics such as hair in our armpits and groins, for example). The changes in the smells we give off before and after puberty might give us clues as to what molecules might be signals" (Wyatt, 2015).

Some evidence for a human pheromone comes from breastfeeding mothers and babies. Nursing in mammals is known to depend on smell (Schaal & Al Aïn, 2014). Human mothers produce a substance from the glands around their nipples. If this secretion, taken from a lactating mother, is put under the nose of a 3-day-old newborn (not their own child), the baby responds with head and mouth movements consistent with nursing behaviour (Doucet et al., 2009). This suggests that one of the compounds in the secreted substance might be a pheromone that encourages nursing behaviour in babies; indeed, the degree to which first-time mothers secrete this substance seems to correlate with the rate of weight gain in the babies in the first days after birth (Doucet et al., 2012).

Sense of Taste

The sense of taste evolved from the sense of smell. Whereas smell analyzes the chemical composition of things outside the body, taste does the same for things taken into the body. One of the primary responsibilities of the chemical sense of taste is identifying things that are bad for you—as in poisonous and lethal. Some aspects of taste perception are genetic, such as an aversion to extreme bitterness (which may indicate poison), and some are learned, such as an aversion to a particular food that once caused nausea. In either case, the direct contact between the tongue and possible foods allows us to anticipate whether something will be harmful or nutritious.

The taste system contains just five main types of taste receptors, corresponding to five primary taste sensations: salt, sour, bitter, sweet, and *umami* (savoury). The first

pheromones Biochemical odourants emitted by other members of an animal's species that can affect its behaviour or physiology.

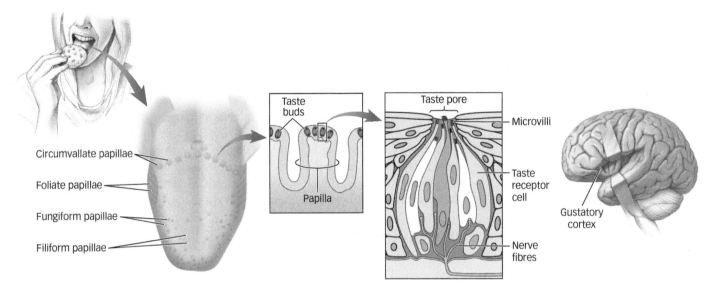

Figure 4.26

A Taste Bud (a) Taste buds stud the bumps (papillae) on the tongue, shown here, as well as the back, sides, and roof of the mouth. (b) Each taste bud contains a range of receptor cells that respond to varying chemical components of foods called tastants. (c) Tastant molecules dissolve in saliva and stimulate the microvilli that form the tips of the taste receptor cells. Each taste bud connects to a cranial nerve that carries taste information to the brainstem, then to the thalamus, and then to the primary gustatory cortex in the brain's frontal lobe.

four are probably familiar to you, but *umami* may not be. The umami receptor was discovered by Japanese scientists who attributed its stimulation to the rich savoury tastes evoked by foods containing a high concentration of protein, such as miso, meats, and cheeses like blue cheese or old cheddar (Yamaguchi, 1998).

The tongue is covered with thousands of small bumps, called *papillae,* which are easily visible to the naked eye. Within most of the papilla are hundreds of **taste buds**, *the organs of taste transduction* (see **FIGURE 4.26**). The mouth contains 5,000 to 10,000 taste buds fairly evenly distributed over the tongue, the roof of the mouth, and the upper throat (Bartoshuk & Beauchamp, 1994; Halpern, 2002). Each taste bud contains 50 to 100 taste receptor cells, and receptors for the different tastes are also pretty evenly distributed—any taste can be detected by any part of the tongue. Taste perception fades with age (Methven et al., 2012; Barragán et al., 2018). This may help explain why young children seem to be "fussy eaters," since they may have greater sensitivity to taste sensations.

Each taste bud contains several types of taste receptor cells whose tips, called *microvilli,* react with *tastant molecules* in food. Just as odours are typically composed of a mixture of odourants, foods usually contain a mixture of tastants. Salt receptors are most strongly activated by sodium chloride (table salt). Sour receptors respond to acids, such as vinegar or lime juice. Bitter, sweet, and umami receptors also respond to tastants that give rise to these tastes in food.

Recent research suggests that there may be a sixth basic taste, fat, that is elicited by fatty acids and is distinct from the five primary taste sensations (Running, Craig, & Mattes, 2015). The researchers noted that the sensation people experience in response to fatty acids is not necessarily consistent with expectations of "fattiness," so they proposed a new word for this taste sensation: *oleogustus.* (*Oleosus* is Latin for "fatty" or "oily," and *gustus* signifies "taste.")

DATA VISUALIZATION

Finding the Best Way to Describe Experimental Data Go to launchpadworks.com.

Taste experiences vary widely across individuals. About 50% of people report a mildly bitter taste in caffeine, saccharine, certain green vegetables, and other substances, whereas roughly 25% report no bitter taste. Members of the first group are called *tasters;* members of the second group are called *nontasters.* The remaining 25% of people are *supertasters,* who report that such substances, especially dark green vegetables, are extremely bitter, to the point of being inedible (Bartoshuk, 2000). Because supertasters tend to avoid fruits and vegetables that contain tastes they experience as extremely bitter,

Fussy eater? Or just too sensitive? Our taste perception declines with age. That can make childhood a time of either savoury delight or sensory overload of taste.

LESLIE BANKS/ISTOCKPHOTO

taste buds The organ of taste transduction.

"We would like to be genetically modified to taste like Brussels sprouts."

they may be at increased health risk for diseases such as colon cancer. On the other hand, because they also tend to avoid fatty, creamy foods, they tend to be thinner and may have decreased risk of cardiovascular disease (Bartoshuk, 2000). There is evidence that genetic factors contribute to individual differences in taste perception (Kim et al., 2003), but much remains to be learned about the specific genes that are involved (Hayes et al., 2008; Reed, 2008).

People also vary dramatically in their tolerance of food textures and spicy food. Some people hate the texture of eggplant ("slimy!") or of tapioca pudding ("frogspawn!"). Some people really love hot spicy food; others do not. In addition to the five (or six) tastes to which receptors in the mouth are sensitive, information about the temperature, spiciness, and texture (mouthfeel) of food is transduced and relayed from the mouth via touch receptors and thermoreceptors such as those discussed earlier.

Perceiving Flavour

Of course, the variety of taste experiences greatly exceeds the five basic taste receptors discussed here. Any food molecules dissolved in saliva evoke specific, combined patterns of activity in the five taste receptor types. Furthermore, taste isn't quite the same thing as flavour. Taste is the contribution made by receptors in your mouth alone. Taste and smell collaborate to produce the complex perception of flavour. Have you ever eaten a meal while suffering through a severe head cold that blocks your sense of smell? In that case, food tastes bland, right?

Food perception is multisensory, involving taste, smell, and texture. Do these different sensory channels combine in one area of the brain to produce the perception of flavour? Or are they each processed separately, such that perception of flavour depends on binding information across systems, rather like visual perception depends on binding information from dorsal and ventral streams? Neuroimaging, particularly fMRI, has been very helpful in letting us get "inside the heads" (literally!) of people while they're eating, to begin to answer this question. This work indicates that areas sensitive to odours from food include not only primary olfactory cortex (near the amygdala) but also primary gustatory (taste) cortex (in the frontal lobe) and the mouth region of primary somatosensory cortex (in the parietal lobe) (Cerf-Ducastel & Murphy, 2001; Small et al., 2005). Indeed, primary olfactory and gustatory cortex are interconnected, and gustatory cortex passes "taste" information directly to olfactory cortex.

One last point about flavour: it is a very easy thing to learn about! In the Learning chapter, we discuss how a strong, lifelong aversion to a food (e.g., hummus) can develop after only one nasty experience with a tainted bowl of it. This makes sense—if something is bad for you once, it probably will be again, and you learn quickly to stay well away. Learned preferences in food are also important in determining flavour, and they depend dramatically on culture and experience. "It's an acquired taste" is something you may have heard about a food you find disgusting: acquired tastes include toasted grasshoppers in Mexico (chapulines); fermented fish in Scandinavia (lutefisk, hakarl, surströmming), fetal ducks still in the shell in Vietnam and Philippines (balut)—even cheese in many parts of the world. One person's "yecch!" is another person's "yummy!"

The full experience of a wine's flavour cannot be appreciated without a finely trained sense of smell. When you raise a glass to your mouth, odourants from the wine enter the nasal cavity via the nostrils, as well as through the back of the throat. Wine aficionados are taught to pull air in over wine held in the mouth: It allows the wine's odourant molecules to enter the nasal cavity through this "back door." The same happens with other foods.

Build to the Outcomes

1. How do the chemical senses differ from the other senses?
2. What roles do various parts of the nose play in the sense of smell?
3. How many odours can humans smell?
4. How do taste and smell contribute to flavour?
5. What is the relationship between smell and emotion?
6. How does smell contribute to social behaviour?
7. Why is the sense of taste an evolutionary advantage?
8. What are the five main types of taste receptors?
9. What are tasters, nontasters, and supertasters?

Chapter Review

Sensation and Perception Are Distinct Activities

- Sensation and perception are critical to survival. Sensation is the simple stimulation of a sense organ, whereas perception organizes, identifies, and interprets sensation at the level of the brain.

- All of our senses depend on the process of transduction, which converts physical signals from the environment into neural signals carried by sensory neurons into the central nervous system.

- In the 19th century, researchers developed psychophysics, an approach to studying perception that measures the strength of a stimulus and an observer's sensitivity to that stimulus. Psychophysicists have developed procedures for measuring an observer's absolute threshold, which is the smallest intensity needed to just barely detect a stimulus, as well as the just noticeable difference (JND), which is the smallest change in a stimulus that can just barely be detected.

- Signal detection theory allows researchers to distinguish between an observer's perceptual sensitivity to a stimulus and criteria for making decisions about that stimulus.

- Sensory adaptation occurs when sensitivity to unchanging stimulation declines over time.

Visual Pathways: Connections Between the Eye and the Brain

- Light travels in waves that pass through several layers in the eye to reach the retina. In a process called accommodation, the eye muscles change the shape of the lens to focus objects at different distances on the retina.

- Two types of photoreceptor cells in the retina transduce light into neural impulses: cones operate under normal daylight conditions and sense colour; rods are active under low-light conditions for night vision. The neural impulses travel along the optic nerve to the brain.

- The retina consists of several layers; the innermost consists of retinal ganglion cells (RGCs) that collect and send signals to the brain. Bundles of RGCs axons form the optic nerve.

- Information encoded by the retina travels to the brain along the optic nerve, which connects to the lateral geniculate nucleus in the thalamus and then to the primary visual cortex (area V1) in the occipital lobe.

- Light striking the retina causes a specific pattern of response in each of three cone types that are critical to colour perception: short-wavelength (bluish) light, medium-wavelength (greenish) light, and long-wavelength (reddish) light. The overall pattern of response across the three cone types results in a unique code for each colour.

- The shapes of objects are perceived when different neurons in the visual cortex fire in response to different orientations of the object's edges.

- Two functionally distinct pathways project from the occipital lobe to visual areas in other parts of the brain. The ventral stream travels into the lower levels of the temporal lobes and includes brain areas that represent an object's shape and identity. The dorsal stream goes from the occipital lobes to the parietal lobes, connecting with brain areas that identify the location and motion of an object.

Visual Perception: Recognizing What We See

- Illusory conjunctions occur when features from separate objects are mistakenly combined. According to feature-integration theory, attention provides the glue necessary to bind features together. The parietal lobe is important for attention and contributes to feature binding.

- Some regions in the occipital and temporal lobes respond selectively to specific object categories, supporting the modular view that specialized brain areas detect particular classes of objects, such as faces or houses or body parts.

- The principle of perceptual constancy holds that even as sensory signals change, perception remains consistent.

- Gestalt principles of perceptual grouping, such as simplicity, closure, and continuity, govern how features are perceptually organized into meaningful objects.

- Depth perception depends on monocular cues, such as familiar size and linear perspective; binocular cues, such as retinal disparity; and motion-based cues, which are based on the movement of the head over time.

- We experience a sense of motion through the differences in the strengths of output from neurons sensitive to motion in different directions. These processes can give rise to illusions such as apparent motion.

- Change blindness and inattentional blindness occur when we fail to notice visible and even salient features of our environment, emphasizing that our conscious visual experience depends on focused attention.

Hearing: More Than Meets the Ear

- Perceiving sound depends on three physical dimensions of a sound wave: The frequency of the sound wave determines the pitch; the amplitude determines the loudness; and differences in the complexity, or mix, of frequencies determine the sound quality, or timbre.

- Auditory pitch perception begins in the ear, which consists of an outer ear that funnels sound waves towards the middle ear, which in turn sends the vibrations to the inner ear, which contains the cochlea. Action potentials from the inner ear travel along an auditory pathway through the thalamus to the primary auditory cortex (area A1) in the temporal lobe.

- Auditory perception depends on both a place code and a temporal code. Our ability to localize sound sources depends critically on the placement of our ears on opposite sides of the head.

- Some hearing loss can be overcome with hearing aids that amplify sound. When hair cells are damaged, a cochlear implant is a possible solution.

The Body Senses: More Than Skin Deep

- Sensory receptors on the body send neural signals to locations in the somatosensory cortex, a part of the parietal lobe, which the brain translates as the sensation of touch. Different locations on the body project sensory signals to different locations in the cortex, and some areas are better at discriminating details.

- The experience of pain depends on signals that travel along two distinct pathways. One pathway sends signals to the somatosensory cortex to indicate the location and type of pain, and another sends signals to the emotional centres of the brain that result in unpleasant feelings that we wish to escape. The experience of pain varies across individuals, which is explained by bottom-up and top-down aspects of the gate-control theory of pain.

- Balance and acceleration depend primarily on the vestibular system but are also influenced by vision.

The Chemical Senses: Adding Flavour

- Our experience of smell, or olfaction, is associated with odorant molecules that bind to sites on specialized olfactory receptors, which converge within the olfactory bulb. The olfactory bulb in turn sends signals to parts of the brain that control drives, emotions, and memories, which helps to explain why smells can have immediate and powerful effects on us.

- Smell is also involved in social behaviour, as illustrated by pheromones, which are related to reproductive behaviour and sexual responses in several species.

- Sensations of taste depend on taste buds, which are distributed across the tongue, the roof of the mouth, and the upper throat, as well as on taste receptors which correspond to the five primary taste sensations of salt, sour, bitter, sweet, and umami.

- Taste experiences vary widely across individuals and, like olfactory experiences, depend in part on cognitive influences.

Key Concept Quiz

1. Sensation involves _____, whereas perception involves _____.
   a. organization; coordination
   b. stimulation; interpretation
   c. identification; translation
   d. comprehension; information

2. What process converts physical signals from the environment into neural signals carried by sensory neurons into the central nervous system?
   a. representation
   b. identification
   c. propagation
   d. transduction

3. The smallest intensity needed to just barely detect a stimulus is called
   a. proportional magnitude.
   b. the absolute threshold.
   c. the just noticeable difference.
   d. Weber's law.

4. Signal detection theory is helpful because it allows researchers to distinguish between:
   a. sensitivity and acuity
   b. perceptual sensitivity and decision criterion
   c. signals and noise
   d. expectations and knowledge.

5. Light striking the retina, causing a specific pattern of response in the three cone types, leads to our ability to see
   a. motion.
   b. colours.
   c. depth.
   d. shadows.

6. Which part of the brain is the location of the primary visual cortex, where encoded information is systematically mapped into a representation of the visual scene?
   a. the thalamus
   b. the lateral geniculate nucleus
   c. the fovea
   d. area V1

7. Our ability to combine visual details so that we perceive unified objects is explained by
   a. feature-integration theory.
   b. illusory conjunction.
   c. synesthesia.
   d. ventral and dorsal streaming.

8. What kind of cues are relative size and linear perspective?
   a. motion-based
   b. binocular
   c. monocular
   d. template

9. The placement of our ears on opposite sides of the head is crucial to our ability to
   a. localize sound sources.
   b. determine pitch.
   c. judge intensity.
   d. recognize complexity.

10. What best explains why smells can have immediate and powerful effects?
    a. the involvement in smell of brain centres for emotions and memories
    b. the vast number of olfactory receptor neurons we have
    c. our ability to detect odours from pheromones
    d. the fact that different odorant molecules produce varied patterns of activity

Don't stop now! Quizzing yourself is a powerful study tool. Go to LaunchPad to access the LearningCurve adaptive quizzing system and your own personalized learning plan. Visit launchpadworks.com.

Key Terms

sensation (p. 124)

perception (p. 124)

transduction (p. 125)

sensory adaptation (p. 125)

psychophysics (p. 126)

absolute threshold (p. 126)

sensitivity (p. 127)

acuity (p. 127)

just noticeable difference (JND) (p. 127)

Weber's law (p. 127)

signal detection theory (p. 128)

visual acuity (p. 130)

retina (p. 131)

accommodation (p. 131)

cones (p. 131)

rods (p. 131)

fovea (p. 132)

blind spot (p. 134)

area V1 (p. 134)

colour-opponent system (p. 136)

visual receptive field (p. 136)

binding problem (p. 138)

parallel processing (p. 139)

illusory conjunction (p. 139)

feature-integration theory (p. 139)

attention (p. 139)

perceptual constancy (p. 141)

perceptual contrast (p. 141)

perceptual organization (p. 141)

monocular depth cues (p. 144)

binocular disparity (p. 146)

apparent motion (p. 148)

spatial acuity (p. 148)

temporal acuity (p. 148)

multisensory (p. 148)

ventriloquist illusion (p. 148)

change blindness (p. 148)

inattentional blindness (p. 149)

pitch (p. 151)

loudness (p. 151)

timbre (p. 152)

cochlea (p. 153)

basilar membrane (p. 153)

travelling wave (p. 153)

inner hair cells (p. 153)

area A1 (p. 154)

place code (p. 155)

temporal code (p. 155)

haptic perception (p. 158)

tactile receptive field (p. 158)

referred pain (p. 160)

gate-control theory (p. 160)

proprioception (p. 161)

vestibular system (p. 161)

olfactory receptor neurons (ORNs) (p. 163)

olfactory bulb (p. 163)

pheromones (p. 164)

taste buds (p. 165)

Changing Minds

1. A friend of yours is taking a class in medical ethics. "We discussed a tough case today," she says. "It has to do with a patient who's been in a vegetative state for several years, and the family has to decide whether to take him off life support. The doctors say he has no awareness of himself or his environment, and he is never expected to recover. But when light is shone in his eyes, his pupils contract. That shows he can sense light, so he has to have some ability to perceive his surroundings, doesn't he?" Without knowing any of the details of this particular case, how would you explain to your friend that a patient might be able to sense light but not perceive it? What other examples from the chapter could you use to illustrate the difference between sensation and perception?

2. In your philosophy class, the professor discusses the proposition that "perception is reality." From the point of view of philosophy, reality is the state of things as they actually exist, whereas perception is how they appear to the observer. What does psychophysics have to say about this issue? What are three ways in which sensory transduction can alter perception, causing perceptions that may differ from absolute reality?

3. A friend comes across the story of an American soldier, Sergeant Leroy Petry, who saved the lives of two of his men. The soldiers were in a firefight in Afghanistan when a live grenade landed at their feet; Petry picked up the grenade and tried to toss it away from the others, but it exploded, destroying his right hand. According to the news report, Petry didn't initially feel any pain; instead, he set about applying a tourniquet to his own arm while continuing to shout orders to his men as the firefight continued. "That's amazingly heroic," your friend says, "but that bit about not feeling the pain—that's crazy. He must just be so tough that he kept going despite the pain." What would you tell your friend? How can the perception of pain be altered?

Answers to Key Concept Quiz

1. b; 2. d; 3. b; 4. b; 5. b; 6. d; 7. a; 8. c; 9. a; 10. a.

LaunchPad features the full e-book of *Psychology*, the LearningCurve adaptive quizzing system, videos, and a variety of activities to boost your learning. Visit LaunchPad at launchpadworks.com.

Consciousness

UNCONSCIOUSNESS IS SOMETHING YOU DON'T REALLY appreciate until you need it. Belle Riskin needed it one day on an operating table, when she awoke just as doctors were pushing a breathing tube down her throat. She felt she was choking, but she couldn't see, breathe, scream, or move. Unable even to blink an eye, she couldn't signal to the surgeons that she was conscious. "I was terrified. Why is this happening to me? Why can't I feel my arms? I could feel my heart pounding in my head. It was like being buried alive, but with somebody shoving something down your throat," she explained later. "I knew I was conscious, that something was going on during the surgery. I had just enough awareness to know I was being intubated" (Groves, 2004).

How could this happen? Anaesthesia for surgery is supposed to leave the patient unconscious, "feeling no pain," yet in this case—and in about 1 in every 20,000 surgical procedures (Pandit et al., 2014)—the patient regains consciousness at some point and even remembers the experience. Some patients remember pain; others remember the clink of surgical instruments in a pan or the conversations of doctors and nurses. This is not how modern surgery is supposed to go, but the problem arises because muscle-relaxing drugs are used to keep the patient from moving involuntarily and making unhelpful contributions to the operation. Yet when the drugs that are given to induce unconsciousness fail to do their job, the patient with extremely relaxed muscles is unable to show or tell doctors that there is a problem.

Waking up in the middle of surgery sounds pretty rough all by itself, but it can cause additional complications. The conscious patient could become alarmed and emotional during the operation, spiking blood pressure and heart rate to dangerous levels. Awareness also might lead to later emotional problems. Fortunately, there are new methods of monitoring wakefulness by measuring the electrical activity of the brain. One system uses

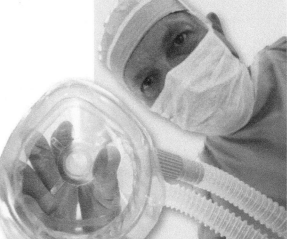

When it's time for surgery, it's great to be unconscious.

sensors attached to the patient's head and gives readings on a scale from 0 (no electrical activity in the brain) to 100 (fully alert), providing a kind of "consciousness meter."

Anesthesiologists using this index deliver anesthetics to keep the patient around 50 for general anaesthesia during surgery. They have found that this system reduces postsurgical reports of consciousness and memory of the surgical experience (Myles et al., 2004), and that letting patients fall below 45 on this index for prolonged periods increases the risk of negative postoperative outcomes, including death (Kertai et al., 2010). One of these devices in the operating room might have helped Belle Riskin settle into the unconsciousness she so sorely needed.

MOST OF THE TIME, OF COURSE, CONSCIOUSNESS IS SOMETHING we cherish. How else could we experience a favourite work of art, the familiar lyrics of our favourite song, the taste of chocolate, or the touch of a loved one's hand? **Consciousness** is *a person's subjective experience of the world and the mind.* Although you might think of consciousness as simply "being awake," the defining feature of consciousness is experience, which you have when you're awake or when you're having a vivid dream. Conscious experience is essential to what it means to be human. The anesthesiologist's dilemma in trying to monitor Belle Riskin's consciousness is a stark reminder, though, that it is impossible for one person to experience another's consciousness.

consciousness A person's subjective experience of the world and the mind.

How can this private world be studied? We'll begin by examining consciousness directly, trying to understand what it is like and how it compares with the mind's *unconscious* processes. Then we'll examine how it departs from normal by exploring altered states: sleep and dreams, intoxication with alcohol and other drugs, hypnosis, and disorders of consciousness resulting from brain damage. Like the traveller who learns the meaning of *home* by roaming far away, we can learn the meaning of *consciousness* by exploring its exotic variations.

The Mysteries of Consciousness

Learning Outcomes

- Explain the two dimensions of mind perception.
- Outline the relationship between brain activity, thinking, and acting.

What does it feel like to be you right now? It probably feels as though you are somewhere inside your head, looking out at the world through your eyes. You can notice the position of your body in your chair as you read or the sounds in the room when you orient yourself towards them. If you shut your eyes, you may be able to imagine things in your mind, even though all the while thoughts and feelings come and go, passing through your imagination. But where are "you," really? And how is it that this theatre of consciousness gives you a view of some things in your world and your mind but not others? The theatre in your mind doesn't have seating for more than one, making it difficult to share what's on your mental screen.

Other sciences, such as physics, chemistry, and biology, have the great luxury of studying *objects,* things that we all can see. Psychology studies objects, too, looking at people and their brains and behaviours, but it has the unique challenge of also trying to make sense of *subjects.* A physicist is not concerned with what it is like to be a neutron, but psychologists hope to understand what it is like to be a human—that is, they seek to understand the subjective perspectives of the people whom they study.

Psychologists hope to include an understanding of **phenomenology**, *how things seem to the conscious person,* in their understanding of mind and behaviour. After all, consciousness is an extraordinary human property. But including phenomenology in psychology brings up mysteries pondered by great thinkers almost since the

phenomenology The study of how things seem to the conscious person.

beginning of thinking. Let's look at two of the more vexing mysteries of consciousness: the problem of other minds and the mind–body problem.

The Problem of Other Minds

One great mystery in psychology is called the **problem of other minds**, *the fundamental difficulty we have in perceiving the consciousness of others*. How do you know that anyone else is conscious? They tell you that they are conscious, of course, and are often willing to describe in depth how they feel, how they think, what they are experiencing, and how good or how bad it all is. But perhaps they are just *saying* these things. There is no clear way to distinguish a conscious person from someone who might do and say all the same things as a conscious person but who is *not* conscious. Philosophers have called this hypothetical nonconscious person a *zombie*, in reference to the living-yet-dead creatures of horror films (Chalmers, 1996). A philosopher's zombie could talk about experiences ("The lights are so bright!") and even seem to react to them (wincing and turning away) but might not be having any inner experience at all. No one knows whether there could be such a zombie, but then again, because of the problem of other minds, none of us will ever know for sure that another person is *not* a zombie.

Even the consciousness meter used by anesthesiologists falls short. It certainly doesn't give the anesthesiologist any special insight into what it is like to be the patient on the operating table; it only predicts whether patients will *say* they were conscious. We simply lack the ability to directly perceive the consciousness of others. In short, *you* are the only thing in the universe that you will ever truly know what it is like to be.

The problem of other minds also means there is no way you can tell if another person's experience of anything is at all like yours. Although you know what the colour red looks like to you, for instance, you cannot know whether it looks the same to other people. Maybe they're seeing what you see as blue and just calling it red in a consistent way. Of course, most people have come to trust each other in describing their inner lives, reaching the general assumption that other human minds are pretty much like their own. But they don't know this for a fact, and they can't know it firsthand.

How do people perceive other minds? Researchers conducting a large online survey asked people to compare the minds of 13 different targets—such as a baby, chimp, or robot—on 18 different mental capacities, such as feeling pain, pleasure, hunger, and consciousness (see **FIGURE 5.1**) (Gray, Gray, & Wegner, 2007).

problem of other minds The fundamental difficulty we have in perceiving the consciousness of others.

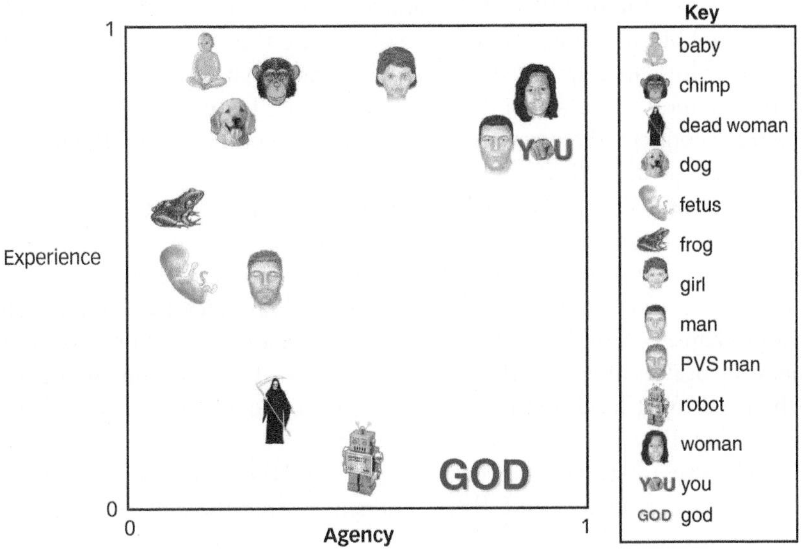

Figure 5.1
Dimensions of Mind Perception
When participants judged the mental capacities of 13 targets, two dimensions of mind perception were discovered (Gray et al., 2007). Participants perceived minds as varying in the capacity for experience (such as abilities to feel pain or pleasure) and in the capacity for agency (such as abilities to plan or exert self-control). They perceived normal adult humans (male, female, or "you," the respondent) to have minds on both dimensions, whereas other targets were perceived to have reduced experience or agency. The man in a persistent vegetative state ("PVS man"), for example, was judged to have only some experience and very little agency. MACMILLAN LEARNING

Key
- baby
- chimp
- dead woman
- dog
- fetus
- frog
- girl
- man
- PVS man
- robot
- woman
- you
- god

Respondents who were judging the mental capacity to feel pain, for example, compared pairs of targets: Is a frog or a dog more able to feel pain? Is a baby or a robot more able to feel pain? When the researchers examined all the comparisons on the different mental capacities with the computational technique of factor analysis (see the Intelligence chapter), they found two dimensions of mind perception. People judge minds according to the capacity for *experience* (such as the ability to feel pain, pleasure, hunger, consciousness, anger, or fear) and the capacity for *agency* (such as the ability for self-control, planning, memory, or thought).

As shown in Figure 5.1, respondents rated some targets as having little experience or agency (the dead woman), others as having experiences but little agency (the baby), and yet others as having both experience and agency (adult humans). Still others were perceived to have agency without experiences (the robot, God). The perception of minds, then, involves more than just whether something has a mind. People appreciate that minds both have experiences and lead us to perform actions.

Ultimately, the problem of other minds is a problem for psychological science. As you'll remember from the Methods chapter, the scientific method requires that any observation made by one scientist should, in principle, be available for observation by any other scientist. But if other minds aren't observable, how can consciousness be a topic of scientific study? One radical solution is to eliminate consciousness from psychology entirely and follow the other sciences into total objectivity by renouncing the study of *anything* mental. This was the solution offered by behaviourism, and it turned out to have its own shortcomings, as you saw in the Psychology: Evolution of a Science chapter. Despite the problem of other minds, modern psychology has embraced the study of consciousness. The astonishing richness of mental life simply cannot be ignored.

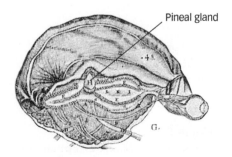

Pineal gland

Figure 5.2

Seat of the Soul Descartes imagined that the seat of the soul—and consciousness—might reside in the pineal gland located behind the third ventricle of the brain. This original drawing from Descartes (1662) shows the pineal gland (H) nicely situated for a soul, right in the middle of the brain.
SCIENCE SOURCE

mind–body problem The issue of how the mind is related to the brain and body.

The Mind–Body Problem

Another mystery of consciousness is the **mind–body problem**, *the issue of how the mind is related to the brain and body.* The French philosopher and mathematician René Descartes (1596–1650) is famous for proposing, among other things, that the human body is a machine made of physical matter but that the human mind or soul is a separate entity made of a "thinking substance." He suggested that the mind has its effects on the brain and body through the pineal gland, a small structure located near the centre of the brain (see **FIGURE 5.2**). In fact, the pineal gland is not even a nerve structure but rather is an endocrine gland, and thus is poorly equipped to serve as a centre of human consciousness. We now know that, far from the tiny connection between mind and brain in the pineal gland that Descartes proposed, the mind and brain are connected everywhere to each other. In other words, "the mind is what the brain does" (Minsky, 1986, p. 287).

But Descartes was right in pointing out the difficulty of reconciling the physical body with the mind. Most psychologists assume that mental events are intimately tied to brain events, such that every thought, perception, or feeling is associated with a particular pattern of activation of neurons in the brain (see the Neuroscience and Behaviour chapter). Thinking about a particular person, for instance, occurs with a unique array of neural connections and activations. If the neurons repeat that pattern, then you must be thinking of the same person; conversely, if you think of the person, the brain activity occurs in that pattern.

One telling set of studies, however, suggests that the brain's activities *precede* the activities of the conscious mind. Researchers measured the electrical activity in the

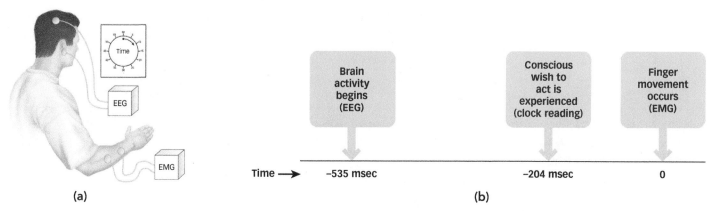

(a)

| Brain activity begins (EEG) | Conscious wish to act is experienced (clock reading) | Finger movement occurs (EMG) |

Time ⟶   −535 msec   −204 msec   0

(b)

Figure 5.3

The Timing of Conscious Will (a) In Benjamin Libet's experiments, the participant was asked to move fingers at will while watching a dot move around the face of a clock to mark the moment at which the action was consciously willed. Meanwhile, EEG sensors timed the onset of brain activation, and EMG sensors timed the muscle movement. (b) The experiment showed that brain activity (EEG) precedes the willed movement of the finger (EMG) but that the reported time of consciously willing the finger to move follows the brain activity.

brains of volunteers by placing sensors on their scalps as they repeatedly decided when to move a hand (Libet, 1985). Participants were also asked to indicate exactly when they consciously chose to move by reporting the position of a dot moving rapidly around the face of a clock just at the point of the decision (**FIGURE 5.3a**). As a rule, the brain begins to show electrical activity about half a second before a voluntary action (535 milliseconds, to be exact) and about one-third of a second (331 milliseconds) before the person's conscious decision to move (as shown in Figure 5.3b). The feeling that you are consciously willing your actions, it seems, may be a result rather than a cause of your brain activity. Although your personal intuition is that you *think* of an action and *then* do it, these experiments suggest that your brain is getting started before *either* the thinking or the doing, paving the way for both thought and action (Haggard & Tsakiris, 2009; Wegner, 2002).

Consciousness has its mysteries, but psychologists like a challenge. Over the past several decades, psychologists have tried to solve this problem by working with computer scientists and others to attempt to create machines that can mimic human consciousness and intelligence. This work has led to the creation of the field of "artificial intelligence" (AI), which refers to the study and use of machines (including computers) that can independently operate in ways that mimic human intelligence and interactions. AI is used increasingly in our daily lives in ways that attempt to mimic the behaviour of human agents—such as through Apple's "Siri" and Amazon's "Alexa." Siri and Alexa already act more like humans than the zombies mentioned earlier (who mostly just grunt and moan), but are they really displaying human-like intelligence?

Back in 1950, Alan Turing famously proposed that to conclude that a machine can exhibit human-like intelligence, it must be able to act in ways that are indistinguishable from humans. His proposed method of demonstrating this, which has come to be called the "Turing test," is by having a person observe a conversation between a person and a computer, such as by reading out their responses to questions posed in that conversation. The machine/computer is said to have passed the test if the observer is unable to accurately determine which is the machine/computer and which is the human.

Over the past several decades, psychological scientists have continued to work towards the development of increasingly sophisticated AI methods in an effort to better understand, and mimic, various aspects of human consciousness, such as the abilities for learning, decision making, attention, memory, and planning for the future (Hassabis et al., 2017). Although there is still much progress to be made, since researchers may not yet be able to know exactly how consciousness

Do Alexa or Siri have human consciousness? How could you find out?

arises from the brain, this has not prevented them from also collecting people's reports of conscious experiences and learning how these reports reveal the nature of consciousness.

Build to the Outcomes

1. Why is it difficult to study consciousness?
2. How does the capacity for experience differ from the capacity for agency?
3. Which comes first: brain activity or conscious thinking?

The Nature of Consciousness

Learning Outcomes

- Describe the four basic properties of consciousness.
- Compare the three levels of consciousness.
- Explain why we can't always control our conscious thoughts.

How would you describe your own consciousness? Researchers examining people's descriptions suggest that consciousness has four basic properties (intentionality, unity, selectivity, and transience); that it occurs on three different levels; and that it includes a range of different contents. Let's examine each of these points in turn.

Four Basic Properties

Researchers have identified four basic properties of consciousness, based on people's reports of conscious experience.

1. Consciousness has *intentionality,* which is the quality of being directed towards an object. Consciousness is always *about* something. Despite all the lush detail you see in your mind's eye, the kaleidoscope of sights and sounds and feelings and thoughts, the object of your consciousness at any one moment is focused on just a small part of all of this. To describe how this works, psychologists refer to three other properties of consciousness: unity, selectivity, and transience.

2. Consciousness has *unity,* which is resistance to division, or the ability to integrate information from all of the body's senses into one coherent whole (see **FIGURE 5.4**). As you read this book, your five senses are taking in a great deal of

Figure 5.4

Bellotto's *Dresden* and Closeup
(*left*) The people on the bridge in the distance look very finely detailed in *View of Dresden with the Frauenkirche* by Bernardo Bellotto (1721–1780). However, when you examine the detail closely (*right*), you discover that the people are made of brushstrokes merely *suggesting* people—an arm here, a torso there. Consciousness produces a similar impression of "filling in," as it seems to consist of extreme detail even in areas that are peripheral (Dennett, 1991).

information. Your eyes are scanning lots of black squiggles on a page (or screen) while also sensing an enormous array of shapes, colours, depths, and textures in your periphery; your hands are gripping a heavy book (or computer); your butt and feet may sense pressure from gravity pulling you against a chair or floor; and you may be listening to music or talking in another room while smelling the odour of freshly made popcorn (or your roommate's dirty laundry). Although your body is constantly sensing an enormous amount of information from the world around you, your brain—amazingly—integrates all of this information into the experience of one unified consciousness (or two, in the case of the split-brain patients described in the Neuroscience and Behaviour chapter).

3. Consciousness has *selectivity,* the capacity to include some objects but not others. You may recall from the Sensation and Perception chapter that, while binding the many sensations around you into a coherent whole, your mind must make decisions about which pieces of information to include and which to exclude. This property is shown through studies of **dichotic listening**, *in which people wearing headphones hear different messages in each ear.* Research participants were instructed to repeat aloud the words they heard in one ear while a different message was presented to the other ear (Cherry, 1953). As a result of focusing on the words they were supposed to repeat, participants noticed little of the second message, often not even realizing that at some point it changed from English to German! So consciousness *filters out* some information. At the same time, participants did notice when the voice in the unattended ear changed from a man's to a woman's, suggesting that the selectivity of consciousness can also work to *tune in* other information.

How does consciousness decide what to tune in and what to filter out? The conscious system is most inclined to select information of special interest to the listener. For example, in what has come to be known as the **cocktail-party phenomenon**, *people tune in one message even while they filter out others nearby.* In the dichotic listening situation, for example, research participants are especially likely to notice if their own name is spoken into the unattended ear (Moray, 1959). Perhaps you, too, have noticed how abruptly your attention is diverted from whatever conversation you are having when someone else within earshot at the party mentions your name. Selectivity is not only a property of waking consciousness: the mind works this way in other states. People are more sensitive to their own name than to others' names, for instance, even during sleep (Oswald, Taylor, & Triesman, 1960). This is why, when you are trying to wake someone, it is best to use the person's name.

4. Consciousness has *transience,* or the tendency to change. Consciousness wiggles and fidgets like a toddler in the seat behind you on an airplane. The mind wanders not just sometimes, but incessantly, from one "right now" to the next "right now" and then on to the next (Wegner, 1997). William James, whom you met way back in the Psychology: Evolution of a Science chapter, famously described consciousness as a "stream" (James, 1890). Prose written in the "stream of consciousness" style illustrates the whirling, chaotic, and constantly changing flow of consciousness. Perhaps because it resembles our own experience of consciousness, this style is widely used, appearing in classic books such as James Joyce's *Ulysses* (1922):

> *I was a Flower of the mountain yes when I put the rose in my hair like the Andalusian girls used or shall I wear a red yes and how he kissed me under the Moorish wall and I thought well as well him as another and then I asked him with my eyes to ask again yes and then he asked me would I yes to say yes my mountain flower and first I put my arms around him yes and drew him down to me so he could feel my breasts all perfume yes and his heart was going like mad and yes I said yes I will Yes*

IMAGE SOURCE PLUS/ALAMY

Participants in a dichotic listening experiment hear different messages played to the right and left ears and may be asked to "shadow" one of the messages by repeating it aloud.

dichotic listening A task in which people wearing headphones hear different messages in each ear.

cocktail-party phenomenon A phenomenon in which people tune in one message even while they filter out others nearby.

The contents of our conscious thoughts are constantly changing, like water in a stream. This might be why we so enjoy the "stream of consciousness" presentation of words used in most popular songs. Black Thought of the musical group The Roots provided a classical example of such a presentation in a radio and online 10-minute freestyle performance so impressive that it was recommended listening by the *New York Times*.

Full consciousness involves a consciousness of oneself, such as thinking about the act of driving while driving a car. How is this different from self-consciousness?

PHOTOMONDO/PHOTODISC/GETTY IMAGES

minimal consciousness A low-level kind of sensory awareness and responsiveness that occurs when the mind inputs sensations and may output behaviour.

full consciousness A level of consciousness in which you know and are able to report your mental state.

Whether or not you have encountered books or stories using stream of consciousness writing, you almost certainly have encountered it in poetry and musical lyrics. For instance, think about the lyrics to your favourite song. Whether you currently are listening to Post Malone, Imagine Dragons, Nas, Ariana Grande, The Roots, or someone else, chances are you will find a lot of songs using a stream of consciousness style. Our own stream of consciousness may flow in this way partly because of the limited capacity of the conscious mind. We humans can hold only so much information in mind at one time, after all, so when we select more information, some of what is currently there must disappear. As a result, our focus of attention keeps changing.

Levels of Consciousness

Consciousness can also be understood as having levels, ranging from minimal consciousness to full consciousness to self-consciousness. These levels of consciousness would probably all register as "conscious" on that wakefulness meter for surgery patients you read about at the beginning of this chapter. The healthy levels of consciousness that psychologists distinguish among involve different qualities of awareness of the world and of the self.

In its minimal form, consciousness is just a connection between the person and the world. When you sense the sun coming in through the window, for example, you might turn towards the light. Such **minimal consciousness** is *a low-level kind of sensory awareness and responsiveness that occurs when the mind inputs sensations and may output behaviour* (Armstrong, 1980). This kind of sensory awareness and responsiveness could even happen when someone pokes you while you're asleep and you turn over. Something seems to register in your mind, at least in the sense that you experience it, but you may not think at all about having had the experience. It could be that animals or, for that matter, even plants can have this minimal level of consciousness. But because of the problem of other minds and the notorious reluctance of animals and plants to talk to us, we can't know for sure that they *experience* the things that make them respond. At least in the case of humans, we can safely assume that there is something it "feels like" to be them and that when they're awake, they are at least minimally conscious.

Human consciousness is often more than minimal, of course, but what exactly gets added? Consider the glorious feeling of waking up on a spring morning as rays of sun stream across your pillow. It's not just that you are having this experience: Being fully conscious means that you are also *aware* that you are having this experience. The critical ingredient that accompanies **full consciousness** is that you *know and are able to report your mental state*. That's a subtle distinction: Being fully conscious means that you are aware of having a mental state while you are experiencing the mental state itself. When you have a hurt leg and mindlessly rub it, for instance, your pain may be minimally conscious. After all, you seem to be experiencing pain because you have acted and are indeed rubbing your leg. It is only when you realize that it hurts, though, that you become fully conscious of the pain.

Have you ever been driving a car and suddenly realized that you don't remember the past 15 minutes of driving? Chances are that you were not unconscious, but instead minimally conscious. When you are completely aware and thinking about your driving, you have moved into the realm of full consciousness. Full consciousness involves not only thinking about things but also thinking about the fact that you are thinking about things (Jaynes, 1976).

Full consciousness involves a certain consciousness of oneself; the person notices the self in a particular mental state. ("Here I am, reading this sentence.") However, this is not quite the same thing as *self*-consciousness. Sometimes consciousness is entirely flooded with the self. ("Not only am I reading this sentence, but I have a pimple on the end of my nose today that makes me feel like I'm guiding a sleigh.") Self-consciousness focuses on the self to the exclusion of almost everything else. William James (1890) and other theorists have suggested that **self-consciousness** is yet another *distinct level of consciousness in which the person's attention is drawn to the self as an object* (Morin, 2006). Most people report experiencing such self-consciousness when they are embarrassed; when they find themselves the focus of attention in a group; when someone focuses a camera on them; or when they are deeply introspective about their thoughts, feelings, or personal qualities.

Self-consciousness brings with it a tendency to evaluate yourself and notice your shortcomings. Looking in a mirror, for example, is all it takes to make people evaluate themselves—thinking not just about their looks, but also about whether they are good or bad in other ways. People go out of their way to avoid mirrors when they've done something they are ashamed of (Duval & Wicklund, 1972). Self-consciousness can certainly spoil a good mood, so much so that a tendency to be chronically self-conscious is associated with depression (Pyszczynski, Holt, & Greenberg, 1987). However, because it makes them self-critical, the self-consciousness that results when people see their own mirror images can make them briefly more helpful, more cooperative, and less aggressive (Gibbons, 1990). Perhaps everyone would be a bit more civilized if mirrors were held up for them to see themselves as objects of their own scrutiny.

Most animals can't follow this path to civilization. The typical dog or cat seems mystified by a mirror, ignoring it or acting as though there is some other critter back there. However, chimpanzees that have spent time with mirrors sometimes behave in ways that suggest they recognize themselves in a mirror. To examine this, researchers painted an odourless red dye over the eyebrow of an anesthetized chimp and then watched when the awakened chimp was presented with a mirror (Gallup, 1977). If the chimp interpreted the mirror image as a representation of some other chimp with an unusual approach to cosmetics, we would expect it just to look at the mirror or perhaps to reach towards it. But the chimp reached towards its *own eye* as it looked into the mirror—not the mirror image—suggesting that it recognized the image as a reflection of itself.

Versions of this experiment have now been repeated with many different animals, and it turns out that, like humans, animals such as chimpanzees and orangutans (Gallup, 1997), possibly dolphins (Reiss & Marino, 2001), and maybe even elephants (Plotnik, de Waal, & Reiss, 2006) and magpies (Prior, Schwartz, & Güntürkün, 2008) recognize their own mirror images. Dogs, cats, crows, monkeys, and gorillas have been tested, too, but don't seem to know they are looking at themselves. Even humans don't have self-recognition right away. Infants don't recognize themselves in mirrors until they've reached about 18 months of age (Lewis & Brooks-Gunn, 1979). The experience of self-consciousness, as measured by self-recognition in mirrors, is limited to a few animals and to humans only after a certain stage of development.

Self-consciousness is a curse and a blessing. Looking in a mirror can make people evaluate themselves on deeper attributes such as honesty as well as superficial ones such as appearance.

A chimpanzee tried to wipe off the red dye on its eyebrow in the Gallup experiment. This suggests that some animals recognize themselves in the mirror.

OKAY, LET ME THINK ALOUD FOR A MINUTE.

THE COST WILL BE $3,000...LOSING FOCUS...MONKEYS ARE FUNNY...MY TONGUE IS DIGESTING IN MY MOUTH.

THAT DIDN'T HELP AS MUCH AS I HAD HOPED.

self-consciousness A distinct level of consciousness in which the person's attention is drawn to the self as an object.

Disorders of Consciousness

So far, we've been talking about normal levels of consciousness during wakefulness, in people with a normal brain. Severe brain damage, caused by illness or accident, can produce a transient or permanent change in the maximum level of consciousness that an individual is capable of. Improvements in medical intensive care over the last few decades mean that more patients are surviving severe brain injury but, as a result, experience either a temporary or permanent *disorder of consciousness*, in which the patient is not able to demonstrate either full consciousness or self-consciousness. Doctors distinguish different *disorders of consciousness*, which can either be transient stages on the road to recovery, or be more permanent conditions.

1. Patients in a *coma* look, at first glance, like they are deeply asleep. Their eyes are closed, they do not communicate, and they do not respond when someone shouts their name or pinches their toe (either of which would generally waken a sleeping person!). They seem to be completely unaware.

2. Patients in a *vegetative state* alternate between an eyes-open and an eyes-closed state: There are regular periods of time in which they appear to be "awake." Patients may move their limbs and eyes, swallow, smile, cry, grunt, moan, or scream, but—and this is key to the diagnosis—none of these behaviours are *produced reliably in response to external stimulation*. In other words, no evidence exists that patients are aware of themselves or their surroundings, as demonstrated by reliable, purposeful responding to sensory stimulation (such as being touched or hearing their name called).

3. Patients in a *minimally conscious state* can respond reliably but somewhat inconsistently to sensory stimulation.

Locked-in syndrome is a rare condition in which patients are fully aware but cannot demonstrate it because they cannot move any voluntary muscles. This is not a disorder of consciousness, but it can easily be mistaken for one. The French journalist Jean-Dominique Bauby wrote *The Diving Bell and the Butterfly* after he suffered a massive stroke that left him with locked-in syndrome. The book was written by Bauby blinking his left eyelid, which he did four hours a day for ten months. Patients with locked-in syndrome can, like Bauby, sometimes move their eyes voluntarily up and down, and they can use this movement to communicate. Some locked-in patients do not have even this minimal control of voluntary muscles.

How do doctors determine whether a patient is aware? Determining level of awareness is difficult, because disorders of consciousness can be transient—as a patient is recovering from brain damage—or they can be permanent. It can be very difficult to observe when a severely injured patient is recovering awareness. Traditionally, physicians observe a patient's behaviour and judge whether the patient is repeatedly able to respond to commands (like "raise your left arm"), or to the sound of his or her name being spoken. If the patient has trouble controlling their body, however, this test can be misleading.

Recently, brain-imaging methods have given researchers and physicians a direct window into brain activity (see The Real World: Anyone for Tennis?). Brain activity is, after all, the wellspring of behaviour—for the left arm to be raised, there first must be a specific pattern of arm-raising activity in the brain. We now know that, out of every 100 people diagnosed as being in a vegetative state using traditional bedside assessment, between 10 and 40 will turn out to be conscious to some degree when they are assessed using these more sensitive measures (Monti et al., 2010), and about a third of patients diagnosed as minimally conscious may be fully conscious (Cruse et al., 2012).

The Real World | Anyone for Tennis?

In 1999, Scott Routley was seriously injured in a car accident that resulted from him pulling out in front of a Sarnia, Ontario, police cruiser. For 12 years, he was considered by doctors to be in a vegetative state: showing periods of apparent eyes-open wakefulness, but without any signs of awareness of himself or his environment and without any apparent ability to communicate. Definitely not (it was thought) in any state to play tennis. This view of Scott changed dramatically when he underwent a series of fMRI scans at the University of Western Ontario.

For many years, Adrian Owen and his colleagues at the University of Western Ontario, working with researchers in Cambridge, UK, and in Liège, Belgium, have been evaluating whether, and how, fMRI can be used to detect signs of consciousness in brain-damaged patients. Traditional bedside measures of awareness rely on the patient being able to make observable movements, which some patients just cannot do, leading to conscious, aware patients being mistaken for vegetative ones. First, the researchers used fMRI to show that two mental imagery tasks reliably activate very different brain regions in healthy "control" individuals. The control group was asked to imagine moving their arms as though swinging a tennis racquet at a ball, which activated motor areas of the brain. Then, they were asked to imagine wandering from room to room in their house, and visualizing what they might see in each place, which activated visual and motor areas (Owen et al., 2006).

Next, the researchers demonstrated that some patients who had been diagnosed as vegetative were also able to reliably generate these distinct patterns. Out of 54 patients diagnosed as vegetative, 5 were able to reliably generate a tennis-playing pattern of activity when asked to imagine playing tennis, and a spatial-navigation pattern of activity when asked to imagine going from room to room in their house. This is voluntary command following—conceptually equivalent to correctly raising your left or right arm when asked to do so—and is a hallmark of agency, which was identified on page 174 as one of the characteristics of conscious awareness (Monti et al., 2010).

When the researchers used this fMRI method with Scott, he was able to reliably generate the tennis and spatial-navigation patterns of activity on command. This indicated, much to the surprise of his doctors, that Scott was not in a vegetative state after all. The researchers went a step further and used this method to ask Scott simple yes-or-no questions. They did this by instructing Scott to imagine playing tennis if he wished to respond *yes* to a question, and to imagine navigating around his house if he wished to respond *no*. The distinct patterns of brain activity for these two tasks could then be interpreted as meaning *yes* or *no*. The researchers started by asking Scott questions to which they knew the answers, such as whether his father's name was Jim (it was). He correctly answered many such questions, indicating that he was fully conscious. The researchers then did something they had never tried with a patient before: They asked Scott

Thirty-nine-year-old Scott Routley was considered to be in a vegetative state for 12 years following a car crash. However, in an experiment conducted by researchers at the University of Western Ontario using fMRI, he was asked to imagine swinging a tennis racquet at a ball. Brain-imaging results showed that the areas of his brain that were activated during this task were the same as those for the control group. This demonstrated that Scott is aware and can answer questions.

a question that only he could know the answer to, "Are you in pain?" Much to everyone's relief, the answering brain activity indicated *no*.

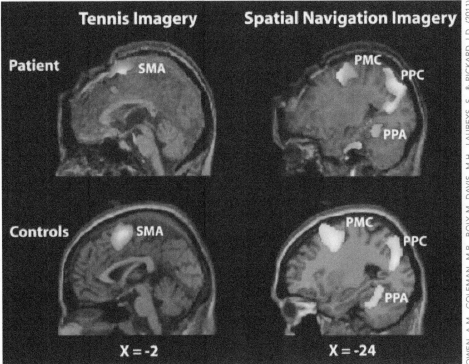

OWEN, A.M., COLEMAN, M.R., BOLY M, DAVIS, M.H., LAUREYS, S., & PICKARD J.D. (2011) DETECTING AWARENESS IN THE VEGETATIVE STATE, SCIENCE, 313, 1402

This image shows the distinct patterns of activity in a healthy control participant and in a brain-damaged patient, resulting from two different mental imagery tasks. The patient, previously diagnosed as being in a vegetative state, was able to follow commands to "imagine playing tennis" or "imagine moving around the rooms of your house," and generated the same patterns as the healthy controls. This ability to reliably engage in purposeful mental activity indicates awareness.

Conscious Contents

What's on your mind? For that matter, what's on everybody's mind? One way to learn what is on people's minds is to ask them, and much research has called on people simply to *think aloud* while in a psychological laboratory. A more modern approach is the use of *experience-sampling* or *ecological momentary assessment (EMA)* techniques, in which people are asked to report their conscious experiences at particular times. Equipped with survey apps loaded onto their smartphone, for example, participants often are asked to record their current thoughts when prompted (e.g., via a push notification) at random times throughout the day (Stone, 2018).

Experience-sampling studies show that consciousness is dominated by the immediate environment—what we see, feel, hear, taste, and smell. What do you experience while actually carrying out the events of your daily life? Researchers who use experience-sampling methods to record the emotions people experience during everyday activities have found interesting results. One study collected data from over 900 working women by asking them to reflect on the events of the past day and record how they felt while engaging in each activity (Kahneman et al., 2004).

Some of the results are as expected. For instance, as shown in **TABLE 5.1**, people score lowest on positive affect when commuting, working, and doing housework. Unfortunately, this is how we spend a large part of our day. The American women in this study reported having the most positive affect while being intimate with another person, although they only did this for 12 minutes of the day. Some less intuitive findings are related to the activities that fell in between the two. In survey studies, parents often report that they are happiest when spending time with their children; but when asked about actual events of the prior day using these daily experience-sampling methods, being with one's children ranked just two ticks above housework and well below other activities such as shopping, watching TV, and making more children.

TABLE 5.1

HOW WAS YOUR DAY? WOMEN'S RATINGS OF LEVEL OF POSITIVE AFFECT AND AMOUNT OF TIME IN DAILY ACTIVITIES

Activities	Mean Affect Rating	
	Positive Affect	Mean Hours/Day
Intimate relations	5.1	0.2
Socializing	4.6	2.3
Relaxing	4.4	2.2
Pray/worship/meditate	4.4	0.4
Eating	4.3	2.2
Exercising	4.3	0.2
Watching TV	4.2	2.2
Shopping	4.0	0.4
Preparing food	3.9	1.1
On the phone	3.9	2.5
Napping	3.9	0.9
Taking care of my children	3.9	1.1
Computer/e-mail/Internet	3.8	1.9
Housework	3.7	1.1
Working	3.6	6.9
Commuting	3.5	1.6

Data from Kahneman et al., 2004.

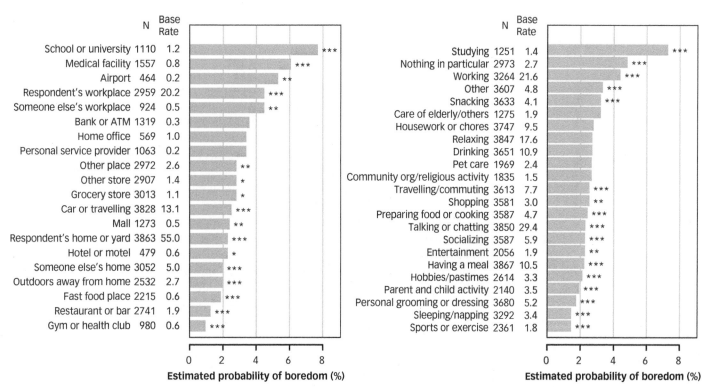

	N	Base Rate			N	Base Rate
School or university	1110	1.2	***	Studying	1251	1.4
Medical facility	1557	0.8	***	Nothing in particular	2973	2.7
Airport	464	0.2	**	Working	3264	21.6
Respondent's workplace	2959	20.2	***	Other	3607	4.8
Someone else's workplace	924	0.5	**	Snacking	3633	4.1
Bank or ATM	1319	0.3		Care of elderly/others	1275	1.9
Home office	569	1.0		Housework or chores	3747	9.5
Personal service provider	1063	0.2		Relaxing	3847	17.6
Other place	2972	2.6	**	Drinking	3651	10.9
Other store	2907	1.4	*	Pet care	1969	2.4
Grocery store	3013	1.1	*	Community org/religious activity	1835	1.5
Car or travelling	3828	13.1	***	Travelling/commuting	3613	7.7
Mall	1273	0.5	**	Shopping	3581	3.0
Respondent's home or yard	3863	55.0	***	Preparing food or cooking	3587	4.7
Hotel or motel	479	0.6	*	Talking or chatting	3850	29.4
Someone else's home	3052	5.0	***	Socializing	3587	5.9
Outdoors away from home	2532	2.7	***	Entertainment	2056	1.9
Fast food place	2215	0.6	***	Having a meal	3867	10.5
Restaurant or bar	2741	1.9	***	Hobbies/pastimes	2614	3.3
Gym or health club	980	0.6	***	Parent and child activity	2140	3.5
				Personal grooming or dressing	3680	5.2
				Sleeping/napping	3292	3.4
				Sports or exercise	2361	1.8

Estimated probability of boredom (%)　　Estimated probability of boredom (%)

Figure 5.5

Situations and Activities Associated with Boredom An experience-sampling study of more than 1 million people revealed the locations and activities associated with the highest (and lowest) probability of being bored. DATA FROM CHIN ET AL. (2016).

Experience-sampling is increasingly being used to study what it is like to be human by focusing on a range of different aspects of conscious experiences. For instance, one recent study used experience-sampling to zoom in on one all too familiar aspect of daily life: boredom (Chin et al., 2017). The authors of this study used experience-sampling to follow 1.1 million people over a 10-day period to better understand, among other things, what situations are most associated with the experience of boredom. As shown in **FIGURE 5.5**, and sadly for you, people reported the highest likelihood of boredom while at school or university—even more so than while in an airport or doctor's office. In terms of activities, people reported the highest likelihood of boredom while studying—an activity that was rated as even more boring than doing nothing at all (fortunately, you have this very stimulating book to keep you from getting bored!).

Daydreams: The Brain Is Always Active

One reason that we often avoid boredom when doing nothing at all is that our mind shifts into a period of *daydreaming,* a state of consciousness in which a seemingly purposeless flow of thoughts comes to mind. When thoughts drift along this way, it may seem as if you are just wasting time. The brain, however, is active even when it has no specific task at hand. The mental work done in daydreaming was examined in an fMRI study of people resting in the scanner (Mason et al., 2007). Usually, people in brain-scanning studies don't have time to daydream much because they are kept busy with mental tasks—scans cost money and researchers want to get as much data as possible for their bucks. But when people are *not* busy, they still show a widespread pattern of activation in many areas of the brain—now known as the *default network* (Gusnard & Raichle, 2001). The study by Mason and colleagues revealed that this network became activated whenever people worked on a mental task that they knew so well that they could daydream while doing it (see **FIGURE 5.6**). The areas of the default network are known to be involved in thinking about social life, about the self, and about the past and future—all the usual haunts of the daydreaming mind (Mitchell, 2006).

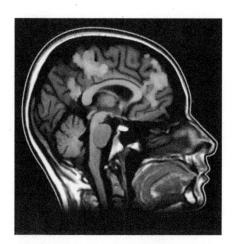

Figure 5.6

The Default Network Activated During Daydreaming An fMRI scan shows that many areas, known as the default network, are active when the person is not given a specific mental task to perform during the scan. DATA FROM SCIENCE FROM WONDERING MINDS, MASON, ET AL., VOL. 315. JANUARY 19, 2007, PP. 393–305.

Efforts to Suppress Current Concerns Can Backfire

The current concerns that populate consciousness can sometimes get the upper hand, transforming daydreams or everyday thoughts into rumination and worry. Thoughts that return again and again, or problem-solving attempts that never seem to succeed, can come to dominate consciousness. When this happens, people may exert **mental control**, *the attempt to change conscious states of mind*. For example, someone troubled by a recurring worry about the future ("What if I can't get a decent job when I graduate?") might choose to try *not* to think about this because it causes too much anxiety and uncertainty. Whenever this thought comes to mind, the person engages in **thought suppression**, the *conscious avoidance of a thought*. This may seem like a perfectly sensible strategy because it eliminates the worry and allows the person to move on to think about something else.

Or does it? The great Russian novelist Fyodor Dostoyevsky (1863/1988, p. 49) remarked on the difficulty of thought suppression: "Try to pose for yourself this task: not to think of a polar bear, and you will see that the cursed thing will come to mind every minute." Inspired by this observation, Daniel Wegner and his colleagues (1987) gave people this exact task in the laboratory. Participants were asked to try not to think about a white bear for 5 minutes while they recorded all their thoughts aloud into a tape recorder. In addition, they were asked to ring a bell if the thought of a white bear came to mind. On average, they mentioned the white bear or rang the bell (indicating the thought) more than once per minute. Thought suppression simply didn't work and instead produced a flurry of returns of the unwanted thought.

What's more, when some research participants later were specifically asked to change tasks and deliberately *think* about a white bear, they became oddly preoccupied with it. A graph of their bell rings in **FIGURE 5.7** shows that for these participants, the white bear came to mind far more often than it did for people who had only been asked to think about the bear from the outset, with no prior suppression. This **rebound effect of thought suppression**, *the tendency of a thought to return to consciousness with greater frequency following suppression*, suggests that attempts at mental control may be difficult indeed. The act of trying to suppress a thought may itself cause that thought to return to consciousness in a robust way.

Go ahead, look away from this book for a minute and try not to think about a white bear.

LARRY WILLIAMS/GETTY IMAGES

mental control The attempt to change conscious states of mind.

thought suppression The conscious avoidance of a thought.

rebound effect of thought suppression The tendency of a thought to return to consciousness with greater frequency following suppression.

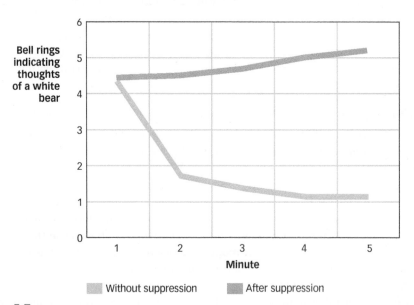

Figure 5.7
Rebound Effect Research participants were first asked to try not to think about a white bear, and then to ring a bell whenever it came to mind. Compared to those who were simply asked to think about a bear without prior suppression, those people who first suppressed the thought showed a rebound of increased thinking about the bear (Wegner et al., 1987).

Processes Outside of Consciousness Can Stymie Attempts at Conscious Control

As with thought suppression, other attempts to steer consciousness in any direction can result in mental states that are precisely the opposite of those desired. How ironic: Trying to consciously achieve one task may produce precisely the opposite outcome! These ironic effects seem most likely to occur when the person is distracted or under stress. People who are distracted while they are trying to get into a good mood, for example, tend to become sad (Wegner, Erber, & Zanakos, 1993), and those who are distracted while trying to relax actually become more anxious than those who are not trying to relax (Wegner, Broome, & Blumberg, 1997). Likewise, an attempt not to overshoot a golf putt, undertaken during distraction, often yields the unwanted overshot (Wegner, Ansfield, & Pilloff, 1998). The theory of **ironic processes of mental control** proposes that such *ironic errors occur because the mental process that monitors errors can itself produce them* (Wegner, 1994a, 2009). The irony about the attempt not to think of a white bear, for instance, is that a small part of the mind is *searching* for the white bear.

This ironic monitoring process is not present in consciousness. After all, trying *not* to think of something would be useless if monitoring the progress of suppression required keeping that target in consciousness. For example, if trying not to think of a white bear meant that you consciously kept repeating to yourself, "No white bear! No white bear!" then you've failed before you've begun: That thought is present in consciousness even as you strive to eliminate it. Rather, the ironic monitor is a process of the mind that works *outside* of consciousness, making us sensitive to all the things we do not want to think, feel, or do so that we can notice and consciously take steps to regain control if these things come back to mind.

As this unconscious monitoring whirs along in the background, it unfortunately increases the person's sensitivity to the very thought that is unwanted. Ironic processes are mental functions that are needed for effective mental control—they help in the process of banishing a thought from consciousness—but they can sometimes yield the very failure they seem designed to overcome. Ironic effects of mental control arise from processes that work outside of consciousness, so they remind us that much of the mind's machinery may be hidden from our view, lying outside the fringes of our experience.

ironic processes of mental control A mental process that can produce ironic errors because monitoring for errors can itself produce them.

Build to the Outcomes

1. What are the limitations to the number of objects that consciousness can take on at one time?
2. How does your mind know which information to allow into consciousness and which to filter out?
3. Which characteristic of full consciousness distinguishes it from minimal consciousness?
4. When do people go out of their way to avoid mirrors?
5. Which animals are also aware of their own reflection in a mirror?
6. What distinguishes vegetative state from coma?
7. What part of the brain is active during daydreaming?
8. Is consciously avoiding a worrisome thought a sensible strategy?

The Unconscious Mind

Many mental processes are unconscious, in the sense that they occur without our experience of them. When we speak, for instance, "We are not really conscious either of the search for words, or of putting the words together into phrases, or of putting the phrases into sentences. . . . The actual process of thinking . . . is not conscious at all . . . only its preparation, its materials, and its end result are consciously perceived" (Jaynes, 1976, p. 41). To put the role of consciousness in perspective, think for a moment about the mental processes involved in simple addition.

Learning Outcome

- Compare Freud's conception of the unconscious with the modern view.
- Explain the dual process perspective.

There are no conscious steps between hearing an easy problem (what's 4 + 5?) and thinking of the answer—unless you have to count on your fingers.

What happens in consciousness between hearing a problem (what's 4 + 5?) and thinking of the answer (9)? Probably nothing—the answer just appears in the mind. But this is a piece of calculation that must take at least a bit of thinking. After all, at a very young age you may have had to solve such problems by counting on your fingers. Now that you don't have to do that anymore (please tell me you don't have to do that anymore), the answer seems to pop into your head automatically, by virtue of a process that doesn't require you to be aware of any underlying steps and, for that matter, doesn't even *allow* you to be aware of the steps. The answer just suddenly appears.

In the early part of the 20th century, when structuralist psychologists such as Edward B. Titchener believed that introspection was the best method of research (see the Psychology: Evolution of a Science chapter), research volunteers trained in describing their thoughts tried to discern what happens when a simple problem brings to mind a simple answer (Watt, 1905). They drew the same blank you probably did. Nothing conscious seems to bridge this gap, but the answer comes from somewhere, and this emptiness points to the unconscious mind. To explore these hidden recesses, we can look at the classical theory of the unconscious, introduced by Sigmund Freud, and then at the modern cognitive psychology of unconscious mental processes.

Freudian Unconscious

The true champion of the unconscious mind was Sigmund Freud. As you read in the Psychology: Evolution of a Science chapter, Freud's psychoanalytic theory viewed conscious thought as the surface of a much deeper mind made up of unconscious processes—but far more than just a collection of hidden processes. Freud described a **dynamic unconscious**—*an active system encompassing a lifetime of hidden memories, the person's deepest instincts and desires, and the person's inner struggle to control these forces.* The dynamic unconscious might contain hidden sexual thoughts about one's parents, for example, or destructive urges aimed at a helpless infant—the kinds of thoughts people keep secret from others and may not even acknowledge to themselves. According to Freud's theory, the unconscious is a force to be held in check by something he called **repression**, *a mental process that removes unacceptable thoughts and memories from consciousness and keeps them in the unconscious.* Freud believed that without repression, a person might think, do, or say every unconscious impulse or animal urge, no matter how selfish or immoral. With repression, these desires are held in the recesses of the dynamic unconscious.

Freud looked for evidence of the unconscious mind in speech errors and lapses of consciousness, or what are commonly called *Freudian slips*. Forgetting the name of someone you dislike, for example, is a slip that seems to have special meaning. Freud believed that errors are not random and instead have some surplus meaning that may appear to have been created by an intelligent unconscious mind, even though the person consciously disavows them. Of course, suggesting that there is special meaning to any one thing a person says, or that there is a pattern to a series of random events is not the same as scientifically predicting and explaining when and why an event should happen. Anyone can offer a reasonable, compelling explanation for an event after it has already happened ("That must have been a Freudian slip!"), but the true work of science is to offer testable hypotheses that can be evaluated based on reliable evidence. Unfortunately, Freud's theories about the unconscious have not been supported by scientific research over the past 100 years.

A Modern View of the Cognitive Unconscious

Modern psychologists share Freud's interest in the impact of unconscious mental processes on consciousness and on behaviour. However, rather than seeing Freud's vision of the unconscious as a teeming menagerie of animal urges and repressed

dynamic unconscious An active system encompassing a lifetime of hidden memories, the person's deepest instincts and desires, and the person's inner struggle to control these forces.

repression A mental process that removes unacceptable thoughts and memories from consciousness and keeps them in the unconscious.

thoughts, the current study of the unconscious mind views it as a rapid, automatic information processor that influences our thoughts, feelings, and behaviours. The **cognitive unconscious** includes *all the mental processes that give rise to a person's thoughts, choices, emotions, and behaviour even though they are not experienced by the person.*

Our Brains Are Wired for Both Fast and Slow Thinking

Modern views of cognition propose that we have two different types of minds wired into our one little brain. **Dual process theories** *suggest that we have two different systems in our brains for processing information: one dedicated to fast, automatic, and unconscious processing; and the other dedicated to slow, effortful, and conscious processing.* The first, which is now commonly referred to as System 1 (Stanovich & West, 2000), is at work when you effortlessly engage in activities such as reading these words; solving problems such as 2 + 2 = ___; and walking down the street, avoiding people, cars, and other obstacles. You use the second, System 2, when you rationally and intentionally work to complete a task, such as answering this chapter's quiz questions, solving problems such as 245 × 32 = ___, and placing an order at a restaurant. These systems, and the important roles they play, are outlined in detail in the psychologist and Nobel laureate Daniel Kahneman's book *Thinking, Fast and Slow* (Kahneman, 2011).

Kahneman (2011) suggests that Systems 1 and 2 are both continuously active whenever we are awake: System 1 helps you efficiently navigate your daily life, and System 2 becomes engaged when more serious mental effort is involved. For instance, if you are walking around campus from one class to another—a walk that you have taken dozens of times—System 1 will guide you. However, if you happen upon a clown holding a fist full of rubber chickens, System 2 may come online to help you resolve this apparent conflict between what System 1 expected and what it observed. In this way, System 2 uses information and inputs from System 1 to help guide your future behaviour.

This dual process perspective is similar in some ways to Freud's idea of the split between the unconscious and the conscious mind. However, dual process theories do not incorporate all of Freud's beliefs about hidden urges, defense mechanisms, Freudian slips, and the like. Instead, they simply propose that we have these two different ways of processing information that draw on different neural pathways. Dual process theories have been used to understand the workings of different cognitive processes, such as attention, learning, and memory (for example, see the discussions of implicit and explicit learning and memory in later chapters on these topics), and continue to guide thinking and research in many different areas of psychology.

The Unconscious Mind: Smart or Not So Smart?

If System 1 can handle only simple tasks, should we think of it as an unintelligent system? Freud attributed great intelligence to the unconscious, believing that it harbours complex motives and inner conflicts and that it expresses these in an astonishing array of thoughts and emotions, as well as psychological disorders (see the Disorders chapter). Contemporary cognitive psychologists wonder whether the unconscious is so smart after all, pointing out that some unconscious processes even seem downright "dumb" (Loftus & Klinger, 1992). For example, the unconscious processes that underlie the perception of subliminal visual stimuli do not seem able to understand the combined meaning of word pairs, although they can understand single words. To the *conscious* mind, for example, a word pair such as *enemy loses* is somewhat positive—it is good to have your enemy lose. However, subliminal presentations of this word pair make people think of negative things, as though the unconscious mind is simply adding together the unpleasantness of the single words *enemy*

cognitive unconscious All the mental processes that give rise to a person's thoughts, choices, emotions, and behaviour even though they are not experienced by the person.

dual process theories Theories that suggest that we have two different systems in our brains for processing information: one dedicated to fast, automatic, and unconscious processing, and the other dedicated to slow, effortful, and conscious processing.

Figure 5.8

Decisions People making roommate decisions who had some time for unconscious deliberation chose better roommates than those who thought about the choice consciously or those who made snap decisions (Dijksterhuis, 2004).

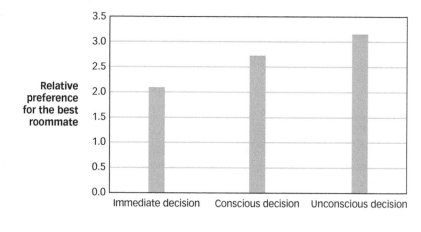

Relative preference for the best roommate

Immediate decision   Conscious decision   Unconscious decision

Choosing a roommate can be like playing the lottery: You win some, you lose some, and then you lose some more.

and *loses* (Greenwald, 1992). So System 1 appears to be able to help us think fast, but it is perhaps not all that bright.

In some cases, however, the unconscious mind can make better decisions than the conscious mind. Participants in an experiment were asked to choose which of three hypothetical people with many different qualities they would prefer as a roommate (Dijksterhuis, 2004). One candidate was objectively better, with more positive qualities, and participants who were given 4 minutes to make a *conscious decision* tended to choose that one. A second group was asked for an *immediate decision* as soon as the information display was over, and a third group was encouraged to reach an *unconscious decision*. This group was also given 4 minutes after the display ended to give their answer (as the conscious group had been given), but during this interval their conscious minds were occupied with solving a set of anagrams. As you can see in **FIGURE 5.8**, the unconscious decision group showed a stronger preference for the good roommate than did the immediate decision or conscious decision groups. Unconscious minds seemed *better able* than conscious minds to sort out the complex information and arrive at the best choice. You sometimes can end up more satisfied with decisions you make after just going with your gut than with the decisions you consciously agonize over.

Build to the Outcomes

1. According to Freud, what is the source of unconscious errors in speech?

2. What is the difference between System 1 and System 2 ways of processing information?

3. What evidence shows that the unconscious mind can be a good decision maker?

Sleep and Dreaming: Good Night, Mind

Learning Outcomes

- Describe the stages of sleep.
- Identify the types of sleep disorders.
- Compare the two leading theories of why we dream.

What's it like to be asleep? Sometimes it's like nothing at all. Sleep can produce a state of unconsciousness in which the mind and brain apparently turn off the functions that create experience: The theatre in your mind is closed. But this is an oversimplification because the theatre seems to reopen during the night for special shows of bizarre cult films—in other words, dreams. Dream consciousness involves a transformation of experience that is so radical it is commonly considered an **altered state of consciousness**: *a form of experience that departs* *significantly from the normal subjective experience of the world and the mind.* Such altered states can be accompanied by changes in thinking, disturbances in the sense of time, feelings of loss of control, changes in emotional expression, alterations in body image and sense of self, perceptual distortions, and changes in meaning or significance (Ludwig, 1966). The world of sleep and dreams, the two topics in this section, provides two unique perspectives on consciousness: a view of the mind without consciousness and a view of consciousness in an altered state.

Sleep

Consider a typical night. As you begin to fall asleep, the busy, task-oriented thoughts of the waking mind are replaced by wandering thoughts and images and odd juxtapositions, some of them almost dreamlike. This pre-sleep consciousness is called the *hypnagogic state.* On some rare nights you might experience a *hypnic jerk,* a sudden quiver or sensation of dropping, as though missing a step on a staircase. No one is quite sure why these happen. Eventually, your presence of mind goes away entirely. Time and experience stop, you are unconscious, and in fact there seems to be no "you" there to have experiences. But then come dreams, whole vistas of a vivid and surrealistic consciousness you just don't get during the day, a set of experiences that occurs with the odd prerequisite that there is nothing "out there" that you are actually experiencing. More patches of unconsciousness may occur, with more dreams here and there. And finally, the glimmerings of waking consciousness return again in a foggy and imprecise form as you enter post-sleep consciousness (the *hypnopompic state*) and then awake, often with bad hair.

Sleep Cycle

The sequence of events that occurs during a night of sleep is part of one of the major rhythms of human life, the cycle of sleep and waking. This **circadian rhythm** is *a naturally occurring 24-hour cycle,* from the Latin *circa* ("about") and *dies* ("day"). Even people sequestered in underground buildings without clocks (known as time-free environments), who are allowed to sleep when they want, tend to have a rest–activity cycle of about 25.1 hours (Aschoff, 1965). This slight deviation from 24 hours is not easily explained (Lavie, 2001), but it seems to underlie the tendency many people have to want to stay up a little later each night and wake up a little later each day. We're 25.1-hour people living in a 24-hour world.

Research Reveals Five Stages of Sleep The sleep cycle is far more than a simple on–off routine, however, since many bodily and psychological processes ebb and flow in this rhythm. In 1929, researchers made EEG (electroencephalograph) recordings of the human brain for the first time (Berger, 1929) (see the Neuroscience and Behaviour chapter). Before this, many people had offered descriptions of their night-time experiences, and researchers knew that there were deeper and lighter periods of sleep, as well as dream periods. But no one had been able to measure much of anything about sleep without waking up the sleeper and ruining it. The EEG recordings revealed a regular pattern of changes in electrical activity in the brain accompanying the circadian cycle. During waking, these changes involve alternating between high-frequency activity (*beta waves*) during alertness and lower-frequency activity (*alpha waves*) during relaxation.

The largest changes in EEG occur during sleep. These changes show a regular pattern over the course of the night that allowed sleep researchers to identify five sleep stages (see **FIGURE 5.9**). In the first stage of sleep, the EEG moves to frequency patterns even lower than alpha waves (*theta waves*). In the second stage of

Dreamers, **by Albert Joseph Moore (1879/1882)** Although their bodies are in the same room, their minds are probably worlds apart—just as it is for you and those who may be sleeping nearby.

altered state of consciousness
A form of experience that departs significantly from the normal subjective experience of the world and the mind.

circadian rhythm A naturally occurring 24-hour cycle.

Figure 5.9

EEG Patterns During the Stages of Sleep The waking brain shows high-frequency beta wave activity, which changes during drowsiness and relaxation to lower-frequency alpha waves. Stage 1 sleep shows lower-frequency theta waves, which are accompanied in stage 2 by irregular patterns called sleep spindles and K complexes. Stages 3 and 4 are marked by the lowest frequencies, delta waves. During REM sleep, EEG patterns return to higher-frequency sawtooth waves that resemble the beta waves of waking.

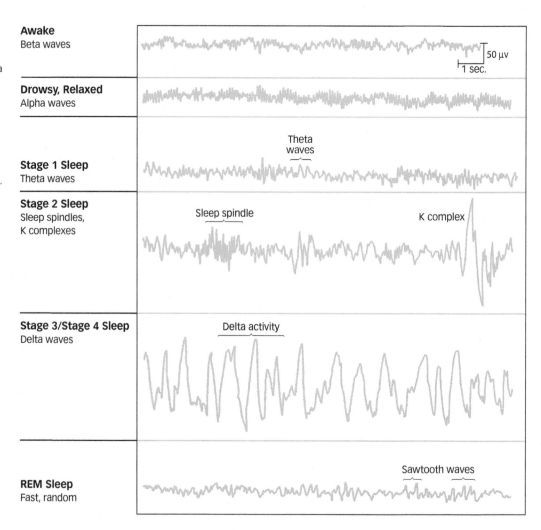

Awake
Beta waves

50 µv

1 sec.

Drowsy, Relaxed
Alpha waves

Stage 1 Sleep
Theta waves

Theta waves

Stage 2 Sleep
Sleep spindles,
K complexes

Sleep spindle

K complex

Stage 3/Stage 4 Sleep
Delta waves

Delta activity

REM Sleep
Fast, random

Sawtooth waves

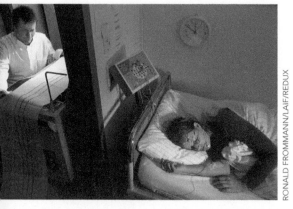

Psychologists learn about what happens when we sleep by collecting EOG, EEG, and other measurements from research volunteers while they sleep in sleep laboratories such as this one.

RONALD FROMMANN/LAIF/REDUX

REM sleep A stage of sleep characterized by rapid eye movements and a high level of brain activity.

electrooculograph (EOG) An instrument that measures eye movements.

sleep, these patterns are interrupted by short bursts of activity called *sleep spindles* and *K complexes,* and the sleeper becomes somewhat more difficult to awaken. The deepest stages of sleep are stages 3 and 4, known as slow-wave sleep, in which the EEG patterns show activity called *delta waves.*

The fifth sleep stage is **REM sleep**, *which is characterized by rapid eye movements and a high level of brain activity,* and during which EEG patterns become high-frequency sawtooth waves, similar to beta waves. This suggests that at this time, the mind is as active as it is during waking (see Figure 5.9). Using an **electrooculograph (EOG)**—*an instrument that measures eye movements*—during sleep, researchers found that sleepers wakened during REM periods reported having dreams much more often than those wakened during non-REM periods (Aserinsky & Kleitman, 1953). During REM sleep, the pulse quickens, blood pressure rises, and there are telltale signs of sexual arousal. At the same time, measurements of muscle movements indicate that the sleeper is very still, except for a rapid side-to-side movement of the eyes. (Watch someone sleeping and you may be able to see the REMs through their closed eyelids. But be careful doing this with strangers down at the bus station.)

Although many people believe that they don't dream much (if at all), some 80% of people awakened during REM sleep report dreams. If you've ever wondered whether dreams actually take place in an instant or whether they take as long to happen as the events they portray might take, the analysis of REM sleep offers an answer. The sleep researchers William Dement and Nathaniel Kleitman (1957) woke volunteers either 5 minutes or 15 minutes after the onset of REM sleep and asked them to

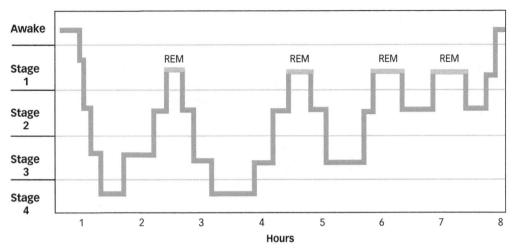

Figure 5.10
Stages of Sleep During the Night
Over the course of a typical night, sleep cycles into deeper stages early on and then more shallow stages later. REM periods become longer in later cycles, and the deeper slow-wave sleep of stages 3 and 4 disappears halfway through the night.

judge, on the basis of the events in the remembered dream, how long they had been dreaming. Sleepers in 92 of 111 cases were correct, suggesting that dreaming occurs in "real time." The discovery of REM sleep has offered many insights into dreaming, but not all dreams occur in REM periods. Some dreams are also reported in other sleep stages, and the dreams that occur at those times are described as less wild than REM dreams and more like normal thinking.

A Typical Night's Sleep Putting EEG and REM data together produces a picture of how a typical night's sleep progresses through cycles of sleep stages (see **FIGURE 5.10**). In the first hour of the night, you fall all the way from waking to the fourth and deepest stage of sleep, the stage marked by delta waves. These slow waves indicate a general synchronization of neural firing, as though the brain is doing one thing at this time rather than many: the neuronal equivalent of "the wave" moving through the crowd at a stadium as lots of individuals move together in synchrony. You then return to lighter sleep stages, eventually reaching REM and dreamland. Note that although REM sleep is lighter than that of lower stages, it is deep enough that you may be difficult to awaken. You then continue to cycle between REM and slow-wave sleep stages every 90 minutes or so throughout the night. Periods of REM last longer as the night goes on, and lighter sleep stages predominate between these periods, with the deeper slow-wave stages 3 and 4 disappearing halfway through the night. Although you're either unconscious or dream-conscious at the time, your brain and mind cycle through a remarkable array of different states each time you have a night's sleep.

Sleep Needs and Deprivation

How Does Sleep Affect You?
Go to launchpadworks.com.

How much do people sleep? The answer depends on the age of the sleeper (Dement, 1999). Newborns will sleep 6 to 8 times in 24 hours, often totaling more than 16 hours. Their napping cycle gets consolidated into "sleeping through the night," usually sometime between 9 and 18 months, but occasionally even later. The typical 6-year-old child might need 11 or 12 hours of sleep, and the progression to less sleep then continues into adulthood, when the average is about 7 to 7.5 hours per night. With aging, people can get along with even a bit less sleep than that. Over a whole lifetime, we get about 1 hour of sleep for every 2 hours we are awake.

This is a lot of sleeping. Could we tolerate less? Monitored by William Dement, Randy Gardner stayed up for 264 hours and 12 minutes (just over 11 days) in 1965 for a science project. When 17-year-old Randy finally did go to sleep, he slept only 14 hours and 40 minutes and awakened essentially recovered (Dement, 1978).

Feats such as this one suggest that sleep might be expendable. This is the thinking behind the classic all-nighter that you may have tried just before a big exam. But, be careful, because, as it turns out, this is not the case. Robert Stickgold and his colleagues (2000) found that when people learning a difficult perceptual task are kept up all night after they have finished practicing the task, their learning of the task is wiped out. Even after two nights of catch-up sleep, they show little indication of their initial training on the task. Sleep following learning appears to be essential for memory consolidation (see Hot Science: Sleep on It, in the Memory chapter). It is as though memories normally deteriorate unless sleep occurs to help keep them in place. Studying all night may help you cram for the exam, but it won't make the material stick, which pretty much defeats the whole purpose.

Sleep turns out to be a necessity rather than a luxury in other ways as well. At the extreme, sleep loss can be fatal. When rats are forced to break Randy Gardner's human waking record and stay awake even longer, they have trouble regulating their body temperature and lose weight although they eat much more than normal. Their bodily systems break down and they die, on average, in 21 days (Rechtschaffen et al., 1983). Shakespeare called sleep "nature's soft nurse," and it is clear that even for healthy young humans, a few hours of sleep deprivation each night can have a cumulative detrimental effect: It reduces mental acuity and reaction time, increases irritability and depression, and increases the risk of accidents and injury (Coren, 1997).

Some researchers have deprived people of different sleep stages selectively by waking them whenever certain stages are detected. Studies of REM sleep deprivation indicate that this part of sleep is psychologically important. Memory problems and excessive aggression are observed in both humans and rats after only a few days of being awakened whenever REM activity starts (Ellman et al., 1991). The brain must value something about REM sleep because REM deprivation causes a rebound of more REM sleep the next night (Brunner et al., 1990). Deprivation from slow-wave sleep (in stages 3 and 4), in turn, has more physical effects, with just a few nights of deprivation leaving people feeling tired, fatigued, and hypersensitive to muscle and bone pain (Lentz et al., 1999).

It's clearly dangerous to neglect the need for sleep. But why would we have such a need in the first place? All animals appear to sleep, although the amount of sleep required varies quite a bit (see **FIGURE 5.11**). Giraffes sleep less than 2 hours daily, whereas brown bats snooze for almost 20 hours. These variations in sleep needs, and the very existence of a need, are hard to explain. Is the

Sleep following learning is essential for memory consolidation. Sleep during class, on the other hand, not so much.

SONDA DAWES/THE IMAGE WORKS

Figure 5.11
Average Daily Sleep Totals All animals and insects seem to require sleep, although in differing amounts. Next time you oversleep and someone accuses you of "sleeping like a baby," you might tell them instead that you were sleeping like a tiger, or a brown bat.

AVERAGE DAILY SLEEP TOTALS

GIRAFFE ELEPHANT HUMAN BOTTLENOSE DOLPHIN CHIMPANZEE RABBIT GERBIL TIGER BROWN BAT

HOURS
0   5   10   15   20
1.9 3.5   8.0 9.7 10.4 11.4 13.1   15.8   19.9

LJERKA ILIC/HERMERA/THINKSTOCK

restoration that happens during the unconsciousness of sleep something that simply can't be achieved during consciousness? Sleep is, after all, potentially costly in the course of evolution. The sleeping animal is easy prey, so the habit of sleep would not seem to have developed so widely across species unless it had significant benefits that made up for this vulnerability. Theories of sleep have not yet determined why the brain and body have evolved to need these recurring episodes of unconsciousness.

Sleep Disorders

In answer to the question "Did you sleep well?" the comedian Stephen Wright said, "No, I made a couple of mistakes." Sleeping well is something everyone would love to do, but for many people, sleep disorders are deeply troubling. The most common disorders that plague sleep include insomnia, sleep apnea, and somnambulism.

Insomnia, *difficulty in falling asleep or staying asleep,* is perhaps the most common sleep disorder. About 30 to 48% of people report symptoms of insomnia, 9 to 15% report insomnia severe enough to lead to daytime complaints, and 6% of people meet criteria for a diagnosis of insomnia, which involves persistent and impairing sleep problems (Bootzin & Epstein, 2011; Ohayon, 2002). Unfortunately, insomnia often is a persistent problem; most people with insomnia experience it for at least a year (Morin et al., 2009).

Insomnia has many potential causes. In some instances, it results from lifestyle choices such as working night shifts (self-induced insomnia), whereas in other cases it occurs in response to depression, anxiety, or some other condition (secondary insomnia). In still other cases, there are no obvious causal factors (primary insomnia). Regardless of type, insomnia can be exacerbated by worrying about insomnia (Blake, Trinder, & Allen, 2018). No doubt you've experienced some nights when sleeping was a high priority, such as before a class presentation or an important interview, and you've found that you were unable to fall asleep. The desire to sleep initiates an ironic process of mental control—a heightened sensitivity to signs of sleeplessness—and this sensitivity interferes with sleep. In fact, participants in an experiment who were instructed to go to sleep quickly became hypersensitive and had more difficulty sleeping than those who were not instructed to hurry (Ansfield, Wegner, & Bowser, 1996). The paradoxical solution for insomnia in some cases, then, may be to give up the pursuit of sleep and instead find something else to do.

Giving up on trying so hard to sleep is probably better than another common remedy—the use of sleeping pills. Although sedatives can be useful for brief sleep problems associated with emotional events, their long-term use is not effective. To begin with, most sleeping pills are addictive. People become dependent on the pills to sleep and may need to increase the dose over time to achieve the same effect. Even in short-term use, sedatives can interfere with the normal sleep cycle. Although they promote sleep, they can reduce the proportion of time spent in REM and slow-wave sleep (Qureshi & Lee-Chiong, 2004), robbing people of dreams and their deepest sleep stages. As a result, the quality of sleep achieved with pills may not be as high as without them, and people may experience side effects such as grogginess and irritability during the day. Finally, stopping the use of sleeping pills suddenly can produce insomnia that is worse than before.

Sleep apnea is *a disorder in which the person stops breathing for brief periods while asleep.* A person with apnea usually snores because apnea involves an involuntary obstruction of the breathing passage. When episodes of apnea occur for over 10 seconds at a time and recur many times during the night, they may cause many awakenings and sleep loss or insomnia. Apnea occurs most often in middle-aged, overweight men (Punjabi, 2008) and may go undiagnosed because it is not easy for the sleeper to notice. Bed partners may be the ones who finally get tired of the snoring and noisy gasping for air when the sleeper's breathing restarts, or the sleeper may

INSOMNIA JEOPARDY

WAYS IN WHICH PEOPLE HAVE WRONGED ME	STRANGE NOISES	DISEASES I PROBABLY HAVE	MONEY TROUBLES	WHY DID I SAY/DO THAT?	IDEAS FOR A SCREENPLAY
$10	$10	$10	$10	$10	$10
$20	$20	$20	$20	$20	$20
$30	$30	$30	$30	$30	$30
$40	$40	$40	$40	$40	$40
$50	$50	$50	$50	$50	$50

R. Chast

insomnia Difficulty in falling asleep or staying asleep.

sleep apnea A disorder in which the person stops breathing for brief periods while asleep.

MATTHEW NOCK

Sleepwalkers in cartoons have their arms outstretched and eyes closed, but that's just for cartoons. A real-life sleepwalker usually walks normally with eyes open, sometimes with a glassy look.

somnambulism (sleepwalking) Occurs when a person arises and walks around while asleep.

narcolepsy A disorder in which sudden sleep attacks occur in the middle of waking activities.

sleep paralysis The experience of waking up unable to move.

night terrors (sleep terrors) Abrupt awakenings with panic and intense emotional arousal.

eventually seek treatment because of excessive sleepiness during the day. Therapies involving weight loss, drugs, sleep masks that push air into the nasal passage, or surgery may solve the problem.

Somnambulism (or **sleepwalking**), occurs when *a person arises and walks around while asleep*. Sleepwalking is more common in children, peaking between the ages of 4 and 8 years, with 15 to 40% of children experiencing at least one episode (Bhargava, 2011). Sleepwalking tends to happen early in the night, usually during slow-wave sleep. Sleepwalkers may awaken during their walk or return to bed without waking, in which case they will probably not remember the episode in the morning. The sleepwalker's eyes are usually open in a glassy stare. Walking with hands outstretched is uncommon except in cartoons. Sleepwalking is not usually linked to any additional problems and is problematic only in that sleepwalkers sometimes engage in strange or unwise behaviours such as urinating in places other than the toilet and leaving the house while still sleeping. People who walk while they are sleeping do not tend to be very coordinated and can trip over furniture or fall down stairs. After all, they're sleeping. Contrary to popular belief, it is safe to wake sleepwalkers or lead them back to bed.

Other sleep disorders are less common. **Narcolepsy** is *a disorder in which sudden sleep attacks occur in the middle of waking activities*. Narcolepsy involves the intrusion of a dreaming state of sleep (with REM) into waking and is often accompanied by unrelenting excessive sleepiness and uncontrollable sleep attacks lasting from 30 seconds to 30 minutes. This disorder appears to have a genetic basis because it runs in families, and it can be treated effectively with medication. **Sleep paralysis** is *the experience of waking up unable to move* and is sometimes associated with narcolepsy. This eerie experience usually happens as you are awakening from REM sleep but before you have regained motor control. This period typically lasts only a few seconds or minutes and can be accompanied by hypnopompic (when awakening) or hypnagogic (when falling asleep) hallucinations in which dream content may appear to occur in the waking world. A very clever series of recent studies suggests that sleep paralysis accompanied by hypnopompic hallucinations of figures being in one's bedroom seems to explain many perceived instances of alien abductions and recovered memories of sexual abuse (aided by therapists who used hypnosis to help the sleepers [incorrectly] piece it all together) (McNally & Clancy, 2005).

Night terrors (or **sleep terrors**) are *abrupt awakenings with panic and intense emotional arousal*. These terrors, which occur most often in children and in only about 2% of adults (Ohayon, Guilleminault, & Priest, 1999), happen most often in non-REM sleep early in the sleep cycle and do not usually have dream content the sleeper can report.

To sum up, a lot happens when we close our eyes for the night. Humans follow a pretty regular sleep cycle, going through the five stages of sleep during the night. Disruptions to that cycle, either from sleep deprivation or sleep disorders, can produce consequences for waking consciousness. But something else happens during a night's sleep that affects our consciousness, both while asleep and when we wake up.

Dreams

The pioneering sleep researcher William C. Dement (1959) said, "Dreaming permits each and every one of us to be quietly and safely insane every night of our lives." Indeed, dreams do seem to have a touch of insanity about them. We experience crazy things in dreams, but even more bizarre is the fact that we are the writers, producers, and directors of the crazy things we experience. Just what are these experiences, and how can they be explained?

Dream Consciousness

Dreams depart dramatically from reality. You may dream of being naked in public, of falling from a great height, of your teeth falling out, or of being chased. These things don't happen much in reality unless you're having a terrible, horrible, no good, very bad day. The quality of consciousness in dreaming is also altered significantly from waking consciousness. Five major characteristics of dream consciousness distinguish it from the waking state (Hobson, 1988).

1. We intensely feel *emotion,* whether it is bliss or terror or love or awe.
2. Dream *thought* is illogical: The continuities of time, place, and person don't apply. You may find you are in one place and then another without any travel in between—or people may change identity from one dream scene to the next.
3. *Sensation* is fully formed and meaningful; visual sensation is predominant, and you may also deeply experience sound, touch, and movement (although pain is uncommon).
4. Dreaming occurs with *uncritical acceptance,* as though the images and events are perfectly normal rather than bizarre.
5. We have *difficulty remembering* the dream after it is over. People often remember dreams only if they are awakened during the dream and even then may lose recall for the dream within just a few minutes of waking. If your waking memory were this bad, you'd be standing around half-naked in the street much of the time, having forgotten your intended destination, clothes, and lunch money.

Not all of our dreams are fantastic and surreal, however. We often dream about mundane topics that reflect prior waking experiences or "day residue." Current conscious concerns pop up (Nikles et al., 1998), along with images from the recent past. A dream may even incorporate sensations experienced during sleep, as when sleepers in one study were led to dream of water when drops were sprayed on their faces during REM sleep (Dement & Wolpert, 1958). The day residue does not usually include episodic memories, that is, complete daytime events replayed in the mind. Instead, dreams that reflect the day's experience tend to single out sensory experiences or objects from waking life. Rather than simply being a replay of that event, dreams often consist of "interleaved fragments of experience" from different times and places that our mind weaves together into a single story (Wamsley & Stickgold, 2011). For instance, after a fun day at the beach with your roommates, your dream that night might include cameo appearances by bouncing beach balls or a flock of seagulls. One study had research participants play the computer game Tetris and found that participants often reported dreaming about the Tetris geometrical figures falling down—even though they seldom reported dreams about being in the experiment or playing the game (Stickgold et al., 2001). Even severely amnesic individuals who couldn't recall playing the game at all reported Tetris-like images appearing in their dreams (Stickgold et al., 2000). The content of dreams takes snapshots from the day rather than retelling the stories of what you have done or seen. This means that dreams often come without clear plots or story lines, so they may not make a lot of sense.

Some of the most memorable dreams are nightmares, and these frightening dreams can wake up the dreamer (Levin & Nielsen, 2009). One set of daily dream logs from university students suggested that the average student has about 24 nightmares per year (Wood & Bootzin, 1990), although some people may have them as often as every night. Children have more nightmares than adults, and people who have experienced traumatic events are inclined to have nightmares that relive those events. Following the 1989 earthquake in the San Francisco Bay area, for example, university students who had experienced the quake reported more nightmares than

Dreams often are quite intense, vivid, and illogical. This can lead to very cool experiences, such as that depicted in this scene from the movie *Inception.*

WARNER BROS/KOBAL/SHUTTERSTOCK

GOETHE HOUSE AND MUSEUM/SNARK/ART RESOURCE, NY

The Nightmare, by Henry Fuseli (1790)
Fuseli depicts not only a mare in this painting but also an incubus—an imp perched on the dreamer's chest that is traditionally associated with especially horrifying nightmares.

those who had not and often reported that the dreams were about the quake (Wood et al., 1992). This effect of trauma may not only produce dreams of the traumatic event: When police officers experience "critical incidents" of conflict and danger, they tend to have more nightmares in general (Neylan et al., 2002).

Dream Theories

Dreams are puzzles that cry out to be solved. How could you not want to make sense out of these experiences? Although dreams may be fantastic and confusing, they are emotionally riveting, filled with vivid images from your own life, and seem very real. The search for dream meaning goes all the way back to biblical figures, who interpreted dreams and looked for prophecies in them. In the Old Testament, the prophet Daniel (a favourite of three of the authors of this book) curried favour with King Nebuchadnezzar of Babylon by interpreting the king's dreams. The question of what dreams mean has been burning since antiquity, mainly because the meaning of dreams is usually far from obvious.

Freud's View: Dreams Hold Meaning In the first psychological theory of dreams, Freud (1900/1965) proposed that dreams are confusing and obscure because the dynamic unconscious creates them precisely *to be* confusing and obscure. According to Freud, dreams represent wishes, and some of these wishes are so unacceptable, taboo, and anxiety-inducing that the mind can express them only in disguised form. Freud believed that many of the most unacceptable wishes are sexual. For instance, he would interpret a dream of a train going into a tunnel as symbolic of sexual intercourse. According to Freud, the **manifest content** of a dream, or *its apparent topic or superficial meaning,* is a smoke screen for its **latent content**, *a dream's true underlying meaning.* The problem with Freud's approach is that any dream has infinite potential interpretations. Finding the "correct" one is a matter of guesswork—and of convincing the dreamer that one interpretation is superior to the others.

Although dreams may not represent elaborately hidden wishes, there is evidence that they do feature the return of suppressed thoughts. Researchers asked volunteers to think of a personal acquaintance and then to spend five minutes before going to bed writing down whatever came to mind (Wegner, Wenzlaff, & Kozak, 2004). Some participants were asked to suppress thoughts of this person as they wrote, others were asked to focus on thoughts of the person, and still others were asked to just write freely about anything. The next morning, participants wrote dream reports. All participants mentioned dreaming more about the person they had named than about other people. But they most often dreamed of the person they named if they were in the group that had been assigned to suppress thoughts of the person the night before. This finding suggests that dreams may indeed harbour unwanted thoughts. Perhaps this is why travellers often dream of getting lost, students often dream of missing tests, and professors often dream of forgetting their lectures.

The Activation–Synthesis Model: The Brain Imposes Meaning on Random Neural Activity Another key theory of dreaming is the **activation–synthesis model** (Hobson & McCarley, 1977). This theory proposes that dreams are produced when the brain attempts to make sense of random neural activity that occurs during sleep. During waking consciousness, the mind is devoted to making sense of the wide range of information that arrives through the senses. You figure out that the odd noise you're hearing during class is your cell phone vibrating, for example, or you realize that the strange smell in the hall outside your room must be from burned popcorn. In the dream state, the mind doesn't have access to external sensations, but it keeps on doing what it usually does: interpreting information. Because that information now comes from neural activations that occur in the now-closed system of the brain, without the continuity provided by the perception of reality, the brain's interpretive mechanisms can run free.

manifest content A dream's apparent topic or superficial meaning.

latent content A dream's true underlying meaning.

activation–synthesis model The theory that dreams are produced when the brain attempts to make sense of random neural activity that occurs during sleep.

This might be why, for example, a person in a dream can sometimes change into someone else. No actual person is being perceived to help the mind keep a stable view. In the mind's effort to perceive and give meaning to brain activation, the person you view in a dream about a grocery store might seem to be a clerk, but then change to be your favourite teacher. The great interest people have in interpreting their dreams the next morning may be an extension of the interpretive activity they've been doing all night.

The Freudian and the activation–synthesis theories differ in the significance they place on the meaning of dreams. In Freud's theory, dreams begin with meaning, whereas in the activation–synthesis theory, dreams begin randomly—but meaning can be added as the mind lends interpretations in the process of dreaming. Dream research has not yet sorted out whether one of these theories or yet another might be the best account of the meaning of dreams.

The Dreaming Brain

What happens in the brain when we dream? Numerous studies have involved fMRI scanning of people's brains during sleep, focusing on the areas of the brain that show changes in activation during REM periods. These studies show that the brain changes that occur during REM sleep correspond with certain alterations of consciousness that occur in dreaming. **FIGURE 5.12** shows some of the patterns of activation and deactivation found in the dreaming brain (Nir & Tononi, 2010; Schwartz & Maquet, 2002).

In dreams there are heights to look down from, dangerous people lurking about, the occasional monster, some minor worries, and at least once in a while that major exam you've forgotten about until you walk into class. These themes suggest that the brain areas responsible for fear or emotion somehow work overtime in dreams, and it turns out that this is clearly visible in fMRI scans. The amygdala is involved in responses to threatening or stressful events, and indeed the amygdala is quite active during REM sleep.

The typical dream is also a visual wonderland, with visual events present in almost all dreams. However, there are fewer auditory sensations, even fewer tactile sensations, and almost no smells or tastes. Moreover, people differ dramatically in how much of each sensation they experience in their dreams, as described in A World of Difference: Dreaming Blind. This dream "picture show" doesn't involve actual perception, of course, just the imagination of visual events. It turns out that the areas of the brain responsible for visual perception are *not* activated during dreaming, whereas the visual association areas in the occipital lobe that are responsible for visual imagery *do* show activation (Braun et al., 1998). Your brain is smart enough to realize that it's not really seeing bizarre images but acts instead as though it's imagining bizarre images.

Freud theorized that dreams represent unacceptable wishes that the mind can only express in disguised form. The activation–synthesis model proposes that dreams are produced when the mind attempts to make sense of random neural activity that occurs during sleep. Suppose you are expecting a visit from an overbearing relative or acquaintance; the night before that person's arrival, you dream that a bus is driven through the living room window of your house. How might Freud have interpreted such a dream? How might the activation–synthesis model interpret such a dream?

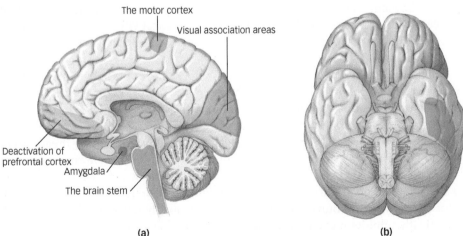

(a)   (b)

Figure 5.12
Brain Activation and Deactivation During REM Sleep Brain areas shaded red are activated during REM sleep; those shaded blue are deactivated. (a) The medial view shows activation of the amygdala, the visual association areas, the motor cortex, and the brain stem, and deactivation of the prefrontal cortex. (b) The ventral view shows activation of other visual association areas and deactivation of the prefrontal cortex (Schwartz & Maquet, 2002).

A World of Difference | Dreaming Blind

What are your dreams like? Are they mostly visual? Do you hear sounds? Do you experience the sense of touch? taste? smell? We all differ in our experience of dreaming, just as we do in our waking life. Most people have the ability to experience all of their senses during dreaming. But what about people who lack the ability to experience one of their senses? What is the experience of dreaming like for those who are blind? Researchers have examined this question by asking people who are blind to keep dream journals each day for several weeks, and comparing their reports of their dreams with those of people with sight. For instance, a study by Meaidi and colleagues (2014) revealed that 100% of dreams among sighted people contain visual impressions, compared with only about 75% of dreams among those who had sight and then lost it ("late blind") and 20% of dreams among those who were born blind ("congenitally blind"). It is perhaps not surprising that people who could never see are less likely to "see" during their dreams, but interesting

that in 20% of their dreams they can see (although these visual impressions occur only in blind individuals who have at least some amount of light perception).

The lack of visual content in the dreams of people who are blind is made up for by a higher percentage of dreams containing auditory and tactile impressions, as shown in the figure.

Unfortunately, those who are congenitally blind also have a much higher frequency of nightmares, which occur in

nearly 25% of their dreams. These nightmares often have the theme that the blind person is doing something wrong (as a result of their lack of sight), which leads to aggressive responses from others (Meaidi et al., 2014). Virtually all of psychology is focused on understanding the waking mind; however, there appear to be a wide range of important individual differences in the experience of the dreaming mind that are just beginning to be understood.

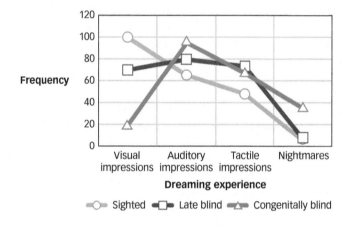

During REM sleep, the prefrontal cortex shows relatively less arousal than it usually does during waking consciousness. What does this mean for the dreamer? As a rule, the prefrontal areas are associated with planning and executing actions, and often dreams seem to be unplanned and rambling. Perhaps this is why dreams often don't have very sensible story lines—they've been scripted by an author whose ability to plan is inactive. One exception to this is seen in the case of *lucid dreaming*, a state in which a person becomes aware that he or she is dreaming while still in a sleep and dream state. Lucid dreams have been described for decades, but are only recently becoming better understood via brain activation studies, which show that people who experience lucid dreams show greater connectivity between the prefrontal cortex and the association areas of the brain that typically are deactivated during sleep (Baird et al., 2018).

Another odd fact of dreaming is that although the eyes are moving rapidly, the body is otherwise very still. During REM sleep, the motor cortex is activated, but spinal neurons running through the brain stem inhibit the expression of this motor activation (Lai & Siegal, 1999). This turns out to be a useful property of brain activation in dreaming; otherwise, you might get up and act out every dream! Individuals suffering from one rare sleep disorder, in fact, lose the normal muscular inhibition accompanying REM sleep and so act out their dreams, thrashing around in bed or stalking around the bedroom (Mahowald & Schenck, 2000). However, most people who are moving during sleep are probably not dreaming. The brain specifically inhibits movement during dreams, perhaps to keep us from hurting ourselves.

Drugs and Consciousness: Artificial Inspiration

The British author of the 1932 dystopian novel *Brave New World,* Aldous Huxley, once wrote of his experiences with the drug mescaline. His book *The Doors of Perception* described the intense experience that accompanied Huxley's departure from normal consciousness. He described "a world where everything shone with the Inner Light, and was infinite in its significance. The legs, for example, of a chair—how miraculous their tubularity, how supernatural their polished smoothness! I spent several minutes—or was it several centuries?—not merely gazing at those bamboo legs, but actually *being* them" (Huxley, 1954, p. 22).

Being the legs of a chair? This probably is better than being the seat of a chair, but it still sounds like an odd experience. Nevertheless, many people seek out such experiences, often through the use of drugs. **Psychoactive drugs** are *chemicals that influence consciousness or behaviour by altering the brain's chemical message system.* You read about several such drugs in the Neuroscience and Behaviour chapter when we explored the brain's system of neurotransmitters. And you will read about them in a different light when we turn to their role in the treatment of psychological disorders in the Treatment chapter. Whether these drugs are used for entertainment, for treatment, or for other reasons, they each exert their influence by increasing the activity of a neurotransmitter (the agonists) or decreasing its activity (the antagonists).

Some of the most common neurotransmitters are serotonin, dopamine, gamma-aminobutyric acid (GABA), and acetylcholine. Drugs alter the functioning of neurotransmitters by preventing them from binding to sites on the postsynaptic neuron, by inhibiting their reuptake to the presynaptic neuron, or by enhancing their binding and transmission. Different drugs can intensify or dull transmission patterns, creating changes in brain electrical activities that mimic natural operations of the brain. For example, a drug such as Valium (benzodiazepine) induces sleep but prevents dreaming and so induces a state similar to slow-wave sleep—that is, what the brain naturally develops several times each night. Other drugs prompt patterns of brain activity that do not occur naturally, however, and their influence on consciousness can be dramatic. Like Huxley, who perceived himself becoming the legs of a chair, people using drugs can have experiences unlike any they might find in normal waking consciousness or even in dreams. To understand these altered states, let's explore how people use and abuse drugs, and examine the major categories of psychoactive drugs.

Drug Use and Addiction

Why do children sometimes spin around until they get dizzy and fall down? There is something strangely attractive about states of consciousness that depart from the norm, and people throughout history have sought out these altered states by

Learning Outcomes

- Explain the dangers of addiction.
- Identify categories of psychoactive drugs and their effects on the body.

psychoactive drugs Chemicals that influence consciousness or behaviour by altering the brain's chemical message system.

MATTHEW NOCK

Why do kids enjoy spinning around until they get so dizzy that they fall down? Even when we are young, there seems to be something enjoyable about altering states of consciousness.

dancing, fasting, chanting, meditating, and ingesting a bizarre assortment of chemicals to intoxicate themselves (Crocq, 2007). People pursue altered consciousness even when there are costs, from the nausea that accompanies dizziness to the life-wrecking obsession with a drug that can come with addiction. In this regard, the pursuit of altered consciousness can be a fatal attraction.

Often, drug-induced changes in consciousness begin as pleasant and spark an initial attraction. Researchers have measured the attractiveness of psychoactive drugs by seeing how hard laboratory animals will work to get them. In one study researchers allowed rats to administer cocaine to themselves intravenously by pressing a lever (Bozarth & Wise, 1985). Rats given free access to cocaine increased their use over the course of the 30-day study. They not only continued to self-administer at a high rate but also occasionally binged to the point of giving themselves convulsions. They stopped grooming themselves and eating until they lost on average almost a third of their body weight. About 90% of the rats died by the end of the study.

Rats are not tiny humans, of course, so such research is not a complete basis for understanding human responses to cocaine. But these results do make it clear that cocaine is addictive and that the consequences of such addiction can be dire. Studies of self-administration of drugs in laboratory animals show that animals will work to obtain not only cocaine but also alcohol, amphetamines, barbiturates, caffeine, opiates (such as morphine and heroin), nicotine, phencyclidine (PCP), MDMA (Ecstasy), and THC (tetrahydrocannabinol, the active ingredient in marijuana). There are some psychoactive drugs that animals won't work for (such as mescaline or the antipsychotic drug phenothiazine), suggesting that these drugs have less potential for causing addiction (Bozarth, 1987).

Dangers of Addiction

People usually do not become addicted to a psychoactive drug the first time they use it. They may experiment a few times, then try again, and eventually find that their tendency to use the drug increases over time. Research suggests that the principles discussed in the Learning chapter apply here—namely, that drug use is initially motivated by *positive reinforcement*, which refers to an increase in the likelihood of a behaviour following the presentation of a reward. In other words, people often try and then repeat the use of psychoactive drugs because those drugs induce a positive psychological state (for reasons described below). Over time, however, some drugs become less rewarding and the motivation to continue to take them is driven by *negative reinforcement*, which refers to an increase in the likelihood of a behaviour following the removal of an aversive state (see **FIGURE 5.13**). That is, people often

Figure 5.13
Drug Addiction Often Occurs as the Motivation to Use Drugs Shifts from Positive to Negative Reinforcement Recent research suggests that people often start out using drugs because of the positive experiences they have as a result. But over time, addiction can result if people continue to use drugs to avoid the unpleasant effects of drug withdrawal (George & Koob, 2017).

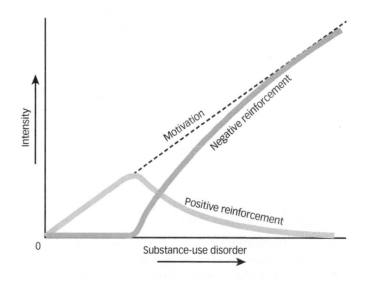

continue to use psychoactive drugs to reduce or eliminate withdrawal symptoms that arise after the drug leaves their system (George & Koob, 2017). Three primary factors are influential in this process:

1. **Drug tolerance** refers to *the tendency for larger drug doses to be required over time to achieve the same effect.* Physicians who prescribe morphine to control pain in their patients are faced with tolerance problems because steadily greater amounts of the drug may be needed to dampen the same pain. With increased tolerance comes the danger of drug overdose; recreational users find they need to use more and more of a drug to produce the same high. But then, if a new batch of heroin or cocaine is more concentrated than usual, or if the user takes the drug in an unfamiliar environment (see The Real World: Understanding Drug Overdoses in the Learning chapter), the "normal" amount the user takes to achieve the same high can be fatal.

2. *Physical dependence* refers to the pain, convulsions, hallucinations, or other unpleasant symptoms that accompany withdrawal from drug use. People who suffer from physical dependence may seek to continue drug use to avoid becoming physically ill. A common example is the "caffeine headache" some people complain of when they haven't had their daily jolt of java.

3. *Psychological dependence* refers to a strong desire to return to the drug even when physical withdrawal symptoms are gone. Drugs can create an emotional need over time that continues to prey on the mind, particularly in circumstances that are reminders of the drug. Some ex-smokers report longing wistfully for an after-dinner smoke, for example, even years after they've successfully quit the habit.

There Are Individual Differences in Risk for Addiction

There continues to be a great deal of debate about the extent to which we should think of addiction as a choice (i.e., a person can simply decide to use drugs or not), or as a disease over which a person has little or no control. Those who suggest that choice plays a prominent role in addiction note that large-scale studies conducted in the 1980s, 1990s, and 2000s consistently show that approximately 75% of those with substance use disorders overcome their addiction, with the biggest drop in use occurring between ages 20 and 30 (Heyman, 2009).

For instance, one classic study of American soldiers who became addicted to heroin while serving in Vietnam during the Vietnam War (1955–1975) found that, years after their return, only 12% remained addicted (Robins et al., 1980). Resuming the activities, attractions, and obligations of normal life, as well as leaving behind the places and faces associated with their old drug habit, made it possible for returning soldiers to quit successfully—or so the argument goes.

On the other hand, those who argue that addiction is a disease note research over the past several decades suggesting that some people have clear genetic, neurobiological, and social predispositions to have deficits in their ability to resist the urge to engage in drug use, even when doing so has extremely negative consequences such as losing one's home or family (Volkow & Boyle, 2018; Volkow, Koob, & McLellan, 2016). Not everyone has these predisposing factors; in fact, studies suggest that even among those who are exposed to drugs of addiction, only about 10% will go on to develop an addiction (Warner et al., 1995). Like the nature-versus-nurture debate more generally, the reality about drug addiction seems not to be an either-or situation. Rather, it seems that most people do not have a genetic, neurobiological, or social predisposition to drug addiction; therefore, even if exposed to addictive

BETTMANN/GETTY IMAGES

Many American soldiers serving in Vietnam became addicted to heroin while there. Robins and colleagues (1980) found that after returning home to the United States, however, the vast majority left their drug habit behind and were no longer addicted.

drug tolerance The tendency for larger doses of a drug to be required over time to achieve the same effect.

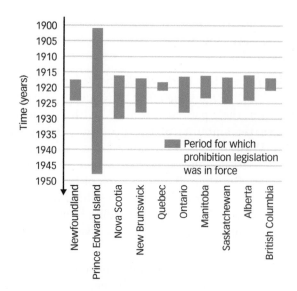

Prohibition legislation in Canada banned the production, storage, transportation, sales, and consumption of the drug alcohol (in the form of beer, wine, and spirits). Prohibition was a provincial matter and occurred at different times in different provinces. Called Canada's "Noble Experiment," Prohibition was always controversial and, as you can see, short-lived. Whereas many provinces had repealed Prohibition legislation by 1925, Prohibition in the United States lasted from 1920 to 1933. Why did the prohibition of alcohol largely fail?

drugs, they will be able to resist their short- or long-term use. However, some people are more strongly predisposed to have difficulties resisting the urge to use drugs—difficulties that, at the extreme end of the spectrum, can take the form of a disease that appears beyond a person's behavioural control.

What's Considered "Addictive" Can Change

Although "addiction" as a concept is familiar to most of us, there is no standard clinical definition of what an addiction actually is. The concept of addiction has been extended to many human pursuits beyond drugs and alcohol, giving rise to such terms as *sex addict*, *gambling addict*, *workaholic*, and, of course, *chocoholic*. Societies react differently at different times. For instance, in the early 17th century, tobacco use was punishable by death in Germany, by castration in Russia, and by decapitation in China (Corti, 1931). Not a good time or place to be a smoker. By contrast, at several points throughout history, marijuana, cocaine, and heroin have all been popular and even recommended as medicines, each without any stigma of addiction attached (Inciardi, 2001).

In Western society today, the use of some drugs is ignored (e.g., caffeine), others regulated (alcohol), others simply taxed (tobacco), and still others subjected to intense prohibition (marijuana, cocaine, and heroin) (see Hot Science: Why Is There an Opioid Epidemic and What Can We Do About It? on page 207 for further discussion of drug use in our society). Rather than viewing *all* drug use as a problem, we need to consider the costs and benefits of such use, as well as establish ways to help people choose behaviours that are informed by this knowledge (Parrott et al., 2005).

Types of Psychoactive Drugs

Four in five North Americans use caffeine in some form every day, but not all psychoactive drugs are this familiar. To learn how both the well-known and lesser-known drugs influence the mind, let's consider several broad categories of drugs: depressants, stimulants, narcotics, hallucinogens, and marijuana. **TABLE 5.2** summarizes what is known about the potential dangers of these different types of drugs.

Depressants

depressants Substances that reduce the activity of the central nervous system.

Depressants are *substances that reduce the activity of the central nervous system*. The most commonly used depressant is alcohol; others include barbiturates,

TABLE 5.2
DANGERS OF DRUGS

Drug	Dangers		
	Overdose (Can taking too much cause death or injury?)	Physical Dependence (Will stopping use make you sick?)	Psychological Dependence (Will you crave it when you stop using it?)
Depressants			
Alcohol	X	X	X
Benzodiazepines/Barbiturates	X	X	X
Toxic inhalants	X	X	X
Stimulants			
Amphetamines	X	X	X
MDMA (Ecstasy)	X		?
Nicotine	X	X	X
Cocaine	X	X	X
Narcotics (opium, heroin, morphine, methadone, codeine)	X	X	X
Hallucinogens (LSD, mescaline, psilocybin, PCP, ketamine)	X		?
Marijuana		?	?

benzodiazepines, and toxic inhalants (such as glue or gasoline). Depressants have a sedative or calming effect, tend to induce sleep in high doses, and can arrest breathing in extremely high doses. Depressants can produce both physical and psychological dependence.

Alcohol Alcohol is king of the depressants, with its worldwide use beginning in prehistory, its easy availability in most cultures, and its widespread acceptance as a socially approved substance. Twenty-two million Canadians, or 80% of the population, report having consumed alcohol in the previous year (Public Health Agency of Canada, 2016). Nineteen percent of (approximately 1 in 5) Canadians aged 12 and over reported being heavy drinkers, meaning that they consumed 5 or more drinks per occasion, at least once a month in the past year (Statistics Canada, 2019c). Young adults (ages 18–34) have higher rates, with 33.5% of men and 23.8% of women reporting that they are heavy drinkers (Statistics Canada, 2019c).

Alcohol's initial effects, euphoria and reduced anxiety, feel pretty positive. As alcohol is consumed in greater quantities, however, drunkenness results, bringing with it slowed reactions, slurred speech, poor judgement, and other reductions in the effectiveness of thought and action. The exact way in which alcohol influences neural mechanisms is still not understood, but, like other depressants, alcohol increases activity of the neurotransmitter GABA (Koob & Volkow, 2016). As you read in the Neuroscience and Behaviour chapter, GABA normally inhibits the transmission of neural impulses, thus one effect of alcohol is as an inhibitor—a chemical that stops the firing of other neurons. Yet people react very differently to alcohol. Some become loud and aggressive, others become emotional and weepy, others become sullen, and still others turn giddy—and the same person can experience each of these effects in different circumstances. How can one drug do all this? Two theories have been offered to account for these variable effects: *expectancy theory* and *alcohol myopia*.

Which theory, expectancy theory or alcohol myopia, views a person's response to alcohol as being (at least partially) learned, through a process similar to observational learning?

expectancy theory The idea that alcohol effects can be produced by people's expectations of how alcohol will influence them in particular situations.

balanced placebo design A study design in which behaviour is observed following the presence or absence of an actual stimulus and also following the presence or absence of a placebo stimulus.

alcohol myopia A condition that results when alcohol hampers attention, leading people to respond in simple ways to complex situations.

1. **Expectancy theory** suggests that *alcohol effects can be produced by people's expectations of how alcohol will influence them in particular situations* (Marlatt & Rohsenow, 1980). So, for instance, if you've watched friends or family drink at weddings and notice that this often produces hilarity and gregariousness, you could well experience these effects yourself should you drink alcohol on a similarly festive occasion. Seeing people get drunk and fight in bars, on the other hand, might lead to aggression after drinking. The expectancy theory has been tested in experiments using a **balanced placebo design**, in which *behaviour is observed following the presence or absence of an actual stimulus and also following the presence or absence of a placebo stimulus*. In such a study, participants are given drinks containing alcohol or a substitute nonalcoholic liquid (adjusted for scent and colour); some people in each group are led to believe they drank alcohol while others are led to believe they did not. These experiments often show that the mere *belief* that one has had alcohol can influence behaviour as strongly as the ingestion of alcohol itself (Goldman, Brown, & Christiansen, 1987).

2. The theory of **alcohol myopia** proposes that *alcohol hampers attention, leading people to respond in simple ways to complex situations* (Steele & Josephs, 1990). This theory recognizes that life is filled with complicated pushes and pulls, and our behaviour is often a balancing act. Imagine that you are really attracted to someone who is dating your friend. Do you make your feelings known or focus on your friendship? The myopia theory holds that when you drink alcohol, your fine judgement is impaired. It becomes hard to appreciate the subtlety of these different options, and the inappropriate response is to veer full tilt one way or the other. In one study on the alcohol myopia theory, men (half of whom were drinking alcohol) watched a video showing an unfriendly woman and then were asked how acceptable it would be for a man to act in a sexually aggressive way towards a woman (Johnson, Noel, & Sutter-Hernandez, 2000). The unfriendly woman seemed to remind them that sex was out of the question, and indeed, men who were drinking alcohol and had seen this video were no more likely to think sexual advances were acceptable than were men who were sober. However, when the same question was asked of a group of men who had seen a video of a *friendly* woman, those who were drinking were more inclined to recommend sexual overtures than those who were not, even when these overtures might be unwanted.

Both the expectancy and myopia theories suggest that people using alcohol will often go to extremes (Cooper, 2006). In fact, it seems that drinking is a major contributing factor to social problems that result from extreme behaviour. Drinking while driving is a major cause of auto accidents. In Canada in 2014, car accidents claimed an estimated 2,297 lives. Based on testing of fatally injured drivers, two in seven deaths resulted from crashes in which the driver tested positive for alcohol, or alcohol and other drugs. Alcohol also has been linked to increased aggression towards others in dozens of studies, including increased likelihood of aggression in general, as well as sexual violence and intimate partner violence (Crane et al., 2015).

Barbiturates, Benzodiazepines, and Toxic Inhalants Compared to alcohol, the other depressants are much less popular but are still widely used and abused. Barbiturates such as Seconal or Nembutal are prescribed as sleep aids and as anesthetics before surgery. Benzodiazepines such as Valium and Xanax are also called minor tranquilizers and are prescribed as antianxiety drugs. These drugs are prescribed by physicians to treat anxiety or sleep problems, but they are dangerous when used in combination with alcohol because they can cause respiratory depression (slowed breathing). Physical dependence is possible because withdrawal from long-term use can produce severe symptoms (including convulsions), and psychological dependence is common as well. Finally, toxic inhalants are perhaps the most alarming substances in this category (Ridenour & Howard, 2012). These drugs are easily accessible, in the vapours of inexpensive household products such as glue, hair spray, nail polish remover, or gasoline. Sniffing or "huffing" vapours from these products can promote temporary effects that resemble drunkenness, but overdoses can be lethal, and continued use holds the potential for permanent neurological damage (Howard et al., 2011). Perhaps because these products are so easily accessible, inhalant abuse often affects children at younger ages, compared to other forms of substance abuse; it is especially common in individuals from minority and economically and socially marginalized groups.

Stimulants

Stimulants are *substances that excite the central nervous system, heightening arousal and activity levels.* They include caffeine, amphetamines, nicotine, cocaine, modafinil, and Ecstasy, some of which sometimes have a legitimate pharmaceutical purpose. Amphetamines (also called *speed*), for example, were originally prepared for medicinal uses and as diet drugs; however, amphetamines such as Methedrine and Dexedrine are widely abused, causing insomnia, aggression, and paranoia with long-term use. Stimulants increase the levels of dopamine and norepinephrine in the brain, thereby inducing higher levels of activity in the brain circuits that depend on these neurotransmitters. As a result, they increase alertness and energy in the user, often producing a euphoric sense of confidence and a kind of agitated motivation to get things done. Stimulants produce physical and psychological dependence, and their withdrawal symptoms involve depressive effects such as fatigue and negative emotions.

Ecstasy (also known as MDMA, "X," or "E"), an amphetamine derivative, is a stimulant, but it has additional effects somewhat like those of hallucinogens. (We'll talk about those shortly.) Ecstasy is particularly known for making users feel empathic and close to those around them. It is used often as a party drug to enhance the group feeling at dance clubs or raves, but it has unpleasant side effects, such as causing jaw clenching and interfering with the regulation of body temperature. The rave culture has popularized pacifiers and juices as remedies for these problems, but users, who have suppressed appetite, thirst, or need to sleep, are highly susceptible to dehydration, heat stroke, and general exhaustion. Although Ecstasy is not as likely as some other drugs to cause physical or psychological dependence, it nonetheless can lead to some dependence. What's more, the impurities sometimes found in street pills can be dangerous (Parrott, 2001). Ecstasy's potentially toxic effect on serotonin neurons in the human brain is under debate, although mounting evidence from animal and human studies suggests that sustained use is associated with damage to serotonergic neurons and potential associated problems with mood, attention and memory, and impulse control (Kish et al., 2010; Urban et al., 2012).

Cocaine is derived from leaves of the coca plant, which has been cultivated by indigenous peoples of the Andes for millennia and chewed as a medication. And yes, the urban legend is true: Coca-Cola did contain cocaine until 1903 and may still use coca leaves to this day (with cocaine removed) as a flavouring—although the company's not telling. (Pepsi-Cola never contained cocaine and is probably made from something brown.) Sigmund Freud tried cocaine and wrote effusively about it for a while. Cocaine (usually snorted) and crack cocaine (smoked) produce exhilaration and euphoria and are seriously addictive, both for humans and the rats you read about earlier in this chapter. Withdrawal takes the form of an unpleasant crash; dangerous side effects of cocaine use include psychological problems (e.g., insomnia, depression, aggression, and paranoia) as well as physical problems (e.g., death from a heart attack or hyperthermia) (Marzuk et al., 1998). Although cocaine has been used for many years as a party drug, its extraordinary potential to create dependence and its potentially lethal side effects should be taken very seriously.

The popularity of nicotine is something of a puzzle, however. This is a drug with almost nothing to recommend it to the newcomer. It usually involves inhaling smoke that doesn't smell that great, at least at first, and there's not much in the way of

stimulants Substances that excite the central nervous system, heightening arousal and activity levels.

Because of the known dangers of smoking cigarettes, many are turning to electronic cigarettes (e-cigarettes) under the assumption that they are a safe alternative. However, an investigation of the chemicals contained in flavoured e-cigarettes revealed that 92% of them contain the dangerous chemical diacetyl, which has been linked to severe and irreversible medical problems such as "popcorn lung" (Allen et al., 2016).

People will often endure significant inconveniences to maintain their addictions, which in the case of smoking means puffing smoke to avoid the withdrawal symptoms that come with quitting.

ANGEL FRANCO/THE NEW YORK TIMES/REDUX PICTURES

a high, either—at best, some dizziness or a queasy feeling. So why do people use it? Tobacco use is motivated far more by the unpleasantness of quitting than by the pleasantness of using. The positive effects people report from smoking—relaxation and improved concentration, for example—come chiefly from relief from withdrawal symptoms (Baker, Brandon, & Chassin, 2004). The best approach to nicotine is to never get started.

Narcotics

Opium, which comes from poppy seeds, and its derivatives heroin, morphine, methadone, and codeine (as well as prescription drugs such as Demerol and Oxycontin) are known as **narcotics** (or **opiates**), *highly addictive drugs derived from opium that relieve pain.* Narcotics induce a feeling of well-being and relaxation that is enjoyable, but they can also induce stupor and lethargy. The addictive properties of narcotics are powerful, and long-term use produces both tolerance and dependence. Because these drugs are often administered with hypodermic syringes, they also introduce the danger of diseases such as hepatitis and HIV when users share syringes. Unfortunately, these drugs are especially alluring because they mimic the brain's own internal relaxation and well-being system.

The brain produces endogenous opioids or endorphins, which are neuropeptides closely related to opiates. As you learned in the Neuroscience and Behaviour chapter, endorphins play a role in how the brain copes internally with pain and stress. These substances reduce the experience of pain naturally. When you exercise for a while and start to feel your muscles burning, for example, you may also find that a time comes when the pain eases—sometimes even *during* exercise. Endorphins are secreted in the pituitary gland and other brain sites as a response to injury or exertion, creating a kind of natural remedy, sometimes referred to as "runner's high," that subsequently reduces pain and increases feelings of well-being. (Recent interesting research suggests that runner's high also seems to be induced in part by activation of the brain's endocannabinoid system—the same one involved in response to smoking marijuana [Fuss et al., 2015]).

When people use narcotics, the brain's endorphin receptors are artificially flooded, however, reducing receptor effectiveness and possibly also depressing the production of endorphins. When external administration of narcotics stops, withdrawal symptoms are likely to occur. Withdrawal symptoms can be especially difficult to cope with when using narcotics, which might partially explain the current opioid epidemic sweeping the United States and Canada (see Hot Science: Why Is There an Opioid Epidemic and What Can We Do About It? for more on this important topic).

Hallucinogens

The drugs that produce the most extreme alterations of consciousness are the **hallucinogens**, *which alter sensation and perception and often cause visual and auditory hallucinations.* These include LSD (lysergic acid diethylamide, or acid), mescaline, psilocybin, PCP (phencyclidine), and ketamine (an animal anesthetic). Some of these drugs are derived from plants (mescaline from peyote cactus, psilocybin or "shrooms" from mushrooms) and have been used by people since ancient times. For example, the ingestion of peyote plays a prominent role in some Native American religious practices. The other hallucinogens are largely synthetic. LSD was first made by the chemist Albert Hofmann in 1938, leading to a rash of experimentation that influenced popular culture in the 1960s. Timothy Leary, at the time a lecturer in the Department of Psychology at Harvard, championed the use of LSD to "turn on, tune in, and drop out"; the Beatles sang of "*Lucy* in the *Sky* with *Diamonds*" (denying, of course, that this might be a reference to LSD); and the wave of interest led many people to experiment with hallucinogens.

narcotics (opiates) Highly addictive drugs derived from opium that relieve pain.

hallucinogens Drugs that alter sensation and perception and often cause visual and auditory hallucinations.

Hot Science | Why Is There an Opioid Epidemic and What Can We Do About It?

Opioids have been around in one form or another for thousands of years. For instance, an early medicine called theriac was used for over 1,500 years to treat a range of illnesses, including anxiety and depression. Its more than 100 ingredients often included things like viper's flesh, roses, and carrots, but the only active ingredient turned out to be opium. Although opium and its derivatives have been consumed in some fashion for some time, our society has seen an absolutely startling rise in the use of opioids in just the past few years. The rate of opioid overdoses has increased dramatically in the past few years, and British Columbia, especially the Lower Mainland, has been among the regions hardest hit (see accompanying figures).

What's the reason for this drastic increase in opioid overdoses? Tragically, this appears to be something of an inside job. Faulty reporting of research in the 1980s and 1990s suggested that the risk of addiction to opioids prescribed for pain relief was low. Pharmaceutical companies pushed this reassuring message about the new opioid drugs they were introducing, and the prescribing of opioids for pain increased sharply in the 1990s. The drugs were subsequently extensively misused: about 10–12% of individuals with prescriptions would become addicted, but the presence of large quantities of these drugs in homes increased access for vulnerable family members, friends, and others. It soon became clear that these drugs could indeed be highly addictive, but by then, addiction and overdose deaths were widespread. Those afflicted had turned to nonprescription forms such as heroin and the powerful synthetic opioid fentanyl.

So, what can be done to turn the tide of this epidemic? Scientists and policy makers are arguing for obvious fixes, such as implementing physician training and policy changes to decrease inappropriately high prescription of these drugs, developing less addictive pain medications, and initiating public education campaigns that alert communities and individuals to the dangers of potential opioid addiction (Volkow et al., 2019). These strategies may help prevent new addictions. Harm from opioid addiction can be reduced through the introduction of supervised consumption facilities, and by making naloxone, a drug that rapidly reverses opioid overdoses, more accessible and easier to use by those without extensive training. What are some other approaches that might be tried?

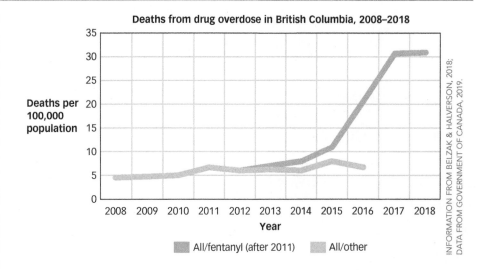

Deaths from drug overdose in British Columbia, 2008–2018

INFORMATION FROM BELZAK & HALVERSON, 2018; DATA FROM GOVERNMENT OF CANADA, 2019.

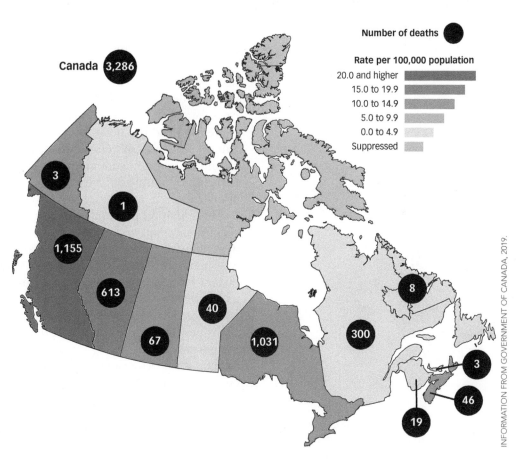

INFORMATION FROM GOVERNMENT OF CANADA, 2019.

ANDREW HERYGERS/HURRAH

Psychedelic art and music of the 1960s were inspired by some visual and auditory effects of drugs such as LSD.

The experiment was not a great success. These drugs produce profound changes in perception. Sensations may seem unusually intense, stationary objects may seem to move or change, patterns or colours may appear, and these perceptions may be accompanied by exaggerated emotions ranging from blissful transcendence to abject terror. These are the "I've-become-the-legs-of-a-chair!" drugs. But the effects of hallucinogens are dramatic and unpredictable, creating a psychological roller-coaster ride that some people find intriguing and others find deeply disturbing. Hallucinogens are the main class of drugs that animals won't work to self-administer, so it is not surprising that in humans these drugs are unlikely to be addictive. Hallucinogens do not induce significant tolerance or dependence, and overdose deaths are rare. Although hallucinogens still enjoy a marginal popularity with people interested in experimenting with their perceptions, they have been more a cultural trend than a dangerous attraction.

Marijuana

Marijuana (or **cannabis**) is *a plant whose leaves and buds contain a psychoactive drug called tetrahydrocannabinol (THC)*. When smoked or eaten, either as is or in concentrated form as *hashish,* this drug produces an intoxication that is mildly hallucinogenic. Users describe the experience as euphoric, with heightened senses of sight and sound and the perception of a rush of ideas. Marijuana affects judgement and short-term memory and impairs motor skills and coordination—making driving a car or operating heavy equipment a poor choice during its use. ("Dude, where's my bulldozer?") Researchers have found that receptors in the brain that respond to THC (Stephens, 1999) are normally activated by a neurotransmitter called *anandamide* that is naturally produced in the brain (Wiley, 1999). Anandamide is involved in the regulation of mood, memory, appetite, and pain perception and has been found to temporarily stimulate overeating in laboratory animals, much as marijuana does in humans (Williams & Kirkham, 1999). Some chemicals found in dark chocolate also mimic anandamide, although very weakly, perhaps accounting for the well-being some people claim they enjoy after a "dose" of chocolate.

The addiction potential of marijuana is not strong because tolerance does not seem to develop, and physical withdrawal symptoms are minimal. Psychological dependence is possible, however, and some people do become chronic users. Marijuana use has been widespread throughout the world throughout recorded history, both as a medicine for pain and/or nausea and as a recreational drug, but its use remains controversial. Marijuana abuse and dependence have been linked with increased risk of depression, anxiety, and other forms of psychopathology. Many people also are concerned that marijuana (along with alcohol and tobacco) is a **gateway drug**, *a drug whose use increases the risk of the subsequent use of more harmful drugs.* The gateway theory has gained mixed support, with recent studies challenging the notion and suggesting that early-onset drug use in general, regardless of type of drug, increases the risk of later drug and mental-health problems (Degenhardt et al., 2008).

In 2014, Canada's leading hospital for mental illness, the Centre for Addiction and Mental Health (CAMH) in Toronto, published evidence-based recommendations concerning cannabis policy in Canada (Centre for Addiction and Mental Health, 2014). It concluded that a public-health approach involving legalization and regulation, such as exists for alcohol and tobacco, would allow for the most control over the risk factors associated with cannabis-related harm. Perhaps this report, as well as the fact that more than 50% of Canadians supported legalization, is why the federal government legalized marijuana in 2018. See Other Voices: Canada's Grand Cannabis Experiment Has Set Scientists Free.

marijuana (cannabis) The leaves and buds of the hemp plant, which contain a psychoactive drug called tetrahydrocannabinol (THC).

gateway drug A drug whose use increases the risk of the subsequent use of more harmful drugs.

Other Voices | Canada's Grand Cannabis Experiment Has Set Scientists Free

When Canada fully legalized recreational cannabis on Oct. 17, the internet giddily reimagined the CN Tower in Toronto peeking out from a thick haze and swapped the flag's red maple leaf for its jagged-edged green cousin. Outsiders might titter about an entire populace turning into potheads, but legalization means some of the country's brightest can now turn their minds to pot.

As the first G-7 nation to slacken cannabis laws, Canada has bolted to the front lines of the plant's methodical scrutiny and investigation. No longer at risk of censure or lacking access to specimens, researchers can transcend the narrow parameters of scientific study once considered acceptable, namely, clinical research, to explore social, biological, genetic and agricultural questions. From botanists to phytochemists, microbiologists to epidemiologists, scientists of all sorts are free to openly pursue a greater quantity and quality of cannabis science than ever before.

Canada's brand-new legislation, the Cannabis Act, replaces a restrictive system that treated researchers like would-be drug dealers. Scientists intending to cultivate their own plants can now simply apply for a specific class of license rather than toil for an exemption from the retrograde Controlled Drugs and Substances Act, which, among other demands, required criminal record checks.

The Canadian government, once unwilling to touch the stuff, has stepped up to properly examine how cannabis affects the body and brain. It's funding 14 new studies and has set aside millions more for research grants that could ask questions like, Will a pregnant mother using cannabis harm her baby's development? Does smoking affect drivers' reaction time behind the wheel? And at what threshold does teenagers' pot consumption become destructive?

With the legal barriers torn down, a path has been cleared for Canadians to stake a global claim in the emerging field of research. New science projects are taking shape in Europe, Israel and Australia, many the fruit of joint ventures with Canadian companies, others made possible only with imported dried medical marijuana and cannabis oil from Canada. The country has become "the de facto source of research-grade cannabis around the world," contends Philippe Lucas, who is the head of research for the Canadian producer Tilray, which has completed exports to 10 countries.

Canada's grand experiment has already been a catalyst for smarter science in the United States, where its federal prohibition has choked research. Although 33 states have relaxed their marijuana laws, only one facility in Mississippi is federally licensed to supply dried cannabis, and its product is often derided by researchers as lackluster.

Enter Tilray, which, in a rare first this September, was approved by the Drug Enforcement Administration to supply cannabis extract from Canada to a California neurologist who's developing a treatment for tremors in the elderly. (Tilray has also built a greenhouse in a Portugal research park, expanding the science into the European Union.) America's cannabis entrepreneurs, however, aren't so keen on the prospective northern pot pipeline. One multistate medical grower has pleaded with President Trump for domestic regulation in a full-page Wall Street Journal ad, fretting that "America is rapidly losing its competitive advantage to Canada!"

Amanda Siebert is a Vancouver-based freelance journalist and author of *The Little Book of Cannabis: How Marijuana Can Improve Your Life.*

As bidding wars replace the drug war, legalization promises empirical evidence for policymakers caught between popular sensibilities and a paucity of data. Canada's statistical agency and the country's health ministry are already gathering information from a newly visible population of cannabis users. The metrics could enable jurisdictions worldwide to devise policy reforms and public health programs that minimize legalization's potentially negative impacts.

The scholarship on cannabis will finally advance now that a developed, Western society has welcomed back an ancient drug plant, says Jonathan Page, a Vancouver-based plant biologist and a leader of the cannabis genome project. Therapeutic marijuana application dates back thousands of years, according to archaeological and historical records.

"Marijuana's hard-won return to the Canadian mainstream suggests that psychoactive plants matter to modern lives and will continue to shape human culture," he said. "Prohibition was just a blip on the timeline of civilization and a dark age for science."

In an age of global paranoia, Canada's decisive leadership has produced a veritable green-field opportunity. It's incumbent on our scientists to do the plowing.

Siebert, A. (2018, November). Canada's Grand Cannabis Experiment Has Set Scientists Free. *New York Times*. Retrieved from https://www.nytimes.com/2018/11/20/opinion/cannabis-science-legal-marijuana-canada.html

Build to the Outcomes

1. What is the allure of altered consciousness?
2. What is the risk associated with increased tolerance to a drug?
3. Identify both physical and psychological drug withdrawal problems.
4. What are the statistics on overcoming addiction?
5. Why do people experience being drunk differently?
6. Do stimulants create dependency?
7. What are some of the dangerous side effects of cocaine use?
8. Why are narcotics especially alluring?
9. What are the effects of hallucinogens?
10. What are the risks of marijuana use?

Hypnosis: Open to Suggestion

hypnosis A social interaction in which one person (the hypnotist) makes suggestions that lead to a change in another person's (the participant's) subjective experience of the world.

posthypnotic amnesia The failure to retrieve memories following hypnotic suggestions to forget.

You may have never been hypnotized, but you have probably heard or read about it. People often describe its wonders with an air of amazement; demonstrations of stage hypnosis make it seem very powerful and mysterious. When you think of hypnosis, you may envision people completely under the power of a hypnotist, who is ordering them to dance like a chicken or perhaps "regress" to early childhood and talk in childlike voices. Many common beliefs about hypnosis are false. **Hypnosis** refers to *a social interaction in which one person (the hypnotist) makes suggestions that lead to a change in another person's (the participant's) subjective experience of the world* (Kirsch et al., 2011). The essence of hypnosis is in leading people to expect that certain things will happen to them that are outside their conscious will (Wegner, 2002).

Induction and Susceptibility

To induce hypnosis, a hypnotist may ask the person being hypnotized to sit quietly and focus on some item, such as a spot on the wall (or a swinging pocket watch), and may then make suggestions to the person about what effects hypnosis will have (e.g., "your eyelids are slowly closing" or "your arms are getting heavy"). Even without hypnosis, some suggested behaviours might commonly happen just because a person is concentrating on them—just thinking about their eyelids slowly closing, for instance, may make many people shut their eyes briefly or at least blink. In hypnosis, however, suggestions may be made—and followed by people in a susceptible state of mind—for very unusual behaviour that most people would not normally do, such as flapping their arms and making loud clucking sounds.

Not everyone is equally hypnotizable. Susceptibility varies greatly. Some highly suggestible people are very easily hypnotized, most people are only moderately influenced, and some people are entirely unaffected by attempts at hypnosis. Susceptibility is not easily predicted by a person's personality traits. A hypnotist will typically test someone's hypnotic susceptibility with a series of suggestions designed to put a person into a more easily influenced state of mind. One of the best indicators of a person's susceptibility is the person's own judgement. So if you think you might be hypnotizable, you may well be (Hilgard, 1965). People respond most strongly to hypnotic suggestions not only when they are highly susceptible, but also when hypnotic suggestions are made very specifically and in the context of hypnotic induction rituals (Landry, Lifshitz, & Raz, 2017).

Hypnotic Effects

From watching stage hypnotism, you might think that the major effect of hypnosis is making people do peculiar things. So what do we actually know to be true about hypnosis? Some impressive demonstrations suggest that real changes occur in those under hypnosis. At the 1849 birthday festivities for Albert, Prince Consort of Queen Victoria, for example, a hypnotized guest was asked to ignore any loud noises and then didn't even flinch when a pistol was fired near his face. These days, hypnotists are discouraged from using firearms during stage shows, but they often have volunteers perform other impressive feats. One common claim for superhuman strength under hypnosis involves asking a hypnotized person to become "stiff as a board" and lie unsupported with shoulders on one chair and feet on another while the hypnotist stands on the hypnotized person's body.

Studies have demonstrated that hypnosis can undermine memory, but with important limitations. People susceptible to hypnosis can be led to experience **posthypnotic amnesia**, *the failure to retrieve memories following hypnotic suggestions to forget.* For instance, Ernest Hilgard (1986) taught a hypnotized person the populations of some remote cities and then suggested that the participant forget

Stage hypnotists often perform an induction on the whole audience and then bring some of the more susceptible members on stage for further demonstrations.

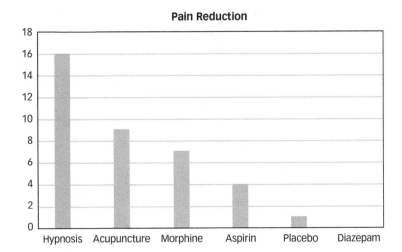

Pain Reduction

Figure 5.14
Hypnotic Analgesia The degree of pain reduction (values represent differences between experimental and control conditions on a self-reported pain scale) reported by people using different techniques for the treatment of laboratory-induced pain. Hypnosis wins (Stern et al., 1977).

the study session; after the session, the person was quite surprised at being able to give the census figures correctly. Asked how he knew the answers, the individual decided he might have learned them from a TV program. Such amnesia can then be reversed in subsequent hypnosis.

Some important research has found that only memories that were lost while under hypnosis can be retrieved through hypnosis. The false claim that hypnosis helps people unearth memories they are not able to retrieve in normal consciousness seems to have surfaced because hypnotized people often make up memories to satisfy the hypnotist's suggestions. For example, Paul Ingram, an American sheriff's deputy accused of sexual abuse by his daughters in the 1980s, was asked by interrogators in session after session to relax and imagine having committed the crimes. He emerged from these sessions having confessed to dozens of horrendous acts of "satanic ritual abuse." These confessions were called into question, however, when the independent investigator Richard Ofshe used the same technique to ask Ingram about a crime that Ofshe had simply made up out of thin air, something of which Ingram had never been accused. Ingram produced a three-page handwritten confession, complete with dialogue (Ofshe, 1992). Still, prosecutors in the case accepted Ingram's guilty plea; he was released only in 2003 after a public outcry and years of work on his defense. After a person claims to remember something, even under hypnosis, it is difficult to convince others that the memory was false (Loftus & Ketchum, 1994).

Hypnosis can lead to measurable physical and behavioural changes in the body. One well-established effect is **hypnotic analgesia**, *the reduction of pain through hypnosis in people who are susceptible to hypnosis.* For example, one classic study (see **FIGURE 5.14**) found that for pain induced in volunteers in the laboratory, hypnosis was more effective than morphine, diazepam (Valium), aspirin, acupuncture, or placebos (Stern et al., 1977). The pain-reducing properties of hypnosis have been demonstrated repeatedly over the years, with recent research from controlled trials suggesting that it can even reduce the experience of pain in brain surgery during which the patient is awake (Frati et al., 2019).

It therefore appears that people under hypnotic suggestion are not merely telling the hypnotist what he or she wants to hear. Rather, they seem to be experiencing what they have been asked to experience.

hypnotic analgesia The reduction of pain through hypnosis in people who are susceptible to hypnosis.

Build to the Outcomes

1. What factors make someone more easily hypnotizable?
2. What type of memory can be retrieved through hypnosis?
3. Can hypnosis be as effective for pain relief as anaesthesia?

Chapter Review

The Mysteries of Consciousness

- People judge mind perception according to the capacities for experience and agency.
- Research suggests that mental activity happens first, paving the way for both conscious thought and action.

The Nature of Consciousness

- Consciousness has four basic properties: intentionality, unity, selectivity, and transience. It can also be understood in terms of levels: minimal consciousness, full consciousness, and self-consciousness.
- Disorders of consciousness result from illness or severe brain damage and include coma, vegetative state, and minimally conscious state. In locked-in syndrome, people can have normal conscious awareness but be unable to signal it behaviourally.
- Conscious contents can include current concerns, daydreams, and unwanted thoughts. Efforts to suppress a thought—such as of a white bear—may backfire as the mind searches for thoughts of that white bear to suppress.

The Unconscious Mind

- Unconscious processes are sometimes understood as expressions of the Freudian dynamic unconscious, but they are more commonly viewed as processes of the cognitive unconscious that create our conscious thought and behaviour.
- The cognitive unconscious is at work when subliminal perception and unconscious decision processes influence thought or behaviour without the person's awareness.

Sleep and Dreaming: Good Night, Mind

- Sleeping and dreaming present a view of the mind in an altered state of consciousness. During a night's sleep, the brain passes in and out of five stages of sleep; most dreaming occurs in the REM sleep stage.
- Sleep needs decrease over the life span, but being deprived of sleep and dreams has psychological and physical costs. Sleep can be disrupted through disorders that include insomnia, sleep apnea, somnambulism, narcolepsy, sleep paralysis, and night terrors.
- Dream consciousness differs from the waking state in that we feel emotion intensely, thought is illogical, and sensation is fully formed and meaningful; images and events occur with uncritical acceptance; and dreams are difficult to remember.
- Theories of dreaming include Freud's psychoanalytic theory and the activation–synthesis model. fMRI studies of the brain while dreaming reveal activations associated with visual imagery, increased sensitivity to emotions such as fear, lessened capacities for planning, and the prevention of motor movement.

Drugs and Consciousness: Artificial Inspiration

- Psychoactive drugs influence consciousness by altering the brain's chemical messaging system and intensifying or dulling the effects of neurotransmitters. Drug tolerance can result in overdose, and physical and psychological dependence can lead to addiction.
- Depressants reduce activity of the central nervous system (CNS); stimulants excite the CNS; narcotics relieve pain; hallucinogens alter sensation and perception; and marijuana is mildly hallucinogenic.

Hypnosis: Open to Suggestion

- Hypnosis is an altered state of consciousness characterized by suggestibility.
- Although many claims for hypnosis overstate its effects, hypnosis can create the experience that one's actions are occurring involuntarily and even relieve pain, suggesting that hypnotic experiences are more than imagination.

Key Concept Quiz

1. Currently, unconscious processes are understood as
   a. a concentrated pattern of thought suppression.
   b. a hidden system of memories, instincts, and desires.
   c. a blank slate.
   d. unexperienced mental processes that give rise to thoughts and behaviour.

2. The _____ unconscious is at work when subliminal and unconscious processes influence thought and behaviour.
   a. minimal
   b. repressive
   c. dynamic
   d. cognitive

3. The cycle of sleep and waking is one of the major patterns of human life called
   a. the circadian rhythm.
   b. the sleep stages.
   c. the altered state of consciousness.
   d. subliminal perception.

4. Sleep needs _____ over the life span.
   a. decrease
   b. increase
   c. fluctuate
   d. remain the same

5. During dreaming, the dreamer _____ changes in emotion, thought, and sensation.
   a. is skeptical of
   b. is completely unconscious of
   c. uncritically accepts
   d. views objectively

6. Which explanation of dreams proposes that they are produced when the mind attempts to make sense of random neural activity that occurs in the brain during sleep?
   a. Freud's psychoanalytic theory
   b. the activation–synthesis model
   c. the cognitive unconscious model
   d. the manifest content framework

7. Psychoactive drugs influence consciousness by altering the effects of
   a. agonists.
   b. neurotransmitters.
   c. amphetamines.
   d. spinal neurons.

8. Tolerance for drugs involves
   a. larger doses being required over time to achieve the same effect.
   b. openness to new experiences.
   c. the initial attraction of drug use.
   d. the decrease of the painful symptoms that accompany withdrawal.

9. Alcohol expectancy refers to
   a. alcohol's initial effects of euphoria and reduced anxiety.
   b. the widespread acceptance of alcohol as a socially approved substance.
   c. alcohol leading people to respond in simple ways to complex situations.
   d. people's beliefs about how alcohol will influence them in particular situations.

10. Hypnosis has been proven to have
    a. an effect on physical strength.
    b. a positive effect on memory retrieval.
    c. an analgesic effect.
    d. an age-regression effect.

 **LearningCurve** macmillan learning

Don't stop now! Quizzing yourself is a powerful study tool. Go to LaunchPad to access the LearningCurve adaptive quizzing system and your own personalized learning plan. Visit launchpadworks.com.

Key Terms

consciousness (p. 172)

phenomenology (p. 172)

problem of other minds (p. 173)

mind–body problem (p. 174)

dichotic listening (p. 177)

cocktail-party phenomenon (p. 177)

minimal consciousness (p. 178)

full consciousness (p. 178)

self-consciousness (p. 179)

mental control (p. 184)

thought suppression (p. 184)

rebound effect of thought suppression (p. 184)

ironic processes of mental control (p. 185)

dynamic unconscious (p. 186)

repression (p. 186)

cognitive unconscious (p. 187)

dual process theories (p. 187)

altered state of consciousness (p. 188)

circadian rhythm (p. 189)

REM sleep (p. 190)

electrooculograph (EOG) (p. 190)

insomnia (p. 193)

sleep apnea (p. 193)

somnambulism (sleepwalking) (p. 194)

narcolepsy (p. 194)

sleep paralysis (p. 194)

night terrors (sleep terrors) (p. 194)

manifest content (p. 196)

latent content (p. 196)

activation–synthesis model (p. 196)

psychoactive drugs (p. 199)

drug tolerance (p. 201)

depressants (p. 202)

expectancy theory (p. 204)

balanced placebo design (p. 204)

alcohol myopia (p. 204)

stimulants (p. 205)

narcotics (opiates) (p. 206)

hallucinogens (p. 206)

marijuana (cannabis) (p. 208)

gateway drug (p. 208)

hypnosis (p. 210)

posthypnotic amnesia (p. 210)

hypnotic analgesia (p. 211)

Changing Minds

1. "I had a really weird dream last night," your friend tells you. "I dreamed that I was trying to fly like a bird but I kept flying into clotheslines. I looked it up online, and dreams where you're struggling to fly mean that there is someone in your life who's standing in your way and preventing you from moving forwards. I suppose that has to be my boyfriend, so maybe I'd better break up with him." Applying what you've read in this chapter, what would you tell your friend about the reliability of dream interpretation?

2. During an early-morning class, you notice your friend yawning, and you ask if he slept well the night before. "On weekdays, I'm in class all day, and I work the night shift," he says. "So I don't sleep much during the week. But I figure it's okay because I make up for it by sleeping late on Saturday mornings." Is it realistic for your friend to assume

that he can balance regular sleep deprivation with rebound sleep on the weekends?

3. You and a friend are watching the 2010 movie *Inception*, starring Leonardo DiCaprio as a corporate spy. DiCaprio's character is hired by a businessman named Saito to plant an idea in the unconscious mind of a competitor while he sleeps. According to the plan, when the competitor awakens, he'll be compelled to act on the idea, to the secret benefit of Saito's company. "It's a cool idea," your friend says, "but it's pure science fiction. There's no such thing as an unconscious mind, and no way that unconscious ideas could influence the way you act when you're conscious." What would you tell your friend? What evidence do we have that the unconscious mind does exist and can influence conscious behaviour?

Answers to Key Concept Quiz

1. d; 2. d; 3. a; 4. a; 5. c; 6. b; 7. b; 8. a; 9. d; 10. c

 **LaunchPad** macmillan learning

LaunchPad features the full e-Book of *Psychology*, the LearningCurve adaptive quizzing system, videos, and a variety of activities to boost your learning. Visit LaunchPad at launchpadworks.com.

Memory

JILL PRICE WAS 12 YEARS OLD when she began to suspect that she possessed an unusually good memory. While she was studying for a seventh-grade science final on May 30, her mind drifted and she became aware that she could recall vividly everything she had been doing on May 30 of the previous year. Remembering specifics of events that occurred a year ago may not seem so extraordinary—you can probably recall what you did for your last birthday or where you spent last Thanksgiving. But can you recall the details of what you did exactly 1 year ago today? Or what you did a week, a month, 6 months, or 6 years before that day? Probably not, but Jill Price can.

Jill can recall clearly and in great detail what has happened to her *every single day since early 1980* (Price & Davis, 2008). This is not just Jill's subjective impression. Dr. James McGaugh, a well-known memory researcher based at the University of California–Irvine, and his colleagues tested Jill's memory over a period of a few years and came up with some shocking results (Parker, Cahill, & McGaugh, 2006). For example, they asked Jill to recall the dates of each Easter from 1980 to 2003, which is a pretty tough task considering that Easter can fall on any day between March 22 and April 15. Even though she had no idea that she would be asked this question, Jill recalled the correct dates quickly and easily; nobody else the researchers tested came close. The researchers also asked Jill about the details of what she had been doing on various randomly chosen dates, and they checked Jill's recall against her personal diary. Again, Jill answered quickly and accurately: *July 1, 1986?*—"I see it all, that day, that month, that summer. Tuesday. Went with (friend's name) to (restaurant name)." *October 3, 1987?*—"That was a Saturday. Hung out at the apartment all weekend, wearing a sling—hurt my elbow." (E. S. Parker et al., 2006, pp. 39–40).

Jill Price can accurately remember just about everything that has happened to her during the past 30 years, as confirmed by her diary.

Researchers still don't understand all the reasons that Jill Price can remember her past so much more fully than the rest of us, but it turns out that Jill is not alone. Jill's extraordinary memory abilities became widely known after a *60 Minutes* story that featured her and Dr. McGaugh. That story elicited a flurry of inquiries to Dr. McGaugh from other people around the world who thought that they, too, possessed the spectacular memory abilities demonstrated by Jill. Although most of them did not, McGaugh and his colleagues (LePort et al., 2012) identified 11 other individuals with "highly superior autobiographical memory" (HSAM) abilities that resemble those they had seen in Jill Price. The researchers discovered differences in the structure of several brain regions known to be involved in memory in the HSAM group compared with a control group. More recent work using functional MRI has revealed that people with HSAM show increased coupling between memory-related brain regions when they recall past experiences (Santangelo et al., 2018). These findings suggest that further study of these unusual individuals might help to unravel the nature of memory more generally.

THE EASE WITH WHICH SOMEONE SUCH AS JILL CAN INSTANTLY REMEMBER HER PAST shouldn't blind us to appreciating how complex that act of remembering really is. Because memory is so remarkably complex, it is also remarkably fragile (Schacter, 1996). We all have had the experience of forgetting something we desperately wanted to remember or of remembering something that never really happened. Why does memory serve us so well in some situations and play such cruel tricks on us in other cases? Is there just one kind of memory, or are there many? These are among the questions that psychologists have asked and answered, and that we'll discuss in this chapter. We'll start by answering the fundamental question: What is memory?

What Is Memory?

memory The ability to store and retrieve information over time.

encoding The process of transforming what we perceive, think, or feel into an enduring memory.

storage The process of maintaining information in memory over time.

retrieval The process of bringing to mind information that has been previously encoded and stored.

Memory *is the ability to store and retrieve information over time.* Even though few of us possess the extraordinary memory abilities of Jill Price and the handful of others with highly superior autobiographical memory, each of us has a unique identity that is intricately tied to the things we have thought, felt, done, and experienced. Memories are the residue of those events, the enduring changes that experience makes in our brains and leaves behind when it passes. If an experience passes without leaving a trace, it might just as well not have happened.

As you've seen in other chapters, the mind's mistakes provide key insights into its fundamental operation, and there is no better illustration of this than in the realm of memory. There are three key functions of memory: **encoding**, *the process of transforming what we perceive, think, or feel into an enduring memory*; **storage**, *the process of maintaining information in memory over time*; and **retrieval**, *the process of bringing to mind information that has been previously encoded and stored.*

Encoding: Transforming Perceptions Into Memories

Bubbles P., a professional gambler with no formal education who spent most of his time shooting craps at local clubs or playing high-stakes poker, had no difficulty rattling off 20 numbers, in either forwards or backwards order, after just a single glance (Ceci, DeSimone, & Johnson, 1992). Most people can listen to a list of numbers and then repeat them from memory—as long as the list is no more than about seven items long. (Try it for yourself using **FIGURE 6.1**.)

How did Bubbles accomplish his astounding feats of memory? For at least 2,000 years, people have thought of memory as a recording device that makes exact copies of the information that comes in through our senses, and then stores those copies for later use. This idea is simple and intuitive. It is also completely incorrect. We make memories by combining information we *already* have in our brains with new information that comes in through our senses. In this way, memory is like cooking; starting from a recipe but improvising along the way, we add old information to new information, mix, shake, and bake, and out pops a memory. Memories are *constructed*, not recorded, and encoding is the process by which we transform what we perceive, think, or feel into an enduring memory. Let's look at three types of encoding processes—semantic encoding, visual imagery encoding, and organizational encoding—and then consider how encoding had possible survival value for our ancestors.

Semantic Encoding

Because memories are a combination of old and new information, the nature of any particular memory depends as much on the old information already in our memories as it does on the new information coming in through our senses. In other words, how we remember something depends on how we think about it at the time. For example, as a professional gambler, Bubbles found numbers unusually meaningful, so when he saw a string of digits, he tended to think about their meanings. However, when Bubbles was tested with materials other than numbers—faces, words, objects, or locations—his memory performance was no better than average. Most of us, unlike Bubbles, can't remember 20 digits, but we can remember 20 experiences (a favourite camping trip, a 16th birthday party, a first day at school, and so on). One reason is that we often think about the meaning behind our experiences, so we semantically encode them without even trying (Craik & Tulving, 1975). **Semantic encoding** *is the process of relating new information in a meaningful way to knowledge that is already stored in memory* (Brown & Craik, 2000).

In a seminal experiment, Toronto researchers Fergus Craik and Endel Tulving presented participants with a series of words and asked them to make one of three types of judgements (Craik & Tulving, 1975):

- *Semantic judgements* required the participants to think about the meaning of the words (Is *hat* a type of clothing?).
- *Rhyme judgements* required the participants to think about the sound of the words (Does *hat* rhyme with *cat*?).
- *Case judgements* required the participants to think about the appearance of the words (Is *HAT* written in uppercase or lowercase?).

Learning Outcomes

- Explain how memory is a construction and not a recording of new information.
- Describe the three main ways that information is encoded into the brain.
- Give reasons why we remember survival-related information so well.

Have you ever wondered why you can remember 20 experiences (your favourite camping trip, your 16th birthday party, your first day at school, etc.) but not 20 digits? One reason is that we often think about the meaning behind our experiences, so we semantically encode them without even trying (Craik & Tulving, 1975).

semantic encoding The process of relating new information in a meaningful way to knowledge that is already stored in memory.

2 8
6 9 1
0 4 7 3
8 7 4 5 4
9 0 2 4 8 1
5 7 4 2 2 9 6
6 4 7 1 9 3 0 4
3 5 6 7 1 8 4 8 5
1 0 2 8 8 3 4 7 2 9
4 7 2 0 8 2 7 4 2 6 4
7 3 1 0 9 3 4 3 5 1 3 8

Figure 6.1

Digit Memory Test How many digits can you remember? Start on the first row and cover the rows below it with a piece of paper. Study the numbers in the row for 1 second and then cover that row back up again. After a couple of seconds, try to repeat the numbers. Then uncover the row to see if you were correct. If so, continue down to the next row, using the same instructions, until you can't recall all the numbers in a row. The number of digits in the last row you can remember correctly is your digit span. Bubbles P. could remember 20 random numbers, or about five rows deep. How did you do?

The type of judgement task influenced how participants thought about each word—what old information they combined with the new—and had a powerful impact on their memories. Those participants who made semantic judgements (i.e., thought about the meaning of the words) had much better memory for the words than did participants who thought about how the words looked or sounded. The results of these and many other studies have shown that long-term retention is greatly enhanced by semantic encoding.

So where does this semantic encoding take place? What's going on in the brain when this type of information processing occurs? Studies reveal that semantic encoding is uniquely associated with increased activity in the lower left part of the frontal lobe and the inner part of the left temporal lobe (**FIGURE 6.2a**) (Demb et al., 1995; Kapur et al., 1994; Wagner et al., 1998). In fact, the amount of activity in each of these two regions during encoding is directly related to whether people later remember an item. The more activity there is in these areas, the more likely the person will remember the information.

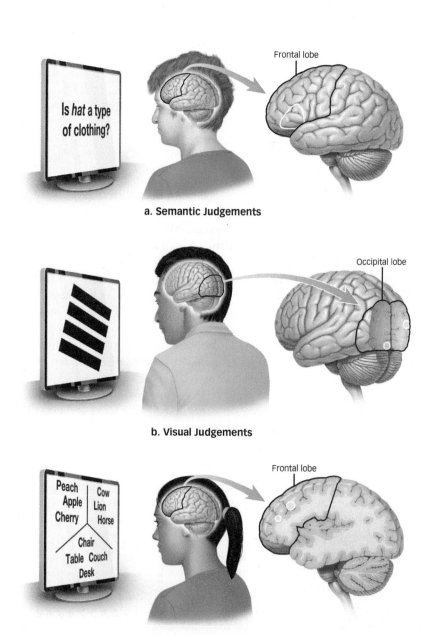

a. Semantic Judgements

b. Visual Judgements

c. Organizational Judgements

Figure 6.2

Brain Activity During Different Types of Judgements fMRI studies reveal that different parts of the brain are active during different types of judgements: (a) During semantic encoding, the lower left frontal lobe is active; (b) during visual imagery encoding, the occipital lobe is active; and (c) during organizational encoding, the upper left frontal lobe is active.

Visual Imagery Encoding

In Athens in 477 BCE, the Greek poet Simonides had just left a banquet when the ceiling collapsed and killed all the people inside. Simonides was able to name every one of the dead simply by visualizing each chair around the banquet table and recalling the person who had been sitting there. Simonides wasn't the first—but he was among the most proficient at it—to use **visual imagery encoding**, *the process of storing new information by converting it into mental pictures.*

Numerous experiments have shown that visual imagery encoding can substantially improve memory. In one experiment, participants who studied lists of words by creating visual images of them later recalled twice as many items as participants who just mentally repeated the words (Schnorr & Atkinson, 1969). Contemporary "memory athletes," who compete in increasingly popular memory championships, typically rely on visual imagery encoding to accomplish astounding feats of memorization (Dresler et al., 2017). Alex Mullen, an American medical student, used visual imagery encoding to memorize the order of a deck of playing cards in under 16 seconds! This world record helped Alex to win the World Memory Championship in 2017.

Why does visual imagery encoding work so well? First, visual imagery encoding does some of the same things that semantic encoding does: When you create a visual image, you relate incoming information to knowledge already in memory. For example, a visual image of a parked car might help you create a link to your memory of your first kiss.

Second, when you use visual imagery to encode words and other verbal information, you end up with two different mental *placeholders* for the items—a visual one and a verbal one—which gives you more ways to remember them than just a verbal placeholder alone (Paivio, 1971, 1986). Visual imagery encoding activates visual processing regions in the occipital lobe (see Figure 6.2b), which suggests that people actually enlist the visual system when forming memories based on mental images (Kosslyn et al., 1993; Pearson & Kosslyn, 2015). Neuroimaging evidence shows that training ordinary people to use visual imagery encoding produces neural changes in visual and memory networks that support enhanced memory performance (Dresler et al., 2017). However, visual imagery encoding requires a great deal of cognitive effort to use successfully, which can limit its practical use for real-world activities such as studying for exams (see page 303 in the Learning chapter).

Organizational Encoding

Have you ever ordered dinner with a group of friends and watched in amazement as your server took the order without writing anything down and yet brought everyone the food they ordered? To find out how this is done, one researcher wired servers in a restaurant with microphones and asked them to think aloud, that is, to say what they were thinking as they walked around all day doing their jobs (Stevens, 1988). Recordings showed that as soon as the server left a customer's table, he or she immediately began *grouping* or *categorizing* the orders into hot drinks, cold drinks, hot foods, and cold foods. The servers remembered their orders by relying on **organizational encoding**, *the process of categorizing information according to the relationships among a series of items.*

For example, suppose you had to memorize the words *peach, cow, chair, apple, table, cherry, lion, couch, horse, desk.* The task seems difficult, but if you organize the items into three categories—fruit (*peach, apple, cherry*), animals (*cow, lion, horse*), and furniture (*chair, table, couch, desk*)—the task becomes much easier. Studies have shown that instructing people to sort items into categories is an effective way to enhance their subsequent recall of those items (Mandler, 1967). Even more complex

Alex Mullen, world memory champion, can quickly remember a deck of playing cards, and much more.

Pen and paper are optional for some servers who have figured out how to use organizational encoding.

visual imagery encoding The process of storing new information by converting it into mental pictures.

organizational encoding The process of categorizing information according to the relationships among a series of items.

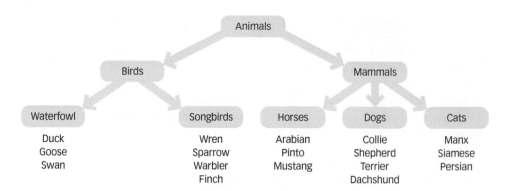

organizational schemes have been used, such as the hierarchy in **FIGURE 6.3** (Bower et al., 1969). People can improve their recall of individual items by organizing them into multiple-level categories, all the way from a general category such as *animals,* through intermediate categories such as *birds* and *songbirds,* down to specific examples such as *wren* and *sparrow.*

Of course, organizational encoding is not just for word lists. In everyday life, we organize our current experiences by segmenting the ongoing flow of events into meaningful units (Kurby & Zacks, 2008). For example, we might segment a shopping trip into event units such as driving to the mall, walking from the parking lot, returning a gift to H&M, checking out the Apple store, and so forth. A recent study showed that when people view movies comprised of everyday activities, segmenting the movie into meaningful event units during encoding enhanced subsequent memory for those events, compared to encoding without event segmentation; and the memory benefit was evident at delays ranging from 10 minutes to one month (Flores et al., 2017).

Just as semantic and visual imagery encoding activate distinct regions of the brain, so, too, does organizational encoding. As you can see in Figure 6.2c, organizational encoding activates the upper surface of the left frontal lobe (Fletcher, Shallice, & Dolan, 1998; Savage et al., 2001). Different types of encoding strategies appear to rely on the activation of different areas of the brain.

Encoding of Survival-Related Information

 DATA VISUALIZATION

Do Men and Women Differ in the Way They Remember Location Information? Go to launchpadworks.com.

Encoding new information is critical to many aspects of everyday life—prospects for attaining your degree would be pretty slim without this ability. According to the evolutionary perspective, which is based on Darwin's principle of natural selection, features of an organism that help it survive and reproduce are more likely than other features to be passed on to subsequent generations (see The Evolution of Psychological Science chapter). Therefore, memory mechanisms that help us survive and reproduce should be preserved by natural selection. Our memory systems should be built in a way that allows us to remember especially well the encoded information that is relevant to our survival, such as sources of food and water and the location of predators.

To test this idea, researchers gave participants three different encoding tasks (Nairne, Thompson, & Pandeirada, 2007). In the first task, a survival-encoding condition, participants were asked to imagine they were stranded in the grasslands of a foreign land without any survival materials. They were told that over the next few months, they would need supplies of food and water and also need to protect themselves from predators. The researchers then showed participants randomly chosen words (e.g., *stone, meadow, chair*) and asked them to rate on a 1–5 scale how relevant each item would be to survival in the hypothetical situation. In a second task, a moving-encoding condition, a second group of participants was asked to imagine that they were planning to move to a new home in a foreign land, and to rate on a 1–5 scale how useful each item might be in helping them set up a new home. In the third task, the pleasantness-encoding condition, a third group was shown the same words and asked to rate on a 1–5 scale the pleasantness of each word.

The findings, displayed in **FIGURE 6.4**, show that participants recalled more words after the survival-encoding task than after either the moving or pleasantness tasks. In later studies, the researchers found that survival encoding resulted in higher levels of recall than several other non–survival-encoding tasks (Nairne, Pandeirada, & Thompson, 2008). Exactly what about survival encoding produces such high levels of memory?

One advantage of encoding survival-related information is that it draws on elements of semantic, visual imagery, and organizational encoding (Burns, Hwang, & Burns, 2011), which together produce high levels of subsequent memory. Also, survival encoding encourages participants to think in detail about the goals they want to achieve and thus engage in extensive planning, which in turn benefits memory and may account for much of the benefit of survival encoding (Bell, Roer, & Buchner, 2015). For example, survival scenarios that *do* involve planning produce superior subsequent memory compared with survival scenarios that do *not* involve planning. It is critical that superior recall is also observed for scenarios that *involve planning but not survival,* such as planning a dinner party (Klein, Robertson, & Delton, 2011). Of course, planning for the future is itself critical for our long-term survival, so these findings are still broadly consistent with the evolutionary perspective that memory is built to enhance our chances of survival (Klein et al., 2011; Schacter, 2012; Suddendorf & Corballis, 2007).

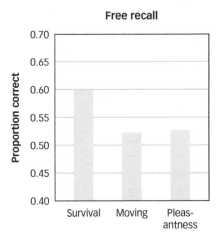

Figure 6.4
Encoding of Survival-Related Information Enhances Later Recall People recall more words after "survival encoding" tasks than after moving or pleasantness-encoding tasks (Nairne et al., 2007). Explain this from your understanding of the three main kinds of encoding discussed in this chapter.

Build to the Outcomes

1. In what way is making a memory like cooking from a recipe?
2. What do we consider when making a semantic judgement?
3. What two factors make visual imagery effective?
4. How might you use organizational encoding to remember material before an exam?
5. What is the evolutionary perspective on encoding survival-related information?

Storage: Maintaining Memories Over Time

Encoding is the process of turning perceptions into memories. But one of the hallmarks of a memory is that you can bring it to mind on Tuesday, not bring it to mind on Wednesday, and then bring it to mind again on Thursday. So where are our memories when we aren't using them? Clearly, those memories are stored in some form in your brain. As pointed out earlier, *storage is the process of maintaining information in memory over time.* There are three major kinds of memory storage: sensory, short-term, and long-term. As these names suggest, the three kinds of storage are distinguished primarily by the amount of time over which a memory is retained.

Sensory Storage

Sensory memory is *a type of storage that holds sensory information for a few seconds or less.* In a series of classic experiments, research participants were asked to remember rows of letters (Sperling, 1960). In one version of the procedure, participants viewed

Learning Outcomes

- Distinguish sensory memory from short-term memory.
- Describe the elements of the model of working memory.
- Explain the interrelationship between memory and the hippocampus.
- Summarize the role of the neural synapse in long-term memory storage.

sensory memory A type of storage that holds sensory information for a few seconds or less.

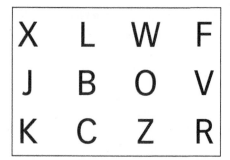

Figure 6.5

Iconic Memory Test When a grid of letters is flashed on screen for only 1/20th of a second, it is difficult to recall individual letters. But if prompted to remember a particular row immediately after the grid is shown, research participants will do so with high accuracy. Sperling used this procedure to demonstrate that although iconic memory stores the whole grid, the information fades away too quickly for a person to recall everything (Sperling, 1960).

iconic memory A fast-decaying store of visual information.

echoic memory A fast-decaying store of auditory information.

short-term memory A type of storage that holds nonsensory information for more than a few seconds but less than a minute.

three rows of four letters each, as shown in **FIGURE 6.5**. The researcher flashed the letters on a screen for just 1/20th of a second. When asked to remember all 12 of the letters they had just seen, participants recalled fewer than half. There were two possible explanations for this:

- People simply couldn't encode all the letters in such a brief period of time.
- People encoded the letters but forgot them while trying to recall everything they had seen.

To test the two ideas, the researcher relied on a clever trick. Just after the letters disappeared from the screen, a tone sounded that cued the participants to report the letters in a particular row. A *high* tone cued participants to report the contents of the top row, a *medium* tone cued participants to report the contents of the middle row, and a *low* tone cued participants to report the contents of the bottom row. When asked to report only a single row, people recalled almost all of the letters in that row! Because the tone sounded after the letters disappeared from the screen and the participants had no way of knowing which of the three rows would be cued, the researcher inferred that virtually all the letters had been encoded. In fact, if the tone was substantially delayed, participants couldn't perform the task because the information had slipped away from their sensory memories. Like the afterimage of a flashlight, the 12 letters flashed on a screen are visual icons, a lingering trace stored in memory for a very short period.

Because we have more than one sense, we have more than one kind of sensory memory. **Iconic memory** is *a fast-decaying store of visual information.* **Echoic memory** is *a fast-decaying store of auditory information.* When you have difficulty understanding what someone has just said, you probably find yourself replaying the last few words—listening to them echo in your "mind's ear," so to speak. What you are actually doing is accessing information that is being held in your echoic memory store. The hallmark of both the iconic and echoic memory stores is that they hold information for a very short time. Iconic memories usually decay in about 1 second or less, and echoic memories usually decay in about 5 seconds (Darwin, Turvey, & Crowder, 1972).

These two sensory memory stores are a bit like doughnut shops: The products come in, they sit briefly on the shelf, and then they are discarded. If you want one, you have to grab it fast. But how to grab it? If information from sensory memory is quickly lost, how do we recall it at all? The key is attention, which brings us to short-term memory (see **FIGURE 6.6**).

Short-Term Storage and Working Memory

A second kind of memory storage is **short-term memory**, which *holds nonsensory information for more than a few seconds but less than a minute.* We need to attend to incoming information for it to enter short-term memory, but as soon as we attend

Figure 6.6

The Flow of Information Through the Memory System Information moves through several stages of memory as it gets encoded, stored, and made available for later retrieval.

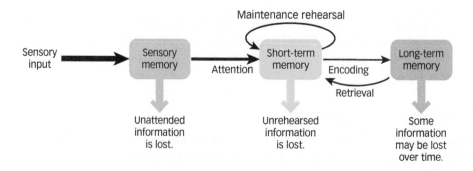

to something else, the information is quickly lost. For example, if someone tells you a telephone number and you pay attention to what they say, you can usually repeat it back with ease—but you will quickly lose the information as soon as your attention focuses on anything else. In one study, research participants were given consonant strings to remember, such as DBX and HLM. After seeing each string, participants were asked to count backwards from 100 by 3 for varying amounts of time and were then asked to recall the consonant strings (Peterson & Peterson, 1959). As shown in **FIGURE 6.7**, memory for the consonant strings declined rapidly, from approximately 80% after a 3-second delay to virtually nothing after a 20-second delay. These results suggest that information can be held in the short-term memory store for about 15 to 20 seconds.

Rehearsal and "Chunking" Strengthen Memory

What if 15 to 20 seconds isn't enough time? What if we need the information for a while longer? We can use a trick that allows us to get around the natural limitations of our short-term memories. **Rehearsal** is *the process of keeping information in short-term memory by mentally repeating it.* If someone gives you a telephone number and you can't immediately enter it into your cell phone or write it down, you say it over and over to yourself until you can. Each time you repeat the number, you are reentering it into short-term memory, giving it another 15 to 20 seconds of shelf life.

Rehearsal can play a role in the **serial position effect**, which refers to the observation that *the first few and last few items in a series are more likely to be recalled than the items in the middle.* Enhanced recall of the first few items in, say, a list of words is called the *primacy effect.* It occurs because these items receive more rehearsals than subsequent items in the middle of the list and thus are more likely to be encoded into long-term storage. Enhanced recall of the last few items is called the *recency effect* and can result from rehearsing items that are still in short-term storage (Atkinson & Shiffrin, 1968). Consistent with this interpretation, classic studies showed that the recency effect—but not the primacy effect—is eliminated when participants count backwards by 3s after the final list item is presented, which prevents them from relying on short-term storage to rehearse the last few items (Glanzer & Cunitz, 1966). However, both primacy and recency effects can be observed in situations that involve only long-term storage, such as recalling details of opera performances over a period of 25 years (Sehulster, 1989) or recalling the order of the seven Harry Potter books (Kelley, Neath, & Surprenant, 2013).

Short-term memory is limited in *how long* it can hold information, as well as in *how much* information it can hold. Not only can most people keep approximately seven numbers in short-term memory, but if they put more new numbers in, then old numbers begin to fall out (Miller, 1956). Short-term memory isn't limited to numbers, of course. It can also hold about seven letters or seven words—even though those seven words contain many more than seven letters. In fact, short-term memory can hold about seven *meaningful items* at once (Miller, 1956). Therefore, one way to increase storage is to group several letters into a single meaningful item. **Chunking** involves *combining small pieces of information into larger clusters or chunks that are more easily held in short-term memory.* Restaurant servers who use organizational encoding (see page 219) to organize customer orders into groups are essentially chunking the information, giving themselves less to remember.

Working Memory Stores and Manipulates Information

Short-term memory was originally conceived as a kind of "place" where information is kept for a limited amount of time. More recently, British researchers have

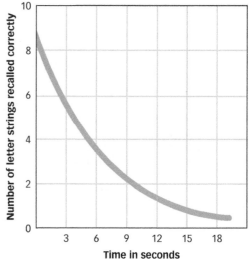

Figure 6.7
The Decline of Short-Term Memory
A 1959 experiment showed how quickly short-term memory fades without rehearsal. On a test for memory of three-letter strings, research participants were highly accurate when tested a few seconds after exposure to each string, but if the test was delayed another 15 seconds, people barely recalled the strings at all (Peterson & Peterson, 1959).

Which of the books in the Harry Potter series are you likely to most easily recall, according to the serial position effect?

rehearsal The process of keeping information in short-term memory by mentally repeating it.

serial position effect The observation that the first few and last few items in a series are more likely to be recalled than the items in the middle.

chunking Combining small pieces of information into larger clusters or chunks that are more easily held in short-term memory.

Figure 6.8
A Refined Model of Working Memory
The working memory system consists of a central executive that controls the flow of information through the system, a visuo-spatial sketchpad and phonological loop that temporarily hold visual/spatial images and verbal/auditory information, respectively, and an episodic buffer that integrates the various kinds of information that are maintained by the visuo-spatial sketchpad and phonological loop. BADDELEY ET AL. (2011)

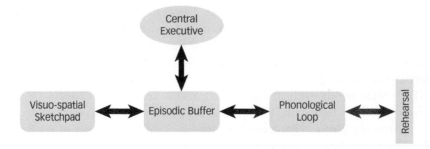

developed and refined a more dynamic model of a limited-capacity memory system, called **working memory**, which refers to *active maintenance of information in short-term storage* (Baddeley & Hitch, 1974). As illustrated in **FIGURE 6.8**, working memory includes two subsystems that store and manipulate information—one for visual images (the *visuo-spatial sketchpad*) and another for verbal information (the *phonological loop*). It also involves an *episodic buffer* that integrates visual and verbal information from the subsystems into a multidimensional code, as well as a *central executive* that coordinates the subsystems and the episodic buffer (Baddeley, 2001; Baddeley, Allen, & Hitch, 2011).

In practical terms, say you were using Google Maps on your phone to walk to a new destination and wanted to keep the arrangement of locations on the map in mind as you contemplated your next move. You'd be relying on your visuo-spatial sketchpad to hold the visual representation of the locations on the map. You might also enlist the phonological loop to hold onto the upcoming street names and rely on your central executive to control mental manipulation of the directions and awareness of the flow of information into and out of memory, all stored for a limited amount of time. In short, the working memory model acknowledges both the limited nature of this kind of memory storage and the activities that are commonly associated with it.

Research conducted in the context of this model has taught us that working memory plays an important role in many aspects of our cognitive lives (Baddeley, 2012). For example, studies of individuals with neurological damage to the phonological loop subsystem of working memory reveal that not only do those individuals have problems holding on to strings of digits and letters for a few seconds, but they also have difficulty learning novel words. This suggests a link between this part of the working memory system and the ability to learn language (Baddeley & Hitch, 2019; Gathercole, 2008).

Brain-imaging studies indicate that the central executive component of working memory depends on regions within the frontal lobe that are important for controlling and manipulating information on a wide range of cognitive tasks (Baddeley, 2001; D'Esposito & Postle, 2015). Children who score low on working memory tasks have difficulty learning new information and performing well in the classroom (Alloway et al., 2009), which has led researchers to focus increasingly on trying to understand the impact of working memory problems on cognitive development (Alloway, 2018).

Researchers only recently have begun to study the episodic buffer. In a typical experiment, people perform tasks in which they need to combine different kinds of information, such as colours, shapes, and sounds, and hold that information over a brief period of time. Evidence from such experiments suggests that the episodic buffer automatically combines separate items into an integrated whole (Baddeley et al., 2011) and is a gateway to long-term memory, which we will discuss at length in the section on explicit memory later in this chapter (see page 236). The episodic buffer plays a role in learning to recognize words, which requires combining visual and verbal information. Recent studies of grade-school children and young adults showed that the ability to link together visual and auditory information and hold it in working

In everyday life, we draw on working memory when using our phones to navigate novel environments.

working memory Active maintenance of information in short-term storage.

memory, a task thought to depend on the episodic buffer, shows marked increases with age and is associated with word recognition skills, even when controlling for the ability to hold the individual items in working memory (Wang & Allen, 2018; Wang et al., 2015). Baddeley and colleagues (2011) have suggested that the episodic buffer also integrates other kinds of sensory information, such as smell and taste (see Figure 6.8), but research is needed to explore this possibility.

Research Is Examining the Link Between Working Memory Training and Cognitive Functioning

Can working memory skills be improved through training, and can such training enhance cognitive functioning? This question has become a hot research topic over the past few years (Klingberg, 2010; Shipstead, Redick, & Engle, 2012; Soveri et al., 2017). In typical studies, participants are first given extensive practice in performing working memory tasks that require the maintenance and manipulation of visual or verbal information. They are then tested on new working memory tasks that have not been specifically trained, as well as on other cognitive tasks (reasoning, comprehension, or paying sustained attention). Some encouraging results have been reported. For example, elementary school students who were trained on several working memory tasks (about 35 minutes/day for at least 20 days over a 5- to 7-week period) showed improvement on other working memory tasks when compared with untrained children (Holmes, Gathercole, & Dunning, 2009). These gains were evident even when the children were tested 6 months after training. There was also some evidence of improvement on math tasks. However, many working memory training studies are inconclusive as to whether the training in particular is responsible for the effects that are observed (Slagter, 2012).

Furthermore, several recent studies have found that working memory training improved performance on the working memory task that was "trained" but did not result in improvements on other cognitive tasks (Redick et al., 2013), including other working memory tasks (De Simoni & von Bastian, 2018). More research will be needed to determine whether working memory training produces any general improvements in cognitive performance and, if so, whether the improvements are large enough to affect performance on everyday cognitive tasks (Au et al., 2015; Redick, 2015; Shipstead et al., 2012). However, the current evidence is consistent with the conclusion that in working memory training studies, people learn specific strategies to perform specific tasks, and not much more than that (De Simoni & von Bastian, 2018; Soveri et al., 2017).

Long-Term Storage

The artist Franco Magnani was born in Pontito, Italy, in 1934. In 1958, he left his village to see the rest of the world and settled in San Francisco in the 1960s. Soon after arriving, Magnani began to suffer from a strange illness. Every night he experienced feverish dreams of Pontito, in which he recalled the village in vivid detail. The dreams soon penetrated his waking life in the form of overpowering recollections, and Magnani decided that the only way to rid himself of these images was to capture them on canvas. For the next 20 years, he devoted much of his time to painting, in exquisite detail, his memories of his beloved village. Many years later, the photographer Susan Schwartzenberg went to Pontito, armed with a collection of Magnani's paintings, and photographed each scene from the perspective of the paintings. As you can see in these two images, the correspondence between the paintings and the photographs was striking (Sacks, 1995; Schacter, 1996).

Many years intervened between Magnani's visual perception and his artistic reconstruction of the village, suggesting that very detailed information can sometimes be stored for a very long time. In contrast to the time-limited sensory and

Even years after leaving home in Pontito, Italy, the painter Franco Magnani was able to create a near-perfect reproduction of what he'd seen there. Magnani's painting (*top*), based on a memory of a place he hadn't seen for years, is remarkably similar to the photograph (*bottom*) Susan Schwartzenberg took of the actual scene.

long-term memory A type of storage that holds information for hours, days, weeks, or years.

anterograde amnesia The inability to transfer new information from the short-term store into the long-term store.

retrograde amnesia The inability to retrieve information that was acquired before a particular date, usually the date of an injury or surgery.

short-term storage stores, **long-term memory** is *a type of storage that holds information for hours, days, weeks, or years.* In contrast to both sensory and short-term storage, long-term memory has no known capacity limits (see Figure 6.6). For example, most people can recall 10,000 to 15,000 words in their native language, tens of thousands of facts (the capital of France is Paris, and 3 × 3 = 9), and an untold number of personal experiences. Just think of all the song lyrics you can recite by heart, and you'll understand that you've got a lot of information tucked away in your long-term memory!

More amazing, people can recall items from long-term memory even if they haven't thought of those items for years. For instance, researchers have found that even 50 years after graduation, people can accurately recognize about 90% of their high-school classmates from yearbook photographs (Bahrick, 2000). Such a feat is more remarkable when you consider that the people in the study probably had not accessed most of this information for years before the experiment.

The Hippocampus as Index: Linking Pieces Into One Memory

Where is long-term memory located in the brain? The clues to answering this question come from individuals who are unable to store long-term memories. In 1953, a 27-year-old man, known then by the initials HM, suffered from intractable epilepsy (Scoville & Milner, 1957). In a desperate attempt to stop the seizures, HM's doctors removed parts of his temporal lobes, including the hippocampus and some surrounding regions (**FIGURE 6.9**). After the operation, HM could converse easily, use and understand language, and perform well on intelligence tests, but he could not remember anything that happened to him after the operation. HM could repeat a telephone number with no difficulty, suggesting that his short-term memory store was just fine (Corkin, 2002, 2013; Hilts, 1995; Squire, 2009). But after information left the short-term store, it was gone forever. For example, he would often forget that he had just eaten a meal or fail to recognize the hospital staff who helped him on a daily basis. Studies of HM and others have shown that the hippocampal region of the brain is critical for putting new information into the long-term store (Clark & Maguire, 2016; Smith et al., 2013). Individuals who have sustained damage to this region suffer from a condition known as **anterograde amnesia**, which is *the inability to transfer new information from the short-term store into the long-term store.* HM's own words best describe what anterograde amnesia must be like: "Right now I'm wondering, have I done or said anything amiss? You see, at this moment everything looks clear to me, but what happened just before? That's what worries me. It's like waking from a dream; I just don't remember" (Milner, 1970).

Some individuals with amnesia also suffer from **retrograde amnesia**, which is *the inability to retrieve information that was acquired before a particular date, usually the date of an injury or surgery.* The fact that HM had much worse anterograde than

Figure 6.9

The Hippocampus Patient HM had his hippocampus and adjacent structures of the medial temporal lobe (indicated by the shaded areas) surgically removed to stop his epileptic seizures (*left*). As a result, he could not remember things that happened after the surgery. Henry Molaison (*right*), better known to the world as patient HM, passed away on December 2, 2008, at the age of 82 at a nursing home near Hartford, Connecticut. Molaison's catastrophic inability to encode new long-term memories was discovered by Montreal psychologist Brenda Milner in 1953; between that time and his death Molaison participated in countless memory experiments. In doing so, he made fundamental contributions to our understanding of memory and the brain (Corkin, 2013).

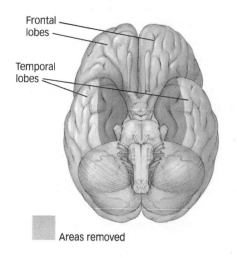

Frontal lobes

Temporal lobes

Areas removed

MACMILLAN LEARNING

retrograde amnesia suggests that the hippocampal region is not the site of long-term memory. Indeed, research has shown that different aspects of a single memory—its sights, sounds, smells, emotional content—are stored in different places in the cortex (Damasio, 1989; Schacter, 1996; Squire & Kandel, 1999). Some psychologists have argued that the hippocampal region acts as a kind of "index" that links together all these otherwise separate bits and pieces so that we remember them as one memory (Schacter, 1996; Squire, 1992; Teyler & DiScenna, 1986). Recent studies support this "index view." fMRI evidence shows that activity in the hippocampus relates to retrieving as a holistic unit the separate elements, such as a person, location, and an object, which were initially encoded by distinct regions in the cortex (Horner et al., 2015). Evidence from hippocampal cell firing patterns in mice also supports the idea that these cells are involved in memory formation and serve as an index that ties together memory contents stored elsewhere (Tanaka et al., 2018).

Over time, however, the hippocampal index may become less necessary. Returning to our cooking analogy, you can think of the hippocampal region index as a printed recipe. The first time you make a pie, you need the recipe to help you retrieve all the ingredients and then mix them together in the right amounts. As you bake more and more pies, though, you don't need to rely on the printed recipe anymore. Similarly, although the hippocampal region index is critical when a new memory is first formed, it may become less important as the memory ages. Another possibility is that the hippocampal index remains involved over long periods of time with some memories (highly detailed recollections of personal experiences, the kinds of memories that give us the feeling that we are almost reliving a past experience), but it does not stay involved in less detailed, more general memories (Harand et al., 2012; Winocur, Moscovitch, & Bontempi, 2010).

In terms of the cooking analogy again, you might need to rely on a recipe each time you cook a complex meal with many details, but not when you cook a simpler meal with a less detailed recipe. Scientists are still debating the extent to which the hippocampal region helps us remember details of our old memories (Bayley et al., 2005; Kirwan et al., 2008; Moscovitch et al., 2016; Squire & Wixted, 2011; Winocur et al., 2010). However, the notion of the hippocampus as an index explains why people such as HM cannot make new memories and why they can remember many old ones.

Consolidation Stabilizes Memories

The idea that the hippocampus becomes less important over time for maintaining memories is closely related to the concept of **consolidation**, *the process by which memories become stable in the brain* (McGaugh, 2000, 2015). Shortly after encoding, memories exist in a fragile state that can be disrupted easily; once consolidation has occurred, they are more resistant to disruption. One type of consolidation operates over seconds or minutes. For example, when someone experiences a head injury in a car crash and later cannot recall what happened during the few seconds or minutes before the crash—but can recall other events normally—the head injury probably prevented consolidation of short-term memory into long-term memory. Another type of consolidation occurs over much longer periods of time—days, weeks, months, and years—and likely involves transfer of information from the hippocampus to more permanent storage sites in the cortex. The operation of this longer-term consolidation process is why individuals who have retrograde amnesia with hippocampal damage can recall memories from childhood relatively normally but are impaired when recalling experiences that occurred just a few years prior to the time they became amnesic (Kirwan et al., 2008; Squire & Wixted, 2011).

How does a memory become consolidated? The act of recalling a memory, thinking about it, and talking about it with others probably contributes to consolidation (Moscovitch et al., 2006). And though you may not be aware of it, consolidation gets a boost from something that you do effortlessly every night: sleep. As explained in Hot Science: Can Sleep Enhance Learning? Yes!, mounting evidence gathered during the past decade indicates that sleep plays an important role in memory consolidation.

consolidation The process by which memories become stable in the brain.

Recalled Memories May Be Disrupted During Reconsolidation

Many researchers have long believed that a fully consolidated memory becomes a permanent fixture in the brain, more difficult to get rid of than a computer virus. But another line of research that has developed rapidly in recent years suggests that things are not so simple. Experiments have shown that even seemingly consolidated *memories can become vulnerable to disruption when they are recalled, thus requiring them to be consolidated again.* This process is called **reconsolidation** (Dudai, 2012; Nader & Hardt, 2009).

Early evidence for reconsolidation came from experiments with rats showing that when animals are cued to retrieve a new memory that was acquired a day earlier, giving the animal a drug (or an electrical shock) that prevents initial consolidation will cause forgetting (Nader, Shafe, & LeDoux, 2000; Sara, 2000). It is critical that if the animal is not actively retrieving the memory, the same drug (or shock) has no effect when given a day after initial encoding. Researchers have produced similar effects using electrical shocks in studies with people (Elsey, Van Ast, & Kindt, 2018; Schiller et al., 2010). This finding is surprising because it was once thought

reconsolidation The process whereby memories can become vulnerable to disruption when they are recalled, thus requiring them to be consolidated again.

Hot Science | Can Sleep Enhance Learning? Yes!

Thinking about pulling an all-nighter before your next big test? Here's a reason to reconsider: Our minds don't simply shut off when we sleep (see the Consciousness chapter). In fact, sleep may be as important to our memories as wakefulness.

Nearly a century ago, Jenkins and Dallenbach (1924) reported that recall of recently learned information is greater immediately after sleeping than after the same amount of time spent awake. But Jenkins and Dallenbach did not think that sleep played an active role in strengthening or consolidating memory. They argued instead that being asleep passively protects us from encountering information that interferes with our ability to remember. As is explained by retroactive interference (page 245), that's a valid argument. However, evidence has accumulated that sleep plays an active role in memory consolidation, doing more than simply protecting us from waking interference (Diekelmann & Born, 2010; Ellenbogen, Payne, & Stickgold, 2006; Vorster & Born, 2015). Sleep selectively enhances the consolidation of memories that reflect the meaning or gist of an experience (Payne et al., 2009), as well as emotionally important memories (Payne et al., 2008, 2015; Payne & Kensinger, 2018), suggesting that sleep helps us remember what's important and discard what's trivial.

Another recent line of evidence shows that memory consolidation during sleep can be enhanced by presenting sounds during sleep that reactivate specific memories, a procedure known as *targeted memory reactivation* (TMR) (Cellini & Capuozzo, 2018; Oudiette & Paller, 2013). Before sleep, participants learned to associate an object, such as a kettle, with a particular location on a screen; they saw a picture of the kettle and also heard its characteristic whistling sound. During a subsequent period of sleep, researchers played for participants the sounds of some of the studied objects in an attempt to reactivate their memories of the object–location associations. In a remarkable result, when tested after awakening, participants showed more accurate memory for the location of the objects whose characteristic sounds were presented during sleep than for the locations of objects whose characteristic sounds were not presented—even though participants were not aware that any sounds had been presented while they slept. Such targeted memory reactivation effects are strongest for those associations that are not well learned initially (Creery et al., 2015).

These findings suggest that it may be possible to use TMR during sleep to boost learning. To examine this possibility,

researchers tested whether TMR could help people acquire new foreign vocabulary (Schreiner & Rasch, 2015). Participants were young adult native German speakers who did not know any items of Dutch vocabulary. While awake in the late evening, all participants learned a series of Dutch words, each paired with their German translation. Some of the participants then slept for 3 hours; one group received TMR in which some of the previously studied Dutch words were presented auditorily, whereas the other group was not exposed to the studied Dutch words while sleeping. After waking up, all participants were given a vocabulary test for the German translation of the Dutch words. Exposure to the Dutch word during sleep improved learning of the German translation during subsequent waking. A later study (Batterink, Westerburg, & Paller, 2017) found similar TMR effects on the learning of novel words by English speakers, although the effects were only observed in participants who obtained a sufficient amount of rapid eye movement sleep (REM; see the Consciousness chapter, pages 187–189).

So when you find yourself nodding off after hours of studying for your exam, the science is on the side of a good night's sleep.

that when memories have been consolidated, drugs or shock that can prevent initial consolidation no longer have any impact. On the contrary, it now appears that each time memories are retrieved, they become vulnerable to disruption and must be reconsolidated.

Disrupting Reconsolidation May Reduce Traumatic Memories

Might it be possible one day to eliminate or modify painful memories by disrupting reconsolidation? Recent research from McGill University suggests it could be. When a traumatic event was reactivated in traumatized individuals who had been given a drug to reduce anxiety, there was a subsequent reduction in traumatic symptoms (Brunet et al., 2008, 2018). However, drugs are not necessary to disrupt reconsolidation of painful memories. Consider the traumatic events of April 15, 2013, when two bombs exploded near the finish line of the Boston Marathon, killing three people and injuring over 250 others. Several months later, researchers asked undergraduates at Boston University (located near the site of the bombing) to recall where they were when they learned of the bombing, what they were doing, and how they felt (Kredlow & Otto, 2015). The students' memories were detailed, and they recalled feeling considerable distress at the time. One minute after this memory reactivation, during the reconsolidation phase when memories are vulnerable to disruption, some students read a negative story, others read either a positive or neutral story, and still others (the control group) did nothing.

The Boston Marathon bombings produced detailed and disturbing memories in people at or near the site of the bombings. However, research shows that the amount of detail in those memories can be reduced by interfering with their reconsolidation.

All the students returned a week later and recalled their memories of the bombing again. Compared with the students in the control group, the students who read a negative story shortly after memory reactivation recalled significantly fewer details about the bombing than they had initially, whereas those who read positive or neutral stories showed smaller, nonsignificant reductions in recalled details. Reading the negative story appeared to interfere with reconsolidation of students' negative memories of the bombing.

Related work using fMRI indicates that disrupting reconsolidation can seemingly eliminate a fear memory in a part of the brain called the *amygdala,* which, as we will learn later in this chapter, plays a key role in emotional memory (Agren et al., 2012). Reconsolidation thus appears to be a key memory process with many important implications.

Memories, Neurons, and Synapses

We've already discussed parts of the brain that are related to memory storage, but we haven't said much about how or where memories are stored. Research suggests that memory storage depends critically on the *spaces* between neurons. You'll recall from the Neuroscience and Behaviour chapter that a *synapse* is the small space between the axon of one neuron and the dendrite of another and that neurons communicate by sending neurotransmitters across these synapses. As it turns out, sending a neurotransmitter across a synapse isn't like sending a toy boat across a pond, because the act of sending actually *changes* the synapse. Specifically, it strengthens the connection between the two neurons, making it easier for them to transmit to each other the next time. As the famous Canadian neuroscientist Donald Hebb said, "Cells that fire together, wire together" (Hebb, 1949).

By studying the sea slug *Aplysia Californica's* extremely simple nervous system, researchers were able to determine that long-term memory storage depends on the growth of new synaptic connections between neurons.

The idea that the connections between neurons are strengthened by their communication, making communication easier the next time, provides the neurological basis for long-term memory—and much of what we know about this comes

Nobel Prize–winning neuroscientist Eric Kandel took a risk and studied the sea slug *Aplysia* based in part on a lesson he had learned from his wife regarding their recent marriage, which encouraged him to trust his intuition: "Denise was confident that our marriage would work, so I took a leap of faith and went ahead. I learned from that experience that there are many situations in which one cannot decide on the basis of cold facts alone—because the facts are often insufficient. One ultimately has to trust one's unconscious, one's instincts, one's creative urge. I did this again in choosing *Aplysia*" (Kandel, 2006, p. 149).

long-term potentiation (LTP) A process whereby repeated communication across the synapse between neurons strengthens the connection, making further communication easier.

from the sea slug *Aplysia.* The story of *Aplysia* and memory is closely linked with the work of the neuroscientist Eric Kandel, who won the Nobel Prize in 2000 for his work with the creature. When Kandel first became interested in *Aplysia* back in the late 1950s, only two researchers in the entire world were studying it. But *Aplysia* was attractive to Kandel because it is relatively uncomplicated and has an extremely simple nervous system consisting of only 20,000 neurons (compared with roughly 100 billion in the human brain), so Kandel followed his intuition and studied *Aplysia* (Kandel, 2006).

When an experimenter stimulates *Aplysia*'s tail with a mild electric shock, the slug immediately withdraws its gill; if the experimenter does it again a moment later, *Aplysia* withdraws its gill even more quickly. If the experimenter comes back an hour later and shocks *Aplysia,* the withdrawal of the gill happens as slowly as it did the first time, as if *Aplysia* can't "remember" what happened an hour earlier (Abel et al., 1995). But if the experimenter shocks *Aplysia* over and over, it does develop an enduring "memory" that can last for days or even weeks. Research suggests that this long-term storage involves the growth of new synaptic connections between neurons (Abel et al., 1995; Kandel, 2006; Squire & Kandel, 1999). Thus, learning in *Aplysia* is based on changes involving the synapses for both short-term storage (enhanced neurotransmitter release) and long-term storage (growth of new synapses). Any experience that results in memory produces physical changes in the nervous system—even if you are a slug.

If you're something more complex than a slug—say, a chimpanzee or your roommate—a similar process of synaptic strengthening happens in the hippocampus, which we've seen is an area crucial for storing new long-term memories. In the early 1970s, researchers applied a brief electrical stimulus to a neural pathway in a rat's hippocampus (Bliss & Lømo, 1973). They found that the electrical current produced a stronger connection between synapses that lay along the pathway and that the strengthening lasted for hours or even weeks. They called this effect **long-term potentiation** (more commonly known as **LTP**), *a process whereby communication across the synapse between neurons strengthens the connection, making further communication easier.* Long-term potentiation has a number of properties that indicate to researchers the important role it plays in long-term memory storage: It occurs in several pathways within the hippocampus; it can be induced rapidly; and it can last for a long time. In fact, drugs that block LTP can turn rats into rodent versions of patient HM: The animals have great difficulty remembering where they've been recently and become easily lost in a maze (Bliss, 1999; Morris et al., 1986).

Build to the Outcomes

1. What evidence from the iconic memory test suggests that all the letters presented to participants were stored in memory before quickly fading?

2. Define iconic memory and echoic memory.

3. Why is it helpful to repeat a telephone number you're trying to remember?

4. How does working memory expand on the idea of short-term memory?

5. What did researchers learn about the role of the hippocampus and memory from HM?

6. Define anterograde amnesia and retrograde amnesia.

7. How does the process of recalling a memory affect its stability?

8. How does building a memory produce a physical change in the nervous system?

Retrieval: Bringing Memories to Mind

There is something fiendishly frustrating about piggy banks. You can put money in them, you can shake them around to assure yourself that the money is there, but you can't easily get the money out. If memories were like pennies in a piggy bank, stored but inaccessible, what would be the point of saving them in the first place? Retrieval is the process of bringing to mind information that has been previously encoded and stored, and it is perhaps the most important of all memory processes (Roediger, 2000; Schacter, 2001a).

Retrieval Cues: Reinstating the Past

One of the best ways to retrieve information from *inside* your head is to encounter information *outside* your head that is somehow connected to it. The information outside your head is called a **retrieval cue**, *external information that is associated with stored information and helps bring it to mind*. Retrieval cues can be incredibly effective. How many times have you said something such as, "I *know* who played the white cop who stood in for the black cop to infiltrate the Ku Klux Klan in *BlacKkKlansman*, but I just can't remember his name," only to have a friend give you a hint ("He was in *The Last Jedi*"), which instantly brings the answer to mind ("Adam Driver!")?

In one experiment, undergraduates studied lists of words, such as *table, peach, bed, apple, chair, grape,* and *desk* (Tulving & Pearlstone, 1966). Later, the students were asked to write down all the words from the list that they could remember. When they were absolutely sure that they had emptied their memory stores of every last word, the experimenters again asked the students to remember the words on the list. This time, however, the experimenters provided retrieval cues, such as "furniture" or "fruit." The students who were sure that they had done all the remembering they possibly could were suddenly able to remember more words. These results suggest that information is sometimes *available* in memory even when it is momentarily *inaccessible* and that retrieval cues help us bring inaccessible information to mind.

In this and many other lab experiments, participants use retrieval cues in a deliberate attempt to recall studied information; in everyday life, however, retrieval cues sometimes spontaneously elicit involuntary memories of past experiences (Berntsen, 2010). Encountering a friend may automatically remind you of the movie you recently saw with her, or hearing a song on the radio may remind you of a concert you attended by that band. Involuntary memories occur even more often in everyday life than memories that we voluntarily try to retrieve (Rasmussen & Bernsten, 2011), underscoring the power of retrieval cues to unlock our personal pasts.

External Context Provides Cues

Hints are one kind of retrieval cue, but they are not the only kind. The **encoding specificity principle** states that *a retrieval cue can serve as an effective reminder when it helps re-create the specific way in which information was initially encoded* (Tulving & Thomson, 1973). External contexts often make powerful retrieval cues (Hockley, 2008). For example, in one study divers learned some words on land and some other words underwater; they recalled the words best when they were tested in the same dry or wet environment in which they had initially learned them, because the environment itself was a retrieval cue (Godden & Baddeley, 1975). Recovering alcoholics often experience a renewed urge to drink when visiting places in which they once drank because those places are retrieval cues. There may even be some wisdom to finding a seat in a classroom, sitting in it for every lecture in that room and then

AP PHOTO/POCONO RECORD, ADAM RICHINS

Retrieval cues are hints that help bring stored information to mind. How does this explain the fact that most students prefer multiple-choice exams to fill-in-the-blank exams?

retrieval cue External information that is associated with stored information and helps bring it to mind.

encoding specificity principle The idea that a retrieval cue can be an effective reminder when it helps re-create the specific way in which information was initially encoded.

sitting in it again when you take the test. The feel of the chair and the sights you see may help you remember the information you learned while you sat there.

Inner States Also Provide Cues

Retrieval cues need not be external contexts—they can also be inner states. **State-dependent retrieval** is *the process whereby information tends to be better recalled when the person is in the same state during encoding and retrieval.* For example, retrieving information when you are in a sad or happy mood increases the likelihood that you will retrieve sad or happy episodes (Eich, 1995). This may be part of the reason why it is so hard to "look on the bright side" when you are feeling down. A person's physiological or psychological state at the time of encoding is associated with the information that is encoded. For instance, being in a good mood affects patterns of electrical activity in parts of the brain responsible for semantic processing, suggesting that mood has a direct influence on semantic encoding (Kiefer et al., 2007). If the person's state at the time of retrieval matches the person's state at the time of encoding, the state itself is a retrieval cue. It is a bridge that connects the moment at which we experience something to the moment at which we remember it. Retrieval cues can even be thoughts themselves, as when one thought calls to mind another, related thought (Anderson et al., 1976).

Matching Encoding and Retrieval Contexts Improves Recall

The encoding specificity principle makes some unusual predictions. For example, you learned earlier that making semantic judgements about a word (e.g., what does *brain* mean?) usually produces a more durable memory for the word than does making rhyme judgements (e.g., what rhymes with *brain*?). Suppose you were shown a cue card of the word *brain* and were then asked to think of a word that rhymes, while your friend was shown the same card and asked to think about what *brain* means. The next day, if we simply asked you both, "Hey, what was that word you saw yesterday?" we would expect your friend to remember it better. However, if instead we asked both of you, "What was that word that rhymed with *train*?" the retrieval cue would match your encoding context better than your friend's, and we would expect you to remember it better than your friend did (Fisher & Craik, 1977). This is a fairly astounding finding. The principle of **transfer-appropriate processing** is *the idea that memory is likely to transfer from one situation to another when the encoding and retrieval contexts of the situations match* (Morris, Bransford, & Franks, 1977; Roediger, Weldon, & Challis, 1989).

Consequences of Retrieval

Human memory differs substantially from computer memory. Simply retrieving a file from my computer doesn't have any effect on the likelihood that the file will open again in the future. Not so with human memory. Retrieval doesn't merely provide a readout of what is in memory; it also changes the state of the memory system in important ways.

Retrieval Can Improve Subsequent Memory

Psychologists have known for some time that the act of retrieval can strengthen a retrieved memory, making it easier to remember that information at a later time (Bjork, 1975). Does this finding surprise you? Probably not. Does studying information twice have the same benefit as retrieving information twice? This finding probably *will* surprise you. It turns out that retrieving information from memory has different effects from studying it again. This point was made dramatically in an experiment in which participants studied brief stories and then either studied them again or were given a test that required retrieving the stories (Roediger & Karpicke, 2006). Participants were then given a final recall test for the stories either 5 minutes,

state-dependent retrieval The process whereby information tends to be better recalled when the person is in the same state during encoding *and* retrieval.

transfer-appropriate processing The idea that memory is likely to transfer from one situation to another when the encoding and retrieval contexts of the situations match.

2 days, or 1 week later. As shown in **FIGURE 6.10**, at the 5-minute delay, studying the stories twice resulted in slightly higher recall than did studying paired with retrieval (testing). In a critical finding, the opposite occurred at the 2-day and 1-week delays: Retrieval produced much higher levels of recall than did an extra study exposure.

A subsequent experiment using foreign vocabulary items also revealed that retrieval of the items produced a much bigger benefit on a delayed vocabulary test than did further study (Karpicke & Roediger, 2008). The benefits of retrieval on subsequent retention occur not only in adults but also in grade school children (Jaeger, Eisenkraemer, & Stein, 2015). Although there are specific situations in which testing produces little or no benefit for subsequent retention (Van Gog et al., 2015), the benefits of retrieval have been documented across many different memory tasks and with both simple and complex materials (Karpicke & Aue, 2015). Furthermore, students are able to learn to use this kind of retrieval practice spontaneously and on their own (Ariel & Karpicke, 2018). These findings have potentially important implications for learning in educational contexts (Karpicke, 2012), which we will explore further in the Learning chapter.

Retrieval Can Also Impair Subsequent Memory

As much as retrieval can help memory, that's not always the case. **Retrieval-induced forgetting** is *a process by which retrieving an item from long-term memory impairs subsequent recall of related items* (Anderson, 2003; Anderson, Bjork, & Bjork, 1994; Murayama et al., 2014).

Let's see how a typical experiment on retrieval-induced forgetting works (Anderson et al., 1994). Participants first studied word pairs consisting of a category name and an example of an item from that category (e.g., *fruit–orange, fruit–apple, tree–elm, tree–birch*). Then they practiced recalling some of the items in response to a category cue and the initial letters of the target item. For instance, for the fruit category participants would practice recalling *orange* to the cue "fruit–or_____," but would not practice recalling *apple*. The general idea was that while they were practicing recall of *orange,* participants suppressed the competitor item *apple*. For other categories (e.g., *trees*), no retrieval practice was given for any of the studied pairs. Later, the participants were given a final test for all the words they initially studied. It was not surprising that on the final test, participants remembered words that they practiced (e.g., *orange*) better than words from categories that they did not practice (e.g., *elm*).

But what happened on the final test to the items such as *apple*, which were not practiced and which participants presumably had to suppress while they practiced recall of related items? Those items were recalled most poorly of all, indicating that retrieving the similar target items (e.g., *orange*) caused subsequent forgetting of the related but suppressed items (e.g., *apple*). In fact, even if you don't successfully retrieve the target item, the act of suppressing the competitors while you attempt to retrieve the target still reduces your ability to retrieve the competitors at a later time (Storm et al., 2006).

Can you think of any examples of how retrieval-induced forgetting could affect memory in everyday life? Here are two. First, retrieval-induced forgetting can occur during conversations: When a speaker selectively talks about some aspects of memories shared with a listener and doesn't mention related information, the listener later has a harder time remembering the omitted events, as does the speaker (Cuc, Koppel, & Hirst, 2007; Hirst & Echterhoff, 2012). This effect occurs even for very important or vivid memories, such as those for major world events (Coman, Manier, & Hirst, 2009). Second, retrieval-induced forgetting can affect eyewitness memory. When witnesses to a staged crime are questioned about some details of the crime scene, their ability to later recall related details that they were not asked about is impaired, compared with that of witnesses who initially were not questioned at all

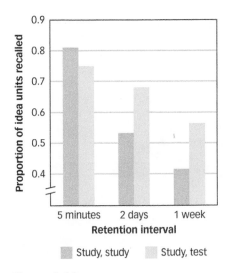

Figure 6.10

Memory Testing Benefits Long-Term Retention With a 5-minute retention interval, the study–study condition results in slightly higher recall. But the results change dramatically with retention intervals of 2 days and 1 week: With these longer delays, the study–test condition yields much higher levels of recall than does the study–study condition (Roediger & Karpicke, 2006).

retrieval-induced forgetting
A process by which retrieving an item from long-term memory impairs subsequent recall of related items.

As part of an experiment, participants wore cameras that took pictures every 15 seconds as the participants toured a museum.

(MacLeod, 2002; Shaw, Bjork, & Handal, 1995). These findings suggest that initial interviews with eyewitnesses should be as complete as possible in order to avoid potential retrieval-induced forgetting of significant details that are not probed during an interview (MacLeod & Saunders, 2008).

Retrieval Can Change Subsequent Memory

In addition to improving and impairing subsequent memory, the act of retrieval also can change what we remember from an experience. In one experiment, participants went on a tour of a museum, where they viewed designated exhibits, each of which contained several different stops (St. Jacques & Schacter, 2013). The participants each wore a camera that, every 15 seconds, automatically took pictures of what was in front of them. Two days later, the participants visited the memory laboratory (in a separate building) for a "reactivation session." Memories of some of the stops were reactivated by showing photos and asking them to rate how vividly they reexperienced what had happened at each stop. The participants were also shown novel photos of *unvisited* stops within the exhibit and were asked to judge how closely these novel photos were related to the photos of the stops they had actually seen in that exhibit. Two days after the reactivation session, the participants were given a memory test.

Participants sometimes incorrectly remembered that the stop shown in the novel photo had been part of the original tour. Most important, participants who tended to make this mistake also tended to have more vivid recollections during the reactivation session. In other words, retrieving and vividly reexperiencing memories of what participants actually did see at the museum led them to incorporate into their memory information that was *not* part of their original experience. This finding may be related to the phenomenon of reconsolidation that we discussed earlier (page 229), where reactivating a memory temporarily makes it vulnerable to disruption and change. At the very least, this finding reinforces the idea that retrieving a memory involves far more than a simple readout of information.

Separating the Components of Retrieval

Before leaving the topic of retrieval, let's look at how the process actually works. There is reason to believe that *trying* to recall an incident and *successfully* recalling one are fundamentally different processes that occur in different parts of the brain (Moscovitch, 1994; Schacter, 1996). For example, regions in the left frontal lobe show heightened activity when people *try* to retrieve information that was presented to them earlier (Oztekin, Curtis, & McElree, 2009; Tulving et al., 1994). This activity may reflect the mental effort of struggling to dredge up the past event (Lepage et al., 2000). However, *successfully* remembering a past experience tends to be accompanied by activity in the hippocampal region (see **FIGURE 6.11**) (Eldridge et al., 2000; Giovanello, Schnyer, & Verfaellie, 2004; Schacter et al., 1996a). Furthermore, successful recall also activates parts of the brain that play a role in processing the sensory features of an experience. For instance, recall of previously heard sounds is accompanied by activity in the auditory cortex (the upper part of the temporal lobe), whereas recall of previously seen pictures is accompanied by activity in the visual cortex (in the occipital lobe) (Wheeler, Petersen, & Buckner, 2000). Although retrieval may seem like a single process, neuroimaging studies suggest that separately identifiable processes are at work.

This finding sheds some light on the phenomenon we just discussed: retrieval-induced forgetting. fMRI evidence indicates that during memory retrieval, regions within the frontal lobe that are involved in retrieval effort play a role in suppressing competitors (Benoit & Anderson, 2012; Kuhl et al., 2007; Wimber et al., 2009). Indeed, repeated attempts to retrieve target items result in a suppression of the specific neural

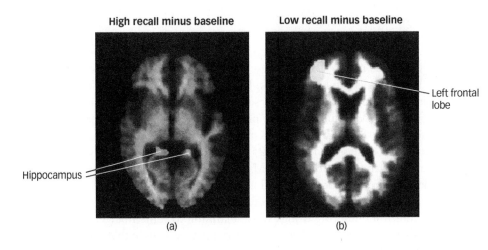

High recall minus baseline

Low recall minus baseline

Hippocampus

Left frontal lobe

(a)

(b)

Figure 6.11
PET Scans of Successful and Unsuccessful Recall (a) When people successfully remembered words they had seen earlier in an experiment (achieving high levels of recall on a test), the hippocampus showed increased activity. (b) When people tried but failed to recall words they had seen earlier (achieving low levels of recall on a test), the left frontal lobe showed increased activity. SCHACTER DL. ALPERT NM, SAVAGE CR. RAUCH SL, ALBERT MS. CONSCIOUS RECOLLECTION AND THE HUMAN HIPPOCAMPAL FORMATION: EVIDENCE FROM POSITRON EMISSION TOMOGRAPHY. PROC NATL ACAD SCI USA 1996; 93: 321–5.

patterns that are uniquely associated with competitors (Wimber et al., 2015). So, for example, when hippocampal activity during retrieval practice signals successful recall of an unwanted competitor, frontal-lobe mechanisms are recruited that help suppress the competitor. Once the competitor is suppressed, the frontal lobe no longer has to work as hard to control retrieval, ultimately making it easier to recall the target item (Kuhl et al., 2007). In addition, successful suppression of an unwanted memory causes reduced activity in the hippocampus (Anderson et al., 2004; Gagnepain, Hulbert, & Anderson, 2017). These findings make sense once we understand the specific roles played by particular brain regions in the retrieval process.

Build to the Outcomes

1. Why are external contexts powerful retrieval cues?

2. How does mood affect memory?

3. Should students spend more time testing themselves on material (retrieval), or studying it over and over?

4. How can retrieval-induced forgetting occur during conversations?

5. How is it possible to remember something you've never seen?

6. How does brain activity differ when you are *trying* to recall an event versus *successfully* recalling it?

Forms of Long-Term Memory: More Than One Kind

In 1977, the British-American neurologist Oliver Sacks interviewed a young man named Greg who had a tumour in his brain that wiped out his ability to remember day-to-day events. One thing Greg could remember, however, was his life during the 1960s in New York's Greenwich Village, years before the tumour formed, when Greg's primary occupation seemed to be attending rock concerts by his favourite band, the Grateful Dead. Greg's memories of those Dead concerts stuck with him over the ensuing years, when he was living in a long-term care hospital and was interviewed regularly by Dr. Sacks. In 1991, Dr. Sacks took Greg to a Dead concert at New York's Madison Square Garden, wondering whether such a momentous event might jolt his memory into action. "That was fantastic," Greg told Dr. Sacks as they left the concert. "I will always remember it.

Learning Outcomes

- Distinguish between explicit memory and implicit memory.

- Give examples of both semantic memories and episodic memories.

- Describe the pros and cons of collaborative memory.

I had the time of my life." But when Dr. Sacks saw Greg the next morning and asked him whether he recalled the previous night's Dead concert at the Garden, Greg drew a blank: "No, I've never been to the Garden" (Sacks, 1995, pp. 76–77).

Although Greg was unable to make new memories, some of the new things that happened to him did seem to leave a mark. For example, Greg did not recall learning that his father had died, but he did seem sad and withdrawn for years after hearing the news. Similarly, HM could not make new memories after his surgery, but if he played a game in which he had to track a moving target, his performance gradually improved with each round (Milner, 1962). Greg could not consciously remember hearing about his father's death, and HM could not consciously remember playing the tracking game, but both showed clear signs of having been permanently changed by experiences that they so rapidly forgot. In other words, they *behaved* as though they were remembering things while claiming to remember nothing at all. This suggests that there must be several kinds of memory—some that are accessible to conscious recall and some that we cannot consciously access (Eichenbaum & Cohen, 2001; Schacter & Tulving, 1994; Schacter, Wagner, & Buckner, 2000; Squire & Kandel, 1999).

Memories can be broken down into two types. **Explicit memory** occurs *when people consciously or intentionally retrieve past experiences*. Recalling last summer's vacation, incidents from a novel you just read, or facts you studied for a test all involve explicit memory. Indeed, anytime you start a sentence with "I remember . . . ," you are talking about an explicit memory. **Implicit memory** occurs when *past experiences influence later behaviour and performance, even without an effort to remember them or an awareness of the recollection* (Graf & Schacter, 1985; Schacter, 1987). Let's look next at both of these.

Implicit Memory

Implicit memories are not consciously recalled, but their presence is "implied" by our actions. Greg's persistent sadness after his father's death, even though he had no conscious knowledge of the event, is an example of implicit memory. So is HM's improved performance on a tracking task that he didn't consciously remember having done before.

The ability to ride a bike or tie your shoelaces or play the guitar are other examples of implicit memory. You may know how to do these things, but you probably can't describe *how* to do them. Such knowledge reflects a particular kind of implicit memory called **procedural memory**, which refers to *the gradual acquisition of skills as a result of practice, or "knowing how" to do things*.

One of the hallmarks of procedural memory is that the things you remember are automatically translated into actions. Sometimes you can explain how it is done (put one finger on the third fret of the E string, one finger . . .), and sometimes you can't (get on the bike and . . . well, uh . . . just balance). The fact that people who have amnesia can acquire new procedural memories suggests that the hippocampal structures that are usually damaged in these individuals may be necessary for explicit memory, but they aren't needed for implicit procedural memory. In fact, it appears that brain regions outside the hippocampal area (including areas in the motor cortex) are involved in procedural memory. The Learning chapter discusses this evidence further, and you will also see that procedural memory is crucial for learning various kinds of motor, perceptual, and cognitive skills.

Priming Makes Some Information More Accessible

Not all implicit memories are procedural or "how to" memories. For example, **priming** refers to *an enhanced ability to think of a stimulus, such as a word or object, as a result of a recent exposure to that stimulus during an earlier study task* (Tulving &

explicit memory The act of consciously or intentionally retrieving past experiences.

implicit memory The influence of past experiences on later behaviour and performance, even without an effort to remember them or an awareness of the recollection.

procedural memory The gradual acquisition of skills as a result of practice, or "knowing how" to do things.

priming An enhanced ability to think of a stimulus, such as a word or object, as a result of a recent exposure to that stimulus during an earlier study task.

Schacter, 1990). In one experiment, university students were asked to study a long list of words, including items such as *avocado, mystery, climate, octopus,* and *assassin* (Tulving, Schacter, & Stark, 1982). Later, explicit memory was tested by showing participants some of these words along with new ones they hadn't seen and asking them which words were on the list. To test implicit memory, participants received word fragments and were asked to come up with a word that fitted the fragment. Try the test yourself:

c h — — — n k   o – t – p — —   — o g – y — — —   — l – m – t e

You probably had difficulty coming up with the answers for the first and third fragments (*chipmunk, bogeyman*) but had little trouble coming up with answers for the second and fourth (*octopus, climate*). Seeing *octopus* and *climate* on the original list made those words more accessible later, during the fill-in-the-blanks test. Just as priming a pump makes water flow more easily, priming the memory system makes some information more accessible. In the fill-in-the-blanks experiment, people showed priming for studied words even when they failed to remember consciously that they had seen them earlier. This suggests that priming is an example of implicit, not explicit, memory.

A truly stunning example of this point comes from a study by Mitchell (2006) in which participants first studied black-and-white line drawings depicting everyday objects. Later, the participants were shown fragmented versions of the drawings that were difficult to identify; some of them depicted objects that they had studied earlier in the experiment, whereas others depicted new objects that they had not studied. Mitchell found that participants correctly identified more fragmented drawings of studied than new objects, and identified more studied objects than did participants in a control group who had never seen the pictures—a clear demonstration of priming (see **FIGURE 6.12**). (This in itself is not so surprising—such priming had been demonstrated by British researchers nearly 40 years earlier [Warrington & Weiskrantz, 1968]). Here's the stunning part: The fragmented drawing test was given 17 years after presentation of the study list! By that time, participants had little or no explicit memory of having seen the drawings, and some had no recollection that they had ever participated in the experiment! "I'm sorry—I really don't remember this experiment at all," said one 36-year-old man who showed a strong priming effect. A 36-year-old woman who showed even more priming stated simply, "Don't remember anything about it" (Mitchell, 2006, p. 929). These observations confirm that priming is an example of implicit memory, and also that priming can persist over very long periods of time.

Procedural Memory and Priming Do Not Rely on the Hippocampus

Because priming is an example of implicit memory, not explicit memory, you'd expect amnesic individuals such as HM and Greg to show priming. In fact, many experiments have shown that amnesic individuals can show substantial priming effects—often as great as healthy, nonamnesic individuals—even though they have no explicit memory for the items they studied (Warrington & Weiskrantz, 1968). These and other similar results suggest that priming, like procedural memory, does not require the hippocampal structures that are damaged in cases of amnesia (Schacter & Curran, 2000).

If the hippocampal region isn't required for procedural memory and priming, which parts of the brain *are* involved? Experiments have revealed that priming is associated with *reduced* activity in various regions of the cortex that are activated when people perform an unprimed task. For instance, when research participants are shown the word stem *mot* _____ or *tab* _____ and are asked to provide the first word that comes to mind, parts of the occipital lobe involved in visual processing and parts of the frontal lobe involved in word retrieval become active. But if people perform the same task after being primed by seeing *motel* and *table*, there's

Musicians such as Janelle Monáe rely heavily on procedural memory to acquire and use the skills they need to play their music at a high level.

ERIKA GOLDRING/GETTY IMAGES

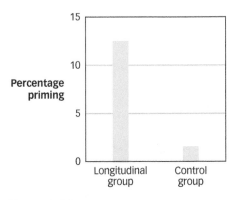

Figure 6.12

Long-Term Priming of Visual Objects Participants who viewed drawings of common objects and were then given a test 17 years later, in which they tried to identify the objects from fragmented drawings (longitudinal group), showed a strong priming effect. In contrast, participants who had not seen the drawings 17 years earlier (control group) showed nonsignificant priming (Mitchell, 2006).

Figure 6.13

Primed and Unprimed Processing of Stimuli Priming is associated with reduced levels of activation in the cortex on a number of different tasks. In each pair of fMRIs, the images on the upper left (a, c) show brain regions in the frontal lobe (a) and occipital/temporal lobe (c) that are active during an unprimed task (in this case, providing a word response to a visual word cue). The images on the lower right within each pair (b, d) show reduced activity in the same regions during the primed version of the same task.

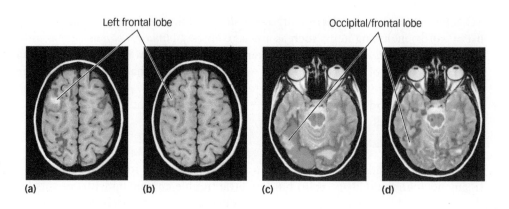

Left frontal lobe   Occipital/frontal lobe

(a)   (b)   (c)   (d)

less activity in these same regions (Buckner et al., 1995; Schott et al., 2005). Something similar happens when people see pictures of everyday objects on two different occasions. On the second exposure to a picture, there's less activity in parts of the visual cortex that were activated by seeing the picture initially. Priming seems to make it easier for parts of the cortex that are involved in perceiving a word or object to identify the item after a recent exposure to it (Schacter, Dobbins, & Schnyer, 2004; Wiggs & Martin, 1998). This suggests that the brain saves a bit of processing time after priming (see **FIGURE 6.13**).

Neuroimaging studies also indicate that different brain systems are involved in two distinct forms of priming: *perceptual priming,* which reflects implicit memory for the sensory features of an item (e.g., the visual characteristics of a word or picture), and *conceptual priming,* which reflects implicit memory for the meaning of a word or how you would use an object. Studies using fMRI indicate that perceptual priming depends primarily on regions towards the back of the brain, such as the visual cortex, whereas conceptual priming depends more on regions towards the front of the brain, such as the frontal lobes (Wig, Buckner, & Schacter, 2009). There is also some evidence that perceptual priming is associated primarily with the right cerebral hemisphere, whereas conceptual priming is associated with the left hemisphere (Schacter, Wig, & Stevens, 2007).

Explicit Memory: Semantic and Episodic

Consider these two questions: (1) What do we remember at 11 a.m. on November 11 every year? (2) What was the most memorable Remembrance Day activity in which you participated during your elementary school years? Most Canadians know the answer to the first question (we honour those who lost their lives in military service), but we all have our own answers to the second. Both of these are explicit memories, consciously or intentionally retrieved from past experiences. But the first one requires you to dredge up a fact that every Canadian schoolchild knows and that is not part of your personal autobiography, while the second requires you to revisit a particular time and place—or episode—from your personal past. These memories are called *semantic* and *episodic* memories, respectively (Tulving, 1972, 1983, 1998) (**FIGURE 6.14**).

- **Semantic memory** is *a network of associated facts and concepts that make up our general knowledge of the world.*
- **Episodic memory** is *the collection of past personal experiences that occurred at a particular time and place.*

Episodic memory is special because it is the only form of memory that allows us to engage in mental time travel, projecting ourselves into the past and revisiting events

semantic memory A network of associated facts and concepts that make up our general knowledge of the world.

episodic memory The collection of past personal experiences that occurred at a particular time and place.

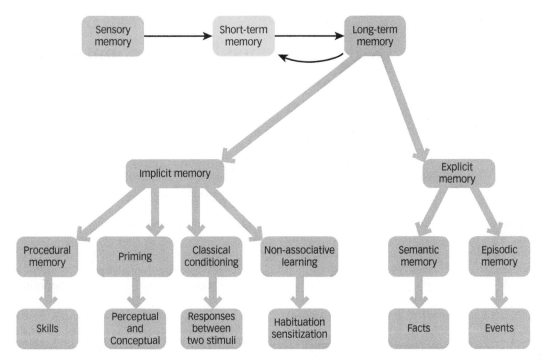

Figure 6.14
Forms of Long-Term Memory Long-term memory consists of explicit and implicit forms, which can be further divided into specific subtypes (see the chapter on Learning for discussion of conditioning, habituation, and sensitization).

that have happened to us. This ability allows us to connect our pasts and our presents to construct a cohesive story of our lives (see A World of Difference: Do We All Reexperience Our Personal Pasts?). People who have amnesia can usually travel back in time and revisit episodes that occurred before they became amnesic, but they are unable to revisit episodes that happened later. For example, Greg couldn't travel back to any time after 1969, because that's when he stopped being able to create new episodic memories. But can people with amnesia create *new* semantic memories?

British researchers have studied three young adults who suffered damage to the hippocampus during birth as a result of difficult deliveries that interrupted oxygen supply to the brain (Brandt et al., 2009; Vargha-Khadem et al., 1997). Their parents noticed that the children could not recall what happened during a typical day, had to be constantly reminded of appointments, and often became lost and disoriented. In view of their hippocampal damage, you might also expect that they would perform poorly in school and might even be classified as learning disabled. Remarkably, however, all three children learned to read, write, and spell; developed normal vocabularies; and acquired other kinds of semantic knowledge that allowed them to perform well in school. On the basis of this evidence, researchers have concluded that the hippocampus is not necessary for acquiring new *semantic* memories.

Remembering why we observe Remembrance Day is an example of semantic memory.

Episodic Memory Contributes to Imagination and Creativity

We've already seen that episodic memory allows us to travel backwards in time, but it turns out that episodic memory also plays a role in allowing us to travel forwards in time. An amnesic Canadian man known by the initials KC provided an early clue. KC could not recollect any specific episodes from his past, and when he was asked to imagine a future episode—such as what he might do tomorrow—he reported a complete "blank" (Tulving, 1985). Consistent with this observation, more recent findings from individuals with hippocampal amnesia reveal that some of them have difficulty imagining new experiences, such as sunbathing on a sandy beach (Hassabis et al., 2007), or events that might happen in their everyday lives (Race, Keane, & Verfaellie, 2011).

A World of Difference | Do We All Reexperience Our Personal Pasts?

Think back to your dinner last night. What did you eat and where? What did the dining room look like? Who else was there? You probably didn't have much difficulty answering these questions and reexperiencing at least a few happenings from dinner last night. But some otherwise high-functioning people seem to lack the ability to vividly reexperience past events, even though they know those events happened. Canadian researchers who recently discovered this condition named it *severely deficient autobiographical memory* (SDAM) (Palombo et al., 2015).

The three SDAM individuals who were studied are each middle-aged adults (one woman, two men) employed at a full-time job; one has a PhD degree. All three perform normally on a standard battery of cognitive tasks that assess general intellectual abilities, and they even perform well on laboratory tests of verbal memory, showing that they can retain information over time. But they each lack the ability to travel back in time and *reexperience* their personal pasts, a hallmark of episodic memory. When tasked with recalling a particular autobiographical memory from everyday life, they recall few episodic details about what happened and are particularly unable to retrieve visual details, which for most people is an integral part of successful episodic recollection.

Given the established link between the hippocampus and successful recollection (page 226), you might expect hippocampal abnormalities in SDAM individuals—and indeed structural MRI scans showed reduced volume in the right hippocampus of SDAM individuals compared with controls (Palombo et al., 2015). Importantly, a more recent study (Palombo et al., 2018) of 30 healthy young adults showed that individual differences in the ability to recall episodic details on the same autobiographical memory task that had been given to the SDAM group are positively correlated with the volume of a particular subregion within the hippocampus known as $DG/CA_{2/3}$ (dentate gyrus/cornu ammonis regions 2 and 3). Previous neuroimaging research had suggested that the $DG/CA_{2/3}$ subregion may be particularly important for episodic memory, and this new research on individual differences provides additional support for that hypothesis.

Something similar happens with aging. When asked either to recall episodes that actually occurred in their pasts or to imagine new episodes that might occur in their futures, older adults provided fewer details about what happened, or what might happen, than did university students (Addis, Wong, & Schacter, 2008; Schacter, Gaesser, & Addis, 2013). Consistent with these findings, neuroimaging studies reveal that a *core network* (Benoit & Schacter, 2015) of brain regions known to be involved in episodic memory—including the hippocampus—shows similarly increased activity when people remember the past and imagine the future (Addis, Wong, & Schacter, 2007; Okuda et al., 2003; Schacter et al., 2012; Szpunar, Watson, & McDermott, 2007) (see **FIGURE 6.15**).

Figure 6.15

Remembering the Past and Imagining the Future Depend on a Common Core Network of Brain Regions A common brain network is activated when people remember episodes that actually occurred in their personal pasts and when they imagine episodes that might occur in their personal futures. This network includes the hippocampus, a part of the medial temporal lobe long known to play an important role in episodic memory (Schacter, Addis, & Buckner, 2008).

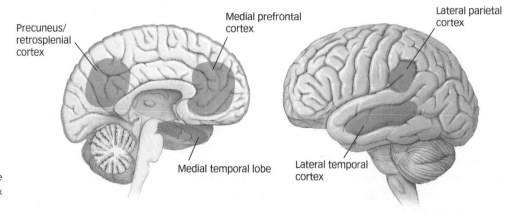

Precuneus/retrosplenial cortex

Medial prefrontal cortex

Lateral parietal cortex

Medial temporal lobe

Lateral temporal cortex

Taken together, these observations strongly suggest that we rely heavily on episodic memory to envision our personal futures (Schacter, Addis, & Buckner, 2008; Szpunar, 2010). Episodic memory is well suited to the task because it is a flexible system that allows us to recombine elements of past experience in new ways, so that we can mentally try out different versions of what might happen (Schacter, 2012; Schacter & Addis, 2007; Suddendorf & Corballis, 2007). For example, when you imagine having a difficult conversation with a friend that will take place in a couple of days, you can draw on past experiences to envision different ways in which the conversation might unfold—and hopefully avoid saying things that, based on past experience, are likely to make the situation worse. After receiving brief training in recalling details of past experience, a procedure known as an *episodic specificity induction* (Schacter & Madore, 2016), people were subsequently better able to imagine different ways in which they could approach a possible future experience, suggesting that increased episodic memory retrieval was responsible for more flexible future imagining (Jing, Madore, & Schacter, 2017). As we'll discuss later, however, this flexibility of episodic memory might also be responsible for some kinds of memory errors (see page 244).

How many unusual uses of a brick can you think of? On the AUT, you would receive credit for coming up with such novel uses as a doorstop, paperweight, or even a weapon.

Imagining the future by recombining elements of past experiences sounds a lot like what psychologists refer to as *divergent creative thinking*: generating creative ideas by combining different types of information in new ways (Guilford, 1967). One common test of divergent creative thinking, the Alternate Uses Task (AUT) (Guilford, 1967), requires participants to generate unusual uses of common objects, such as a brick.

When people perform the AUT during an fMRI scan, parts of the core brain network that supports episodic memory and future imagining, including the hippocampus, show increased activity (Beaty et al., 2016, 2018; Benedek et al., 2014), suggesting that episodic memory may contribute to divergent creative thinking. In findings consistent with this idea, amnesic patients with hippocampal damage and episodic memory deficits perform poorly on tests that tap divergent creative thinking (Duff et al., 2013). Finally, a recent study of healthy young adults revealed that brief training in retrieving details from episodic memory using the episodic specificity induction discussed above enhances divergent creative thinking on the AUT (Madore, Addis, & Schacter, 2015). Training in how to recall episodic details led participants to rely more on their episodic memories during the AUT, helping them recombine information in novel ways and come up with more unusual uses for objects. fMRI evidence revealed that this episodic induction effect is accompanied by increased activity in the hippocampus, as well as increased coupling between the core brain network that supports episodic processing and an executive network that supports working memory and related control functions (Madore et al., 2019). This finding fits well with other evidence indicating that coupling between core and executive networks is a signature feature of divergent creative thinking (Beaty et al., 2016, 2018).

Collaborative Memory: Social Influences on Remembering

So far, we've focused mainly on memory in individuals functioning on their own. But remembering also serves important social functions, which is why we get together with family to talk about old times, or share our memories with friends by posting our vacation photos on Instagram. And we are quick to communicate our memories to others: In a diary study in which university students recorded a memorable event each day for a week, they disclosed 62% of these events to others before the end of the day on which the event occurred (Pasupathi, McLean, & Weeks, 2009). Sharing memories with others can strengthen them (Hirst & Echterhoff, 2012), but we've already seen that talking about some aspects of a memory, yet omitting other related events, can also produce retrieval-induced *forgetting* (see page 233) (Coman et al., 2009; Cuc et al., 2007). Psychologists have become increasingly interested in how people remember in groups, which is now referred to as *collaborative memory* (Meade et al., 2018; Rajaram, 2011).

Groups Can Recall More Than a Single Individual, But Less Than Multiple Individuals Working on Their Own

In a typical collaborative memory experiment, participants first encode a set of target materials, such as a list of words, on their own (just as in the traditional memory experiments that we've already considered). Things start to get interesting at the time of retrieval, when participants work together in small groups (usually two or three participants) to try to remember the target items. The number of items recalled by this group can then be compared with the number of items recalled by individuals who are trying to recall items on their own, without any help from others. The collaborative group typically recalls more target items than any individual (Hirst & Echterhoff, 2012; Weldon, 2001), suggesting that collaboration benefits memory. That makes a lot of sense and generally fits with our intuitions about what should happen in such a situation (Rajaram, 2011). For example, Tim might recall an item that Emily forgot, and Eric might remember items that neither Tim nor Emily recalled, so the sum total of the group will exceed what any one person can recall.

But things get really interesting when we compare the performance of the collaborative group with the performance of what is called a *nominal group*: the combined recall of several individuals recalling target items on their own. Let's consider a nominal group of three compared with a collaborative group of three. In the nominal group, let's assume that after studying a list of eight words, Tim recalls items 1, 2, and 8, Emily recalls items 1, 4, and 7, and Eric recalls items 1, 5, 6, and 8. Functioning on their own, Tim, Emily, and Eric recalled in combination seven of the eight items that were presented. (Nobody recalled item 3.) The surprising finding now reported by many studies is that the collaborative group typically recalls fewer items than the nominal group; that is, when they remember together, Tim, Emily, and Eric will come up with fewer total items than when they remember on their own (Basden et al., 1997; Hirst & Echterhoff, 2012; Rajaram, 2011; Rajaram & Pereira-Pasarin, 2010; Weldon, 2001). This negative effect of group recall on memory is known as *collaborative inhibition*: The same number of individuals working together recall fewer items than they would on their own.

What's going on here? Most people believe, on the basis of intuition, that working together should increase rather than decrease recall (Rajaram, 2011). Why does it turn out otherwise? One possibility is that, in a group, some individuals are prone to "social loafing": They let others do the work and don't pull their own weight. Although social loafing is well known to occur in groups (Karau & Williams, 1993), memory researchers have tested this account of collaborative inhibition and rejected it (Barber, Rajaram, & Fox, 2012).

Remembering as a collaborative group leads to greater recall than any single member of the group would achieve alone, but less than that produced by a nominal group of individuals remembering on their own.

The Real World | Is Google Hurting Our Memories?

Take some time to try to answer a simple question before returning to reading this box: What country has a national flag that is not rectangular? Now let's discuss what went through your mind as you searched for an answer. (The correct answer is Nepal.) Did you start thinking about the shapes of national flags? Take a mental walk through a map of the world? Or did you think instead about computers—more specifically, about typing the question into Google? There probably was a time not too long ago when most people would have tried to conjure up images of national flags or take a mental world tour, but research conducted in the lab of one of your textbook authors indicates that nowadays, most of us think about computers and Google searches when confronted with questions of this kind (Sparrow, Liu, & Wegner, 2011).

Sparrow and colleagues found that after people were given difficult general-knowledge questions, they were slower to name the colour in which a computer-related word (e.g., Google, Internet, Yahoo) was printed than the colour in which a noncomputer-related word (e.g., Nike, table, Yoplait) was printed. This suggests that after being given difficult questions, these people were thinking about things related to computers, which interfered with their ability to name the colour in which the word was printed. The

researchers concluded that we are now so used to searching for information on Google when we don't immediately know the answer to a question that we immediately think of computers, rather than searching our memories.

Thinking about computers when faced with a tough question makes sense: We will probably come up with the answer more quickly if we do a Google search than if we think about what different flags look like. But this result also raises troubling questions: Is reliance on computers and the Internet having an adverse effect on human memory? If we rely on Google for answers, are we unknowingly making our memories obsolete? More recent research has shown that when people are instructed to use the Internet to answer difficult trivia questions, they are later more likely to use the Internet to also answer easier trivia questions (Storm, Stone, & Benjamin, 2017), suggesting that we are prone to becoming increasingly reliant on Google and other Internet sources the more we use them, and less reliant on our own memories.

However, this reliance may produce some benefits. For example, even though participants had a harder time remembering bits of trivia that they typed into a computer when they were told that the computer would save their answers

than when they were told that the answers would be erased, people often remembered where they saved the answers even when they did not remember the information itself (Sparrow et al., 2011). More recent research has shown that saving information to a computer can take some of the load off people's own memories. When participants saved a PDF file containing a word list to the computer and didn't try to remember the words themselves, they remembered more words from a second PDF file presented a few seconds later than they remembered in the first file (Storm & Stone, 2015).

Taken together, the findings from these studies indicate that offloading our memories to computers has both costs and benefits (for related observations, see the discussion of prospective memory on page 247). Sparrow and colleagues (2011) suggested that people may be adapting their memories to the demands of new technology, relying on computers in a way that is similar to how we sometimes rely on other people (friends, family members, or colleagues) to remember things that we may not remember ourselves. This is similar to what we discussed as *collaborative memory*, and just as collaborative remembering with other people has both helpful and harmful effects, so does collaborative remembering with our computers.

A more likely explanation is that when recalling items together, the retrieval strategies used by individual members of the group disrupt those used by others (Basden et al., 1997; Hirst & Echterhoff, 2012; Rajaram, 2011). For instance, suppose that Tim goes first and recalls items in the order that they were presented. This retrieval strategy may be disruptive to Emily, who prefers to recall the last item first and then work backwards through the list. Interesting recent research indicates that the negative effects of collaborative inhibition on memory persist even when individual members of a group later try to recall studied items on their own, without the disruption of retrieval strategies by other group members (Barber, Harris, & Rajaram, 2015). These findings suggest that collaborative inhibition produces a lasting reduction in the accessibility of individuals' memories.

Collaborative Recall Has Other Benefits

Despite the effects of collaborative inhibition, when individuals recall information together in a group, they are exposed to items recalled by others that they may not recall themselves. This exposure improves their memory when they are retested at a later time (Blumen & Rajaram, 2008). And when group members discuss what they have recalled, they can help each other to correct and reduce memory errors (Ross, Blatz, & Schryer, 2008). These observations fit with earlier work showing that couples in close relationships often rely on collaborative remembering (also called *transactive memory*) (Wegner, Erber, & Raymond, 1991), whereby each member of the couple remembers certain kinds of information that they can share with the other. (Can you rely on your computer for collaborative remembering? See The Real World: Is Google Hurting Our Memories?). So the next time you are sharing memories of a past activity with friends, you will be shaping your memories for both better and worse.

Build to the Outcomes

1. What is the type of memory in which you just "know how" to do something?
2. How does priming make memory more efficient?
3. What parts of the brain are involved for procedural memory and priming?
4. What form of memory is like a time machine to our past?
5. How does episodic memory help us imagine our futures?
6. Why does a collaborative group typically recall fewer items than a nominal group?

Memory Failures: The Seven "Sins" of Memory

Learning Outcomes

- Identify each of the memory "sins."
- Describe possible benefits of each memory "sin."

NATIONAL LIBRARY OF MEDICINE/SCIENCE PHOTO LIBRARY/ SCIENCE SOURCE

Wilder Penfield was, during his lifetime, called "the greatest living Canadian" for his contributions to the surgical treatment of neurological disorders, including epilepsy. His research into the functions of the living brain greatly expanded scientific knowledge of the brain.

You probably haven't given much thought to breathing today, and the reason is that from the moment you woke up, you've been doing it effortlessly and well. But the moment breathing fails, you are reminded of just how important it is. Memory is like that. Every time we see, think, notice, imagine, or wonder, we are drawing on our ability to use information stored in our brains, but it isn't until this ability fails that we become acutely aware of just how much we should treasure it. Such memory errors—the seven "sins" of memory—cast similar illumination on how memory normally operates and how often it operates well (Schacter, 1999, 2001b). We'll discuss each of the seven "sins" in detail below.

1. Transience

Wilder Penfield, a Canadian neurosurgeon, founded the Montreal Neurological Institute; he also developed the effective surgical treatment of epilepsy. Before he operated on a patient, he would stimulate regions of his or her brain with electrical probes while the patient was awake on the operating table (under only local anaesthesia). His original intent was to identify the regions of the brain responsible for generating the seizures, but in the process he found that he was able to create detailed maps of the functioning of the human cortex. Stimulation in one area caused the left hand to twitch, while stimulating another area caused the patient to report a tingling in his or her right leg. Many of the patient reports of these experiences of stimulation had the character of amazingly detailed, vivid memories. For example, a patient might hear the voice of a cousin in Africa, or see a man and dog walking along a road near his place in the country. During such experiences, the patient was simultaneously aware of being in the operating room.

These "memories" (as they seemed to be) were so detailed that, to Penfield, it seemed as though the cortex must contain a permanent record of all past experience (Penfield & Perot, 1963). In fact, only a small minority of his patients reported such experiences, and whether or not they are memories is impossible to know—it now seems very likely that they were not memories at all. Contrary

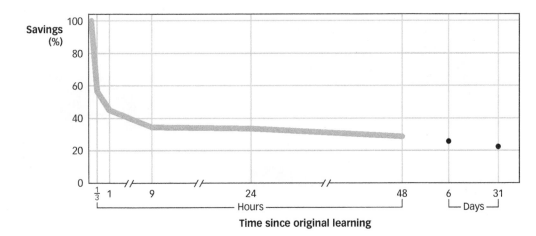

Figure 6.16
The Curve of Forgetting
Hermann Ebbinghaus measured his retention at various delay intervals after he studied lists of nonsense syllables. He measured retention in percent savings, that is, the percentage of time he needed to relearn the list compared with the time he needed to learn it initially.

to what Penfield believed, we now know that memories can and do degrade with time. The culprit here is **transience**: *forgetting what occurs with the passage of time*. Transience occurs during the storage phase of memory, after an experience has been encoded and before it is retrieved. You've already seen the workings of transience—rapid forgetting—in sensory storage and short-term storage. Transience also occurs in long-term storage, as was first illustrated in the late 1870s by Hermann Ebbinghaus, a German philosopher who, after studying lists of nonsense syllables, measured his own memory for those syllables at different delays (Ebbinghaus, 1885/1964). Ebbinghaus charted his recall of the syllables over time, creating the forgetting curve shown in **FIGURE 6.16**. He noted a rapid drop-off in retention during the first few tests, followed by a slower rate of forgetting on later tests—a general pattern confirmed by many subsequent memory researchers (Wixted & Ebbensen, 1991). So, for example, when English-speakers were tested for memory of Spanish vocabulary acquired during high school or undergraduate courses taken 1 to 50 years earlier, there was a rapid drop-off in memory during the first 3 years after the students' last class, followed by tiny losses in later years (Bahrick, 1984, 2000). In all these studies, memories didn't fade at a constant rate as time passed; most forgetting happened soon after an event occurred, with increasingly less forgetting as more time passed.

Not only do we forget memories with the passage of time but the quality of our memories also changes. At early time points on the forgetting curve—minutes, hours, and days—memory preserves a relatively detailed record, allowing us to reproduce the past with reasonable if not perfect accuracy. But with the passing of time, we increasingly rely on our general memories for what usually happens and attempt to reconstruct the details by inference and even sheer guesswork. Transience involves a gradual switch from specific to more general memories (Brewer, 1996; Eldridge, Barnard, & Bekerian, 1994; Thompson et al., 1996).

In one early study, British research participants read a brief Native American folktale that contained odd imagery and unfamiliar plots, then recounted it as best they could after a delay (Bartlett, 1932). The readers made interesting but understandable errors, often eliminating details that didn't make sense to them or adding elements to make the story more coherent. As the specifics of the story slipped away, the general meaning of the events stayed in memory, but usually with elaborations and embellishments that were consistent with the readers' culture and worldview. Because the story was unfamiliar to the readers, they raided their stores of general information and patched together a reasonable recollection of what *probably* happened.

transience Forgetting what occurs with the passage of time.

First memories are seen later in cultures that place less emphasis on talking about the past.

Yo-Yo Ma with his $2.5 million cello. The famous cellist lost the instrument when he absentmindedly forgot that he'd placed it in a taxicab's trunk minutes earlier.

retroactive interference Situations in which information learned later impairs memory for information acquired earlier.

proactive interference Situations in which information learned earlier impairs memory for information acquired later.

absentmindedness A lapse in attention that results in memory failure.

Yet another way that memories can be forgotten is by interference from other memories. For example, if you carry out the same activities at work each day, by the time Friday rolls around, it may be difficult to remember what you did on Monday because later activities blend in with earlier ones. This is an example of **retroactive interference**, *situations in which later learning impairs memory for information acquired earlier* (Postman & Underwood, 1973). **Proactive interference**, in contrast, refers to *situations in which earlier learning impairs memory for information acquired later*. For instance, if you use the same parking lot each day at work or at school, you've probably gone out to find your car and then stood there confused by the memories of having parked it on previous days.

Finally, one of the most common types of forgetting over time is that most of us have few or no memories from the first few years of life, due to *childhood amnesia*, or *infantile amnesia*. On average, an individual's first memory dates to about 3 to 3½ years of age (Dudycha & Dudycha, 1933; Waldfogel, 1948), with women reporting slightly earlier first memories (3.07 years of age) than men (3.4 years) (Howes, Siegel, & Brown, 1993). These estimates are based on individuals from Western (i.e., North American and European) cultures, which emphasize talking about the past. First memories are seen at even later ages in Asian cultures that place less emphasis on talking about the past, such as Korea and China (MacDonald, Uesiliana, & Hayne, 2000; Mullen, 1994; Peterson, Wang, & Hou, 2009). Culture may thus impact how long our memories last.

2. Absentmindedness

The great cellist Yo-Yo Ma put his treasured $2.5 million instrument in the trunk of a taxicab in New York City and then rode to his destination. After a 10-minute trip, he paid the driver and left the cab, forgetting his cello. Minutes later, Ma realized what he had done and called the police. Fortunately, they tracked down the taxi and recovered the instrument within hours (Finkelstein, 1999). But how had the celebrated cellist forgotten about something so important that had occurred only 10 minutes earlier? Transience is not a likely culprit. As soon as Mr. Ma realized what he'd done with his instrument, he recalled where he had put it. This information had not disappeared from his memory (which is why he was able to tell the police where the cello was). Instead, Yo-Yo Ma was a victim of **absentmindedness**, *a lapse in attention that results in memory failure*.

What makes people absentminded? One common cause is lack of attention. Attention plays a vital role in encoding information into long-term memory. Without proper attention, material is much less likely to be stored properly and recalled later. In studies of divided attention, research participants are given materials to remember, such as a list of words, a story, or a series of pictures. At the same time, they are required to perform an additional task that draws their attention away from the material. For example, participants in one study listened to lists of 15 words for a later memory test (Craik et al., 1996). They were allowed to pay full attention to certain lists, but while hearing other lists they had to simultaneously view a visual display that contained four boxes; they were told to press different keys to indicate where an asterisk was appearing and disappearing. On a later test, participants recalled far fewer words from the list they had heard while their attention was divided.

There Is Less Activity in the Left Frontal Lobe When Attention Is Divided

What happens in the brain when attention is divided? As we saw earlier, greater activity in the lower left frontal region during encoding is associated with better memory. But participants show less activity in the lower left frontal lobe when their attention is divided (Shallice et al., 1994). Dividing attention, then, prevents the lower left frontal lobe from playing its normal role in semantic encoding, and the result is absentminded forgetting. Divided attention also leads to less hippocampal involvement in encoding (Kensinger, Clarke, & Corkin, 2003; Uncapher & Rugg, 2008). Given the importance of the hippocampus to episodic memory, this finding may help to explain why absentminded forgetting is sometimes so extreme, as when we forget where we put our keys or glasses only moments earlier.

We Don't Always Remember to Remember

Another common cause of absentmindedness is forgetting to carry out actions that we plan to do in the future. On any given day, you need to remember the times and places that your classes meet, you need to remember with whom and where you are having lunch, you need to remember which grocery items to pick up for dinner, and you need to remember which page of this book you were on when you fell asleep. In other words, you have to remember to remember, which is called **prospective memory**, *remembering to do things in the future* (Einstein & McDaniel, 1990, 2005).

Failures of prospective memory are a major source of absentmindedness in everyday life (Dismukes, 2012). Avoiding these problems often requires having a cue available at the very moment you need to remember to carry out an action. For example, air traffic controllers must sometimes postpone an action, such as granting a pilot's request to change altitude, but remember to carry out that action a few minutes later when conditions change. In a simulated air traffic control experiment, researchers provided controllers with electronic signals to remind them to carry out a deferred request 1 minute later. The reminders were made available either during the 1-minute waiting period or at the time the controller needed to act on the deferred request. The controllers' memory for the deferred action improved only when the reminder was available at the time needed for retrieval. Providing the reminder during the waiting period did not help (Vortac, Edwards, & Manning, 1995). An early reminder, then, is no reminder at all.

Because external reminders are so important for enhancing prospective memory, and thereby reducing absentminded memory errors, it is perhaps not surprising in this era of smartphones and Google Calendar that we are increasingly relying on external devices to remind us to carry out future tasks in everyday life, a process referred to as *intention offloading* (Risko & Gilbert, 2016). People are particularly likely to engage in intention offloading when task demands are high and when they lack confidence in their memory abilities, but this self-initiated reliance on external reminders improves prospective memory performance (Gilbert, 2015).

Prospective memory failures are especially common after brain injuries, so it is important to determine whether novel kinds of external reminders, such as Google Calendar, can help brain-injured patients who suffer from high rates of absentminded forgetting. One study of 12 patients who had serious memory impairments

Talking on a cell phone while driving is a common occurrence and an example of divided attention in everyday life; texting is even worse. Texting while driving can be dangerous, and is illegal, entailing hefty fines and even license suspension in Canada.

External memory aids such as Google Calendar can enhance prospective memory in healthy individuals, as well as in patients experiencing memory deficits attributable to traumatic brain injury or Alzheimer's disease.

prospective memory Remembering to do things in the future.

as a consequence of various kinds of brain injuries showed that training these patients to use Google Calendar to set reminders improved their prospective memory performance in everyday life more than did training them to use a diary (McDonald et al., 2011). More recent case studies of patients with memory problems resulting from traumatic brain injury (Baldwin & Powell, 2015) and Alzheimer's disease (El Haj, Gallouj, & Antoine, 2017) have shown positive effects on everyday prospective memory from training the patients to use Google Calendar synched to their smartphones. These advantages of technology for improving prospective memory failures are balanced by the costs discussed in The Real World: Is Google Hurting our Memories?

3. Blocking

Have you ever tried to recall the name of a famous movie actor or a book you've read—and felt that the answer was on the tip of your tongue, rolling around in your head *somewhere* but just out of reach at that moment? This tip-of-the-tongue experience is a classic example of **blocking**, *a failure to retrieve information that is available in memory even though you are trying to produce it*. The sought-after information has been encoded and stored, and a cue is available that would ordinarily trigger recall of it. The information has not faded from memory, and you aren't forgetting to retrieve it. Rather, you are experiencing a full-blown retrieval failure, which makes this memory breakdown especially frustrating. Researchers have described the tip-of-the-tongue state, in particular, as "a mild torment, something like [being] on the brink of a sneeze" (Brown & McNeill, 1966, p. 326).

Blocking occurs especially often for the names of people and places (Cohen, 1990; Semenza, 2009; Valentine, Brennen, & Brédart, 1996). Why? Because their links to related concepts and knowledge are weaker than for common names. That somebody's last name is Baker doesn't tell us much about the person, but saying that he *is* a baker does. To illustrate this point, researchers showed people pictures of cartoon and comic strip characters, some with descriptive names that highlight key features of the character (e.g., Grumpy, Snow White, Scrooge) and others with arbitrary names (e.g., Aladdin, Mary Poppins, Pinocchio) (Brédart & Valentine, 1998). Even though the two types of names were equally familiar to participants in the experiment, they blocked less often on the descriptive names than on the arbitrary names.

Although it's frustrating when it occurs, blocking is a relatively infrequent event for most of us. However, it occurs more often as we grow older, and it is a very common complaint among people in their 60s and 70s (Burke et al., 1991; Schwartz, 2002). Even more striking, some individuals with brain damage live in a nearly perpetual tip-of-the-tongue state (Semenza, 2009). One such individual could recall the names of only 2 of 40 famous people when she saw their photographs, compared with 25 of 40 for healthy volunteers in the control group (Semenza & Zettin, 1989). Yet she could still recall correctly the occupations of 32 of these people—the same number as healthy people could recall. This case and similar ones have given researchers important clues about what parts of the brain are involved in retrieving proper names. Name blocking usually results from damage to parts of the left temporal lobe on the surface of the cortex, most often as a result of a stroke. In fact, studies that show strong activation of regions within the temporal lobe when people recall proper names support this idea (Damasio et al., 1996; Gorno-Tempini et al., 1998).

AP PHOTO/CRAIG RUTTLE

Those who attend a Santa Claus Parade will easily recall this character's name, closely associated with a grumpy attitude: The Grinch!

blocking A failure to retrieve information that is available in memory even though you are trying to produce it.

4. Memory Misattribution

In 1971, musician George Harrison (formerly of The Beatles) had a huge hit worldwide with the song "My Sweet Lord." Because of its similarity to the earlier Chiffons hit "He's So Fine" (written by Ronnie Mack), Harrison was sued. In 1976, the court found that he had "subconsciously" copied the earlier song, but that the lack of awareness was not a mitigating factor—the court recommended that he pay \$U.S. 1.6 million in damages to the copyright owner of "He's So Fine" (equivalent to about \$8.7 million in today's Canadian dollars). Harrison was a victim of **memory misattribution**, *assigning a recollection or an idea to the wrong source* (see **FIGURE 6.17**).

Memory misattribution errors are a primary cause of eyewitness misidentifications. The memory researcher Donald Thomson was accused of rape on the basis of the victim's detailed recollection of his face, although he was eventually cleared when it turned out he had an airtight alibi. At the time of the rape, Thomson was giving a live television interview on the subject of distorted memories! The victim had been watching the show just before she was assaulted and misattributed her memory of Thomson's face to the rapist's face (Schacter, 1996; Thomson, 1988). Thomson's case, though dramatic, is not an isolated occurrence: Faulty eyewitness memory was a factor in more than 75% of the first 250 cases in which individuals were shown to be innocent through DNA evidence after being convicted of crimes they did not commit (Garrett, 2011) (see Other Voices: Memories Inside Out).

Figure 6.17
Memory Misattribution George Harrison committed a memory misattribution when he thought that he had composed a melody that had already been created by someone else; that mistake cost him nearly 9 million dollars. He still found reasons to smile, though.

Correct Memories Can Be Attributed to the Wrong Source

Part of memory is knowing where our memories came from. This is known as **source memory**, *recall of when, where, and how information was acquired* (Johnson, Hashtroudi, & Lindsay, 1993; Mitchell & Johnson, 2009; Schacter, Harbluk, & McLachlan, 1984). People sometimes correctly recall a fact they learned earlier or accurately recognize a person or object they have seen before but misattribute the source of this knowledge—just as happened to the rape victim in the Donald Thomson incident (Davies, 1988). Such misattribution could be the cause of déjà vu experiences, when you suddenly feel that you have been in a situation before even though you can't recall any details. A present situation that is similar to a past experience may trigger a general sense of familiarity that is mistakenly attributed to having been in the exact situation previously (Brown, 2004; Reed, 1988; see Hot Science: Déjà Vu: Can We Predict the Future?).

Individuals with damage to the frontal lobes are especially prone to memory misattribution errors (Schacter et al., 1984; Shimamura & Squire, 1987). This is probably because the frontal lobes play a significant role in effortful retrieval processes, which are required to dredge up the correct source of a memory. These individuals sometimes produce bizarre misattributions. In 1991, a British photographer in his mid-40s known as MR was overcome with feelings of familiarity about people he didn't know. He kept asking his wife whether each new passing stranger was "somebody"—a screen actor, television news announcer, or local celebrity. MR's feelings were so intense that he often could not resist approaching strangers and asking whether they were indeed famous celebrities. When given formal tests, MR recognized the faces of actual celebrities as accurately as did healthy volunteers in the control group. But MR also "recognized" more than 75% of unfamiliar faces, whereas healthy volunteers hardly ever did. Neurological exams revealed that MR suffered from multiple sclerosis, which had caused damage to his frontal lobes (Ward et al., 1999).

memory misattribution Assigning a recollection or an idea to the wrong source.

source memory Recall of when, where, and how information was acquired.

Other Voices | Memories Inside Out

There's a good chance that sometime during the summer of 2015 you saw and enjoyed the hit Pixar movie *Inside Out*, which portrays the emotional struggles of the 11-year-old Riley after her family moves to a new home by drawing on psychological research that distinguishes among basic emotions (see the chapter on Emotion and Motivation, pp. 308–347). The movie also delved into Riley's memories and provided some realistic insights into how memories can be used to regulate emotions. But as Karen Daniel points out in an opinion piece published when the movie opened, the film's depiction of memory ignored some key findings and ideas from psychological research on memory, with potentially serious consequences:

Let me begin by saying that I love, love, love Pixar movies. Like many adults, I began watching them as part of my parental duties. There was a time when I could recite all the dialogue from *Monsters Inc.* and the first two *Toy Story* films.

It was thus with great anticipation that I tuned in to a radio interview of Pete Docter, the director of the latest Pixar release, *Inside Out*. What a fabulous idea: animating the emotions inside the mind of an 11-year-old child named Riley who is undergoing a major life transition. Docter explained that he researched many aspects of psychology to make the film accurate. When it came to human memory, however, Docter departed from science for the sake of the story line.

As shown in a trailer for *Inside Out*, Riley's memories are portrayed as mini-animations safely preserved inside little globes, which can be pulled out and replayed exactly the way they happened. The character Joy explains that certain of these globes contain "core memories" that form the basis of Riley's personality. This representation of memory is essential to the plot but is not true, as Docter candidly admitted.

I couldn't help but cringe. Given the wide appeal of Pixar movies, a new generation may grow up internalizing the profoundly false notion that memory works like a video recording and that perfect memories of events can be recalled at will. In reality, memory is fallible, malleable, and subject to suggestion and distortion. Docter noted that learning this was a revelation to him, even though he chose not to depict memory that way in *Inside Out*.

One may ask, "Who cares? It's just a movie." In the world of criminal justice, it matters a great deal. One of the most critical moments in a criminal trial is when a victim or witness points at the defendant and declares, "I will never forget that face." The witness usually professes complete certainty, and the prosecutor highlights this as proof of the defendant's guilt—even though experts tell us courtroom certainty does not necessarily correlate to accuracy.

In fact, mistaken identification is a leading cause of conviction of the innocent. Myriad factors that are not necessarily obvious to the average person can affect the reliability of an eyewitness identification, such as distractions at the time of the event, lapse of time, post-event discussions with police, and limitations inherent in cross-racial identifications. Expert witnesses can help explain these factors, but most judges exclude expert testimony on the ground [sic] that eyewitness identifications are a matter of "common sense" and expert

Karen L. Daniel is the director of the Center on Wrongful Convictions at Northwestern University School of Law.

assistance is not necessary. (The Illinois Supreme Court is now reviewing a case that challenges this approach.)

Which brings us back to *Inside Out*. Absent the input of an expert, jurors are left to draw on personal experiences in evaluating testimony. Today's children (and their parents) may become tomorrow's jurors who believe, incorrectly, that memories are stored intact, and that witnesses can simply compare the pictures within their little memory globes to the person sitting at the defendant's table. Docter explained that this comports with most people's sense of how memory works—which is why relying on "common sense" in criminal trials falls short.

We can never entirely eliminate human error from the justice system, but overconfidence in witnesses and misunderstanding by factfinders leads to many wrongful convictions. Let's enjoy Pixar's new film, but when we return from the movie theater, let's ensure that those charged with deciding guilt or innocence in the courtroom are armed with scientific information about eyewitness identifications rather than with the snow globe concept of memory.

Daniel, K. (2015, June 16). Pixar movie teaches future jurors wrong lesson on memory. *Chicago Sun-Times*.

As Daniel and the text point out, faulty eyewitness memories are frequently at work in wrongful convictions. It would be unfortunate if the naive view of memory communicated by *Inside Out* has a lasting influence on any prospective jurors. On a more encouraging note, there are signs that some of the important findings regarding memory's fallibility, such as the seven sins of memory that you are learning about in this chapter, are being communicated to participants in the legal system. For example, in 2014 the United States' National Academy of Sciences published a report written by a distinguished committee composed of experts in both psychology and law titled *Identifying the Culprit: Assessing Eyewitness Identification*, which is intended to convey the findings of psychological research on eyewitness memory to participants in the legal system. Though no doubt many more people saw *Inside Out* than will read this important report, it seems likely that accurate characterizations of memory research such as those contained in the National Academy of Sciences' report will ultimately be more influential in the courtroom than the entertaining though misleading depictions of Riley's memory globes.

Psychologists call MR's type of memory misattribution **false recognition**, *a feeling of familiarity about something that hasn't been encountered before.*

The subjective experience for MR, as in everyday déjà vu experiences, is characterized by a strong sense of familiarity without any recall of associated details. Other individuals with neurological damage exhibit a recently discovered type of memory misattribution called *déjà vécu*: They feel strongly—but mistakenly—that they have already lived through an experience and remember the details of what happened (Moulin et al., 2005). For example, when watching television, one such individual was certain that he recalled seeing each show before, even when he was watching an entirely new episode. When he went shopping, he constantly thought it was unnecessary to buy needed items because he remembered having done so already. Although the basis of this strange disorder is not well understood, it probably involves disruption to parts of the temporal lobe that normally generate a subjective feeling of remembering (Moulin et al., 2005) as well as parts of the frontal lobe that are involved in source memory (Craik et al., 2014; Moulin, 2013).

Memory Misattribution Happens to Us All

We are all vulnerable to memory misattribution. Take the following test and there is a good chance that you will experience false recognition for yourself. First, study the two lists of words presented in **TABLE 6.1** by reading each word for about 1 second. When you are done, return to this paragraph for more instructions, but don't look back at the table! Now try to recognize which of the following words appeared in the list you just studied: *taste, bread, needle, king, sweet, thread.* If you think that *taste* and *thread* were on the lists you studied, you're right. And if you think that *bread* and *king* weren't on those lists, you're also right. But if you think that *needle* or *sweet* appeared in the lists, you're dead wrong.

Most people make exactly the same mistake, claiming with confidence that they saw *needle* and *sweet* on the list. This occurs because all the words in the lists are associated with *needle* or *sweet*. Seeing each word in the study list activates related words. Because *needle* and *sweet* are related to all of the associates, they become more activated than other words—so highly activated that only minutes later, people swear that they actually studied the words (Deese, 1959; Gallo, 2006, 2010; Roediger & McDermott, 1995, 2000). This error is extremely powerful: even people with "highly superior autobiographical memory" (see chapter opening), who have an extraordinary ability to recall everyday experiences accurately, are as susceptible to this type of memory misattribution as the rest of us (Patihis et al., 2013). In fact, neuroimaging studies show that many of the same brain regions are active during false recognition and true recognition, including the hippocampus (Cabeza et al., 2001; Schacter et al., 1996b).

Similar results are obtained when people view a series of common objects (e.g., cars, umbrellas) and then are later shown a new object that looks like one they saw earlier: They often falsely recognize the similar new item, and many of the same brain regions become active during this kind of false recognition as during true recognition (Gutchess & Schacter, 2012; Slotnick & Schacter, 2004).

However, false recognition can be reduced (Schacter, Israel, & Racine, 1999). For example, when participants are given a choice between an object that they actually saw (e.g., a car) and a visually similar new object (a different car that looks like the one they saw), they almost always choose the car that they actually saw and thus avoid making a false recognition error (Guerin et al., 2012a, 2012b). This finding suggests that false recognition occurs, at least in part, because participants, when presented with a similar new object on its own, don't recollect specific details about

TABLE 6.1

FALSE RECOGNITION

sour	thread
candy	pin
sugar	eye
bitter	sewing
good	sharp
taste	point
tooth	prick
nice	thimble
honey	haystack
soda	pain
chocolate	hurt
heart	injection
cake	syringe
tart	cloth
pie	knitting

false recognition A feeling of familiarity about something that hasn't been encountered before.

Hot Science | Déjà Vu: Can We Predict the Future?

Pat Long, a journalist based in London, U.K., began to notice something odd about his memory: He had intense feelings of having previously lived through a current experience despite realizing that he almost certainly had not. These feelings of déjà vu occurred as many as 10 times per day and were associated with the onset of epileptic seizures caused by a tumour in his brain (Long, 2017). Previous reports had linked frequent sensations of déjà vu with epileptic seizures, but many people without epilepsy have had similar, if less frequent, experiences: Surveys indicate that roughly two-thirds of people have experienced déjà vu at least once (Brown, 2004). Yet déjà vu is not only about the past: Surveys also indicate that déjà vu is often accompanied by a feeling that one knows exactly what is going to happen next (Brown, 2004). Indeed, Pat Long referred to his own déjà vu experience as "a feeling of precognition." But do we actually know what is going to happen next when we experience déjà vu?

Cleary and Claxton (2018) recently addressed this question using an innovative virtual-reality procedure developed in earlier research (Cleary et al., 2012) to induce déjà vu in the lab. Participants navigated through a virtual reality video sequence of places, among them scene (a). After this encoding phase, participants were shown novel scenes, half of which depicted a configuration similar to a previously viewed scene (as scene (b) does in relation to scene (a)), and half of which were not configurally similar to any previously presented scenes. When participants were unable to recall a configurally similar scene to the one they were viewing, they were nonetheless more likely to claim an experience of déjà vu (defined by them as "a feeling of having been somewhere or done something before, despite knowing that the current situation is new") than when a scene did not depict a similar configuration to a previously viewed scene. This finding replicated earlier work by Cleary and colleagues (2012) and shows that the experience of déjà vu can be driven by configural overlap between a novel scene and a previously viewed scene that participants do not recall.

To investigate the feeling of what happens next, Cleary and Claxton (2018) added an important new twist to the earlier procedure. Because in the encoding phase, participants had viewed the images as a video, they had seen many turns that could prime a sense of what might happen next. When participants saw the novel scenes during the test phase, they were told that "Without knowing why, you may also feel a sense of which way to turn next. Indicate which way to turn. Press L for Left and R for Right." Would participants claim to have a feeling of which way to turn next more frequently when they reported an experience of déjà vu to a novel, configurally similar scene than when they did not report an experience of déjà vu to this kind of scene? The answer was a resounding "yes." But did participants *actually* know the correct way to turn? The answer was a resounding "no": Participants could not accurately predict what the next turn would be when shown a novel, configurally similar scene, despite feeling that they knew it.

These findings led Cleary and Claxton to characterize déjà vu as "an illusion of prediction." This idea fits well with research discussed earlier in the chapter (pages 239–241), indicating a close link between memory and thinking about the future. It may also help Pat Long understand that while the "feeling of precognition" that characterizes his déjà vu experiences is shared by others, that feeling does not contain reliable information about what the future has in store for him.

A)

B)

the object they actually studied; rather, they need to retrieve these details in order to indicate correctly that the similar object is new. Yet this information is available in memory, as shown by the ability of participants to choose correctly between the studied object and the visually similar new object. When people experience a strong sense of familiarity about a person, object, or event but lack recollection of specific details, a potentially dangerous recipe for memory misattribution is in place—both in the laboratory and in real-world situations involving eyewitness memory. Understanding this point may be a key to reducing the dangerous consequences of misattribution in eyewitness testimony.

5. Suggestibility

On October 4, 1992, an El Al cargo plane crashed into an apartment building in a southern suburb of Amsterdam, killing 39 residents and all 4 members of the airline crew. The disaster dominated news in the Netherlands for days as people viewed footage of the crash scene and read about the catastrophe. Ten months later, Dutch psychologists asked a simple question of university students: "Did you see the television film of the moment the plane hit the apartment building?" Fifty-five percent answered yes (Crombag, Wagenaar, & Van Koppen, 1996). All of this might seem perfectly normal except for one key fact: There was no television film of the moment when the plane actually crashed. The researchers had asked a suggestive question, one that implied that television film of the crash had been shown. Respondents may have viewed television film of the *postcrash* scene, and they may have read, imagined, or talked about what might have happened when the plane hit the building, but they most definitely did not see it. The suggestive question led participants to misattribute information from these or other sources to a film that did not exist. **Suggestibility** is the *tendency to incorporate misleading information from external sources into personal recollections.*

In 1992, an El Al cargo plane crashed into an apartment building in a suburb of Amsterdam. When Dutch psychologists asked students if they had seen the television film of the plane crashing, a majority said they had. In fact, no such footage exists (Crombag et al., 1996).

If misleading details can be implanted in people's memories, is it also possible to suggest entire episodes that never occurred? The answer seems to be yes (Loftus, 1993, 2003). In one study, the research participant, a teenager named Chris, was asked by his older brother, Jim, to try to remember the time Chris had been lost in a shopping mall at age 5. He initially recalled nothing, but after several days, Chris produced a detailed recollection of the event. He recalled that he "felt so scared I would never see my family again" and remembered that a kindly old man wearing a flannel shirt found him crying (Loftus, 1993, p. 532). But according to Jim and other family members, Chris was never lost in a shopping mall. Of 24 participants in a larger study on implanted memories, approximately 25% falsely remembered being lost as a child in a shopping mall or in a similar public place (Loftus & Pickrell, 1995).

In response to suggestions, people develop false memories for some of the same reasons memory misattribution occurs. We do not store all the details of our experiences in memory, making us vulnerable to accepting suggestions about what might have happened or should have happened. In addition, visual imagery plays an important role in constructing false memories (Goff & Roediger, 1998). Asking people to imagine an event like spilling punch all over the bride's parents at a wedding increases the likelihood that they will develop a false memory of it (Hyman & Pentland, 1996). Social pressure can also enhance suggestibility, as in cases in which people falsely confess to crimes they did not commit after repeated interrogations by authority figures such as police who are convinced of their guilt and press for a confession (Kassin, 2015). In some instances, these wrongly accused individuals develop false memories of the crime (Kassin, 2007).

All of these factors were operating in a recent study that provides some of the most dramatic evidence for the misleading effects of suggestion. Consider the

suggestibility The tendency to incorporate misleading information from external sources into personal recollections.

following question: Did you ever commit a crime when you were between the ages of 11 and 14 years old? Assuming that you did not, do you think that you could ever be convinced that you did? Shaw and Porter (2015) asked university students about an experience that actually occurred between ages 11 and 14, and also about a crime that they supposedly committed during those years (theft, assault, or assault with a weapon). Although none of the students had actually committed any crimes, during three separate interviews, the experimenters required them repeatedly to imagine that they did. The researchers also applied social pressure techniques, such as telling students that their parents or caregivers said they had committed the crime and stating that most people can retrieve seemingly lost memories if they try hard enough. By the end of the third interview, 70% of the students came to believe that they had committed the crime, and some of them even developed detailed false memories of having done so (Shaw & Porter, 2015; Wade, Garry, & Pezdek, 2018).

Studies such as these can help us understand the key role that suggestibility played in a controversy that arose during the 1980s and 1990s, concerning the accuracy of childhood memories that people recalled during psychotherapy. One highly publicized example involved a woman named Diana Halbrooks (Schacter, 1996). After a few months in psychotherapy, she began recalling disturbing incidents from her childhood—for example, that her mother had tried to kill her and that her father had abused her sexually. Although her parents denied these events had ever occurred, her therapist encouraged her to believe in the reality of her memories. Eventually, Diana Halbrooks stopped therapy and came to realize that the "memories" she had recovered were inaccurate.

How could this have happened? A number of the techniques used by psychotherapists to try to pull up forgotten childhood memories are clearly suggestive (Poole et al., 1995). Importantly, memories that people remember spontaneously on their own are corroborated by other people at about the same rate as the memories of individuals who never forgot their abuse, whereas memories recovered in response to suggestive therapeutic techniques are virtually never corroborated by others (McNally & Geraerts, 2009).

6. Bias

In 2000, the outcome of a very close United States presidential race between George W. Bush and Al Gore was decided by the U.S. Supreme Court 5 weeks after the election had taken place. The day after the election (when the result was still in doubt), supporters of Bush and Gore were asked to predict how happy they would be after the outcome of the election was determined (Wilson, Meyers, & Gilbert, 2003). These same respondents reported how happy they felt with the outcome on the day after Al Gore conceded. And 4 months later, the participants recalled how happy they had been right after the election was decided.

Bush supporters, who eventually enjoyed a positive result (their candidate took office), were understandably happy the day after the Supreme Court's decision. However, their retrospective accounts *over*estimated how happy they were at the time. Conversely, Gore supporters were not pleased with the outcome. But when polled 4 months after the election was decided, Gore supporters *over*estimated how unhappy they actually were at the time of the result. In both groups, recollections of happiness were at odds with existing reports of their actual happiness at the time (Wilson et al., 2003).

These results illustrate the problem of **bias**, *the distorting influences of present knowledge, beliefs, and feelings on recollection of previous experiences.* Sometimes what people remember from their pasts says less about what actually happened than about what they think, feel, or believe now about themselves or others

bias The distorting influences of present knowledge, beliefs, and feelings on recollection of previous experiences.

(Levine et al., 2018). Researchers have also found that our current moods can bias our recall of past experiences (Bower, 1981; Buchanan, 2007; Eich, 1995). So, in addition to helping you recall actual sad memories (as you saw earlier in this chapter), a sad mood can also bias your recollections of experiences that may not have been so sad. *Consistency bias* is the bias to reconstruct the past to fit the present. One researcher asked people in 1973 to rate their attitudes towards a variety of controversial social issues, including legalization of marijuana, women's rights, and aid to minorities (Marcus, 1986). They were asked to make the same rating again in 1982 and also to indicate what their attitudes had been in 1973. Researchers found that participants' recollections in 1982 of their 1973 attitudes were more closely related to what they believed in 1982 than to what they had actually said in 1973.

Whereas consistency bias exaggerates the similarity between past and present, *change bias* is the tendency to exaggerate differences between what we feel or believe now and what we felt or believed in the past. In other words, *change biases* also occur. For instance, most of us would like to believe that our romantic attachments grow stronger over time. In one study, dating couples were asked once a year for 4 years to assess the present quality of their relationships and to recall how they felt in past years (Sprecher, 1999). Couples who stayed together for the 4 years recalled that the strength of their love had increased since they last reported on it. Yet their actual ratings at the time did not show any increases in love and attachment. In an objective sense, the couples did not love each other more today than yesterday. But they did from the subjective perspective of memory.

A special case of change bias is *egocentric bias*, the tendency to exaggerate the change between present and past in order to make ourselves look good in retrospect. For example, students sometimes remember feeling more anxious before taking an exam than they actually reported at the time (Keuler & Safer, 1998), and blood donors sometimes recall being more nervous about giving blood than they actually were (Breckler, 1994). In both cases, change biases colour memory and make people feel that they behaved more bravely or courageously than they actually did. Similarly, when university students tried to remember high school grades and their memories were checked against their actual transcripts, they were highly accurate for grades of A (89% correct) and extremely inaccurate for grades of D (29% correct) (Bahrick, Hall, & Berger, 1996). The same kind of egocentric bias occurs with memory for university grades: 81% of errors inflated the actual grade, and this bias was evident even when participants were asked about their grades soon after graduation (Bahrick, Hall, & DaCosta, 2008). People were remembering the past as they wanted it to be rather than the way it actually was.

7. Persistence

The artist Melinda Stickney-Gibson awoke in her apartment to the smell of smoke. She jumped out of bed and saw black plumes rising through cracks in the floor. Raging flames had engulfed the entire building, and she had no chance to escape except by jumping from her third-floor window. Shortly after she crashed to the ground, the building exploded into a brilliant fireball. Although she survived the fire and the fall, Melinda became overwhelmed by memories of the fire. When she sat down in front of a blank canvas to start a new painting, her memories of that awful night intruded. Her paintings, which were previously bright, colourful abstractions, became dark meditations that included only black, orange, and ochre—the colours of the fire (Schacter, 1996).

How happy do you think you'd be if the candidate you supported won an election? Do you think you'd accurately remember your level of happiness if you recalled it several months later? Chances are good that bias in the memory process would alter your recollection of your previous happiness. Indeed, 4 months after they heard the outcome of the 2000 U.S. presidential election, supporters of George W. Bush (*left*) overestimated how happy they were, whereas the supporters of Al Gore (*right*) overestimated how unhappy they were.

The way each member of this happy couple recalls earlier feelings towards the other depends on how each currently views their relationship.

Some events are so emotionally charged that we form unusually detailed memories of when and where we heard about them. Examples include Paul Henderson's winning goal in the 1972 hockey series that Team Canada played against the Soviet Union, and the terrorist attacks in the United States on September 11, 2001. These flashbulb memories generally persist much longer than memories for more ordinary events.

persistence The intrusive recollection of events that we wish we could forget.

flashbulb memories Detailed recollections of when and where we heard about shocking events.

Melinda Stickney-Gibson's experiences illustrate memory's seventh and most deadly sin, **persistence:** *the intrusive recollection of events that we wish we could forget.* Melinda's experience is far from unique; persistence frequently occurs after disturbing or traumatic incidents, such as the fire that destroyed her home. Although being able to recall memories quickly is usually considered a good thing, in the case of persistence, that ability mutates into an unwelcome burden.

Emotional Experiences Are Easiest to Remember

Emotional experiences tend to be better remembered than nonemotional ones. For instance, memory for unpleasant pictures, such as mutilated bodies, or pleasant ones, such as attractive men and women, is more accurate than for emotionally neutral pictures, such as household objects (Ochsner, 2000). Emotional arousal seems to focus our attention on the central features of an event. In one experiment, people who viewed an emotionally arousing sequence of slides involving a bloody car accident remembered more of the central themes and fewer peripheral details than people who viewed a nonemotional sequence (Christianson & Loftus, 1987).

Intrusive memories are undesirable consequences of emotional experiences because emotional experiences generally lead to more vivid and enduring recollections than nonemotional experiences do. One line of evidence comes from the study of **flashbulb memories**, which are *detailed recollections of when and where we heard about shocking events* (Brown & Kulik, 1977). For example, most North Americans born in the 1980s or earlier can recall exactly where they were and how they heard about the September 11, 2001, terrorist attacks in which passenger aircraft were deliberately flown into the World Trade Center in New York City— almost as if a mental flashbulb had gone off automatically and recorded the event in long-lasting and vivid detail (Kvavilashvili et al., 2009). Several studies have shown that flashbulb memories are not always entirely accurate, but they are generally better remembered than mundane news events from the same time (Larsen, 1992; Neisser & Harsch, 1992). Enhanced retention of flashbulb memories is partly attributable to the emotional arousal elicited by events such as the 9/11 terrorist attacks, and partly attributable to the fact that we tend to talk and think a lot about these experiences. Recall that semantic encoding enhances memory: When we talk about flashbulb experiences, we elaborate on them and thus further increase the memorability of those aspects of the experience that we discuss (Hirst et al., 2009, 2015).

The Amygdala Plays a Role

Why do our brains succumb to persistence? A key player in the brain's response to emotional events is a small, almond-shaped structure called the *amygdala*, shown in **FIGURE 6.18**. The amygdala influences hormonal systems that kick into high gear when we experience an arousing event; these stress-related hormones, such as adrenaline and cortisol, mobilize the body in the face of threat—and they also enhance memory for the experience. Damage to the amygdala does not result in a general memory deficit. Individuals with amygdala damage, however, do not remember emotional events any better than they remember nonemotional events (Cahill & McGaugh, 1998).

Consider what happened when research participants viewed a series of photographic slides that began with a mother walking her child to school and later included an emotionally arousing event: the child being hit by a car. When tested later, the participants remembered the arousing event better than the mundane ones. But individuals with amygdala damage remembered the mundane and emotionally arousing events equally well (Cahill & McGaugh, 1998). Neuroimaging studies show that when healthy people view a slide sequence that includes an emotionally arousing event, the level of activity in the amygdala at the time they see it is a good predictor of their subsequent memory for the slide. When there is heightened activity in the amygdala as people watch emotional events, there's a better chance that they will recall those events on a later test (Cahill et al., 1996; Kensinger & Schacter, 2005, 2006). And when people are given a drug that interferes with the amygdala-mediated release of stress hormones, their memory for the emotional sections is no better than their memory for the mundane sections (Lonegran et al., 2013).

In many cases, there are clear benefits to forming strong memories for highly emotional events, particularly those that are life-threatening. In the case of persistence, though, such memories may be too strong—strong enough to interfere with other aspects of daily life.

Are the Seven "Sins" Vices or Virtues?

You may have concluded that evolution has burdened us with an extremely inefficient memory system so prone to error that it often jeopardizes our well-being. Not so. The seven sins are the price we pay for the many benefits that memory provides, the occasional result of the normally efficient operation of the human memory system (Schacter, 2001b).

Consider transience, for example. Wouldn't it be great to remember all the details of every incident in your life, no matter how much time had passed? Not necessarily: If we didn't gradually forget information over time, our minds would be cluttered with details that we no longer need, such as an old phone number (Bjork, 2011; Bjork & Bjork, 1988; Norby, 2015). Information that we use infrequently is less likely to be needed in the future than is information we use more frequently over the same period (Anderson & Schooler, 1991, 2000). Also, relieving ourselves of outdated information can enhance our ability to make decisions based on memory (Richards & Frankland, 2017). Memory, in essence, makes a bet that when we haven't used information recently, we probably won't need it in the future. We win this bet more often than we lose it, making transience an adaptive property of memory.

Similarly, absentmindedness and blocking can be frustrating, but they are side effects of our memory's usually successful attempt to sort through incoming information, preserving details that are worthy of attention and recall while discarding those that are less worthy.

Memory misattribution and suggestibility both occur because we often fail to recall the details of exactly when and where we saw a face or learned a fact. Our memories carefully record such details only when we think we may need them later, and most of the time we are better off for it. Furthermore, we often use memories to anticipate possible future events. As discussed earlier, memory is flexible, allowing us to recombine elements of past experience in new ways, so that we can mentally try out different versions of what might happen. Researchers have hypothesized that this very flexibility—a strength of memory—may sometimes produce misattribution errors in which elements of past experience are miscombined (Schacter & Addis, 2007; Schacter, Guerin, & St. Jacques, 2011). Recent studies provide experimental evidence that supports this hypothesis (Carpenter & Schacter, 2017; Dewhurst et al., 2016).

Bias skews our memories so that we depict ourselves in an overly favourable light, but it can also produce the benefit of contributing to our overall sense of contentment. Holding positive illusions about ourselves can lead to greater psychological well-being (Taylor, 1989). Although persistence can cause us to be haunted by traumas that we'd be better off forgetting, overall, it is probably adaptive to remember threatening or traumatic events that could pose a threat to survival.

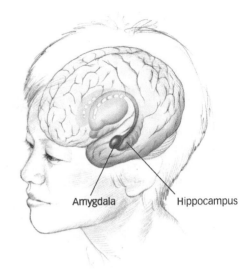

Figure 6.18
The Amygdala's Influence on Memory The amygdala, located next to the hippocampus, responds strongly to emotional events. Individuals with amygdala damage are unable to remember emotional events any better than they can remember nonemotional ones (Cahill & McGaugh, 1998) REPUBLISHED BY PERMISSION OF MACMILLAN PUBLISHERS LTD. FROM NATURE NEUROSCIENCE, A SENSORY SIGNATURE THAT DISTINGUISHES TRUE FROM FALSE MEMORIES, SLOTNICK & SCHACTER, 7(61), 2004. PERMISSIONS CONVEYED THROUGH COPYRIGHT CLEARANCE CENTER, INC.

Although each of the seven sins can cause trouble in our lives, each has an adaptive side as well. You can think of the seven sins as costs we pay for benefits that allow memory to work as well as it does most of the time.

Build to the Outcomes

1. How might general memories come to distort specific memories?
2. How is memory affected for someone whose attention is divided?
3. Why is Snow White's name easier to remember than Mary Poppins's?
4. What can explain a déjà vu experience?
5. How can eyewitnesses be misled?
6. How does your current outlook colour your memory of a past event?
7. How does emotional trauma affect memory?
8. How are we better off with imperfect memories?

Chapter Review

Encoding: Transforming Perceptions Into Memories

- Encoding is the process of transforming the information received through our senses into a lasting memory.

- A new memory is made and automatically semantically encoded when new information mixes with old information that already has meaning to us.

- Semantic encoding is characterized by relating new information to previous knowledge in a meaningful way.

- Visual imagery encoding also relates new information to previous knowledge but features both a visual and a verbal placeholder.

- Organizational encoding is a process of finding relationships between items to make them easier to retrieve.

- Encoding information with respect to its survival value is a particularly effective method for increasing subsequent recall, perhaps because our memory systems have evolved in a way that allows us to remember especially well information that is relevant to our survival, and perhaps because survival scenarios used in memory experiments draw on elements of semantic, visual imagery, and organizational encoding, as well as require extensive planning.

Storage: Maintaining Memories Over Time

- Because research participants could recall the same number of letters from any row of the grid, the iconic memory test suggests that sensory memory holds information for a second or two. "Rehearsal" helps keep memories in short-term storage, and "chunking" combines information into a single, meaningful item.

- Working memory is the active maintenance of information in short-term storage, where information is retained for about 15 to 20 seconds. A model of working memory describes the subsystems that store and manipulate visual and verbal information, the episodic buffer that integrates information, and the central executive that coordinates them.

- The hippocampus functions as an index to put information into long-term memory, but evidence from amnesiacs indicates that it is not the site of long-term memory storage.

- The act of recalling, thinking, and talking about a memory leads to consolidation. Sleep also is an important factor. However, when memories are retrieved, they may also become vulnerable to disruption.

- Memory storage depends on changes in synapses, and long-term potentiation (LTP) increases synaptic connections.

Retrieval: Bringing Memories to Mind

- Whether or not we remember a past experience depends on whether retrieval cues are available to trigger recall. Retrieval cues are effective when they are given in the same context as when we encoded an experience. Moods and inner states can become retrieval cues.

- Retrieving information from memory has consequences for later remembering. Retrieval improves subsequent memory of the retrieved information, as the benefits of testing on later recall show. However, fMRI evidence shows that regions of the frontal lobe involved with retrieving information also play a role in suppressing related information that is not retrieved. This finding underscores the importance of eyewitness interviews being as complete as possible.

- Research shows that retrieving and vividly reexperiencing memories of objects that were seen makes memory vulnerable to disruption, such that unseen objects may be wrongly incorporated into the memory.

- Retrieval can be separated into the effort we make while trying to remember what happened in the past, and the successful recovery of stored information. Neuroimaging studies suggest that trying to remember activates the left frontal lobe, whereas successful recovery of stored information activates the hippocampus and regions in the brain related to the sensory aspects of an experience.

Forms of Long-Term Memory: More Than One Kind

- Long-term memory consists of several different forms.

- Implicit memory refers to the unconscious influence of past experiences on later behaviour and performance, such as procedural memory and priming. Procedural memory involves the acquisition of skills as a result of practice, and priming is a change in the ability to recognize or identify an object or a word as the result of past exposure to it. People who have amnesia are able to retain implicit memory, including procedural memory and priming, but they lack explicit memory.

- Explicit memory is the act of consciously or intentionally retrieving past experiences. Episodic memory is the collection of personal experiences from a particular time and place; it allows us both to recollect the past and imagine the future. Semantic memory is a networked, general, impersonal knowledge of facts, associations, and concepts.

- Collaborative memory refers to remembering in groups. Collaborative remembering can both impair memory (collaborative inhibition) and enhance it by exposing people to new information and helping to correct errors.

Memory Failures: The Seven "Sins" of Memory

- Memory's mistakes can be classified into seven "sins."

- Transience is reflected by a rapid decline in memory, followed by more gradual forgetting. With the passing of time, memory switches from detailed to general. Both decay and interference contribute to transience.

- Absentmindedness results from failures of attention, shallow encoding, and the influence of automatic behaviours; it is often associated with forgetting to do things in the future.

- Blocking occurs when stored information is temporarily inaccessible, as when information is on the "tip of the tongue."

- Memory misattribution happens when we experience a sense of familiarity but don't recall, or we mistakenly recall, the specifics of when and where an experience occurred. Misattribution can result in eyewitness misidentification or false recognition. Individuals suffering from frontal lobe damage are especially susceptible to false recognition.

- Suggestibility gives rise to implanted memories of small details or entire episodes. Suggestive techniques such as hypnosis or visualization can promote vivid recall of suggested events, and therapists' use of suggestive techniques may be responsible for some individuals' false memories of childhood traumas. Bias reflects the influence of current knowledge, beliefs, and feelings on memory of past experiences.

- Bias can lead us to make the past consistent with the present, to exaggerate changes between past and present, or to remember the past in a way that makes us look good.

- Persistence reflects the fact that emotional arousal generally leads to enhanced memory, whether we want to remember an experience or not. Persistence is partly attributable to the operation of hormonal systems influenced by the amygdala. Although each of the seven sins can cause trouble in our lives, each has an adaptive side as well.

- You can think of the seven "sins" as costs we pay for benefits that allow memory to work as well as it does most of the time.

Key Concept Quiz

1. Encoding is the process
   a. by which we transform what we perceive, think, or feel into an enduring memory.
   b. of maintaining information in memory over time.
   c. of bringing to mind information that has been previously stored.
   d. through which we recall information previously learned but have forgotten.

2. What is the process of relating new information in a meaningful way to knowledge that is already in memory?
   a. spontaneous encoding
   b. organization encoding
   c. semantic encoding
   d. visual imagery encoding

3. What kind of memory storage holds information for a second or two?
   a. retrograde memory
   b. working memory
   c. short-term memory
   d. sensory memory

4. The process by which memories become stable in the brain is called
   a. consolidation.
   b. long-term memory.
   c. iconic memory.
   d. hippocampal indexing.

5. Long-term potentiation occurs through
   a. the interruption of communication between neurons.
   b. the strengthening of synaptic connections.
   c. the reconsolidation of disrupted memories.
   d. sleep.

6. The increased likelihood of recalling a sad memory when you are in a sad mood is an illustration of
   a. the encoding specificity principle.
   b. state-dependent retrieval.
   c. transfer-appropriate processing.
   d. memory accessibility.

7. Neuroimaging studies suggest that *trying* to remember activates the
   a. left frontal lobe.
   b. hippocampal region.
   c. occipital lobe.
   d. upper temporal lobe.

8. The act of consciously or intentionally retrieving past experiences is
   a. priming.
   b. procedural memory.
   c. implicit memory.
   d. explicit memory.

9. Remembering a family reunion that you attended as a child illustrates
   a. semantic memory.
   b. procedural memory.
   c. episodic memory.
   d. perceptual priming.

10. Eyewitness misidentification or false recognition is most likely a result of
    a. memory misattribution.
    b. suggestibility.
    c. bias.
    d. retroactive interference.

LearningCurve macmillan learning

Don't stop now! Quizzing yourself is a powerful study tool. Go to LaunchPad to access the LearningCurve adaptive quizzing system and your own personalized learning plan. Visit launchpadworks.com.

Key Terms

memory (p. 216)
encoding (p. 216)
storage (p. 216)
retrieval (p. 216)
semantic encoding (p. 217)
visual imagery encoding (p. 219)
organizational encoding (p. 219)
sensory memory (p. 221)
iconic memory (p. 222)
echoic memory (p. 222)
short-term memory (p. 222)
rehearsal (p. 223)

serial position effect (p. 223)
chunking (p. 223)
working memory (p. 224)
long-term memory (p. 226)
anterograde amnesia (p. 226)
retrograde amnesia (p. 226)
consolidation (p. 227)
reconsolidation (p. 228)
long-term potentiation (LTP) (p. 230)
retrieval cue (p. 231)
encoding specificity principle (p. 231)

state-dependent retrieval (p. 232)
transfer-appropriate processing (p. 232)
retrieval-induced forgetting (p. 233)
explicit memory (p. 236)
implicit memory (p. 236)
procedural memory (p. 236)
priming (p. 236)
semantic memory (p. 238)
episodic memory (p. 238)
transience (p. 245)
retroactive interference (p. 246)

proactive interference (p. 246)
absentmindedness (p. 246)
prospective memory (p. 247)
blocking (p. 248)
memory misattribution (p. 249)
source memory (p. 249)
false recognition (p. 251)
suggestibility (p. 253)
bias (p. 254)
persistence (p. 256)
flashbulb memories (p. 256)

Changing Minds

1. A friend of yours lost her father to cancer when she was a very young child. "I really wish I remembered him better," she says. "I know all the memories are locked in my head. I'm thinking of trying hypnotism to unlock some of those memories." You explain that we don't, in fact, have stored memories of everything that ever happened to us locked in our heads. What examples could you give of ways in which memories can be lost over time?

2. Your older cousin has a very vivid memory of sitting with his parents in the living room on September 11, 2001, watching live TV as the Twin Towers of the World Trade Center in New York City fell during the terrorist attacks. "I remember my mother was crying," he says, "and that scared me more than the pictures on the TV." Later, he discusses the events of 9/11 with his mother—and is stunned when she assures him that he was actually in school on the morning of the attacks and was only sent home at lunchtime, after the towers had fallen. "I don't understand," he tells you afterward. "I think she must be confused, because I have a perfect memory of that morning." Assuming your aunt is recalling events correctly, how would you explain to your cousin the ways in which his snapshot memory could be wrong? What memory sin might be at work?

3. You ask one of your psychology classmates if she wants to form a study group to prepare for an upcoming exam. "No offence," she says, "but I can study the material best by just reading the chapter eight or nine times, and I can do that without a study group." What's wrong with your classmate's study plan? In what ways might the members of a study group help each other learn more effectively?

4. You and a friend go to a party where you meet a lot of new people. After the party, your friend says, "I liked a lot of the people we met, but I'll never remember all their names. Some people just have a good memory, and some don't, and there's nothing I can do about it." What advice could you give your friend to help him remember the names of people he meets at the next party?

5. A friend of yours who is taking a criminal justice class reads about a case in which the conviction of an accused murderer was later overturned on the basis of DNA evidence. "It's a travesty of justice," she says. "An eyewitness clearly identified the man by picking him out of a lineup and then identified him again in court during the trial. No results from a chemistry lab should count more than eyewitness testimony." What is your friend failing to appreciate about eyewitness testimony? What sin of memory could lead an eyewitness to honestly believe she is identifying the correct man when she is actually making a false identification?

Answers to Key Concept Quiz

1. a; 2. c; 3. d; 4. a; 5. b; 6.b; 7. a; 8. d; 9. c; 10. a.

LaunchPad features the full e-Book of *Psychology*, the LearningCurve adaptive quizzing system, videos, and a variety of activities to boost your learning. Visit LaunchPad at launchpadworks.com.

Learning

JENNIFER, A 45-YEAR-OLD AMERICAN MILITARY NURSE, lived quietly in a rural area of the United States with her spouse of 21 years and their two children before she served 19 months abroad during the Iraq war. In Iraq, she provided care to soldiers from different countries as well as to Iraqi civilians, prisoners, and militant extremists. Jennifer served 4 months of her assignment in a prison hospital near Baghdad, where she witnessed many horrifying events. The prison was the target of relentless mortar fire, resulting in numerous deaths and serious casualties, including bloody injuries and loss of limbs. Jennifer worked 12- to 14-hour shifts, trying to avoid incoming fire while tending to some of the most gruesomely wounded cases. She frequently encountered the smell of burned flesh and the sight of "young, mangled bodies" as part of her daily duties (Feczer & Bjorklund, 2009, p. 285).

This repetitive trauma took a toll on Jennifer; when she returned home, it became evident that she had not left behind her war experiences. Jennifer thought about them repeatedly, and they profoundly influenced her reactions to many aspects of everyday life. The sight of blood or the smell of cooking meat made her sick to her stomach, to the point that she had to stop eating meat. The previously innocent sound of a helicopter approaching, which in Iraq signalled that new wounded bodies were about to arrive, now created in Jennifer heightened feelings of fear and anxiety. She regularly awoke from nightmares concerning the most troubling aspects of her Iraq experiences, such as tending to soldiers with multiple amputations. In the words of the authors who described her case, Jennifer was "forever changed" by her Iraq experiences (Feczer & Bjorklund, 2009). That is one reason why Jennifer's story is a compelling, though disturbing, introduction to the topic of learning.

During the 4 months that she served at a prison hospital near Baghdad during the Iraq war, Jennifer learned to associate the sound of an arriving helicopter with wounded soldiers. That learned association had a long-lasting influence on her.

Much of what happened to Jennifer after she returned home reflects the operation of a kind of learning based on association. Sights, sounds, and smells in Iraq had become associated with negative emotions in a way that created an enduring bond, such that encountering similar sights, sounds, and smells at home elicited similarly intense negative feelings.

LEARNING IS SHORTHAND FOR A COLLECTION OF DIFFERENT TECHNIQUES, procedures, and outcomes that produce changes in an organism's behaviour. Learning psychologists have identified and studied as many as 40 different types of learning. In this chapter, we'll discuss the development and basic psychological principles behind two major approaches to learning: classical conditioning and operant conditioning. We'll then move on to see that some important kinds of learning occur when we simply watch others and that such observational learning plays an important role in the cultural transmission of behaviour. Next, we'll discover that some types of learning can occur entirely outside of awareness. We'll conclude with a discussion of learning in a context that should matter a lot to you: the classroom. We kick off the chapter, however, with some basic insights and definitions.

What Is Learning?

Learning Outcomes

- Define learning.
- Identify how even the simplest organisms appear to learn.

Despite the many different kinds of learning that psychologists have discovered, there is a basic principle at the core of all of them. **Learning** involves *the acquisition, from experience, of new knowledge, skills, or responses that results in a relatively permanent change in the state of the learner.* This definition emphasizes these key ideas:

- Learning is based on experience.
- Learning produces changes in the organism.
- These changes are relatively permanent.

Think about Jennifer's time in Iraq and you'll see all of these elements: Experiences that led to associating the sound of an approaching helicopter with the arrival of wounded soldiers changed the way Jennifer responded to certain situations in a way that lasted for years.

Learning can also occur in much simpler, nonassociative forms. You are probably familiar with the phenomenon of **habituation**, *a general process in which repeated or prolonged exposure to a stimulus results in a gradual reduction in responding.* If you've ever lived under the flight path of your local airport, near railroad tracks, or by a busy highway, you've probably noticed the deafening roar of a Boeing 737 coming in for a landing, the clatter of a train speeding down the track, or the sound of traffic when you first moved in. You probably also noticed that, after a while, the roar wasn't quite so deafening anymore and eventually you were able to ignore the sounds of the planes, trains, or automobiles in your vicinity. This welcome reduction in responding reflects the operation of habituation.

Habituation occurs even in the simplest organisms. For example, in the Memory chapter you learned about the sea slug *Aplysia*, studied in detail by Nobel Prize winner Eric Kandel (2006). Kandel and his colleagues showed clearly that *Aplysia* exhibits habituation: When lightly touched, the sea slug initially withdraws its gill, but the response gradually weakens after repeated light touches. In addition, *Aplysia* also exhibits another simple form of learning known as **sensitization**, which

learning The acquisition, from experience, of new knowledge, skills, or responses that results in a relatively permanent change in the state of the learner.

habituation A general process in which repeated or prolonged exposure to a stimulus results in a gradual reduction in responding.

sensitization A simple form of learning that occurs when presentation of a stimulus leads to an increased response to a later stimulus.

occurs when *presentation of a stimulus leads to an increased response to a later stimulus*. For example, Kandel found that after receiving a strong shock, *Aplysia* showed an increased gill-withdrawal response to a light touch. In a similar manner, people whose houses have been broken into may later become hypersensitive to late-night sounds that wouldn't have bothered them previously.

Although these simple kinds of learning are important, in this chapter we'll focus on more complex kinds of learning that psychologists have studied intensively. As you'll recall from The Evolution of Psychological Science chapter, a sizeable chunk of psychology's history was devoted to behaviourism, with its insistence on measuring only observable, quantifiable behaviour and its dismissal of mental activity as irrelevant and unknowable. Behaviourism was the major outlook of most psychologists working from the 1930s through the 1950s, the period during which most of the fundamental work on learning theory took place.

You might find the intersection of behaviourism and learning theory a bit surprising. After all, at one level, learning seems abstract: Something intangible happens to you, and you think or behave differently thereafter. It seems logical that you'd need to explain this transformation in terms of a change in mental outlook. However, most behaviourists argued that learning's "permanent change in experience" could be demonstrated equally well in almost any organism: rats, dogs, pigeons, mice, pigs, or humans. From this perspective, behaviourists viewed learning as a purely behavioural activity requiring no mental activity.

In many ways, the behaviourists were right. Much of what we know about how organisms learn comes directly from the behaviourists' observations of behaviours. However, they also overstated their case. We need to address some important cognitive considerations (i.e., elements of mental activity) in order to understand the learning process.

How might psychologists use the concept of habituation to explain the fact that today's action movies, like *Venom*, tend to show much more graphic violence than movies of the 1980s, which in turn tended to show more graphic violence than movies of the 1950s?

Build to the Outcomes

1. What are the key ideas that support the definition of learning?

2. How do habituation and sensitization occur?

Classical Conditioning: One Thing Leads to Another

The American psychologist John B. Watson kick-started the behaviourist movement in the early 20th century, arguing that psychologists should "never use the terms *consciousness, mental states, mind, content, introspectively verifiable, imagery*, and the like" (Watson, 1913, p. 166). Watson's firebrand stance was fuelled in large part by the work of a Russian physiologist, Ivan Pavlov (1849–1936). Ironically, however, although Pavlov respected the behaviourist approach, he did not deny the importance of subjective experience and in fact was deeply interested in understanding consciousness and related mental states (Todes, 2014).

Pavlov was awarded the Nobel Prize in Physiology in 1904 for his work on the salivation of dogs. He studied the digestive processes of laboratory animals by surgically implanting test tubes into the cheeks of dogs to measure their salivary responses to different kinds of foods. Serendipitously, his explorations into spit and drool revealed the mechanics of one form of learning, which came to be called classical conditioning. **Classical conditioning** occurs *when a neutral stimulus produces a response after*

Learning Outcomes

- Describe the process of classical conditioning.

- Explain how cognitive, neural, and evolutionary aspects influence our understanding of classical conditioning.

classical conditioning A type of learning that occurs when a neutral stimulus produces a response after being paired with a stimulus that naturally produces a response.

being paired with a stimulus that naturally produces a response. In his classic experiments, Pavlov showed that dogs learned to salivate to neutral stimuli such as a buzzer or a metronome after the dogs had associated that stimulus with another stimulus that naturally evokes salivation, such as food.

When Pavlov's findings first appeared in the scientific and popular literature (Pavlov, 1923a, 1923b), they produced a flurry of excitement because psychologists now had demonstrable evidence of how conditioning produced learned behaviours. This was the kind of behaviourist psychology John B. Watson was proposing: An organism experiences events or stimuli that are observable and measurable, and scientists can directly observe and measure changes in that organism. Dogs learned to salivate to the sound of a buzzer or metronome, and there was no need to resort to explanations about what the dog wanted, or how the animal thought about the situation. In other words, there was no need to consider the mind in this classical conditioning paradigm, which appealed to Watson and the behaviourists. Pavlov also appreciated the significance of his discovery, and he embarked on a systematic investigation of the mechanisms of classical conditioning. Let's take a closer look at some of these principles. (As The Real World: Understanding Drug Overdoses shows, these principles also help explain how drug overdoses occur.)

The Basic Principles of Classical Conditioning

Pavlov's basic experimental setup involved cradling dogs in a harness to administer the foods and to measure the salivary response, as shown in **FIGURE 7.1**. He noticed that dogs that had previously been in the experiment began to produce a kind of "anticipatory" salivary response as soon as they were put in the harness, even before any food was presented. Pavlov and his colleagues regarded these responses as annoyances at first because they interfered with collecting naturally occurring salivary secretions. In reality, the dogs were behaving in line with the basic elements of classical conditioning:

- When the dogs were initially presented with a plate of food, they began to salivate. No surprise here—placing food in front of most animals will launch the salivary process. Pavlov called the presentation of food an **unconditioned stimulus (US)**, *something that reliably produces a naturally occurring reaction in an organism* (see **FIGURE 7.2a**). He called the dogs' salivation an **unconditioned response (UR)**, *a reflexive reaction that is reliably produced by an unconditioned stimulus.*

unconditioned stimulus (US) Something that reliably produces a naturally occurring reaction in an organism.

unconditioned response (UR) A reflexive reaction that is reliably produced by an unconditioned stimulus.

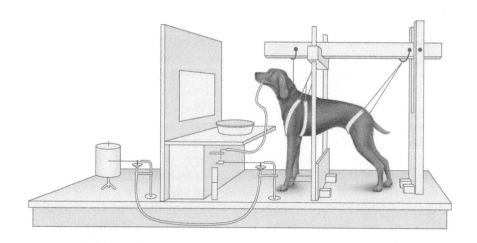

Figure 7.1

Pavlov's Apparatus for Studying Classical Conditioning Using a metronome or a buzzer, Pavlov presented auditory stimuli to the dogs. Visual stimuli could be presented on the screen.

The Real World | **Understanding Drug Overdoses**

All too often, police are confronted with a perplexing problem: the sudden death of addicts from a drug overdose. The problem exists worldwide, has increased substantially during the past decade (Martins et al., 2015), and is receiving increasing attention because of the opioid epidemic in the United States (Lyden & Binswanger, 2019). These deaths are puzzling for at least three reasons: The victims are often experienced drug users; the dose taken is usually not larger than what they usually take; and the deaths tend to occur in unusual settings. Experienced drug users are just that: experienced! So you'd think that the chances of an overdose would be lower than usual.

McMaster neuroscientist Shepard Siegel realized that classical conditioning provides some insight into how these deaths occur (Siegel, 2016). First, when classical conditioning takes place, the conditioned stimulus (CS) is more than a simple buzzer or tone: It also includes the overall *context* within which the conditioning takes place. Indeed, Pavlov's dogs often began to salivate even as they approached the experimental apparatus. Second, many conditioned responses (CRs) are compensatory reactions to the unconditioned stimulus (US). Heroin, for example, slows down a person's breathing rate, so the body responds with a compensatory reaction that speeds up breathing in order to maintain a state of balance, or homeostasis, a critically important CR.

These two finer points of classical conditioning help explain the seeming paradox of fatal heroin overdoses in experienced drug users (Siegel, 1984, 2016). When the drug is injected, the entire setting (the drug paraphernalia, the room, the lighting, the addict's usual companions) functions as the CS, and the addict's brain reacts to the heroin by secreting neurotransmitters that counteract its effects. Over time, this protective physiological response becomes part of the CR, and like all CRs, it occurs in the presence of the CS but prior to the actual administration of the drug. These

Although supervised drug-injection facilities such as Vancouver's Insite (shown here) are controversial, they are safe places for addicts to use drugs. In addition to providing clean needles and access to health care, the consistent environment becomes part of the addict's CS. Without such legal sites, addicts may be pushed to use drugs in new situations when illegal sites are closed down, contributing to overdoses and fatalities.

compensatory physiological reactions are also what make drug abusers take increasingly larger doses to achieve the same effect. Ultimately, these reactions produce *drug tolerance,* discussed in the Consciousness chapter.

On the basis of these principles of classical conditioning, taking drugs in a new environment can be fatal for a longtime drug user. If an addict injects the usual dose in a setting that is sufficiently novel or where he or she has never taken heroin before, the CS is now altered, such that the physiological compensatory CR that usually has a protective function either does not occur or is substantially decreased (Siegel et al., 2000). As a result, the addict's usual dose becomes an overdose, and death often results. Addicts intuitively may stick with the crack houses, drug dens, or "shooting galleries" with which they're familiar for just this reason.

This effect has also been shown experimentally: Rats that have had extensive experience with morphine in one setting were much more likely to survive dose increases in that same setting than in

a novel one (Siegel, 1976; Siegel et al., 2000). This same basic effect occurs with a variety of drugs. For example, university students show less tolerance for the intoxicating effects of alcohol when they consume it in the presence of a novel cue (a peppermint-flavoured drink) than a familiar one (a beer-flavoured drink) (Siegel, 2005).

Understanding these principles has also led to treatments for drug addiction. For instance, the addict can experience the brain's compensatory response to a drug—when elicited by the familiar contextual cues ordinarily associated with drug taking that constitute the CS—as withdrawal symptoms. In *cue exposure therapies,* an addict is exposed to drug-related cues without being given the usual dose of the drug itself, eventually resulting in extinction of the association between the contextual cues and the effects of the drug. After such treatment, encountering familiar drug-related cues will no longer result in the compensatory response linked to withdrawal symptoms, thereby making it easier for a recovering addict to remain abstinent (Siegel, 2005).

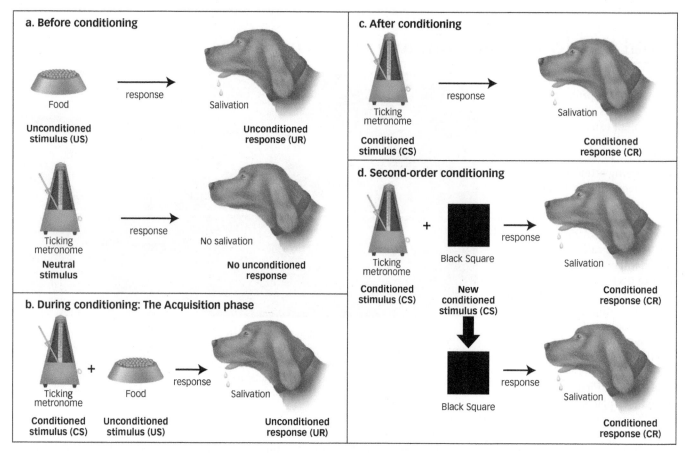

Figure 7.2

The Elements of Classical Conditioning
(a) Before conditioning, the dog salivates in response to food, the unconditioned stimulus (US), but not to the ticking of a metronome. (b) During conditioning, the food is paired with the ticking metronome, which becomes a conditioned stimulus (CS). (c) After conditioning, the ticking metronome, now a conditioned stimulus (CS), can produce salivation. (d) In second-order conditioning, the ticking metronome can be used to condition a new stimulus, such as a black square.

acquisition The phase of classical conditioning when the CS and the US are presented together.

conditioned stimulus (CS)
A previously neutral stimulus that produces a reliable response in an organism after being paired with a US.

conditioned response (CR)
A reaction that resembles an unconditioned response but is produced by a conditioned stimulus.

- Then Pavlov paired the presentation of food with the sound of the ticking of a metronome, a buzzer, the humming of a tuning fork, or the flash of a light (Pavlov, 1927). This period is called **acquisition**, *the phase of classical conditioning when the CS and the US are presented together* (see Figure 7.2b).

- Nothing in nature would make a dog salivate to the sound of a metronome or a buzzer. However, when the CS (the sound of the metronome) is paired over time with the US (the food), the animal will learn to associate food with the sound, and eventually the CS is sufficient to produce a response, or salivation. Sure enough, Pavlov found that the dogs ultimately salivated to these sounds and flashes, each of which had become a **conditioned stimulus (CS)**, *a previously neutral stimulus that produces a reliable response in an organism after being paired with a US*. This response resembles the UR, but Pavlov called it the **conditioned response (CR)**, *a reaction that resembles an unconditioned response but is produced by a conditioned stimulus*. In this example, the dogs' salivation (CR) was eventually prompted by the sound of the metronome (CS) alone because the sound of the metronome and the food (US) had been associated so often in the past (see Figure 7.2c).

Consider your own dog (or cat). Does your dog always know when dinner's coming, preparing just short of pulling up a chair and tucking a napkin into her collar? It's as though she has one eye on the clock every day, waiting for the dinner hour. Alas, your dog is no clock-watching wonder hound. Instead, for her the presentation of food (the US) has become associated with a complex CS—your getting up, moving into the kitchen, opening the cabinet, working the can opener—such that the CS alone signals to your dog that food is on the way, therefore initiating the CR of her getting ready to eat. And classical conditioning isn't just for dogs. When you hear your smartphone ring announcing the arrival of a new text, you may not salivate but you probably feel like you've got to check it right away—and you might even experience anxiety if you are in a situation in which you can't. Socially important information from friends and others contained in prior texts (the US) has become associated with the text message sound on your phone (the CS), so that the CS alone signals that important information may be on the way, thus initiating the phone-checking CR.

After conditioning has been established, a phenomenon called **second-order conditioning**, which is *a type of learning whereby a CS is paired with a stimulus that became associated with the US in an earlier procedure*, can be demonstrated. For instance, in an early study, Pavlov repeatedly paired a new CS, a black square, with the now reliable tone. After a number of training trials, his dogs produced a salivary response to the black square, even though the square itself had never been directly associated with the food (see Figure 7.2d).

Acquisition, Extinction, and Spontaneous Recovery

Remember when you first got your dog? Chances are she didn't seem too smart, especially the way she stared at you vacantly as you went into the kitchen, not anticipating that food was on the way. During the initial phase of the acquisition period of classical conditioning, typically there is a gradual increase in learning: It starts low, rises rapidly, and then slowly tapers off, as shown on the left side of the first panel of **FIGURE 7.3**. Pavlov's dogs gradually increased their amount of salivation over several trials of pairing a tone with the presentation of food; similarly, your dog eventually learned to associate your kitchen preparations with the subsequent appearance of food. After learning has been established, in the second-order phase, the CS by itself will reliably elicit the CR.

After Pavlov and his colleagues had explored the process of acquisition extensively, they turned to the next logical question: What would happen if they continued to present the CS (metronome ticking) but stopped presenting the US (food)? Repeatedly presenting the CS without the US produces exactly the result you might imagine. As shown on the right side of the first panel in Figure 7.3, behaviour declines abruptly and continues to drop until eventually the dog ceases to salivate

Second-order conditioning helps explain why some people desire money to the point that they hoard it and value it even more than the objects it purchases. Money is initially used to purchase objects that produce gratifying outcomes, such as an expensive car. Although money is not directly associated with the thrill of driving a new sports car, through second-order conditioning, money can become linked with this type of desirable reward.

second-order conditioning A type of learning whereby a CS is paired with a stimulus that became associated with the US in an earlier procedure.

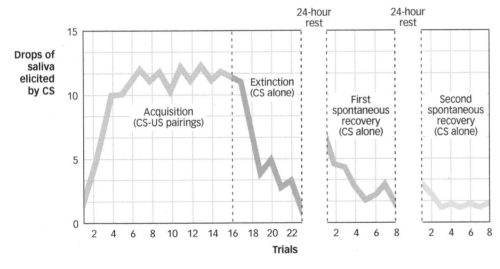

Figure 7.3

Acquisition, Extinction, and Spontaneous Recovery In classical conditioning, the CS is originally neutral and elicits no specific response. As an example, after several trials pairing the CS with the US, the CS alone comes to elicit the salivary response (the CR). Learning tends to take place fairly rapidly and then levels off as stable responding develops. In extinction, the CR diminishes quickly until it no longer occurs. A rest period, however, is typically followed by spontaneous recovery of the CR. In fact, a well-learned CR may show spontaneous recovery after more than one rest period even without any additional learning trials.

to the sound of the tone. This process is called **extinction**, *the gradual elimination of a learned response that occurs when the CS is repeatedly presented without the US.* This term was introduced because the conditioned response is "extinguished" and no longer observed. Having established that he could produce learning through conditioning and then extinguish it, Pavlov wondered if this elimination of conditioned behaviour was permanent. Is a single session of extinction sufficient to knock out the CR completely? Or is there some residual change in the dog's behaviour such that the CR might reappear?

To explore this question, Pavlov extinguished the classically conditioned salivation response and then allowed the dogs to have a short rest period. When they were brought back to the lab and presented with the CS again, they displayed **spontaneous recovery**, *the tendency of a learned behaviour to recover from extinction after a rest period.* This phenomenon is shown in the middle panel in Figure 7.3. Notice that this recovery takes place even though there have not been any additional associations between the CS and US. Some spontaneous recovery of the conditioned response even takes place in what is essentially a second extinction session after another period of rest (see the right-hand panel in Figure 7.3). Clearly, extinction had not completely erased the learning that had been acquired. The ability of the CS to elicit the CR was weakened, but it was not eliminated.

Generalization and Discrimination

Do you think your dog will be stumped, unable to anticipate the presentation of her food, if you get a new can opener? Will you need to establish a whole new round of conditioning with this modified CS?

Probably not. It wouldn't be very adaptive for an organism if each little change in the CS–US pairing required an extensive regimen of new learning. Rather, the phenomenon of **generalization** tends to take place: *The CR is observed even though the CS is slightly different from the CS used during acquisition.* In other words, the conditioning generalizes to stimuli that are similar to the CS used during the original training. As you might expect, the more the new stimulus changes, the less conditioned responding is observed—which means that if you replaced a manual can opener with an electric can opener, your dog would probably show a much weaker conditioned response (Pearce, 1987; Rescorla, 2006).

When an organism generalizes to a new stimulus, two things are happening. First, by responding to the new stimulus used during generalization testing, the organism demonstrates that it recognizes the similarity between the original CS and the new stimulus. Second, by displaying a *diminished* response to that new stimulus, it also tells us that it notices a difference between the two stimuli. In the second case, the organism shows **discrimination**, *the capacity to distinguish between similar but distinct stimuli.* Generalization and discrimination are two sides of the same coin. The more organisms show one, the less they show the other, and training can modify the balance between the two.

Conditioned Emotional Responses: The Case of Little Albert

Before you conclude that classical conditioning is merely a sophisticated way to train your dog, let's revisit the larger principles of Pavlov's work. Classical conditioning demonstrates that scientists can achieve durable, substantial changes in behaviour simply by setting up the proper conditions. It was this kind of simplicity that appealed to behaviourists. In fact, Watson and his followers thought that it was possible to develop general explanations of pretty much *any* behaviour of *any* organism, based on classical conditioning principles. As a step in that direction, Watson embarked

extinction The gradual elimination of a learned response that occurs when the CS is repeatedly presented without the US.

spontaneous recovery The tendency of a learned behaviour to recover from extinction after a rest period.

generalization The CR is observed even though the CS is slightly different from the CS used during acquisition.

discrimination The capacity to distinguish between similar but distinct stimuli.

on a controversial study with his research assistant Rosalie Rayner (Watson & Rayner, 1920).

To support his contention that even complex behaviours were the result of conditioning, Watson enlisted the assistance of 9-month-old "Little Albert." Albert was a healthy, well-developed child and, by Watson's assessment, was "stolid and unemotional" (Watson & Rayner, 1920, p. 1). Watson wanted to see if such a child could be classically conditioned to experience a strong emotional reaction—namely, fear. Here's how he proceeded:

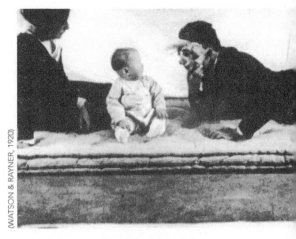

- Watson presented Little Albert with a variety of stimuli: a white rat, a dog, a rabbit, various masks, and a burning newspaper. Albert reacted in most cases with curiosity or indifference, and he showed no fear of any of the items.

- Watson also established that something *could* make Albert afraid. While Albert was watching Rayner, Watson unexpectedly struck a large steel bar with a hammer, producing a loud noise. Predictably, this caused Albert to cry, tremble, and be generally displeased.

- Watson and Rayner then led Little Albert through the acquisition phase of classical conditioning. Albert was presented with a white rat. As soon as he reached out to touch it, the steel bar was struck. This pairing occurred again and again over several trials. Eventually, the sight of the rat alone caused Albert to recoil in terror, crying and clamouring to get away from it. In this situation, a US (the loud sound) was paired with a CS (the presence of the rat) such that the CS all by itself was sufficient to produce the CR (a fearful reaction).

- Little Albert also showed stimulus generalization. The sight of a white rabbit, a seal-fur coat, and a Santa Claus mask produced the same kinds of fear reactions in the infant.

John Watson and Rosalie Rayner show Little Albert an unusual bunny mask. Why isn't the mere presence of these experimenters a conditioned stimulus in itself?

What was Watson's goal in all this? First, he wanted to show that a relatively complex reaction could be conditioned using Pavlovian techniques. Second, he wanted to show that emotional responses such as fear and anxiety could be produced by classical conditioning and therefore need not be the product of deeper unconscious processes or early life experiences as Freud and his followers had argued (see The Evolution of Psychological Science chapter). Instead, Watson proposed that fears could be learned, just like any other behaviour. Third, Watson wanted to confirm that conditioning could be applied to humans as well as to other animals. This study was controversial in its cavalier treatment of a young child, especially given that Watson and Rayner did not follow up with Albert or his mother during the ensuing years (Harris, 1979). Modern ethical guidelines that govern the treatment of research participants ensure that this kind of study could not be conducted today.

The kind of conditioned fear responses that were at work in Little Albert's case were also important in the chapter-opening case of Jennifer, who experienced fear and anxiety when hearing the previously innocent sound of an approaching helicopter as a result of her experiences in Iraq. Indeed, a therapy that has proven effective in dealing with such trauma-induced fears is based directly on principles of classical conditioning: Individuals are repeatedly exposed to conditioned stimuli associated with their trauma in a safe setting, in an attempt to extinguish the conditioned fear response (Bouton, 1988; Rothbaum & Schwartz, 2002). However, conditioned emotional responses include much more than just fear and anxiety responses.

Advertisers, for example, understand that conditioned emotional responses can include various positive emotions that they would like potential customers to associate with their products, which may be why attractive women are commonly involved in ads for products geared towards young males, including beer and sports cars. Even the warm and fuzzy feelings that envelop you when hearing a song that you used to listen to with a former boyfriend or girlfriend are a type of conditioned emotional response.

What response do you think the advertisers of Pepsi are looking for when they feature Sofia Vergara in an ad?

A Deeper Understanding of Classical Conditioning

As a form of learning, classical conditioning could be reliably produced: It had a simple set of principles and applications to real-life situations. In short, classical conditioning offered a good deal of utility for psychologists who sought to understand the mechanisms that underlie learning, and it continues to do so today.

Like a lot of strong starters, though, classical conditioning has been subjected to deeper scrutiny in order to understand exactly how, when, and why it works. Let's examine three areas that zero in on the mechanisms of classical conditioning: the cognitive, neural, and evolutionary elements.

The Cognitive Elements of Classical Conditioning

As we've seen, Pavlov's work was a behaviourist's dream come true. In this view, conditioning is something that *happens* to a dog, a rat, or a person, apart from what the organism thinks about the conditioning situation. However, although the dogs salivated when their feeders approached (see The Evolution of Psychological Science chapter), they did not salivate when Pavlov approached. Eventually, someone was bound to ask an important question: *Why not?* After all, Pavlov also delivered the food to the dogs, so why didn't *he* become a CS? Indeed, if Watson was present whenever the unpleasant US was sounded, why didn't Little Albert come to fear *him*?

Somehow, Pavlov's dogs were sensitive to the fact that Pavlov was not a *reliable* indicator of the arrival of food. Pavlov was linked with the arrival of food, but he was also linked with other activities that had nothing to do with food, including checking on the apparatus, bringing the dog from the kennel to the laboratory, and standing around talking with his assistants.

Robert Rescorla and Allan Wagner (1972) were the first to theorize that classical conditioning occurs when an animal has learned to set up an *expectation*. The sound of a metronome, because of its systematic pairing with food, set up this cognitive state for the laboratory dogs; Pavlov, because of the lack of any reliable link with food, did not. In fact, in situations such as this, many responses are actually being conditioned. When the metronome ticks, the dogs also wag their tails, make begging sounds, and look towards the food source (Jenkins et al., 1978). In short, what is really happening is something like the situation shown in **FIGURE 7.4**.

The Rescorla–Wagner model introduced a cognitive component that accounted for a variety of classical conditioning phenomena that were difficult to understand from a simple behaviourist point of view. For example, the model predicted that conditioning would be easier when the CS was an *unfamiliar* event than when it was familiar. The reason is that familiar events, being familiar, already have expectations

Figure 7.4

Expectation In Classical Conditioning In the Rescorla–Wagner model of classical conditioning, a CS sets up an expectation. The expectation in turn leads to an array of behaviours associated with the presence of the CS.

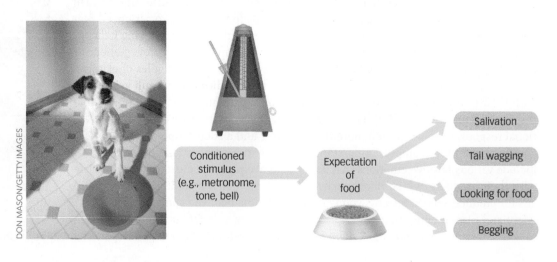

DON MASON/GETTY IMAGES

Conditioned stimulus (e.g., metronome, tone, bell) → Expectation of food → Salivation / Tail wagging / Looking for food / Begging

associated with them, making new conditioning difficult. In short, classical conditioning might appear to be a primitive process, but it is actually quite sophisticated and incorporates a significant cognitive element.

The Neural Elements of Classical Conditioning

Pavlov saw his research as providing insights into how the brain works. After all, he was trained in medicine, not psychology, and was a bit surprised when psychologists became excited by his findings. Recent research has clarified some of what Pavlov hoped to understand about conditioning and the brain.

A series of pioneering experiments conducted across several decades by Richard Thompson and his colleagues focused on classical conditioning of eyeblink responses in rabbits. In the most basic type of eyeblink conditioning, the CS (a tone) is immediately followed by the US (a puff of air), which elicits a reflexive eyeblink response. After many CS–US pairings, the eyeblink response occurs in response to the CS alone. Thompson and colleagues showed convincingly that the cerebellum is critical for the occurrence of eyeblink conditioning (Thompson, 2005). Studies of people with lesions to the cerebellum supported these findings by demonstrating impaired eyeblink conditioning (Daum et al., 1993). Rounding out the picture, more recent neuroimaging findings in healthy young adults show activation in the cerebellum during eyeblink conditioning (Cheng et al., 2008). As you learned in the Neuroscience and Behaviour chapter, the cerebellum is part of the hindbrain and plays an important role in motor skills and learning.

In addition to eyeblink conditioning, fear conditioning has been extensively studied. Also in the Neuroscience and Behaviour chapter, you saw that the amygdala plays an important role in the experience of emotion, including fear and anxiety. So it should come as no surprise that the amygdala, particularly an area known as the *central nucleus,* is also critical for emotional conditioning.

Consider a rat that is conditioned to a series of CS–US pairings in which the CS is a tone and the US is a mild electric shock. When rats experience sudden painful stimuli in nature, they show a defensive reaction, known as *freezing,* in which they crouch down and sit motionless. In addition, their autonomic nervous systems go to work: Heart rate and blood pressure increase, and various hormones associated with stress are released. When fear conditioning takes place, these two components—one behavioural and one physiological—occur, except that now they are elicited by the CS.

The central nucleus of the amygdala plays a role in producing both of these outcomes through two distinct connections with other parts of the brain. If connections linking the amygdala to the midbrain are disrupted, the rat does not exhibit the behavioural freezing response. If the connections between the amygdala and the hypothalamus are severed, the autonomic responses associated with fear cease (LeDoux et al., 1988). Hence, the action of the amygdala is an essential element in fear conditioning, and its links with other areas of the brain are responsible for producing specific features of conditioning (Bentz & Schiller, 2015). The amygdala is involved in fear conditioning in people as well as in rats and other animals (Olsson & Phelps, 2007; Phelps & LeDoux, 2005).

The Evolutionary Elements of Classical Conditioning

In addition to this cognitive component, evolutionary mechanisms also play an important role in classical conditioning. As you learned in The Evolution of Psychological Science chapter, evolution and natural selection go hand in hand with adaptiveness: Behaviours that are adaptive allow an organism to survive and thrive in its environment. In the case of classical conditioning, psychologists began to appreciate how this type of learning could have adaptive value. Much research exploring this adaptiveness has focused on conditioned food aversions, primarily taste aversions.

Under certain conditions, people may develop taste aversions. This serving of hummus looks inviting and probably tastes delicious, but at least one psychologist avoids all hummus like the plague.

Consider this example: A psychology professor was once on a job interview in southern California, and his hosts took him to lunch at a Middle Eastern restaurant. Suffering from a case of bad hummus, he was up all night long and developed a life-long aversion to hummus.

On the face of it, this looks like a case of classical conditioning, but there are several peculiar aspects to this case. The hummus was the CS, a bacterium or some other source of toxicity was the US, and the resulting nausea was the UR. The UR (the nausea) became linked to the once-neutral CS (the hummus) and became a CR (an aversion to hummus). However, all of the psychologist's hosts also ate the hummus, yet none of them reported feeling ill. It's not clear, then, what the US was; it couldn't have been anything that was actually in the food. What's more, the time between the hummus and the distress was several hours; usually, a response follows a stimulus fairly quickly. Most baffling, this aversion was cemented with a single acquisition trial. It usually takes several pairings of a CS and US to establish learning.

These peculiarities are not so peculiar from an evolutionary perspective. Any species that forages or consumes a variety of foods needs to develop a mechanism by which it can learn to avoid any food that once made it ill. To have adaptive value, this mechanism should have several properties:

- Rapid learning should occur in perhaps one or two trials. If learning takes more trials than this, the animal could die from eating a toxic substance.

- Conditioning should be able to take place over very long intervals, perhaps up to several hours. Toxic substances often don't cause illness immediately, so the organism would need to form an association between the food and the illness over a longer term.

- The organism should develop the aversion to the smell or taste of the food rather than its ingestion. It's more adaptive to reject a potentially toxic substance based on smell alone than it is to ingest it.

- Learned aversions should occur more often with novel foods than with familiar ones. It is not adaptive for an animal to develop an aversion to everything it has eaten on the particular day it got sick. Our psychologist friend didn't develop an aversion to the Coke he drank with lunch or the scrambled eggs he had for breakfast that day; however, the sight and smell of hummus do make him uneasy.

A Modern Application

John Garcia and his colleagues illustrated the adaptiveness of classical conditioning in a series of studies with rats (Garcia & Koelling, 1966). They used a variety of CSs (visual, auditory, tactile, taste, and smell) and several different USs (injection of a toxic substance, radiation) that caused nausea and vomiting hours later. The researchers found weak or no conditioning when the CS was a visual, auditory, or tactile stimulus, but a strong food aversion developed with stimuli that had a distinct taste and smell.

This research had an interesting application. It led to the development of a technique for dealing with an unanticipated side effect of radiation and chemotherapy: Cancer patients who experience nausea from their treatments often develop aversions to foods they ate before the therapy. Broberg and Bernstein (1987) reasoned that, if the findings with rats generalized to humans, a simple technique should minimize the negative consequences of this effect. They gave their patients an unusual food (coconut- or root-beer-flavoured candy) at the end of the last meal before undergoing treatment. Sure enough, the conditioned food aversions that the patients developed were overwhelmingly for one of the unusual flavours and not for any of the other foods in the meal. Other than any root beer or coconut fanatics among the sample, patients were spared from developing aversions to common foods that they were more likely to eat.

Studies such as these suggest that evolution has provided each species with a kind of **biological preparedness**, *a propensity for learning particular kinds of associations over other kinds,* such that some behaviours are relatively easy to condition in some species but not in others. For example, the taste and smell stimuli that produce food aversions in rats do not work with most species of birds. Birds depend primarily on visual cues for finding food and are relatively insensitive to taste and smell. However, as you might guess, it is relatively easy to produce a food aversion in birds using an unfamiliar visual stimulus as the CS, such as a brightly coloured food (Wilcoxon, Dragoin, & Kral, 1971). Indeed, most researchers agree that conditioning works best with stimuli that are biologically relevant to the organism (Domjan, 2005).

Build to the Outcomes

1. Why do some dogs seem to know when it's dinnertime?
2. If both an unconditioned and conditioned stimulus can produce the same effect, what is the difference?
3. What is second-order conditioning?
4. How does a conditioned behaviour change when the unconditioned stimulus is removed?
5. Why are generalization and discrimination "two sides of the same coin"?
6. Why did Little Albert fear the rat?
7. How does the role of expectation in conditioning challenge behaviourist ideas?
8. What is the role of the amygdala in fear conditioning?
9. How has cancer patients' discomfort been eased by our understanding of food aversions?

Operant Conditioning: Reinforcements from the Environment

The study of classical conditioning is the study of behaviours that are *reactive*. Most animals don't voluntarily salivate or feel spasms of anxiety; rather, they exhibit these responses involuntarily during the conditioning process. Involuntary behaviours make up only a small portion of our behavioural repertoires. The remainder are behaviours that we voluntarily perform. We engage in these voluntary behaviours in order to obtain rewards and avoid punishment; understanding them is essential to developing a complete picture of learning. Because classical conditioning has little to say about these voluntary behaviours, we turn now to a different form of learning: **operant conditioning**, *in which the consequences of an organism's behaviour determine whether it will repeat that behaviour in the future.* The study of operant conditioning is the exploration of behaviours that are *active*.

Learning Outcomes

- Describe the process of operant conditioning.
- Explain how behavioural, cognitive, neural, and evolutionary aspects influence our understanding of operant conditioning.

The Development of Operant Conditioning: The Law of Effect

The study of how active behaviour affects the environment began at about the same time as classical conditioning. In fact, Edward L. Thorndike (1874–1949) first examined active behaviours back in the 1890s, before Pavlov published his findings. Thorndike's research focused on *instrumental behaviours,* that is, behaviour that required an organism to *do* something, such as solve a problem or otherwise

biological preparedness A propensity for learning particular kinds of associations over other kinds.

operant conditioning A type of learning in which the consequences of an organism's behaviour determine whether it will repeat that behaviour in the future.

Figure 7.5
Thorndike's Puzzle Box In Thorndike's original experiments, food was placed just outside the door of the puzzle box, where the cat could see it. If the cat triggered the appropriate lever, the door would open and the cat could get out.

manipulate elements of its environment (Thorndike, 1898). For example, Thorndike completed several experiments using a puzzle box, which was a wooden crate with a door that would open when a concealed lever was moved in the right way (see **FIGURE 7.5**). A hungry cat placed in a puzzle box would try various behaviours to get out—scratching at the door, meowing loudly, sniffing the inside of the box, putting its paw through the openings—but only one behaviour opened the door and led to food: tripping the lever in just the right way. After the cat earned its reward, Thorndike placed it back in the puzzle box for another round. Don't get the wrong idea. Thorndike probably *really liked* cats. Far from teasing them, he was after an important behavioural principle.

Fairly quickly, the cats became quite skilled at triggering the lever for their release. Notice what's going on. At first, the cat enacts any number of likely (yet ultimately ineffective) behaviours, but only one behaviour leads to freedom and food. Over time, the ineffective behaviours become less and less frequent, and the one instrumental behaviour (going right for the latch) becomes more frequent (see **FIGURE 7.6**). From these observations, Thorndike developed the **law of effect**, the principle that

law of effect The principle that behaviours that are followed by a "satisfying state of affairs" tend to be repeated, whereas those that produce an "unpleasant state of affairs" are less likely to be repeated.

Figure 7.6
The Law of Effect Thorndike's cats displayed trial-and-error behaviour when trying to escape from the puzzle box. For example, they made lots of irrelevant movements and actions until, over time, they discovered the solution. Once they figured out which behaviour was instrumental in opening the latch, they stopped all other ineffective behaviours and escaped from the box faster and faster.

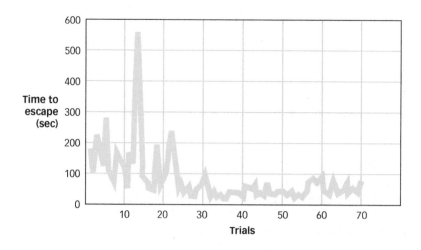

behaviours that are followed by a "satisfying state of affairs" tend to be repeated, whereas those that produce an "unpleasant state of affairs" are less likely to be repeated.

The circumstances that Thorndike used to study learning were very different from those used in classical conditioning research. Remember that in classical conditioning experiments, the US occurred on every training trial, no matter what the animal did. Pavlov delivered food to the dog whether it salivated or not. But in Thorndike's work, the behaviour of the animal determined what happened next. If the behaviour was "correct" (i.e., the animal triggered the latch), the animal was rewarded with food. Incorrect behaviours produced no results, and the animal was stuck in the box until it performed the correct behaviour. Although different from classical conditioning, Thorndike's work resonated with most behaviourists at the time: It was still observable, quantifiable, and free from explanations involving the mind (Galef, 1998).

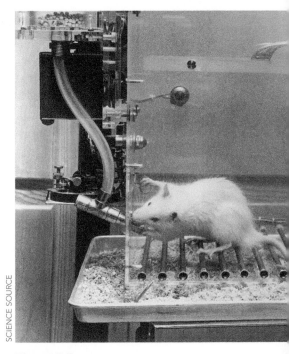

Figure 7.7
Skinner Box This is a typical Skinner box, or operant conditioning chamber. A rat, pigeon, or other suitably sized animal is placed in this environment and observed during learning trials that apply operant conditioning principles.

B. F. Skinner: The Role of Reinforcement and Punishment

Several decades after Thorndike's work, B. F. Skinner (1904–1990) coined the term **operant behaviour** to refer to *behaviour that an organism performs that has some impact on the environment.* In Skinner's system, all of these emitted behaviours "operated" on the environment in some manner, and the environment responded by providing events that either strengthened those behaviours (i.e., they *reinforced* them) or made them less likely to occur (i.e., they *punished* them). Skinner's elegantly simple observation was that most organisms do *not* behave like a dog in a harness, passively waiting to receive food no matter what the circumstances. Rather, most organisms are like cats in a box, actively engaging the environment in which they find themselves to reap rewards (Skinner, 1938, 1953).

In order to study operant behaviour scientifically, Skinner developed a variation on Thorndike's puzzle box. The *operant conditioning chamber,* or *Skinner box,* as it is commonly called (shown in **FIGURE 7.7**), allows a researcher to study the behaviour of small organisms in a controlled environment.

Skinner's approach to the study of learning focused on *reinforcement* and *punishment.* These terms, which have commonsense connotations, turned out to be rather difficult to define. For example, some people love roller coasters, whereas others find them horrifying; the chance to go on one will be reinforcing for one group but punishing for another. Dogs can be trained with praise and a good belly rub—procedures that are nearly useless for most cats. Skinner settled on a neutral definition that would characterize each term by its effect on behaviour. Therefore, a **reinforcer** is *any stimulus or event that increases the likelihood of the behaviour that led to it,* whereas a **punisher** is *any stimulus or event that decreases the likelihood of the behaviour that led to it.*

Whether a particular stimulus acts as a reinforcer or a punisher depends in part on whether it increases or decreases the likelihood of a behaviour. Presenting food is usually reinforcing and it produces an increase in the behaviour that led to it; removing food is often punishing and leads to a decrease in the behaviour. Turning on an electric shock is typically punishing (and decreases the behaviour that led to it); turning it off is rewarding (and increases the behaviour that led to it).

To keep these possibilities distinct, Skinner used the term *positive* for situations in which a stimulus was presented and *negative* for situations in which it was removed. Consequently, as shown in **TABLE 7.1**, there is *positive reinforcement* (a stimulus is presented that increases the likelihood of a behaviour) and a *negative reinforcement* (a stimulus is removed that increases the likelihood of a behaviour), as well as *positive punishment* (a stimulus is administered that reduces the likelihood of a behaviour) and a *negative punishment* (a stimulus is removed that decreases the likelihood of a behaviour).

B. F. Skinner with one of his many research participants.

operant behaviour Behaviour that an organism performs that has some impact on the environment.

reinforcer Any stimulus or event that increases the likelihood of the behaviour that led to it.

punisher Any stimulus or event that decreases the likelihood of the behaviour that led to it.

TABLE 7.1

REINFORCEMENT AND PUNISHMENT

	Increases the Likelihood of Behaviour	Decreases the Likelihood of Behaviour
Stimulus is presented	Positive reinforcement: Parents buy teen a new car as a reward for safe driving.	Positive punishment: Parents assign difficult new chores after teen is stopped for speeding.
Stimulus is removed	Negative reinforcement: Parents reduce restrictions on where teen can drive as a reward for safe driving.	Negative punishment: Parents suspend driving privileges after teen is stopped for speeding.

Here the words *positive* and *negative* mean, respectively, something that is *added* or something that is *taken away*; they do not mean "good" or "bad" as they do in everyday speech.

These distinctions can be confusing at first; after all, "negative reinforcement" and "punishment" both sound like they should be "bad" and produce the same type of behaviour. However, negative reinforcement, for example, does not involve administering something that decreases the likelihood of a behaviour; it's the *removal* of something, such as a shock, that increases the likelihood of a behaviour.

For instance, new parents are highly trainable by their babies—and they quickly learn to repeat behaviours that stop their little bundle of joy from crying (such as bouncing the baby a certain way, swinging the baby in her car seat at a certain rate, or pulling goofy faces). The baby is providing negative reinforcement that encourages these behaviours.

Reinforcement is generally more effective than punishment in promoting learning, for many reasons (Gershoff, 2002). One reason is that punishment signals that an unacceptable behaviour has occurred, but it doesn't specify what should be done instead. Scolding a young child for starting to run into a busy street certainly stops the behaviour, but it doesn't promote any kind of learning about the *desired* behaviour.

Primary and Secondary Reinforcement and Punishment

Reinforcers and punishers often gain their functions from basic biological mechanisms. A pigeon that pecks at a target in a Skinner box is usually reinforced with food pellets, just as an animal that learns to escape a mild electric shock has avoided the punishment of tingly paws. Food, comfort, shelter, and warmth are examples of *primary reinforcers* because they help satisfy biological needs or desires. However, the vast majority of reinforcers or punishers in our daily lives have little to do with biology: Verbal approval, a bronze trophy, or money all serve powerful reinforcing functions, yet none of them taste very good or help keep you warm at night. The point is, we learn to perform a lot of behaviours on the basis of reinforcements that have little or nothing to do with biological satisfaction.

These *secondary reinforcers* derive their effectiveness from their associations with primary reinforcers through classical conditioning. For example, money starts out as a neutral CS that, through its association with primary USs such as acquiring food or shelter, takes on a conditioned emotional element. Flashing lights, originally a neutral CS, acquire powerful negative elements through association with a speeding ticket and a fine.

Immediate Versus Delayed Reinforcement and Punishment

A key determinant of the effectiveness of a reinforcer is the amount of time between the occurrence of a behaviour and the reinforcer: The more time elapses, the less effective the reinforcer (Lattal, 2010; Renner, 1964). This was

MICHELLE SELESNICK/MOMENT/GETTY IMAGES

Negative reinforcement involves the removal of something unpleasant from the environment. When Daddy stops the car, he gets a reward: His little monster stops screaming. However, from the perspective of the child, this is positive reinforcement. The child's tantrum results in something positive added to the environment—stopping for a snack.

Figure 7.8

Delay of Reinforcement Rats pressed a lever in order to obtain a food reward. Researchers varied the amount of time between the lever press and the delivery of food reinforcement. The number of lever presses declined substantially with longer delays.

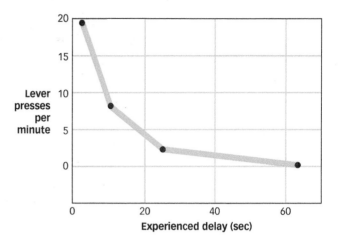

dramatically illustrated in experiments with hungry rats in which food reinforcers were given at varying times after a rat pressed a lever (Dickinson, Watt, & Griffiths, 1992). Delaying reinforcement by even a few seconds led to a reduction in the number of times the rat subsequently pressed the lever, and extending the delay to a minute rendered the food reinforcer completely ineffective (see **FIGURE 7.8**). The most likely explanation for this effect is that delaying the reinforcer made it difficult for the rats to figure out exactly what behaviour they needed to perform in order to obtain it. In the same way, parents who wish to use a piece of candy to reinforce their children for playing quietly should provide the candy while the child is still playing quietly; waiting until later, when the child may be engaging in other behaviours—perhaps making a racket with pots and pans—will make it more difficult for the child to link the reinforcer with the behaviour of playing quietly (Powell et al., 2009).

The greater potency of immediate versus delayed reinforcers may help us appreciate why it can be difficult to engage in behaviours that have long-term benefits. The smoker who desperately wants to quit smoking will be reinforced immediately by the feeling of relaxation that results from lighting up, but she may have to wait years to be reinforced with the better health that results from quitting; the dieter who sincerely wants to lose weight may easily succumb to the temptation of a chocolate sundae that provides reinforcement now, rather than waiting weeks or months for the reinforcement (looking and feeling better) that would be associated with losing weight.

Similar considerations apply to punishment: As a general rule, the longer the delay between a behaviour and the administration of punishment, the less effective the punishment will be in suppressing the targeted behaviour (Kamin, 1959; Lerman & Vorndran, 2002). The reduced effectiveness of delayed punishment can be a serious problem in nonlaboratory settings because in everyday life, it is often difficult to administer punishment immediately or even soon after a problem behaviour has occurred (Meindl & Casey, 2012). For example, a parent whose child misbehaves at a shopping mall may be unable to punish the child immediately with a time-out because it is impractical in the mall setting. Some problem behaviours, such as cheating, can be difficult to detect immediately, therefore punishment is necessarily delayed. Research in both the laboratory and everyday settings suggests several strategies for increasing the effectiveness of delayed punishment, including increasing the severity of the punishment or attempting to bridge the gap between the behaviour and the punishment with verbal instructions (Meindl & Casey, 2012). The parent in the shopping mall, for instance, might tell the misbehaving child exactly when and where a later time-out will occur.

Suppose you are the mayor of a suburban town, and you want to institute some new policies to decrease the number of drivers who speed on residential streets. How might you use punishment to decrease the undesirable behaviour (speeding)? How might you use reinforcement to increase the desirable behaviour (safe driving)? Thinking about the principles of operant conditioning you read about in this section, which approach do you think might be most fruitful?

The Basic Principles of Operant Conditioning

After establishing how reinforcement and punishment produced learned behaviour, Skinner and other scientists began to expand the parameters of operant conditioning. This took the form of investigating some phenomena that were well known in classical conditioning—such as discrimination, generalization, and extinction—as well as some practical applications, such as how best to administer reinforcement or how to produce complex learned behaviours in an organism. Let's look at some of these basic principles of operant conditioning.

Discrimination, Generalization, and the Importance of Context

We all take off our clothes at least once a day, but usually not in public. We scream at rock concerts, but not in libraries. We say, "Please pass the gravy," at the dinner table, but not in a classroom. Although these observations may seem like nothing more than common sense, Thorndike was the first to recognize the underlying message: Learning takes place *in contexts,* not in the free range of any plausible situation. As Skinner rephrased it later, most behaviour is under *stimulus control,* which develops when a particular response occurs only when an appropriate *discriminative stimulus* (one that indicates that a response will be reinforced) is present.

Skinner (1972) discussed this process in terms of a "three-term contingency": In the presence of a *discriminative stimulus* (classmates drinking coffee together in Starbucks), a *response* (joking comments about a psychology professor's increasing waistline and receding hairline) produces a *reinforcer* (laughter among classmates). The same response in a different context—say, the professor's office—would most likely produce a very different outcome.

Stimulus control, perhaps not surprisingly, shows both discrimination and generalization effects similar to those we saw with classical conditioning. To demonstrate this, researchers used either a painting by the French impressionist Claude Monet or one of Pablo Picasso's paintings from his cubist period for the discriminative stimulus (Watanabe, Sakamoto, & Wakita, 1995). Participants in the experiment were reinforced only if they responded when the appropriate painting was presented.

After training, the participants discriminated appropriately: Those trained with the Monet painting responded when other paintings by Monet were presented, and those trained with a Picasso painting reacted when other cubist paintings by Picasso were shown. And as you might expect, Monet-trained participants did not react to Picassos, and Picasso-trained participants did not respond to Monets. What's more, the research participants showed that they could generalize *across* painters as long as they were from the same artistic tradition. Those trained with Monet responded appropriately when shown paintings by Auguste Renoir (another French impressionist), and the Picasso-trained participants responded to artwork by the cubist painter Henri Matisse, despite never having seen those paintings before.

If these results don't seem particularly startling to you, it might help to know that the research participants were pigeons that were trained to key-peck to these various works of art. Stimulus control, and its ability to foster stimulus discrimination and stimulus generalization, is effective even if the stimulus has no meaning to the respondent.

In research on stimulus control, participants trained with Picasso paintings, such as the one on the left, responded to other paintings by Picasso or even to paintings by other cubists. Participants trained with Monet paintings, such as the one at the right, responded to other paintings by Monet or by other French impressionists. An interesting detail: The participants in this study were pigeons.

Extinction

As in classical conditioning, operant behaviour undergoes extinction when the reinforcements stop. Pigeons cease pecking at a key if food is no longer presented following that behaviour. You wouldn't put more money into a vending machine if it failed to give you its promised candy bar or soda. Warm smiles that are greeted with scowls and frowns will quickly disappear. On the surface, extinction of operant behaviour looks like that of classical conditioning: The response rate drops off fairly rapidly and, if a rest period is provided, spontaneous recovery is typically seen.

However, there is an important difference. As noted, in classical conditioning, the US occurs on *every* trial, no matter what the organism does. In operant conditioning, the reinforcements occur *only* when the proper response has been made, and they don't always occur even then. Not every trip into the forest produces nuts for a squirrel, auto salespeople don't sell to everyone who takes a test drive, and researchers run many experiments that do not work out and thus never get published. Yet these behaviours don't weaken and gradually extinguish. In fact, they typically become stronger and more resilient. Curiously, then, extinction is a bit more complicated in operant conditioning than in classical conditioning because it depends, in part, on how often reinforcement is received. In fact, this principle is an important cornerstone of operant conditioning that we'll examine next.

Schedules of Reinforcement

Skinner was intrigued by the apparent paradox surrounding extinction, and in his autobiography, he described how he began studying it (Skinner, 1979). He had been laboriously rolling ground rat meal and water to make food pellets to reinforce the rats in his early experiments. It occurred to him that perhaps he could save time and effort by not giving his rats a pellet for every bar press but instead delivering food on some intermittent schedule. The results of this hunch were dramatic. Not only did the rats continue bar pressing, but they also shifted the rate and pattern of bar pressing depending on the timing and frequency of the presentation of the reinforcers. Unlike in classical conditioning, where the sheer *number* of learning trials was important, the *pattern* with which reinforcements appeared was crucial in operant conditioning.

Skinner explored dozens of what came to be known as *schedules of reinforcement* (Ferster & Skinner, 1957) (see **FIGURE 7.9**). The two most important are *interval schedules,* based on the time intervals between reinforcements, and *ratio schedules,* based on the ratio of responses to reinforcements.

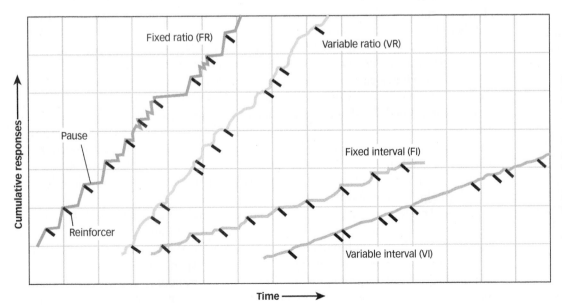

Figure 7.9
Reinforcement Schedules
Different schedules of reinforcement produce different rates of response. These lines represent the number of responses that occur under each type of reinforcement. The black slash marks indicate when reinforcement was administered. Notice that ratio schedules tend to produce higher rates of responding than do interval schedules, as shown by the steeper lines for fixed-ratio and variable-ratio reinforcement.

Interval Schedules Students cramming at the last minute for an exam often show the same kind of behaviour as pigeons being reinforced under a fixed-interval schedule. Radio stations offer tickets to hopeful concert goers on a less predictable, variable-interval schedule of reinforcement.

fixed-interval (FI) schedule An operant conditioning principle whereby reinforcers are presented at fixed time periods, provided that the appropriate response is made.

variable-interval (VI) schedule An operant conditioning principle whereby a behaviour is reinforced on the basis of an average time that has expired since the last reinforcement.

fixed-ratio (FR) schedule An operant conditioning principle whereby reinforcement is delivered after a specific number of responses have been made.

variable-ratio (VR) schedule An operant conditioning principle whereby the delivery of reinforcement is based on a particular average number of responses.

intermittent reinforcement An operant conditioning principle whereby only some of the responses made are followed by reinforcement.

Interval Schedules Under a **fixed-interval (FI) schedule**, *reinforcers are presented at fixed time periods, provided that the appropriate response is made.* For example, on a 2-minute fixed-interval schedule, a response will be reinforced, but only after 2 minutes have expired since the last reinforcement. Rats and pigeons in Skinner boxes produce predictable patterns of behaviour under these schedules. They show little responding right after the presentation of the reinforcement, but as the next time interval draws to a close, they show a burst of responding. Many students behave exactly like this. They do relatively little work until just before the upcoming exam, then engage in a burst of reading and studying.

Under a **variable-interval (VI) schedule**, *a behaviour is reinforced on the basis of an average time that has expired since the last reinforcement.* For instance, on a 2-minute variable-interval schedule, responses will be reinforced every 2 minutes, *on average,* but not after each 2-minute period. Variable-interval schedules typically produce steady, consistent responding because the time until the next reinforcement is less predictable. Such schedules are not encountered that often in real life, although one example might be radio promotional giveaways, such as tickets to rock concerts. The reinforcement—getting the tickets—might average out to once an hour across the span of the broadcasting day, but the presentation of the reinforcement is variable: It might come early in the 10 o'clock hour, later in the 11 o'clock hour, immediately into the 12 o'clock hour, and so on.

Both fixed-interval schedules and variable-interval schedules tend to produce slow, methodical responding because the reinforcements follow a time scale that is independent of how many responses occur. It doesn't matter if a rat on a fixed-interval schedule presses a bar 1 time during a 2-minute period or 100 times: The reinforcing food pellet won't drop out of the chute until 2 minutes have elapsed, regardless of the number of responses.

Ratio Schedules Under a **fixed-ratio (FR) schedule**, *reinforcement is delivered after a specific number of responses have been made.* One schedule might present reinforcement after every fourth response, and a different schedule might present reinforcement after every 20 responses; the special case of presenting reinforcement after each response is called *continuous reinforcement,* and it's what drove Skinner to investigate these schedules in the first place. Notice that, in each example, the ratio of reinforcements to responses, once set, remains fixed.

There are many situations in which people, sometimes unknowingly, find themselves being reinforced on a fixed-ratio schedule: Book clubs often give you a freebie after a set number of regular purchases; pieceworkers get paid after making a fixed number of products; and some credit card companies return to their customers a percentage of the amount charged. When a fixed-ratio schedule is operating, it is possible, in principle, to know exactly when the next reinforcer is due.

Under a **variable-ratio (VR) schedule**, *the delivery of reinforcement is based on a particular average number of responses.* Slot machines in a modern casino pay off on variable-ratio schedules that are determined by the random number generator controlling the play of the machines. A casino might advertise that its machines pay off on "every 100 pulls, on average," which could be true. However, one player might hit a jackpot after 3 pulls on a slot machine, whereas another player might not hit a jackpot until after 80 pulls. The ratio of responses to reinforcements is variable, which probably helps casinos stay in business.

It should come as no surprise that variable-ratio schedules produce slightly higher rates of responding than fixed-ratio schedules, primarily because the organism never knows when the next reinforcement is going to appear. What's more, the higher the ratio, the higher the response rate tends to be: A 20-response variable-ratio schedule will produce considerably more responding than a 2-response variable-ratio schedule will. When schedules of reinforcement provide **intermittent reinforcement**, *whereby only some of the responses made are followed by reinforcement,* they produce

JEFF HOLT/BLOOMBERG VIA GETTY IMAGES

STOCKBROKER/MBI/ALAMY

Ratio Schedules These pieceworkers in a textile factory get paid according to a fixed-ratio schedule: They receive payment after sewing some set number of shirts. Slot machines in casinos pay out following a variable-ratio schedule. This helps explain why some gamblers feel incredibly lucky, whereas others can't believe they can play a machine for so long without winning a thing.

behaviour that is much more resistant to extinction than does a continuous reinforcement schedule. One way to think about this effect is to recognize that the more irregular and intermittent a schedule is, the more difficult it becomes for an organism to detect when it has actually been placed on extinction.

For instance, if you've just put a toonie into a vending machine that, unknown to you, is broken, no can of pop comes out. Because you're used to getting your drinks on a continuous reinforcement schedule—one toonie produces one can of pop—this abrupt change in the environment is easy to notice, and you are unlikely to put additional money into the machine: You'd quickly show extinction. However, if you've put your dollar into a slot machine that, unknown to you, is broken, do you stop after one or two plays? Almost certainly not. If you're a regular slot player, you're used to going for many plays in a row without winning anything, so it's difficult to tell that anything is out of the ordinary. Under conditions of intermittent reinforcement, all organisms will show considerable resistance to extinction and continue for many trials before they stop responding. This effect has been observed even in infants (Weir et al., 2005).

This relationship between intermittent reinforcement schedules and the robustness of the behaviour they produce is called the **intermittent reinforcement effect**, *the fact that operant behaviours that are maintained under intermittent reinforcement schedules resist extinction better than those maintained under continuous reinforcement.* In one extreme case, Skinner gradually extended a variable-ratio schedule until he managed to get a pigeon to make an astonishing 10,000 pecks at an illuminated key for one food reinforcer! Behaviour maintained under a schedule like this is virtually immune to extinction.

ELENATHEWISE/ISTOCK/GETTY IMAGES

Imagine you own an insurance company, and you want to encourage your salespeople to sell as many policies as possible. You decide to give them bonuses according to the number of policies they sell. How might you set up a system of bonuses using a fixed-ratio schedule? Using a variable-ratio schedule? Which system do you think would encourage your salespeople to work harder, in terms of making more sales?

Shaping Through Successive Approximations

Have you ever been to a dolphin show at an aquarium and wondered how the dolphins learn to jump up in the air, twist around, splash back down, do a somersault, and then jump through a hoop, all in one smooth motion? Well, they don't. Wait—of course they do—you've seen them. It's just that they don't learn to do all those complex aquabatics in *one* smooth motion. Rather, elements of their behaviour are shaped over time until the final product looks like one smooth motion.

Skinner noted that the trial-by-trial experiments of Pavlov and Thorndike were rather artificial. Behaviour rarely occurs in fixed frameworks in which a stimulus is presented and then an organism has to engage in some activity or another. We are continuously acting and behaving, and the world around us reacts in response to our actions. Most of our behaviours, then, are the result of **shaping**, *learning that results from the reinforcement of successive steps to a final desired behaviour.* The outcomes of one set of behaviours shape the next set of behaviours, whose outcomes shape the next set of behaviours, and so on. For example, parents use shaping to teach young children skills such as walking or riding a bike by reinforcing successive behaviours that are needed to attain the complex goal behaviour.

intermittent reinforcement effect The fact that operant behaviours that are maintained under intermittent reinforcement schedules resist extinction better than those maintained under continuous reinforcement.

shaping Learning that results from the reinforcement of successive steps to a final desired behaviour.

Skinner realized the potential power of shaping when, one day in 1943, he was working on a wartime project sponsored by General Mills in a lab on the top floor of a flour mill where pigeons frequently visited (Peterson, 2004). In a lighthearted moment, Skinner and his colleagues decided to see whether they could teach the pigeons to "bowl" by swiping with their beaks at a ball that Skinner had placed in a box along with some pins. Nothing worked until Skinner decided to reinforce any response even remotely related to a swipe, such as merely looking at the ball. "The result amazed us," Skinner recalled. "In a few minutes the ball was caroming off the walls of the box as if the pigeon had been a champion squash player" (Skinner, 1958, p. 974).

Skinner applied this insight in his later laboratory research. For instance, he noted that if you put a rat in a Skinner box and wait for it to press the bar, you could end up waiting a very long time: Bar pressing just isn't very high in a rat's natural hierarchy of responses. However, it is relatively easy to shape bar pressing. Watch the rat closely: If it turns in the direction of the bar, deliver a food reward. This will reinforce turning towards the bar, making such a movement more likely. Now wait for the rat to take a step towards the bar before delivering food; this will reinforce moving towards the bar. After the rat walks closer to the bar, wait until it touches the bar before presenting the food. Notice that none of these behaviours is the final desired behaviour (reliably pressing the bar). Rather, each behaviour is a *successive approximation* to the final product, or a behaviour that gets incrementally closer to the overall desired behaviour. In the dolphin example—and indeed, in many instances of animal training in which relatively simple animals seem to perform astoundingly complex behaviours—you can think through how each smaller behaviour is reinforced until the overall sequence of behaviour is performed reliably.

Superstitious Behaviour

Everything we've discussed so far suggests that one of the keys to establishing reliable operant behaviour is the correlation between an organism's response and the occurrence of reinforcement. In the case of continuous reinforcement, when every

B. F. Skinner shaping a dog named Agnes. By reinforcing Agnes for touching successively higher lines on the wall, Skinner taught Agnes a pretty neat trick: after 20 minutes of shaping, Agnes wandered in, stood on her hind legs, and jumped straight to the top line.

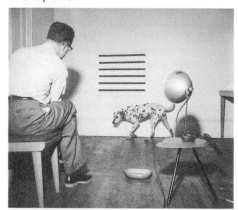
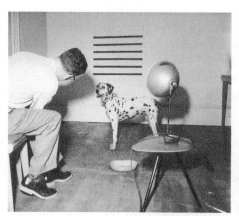
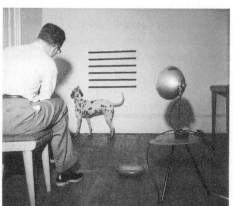
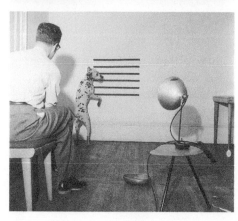
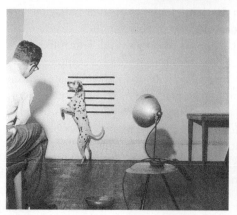
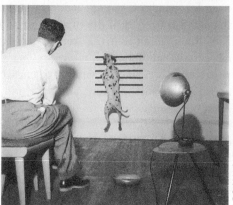

response is followed by the presentation of a reinforcer, there is a one-to-one, or perfect, correlation. In the case of intermittent reinforcement, the correlation is weaker (i.e., not every response is met with the delivery of reinforcement), but it's not zero. As you read in the Methods in Psychology chapter, however, just because two things are correlated (i.e., they tend to occur together in time and space) doesn't imply that there is causality (i.e., the presence of one reliably causes the other to occur).

Skinner (1948) designed an experiment that illustrates this distinction. He put several pigeons in Skinner boxes, set the food dispenser to deliver food every 15 seconds, and left the birds to their own devices. Later he returned and found the birds engaging in odd, idiosyncratic behaviours, such as pecking aimlessly in a corner or turning in circles. He referred to these behaviours as "superstitious" and offered a behaviourist analysis of their occurrence. The pigeons, he argued, were simply repeating behaviours that had been accidentally reinforced. That is, a pigeon that just happened to have pecked randomly in the corner when the food showed up had connected the delivery of food to that behaviour. Because this pecking behaviour was reinforced by the delivery of food, the pigeon was likely to repeat it. Now pecking in the corner was more likely to occur, and it was more likely to be reinforced 15 seconds later when the food appeared again. For each pigeon, the behaviour that is reinforced would most likely be whatever the pigeon happened to be doing when the food was first delivered. Skinner's pigeons acted as though there was a causal relationship between their behaviours and the appearance of food when it was merely an accidental correlation.

Although some researchers questioned Skinner's characterization of these behaviours as superstitious (Staddon & Simmelhag, 1971), later studies have shown that reinforcing adults or children using schedules in which reinforcement is not contingent on their responses can produce seemingly superstitious behaviour. It seems that people, like pigeons, behave as though there's a correlation between their responses and reward when in fact the connection is merely accidental (Bloom et al., 2007; Mellon, 2009; Ono, 1987; Wagner & Morris, 1987).

Baseball players who play well on days they happened not to have showered may continue that tradition, mistaking the accidental correlation between poor personal hygiene and a good day at bat as somehow causal. This "stench causes home runs" hypothesis is just one of many examples of human superstitions (Gilbert et al., 2000; Radford & Radford, 1949).

A Deeper Understanding of Operant Conditioning

Like classical conditioning, operant conditioning also quickly proved to be a powerful approach to learning. But Skinner, like Watson before him, was satisfied to observe an organism perform a learned behaviour; he didn't look for a deeper explanation of mental processes (Skinner, 1950). In this view, an organism behaved in a certain way in response to stimuli in the environment, not because the animal in question wanted, wished, or willed anything. However, some research on operant conditioning digs deeper into the underlying mechanisms that produce the familiar outcomes of reinforcement. As we did with classical conditioning earlier in this chapter, let's examine three elements that expand our view of operant conditioning: the cognitive, neural, and evolutionary elements of operant conditioning.

The Cognitive Elements of Operant Conditioning

Edward Chace Tolman (1886–1959) was one of the first researchers to question Skinner's strictly behaviourist interpretation of learning and was the strongest early advocate of a cognitive approach to operant learning. Tolman argued that there was more to learning than just knowing the circumstances in the environment (the properties of the stimulus) and being able to observe a particular outcome (the reinforced response). Instead, Tolman proposed that an animal established a means–ends relationship. That is, the conditioning experience produced knowledge or a belief that in this particular situation, a specific reward (the end state) will appear if a specific response (the means to that end) is made.

Tolman's means–ends relationship may remind you of the Rescorla–Wagner model of classical conditioning. Rescorla argued that the CS functions by setting

Edward Chace Tolman advocated a cognitive approach to operant learning and provided evidence that in maze-learning experiments, rats develop a mental picture of the maze, which he called a cognitive map.

latent learning A process in which something is learned, but it is not manifested as a behavioural change until sometime in the future.

cognitive map A mental representation of the physical features of the environment.

up an expectation about the arrival of a US, and expectations most certainly involve cognitive processes. In both Rescorla's and Tolman's theories, the stimulus does not directly evoke a response; rather, it establishes an internal cognitive state that then produces the behaviour. These cognitive theories of learning focus less on the stimulus–response (SR) connection and more on what happens in the organism's mind when faced with the stimulus. During the 1930s and 1940s, Tolman and his students conducted studies that focused on *latent learning* and *cognitive maps*, two phenomena that strongly suggest that simple S–R interpretations of operant learning behaviour are inadequate.

Latent Learning and Cognitive Maps In **latent learning**, *something is learned, but it is not manifested as a behavioural change until sometime in the future.* Latent learning can easily be established in rats and it occurs without any obvious reinforcement, a finding that posed a direct challenge to the then-dominant behaviourist position that all learning required some form of reinforcement (Tolman & Honzik, 1930a).

Tolman gave three groups of rats access to a complex maze every day over a span of 17 days. The control group never received any reinforcement for navigating the maze. They were simply allowed to run around until they reached the goal box at the end of the maze. In **FIGURE 7.10**, you can see that over the 17 days of the study, the control group (in green) got a little better at finding their way through the maze, but not by much. A second group of rats received regular reinforcements; when they reached the goal box, they found a small food reward there. Not surprisingly, these rats showed clear learning, as can be seen in blue in Figure 7.10. A third group was treated exactly like the control group for the first 10 days and then rewarded for the last 7 days. This group's behaviour (in orange) was quite striking. For the first 10 days, they behaved like the rats in the control group. However, during the final 7 days, they behaved a lot like the rats in the second group, which had been reinforced every day. Clearly, the rats in this third group had learned a lot about the maze and the location of the goal box during those first 10 days even though they had not received any reinforcements for their behaviour. In other words, they showed evidence of latent learning.

These results suggested to Tolman that beyond simply learning "start here, end here," his rats had developed a sophisticated mental picture of the maze. Tolman called this a **cognitive map**, *a mental representation of the physical features of the environment.* Tolman thought that the rats had developed a mental picture of the maze, along the lines of "make two lefts, then a right, then a quick left at the corner," and he devised several experiments to test that idea (Tolman & Honzik, 1930b; Tolman, Ritchie, & Kalish, 1946).

Further Support for Cognitive Explanations One simple experiment provided support for Tolman's theories and wreaked havoc with the noncognitive explanations offered by staunch behaviourists. Tolman trained a group of rats in the maze shown

Figure 7.10

Latent Learning Rats in a control group that never received any reinforcement (green curve) improved at finding their way through the maze over 17 days, but not by much. Rats that received regular reinforcements (blue curve) showed fairly clear learning; their error rate decreased steadily over time. Rats in the latent learning group (orange curve) were treated exactly like the control group rats for the first 10 days and then like the regularly rewarded group for the last 7 days. Their dramatic improvement on day 12 shows that these rats had learned a lot about the maze and the location of the goal box even though they had never received reinforcements.

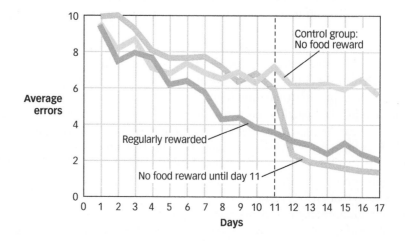

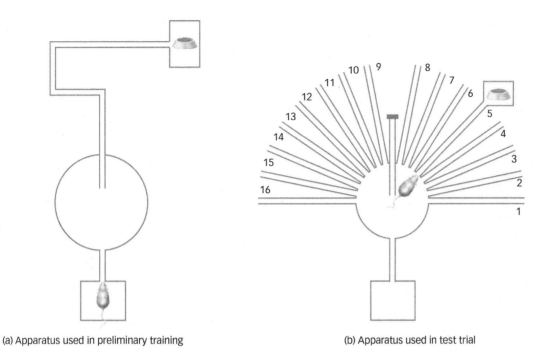

(a) Apparatus used in preliminary training

(b) Apparatus used in test trial

Figure 7.11
Cognitive Maps (a) Rats trained to run from a start box to a goal box in the maze on the left mastered the task quite readily. When those rats were then placed in the maze on the right (b), in which the main straightaway had been blocked, they did something unusual. Rather than simply backtracking and trying the next closest runway (i.e., one of those labelled 8 or 9 in the figure), which would be predicted by stimulus generalization, the rats typically chose runway 5, which led most directly to where the goal box had been during their training. The rats had formed a cognitive map of their environment and knew where they needed to end up spatially, relative to where they began.

in **FIGURE 7.11a**. As you can see, rats run down a straightaway, take a left, a right, a long right, ending up in the goal box at the end of the maze. Because we're looking at it from above, we can see that the rat's position at the end of the maze, relative to the starting point, is diagonal to the upper right. Of course, all that the rat in the maze sees is the next set of walls and turns until it eventually reaches the goal box. Nonetheless, rats learned to navigate this maze without error or hesitation after about four nights. Clever rats. But they were cleverer than you think.

After the rats had mastered the maze, Tolman changed things around a bit and put them in the maze shown in Figure 7.11b. The goal box was still in the same place relative to the start box. However, many alternative paths now spoked off the main platform, and the main straightaway that the rats had learned to use was blocked. Most behaviourists would predict that the rats in this situation—running down a familiar path only to find it blocked—would show stimulus generalization and pick the next closest path, such as one immediately adjacent to the straightaway. This is not what Tolman observed. When faced with the blocked path, the rats instead ran all the way down the path that led directly to the goal box. The rats had formed a sophisticated cognitive map of their environment and behaved in a way that suggested they were successfully following that map after the conditions had changed. Latent learning and cognitive maps suggest that operant conditioning involves an animal's doing much more than responding to a stimulus. Tolman's experiments strongly suggest that there is a cognitive component, even in rats, to operant learning.

Learning to Trust: For Better or Worse Cognitive factors also played a key role in an experiment that examined learning and brain activity (using fMRI) in people who played a "trust" game with a fictional partner (Delgado, Frank, & Phelps, 2005). On each trial, a participant could either keep a $1 reward or transfer the reward to a partner, who would receive $3. The partner could then either keep the $3 or share half of it with the participant. When playing with a partner who was willing to share the reward, the participant would be better off transferring the money, but when playing with a partner who did not share, the participant would be better off keeping the reward in the first place. Participants in such experiments typically find out who is trustworthy on the basis of trial-and-error learning during the game, transferring more money to partners who reinforce them by sharing.

In the study by Delgado and colleagues, participants were given detailed descriptions of their partners as either trustworthy, neutral, or suspect. Even though, during the game itself, the sharing behaviour of the three types of partners did not differ—they each reinforced participants to the same extent through sharing—the participants' cognitions about their partners had powerful effects. Participants transferred more money to the trustworthy partner than to the others, essentially ignoring the trial-by-trial feedback that would ordinarily shape their playing behaviour, thus reducing the amount of reward they received. Highlighting the power of the cognitive effect, signals in a part of the brain that ordinarily distinguishes between positive and negative feedback were evident only when participants played with the neutral partner; these feedback signals were absent when participants played with the trustworthy partner and decreased when participants played with the suspect partner.

These kinds of effects might help us understand otherwise perplexing real-life cases such as that of the American con artist Bernard Madoff, who in March 2009 pleaded guilty to swindling numerous investors out of billions of dollars in a highly publicized case that attracted worldwide attention. Madoff had been the chairman of the NASDAQ stock exchange and seemed to his investors an extremely trustworthy figure with whom they could safely invest their money. Those powerful cognitions might have caused investors to miss danger signals that otherwise would have led them to learn about the true nature of Madoff's operation. If so, the result was one of the most expensive failures of learning in modern history.

The Neural Elements of Operant Conditioning

Soon after psychologists came to appreciate the range and variety of things that could function as reinforcers, they began looking for underlying brain mechanisms that might account for these effects. The first hint of how specific brain structures might contribute to the process of reinforcement arose from the discovery of what came to be called *pleasure centres*. McGill researchers James Olds and Peter Milner inserted tiny electrodes into different parts of a rat's brain and allowed the animal to control electric stimulation of its own brain by pressing a bar. They discovered that some brain areas, particularly those in the limbic system (see the Neuroscience and Behaviour chapter), produced what appeared to be intensely positive experiences: The rats would press the bar repeatedly to stimulate these structures. The researchers observed that these rats would ignore food, water, and other life-sustaining necessities for hours on end simply to receive stimulation directly in the brain. They then called these parts of the brain pleasure centres (Olds, 1956) (see **FIGURE 7.12**).

In the years since these early studies, researchers have identified a number of structures and pathways in the brain that deliver rewards through stimulation (Wise, 1989, 2005). The neurons in the *medial forebrain bundle,* a pathway that meanders its way from the midbrain through the *hypothalamus* into the *nucleus accumbens,* are the most susceptible to stimulation that produces pleasure. This is not surprising because psychologists have identified this bundle of cells as crucial to behaviours that clearly involve pleasure, such as eating, drinking, and engaging in sexual activity. Second, the neurons all along this pathway and especially those in the nucleus accumbens itself are all *dopaminergic* (i.e., they secrete the neurotransmitter *dopamine*). Remember from the Neuroscience and Behaviour chapter that higher levels of dopamine in the brain are usually associated with

Bernard Madoff, shown here leaving a court hearing in March 2009, pleaded guilty to fraud after swindling billions of dollars from investors who trusted him.

Figure 7.12

Pleasure Centres in the Brain The nucleus accumbens, medial forebrain bundle, and hypothalamus are all major pleasure centres in the brain.

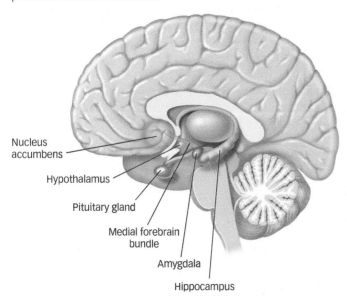

Nucleus accumbens

Hypothalamus

Pituitary gland

Medial forebrain bundle

Amygdala

Hippocampus

positive emotions. During recent years, several competing hypotheses about the precise role of dopamine have emerged, including the idea that dopamine is more closely linked with the expectation of reward than with reward itself (Fiorillo, Newsome, & Schultz, 2008; Schultz, 2016) or that dopamine is more closely associated with wanting or even *craving* something rather than simply liking it (Berridge, 2007).

Whichever view turns out to be correct, researchers have found good support for a reward centre in which dopamine plays a key role. First, as you've just seen, rats will work to stimulate this pathway at the expense of other basic needs (Olds & Fobes, 1981). However, if drugs that block the action of dopamine are administered to the rats, they cease stimulating the pleasure centres (Stellar, Kelley, & Corbett, 1983). Second, drugs such as cocaine, amphetamine, and opiates, activate these pathways and centres (Moghaddam & Bunney, 1989), but dopamine-blocking drugs dramatically diminish their reinforcing effects (White & Milner, 1992). Third, fMRI studies show increased activity in the nucleus accumbens in heterosexual men looking at pictures of attractive women (Aharon et al., 2001) and in individuals who believe they are about to receive money (Cooper et al., 2009; Knutson et al., 2001). Finally, rats that are given primary reinforcers (e.g., food or water) or that are allowed to engage in sexual activity show increased dopamine secretion in the nucleus accumbens—but only if they are hungry, thirsty, or sexually aroused (Damsma et al., 1992).

This last finding is exactly what we might expect, given our earlier discussion of the complexities of reinforcement. After all, food tastes a lot better when we are hungry, and sexual activity is more pleasurable when we are aroused. The biological structures that underlie rewards and reinforcements probably evolved to ensure that species engaged in activities to help their survival and reproduction. (For more on the relationship between dopamine and Parkinson's, see Hot Science: Dopamine and Reward Learning: From Parkinson's Disease to Gambling.)

The Evolutionary Elements of Operant Conditioning

As you'll recall, classical conditioning has an adaptive value that has been fine-tuned by evolution. Not surprisingly, we can also view operant conditioning from an evolutionary perspective. This viewpoint grew out of a set of curious observations from the early days of conditioning experiments. Several behaviourists who were using simple T mazes, such as the one shown in **FIGURE 7.13**, to study learning in rats discovered that if a rat found food in one arm of the maze on the first trial of the day, it typically ran down the *other* arm on the very next trial. A staunch behaviourist wouldn't expect the rats to behave this way. After all, the rats in these experiments were hungry, and they had just been reinforced for turning in a particular direction. According to operant conditioning, this should *increase* the likelihood of their turning in that same direction, not reduce it. With additional trials, the rats eventually learned to go to the arm with the food, but they had to learn to overcome this initial tendency to go the wrong way. How can we explain this?

What was puzzling from a behaviourist perspective makes sense when viewed from an evolutionary perspective. Rats are foragers, and like all foraging species, they have evolved a highly adaptive strategy for survival. They move around in their environment, looking for food. If they find it somewhere, they eat it (or store it) and then go look somewhere else for more. If they do not find food, they forage in another part of the environment. So if the rat just found food in the *right* arm of a T maze, the obvious place to look next time is the *left* arm. The rat knows that there isn't any more food in the right arm because it just ate the food it found there! Indeed, foraging animals such as rats have well-developed spatial representations that allow them to search their environment efficiently. If given the opportunity to explore a complex

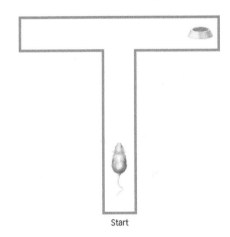

Start

Figure 7.13

A Simple T Maze When rats find food in the right arm of a typical T maze, on the next trial, they will often run to the left arm of the maze. This contradicts basic principles of operant conditioning: If the behaviour of running to the right arm is reinforced, it should be more likely to occur again in the future. However, this behaviour is perfectly consistent with a rat's evolutionary preparedness. Like most foraging animals, rats explore their environments in search of food and seldom return to where food has already been found. If the rat already has found food in the right arm of the T maze, it quite sensibly will search the left arm next to see if more food is there.

Hot Science | Dopamine and Reward Learning: From Parkinson's Disease to Gambling

The neurotransmitter dopamine plays an important role in reward-based learning, especially *reward prediction error*, the difference between the actual reward received and the amount of predicted or expected reward. For example, when an animal presses a lever and receives an unexpected food reward, a *positive* prediction error occurs (a better-than-expected outcome), and the animal learns to press the lever again. By contrast, when an animal expects to receive a reward from pressing a lever but does not receive it, a *negative* prediction error occurs (a worse-than-expected outcome), and the animal subsequently will be less likely to press the lever again. Reward prediction error can thus be a kind of "teaching signal" that helps the animal learn to behave in a way that maximizes reward.

In pioneering studies linking reward prediction error to dopamine, Wolfram Schultz and his colleagues recorded activity in dopamine neurons located in the reward centres of a monkey's brain. They found that those neurons showed increased activity when the monkey received unexpected juice rewards but showed decreased activity when the monkey did not receive expected juice rewards. This suggests that dopamine neurons play an important role in generating the reward prediction error (Schultz, 2016; Schultz, Dayan, & Montague, 1997). Schultz and his colleagues' observations have been backed up by studies that use neuroimaging techniques to show that human brain regions involved in reward-related learning also produce reward prediction error signals and that dopamine is involved in generating those signals (Howard & Kahnt, 2018; Pessiglione et al., 2006).

Recent research has shown that these findings have important implications for people with Parkinson's disease, which involves movement disorders and loss of neurons that produce dopamine. As you learned in the Neuroscience and Behaviour chapter, the drug L-dopa is often used to treat Parkinson's disease because it spurs surviving neurons to produce more dopamine.

Several studies report that reward-related learning can be impaired in individuals with Parkinson's (Dagher & Robbins, 2009; Skvortsova et al., 2017), and others provide evidence that when individuals with Parkinson's perform reward-related learning tasks, the reward prediction error signal is disrupted (Meder et al., 2018; Schonberg et al., 2009). There is also evidence that Parkinson's treatment drugs can interfere with reward-related learning and the reward prediction error signal (García-García, Zeighami, & Dagher, 2017; Rutledge et al., 2009).

These results may relate to another intriguing feature of Parkinson's disease: Some individuals with the disease develop serious problems with compulsive gambling, shopping, and related impulsive behaviours. Such problems seem to be largely the consequence of Parkinson's drugs that stimulate dopamine receptors (Ahlskog, 2011; Weintraub, Papay, & Siderowf, 2013). Indeed, neuroimaging studies have provided evidence of increased dopamine responses to reward cues in Parkinson's patients who develop problems with compulsive gambling as a consequence of drugs that stimulate dopamine receptors (Clark & Dagher, 2014).

These findings linking dopamine and risk-taking behaviours such as gambling may have more general implications. In

Recent findings suggest that boosting dopamine levels increases propensity to gamble.

a study by Rigoli et al. (2016), healthy adults performed a task in which they could either choose a guaranteed monetary reward or take a gamble by choosing an option in which they would receive double the guaranteed reward or nothing at all. The researchers examined the effect of boosting dopamine levels on performance of this task by administering L-dopa to the participants in one experimental session, versus administering a placebo to the same participants in a separate session. Importantly, administering L-dopa increased participants' overall propensity to gamble when performing the choice task.

Although much remains to be learned about how dopamine impacts reward learning and cognition more generally (Martins, Mehta, & Prada, 2017; Westbrook & Frank, 2018), future studies that combine drug manipulations, neuroimaging, and controlled learning paradigms should have important scientific and practical implications.

environment such as the multi-arm maze shown in **FIGURE 7.14**, rats will systematically go from arm to arm collecting food, rarely returning to an arm they have previously visited (Olton & Samuelson, 1976).

Two of Skinner's former students, Keller Breland and Marian Breland, were among the first researchers to discover that it wasn't just rats in T mazes that presented a problem for behaviourists (Breland & Breland, 1961). The Brelands pointed

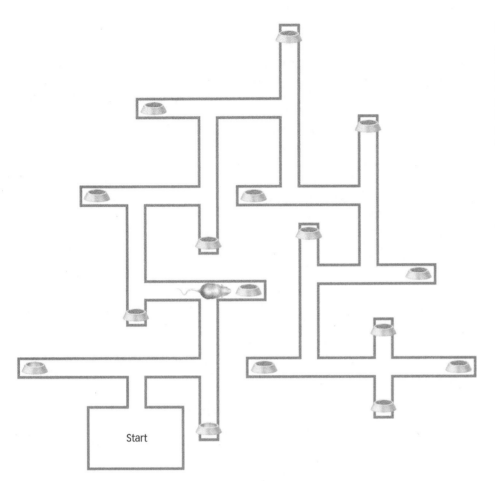

Figure 7.14
A Complex T Maze Like many other foraging species, rats placed in a complex T maze such as this one show evidence of their evolutionary preparedness. These rats will systematically travel from arm to arm in search of food, never returning to arms they have already visited.

Start

out that psychologists and the organisms they study often seemed to "disagree" on what the organisms should be doing. Their argument was simple: When this kind of dispute develops, the animals are always right, and the psychologists had better rethink their theories.

The Brelands, who made a career out of training animals for commercials and movies, often used pigs because pigs are surprisingly good at learning all sorts of tricks. However, they discovered that it was extremely difficult to teach a pig the simple task of dropping coins in a box. Instead of depositing the coins, the pigs persisted in rooting with them as if they were digging them up in soil, tossing them in the air with their snouts and pushing them around. The Brelands tried to train raccoons at the same task, with different but equally dismal results. The raccoons spent their time rubbing the coins between their paws instead of dropping them in the box.

The misbehaviour of organisms: Pigs are biologically predisposed to root out their food, just as raccoons are predisposed to wash their food. Trying to train either species to behave differently can prove to be an exercise in futility.

Having learned the association between the coins and food, the animals began to treat the coins as stand-ins for food. Pigs are biologically predisposed to root out their food, and raccoons have evolved to clean their food by rubbing it with their paws. That is exactly what each species of animal did with the coins.

The Brelands' work shows that all species, including humans, are biologically predisposed to learn some things more readily than others and to respond to stimuli in ways that are consistent with their evolutionary history (Gallistel, 2000). Such adaptive behaviours, however, evolved over extraordinarily long periods and in particular environmental contexts. If those circumstances change, some of the behavioural mechanisms that support learning can lead an organism astray. Raccoons that associated coins with food failed to follow the simple route to obtaining food by dropping the coins in the box; "nature" took over and they wasted time rubbing the coins together. The point is that, although much of every organism's behaviour results from predispositions sharpened by evolutionary mechanisms, these mechanisms sometimes can have ironic consequences.

Build to the Outcomes

1. What is the law of effect?
2. What do "positive" and "negative" mean in operant conditioning?
3. Why is reinforcement more constructive than punishment in learning a desired behaviour?
4. What are primary and secondary reinforcers?
5. How does the concept of delayed reinforcement relate to difficulties with quitting smoking?
6. What does it mean to say that learning takes place in contexts?
7. How is the concept of extinction different in operant conditioning than in classical conditioning?
8. How does a radio station use scheduled reinforcements to keep you listening?
9. How do ratio schedules work to keep you spending your money?
10. How can operant conditioning produce complex behaviours?
11. What are cognitive maps? Why are they a challenge to behaviourism?
12. How do specific brain structures contribute to the process of reinforcement?
13. What explains a rat's behaviour in a T maze?

Observational Learning: Look at Me

Learning Outcomes

- Explain the social, cultural, and evolutionary aspects of observational learning.

- Compare evidence of observational learning in animals raised among humans with that in animals raised in the wild.

- Explain the neural elements of observational learning.

observational learning A process in which an organism learns by watching the actions of others.

Four-year-old Rodney and his 2-year-old sister Margie had always been told to keep away from the stove, which is good advice for any child and many an adult. Being a mischievous imp, however, Rodney decided one day to heat up a burner and place his hand over it until the singeing of his flesh led him to recoil, shrieking in pain. Rodney was more scared than hurt, really—and no one hearing this story doubts that he learned something important that day. But little Margie, who stood by watching these events unfold, *also* learned the same lesson. Rodney's story is a behaviourist's textbook example: The administration of punishment led to a learned change in his behaviour. But how can we explain Margie's learning? She received neither punishment nor reinforcement—indeed, she didn't even have direct experience with the wicked appliance—yet it's arguable that she's just as likely to keep her hands away from stoves in the future as Rodney is.

Margie's is a case of **observational learning**, in which *an organism learns by watching the actions of others*. Observational learning challenges behaviourism's reinforcement-based explanations of classical and operant conditioning, but there is no doubt that this type of learning produces changes in behaviour. In all societies, appropriate social behaviour is passed on from generation to generation largely through observation (Bandura, 1965). The rituals and behaviours that are a part of our culture are acquired by each new generation, not only through deliberate training of the young but also through young people observing the patterns of behaviours of their elders and each other (Flynn & Whiten, 2008).

Tasks such as using chopsticks or operating a TV's remote control are more easily acquired if we watch these activities being carried out before we try them ourselves. Even complex motor tasks, such as performing surgery, are learned in part through extensive observation and imitation of models. And anyone who is about to undergo surgery is grateful for observational learning. Just the thought of a generation of surgeons acquiring their surgical techniques through the trial-and-error methods that Thorndike studied, or the shaping of successive approximations that captivated Skinner, would make any of us very nervous.

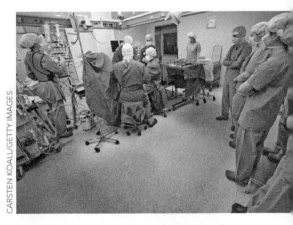

Happily, recent research on observational learning in surgeons and other medical professionals is providing useful new information about how to optimize learning from watching others (Cordovani & Cordovani, 2016; Harris et al., 2018).

Observational Learning In Humans

In a series of studies that have become landmarks in psychology, Canadian psychologist Albert Bandura and his colleagues investigated the parameters of observational learning (Bandura, Ross, & Ross, 1961; for additional discussion of Bandura's work, see the Social Psychology chapter). The researchers escorted individual preschoolers into a play area, where they found a number of desirable toys that 4-year-olds typically like. An adult *model*—someone whose behaviour might be a guide for others—was then led into the room and seated in the opposite corner, where among other toys was a Bobo doll, which is a large, inflatable plastic toy with a weighted bottom that allows it to bounce back upright when knocked down. The adult played quietly for a bit but then started aggressing towards the Bobo doll, knocking it down, jumping on it, hitting it with a toy mallet, kicking it around the room, and yelling "Pow!" and "Kick him!" When the children who observed these actions were later allowed to play with a variety of toys, including a child-size Bobo doll, they were more than twice as likely to interact with it in an aggressive manner as a group of children who hadn't observed the aggressive model.

So what? Kids like to break stuff, and after all, Bobo dolls are made to be punched. Also, children in both groups had been to some extent biased towards aggressive behaviour just before being given the opportunity to play with the Bobo doll: The experimenter had stopped them from playing with some especially attractive toys, which she said were reserved for other children. As **FIGURE 7.15** shows, the degree of imitation displayed by the children who had initially observed the aggressive model was startling. In fact, the adult model purposely used novel behaviours such as hitting the doll with the toy mallet or throwing it up in the air, so that the researchers could distinguish aggressive acts that were clearly the result of observational learning.

The children in these studies also showed that they were sensitive to the consequences of the actions they observed. When they saw the adult models being punished for behaving aggressively, the children showed considerably less aggression. When the children observed a model being rewarded and praised for aggressive behaviour, they displayed an increase in aggression (Bandura, Ross, & Ross, 1963). The observational learning seen in Bandura's studies has implications for social learning and cultural transmission of behaviours, norms, and values (Bandura, 1977, 1994).

Research with children has shown that observational learning is well suited to seeding behaviours that can spread widely across a culture through a process called a **diffusion chain**, whereby *individuals initially learn a behaviour by observing another individual perform that behaviour, and then become models from which other individuals learn the behaviour* (Flynn, 2008; Flynn & Whiten, 2008). Experiments investigating the operation of diffusion chains in preschool-age children have used a procedure in which a child (B) observes an adult model (A) performing a target act, such as using a novel tool to obtain a reward. Then, B becomes a model for another child, C, who watches B perform the target act, followed by child D observing C

diffusion chain A process whereby individuals initially learn a behaviour by observing another individual perform that behaviour, and then become models from which other individuals learn the behaviour.

© ALBERT BANDURA, DEPT. OF PSYCHOLOGY, STANFORD UNIVERSITY

Figure 7.15

Beating Up Bobo Children who were exposed to an adult model who behaved aggressively towards a Bobo doll were likely to behave aggressively towards the doll themselves. This behaviour occurred in the absence of any direct reinforcement. Observational learning was responsible for producing the children's behaviours.

Coaches rely on observational learning when they demonstrate techniques to athletes.

AP PHOTO/ROBERT F. BUKATY

perform the target act, and so forth. The evidence to date indicates that children can learn how to use a novel tool by observing an adult model use that tool; more importantly, they can then become effective models for other children to learn how to use that tool.

Initial studies of diffusion chains showed that behaviours such as novel tool use could be spread accurately across 10 children (Flynn & Whiten, 2008; Horner et al., 2006). More recent work indicates faithful transmission of tool use across a diffusion chain comprising 20 children (Hopper et al., 2010). These findings of transmission across multiple "cultural generations" underscore that observational learning is well suited for transmission through a diffusion chain and thus a potentially powerful means of influencing a culture (Legare & Nielsen, 2015).

Observational learning is important in many domains of everyday life. Sports provide a good example. Coaches in just about all sports rely on observational learning when demonstrating critical techniques and skills for their players, and athletes also have numerous opportunities to observe other athletes perform. Studies of varsity- and recreational-level athletes in both team and individual sports indicate that they all report relying heavily on observational learning to improve their performance of critical skills in their respective sports, with varsity athletes reporting an even greater reliance on observational learning than recreational athletes (Wesch, Law, & Hall, 2007). But can merely observing a skill result in an improvement in performing that skill without actually practicing it? A number of studies have shown that observing someone else perform a motor task, ranging from reaching for a target to pressing a sequence of keys, can produce robust learning in the observer. In fact, observational learning sometimes results in just as much learning as practicing the task itself (Heyes & Foster, 2002; Mattar & Gribble, 2005; Vinter & Perruchet, 2002).

Observational learning is especially effective when people can observe both experts and novices perform a task, because they can learn to avoid making the same errors the novices made (Andrieux & Prouteau, 2014). Recent research has also shown that although interrupting performance of a motor task impairs learning during physical practice, it has no impact on observational learning of the interrupted task (Badets, Boudin, & Michelet, 2018), suggesting that observational learning can be more flexible than physical motor learning.

Observational Learning in Animals

Humans aren't the only creatures capable of learning through observing. A wide variety of species learn by observing. In one study, for example, pigeons watched other pigeons get reinforced for either pecking at the feeder or stepping on a bar. When placed in the box later, the pigeons tended to use whatever technique they had observed the other pigeons use earlier (Zentall, Sutton, & Sherburne, 1996).

In an interesting series of studies, researchers showed that laboratory-raised rhesus monkeys that had never seen a snake would develop a fear of snakes simply by observing the fear reactions of other monkeys (Cook & Mineka, 1990; Mineka & Cook, 1988). In fact, the fear reactions of these lab-raised monkeys were so authentic and pronounced that they could be models for still *other* lab-raised monkeys, creating a kind of observational learning "chain" that resembles the diffusion chains seen in young children that we discussed earlier. Indeed, more recent studies have provided evidence that other behaviours acquired through observational learning among chimpanzees can be transmitted along such diffusion chains, such as ways to search for food (Horner et al., 2006; Whiten, 2017). These findings highlight that diffusion chains are not unique to humans and indeed contribute to behaviours that are critical for survival (Whiten & van de Waal, 2018).

The results on fear learning also support our earlier discussion of how each species has evolved particular biological predispositions for specific behaviours. Virtually every rhesus monkey raised in the wild has a fear of snakes, which strongly suggests that such a fear is one of this species' predispositions. This research also helps explain why some phobias that humans suffer from, such as fear of heights (acrophobia) or of enclosed spaces (claustrophobia), are so common, even in people who have never had unpleasant experiences in these contexts (Mineka & Ohman, 2002). The fears may emerge not from specific conditioning experiences but from observing and learning from the reactions of others.

Monkeys can learn to fear snakes through observational learning if they see another monkey reacting with fear to the sight of a snake. But monkeys cannot be trained to fear flowers through observational learning—no matter how many times they watch another monkey who has been conditioned to fear the same flower. How does the principle of biological preparedness account for this finding?

Monkeys and Chimpanzees Can Learn to Use Tools Through Observation

One of the most important questions about observational learning in animals concerns whether monkeys and chimpanzees can learn to use tools by observing tool use in others, which we've already seen that young children can accomplish. In one of the first controlled studies to examine this issue, chimpanzees observed a model (the experimenter) use a metal bar shaped like a T to pull items of food towards them (Tomasello et al., 1987). Compared with a group that did not observe any tool use, these chimpanzees showed more learning when later performing the task themselves. However, the researchers noted that the chimpanzees hardly ever used the tool in the exact same way that the model did.

So, in a later experiment, they introduced a novel twist (Nagell, Olguin, & Tomasello, 1993). In one condition, a model used a rake in its normal position (with the teeth pointed towards the ground) to capture a food reward—but this method was rather inefficient because the teeth were widely spaced, and the food sometimes slipped between them. In a second condition, the model flipped over the rake, so that the teeth were pointed up and the flat edge of the rake touched the ground—a more effective procedure for capturing the food. Both groups that observed tool use performed better when trying to obtain the food themselves than did a control group that did not observe a model use the tool. However, the chimpanzees who observed the more efficient procedure did not use it any more often than did those who observed the less efficient procedure—the two groups performed identically. By contrast, 2-year-old children exposed to the same conditions used the rake in the exact same way that each of the models did in the two observational learning conditions. The chimpanzees seemed only to be learning that the tool could be used to obtain food, whereas the children learned something specific about how to use the tool.

Chimpanzees Raised with Humans Learn to Imitate Exact Actions

The chimpanzees in these studies had been raised by their mothers in the wild. In a related study, the researchers asked whether chimpanzees who had been raised in environments that also included human contact could learn to imitate the exact actions performed by a model (Tomasello, Savage-Rumbaugh, & Kruger, 1993). The answer was a resounding yes: Chimpanzees raised in a more humanlike environment showed more specific observational learning than did those who had been reared by their mothers and performed similarly to human children. This finding led Tomasello and colleagues (1993) to put forth what they termed the *enculturation hypothesis:* Being raised in a human culture has a profound effect on the cognitive abilities of chimpanzees, especially their ability to understand the intentions of others when performing tasks such as using tools, which in turn increases their observational learning capacities. Others have criticized this hypothesis (Bering, 2004), noting that there is relatively little evidence in support of it beyond the results of the Tomasello et al. study (1993).

However, more recent research has found something similar in capuchin monkeys, who are known for their tool use in the wild, such as employing branches or stone hammers to crack open nuts (Boinski, Quatrone, & Swartz, 2000; Fragaszy et al., 2004) or using stones to dig up buried roots (Moura & Lee, 2004). Fredman and Whiten (2008) studied monkeys who had been reared in the wild by their mothers or by human families in Israel as part of a project to train the monkeys to aid quadriplegics. A model demonstrated two ways of using a screwdriver to gain access to a food reward hidden in a box. Some monkeys observed the model poke through a hole in the centre of the box, whereas others watched him pry open the lid at the rim of the box (see **FIGURE 7.16**). A control group did not observe any use of the tool. Both mother-reared and human-reared monkeys showed evidence of observational learning compared with those in the control group, but the human-reared monkeys carried out the exact action they had observed more often than did the mother-reared monkeys.

Although this evidence implies that there is a cultural influence on the cognitive processes that support observational learning, the researchers noted that the effects on observational learning could be attributed to any number of influences on the human-reared monkeys, including more experience with tools, more attention to a model's behaviour, or, as originally suggested by Tomasello et al. (1993), increased sensitivity to the intentions of others. Thus, more work is needed to understand the exact nature of those processes (Damerius et al., 2017; Mesoudi et al., 2015; Tomasello & Call, 2004).

Neural Elements of Observational Learning

Observational learning involves a neural component as well. As you read in the Neuroscience and Behaviour chapter, *mirror neurons* are a type of cell found in the brains of primates (including humans). They fire when an animal performs an action, as when a monkey reaches for a food item. More important, however, mirror neurons

Figure 7.16

Observational Learning Monkeys who had been reared in the wild by their mothers or reared by human families watched a model either (*top*) poke a screwdriver through a hole in the centre of a box to obtain a food reward or (*bottom*) pry open the lid to obtain the reward. Both groups showed some evidence of observational learning, but the human-reared monkeys were more likely to carry out the exact action they had watched.

also fire when an animal watches someone *else* perform the same specific task (Rizzolatti & Craighero, 2004). Although this "someone else" is usually a fellow member of the same species, some research suggests that mirror neurons in monkeys also fire when they observe humans performing an action (Fogassi et al., 2005). For example, monkeys' mirror neurons fired when they observed humans grasping for a piece of food, either to eat it or to place it in a container.

Mirror neurons, then, may play a critical role in the imitation of behaviour as well as the prediction of future behaviour (Rizzolatti, 2004). Mirror neurons are thought to be located in specific subregions in the frontal and parietal lobes, and there is evidence that individual subregions respond most strongly to observing certain kinds of actions (see **FIGURE 7.17**). If appropriate neurons fire when an animal sees another animal performing an action, it could indicate an awareness of intentionality or that the animal is anticipating a likely course of future actions. Although the exact functions of mirror neurons continue to be debated (Hickok, 2009, 2014; Rizzolatti & Rozzi, 2018), both of these elements—rote imitation of well-understood behaviours and an awareness of how behaviour is likely to unfold—contribute to observational learning.

Studies of observational learning in healthy adults have shown that watching someone else perform a task engages some of the same brain regions that are activated when people actually perform the task themselves. Do you consider yourself a good dancer? Have you ever watched someone who is a good dancer—a friend or maybe a celebrity on *Dancing with the Stars*—in the hopes of improving your own dance-floor moves? In one fMRI study, participants performed two tasks for several days prior to scanning: practicing dance sequences to unfamiliar techno-dance songs and watching music videos of other dance sequences accompanied by unfamiliar techno-dance songs (Cross et al., 2009). The participants were then scanned while viewing videos of sequences that they had previously danced or watched, as well as videos of sequences they had not danced or watched (untrained sequences).

Analysis of the fMRI data revealed that in comparison with the untrained sequences, viewing the previously danced or watched sequences recruited largely similar brain networks, including regions considered part of the mirror neuron system, as well as a couple of brain regions that showed more activity for previously danced than watched videos. The results of a surprise dancing test given to participants after the conclusion of scanning showed that performance was better on sequences previously watched than on the untrained sequences, demonstrating significant observational learning; but performance was best of all on the previously danced sequences (Cross et al., 2009). So although watching *Dancing with the Stars* might indeed improve your dancing skills, practicing on the dance floor should help even more.

Related evidence indicates that observational learning of some motor skills relies on the motor cortex, which is known to be critical for motor learning. For example, when participants watch another individual engage in a task that involves making a complex reaching movement, significant observational learning occurs (Mattar & Gribble, 2005). To examine whether the observational learning depends on the motor cortex, researchers applied transcranial magnetic stimulation (TMS) to the motor cortex just after participants observed performance of the reaching movement. (As you learned in the Neuroscience and Behaviour chapter, TMS results in a temporary disruption in the function of the brain region to which it is applied.) In a striking finding, applying TMS to the motor cortex greatly reduced the amount of observational learning, whereas applying TMS to a control region outside the motor cortex had no effect on observational learning (Brown, Wilson, & Gribble, 2009).

These findings indicate that some kinds of observational learning are grounded in brain regions that are essential for action. When one organism patterns its actions on another organism's behaviours, learning is speeded up, and potentially dangerous errors (think of Margie, who won't burn her hand on the stove) are prevented.

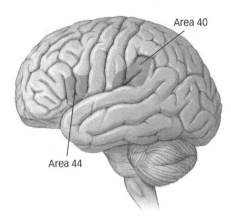

Figure 7.17

Mirror Neuron System Regions in the frontal lobe (area 44) and parietal lobe (area 40) are thought to be part of the mirror neuron system in humans.

Observing skilled dancers, such as this energetic pair on *So You Think You Can Dance*, engages many of the same brain regions as does actual dance practice, and can produce significant learning.

Build to the Outcomes

1. What is observational learning?
2. Why might a younger sibling appear to learn faster than a firstborn?
3. What did the Bobo doll experiment show about children and aggressive behaviour?
4. What is a diffusion chain?
5. What are the cognitive differences between chimpanzees raised among humans and those raised in the wild?
6. What do mirror neurons do?

Implicit Learning: Under the Radar

Learning Outcomes

- Explain why language studies led to studies of implicit learning.

- Outline the number of ways that implicit and explicit learning differ.

It's safe to assume that people are sensitive to the patterns of events that occur in the world around them. Most people don't stumble through life, thoroughly unaware of what's going on. Okay, maybe your roommate does. But people usually are attuned to linguistic, social, emotional, or sensorimotor events in the world around them—so much so that they gradually build up internal representations of those patterns that they acquired without explicit awareness. This process is often called **implicit learning**, or *learning that takes place largely independent of awareness of both the process and the products of information acquisition.* Because it occurs without our awareness, implicit learning is knowledge that sneaks in "under the radar."

Habituation, which we discussed at the outset of this chapter, is a very simple kind of implicit learning in which repeated exposure to a stimulus results in a reduced response. Habituation occurs even in a simple organism such as *Aplysia,* which lacks the brain structures necessary for explicit learning, such as the hippocampus (Eichenbaum, 2008; Squire & Kandel, 1999). In contrast, some forms of learning start out explicitly but become more implicit over time. When you first learned to drive a car, for example, you probably devoted a lot of attention to the many movements and sequences that you needed to carry out simultaneously. ("Step lightly on the accelerator while you push the turn indicator, and look in the rearview mirror while you turn the steering wheel.") That complex interplay of motions is now probably quite effortless and automatic for you. Explicit learning has become implicit over time.

These distinctions in learning might remind you of similar distinctions in memory, and for good reason. In the Memory chapter, you read about the differences between *implicit* and *explicit* memories. Do implicit and explicit learning mirror implicit and explicit memory? It's not that simple, but it is true that learning and memory are inextricably linked. Learning produces memories, and, conversely, the existence of memories implies that knowledge was acquired, that experience was registered and recorded in the brain, or that learning has taken place.

Ten years ago, no one knew how to type using their thumbs; now just about all teenagers do it automatically.

MARY ALTAFFER/AP IMAGES

implicit learning Learning that takes place largely independent of awareness of both the process and the products of information acquisition.

Cognitive Approaches to Implicit Learning

Psychologists became interested in implicit learning when researchers began to investigate how children learn language and social conduct (Reber, 1967). Most children, by the time they are 6 or 7 years old, are fairly sophisticated in terms of linguistics and social behaviour. Yet most children reach this state with very little explicit awareness that they have learned something, and with equally little awareness of what it was they actually learned. For example, although children are often given explicit rules of social conduct ("Don't chew with your mouth open"), they learn through experience how to behave in a civilized way. They're probably not aware of when or how they learned a particular course of action and may not even be able to state the general principle underlying their behaviour. Yet most kids have learned not to eat with their feet, to listen when they are spoken to, and not to kick the dog.

What Research in the Lab Shows

To investigate implicit learning in the laboratory, researchers, in early studies, showed participants 15- or 20-letter strings and asked them to memorize them. The letter strings, which at first glance look like nonsense syllables, were actually formed using a complex set of rules called an *artificial grammar* (see **FIGURE 7.18**). Participants were not told anything about the rules, but, with experience, they gradually developed a vague, intuitive sense of the "correctness" of particular letter groupings. Once these letter groups became familiar to the participants, they processed them more rapidly and efficiently than the "incorrect" letter groupings (Reber, 1967, 1996).

Take a look at the letter strings shown in Figure 7.18. Those on the left are correct and follow the rules of the artificial grammar; those on the right all violate the rules. The differences are pretty subtle, and if you haven't been through the learning phase of the experiment, both sets look a lot alike. In fact, each nongrammatical string has only a single letter violation. Research participants were asked to classify new letter strings according to whether they follow the rules of the grammar. People turn out to be quite good at this task (usually they get 60–70% correct), but they are unable to provide much in the way of explicit awareness of the rules and regularities that they are using. The experience is similar to coming across a sentence with a grammatical error. You are immediately aware that something is wrong, and you can certainly make the sentence grammatical, but unless you are a trained linguist, you'll probably find it difficult to articulate which rules of English grammar were violated or which rules you used to repair the sentence.

Other studies of implicit learning have used a *serial reaction time* task (Nissen & Bullemer, 1987). Here, research participants are presented with five small boxes on a computer screen. Each box lights up briefly; when that happens the participant is asked to press the button just beneath that box as quickly as possible. Like the artificial grammar task, the sequence of lights appears to be random but in fact follows a pattern. Research participants eventually get faster with practice as they learn to anticipate which box is most likely to light up next. But if asked, they are generally unaware that there is a pattern to the lights.

Implicit learning has some characteristics that distinguish it from explicit learning. For example, when asked to carry out implicit tasks, people differ relatively little from one another; but on explicit tasks (e.g., conscious problem solving), they show large differences across individuals (Reber et al., 1991). Implicit learning also seems to be unrelated to IQ: People with high scores on standard intelligence tests are no better at implicit learning tasks, on average, than those whose scores are more modest (Reber & Allen, 2000). Perhaps even more striking, recent evidence indicates that at least one form of implicit learning is *enhanced* in autistic adults whose IQs are matched to those of nonautistic adults (see A World of Difference: Implicit Learning in Autism Spectrum Disorder).

Implicit learning changes little across the life span. Researchers discovered well-developed implicit learning of complex, rule-governed auditory patterns in 8-month-old infants (Saffran, Aslin, & Newport, 1996). Infants listened to streams of speech that contained experimenter-defined nonsense words. For instance, the infants might hear a sequence such as "bidakupadotigolabubidaku," which contains the nonsense word *bida*. The infants weren't given any explicit clues as to which sounds were "words" and which were not, but after several repetitions, the infants showed signs that they had learned the novel words. Infants tend to prefer novel information, and they spent more time listening to novel nonsense words that had not been presented earlier than to the nonsense words such as *bida* that had been presented. It was remarkable that the infants in this study were as good at learning these sequences as university students.

Grammatical Strings	Nongrammatical Strings
VXJJ	VXTJJ
XXVT	XVTVVJ
VJTVXJ	VJTTVTV
VJTVTV	VJTXXVJ
XXXXVX	XXXVTJJ

Figure 7.18

Artificial Grammar and Implicit Learning These are examples of letter strings formed by an artificial grammar. Research participants are exposed to the rules of the grammar and are later tested on new letter strings. Participants show reliable accuracy at distinguishing the valid, grammatical strings from the invalid, nongrammatical strings—even though they usually can't explicitly state the rule they are following when making such judgments. Using an artificial grammar is one way of studying implicit learning (Reber, 1996).

A World of Difference | Implicit Learning in Autism Spectrum Disorder

As pointed out elsewhere in this chapter, implicit learning generally doesn't differ much among individuals. But recent research has uncovered a striking exception. In the Psychological Disorders chapter, you will become acquainted with a condition known as autism spectrum disorder (ASD).

People with ASD have communication problems and engage in repetitive and restricted behaviours. But they also have some intriguing strengths, such as normal or even superior visuospatial abilities, relative to impaired verbal abilities (Caron et al., 2006). This pattern is clearest in situations in which the task is to focus on parts or local details of a visual display, as opposed to the "big picture" of how all the parts fit together (Happé & Frith, 2006; Rondan & Deruelle, 2004).

Roser and colleagues (2015) recently sought to test this in an implicit learning experiment. Participants viewed a series of nine-box grids, each containing a pair of visual shapes (the three grids in the image at top right were taken from a longer series). Unknown to the participants, the pairs of visual shapes always appeared in a particular spatial relationship to one another: shapes 1 and 2 always side by side; shapes 3 and 4 always diagonally apart; and shape 5 always above shape 6 (these constant spatial relationships are shown in the bottom grid; participants never saw this grid). During the learning phase of the experiment, participants were shown hundreds of grids containing different combinations of these shapes and were instructed simply to look at the shapes in the grids, which appeared for about 3 seconds each.

After viewing the grids, participants were asked a series of questions designed to probe their *explicit* awareness of the spatial relationships among the shapes they had seen:

1. Can you tell me anything about the things you have just seen?

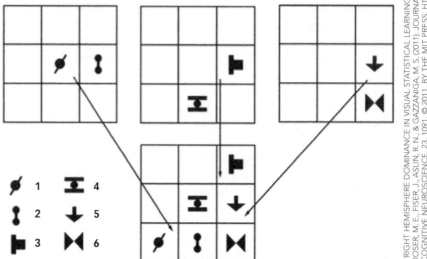

"RIGHT HEMISPHERE DOMINANCE IN VISUAL STATISTICAL LEARNING" BY ROSER, M. E., FISER, J., ASLIN, R. N., & GAZZANIGA, M. S. (2011), JOURNAL OF COGNITIVE NEUROSCIENCE, 23, 1091. © 2011, BY THE MIT PRESS. HTTP://WWW.MITPRESSJOURNALS.ORG/DOI/ABS/10.1162/JOCN.2010.21508#. VZDMI9DLR28. REPRINTED BY PERMISSION OF MIT PRESS JOURNALS

2. Did you notice anything about the arrangement of the shapes in the grid?
3. Did you notice any regularity in the arrangement of the shapes?
4. Did you notice any shapes that were associated in any way with any other shapes?
5. Did you notice that shapes always appeared in pairs in the same spatial arrangement?

Almost all of the ASD and control participants said "no" to all five questions; only a few were aware that some shapes appeared consistently with others; and none were aware of the exact spatial relationships in any shape pairs.

To test whether participants showed *implicit* learning of the spatial relationships within target pairs, the experimenters gave a test consisting of grids that contained pairs of objects, some in the same spatial relationship as during the learning phase, and others in a different spatial relationship. On this test, all participants showed evidence of implicit learning; that is, they chose the shapes depicted in the correct spatial relationships significantly more often than would

be expected on the basis of chance. In a striking finding, adults with ASD performed at a significantly higher level than adults without ASD, whereas 13-year-old children with ASD performed at about the same level as 13-year-old children without ASD.

Roser and colleagues (2015) suggest that adults with ASD outperformed adults without ASD because when they viewed the grids during the learning phase of the experiment, they naturally focused more on the local relationships between individual pairs of objects, rather than taking in the entire display; thus, they implicitly learned more about the recurring spatial relationships of the object pairs. The authors believe that the ASD children have this same tendency but did not show superior implicit learning because this tendency is not yet as fully developed in them as in the ASD adults. Because several other studies show largely intact implicit learning in ASD (Zwart et al., 2018), an intriguing question for future research concerns whether spared or enhanced capacities for implicit learning could be exploited to help individuals with ASD in everyday life.

At the other end of the life span, researchers have found that implicit learning abilities extend well into old age. These abilities tend to be less affected by aging than are explicit learning abilities (Howard & Howard, 1997), although recent research indicates that implicit learning is not completely preserved in older adults (Stillman, Howard, & Howard, 2016).

Implicit Learning Is Resistant to Some Disorders That Affect Explicit Learning

Implicit learning is remarkably resistant to various disorders that are known to affect explicit learning (Reber, 2013). A group of patients suffering from various psychoses were so severely impaired that they could not solve simple problems that university students had little difficulty with. Yet those patients were able to solve an artificial grammar learning task about as well as these students (Abrams & Reber, 1988). Other studies have found that profoundly amnesic patients not only show normal implicit memories but also display virtually normal implicit learning of artificial grammar (Knowlton, Ramus, & Squire, 1992). In fact, they made accurate judgments about novel letter strings even though they had essentially no explicit memory of having been in the learning phase of the experiment!

In contrast, several studies have shown that dyslexic children who fail to acquire reading skills despite normal intelligence and good educational opportunities exhibit deficits in implicit learning of artificial grammars (Pavlidou, Williams, & Kelly, 2009) and motor and spatial sequences on the serial reaction time task (Bennett et al., 2008; Orban, Lungu, & Doyon, 2008; Stoodley et al., 2008). These findings suggest that problems with implicit learning play an important role in developmental dyslexia and need to be taken into account in the development of remedial programs (Stoodley et al., 2008).

Implicit and Explicit Learning Use Distinct Neural Pathways

The fact that individuals suffering amnesia show intact implicit learning strongly suggests that the brain structures that underlie implicit learning are distinct from those that underlie explicit learning. As we learned in the Memory chapter, amnesic individuals are characterized by lesions to the hippocampus and nearby structures in the medial temporal lobe; thus, researchers have concluded that these regions are not necessary for implicit learning (Bayley, Frascino, & Squire, 2005). What's more, it appears that distinct regions of the brain may be activated depending on how people approach a task (Reber, 2013).

For example, in one study, participants saw a series of dot patterns, each of which looked like an array of stars in the night sky (Reber et al., 2003). Actually, all the stimuli were constructed to conform to an underlying prototypical dot pattern. The dots, however, varied so much that it was virtually impossible for a viewer to guess that they all had this common structure. Before the experiment began, half of the participants were told about the existence of the prototype; in other words, they were given instructions that encouraged explicit processing. The others were given standard implicit learning instructions: They were told nothing other than to attend to the dot patterns.

The participants were then scanned as they made decisions about new dot patterns, attempting to categorize them according to whether or not they conformed to the prototype. Interestingly, both groups performed equally well on this task, correctly classifying about 65% of the new dot patterns. However, the brain scans revealed that the two groups made these decisions using very different parts of

Implicit learning, which is involved in acquiring and retaining the skills needed to ride a bicycle, tends to decline less in old age than explicit learning.

Figure 7.19

Implicit and Explicit Learning Activate Different Brain Areas Research participants were scanned with fMRI while engaged in either implicit learning or explicit learning about the categorization of dot patterns. The occipital region (in blue) showed decreased brain activity after implicit learning. The areas in yellow, orange, and red showed increased brain activity during explicit learning, including the left temporal lobe (*far left*), the right frontal lobe (*second from left* and *second from right*), and the parietal lobe (*second from right* and *far right*) (Reber et al., 2003).

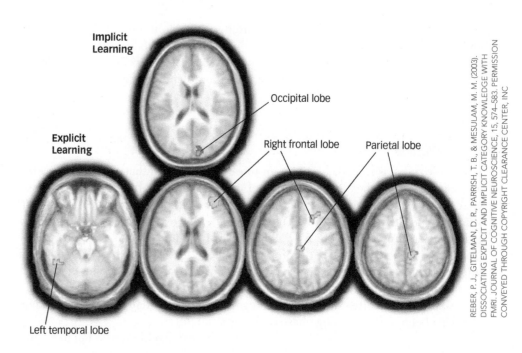

REBER, P. J., GITELMAN, D. R., PARRISH, T. B., & MESULAM, M. M. (2003). DISSOCIATING EXPLICIT AND IMPLICIT CATEGORY KNOWLEDGE WITH FMRI. JOURNAL OF COGNITIVE NEUROSCIENCE, 15, 574–583. PERMISSION CONVEYED THROUGH COPYRIGHT CLEARANCE CENTER, INC

their brains (see **FIGURE 7.19**). Participants who were given the explicit instructions showed *increased* brain activity in the prefrontal cortex, parietal cortex, hippocampus, and a variety of other areas known to be associated with the processing of explicit memories. Those given the implicit instructions showed *decreased* brain activation primarily in the occipital region, which is involved in visual processing. This finding suggests that participants recruited distinct brain structures in different ways, depending on whether they were approaching the task using explicit or implicit learning.

Other studies have begun to pinpoint the brain regions that are involved in two of the most commonly tested implicit learning tasks: artificial grammar learning and sequence learning on the serial reaction time task. Several fMRI studies have shown that Broca's area—which, as you learned in the Neuroscience and Behaviour chapter, plays a key role in language production—is turned on during artificial grammar learning (Forkstam et al., 2006; Petersson, Forkstam, & Ingvar, 2004). Furthermore, activating Broca's area by applying electrical stimulation to the overlying scalp enhances implicit learning of artificial grammar, most likely by facilitating acquisition of grammatical rules (De Vries et al., 2010). In contrast, the motor cortex appears critical for sequence learning on the serial reaction time task. When the motor cortex was temporarily disabled by the application of a recently developed type of TMS that lasts for a long time (so that participants can perform the task without having TMS constantly applied while they are doing so), sequence learning was abolished (Wilkinson et al., 2010).

Build to the Outcomes

1. What is the difference between implicit learning and explicit learning?

2. How are learning and memory linked?

3. How can you learn something without being aware of it?

4. Why are tasks learned implicitly difficult to explain to others?

5. What technology shows that implicit learning and explicit learning are associated with separate structures of the brain?

Learning in the Classroom

In this chapter, we've considered several different types of learning from behavioural, cognitive, evolutionary, and neural perspectives. Yet it may seem strange to you that we haven't discussed the kind of learning to which you are currently devoting much of your life: learning in educational settings such as the classroom. During the past several years, psychologists have published a great deal of work specifically focused on enhancing learning in educational settings. Let's consider what some of this research says about learning techniques and then turn to the equally important topic of exerting control over learning processes.

Learning Outcomes

- Explain why distributed practice and practice testing are effective study techniques.

- Describe how judgments of learning (JOLs) impact learning.

Techniques for Learning

Students use a wide variety of study techniques in attempts to improve their learning. Popular techniques—ones that you might use yourself—include highlighting and underlining, rereading, summarizing, and visual imagery mnemonics (Annis & Annis, 1982; Wade, Trathen, & Schraw, 1990). How effective are these and other techniques? A team of psychologists who specialize in learning published a comprehensive analysis of research concerning 10 learning techniques that students use (Dunlosky et al., 2013). They considered the usefulness of each technique across four main variables: learning conditions (e.g., how often and in what context the technique is used), materials to be learned (e.g., texts, math problems, concepts), student characteristics (e.g., age and ability level), and outcome measures (e.g., rote retention, comprehension, problem solving). On the basis of the picture that emerged across these four variables, Dunlosky and colleagues evaluated the overall usefulness of each technique and classified it as high, moderate, or low utility (**TABLE 7.2**).

Despite their popularity, highlighting, rereading, summarizing, and visual imagery mnemonics (which encompasses keyword mnemonic and imagery for the text) all received a low utility assessment. That doesn't mean these techniques have no value whatsoever for improving learning, but it does indicate that each one has significant limitations and that students could better spend their time using other approaches—a reason that none of these techniques appeared in the Six Tips For Reading This Textbook section of the Preface. We also discussed some material related to these techniques in the Memory chapter (see pages 214–261). Because distributed practice, interleaved practice, and practice testing are the most successful techniques, let's take a deeper look at them now (see also Other Voices: Learning at Jiffy Lube University).

TABLE 7.2

EFFECTIVENESS OF STUDY TECHNIQUES

High Effectiveness	Moderate Effectiveness	Low Effectiveness
Practice testing	Elaborative interrogation	Summarization
Distributed practice	Self-explanation Interleaved practice	Highlighting/underlining Keyword mnemonic
		Imagery for text
		Rereading

Other Voices | Learning at Jiffy Lube University

The study techniques we reviewed in this chapter on learning in the classroom can help improve academic performance. But these techniques also have broader applications outside the classroom, in situations where people need to acquire new knowledge and skills. One of the most important everyday applications of learning techniques involves training to perform a job. In an excellent 2014 book called *Make It Stick: The Science of Successful Learning*, which elaborates on several of the key techniques and ideas we have discussed in this section, the writer Peter C. Brown and the cognitive psychologists Henry L. Roediger III and Mark A. McDaniel tell the story of Jiffy Lube University. This is an educational program in which the well-known service-garage business has incorporated practice testing, distributed practice, and other learning techniques to aid in training employees:

If you don't expect innovations in training to spring from your local service garage, Jiffy Lube may surprise you. An integrated suite of educational courses under the felicitous name Jiffy Lube University is helping the company's franchises win customers, reduce employee turnover, broaden their service offerings, and boost sales.

Jiffy Lube is a network of more than two thousand service centres in the United States and Canada that provide oil changes, tire rotation, and other automotive services. Although the company is a subsidiary of Shell Oil Company, every outlet is owned and operated by an independent franchisee, who hires employees to serve customers.

The rapid-oil-change business, like most others, has had to adjust to changes in the marketplace and advances in technology. Synthetic lubricants have made oil changes less frequent, and because cars have become more complicated, garage employees need higher levels of training to understand diagnostic codes and provide appropriate services.

No employee may work on a customer's car until he or she has been certified as proficient. For this, they enter Jiffy Lube University, a Web-based learning platform. Certification starts with interactive e-learning, with frequent quizzing and feedback to learn what a particular job entails and how it's to be performed. When employees score 80 percent or better on an exam, they are eligible to begin training on the job, practicing new skills by following a written guide that breaks each service activity into its component steps. The steps may number as many as thirty and are performed as part of a team, often involving call and response (for example, between a technician working from the top side of an engine and another underneath). A supervisor coaches the employee and rates his or her performance on each step. When the technician demonstrates mastery, certification is recorded in his or her permanent file, signed by the supervisor. Technicians must recertify every two years to keep their mastery up to snuff and adapt to operational and technical changes. Higher-level jobs for advanced services like brake repair or running engine diagnostics are trained in the same manner.

The e-learning and on-the-job training are active learning strategies that incorporate various forms of quizzing, feedback, and spaced and interleaved practice. All progress is displayed by computer on a virtual "dashboard" that provides an individualized

learning plan, enabling an employee to track his or her performance, focus on skills that need to be raised, and monitor his or her progress against the company's completion schedule. Jiffy Lube employees are typically eighteen to twenty-five years old and filing for their first jobs. As a technician is certified in one job, he or she begins training in another, until he or she has trained in all store positions, including management.

Ken Barber, Jiffy Lube International's manager of learning and development, says training has to be engaging in order to hold employees' attention. At the time we spoke, Barber was putting the finishing touches on a computer-based simulation game for company managers called "A Day in the Life of a Store Manager." The service centre manager is confronted with various challenges and is required to select among a range of possible strategies for resolving them. The manager's choices determine how the game unfolds, providing feedback and the opportunity to strive for better outcomes, sharpening decision-making skill.

In the six years since Jiffy Lube University was launched, it has received many accolades from the training profession and earned accreditation by the American Council on Education. Employees who progress through training in all job certifications can enroll at a postsecondary institution with seven hours of college credit under their belts. Since the program's beginning, employee turnover has dropped and customer satisfaction has increased.

"For most employees of a Jiffy Lube franchisee, this is a way into the workforce, and the training curriculum helps them to grow and expand their knowledge," Barber says. "It helps them find a path to success."

Peter C. Brown is a writer in St. Paul, Minnesota, USA. Henry L. Roediger III and Mark A. McDaniel are both professors of psychology at Washington University in St. Louis, Missouri, USA.

From the results thus far, Jiffy Lube University appears to be a big success. It is notable that, in addition to incorporating the learning techniques described in this chapter, Jiffy Lube University combines e-learning based on a Web platform with actual on-the-job training. The use of e-learning, also referred to as online learning, has expanded rapidly in recent years, and debates about its effectiveness have been spirited (Brooks, 2012; Koller, 2011). Jiffy Lube's successful combination of e-learning and live learning fits with earlier evidence that indicates that combining these two formats may be especially effective (Means et al., 2010).

And Jiffy Lube isn't the only company to make use of effective learning techniques. Brown, Roediger, and McDaniel also summarize successful training programs developed by Farmers Insurance, Andersen Windows and Doors, and other companies. So after you complete your studies and enter the workforce, don't be surprised if you find yourself applying practice testing, distributed practice, and related study techniques and principles that promote effective learning.

Peter C. Brown, Henry L. Roediger III, and Mark A. McDaniel, *Make It Stick: The Science of Successful Learning* (Cambridge, MA: Harvard University Press), 245–246.

Distributed Practice

Cramming for exams—that is, neglecting to study for an extended period of time and then studying intensively just before an exam (Vacha & McBride, 1993)—is a common occurrence in educational life. Surveys of students across a range of universities indicate that anywhere from about 25% to as many as 50% of students report that they rely on cramming (McIntyre & Munson, 2008). Although cramming is better than not studying at all, when students cram for an exam, they repeatedly study the information to be learned with little or no time between repetitions, a procedure known as *massed practice.* Such students are thus denying themselves the benefits of *distributed practice,* which involves spreading out study activities so that more time intervenes between repetitions of the information to be learned. (Furthermore, students who rely on cramming are also inviting some of the health and performance problems associated with procrastination that we will address in the Stress and Health chapter.)

The benefits of distributed practice relative to massed practice have been known for a long time; in fact, Ebbinghaus (1885/1964) first reported them in his classic studies concerning retention of nonsense syllables (see the Memory chapter). What's most impressive is just how widespread the benefits of distributed practice are: They have been observed for numerous different kinds of materials, including foreign vocabulary, definitions, and face–name pairs, and they have been demonstrated not only in university students but also in children, older adults, and individuals with memory problems due to brain damage (Dunlosky et al., 2013). A review of 254 separate studies involving more than 14,000 participants concluded that, on average, participants retained 47% of studied information after distributed practice, compared with 37% after massed practice (Cepeda et al., 2006). Several recent studies have also shown that distributed practice can improve long-term retention of actual classroom learning in student populations, including eighth-graders and university students (Rohrer, 2015).

Despite all the evidence indicating that distributed practice is an effective learning strategy, we still don't fully understand why that is so. One promising idea is that when we engage in massed practice, retrieving recently studied information is relatively easy, whereas during distributed practice, it is more difficult to retrieve information that we studied less recently. More difficult retrievals benefit subsequent learning more than easy retrievals, what psychologists call "desirable difficulties" (Bjork & Bjork, 2011). Whatever the explanation for the effects of distributed practice, there is no denying its benefits for students.

Interleaved Practice

Researchers have also discovered some novel benefits of the closely related technique of *interleaved practice,* a practice schedule that mixes different kinds of problems or materials within a single study session. Dunlosky et al. (2013) assigned interleaved practice a moderate utility assessment, but recent research suggests that it may be particularly effective for learning mathematics. Rohrer, Dedrick, and Stershic (2015) gave seventh-grade students practice math problems over a three-month period. The first group of students were given problems in the traditional blocked form; they practiced a set of similar problems that all required the same solution. The second group of students received problems in interleaved form; they practiced a mixture of different kinds of problems that each required distinct strategies.

The interleaved practice group scored higher than the blocked practice group on surprise tests given 1 day or 30 days after the conclusion of practice. The researchers suggested that interleaved practice was more effective because it requires students to choose a strategy according to the nature of individual problems (as students must do on a test), whereas during blocked practice, students could repeatedly apply the same strategy without having to select among possible strategies.

AGE FOTOSTOCK/SUPERSTOCK

Studying well in advance of an exam, allowing for breaks and distribution of study time, will generally produce a better outcome than cramming at the last minute.

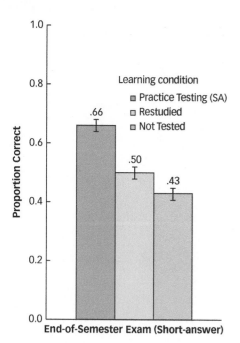

Figure 7.20

In a classroom study, 7th-grade science students received short-answer practice tests for some learning units, restudied other learning units, and received no practice tests or restudy for other units. On a short-answer exam at the end of the semester, practice testing produced significantly higher scores (McDermott et al., 2014).

Practice Testing

Practice testing, like distributed practice, has proven useful across a wide range of materials, including learning of stories, facts, vocabulary, and lectures (Karpicke & Aue, 2015; Roediger & Karpicke, 2018; see also the LearningCurve system associated with this text, which uses practice testing). As you learned in the Memory chapter, practice testing is effective, in part, because actively retrieving an item from memory during a test improves subsequent retention of that item more efficiently than simply studying it again (Roediger & Karpicke, 2006). Yet when asked about their preferred study strategies, students indicated by a wide margin that they prefer rereading materials to testing themselves (Karpicke, 2012).

The benefits of testing tend to be greatest when the test is difficult and requires considerable retrieval effort (Pyc & Rawson, 2009), also consistent with the desirable difficulties hypothesis (Bjork & Bjork, 2011). Not only does testing increase verbatim learning of the exact material that is tested but it can also enhance the *transfer* of learning from one situation to another (Carpenter, 2012; Pan & Rickard, 2018). For example, if you are given practice tests with short-answer questions, such testing improves later performance on both short-answer and multiple-choice questions more than restudying does (Kang, McDermott, & Roediger, 2007). Testing also improves the ability to draw conclusions from the studied material, which is an important part of learning and often critical to performing well in the classroom (Karpicke & Blunt, 2011). Also important, studies of students' performance in actual classrooms reveal benefits of practice testing that are similar to those observed in the laboratory (McDaniel et al., 2013; McDermott et al., 2014) (see **FIGURE 7.20**).

Testing Aids Attention

Recent research conducted in the laboratory of one of your textbook authors highlights yet another benefit of testing: Including brief tests during a lecture can improve learning by reducing the mind's tendency to wander (Szpunar, Khan, & Schacter, 2013). How often have you found your mind wandering—thinking about your evening plans, recalling a scene from a movie, or texting a friend—in the midst of a lecture that you know you ought to be attending to carefully? It's probably happened more than once. Research indicates that students' minds wander frequently during classroom lectures (Bunce, Flens, & Neiles, 2011; Lindquist & McLean, 2011; Wilson & Korn, 2007). Such mind wandering critically impairs learning of the lecture material (Risko et al., 2012; Wammes et al., 2016). In the study by Szpunar and colleagues (2013), participants watched a videotaped statistics lecture that was divided into four segments. All of the participants were told they might or might not be tested after each segment; they were also encouraged to take notes during the lectures.

- Participants in the *tested* group received brief tests on each segment.
- Participants in the *nontested* group did not receive a test until after the final segment. (They worked on arithmetic problems after each of the earlier segments.)
- Participants in a *restudy* group were shown, but not tested on, the same material as the tested group after each segment.

At random times during the lectures, participants in all groups were asked about whether they were paying attention to the lecture or whether their minds were wandering off to other topics. Participants in the nontested and restudy groups indicated that their minds wandered in response to about 40% of the inquiries; but, in the tested group, the incidence of mind wandering was cut in half, to about 20%. Participants in the tested group took significantly more notes during the lectures and retained significantly more information from the lecture on a final test than did participants in the other two groups, who performed similarly on this test. Participants in the tested group were also less anxious about the final test than those in the other groups.

These results indicate that part of the value of testing comes from encouraging people to sustain attention to a lecture in a way that discourages task-irrelevant activities such as mind wandering, and encourages task-relevant activities such as note taking. A subsequent study using a similar design (Jing, Szpunar, & Schacter, 2016) showed that when participants in the tested group did mind-wander, they tended to think about other parts of the lecture, whereas participants in the restudy group mind-wandered about topics that were unrelated to the lecture (i.e., day-to-day happenings in their own lives). The tested group not only showed enhanced verbatim recall of lecture material, but also showed an increased ability to integrate information from different parts of the lecture.

Because these benefits of testing were observed in response to a videotaped lecture, they apply most directly to online learning, where taped lectures are the norm (Breslow et al., 2013; Schacter & Szpunar, 2015), but there is every reason to believe that the results would apply to live classroom lectures as well, especially in light of the evidence we just discussed that practice testing enhances classroom performance.

Control of Learning

It's the night before the final exam in your introductory psychology course. You've put in a lot of time reviewing your course notes and the material in this textbook, and you feel that you have learned most of it pretty well. You are in the home stretch with little time left, and you've got to decide whether to devote those precious remaining minutes to studying psychological disorders or social psychology. How do you make that decision? What are its potential consequences? An important part of learning involves assessing how well we know something and how much more time we need to devote to studying it.

Experimental evidence shows that people's judgments about what they have learned play a critical role in guiding further study and learning (Dunlosky & Thiede, 2013; Metcalfe, 2009). These subjective assessments, which psychologists refer to as *judgments of learning* (JOLs), have a causal influence on learning: People typically devote more time to studying items that they judge they have not learned well (Metcalfe & Finn, 2008; Son & Metcalfe, 2000).

The finding that JOLs are causally related to decisions about how much to study a particular item is important because JOLs are sometimes inaccurate (Castel, McCabe, & Roediger, 2007). For example, after you read and reread a chapter or article in preparation for a test, the material will likely feel quite familiar, and that feeling may convince you that you've learned the material well enough that you don't need to study it further. However, the feeling of familiarity can be misleading: It may be the result of a low-level process such as perceptual priming (see the Memory chapter) and not the kind of learning that will necessary to perform well on an exam (Bjork & Bjork, 2011).

Similarly, research has shown that students are sometimes overconfident in judging how well they have learned definitions of new terms and thus fail to study them effectively (Dunlosky & Rawson, 2012). Practice testing can help reduce this kind of overconfidence (Soderstrom & Bjork, 2014). Therefore, one way to avoid being fooled by misleading subjective impressions when studying for an exam is to test yourself from time to time under exam-like conditions; in the case of learning definitions, carefully compare your answers to the actual definitions.

DATA VISUALIZATION

Do People Differ in How They Learn?
Go to launchpadworks.com.

So if you are preparing for the final exam in this course and need to decide whether to devote more time to studying psychological disorders or social psychology, try to exert control over your learning by testing yourself on material from those two chapters; you can use the results of those tests to help you decide which chapter requires further work. Heed the conclusion from researchers (Bjork, Dunlosky, and Kornell, 2013) that becoming a more sophisticated and effective learner requires understanding: (1) key features of learning and memory; (2) effective learning techniques; (3) how to monitor and control one's own learning; and (4) biases that can undermine judgements of learning.

Build to the Outcomes

1. What are the most and least effective study techniques?

2. What are the benefits of distributed practice?

3. Why does a difficult practice test have the greatest benefit?

4. How does taking practice tests help focus a wandering mind?

5. In what ways can JOLs be misleading?

Chapter Review

What Is Learning?

- Learning involves the acquisition of new knowledge, skills, and responses. It is based on experience and produces a change in the organism, and that change is relatively permanent.

- Even the simplest organisms exhibit simple forms of learning known as habituation and sensitization.

Classical Conditioning: One Thing Leads to Another

- Classical conditioning can be thought of as an exercise in pairing a neutral stimulus with a meaningful event or stimulus. Ivan Pavlov's initial work paired a neutral tone (a conditioned stimulus, CS) with a meaningful act: the presentation of food to a hungry animal (an unconditioned stimulus, US). As he and others demonstrated, the pairing of a CS and a US during the acquisition phase of classical conditioning eventually allows the CS, all by itself, to elicit a response called a conditioned response (CR).

  ○ *In second-order conditioning, the CS can be paired with a new neutral stimulus to elicit a response.*

  ○ *The conditioned response will decline in a process called extinction if the CS is repeatedly presented without the US, although spontaneous recovery can occur after a rest period.*

  ○ *Conditioning generalizes to similar stimuli, which indicates an ability to discriminate between them.*

- Classical conditioning was embraced by behaviourists such as John B. Watson, who believed that higher-level functions, such as thinking or awareness, did not need to be invoked to understand behaviour. Later researchers showed, however, that the underlying mechanism of classical conditioning is more complex (and more interesting) than the simple association between a CS and a US.

- Classical conditioning involves setting up expectations and is sensitive to the degree to which the CS is a genuine predictor of the US, indicating that classical conditioning can involve some degree of cognition. The cerebellum plays an important role in eyeblink conditioning, whereas the amygdala is important for fear conditioning.

- The evolutionary aspects of classical conditioning show that each species is biologically predisposed to acquire particular CS–US associations on the basis of its evolutionary history. In short, classical conditioning is not an arbitrary mechanism that merely forms associations. Rather, it is a sophisticated mechanism that evolved precisely because it has adaptive value.

Operant Conditioning: Reinforcements from the Environment

- Operant conditioning has at its root the law of effect and is a process by which behaviours are reinforced and therefore become more likely to occur. Positive and negative reinforcement increase the likelihood of behaviour; positive and negative punishment decrease the likelihood of behaviour.

  ○ *Secondary reinforcers can derive their effectiveness from associations with primary reinforcers.*

  ○ *Delayed reinforcement or punishment is less effective than immediate reinforcement or punishment.*

  ○ *Reinforcements occur only when the proper response has been made, but not every time, as evidenced by varying schedules of reinforcement.*

  ○ *Complex behaviours are shaped through reinforcement of successive steps.*

- Like John B. Watson, B. F. Skinner tried to explain behaviour without considering cognitive, neural, or evolutionary mechanisms. However, as with classical conditioning, this approach turned out to be incomplete.
  - *Operant conditioning has clear cognitive components: Organisms behave as though they have expectations about the outcomes of their actions and adjust their actions accordingly. Cognitive influences can sometimes override the trial-by-trial feedback that usually influences learning.*
  - *Studies with both animals and people highlight the operation of a neural reward centre that affects learning.*
  - *The associative mechanisms that underlie operant conditioning have their roots in evolutionary biology. Some things are relatively easy to learn, whereas others are difficult; the history of the species is usually the best clue as to which will be which.*

Observational Learning: Look at Me

- Observational learning is based on cognitive mechanisms such as attention, perception, memory, and reasoning. But observational learning also has roots in evolutionary biology and for the most basic of reasons: It has survival value. Observational learning is an important process by which species gather information about the world around them.
- Observational learning has important social and cultural consequences because it appears to be well suited to transmission of novel behaviours across individuals.
- Chimpanzees and monkeys can benefit from observational learning, supporting the idea that each species evolved particular biological predispositions.
- The mirror neuron system becomes active during observational learning, and many of the same brain regions are active during both observation and performance of a skill.

Observational learning is closely tied to parts of the brain that are involved in action.

Implicit Learning: Under the Radar

- In general, children are linguistically and socially sophisticated by age 6 or 7, but without awareness of how they have learned.
- Implicit learning is a process that detects, learns, and stores patterns without the application of explicit awareness by the learner. Simple behaviours such as habituation can reflect implicit learning, but complex behaviours, such as language use or socialization, can also be learned through an implicit process.
- Tasks that have been used to document implicit learning include artificial grammar and serial reaction time tasks.
- Implicit and explicit learning differ from each other in a number of ways: There are fewer individual differences in implicit than explicit learning; psychotic and amnesic patients with explicit learning problems can exhibit intact implicit learning; and neuroimaging studies indicate that implicit and explicit learning recruit different brain structures, sometimes in different ways.

Learning in the Classroom

- Research on learning techniques indicates that some popular study methods, such as highlighting, underlining, and rereading, have low utility, whereas other techniques, such as practice testing and distributed practice, have high utility.
- Practice testing improves retention and transfer of learning and can also enhance learning and reduce mind wandering during lectures.
- Judgements of learning play a causal role in determining what material to study, but they can be misleading.

Key Concept Quiz

1. In classical conditioning, a conditioned stimulus is paired with an unconditioned stimulus to produce
   a. a neutral stimulus.
   b. a conditioned response.
   c. an unconditioned response.
   d. another conditioned stimulus.

2. What occurs when a conditioned stimulus is no longer paired with an unconditioned stimulus?
   a. generalization
   b. spontaneous recovery
   c. extinction
   d. acquisition

3. What did Watson and Rayner seek to demonstrate about behaviourism through the Little Albert experiments?
   a. Conditioning involves a degree of cognition.
   b. Classical conditioning has an evolutionary component.
   c. Behaviourism alone cannot explain human behaviour.
   d. Even sophisticated behaviours such as emotion are subject to classical conditioning.

4. Which part of the brain is involved in the classical conditioning of fear?
   a. the amygdala
   b. the cerebellum
   c. the hippocampus
   d. the hypothalamus

5. After having a bad experience with a particular type of food, people can develop a lifelong aversion to that food. This suggests that conditioning has a(n) _____ aspect.
   a. cognitive
   b. evolutionary
   c. neural
   d. behavioural

6. Which of the following mechanisms have no role in Skinner's approach to behaviour?
   a. cognitive
   b. neural
   c. evolutionary
   d. all of the above

7. Latent learning provides evidence for a cognitive element in operant conditioning because it
   a. occurs without any obvious reinforcement.
   b. requires both positive and negative reinforcement.
   c. points towards the operation of a neural reward centre.
   d. depends on a stimulus–response relationship.

8. Neural research indicates that observational learning is closely tied to brain areas that are involved in
   a. memory.
   b. vision.
   c. action.
   d. emotion.

9. What kind of learning takes place largely independent of awareness of both the process and the products of information acquisition?
   a. latent learning
   b. implicit learning
   c. observational learning
   d. conscious learning

10. Which study strategy has been shown to be the most effective?
   a. highlighting text
   b. rereading
   c. summarizing
   d. taking practice tests

 **LearningCurve** macmillan learning   Don't stop now! Quizzing yourself is a powerful study tool. Go to LaunchPad to access the LearningCurve adaptive quizzing system and your own personalized learning plan. Visit launchpadworks.com.

Key Terms

learning (p. 264)

habituation (p. 264)

sensitization (p. 264)

classical conditioning (p. 265)

unconditioned stimulus (US) (p. 266)

unconditioned response (UR) (p. 266)

acquisition (p. 268)

conditioned stimulus (CS) (p. 268)

conditioned response (CR) (p. 268)

second-order conditioning (p. 269)

extinction (p. 270)

spontaneous recovery (p. 270)

generalization (p. 270)

discrimination (p. 270)

biological preparedness (p. 275)

operant conditioning (p. 275)

law of effect (p. 276)

operant behaviour (p. 277)

reinforcer (p. 277)

punisher (p. 277)

fixed-interval (FI) schedule (p. 282)

variable-interval (VI) schedule (p. 282)

fixed-ratio (FR) schedule (p. 282)

variable-ratio (VR) schedule (p. 282)

intermittent reinforcement (p. 282)

intermittent reinforcement effect (p. 283)

shaping (p. 283)

latent learning (p. 286)

cognitive map (p. 286)

observational learning (p. 292)

diffusion chain (p. 293)

implicit learning (p. 298)

Changing Minds

1. A friend is taking a class in childhood education. "Back in the old days," she says, "teachers used physical punishment, but of course that's not allowed anymore. Now, a good teacher should only use reinforcement. When children behave, teachers should provide positive reinforcement, like praise. When children misbehave, teachers should provide negative reinforcement, like scolding or withholding privileges." What is your friend misunderstanding about reinforcement? Can you give better examples of how negative reinforcement could be applied productively in an elementary school classroom?

2. A friend of your family is trying to train her daughter to make her bed every morning. You suggest trying positive reinforcement. A month later, the woman reports back to you. "It's not working very well," she says. "Every time Vicky makes her bed, I put a gold star on the calendar, and at the end of the week, if there are

seven gold stars, I give her a reward—a piece of licorice. But so far, she's earned the licorice only twice." How could you explain why the desired behaviour—bed making—might not increase as a result of this reinforcement procedure?

3. While studying for the psych exam, you ask your study partner to provide a definition of classical conditioning. "In classical conditioning," he says, "there's a stimulus, the CS, that predicts an upcoming event, the US. Usually it's something bad, like an electric shock, nausea, or a loud, frightening noise. The learner makes a response, the CR, in order to prevent the US. Sometimes, the US is good, like food for Pavlov's dogs, and then the learner makes the response in order to earn the US." What's wrong with this definition?

4. One of your classmates announces that he liked the last chapter (on memory) better than the current chapter

on learning. "I want to be a psychiatrist," he says, "so I mostly care about human learning. Conditioning might be a really powerful way to train animals to push levers or perform tricks, but it really doesn't have much relevance to how humans learn things." How similar is learning in humans and other animals? What real-world examples can you provide to show that conditioning does occur in humans?

Answers to Key Concept Quiz

1. b; 2. c; 3. d; 4. a; 5. b; 6. d; 7. a; 8. c; 9. b; 10. d.

LaunchPad features the full e-book of *Psychology*, the LearningCurve adaptive quizzing system, videos, and a variety of activities to boost your learning. Visit LaunchPad at launchpadworks.com.

Emotion and Motivation

LEONARDO DOES WHAT YOU'D EXPECT A 5-YEAR-OLD CHILD TO DO. He builds towers of blocks, does puzzles, and plays guessing games. But unlike most children, Leonardo isn't proud when he solves a puzzle or angry when he loses a game. That's because Leonardo has an unusual condition that has made him incapable of experiencing normal human emotions. He does not feel joy or sorrow, delight or despair, shame, envy, annoyance, excitement, gratitude, or regret. Never once has he laughed or cried.

Leonardo's condition has had profound consequences. For instance, interacting with people is quite challenging, and to do it, Leonardo has had to learn how to make just the right facial expression at just the right time—to pull his mouth into a smile when his interaction partner says something nice to him, or to raise his eyebrow once in a while to signal his interest in what they are saying. When his mother comes into the room, Leonardo knows that he is supposed to smile at her, and so he does. She's proud that he has mastered this trick, but she is also keenly aware of the fact that when Leonardo smiles he is simply "making faces" and that he is not actually *feeling* happy to see her. Most mothers would be bothered by this, but not Cynthia Breazeal. In fact, she's delighted. Because despite Leonardo's limitations, she still thinks he is the cutest robot she ever designed.

Most children experience happiness, fear, surprise, and anger. But Leonardo cannot experience these or any other emotions.

SAM OGDEN/SCIENCE SOURCE

Leonardo and his "mom," robot designer and MIT professor Cynthia Breazeal.

THAT'S RIGHT. LEONARDO IS A ROBOT. He can see and hear, he can remember and reason. But despite his lovable smile and knowing wink, he can't feel a thing—and that makes him infinitely different from us. Our ability to love and to hate, to be amused and annoyed, to feel elated and devastated, is a defining feature of our humanity, and a person who couldn't feel these emotions would seem a lot like a robot to the rest of us. But what exactly are emotions? And why are they so essential? In this chapter, we'll explore these questions. We'll start by discussing the nature of emotions and seeing how they relate to the states of our bodies and our brains. Next, we'll see how people express their emotions and how they use those expressions to communicate with each other. We'll then examine the essential role that emotions play in motivation—how they inform us and how they compel us to do everything from making war to making love. Finally, we'll discuss a few of our most powerful motivations—those we share with other animals and those that make us uniquely human.

The Nature of Emotion

Learning Outcomes

- Understand how and why psychologists "map" feelings.
- Distinguish between appraisals and action tendencies.
- Explain the roles that the body and brain play in producing emotions.

LEVRANII/SHUTTERSTOCK

It is almost impossible not to feel something when you look at this photograph, but it is almost impossible to say exactly what you are feeling.

Are you alive? You probably answered that question quickly and in the affirmative. At least we hope so. But what exactly does the word *alive* mean? Alive is not a *thing* you can point to. Rather, it is a *state* that an entity may or may not be in—a state that is defined by many features, such as the capacity for reproduction, growth, metabolic activity, and so on. Some entities (such as you) have all these features and so are clearly alive; other entities (such as rocks) have none of these features and so are clearly not alive; and some entities (such as viruses) have a few of these features but not others, which makes it a bit more difficult to say whether they are alive or not.

Similarly, an emotion is not a thing. There is no place in the brain where it resides and no single way to measure it (Mauss & Robinson, 2009). Rather, an **emotion** is *a temporary state that includes unique subjective experiences and physiological activity, and that prepares people for action.* An emotion has many distinct features (Mauss et al., 2005). Its mental features include what a person thinks, feels, and is prepared to do; and its physical features include the activity of both the body and the brain. When a person's state at a particular moment in time has most or all of these features, we say that person is "experiencing an emotion." What are these features? Let's start by examining the mental ones.

The Emotional Mind

People all over the planet experience an emotion that has no name in English, but that in Sanskrit is called *kama muta* (Zickfeld et al., 2019). When people experience this emotion, they say they are feeling "moved to tears" or "touched." They describe the experience as "stirring" or "heart-warming." You've probably felt this emotion yourself, but how would you describe it to someone who hasn't felt it? You might try telling them about the circumstances that trigger this emotion (seeing someone do something that bonds them to others, such as making a sacrifice or giving a gift), or you might try telling them about what happens to your body when you experience it (your eyes get moist, your chest gets warm, and your throat gets tight). But in the end, both descriptions would fall a bit flat because one of the essential features of

	St John's	Halifax	Ottawa	Winnipeg	Whitehorse	Victoria
St John's	0	1,484	2,727	4,802	8,109	7,506
Halifax	1,484	0	1,435	3,510	6,814	6,214
Ottawa	2,727	1,435	0	2,146	5,385	4,429
Winnipeg	4,802	3,510	2,146	0	3,292	2,378
Whitehorse	8,109	6,814	5,385	3,292	0	2,484
Victoria	7,506	6,214	4,429	2,378	2,484	0

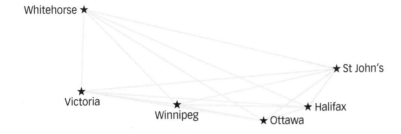

Figure 8.1
From Distances to Maps Knowing the distances between things—like cities, for example—allows us to draw a map that reveals the dimensions on which they vary.

kama muta is the *feeling* of it—and trying to explain a feeling to someone who hasn't had it is a bit like trying to explain *green* to a person who was born blind. It *feels* like something to be moved to tears, and what it feels like is one of the emotion's defining features (Heavey, Hurlburt, & Lefforge, 2012).

Feelings

If we can't easily describe our feelings, then how can we study them scientifically? One way is by capitalizing on the fact that even though we can't always say *what* we are feeling, we usually can say how *close* one feeling is to another ("Kama muta is more like happiness than anger"). That's good news, because knowing how close a bunch of things are allows scientists to map them! Consider the table in **FIGURE 8.1** that lists the distance between—or "closeness" of—six Canadian cities. If you tried to draw a map using the numbers in the table, you would be *forced* to draw a map of Canada, just like the one beneath the table. If you don't believe it, just try moving Winnipeg. You can't. If you move Winnipeg even a hair to the right, it will suddenly be too close to Ottawa and too far from Victoria. Winnipeg is in the *one and only spot* that allows it to be exactly 2,146 km from Ottawa and 2,378 km from Victoria, while still being 3,292 km from Whitehorse—and the same is true of every other city on the map. So what does this have to do with feelings? When people say how close two feelings are, they are essentially estimating the "distance" between them, which allows psychologists to draw a map of the feeling-scape. The map of emotions, shown in **FIGURE 8.2**, is the one that human beings most commonly produce.

Of course, no one spends a summer vacation driving from Glad to Excited, so who needs a map of the feeling-scape? We do, because maps don't merely show us where things are located; they also reveal the *dimensions* on which those locations vary. For example, the map in Figure 8.1 reveals that cities' locations vary on exactly two dimensions, which we call longitude (the east–west dimension) and latitude (the north–south dimension). Now look at Figure 8.2, which shows that feelings vary on two dimensions as well: *valence* (how positive the feeling is) and *arousal* (how energetic the feeling is). Although some researchers have produced more complex maps of the feeling-scape (Cowen & Keltner, 2017), decades of research suggest that the feelings of people all over the world can be fairly well described by each feeling's unique location on this simple two-dimensional map (Russell, 1980; Watson & Tellegen, 1985; Yik, Russell, & Steiger, 2011).

emotion A temporary state that includes unique subjective experiences and physiological activity, and that prepares people for action.

Figure 8.2

Two Dimensions of Emotion Just as the locations of cities vary on two dimensions called longitude and latitude, emotional experiences vary on two dimensions called valence and arousal.

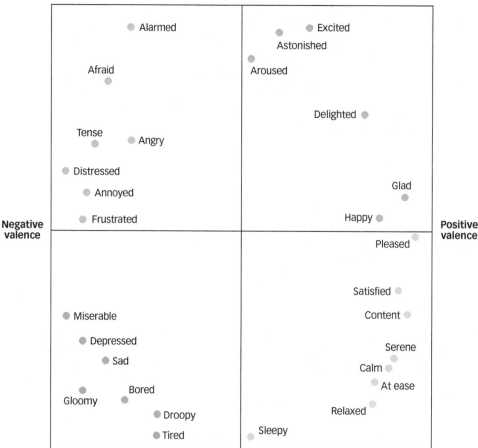

Appraisals and Action Tendencies

One feature of an emotion, then, is what it feels like. Another is where it comes from and what it leads to. Emotions rarely come out of nowhere; rather, they are reactions to events in the world. You see a man with a gun running towards you, and your reaction is fear. You see a little boy bending down to pick a flower for his mother and your reaction is kama muta. And yet, if the man were a policeman who was coming to your rescue, your reaction would be relief, and if the little boy was visiting his mother's grave, your reaction would be sorrow.

Our emotions are responses, but they are not responses to events so much as to our interpretation of those events. Psychologists use the word **appraisal** to refer to *conscious or unconscious evaluations and interpretations of the emotion-relevant aspects of a stimulus or event* (Arnold, 1960; Blascovich & Mendes, 2000; Ellsworth & Scherer, 2003; Lazarus, 1984; Roseman, 1984; Roseman & Smith, 2001; Scherer, 1999, 2001). Research suggests that we naturally appraise events on a number of dimensions, such as the event's self-relevance ("Does this affect me?") and importance ("Does this matter?"), our ability to cope with the event ("Can I handle this?") and to control it ("Can I change this?"), and others. How we answer these questions—that is, how we appraise the events—influences the emotions we experience.

Because emotions are responses to appraisals, different people can have different emotional reactions to precisely the same event. For instance, in one study (Siemer, Mauss, & Gross, 2007), participants were asked to perform a demanding task ("Count backward in steps of 7 from 18,652"), and each time they tried, the experimenter gave them increasingly snarky feedback about their performance ("You aren't speaking loudly enough" or "Stop moving around so much"). After they had attempted the task three times, the experimenter explained with great annoyance

appraisal Conscious or unconscious evaluations and interpretations of the emotion-relevant aspects of a stimulus or event.

that the participant's performance had been worthless and that she was terminating the task. How did participants respond to this event? It depended on how they appraised it. Those who thought the problem was the experimenter's fault ("She didn't *tell* me I was supposed to sit still") felt amused or angry, whereas those who thought the problem was their own fault ("I should know better than to wiggle in my chair") felt guilty, ashamed, or sad.

Emotions follow from appraisals and they produce **action tendencies**, which are *a readiness to engage in a specific set of emotion-relevant behaviours* (Frijda, Kuipers, & ter Schure, 1989). For example, have you ever noticed that when you are frightened by a sudden loud noise, you instantly stop moving? Why? Because the emotional state called fear produces an action tendency called "freezing" (Roelofs, 2017). Similarly, if you've ever gotten into a heated argument with someone, you may have noticed yourself inching *towards* that person rather than away, because the emotional state called anger produces an action tendency called "approach" (Carver & Harmon-Jones, 2009). And when you are surfing the web and accidentally come across a picture that is vile and repulsive, you momentarily close your eyes and turn your head to the side because the emotional state called "disgust" produces an action tendency called "avoidance" (Chapman et al., 2009). Each of these action tendencies makes a good deal of evolutionary sense: When a bear growls at you, you *should* stand still; when an enemy threatens, you *should* move forwards to stop him; and when you see something totally gross, you *should* move away before you catch something. Action tendencies remind us that emotions are adaptive states that nature designed to ensure our survival—and perhaps the survival of other species (see Other Voices: Do Dogs Feel Emotions Like Hope and Guilt?).

The Emotional Body

Speaking of bears, what do you think would happen if you walked into your kitchen right now and saw one nosing through the garbage can? You'd feel afraid, of course. Really very highly afraid. Then your heart would start pounding, you'd begin to breathe heavily, and the muscles in your legs would tense as they prepared you to do some of that fleeing you've heard so much about. In short, you *first* would feel fear and *then* your body would respond. Right? Not according to William James. In the late 19th century, James suggested that the feeling of fear does not cause these bodily responses, but, rather, these bodily responses cause the feeling of fear:

> Our natural way of thinking about these coarser emotions is that the mental perception of some fact excites the mental affection called the emotion, and that this latter state of mind gives rise to the bodily expression. My theory, on the contrary, is that the bodily changes follow directly the perception of the exciting fact, and that our feeling of the same changes as they occur *is* the emotion. Common-sense says, we lose our fortune, are sorry and weep; we meet a bear, are frightened and run; we are insulted by a rival, are angry and strike. The hypothesis here to be defended says that this order of sequence is incorrect . . . and that the more rational statement is that we feel sorry because we cry, angry because we strike, afraid because we tremble. (James, 1890, Vol. 2, p. 449)

According to James, first you see the bear (the "exciting fact"), which instantly causes your heart to start pounding (the "bodily changes"), and *then* you have the feeling called fear, which is nothing more than *your perception of your body's response*. The psychologist Carl Lange suggested something similar at about the same time, so this idea became known as the **James–Lange theory** of emotion, which states that *feelings are simply the perception of one's own physiological responses to a stimulus*. According to this theory, our feelings are the consequence—and not the cause—of our body's reactions to events in the world, such as the sudden appearance of bears in our kitchens.

This theory is original, elegant, and provocative—but as the physiologists Walter Cannon and Philip Bard noted, it can't possibly be right. Although Cannon and Bard

action tendencies A readiness to engage in a specific set of emotion-related behaviours.

James–Lange theory The theory that feelings are simply the perception of one's own physiological responses to a stimulus.

Other Voices ┊ **Do Dogs Feel Emotions Like Hope and Guilt?**

This chapter is about emotions in people, but we are not alone in experiencing emotions. Dr. Frans de Waal, a primatologist, has spent his career studying our primate relations and other animals, and he thinks that we should consider emotions not just across cultures, but across species. Here's what he has to say:

> Like organs, the emotions evolved over millions of years to serve essential functions. Their usefulness has been tested again and again, giving them the wisdom of ages. They nudge us to do what is best for us. Some emotions may be more developed in humans, or apply to a wider range of circumstances, but none is fundamentally new.
>
> . . .
>
> Open your front door and tell your dog that you are going out for a walk, then close the door and return to your seat. Your dog, who had been barking and wriggling with excitement, now slinks back to his basket and puts his head down on his paws. You have just witnessed both hope and disappointment in another species. . . .
>
> You may say that it is impossible to know what a dog feels. True, yet his behaviour clearly reflects an abrupt change in his emotional state. Expressed in the body, these states are perfectly observable and measurable even if the associated private experiences are not.
>
> In fact, the possibility of animal hope was experimented upon nearly a century ago by the psychologist Otto Tinklepaugh. He first let a monkey watch a banana being hidden under a cup, then allowed her into the room where this had been done. If she found the banana, everything proceeded smoothly. But if the experimenter had surreptitiously replaced the banana with a piece of lettuce, the monkey would frantically look around, lifting up the cup, while shrieking at the experimenter. Her expectations had been violated, for which she rightly blamed the sneaky experimenter.
>
> We share so many so-called secondary emotions with other species that the whole concept is questionable. There is one exception, though, which keeps being proposed as definitely cultural: guilt.
>
> This is despite the many dog owners who seem to recognize it in their pets when they hide under the table after a transgression. One expert in animal cognition at Barnard, Alexandra Horowitz, tested this out by having dogs meet an angry owner both when they had not broken any rules and when they had; she also had them meet a relaxed owner in the same two situations. Dr. Horowitz concluded that whether dogs take on a guilty look—lowered gaze, ears pressed back, tail rapidly beating between the legs—is unrelated to whether or not they followed orders. If the owner scolds them, they look extremely guilty. If

> the owner doesn't, they still sometimes look like this, but less often.
>
> One problem, however, is that our rules are of our own making, such as "Don't jump on that couch!" or "Keep your nails off my leather chair!" It must be as tough for our pets to grasp these prohibitions as it was for me to understand why I couldn't chew gum in Singapore.
>
> It would be better to test behaviour that is wrong by almost any standard, including that of their own species. The Austrian ethologist Konrad Lorenz gave one of my favourite examples, about his dog, Bully, who broke the fundamental rule never to bite your superior.
>
> Humans don't need to teach this rule, and indeed Bully had never been punished for it. The dog bit his master's hand when Dr. Lorenz tried to break up a dogfight. Even though Dr. Lorenz petted him right away, Bully suffered a complete nervous breakdown. For days, he was virtually paralyzed and ignored his food. He would lie on the rug breathing shallowly, occasionally interrupted by a deep sigh. He had violated a natural taboo, which among ancestral canines could have had the worst imaginable consequences, such as expulsion from the pack.
>
> Among the primates, the most suggestive cases of remorse concern bonobos. These apes are as close to us as chimpanzees, but far more peaceful and gentle, which means that they almost never hurt one another. Whereas in most primates reconciliation after a fight is typically sought by the subordinate party, in bonobos it is the dominant animal that seeks to make amends, especially if he has inflicted an injury. He may return to his victim and unerringly reach for the exact same toe that he has bitten and carefully inspect the damage. He obviously knows precisely what he has done and where. Then he spends half an hour or more licking and cleaning the wound that he himself inflicted.
>
> . . .
>
> For the longest time, science has depicted animals as stimulus–response machines while declaring their inner lives barren. This has helped us sustain our customary "anthropodenial": the denial that we are animals. We like to see ourselves as special, but whatever the difference between humans and animals may be, it is unlikely to be found in the emotional domain.

Dr. Frans de Waal is a Dutch/American biologist. He is a professor at Emory University in Georgia, USA, and the author of numerous books on primate social behaviour.

Excerpt from "Your dog feels as guilty as she looks," Opinion, *New York Times*, Mar 9 2019.

had their own incorrect ideas about emotions (which they thought occurred at the same time as, but independently of, physiological activity), they correctly noted that the James–Lange theory was at odds with three basic facts.

- First, some of our emotional experiences happen *before* our bodily responses do. People *feel* embarrassed at precisely the moment their pants fall down in public, but the bodily response called "blushing" takes a full 15 to 30 seconds to occur. How could embarrassment simply be "the perception of blushing" if the feeling happens first?

- Second, all sorts of things can cause bodily responses without also causing emotions. When your bedroom gets hot, your heart naturally starts to beat a bit faster, yet you don't feel afraid of your pillow, do you? If fear were merely "the perception of a rapid heartbeat," then why wouldn't you be scared every time your roommate cranked the thermostat?

- Third, for the James–Lange theory to work, every human emotion would have to be associated with a unique set of bodily responses—that is, every emotion would have to have a unique "physiological fingerprint," so to speak (Clark-Polner, Johnson, & Barrett, 2017; Siegel et al., 2018). And they don't! Different emotional experiences are sometimes associated with the same set of bodily responses, and different bodily responses are sometimes associated with the same emotional experience.

The James–Lange theory was broken from the start, and nearly a century later, psychologists Stanley Schachter and Jerome Singer (1962) tried to repair it. Like James and Lange, Schachter and Singer believed that our emotional experiences are based on our perceptions of our body's reactions. But instead of suggesting that a specific set of bodily responses correspond to each and every unique emotional experience, they proposed that there is just one bodily response (which they called "undifferentiated physiological arousal") and that how people interpret this response determines which emotion they experience (**FIGURE 8.3**). Their **two-factor theory of emotion** stated that *stimuli trigger a general state of physiological arousal, which is then interpreted as a specific emotion.*

According to this theory, when you see a bear in your kitchen, your body instantly goes on red alert—your heart pounds, your muscles tense, and you start breathing like a marathon runner. Your mind notices this heightened physiological arousal and seeks to interpret it. It looks around the room, sees a bear, and, knowing something about how much bears like to eat people, it concludes the bear is causing you to feel fear. But, according to the two-factor theory, if you had seen a pair of cute kittens instead of a bear, your mind would have drawn a completely different conclusion—for instance, that you were feeling *delight*. The two-factor theory suggests that we have just one bodily response to all emotionally relevant stimuli, but that we interpret that response differently on different occasions. Different emotions are simply different interpretations of the same physiological reaction.

How has the two-factor theory fared? Although Schachter and Singer's experiments were disastrously flawed by modern standards (Cotton, 1981), at least one of their

two-factor theory of emotion The theory that stimuli trigger a general state of physiological arousal which is then interpreted as a specific emotion.

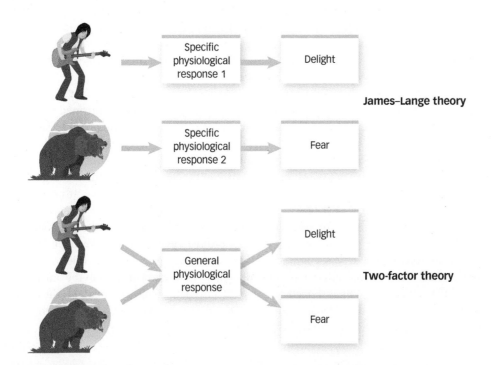

James–Lange theory

Two-factor theory

Figure 8.3
Classic Theories of Emotion The James–Lange theory suggests that different stimuli (e.g., your favourite singer and a growling bear) trigger different physiological responses that are then experienced as different emotions. The two-factor theory suggests that different stimuli trigger the same general physiological response, which is interpreted or "labelled" differently under different circumstances. Research suggests that neither of these classic theories is quite right.

theory's key claims has been largely supported by more rigorous testing: Under some circumstances, people make inferences about the causes of their physiological arousal, and those inferences can influence the emotions they experience. For instance, after exercising, people are more sexually attracted to potential romantic partners, as though they were interpreting their exercise-induced arousal as lust (Cantor, Zillmann, & Bryant, 1975; Dutton & Aron, 1974; White, Fishbein, & Rutsein, 1981; White & Kight, 1984). Is it possible that exercise just makes people horny? No, because after exercising, the same people behave more aggressively towards potential enemies, as though under these circumstances they were interpreting their exercise-induced arousal as anger (Zillmann & Bryant, 1974). In one study (Lindquist & Barrett, 2008), participants either were or were not led to think about fear, and then either were or were not exposed to highly arousing music. The experimenters then measured how fearful the participants themselves felt by asking whether they'd be willing to do a whole bunch of scary things. Results showed that participants felt afraid only when they had thought about fear *and* been aroused by music (see also Sinclair et al., 1994).

Although research suggests that a single bodily response can sometimes give rise to different emotional experiences, research has not been so kind to the two-factor theory's claim that different emotional experiences are *nothing but* different interpretations of a single bodily response. For example, research shows that anger, fear, and sadness all produce a higher heart rate than disgust does; fear and disgust produce higher galvanic skin response (sweating) than sadness or anger do; and anger produces a larger increase in finger temperature than fear does (Christie & Friedman, 2004; Ekman, Levenson, & Friesen, 1983; Kreibig, 2010; Levenson, Ekman, & Friesen, 1990; Levenson et al., 1991, 1992; Shiota et al., 2011; Stemmler, Aue, & Wacker, 2007). It seems rather unlikely (as James and Lange maintained) that every human emotion has its own unique "physiological fingerprint," but it seems even more unlikely (as Schachter and Singer maintained) that every human emotion has precisely the same physiological fingerprint. The truth is probably somewhere in the middle, and modern researchers are working to determine exactly where in the middle it lies.

The Emotional Brain

In the late 1930s, two researchers made an accidental discovery (Klüver & Bucy, 1937, 1939). A few days after performing brain surgery on a monkey named Aurora, they noticed that she was acting strangely. First, she would eat just about anything and have sex with just about anyone—as though she could no longer distinguish between good and bad food, or between good and bad mates. Second, she was absolutely fearless and unflappable, remaining perfectly calm when she was handled by researchers or even when confronted by snakes, both of which monkeys generally don't much like. What had happened to Aurora?

As it turned out, during the surgery, the researchers had accidentally damaged a structure in Aurora's brain called the *amygdala,* and subsequent studies confirmed that the amygdala often plays an important role in producing emotions (Cunningham & Brosch, 2012). For example, researchers surgically altered a monkey's brain so that visual information entering the monkey's left eye was transmitted to its amygdala, but visual information entering its right eye was not (Downer, 1961). When the monkey saw a threatening stimulus with only its left eye, it responded with fear and alarm; but when it saw a threatening stimulus with only its right eye, it remained calm and unruffled. Studies of human beings have shown similar effects. For instance, most people have better memory for emotionally evocative words such as *death* or *vomit* than for ordinary words such as *box* or *chair,* but this is not true of people whose amygdalae have been damaged (LaBar & Phelps, 1998) or who have been given drugs that temporarily impair neurotransmission in the amygdala (van Stegeren et al., 1998). Although people with amygdala damage do not feel fear when they *see* a threat, they do feel fear when they *experience* a threat—for example, when they suddenly find they can't breathe (Feinstein et al., 2013).

The tourist and the tiger have something in common: each has an amygdala that is working at lightning speed to decide whether the other is a threat. Let's hope the tourist's amygdala is working a little faster.

AP PHOTO/DAVID LONGSTREATH

Together, these findings provide clues about what the amygdala does. Before an animal feels fear, it must know that there is something to be afraid of—in other words, it must generate an appraisal. The amygdala seems to play a part in that, helping to determine whether stimuli are emotionally relevant. In his work on rats, the psychologist Joseph LeDoux discovered that information about a stimulus enters the eye and is then simultaneously transmitted along two different routes: a "fast pathway" that goes from the eye to the thalamus and then directly to the amygdala (shown in green in **FIGURE 8.4**), and a "slow pathway" that goes from the eye to the thalamus and then *to the cortex* and *then* to the amygdala (shown in red in Figure 8.4). As such, when you see a bear in your kitchen, information about the bear arrives at your amygdala and at your cortex at about the same time. While your cortex conducts a relatively slow, full-scale investigation of the information ("This seems to be an animal, probably a mammal, maybe a member of the genus *Ursus . . .*"), your amygdala uses the information quickly to answer a simple question: "Is this stimulus relevant to my survival?" If your amygdala's answer to that question is yes, it helps produce the bodily responses that, when your cortex is finally done with its investigation, you will come to call *fear*.

LeDoux's research shows how we get scared. So how do we stop? As Figure 8.4 shows, your amygdala receives information directly from your thalamus via the fast pathway (shown in green), but it also receives information from your cortex via the slow pathway (shown in red). This latter connection allows your cortex to "talk" to your amygdala—and one of the things it sometimes says is, "Chill out!" Once the cortex has finished its full-scale investigation of the information it has received, this connection allows the cortex to *downregulate* the amygdala, which is just a fancy way of saying that the cortex tells the amygdala to reduce its activity. In a sense, the amygdala's job is to hit the emotional gas pedal, and the cortex's job is to hit the brakes. That's why both adults who have cortical damage and children (whose cortices are not yet well developed) often have trouble inhibiting their emotional responses (Cohen et al., 2016; Stuss & Benson, 1986). When people are asked to make themselves feel sad, afraid, or angry, they show increased activity in the amygdala and decreased activity in the cortex (Damasio et al., 2000); but, when they are asked to make themselves *not* feel these emotions, they show increased cortical activity and decreased amygdala activity (Ochsner et al., 2002).

Does all of this mean that the amygdala is the brain's "fear centre?" If only the brain were that simple! Although specific areas of the brain do seem to play special roles in the production of specific emotions—the anterior insula in disgust, the orbitofrontal cortex in anger, the anterior cingulate cortex in sadness—the fact is that the brain simply does not have different "centres" for different emotions (Lindquist et al., 2012). The amygdala's precise role in producing fear is complicated and still not very well understood (Phelps & LeDoux, 2005). There are times when the amygdala is highly active but that people do not report feeling afraid, just as there are times when it is not highly active but people do report feeling afraid (Feinstein et al., 2013). What's more, the amygdala appears to play a role in emotions other than fear (Phelps, 2006). The bottom line is that we don't know exactly what the amygdala does, but we do know that the cortex and the amygdala—as well as other limbic and non-limbic structures—work together in complex ways to produce the reactions of the body and the experiences of the mind that together constitute an emotion.

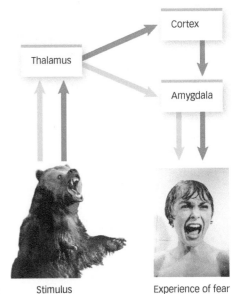

Stimulus   Experience of fear

Figure 8.4
The Fast and Slow Pathways of Fear Information about a stimulus takes two routes simultaneously through the brain: the "fast pathway" (shown in green), which runs from the thalamus directly to the amygdala, and the "slow pathway" (shown in red), which runs from the thalamus to the cortex and then to the amygdala. Because the amygdala receives information from the thalamus before it receives information from the cortex, a person can be afraid of something before he or she knows what it is. BEAR: JIM ZUCKERMAN/GETTY IMAGES; WOMAN: SNAP/SHUTTERSTOCK

Build to the Outcomes

1. What are the two dimensions on which feelings vary?
2. What is the difference between an appraisal and an action tendency?
3. What are some problems with the James–Lange theory?
4. How did the two-factor theory build on earlier theories?
5. How do the amygdala and cortex interact to produce fear?

Emotional Communication

Leonardo is a robot so he can't experience emotions. But he can smile and frown, wink and nod. Indeed, humans who interact with Leonardo quickly forget that he is a machine precisely because he is so good at *expressing* emotions that he isn't actually experiencing. An **emotional expression** is *an observable sign of an emotional state,* and, although robots can be taught to exhibit them, human beings do so naturally. Our emotions influence the way we talk—from our intonation and inflection to the volume and duration of our speech—which is why observers can guess our emotional state from our voice alone (Banse & Scherer, 1996; Cordaro et al., 2016; Frick, 1985; Sauter et al., 2010). They can also guess our emotional state from the direction of our gaze, the rhythm of our gait, or from the way we touch them on the arm (Dael, Mortillaro, & Scherer, 2012; Dittrich et al., 1996; Hertenstein et al., 2009; Parkinson et al., 2017; Wallbott, 1998). In some sense, we are all walking, talking advertisements for what's going on inside us.

Of course, no part of our bodies is more exquisitely designed for communicating our emotional state than is our face (Jack & Schyns, 2017). Beneath the skin of your face lie 43 muscles that are capable of creating more than 10,000 unique configurations that enable you to convey information about your emotional state with an astonishing degree of subtlety and specificity (Campos et al., 2013; Ekman, 1965) (see **FIGURE 8.5**). The psychologists Paul Ekman and Wallace Friesen (1971) identified 46 unique muscle configurations or "action units" whose names (e.g., cheek puffer, chin raiser, lip corner puller) pretty much say it all. Research shows that some (though not all) of these action units are reliably associated with specific emotional states (Davidson et al., 1990; Mehu & Scherer, 2015). For example, when you feel happy, your *zygomaticus major* (a muscle that pulls your lip corners up) and your *orbicularis oculi* (a muscle that crinkles the outside edges of your eyes) produce a unique facial expression that psychologists describe as "action units 6 and 12" but that you probably just call smiling (Ekman & Friesen, 1982; Martin et al., 2017).

Communicative Expression

Why are our emotions written all over our faces? In 1872, Charles Darwin published *The Expression of the Emotions in Man and Animals,* in which he speculated about the evolutionary significance of emotional expression. Darwin noticed that human and nonhuman animals share certain postures and facial expressions, and he suggested that these "displays" were meant to communicate information about internal states. It isn't hard to see how such communications might be useful (Shariff & Tracy, 2011; Tracy, Randles, & Steckler, 2015). If a dominant animal can bare its teeth and communicate the message "I am angry," and if a subordinate animal can lower its head and communicate the message "I am afraid," then the two can establish a pecking order without any actual pecking. Darwin suggested that emotional expressions are a convenient way for one animal to let another animal know how it is feeling and therefore how it is prepared to act—that is, what its action tendencies might be. Darwin thought that emotional expressions were a bit like the words of a nonverbal language.

The Universality of Expression

Of course, a language doesn't work unless everybody speaks the same one, and that's what led Darwin to advance the **universality hypothesis**, which suggests that *all emotional expressions mean the same thing to all people in all places at all times.* Darwin believed that every human being naturally expresses happiness with a smile and that, as a result, every human being naturally understands that a smile signifies happiness. Emotional expression is a language that is universally spoken and universally understood.

emotional expression An observable sign of an emotional state.

universality hypothesis The theory that all emotional expressions mean the same thing to all people in all places at all times.

DU, S., TAO, Y., & MARTINEZ, A. M. (2014). COMPOUND FACIAL EXPRESSIONS OF EMOTION. PROCEEDINGS OF THE NATIONAL ACADEMY OF SCIENCES, 111(15), E1454- E1462. IMAGE COURTESY OF ALEIX M. MARTINEZ

Happy	Sad	Fearful	Angry	Surprised
Disgusted	Happily surprised	Happily disgusted	Sadly fearful	Sadly angry
Sadly surprised	Sadly disgusted	Fearfully angry	Fearfully surprised	Fearfully disgusted
Angrily surprised	Angrily disgusted	Disgustedly surprised	Hatred	Awed

Figure 8.5
Human observers can identify at least 20 distinct facial expressions of emotion, such as those indicated here.

Evidence suggests that Darwin was . . . well, not exactly right. Some facial expressions do seem to be universal. For instance, people who have never seen a human face make the same facial expressions as those who have: Congenitally blind people smile when they are happy (Galati, Scherer, & Ricci-Bitt, 1997; Matsumoto & Willingham, 2009), and 2-day-old infants make a disgust face when bitter chemicals are put in their mouths (Steiner, 1973, 1979). People are quite good at identifying the meaning of the emotional expressions made by members of their own cultures, but they are also pretty good (though not as good) at identifying the meaning of the emotional expressions made by members of other cultures (Ekman & Friesen, 1971; Elfenbein & Ambady, 2002; Frank & Stennet, 2001; Haidt & Keltner, 1999). In the 1950s, researchers took photographs of Westerners expressing anger, disgust, fear, happiness, sadness, and surprise and showed them to members of the South Fore, a people who lived a Stone Age existence in the highlands of Papua New Guinea and who at that point had had little contact with the modern world. When the researchers asked these participants to match each photograph to a word (such as "happy" or "afraid"), they found that the South Fore made matches that were very similar to those made by Americans.

Nobuyuki Tsujii (shown here) is a classical pianist who won the prestigious Van Cliburn International Piano Competition. Although he was born blind and has never seen a facial expression, winning a million-dollar prize immediately gave rise to a million-dollar smile.

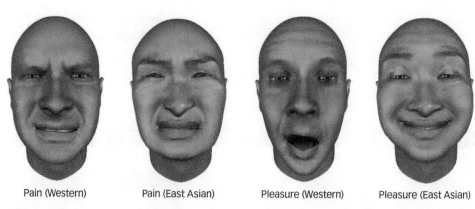

Pain (Western) Pain (East Asian) Pleasure (Western) Pleasure (East Asian)

Figure 8.6

The Faces of Pain and Pleasure Westerners and East Asians agree about how the face expresses the experience of intense physical pain, but they disagree about how it expresses the experience of intense physical pleasure. For instance, East Asians expect the physical pleasure of orgasm to produce an expression that is a lot like the expression of happiness, but Westerners expect it to produce an expression that is a lot like the expression of surprise. DISTINCT FACIAL EXPRESSIONS REPRESENT PAIN AND PLEASURE ACROSS CULTURES. CHAONA CHEN, ET AL. PNAS OCT 2018, 115 (43). COPYRIGHT 2018, NATIONAL ACADEMY OF SCIENCES.

The majority of psychologists believe that the facial displays of at least five emotions—*anger, disgust, fear, happiness,* and *sadness*—are clearly universal (Ekman, 2016) and that a few other emotions—such as *embarrassment, surprise, amusement, guilt, shame,* and *pride*—may be universal as well (Keltner, 1995; Keltner & Buswell, 1996; Keltner & Haidt, 1999; Keltner & Harker, 1998; Tracy et al., 2013). Other psychologists think the majority is wrong (Gendron, Crivelli, & Barrett, 2018). Research on members of an isolated tribe called the Himba suggests that these people match faces to emotion words just as Americans do, but that when they are instead asked to match faces to other faces that are "feeling the same way," they produce matches that are unlike those produced by their American counterparts (Gendron et al., 2014). Research also suggests that some emotional expressions—such as shame, happiness, and sadness—have distinct cultural "accents" (Elfenbein, 2007) (see **FIGURE 8.6**). Studies such as these suggest that the universality hypothesis has been overstated. It seems safe to say that human beings show considerable agreement about the emotional meaning of many facial expressions, but this agreement is short of being universal (Cordaro et al., 2018).

The Cause and Effect of Expression

Members of different cultures express many of their emotions in the same way. But why? They don't all speak the same language, so why should they smile the same smile or frown the same frown? The answer is that words are *symbols*, and facial expressions are *signs*. Symbols are arbitrary designations that have no causal relationship with the things they symbolize: English speakers use the word *cat* to indicate a particular animal, but there is nothing about felines that actually *causes* this particular sound to pop out of our mouths, which is why we aren't surprised when other human beings make entirely different sounds—such as *popoki* or *gatto*—to indicate a furry pet that thinks it is better than you. But facial expressions are not arbitrary symbols of the emotions they convey. They are signs of those emotions because, unlike symbols, signs are *caused* by the things they signify. The emotion called happiness *causes* the contraction of the zygomatic major, and therefore that contraction is a sign of that emotion in the same way that a footprint in the snow is a sign that someone walked there.

COURTESY OF SCOTT FAHLMAN

On September 19, 1982, Scott Fahlman posted a message to a brand-new thing called "the world wide web" which read, "I propose the following character sequence for joke markers: :-) Read it sideways." And so the emoticon was born. Fahlman's smile is a sign of happiness, whereas his emoticon is a symbol.

Just as a symbol (*cat*) can have more than one meaning ("a small domesticated carnivorous mammal" or "a brand of heavy machinery"), so too can a sign. Look at the face of the man in **FIGURE 8.7**. Is he experiencing great joy or great sorrow? It's hard to tell because these two very different emotions often produce the same facial expression. So in everyday life, how do we manage to tell them apart? The answer is *context*. When a man says, "My cat ate a mouse," the context of the sentence suggests that he is referring to his pet and not his front-end loader. Similarly, the context in which a facial expression occurs can tell us what that expression means (Aviezer et al., 2008; Barrett, Mesquita, & Gendron, 2011; Kayyal, Widen, & Russell, 2015; Reschke et al., 2019). You may be uncertain about whether the man in Figure 8.7 is feeling sorrow or joy, but if you turn to **FIGURE 8.9** on page 329 and see his face in the context of his body, and in the context of the things going on around him, you will instantly know what he is feeling. Indeed, when you return to this page (and please do come back soon because we miss you already), you will wonder how you could ever have been uncertain.

Emotions cause emotional expressions—but it can also work the other way around. The **facial feedback hypothesis** (Adelmann & Zajonc, 1989; Izard, 1971; Tomkins, 1981) suggests that *emotional expressions can cause the emotional experiences they typically signify*. For instance, studies show that under the right circumstances, people feel happier when they are asked to hold a pencil in their teeth (which causes contraction of the zygomaticus major) than when they are asked to hold a pencil in their lips (Strack, Martin, & Stepper, 1988; see also Marsh, Rhoads, & Ryan, 2018; Noah, Schul, & Mayo, 2018; Strack, 2016). Similarly, when people are instructed to arch their brows (an expression of surprise), they find facts more surprising, and when they are instructed to wrinkle their noses (an expression of disgust), they find odours less pleasant (Lewis, 2012). These things happen because facial expressions and emotional states become strongly associated with each other over time (Ding! Remember Pavlov?), and eventually each has the power to bring about the other. These effects are not limited to the face: People feel more assertive when instructed to make a fist (Schubert & Koole, 2009) and more confident when instructed to stand with their legs spread and their hands on their hips (Carney, Cuddy, & Yap, 2010). And when people are instructed to extend their middle fingers (an expression of . . . well, you know) they rate other people more negatively (Chandler & Schwarz, 2009).

The fact that emotional expressions can cause the emotional experiences they signify may help explain why people are so good at recognizing the emotional expressions of others. When people interact, they unconsciously mimic their interaction partner's body postures and facial expressions (Chartrand & Bargh, 1999; Dimberg, 1982). When our interaction partners smile, we smile, too—even if just a little and even if we don't realize we are doing it (Foroni & Semin, 2009). The tendency to ape the facial expressions of our interaction partners is so natural that, yes, even apes do it (Davila Ross, Menzler, & Zimmermann, 2008). Our mimicry of others may have a hidden benefit: Because facial expressions can cause us to experience the emotions they signify, mimicking our interaction partner's expressions can cause us to *feel* what our partners are feeling, which makes it easy for us to identify our partner's emotions. If your friend's frown makes you frown, and your frown makes you feel sad, then you don't have to think very hard to know what your friend is feeling.

Is there any evidence to suggest that people do, in fact, use their own emotions to identify the emotions of others? There is. First, people find it difficult to identify other people's emotions when they are unable to make facial expressions of their own—for instance, if their facial muscles have been paralyzed with Botox (Niedenthal et al., 2005). People also find it difficult to identify other people's

Figure 8.7
Two Emotions, One Expression Without any context, it is difficult to know if this man is feeling sorrow or joy.

Jonathan Kalb is an American theatre professor who contracted Bell's palsy and lost the ability to make a smile. "For the past thirteen years, my smile has been an incoherent tug-of-war between a grin on one side and a frown on the other: an expression of joy spliced to an expression of horror. . . . The worst effect of my damaged smile is that it can dampen my experience of joy. . . . my brain doesn't receive the same feedback messages that normal people receive from their smiles, which reinforce their happy feelings as well as relaying them. I've been devastated by the loss" (Kalb, 2015).

facial feedback hypothesis The theory that emotional expressions can cause the emotional experiences they typically signify.

emotions when they are unable to *experience* emotions of their own (Hussey & Safford, 2009; Pitcher et al., 2008). For example, some people with amygdala damage don't feel fear and anger, and as a result, they are typically poor at recognizing the expressions of those emotions in others (Adolphs, Russell, & Tranel, 1999). On the flip side, the people who are naturally talented at figuring out what others are feeling also tend to be natural mimics (Sonnby-Borgstrom, Jonsson, & Svensson, 2003), and their mimicry pays off: Negotiators who mimic the facial expressions of their opponents earn more money than those who don't (Maddux, Mullen, & Galinsky, 2008).

Deceptive Expression

Our emotional expressions can communicate our true feelings—or not. When a friend makes a sarcastic remark about your hairstyle, you may express your contempt with an arched brow or an exaggerated eye roll; but when your grandmother makes the same remark, you swallow hard and fake a smile. You know that it is okay to show a bit of contempt for a friend but not for a grandparent, and this knowledge is called a **display rule**, which is *a norm for the appropriate expression of emotion* (Ekman, 1972; Ekman & Friesen, 1968). Obeying display rules requires using several techniques, which most of us have mastered:

- *Intensification* involves exaggerating the expression of emotion, as people do when pretending to be delighted by an unwanted gift. ("A bow tie with little pictures of Keanu Reeves! Thanks, Dad. It's just what I always wanted!")

- *Deintensification* involves muting the expression of one's emotion, as athletes do when they lose their events but try not to look too disappointed. ("No, really, I'm perfectly fine with the silver medal. It matches my belt buckle.")

- *Masking* involves expressing one emotion while feeling another, as a judge does when she tries to seem interested in, rather than contemptuous of, a lawyer's argument. ("So you are saying that your client simply did not realize that the bank belonged to someone else?")

- *Neutralizing* involves showing no expression of the emotion one is feeling, as when a card player tries to keep a "poker face" despite having been dealt a winning hand. ("Four aces. Ho hum. Nice weather we're having.")

Although people in different cultures use the same techniques, they use them in the service of different display rules. In one study, Japanese and American university students watched an unpleasant video of car accidents and amputations (Ekman, 1972; Friesen, 1972). When the students didn't know that the experimenters were observing them, Japanese and American students showed similar facial expressions of disgust; but when they knew the experimenters were observing them, the Japanese students masked their disgust with pleasant expressions and the American students did not. Why? Because in Japan it is considered rude to display negative emotions in the presence of a respected person, so Japanese tend to mask or neutralize their expressions when being observed. The fact that different cultures have different display rules may be one of the reasons that people are generally better at recognizing the facial expressions of members of their own cultures (Elfenbein & Ambady, 2002) (see A World of Difference: Say Cheese).

Of course, our attempts to obey our culture's display rules don't always work out. Anyone who has ever watched the members of a losing team in a hockey or basketball game congratulate the winners knows that voices, bodies, and faces often betray

Can you tell what this man is feeling? He hopes not. John Cynn is an American poker player who does not want other players to know how he feels about his cards. In 2018, he won the World Series of Poker championship and took home $8.8 million, so he seems to be doing a good job.

display rule A norm for the appropriate expression of emotion.

A World of Difference | **Say Cheese**

Canada is one of the most culturally diverse countries in the world. About one in five Canadians was born elsewhere, and those born here can also belong to different distinct cultures. Different cultures have different display rules—different ways of nonverbally expressing emotions—which suggests that Canadians with different backgrounds should have trouble "reading" their neighbours. And yet, they don't seem to. How come?

Wood, Rychlowska, and Niedenthal (2016) analyzed data from 92 scientific papers that had measured the accuracy with which people from 82 different cultures could recognize the emotional expressions of people from other cultures. First, the researchers used historical, genetic, and sociological data to compute the cultural diversity of each of the 82 cultures. Nations such as Brazil and the United States scored high in diversity, whereas nations such as Japan and Ethiopia scored low (see the map above). Second, they computed how easily the facial expressions of people from each of these cultures could be recognized by people from other cultures. When they compared these two measures, they found a positive correlation (see the graph to the right). The more diverse a culture is, the more easily the facial expressions of its members can be understood by members of other cultures. Why might that be the case?

The researchers suggest that in nations with little cultural diversity, people can communicate with subtle expressions—a slightly raised eyebrow or the fleeting flare of a nostril—because everyone knows and follows the same display rules. But in diverse nations, people of different backgrounds follow different sets of rules, so to communicate with each other, they have learned to use expressions that are so perfectly clear that they can be accurately recognized by any human on the planet.

▲ The diversity of cultures: Darker colours indicate greater cultural diversity.

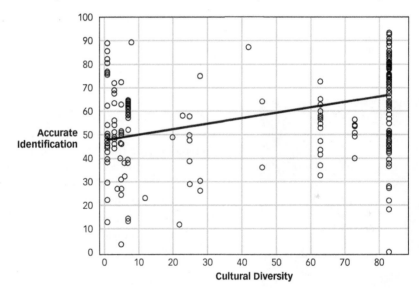

▲ Diversity and accuracy: Each circle in this figure represents one of the 82 cultures.

a person's true emotional state. Darwin noted that "those muscles of the face which are least obedient to the will, will sometimes alone betray a slight and passing emotion" (1899/2007, p. 64), and Darwin was right. The so-called *reliable muscles* are those that people cannot easily control, and they do provide clues to the sincerity of an expression. For instance, most people can easily control the *zygomaticus major* muscles that raise the corners of the mouth but not the *orbicularis oculi* muscles that crinkle the corners of the eyes, which is why eye crinkles are a good clue to the

Figure 8.8

How Reliable Are the Reliable Muscles?
Real smiles (*left*) are often accompanied by a crinkling of the eye corners, and fake smiles (*right*) are not. Eye crinkles are reliable signs—but not perfectly reliable signs—of happiness. Happy people don't always crinkle their eyes (Crivelli et al., 2015), and although most people can't fake the crinkle, some can (Gunnery et al., 2013).

The polygraph was invented in 1921 by a police officer named John Augustus Larson, and it has been in widespread use ever since. The machine measures a person's blood pressure, pulse, respiration rate, and skin conductivity during questioning. Does it work? "Like most junk science that just won't die (graphology, astrology and homeopathy come to mind), because of the usefulness or profit their practitioners enjoy, the polygraph stays with us." Those words were written by Aldrich Ames (shown above), a former CIA agent who is currently serving a life sentence in prison for selling state secrets to the Russian government. Ames passed several polygraph exams before he was caught, and claims that fooling the machine is easy.

sincerity of a smile (see **FIGURE 8.8**). Sincere expressions also tend to be symmetrical, to last between a half second and 5 seconds, and to start and end smoothly. That's why asymmetrical expressions that are too short or too long and that have abrupt onsets or offsets are likely to be insincere (Ekman, 2003).

Lying

Sometimes people lie with their smiles, but just as often they lie with their words. Research shows that telling lies affects both our verbal and nonverbal behaviour (DePaulo et al., 2003). Liars tend to speak more slowly, take longer to respond to questions, and often respond with less detail than do people who are telling the truth. Liars tend to be less fluent, less engaging, more uncertain, tenser, and less pleasant than truth-tellers. Oddly enough, one of the signs that a person is lying is that his or her performance tends to be just a little too *good*. A liar's speech often lacks the small imperfections that a truth-teller's speech contains. People who are telling the truth include superfluous details ("I noticed that the robber was wearing the same shoes that I saw on sale last week at Aldo and I found myself wondering what he paid for them"), they correct themselves ("He was six feet tall . . . well, no, actually more like six-two"), and they express self-doubt ("I think he had blue eyes, but I'm really not sure"). Liars are less likely to do any of these things.

Given the observable differences between truth-tellers and liars, you might think that people would be pretty good at distinguishing one from another. But you'd be wrong. In most cases, participants in lie-detection experiments don't perform much better than chance (Bond & DePaulo, 2006; cf. ten Brinke, Vohs, & Carney, 2016). One reason is that people have a tendency to believe that others are telling truth, which explains why they tend to mistake liars for truth-tellers much more often than they mistake truth-tellers for liars (Gilbert, 1991). A second reason is that people don't know what to look for when trying to detect lies (Vrij et al., 2011). For instance, people believe that fast talking is a sign of lying when in fact it isn't, and they don't realize that slow talking is a sign of lying when often it is. Not only are people fairly bad lie detectors, but they also don't seem to know they are fairly bad lie detectors: The correlation between a person's ability to detect lies and the person's confidence in that ability is essentially zero (DePaulo et al., 1997).

When we humans can't do something very easily—such as adding huge numbers or lifting huge rocks—we often turn the job over to a machine. Can machines detect lies better than we can? Although several companies claim that they can use brain scans to detect lies, the scientific evidence suggests that they may not . . . um, be telling the truth. At present, at least, brain scans cannot tell us with much accuracy whether or not a person is lying (Farah et al., 2014). But what about the traditional lie-detecting machine—the polygraph? As you probably know, a polygraph measures a variety of physiological responses that are associated with stress, which people often feel when they are afraid of being caught in a lie. So can it actually detect lies? Well, yes, a polygraph can detect lies with better-than-chance accuracy. But that's not very helpful, because while the polygraph's error rate is not 100%, it is far too high to be useful.

To illustrate this, imagine that 10 of the 10,000 people coming through an airport are terrorists. The authorities decide to hook every one of them up to a polygraph and ask them, "Are you a terrorist?" to which all of them say "No." If the polygraph were set to *maximum* sensitivity, it would catch 8 of the 10 terrorists in a lie. Not bad, huh? Yes—*very* bad! Because it would also mistakenly "catch" 1,598 innocent people! If the polygraph were instead set to *minimum* sensitivity, it would mistakenly "catch" just 39 innocent people, but it would also catch only 2 of the 10 terrorists. And even these numbers are optimistic because they assume that terrorists can't fool a polygraph, which, in fact, people can be trained to do. No wonder the National Research Council of the American National Academy of Sciences (2003) warned against its use. "The history of polygraphy offers tragic reminders of the cost, in national security and human life, of overreliance on an apparently

REUTERS/FAYAZ AZIZ

Figure 8.9
What Do You Think Now? This Pakistani man is being led away from the scene of the suicide bombing that killed his father. Now that you see the sorrow in his face, is it hard to imagine how you could ever have thought he might be feeling joy?

high-tech but inaccurate method for detecting deception" (Farah et al., 2014, p. 23). In short, neither people nor machines are particularly good at lie detection, which is probably why lying remains such a popular human sport.

Build to the Outcomes

1. What is the difference between a sign and a symbol?
2. What evidence suggests that facial expressions of emotion are or are not universal?
3. What are display rules?
4. What features distinguish between sincere and insincere facial expressions?
5. What is the problem with using a polygraph to detect liars in the real world?

The Nature of Motivation

Leonardo is a robot, so he does what he is commanded to do, but nothing more. Because he doesn't have wants and urges—doesn't crave friendship or desire chocolate or hate homework—he doesn't initiate his own behaviour. He is reactive rather than proactive, a responder rather than an originator. The spark that you have but that Leonardo lacks is called **motivation**, which refers to *the internal causes of purposeful behaviour.* You eat because you feel hungry and you sleep because you feel tired. You find friends because you feel lonely, you ditch friends because you feel bored. Everything you do, you do for a reason—but what are those reasons? And where do they come from? And how do they get you to act on them?

Instincts

When a newborn baby is given a drop of sugar water, she smiles, and when given a cheque for $10,000, she acts like she couldn't care less. By the time that baby goes to university, these responses pretty much reverse. It seems clear that nature endows us with certain motivations and that experience endows us with others. William James (1890) called the natural tendency to seek a particular goal an *instinct,* which he defined as "the faculty of acting in such a way as to produce certain ends, without foresight of the ends, and without previous education in the performance" (p. 383). According to James, nature hardwired people, penguins, parrots, and puppies to want certain things without being taught to want them, and to execute the

Learning Outcomes

- Explain what's right and what's wrong with the concept of instinct.
- Describe the concept of drive and the role it plays in homeostasis.
- Explain the hedonic principle and how it influences emotion regulation.

motivation The internal causes of purposeful behaviour.

All animals are born with instincts. In the annual running of the bulls in Pamplona, Spain, no one has to teach the bulls to chase the runners, and no one has to teach the runners to flee.

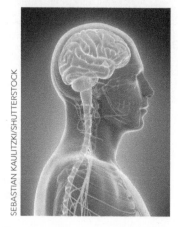

A thermostat is a homeostatic device. It monitors the temperature of a room and, when necessary, initiates corrective action to restore equilibrium. The human brain comes with a similar homeostatic device called the hypothalamus, which monitors the temperature of the body. The word "homeostasis" was coined in 1926 by the physiologist Walter Cannon, who called it "the wisdom of the body."

behaviours that produce these things without ever thinking about it. He and other psychologists of his time tried to make a list of what those things were.

They were a little too successful. In just a few decades of list-making, their list of instincts had grown to contain nearly 6,000 entries, including some rather exotic ones such as "the instinct to be secretive" and "the instinct to grind one's teeth." Some researchers complained that the term suffered from "a great variety of usage and the almost universal lack of critical standards" (Bernard, 1924, p. 21), and others worried that attributing the tendency for people to affiliate to an "affiliation instinct" was not really saying much—that it was more of a description than an explanation (Ayres, 1921; Dunlap, 1919; Field, 1921). By 1930, the term had fallen out of fashion, in part because it didn't really seem to explain anything, but also because it flew in the face of Western psychology's hot new trend—behaviourism—which you learned about in The Evolution of Psychological Science and Learning chapters.

Behaviourists rejected the concept of instinct on two grounds. First, they believed that behaviours were fully explained by the external stimuli that elicited them and that there was no need to posit hypothetical internal states; and second, behaviourists believed that complex behaviours were learned, not hard-wired. Instincts violated these maxims. They were inborn and internal, and therefore of little theoretical value.

Drives

Behaviourists didn't have much use for internal states, but that made it difficult for them to explain certain phenomena. For example, if all behaviour is simply a response to an external stimulus, then why does a rat that is sitting quietly in its cage suddenly get up and start wandering around, looking for food? Nothing in the environment has changed, so why has the rat's behaviour changed? What visible, measurable, external stimulus is the wandering rat responding to? The obvious answer is that the rat is not responding to an external stimulus but to an internal stimulus, which meant that psychologists were going to have to talk about what happens *inside* a rat if they were going to explain its behaviour. But how could they do that without talking about a rat's "beliefs" and "desires?"

By talking about thermostats. When a thermostat senses that the room is too cold, it sends a signal to the furnace to take corrective action—that is, to fire itself up and start blowing heat into the room. Later, when the thermostat senses that the room has reached the optimal temperature, it sends a signal to the furnace to terminate its action—that is, to turn itself off and stop blowing heat. When a room is at the optimal temperature, a thermostat is said to be in *equilibrium* (from the Latin words for "equal" and "balance"). It isn't telling the furnace to turn itself on or to shut itself off. It's just hanging out there on the wall, happily doing nothing. **Homeostasis** is *the tendency for a system to take action to keep itself in equilibrium,* which is why a thermostat is said to be a "homeostatic device."

The brain and body work the same way. The brain monitors the body—its hydration, its glucose levels, its temperature, and so on. When it senses that the body is in disequilibrium, it sends a signal to initiate a corrective action such as drinking, eating, shivering, and so on. When later it senses that equilibrium has been restored, it sends a signal to terminate those actions. The language of equilibrium and homeostasis provides a convenient way for behaviourists to talk about the inside of a rat without talking about its beliefs and desires. According to Clark Hull, one of the most important behaviourists of his day, disequilibrium produces a "need," which Hull called a "drive," and his **drive-reduction theory** suggested that *the primary motivation of all organisms is to reduce their drives.* According to this theory, animals are not actually motivated to eat and don't actually find food rewarding. Rather, they are motivated to reduce their drive for food, and it is the reduction of this drive that they find rewarding. A reinforcement is simply any "substance or commodity in the environment which satisfies a need, i.e., which reduces a drive" (Hull, 1943, p. 131).

Although the words *instinct* and *drive* are no longer widely used in psychology, both concepts still have something to teach us. The concept of instinct reminds us that nature endows us with certain desires, and the concept of drive reminds us that our actions are often attempts to fulfill them. So what *kinds* of desires do we have?

The Hedonic Principle

It is no coincidence that the words *emotion* and *motivation* share a common Latin root (*movere*, which means "to move") because, of all the many things that people are moved to do, or motivated to do, or driven to do, or want to do, experiencing positive emotion and avoiding negative emotion is chief among them. The **hedonic principle** is the claim that *people are primarily motivated to experience pleasure and avoid pain,* and that claim has a very long history. The ancient Greek philosopher Aristotle thought the hedonic principle explained everything there was to explain about human motivation: "It is for the sake of this that we all do all that we do," he wrote. Although we want many things, from peace and prosperity to health and security, we want them for just one reason: They make us happy. "Are these things good for any other reason except that they end in pleasure, and get rid of and avert pain?" asked Plato. "Are you looking to any other standard but pleasure and pain when you call them good?" In other words, feeling good is our *raison d'être*—our reason for being. Even when we purposefully do things that feel bad, such as paying the dentist to drill our teeth or waking up early for a boring class, we are doing these things because we believe they will make us feel even better later (Michaela et al., 2009; Miyamoto, Ma, & Petermann, 2014; Tamir & Ford, 2012; Tamir et al., 2015).

So how do we accomplish that goal? **Emotion regulation** refers to *the strategies people use to influence their own emotional experience.* Nine out of 10 people report that they attempt to regulate their emotional experience at least once a day (Gross, 1998), and they report more than a thousand different strategies for doing so (Parkinson & Totterdell, 1999). Some of these strategies are behavioural (e.g., avoiding situations that trigger unwanted emotions) and some are cognitive (e.g., recruiting memories that trigger the desired emotion) (Webb, Miles, & Sheeran, 2012), but regardless of how they work, people seem to have a poor understanding of which are most effective (Heiy & Cheavens, 2014; Troy et al., 2018).

For example, most people think that *suppression,* which involves inhibiting the outward signs of an emotion, is an effective way to regulate their emotional state. *If you're glum, just stand up straight, keep a stiff upper lip, and you'll jolly well feel better in no time!* Except that it isn't true (Gross, 2002; Kalokerinos, Greenaway, & Denson, 2015). Not only is suppression a relatively ineffective way to regulate emotions, but it also requires a lot of effort and therefore makes it harder for people to function successfully in their everyday lives (Franchow & Suchy, 2015). On the other hand, most people think that *affect labelling,* which involves putting one's feelings into words, has little or no impact on their emotions. But in fact, affect labelling turns out to be quite an effective way to reduce the intensity of emotional states (Lieberman et al., 2011; Torre & Lieberman, 2018) (see **FIGURE 8.10**).

One of the best strategies for emotion regulation is **reappraisal**, which involves *changing one's emotional experience by changing the way one thinks about the emotion-eliciting stimulus* (Gross, 1998). In one study, participants who watched a video of a circumcision that was described as a joyous religious ritual had slower heart rates and reported less distress than did participants who watched the same video but did not hear that description (Lazarus & Alfert, 1964). In another study, participants' brains were scanned as they saw photos that induced negative emotions, such as a photo of a woman crying during a funeral. Some participants were then asked to reappraise the

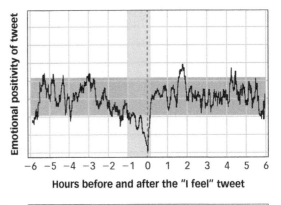

Hours before and after the "I feel" tweet

> **Daniel Gilbert** ✔ @ DanTGilbert . Feb 20 ⌄
> I feel sad because the Patriots always win, which makes my friends jealous so they hate me.

Figure 8.10

Labelling Affect with 140 Characters Fan and colleagues (2019) analyzed the emotional content of the tweets of nearly 75,000 twitter users over time and discovered that when a user's tweet contains the sentence "I feel _____" followed by a negative emotion word, within an hour their tweets begin to contain much more positive emotion words. One interpretation of this finding is that labelling their negative emotions helped users overcome them.

homeostasis The tendency for a system to take action to keep itself in equilibrium.

drive-reduction theory A theory suggesting that the primary motivation of all organisms is to reduce their drives.

hedonic principle The claim that people are motivated to experience pleasure and avoid pain.

emotion regulation The strategies people use to influence their own emotional experiences.

reappraisal The process of changing one's emotional experience by changing the way one thinks about the emotion-eliciting stimulus.

picture, for example, by imagining that the woman in the photo was at a wedding rather than a funeral. The results showed that when participants initially saw the photo, their amygdalae were activated; but when they reappraised the picture, their cortices were activated and moments later their amygdalae were deactivated (Ochsner et al., 2002). In other words, participants were able to downregulate the activity of their own amygdalae simply by thinking about the photo in a different way.

Reappraisal is a skill. Like most skills, it can be learned (Denny & Ochsner, 2014; Smith et al., 2018), and like most skills, some people are naturally better at it than others (Malooly, Genet, & Siemer, 2013). People who are especially good at reappraisal tend to be both mentally and physically healthier (Davidson, Putnam, & Larson, 2000; Gross & Muñoz, 1995), and to have better relationships with their parents (Cooke et al., 2018) and romantic partners (Bloch, Haase, & Levenson, 2014). This should not be surprising, given that reappraisal is one of the skills that therapists commonly try to teach people who are dealing with emotional problems (Jamieson, Nock, & Mendes, 2013). On the other hand, this skill has a dark side: People who are good at changing how they see things in order to feel better about the things they see can be less compassionate towards those who are suffering (Cameron & Payne, 2011). Given how effective reappraisal is, you might expect people to do it all the time, but you'd be wrong (Heiy & Cheavens, 2014). People tend to underutilize reappraisal in part because it is a strategy that requires some effort to implement (Milyavsky et al., 2019), which may also explain why people are even less inclined to use reappraisal as they age (Scheibe, Sheppes, & Staudinger, 2015).

Build to the Outcomes

1. How are emotions and motivations related?
2. Why did psychologists abandon the concept of instinct?
3. What is drive-reduction theory?
4. What is homeostasis?
5. What is the hedonic principle?
6. What are the best and worst strategies for emotion regulation?

The Motivated Body

Learning Outcomes

- Describe Maslow's hierarchy of needs.
- Explain how hunger signals get turned on and off.
- Identify the common eating disorders.
- Understand what causes obesity and how it can be prevented.
- Describe the role that hormones play in sexual interest.
- Describe the human sexual response cycle.

People like to feel good. How do they do it? What are the things that bring positive emotions about? The psychologist Abraham Maslow (1954) believed that people feel good when their needs are met, and he suggested that the list of human needs could be organized by how "pressing" each of them was. Maslow designed a hierarchy (see **FIGURE 8.11**) with the most pressing human needs at the bottom and the least pressing needs at the top, and suggested that as a rule, people do not experience a need until the needs below it are met. According to Maslow, people are motivated to experience intellectual fulfillment and moral clarity, but they do not experience this need until their more basic needs for food, water, and sleep are met. In Maslow's hierarchy, the most pressing needs are those we share with other animals, such as the need to eat and the need to mate (Kenrick et al., 2010), so let's begin our exploration of specific motivations at the bottom of the pyramid and then work our way up. Let's start by examining one of the most basic of all needs—a need you had recently and will have again soon.

Hunger

Animals convert matter into energy by eating, and the drive to eat is called *hunger*. But what exactly is hunger and how is it produced? At every moment, your body is sending reports to your brain about its current energy state. If your body has insufficient energy (i.e., if it is in disequilibrium), it sends an *orexigenic* signal to your brain telling it to switch hunger on, and if your body has sufficient energy, it sends an *anorexigenic* signal to your brain telling it to switch hunger off (Gropp et al., 2005). No one knows precisely what these signals are or how they are sent and received, but research has identified a few candidates.

Ghrelin is a hormone that is produced in the stomach and appears to be one of the orexigenic signals that tells the brain to switch hunger on (Inui, 2001; Nakazato et al., 2001). When people are injected with ghrelin, they become intensely hungry and eat about 30% more than usual (Wren et al., 2001). Interestingly, ghrelin also binds to neurons in the hippocampus and temporarily improves learning and memory (Diano et al., 2006), perhaps so that we become just a little bit better at locating food when our bodies need it most. *Leptin* is a chemical secreted by fat cells, and it is an anorexigenic signal that tells the brain to switch hunger off. It seems to do this by making food less rewarding (Farooqi et al., 2007). People who are born with a leptin deficiency have trouble controlling their appetites (Montague et al., 1997). For example, in 2002, medical researchers reported on the case of a 9-year-old girl who weighed 200 pounds, but after just a few leptin injections, she reduced her food intake by 84% and attained normal weight (Farooqi et al., 2002). Some researchers think the idea that chemicals turn hunger on and off is far too simple. In fact, they argue, there is no general drive called *hunger,* but rather, there are many different hungers, each of which is a response to a unique nutritional deficit and each of which is switched on by a unique chemical messenger (Rozin & Kalat, 1971). For example, rats that are deprived of protein will seek proteins while turning down fats and carbohydrates, suggesting that they are experiencing a specific "protein hunger" and not a general hunger (Rozin, 1968).

We do not know whether hunger is one signal or many, but we do know that the primary receiver of these signals is the hypothalamus. Different parts of the hypothalamus receive different signals (see **FIGURE 8.12**). The *lateral hypothalamus* receives orexigenic signals, and when it is destroyed, animals sitting in a cage full of food will starve themselves to death. The *ventromedial hypothalamus* receives anorexigenic signals, and when it is destroyed, animals will gorge themselves to the point of illness and obesity (Miller, 1960; Steinbaum & Miller, 1965). These two structures were once thought to be the "hunger centre" and the "satiety centre" of the brain, but this view turned out to be far too simple (Woods et al., 1998). Hypothalamic structures clearly play an important role in turning hunger on and off, but the precise way in which they execute these functions remains poorly understood (Stellar & Stellar, 1985).

Eating Disorders

Feelings of hunger tell most of us when to start and stop eating. But for the estimated 113,000 Canadians who have eating disorders (Statistics Canada, 2019f), eating is a much more complicated affair (Hoek & van Hoeken, 2003; Hudson et al., 2006).

- The most common eating disorder is **binge eating disorder** (or **BED**), which is *an eating disorder characterized by recurrent and uncontrolled episodes of consuming a large number of calories in a short time.* People with BED quickly consume large quantities of food over a period of just a few hours, often at night. They frequently report feeling a lack of control over their own behaviour—a sense that they "just can't stop eating."

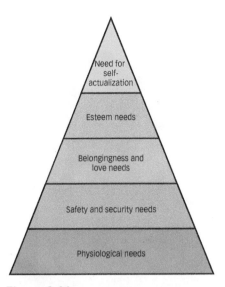

Figure 8.11
Maslow's Hierarchy of Needs The psychologist Abraham Maslow believed that needs form a hierarchy, with physiological needs at the bottom and self-actualization needs at the top.

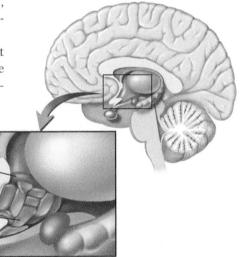

Figure 8.12
Hunger, Satiety, and the Hypothalamus The hypothalamus comprises many parts. In general, the lateral hypothalamus receives the signals that turn hunger on and the ventromedial hypothalamus receives the signals that turn hunger off.

binge eating disorder (BED) An eating disorder characterized by recurrent and uncontrolled episodes of eating a large number of calories in a short time.

The model Yityish Aynaw was crowned Miss Israel in 2013, the same year that Israel became the first nation to ban advertisements showing models whose body mass index is below 18.5. In the years since, Italy, Spain, and France have all passed similar laws.

- The second most common eating disorder is **bulimia nervosa**, which is *an eating disorder characterized by binge eating followed by compensatory behaviour*. People with bulimia also binge, but then they take actions to compensate for their eating, such as fasting, excessive exercising, taking diuretics or laxatives, or even inducing vomiting to purge the food from their bodies. People with BED or bulimia are caught in a cycle: They eat to ease negative emotions such as sadness and anxiety, but then concern about weight gain leads them to experience negative emotions such as guilt and self-loathing (Sherry & Hall, 2009; cf. Haedt-Matt & Keel, 2011).

- The third most common eating disorder is **anorexia nervosa**, which is *an eating disorder characterized by an intense fear of being overweight and a severe restriction of food intake*. People with anorexia tend to have a distorted body image that leads them to believe they are overweight when they may actually be emaciated. They tend to be high-achieving perfectionists who see their severe control of eating as a triumph of will over impulse. Anorexia is often fatal: It literally leads people to starve themselves to death.

What causes these eating disorders? Many things, from the genetic (Zerwas & Bulik, 2011) to the experiential (Inniss, Steiger, & Bruce, 2011) to the psychological (Klump et al., 2004). Culture may play a role as well (Hogan & Strasburger, 2008). For example, women with anorexia typically believe that thinness equals beauty, and it isn't hard to understand where that idea comes from. The average Canadian woman is 161 cm and weighs 70 kg (Statistics Canada, 2015), but the average fashion model is 180 cm and weighs 53 kg (Rosenbaum, 2016) (see **FIGURE 8.13**). Perhaps it is not surprising then that most university-age women report wanting to be thinner than they are (Rozin, Trachtenberg, & Cohen, 2001); that nearly 20% report being *embarrassed* to be seen buying chocolate (Rozin, Bauer, & Catanese, 2003); and that the more attractive their dinner date is, the fewer calories they consume at the restaurant (Baker, Strickland, & Fox, 2019). Although North American women's satisfaction with their bodies has increased in the last 30 years (Karazsia, Murnen, & Tylka, 2017), the pressure to be thin remains strong.

With all that said, anorexia is not just "vanity run amok" (Striegel-Moore & Bulik, 2007). Most researchers believe that there are biological and genetic components to this illness as well. For example, although anorexia primarily affects women, men have a sharply increased risk of becoming anorexic if they have a female twin who has the disorder (Procopio & Marriott, 2007), suggesting that anorexia may have something to do with prenatal exposure to female hormones.

Figure 8.13

The Real and the Ideal These body simulations were made using the BMI Visualizer (http://www.bmivisualizer.com/), and, as you can see, the average Canadian woman (*left*) and the average fashion model (*right*) don't look very much alike.

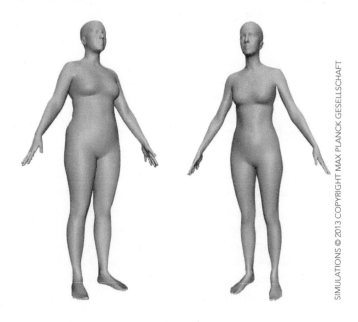

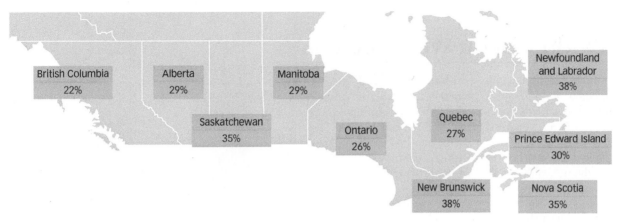

British Columbia 22%

Alberta 29%

Manitoba 29%

Newfoundland and Labrador 38%

Saskatchewan 35%

Ontario 26%

Quebec 27%

Prince Edward Island 30%

New Brunswick 38%

Nova Scotia 35%

Figure 8.14
The Geography of Obesity The map shows the proportion of the adult population who were obese in the 10 provinces of Canada in 2016–2017. Obesity rates are particularly high in the Atlantic provinces. DATA FROM STATISTICS CANADA, 2018a.

Obesity

Bulimia and anorexia are serious problems, but they affect a small fraction of the world's population. The most pervasive eating-related problem today is obesity. Currently, 61% of adults in Canada are overweight or obese: 35% are overweight, 25% are obese (Statistics Canada, 2019d). To give you a sense of what this means, "overweight" for a person who is 170 cm tall (5 feet, 6 inches) would be 73 kg (161 pounds), and "obese" would be 87 kg (192 pounds) or more. Rates of obesity across the country vary substantially, but are increasing everywhere (see **FIGURE 8.14**). Rates of unhealthy weight are increasing among children and adolescents as well. In 1978, fewer than 15% of adolescents were overweight or obese—by 2015, 32% were (Statistics Canada, 2019d). The problem is not unique to North America: Nearly 30% of the world's population is overweight or obese, and no country has reduced its obesity rate in the last three decades (Ng et al., 2014).

Obesity is defined as having a body mass index (BMI) of 30 or greater. You can compute your BMI simply by typing "BMI Calculator" into Google, but the odds are that you won't like what you learn. Although BMI is a better predictor of mortality for some people than for others (Romero-Corral et al., 2006; van Dis et al., 2009), most researchers agree that an extremely high BMI comes with a cost. Obesity and related illnesses cost the Canadian health care system about $4 billion annually (Eisenberg et al., 2011; Public Health Agency of Canada and Canadian Institute for Health Information, 2009). Arguably more important is the cost of lives: Affected adults appear to die 3 to 7 years earlier than individuals at a healthy weight (Peeters et al., 2003). In addition to the health risks, obese people tend to have lower psychological well-being, lower self-esteem, and lower quality of life, and are viewed more negatively by others (Gallup, 2014a; Hebl & Heatherton, 1997; Kolotkin, Meter, & Williams, 2001; Sutin, Stephan, & Terracciano, 2015). Obese women earn about 7% less than their nonobese counterparts (Lempert, 2007), and the stigma of obesity is so powerful that average-weight people are viewed negatively if they have a relationship with someone who is obese (Hebl & Mannix, 2003). All of this is true, but sad. As one scientist noted, we need "a war on obesity, not the obese" (Friedman, 2003).

Obesity's Causes

Obesity seems to have many causes. It is highly heritable (Allison et al., 1996), which may explain why a disproportionate amount of the weight gained by Canadians in the past few decades has been gained by those who were already the heaviest (Flegal & Troiano, 2000) and by those who score high on heritable personality traits such as impulsivity (Stevenson, 2017). Some studies suggest that toxins in the environment can disrupt the functioning of the endocrine system and predispose people to obesity (Grün & Blumberg, 2006; Newbold et al., 2005), some suggest that obesity can be

bulimia nervosa An eating disorder characterized by binge eating followed by compensatory behaviour.

anorexia nervosa An eating disorder characterized by an intense fear of being overweight and a severe restriction of food intake.

The Real World | Get It While You Can

Scientists have known for some time that children who grow up in low-SES (socioeconomic status) households are at increased risk of becoming obese adults. But why? The typical explanation is that these children have limited access to healthy foods and so they eat the unhealthy foods that are available to them, which eventually cause them to become obese. But recent research suggests that this isn't the whole story: Growing up in poverty doesn't just influence *what* people eat, but *when*.

A team of psychologists (Hill et al., 2016) invited university students to their laboratory and asked them to drink either sparkling water or a high-calorie soft drink that raised their blood sugar levels and reduced their hunger. Then they asked the students to rate the taste of some cookies and told them they could sample as many cookies as they wished in order to make their ratings. How many cookies did the two groups of students sample?

That depended on whether the students had grown up in a high-SES or low-SES household. Students who had grown up in high-SES households ate far fewer cookies after drinking soda than after drinking water, suggesting that their decisions about how many cookies to eat were based on how hungry they felt at the moment. But students who had grown up in low-SES households ate just as many cookies when they were not hungry as when they were hungry. Interestingly, the students' *current* SES had no effect on the number of cookies they ate; only their *childhood* SES did.

What do these results mean? Children who grow up in poverty cannot always count on having steady access to food, so they

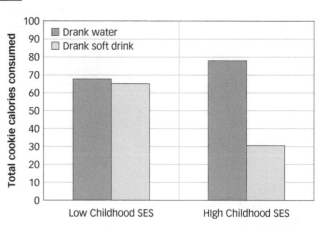

learn to eat when food is available and not to wait until they are hungry. *The cookies are here now and there is no guarantee there will be more later, so get them while you can.* The lessons of childhood do not simply disappear when we become adults, and this research suggests that the relationships we establish with food early on may have enduring consequences for our health.

RENE VAN BAKEL/ASABLANCA VIA GETTY IMAGES

Sea turtles suffer from evolutionary mismatch. When their eggs hatch on the beach at night, the hatchlings move towards the light. This tendency was adaptive in the turtle's ancestral environment because the ocean, which reflects moonlight, was the brightest thing around. But now the trait is maladaptive because hatchlings are lured away from the ocean by the lights of human habitats, where they inevitably perish.

evolutionary mismatch The idea that traits that were adaptive in an ancestral environment may be maladaptive in a modern environment.

caused by a dearth of "good bacteria" in the gut (Liou et al., 2013), some suggest that obesity can result from everyday wear-and-tear on the hippocampus (Stevenson & Francis, 2017), and some suggest that the brains of obese people are simply more sensitive to rewards (Stice & Yokum, 2016). Whatever the causes, obese people are often leptin-resistant (i.e., their brains do not respond to the chemical signal that tells the brain to shut hunger off), and even leptin injections don't seem to help (Friedman & Halaas, 1998; Heymsfield et al., 1999).

But in most cases, the cause of obesity isn't much of a mystery: We simply exercise too little and eat too much. We eat when we are hungry, but we also eat when we are sad or anxious, when it is convenient, or when everyone else is doing it (Herman, Roth, & Polivy, 2003) (see The Real World: Get It While You Can). Sometimes we eat simply because the clock tells us to do so, which is why people with amnesia will happily eat a second lunch shortly after finishing an unremembered first one (Rozin et al., 1998).

DATA VISUALIZATION

Have BMI and Food Consumption Changed Over Time?
Go to launchpadworks.com.

Why do we overeat? After all, we don't breathe ourselves sick or sleep ourselves sick, so why do we eat ourselves sick? **Evolutionary mismatch** refers to the idea that *traits that were adaptive in an ancestral environment may be maladaptive in a modern environment* (Mayr, 1942; Riggs, 1993). Hundreds of thousands of years ago, the main food-related problem facing our ancestors was starvation, and humans evolved two strategies to avoid it. First, we developed a strong attraction to foods that provide large amounts of energy per bite, which is why most of us prefer cheeseburgers and milkshakes to spinach and tea (see Hot Science: This Is Your Brain on Goldfish). Second, we developed an ability to store excess food energy in the form of fat, which enabled us to eat more than we needed when food was plentiful and then live off our

Hot Science | **This Is Your Brain on Goldfish**

Are there more calories in an avocado or a Snickers bar? If you are like most people, you aren't really sure—but you know that an avocado is a fruit (healthy healthy!) and that a Snickers bar is a candy (naughty naughty!), so you'd probably guess that the latter has more calories. And you'd be wrong, because an avocado has about 50% more calories than a Snickers bar. Holy guacamole!

Don't feel bad. When it comes to estimating the caloric content of foods, most people haven't got a clue. But research suggests that people's brains may know things that the people who own them don't.

Researchers at the Montreal Neurological Institute of McGill University (Tang, Fellows, & Dagher, 2014) showed participants photos of 50 food items—from apples to Pop-Tarts, from quinoa to Goldfish—and then measured three things. First, they asked the participants to estimate how many calories each of the food items contained. Second, they asked the participants how much they would pay to

eat each of the food items. And third, they used fMRI to measure the activity in the participants' brains as they stared at the food item. What did the researchers find?

Panel A of the accompanying figure shows the correlation between the actual caloric density (the number of calories per gram) of each food item and the participants' estimates of caloric density. If the line looks flat, then you've got good eyes. That utterly flat line indicates that the correlation between these two measures was zero. In other words, the participants were completely unable to say which foods were calorie-rich and which were calorie-poor.

But now look at Panel B. That's the correlation between the actual caloric density of the food item and how much the participants wanted to eat it, as measured by their willingness to part with their hard-earned cash in order to get a bite. That line has a positive slope, which means that participants were willing to pay more for the opportunity to eat foods that were calorie-rich than calorie-poor.

Finally, when the researchers examined the data from the brain scans, they discovered that neural activity in the ventromedial prefrontal cortex (an area of the brain that is involved in computing the value of a stimulus) was (1) uncorrelated with participants' guesses about caloric content; but (2) positively correlated with actual caloric content. In other words, the participants *wanted* to eat calorie-rich food, and *their brains responded positively* to calorie-rich food—yet the participants themselves could not say which foods were rich in calories!

People have been counting the calories in food for just a few decades, but their brains have been wanting and valuing food for millions of years. It appears that evolution has wired our brains to detect and delight in the calorie-rich foods that can best fuel them, even if we don't consciously know which foods those are. If you want to know how many calories are in that bagel or banana, just ask yourself how much you'd like to have a bite.

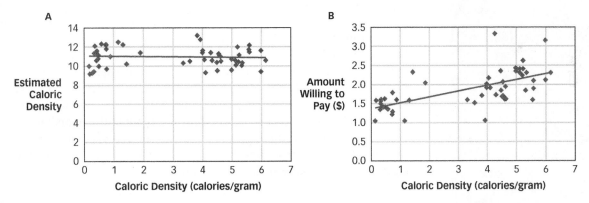

Panel A shows the correlation between participants' estimates of the caloric density and the actual caloric density of the food items. Panel B shows the correlation between the amount participants were willing to pay to eat the food items and the actual caloric density of the food items.

reserves when food was scarce. These two adaptations allowed our species to survive in a world in which calorie-rich food was available only rarely, and the problem is that we don't live in that world anymore (Li, van Vugt, & Colarelli, 2018). Instead, we live in a world in which the calorie bombs of modern technology—from chocolate cupcakes to sausage pizzas—are inexpensive and readily available (Simpson & Raubenheimer, 2014). As one research team noted, "We evolved on the savannahs of Africa; we now live in Candyland" (Power & Schulkin, 2009). To make matters worse, many of Candyland's foods tend to be high not only in calories but in saturated fat, which has the paradoxical effect of making the brain *less* sensitive to some of the chemical messengers that tell it to shut hunger off (Benoit et al., 2009).

Actor and comedian Jonah Hill (*left*, in 2007; *right*, in 2018) has lost and gained weight many times in his career. In a recent interview with Ellen DeGeneres, he said, "I spent most of my young adult life listening to people say I was fat, gross, and unattractive, and it's only in the last four years . . . that I've started to understand how much that hurt and got into my head."

One reason that obesity rates are rising is that "normal portions" keep getting larger. When researchers analyzed 52 depictions of The Last Supper that were painted between the years 1000 and 1800, they found that the average plate size had increased by 66% (Wansink & Wansink, 2010).

metabolism The rate at which the body uses energy.

Conquering Obesity

Our brains and bodies evolved for a very different world than this one, which is why it is so easy for us to bulk up and so hard for us to slim down. Just as our bodies seek weight gain, they resist weight loss, and they do this in two ways.

- First, when we gain weight, we experience an increase in both the size and the number of fat cells in our bodies (usually in our abdomens if we are male and in our thighs and buttocks if we are female). When we lose weight, the *size* of our fat cells decreases, but the *number* does not. Once our bodies have added a fat cell, that cell is with us pretty much forever. It may become smaller when we lose weight, but it is unlikely to die. It's always there, just waiting to be re-enlarged.

- Second, our bodies respond to dieting by decreasing our **metabolism**, which is *the rate at which the body uses energy*. When our bodies sense that there is a famine (which is what they conclude when we refuse to feed them), they decrease their caloric requirements by finding more efficient ways to turn food into fat. This was a great trick for our ancestors, but it is a real problem for us. When rats are overfed, then put on diets, then overfed again, then put on diets again, they gain weight faster and lose weight more slowly the second time around, which suggests that with each round of dieting, their bodies become increasingly efficient at converting food to fat (Brownell et al., 1986).

All of this explains why avoiding obesity is easier than overcoming it (Casazza et al., 2013). And avoiding it is exactly what some psychologists are trying to help people do by using small interventions that have a big impact—interventions commonly known as *nudges* (Thaler & Sunstein, 2008). For instance, one study showed that placing hard-boiled eggs just a few inches away from the more healthful ingredients in a salad bar led people to eat 10% fewer eggs (Rozin et al., 2011). Ten percent of an egg may not sound like much to you, but if you are a person who eats two eggs every day, cutting that amount by just 10% would allow you to lose about 1.5 pounds every year, which would make you the slimmest person at your 25th high school reunion.

Other nudges have been shown to be equally successful: People are less likely to order a sugary soft drink when it appears in the middle of the menu than at the top or bottom (Dayan & Bar-Hillel, 2011); they eat less when they are given a large fork than a small one (Mishra, Mishra, & Masters, 2012); they take less cake when they have to cut it themselves (Hagen, Krishna, & McFerran, 2016); and when they mix foods—such as granola and yogurt—they use more of the ingredient they put in the bowl first and less of the ingredient they put on top of it (Bschaden et al., 2019). These and many other studies show that small changes to the environment can make big differences to our waistlines (Cadario & Chandon, 2019).

Sexual Desire

Food motivates us because without it we die. Although sex is not essential to our personal survival, it is essential to the survival of our DNA, and that's why evolution has wired sexual desire into almost everybody's brain. The general wiring scheme is simple: Glands secrete hormones that travel through the blood to the brain and stimulate our sexual interest. But the details of the wiring scheme are complicated: Which hormones trigger which parts of the brain, and what triggers the launch in the first place?

Three hormones appear to play key roles. The hormone *dihydroepiandosterone* (DHEA) seems to be involved in the initial onset of sexual desire. Both boys and girls begin producing this slow-acting hormone at about the age of 6, which may help to explain why boys and girls both experience their initial sexual interest at about the age of 10, despite the fact that boys reach puberty much later than girls do. Two other hormones have more sex-specific effects. Both males and females produce *testosterone* and *estrogen,* but males produce more of the former and females produce more of the latter. As you will learn in the Development chapter, these two hormones are largely responsible for the physical and psychological changes that characterize puberty. But are they also responsible for sexual desire in adults?

The answer is yes—as long as those adults are mice. Testosterone regulates sexual desire in male mice and estrogen regulates both sexual desire and fertility in female mice, and the same is true for most mammals. That's why most female mammals have little or no interest in sex except when their estrogen levels are high, which happens when they are ovulating or "in estrus." But humans are different. The level of estrogen in a woman's body changes dramatically over the course of her monthly menstrual cycle, yet her sexual desire changes little. Somewhere in the course of our evolution, women's sexual interest became independent of their ovulatory cycles, and some scientists believe that this happened because having full-time sexual interests gave women an evolutionary advantage by making it difficult for men to know whether a woman was ovulating.

Why was this an advantage? Most male mammals guard their mates jealously when their mates are ovulating, but then go off in search of other receptive females when their mates are not. If a male cannot use his mate's sexual receptivity as information about when she was ovulating, then he has no choice but to hang around and guard her all the time. This is a considerable advantage for females who are trying to keep their mates at home so that they will contribute to the rearing of young. No one knows if this is in fact the reason why human females remain interested in sex even when they are not ovulating, but it is a compelling explanation for why this tendency—which is unusual in the animal kingdom—might have evolved.

Hormonally, then, female humans are a lot more complicated than female rats. But if estrogen is not the hormonal basis of a woman's sex drive, then what is? Two pieces of evidence suggest that the answer is testosterone—the same hormone that drives male sexuality. First, men naturally have more testosterone than women do, and they generally have stronger sex drives. Men are more likely than women to think about sex, have sexual fantasies, seek sex and sexual variety (whether positions or partners), masturbate, want sex at an early point in a relationship, sacrifice other things for sex, have permissive attitudes towards sex, and complain about low sex drive in their partners (Baumeister, Cantanese, & Vohs, 2001). Second, when women are given testosterone, their sex drives increase. These facts suggest that testosterone may be the hormonal basis of sexual motivation in both men and women.

Sexual Behaviour

Men and women may have different levels of sexual drive on average, but their physiological responses during sex seem to have a lot in common. Prior to the 1960s, data on human sexual behaviour consisted primarily of people's answers to questions about their sex lives, and you may have noticed that this is a topic about which people don't always tell the truth. William Masters and Virginia Johnson changed all that by conducting groundbreaking studies in which they actually measured the physical responses of hundreds of volunteers as they masturbated or had sex in a laboratory (Masters & Johnson, 1966). Their work was controversial at the time, but it led to a much deeper scientific understanding of the **human sexual response cycle**, which comprises *the stages of physiological arousal during sexual activity* (see **FIGURE 8.15**). The human sexual response cycle has four phases:

- During the *excitement phase,* muscle tension and blood flow increase in and around the sexual organs, heart and respiration rates increase, and blood pressure rises. Both men and women may experience erect nipples and a "sex flush" on the skin of the upper body and face. A man's penis typically becomes erect or partially erect and his testicles draw upward, while a woman's vagina typically becomes lubricated and her clitoris becomes swollen.

- During the *plateau phase,* heart rate and muscle tension increase further. A man's urinary bladder closes to prevent urine from mixing with semen, and muscles at the base of his penis begin a steady rhythmic contraction. A man's Cowper gland

MICHAEL NICHOLS/NATIONAL GEOGRAPHIC/GETTY IMAGES

JUPITERIMAGES/STOCKBYTE/GETTY IMAGES

The red colouration on the female gelada's chest (*top photo*) indicates that she is ovulating and amenable to sex. Her mate therefore knows exactly when to guard her (to make sure that other males do not inseminate her) and when to go off in search of other mating opportunities. In contrast, the sexual interest of a female human (*bottom*) is not limited to a particular time in her ovulatory cycle; therefore, her behaviour does not provide a clue to her fertility.

human sexual response cycle The stages of physiological arousal during sexual activity.

Figure 8.15

The Human Sexual Response Cycle The pattern of the sexual response cycle is quite similar for men and for women. Both men and women go through the excitement, plateau, orgasm, and resolution phases, although the timing of their responses may differ.

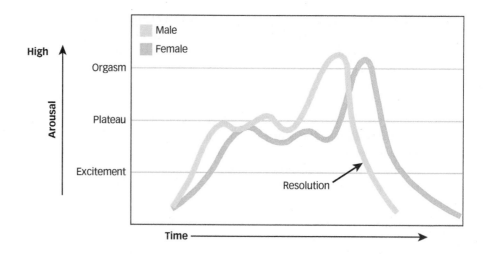

may secrete a small amount of lubricating fluid (which, by the way, often contains enough sperm to cause pregnancy). A woman's clitoris may withdraw slightly, and her vagina may become more lubricated. Her outer vagina may swell, and her muscles may tighten and reduce the diameter of the opening of the vagina.

- During the *orgasm phase,* breathing becomes extremely rapid and the pelvic muscles begin a series of rhythmic contractions. Both men and women experience quick cycles of muscle contraction of the anus and lower pelvic muscles, and women often experience uterine and vaginal contractions as well. During this phase, men ejaculate about 2 to 5 millilitres of semen (depending on how long it has been since their last orgasm and how long they were aroused prior to ejaculation). Ninety-five percent of heterosexual men and 69% of heterosexual women reported having an orgasm during their last sexual encounter (Richters et al., 2006). However, roughly 15% of women never experience orgasm, fewer than half experience orgasm from intercourse alone, and roughly half report having "faked" an orgasm at least once (Wiederman, 1997). The frequency with which women have orgasms seems to have a genetic component (Dawood et al., 2005). And it probably goes without saying that when men and women have orgasms, they typically experience them as intensely pleasurable.

- During the *resolution phase,* muscles relax, blood pressure drops, and the body returns to its resting state. Most men and women experience a *refractory period,* during which further stimulation does not produce excitement. This period may last from minutes to days and is typically longer for men than for women.

Although sex is generally a prerequisite for reproduction, the vast majority of sexual acts are not intended to produce babies. University students, for example, are rarely aiming to get pregnant, but they often do aim to have sex—and when they get what they are aiming for, they feel happier and find life to be more meaningful in the following days (Kashdan et al., 2018). Students report a wide variety of reasons for having sex. They have it because they are *physically attracted* to a partner ("Alex has beautiful eyes"), to increase *emotional connection* ("I wanted to communicate at a deeper level"), to *alleviate insecurity* ("It was the only way Alex would spend time with me"), as a *means to an end* ("I wanted to be popular"), or for more than one of these reasons (Meston & Buss, 2007).

Although men are more likely than women to report having sex for purely physical reasons, **TABLE 8.1** shows that men and women don't differ dramatically in their most frequent reasons. It is worth noting that not all sex is motivated by any of these reasons: About half of university-age women and a quarter of university-age men report having unwanted sexual activity in a relationship (O'Sullivan & Allgeier, 1998). We will have much more to say about sexual attraction and relationships in the Social Psychology chapter.

TABLE 8.1

TOP 10 REASONS WHY WOMEN AND MEN REPORT HAVING SEX

	Women	Men
1	I was attracted to the person.	I was attracted to the person.
2	I wanted to experience the physical pleasure.	It feels good.
3	It feels good.	I wanted to experience the physical pleasure.
4	I wanted to show my affection to the person.	It's fun.
5	I wanted to express my love for the person.	I wanted to show my affection to the person.
6	I was sexually aroused and wanted the release.	I was sexually aroused and wanted the release.
7	I was "horny."	I was "horny."
8	It's fun.	I wanted to express my love for the person.
9	I realized I was in love.	I wanted to achieve an orgasm.
10	I was "in the heat of the moment."	I wanted to please my partner.

Information from Meston & Buss, 2007.

Build to the Outcomes

1. Why do some motivations take precedence over others?
2. What purpose does hunger serve?
3. What causes BED, bulimia, and anorexia?
4. What causes obesity?
5. Why is dieting so difficult and ineffective?
6. Which hormones regulate sexual interest in men and in women?
7. What is the human sexual response cycle?
8. Why do people have sex?

The Motivated Mind

Survival and reproduction are every animal's first order of business, so it is no surprise that we are strongly motivated by food and sex. But humans are motivated by other things, too. Yes, we crave kisses of both the chocolate and romantic variety, but we also crave friendship and respect, security and certainty, wisdom and meaning, and a whole lot more. Our psychological motivations can be every bit as powerful as our biological motivations, but they differ in two important ways.

First, although we share our biological motivations with most other animals, our psychological motivations appear to be unique. Chimps and rabbits and robins and turtles are all motivated to have sex, but only human beings seem motivated to imbue the act with deeper meaning. Second, although our biological motivations are of a few basic kinds—food, sex, oxygen, sleep, and a handful of other things—our psychological motivations are virtually limitless. The things we care about feeling and thinking, knowing and believing, having and being are just so numerous and varied that no psychologist has ever been able to make a complete list of them (Hofmann, Vohs, & Baumeister, 2012). Nonetheless, even if you looked at an incomplete list, you'd quickly notice that psychological motivations vary on three key dimensions: Some are extrinsic and others are intrinsic, some are conscious and others are unconscious, and some lead us to approach while others lead us to avoid. Let's examine each of these dimensions in turn.

Learning Outcomes

- Explain the advantages of intrinsic and extrinsic motivations.
- Explain how rewards and threats can backfire.
- Explain when people become conscious of their motivations.
- Explain how we know that avoidance motivation is more powerful than approach motivation.

Mohammed Bouazizi was a fruit seller. In 2010, he set himself on fire to protest his treatment by the Tunisian government, and his dramatic suicide ignited the revolution that came to be known as the Arab Spring. Clearly, psychological needs—such as the need for justice—can be even more powerful than biological needs.

Intrinsic Versus Extrinsic

Eating a potato chip and taking a psychology exam are different in many ways. One makes you chubby while the other makes you crabby, one requires that you move your lips while the other requires that you don't, and one is so pleasant that you'd pay to have it while the other is so unpleasant that you'd pay not to. But the most significant difference between these activities is that one is a means to an end and the other is an end in itself. An **intrinsic motivation** is *a motivation to take actions that are themselves rewarding.* When we eat a potato chip because it tastes good, ride a bicycle because it feels good, or listen to music because it sounds good, we are intrinsically motivated. These activities don't *have* a payoff because they *are* a payoff.

Conversely, an **extrinsic motivation** is *a motivation to take actions that lead to reward.* When we floss our teeth so we can avoid gum disease, when we work hard for money so we can pay our rent, and when we take a psychology exam so we can get a university degree that will allow us to earn enough money to buy dental floss and pay rent, we are extrinsically motivated. None of these things is a source of pleasure in and of itself, but all can increase pleasure in the long run.

Extrinsic Motivation

Extrinsic motivation gets a bad rap. Canadians tend to believe that people should "follow their hearts" and "do what they love," and we feel sorry for students who choose courses just to please their parents and for parents who choose jobs just to earn a pile of money. But the fact is that our ability to engage in behaviours that are unrewarding in the present because we believe they will bring greater rewards in the future is one of our species' most significant talents—and no other species can do it quite as well as we can (Gilbert, 2006). Researchers who study how well people can put off pleasure, or "delay gratification" (Ayduk et al., 2007; Mischel et al., 2004), typically give participants a choice between getting something they want right now (e.g., a scoop of ice cream today) or getting more of what they want later (e.g., two scoops of ice cream tomorrow). Waiting for ice cream in a study like this is a lot like taking an exam or flossing: It isn't much fun, but you might do it because you know that if you are patient, you will reap greater rewards in the end. Studies show that 4-year-old children who can delay gratification are judged to be more intelligent and socially competent 10 years later and have higher university admissions test scores when they enter university (Mischel, Shoda, & Rodriguez, 1989). In fact, the ability to delay gratification is a better predictor of a child's grades in school than is the child's IQ (Duckworth & Seligman, 2005). Apparently, there is something to be said for extrinsic motivation.

Intrinsic Motivation

There is a lot to be said for intrinsic motivation, too (Patall, Cooper, & Robinson, 2008). People work harder when they are intrinsically motivated, they enjoy what they do more, and they do it more creatively. Both kinds of motivation have advantages, which is why many of us try to build lives in which we are both intrinsically and extrinsically motivated by the same activity—lives in which we are paid the big bucks for doing exactly what we like to do best. Who hasn't fantasized about becoming an artist or an athlete or Drake's personal party planner?

Alas, research suggests that it is difficult to get paid for doing what you love and still end up loving what you do because rewards can undermine intrinsic motivation (Deci, Koestner, & Ryan, 1999; Henderlong & Lepper, 2002). For example, in one study, university students who were intrinsically motivated to complete a puzzle either were paid to complete it or completed it for free. Those who received money were less likely to play with the puzzle later on (Deci, 1971). In a similar study, children who were intrinsically motivated to draw with coloured markers were either promised or not promised a reward. Those who were promised the reward were less

intrinsic motivation A motivation to take actions that are themselves rewarding.

extrinsic motivation A motivation to take actions that lead to reward.

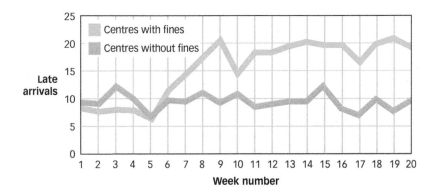

Figure 8.16

When Threats Backfire Threats can cause behaviours that were once intrinsically motivated to become extrinsically motivated. Day care centres that instituted fines for late-arriving parents saw an increase in the number of parents who arrived late.

likely to use the markers later (Lepper, Greene, & Nisbett, 1973). It appears that under some circumstances, people interpret rewards as information about the intrinsic goodness of an activity ("If they had to pay me to do that puzzle, it couldn't have been a very fun one"), which means that rewards can sometimes undermine intrinsic motivation.

Threats can have the same effect. For example, when a group of day care centres got fed up with parents who picked up their children late, some instituted a small financial penalty for tardiness. As **FIGURE 8.16** shows, the financial penalty did not decrease tardiness—it *increased* it (Gneezy & Rustichini, 2000). Why? Because most parents were already intrinsically motivated to pick up their kids on time. But when the day care centres started punishing them for their tardiness, the parents became *extrinsically* motivated to pick up their children on time—and because the price of tardiness wasn't particularly high, they decided to pay a small financial penalty in order to leave their children in day care for an extra hour. When threats and rewards change intrinsic motivation into extrinsic motivation, unexpected consequences can follow.

Conscious Versus Unconscious

When prizewinning artists and scientists are asked to explain how they achieved greatness, they typically say things like "I wanted to liberate colour from form" or "I wanted to rid the world of smallpox." They almost never say things like "I wanted to exceed my father's accomplishments, thereby proving to my mother that I was worthy of her love." Prizewinners can articulate their **conscious motivations**, which are *motivations of which people are aware*, but by definition they have trouble articulating their **unconscious motivations**, which are *motivations of which people are not aware* (Aarts, Custers, & Marien, 2008; Bargh et al., 2001; Hassin, Bargh, & Zimerman, 2009).

Everyone has unconscious motivations. For instance, people vary in their **need for achievement**, which is *the motivation to solve worthwhile problems* (McClelland et al., 1953). This basic motivation is unconscious and thus must be measured with special techniques such as the Thematic Apperception Test, which presents people with a series of drawings and asks them to tell stories about them. The amount of "achievement-related imagery" in the person's story ostensibly reveals the person's unconscious need for achievement. (You'll learn more about these sorts of tests in the Personality chapter.) Although there has been a great deal of controversy about the validity and reliability of measures such as these (Lilienfeld, Wood, & Garb, 2000; Tuerlinckx, De Boeck, & Lens, 2002), research shows that a person's responses on this test do reliably predict the person's behaviour in certain circumstances (Khalid, 1991). Research also suggests that this motivation can be primed in

conscious motivations Motivations of which people are aware.

unconscious motivations Motivations of which people are not aware.

need for achievement The motivation to solve worthwhile problems.

It seems fair to speculate that Elon Musk is high in the need for achievement. The 49-year-old billionaire has built numerous companies, from PayPal and Tesla to SpaceX and Hyperloop, and he intends to build more. "I think it is possible for ordinary people to choose to be extraordinary," he said. "You should not give up unless you are forced to give up."

much the same way that thoughts and feelings can be primed. For example, when words such as *achievement* are presented on a computer screen so rapidly that people cannot consciously perceive them, those people will work especially hard to solve a puzzle (Bargh et al., 2001) and will feel especially unhappy if they fail (Chartrand & Kay, 2006).

What determines whether we are conscious of our motivations? Most actions have more than one motivation, and the ease or difficulty of performing the action sometimes determines which of these motivations we will be aware of (Vallacher & Wegner, 1985, 1987). When actions are easy (e.g., screwing in a light bulb), we are aware of our most *general motivations* (e.g., to be helpful), but when actions are difficult (e.g., wrestling with a light bulb that is stuck in its socket), we are aware of our more specific motivations (e.g., to get the threads aligned). People usually are aware of the general motivations for their behaviour and become aware of their more specific motivations only when they encounter problems. For example, participants in one study drank coffee from a normal mug or from a mug that had a heavy weight attached to the bottom, which made the mug difficult to manipulate. When asked what they were doing, those who were drinking from the normal mug explained that they were "satisfying needs," whereas those who were drinking from the weighted mug explained that they were "swallowing" (Wegner et al., 1984). The ease with which we can execute an action is one of many factors that determine which of our motivations we are conscious of.

Approach Versus Avoidance

The poet James Thurber (1956) wrote: "All men should strive to learn before they die / What they are running from, and to, and why." As these lines remind us, the hedonic principle actually describes two distinct motivations: one that makes us "run to" pleasure and another that makes us "run from" pain. Psychologists—being a bit less poetic and a lot more precise—call these **approach motivation**, which is *the motivation to experience positive outcomes*, and **avoidance motivation**, which is *the motivation to avoid experiencing negative outcomes*. Pleasure and pain may be two sides of the same coin, but they *are* two sides. Pleasure is not just the lack of pain, and pain is not just the lack of pleasure. Pleasure and pain are distinct experiences, each of which is associated with distinct patterns of activity in different regions of the brain (Davidson et al., 1990; Gray, 1990).

But which is more powerful? Research suggests that, all else being equal, avoidance motivation tends to be the stronger of the two. This is easy to illustrate: Would you bet on a coin flip that will pay you $100 if it comes up heads but will require you to pay $80 if it comes up tails? Mathematically speaking, this should be an extremely attractive wager, because the potential gain is larger than the equally likely potential loss. And yet, most people refuse this bet because they expect the pain of losing $80 to be stronger than the pleasure of winning $100. **Loss aversion** is *the tendency to care more about avoiding losses than about achieving equal-size gains* (Kahneman & Tversky, 1979, 1984), and its effects can be dramatic.

Grocery stores in the Washington, DC, area tried to motivate their customers to reuse their shopping bags by giving them a 5-cent bonus whenever they did (a financial gain), or by taxing them whenever they didn't (a financial loss), or by doing neither or both of these things. As **FIGURE 8.17** shows, the prospect of losing money had a large impact on shoppers' behaviour, but the prospect of gaining the same amount of money had no impact at all (Homonoff, 2013). People, it seems, are unusually anxious about losing what they have, which is why they display reduced loss aversion after taking drugs that reduce fear and anxiety (Sokol-Hessner et al., 2015) and increased loss aversion after being exposed to stimuli that increase fear and anxiety (Schulreich, Gerhardt, & Heekeren, 2016).

approach motivation The motivation to experience positive outcomes.

avoidance motivation The motivation to avoid experiencing negative outcomes.

loss aversion The tendency to care more about avoiding losses than about achieving equal-size gains.

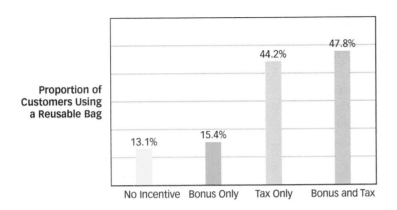

Figure 8.17
The Power of Loss Avoidance motivation is typically more powerful than approach motivation. Shoppers in the Washington, D.C., area were highly motivated to reuse their bags to avoid a 5-cent tax, but they were entirely unmotivated to reuse their bags to get a 5-cent bonus. (Homonoff, 2013).

Because people expect the pain of a loss to outweigh the pleasure of a gain, they typically take more risks to avoid the former than to achieve the latter. For instance, what would you do if you knew that a terrible disease was going to kill 600 students at your school, and you were the one who was in charge of deciding whether to administer Vaccine A (which would save exactly 200 students) or Vaccine B (which has a one-third chance of saving everybody and a two-thirds chance of saving nobody)? When people are asked this question, about three-quarters of them decide to play it safe and select Vaccine A. And yet, when people are given a choice between Vaccine C (which would allow exactly 400 students to die) and Vaccine D (which has a one-third chance of allowing no one to die and a two-thirds chance of allowing everyone to die), about three-quarters of them decide to take the risk and select Vaccine D (Tversky & Kahneman, 1981). As **FIGURE 8.18** shows, Vaccines A and C are actually identical, as are Vaccines B and D. Indeed, the only difference is that A and B are *described* in terms of lives gained, whereas C and D are *described* in terms of lives lost. Those descriptions matter a lot, leading people to take risks in one case but not in another. It is worth noting that monkeys also take risks to avoid losses but not to achieve gains (Lakshminarayanan, Chen, & Santos, 2011), which suggests that you probably should not put one in charge of your major medical decisions.

Figure 8.18
When Do We Take Risks? Loss aversion leads people to take risks and to avoid losses (most people choose Vaccine D over C) but not to achieve gains (most people choose Vaccine A over B).

Without vaccine, 600 students will die...

Vaccine A	Vaccine B
200 will definitely live!	1/3 chance that everyone will live & 2/3 chance that no one will live

Vaccine C	Vaccine D
400 will definitely die!	1/3 chance that no one will die & 2/3 chance that everyone will die

Although avoidance motivation is stronger than approach motivation, on average, the relative strength of these two tendencies does differ from person to person. A person's agreement or disagreement with each of the statements shown in **TABLE 8.2** turns out to be a pretty good measure of that person's approach and avoidance tendencies (Carver & White, 1994). Research shows that people who tend to agree with the statements are happier when rewarded than those who disagree, and that those who tend to disagree with the statements are more anxious when threatened than those who disagree (Carver, 2006).

Just as some people seem to be more responsive to rewards than to punishments (and vice versa), some people tend to think about their behaviours as attempts to get rewards rather than to avoid punishment (and vice versa). People who have a *promotion focus* tend to think in terms of achieving gains, whereas people who have a *prevention focus* tend to think in terms of avoiding losses (Higgins, 1997). In one study, participants were given an anagram task. Some were told that they would be paid $4 for the experiment, but they could earn an extra dollar by finding 90% or more of all the possible words. Others were told that they would be paid $5 for the experiment, but they could avoid losing a dollar by not missing more than 10% of all the possible words. People who had a promotion focus performed better in the first case than in the second, but people who had a prevention focus performed better in the second case than in the first (Shah, Higgins, & Friedman, 1998).

So what is the one thing that virtually every human being wants to avoid? Death, of course. All animals strive to stay alive, but only human beings know that all that striving is ultimately in vain, because no matter what you do, eventually you will die. Some psychologists have suggested that this knowledge creates a uniquely human "existential terror"

TABLE 8.2
MEASURING APPROACH AND AVOIDANCE TENDENCIES
If you agree with these statements, you probably have a strong approach motivation, and if you disagree you probably have a strong avoidance motivation
I go out of my way to get things I want.
When I'm doing well at something, I love to keep at it.
I'm always willing to try something new if I think it will be fun.
When I get something I want, I feel excited and energized.
When I want something, I usually go all-out to get it.
I will often do things for no other reason than that they might be fun.
If I see a chance to get something I want, I move on it right away.
When I see an opportunity for something I like, I get excited right away.
I often act on the spur of the moment.
When good things happen to me, it affects me strongly.
If something bad is about to happen to me, I usually experience fear or nervousness.
Criticism or scolding hurts me quite a bit.
I feel pretty worried or upset when I think or know somebody is angry at me.
If I think something unpleasant is going to happen, I usually get pretty "worked up."
I feel worried when I think I have done poorly at something important.
I have quite a few fears compared to my friends.
I worry about making mistakes.

Information from Carver & White, 1994.

that much of human behaviour is an attempt to manage. **Terror management theory** is *a theory about how people respond to knowledge of their own mortality* and it suggests that one way in which people cope with knowledge of their own mortality is by developing a *cultural worldview,* which is a shared set of beliefs about what is good and right and true (Greenberg, Solomon, & Arndt, 2008; Solomon, Greenberg, & Pyszczynski, 2004). These beliefs allow people to see themselves as more than mortal animals because they inhabit a world of meaning in which they can achieve symbolic immortality (e.g., by leaving a great legacy or having children) and perhaps even literal immortality (e.g., by being pious and earning a spot in the afterlife). According to this theory, a cultural worldview is a kind of shield that buffers people against the overwhelming anxiety that certain knowledge of their own mortality elicits.

If that's true, then people who are reminded of their mortality should be especially motivated to hang on to their cultural worldviews. In the last 20 years, this *mortality salience hypothesis* has been supported by the results of nearly 400 studies. Those results show that when people are reminded of death (often in very subtle ways, such as by flashing the word *death* for just a few milliseconds in a laboratory, or by stopping people on a street corner that happens to be near a graveyard), they are more likely to praise and reward those who share their cultural worldviews, derogate and punish those who don't, value their spouses and defend their countries, feel disgusted by "animalistic" behaviours such as breast-feeding, and so on. All of these responses are presumably ways of shoring up their cultural worldviews, thereby protecting themselves from the existential terror that reminders of mortality create.

terror management theory The theory that people respond to the knowledge of their own mortality by developing a cultural worldview.

Build to the Outcomes

1. What are intrinsic and extrinsic motivations?
2. Why should people delay gratification?
3. Why do rewards sometimes backfire?
4. What makes people conscious of their motivations?
5. What is loss aversion?
6. What are the consequences of mortality salience?

Chapter Review

The Nature of Emotion

- Feelings are difficult to describe, but psychologists have identified two underlying dimensions: arousal and valence.

- Emotions are reactions to the person's interpretation or appraisal of an event, and they give rise to action tendencies, which prepare people to act in particular ways that make evolutionary sense.

- Psychologists have spent more than a century trying to understand how emotional experience and physiological activity are related. The James–Lange theory suggests that a stimulus triggers a specific bodily reaction that produces an emotional experience, and the two-factor theory suggests that a stimulus triggers general physiological arousal which is then interpreted as a specific emotion. Neither of these theories is entirely right, but each has elements that are supported by research.

- Emotions are produced by the complex interaction of many brain areas, including the cortex and limbic structures such

as the amygdala. Information about a stimulus is sent simultaneously to the amygdala (which plays a role in the rapid appraisal of the stimulus) and the cortex (which conducts a slower and more comprehensive analysis of the stimulus). Depending on the results of that analysis, the cortex may downregulate the amygdala.

Emotional Communication

- The voice, the body, and the face all communicate information about a person's emotional state. Research suggests that some emotional expressions may be universal.

- Emotions cause expressions, but expressions can also cause emotions. Emotional mimicry allows people to experience and hence identify the emotions of others.

- People follow display rules that tell them when and how to express emotion. Different cultures have different display rules, but people follow them by using the same basic techniques.

- There are reliable differences between sincere and insincere expressions, but people are generally poor at telling them apart. The same is true of verbal lies. The polygraph detects lies at a better-than-chance rate, but its error rate is far too high to make it useful.

The Nature of Motivation

- All organisms are born with some motivations and acquire others through experience, but calling these motivations "instincts" describes them without explaining how they operate. Drive-reduction theory explains how they operate by suggesting that disequilibrium of the body produces drives that organisms are motivated to reduce. Neither instinct nor drive are widely used concepts in modern psychology, but both have something useful to teach us.

- The hedonic principle suggests that people are motivated to experience pleasure and avoid pain and that this basic motivation underlies all others. One of the ways people achieve this goal is by using different strategies to regulate their emotions. Research shows that people don't always use the most effective strategies: for example, affect labelling (which involves naming and describing one's emotions) and reappraisal (which involves changing the way one thinks about the emotion-eliciting event) are both effective but underutilized.

The Motivated Body

- Physiological motivations generally take precedence over psychological motivations in Maslow's "hierarchy of needs." One of the most basic physiological motivations is hunger, which is the result of the complex interplay between different kinds of chemical messengers.

- Eating disorders and obesity have genetic, experiential, environmental, psychological, and cultural origins—all of which are difficult to overcome. Obesity is the most common eating-related problem in the world, and it is easier to prevent than to remedy. Dieting is generally ineffective because our bodies store excess food energy as fat as a defence against times of food scarcity, and our metabolism slows as a response to reduced calories.

- Unlike most other mammals, the sex drives of male and female humans are both regulated by testosterone. Men and women experience roughly the same sequence of physiological events during sex, and they engage in sex for many of the same reasons.

The Motivated Mind

- People have many psychological motivations that vary on three key dimensions, one of which is the intrinsic–extrinsic dimension. Research shows that intrinsic motivations can be undermined by extrinsic rewards and punishments.

- People are not always conscious of their motivations. They tend to be conscious of their most general motivations and become conscious of their more specific motivations only when they encounter difficulty carrying out their actions.

- The fact that avoidance motivation is generally more powerful than approach motivation leads people to be loss-averse. Death is the ultimate loss, and people develop cultural worldviews to protect themselves against the anxiety that knowledge of their mortality produces.

Key Concept Quiz

1. Feelings can be described by their location on the two dimensions of
   a. motivation and emotion.
   b. arousal and valence.
   c. instinct and drive.
   d. pain and pleasure.

2. Which theory suggests that emotions are people's interpretations of their own general physiological arousal?
   a. terror management theory
   b. the James–Lange theory
   c. the two-factor theory
   d. drive-reduction theory

3. Which brain structure is most directly involved in the rapid appraisal of whether a stimulus is good or bad?
   a. the cortex
   b. the lateral hypothalamus
   c. the amygdala
   d. the ventromedial hypothalamus

4. _____ is an emotion-regulation strategy that involves thinking about events in new ways.
   a. Affect labelling
   b. Intensification
   c. Suppression
   d. Reappraisal

5. _____ is the idea that emotional expressions can cause emotional experiences.
   a. Homeostasis
   b. Evolutionary mismatch
   c. The universality hypothesis
   d. The facial feedback hypothesis

6. Pretending to experience one emotion when you are really experiencing a completely different one is an example of _____.
   a. deintensification
   b. masking
   c. neutralizing
   d. intensification

7. The hedonic principle states that
   a. smiles mean the same thing in every culture.
   b. people are primarily motivated to experience pleasure and avoid pain.
   c. organisms are motivated to reduce their drives.
   d. some motivations are hard-wired by nature.

8. An unlearned motivation has been called
   a. an instinct.
   b. an action tendency.
   c. homeostasis.
   d. an appraisal.

9. According to Maslow, our most basic needs are
   a. self-actualization and self-esteem.
   b. shared with other animals.
   c. not experienced until higher needs are met.
   d. belongingness and love.

10. Which statement is true?
   a. Men and women engage in sex for many of the same reasons.

   b. Boys and girls experience initial sexual interest at very different ages.
   c. The sequence of physiological arousal for men and women differs dramatically.
   d. The human male sex drive is regulated by testosterone, whereas the human female sex drive is regulated by estrogen.

 **LearningCurve** macmillan learning   Don't stop now! Quizzing yourself is a powerful study tool. Go to LaunchPad to access the LearningCurve adaptive quizzing system and your own personalized learning plan. Visit launchpadworks.com.

Key Terms

emotion (p. 314)

appraisal (p. 316)

action tendencies (p. 317)

James–Lange theory (p. 317)

two-factor theory of emotion (p. 319)

emotional expression (p. 322)

universality hypothesis (p. 322)

facial feedback hypothesis (p. 325)

display rule (p. 326)

motivation (p. 329)

homeostasis (p. 330)

drive-reduction theory (p. 330)

hedonic principle (p. 331)

emotion regulation (p. 331)

reappraisal (p. 331)

binge eating disorder (BED) (p. 333)

bulimia nervosa (p. 334)

anorexia nervosa (p. 334)

evolutionary mismatch (p. 336)

metabolism (p. 338)

human sexual response cycle (p. 339)

intrinsic motivation (p. 342)

extrinsic motivation (p. 342)

conscious motivations (p. 343)

unconscious motivations (p. 343)

need for achievement (p. 343)

approach motivation (p. 344)

avoidance motivation (p. 344)

loss aversion (p. 344)

terror management theory (p. 347)

Changing Minds

1. While watching the news, you and a friend hear about a celebrity who punched a fan in a restaurant. "I just lost it," the celebrity said. "I saw what I was doing, but I just couldn't control myself." According to the news, the celebrity was sentenced to anger management classes. "I'm not excusing the violence," your friend says, "but I'm not sure anger management classes are very useful. I mean, you can't *control* your emotions. They just *happen*." What evidence would you use to explain to your friend why they are wrong?

2. One of your friends has just been dumped by his boyfriend, and he's devastated. He's spent days in his room, refusing to go out. You and your roommate decide to keep a close eye on him during this tough time. "Negative emotions are so destructive," your roommate says. "We'd all be better off without them." How would you convince your roommate that negative emotions are actually critical for our survival?

3. A friend is majoring in education. "We learned today about several cities, including New York and Chicago, that tried giving cash rewards to students who passed their classes or did well on achievement tests. That's bribing kids to get good grades, and as soon as you stop paying them, they'll stop studying." Your friend is assuming that extrinsic motivation undermines intrinsic motivation. In what ways is the picture more complicated?

4. One of your friends is a gym rat who spends all his free time working out and is very proud of his ripped abs. His roommate is obese. "I keep telling him to diet and exercise," your friend says, "but he never loses any weight. If he just had a little more willpower, he could slim down." What would you tell your friend? What makes it so hard for people to lose weight?

Answers to Key Concept Quiz

1. b; 2. c; 3. c; 4. d; 5. d; 6. b; 7. b; 8. a; 9. b; 10. a.

 **LaunchPad** macmillan learning   LaunchPad features the full e-book of *Psychology*, the LearningCurve adaptive quizzing system, videos, and a variety of activities to boost your learning. Visit LaunchPad at launchpadworks.com.

group online
connect
friend
digital
net
profile like
thum
like
page
go media work
@notify trend share flow
home chat photo letter
www
socialize net
friend
online
social internet
message
nice
like
post info
@ like friend :)
message
invitation
message play :0)
all comm
connect tag
notify
group search
status application
subscribe
timeline fun
follow updates
share
confirm
network
nice
digital thumb
friend
profile like
go media work
trend share flow
home
friend
socialize net
online
message
nice
like
post
@ like friend :)
network invitation
message play :0)

Language and Thought

AN ENGLISH BOY NAMED CHRISTOPHER showed an amazing talent for languages. By the age of 6, he had learned French from his sister's schoolbooks; he acquired Greek from a textbook in only 3 months. His talent was so prodigious that grown-up Christopher could converse fluently in 16 languages. When tested on English–French translations, he scored as well as a native French speaker. Presented with a made-up language, he figured out the complex rules easily, even though advanced language students found them virtually impossible to decipher (Smith & Tsimpli, 1995).

If you've concluded that Christopher is extremely smart, perhaps even a genius, you're wrong. His scores on standard intelligence tests are far below normal. He fails simple cognitive tests that 4-year-old children pass with ease, and he cannot even learn the rules for simple games like tic-tac-toe. Despite his talent, Christopher lives in a halfway house because he does not have the cognitive capacity to make decisions, reason, or solve problems in a way that would allow him to live independently.

CHRISTOPHER'S STRENGTHS AND WEAKNESSES offer compelling evidence that cognition is composed of distinct abilities. People who learn languages with lightning speed are not necessarily gifted at decision making or problem solving. People who excel at reasoning may have no special ability to master languages. In this chapter, you will learn about five key higher cognitive functions: acquiring and using language, forming concepts and categories, making decisions, solving problems, and reasoning. We excel at these functions compared with other animals, and they help define who we are as a species. We'll learn about each of these abilities by examining evidence that reveals their unique psychological characteristics, and we'll learn about their distinct neural underpinnings by considering

Christopher absorbed languages quickly from textbooks, yet he completely failed simple tests of other cognitive abilities.

individuals with brain lesions, as well as neuroimaging studies. But despite clear differences among them, these five cognitive abilities have something important in common: They are critical to our functioning in just about all aspects of our everyday existence—including work, school, and personal relationships—and as we've just seen with Christopher, impairment of these cognitive abilities can result in major and lasting disruptions to our lives.

Language and Communication: From Rules to Meaning

Learning Outcomes

- Describe the basic characteristics of language.
- Explain the milestones of language development.
- Compare the behaviourist, nativist, and interactionist theories of language development.

language A system for communicating with others using signals that are combined according to rules of grammar and that convey meaning.

grammar A set of rules that specify how the units of language can be combined to produce meaningful messages.

Most social species have systems of communication that allow them to transmit messages to each other. Honeybees communicate the location of food sources by means of a "waggle dance" that indicates both the direction and distance of the food source from the hive (Kirchner & Towne, 1994; Von Frisch, 1974). Vervet monkeys have three different warning calls that uniquely signal the presence of their main predators: a leopard, an eagle, and a snake (Cheney & Seyfarth, 1990). A leopard call provokes monkeys to climb higher into a tree; an eagle call makes them look up into the sky; and a snake signal makes them look down. Each different warning call conveys a particular meaning and functions like a word in a simple language.

Language is *a system for communicating with others using signals that are combined according to rules of grammar and that convey meaning.* **Grammar** is *a set of rules that specify how the units of language can be combined to produce meaningful messages.* Language allows individuals to exchange information about the world, coordinate group action, and form strong social bonds.

Human language may have evolved from signaling systems used by other species. However, three striking differences distinguish human language from vervet monkey yelps, for example. First, the complex structure of human language distinguishes it from simpler signaling systems. Most humans can express a wide range of ideas and concepts, as well as generate an essentially infinite number of novel sentences.

Honeybees communicate with each other about the location of food by doing a waggle dance that indicates the direction and distance of food from the hive.

Second, humans use words to refer to intangible things, such as *unicorn* or *democracy*. These words could not have originated as simple alarm calls. Third, we use language to name, categorize, and describe things to ourselves when we think, which influences how knowledge is organized in our brains. It's doubtful that honeybees consciously think, "I'll fly north today to find more honey so the queen will be impressed!"

In this section, we'll examine the elements of human language that contribute to its complex structure. We'll consider the ease with which we acquire language despite this complexity, and how both biological and environmental influences shape language acquisition and use.

The Complex Structure of Human Language

Compared with other forms of communication, human language is a relatively recent evolutionary phenomenon, emerging as a spoken system no more than 1 to 3 million years ago and as a written system as recently as 6,000 years ago. There are approximately 4,000 human languages, which linguists have grouped into about 50 language families (Nadasdy, 1995). Despite their differences, all of these languages share a basic structure involving a set of sounds and rules for combining those sounds to produce meanings.

Basic Characteristics

The smallest units of sound that are recognizable as speech rather than as random noise are called **phonemes**. These building blocks of spoken language differ in how they are produced. For example, when you say *ba,* your vocal cords start to vibrate as soon as you begin the sound, but when you say *pa,* there is a 60-millisecond lag between the time you start the *p* sound and the time your vocal cords start to vibrate. *B* and *p* are classified as separate phonemes in English because they differ in the way they are produced by the human speaker.

Every language has **phonological rules** that *indicate how phonemes can be combined to produce speech sounds.* For example, the initial sound *ts* is acceptable in German but not in English. Typically, people learn these phonological rules without instruction, and if the rules are violated, the resulting speech sounds odd.

Phonemes are combined to make **morphemes**, *the smallest meaningful units of language* (see **FIGURE 9.1**). For example, your brain recognizes the *d* sound you make

phoneme The smallest unit of sound that is recognizable as speech rather than as random noise.

phonological rules A set of rules that indicate how phonemes can be combined to produce speech sounds.

morphemes The smallest meaningful units of language.

Figure 9.1

Units of Language A sentence—the largest unit of language—can be broken down into progressively smaller units: phrases, morphemes, and phonemes. In all languages, phonemes and morphemes form words, which can be combined into phrases and ultimately into sentences.

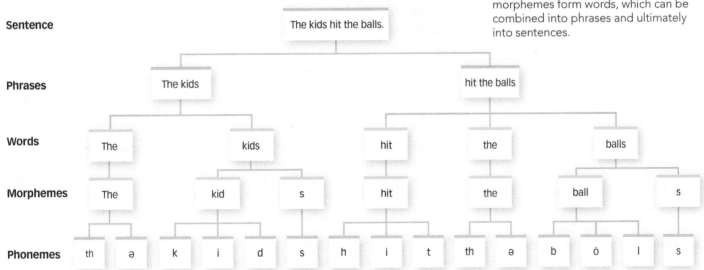

Figure 9.2

Syntactic Rules Syntactic rules indicate how words can be combined to form sentences. Every sentence must contain one or more nouns, which can be combined with adjectives or articles to create a noun phrase. A sentence also must contain one or more verbs, which can be combined with noun phrases, adverbs, or articles to create a verb phrase.

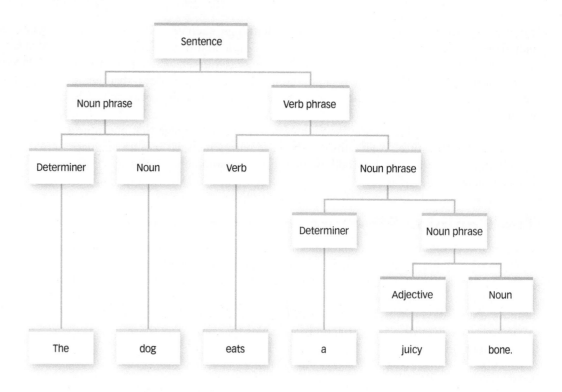

at the beginning of *dog* as a speech *sound,* but it carries no particular meaning. The morpheme *dog,* on the other hand, is recognized as an element of speech that carries meaning. Adding *s* to *dog* (*dogs*) changes the meaning of the word, so here *s* functions as a morpheme.

All languages have grammar rules that generally fall into two categories: rules of morphology and rules of syntax. **Morphological rules** *indicate how morphemes can be combined to form words.* Some morphemes—content morphemes and function morphemes—can stand alone as words. *Content morphemes* refer to things and events (e.g., "cat," "dog," "take"). *Function morphemes* serve grammatical functions, such as tying sentences together ("and," "or," "but") or indicating time ("when"). Many function morphemes are not words on their own—they get added to content morphemes (as a prefix or suffix) to change meaning. Here are three examples: (1) Adding *-s* to many nouns makes them plural (e.g., "cat, cats"). (2) Adding *-en* to "take" creates an adjective from a verb ("taken"). (3) Adding *re-* to the beginning of many verbs creates the idea of a second attempt (e.g., "redo," "retake," "relive," "relearn"). About half of the morphemes in human languages are function morphemes, and it is the function morphemes that make human language grammatically complex enough to permit us to express abstract ideas rather than simply to point verbally to real objects in the here and now.

Content and function morphemes can be combined and recombined to form an infinite number of new sentences, which are governed by syntax. **Syntactic rules** *indicate how words can be combined to form phrases and sentences.* A simple syntactic rule in English is that every sentence must contain one or more nouns, which may be combined with adjectives or articles to create noun phrases (see **FIGURE 9.2**). A sentence also must contain one or more verbs, which may be combined with adverbs or articles to create verb phrases. So, the utterance "dogs bark" is a full sentence, but "the big grey dog over by the building" is not.

Language Development

Language is a complex cognitive skill, yet we can carry on complex conversations with playmates and family even before we begin school. Three characteristics

morphological rules A set of rules that indicate how morphemes can be combined to form words.

syntactic rules A set of rules that indicate how words can be combined to form phrases and sentences.

of language development are worth bearing in mind. First, children learn language at an astonishingly rapid rate. The average 1-year-old has a vocabulary of 10 words. This tiny vocabulary expands to over *10,000* words in the next 4 years, requiring the child to learn, on average, about 6 or 7 new words *every day*. Second, children make few errors while learning to speak, and as we'll see shortly, the errors they do make usually result from applying, but overregularizing, grammatical rules they've learned. This is an extraordinary feat. There are over 3 *million* ways to rearrange the words in any 10-word sentence, but only a few of these arrangements will be both grammatically correct and meaningful (Bickerton, 1990). Third, children's *passive mastery* of language develops faster than their *active mastery*. At every stage of language development, children understand language better than they speak it.

Distinguishing Speech Sounds

At birth, infants can distinguish among all of the contrasting sounds that occur in all human languages. Within the first 6 months of life, they lose this ability and, like their parents, can only distinguish among the contrasting sounds in the language they hear being spoken around them. For example, two distinct sounds in English are the *l* sound and the *r* sound, as in *lead* and *read*. These sounds are not distinguished in Japanese; instead, the *l* and *r* sounds fall within the same phoneme. Japanese adults cannot hear the difference between these two phonemes, but American adults can distinguish between them easily—and so can Japanese infants. By the same token, American speakers do not hear many of the contrasts that are common in Japanese.

In one study, researchers constructed a tape of a voice saying "la-la-la" or "ra-ra-ra" repeatedly (Eimas et al., 1971). They rigged a pacifier so that whenever an infant sucked on it, a tape player that broadcast the "la-la" tape was activated. When the "la-la" sound began playing in response to their sucking, the infants were delighted and kept sucking on the pacifier to keep the "la-la" sound playing. After a while, they began to lose interest, and sucking frequency declined to about half of its initial rate. At this point, the experimenters switched the tape so that "ra-ra" was repeatedly played. The Japanese infants began sucking again with vigor, indicating that they could hear the difference between the old, boring "la" sound and the new, interesting "ra" sound.

Infants can distinguish among speech sounds, but they cannot produce them dependably and so must rely mainly on cooing (i.e., simple vowel-like sounds, such as *ah-ah*), cries, laughs, and other vocalizations to communicate. Between the ages of about 4 and 6 months, they begin to babble speech sounds. Babbling involves combinations of vowels and consonants that sound like real syllables but are meaningless. Regardless of the language they hear spoken, all infants go through the same babbling sequence. For example, *d* and *t* appear in infant babbling before *m* and *n*. Even deaf infants babble sounds they've never heard, and they do so in the same order as hearing infants do (Ollers & Eilers, 1988). This is evidence that infants aren't simply imitating the sounds they hear; rather, it suggests that babbling is a natural part of the language development process. Recent research has shown that babbling serves as a signal that the infant is in a state of focused attention and ready to learn (Goldstein et al., 2010). Deaf infants don't babble as much, however, and their babbling starts later than that of hearing infants (at 11 months rather than 6 months).

For vocal babbling to continue, though, infants must be able to hear themselves. In fact, delayed babbling or the cessation of babbling merits testing for possible hearing difficulties. Babbling problems can lead to speech impairments, but they do not necessarily prevent language acquisition. McGill University researchers discovered that deaf infants whose parents communicate using American Sign Language (ASL)

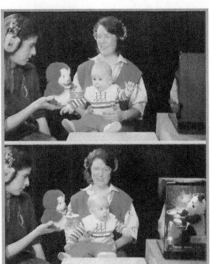

In this videotaped test, the infant watches an animated toy animal while a single speech sound is repeated. After a few repetitions, the sound changes and then the display changes, and then they both change again. If the infant switches her attention when the sound changes, she is anticipating the new display, which demonstrates that she can discriminate between the sounds.

COURTESY DR. PATRICIA K KUHL, UW INSTITUTE FOR LEARNING AND BRAIN SCIENCES

TABLE 9.1

LANGUAGE MILESTONES

Average Age	Language Milestones
0–4 months	Can tell the difference between all possible speech sounds (phonemes); coos, especially in response to speech.
4–6 months	Babbles consonants.
6–10 months	Understands some words and simple requests; can no longer reliably distinguish sounds that are not used in their native language.
10–12 months	Begins to use single words.
12–18 months	Has vocabulary of 30–50 words (simple nouns, adjectives, and action words).
18–24 months	Two-word phrases are ordered according to syntactic rules; vocabulary consists of 50–200 words; understands rules.
24–36 months	Has vocabulary of about 1,000 words; produces phrases and incomplete sentences.
36–60 months	Vocabulary grows to more than 10,000 words; produces full sentences; shows mastery of grammatical morphemes (such as *-ed* for past tense) and function words (such as *the, and, but*); can form questions and negations.

Deaf infants who learn sign language from their parents start babbling with their hands around the same time that hearing infants babble vocally.

fast mapping The process whereby children map a word onto an underlying concept after only a single exposure.

telegraphic speech Speech that is devoid of function morphemes and consists mostly of content words.

begin to babble with their hands at the same age that hearing children begin to babble vocally—between 4 and 6 months (Petitto & Marentette, 1991). Their babbling consists of sign language syllables that are the fundamental components of ASL.

Language Milestones

At about 10 to 12 months of age, infants begin to utter (or sign) their first words. By 18 months, they can say about 50 words and can understand several times more than that. Toddlers generally learn nouns before verbs, and the nouns they learn first are names for everyday, concrete objects (e.g., chair, table, milk) (see **TABLE 9.1**). At about this time, their vocabularies undergo explosive growth. By the time the average child begins school, a vocabulary of 10,000 words is not unusual. (These averages may differ for children in low- and high-income families, as discussed in The Real World: Exploring the 30-Million-Word Gap.) By fifth grade, the average child knows the meanings of 40,000 words. By university, the average student's vocabulary is about 200,000 words. **Fast mapping,** *the process whereby children map a word onto an underlying concept after only a single exposure,* enables them to learn at this rapid pace (Kan & Kohnert, 2008; Mervis & Bertrand, 1994). This astonishingly easy process contrasts dramatically with the effort required later to learn other concepts and skills, such as arithmetic or writing.

Around 24 months, children begin to form two-word sentences, such as "More milk" or "Throw ball." Such sentences are referred to as **telegraphic speech** because they are *devoid of function morphemes and consist mostly of content words.* Yet despite the absence of function words, such as prepositions or articles, these two-word sentences tend to be grammatical; the words are ordered in a manner consistent with the syntactic rules of the language the children are learning to speak. So, for example, toddlers will say "Throw ball" rather than "Ball throw" when they want you to throw the ball to them, and they will say "More milk" rather than "Milk more" when they want you to give them more milk. With these seemingly primitive expressions, 2-year-olds show that they have already acquired an appreciation of the syntactic rules of the language they are learning.

The Real World | Exploring the 30-Million-Word Gap

An early study of the language development of 1- to 2-year-old children in American families at different levels of socioeconomic status (SES)—ranging from families on welfare (low SES) to working class (middle SES) and professional (high SES)—produced stunning results: By the time they reached age 3, children in high-SES families were exposed to millions more words than were children in lower-SES families (Hart & Risley, 1995). This came to be widely known as the "30-million-word gap." The researchers also found that these early language differences were highly predictive of how these children performed as third graders on various language and cognitive tests.

Since that time, the 30-million-word gap has become widely known. Awareness of the gap has led to increased appreciation of the importance of SES differences in early language development, as well as attempts to increase language exposure in low-SES children. Learning more about the origins and nature of the gap is critical to devising effective methods to reduce it, and psychologists have made some important discoveries during the past few years. For example, Fernald, Marchman, and Weisleder (2013) found significant differences between low- and high-SES children as young as 18 months of age: Low-SES children had smaller vocabularies than high-SES children, and they were also slower and less accurate in moving their eyes to the object named by the speaker than were high-SES children. By the age of 24 months, language abilities in the low-SES children were already about six months behind those in the high-SES children.

What exactly produces these troubling lags in low-SES children? A recent study by American researcher Kathy Hirsh-Pasek

Quantity and quality of communication between a parent and a child is an essential factor in language development.

and colleagues (2015) provides evidence that in addition to the sheer number of words that low-SES children are exposed to, the *quality* of early communications makes an important contribution. Hirsh-Pasek and her associates focused on 24-month-old children from low-SES families, using video records of mother–child interactions while they played with items from three different boxes (a storybook, toy stove/cooking accessories, and a dollhouse). The researchers assessed the quantity of words used during these interactions and also the quality of the communications, such as how coordinated the mother–child interactions were (e.g., taking turns), and how often they were jointly engaged in a task (e.g., when playing with the dollhouse, the child produced the word "baby" with a gesture indicating sleep, and the mother placed the figure on the bed).

A year later, the researchers assessed the children's language abilities using scales that were developed to detect changes in language development in young children. Consistent with earlier studies, Hirsh-Pasek and colleagues found that the quantity of words used by the mother during the play task was associated with her child's language performance a year later. (More words from the mother predicted higher performance by the child.) Importantly, though, they also found that the rated quality of communication during the play task was an even stronger predictor of language performance a year later. The findings thus suggest that to counter some of the negative consequences with the 30-million-word gap, it will be important to take into account and improve the quality of communications between parents and children in low-SES families.

The Emergence of Grammatical Rules

Evidence of the ease with which children acquire grammatical rules comes from some interesting errors that children make while forming sentences. If you listen to average 2- or 3-year-old children speaking, you may notice that they use the correct past-tense versions of common verbs, as in the expressions "I ran" and "You ate." By the age of 4 or 5, the same children will be using incorrect forms of these verbs, saying such things as "I runned" or "You eated," forms most children are unlikely ever to have heard (Prasada & Pinker, 1993). The reason is that very young children memorize the particular sounds (i.e., words) that express what they want to communicate. But as children acquire the grammatical rules of their language, they tend to *overregularize*. For example, if a child *overregularizes* the rule that past tense is indicated by *-ed*, then *run* becomes *runned* or even *ranned* instead of *ran*.

These errors show that language acquisition is not simply a matter of imitating adult speech. Instead, children acquire grammatical rules by listening to the speech around them and using those rules to create verbal forms they've never heard. They manage this without explicit awareness of the grammatical rules they've learned. In fact, few children or adults can articulate the grammatical rules of their native language, yet the speech they produce obeys these rules.

By about 3 years of age, children begin to generate complete simple sentences that include function words (e.g., "Give me *the* ball" and "That belongs *to* me"). The sentences increase in complexity over the next 2 years. By the time children are 4 to 5 years of age, many aspects of the language acquisition process are complete. As children continue to mature, their language skills become more refined, with added appreciation of subtler communicative uses of language, such as humour, sarcasm, or irony.

Language Development and Cognitive Development

Language development typically unfolds as a sequence of steps in which children achieve one milestone before moving on to the next. Nearly all infants begin with one-word utterances before progressing to telegraphic speech and then to simple sentences that include function morphemes. It's hard to find solid evidence of infants launching immediately into speaking in sentences—even though you may occasionally hear reports of such feats from proud parents, including possibly your own! There are two possible explanations for this:

- The orderly progression could result from general cognitive development that is unrelated to experience with a specific language (Shore, 1986; Wexler, 1999). For example, perhaps infants begin with one- and then two-word utterances because their short-term memories are so limited that initially they can hold in mind only a word or two; additional cognitive development might be necessary before they have the capacity to put together a simple sentence.

- By contrast, the orderly progression might depend on experience with a specific language, reflecting a child's emerging knowledge of that language (Bates & Goodman, 1997; Gillette et al., 1999).

These two possibilities are difficult to tease apart, but recent research has begun to do so using a novel strategy: examining the acquisition of English by internationally adopted children who did not know any English prior to adoption (Snedeker, Geren, & Shafto, 2007, 2012). Although most of those adoptees were infants or toddlers, a significant proportion were preschoolers. Studying the acquisition of English in such an older adoptee provides a unique opportunity to explore the relationship between language development and cognitive development. If the orderly sequence of milestones that characterizes the acquisition of English by non-adopted infants is a by-product of general cognitive development, then different patterns should be observed in older internationally adopted children, who are more advanced cognitively than infants. However, if the milestones of language development are critically dependent on experience with a specific language—English—then language learning in older adopted children should show the same orderly progression as seen in infants.

Snedeker and colleagues (2007) examined preschoolers ranging from 2½ to 5½ years old, 3 to 18 months after they were adopted from China. They did so by mailing materials to parents, who periodically recorded language samples in their homes and also completed questionnaires concerning specific features of language observed in their children. These data were compared with similar data obtained from monolingual infants. The main result was clear-cut: Language acquisition in preschool-age adopted children showed the same orderly progression of milestones that characterizes infants' language learning. These children began with one-word utterances before moving on to simple word combinations. Furthermore, their vocabulary, just like that of infants, was initially dominated by nouns, and they produced few function morphemes.

These results indicate that some of the key milestones of language development depend on experience with English. However, the adopted children did add new words to their vocabularies more quickly than infants did, perhaps reflecting an influence of general cognitive development. Overall, though, the main message from this study is that observed shifts in early language development reflect specific characteristics of language learning rather than general limitations of cognitive development. A later study by Snedeker and colleagues (2012) provided additional support for this general conclusion, but also produced new evidence for a role of cognitive development in specific aspects of language. For example, adopted preschoolers acquire words that refer to the past or the future—such as *tomorrow, yesterday, before,* or *after*—much more quickly than do infants, perhaps reflecting that infants have difficulty representing these abstract concepts and therefore take longer to learn the words than more cognitively sophisticated preschoolers.

Chinese preschoolers who are adopted by English-speaking parents progress through the same sequence of linguistic milestones as do infants born into English-speaking families, suggesting that these milestones reflect experience with English in particular rather than general cognitive development.

Theories of Language Development

We know a good deal about how language develops, but what underlies the process? The language acquisition process has been the subject of considerable controversy and (at times) angry exchanges among scientists coming from three different approaches: behaviourist, nativist, and interactionist.

Behaviourist Explanations

According to B. F. Skinner's behaviourist explanation of language learning, we learn to talk in the same way we learn any other skill: through reinforcement, shaping, extinction, and the other basic principles of operant conditioning that you read about in the Learning chapter (Skinner, 1957). As infants mature, they begin to vocalize. Those vocalizations that are not reinforced gradually diminish, and those that are reinforced remain in the developing child's repertoire. So, for example, when an infant gurgles "prah," most parents are pretty indifferent. However, a sound that even remotely resembles "da-da" is likely to be reinforced with smiles, whoops, and cackles of "Goooood baaaaaby!" by doting parents. Maturing children also imitate the speech patterns they hear. Then parents or other adults shape the children's speech patterns by reinforcing those that are grammatical and ignoring or punishing those that are ungrammatical. "I no want milk" is likely to be squelched by parental clucks and titters, whereas "No milk for me, thanks" will probably be reinforced.

The behavioural explanation is attractive because it offers a simple account of language development, but this theory cannot account for many fundamental characteristics of language development (Chomsky, 1986; Pinker, 1994; Pinker & Bloom, 1990).

Though behaviourist explanations are widely discredited, parents do indeed reinforce the sounds "da-da" and "ma-ma."

Nativist Explanations

The study of language and cognition underwent an enormous change in the 1950s, when the linguist Noam Chomsky (1957, 1959) published a blistering reply to the behaviourist approach. According to Chomsky, language-learning capacities are built into the brain, which is specialized to acquire language rapidly through simple exposure to speech. This **nativist theory** holds that *language development is best explained as an innate, biological capacity.* According to Chomsky, the human brain is equipped with a **universal grammar**, *a collection of processes that facilitate language learning.* Language processes naturally emerge as the infant matures, provided the infant receives adequate input to maintain the acquisition process.

nativist theory The view that language development is best explained as an innate, biological capacity.

universal grammar A collection of processes that facilitate language learning.

Language Ability Is Partly Separate From General Intelligence Christopher's story is consistent with the nativist view of language development: His genius for language acquisition, despite his low overall intelligence, indicates that language capacity can be somewhat distinct from other mental capacities. Other individuals show the opposite pattern: Some people with normal or nearly normal intelligence can find certain aspects of human language difficult or impossible to learn. This condition is known as **genetic dysphasia**, *a syndrome characterized by an inability to learn the grammatical structure of language despite having otherwise normal intelligence.* Genetic dysphasia tends to run in families, and a single dominant gene has been implicated in its transmission (Gontier, 2008; Gopnik, 1990a, 1990b; Vargha-Khadem et al., 2005). Consider some sentences generated by children with the disorder:

She remembered when she hurts herself the other day.
Carol is cry in the church.

Notice that the ideas these children are trying to communicate are intelligent. Their problems with grammatical rules persist even if they receive special language training. When asked to describe what she did over the weekend, one child wrote, "On Saturday I watch TV." Her teacher corrected the sentence to "On Saturday, I watch*ed* TV," drawing attention to the *-ed* rule for describing past events. The following week, the child was asked to write another account of what she did over the weekend. She wrote, "On Saturday I wash myself and I watched TV and I went to bed." Notice that although she had memorized the past-tense forms *watched* and *went*, she could not generalize the rule to form the past tense of another word (*washed*).

As predicted by the nativist view, studies of people with genetic dysphasia suggest that normal children learn the grammatical rules of human language with ease in part because they are "wired" to do so. This biological predisposition to acquire language explains why newborn infants can distinguish contrasts among phonemes that occur in all human languages—even phonemes they've never heard spoken. If we learned language through imitation, as behaviourists theorized, infants would distinguish only the phonemes they'd actually heard. The nativist theory also explains why deaf infants babble speech sounds they have never heard and why the pattern of language development is similar in children throughout the world. These characteristics of language development are just what would be expected if our biological heritage provided us with the broad mechanics of human language.

Language Is Harder to Learn After Puberty Sets In Also consistent with the nativist view is evidence that language can be acquired only during a restricted period of development, as has been observed with songbirds. If young songbirds are prevented from hearing adult birds sing during a particular period in their early lives, they do not learn to sing. A similar mechanism seems to affect human language learning, as illustrated by the tragic case of Genie (Curtiss, 1977). At the age of 20 months, Genie was tied to a chair by her parents and kept in virtual isolation. Her father forbade Genie's mother and brother to speak to her, and he himself only growled and barked at her. She remained in this brutal state until the age of 13 when her mother finally sought help for her. Genie's life improved substantially, and she received years of language instruction, but it was too late. Her language skills remained extremely primitive. She developed a basic vocabulary and could communicate her ideas, but she could not grasp the grammatical rules of English.

Similar cases have been reported, with a common theme: Once puberty is reached, acquiring language becomes extremely difficult (Brown, 1958). Data from studies of language acquisition in immigrants support this conclusion. In one study, researchers found that the proficiency with which immigrants spoke English depended not on how long they'd lived in the United States but on their age at immigration (Johnson & Newport, 1989). Those who arrived as children were the most proficient, whereas among those who immigrated after puberty, proficiency showed a significant decline regardless of the

"GOT IDEA. TALK BETTER. COMBINE WORDS. MAKE SENTENCES."

genetic dysphasia A syndrome characterized by an inability to learn the grammatical structure of language despite having otherwise normal intelligence.

number of years immigrants were in their new country. More recent work using fMRI shows that acquiring a second language early in childhood (between 1 and 5 years of age) results in very different representation of that language in the brain than does acquiring that language much later (after 9 years of age) (Bloch et al., 2009). Further, a child's first language appears to leave lasting traces in the brain, even when that language is no longer used after infancy. McGill University researchers used fMRI to study teenagers who had been adopted from China as infants by French-speaking parents. These teens were French-speaking and did not consciously remember any Chinese at all. Activation in the brains of these teens to Chinese speech sounds was more similar to that of native Chinese-speaking teens who continued to use the language, than it was to French-speaking teens who had never been exposed to Chinese (Pierce et al., 2014).

Immigrants who learn English as a second language are more proficient if they start to learn English before puberty rather than after.

Interactionist Explanations

Nativist theories are often criticized because they do not explain *how* language develops; they merely explain why. A complete theory of language acquisition requires an explanation of the processes by which the innate, biological capacity for language combines with environmental experience. The interactionist approach holds that although infants are born with an innate ability to acquire language, social interactions play a crucial role in language. Interactionists point out that parents tailor their verbal interactions with children in ways that simplify the language acquisition process: They speak slowly, enunciate clearly, and use simpler sentences than they do when speaking with adults (Bruner, 1983; Farrar, 1990).

Further evidence of the interaction of biology and experience comes from a fascinating study of the creation of a new language by deaf children (Senghas, Kita, & Ozyurek, 2004). Prior to about 1980, deaf children in Nicaragua stayed at home and usually had little contact with other deaf individuals. In 1981, some deaf children began to attend a new vocational school. At first, the school did not teach a formal sign language, and none of the children had learned to sign at home, but the children gradually began to communicate using hand signals they themselves invented.

Over the past 30 years, their sign language has developed considerably (Pyers et al., 2010), and researchers have studied this new language for the telltale characteristics of languages that have evolved over much longer periods. For instance, mature languages typically break down experience into separate components. When we describe something in motion, such as a rock rolling down a hill, our language separates the type of movement (rolling) and the direction of movement (down). If we simply made a gesture, however, we would use a single continuous downward movement to indicate this motion. This is exactly what the first children to develop the Nicaraguan sign language did. But younger groups of children, who have developed the sign language further, use separate signs to describe the direction and the type of movement—a defining characteristic of mature languages. That the younger children did not merely copy the signs from the older users suggests that a predisposition exists to use language to dissect our experiences. Thus, their acts of creation nicely illustrate the interplay of nativism (the predisposition to use language) and experience (growing up in an insulated deaf culture).

How does the evolution of the Nicaraguan deaf children's sign language support the interactionist explanation of language development?

Build to the Outcomes

1. What are language and grammar?

2. What are the distinctions between human language and animal communication?

3. Is the meaning of a sentence more memorable than how the sentence is worded?

4. What language ability do infants have that adults do not?

5. What are the language milestones?

6. How do children learn and use grammatical rules?

7. What is the role of cognitive development in acquiring language?

8. How do behaviourists, nativists, and interactionists explain language development?

Language Development and the Brain

Learning Outcomes

- Describe the language centres of the brain.

- Identify cognitive advantages and disadvantages for bilingual children.

- Explain what has been learned from language studies with nonhuman primates.

As the brain matures, specific neurological structures become specialized, which allows language to develop (Kuhl, 2010; Kuhl & Rivera-Gaxiola, 2008). Where, then, are the language centres of the brain?

Broca's Area and Wernicke's Area of the Brain

In early infancy, language processing is distributed across many areas of the brain. But language processing gradually becomes more and more concentrated in two areas: Broca's area and Wernicke's area, which are sometimes referred to as the language centres of the brain. These areas are connected to one another by a pathway known as the arcuate fasciculus; they are also interconnected with many other brain regions, as language is a complex process that cannot be simply localized to these two parts of the brain. Nonetheless, as the brain matures, Broca's and Wernicke's areas become increasingly specialized for language, so much so that damage to those areas results in a serious condition called **aphasia**, *difficulty in producing or comprehending language.*

Broca's area is located in the left frontal cortex and is involved in the production of the sequential patterns in vocal and sign languages (see **FIGURE 9.3**). As you saw in The Evolution of Psychological Science chapter, Broca's area is named after the French physician Paul Broca, who first reported on speech problems resulting from damage to a specific area of the left frontal cortex (Broca, 1861, 1863). Individuals with damage to this area, which results in *Broca's aphasia*, understand language relatively well, but they have increasing comprehension difficulty as grammatical structures get more complex. Their real struggle, though, is with speech production. Typically, they speak in short, staccato phrases that consist mostly of content morphemes (e.g., *cat, dog*). Function morphemes (e.g., *and, but*) are usually missing, and grammatical structure is impaired. A person with Broca's aphasia might say something like "Ah, Monday, uh, Casey park. Two, uh, friends, and, uh, 30 minutes."

Wernicke's area, located in the left temporal cortex, is involved in language comprehension (whether spoken or signed). The German neurologist Carl Wernicke first described the area that bears his name after observing speech difficulty in patients who had sustained damage to the left posterior temporal cortex (Wernicke, 1874). Individuals with *Wernicke's aphasia* differ from those with Broca's aphasia in two ways: They can produce grammatical speech, but it tends to be meaningless, and they have considerable difficulty comprehending language. A person suffering from Wernicke's aphasia might say something like "Feel very well. In other words, I used to be able to work cigarettes. I don't know how. Things I couldn't hear from are here."

In normal language processing, Wernicke's area is highly active when we make judgements about word meaning, and damage to this area impairs comprehension of spoken and signed language, although the ability to identify nonlanguage sounds is unimpaired. For example, Japanese can be written using symbols that, like the English alphabet, represent speech sounds, or by using pictographs that, like Chinese pictographs, represent ideas. Japanese persons who suffer from Wernicke's aphasia encounter difficulties in writing and understanding the symbols that represent speech sounds but not pictographs (Sasanuma, 1975).

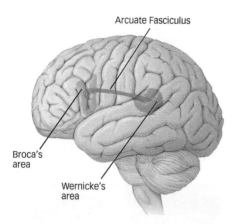

Arcuate Fasciculus

Broca's area

Wernicke's area

Figure 9.3

Broca's and Wernicke's Areas Neuroscientists study people who have brain damage in order to better understand how the brain typically operates. When Broca's area is damaged, people have a hard time producing sentences (but speech, when produced, is meaningful). When Wernicke's area is damaged, people can produce sentences, but the sentences tend to be meaningless. The arcuate fasciculus connects the two areas.

Involvement of the Right Cerebral Hemisphere

As important as Broca's and Wernicke's areas are for language, they are not the entire story. Four kinds of evidence indicate that the right cerebral hemisphere also contributes to language processing, especially to language comprehension (Jung-Beeman, 2005).

aphasia Difficulty in producing or comprehending language.

First, when words are presented to the right hemisphere of healthy participants using divided visual field techniques (see the Neuroscience and Behaviour chapter), the right hemisphere shows some capacity for processing meaning. Second, individuals with damage to the right hemisphere sometimes have subtle problems with language comprehension. Third, a number of neuroimaging studies have revealed evidence of right-hemisphere activation during language tasks. Fourth, and most directly related to language development, some children who have had their entire left hemispheres removed during childhood as a treatment for epilepsy can recover many of their language abilities (Bulteau et al., 2015).

Bilingualism and the Brain

Research on the effects of bilingualism on the brain has shown mixed results. Early studies of bilingual children seemed to suggest that bilingualism slows or interferes with normal cognitive development. When compared with monolingual children, bilingual children performed more slowly when processing language, and their IQ scores were lower. A reexamination of these studies, however, revealed several crucial flaws. First, the tests were given in English even when that was not the children's primary language. Second, the bilingual participants were often first- or second-generation immigrants whose parents were not proficient in English. Finally, the bilingual children came from lower socioeconomic backgrounds than the monolingual children (Andrews, 1982).

Later studies controlled for these factors and revealed a very different picture, indicating that bilingual and monolingual children in Montreal, where bilingualism is common, do not differ significantly in the course and rate of many aspects of their language development (Nicoladis & Genesee, 1997). In fact, several studies showed that middle-class children who are fluent in two languages score higher than monolingual children on several measures of cognitive functioning, including executive control capacities such as the ability to prioritize information and flexibly focus attention (Bialystok, 1999, 2009; Bialystok, Craik, & Luk, 2012). The idea here is that bilingual individuals benefit from exerting executive control in their daily lives when they attempt to suppress the language that they don't want to use. However, a number of recent studies have failed to replicate the beneficial effects of bilingualism on these cognitive tasks. Replication failures have been reported for children (Duñabeitia et al., 2014), young adults (Paap & Sawi, 2014; von Bastian, Souza, & Gade, 2016), and old adults (Kirk et al., 2014), although the evidence for a bilingual advantage in executive functioning appears to be stronger in old adults and children than in young adults (Bialystok, 2017). However, a recent comprehensive analysis of both published and unpublished studies revealed little to no evidence of a bilingual advantage in executive function (Lehtonen et al., 2018).

Nonetheless, bilingualism may have benefits much later in life: Evidence indicates that bilingual individuals tend to have a later onset of Alzheimer's disease than monolingual individuals do, perhaps reflecting the fact that during their lives they have built up a greater amount of back-up cognitive ability, or "cognitive reserve" (Schweizer et al., 2012; Woumans et al., 2015). These benefits are more consistently supported by research (Guzmán-Vélez & Tranel, 2015; Klein, Christie, & Parkvail, 2016). Furthermore, these findings are consistent with research showing that learning a second language produces lasting changes in the brain (Mechelli et al., 2004; Stein et al., 2009). For example, the grey matter in a part of the left parietal lobe that is involved in language is denser in bilingual than in monolingual individuals, and the increased density is most pronounced in those who are most proficient in using their second language (Mechelli et al., 2004; see **FIGURE 9.4**).

Failures to replicate have led to a fierce but as yet unresolved debate about why a bilingual advantage that initially appeared to be robust has been cast in doubt by more recent studies (Bialystok, 2017; Lehtonen et al., 2018; Paap, Johnson, & Sawi, 2015; Valian, 2015). Given the theoretical and practical importance of understanding

Japanese individuals who suffer from Wernicke's aphasia can still understand pictographs like these, even though they have difficulty understanding speech sounds.

Figure 9.4

Bilingualism Alters Brain Structure
Learning a second language early in life increases the density of grey matter in the brain. Panel (a) shows a view of the lower left parietal region, which has denser grey matter in bilingual individuals relative to monolingual individuals. (b) As proficiency in a second language increases, so does the density of grey matter in the lower parietal region. People who acquired a second language earlier in life were also found to have denser grey matter in this region. Interestingly, this area corresponds to the same area that is activated during verbal fluency tasks (Mechelli et al., 2004).

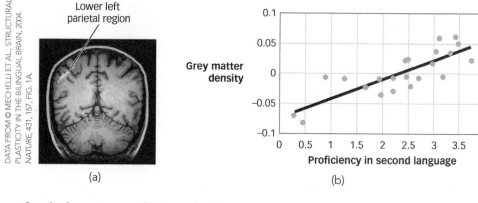

DATA FROM © MECHELLI ET AL., STRUCTURAL PLASTICITY IN THE BILINGUAL BRAIN, 2004. NATURE, 431, 157, FIG. 1A.

Lower left parietal region

(a)

Grey matter density

Proficiency in second language

(b)

© FRIENDS OF WASHOE, CHIMPANZEE & HUMAN COMMUNICATION INSTITUTE, CENTRAL WASHINGTON UNIVERSITY

Allen and Beatrix Gardner used sign language to teach the female chimpanzee Washoe about 160 words. Washoe could also construct simple sentences and combine words in novel ways.

if and why any type of bilingual advantage exists, it seems certain that researchers will continue to try to pin down which benefits are real and which are not.

Can Other Species Learn Human Language?

The human vocal tract and the extremely nimble human hand are better suited to human language than are the throats and paws of other species. Nonetheless, attempts have been made to teach nonhuman animals, particularly apes, to communicate using human language.

Early attempts to teach apes to speak failed dismally because their vocal tracts cannot accommodate the sounds used in human languages (Hayes & Hayes, 1951). Later attempts to teach apes human language have met with more success, including teaching them to use American Sign Language and computer-monitored keyboards that display geometric symbols that represent words. Allen and Beatrix Gardner were the first to use ASL with apes (Gardner & Gardner, 1969). The Gardners worked with a young female chimpanzee named Washoe as though she were a deaf child, signing to her regularly, rewarding her correct efforts at signing, and assisting her acquisition of signs by manipulating her hands in a process referred to as *molding*. In 4 years, Washoe learned approximately 160 words and could construct simple sentences, such as "More fruit." She also formed novel word constructions such as "water bird" for "duck." After a fight with a rhesus monkey, she signed, "dirty monkey!" This constituted a creative use of the term because she had only been taught the use of *dirty* to refer to soiled objects.

Other chimpanzees were immersed in ASL in a similar fashion, and Washoe and her companions were soon signing to each other, creating a learning environment conducive to language acquisition. One of Washoe's cohorts, a chimpanzee named Lucy, learned to sign "drink fruit" for watermelon. When Washoe's second infant died, her caretakers arranged for her to adopt an infant chimpanzee named Loulis.

In a few months, young Loulis, who was not exposed to human signers, learned 68 signs simply by watching Washoe communicate with the other chimpanzees. People who have observed these interactions and are themselves fluent in ASL report little difficulty in following the conversations (Fouts & Bodamer, 1987). One such observer, a *New York Times* reporter who spent some time with Washoe, reported, "Suddenly I realized I was conversing with a member of another species in my native tongue."

Other researchers have taught bonobo chimpanzees to communicate using a geometric keyboard system (Savage-Rumbaugh, Shanker, & Taylor, 1998). Their star pupil, Kanzi, learned the keyboard system by watching researchers try to teach his mother. Like Loulis, young Kanzi picked up the language relatively easily (his mother never did learn the system), suggesting that like humans, birds, and other species, apes experience a critical period for acquiring communicative systems.

Kanzi has learned hundreds of words and has combined them to form thousands of word combinations. Also as in human children, his passive mastery of language appears to exceed his ability to produce language. In one study, researchers tested 9-year-old Kanzi's understanding of 660 spoken sentences. These grammatically complex sentences asked him to perform simple actions, such as "Go get the balloon that's in the microwave" and "Pour the Perrier into the Coke." Some sentences were also potentially misleading, such as "Get the pine needles that are in the refrigerator," when there were pine needles in clear view on the floor. Impressively, Kanzi correctly carried out 72% of the 660 requests (Savage-Rumbaugh & Lewin, 1996).

These results indicate that apes can acquire sizable vocabularies, string words together to form short sentences, and process sentences that are grammatically complex. Their skills are especially impressive because human language is hardly their normal means of communication. Research with apes also suggests that the neurological "wiring" that allows us to learn language overlaps to some degree with theirs (and perhaps with that of other species).

Equally informative are the limitations apes exhibit when learning, comprehending, and using human language:

- *Limited vocabularies.* As mentioned, Washoe's and Kanzi's vocabularies number in the hundreds, but an average 4-year-old human child has a vocabulary of approximately 10,000 words.

- *Limited conceptual repertoire.* Apes primarily sign and respond to names for concrete objects and simple actions. Apes (and several other species) have the ability to map arbitrary sounds or symbols onto objects and actions, but learning, say, the meaning of the word *economics* would be difficult for Washoe or Kanzi. In other words, apes can learn signs for concepts they understand, but the words they can master are smaller and simpler than those that humans understand.

- *Limited understanding of grammar.* The third and perhaps most important limitation is the complexity of grammar that apes can use and comprehend. Apes can string signs together, but their constructions rarely exceed three or four words, and when they do, they are rarely grammatical. Comparing the grammatical structures produced by apes with those produced by human children highlights the complexity of human language as well as the ease and speed with which we generate and comprehend it.

Kanzi, a young male bonobo chimpanzee, learned hundreds of words and word combinations through a keyboard system as he watched researchers try to teach his mother.

"He says he wants a lawyer."

Build to the Outcomes

1. How does language processing change the brain as the child matures?

2. What are the Broca and Wernicke's areas?

3. How does bilingualism influence brain structure?

4. What do studies of apes and language teach us about humans and language?

Language and Thought: How Are They Related?

Language is such a dominant feature of our mental world that it is tempting to equate language with thought. Some theorists have even argued that language is simply a means of expressing thought. Benjamin Whorf (1956), on the other hand, championed the **linguistic relativity hypothesis,** *the idea that language shapes the nature of thought.* Whorf was an engineer who studied language in his spare time and was especially interested in Native American languages. The most frequently cited example of linguistic relativity comes from the Inuit in Canada. Their language has many different terms for frozen white flakes of precipitation, for which we use the word *snow.* Whorf believed that because they have so many terms for snow, the Inuit perceive and think about snow differently than do English speakers. However, Whorf has been criticized for the anecdotal nature of his observations (Pinker, 1994).

Learning Outcome

- Describe the evidence that both supports and discounts the linguistic relativity hypothesis.

linguistic relativity hypothesis The idea that language shapes the nature of thought.

The Inuit of Canada use many different terms for snow, leading Benjamin Whorf (1956) to propose that the Inuit think about snow differently than do English-speakers.

Language and Colour Processing: Differing Results

Eleanor Rosch (1973) cast doubt on Whorf's hypothesis with studies of the Dani, an isolated agricultural tribe living in New Guinea. They have only two terms for colours, which roughly refer to "dark" and "light." If Whorf's hypothesis were correct, you would expect the Dani to have problems perceiving and learning different shades of colour. But in Rosch's experiments, they learned shades of colour just as well as people who have many more colour terms in their first language.

However, more recent evidence shows that language may indeed influence colour processing (Roberson et al., 2004). Researchers compared English children with African children from a cattle-herding tribe in Namibia known as the Himba. The English have 11 basic colour terms, but the Himba, who are largely isolated from the outside world, have only five. For example, they use the term *serandu* to refer to what English speakers would call red, pink, or orange. Researchers showed a series of coloured tiles to each child and then asked the child to choose one colour from an array of 22 different colours. The youngest children, both English and Himba, who knew few or no colour names, tended to confuse similar colours. But as the children grew and acquired more names for colours, their choices increasingly reflected the colour terms they had learned. English children made fewer errors matching tiles that had English colour names; Himba children made fewer errors for tiles with colour names in Himba. These results reveal that language can indeed influence how children think about colours.

Similar effects have been observed in adults. Consider the row of 20 blue rectangles shown in **FIGURE 9.5**, which you'll easily see change gradually from lightest blue on the left to darkest blue on the right. What you might not know is that in Russian, there are different words for light blue (*goluboy*) and dark blue (*siniy*). Researchers investigated whether Russian speakers would respond differently to patches of blue when they fell into different linguistic categories rather than into the same linguistic category (Winawer et al., 2007). Russian speakers as well as English speakers, on average, classified rectangles 1 through 8 as light blue and 9 through 20 as dark blue, but only Russian speakers used different words to refer to the two classes of blue. In the same experimental task, participants were shown three blue squares, as in the lower part of Figure 9.5, and were asked to pick which of the two bottom blue squares among the three matched the colours of the top square. Russian speakers responded more quickly when one of the bottom squares was *goluboy* and the other was *siniy* than when both bottom squares were *goluboy* or both were *siniy*, whereas English speakers took about the same amount of time to respond in the two conditions (Winawer et al., 2007). As with children, language can affect how adults think about colours. Some striking recent evidence bearing on this issue is discussed in A World of Difference: Language and Perception: Is There a Dominant Sense?

Figure 9.5

Language Affects How We Think About Colour Unlike English, the Russian language has different words for light blue and dark blue. Russian speakers who were asked to pick which of the two bottom squares matched the colour of the single square above responded more quickly when one of the bottom squares was called *goluboy* (light blue) and the other was called *siniy* (dark blue) than when both were referred to by the same name. English speakers took about the same amount of time.

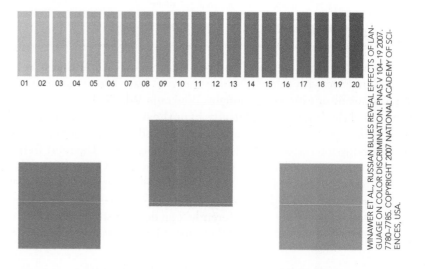

A World of Difference | Language and Perception: Is There a Dominant Sense?

Do you find it easier to describe a colour than an odour? Or a sound versus a taste? Philosophers and linguists have long maintained that visual experience is most accessible to language, that hearing is nearly as accessible, and that touch, taste, and smell are the least accessible (Howes, 2005; San Roque et al., 2015). This makes sense intuitively: When we see a banana and are asked about its colour, most of us will say that it is yellow, yet there will probably be less agreement when people try to describe the odour that comes from peanut butter. But is this hierarchy a universal feature of all languages? Or does the accessibility of the five senses to linguistic description differ across languages?

Majid and colleagues (2018) recently reported an ambitious study to address this fascinating question. They assembled a large group of researchers who were studying 20 different languages across the globe (see figure). Most of these were spoken languages, but three signed languages were also included. The researchers asked users of all languages to describe a variety of sensory stimuli: colours and shapes for vision; sounds that varied in pitch, loudness, and tempo for audition (except for the signers, of course); surfaces varying in roughness and smoothness for touch; sweet, salty, bitter, and umami stimuli for taste; and common scents such as smoke or onion for smell. The researchers came up with a measure of the diversity of names used to describe each stimulus (*codability*) for each of the five senses. A high codability score would mean that people tend to use the same terms to describe a particular stimulus; a low codability score would mean that people use diverse terms to describe that stimulus.

For English, the results lined up well with traditional thinking: Vision and sound had the highest codability scores, followed by touch and taste, with smell having the lowest codability scores. Was this ordering universal across languages? The answer, for the most part, was a resounding "no." For example, in contrast to English speakers and users of American Sign Language, individuals who spoke Yélî Dnye or signed Kata Kolok had extremely low visual codability scores. Codability scores for speakers of Farsi, Lao, and several other languages were highest for taste. There was, however, one nearly universal finding: Smell consistently had the lowest codability scores across virtually all languages.

These results raise intriguing and fundamental questions about the relationship between language and sensory experience: Why is it that different languages seem to be more or less attuned to different sensory domains? And why is smell, in contrast to the other senses, consistently poorly coded in language? Something to think about next time you see a banana or smell something that might or might not be peanut butter.

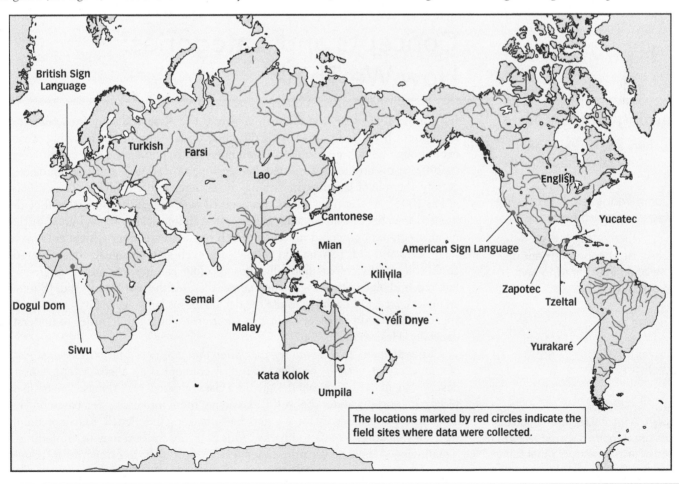

The locations marked by red circles indicate the field sites where data were collected.

Was Whorf "Half Right"?

DATA VISUALIZATION

How Do Subtle Language Changes Influence Decisions? Go to launchpadworks.com.

Bear in mind, however, that either thought or language ability can be severely impaired while the capacity for the other is relatively spared, as illustrated by the case of Christopher, which you read about earlier in this chapter—and as we'll see again in the next section. These kinds of observations have led some researchers to suggest that Whorf was only "half right" in his claims about the effect of language on thought (Regier & Kay, 2009). Others suggest that, consistent with this idea, it is overly simplistic to talk in general terms about whether language influences thought and that researchers need to be more specific about the exact ways in which language influences thought. For example, Wolff & Holmes (2011) rejected the idea that language entirely determines thought. But they also pointed out that there is considerable evidence that language can *influence* thought both by highlighting specific properties of concepts and by allowing us to formulate verbal rules that help solve problems. Thus, recent research has started to clarify the ways in which the linguistic relativity hypothesis is right and the ways in which it is wrong.

Build to the Outcomes

1. What is the linguistic relativity hypothesis?
2. How does language influence our understanding of colour?

3. What does the fact that impaired language does not mean impaired thought (and vice versa) suggest about the relationship between the two?

Concepts and Categories: How We Think

Learning Outcomes

- Identify why concepts are fundamental to our ability to think.

- Compare the family prototype and exemplar theories of concepts.

- Describe the involvement of the brain in organizing and processing concepts.

In October 2000, a 69-year-old man known by the initials JB went for a neurological assessment because he was having difficulty understanding the meaning of words, even though he still performed well on many other perceptual and cognitive tasks. In 2002, as his problems worsened, he began participating in a research project concerning the role of language in naming, recognizing, and classifying colours (Haslam et al., 2007). As the researchers observed JB over the next 15 months, they documented that his colour language deteriorated dramatically; he had great difficulty naming colours and could not even match objects with their typical colours (e.g., strawberry and red, banana and yellow). Yet even as his language deteriorated, JB could still classify colours normally, sorting colour patches into groups of green, yellow, red, and blue in the exact same manner that healthy participants did. JB retained an intact *concept* of colours despite the decline of his language ability—a finding that suggests we need to look at factors in addition to language in order to understand concepts (Haslam et al., 2007).

Concept refers to a *mental representation that groups or categorizes shared features of related objects, events, or other stimuli.* A concept is an abstract representation, description, or definition that designates a class or category of things. The brain organizes our concepts about the world, classifying them into categories based on shared similarities. Our category for *dog* may be something like "small, four-footed animal with fur that wags its tail and barks." Our category for *bird* may be something like "small winged, beaked creature that flies." We form these categories in large part

concept A mental representation that groups or categorizes shared features of related objects, events, or other stimuli.

by noticing similarities among objects and events that we experience in everyday life. For example, your concept of a chair might include such features as sturdiness, relative flatness, and an object that you can sit on. That set of attributes defines a category of objects in the world—desk chairs, recliner chairs, flat rocks, bar stools, and so on—that can all be described in that way.

Concepts are fundamental to our ability to think and make sense of the world. We'll first compare various theories that explain the formation of concepts and then consider studies that link the formation and organization of concepts to the brain. As with other aspects of cognition, we can gain insight into how concepts are organized by looking at some instances in which they are rather disorganized. We'll encounter some unusual disorders that help us understand how concepts are organized in the brain.

There is family resemblance between family members despite the fact that there is no defining feature that they all have in common. Instead, there are shared common features. Someone who also shares some of those features may be categorized as belonging to the family.

Psychological Theories of Concepts and Categories

Early psychological theories described concepts as rules that specify the necessary and sufficient conditions for membership in a particular category. A *necessary condition* is something that must be true of the object in order for it to belong to the category. For instance, suppose you were trying to determine whether an unfamiliar animal was a dog. It is necessary that the creature be a mammal; otherwise it doesn't belong to the category *dog* because all dogs are mammals. A *sufficient condition* is something that, if it is true of the object, proves that it belongs to the category. Suppose someone told you that the creature was a German shepherd and you know that a German shepherd is a type of dog. *German shepherd* is a sufficient condition for membership in the category *dog*.

Most natural categories, however, cannot be so easily defined in terms of this classical approach of necessary and sufficient conditions. For example, what is your definition of *dog*? Can you come up with a rule of "dogship" that includes all dogs and excludes all non-dogs? Most people can't, but they still use the term *dog* intelligently, easily classifying objects as dogs or non-dogs. Two major theories seek to explain how people perform these acts of categorization.

Prototype theory, which can be traced to the pioneering experimental studies of Eleanor Rosch and her colleagues (Rosch, 1973, 1975; Rosch & Mervis, 1975), is based on *the "best" or "most typical" member of a category.* A prototype possesses many (or all) of the most characteristic features of the category. For North Americans, the prototype of the *bird* category would be something like a wren: a small animal with feathers and wings that flies through the air, lays eggs, and migrates (see **FIGURE 9.6**). If you lived in Antarctica, your prototype of a bird might be a penguin: a small animal that has flippers, swims, and lays eggs. According to *prototype theory,* if your prototypical bird is a robin, then a canary would be considered a better example of a bird than would an ostrich, because a canary has more features in common with a robin than an

prototype theory The concept that we classify new objects by comparing them to the "best" or "most typical" member (the *prototype*) of a category.

Properties	Generic bird	Wren	Blue heron	Golden eagle	Domestic goose	Penguin
Flies regularly	✔	✔	✔	✔		
Sings	✔	✔	✔			
Lays eggs	✔	✔	✔	✔	✔	✔
Is small	✔	✔				
Nests in trees	✔	✔				

Figure 9.6

Critical Features of a Category We tend to think of a generic bird as possessing a number of critical features, but not every bird possesses all of those features. In North America, a wren is a better example of a bird than a penguin or an ostrich.

ostrich does. People make category judgements by comparing new instances with the category's prototype. This contrasts with the classical approach to concepts in which something either is or is not an example of a concept (i.e., it either does or does not belong in the category *dog* or *bird*).

Exemplar theory holds that *we make category judgements by comparing a new instance with stored memories for other instances of the category* (Medin & Schaffer, 1978). Imagine that you're out walking in the woods, and from the corner of your eye you spot a four-legged animal that might be a wolf or a coyote but that reminds you of your cousin's German shepherd. You figure it must be a dog and continue to enjoy your walk rather than fleeing in a panic. You probably categorized this new animal as a dog because it bore a striking resemblance to other dogs you've encountered; in other words, it was a good example (or an *exemplar*) of the category *dog*. Exemplar theory does a better job than prototype theory of accounting for certain aspects of categorization (Ashby & Rosedahl, 2017; Nosofsky, Sanders, & McDaniel, 2018), especially in that we recall not only what a *prototypical* dog looks like but also what *specific* dogs look like. **FIGURE 9.7** illustrates the difference between prototype theory and exemplar theory.

exemplar theory The concept that we make category judgements by comparing a new instance with stored memories of other instances of the category.

Figure 9.7
Prototype Theory and Exemplar Theory According to prototype theory, we classify new objects by comparing them to the "prototype" (or most typical) member of a category. According to exemplar theory, we classify new objects by comparing them with all category members.

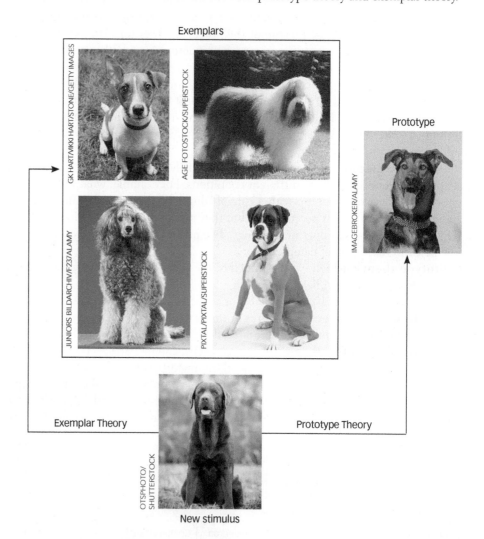

Concepts, Categories, and the Brain

Studies that have attempted to link concepts and categories to the brain have helped make sense of the theories we have just considered. For example, in one set of studies (Marsolek, 1995), participants classified prototypes faster when the stimuli were presented to the right visual field, meaning that the left hemisphere received the input first. (See the Neuroscience and Behaviour chapter for a discussion of how the two hemispheres of the brain receive input from the outside world.) In contrast, participants classified previously seen exemplars faster when images were presented to the left visual field (meaning that the right hemisphere received the input first). These results suggest a role for both exemplars and prototypes: The left hemisphere is primarily involved in forming prototypes, and the right hemisphere is mainly active in recognizing exemplars.

More recently, researchers using neuroimaging techniques have also concluded that we use both prototypes and exemplars when forming concepts and categories. The visual cortex is involved in forming prototypes, whereas the prefrontal cortex and basal ganglia are involved in learning exemplars (Ashby & Ell, 2001; Ashby & O'Brien, 2005). This evidence suggests that exemplar-based learning involves analysis and decision making (prefrontal cortex), whereas prototype formation is a more holistic activity involving image processing (visual cortex).

Category-Specific Deficit

Some of the most striking evidence linking concepts and categories with the brain originated in a pioneering study of an odd case. Two neuropsychologists (Warrington & McCarthy, 1983) described a man with brain damage who could not recognize a variety of human-made objects or retrieve any information about them, but whose knowledge of living things and foods was perfectly normal. In the following year, neuropsychologists (Warrington & Shallice, 1984) reported on four individuals with brain damage who exhibited the reverse pattern: They could recognize information about human-made objects, but their ability to recognize information about living things and foods was severely impaired. Over 100 similar cases have since been reported (Martin & Caramazza, 2003). These unusual cases became the basis for a syndrome called **category-specific deficit**, *an inability to recognize objects that belong to a particular category, although the ability to recognize objects outside the category is undisturbed.*

Category-specific deficits like these have been observed even when the brain trauma that produces them occurs shortly after birth. Two researchers reported the case of Adam, a 16-year-old boy who suffered a stroke a day after he was born (Farah & Rabinowitz, 2003). Adam has severe difficulty recognizing faces and other biological objects. When shown a picture of a cherry, he identified it as "a Chinese yo-yo." When shown a picture of a mouse, he identified it as an owl. He made errors like these on 79% of the animal pictures and 54% of the plant pictures he was shown. In contrast, he made errors only 15% of the time when identifying pictures of nonliving things, such as spatulas, brooms, and cigars. What's so important about this case? The fact that 16-year-old Adam exhibited category-specific deficits despite suffering a stroke when he was only 1 day old strongly suggests that the brain is "prewired" to organize perceptual and sensory inputs into broad-based categories, such as living and nonliving things.

The type of category-specific deficit suffered depends on where the brain is damaged. Deficits usually result when an individual suffers a stroke or other trauma to areas in the left hemisphere of the cerebral cortex (Mahon & Caramazza, 2009). Damage to the front part of the left temporal lobe results in difficulty identifying humans; damage to the lower left temporal lobe results in difficulty identifying animals; damage to the region where the temporal lobe meets the occipital and parietal lobes impairs the ability to retrieve names of tools (Damasio et al., 1996). Similarly, when healthy people undertake the same task, imaging studies have demonstrated that the same regions of the brain are more active during naming of tools than during naming of animals and vice versa, as shown in **FIGURE 9.8** (Martin, 2007; Martin & Chao, 2001).

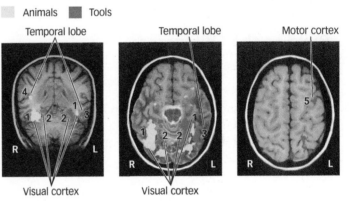

Figure 9.8

Brain Areas Involved in Category-Specific Processing Participants were asked to silently name pictures of animals and tools while they underwent fMRI scanning. The fMRIs revealed greater activity in the areas in yellow when participants named animals, and areas in purple showed greater activity when participants named tools. Specific regions indicated by numbers include areas within the visual cortex (1, 2), parts of the temporal lobe (3, 4), and the motor cortex (5). Note that the images are left/right reversed.

category-specific deficit
A neurological syndrome characterized by an inability to recognize objects that belong to a particular category, although the ability to recognize objects outside the category is undisturbed.

Touch is one way that blind individuals could develop category-preferential brain responses.

Are Our Brains Prewired?

How do particular brain regions develop category preferences for objects such as tools or animals? One possibility is that these preferences develop from the specific visual experiences that individuals have during the course of their lives. An alternative possibility is suggested by the study of Adam that we just considered: The brain may be prewired such that particular regions respond more strongly to some categories than to others. A recent study tested these ideas by examining the activity of category-preferential regions in adults who have been blind since birth (Mahon et al., 2009). While in the fMRI scanner, blind and sighted individuals each heard a series of words, including some words that referred to animals and others that referred to tools. For each word, participants made a judgement about the size of the corresponding object. The critical finding was that category-preferential regions showed highly similar patterns of activity in the blind and sighted individuals. In both groups, for example, regions in the visual cortex and temporal lobe responded to animals and tools in much the same manner as that shown in Figure 9.8.

These results provide compelling evidence that category-specific organization of visual regions does not depend on an individual's visual experience. The category-specific organization conceivably could have arisen from interactions with objects that blind individuals have had that involved senses other than vision, such as touch (Peelen & Kastner, 2009). However, when these results are combined with the observations of Adam, the simplest explanation may be that category-specific brain organization is innately determined (Bedny & Saxe, 2012; Mahon et al., 2009).

Build to the Outcomes

1. What are concepts?
2. Why are concepts useful to us?
3. What are necessary and sufficient conditions in forming concepts?
4. How do the prototype and exemplar theories differ?
5. How do prototypes and exemplars relate to each other?
6. What evidence suggests that the brain is "prewired" to organize perceptual and sensory inputs?
7. What is the role of vision in category-specific organization?

Decision Making: Rational and Otherwise

rational choice theory The classical view that we make decisions by determining how likely something is to happen, judging the value of the outcome, and then multiplying the two.

We use categories and concepts to guide the hundreds of decisions and judgements we make during the course of an average day. Some decisions are easy (what to wear; what to eat for breakfast; whether to walk, ride a bicycle, or drive to class) and some are more difficult (which car to buy, which apartment to rent, who to hang out with on Friday night, and even which job to take after graduation). Some decisions are based on sound judgements. Others are not.

The Rational Ideal

Economists contend that if we are rational thinkers, free to make our own decisions, we will behave as predicted by **rational choice theory**: *We make decisions by determining how likely something is to happen, judging the value of the outcome, and then multiplying the two* (Edwards, 1955). This means that our judgements will vary depending on the value we assign to the possible outcomes. Suppose, for example, you were asked to choose between a 10% chance of gaining $500 and a 20% chance of gaining $2,000. The rational person would choose the second alternative because the expected payoff is $400 ($2,000 × 20%), whereas the first offers an expected gain of only $50 ($500 × 10%). Selecting the option with the highest expected value seems so straightforward that many economists accept the basic ideas in rational choice theory. But how well does this theory describe decision making in our everyday lives? In many cases, the answer is: not very well.

The Irrational Reality

Is the ability to classify new events and objects into categories always a useful skill? Alas, no. These strengths of human decision making can turn into weaknesses when certain tasks inadvertently activate these skills. In other words, the same principles that allow cognition to occur easily and accurately can pop up to bedevil our decision making.

Judging Frequencies and Probabilities

Consider the following list of words:

block table block pen telephone block disk glass table block telephone block watch table candy

You probably noticed that the words *block* and *table* occur more frequently than the other words do. In fact, studies have shown that people are quite good at estimating *frequency,* simply the number of times something will happen. This skill matters quite a bit when it comes to decision making. In contrast, we perform poorly on tasks that require us to think in terms of *probabilities,* or the likelihood that something will happen.

Even with probabilities, however, performance varies depending on how the problem is described. In one experiment, 100 physicians were asked to predict the incidence of breast cancer among women whose mammogram screening tests showed possible evidence of breast cancer. The physicians were told to take into consideration the rarity of breast cancer (1% of the population at the time the study was done) and radiologists' record in diagnosing the condition (correctly recognized only 79% of the time and falsely diagnosed almost 10% of the time). Of the 100 physicians, 95 estimated the probability that cancer was present to be about 75%! The correct answer was 8%. The physicians apparently had difficulty taking into account that much information when making their decision (Eddy, 1982). Similar dismal results have been reported with a number of medical screening tests (Hoffrage & Gigerenzer, 1996; Windeler & Kobberling, 1986).

However, dramatically different results were obtained when the study was repeated using *frequency* information instead of *probability* information. Stating the problem as "10 out of every 1,000 women actually have breast cancer" instead of "1% of women actually have breast cancer" led 46% of the physicians to derive the right answer, compared with only 8% who came up with the right answer when the problem was presented using probabilities (Hoffrage & Gigerenzer, 1998). This finding suggests, at a minimum, that when seeking advice (even from a highly skilled decision maker), make sure your problem is described using frequencies rather than probabilities.

Availability Bias

Take a look at the list of names in **FIGURE 9.9.** Now look away from the book and estimate the number of male names and female names in the figure. Did you notice that some of the women on the list are famous and none of the men are? Was your estimate off because you thought the list contained more women's names than men's names (Tversky & Kahneman, 1973, 1974)? The reverse would have been true if you had looked at a list with the names of famous men and unknown women because people typically fall prey to **availability bias**: *Items that are more readily available in memory are judged as having occurred more frequently.*

People don't always make rational choices. When a lottery jackpot is larger than usual, more people will buy lottery tickets, thinking that they might well win big. However, more people buying lottery tickets reduces the likelihood of any one person winning the lottery. Ironically, people have a better chance at winning a lottery with a relatively small jackpot.

Jennifer Aniston	Robert Kingston
Judy Smith	Gilbert Chapman
Frank Carson	Gwyneth Paltrow
Elizabeth Taylor	Martin Mitchell
Daniel Hunt	Thomas Hughes
Henry Vaughan	Michael Drayton
Agatha Christie	Julia Roberts
Arthur Hutchinson	Hillary Clinton
Jennifer Lopez	Jack Lindsay
Allen Nevins	Richard Gilder
Jane Austen	George Nathan
Joseph Litton	Britney Spears

Figure 9.9

Availability Bias Looking at this list of names, estimate the number of women's and men's names.

availability bias The concept that items that are more readily available in memory are judged as having occurred more frequently.

The availability bias affects our estimates because memory strength and frequency of occurrence are directly related. Frequently occurring items are remembered more easily than *in*frequently occurring items, so you naturally conclude that items for which you have better memory must also have been more frequent. Unfortunately, better memory in this case was due not to greater *frequency* but to greater *familiarity*.

Shortcuts such as the availability bias are sometimes referred to as **heuristics**, *fast and efficient strategies that may facilitate decision making but do not guarantee that a solution will be reached*. Heuristics are mental shortcuts that are often—but not always—effective when approaching a problem (Swinkels, 2003). In contrast, an **algorithm** is *a well-defined sequence of procedures or rules that guarantees a solution to a problem*. Consider, for example, two approaches to constructing a PowerPoint presentation involving features you rarely use, such as inserting movies and complex animations: (1) You try to remember what you did the last time you tried to do a similar presentation; and (2) you follow a set of step-by-step directions that you wrote down the last time you did something similar, which tells you exactly how to insert movies and build complex animations.

The first procedure is an intelligent heuristic that may be successful, but you could continue searching your memory until you finally run out of time or patience. The second strategy is a series of well-defined steps that, if properly executed, will guarantee a solution.

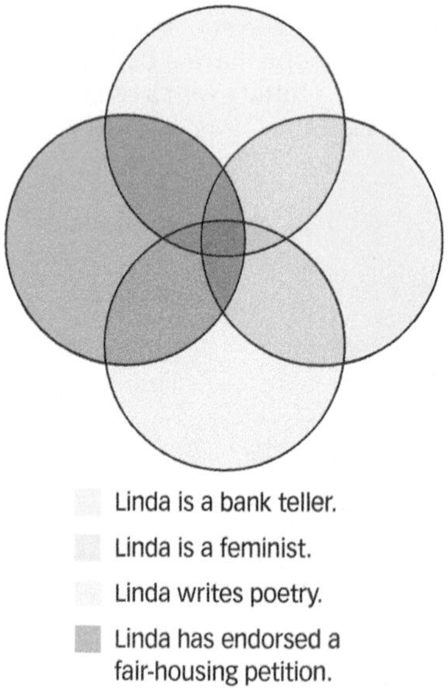

The Conjunction Fallacy

The availability bias illustrates a potential source of error in human cognition. Unfortunately, it's not the only one. Consider the following description:

> Linda is 31 years old, single, outspoken, and very bright. In university, she majored in philosophy. As a student, she was deeply concerned with issues of discrimination and social justice and also participated in antinuclear demonstrations.

Which state of affairs is more probable?

a. Linda is a bank teller.

b. Linda is a bank teller and is active in the feminist movement.

In one study, 89% of participants rated option b as more probable than option a (Tversky & Kahneman, 1983), although that's logically impossible. Let's say there's a 20% chance that Linda is a bank teller; after all, there are plenty of occupations she might hold. Independently, let's say there's also a 20% chance that she's active in the feminist movement; she probably has lots of interests. The joint probability that *both* things are true simultaneously is the product of their separate probabilities. In other words, the 20% chance that she's a teller multiplied by the 20% chance that she's in the feminist movement produces a 4% chance that *both* things are true at the same time (.20 × .20 = .04, or 4%). The combined probability of events is always less than the independent probability of each event; therefore, it's always *more* probable that any one state of affairs is true than is a set of events simultaneously.

This situation is called the **conjunction fallacy** because *people think that two events are more likely to occur together than either individual event alone*. The fallacy is that when people are given more and more pieces of information, they think there's a higher probability that all are true. In actuality, the probability diminishes rapidly. Judging by her description, do you think Linda also voted for the liberal candidate in the last election? Do you think she also writes poetry? Do you think she's also signed her name to fair-housing petitions? With each additional bit of information, you probably think you're getting a better and better description of Linda, but as you can see in **FIGURE 9.10**, the likelihood of *all* those events being true *at the same time* is very small.

- Linda is a bank teller.
- Linda is a feminist.
- Linda writes poetry.
- Linda has endorsed a fair-housing petition.

Figure 9.10

The Conjunction Fallacy People often think that with each additional bit of information, the probability that all the facts are simultaneously true of a person increases. In fact, the probability decreases dramatically. Notice how the intersection of *all* these possibilities is much smaller than the area of any one possibility alone.

heuristic A fast and efficient strategy that may facilitate decision making but does not guarantee that a solution will be reached.

algorithm A well-defined sequence of procedures or rules that guarantees a solution to a problem.

conjunction fallacy Thinking that two events are more likely to occur together than either individual event alone.

Representativeness Heuristic

Think about the following situation: A panel of psychologists wrote 100 descriptions based on interviews with engineers and lawyers. THE DESCRIPTIONS WERE OF 70 ENGINEERS AND 30 LAWYERS. You will be shown a random selection of these descriptions. Read each one and then pause and decide if it is more likely that the person is an engineer or a lawyer. Note your decision and read on.

1. Jack enjoys reading books on social and political issues. During the interview, he displayed particular skill at argument.

2. Tom is a loner who enjoys working on mathematical puzzles during his spare time. During the interview, his speech remained fairly abstract and his emotions were well controlled.

3. Harry is a bright man and an avid racquetball player. During the interview, he asked many insightful questions and was very well spoken.

Research participants read a series of descriptions like these and were then asked to judge the likelihood that the person described was a lawyer or an engineer (Kahneman & Tversky, 1973). Remember, of the descriptions, 70 were engineers and 30 were lawyers. If participants took this proportion into consideration, their judgements should have reflected the fact that there were more than twice as many engineers as lawyers. But researchers found that, instead of using this information, people based their judgements solely on how closely the description matched their own concepts of lawyers and engineers. So the majority of participants thought descriptions such as #1 were more likely to be lawyers, whereas descriptions such as #2 were more likely to be engineers and that descriptions such as #3 could be either.

Consider participants' judgements about Harry. His description doesn't sound like a lawyer's or an engineer's, so most people said he was *equally likely* to hold either occupation. But the pool contains more than twice as many engineers as lawyers, so it is far *more* likely that Harry is an engineer. People seem to ignore information about *base rate,* or the existing probability of an event, basing their judgements on similarities to categories. Researchers call this the **representativeness heuristic**: *making a probability judgement by comparing an object or event with a prototype of the object or event* (Kahneman & Tversky, 1973). Thus, the probability judgements were skewed towards the participants' prototypes of lawyer and engineer. The greater the similarity, the more likely the people in the descriptions were judged to be members of that category despite the existence of much more useful base rates.

Heuristics such as availability, representativeness, or the conjunction fallacy highlight both the strengths and weaknesses of the way we think. We are very good at forming categories based on prototypes and making classification judgements on the basis of similarity to prototypes. Judging probabilities is not our strong suit. As we saw earlier in this chapter, the human brain easily processes frequency information, so decision-making performance can usually be improved if probability problems are reframed using frequencies.

Framing Effects

You've seen that, according to rational choice theory, our judgements will vary depending on the value we place on the expected outcome. So how effective are we at assigning value to our choices? Studies show that **framing effects**, which occur when *people give different answers to the same problem depending on how the problem is phrased (or framed),* can influence the assignment of value.

For example, if people are told that a particular drug has a 70% effectiveness rate, they're usually pretty impressed: getting what ails you cured 70% of the time by using

representativeness heuristic A mental shortcut that involves making a probability judgement by comparing an object or event with a prototype of the object or event.

framing effects A bias whereby people give different answers to the same problem depending on how the problem is phrased (or framed).

sunk-cost fallacy A framing effect in which people make decisions about a current situation on the basis of what they have previously invested in the situation.

optimism bias A bias whereby people believe that, compared with other individuals, they are more likely to experience positive events and less likely to experience negative events in the future.

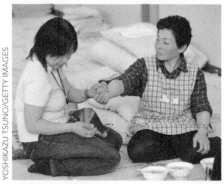

Different cultures show different levels of optimism bias, which may be a clue to understanding its origins.

the drug sounds like a good deal. Tell them instead that a drug has a 30% failure rate—that 30% of the time the drug does no good—and they typically perceive it as risky, potentially harmful, and something to be avoided. Notice that the information is the same: A 70% effectiveness rate means that 30% of the time, it's ineffective. The way the information is framed, however, leads to substantially different conclusions (Tversky & Kahneman, 1981).

One of the most striking framing effects is the **sunk-cost fallacy**, which occurs when *people make decisions about a current situation on the basis of what they have previously invested in the situation.* Imagine waiting in line for 3 hours, paying $100 for a ticket to the Warped Tour to see your favourite bands, and waking on the day of the outdoor concert to find that it's bitterly cold and rainy. If you go, you'll feel miserable. But you go anyway, reasoning that the $100 you paid for the ticket and the time you spent in line will have been wasted if you stay home.

Notice that you have two choices: (1) Spend $100 and stay comfortably at home; or (2) spend $100 and endure many uncomfortable hours in the rain. The $100 is gone in either case: It's a sunk cost, irretrievable at the moment of your decision. But the way you framed the problem created a problem: Because you invested time and money, you feel obligated to follow through, even though it's something you no longer want. If you can turn off this feeling and ask yourself if you'd rather spend $100 to be comfortable or spend it to be miserable, the smart choice is clear: Stay home and watch the live stream of the show!

Even the National Basketball Association (NBA) is guilty of a sunk-cost fallacy. Coaches should play their most productive players and keep them on the team longer, but they don't. The most *expensive* players are given more time on court and are kept on the team longer than cheaper players, even if the costly players are not performing up to par (Staw & Hoang, 1995). Coaches act to justify their team's investment in an expensive player rather than recognize the loss. Framing effects can be costly, but they can also be exploited to increase wealth (see Hot Science: Can Framing Effects Make You Rich?).

Optimism Bias

In addition to heuristics and the biases we've just considered, human decision making often reflects the effects of **optimism bias**: *People believe that, compared with other individuals, they are more likely to experience positive events and less likely to experience negative events in the future* (Sharot, 2011). For example, people believe they are more likely than others to own their own homes and live a long life and that they are less likely to have a heart attack or a drinking problem (Weinstein, 1980). Although optimism about the future is often a good thing for our mental and physical health—optimistic individuals are usually well adjusted psychologically and are able to handle stress well (Nes & Sergerstrom, 2006)—too much optimism can be detrimental because it may prevent us from taking the necessary steps to achieve our goals. Thus, overly optimistic individuals may think that they can attain a goal even when they lack the ability to achieve it, as exemplified by the finding that higher levels of optimism can be associated with lower levels of academic achievement (Sweeny, Carroll, & Shepperd, 2006).

Several studies have found that optimism bias is greater in North Americans than in individuals from eastern cultures such as Japan (Heine & Lehman, 1995; Klein & Helweg-Larsen, 2002). One study examined optimism bias concerning the risk of natural disasters and terrorist attacks in American, Japanese, and Argentinean mental health workers who had received training in responding to such events (Gierlach, Blesher, & Beutler, 2010). Although participants in all three countries judged that they were at lower risk of experiencing a disaster than others in their country,

Hot Science | Can Framing Effects Make You Rich?

Financial experts agree that it is critically important to save money for future needs, yet nearly 40% of American adults report having no retirement savings (Martin, 2018). Researchers refer to this as a retirement savings crisis (Benartzi & Thaler, 2013). For three consecutive years (2016–2018), the financial services company Bankrate.com asked American adults about their financial regrets. Each year, the biggest financial regret was not saving for retirement, followed by not saving for an emergency, yet only about half of those with a financial regret said they had a plan to address it (Tepper, 2018). Finding ways to help people save more could thus contribute to their financial health and likely relieve some psychological distress. Recent research suggests that one possible avenue is to use framing effects.

How to accomplish this objective? A clue comes from an intriguing effect known as an *illusion of wealth* (Goldstein, Hershfield, & Benartzi, 2016). Goldstein and colleagues (2016) questioned nearly 1,000 adults on how adequate various amounts of wealth would be in retirement. They framed the amounts either as a lump sum (e.g., $100,000) or as an equivalent amount of monthly payments for life (e.g., $500/per month). For relatively small amounts, the researchers

uncovered evidence that people value the lump sum more than the equivalent amount divided and paid out per month. They surmised that when framed as a monthly payment, the amount is small enough that people can see how little it would actually purchase, but the lump sum seems substantial.

Flipping this around, Hershfield, Shu, and Benartzi (2019) reasoned that it may be more psychologically painful to *part* with a lump sum than an equivalent amount of money meted out in smaller amounts. For example, people might be more reluctant to commit to saving $150/month than $5/day, because they see the lump sum as more valuable, even though the amount they are parting with per month is the same.

To test their hypothesis in a real-world context, Hershfield and colleagues conducted a study in collaboration with the financial company Acorns, which allows people to invest spare change or larger amounts of money to an online account through a smartphone app (for details, go to www.acorns.com). In the Hershfield et al. study, new users who had just established an account at Acorns (young adults with a mean age of about 32 years) were assigned to different savings conditions. In each of three conditions,

approximately 1,800 users were asked if they wanted to sign up to deposit $150 each month, but the framing varied across conditions, from $5/day to $35/week to $150/month.

If people find it psychologically more painful to part with the larger sum than equivalent smaller amounts, then more users should sign up for the daily deposits than for the weekly and monthly deposits. This is exactly what Hershfield and colleagues found: 29% of users signed up when given the daily framing, compared with 10% for the weekly framing and only 7% for the monthly framing. There was also evidence that more people in the daily framing remained in the program one month longer than in the other two conditions. In two other conditions involving smaller deposit amounts, framing was varied from $7/week to $30/month, with the same key result as in the other conditions: many more sign-ups for the weekly (40%) than for the monthly (22%) framing.

These results suggest that there is a way to avoid financial regrets that loom large for too many people later in life: Put away a small amount of money—small enough that parting with it doesn't cause psychological pain—as frequently as possible.

---

optimism bias was strongest in the American sample. Cultural differences such as these may eventually help us understand why optimism bias occurs.

Why Do We Make Decision-Making Errors?

As you have seen, everyday decision making seems riddled with errors and shortcomings. Our decisions vary wildly, depending on how a problem is presented (e.g., framed in terms of frequencies versus probabilities or in terms of losses rather than savings). We also seem to be prone to fallacies, such as the sunk-cost fallacy, the conjunction fallacy, or optimism bias. Psychologists have developed several theories to explain why everyday decision making suffers from these failings. We'll review the most influential theory, known as *prospect theory*.

According to a totally rational model of inference, people should make decisions that maximize value; in other words, they should seek to increase what psychologists and economists call *expected utility*. We face decisions like this every day. If you are making a decision that involves money, and if money is what you value, then you should choose the outcome that is likely to bring you the most money. For

prospect theory The theory that people choose to take on risk when evaluating potential losses and avoid risks when evaluating potential risks.

instance, when deciding which of two apartments to rent, you'd compare the monthly expenses for each and choose the one that leaves more money in your pocket.

As you have seen, however, people often make decisions that are inconsistent with this simple principle. The question is, why? To explain these effects, Amos Tversky and Daniel Kahneman (1992) developed **prospect theory**, which proposes that *people choose to take on risks when evaluating potential losses and to avoid risks when evaluating potential gains.* These decision processes take place in two phases:

- First, people simplify available information. So in a task such as choosing an apartment, they tend to ignore a lot of potentially useful information because apartments differ in so many ways (the closeness of restaurants, the presence of a swimming pool, the colour of the carpet, and so forth). Comparing each apartment on each factor is simply too much work; focusing only on differences that matter is more efficient.

- In the second phase, people choose the prospect that they believe offers the best value. This value is personal and may differ from an objective measure of "best value." For example, you might choose the apartment with higher rent because you can walk to eight great bars and restaurants.

Prospect theory makes other assumptions that account for people's choice patterns. One assumption, called the *certainty effect,* suggests that when making decisions, people give greater weight to outcomes that are a sure thing. When deciding between playing a lottery with an 80% chance of winning $4,000 or receiving $3,000 outright, most people choose the $3,000, even though the expected value of the first choice is $200 more ($4,000 × 80% = $3,200)! Apparently, people weigh certainty much more heavily than expected payoffs when making choices.

Prospect theory also assumes that, in evaluating choices, people compare them with a reference point. For instance, suppose you're still torn between two apartments. The $400 monthly rent for apartment A is discounted $10 if you pay before the fifth of the month. A $10 surcharge is tacked onto the $390 per month rent for apartment B if you pay after the fifth of the month. Although the apartments are objectively identical in terms of cost, different reference points may make apartment A seem psychologically more appealing than apartment B.

Furthermore, prospect theory also assumes that people are more willing to take risks to avoid losses than to achieve gains. Given a choice between a definite $300 rebate on your first month's rent or spinning a wheel that offers an 80% chance of getting a $400 rebate, you'll most likely choose the lower sure payoff over the higher potential payoff ($400 × 80% = $320). However, given a choice between a sure fine of $300 for damaging an apartment or spinning a wheel that has an 80% chance of a $400 fine, most people will choose the higher potential loss over the sure loss. This asymmetry in risk preferences shows that we are willing to take on risk if we think it will ward off a loss, but we're risk averse if we expect to lose some benefits.

Decision Making and the Brain

A man identified as Elliot was a successful businessman, husband, and father prior to developing a brain tumour. After surgery, his intellectual abilities seemed intact, but he was unable to differentiate between important and unimportant activities and would spend hours doing mundane tasks. He lost his job and got involved in several risky financial ventures that bankrupted him. He had no difficulty discussing what had happened, but his descriptions were so detached and dispassionate that it seemed as though his abstract intellectual functions had become dissociated from his social and emotional abilities.

Research confirms that this interpretation of Elliot's downfall is right on track in terms of the effects of his brain tumour. In one study, researchers looked at how healthy volunteers differed from people with prefrontal lobe damage on a gambling task that involves risky decision making (Bechara et al., 1994, 1997). Four decks of cards were placed face down, and participants were required to make 100 selections of cards that specified an amount of play money they could win or lose. Two of the decks usually provided large payoffs or large losses, whereas the other two provided smaller payoffs and losses. While playing the game, the participants' galvanic skin responses (GSRs) were recorded to measure heightened emotional reactions.

The performance of players with prefrontal lobe damage mirrored Elliot's real-life problems: They selected cards equally from the riskier and the safer decks, leading most players to eventually go bankrupt. At first, the healthy volunteers also selected from each deck equally, but they gradually shifted to choosing primarily from the safer decks. This difference in strategy occurred even though both groups showed strong emotional reactions to big gains and losses, as measured by their comparable GSR scores. The two groups differed in one important way, however. As the game progressed, the healthy participants began to show anticipatory emotional reactions when they even *considered* choosing a card from the risky deck. Their GSR scores jumped dramatically even before they were able to say that some decks were riskier than others (Bechara et al., 1997). The participants with prefrontal damage didn't show these anticipatory feelings when they were thinking about selecting a card from the risky deck. Apparently, their emotional reactions did not guide their thinking, so they continued to make risky decisions, as shown in **FIGURE 9.11**.

Further studies of the participants with prefrontal damage suggest that their risky decision making grows out of insensitivity to the future consequences of their behaviour (Naqvi, Shiv, & Bechara, 2006). Unable to think beyond immediate

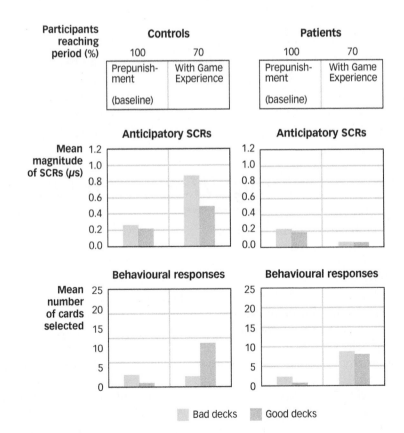

Figure 9.11

The Neuroscience of Risky Decision Making In a study of risky decision making, researchers compared healthy participants' (the control group) choices to those made by people with damage to the prefrontal cortex. Participants played a game in which they selected a card from one of four decks. Two of the decks were made up of riskier cards, that is, cards that provided large payoffs or large losses. The other two decks contained safer cards—those with much smaller payoffs and losses. At the beginning of the game, both groups chose cards from the two decks with equal frequency. Over the course of the game, however, the healthy controls avoided the bad decks and showed large emotional responses (SCRs, or skin conductance responses) when they even considered choosing a card from a risky deck. Participants with prefrontal brain damage, on the other hand, continued to choose cards from the two decks with equal frequency and showed no evidence of emotional learning; they eventually went bankrupt. DATA FROM BECHARA ET AL., 1997.

consequences, they could not shift their choices in response to a rising rate of losses or a declining rate of rewards (Bechara, Tranel, & Damasio, 2000). Interestingly, substance-dependent individuals, such as alcoholics and cocaine addicts, act the same way. Most perform as poorly on the gambling task as do individuals with prefrontal damage (Bechara et al., 2001). More recent work has extended these impairments on the gambling task across cultures to Chinese adolescents with binge-drinking problems (Johnson et al., 2008).

These findings have potentially important implications for such everyday issues as road safety. A recent study focused on people who had been convicted of driving while impaired with alcohol (DUI). Offenders who performed poorly on the gambling task were much more likely to commit repeated DUI offenses than those who performed well on the gambling task (Bouchard, Brown, & Nadeau, 2012). Related recent work has documented gambling-task impairments in binge eaters, another group who demonstrate an insensitivity to the future consequences of behaviour (Danner et al., 2012).

Neuroimaging studies of healthy individuals have provided evidence that fits well with the earlier studies of individuals with damage to the prefrontal cortex: During the gambling task, an area in the prefrontal cortex is activated when participants make risky decisions as compared to safe decisions. Indeed, the activated region is in the part of the prefrontal cortex that is typically damaged in participants who perform poorly on the gambling task; greater activation in this region is correlated with better task performance in healthy individuals (Fukui et al., 2005; Lawrence et al., 2009). Taken together, the neuroimaging and lesion studies show clearly that aspects of risky decision making depend critically on the contributions of the prefrontal cortex.

Build to the Outcomes

1. What is the importance of rational choices in decision making?
2. Why is a better decision more likely when we consider frequency, rather than the likelihood that something will happen (probability)?
3. How are strength of memory and frequency of occurrence related?
4. How can more information sometimes lead people to wrong conclusions?
5. What can cause people to ignore the base rate of an event?
6. How does framing a problem differently influence one's answer?
7. Why will most people take more risks to avoid losses than to make gains?
8. What role does the prefrontal cortex play in risky behaviour?

Problem Solving: Working It Out

Learning Outcomes

- Compare the means–ends analysis and analogical problem-solving approaches.
- Explain the factors that lead to, or inhibit, creativity and insight.

You have a problem when you find yourself in a place where you don't want to be. In such circumstances, you try to find a way to change the situation so that you end up in a situation you *do* want. Let's say that it's the night before a test, and you are trying to study but just can't settle down and focus on the material. This is a situation you don't want, so you try to think of ways to help yourself focus. You might begin with the material that most interests you, or provide yourself with rewards, such as a music break or a trip to the refrigerator. If these activities enable you to get down to work, your problem is solved.

Two major types of problems complicate our daily lives. The first and most frequent is the *ill-defined problem,* one that does not have a clear goal or well-defined path(s) to a solution. Your study block is an ill-defined problem: Your goal isn't clearly defined (i.e., somehow get focused), and the solution path for achieving the goal is even less clear (i.e., there are many ways to gain focus). Most everyday problems (being a better person, finding that special someone, achieving success) are ill defined. In contrast, a *well-defined problem* is one with clearly specified goals and clearly defined solution paths. Examples include following a clear set of directions to get to school, solving simple algebra problems, or playing a game of chess.

Means–Ends Analysis

In 1945, the German psychologist Karl Duncker reported some important studies of the problem-solving process. He presented people with ill-defined problems and asked them to "think aloud" while solving them (Duncker, 1945). On the basis of what people said about how they solve problems, Duncker described problem solving in terms of **means–ends analysis**, *a process of searching for the means or steps to reduce the differences between the current situation and the desired goal*. This process usually took the following steps:

Even though it may not be easy to put together this model, having instructions for assembly makes it a well-defined problem.

1. Analyze the goal state (i.e., the desired outcome you want to attain).
2. Analyze the current state (i.e., your starting point, or the current situation).
3. List the differences between the current state and the goal state.
4. Reduce the list of differences by

   - Direct means (a procedure that solves the problem without intermediate steps).
   - Generating a subgoal (an intermediate step on the way to solving the problem).
   - Finding a similar problem that has a known solution.

Consider, for example, one of Duncker's problems:

A patient has an inoperable tumour in his abdomen. The tumour is inoperable because it is surrounded by healthy but fragile tissue that would be severely damaged during surgery. How can the patient be saved?

The *goal state* is a patient without the tumour and with undamaged surrounding tissue. The *current state* is a patient with an inoperable tumour surrounded by fragile tissue. The *difference* between these two states is the tumour. A *direct-means solution* would be to destroy the tumour with X-rays, but the required X-ray dose would destroy the fragile surrounding tissue and possibly kill the patient. A *subgoal* would be to modify the X-ray machine to deliver a weaker dose. After this subgoal is achieved, a direct-means solution could be to deliver the weaker dose to the patient's abdomen. But this solution won't work either: The weaker dose wouldn't damage the healthy tissue but also wouldn't kill the tumour. So, what to do? Find a similar problem that has a known solution. Let's see how this can be done.

Analogical Problem Solving

When we engage in **analogical problem solving**, we attempt to *solve a problem by finding a similar problem with a known solution and applying that solution to the current problem*. Consider the following story:

An island surrounded by bridges is the site of an enemy fortress. The massive fortification is so strongly defended that only a very large army could capture it. Unfortunately, the bridges would collapse under the weight of such a huge force. So a clever general divides the army into several smaller units and sends the units over different bridges, timing the crossings so that the many streams of soldiers converge on the fortress at the same time, and the fortress is taken.

Does this story suggest a solution to the tumour problem? It should. Removing a tumour and attacking a fortress are very different problems, but the two problems are analogous because they share a common structure: The *goal state* is a conquered fortress with undamaged surrounding bridges. The *current state* is an occupied fortress surrounded by fragile bridges. The *difference* between the two states is the occupying enemy.

means–ends analysis A process of searching for the means or steps to reduce differences between the current situation and the desired goal.

analogical problem solving The process of solving a problem by finding a similar problem with a known solution and applying that solution to the current problem.

Figure 9.12

Analogical Problem Solving Just as smaller, lighter battalions can reach the fortress without damaging the bridges, many small X-ray doses can destroy the tumour without harming the delicate surrounding tissue. In both cases, the additive strength achieves the objective. Did this solution occur to you after reading the fortress story? In studies that have used the tumour problem, only 10% of participants spontaneously generated the correct solution. This percentage rose to 30% if participants read the island fortress problem or another analogous story. However, the success rate climbed dramatically to 75% among participants who had a chance to read more than one analogous problem or were given a deliberate hint to use the solution to the fortress story (Gick & Holyoak, 1980).

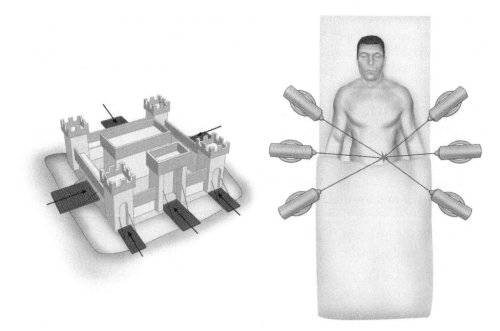

The *solution* is to divide the required force into smaller units that are light enough to spare the fragile bridges and send them down the bridges simultaneously so that they converge on the fortress. The combined units will form an army strong enough to take the fortress (see **FIGURE 9.12**).

This analogous problem of the island fortress suggests the following direct-means solution to the tumour problem:

> Surround the patient with X-ray machines and simultaneously send weaker doses that converge on the tumour. The combined strength of the weaker X-ray doses will be sufficient to destroy the tumour, but the individual doses will be weak enough to spare the surrounding healthy tissue.

Why was the fortress problem so ineffective by itself? Problem solving is strongly affected by superficial similarities between problems, and the relationship between the tumour and fortress problems lies deep in their structure (Catrambone, 2002).

Creativity and Insight

Analogical problem solving shows us that successfully solving a problem often depends on learning the principles that underlie a particular type of problem and also that solving lots of problems improves our ability to recognize certain problem types and generate effective solutions. Some problem solving, however, seems to involve brilliant flashes of insight and creative solutions that have never before been tried. Creative and insightful solutions often rely on restructuring a problem so that it turns into a problem you already know how to solve (Cummins, 2012).

Genius and Insight

Consider the exceptional mind of the mathematician Friedrich Gauss (1777–1855). One day, Gauss's elementary schoolteacher asked the class to add up the numbers 1 through 10. While his classmates laboriously worked their sums, Gauss had a flash of insight that caused the answer to occur to him immediately. Gauss imagined the numbers 1 through 10 as weights lined up on a balance beam, as shown in **FIGURE 9.13**. Starting at the left, each "weight" increases by 1. For the beam to balance, each weight on the left must be paired with a weight on the right. You can see this by starting at the middle and noticing that $5 + 6 = 11$, then moving

Figure 9.13

Genius and Insight Young Friedrich Gauss imagined the scheme shown here and quickly reduced a laborious addition problem to an easy multiplication task. Gauss's early insight later led him to realize an intriguing truth: This simple solution generalizes to number series of any length. INFORMATION FROM WETHEIMER, 1945/1982.

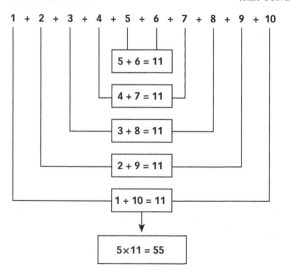

outward, $4+7=11$, $3+8=11$, and so on. This produces five number pairs that add up to 11. Now the problem is easy: Multiply. Gauss's genius lay in restructuring the problem in a way that allowed him to notice a very simple and elegant solution to an otherwise tedious task—a procedure, by the way, that generalizes to series of any length.

According to Gestalt psychologists, insights such as these reflect a spontaneous restructuring of a problem. A sudden flash of insight contrasts with incremental problem-solving procedures whereby one gradually gets closer and closer to a solution. Early researchers studying insight found that people were more likely to solve a non-insight problem if they felt they were gradually getting "warmer" (incrementally closer to the solution). But whether someone felt "warm" did not predict the likelihood of their solving an insight problem (Metcalfe & Wiebe, 1987). The solution for an insight problem seemed to appear out of the blue, regardless of what the participant felt.

Later research suggested that unconscious processes contribute to performance on insight problem–solving tasks (Bowers et al., 1990). In one study, research participants were shown paired, three-word series like those in **FIGURE 9.14** and asked to find a fourth word that was associated with the three words in each series. However, only one series in each pair had a common associate. Solvable series were termed *coherent,* whereas those with no solution were called *incoherent.*

Even if participants couldn't find a solution, they could reliably decide, more than by chance alone, which of the pairs was coherent. However, if insightful solutions only occur in a sudden, all-or-nothing manner, their performance should have been no better than chance. Thus, the findings suggest that insight problem solving may be impacted by processing that occurs outside of conscious awareness. The process works something like this: The pattern of clues that constitute a problem unconsciously activates relevant information in memory. Activation then spreads through the memory network, recruiting additional relevant information (Bowers et al., 1990). When sufficient information has been activated, it crosses the threshold of awareness, and we experience a sudden flash of insight into the problem's solution.

Finding a connection between the words *strawberry* and *traffic* might take some time, even for someone motivated to figure out how they are related. But if the word *strawberry* activates *jam* in long-term memory (see the Memory chapter), and the activation spreads from *strawberry* to *traffic*, the solution to the puzzle may suddenly spring into awareness without the thinker's knowing how it got there.

Sudden Insight and the Brain

The "aha!" moment that accompanies a sudden flash of insight highlights that solving a problem based on insight *feels* radically different from solving it through step-by-step analysis or trial and error. This difference in subjective experience suggests that something different is going on in the brain when we solve a problem using insight instead of analytic strategies (Kounios & Beeman, 2009).

To examine brain activity associated with insight, researchers used a procedure called *compound remote associates* that is similar in some respects to the three-word problems displayed in Figure 9.14. Each compound remote associates problem consists of three words, such as *crab, pine,* and *sauce.* Sometimes people solve these problems with a flash of insight: The solution word (*apple!*) suddenly pops into their minds, seemingly out of nowhere. Other times, people solve the problem by using analytic strategies that involve trying out different alternatives by generating a compound word for *crab* and then assessing whether that word fits *pine* and *sauce. Crab-grass* works, but *grass* doesn't work with *pine* and *sauce. Crabapple?* Problem solved.

Participants are instructed to press a button the moment a solution comes to mind, then describe whether they arrived at the solution via insight or through an analytic strategy. In an initial study, researchers used the electroencephalograph (EEG); (see the Neuroscience and Behaviour chapter) to measure brain electrical

Coherent	Incoherent
Playing	Still
Credit	Pages
Report	Music
Blank	Light
White	Folk
Lines	Head
Ticket	Town
Shop	Root
Broker	Car
Magic	House
Plush	Lion
Floor	Butter
Base	Swan
Snow	Army
Dance	Mask
Gold	Noise
Stool	Foam
Tender	Shade

INFORMATION FROM BOWERS ET AL., 1990.

Figure 9.14

Insightful Solutions Are Really Incremental Participants were asked to find a fourth word that was associated with the other three words in each series. Even if they couldn't find a solution, they could reliably choose which series of three words were solvable and which were not. Try to solve these. (The answers are on page 384.)

Louis Pasteur realized that sudden scientific insights don't just happen out of the blue; they depend on a prepared mind to take advantage of opportunity.

Answers to Figure 9.14
Solutions:
Card, paper, pawn, carpet, ball, bar

functional fixedness The tendency to perceive the functions of objects as unchanging.

activity as participants attempted to solve the problems. What they observed was striking: Beginning about one-third of a second before participants came up with a solution, there was a sudden and dramatic burst of high-frequency electrical activity (40 cycles per second, or gamma band) for problems solved via insight, but not for problems solved via analytic strategies (Jung-Beeman et al., 2004). This activity was centred over the front part of the right temporal lobe, slightly above the right ear. When the researchers performed a similar study using fMRI to measure brain activity, they found that this right temporal area was the only region in the entire brain that showed greater activity for insight solutions than for solutions based on analytic strategies.

The great French scientist Louis Pasteur once stated, "Chance favors only the prepared mind." Inspired by this observation, researchers asked whether brain activity occurring just before presentation of a problem influenced whether that problem was solved via insight or analytic strategies (Kounios et al., 2006). It did. In the moments before a problem was solved with an insight solution, there was increased activity deep in the frontal lobes, in a part of the brain known as the anterior cingulate, which controls cognitive processes, such as the ability to switch attention from one thing to another. The researchers suggested that this increased activity in the anterior cingulate enabled participants to attend to and detect associations that were only weakly activated, perhaps at a subconscious level, and that facilitated sudden insight.

The results of these studies suggest that the familiar image of a lightbulb turning on in your head when you experience an "aha!" moment is on the mark. Those moments are accompanied by something like an electrical power surge in the brain, and the increasing amount of research on creative insight and the brain (Beaty et al., 2016; Kounios & Beeman, 2015) should tell us much more about how to turn on the mental lightbulb and keep it burning bright.

Functional Fixedness

Sudden insights occur relatively infrequently. One reason for their rarity is that problem solving (like decision making) suffers from framing effects. In problem solving, framing tends to limit the types of solutions that occur to us. **Functional fixedness**—*the tendency to perceive the functions of objects as unchanging*—is a process that constricts our thinking. Look at **FIGURES 9.15** and **9.16** and see if you can solve the problems before reading on. In Figure 9.15, your task is

Figure 9.15

Functional Fixedness and the Candle Problem How can you use these objects—a box of matches, thumbtacks, and a candle—to mount the candle on the wall so that it illuminates the room? Give this problem some thought before you check the answer in Figure 9.18 on page 386.

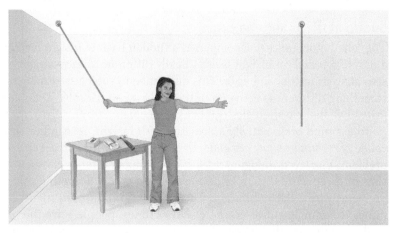

Figure 9.16

Functional Fixedness and the String Problem The strings hanging from hooks on either side of the ceiling are long enough to be tied together, but they are positioned too far apart to reach one while holding on to the other. Using the tools shown on the table (nails, matches, and a hammer), how can you accomplish the task? Compare your answer with that in Figure 9.19 on page 386.

to illuminate a dark room using the following objects: some thumbtacks, a box of matches, and a candle. In Figure 9.16, your task is to use the items on the table to find a way to hold on to a string hanging from the ceiling and at the same time reach a second string that is too far away to grasp.

Difficulty with solving these problems derives from our tendency to think of the objects only in terms of their normal, typical, or "fixed" functions. We don't think to use the matchbox for a candleholder because boxes typically hold matches, not candles. Similarly, using the hammer as a pendulum weight doesn't spring to mind because hammers are typically used to pound things. Did functional fixedness prevent you from solving these problems? (The solutions are shown in **FIGURES 9.18** and **9.19**.)

Sometimes framing limits our ability to generate a solution. Before reading on, look at **FIGURE 9.17**. Without lifting your pencil from the page, try to connect all nine dots with only four straight lines. To solve this problem, you must allow the lines you draw to extend outside the imaginary box that surrounds the dots (see **FIGURE 9.20**). This constraint resides not in the problem but in the mind of the problem solver (Kershaw & Ohlsson, 2004). Despite the apparent sudden flash of insight that seems to yield a solution to problems of this type, research indicates that the thought processes people apply when solving even this type of insight problem are best described as an incremental, means–ends analysis (MacGregor, Ormerod, & Chronicle, 2001).

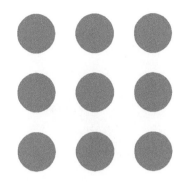

Figure 9.17
The Nine-Dot Problem Connect all nine dots with four straight lines without lifting your pencil from the paper. Compare your answer with those in Figure 9.20 on page 386.

Build to the Outcomes

1. What is the difference between an ill-defined and a well-defined problem?
2. What are the steps in the means–ends analysis process of problem solving?
3. What is analogical problem solving?
4. What is the role of the unconscious in flashes of insight?
5. What is functional fixedness?

Reasoning: Truth and Validity

Reasoning is *a mental activity that consists of organizing information or beliefs into a series of steps in order to reach conclusions.* We rely on logic to assess the results of the reasoning process. Logic is a system of rules that specifies which conclusions follow from a set of statements. To put it another way, if you know that a given set of statements is true, logic will tell you which other statements *must* also be true. If the statement "Jack and Jill went up the hill" is true, then according to the rules of logic, the statement "Jill went up the hill" must also be true. Accepting the truth of the first statement while denying the truth of the second statement would be a contradiction. Logic is a tool for evaluating reasoning, but it should not be confused with the process of reasoning itself. Equating logic and reasoning would be like equating carpenter's tools (logic) with building a house (reasoning).

These considerations highlight that there is a fundamental distinction in reasoning between the *truth* of statements and the *validity* of an argument. If statements are true and an argument is valid (i.e., logical), then sound conclusions will be reached. But even if statements are true, a faulty argument will produce invalid conclusions. For example, the statements that "All football players are athletes" and "LeBron James is an athlete" are true, but the conclusion that "LeBron James is a football player" is not true because the argument relating the two statements is invalid.

Learning Outcome

- Explain the distinction between truth and validity in reasoning, as well as how it links to belief biases and illusions of truth in the lab and in everyday life.

reasoning A mental activity that consists of organizing information or beliefs into a series of steps in order to reach conclusions.

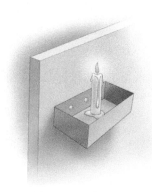

Figure 9.18
The Solution to the Candle Problem
What makes this problem difficult is that the usual function of the box (to hold matches) interferes with recognizing that it can be tacked to the wall to serve as a candleholder.

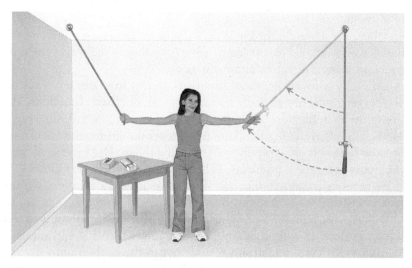

Figure 9.19
The Solution to the String Problem
The usual function of the hammer (to pound things) interferes with recognizing that it can also serve as a weighted pendulum to swing the string into the person's grasp.

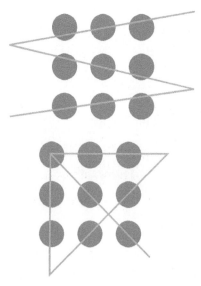

Figure 9.20
Two Solutions to the Nine-Dot Problem Solving this problem requires "thinking outside the box"—that is, going outside the imaginary box implied by the dot arrangement. The limiting box isn't really there; it is imposed by the problem solver's perceptual set.

belief bias The idea that people's judgements about whether to accept conclusions depend more on how believable the conclusions are than on whether the arguments are logically valid.

syllogistic reasoning Determining whether a conclusion follows from two statements that are assumed to be true.

Belief Bias

The distinction between truth and validity can help us understand why people are sometimes prone to failures in reasoning, as illustrated by **belief bias**, which is that *people's judgements about whether to accept conclusions depend more on how believable the conclusions are than on whether the arguments are logically valid* (Evans, Barston, & Pollard, 1983). For example, **syllogistic reasoning** assesses *whether a conclusion follows from two statements that are assumed to be true,* as in the LeBron James example. Consider the two following syllogisms, evaluate the argument, and ask yourself whether or not the conclusions must be true if the statements are true:

Syllogism 1

    Statement 1: No cigarettes are inexpensive.

    Statement 2: Some addictive things are inexpensive.

    Conclusion: Some addictive things are not cigarettes.

Syllogism 2

    Statement 1: No addictive things are inexpensive.

    Statement 2: Some cigarettes are inexpensive.

    Conclusion: Some cigarettes are not addictive.

If you're like most people, you probably concluded that the argument is valid in Syllogism 1 but flawed in Syllogism 2. Indeed, researchers found that nearly 100% of participants accepted the first conclusion as valid, but fewer than half accepted the second (Evans et al., 1983). But notice that the syllogisms are in exactly the same form. This form of syllogism is valid, so both conclusions are valid given that the two statements are true. Evidently, the believability of the conclusions influences people's judgements.

These findings suggest that it is difficult for people to inhibit their pre-existing knowledge and beliefs when reasoning about syllogisms. Children and older adults are known to have difficulties inhibiting knowledge and beliefs that are activated by a task even when they are not needed for performing the task (Bédard et al., 2002; Christ et al., 2001). Consistent with a role for inhibitory processing in overcoming belief bias, 12-year-old children and older adults (65+ years) performed worse than young adults (20 years old) when they reasoned about syllogisms that require inhibition of pre-existing beliefs to come to a correct conclusion; on the other hand, there was no effect of age on reasoning about syllogisms that do not require such inhibitory processing (De Neys & Van Gelder, 2009).

Research using fMRI provides additional insights into how pre-existing knowledge and inhibitory processes impact belief biases on reasoning tasks (Goel & Dolan, 2003; Goel, 2007). In *belief-laden* trials, participants' brains were scanned while they reasoned about syllogisms that could be influenced by knowledge that affected the believability of the conclusions. In *belief-neutral* trials, syllogisms contained obscure terms whose meaning was unknown to participants, as in the following example:

Syllogism 3

Statement 1: No codes are highly complex.

Statement 2: Some quipu are highly complex.

Conclusion: No quipu are codes.

Belief-neutral reasoning activated different brain regions than did belief-laden reasoning. Activity in a part of the left temporal lobe that's involved in retrieving and selecting facts from long-term memory increased during belief-laden reasoning. In contrast, during belief-neutral reasoning, that part of the brain showed little activity while parts of the parietal lobe that are involved in mathematical reasoning and spatial representation showed greater activity. Critically, in belief-laden reasoning trials in which conclusions conflicted with people's pre-existing knowledge (as in Syllogism 2 above), the right prefrontal cortex—a region known to be involved in inhibitory processing—showed increased activity. This finding is consistent with the evidence from children and older adults that indicates that inhibitory processing is critically important for resisting belief bias.

Although the evidence we've considered regarding belief bias comes from controlled laboratory tasks, the phenomenon has important real-world implications. For example, despite a near-universal scientific consensus that climate change is a genuine phenomenon, a significant minority of the population (around 20% in the United States) deny the existence of climate change (Lewandowsky, Oberauer, & Gignac, 2013). Denial of climate change, in turn, is linked to strong belief in free markets (whose operation could be threatened by steps taken to counter climate change) and in conspiracy theories (e.g., the Apollo moon landing never happened—it was staged in a Hollywood film studio). These findings highlight that belief biases can impact assessment of critically important scientific findings.

Battling the causes of climate change could be undermined by belief bias.

The Illusion of Truth

People sometimes are misled regarding the truth of a statement because they reason about truth on the basis of influences other than a valid argument. This is illustrated by the **illusory truth effect**, which occurs *when repeated exposure to a statement increases the likelihood that people will judge the statement to be true* (Hasher, Goldstein, & Toppino, 1977). Repeated exposure increases the familiarity of a statement, which is mistakenly accepted as evidence that the statement is true (Begg, Anas, & Farinacci, 1992; Fazio et al., 2015).

A striking everyday example of the illusory truth effect comes from recent research on "fake news"—made-up news stories that are presented as factual (see Other Voices: Why Do People Fall for Fake News?). Fake news became a topic of intense concern

illusory truth effect An error in reasoning that occurs when repeated exposure to a statement increases the likelihood that people will judge that statement to be true.

Other Voices | Why Do People Fall for Fake News?

In our discussion of the illusion of truth, we saw that prior exposure to a fake news story increased estimates of the story's accuracy. Here two of the researchers who produced that finding (Gordon Pennycook of the University of Regina, and David Rand of the Massachusetts Institute of Technology) discuss the importance of reasoning processes in combatting susceptibility to fake news.

Gordon Pennycook (*left*) is an assistant professor at the Hill & Levene Schools of Business at the University of Regina, in Saskatchewan. David Rand (*right*) is an associate professor at the Sloan School of Management and the Department of Brain and Cognitive Sciences at the Massachusetts Institute of Technology.

What makes people susceptible to fake news and other forms of strategic misinformation? And what, if anything, can be done about it? . . .

The good news is that psychologists and other social scientists are working hard to understand what prevents people from seeing through propaganda. The bad news is that there is not yet a consensus on the answer. Much of the debate among researchers falls into two opposing camps. One group claims that our ability to reason is hijacked by our partisan convictions: that is, we're prone to rationalization. The other group—to which the two of us belong—claims that the problem is that we often fail to exercise our critical faculties: that is, we're mentally lazy. . . .

The rationalization camp, which has gained considerable prominence in recent years, is built around a set of theories contending that when it comes to politically charged issues, people use their intellectual abilities to persuade themselves to believe what they want to be true rather than attempting to actually discover the truth. According to this view, political passions essentially make people unreasonable, even—indeed, especially—if they tend to be good at reasoning in other contexts. (Roughly: The smarter you are, the better you are at rationalizing.)

Some of the most striking evidence used to support this position comes from an influential 2012 study in which the law professor Dan Kahan and his colleagues found that the degree of political polarization on the issue of climate change was greater among people who scored higher on measures of science literary and numerical ability than it was among those who scored lower on these tests. Apparently, more "analytical" Democrats were better able to convince themselves that climate change was a problem, while more "analytical" Republicans were better able to convince themselves that climate change was not a problem. . . .

The implications here are profound: Reasoning can exacerbate the problem, not provide the solution, when it comes to partisan disputes over facts. . . .

But this "rationalization" account, though compelling in some contexts, does not strike us as the most natural or most common explanation of the human weakness for misinformation. We believe that people often just don't think critically enough about the information they encounter.

A great deal of research in cognitive psychology has shown that a little bit of reasoning goes a long way towards forming accurate beliefs. For example, people who think more analytically (those who are more likely to exercise their analytic skills and not just trust their "gut" response) are less superstitious, less likely to believe in conspiracy theories and less receptive to seemingly profound but actually empty assertions (like "Wholeness quiets infinite phenomena"). This body of evidence suggests that the main factor explaining the acceptance of fake news could be cognitive laziness, especially in the context of social media, where news items are often skimmed or merely glanced at.

To test this possibility, we recently ran a set of studies in which participants of various political persuasions indicated whether they believed a series of news stories. We showed them real headlines taken from social media, some of which were true and some of which were false. We gauged whether our participants would engage in reasoning or "go with their gut" by having them complete something called the cognitive reflection test, a test widely used in psychology and behavioral economics. It consists of questions with intuitively compelling but incorrect answers, which can be easily shown to be wrong with a modicum of reasoning. (For example: "If you're running a race and you pass the person in second place, what place are you in?" If you're not thinking you might say "first place," when of course the answer is second place.)

We found that people who engaged in more reflective reasoning were better at telling true from false, regardless of whether the headlines aligned with their political views. (We controlled for demographic facts such as level of education as well as political leaning.) . . .

Our results strongly suggest that somehow cultivating or promoting our reasoning abilities should be part of the solution to the kinds of partisan misinformation that circulate on social media. . . .

This is not just an academic debate; it has real implications for public policy. Our research suggests that the solution to politically charged misinformation should involve devoting resources to the spread of accurate information and to training or encouraging people to think more critically. You aren't doomed to be unreasonable, even in highly politicized times. Just remember that this is also true of people you disagree with.

To put in action Pennycook and Rand's advice in your own life, keep in mind the distinction between truth and validity, and the lessons you've learned about why people are prone to belief biases and the illusions of truth.

during the 2016 presidential election because planted fake stories appeared frequently on social media sites such as Facebook and attracted at least as much attention as did real news stories (Silverman et al., 2016). Researchers Pennycook, Cannon, and Rand (2018) asked participants to judge the accuracy of fake news stories that had actually been posted on Facebook. They found that just a single prior exposure to one of these stories increased participants' estimates of the stories' accuracy, even when the stories were implausible and flagged as contested by fact checkers. The only stories that were not influenced by this illusory truth effect were completely implausible ones that could be easily judged as false (e.g., "The Earth is a perfect square"). Here, we can see the danger of assessing truth without relying on a valid argument: Simply repeating a statement does not make it true.

Build to the Outcomes

1. What is reasoning?
2. Summarize the distinction between truth and validity in reasoning.
3. What is the role of belief bias in syllogistic reasoning?
4. What is the basis of the illusory truth effect?
5. How does the distinction between truth and validity apply to everyday life?

Chapter Review

Language and Communication: From Rules to Meaning

- Human language is characterized by a complex organization—from phonemes to morphemes to phrases and finally to sentences.

- Children can distinguish between all contrasting sounds of human language, but they lose that ability within the first year. Vocal babbling occurs at about 4 to 6 months, and first words are uttered or signed by 10 to 12 months. Sentences emerge around 24 months.

- Children acquire grammatical rules in development, even without being taught explicitly.

- The behaviourist explanation for language learning is based on operant conditioning, whereas nativists hold that humans are biologically predisposed to process language. Interactionists explain it as both a biological and a social process.

Language Development and the Brain

- Our abilities to produce and comprehend language depend on distinct but interacting regions of the brain, with Broca's area critical for language production and Wernicke's area critical for comprehension.

- Bilingual and monolingual children show similar rates of language development. Some bilingual children show greater executive control capacities, such as the ability to prioritize information and flexibly focus attention, but this finding has proven difficult to replicate in recent research. Bilinguals do tend to have a later onset of Alzheimer's disease.

- Nonhuman primates can learn new vocabulary and construct simple sentences, but there are significant limitations on the size of their vocabularies and the grammatical complexity they can handle.

Language and Thought: How Are They Related?

- The linguistic relativity hypothesis maintains that language shapes the nature of thought.

- Recent studies on colour processing point to an influence of language on thought.

- However, either language or thought may be impaired while the other is not, suggesting that language and thought are to some extent separate.

Concepts and Categories: How We Think

- We organize knowledge about objects, events, or other stimuli by creating concepts, prototypes, and exemplars.

- We acquire concepts using processes suggested by two theories: Prototype theory uses the most typical member of a category to assess new items; exemplar theory states that we compare new items with stored memories of other members of the category.

- Neuroimaging studies have shown that prototypes and exemplars are processed in different parts of the brain.

- Studies of people with cognitive and visual deficits have shown that the brain organizes concepts into distinct categories, such as living things and human-made things; the studies also suggest that visual experience is not necessary for the development of such categories.

Decision Making: Rational and Otherwise

- Human decision making often departs from a completely rational process. The mistakes that accompany this departure tell us a lot about how the human mind works.

- The values we place on outcomes weigh so heavily in our judgements that they sometimes overshadow objective evidence. When people are asked to make probability judgements, they will turn the problem into something they know how to solve, such as judging memory strength, judging similarity to prototypes, or estimating frequencies. This can lead to errors of judgement.

- When a problem fits our mental algorithms, we show considerable skill at making appropriate judgements. In making a judgement about the probability of an event, performance can vary dramatically.

- Because we feel that avoiding losses is more important than achieving gains, framing effects can affect our choices. Emotional information also strongly influences our decision making, even when we are not aware of it. Although this influence can lead us astray, it often is crucial for making decisions in everyday life.

- The prefrontal cortex plays an important role in decision making, and patients with prefrontal damage make more risky decisions than do non-brain-damaged individuals.

Problem Solving: Working It Out

- Like concept formation and decision making, problem solving is a process in which new inputs (in this case, problems) are interpreted in terms of old knowledge. Problems may be ill defined or well defined, leading to less obvious or more obvious solutions.

- The solutions we generate depend as much on the organization of our knowledge as on the objective characteristics of the problems we face. Means–ends analysis and analogical problem solving offer pathways to effective solutions, although we often frame things in terms of what we already know and already understand.

- Sometimes, as in the case of functional fixedness, that knowledge can restrict our problem-solving processes, making it difficult to reach solutions that should be easy to find.

Reasoning: Truth and Validity

- A fundamental distinction in human reasoning concerns the *truth* of statements and the *validity* of an argument. The success of human reasoning requires both true statements and valid arguments about them in order to reach sound conclusions.

- Belief bias describes a distortion of judgements about conclusions of arguments, causing people to focus on the believability of the conclusions rather than on the logical connections between the premises. This bias is exaggerated when people fail to inhibit pre-existing knowledge and beliefs.

- The illusory truth effect occurs when repeated exposure to a statement increases the likelihood that people will judge the statement to be true, even when it is false.

- Belief bias and the illusory truth effect both have potentially important real-world implications, as illustrated by how beliefs impact assessments of climate change and how exposure to fake news stories impacts assessment of their accuracy.

Key Concept Quiz

1. The combining of words to form phrases and sentences is governed by
   a. phonological rules.
   b. morphological rules.
   c. structural rules.
   d. syntactic rules.

2. Language development as an innate, biological capacity is explained by
   a. fast mapping.
   b. behaviourism.
   c. nativist theory.
   d. interactionist explanations.

3. Damage to the brain region called Broca's area results in
   a. failure to comprehend language.
   b. difficulty in producing grammatical speech.
   c. the reintroduction of infant babbling.
   d. difficulties in writing.

4. The linguistic relativity hypothesis maintains that
   a. language and thought are separate cognitive phenomena.
   b. words have different meanings to different cultures.

   c. human language is too complex for nonhuman animals to acquire.
   d. language shapes the nature of thought.

5. The "most typical" member of a category is a(n)
   a. prototype.
   b. exemplar.
   c. concept.
   d. definition.

6. Which theory of how we form concepts is based on our judgement of features that appear to be characteristic of category members but may not be possessed by every member?
   a. prototype theory
   b. family resemblance theory
   c. exemplar theory
   d. heuristic theory

7. The inability to recognize objects that belong to a particular category, even when the ability to recognize objects outside the category is undisturbed, is called
   a. category-preferential organization.
   b. cognitive-visual deficit.
   c. category-specific deficit.
   d. aphasia.

8. People give different answers to the same problem, depending on how the problem is phrased, because of
   a. the availability bias.
   b. the conjunction fallacy.
   c. the representativeness heuristic.
   d. framing effects.

9. Miranda decides on a goal, analyzes her current situation, lists the differences between her current situation and her goal, then settles on strategies to reduce those differences. Miranda is engaging in

   a. means–ends analysis.
   b. analogical problem solving.
   c. capitalizing on insight.
   d. functional fixedness.

10. What kind of reasoning is aimed at deciding on a course of action?
    a. theoretical
    b. belief
    c. syllogistic
    d. practical

 Don't stop now! Quizzing yourself is a powerful study tool. Go to LaunchPad to access the LearningCurve adaptive quizzing system and your own personalized learning plan. Visit launchpadworks.com.

Key Terms

language (p. 352)
grammar (p. 352)
phoneme (p. 353)
phonological rules (p. 353)
morphemes (p. 353)
morphological rules (p. 354)
syntactic rules (p. 354)
fast mapping (p. 356)
telegraphic speech (p. 356)
nativist theory (p. 359)

universal grammar (p. 359)
genetic dysphasia (p. 360)
aphasia (p. 362)
linguistic relativity hypothesis (p. 365)
concept (p. 368)
prototype theory (p. 369)
exemplar theory (p. 370)
category-specific deficit (p. 371)

rational choice theory (p. 372)
availability bias (p. 373)
heuristic (p. 374)
algorithm (p. 374)
conjunction fallacy (p. 374)
representativeness heuristic (p. 375)
framing effects (p. 375)
sunk-cost fallacy (p. 376)

optimism bias (p. 376)
prospect theory (p. 378)
means–ends analysis (p. 381)
analogical problem solving (p. 381)
functional fixedness (p. 384)
reasoning (p. 385)
belief bias (p. 386)
syllogistic reasoning (p. 386)
illusory truth effect (p. 387)

Changing Minds

1. You mention to a friend that you've just learned that the primary language we learn can shape the way that we think. Your friend says that people are people everywhere and that this can't be true. What evidence could you describe to support your point?

2. In September 2011, *Wired* magazine ran an article discussing the fourth-down decisions of National Football League coaches. On fourth down, a coach can choose to play aggressively and go for a first down (or even a touchdown), or the coach can settle for a punt or a field goal, which are safer options but result in fewer points than a touchdown. Statistically, the riskier play results in greater point gain, on average, than playing it safe. But in reality, coaches choose the safer plays over 90% of the time. Reading this article, one of your friends is incredulous. "Coaches aren't stupid, and they want to win," he says. "Why would they always make the wrong decision?" Your friend is assuming that humans are rational decision makers. In what ways is your friend wrong? What might be causing the football coaches to make irrational decisions?

Answers to Key Concept Quiz

1. d; 2. c; 3. b; 4. d; 5. a; 6. b; 7. c; 8. d; 9. a; 10. d.

 LaunchPad features the full e-Book of Psychology, the LearningCurve adaptive quizzing system, videos, and a variety of activities to boost your learning. Visit LaunchPad at launchpadworks.com.

Intelligence

WHEN ANNE MCGARRAH DIED at the age of 57, she had lived more years than she could count. That's because Anne couldn't count at all. Like most people with Williams syndrome, she couldn't add 3 and 7, couldn't make change for a dollar, and couldn't distinguish right from left. Her cognitive ability was so impaired that she was unable to care for herself or hold a full-time job. So what did she do with her time?

> I love to read. Biographies, fiction, novels, different articles in newspapers, articles in magazines, just about anything. I just read a book about a young girl—she was born in Scotland—and her family who lived on a farm. . . . I love listening to music. I like a little bit of Beethoven, but I specifically like Mozart and Chopin and Bach. I like the way they develop their music—it's very light, it's very airy, and it's very cheerful music. I find Beethoven depressing. (Finn, 1991, p. 54)

People with Williams syndrome are often unable to tie their own shoes or make their own beds, but, as Anne's words suggest, they often have an unusual flair for language and music. Williams syndrome is caused by the absence of just a few genes on a single chromosome, and no one knows how this tiny genetic glitch can so profoundly impair people's general cognitive abilities and yet leave them with a few extraordinary talents. So here's the question: Was Anne McGarrah intelligent?

THAT'S A TOUGH ONE. IT SEEMS ODD TO SAY that someone is intelligent when they can't do simple addition, but it seems equally odd to say that someone is not intelligent when they know the difference between baroque counterpoint and 19th-century romanticism. In a world of Albert Einsteins and Homer Simpsons, we'd have no trouble distinguishing the geniuses from the dullards. But ours is a world of people like Anne McGarrah and people like us: people who are

People with Williams syndrome have diminished cognitive abilities, but often have unusual gifts for music and language. Gabrielle Marion-Rivard is a singer and actress who has Williams syndrome. She won the Canadian Screen Award for Best Actress in 2014.

sometimes brilliant, often bright, usually competent, and occasionally dimmer than broccoli. So what is this thing called intelligence?

More than 20 years ago, a large group of scientific experts came together to answer this question. They concluded that intelligence involves . . .

> the ability to reason, plan, solve problems, think abstractly, comprehend complex ideas, learn quickly, and learn from experience. It is not merely book learning, a narrow academic skill, or test-taking smarts. Rather it reflects a broader and deeper capability for comprehending our surroundings—"catching on," "making sense" of things, or "figuring out" what to do. (Gottfredson, 1997, p. 13)

In short, **intelligence** is *the ability to use one's mind to solve novel problems and learn from experience,* and for more than a century, psychologists have been asking four questions about this remarkable ability: *How* can intelligence be measured? *What* exactly is intelligence? *Where* does intelligence come from? *Why* are some people more intelligent than others? As you will see, we now have good answers to all of these questions, but they did not come without controversy.

intelligence The ability to use one's mind to solve novel problems and learn from experience.

How Can Intelligence Be Measured?

Learning Outcomes

- Define intelligence.
- Explain how and why intelligence tests were developed.
- Explain why intelligence matters.

Few things are more dangerous than a man with a mission. In the 1920s, the psychologist Henry Goddard administered intelligence tests to arriving Europeans at Ellis Island, the main immigration gateway to the United States, and concluded that the overwhelming majority of Jews, Hungarians, Italians, and Russians were "feebleminded." Goddard also used his tests to identify feebleminded American families (whom, he claimed, were largely responsible for the nation's social problems) and suggested that the government should segregate them in isolated colonies and "take away from these people the power of procreation" (Goddard, 1913, p. 107). The United States subsequently passed laws restricting the immigration of people from southern and eastern Europe, and the majority of U.S. states passed laws requiring the sterilization of "mental defectives." Although Canada did not exclude immigrants to the same degree as the United States did, sterilization laws were also passed in British Columbia and Alberta in the 1920s. In Alberta, an amendment in 1937 allowed for the sterilization of "mental defectives" without their consent, and this law stayed on the books until 1972. Over 2800 procedures were performed in total, including 50 the last year the law remained in effect.

From Goddard's day to our own, intelligence tests have been used to rationalize prejudice and discrimination on the basis of race, religion, and nationality. Although intelligence testing has achieved many notable successes, its history is marred by more than its share of fraud and disgrace (Chorover, 1980; Lewontin, Rose, & Kamin, 1984). The fact that intelligence tests have sometimes been used for detestable purposes is especially ironic because, as you are about to see, those tests were originally developed for the noblest of purposes: to help underprivileged children succeed in school.

The Intelligence Quotient

Towards the end of the 19th century, France instituted a sweeping set of social reforms that for the first time required all boys and girls between the ages of 6 and 13 to attend school. This was nice in theory but difficult in practice because, as it turned out, not all children of the same age were equally prepared to learn. So the government appointed a small group of experts to figure out how mandatory public education might actually work. Some of the experts argued that psychiatrists should examine every French child and that the government should build special schools for the "slow-witted" ones—or better yet, send them to asylums. But one of the experts, a psychologist named Alfred Binet, disagreed. He believed that the government

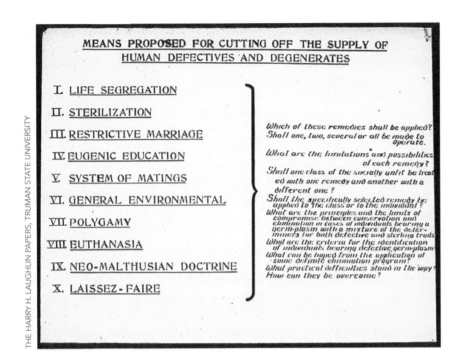

THE HARRY H. LAUGHLIN PAPERS, TRUMAN STATE UNIVERSITY

During the early 20th century, so-called eugenics laws were passed in several countries, including Canada, the United States, and, notoriously, Germany. These laws took many forms but generally required the involuntary sterilization of people with perceived low intelligence. Nazi Germany took this much further, and the policies of the Nazis to kill all "undesirable" people, including the mentally ill, homosexuals, and, especially Jews, culminated in the Holocaust. After World War II, eugenics was less popular and eventually was discredited entirely.

should rely not on the subjective evaluations of parents, teachers, or psychiatrists, but rather, it should use an objective method to determine the learning capabilities of each child. Those who needed extra help, he argued, should not be put in asylums, but placed in special classrooms alongside their peers (Nicolas et al., 2013).

To make proper placement possible, Binet and Simon created a series of tasks that "bright" children could perform well and that "slow" children could not. These tasks included solving logic problems, remembering words, copying pictures, distinguishing edible and inedible foods, making rhymes, and answering questions such as "Before deciding something important, what should you do?" Binet and Simon assembled 30 of these tasks into a test that they suggested could measure a child's "natural intelligence." What did they mean by that phrase?

> We here separate natural intelligence and instruction . . . by disregarding, insofar as possible, the degree of instruction which the subject possesses. . . . We give him nothing to read, nothing to write, and submit him to no test in which he might succeed by means of rote learning. In fact, we do not even notice his inability to read if a case occurs. It is simply the level of his natural intelligence that is taken into account. (Binet, 1905).

In other words, Binet and Simon designed their test to measure a child's *aptitude* for learning, independent of the child's prior educational *achievement*. Moreover, they designed it to allow psychologists to estimate a student's "mental level" simply by computing the average test score of many students in different age groups, and then finding the age group whose average test score best matched the test score of the particular student. For example, a 10-year-old child whose test score was about the same as the average test score of all 8-year-olds was said to have the mental level of an 8-year-old and thus to need remedial education.

About a decade later, the German psychologist William Stern (1914) suggested that this *mental level* could actually be thought of as the child's *mental age* and that the best way to determine whether a child was developing normally was simply to compute the ratio of the child's mental age to the child's physical age. Thus was born the *intelligence quotient,* or what most of us just call IQ. Initially, psychologists computed **ratio IQ**, which is *a statistic obtained by dividing a person's mental age by the person's physical age and then multiplying the quotient by 100.* According to this formula, a 10-year-old child whose test score is about the same as the average 10-year-old child's test score has a ratio IQ of 100

ratio IQ A statistic obtained by dividing a person's mental age by the person's physical age and then multiplying the quotient by 100.

SOLENT NEWS/SHUTTERSTOCK

At 4 years old, Heidi Hankins became one of the youngest people ever admitted to Mensa, an organization for people with unusually high IQs. Heidi's IQ is 159—about the same as Albert Einstein's.

because $(10/10) \times 100 = 100$. But a 10-year-old child whose test score is about the same as the average 8-year-old child's test score has a ratio IQ of 80 because $(8/10) \times 100 = 80$.

This computation sounds simple, and it is. But there's a problem with it. Intelligence increases dramatically in the first decade or so of life and then levels off. As you probably know from your own experience, the intellectual difference between a 10-year-old and a 5-year-old is quite dramatic, but the intellectual difference between a 40-year-old and a 35-year-old is not. This makes ratio IQ scores problematic. For example, a 7-year-old who performs on an intelligence test like a 14-year-old does will have a whopping ratio IQ score of 200—and that's okay, because any 7-year-old who can do algebra is probably pretty smart. But a 20-year-old who performs like a 40-year-old isn't necessarily super smart, yet he will also have a ratio IQ of 200, which doesn't make sense at all.

Psychologists quickly realized that comparing mental age to chronological age works fairly well for kids but not for adults, because adults of different ages simply don't have remarkably different intellectual capacities (Ackerman, 2017). To solve this problem, psychologists began to measure intelligence by computing **deviation IQ**, which is *a statistic obtained by dividing a person's test score by the average test score for people of that age and then multiplying the quotient by 100.* So, instead of comparing a person's mental age to her physical age, the deviation IQ score compares her performance to the performance of others of the same age. A 20-year-old who scores the same as the average 20-year-old has a deviation IQ of 100. The nice thing about the deviation IQ is that a 20-year-old whose test performance is similar to that of the average 40-year-old is no longer mistakenly labelled a genius. When you hear people talk about IQ scores today, they are almost always talking about deviation IQ.

The Intelligence Test

Most modern intelligence tests have their roots in the test that Binet and Simon developed more than a century ago. For instance, the *Stanford–Binet Intelligence Scale* is based on Binet and Simon's original test and was initially updated by Stanford University professor Lewis Terman (whom you will encounter again later in this chapter). The most widely used modern intelligence tests are the *Wechsler Adult Intelligence Scale* (WAIS) and the *Wechsler Intelligence Scale for Children* (WISC). The psychologist David Wechsler worked with the U.S. army during World War I to develop tests to screen new recruits. Like Binet and Simon's original test, the WAIS and the WISC measure intelligence by asking people to answer questions and solve problems. Test takers are required to see similarities and differences between ideas and objects, to draw inferences from evidence, to work out and apply rules, to remember and manipulate material, to construct shapes, to articulate the meaning of words, to recall general knowledge, to explain practical actions in everyday life, to use numbers, to attend to details, and so forth. In the spirit of Binet and Simon's early test, none of the tests requires writing words. Some sample problems from the WAIS are shown in **TABLE 10.1**.

These sample problems may look to you like fun and games (perhaps without the fun part), but decades of research show that a person's performance on tests like the WAIS predict an astonishing number of important life outcomes (Borghans et al., 2016; Deary, Batty, & Gale, 2008; Deary et al., 2008; Der, Batty, & Deary, 2009; Leon et al., 2009; Richards et al., 2009; Rushton & Templer, 2009).

For example, intelligence test scores are excellent predictors of income. One study compared siblings who had significantly different IQs and found that the less intelligent sibling earned roughly half of what the more intelligent sibling earned over the course of their lifetimes (Murray, 2002) (see **FIGURE 10.1**). One reason for this is that intelligent people have a variety of traits that promote economic success. For

deviation IQ A statistic obtained by dividing a person's test score by the average test score for people of that age and then multiplying the quotient by 100.

TABLE 10.1

THE TESTS AND CORE SUBTESTS OF THE WECHSLER ADULT INTELLIGENCE SCALE IV

WAIS-IV Test	Core Subtest	Questions and Tasks
Verbal comprehension test	Vocabulary	The test taker is asked to tell the examiner what certain words mean. For example: *chair* (easy), *hesitant* (medium), and *presumptuous* (hard).
	Similarities	The test taker is asked what 19 pairs of words have in common. For example: In what way are an apple and a pear alike? In what way are a painting and a symphony alike?
	Information	The test taker is asked several general knowledge questions. These cover people, places, and events. For example: How many days are in a week? What is the capital of France? Name three oceans. Who wrote *The Inferno*?
Perceptual reasoning test	Block design	The test taker is shown 2-D patterns made up of red and white squares and triangles and is asked to reproduce these patterns using cubes with red and white faces.
	Matrix reasoning	The test taker is asked to add a missing element to a pattern so that it progresses logically. For example: Which of the four symbols at the bottom goes in the empty cell of the table? 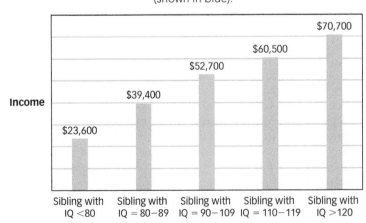
	Visual puzzles	The test taker is asked to complete visual puzzles like this one: "Which three of these pictures go together to make this puzzle?"
Working memory test	Digit span	The test taker is asked to repeat a sequence of numbers. Sequences run from two to nine numbers in length. In the second part of this test, the sequences must be repeated in reversed order. An easy example is to repeat 3-7-4. A harder one is 3-9-1-7-4-5-3-9.
	Arithmetic	The test taker is asked to solve arithmetic problems, progressing from easy to difficult ones.
Processing speed test	Symbol search	The test taker is asked to indicate whether one of a pair of abstract symbols is contained in a list of abstract symbols. There are many of these lists, and the test taker does as many as he or she can in 2 minutes.
	Coding	The test taker is asked to write down the number that corresponds to a code for a given symbol (e.g., a cross, a circle, and an upside-down T) and does as many as he or she can in 90 seconds.

instance, they are more patient, they are better at calculating risk, and they are better at predicting how other people will act and how they should respond (Burks et al., 2009). But the main reason that intelligent people earn much more money than their less intelligent counterparts (or siblings!) is that they get more education (Deary et al., 2005; Nyborg & Jensen, 2001).

In fact, a person's IQ is a better predictor of the amount of education he or she will receive than is that person's social class (Deary, 2012; Deary et al., 2005). Intelligent people not only spend more time in school but also perform better when they're there (Roth et al., 2015). The correlation between IQ and academic performance is roughly $r = .50$ across a wide range of people and situations. The relationship between IQ and performance continues after school ends. Intelligent people perform so much better at their jobs that one pair of researchers concluded that "for hiring employees without previous experience in the job, the most valid measure of future performance and learning is general mental ability" (Schmidt & Hunter, 1998, p. 262).

Figure 10.1

Income and Intelligence Among Siblings
This graph shows the average annual salary of a person who has an IQ of 90–109 (shown in pink) and of his or her siblings who have higher or lower IQs (shown in blue).

Income

Sibling with IQ <80	Sibling with IQ = 80–89	Sibling with IQ = 90–109	Sibling with IQ = 110–119	Sibling with IQ >120
$23,600	$39,400	$52,700	$60,500	$70,700

Intelligent people aren't just wealthier, they are healthier as well. Researchers who have followed millions of people over decades have found a strong correlation between intelligence and both health and longevity (Calvin et al., 2011; Wraw et al., 2015). Intelligent people are less likely to smoke and drink alcohol and are more likely to exercise and eat well (Batty et al., 2007; Ciarrochi, Heaven, & Skinner, 2012; Weiser et al., 2010). Not surprisingly, they also live longer. In fact, every 15-point increase in a young person's IQ is associated with a 24% decrease in his or her risk of death from a wide variety of causes, including cardiovascular disease, suicide, homicide, and accidents (Calvin et al., 2011).

Health and wealth are related, of course, and some data suggest that intelligence promotes longevity by allowing people to succeed in school, which allows them to get better jobs, which allows them to earn more money, which allows them to avoid illnesses such as cardiovascular disease (Deary, Weiss, & Batty, 2011; Jokela et al., 2009). However it happens, the bottom line is clear: Intelligence matters for almost everything people value (see A World of Difference: Equality in Smartland).

A World of Difference • Equality in Smartland

Being smart and being happy are pretty nice things, so it doesn't seem fair that the people who have a whole lot of one should also have more than their fair share of the other. But (sigh) they do. Smart people have better health, better jobs, and better relationships; so, predictably, they tend to be happier as well. What's true at the individual level is also true at the national level. Scientists have long known that a nation's average IQ scores and average happiness scores are positively correlated: Happy nations have smart citizens and smart nations have happy citizens. Go, Denmark!

But recently, scientists have discovered that the relationship between national happiness and national intelligence is more interesting than anyone had realized. Nikolaev and Salahodjaev (2016) gathered data on the intelligence and happiness of the citizens of 81 countries. As expected, they found a positive correlation between a nation's average IQ and its average happiness. But in addition to calculating the mean of each nation's happiness scores, they also calculated the standard deviation, which (as you know from the Methods in Psychology chapter) measures the dispersion of scores around a mean. Just as the mean of a set of happiness scores provides a rough index of a

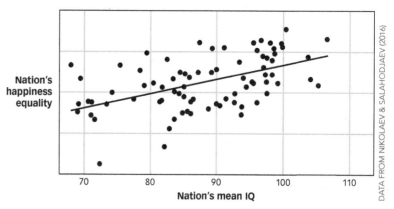

Each dot represents a nation. The positive correlation indicates that the smarter a nation is, the more "happiness equality" it has.

nation's happiness, the standard deviation provides a rough index of a nation's "happiness equality." If most citizens are about equally happy, then the standard deviation is low and happiness equality is high. But if many citizens are ecstatic and many are despondent, then the standard deviation is high and happiness equality is low.

When the researchers computed the correlation between IQ and happiness equality, they discovered something that no one had noticed before: Nations with smart citizens do not just have more happiness, they also have more happiness equality (see the

accompanying graph). In other words, if two nations have the same average happiness, the smarter one tends to distribute that happiness more equally among its citizens. Correlations must always be interpreted with caution, of course, but this one is intriguing and begs for explanation. One explanation is that intelligent people spread happiness to others. Another explanation is that the social policies that give rise to happiness equality also foster intelligence. Whether either, both, or neither of these explanations turns out to be right, it seems clear that smart people are about as happy as their neighbours.

1. Why were intelligence tests originally developed?
2. What is an intelligence quotient (IQ)?
3. How do ratio IQ and deviation IQ differ?
4. What important life outcomes do intelligence test scores predict?

What Is Intelligence?

James Franco is a remarkably talented actor, which is why he won Golden Globe Awards for his performances in the 2017 film *The Disaster Artist* and the 2001 film *James Dean* and was nominated for an Academy Award for Best Actor for his performance in the riveting 2010 film *127 Hours* (in which he played a trapped hiker who cuts off his own arm with a pocket knife. Really. You have to see it.) So when Franco released his first book of poetry in 2014, he was probably surprised to learn from critics that his writing—well, there's really no way to say this nicely—sucks. The *New York Times* said his work was "aggressively lazy" and the *Telegraph* said it was "hard to forgive." The *Boston Globe* said that reading his book was "like being trapped on a date with a chronic mansplainer whose deepest fear is silence." Other critics were less kind.

Franco's excellence on the screen and his mediocrity on the page are equally difficult to deny—and clearly show that these two artistic endeavours require different abilities that are not necessarily possessed by the same individual. But if acting and writing require different abilities, then what does it mean to say that someone has artistic talent? Is "artistic talent" just an aggressively lazy phrase that actually means nothing or does it refer to something measurable and real? The science of intelligence has grappled with a similar question for more than a century. Intelligence test scores predict important outcomes, from academic success to longevity, but is that because they measure a real ability called intelligence?

A Hierarchy of Abilities

If there really is an ability called intelligence that enables people to perform a variety of intelligent behaviours, then those who have this ability should do well at just about everything, and those who lack it should do well at just about nothing. In other words, if intelligence is a single, general ability, then there should be a very strong positive correlation between people's performances on many different kinds of tests. This is precisely the hypothesis that the psychologist Charles Spearman (1904) set out to examine at the start of the 20th century. He began by measuring how well school-age children could discriminate small differences in colour, auditory pitch, and weight, and he then computed the correlation between these scores and the children's grades in different academic subjects. He immediately noticed two things.

First, Spearman noticed that performances on these different tests were positively correlated, which is to say that children who performed well on one test (e.g., distinguishing the musical notes C# and D) tended to perform well on other tests (e.g., solving algebraic equations). Some psychologists have called this finding "the most replicated result in all of psychology" (Deary, 2000, p. 6), and it may well be. Indeed, there is even a strong positive correlation between

Learning Outcomes

- Explain how the three-level hierarchy of intelligence confirms both Spearman and Thurstone's conclusions.

- Identify the strengths and weaknesses of the data-based and theory-based approaches to measuring abilities.

- Describe how the concept of intelligence differs across cultures.

Social psychologist Jennifer Richeson received a so-called "genius award" from the MacArthur Foundation for her research on the dynamics of interracial interaction. Spearman's notion of *g* suggests that because she's really good at psychology, she's probably pretty good at most other things too.

two-factor theory of intelligence Spearman's theory suggesting that a person's performance on a test is due to a combination of general ability and skills that are specific to the test.

performances on different kinds of cognitive tests in mice (Matzel et al., 2003) and in dogs (Arden & Adams, 2016)! Second, Spearman noticed that although performances on different tests were positively correlated, they were not *perfectly* correlated. In other words, the child who had the very highest score on one test didn't necessarily have the very highest score on every test. Spearman combined these two facts into his **two-factor theory of intelligence**, which suggests that *a person's performance on a test is due to a combination of general ability and skills that are specific to the test.* Spearman referred to general ability as *g* and to specific ability as *s*.

As sensible as Spearman's theory was, not everyone agreed with it. Louis Thurstone (1938) noticed that although the correlations between performances on different tests were all *positive,* they were much *stronger* when the tests had something in common. For example, performances on a verbal test were more strongly correlated with scores on another verbal test than with scores on a perceptual test. Thurstone took this "clustering of correlations" to mean that there was actually no such thing as general ability; rather, there were a few stable and independent mental abilities—such as perceptual ability, verbal ability, and numerical ability. Thurstone called these the *primary mental abilities* and argued that they were neither general like *g* (e.g., a person might have strong verbal abilities and weak numerical abilities), nor specific like *s* (e.g., a person who had strong verbal abilities tended both to speak and read well). In essence, Thurstone argued that just as we have games called *hockey* and *basketball* but no game called *athletics,* so we have abilities such as verbal ability and perceptual ability but no general ability called intelligence. **TABLE 10.2** shows the primary mental abilities that Thurstone identified.

For more than half a century, psychologists debated the existence of *g*. Then, in the 1980s, a new mathematical technique called *confirmatory factor analysis* brought the debate to a quiet close by revealing that Spearman and Thurstone had both been right, but each in his own way. Specifically, this new technique showed that the correlations between scores on different tests are best described by a three-level hierarchy (see **FIGURE 10.2**) with a *general factor* (much like Spearman's *g*) at the top, *specific factors* (much like Spearman's *s*) at the bottom, and a set of factors called *group factors* (much like Thurstone's *primary mental abilities*) in the middle (Gustafsson, 1984). A reanalysis of massive amounts of data collected over 60 years from more than 130,000 people has shown that almost every study done since the early 1900s can be described by a three-level hierarchy of this kind (Carroll, 1993). This hierarchy suggests that people have a very general ability called intelligence, which is made up of a small set of middle-level abilities, which are made up of

TABLE 10.2	
THURSTONE'S PRIMARY MENTAL ABILITIES	
Primary Mental Ability	**Description**
Word fluency	Ability to solve anagrams and to find rhymes, etc.
Verbal comprehension	Ability to understand words and sentences
Numerical ability	Ability to make mental and other numerical computations
Spatial visualization	Ability to visualize a complex shape in various orientations
Associative memory	Ability to recall verbal material, learn pairs of unrelated words, etc.
Perceptual speed	Ability to detect visual details quickly
Reasoning	Ability to induce a general rule from a few instances

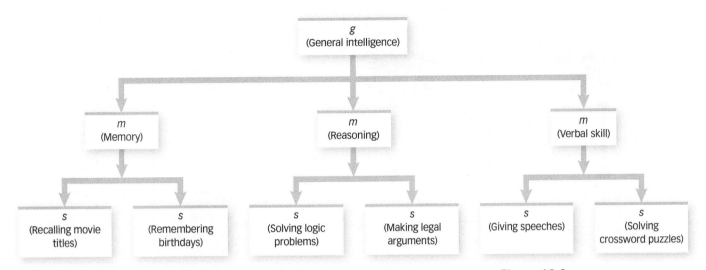

Figure 10.2

A Three-Level Hierarchy Most intelligence test data are best described by a three-level hierarchy with general intelligence (*g*) at the top, specific abilities (*s*) at the bottom, and a small number of middle-level abilities (*m*) (sometimes called group factors) in the middle.

a large set of specific abilities that are unique to particular tasks. Although this resolution to a half century of debate is not particularly exciting, it appears to have the compensatory benefit of being true.

The Middle-Level Abilities

James Franco's acting is better than his writing, but the fact is that he does both of these things much better than most people can do either one. His specific abilities have allowed him to be more successful at one of these artistic endeavours than the other, but his general ability has allowed him to outperform 99% of the world's population on both. Franco clearly has many specific abilities (memorizing lines) and a general ability (artistic talent), but it is not so easy to say precisely what his middle-level abilities were. Should we draw a distinction between screen presence and dramatic timing or between creative insight and physical expressiveness? Should we describe his talent as a function of three middle-level abilities, or 4 or 6 or 92.5?

Similar questions arise when we consider intelligence. Most psychologists agree that there are very specific mental abilities, as well as a very general mental ability and that the really hard problem is to characterize accurately the middle-level abilities that lie between them. Some psychologists have taken a *data-based approach* to the problem by starting with people's responses on intelligence tests and then looking to see what kinds of independent clusters these responses form. Other psychologists have taken a *theory-based approach* to this problem by starting with a broad survey of human abilities and then looking to see which of these abilities intelligence tests measure—or fail to measure. These approaches have led to rather different suggestions about the best way to characterize the middle-level abilities that constitute intelligence.

The Data-Based Approach

One way to determine the nature of the middle-level abilities is to start with the data and go where they lead us. Just as Spearman and Thurstone did, we could compute the correlations between people's performances on a large number of tests and then see how those correlations cluster. For example, imagine that we tested how well a large group of people could (1) balance teacups, (2) understand Shakespeare, (3) swat flies, and (4) sum the whole numbers between 1 and 1,000. Now imagine that we computed the correlations between scores on each of these tests and observed a pattern of correlations like the one shown in **FIGURE 10.3a**. What would this pattern tell us?

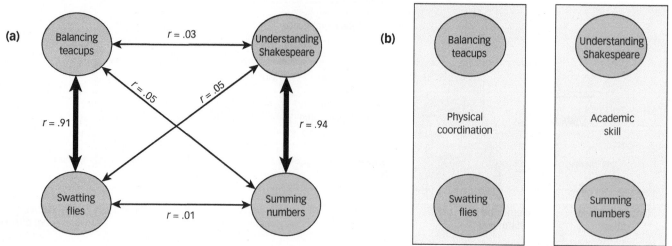

Figure 10.3

Patterns of Correlation Can Reveal Middle-Level Abilities The pattern of correlations shown in part (a) suggests that these four specific abilities can be thought of as instances of the two middle-level abilities, physical coordination and academic skill, as shown in part (b).

This pattern suggests that a person who can swat flies well can also balance teacups well and that a person who can understand Shakespeare well can also sum numbers well. But it also suggests that a person who can swat flies well and balance teacups well may or may not be able to sum numbers or understand Shakespeare well. From this pattern, we could conclude that there are two middle-level abilities (shown in Figure 10.3b), which we might call *physical coordination* (the ability that allows people to swat flies and balance teacups) and *academic skill* (the ability that allows people to understand Shakespeare and sum numbers). In other words, some people are really good at the specific tasks of fly swatting and teacup balancing because they have a middle-level ability called physical coordination, but this middle-level ability is unrelated to the other middle-level ability, academic skill, which is why these people are not necessarily good at summing numbers or understanding Shakespeare. As this example shows, simply by examining the pattern of correlations between different tests, we can discover the nature and number of the middle-level abilities.

Of course, in the real world, there are far more than four specific skills measured by four specific tests. So what kinds of patterns do we observe when we compute the correlations between *all* the many tests of mental ability that psychologists have actually used? This is precisely what the psychologist John Carroll (1993) set out to discover in his landmark analysis of intelligence test scores from nearly 500 studies conducted over a half century. And what Carroll discovered was that there are not three middle-level abilities—nor 4 nor 6 nor 92.5. Rather, there are eight, namely: *memory and learning, visual perception, auditory perception, retrieval ability, cognitive speediness, processing speed, crystallized intelligence,* and *fluid intelligence*.

Although most of the abilities on this list are self-explanatory, the last two are not (Horn & Cattell, 1966). **Crystallized intelligence** refers to the *ability to apply knowledge that was acquired through experience,* and it is generally measured with tests of vocabulary and factual information. **Fluid intelligence** refers to the *ability to solve and reason about novel problems,* and it is generally measured with tests that present people with abstract problems in new domains that must be solved under time pressure (see **FIGURE 10.4**). Problems that require crystallized or fluid intelligence appear to activate different networks in the brain (Barbey, 2018), which may explain why impairment of one kind of intelligence does not always lead to impairment of the other. For example, both autism and Alzheimer's disease impair crystallized intelligence more than fluid intelligence, whereas damage to the prefrontal cortex impairs fluid intelligence more than crystallized intelligence (Blair, 2006).

crystallized intelligence The ability to apply knowledge that was acquired through experience.

fluid intelligence The ability to solve and reason about novel problems.

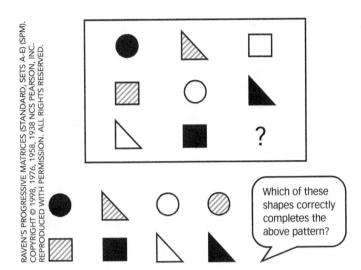

> Which of these shapes correctly completes the above pattern?

Figure 10.4

Measuring Fluid Intelligence Problems like this one from Raven's Progressive Matrices Test (Raven, Raven, & Court, 2004) measure fluid intelligence rather than crystallized intelligence.

The Theory-Based Approach

Not everyone agrees that there are precisely eight middle-level abilities, though you will be pleased to know that the reasons have nothing to do with math. The data-based approach discovers middle-level abilities by analyzing the correlations between performances on intelligence tests. The good thing about this approach is that its conclusions are based on hard evidence; the bad thing is that this approach is incapable of discovering any middle-level ability that the hard evidence doesn't happen to provide (Stanovich, 2009). For example, if an intelligence test does not ask people to find three new uses for an origami fish or to answer the question "What is the question you thought you'd be asked but weren't?" then no analysis of those tests' scores will ever reveal a middle-level ability called *imagination*. Are there any middle-level abilities to which the data-based approach has been blind?

The psychologist Robert Sternberg (1999, 2006) thinks so. He has argued that because standard intelligence tests present clearly defined problems that have one right answer, and then supply all the information needed to solve them, they can measure only *analytic intelligence,* which is the ability to identify and define problems and to find strategies for solving them. But in everyday life, people find themselves in situations in which they must *formulate* the problem, find the information needed to solve it, and then choose among multiple right answers. These situations require *creative intelligence,* which is the ability to generate solutions that other people do not, as well as *practical intelligence,* which is the ability to implement these solutions in everyday settings. In one study, workers at milk-processing plants developed complex strategies for efficiently combining partially filled cases of milk. Not only did they outperform highly educated white-collar workers, but their performance was unrelated to their scores on intelligence tests, suggesting that practical and analytic intelligence are not the same thing (Scribner, 1984). Sternberg has argued that tests of practical intelligence are actually better than tests of analytic intelligence at predicting a person's job performance (cf. Brody, 2003; Gottfredson, 2003).

Two items from a test of emotional intelligence (Mayer et al, 2008). Item 1 measures the accuracy with which a person can read emotional expressions (*left*). Item 2 measures the ability to predict emotional responses to events (*right*). The correct answer on both items is a.

1.

Emotion	Select one:
a. Happy	O
b. Angry	O
c. Fearful	O
d. Sad	O

2.

Tom felt worried when he thought about all the work he needed to do. He believed he could handle it—if only he had the time. When his supervisor brought him an additional project, he felt _____. (Select the best choice.)

Emotion	Select one:
a. Frustrated and anxious	O
b. Content and calm	O
c. Ashamed and accepting	O
d. Sad and guilty	O

Of course, not all of the problems that intelligence enables us to solve are analytical, practical, or creative. For instance, how do you tell a friend that she talks too much without hurting her feelings? How do you cheer yourself up after failing a test? How do you know whether you are feeling anxious or angry? The psychologists John Mayer and Peter Salovey define **emotional intelligence** as *the ability to reason about emotions and to use emotions to enhance reasoning* (Mayer, Roberts, & Barsade, 2008; Salovey & Grewal, 2005). Emotionally intelligent people know what kinds of emotions a particular event will trigger; they can identify, describe, and manage their emotions; they know how to use their emotions to improve their decisions; and they can identify other people's emotions from facial expressions and tones of voice. Furthermore, they do all this quite easily, which is why emotionally intelligent people show *less* neural activity when solving emotional problems than emotionally unintelligent people do (Jausovec & Jausovec, 2005; Jausovec, Jausovec, & Gerlic, 2001).

Emotional intelligence is also quite important for social relationships. Emotionally intelligent people have better social skills and more friends (Eisenberg et al., 2000; Mestre et al., 2006; Schultz, Izard, & Bear, 2004), they are judged to be more competent in their interactions (Brackett et al., 2006), and they have better romantic relationships (Brackett, Warner, & Bosco, 2005) and workplace relationships (Elfenbein et al., 2007; Lopes et al., 2006). Given all this, it isn't surprising that emotionally intelligent people tend to be happier (Brackett & Mayer, 2003; Brackett et al., 2006), healthier (Mikolajczak et al., 2015), and more satisfied with their lives (Ciarrochi, Chan, & Caputi, 2000; Mayer, Caruso, & Salovey, 1999). Accumulating evidence suggests that emotional intelligence is indeed one of the middle-level abilities that the data-based approach has missed (MacCann et al., 2014).

The data-based approach is also blind to middle-level abilities that are valued in cultures where intelligence tests are not common. For instance, Westerners regard people as intelligent when they speak quickly and often, but Africans regard people as intelligent when they are deliberate and quiet (Irvine, 1978).

emotional intelligence The ability to reason about emotions and to use emotions to enhance reasoning.

The Hungarian chess grandmaster Judit Polgar (*left*) and the Korean actress Ryu Si-Hyeon (*right*) both have genius-level IQs. But their cultures construe intelligence differently. Westerners tend to think of intelligence as an individual's ability to engage in rational thinking, but Easterners tend to think of it as the ability to recognize contradictions and complexities.

AP PHOTO/KEYSTONE/PETER SCHNEIDER

PARK SEA-YEON/EPA/ALAMY

The Confucian tradition's conception of intelligence emphasizes flexibility in thinking and the ability to identify wisdom in others (Pang, Esping, & Plucker, 2017), the Taoist tradition emphasizes humility and self-knowledge; and the Buddhist tradition emphasizes determination and mental effort (Yang & Sternberg, 1997). Unlike Western societies, many African and Asian societies conceive of intelligence as including social responsibility and cooperativeness (Azuma & Kashiwagi, 1987; Serpell, 1974; White & Kirkpatrick, 1985). In Zimbabwe, the word for "intelligence" is *ngware,* which means to be wise and cautious in social relationships (Sternberg & Grigorenko, 2004).

Some researchers take all this to mean that different cultures have radically different conceptualizations of intelligence, but others are convinced that what appear to be differences in the conceptualization of intelligence are really just differences in language. They argue that every culture values the ability to solve important problems and that what really distinguishes cultures is the *kinds* of problems that are considered important.

Build to the Outcomes

1. What was the debate between Spearman and Thurstone and how was it resolved?

2. What approaches have been used to assess middle-level abilities?

3. How does fluid intelligence differ from crystallized intelligence?

4. What are some of the skills of emotionally intelligent people?

5. What are the common threads between conceptualizations of intelligence across cultures?

Where Does Intelligence Come From?

No one is born knowing calculus, and no one has to be taught how to blink. Some things are learned, others are not. But almost all of the really *interesting* things about people are a joint product of the experiences they have had and the characteristics with which they were born. Intelligence is one of those really interesting things, and it is influenced both by nature and by nurture. Let's examine these in turn.

Learning Outcomes

- Describe the influence of genes on intelligence.
- Explain how environmental factors influence intelligence.

Genetic Influences on Intelligence

The notion that intelligence is somehow "in the blood" has been with us for a very long time. As early as 380 BCE, the philosopher Plato suggested that people are born with innate aptitudes that make them good rulers, good soldiers, or good tradesmen. But it wasn't until late in the 19th century that this idea became the subject of scientific inquiry. Sir Francis Galton was a half cousin of Charles Darwin, and his contributions to science ranged from meteorology to fingerprinting. He was also the father of eugenics—the idea that humankind should be improved by controlled breeding—which was seized upon by the Nazis as a rationale for exterminating millions of people during World War II. Despite the horrors that his work inspired, Galton did careful genealogical studies of eminent families, collected measurements from over 12,000 people, and concluded that intelligence was largely inherited. Was he right?

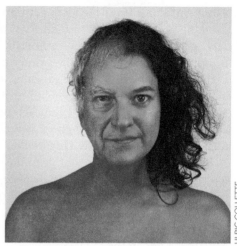

These photos, taken from the "Genetic Portraits" series by Quebec City artist Ulric Collette, were made by blending the face of a 32-year-old woman with the face of her mother (*left*) and the face of her father (*right*). Because physical appearance is highly heritable, the resemblance between family members can often be quite striking. If intelligence is highly heritable, then it too should be similar among family members. Is it?

Tamara Rabi and Adriana Scott were 20 years old when they met for the first time in a McDonald's parking lot in New York. "I'm just standing there looking at her," Adriana recalled. "It was a shock. I saw me" (Gootman, 2003). It turned out that the two women were identical twins who had been separated at birth and adopted by different families. By coincidence, both families lived in the New York area and sent their daughters to colleges just a few miles apart.

fraternal (dizygotic) twins Siblings who develop from two different eggs that were fertilized by two different sperm.

identical (monozygotic) twins Siblings who develop from the splitting of a single egg that was fertilized by a single sperm.

Genetic Relatedness

Although intelligence does appear to "run in families," that isn't very good evidence of genetic influence because family members share experiences as well as genes. Parents and children typically live in the same house and eat the same foods; siblings often go to the same schools, watch the same TV shows and movies; and so on. Family members may have similar levels of intelligence because they share genes, because they share environments, or both. If we want to know how much influence each of these factors has on intelligence, we need to measure and compare the intelligence scores of people who share one, both, or neither. For example, siblings who are raised together share both genes and environments; siblings who are separated at birth and raised by different families share genes but not environments; and adopted children who are raised together share environments but not genes.

Furthermore, different kinds of siblings share different amounts of their genes. Siblings who were born at different times share, on average, about 50% of their genes. And so do **fraternal** (or **dizygotic**) **twins**, who are *siblings who develop from two different eggs that were fertilized by two different sperm.* On the other hand, **identical** (or **monozygotic**) **twins** are *siblings who develop from the splitting of a single egg that was fertilized by a single sperm,* and they share 100% of their genes. By comparing people who have different combinations of shared genes and environments, and different degrees of genetic relatedness, psychologists have been able to assess the influence of genes on intelligence.

That influence is extremely powerful. For example, the IQs of biologically unrelated children raised in the same household are only modestly correlated ($r = .32$). In contrast, the IQs of identical twins are much more highly correlated—and that's true even when those twins were raised in different households (Bouchard & McGue, 2003). Indeed, if you look at **TABLE 10.3**, you'll see that identical twins who were raised apart have more similar IQs ($r = .78$) than do fraternal twins who were raised together ($r = .60$). These patterns of correlation suggest that genes play an important role in determining intelligence—and that shouldn't surprise you. After all, intelligence is influenced by the structure and function of the brain, and the structure and function of the brain are influenced by the genes that provide the blueprint for it. Indeed, given that genes influence just about every other human trait (Polderman et al., 2015), it would be rather remarkable if they *didn't* influence intelligence.

TABLE 10.3

INTELLIGENCE TEST CORRELATIONS BETWEEN PEOPLE WITH DIFFERENT RELATIONSHIPS

Relationship	Shared Environment	Shared Genes (%)	Correlation Between Intelligence Test Scores (r)
Twins			
Identical twins ($n = 4,672$)	yes	100	.86
Identical twins ($n = 93$)	no	100	.78
Fraternal twins ($n = 5,533$)	yes	50	.60
Parents and Children			
Parent–biological child ($n = 8,433$)	yes	50	.42
Parent–biological child ($n = 720$)	no	50	.24
Nonbiological parent–adopted child ($n = 1,491$)	yes	0	.19
Siblings			
Biological siblings (2 parents in common) ($n = 26,473$)	yes	50	.47
Nonbiological siblings (no parents in common) ($n = 714$)	yes	0	.32
Biological siblings (2 parents in common) ($n = 203$)	no	50	.24

Information from Plomin et al., 2001, p. 168.

The Heritability Coefficient: Measuring the Influence of Genes on IQ

Genes exert a powerful influence on intelligence—but exactly how powerful? The **heritability coefficient** (commonly denoted as h^2) is *a statistic that describes the proportion of the difference between people's IQ scores that can be explained by differences in their genes.* When the data from numerous studies of children and adults are analyzed together, the heritability of intelligence is somewhere between .5 and .7, which is to say that roughly 50% to 70% of the difference between people's intelligence test scores is due to genetic differences between those people (Plomin & Spinath, 2004; Plomin et al., 2013; cf. Chabris et al., 2012).

Most people misunderstand the heritability coefficient, so let's make sure you aren't one of them. First, the heritability coefficient h^2 is *not* the same as the correlation coefficient r. Yes, both are quite efficient, but that's where the similarity ends. Second, many people who hear that "the heritability of intelligence is roughly .5" think this means that roughly half of *their* intelligence is due to their genes and half is due to their experiences. That is completely wrong, and to understand why, consider the rectangles in **FIGURE 10.5**. These rectangles have the same heights but different widths, so they have different areas. (Remember high school geometry? $A = H \times W$.) So if you were asked how much of the difference in their areas was due to differences in their widths, you would say that all of it was—100%—and if you were asked to say how much of the difference in their areas was due to differences in their heights you would say that none of it was—0%.

DEANNE FITZMAURICE

Small genetic differences can make a big difference. A single gene on chromosome 15 determines whether a dog will be too small for your pocket or too large for your garage.

heritability coefficient A statistic (commonly denoted as h^2) that describes the proportion of the difference between people's IQ scores that can be explained by differences in their genes.

Figure 10.5

Questions With and Without Answers
These rectangles differ in area. The question "How much of the difference in their areas is due to differences in their widths, and how much is due to differences in their heights?" has an answer. But the question "How much of rectangle A's area is due to width and how much is due to height?" does not.

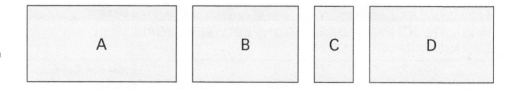

Well done. Your answers about the *differences between the rectangles* are correct. Now try to answer a different question: How much of rectangle A's area is due to its height, and how much is due to its width? This question is nonsense because an *individual* rectangle's area is a product of *both* its height and its width, so it can't be "due to" one of these more or less than it is "due to" the other.

Now let's apply this wisdom to the problem of intelligence. If you measured the intelligence of every person at a hockey game and were then asked to say how much of the *difference in their intelligence scores* was due to differences in their genes, the fact that h^2 is between .5 and .7 would allow you to guess that the answer is between 50% and 70%. But if someone pointed to the annoying guy in Row 17, Seat 4, and asked how much of *his* intelligence was due to his genes, the right answer would be, "You didn't read the textbook very carefully, did you?" This question is nonsense because the intelligence of a particular person is a joint product of both genes and experience—just as the area of a particular rectangle is a joint product of its height and width—thus, it cannot be "due to" one of these things or the other.

The heritability coefficient tells us how big a role genes play in *interpersonal differences* in intelligence, so its value changes depending on the particular persons we measure. For example, the heritability of intelligence among high-income children in the United States is about .72 and among low-income children about .10 (Turkheimer et al., 2003; cf. Figlio et al., 2017). Why should that be? High-income children in America have fairly similar environments—they all have pretty nice homes with lots of books, plenty of free time, ample nutrition—so differences in their intelligence must be due to the one and only factor that distinguishes them from each other: their genes.

Conversely, poor children in America have very different environments—some have books and free time and ample nutrition, but others have little or none of these—so differences in their intelligence may be due to either of the two factors that distinguish them from each other: their genes and their environments (Tucker-Drob et al., 2010). This may be why intelligence is not equally heritable among high- and low-income children in America but is equally heritable among high- and low-income children in more socioeconomically equitable places like Western Europe and Australia, where both high- and low-income citizens have more equal amounts of nutrition and leisure, more equal access to books, and so on (Bates et al., 2016; Tucker-Drob & Bates, 2016).

The value of the heritability coefficient also changes depending on the age of the people being measured. For example, the heritability of intelligence is higher among adults than among children (see **FIGURE 10.6**), and it is higher among older children than younger children. Indeed, in infancy, genes account for less than 25% of the interpersonal differences in intelligence, but by adolescence they account for about 70% (Haworth et al., 2010). Why? One possibility is that the environments of older people are more similar than the environments of younger people, and when environments don't differ much across people, then differences in their intelligence scores must be due to the one thing that does differ: their genes. It may seem paradoxical, but in a science-fictional world of clones, in which all humans were genetically identical, the heritability of intelligence would be zero because environments would be the only thing that distinguished one clone from another.

Some research suggests that IQ is more heritable among higher-income children, perhaps because their environments are so similar. If there are fewer differences in their environments, then differences in their IQs are more likely to be due to differences in their genes.

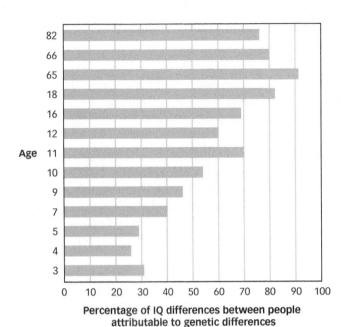

Figure 10.6
Age and Heritability of Intelligence The heritability of intelligence generally increases with the age of the sample measured.

Does that mean that in a science-fictional world in which humans were genetically different but lived in identical houses and received identical meals, educations, parental care, and so on, the heritability coefficient would be 1.00? Not likely, and that's because two people who live in the same household will share *some* of their experiences but not *all* of their experiences. The **shared environment** refers to *features of the environment that are experienced by all relevant members of a household.* For example, siblings raised in the same household usually get about the same nutrition, have about the same access to books, and so on. The **nonshared environment** refers to *features of the environment that are not experienced by all relevant members of a household.* Siblings raised in the same household usually have different friends and different teachers, contract different illnesses, and so on. This may explain why the correlation between the IQ scores of siblings is greater if they are close to each other in age: Similar-aged siblings are more likely to have the same teacher, contract the same illnesses at the same time, and so on (Sundet, Eriksen, & Tambs, 2008).

Environmental Influences on Intelligence

Every individual should have an equal chance to succeed in life, and one of the reasons that some people get nervous when they hear about genetic influences on intelligence is that they mistakenly believe that our genes are our destinies—that "genetic" is a synonym for "unchangeable" (Pinker, 2003). But that isn't true because traits that are strongly influenced by genes may also be strongly influenced by the environment. For example, height is a highly heritable trait, which is why tall parents tend to have tall children. But that doesn't mean that height is unchangeable. In 1848, 25% of all Dutch men were rejected by the military because they were less than 5' 2" tall, but because of changes in nutrition, the average Dutch man today is over 6' tall (Max, 2006). The average height of South Korean boys has increased by more than 16 cm in the last century (NCD Risk Factor Collaboration, 2016). Genes may explain why two people who have the same diet differ in height—that is, why Chang-sun is taller than Kwan-ho and why Thijs is taller than Daan—but they do not dictate how tall any of these boys

shared environment Features of the environment that are experienced by all relevant members of a household.

nonshared environment Features of the environment that are not experienced by all relevant members of a household.

First-born children tend to be more intelligent than their later-born siblings. But when a first-born child dies in infancy and the second-born child becomes the oldest child in the family, that second-born child ends up being just as intelligent as the average first-born child (Kristensen & Bjerkedal, 2007). This suggests that first-borns are smarter than their siblings not for biological reasons but because they experience a different family environment.

will actually grow up to be. Is intelligence like height in this regard? Alfred Binet (1909) thought so:

> A few modern philosophers . . . assert that an individual's intelligence is a fixed quantity that cannot be increased. We must protest and react against this brutal pessimism. . . . With practice, training, and above all method, we manage to increase our attention, our memory, our judgment, and literally to become more intelligent than we were before. (p. 141)

Binet was right. As **FIGURE 10.7** shows, intelligence clearly changes over time (Owens, 1966; Schaie, 1996, 2005; Schwartzman, Gold, & Andres, 1987). For most people, the direction of this change is upwards between adolescence and middle age and then downwards thereafter (cf. Ackerman, 2014). The sharpest decline occurs in old age (Kaufman, 2001; Salthouse, 1996a, 2000; Schaie, 2005) and may be due to a general decrease in the brain's processing speed (Salthouse, 1996b; Zimprich & Martin, 2002). These age-related declines are more evident in some domains than in others. For example, on tests that measure vocabulary, general information, and verbal reasoning, people show only small changes from age 18 to 70; but on tests that are timed, have abstract material, involve making new memories, or require reasoning about spatial relationships, most people show marked declines in performance after middle age (Avolio & Waldman, 1994; Lindenberger & Baltes, 1997; Rabbitt et al., 2004; Salthouse, 2001).

The brain is still growing and changing during adolescence, and intelligence can change quite dynamically as well in this time period. Figure 10.7 shows central tendency (see the Methods in Psychology chapter) across a large group. The apparent stability in average IQ from 16–19 years of age (see the two leftmost groups in Figure 10.7) masks the fact that IQ can change quite a lot in individuals over this approximate time period; changes in IQ within individuals over this time are also linked to structural changes in the brain (Ramsden et al., 2011; see The Real World: Is IQ Stable in Adolescence?).

DATA VISUALIZATION

How Do Nature and Nurture Influence Intelligence? Go to launchpadworks.com.

Not only does intelligence change over the life span, but it also changes over generations (see **FIGURE 10.8**). The *Flynn effect* refers to the fact that the average IQ score today is roughly 30 points higher than it was a century ago (Dickens & Flynn, 2001; Flynn, 2012; cf. Lynn, 2013). This is a striking number. It means that the average person today is smarter than 95% of the people who were alive in 1900! Why is each generation outscoring the one before it? Some researchers give the credit to improved nutrition, schooling, and parenting (Baker et al., 2015; Lynn, 2009; Neisser, 1998), whereas others suggest that the least intelligent people got left out of the mating game (Mingroni, 2007). But most scientists believe that the industrial and technological revolutions have changed the nature of daily living such that people now spend more and more time solving precisely the kinds of abstract problems that

Figure 10.7
Intelligence Changes Over Time
Intelligence changes over the lifespan, rising early, peaking in middle age, and declining thereafter.

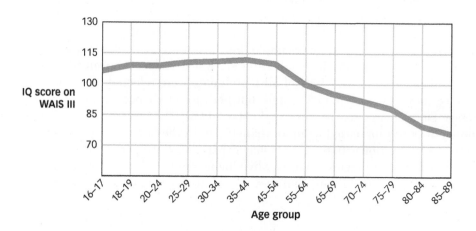

The Real World : **Is IQ Stable in Adolescence?**

Now, Albert Einstein is revered for his intellect. As a young child, however, he was slow to learn to talk, and his family nickname was "the dopey one." Clearly, something changed between his childhood and his 40s, when he was awarded the Nobel Prize in Physics.

Figure 10.7 shows that IQ changes over the adult lifespan, but only very slowly. And, in general, IQ seems to be pretty stable. IQ measurements made at different points in a person's life tend to correlate well, and, as discussed in the text, can predict life outcomes such as life span and wealth. But even quite strong correlations may mask a lot of individual variability. As discussed in the Methods in Psychology chapter, a reasonably strong correlation, like 0.5, can be obtained even if there are exceptions to the "rule" (in this case, that IQ is constant).

In an important study (Ramsden et al., 2011), Ramsden and colleagues studied variation in IQ over time in a group of British teenagers aged 12–20. The researchers used standardized tests to measure IQ twice, about 3 years apart, and they found that the teenagers' scores were surprisingly variable. The scatter plot in part a of the accompanying figure shows how IQ measured at Time 1 (on the x axis) relates to IQ measured at Time 2 (on the y axis). If the scores are identical, they fall on the red line; but, most of the data are not on the red line. The two time points correlate at 0.6, which is reasonably strong, but there is still much individual variability.

The same data are shown in a different way in part b of the accompanying figure. Each coloured line shows measured IQ for an individual at a young age (Time 1), and then about 3 years later (Time 2). As you can see, on average, IQ rises slightly over time, which is consistent with known increases in IQ with maturation. However, IQ dropped in some participants and increased in others. In 11 of the 33 participants, scores changed quite dramatically;

for example, someone with an IQ in the Very High range (scores of 120–129) at Time 1 may have had an IQ in the Average range (scores of 90–109) at Time 2, or vice versa.

You might wonder (and you'd be right to wonder!) whether this variation is just random. As you learned in the Methods in Psychology chapter, if a test is used to measure the same property at different times and gives similar results each time, it is reliable. If repeating the test yields a different measurement (assuming the property has not changed), the test is not reliable. Maybe IQ tests are just not perfectly reliable. After all, people are generally brighter when they are rested and relaxed, as compared to when they are tired, hungry, distracted, or stressed. Situational differences are undoubtedly part of the reason why scores vary, but they don't explain the variation entirely. Why not? *Because brain structure also changed between Time 1 and Time 2, in ways that related systematically to the changes in IQ.*

As you've learned, IQ is a composite measure of performance across many domains, including verbal and nonverbal (spatial and sensorimotor) domains. The researchers found that changes in grey matter volume in a region of the left frontal lobe

were important for speech production, which is correlated with the verbal subscale score. If verbal IQ increased over time, so had the grey matter volume in this area; if verbal IQ decreased over time, so had the grey matter volume. Because the amount of grey matter in a region is thought to reflect, at least in part, the number and density of neurons in a region, the presence of more grey matter suggests that more neurons are present. The implication is that, even in adolescence, local brain regions are growing (or shrinking) over time.

Changes on the nonverbal subscale of the IQ test from Time 1 to Time 2 also correlated with grey matter volume, but in a motor region of the brain. Again, increases in nonverbal IQ were associated with increases in volume in this region, and decreases in nonverbal IQ were associated with decreases in volume.

The work by Ramsden and colleagues suggests that the brain is surprisingly plastic in adolescence. People's intelligence, relative to that of their peers, can increase or decrease in the teenage years. Perhaps the class smarty-pants you remember from grade 7 has since sunk back into the crowd, and the dopey kid in the back row has since become a rocket scientist.

(a)

The relationship in two measurements of a person's IQ

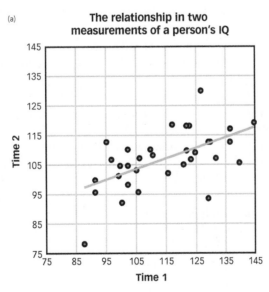

(b)

Full-scale IQ at two time points

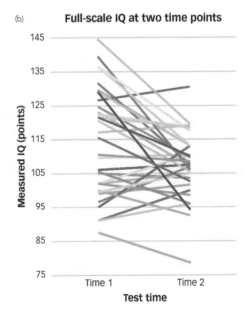

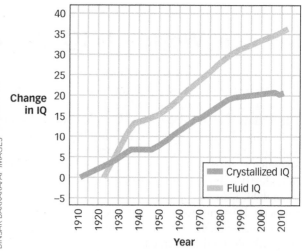

Figure 10.8

The Flynn Effect 105-year-old Khatijah (front row, second from right) sits with five generations of her family. As the graph shows, human intelligence has been increasing across generations for at least the last century, though some recent studies suggest that this increase may recently have ended. INFORMATION FROM PIETSCHNIG & VERACEK, 2015.

intelligence tests include—and as we all know, practice makes perfect (Bordone, Scherbov, & Steiber, 2015; Bratsberg & Rogeberg, 2018; Flynn, 2012).

This could explain why these generational increases are nearly twice as large for fluid intelligence as they are for crystalized intelligence (Pietschnig & Voracek, 2015). Research on how well people can estimate other people's IQs shows that people tend to think their own children are smarter than their own grandparents—and the Flynn effect suggests that they are right (Furnham, 2001)! It is worth noting that some very recent evidence suggests that the increase in IQ across generations has recently come to a halt (Dutton, van der Linden, & Lynn, 2016). Time will tell.

The fact that intelligence changes over the life span and across generations shows that it is by no means a "fixed quantity that cannot be increased" (Binet, 1909, p. 141). Our genes may determine the range in which our IQ is likely to fall, but our experiences determine the point in that range at which it actually does fall (Hunt, 2011) (see **FIGURE 10.9**). As you are about to see, two of the most powerful intelligence-altering experiences involve economics and education.

Economics: Poverty Is Intelligence's Enemy

Maybe money can't buy love, but it can buy intelligence. One of the best predictors of a person's intelligence is the material wealth of the family in which he or she was raised—what psychologists call *socioeconomic status* (SES). Studies suggest that being raised in a high-SES family rather than a low-SES family is worth between 12 and 18 IQ points (Nisbett, 2009; van IJzendoorn, Juffer, & Klein Poelhuis, 2005). For instance, one study compared pairs of siblings who were born to low-SES parents. In each case, one of the siblings was raised by his or her low-SES parents, and the other was adopted and raised by a high-SES family. On average, the child who had been raised by high-SES parents had an IQ that was 14 points higher than his or her sibling (Schiff et al., 1978). Although these siblings had similar genes, they ended up with dramatically different IQs simply because one was raised in a wealthier household. High-SES and low-SES children have different IQs at the age of 2, and by the age of 16 the size of difference between them nearly triples (von Stumm & Plomin, 2015).

Exactly how does SES influence intelligence? One way is by influencing the brain itself. Low-SES children have poorer nutrition and medical care, they experience greater daily stress, and they are more likely to be exposed to environmental toxins such as air pollution and lead—all of which can impair brain development (Ash & Boyce, 2018; Chen, Cohen, & Miller, 2010; Evans, 2006; Hackman & Farah, 2008). The fact that low SES can impair a child's brain development may explain why children who experience poverty in early childhood are less intelligent than those who experience poverty in middle or late childhood (Duncan et al., 1998).

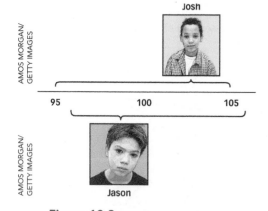

Figure 10.9

Genes and Environment Genes establish the range in which a person's intelligence *may* fall, but environment determines the point in that range at which the person's intelligence *will* fall. Although Jason's genes give him a better chance to be smart than Josh's genes do, differences in their diets could easily cause Josh to have a higher IQ than Jason.

SES affects the brain, and it also affects the environment in which that brain lives and learns. Intellectual stimulation increases intelligence (Nelson et al., 2007), and research shows that high-SES parents are more likely to provide it (Nisbett, 2009). For instance, high-SES parents are more likely to read to their children and to connect what they are reading to the outside world ("Billy has a rubber ducky. Who do you know who has a rubber ducky?") (Heath, 1983; Lareau, 2003). When high-SES parents talk to their children, they tend to ask stimulating questions such as "Do you think a ducky likes to eat grass?", whereas low-SES parents tend to give instructions such as "Please put your ducky away" (Hart & Risley, 1995). Differences in access to books and educational opportunities in the home environment may explain why children from low-SES families show a decrease in intelligence during the summer when school is not in session, whereas children from the very highest SES families actually show an increase (Burkham et al., 2004; Cooper et al., 1996). Clearly, poverty is the enemy of intelligence (Evans & Kim, 2012).

Education: School Is Intelligence's Friend

Alfred Binet believed that if poverty was intelligence's enemy, then education was its friend. And he was right about that, too. The correlation between the amount of formal education a person receives and his or her intelligence is somewhere in the range of $r = .55$ to .90 (Ceci, 1991; Neisser et al., 1996). One reason this correlation is so large is that smart people tend to stay in school, but the other reason is that school makes people smarter (Ceci & Williams, 1997). When schooling is delayed because of war, political strife, or the simple lack of qualified teachers, children show a measurable decline in intelligence (Nisbett, 2009). The best estimate to date suggests that each additional year of education raises a person's IQ by 1 to 5 points (Ritchie & Tucker-Drob, 2018).

Does this mean that anyone can become a lifelong genius just by showing up for class? Unfortunately not. Although education does increase intelligence, its effects tend to vanish when education ends (Protzko, 2015, 2016). For example, prekindergarten programs for low-SES children tend to raise their IQs, but the effects fade once these children leave their intellectually enriched environments and go to elementary school. On the other hand, a few intensive education programs have produced longer-lasting gains. For instance, an experiment conducted in the 1970s allowed low-SES children in an American community to enroll in a full-time preschool program that focused on developing their cognitive, linguistic, and social skills in small classes of about six students total (Campbell et al., 2002). Compared with a control group, in the same community, those children showed IQ gains that were still measurable at the age of 21 (though it appears that girls benefited far more than boys) (Anderson, 2008).

Although education does not always produce long-lasting increases in intelligence, it does seem to produce long-lasting increases in other important skills such as reasoning. In terms of just about every important outcome—from health to wealth to happiness—the difference between an illiterate person with an IQ of 100 and a literate person with an IQ of 101 is much larger than a single IQ point would suggest.

Gene–Environment Interactions

Genes and environments clearly influence intelligence. But how? Does each of them exert an independent effect, or do they somehow work together? The answer is yes—they do both! Genes and environments do indeed have direct and independent effects on the brain. For example, most embryos have 23 pairs of chromosomes—one set of 23 inherited from their mother and one set inherited from their father. But about 1 in every 700 embryos has an extra 21st chromosome, and these embryos become children with "trisomy 21," also known as

To encourage low-SES parents to talk more to their children, the city of Providence, Rhode Island, created a program called "Providence Talks." Once a month, a child wears a small recording device for the day, which allows a computer to calculate how many words she spoke, how many were spoken by adults in her vicinity, and how many conversational exchanges she experienced. A caseworker then visits her parent and provides a progress report.

Down syndrome. That extra 21st chromosome holds about 250 genes, and one or more of those genes impairs the development of the embryos' brains and lowers intelligence. Similarly, the environment can directly affect brain development. Environmental toxins such as mercury can kill brain cells and alter the cells' ability to migrate and proliferate, which can lead to lower intelligence (Lanphear, 2015). So yes, both genes and environments can directly and independently influence intelligence.

But you knew that. What you may not have known is that genes and environments can interact in fascinating ways. For instance, a person can *have* a gene, but the environment can determine whether that gene will or will not play an active role in producing proteins. When a gene does play an active role, biologists say it is being "expressed," and the environment can determine whether expression takes place. As you read in the Neuroscience and Behaviour chapter, epigenetics refers to environmentally induced changes to a gene that can alter its expression. You can think of a gene as a little switch that the environment can turn to the *on* or *off* position. If the environment turns it on, then the gene plays a role in the production of proteins that influence both the development and function of the brain; if the environment turns it off, then the gene is silent and does nothing—as if it weren't even there. Scientists have discovered more than 50 genes that can influence intelligence (Sniekers et al., 2017), and whether a person *has* these genes depends on his or her parents, but whether these genes are *expressed* may depend on the experiences the person has.

In addition to epigenetics, there is another way in which genes and environments can interact to influence intelligence: Genes can cause people to be drawn towards or away from particular environments (Dickens & Flynn, 2001; Nisbett, 2009; Plomin et al., 2001; Tucker-Drob, Briley, & Harden, 2013). For example, personality traits such as extraversion are heritable (Polderman et al., 2015). If a particular set of genes makes people more outgoing and more sociable, then those genes may cause some people to enjoy the company of their peers more than others, which may cause them to stay in school longer, which may cause them to become smarter. Those genes would not be playing a direct role in promoting intelligence, but rather, they would be playing an indirect role by "pushing" people into the environments that promote their intelligence and "pulling" them away from environments that don't.

The fact that genes and environments can interact challenges the way most of us think about them. For instance, if a gene that lowers intelligence by impairing brain function is normally switched off, but in Jean's case it was switched on by the stress of his impoverished environment, should we attribute Jean's low intelligence to his "low intelligence gene" or to his "stressful environment"? If Anaya has a gene that causes her to be extraverted, which causes her to join all the clubs at school, which causes her to read more books and attend more lectures, should we attribute her high intelligence to her "extraversion gene" or to her extra education? These questions highlight the fact that genes and environments work together in complex ways that scientists are just beginning to understand, which is why the obvious distinction between nature and nurture is becoming less obvious every day (see Hot Science: Brains Wide Open).

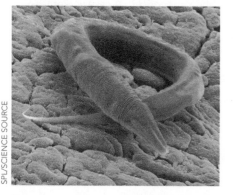

Roundworms that have the NPR-1 gene get fewer infections than those that don't. But this gene does not directly influence the functioning of the immune system. Rather, it causes roundworms to "dislike" the kinds of environments where bacteria hang out. Similarly, genes may influence intelligence not by directly influencing the functioning of the brain, but by causing people to gravitate towards or away from particular environments.

Build to the Outcomes

1. What do twin studies teach us about the influence of genes and environments on intelligence?
2. What is the heritability coefficient?
3. Why is heritability of intelligence higher among wealthy people than poor people?
4. What are the most important environmental influences on intelligence?
5. How do genes and environments interact to influence intelligence?

Hot Science | **Brains Wide Open**

One of the things that makes our species so smart is that our brains are designed to be programmed by our environments. Turtles, lizards, and houseflies are all prewired by evolution to react in very specific ways to very specific stimuli. But mammalian brains—and especially human brains—are built to be *environmentally sensitive*, which means that humans are born with the minimal amount of hardwiring and are instead wired by their experiences in the world in which they find themselves. This is one of the things that allows human beings to function so effectively in a wide variety of physical and cultural environments.

But the brain's remarkable openness to experience doesn't last forever. After the age of 18 or so, the brain is never again as environmentally sensitive as it was in childhood. If the brain's environmental sensitivity is one of the things that makes our species so smart, it stands to reason that the smartest people among us might have brains that remain environmentally sensitive for longer than usual. Is that true?

That's what Brant and colleagues (2013) set out to discover. They examined data from nearly 11,000 sets of monozygotic (MZ) and dizygotic (DZ) twins who had taken IQ tests sometime between infancy and adulthood. Using sophisticated mathematical techniques, they computed the extent to which differences in IQ scores at each age had been influenced by genes or by the environment. What they found was fascinating. Children's brains were relatively open to environmental influence, while adult's brains were relatively closed—but the point at which the closing happened was different for high-IQ people than for low-IQ people. Whereas the brains of low-IQ people closed by early adolescence, the brains of high-IQ people remained open to influence well into adolescence.

The accompanying graph shows the magnitude of both environmental and genetic influences at different ages. As indicated, the brains of high-IQ adolescents remained as sensitive as the brains of children, but the brains of low-IQ adolescents were as insensitive as the brains of adults. Whether you look at the effect of genes (in orange) or the effect of environment (in purple), you'll notice that the high- and low-IQ people start in the same place and end in the same place, but they get there at different speeds—specifically, low-IQ people get there faster.

No one knows why the brains of high-IQ people remain sensitive to the environment for longer, and no one knows if this is a cause or a consequence of their intelligence. All we know is that the longer the brain retains its childlike openness to experience, the more effectively it functions for the rest of its life.

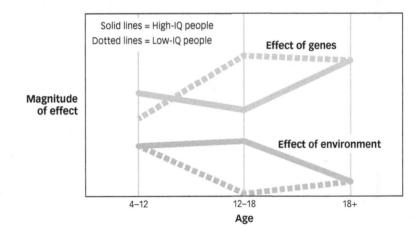

Solid lines = High-IQ people
Dotted lines = Low-IQ people

Effect of genes

Effect of environment

Magnitude of effect

4–12   12–18   18+

Age

Who Is Most Intelligent?

Individual Differences in Intelligence

Intelligence is a prized trait, and some people have more or less of it than others. The average IQ is 100, and 68% of us have IQs between 85 and 115 (see **FIGURE 10.10**). The people who score well above this large middle range are said to be *intellectually gifted,* and the people who score well below it are said to be *intellectually disabled.* Although these people live at opposite ends of the intelligence continuum, they do have one thing in common: They are more likely to be male than female. Males and females have the same average IQ, but the distribution of males' IQ scores is wider and more variable than the distribution of females' IQ scores, which means that there are more males than females at both the very top and the very bottom of the IQ range (Hedges & Nowell, 1995; Lakin, 2013; Wai, Putallaz, & Makel, 2012). Some of this difference is due to the different ways in which boys and girls are socialized. Whether any of this difference is

Learning Outcomes

- Describe myths about the intellectually gifted and the intellectually disabled.

- Explain what is and is not known about between-group differences in intelligence.

- Identify ways in which intelligence can be enhanced.

LEE FOSTER/ALAMY

The artist Vincent van Gogh was the iconic "tortured genius." But data suggest that low intelligence, not high intelligence, is most strongly associated with mental illness.

due to innate biological differences between males and females remains a hotly debated issue in psychology (Ceci, Williams, & Barnett, 2009; Nisbett et al., 2012; Spelke, 2005).

Those of us who occupy the large middle of the intelligence distribution tend to have a number of misconceptions about those who live at the extremes. For example, movies often portray the "tortured genius" as a person (usually a male person) who is brilliant, creative, misunderstood, despondent, and more than a little bit weird. Although some psychologists believe there is a link between creative genius and certain forms of psychopathology (Gale et al., 2012; Jamison, 1993; cf. Schlesinger, 2012; Simonton, 2014), for the most part Hollywood has the relationship between intelligence and mental illness backwards: People with very high intelligence are *less* susceptible to mental illness than are people with very low intelligence (Dekker & Koot, 2003; Didden et al., 2012; Walker et al., 2002). Indeed, a 15-point *decrease* in IQ at age 20 is associated with a 50% *increase* in the risk of later hospitalization for schizophrenia, mood disorder, and alcohol-related disorders (Gale et al., 2010), as well as for personality disorders (Moran et al., 2009). Just as intelligence seems to buffer people against physical illness, so it seems to buffer people against mental illness as well.

Gifted children are rarely gifted in all departments, but instead have gifts in particular domains such as math, language, or music (Achter, Lubinski, & Benbow, 1996; Makel et al., 2016). Because gifted children tend to be single-gifted, they also tend to be single-minded, displaying a "rage to master" the domain in which they excel. As one psychologist noted, "One cannot tear these children away from activities in their area of giftedness, whether they involve an instrument, a computer, a sketch pad, or a math book. These children . . . can focus so intently on work in this domain that they lose sense of the outside world" (Winner, 2000, p. 162). Some research suggests that what most clearly distinguishes gifted children from their less gifted peers is the sheer amount of time they spend engaged in their domain of excellence (Ericsson & Charness, 1999), which suggests that a part of nature's gift may simply be the capacity for passionate devotion to a single activity (cf. Hambrick et al., 2013; Mayer et al., 1989). This passionate devotion may explain why gifted children are much more likely to become high-achieving adults (Lubinski, 2016).

On the other end of the intelligence spectrum are people with intellectual disabilities, which can range from mild (50 < IQ < 69) to moderate (35 < IQ < 49) to severe (20 < IQ < 34) to profound (IQ < 20). About 70% of people with IQs in this range are male. Two of the most common causes of intellectual disability are Down syndrome (caused by the presence of a third copy of chromosome 21) and fetal alcohol syndrome (caused by a mother's excessive alcohol use during pregnancy). The intellectual disabilities associated with these two causes tend to be quite general, and people who have them typically show impaired performance on most or all cognitive tasks. There are many myths about the intellectually disabled, but perhaps the most pervasive is that they are unhappy. The fact is that nearly all people with Down syndrome are happy with their lives, like who they are, and like how they look (Skotko, Levine, & Goldstein, 2011b). Their siblings are proud of them and feel that their relationships have made them "better people," and they do not wish that their sibling with Down syndrome were any different (Skotko, Levine, & Goldstein, 2011a).

Figure 10.10

The Normal Curve of Intelligence
Deviation IQ scores produce a normal curve. This graph shows the percentage of people who score in each range of IQ.

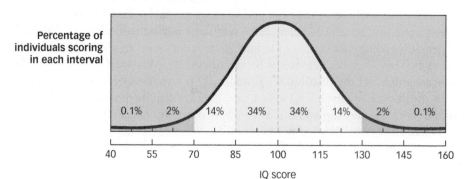

Percentage of individuals scoring in each interval

0.1%   2%   14%   34%   34%   14%   2%   0.1%

40   55   70   85   100   115   130   145   160

IQ score

People with intellectual disabilities face many challenges, but being misunderstood by those who don't know them is among the most difficult.

Group Differences in Intelligence

Eugenics is the idea that the intelligence of humankind can and should be improved by controlled breeding. George Bernard Shaw, Theodore Roosevelt, Margaret Sanger, Calvin Coolidge, and Oliver Wendell Holmes Jr. were all early supporters of eugenics, which was "hugely popular in America and Europe among the 'better sort' before Hitler gave it a bad name" (Lemann, 1999).

The Stanford University professor Lewis Terman (whom you encountered earlier in this chapter) was also a supporter of eugenics. In the early 1900s, he improved on Binet and Simon's work and produced the intelligence test that today is known as the Stanford–Binet Intelligence Scale. One of the things Terman discovered when he gave people his intelligence test was that American White people performed better than American non-White people. Terman did not need evidence to know why: "Are the inferior races really inferior, or are they merely unfortunate in their lack of opportunity to learn?" he asked, and then answered unequivocally: "Their dullness seems to be racial, or at least inherent in the family stocks from which they come" (Terman, 1916, pp. 91–92).

A century later, Terman's words make most of us cringe. But which words are the cringe-worthy ones? Terman claimed that (1) intelligence is influenced by genes, (2) members of some racial groups score better than others on intelligence tests, and (3) members of some racial groups score better than others on intelligence tests *because* of differences in their genes. Virtually all modern scientists who study intelligence consider Terman's first two claims to be well-established facts: Intelligence *is* influenced by genes, and some groups *do* perform better than others on intelligence tests. But Terman's third claim—that differences in genes are the *reason* why some groups outperform others—is *not* an established fact. In fact, it is a controversial conjecture that has been the subject of acrimonious debate. What does science have to tell us about it?

Before answering that question, let's be clear about one thing: Group differences in intelligence are not inherently problematic. No one is troubled by the possibility that this year's winners of the Nobel Prize in Physics are on average more intelligent than this year's winners of the Super Bowl, or that people who graduate from university are on average more intelligent than people who never attended school. On the other hand, most of us *are* troubled by the possibility that people of one gender, race, or nationality may be more intelligent than people of another. Intelligence is a valuable trait, and it doesn't seem fair for some people to have more of it than others simply because of an accident of birth or geography.

But fair or not, they do. Women routinely outscore men on tests that require rapid access to and use of semantic information, production and comprehension of complex prose, fine motor skills, and perceptual speed of verbal intelligence. Men routinely outscore women on tests that require transformations in visual or spatial memory, certain motor skills, spatiotemporal responding, and fluid reasoning in abstract mathematical and scientific domains (Halpern et al., 2007; Nisbett et al., 2012). In the United States, Asians routinely outscore Whites who routinely outscore Blacks on standard intelligence tests (Neisser et al., 1996; Nisbett et al., 2012). Although the average difference between groups is considerably less than the average difference within groups (groups overlap a lot), there is no doubt that some groups outperform others—and the interesting and important question is why?

Tests and Test Takers

One possibility is that there is something wrong with the tests. In fact, the earliest intelligence tests did ask questions whose answers were more likely to be known by members of one group (usually White Europeans) than by members of another. For example, one of Binet and Simon's questions was this: "When anyone has offended you and asks you to excuse him, what ought you to do?" Binet and Simon were looking for answers such as "accept the apology like a gentleman or explain why it is insufficient."

Isabella Springmuhl Tejada is a fashion designer who has Down syndrome. Her work has been showcased during London Fashion Week, and the British Broadcasting Corporation (BBC) voted her one of the 100 most inspiring and innovative women of 2016.

These students are writing the Medical College Admission Test (MCAT). When people are asked about their race before taking a test, their performance can be affected.

FUSE/GETTY IMAGES

Answers such as "challenge him to a fight" or "demand three goats" would have been counted as wrong despite the fact that in some cultures those answers would have been right. Early intelligence tests were clearly culturally biased, but those tests have come a long way in a century, and one would have to look hard to find such blatantly biased questions on a modern intelligence test (Suzuki & Valencia, 1997). Moreover, group differences emerge even on those portions of intelligence tests that measure nonverbal skills, such as Raven's Progressive Matrices Test (see Figure 10.4).

Of course, even when test *questions* are unbiased, testing *situations* may not be. For example, studies show that African American students (but not European American students) perform more poorly on tests if they are asked to report their race at the top of the answer sheet, presumably because doing so leads them to feel anxious about confirming racial stereotypes (Steele & Aronson, 1995), and anxiety naturally interferes with test performance (Reeve, Heggestad, & Lievens, 2009). **Stereotype threat** is *the fear of confirming the negative beliefs that others may hold* (Aronson & Steele, 2004; Schmader, Johns, & Forbes, 2008; Walton & Spencer, 2009), and it can influence people's test performances. When Asian American women are reminded of their gender, they perform poorly on tests of mathematical skill if they are aware of stereotypes suggesting that women can't do math; but when the same women are instead reminded of their ethnicity, they perform well on such tests if they are aware of stereotypes suggesting that Asians are especially good at math (Gibson, Losee, & Vitiello, 2014; Shih, Pittinsky, & Ambady, 1999). Indeed, when women read an essay suggesting that mathematical ability is strongly influenced by genes, they perform more poorly on subsequent math tests (Dar-Nimrod & Heine, 2006). Findings such as these remind us that the situations in which intelligence tests are administered can affect members of different groups differently and may cause group differences in *performance* that do not reflect group differences in actual *intelligence*.

Environments and Genes

Biases in the testing situation may explain some of the between-group differences in intelligence test scores, but probably not all. If we assume that some of these differences reflect real differences in the abilities that intelligence tests are meant to measure, then what accounts for these ability differences?

There is broad agreement among scientists that environment plays a major role. For example, African American children have lower birth weights, poorer diets, higher rates of chronic illness, and poorer medical care; attend worse schools; and are three

stereotype threat The fear of confirming the negative beliefs that others may hold.

times more likely than European American children to live in single-parent households (Acevedo-Garcia et al., 2007; National Center for Health Statistics, 2016a). African American households have lower incomes, and studies show that children in families earning more than $100,000 per year are nearly 50% more likely to be in excellent health than are children in families earning less than $35,000 per year (National Center for Health Statistics, 2016b). Given the vast differences between the SES of European Americans and African Americans, it isn't very surprising that African Americans score, on average, 10 points lower on IQ tests than do European Americans.

Which brings us to the question that has caused so much controversy over the last century: Do genes play any role in group differences like this one? There are uninformed people on every side of this issue and most of them seem to have Twitter accounts. But so far, scientists have not found any facts about group differences that require a genetic explanation. They have, however, found several facts that make such an explanation unlikely. For example, the average African American has about 20% European genes; and yet, those who have more of these genes are no smarter than those who have fewer, which is not what we'd expect if European genes made people smart (Loehlin, 1973; Nisbett et al., 2012; Scarr et al., 1977). Similarly, African American children and mixed-race children have different amounts of European genes; and yet, when they are adopted into middle-class families, their IQs don't differ (Moore, 1986), which is once again not what we'd expect if European genes made people smart. These facts do not prove that there is no genetic basis of the between-group differences in intelligence, but they do make that possibility less plausible.

What would it take to prove that intelligence differences—or any other psychological differences—between groups have a genetic origin? It would take the kind of evidence that scientists often find when they study the *physical* differences between groups. For instance, people who have hepatitis C are often given a prescription for antiviral drugs, and European Americans typically benefit more from this treatment than African Americans do. Physicians once thought this was because European Americans were more likely to *take* the medicine they were given, but then scientists discovered a gene that makes people unresponsive to these antiviral drugs—and guess what? African Americans are *more* likely than European Americans to have that gene for unresponsiveness (Ge et al., 2009). This kind of evidence of genetic differences between groups is exactly what's lacking in the debate on group differences in intelligence. The best research suggests that intelligence is not strongly influenced by a single gene but is instead weakly influenced by a very large number of genes (Davies et al., 2011). Unless researchers can isolate those genes and then show that they are more prevalent in one group than another, most scientists are unlikely to embrace a genetic explanation of between-group differences in intelligence.

Improving Intelligence

Intelligence can be improved—by money, for example, and by education. But most people can't just snap their fingers and become wealthier, and education takes time. Is there anything that average parents can do to raise their child's IQ? Researchers recently analyzed the data from all the high-quality scientific studies on this question that have been performed over the last few decades (Protzko, Aronson, & Blair, 2013); and they found four things that seem to reliably raise a child's intelligence. First, supplementing the diets of pregnant women and neonates with long-chain polyunsaturated fatty acids (substances found in breast milk) appears to raise children's IQ by up to 4 points (Boutwell, Young, & Meldrum, 2018). Second, enrolling low-SES infants in so-called early educational interventions tends to raise their IQ by about 6 points. Third, reading to children in an interactive manner raises their IQ by about 6 points. Fourth, sending children to preschool raises their IQ by about 6 points. In short, there do seem to be some things parents can do to make their kids smarter.

Parents are constantly looking for things they can do to make their kids smarter. Some studies suggest that learning to play a musical instrument can increase a child's intelligence (Protzko, 2017), while others suggest that musical training and intelligence are not causally related (Sala & Gobet, 2018).

Other Voices : **Not By Intelligence Alone**

Intelligence matters. But is it all that matters? Professor Barry Schwartz thinks not. He believes that intelligence alone cannot make us happy, productive, and successful citizens unless it is combined with a list of "intellectual virtues" that enable us to *use* our intelligence properly. In his view, universities should focus less on teaching students *what* to think and focus more on teaching students *how* to think by demonstrating and instilling nine key intellectual virtues. What are they?

Knowing how to think demands a set of cognitive skills— quantitative ability, conceptual flexibility, analytical acumen, expressive clarity. But beyond those skills, learning how to think requires the development of a set of intellectual virtues that make good students, good professionals, and good citizens . . .

Love of truth. Students need to love the truth to be good students . . . It has become intellectually fashionable to attack the very notion of truth. You have your truth, and I have mine. You have one truth today, but you may have a different one tomorrow. Everything is relative, a matter of perspective. People who claim to know the "truth," it is argued, are in reality just using their positions of power and privilege to shove their truth down other people's throats.

This turn to relativism is in part a reflection of something good and important that has happened to intellectual inquiry. People have caught on to the fact that much of what the intellectual elite thought was the truth *was* distorted by limitations of perspective. Slowly the voices of the excluded have been welcomed into the conversation. And their perspectives have enriched our understanding. But the reason they have enriched our understanding is that they have given the rest of us an important piece of the truth that was previously invisible to us. Not *their* truth, but *the* truth. It is troubling to see how quickly an appreciation that each of us can attain only a partial grasp of the truth degrades into a view that there really isn't any truth out there to be grasped . . .

Honesty. Honesty enables students to face the limits of what they themselves know; it encourages them to own up to their mistakes. And it allows them to acknowledge uncongenial truths about the world . . .

Fair-mindedness. Students need to be fair-minded in evaluating the arguments of others . . .

Humility. Humility allows students to face up to their own limitations and mistakes and to seek help from others . . .

Perseverance. Students need perseverance, since little that is worth knowing or doing comes easily . . .

Courage. Students need intellectual courage to stand up for what they believe is true, sometimes in the face of disagreement from others, including people in authority, like their professors. And they need courage to take risks, to pursue intellectual paths that might not pan out.

Good listening. Students can't learn from others, or from their professors, without listening. It takes courage to be a good listener, because good listeners know that their own views of the world, along with their plans for how to live in it, may be at stake whenever they have a serious conversation.

Perspective-taking and empathy. It may seem odd to list perspective-taking and empathy as intellectual virtues, but it takes a great deal of intellectual sophistication to get perspective-taking right. Young children "feel" for a peer who is upset but are clueless about how to comfort her. They try to make a crying child feel better by doing what would make them feel better. And teachers, at all levels, must overcome "the curse of knowledge." If they can't remind themselves of what they were like before they understood something well, they will be at a loss to explain it to their students. Everything is obvious once you know it . . .

Wisdom. Finally, students need what Aristotle called practical wisdom. Any of the intellectual virtues I've mentioned can be carried to an extreme. Wisdom is what enables us to find the balance (Aristotle called it the "mean") between timidity and recklessness, carelessness and obsessiveness, flightiness and stubbornness, speaking up and listening up, trust and skepticism, empathy and detachment. Wisdom is also what enables us to make difficult decisions when intellectual virtues conflict. Being empathetic, fair, and open-minded often rubs up against fidelity to the truth. Practical wisdom is the master virtue . . .

Cultivation of intellectual virtues is not in conflict with training in specific occupations. On the contrary, intellectual virtues will help to create a work force that is flexible, able to admit to and learn from mistakes, and open to change. People with intellectual virtues will be persistent, ask for help when they need it, provide help when others need it, and not settle for expedient but inaccurate solutions to tough problems . . . Workplaces need people who have intellectual virtues, but workplaces are not in a good position to instill them. Colleges and universities should be doing this training for them.

Barry Schwartz is the Dorwin Cartwright Professor of Social Theory and Social Action at Swarthmore College. He is the author of numerous books including *The Paradox of Choice* (2004) and *Practical Wisdom: The Right Way to Do the Right Thing* (2010).

Schwartz believes that without a love of truth, honesty, fair-mindedness, and the rest, intelligence itself just can't get us very far. Is he right? And if so, can these virtues be taught? How? Is his list complete, and if not, what's missing? These are difficult but important questions which, if you believe Schwartz, will never be answered by intelligence alone.

Maybe pills can also make us smarter. **Cognitive enhancers** are *drugs that improve the psychological processes that underlie intelligent performance.* Stimulants such as Ritalin and Adderall can enhance cognitive performance (Elliott et al., 1997; Halliday et al., 1994; McKetin et al., 1999), temporarily improving people's ability to focus attention, manipulate information in working memory, and flexibly control their responses (Sahakian & Morein-Zamir, 2007). Cognitive performance can also be enhanced by a drug such as Modafinal (Ingvar et al., 1997), which has been shown to improve short-term memory and planning abilities (Turner et al., 2003). All these drugs enhance cognitive performance, but they can also have damaging side effects and lead to abuse.

In the near future, cognitive enhancement may be achieved not with chemicals that alter the brain's function, but with techniques that alter its actual structure. By manipulating the genes that guide hippocampal development, for instance, scientists have created a strain of "smart mice" that have extraordinary memory and learning abilities, (Tang et al., 1999, p. 64), and new "gene-editing" techniques may allow these animals to pass their genetic modifications on to their young. Although no one has yet developed a safe and powerful "smart pill" or a gene-editing technique that enhances intelligence in mammals, many experts believe that both of these things will happen in the very near future (Farah et al., 2004; Rose, 2002; Turner & Sahakian, 2006).

Do we want to live in a world in which a highly prized human attribute such as intelligence can be purchased, rather than being earned or endowed by nature? That's a question we will all soon be asking, and we will need a whole lot of intelligence to answer it.

> **cognitive enhancers** Drugs that improve the psychological processes that underlie intelligent performance.

Build to the Outcomes

1. What are the most common misconceptions about the intellectually gifted and the intellectually disabled?

2. What one thing most clearly distinguishes gifted children from other children?

3. How can the testing situation affect a person's performance on an IQ test?

4. What evidence suggests that genes are unlikely to be the cause of between-group differences in intelligence?

5. In what physical and chemical ways can intelligence be enhanced? What ethical questions are raised?

Chapter Review

How Can Intelligence Be Measured?

- *Intelligence* is the ability to use one's mind to solve problems and learn from experience. Binet and Simon developed a test that was meant to measure a child's natural aptitude for learning, independent of previous experience.

- Intelligence tests produce a score known as an *intelligence quotient,* or IQ. *Ratio IQ* is the ratio of a person's mental to physical age. *Deviation IQ* is the deviation of an adult's test score from the average adult's test score. Deviation IQ is the more common method for estimating intelligence.

- Intelligence test scores predict many important life outcomes, such as scholastic performance, job performance, health, and wealth.

What Is Intelligence?

- People who score well on one test of mental ability *tend to* score well on others, which suggests that each person has

a particular level of general intelligence (*g*). Yet the person who scores highest on one test doesn't necessarily score highest on every other test, which suggests that different people have different specific abilities (*s*).

- Most intelligence test data can be described by a three-level hierarchy, revealing several *middle-level abilities* between *g* and *s*.

- The *data-based approach* suggests that there are eight middle-level abilities.

- The *theory-based approach* suggests that there may be middle-level abilities that standard intelligence tests don't measure, such as practical, creative, and emotional intelligence.

- While all cultures value the intellectual ability to solve problems, non-Western cultures sometimes include social responsibility and cooperation in their definitions of intelligence.

Where Does Intelligence Come From?

- The IQs of MZ twins (who share 100% of their genes) are more highly correlated than are the IQs of DZ twins (who share 50% of their genes), suggesting that genes have a powerful influence on intelligence.

- The heritability coefficient (h^2) tells us how much of the difference between the IQ scores of different people is due to differences in their genes, but it does not tell us anything about individuals.

- Environments can influence intelligence. SES and education can both be powerful influences on IQ, though the effects of education are sometimes short-lived.

- Whether or not a person has a specific gene depends on that person's parents, but environmental factors can determine whether that gene is expressed.

Who Is Most Intelligent?

- Intelligence is correlated with mental health, and gifted children are as well-adjusted as their peers. Despite the myth, people with intellectual disabilities are typically happy with themselves and their lives.

- Some groups outscore others on intelligence tests. This may happen in part because testing situations can impair the performance of some groups more than others, and in part because low-SES environments have an adverse impact on intelligence. There is no compelling evidence to suggest that this is due to the genetic differences between the groups.

- Human intelligence can be increased by a variety of means, from preschool to mental exercise to pharmaceuticals. Some of these methods carry greater risks, and raise more difficult ethical questions, than others.

Key Concept Quiz

1. Intelligence tests were originally developed
   a. to help place children in the most appropriate classroom.
   b. to measure educational achievement rather than aptitude.
   c. by governments that wanted to halt immigration.
   d. in Russia.

2. Intelligence tests have been shown to be predictors of
   a. academic performance.
   b. mental health.
   c. physical health.
   d. all of the above.

3. People who score well on one test of mental ability usually score well on others, suggesting that
   a. tests of mental ability are perfectly correlated.
   b. intelligence cannot be measured meaningfully.
   c. there is a general ability called intelligence.
   d. intelligence is genetic.

4. Most scientists now believe that intelligence is best described
   a. as a set of group factors.
   b. by a two-factor framework.
   c. as a single, general ability.
   d. by a three-level hierarchy.

5. Standard intelligence tests typically measure
   a. analytic intelligence.
   b. practical intelligence.
   c. creative intelligence.
   d. all of the above.

6. Intelligence is influenced by
   a. genes alone.
   b. genes and environment.
   c. environment alone.
   d. neither genes nor environment.

7. The heritability coefficient is a statistic that describes how much of the difference between different people's intelligence scores can be explained by
   a. the nature of the specific test.
   b. differences in their environment.
   c. differences in their genes.
   d. their age at the time of testing.

8. Intelligence changes
   a. over the life span and across generations.
   b. over the life span but not across generations.
   c. across generations but not over the life span.
   d. neither across generations nor over the life span.

9. A person's socioeconomic status has a(n) _____ effect on intelligence.
   a. powerful
   b. negligible
   c. unsubstantiated
   d. unknown

10. About which of these statements is there a broad agreement among scientists?
    a. Differences in the intelligence test scores of different ethnic groups are clearly due to genetic differences between those groups.
    b. Differences in the intelligence test scores of different ethnic groups are caused in part by factors such as low birth weight and poor diet, which are more prevalent in some groups than in others.
    c. Differences in the intelligence test scores of different ethnic groups always reflect real differences in intelligence.
    d. Genes that are strongly associated with intelligence have been found to be more prevalent in some ethnic groups than in others.

LearningCurve
macmillan learning

Don't stop now! Quizzing yourself is a powerful study tool. Go to LaunchPad to access the LearningCurve adaptive quizzing system and your own personalized learning plan. Visit launchpadworks.com.

Key Terms

intelligence (p. 394)

ratio IQ (p. 395)

deviation IQ (p. 396)

two-factor theory of
    intelligence (p. 400)

crystallized intelligence
    (p. 402)

fluid intelligence (p. 402)

emotional intelligence
    (p. 404)

fraternal (dizygotic) twins
    (p. 406)

identical (monozygotic) twins
    (p. 406)

heritability coefficient (p. 407)

shared environment (p. 409)

nonshared environment
    (p. 409)

stereotype threat (p. 418)

cognitive enhancers (p. 421)

Changing Minds

1. In biology class, the topic turns to genetics. The professor describes how scientists used gene editing to make a smarter mouse. Your classmate turns to you. "I knew it," she said. "There's a 'smart gene' after all. Some people have it, and some people don't, and that's why some people are intelligent, and some people aren't." What would you tell her about the role genetics plays in intelligence and about the way in which genes affect it?

2. One of your friends tells you about his sister. "We're very competitive," he says. "But she's smarter. We both took IQ tests when we were kids, and she scored 104, but I only scored 102." What would you tell your friend about the relationship between IQ scores and intelligence?

3. A new survey shows that in mathematics departments all over the country, tenured male professors outnumber tenured female professors by about 9 to 1. One of your friends says, "But it's a fact—girls just don't do as well as boys at math, so it's not surprising that fewer girls choose math-related careers." Considering what you've read in this chapter about group differences in intelligence, how might you explain this fact to your friend?

4. One of your cousins has a young son, and she's very proud of the boy's accomplishments. "He's very smart," she says. "I know this because he has a great memory: He gets 100% on all his vocabulary tests." What kind of intelligence do vocabulary tests measure? Although these skills are important for intelligence, what other abilities contribute to an individual's overall intelligence?

Answers to Key Concept Quiz

1. a; 2. d; 3. c; 4. d; 5. a; 6. b; 7. c; 8. a; 9. a; 10. b.

Development

HIS MOTHER CALLED HIM ADI and showered him with affection, but his father was not so kind. His sister later recalled that Adi "got his sound thrashing every day. . . . How often on the other hand did my mother caress him and try to obtain with her kindness what my father could not obtain with his harshness." Although Adi's father wanted him to become a civil servant, Adi's true love was art, and his mother quietly encouraged that gentle interest. When Adi was just 18 years old, his mother was diagnosed with terminal cancer, and his sister noted that Adi "spoiled my mother during this time of her life with overflowing tenderness. He was indefatigable in his care for her, wanted to comply with any desire she could possibly have and did all to demonstrate his great love for her."

Adi was heartbroken when his mother died, but he had little time for grieving. As he later wrote, "Poverty and hard reality compelled me to make a quick decision. I was faced with the problem of somehow making my own living." In defiance of his father, Adi decided to make his living as an artist. He applied to art school but was flatly rejected, and so— motherless, homeless, and penniless—Adi wandered the streets for years, sleeping on park benches, living in shelters, and eating in soup kitchens, all the while trying desperately to sell his sketches and watercolours, and sometimes trading them for food.

But this is not the story of a forgotten artist. Indeed, just 10 years after his mother died, Adi had achieved a degree of fame that few artists have ever known. Today, collectors from all over the world compete at auctions to buy his paintings, which rarely come up for sale. The largest collection of his work is not in the hands of any private citizen or museum but is instead owned by the U.S. government, which keeps the collection under lock and key, in a windowless room in Washington, DC, where few people

Adi painted in many styles, including the precise and well-structured watercolour shown here. In 2013, one of his paintings sold at auction for $40,000.

have ever been allowed to visit. Marylou Gjernes, the longtime curator of this collection, once remarked, "I often looked at them and wondered, 'What if? What if he had been accepted into art school? Would World War II have happened?'" Why would the curator ask such a question? Because although the artist's mother called him Adi, the rest of us know him as Adolf Hitler.

WHY IS IT SO DIFFICULT TO IMAGINE ONE OF THE WORST mass murderers of the 20th century as a gentle child who loved to draw, as a compassionate adolescent who cared for his ailing mother, or as a dedicated young adult who suffered for the sake of his art? After all, *you* didn't start out as the person you are today. You are utterly different from the baby you once were, and utterly different from the elderly person you will someday become—so different, in fact, that people who saw just one of these versions of you would probably be unable to recognize the other. From birth to infancy, from childhood to adolescence, from young adulthood to old age, human beings are transformed by time. They experience dramatic changes in the way they look, think, feel, and act, but they also display some surprising consistencies. **Developmental psychology** is *the study of continuity and change across the life span,* and in the last century, developmental psychologists have discovered some truly amazing things about our metamorphosis.

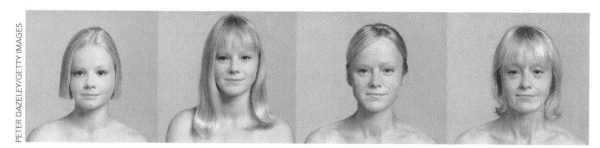

PETER DAZELEY/GETTY IMAGES

Throughout the lifespan, human beings show both continuity and change in how they look, think, feel, and behave.

developmental
psychology The
study of continuity and
change across the
life span.

The story of our development starts where we do: at conception. First we'll examine the 9-month period between conception and birth and see how prenatal events set the stage for so much of what's to come. Then we'll examine infancy and childhood, the periods during which children learn how to think about the world and their relationship to it, understand and bond with others, and tell the difference between right and wrong. Next, we'll examine a relatively new invention called adolescence, which is the stage at which children become both independent and sexual creatures. Finally, we'll examine adulthood, the stage at which people typically leave their parents, find mates, and have children of their own.

Prenatality: A Womb With a View

Most of us calculate our age by counting our birthdays, but the fact is that on the day we are born we are already 9 months old. The *prenatal stage* of development ends with birth, but it begins 9 months earlier when about 200 million sperm set out on a journey from a woman's vagina, through her uterus, and to her fallopian tubes. Many are called, but few are chosen. Some of the sperm don't swim vigourously enough to make any progress, and others get stuck in a kind of spermatozoidal traffic jam in which too many sperm head in the same direction at the same time. Of those that do manage to make their way through the uterus, many sperm take the wrong turn and end up in the fallopian tube that does not contain an egg. When all is said and done, only one out of every million sperm manages to find the correct fallopian tube, get close to an egg, and then release digestive enzymes that erode the egg's protective outer coating. The moment the first sperm does this, the egg releases a chemical that reseals its coating and keeps all the other sperm from entering. After triumphing over 199,999,999 of its fellow travellers, this single successful sperm sheds its tail and fertilizes the egg. About 12 hours later, the egg merges with the nucleus of the sperm, and the prenatal development of a unique human being begins.

Prenatal Development

A *zygote* is a fertilized egg that contains genetic material from both the egg and the sperm, and its brief lifetime is called the **germinal stage**, which is *the 2-week period that begins at conception*. During this stage, the one-celled zygote divides into two cells that then divide into four cells that then divide into eight cells, and so on. By the time an infant is born, its body contains trillions of cells, each of which came from the original zygote. During the germinal stage, the zygote migrates down the fallopian tube and implants itself in the wall of the uterus. This is a difficult journey, and about half of zygotes don't complete it, either because they are defective or because they implant themselves in an inhospitable part of the uterus. Male zygotes are especially unlikely to complete this journey and no one understands why, though several comedians have suggested it's because male zygotes are especially unwilling to stop and ask for directions.

The moment the zygote successfully implants itself in the uterine wall, it loses its old name and earns a new one: *embryo*. The **embryonic stage** is *a period that starts at about the 2nd week after conception and lasts until about the 8th week* (see **FIGURE 11.1**). During this stage, the implanted embryo continues to divide, and its cells begin to differentiate. Although it is only an inch long, the embryo already has arms, legs, and a beating heart. It also has the beginnings of female reproductive

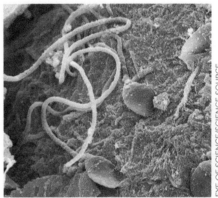

EYE OF SCIENCE/SCIENCE SOURCE

This electron micrograph shows several human sperm, one of which is fertilizing an egg. Contrary to what many people think, fertilization does not happen right away. It typically happens 1 to 2 days after intercourse, but can happen as many as 5 days later.

germinal stage The 2-week period of prenatal development that begins at conception.

embryonic stage The period of prenatal development that lasts from the 2nd week until about the 8th week.

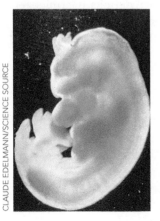

CLAUDE EDELMANN/SCIENCE SOURCE

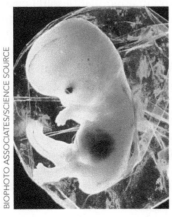

BIOPHOTO ASSOCIATES/SCIENCE SOURCE

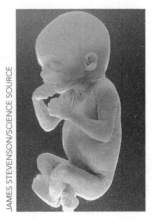

JAMES STEVENSON/SCIENCE SOURCE

Figure 11.1

Prenatal Development Humans undergo dramatic changes during the 9 months of prenatal development. These images show an embryo at 30 days (about the size of a poppyseed), an embryo at 8 weeks (about the size of a raspberry), and a fetus at 5 months (about the size of a banana).

This chimp and boy share a deep interest in dirt, bugs, and leaves. But one difference between them is that a newborn chimp's brain will not quite double in size while a newborn human's brain will quadruple!

This child has some of the telltale facial features associated with fetal alcohol syndrome (FAS): short eye openings, a flat midface, a flat ridge under the nose, a thin upper lip, and an underdeveloped jaw.

fetal stage The period of prenatal development that lasts from about the 9th week until birth.

myelination The formation of a fatty sheath around the axons of a neuron.

teratogen Any substance that passes from mother to unborn child and impairs development.

fetal alcohol syndrome (FAS) A developmental disorder that stems from heavy alcohol use by the mother during pregnancy.

organs, and if it is a male embryo, it begins to produce a hormone called testosterone that will masculinize those organs.

The embryo doesn't have a lot of time to get used to its new name, however, because at about 9 weeks it becomes a *fetus*. The **fetal stage** is *a period that lasts from about the 9th week after conception until birth*. The fetus has a skeleton and muscles that make it capable of movement. It develops a layer of insulating fat beneath its skin, and its digestive and respiratory systems mature. During the fetal stage, brain cells begin to generate axons and dendrites that allow them to communicate with other brain cells. They also begin to undergo a process (described in the Neuroscience and Behaviour chapter) known as **myelination**, which is *the formation of a fatty sheath around the axons of a neuron*. Just as plastic sheathing insulates the wires in a kitchen appliance, myelin insulates the neurons in the brain, preventing the leakage of the signals that travel along the axon. Myelination starts during the fetal stage, but it doesn't end until adulthood.

The human brain grows rapidly during the fetal period, but unlike the brains of other primates, it does not come close to achieving its adult size. A newborn chimpanzee's brain is nearly 60% of its adult size, but a newborn human's brain is only 25% of its adult size, which is to say that 75% of a human's brain development occurs after birth. Why are humans born with such underdeveloped brains? First, humans have really big heads, and if a newborn baby's head were anywhere close to its adult size, then the baby could never pass through its mother's birth canal. Second, one of our species' greatest talents is its ability to adapt to a wide range of novel environments that differ in climate, social structure, and so on. So, rather than arriving in the world with a highly developed brain that may or may not meet the requirements of its environment, human beings arrive with underdeveloped brains that do much of their developing *within* the very environments in which they ultimately must function, thereby gaining the unique capacities that each environment requires.

Prenatal Environment

The word *environment* probably makes you think of green fields and blue skies. But the womb is also an environment, and it has a powerful impact on development (Coe & Lubach, 2008; Glynn & Sandman, 2011; Wadhwa, Sandman, & Garite, 2001). Although a woman's bloodstream is separated from the bloodstream of her unborn child by the placenta, many substances can pass through the placenta. A **teratogen** is *any substance that passes from mother to unborn child and impairs development*.

Teratogens include the mercury in fish, the lead in water, and the paint dust in air, but the most common teratogens are substances that have their very own advertising campaigns. **Fetal alcohol syndrome (FAS)** is *a developmental disorder that stems from heavy alcohol use by the mother during pregnancy* and children born with FAS have a variety of brain abnormalities and cognitive deficits (Carmichael Olson et al., 1997; Streissguth et al., 1999). One study that followed children born with FAS for 25 years found that by the age of 14, a stunning 60% had been suspended or expelled from school (Streissguth, 2007). Although some studies suggest that light drinking does not harm the fetus, there is little consensus about how much drinking is "light" (Warren & Hewitt, 2009). On the other hand, everyone agrees that "none" is a perfectly safe amount.

Tobacco is the other common teratogen, and there is no debate about its effects. Approximately 10% of women in Canada smoke during pregnancy (Al-Sahab et al., 2010), and 11% are exposed to secondhand smoke during pregnancy (Crane et al., 2011). Both maternal smoking and secondhand smoke have been associated with a higher risk of stillbirth and infant death before the first birthday, as well as lower birth weight (birth weight being a general indicator of the health of a baby) and a smaller head circumference (Crane et al., 2011; Horta et al., 1997).

Exactly how dangerous is smoking during pregnancy? Very! Research suggests that smoking during pregnancy increases a woman's odds of having a stillborn child by a whopping 47% (Marufu et al., 2015).

The things a pregnant woman ingests can harm her unborn child, but so too can the things she *fails* to ingest. Women who don't get enough nutrition during pregnancy have children who are at increased risk for a variety of physical and mental illnesses (Neugebauer, Hoek, & Susser, 1999; Susser, Brown, & Matte, 1999). It is worth noting that the embryo is more vulnerable to the effects of teratogens and malnutrition than is the fetus but that structures such as the central nervous system are vulnerable throughout the entire prenatal period.

The prenatal environment is rich with chemicals that affect the unborn child, but it is also rich with information. The fetus can hear its mother's heartbeat, the gastrointestinal sounds associated with her digestion, and her voice. Newborns will suck a nipple more vigorously when they hear the sound of their mother's voice than when they hear the voice of a female stranger (Querleu et al., 1984), indicating that even at birth they are already more familiar with the former. Newborns who listen to strangers speaking two languages will suck more vigorously when they hear words from their mother's native language, indicating that they are already familiar with the tempo and rhythm of their mother's speech (Byers-Heinlein, Burns, & Werker, 2010). What unborn children hear in the womb even influences the sounds they make themselves. French newborns cry with a rising pitch and German newborns cry with a falling pitch, mimicking the cadence of their mother's native tongue (Mampe et al., 2009). Clearly, the fetus is listening.

Build to the Outcomes

1. What are the three stages of prenatal development?
2. What is the adaptive benefit of being born with an underdeveloped brain?
3. How does the uterine environment affect the unborn child?
4. What evidence suggests that "the fetus is listening"?

Infancy and Childhood: Perceiving, Doing, and Thinking

Newborn babies don't look like they can do much more than poop, burp, sleep, and cry. But looks can be deceiving. **Infancy** is *the stage of development that begins at birth and lasts between 18 and 24 months,* and in the last few decades, researchers have discovered that much more is going on inside the infant than meets the untrained eye.

Perceptual Development

New parents might not stand around the crib and make goofy faces if they realized that their babies can't see them. Newborns have a limited range of vision, and the amount of detail they can see from 6 metres away is roughly equivalent to the amount of detail that you can see from 183 metres away (Banks & Salapatek, 1983). On the other hand, newborns can see things that are 20 to 30 centimetres away, which just so happens to be the distance between a mother's face and her nursing infant's eyes.

But wait. How do psychologists know what a newborn can and can't see? Recall from the Learning chapter that *habituation* is the tendency for organisms to respond

Learning Outcomes

- Describe the evidence suggesting that newborns can see.
- Explain the two rules of motor development.
- Outline the stages of Piaget's theory of cognitive development.
- Differentiate between egocentrism and theory of mind.
- Describe the key skills that allow infants to learn from others.

infancy The stage of development that begins at birth and lasts between 18 and 24 months.

Figure 11.2

Infants Track Social Stimuli When newborns see the stimuli in the left panel, they will track the shapes with facial features (*left*) longer than the shapes with scrambled facial features (*middle*) or no facial features (*right*). When fetuses see the stimuli in the right panel, they are more likely to turn their heads towards the face-like configuration (*left*) than the other configuration (*right*). (*LEFT*) RESEARCH FROM JOHNSON ET AL, 1991; (*RIGHT*) RESEARCH FROM REID ET AL, 2017.

(a)
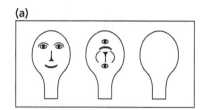

(b)
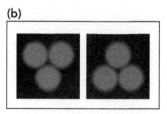

Infants mimic the facial expressions of adults—and vice versa, of course!

less intensely to a stimulus each time it is presented. So if a newborn habituates to a visual stimulus, that means he or she must have been able to see it. If newborns are shown an object over and over again, they will stare a lot at first and then less and less each time the object is presented. If the object is then rotated 90°, the newborns will begin staring at it again (Slater, Morison, & Somers, 1988). So yes, newborns can see objects, and the objects to which they are especially attentive are those that look like faces (Biro et al., 2014). For example, newborns in one study were shown a shape that either had facial features, scrambled facial features, or no facial features (see **FIGURE 11.2a**). When the shape was moved across their fields of vision, the newborns tracked the movement with their eyes—but they tracked the moving shape that had facial features longer than they tracked either of the others (Johnson et al., 1991; cf. Kwon et al., 2016). Some studies suggest that even the fetus attends to facial features (see **FIGURE 11.2b**). When lights were shined through pregnant women's abdomens, their fetuses were more likely to turn towards the lights that were configured like a human face (Reid et al., 2017).

Infants don't just attend to human objects—they also respond to them. In one study, researchers got very close to two groups of newborn infants. They stuck out their tongues in front of one group and pursed their lips in front of the other. Did the newborns see them? Yes, and not only that, but the newborns in the first group stuck out their own tongues more often than did the newborns in the second group; and the newborns in the second group pursed their lips more often than did the newborns in the first group (Meltzoff & Moore, 1977; cf. Oostenbroek et al., 2016, and Meltzoff et al., 2018). It doesn't take newborns long to learn this trick: They have been shown to mimic facial expressions in their very first *hour* of life (Reissland, 1988). Clearly, babies are watching—and what they are watching most closely is us!

Motor Development

Infants can use their eyes and ears right away, but they have to spend some time learning to use their other parts. **Motor development** is *the emergence of the ability to execute physical actions* such as reaching, grasping, crawling, and walking. Infants can do a bit of this at birth because they are born with a small set of **motor reflexes**, which are *motor responses that are triggered by specific patterns of sensory stimulation*. For example, the *rooting reflex* causes infants to move their mouths towards any object that touches their cheek, and the *sucking reflex* causes them to suck any object that enters their mouth. Together, these two reflexes allow newborn infants to find their mother's nipple and begin feeding—a behaviour so vitally important that nature took no chances and hard-wired it into every one of us. Interestingly, these and other reflexes that are present at birth seem to disappear in the first few months as infants learn to execute more sophisticated motor behaviour.

The development of these more sophisticated behaviours tends to obey two general rules. The first is the **cephalocaudal rule** (or the "top-to-bottom" rule), which describes *the tendency for motor skills to emerge in sequence from the head to the feet*. Infants tend to gain control over their heads first, their arms and trunks next, and their legs last. A young infant who is placed on her stomach

motor development The emergence of the ability to execute physical actions.

motor reflexes Motor responses that are triggered by specific patterns of sensory stimulation.

cephalocaudal rule The "top-to-bottom" rule that describes the tendency for motor skills to emerge in sequence from the head to the feet.

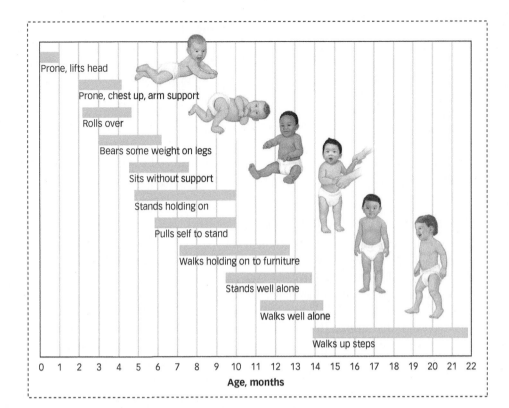

Figure 11.3
Motor Development Infants learn to control their bodies from head to feet and from centre to periphery. These skills do not emerge on a strict time-table, but they do emerge in a strict sequence.

may lift her head and her chest by using her arms for support, but she typically has little control over her legs. The second rule is the **proximodistal rule** (or the "inside-to-outside" rule), which describes *the tendency for motor skills to emerge in sequence from the centre to the periphery.* Infants learn to control their trunks before their elbows and knees, which they learn to control before their hands and feet (see **FIGURE 11.3**). Although motor skills develop in an orderly sequence, they do not develop on a strict timetable. Rather, the timing of these skills is influenced by many factors, such as the infant's incentive for reaching, body weight, muscular development, and general level of activity. Some evidence suggests that the early emergence of certain motor skills is associated with greater intelligence in adulthood (Flensborg-Madsen & Mortensen, 2018).

For adults, perceptual and motor skills work seamlessly together. But children take a while to learn to act on what they see. When infants or young children are allowed to play with an object such as a slide or a car and are then given a miniature version of the object, they will often make a *scale error* by treating the miniature object as though it were the regular-sized one—for instance, they'll try to get inside the miniature car or slide down the miniature slide (DeLoache, Uttal, & Rosengren, 2004) (see **FIGURE 11.4**). Although the children can *see* that

Motor skills develop through practice. In just 1 hour in a playroom, the average 12- to 19-month-old infant takes 2,368 steps, travels 0.4 miles, and falls 17 times (Adolph et al., 2012).

proximodistal rule The "inside-to-outside" rule that describes the tendency for motor skills to emerge in sequence from the centre to the periphery.

Figure 11.4
Scale Errors (a) This 21-month-old child has made a scale error by attempting to slide down a miniature slide. (b) This 24-month-old child has opened the door to the miniature car and is repeatedly trying to force his foot inside the car.

(a)

(b)

the miniature objects are small (which is why they bend down to touch them), their perceptual knowledge of the object's size is not yet coordinated with their motor behaviour, so they try to do with the miniature object what they would normally do with the regular-sized object. The perceptual system that is responsible for the identification of objects is neurologically separate from the motor system that is responsible for the control of movements, which is why certain kinds of brain damage can cause these two systems to become dis-coordinated in adults. (See the section "Pathways for What, Where, and How" in the Sensation and Perception chapter.) The same two systems appear to be not-yet-coordinated in infants and young children.

Cognitive Development

Infants can see and hear and move their bodies. So can houseflies. The question is whether infants can do the thing that makes humans so special: Can they think? In the first half of the 20th century, a Swiss biologist named Jean Piaget became interested in this question and so began to study **cognitive development**, which is *the process by which infants and children gain the ability to think and understand.* Piaget suggested that during this process, infants and children learn three essential things: how the physical world works, how their own minds work, and how other people's minds work. Let's see how they achieve these understandings.

Discovering the World

Piaget (1954) suggested that cognitive development occurs in four discrete stages: the sensorimotor stage, the preoperational stage, the concrete operational stage, and the formal operational stage (see **TABLE 11.1**). The **sensorimotor stage** is *a stage of cognitive development that begins at birth and lasts through infancy.* As the word *sensorimotor* suggests, infants at this stage are mainly busy using their ability to *sense* (perceptual skills) and their ability to *move* (motor skills) to acquire information about the world.

By actively exploring their environments with their eyes, mouths, and fingers, infants begin to construct **schemas**, which are *theories about the way the world works.* As every scientist knows, the good thing about theories is that they allow us to predict what will happen next. If an infant learns that tugging at a stuffed animal brings the toy closer, then that observation is incorporated into the infant's theory about how physical objects behave ("Things come closer if I pull them"), and the infant can later use that theory when she wants a different object to come closer, such as a rattle or a ball. Piaget called this **assimilation**, which happens when *infants apply their schemas in novel situations.* Of course, if the infant applies this theory to the family cat, the cat is likely to sprint in the opposite direction. Infants' theories about

Jean Piaget (1896–1980) was the father of modern developmental psychology, as well as the last man who actually looked cool wearing a beret.

cognitive development The process by which infants and children gain the ability to think and understand.

sensorimotor stage A stage of cognitive development that begins at birth and lasts through infancy, during which infants acquire information about the world by sensing it and moving around within it.

schemas Theories about the way the world works.

assimilation The process by which infants apply their schemas in novel situations.

<table>
<tr><td colspan="2">TABLE 11.1</td></tr>
<tr><td colspan="2">PIAGET'S FOUR STAGES OF COGNITIVE DEVELOPMENT</td></tr>
<tr><td>Stage</td><td>Characteristic</td></tr>
<tr><td>Sensorimotor
(Birth–2 years)</td><td>Infant experiences the world by sensing it and moving in it, develops schemas, begins to act intentionally, and shows evidence of understanding object permanence.</td></tr>
<tr><td>Preoperational
(2–6 years)</td><td>Child acquires motor skills but does not understand conservation of physical properties. Child begins this stage by thinking egocentrically but ends with a basic understanding of other minds.</td></tr>
<tr><td>Concrete operational
(6–11 years)</td><td>Child can think logically about physical objects and events and understands conservation of physical properties.</td></tr>
<tr><td>Formal operational
(11 years and up)</td><td>Child can think logically about abstract propositions and hypotheticals.</td></tr>
</table>

the world are sometimes disconfirmed by experience, which causes infants to take special notice (Stahl & Feigenson, 2015) and to adjust their theories ("Inanimate things come closer when I pull them, but animate things just hiss and run"). Piaget called this **accommodation**, which happens when *infants revise their schemas in light of new information.*

What kinds of theories or schemas do infants develop, apply, and adjust? Piaget suggested that infants are surprisingly clueless about some of the most basic properties of the physical world and must acquire information about those properties through experience. For example, when you put your shoes in the closet, you know that they are still there even after you close the closet door, and you would be surprised if you opened the door a moment later and found the closet empty. But according to Piaget, this wouldn't surprise an infant because infants do not yet have an understanding of **object permanence**, which refers to *the fact that objects continue to exist even when they are not visible.* Piaget noted that in the first few months of life, infants act as though objects stop existing the moment they are out of sight. For instance, a 2-month-old infant will track a moving object with her eyes, but once the object leaves her visual field, she will not search for it. Put the shoes in the closet and close the door and—poof!—the infant acts as if they no longer exist.

But does this really mean that infants don't realize that objects have permanence? To answer this question definitively, of course, we'd have to know what infants are thinking, which Piaget considered impossible: "The child's first year of life is unfortunately still an abyss of mysteries for the psychologist. If only we could know what is going on in a baby's mind while observing him in action, we could certainly understand everything there is to psychology" (Piaget, 1927/1977, p. 199). But there's nothing scientists love more than an abyss of mysteries, and during the 1960s, the psychologist Robert Fantz (1964) developed an ingenious technique for finding out what is "going on in a baby's mind." The logic of his *preferential looking time* technique is simple. Check out the objects in **FIGURE 11.5**. The odds are good that you looked longer at the one on the left than the one on the right. Why? Because the object on the left is an "impossible object." You found it interesting precisely because it violates your beliefs about how the physical world works. Now, here's the cool part: Because you naturally stare longer at things that violate your beliefs, psychologists can use the duration of your stare to figure out what your beliefs must be! Your mind is no longer an abyss of mysteries. It is open to investigation.

When psychologists used this simple technique with infants, they quickly discovered that infants know more about object permanence than Piaget suspected. For instance, in one study, infants were shown a miniature drawbridge that flipped up and

During the sensorimotor stage, infants explore with their hands and mouths, learning important lessons about the physical world such as "Guacamole falls down, not up."

accommodation The process by which infants revise their schemas in light of new information.

object permanence The fact that objects continue to exist even when they are not visible.

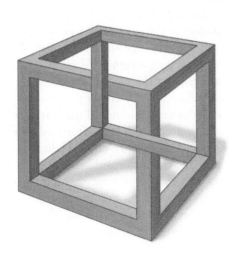 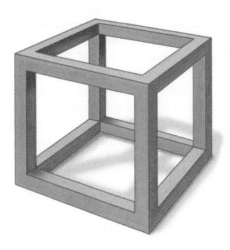

Figure 11.5
BUT . . . THAT'S IMPOSSIBLE! Which of these pictures did you look at longer? What does that reveal about your theory of the physical world?

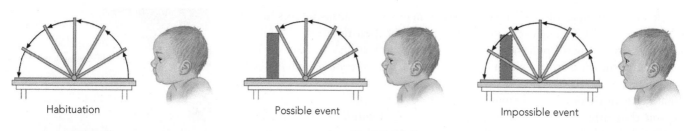

Habituation   Possible event   Impossible event

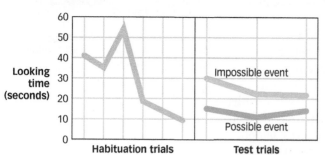

Figure 11.6

The Impossible Event During the habituation trials, infants watch a drawbridge flip back and forth with nothing in its path until they grow bored. During the test trials, a box is placed behind the drawbridge, and the infants are shown either a possible event (in which the motion of the drawbridge is impeded) or an impossible event (in which the motion of the drawbridge is not impeded). The graph shows the infants' looking times during the habituation trials and the test trials. As you can see, during the test trials, the infants' interest was reawakened by the impossible event but not by the possible event (Baillargeon, Spelke, & Wasserman, 1985).

down (see **FIGURE 11.6**). These were the "habituation trials." Once the infants got used to this, they watched as a solid box was placed behind the drawbridge—in the path of the drawbridge, but out of the infant's sight. Some infants then saw a *possible* event: The drawbridge began to flip and then it suddenly stopped, as if its motion was being impeded by the unseen solid box. Other infants saw an *impossible* event: The drawbridge began to flip—and then it didn't stop, as if its motion was unimpeded by the unseen solid box. So what did infants do? Four-month-old infants stared longer at the impossible event than at the possible event (Baillargeon, Spelke, & Wasserman, 1985). The only thing that made the impossible event impossible was the fact that an unseen box should have—but didn't—impede the motion of the drawbridge, which means that the infants must have realized that the box continued to exist even when it could no longer be seen. These and other studies suggest that infants acquire an understanding of object permanence much earlier than Piaget suspected (Shinskey & Munakata, 2005; Wang & Baillargeon, 2008).

Discovering the Mind

The long period following infancy is called **childhood**, which is *the stage of cognitive development that begins at about 18 to 24 months and lasts until about 11 to 14 years.* According to Piaget, people enter childhood at one stage of cognitive development and leave at another. They enter at the **preoperational stage**, which is *the stage of cognitive development that begins at about 2 years and ends at about 6 years, during which children develop a preliminary understanding of the physical world.* They exit at the **concrete operational stage**, which is *the stage of cognitive development that begins at about 6 years and ends at about 11 years, during which children learn how actions, or operations, can transform the concrete objects of the physical world.*

The difference between these stages is nicely illustrated by one of Piaget's clever experiments, in which he showed children a row of cups and asked them to place an egg in each. Preoperational children were able to do this, and afterwards they readily agreed that there were just as many eggs as there were cups. Then Piaget removed the eggs and spread them out in a long line that extended beyond the row of cups. Preoperational children incorrectly claimed that there were now more eggs than cups, pointing out that the row of eggs was longer than the row of cups and hence there must be more of them. Concrete operational children, on the other hand, correctly reported that the number of eggs did not change when they were

childhood The stage of development that begins at about 18 to 24 months and lasts until about 11 to 14 years.

preoperational stage The stage of cognitive development that begins at about 2 years and ends at about 6 years, during which children develop a preliminary understanding of the physical world.

concrete operational stage The stage of cognitive development that begins at about 6 years and ends at about 11 years, during which children learn how various actions, or *operations*, can transform the concrete objects of the physical world.

merely spread out in a longer line. They understood that *quantity* is a property of a set of concrete objects that does not change when an operation such as *spreading out* alters the set's appearance (Piaget, 1954). Piaget called the child's insight **conservation**, which is *the understanding that the quantitative properties of an object are invariant, despite changes in the object's appearance.*

Why don't preoperational children grasp the notion of conservation? Adults naturally distinguish between the subjective and the objective, between appearances and realities, between the way things look and the way things are. We know that a wagon can *be* red but *look* grey at dusk, and that a highway can *be* dry but *look* wet in the heat. Visual illusions delight us precisely because we know that they look one way but are really another. Preoperational children don't make this distinction. They assume that things are as they seem, that what's in their minds is also in the world, and that when something *looks* grey or wet it must *be* grey or wet. As they move from the preoperational to the concrete operational stage, they come to realize that the way the world *appears* and the way the world *is* are sometimes very different things.

Once children have this epiphany, they can suddenly solve problems that require them to ignore an object's subjective appearance (cf. Deák, 2006; Lane et al., 2014). They can understand that when a ball of clay is rolled, stretched, or flattened, it is still the same amount of clay despite the fact that it looks larger in one form than in another. They can understand that when water is poured from a short, wide beaker into a tall, thin cylinder, it is still the same amount of water despite the fact that the water level in the tall cylinder is higher. They can understand that when a sponge is painted grey to look like a rock, it is still a sponge despite its appearance. In short, they understand that certain operations—such as squishing, pouring, and spreading out—can change what an object *looks* like without changing what the object *is* like.

Children learn to solve physical problems at the concrete operational stage, and they learn to solve nonphysical problems at the **formal operational stage**, which is *the final stage of cognitive development that begins around the age of 11, during which children learn to reason about abstract concepts.* Childhood ends when formal operations begin, and people who move on to this stage (and Piaget believed that some people never do) are able to reason systematically about abstract concepts such as *liberty* and *love* and about hypotheticals and counterfactuals—about events that have not yet happened and about events that might have happened but didn't. There are no concrete objects in the world to which the words *liberty* and *love* refer, yet people at the formal operational stage can think and reason about such concepts in the same way that a concrete operational child can think and reason about squishing and folding. The ability to generate, consider, reason about, or mentally "operate on" abstract concepts is the hallmark of formal operations.

Discovering Other Minds

As children develop, they discover their own minds. But they also discover the minds of others. Because preoperational children don't fully grasp the fact that they have minds that mentally represent objects, they also don't fully grasp the fact that other people have minds that may mentally represent the same objects in different ways. That's why preoperational children mistakenly expect others to see the world as they do. When 3-year-old children are asked what a person on the opposite side of a table is seeing, they typically claim that the other person sees what they themselves see (see **FIGURE 11.7**). **Egocentrism** is *the failure to understand that the world appears different to different people.* Egocentrism is a hallmark of the preoperational stage, and it reveals itself in a variety of interesting ways.

When preoperational children are shown two equal-size glasses filled with equal amounts of liquid, they correctly say that neither glass "has more." But when the contents of one glass are poured into a taller, thinner glass, they incorrectly say that the taller glass now "has more." Concrete operational children don't make this mistake, because they recognize that operations such as pouring change the appearance of the liquid but not its actual volume.

According to Piaget, people cannot reason about abstract concepts such as freedom and justice until they reach the formal operational stage. But they can still hold signs!

conservation The understanding that the quantitative properties of an object are invariant despite changes in the object's appearance.

formal operational stage The final stage of cognitive development that begins around the age of 11, during which children learn to reason about abstract concepts.

egocentrism The failure to understand that the world appears different to different people.

Figure 11.7

Egocentrism Pre-operational children mistakenly believe that others share their points of view. The child can see the tree, but when asked what the adult sees, she will say "a tree." The child doesn't seem to realize that although she can see the tree, the adult cannot.

Perceptions and Beliefs Just as 3-year-old children fail to realize that other people don't always see what they see, they also fail to realize that other people don't always know what they know. This fact has been demonstrated in numerous studies using the *false-belief task* (Wimmer & Perner, 1983). In the standard version of this task, children see a puppet named Maxi deposit some chocolate in a cupboard and then leave the room. A second puppet arrives a moment later, finds the chocolate, and moves it to a different cupboard. The children are then asked where Maxi will look for the chocolate when he returns: in the first cupboard where he initially put it, or in the second cupboard, where the children know it currently is?

Most 5-year-olds realize that Maxi will search the first cupboard because Maxi did not see what the children saw—namely, that the chocolate was moved. But 3-year-olds typically claim that Maxi will look in the second cupboard. Why? Because that's where *the children* know the chocolate is—and they assume that what they know, everyone knows! Children are able to give the right answer in the false-belief task somewhere between the ages of 4 and 6 (Callaghan et al., 2005), though children in some cultures are able to give it earlier than children in others (Liu et al., 2008).

Some researchers, however, think the false-belief task, like Piaget's test for object permanence, doesn't allow very young children to demonstrate their true abilities (Scott & Baillargeon, 2017), and several studies have shown that even infants can perform surprisingly well when given modified versions of the false-belief task that make it easier for them to respond (Baillargeon, Scott, & He, 2010; Onishi & Baillargeon, 2005; Rubin-Fernandez & Geurts, 2012; Senju et al., 2011; Southgate, Senju, & Csibra, 2007; but see Kulke et al., 2018). Even chimpanzees, bonobos, and orangutans can perform the modified versions of this task (Krupenye et al., 2016). Of course, infants and great apes may not arrive at the right answer the same way that older children do, namely, by truly understanding that others can have beliefs that differ from their own (Apperly & Butterfill, 2009; Low & Watts, 2013). Still, whatever it is they are doing, their performances are impressive, and it seems clear that the age at which children acquire some rudimentary understanding of other minds is lower than Piaget suspected.

Desires and Emotions Different people have different perceptions and beliefs. They also have different desires and emotions. Do children understand that these aspects of other people's mental lives can differ from their own? Infants do seem to understand that people have desires that guide their behaviour (Liu et al., 2017) and that other people's desires can differ from their own. For example, a 2-year-old who

When small children are told to hide, they sometimes cover their eyes. Because they can't see you, they assume that you can't see them (Russell, Gee, & Bullard, 2012).

likes dogs can understand that other children don't like dogs and can correctly predict that other children will avoid dogs that the child herself would approach. When 18-month-old toddlers see an adult express disgust while eating a food that the toddlers enjoy, they hand the adult a different food, as if they understand that different people have different tastes (Repacholi & Gopnik, 1997). Interestingly, young children seem to understand other people's desires best when their own desires have already been fulfilled and are not competing for their attention (Atance, Bélanger, & Meltzoff, 2010).

In contrast, children take a much longer time to understand that other people may have emotional reactions unlike their own. When 5-year-olds hear a story in which Little Red Riding Hood knocks on her grandmother's door, unaware that a wolf is inside waiting to devour her, they realize that Little Red Riding Hood does not know what they know; nonetheless, they expect Little Red Riding Hood to feel what they feel, namely, afraid (Bradmetz & Schneider, 2004; de Rosnay et al., 2004; Harris et al., 1989). When asked where Maxi will look for the chocolate that was moved while Maxi was out of the room, they correctly say that Maxi will look in the original location, but they incorrectly say that Maxi feels sad. It is only at about 6 years of age that children come to understand that because they and others have different knowledge, they and others may also experience different emotions in the same situation.

Theory of Mind Clearly, children have a whole lot to learn about how the mind works—and most of them eventually do. The vast majority of children ultimately come to understand that they and others have minds and that these minds represent the world in different ways. Once children understand these things, they are said to have acquired a **theory of mind**, which is *the understanding that the mind produces representations of the world and that these representations guide behaviour.*

The age at which most children acquire a theory of mind appears to be influenced by a variety of factors, such as the number of siblings the child has, the frequency with which the child engages in pretend play, whether the child has an imaginary companion, the socioeconomic status of the child's family, and even culture (see A World of Difference: That's the Dumbest Thing I Never Heard!). But, of all the factors researchers have studied, language seems to be the most important (Astington & Baird, 2005). Children's language skills are an excellent predictor of how well they perform on false-belief tasks (Happé, 1995). The way caregivers talk to children is also a good predictor of how well children perform on these tasks. Perhaps not surprisingly, children whose caregivers frequently talk about thoughts and feelings tend to be good at understanding beliefs and belief-based emotions. Some psychologists speculate that children benefit from hearing psychological words such as *think, know,* and *want* (Ruffman et al., 2018). Others suggest that children benefit from the grammatically complex sentences that typically contain these psychological words. And still others believe that caregivers who use psychological words are also more effective in getting children to reflect on mental states.

Whatever the explanation, it is clear that language—and especially language about thoughts and feelings—is an important tool for helping children make sense of their own and others' minds (Harris, de Rosnay, & Pons, 2005). This fact also helps explain why deaf children whose parents do not know sign language are slow to acquire a theory of mind (DeVilliers, 2005; Peterson & Siegal, 1999; Peterson et al., 2016; Pyers & Senghas, 2009).

Another group of children who are slow to acquire a theory of mind are those with *autism,* a disorder we'll cover in more depth in the Disorders chapter. Children with autism often have difficulty communicating with other people and making friends, and some psychologists have suggested that this is because they have

JOACHIM LADEFOGED/VII/REDUX

People with autism often have an unusual ability to concentrate on small details, words, and numbers for extended periods of time. Thorkil Sonne (*right*) started a company called Specialisterne.com, which places people who have autism—such as his son Lars (*left*)—at jobs that they can do better than more "neurotypical" people can.

theory of mind The understanding that the mind produces representations of the world and that these representations guide behaviour.

A World of Difference • That's the Dumbest Thing I Never Heard!

Everyone sees the world a bit differently. That's obvious to you. But it isn't obvious to a 2-year-old child, who naturally assumes that her view is everyone else's view as well. As children develop, they acquire a theory of mind, and one component of that theory is the realization that other people may believe things that the child doesn't, and may not believe things that the child does.

But where does that realization come from? Does a lightbulb just switch on at some point, leaving the child permanently illuminated? Piaget didn't think so. He thought children came to this realization in the course of their social interactions, where they inevitably encountered disagreement. A child says, "That dog is mean," and his father replies, "No, he's very nice." A playmate says, "My house is red," and another responds, "You're wrong. It's blue!" All of the disagreement that children hear eventually leads them to understand that different people have different beliefs about the world.

Although being disagreeable is a popular pastime in Western societies, not all cultures appreciate a good argument. For instance, many Eastern cultures encourage respect for one's elders and family harmony, and they encourage people to avoid interpersonal conflict. In such cultures, if a person doesn't have something agreeable to say, they often say nothing at all. Thus, children who grow up in these cultures do not normally hear people challenging each other's beliefs. So how do they come to understand that different people *have* different beliefs?

The answer seems to be: s-l-o-w-l-y! For example, in one study, 77% of Australian preschoolers understood that different people have different beliefs, but only 47% of Iranian preschoolers understood the same (Shahaeian et al., 2011). Were the Iranian children just slow learners? Nope. In fact, they were just as likely as the Australian children to have acquired other components of a theory of mind—for instance, the realization that different people *like* different things—and they were even *more* likely than the Australian children to realize that people know what they see and not what they don't. Iranian preschoolers appear to learn just as fast as Australian preschoolers do, but it takes them a bit longer to understand that people have different beliefs because they are exposed to fewer debates about them. The pattern seen in Australia is also seen in the United States, and the pattern seen in Iran is also seen in China, suggesting that this may be a stable difference between Western and Eastern cultures (Wellman et al., 2006).

In the end, of course, everyone comes to realize that human beings don't always see eye to eye. But people who live in places where they are encouraged to speak their

When parents debate the best way to get a bike into a car, their children learn that people have different beliefs. For example, Mom believes that Dad should shut up, and Dad doesn't. But he will. Probably soon.

minds and air their differences in public seem to figure that out a bit earlier than most. At least that's what research suggests. Do you agree? Well, why not? What's the matter with you anyway?

---

trouble acquiring a theory of mind (Frith, 2003). They find it difficult to understand the inner lives of other people (Dawson et al., 2007; Peterson et al., 2016), are slow to recognize that other people can believe what they don't believe themselves (Baron-Cohen, Leslie, & Frith, 1985; Senju et al., 2009), and have trouble understanding belief-based emotions such as embarrassment and shame (Baron-Cohen, 1991; Heerey, Keltner, & Capps, 2003). Interestingly, children with autism (and other children who have not yet acquired a theory of mind) are not susceptible to the phenomenon of "contagious yawning," which apparently requires that one be able to imagine what the yawner herself is experiencing (Platek et al., 2003; Senju et al., 2007).

Piaget Remixed Cognitive development is a long, strange trip, and Piaget's ideas about it were nothing short of groundbreaking. Few psychologists have had such a profound and enduring impact. But while some of his ideas have held up quite well, in the last few decades psychologists have discovered two general ways in which Piaget got it wrong. First, Piaget thought that children graduated from one stage to another in the same way that they graduated from kindergarten to first grade: A child is in kindergarten *or* first grade, he is never in both, and there is an exact moment of transition to which anyone can point. Modern psychologists see development as a more fluid, continuous, and less step-like progression than Piaget believed it to be. Children who are making the transition between stages may perform more mature behaviours one day and less mature behaviours the next. In a sense, cognitive development is more like the gradual change of seasons than it is like graduation day.

The second thing about which Piaget was mistaken was the ages at which these transitions occur. By and large, they happen *earlier* than he realized (Gopnik, 2012). For example, Piaget suggested that infants had no sense of object permanence because they did not actively search for objects that were moved out of their sight. But when researchers use experimental procedures that allow infants to "show what they know," even 4-month-olds display a sense of object permanence. Piaget also suggested that it takes many years until children can overcome their egocentrism enough to realize that others do not know what they know, but new experimental procedures have detected some evidence of this understanding in 13-month-old infants (Baillargeon et al., 2010). Every year, clever researchers find new ways of testing infants and children, and every year, textbook authors must lower the age at which cognitive milestones are achieved. Don't be too surprised if in the coming years, someone discovers that zygotes can do algebra.

Development is not the step-like progression that Piaget imagined. Children who are making the transition between stages may act more mature one day and less mature the next.

Discovering Our Cultures

Piaget saw the child as a lone scientist who goes out into the world and makes observations, develops theories, and revises those theories in light of disconfirming evidence. But scientists rarely go it alone. Rather, they receive training from more experienced scientists, inherit the theories and methods of their forebears, and seek each other's opinions. According to the Russian psychologist Lev Vygotsky, children do the same thing. Vygotsky was born in 1896—the same year as Piaget—but unlike Piaget, he believed that cognitive development was largely the result of the child's interaction with members of her own culture rather than her interaction with rocks, paper, scissors, and other concrete objects. Vygotsky didn't think it made sense to divide the universe of skills into those that a child has and has not yet acquired. He noted that between the things a child can do and the things a child cannot do lies a *zone of proximal development*, which refers to the range of things children cannot do by themselves but can do with guidance and instruction. For example, most infants cannot open a jar on their own, but they can learn to open a jar if an adult shows them how.

Vygotsky also noted that *cultural tools*, such as language and counting systems, exert a strong influence on cognitive development (Vygotsky, 1978). For instance, in both English and Chinese, the numbers beyond 20 are named by a decade (twenty) that is followed by a digit (one), and their names follow a logical pattern (twenty-one, twenty-two, twenty-three, etc.). In Chinese, the numbers from 11 to 19 are constructed the same way (ten-one, ten-two, ten-three . . .). But in English, the names of the numbers between 11 and 19 either reverse the order of the decade and the digit (sixteen, seventeen) or are just plain arbitrary (eleven, twelve). The difference in the regularity of these two systems makes a big difference to the children who must learn them. The fact that 12 is a 10 plus a 2 is obvious to the Chinese-speaking child, who actually calls the number "ten-two," but not so obvious to the English-speaking child, who calls it "twelve."

In one study, children from many countries were asked to hand an experimenter a certain number of bricks. Some of the bricks were single, and some were glued together in strips of 10. When Asian children were asked to hand the experimenter 26 bricks, they tended to hand over two strips of 10 plus six singles.

As Vygotsky pointed out, children are not lone explorers who discover the world for themselves; rather, they are members of families, communities, and societies that teach them much of what they need to know.

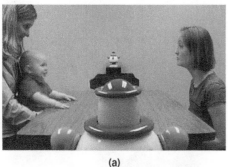

(a)

(b)

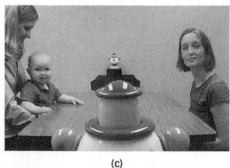

(c)

Figure 11.8

Joint Attention Joint attention allows children to learn from others. When a 12-month-old infant interacts with an adult (a) who then looks at an object (b), the infant will typically look at the same object (c)—but only when the adult's eyes are open (Meltzoff et al., 2009).

Non-Asian children used the clumsier strategy of counting out 26 single bricks (Miura et al., 1994). Results such as these suggest that the regularity of the counting system that children inherit can promote or discourage their discovery of basic mathematical facts (Gordon, 2004; Imbo & LeFevre, 2009).

Human children can take advantage of the accumulated wisdom of their species because unlike most other animals, they have three essential skills that allow them to learn from others (Meltzoff et al., 2009; Striano & Reid, 2006; Whiten, 2017):

1. If an adult turns her head to the left, 3-month old infants and 9-month-old infants will look to the left. But if the adult first closes her eyes and then looks to the left, the younger infant will look to the left, but the older infant will not (Brooks & Meltzoff, 2002). This suggests that younger infants are following the adult's head movements but that older infants are following her gaze. That is, they are trying to see what they think she is seeing (Rossano, Carpenter, & Tomasello, 2012). The ability to focus on what another person is focused on, known as *joint attention,* is a prerequisite for learning what others have to teach us (Sodian & Kristen-Antonow, 2015) (see **FIGURE 11.8**).

2. Infants are natural mimics who often do what they see adults do (Jones, 2007). This tendency is known as *imitation.* Children imitate adults so precisely that they even copy parts of their actions that they know to be pointless, a phenomenon called *overimitation* (Lyons, Young, & Keil, 2007; Simpson & Riggs, 2011). But they don't copy parts of their actions that they know to be wrong. When an 18-month-old sees an adult's hand slip as the adult tries to pull the lid off a jar, the child won't copy the slip but will instead perform the *intended* action of removing the lid (Meltzoff, 1995, 2007; Yu & Kushnir, 2014).

3. An infant who approaches a new toy will often stop and look back to examine her mother's face for cues about whether Mom thinks the toy is or isn't dangerous. The ability to use another person's reactions as information about how they should think about the world is known as *social referencing* (Kim, Walden, & Knieps, 2010; Walden & Ogan, 1988). This is just one of the many instances in which children rely on adults to tell them what they should and shouldn't fear.

Joint attention ("I see what you see"), imitation ("I do what you do"), and social referencing ("I think what you think") are three of the basic abilities that allow infants to learn from other members of their species and to discover things about the world that they might never discover alone (Heyes, 2016).

Build to the Outcomes

1. How does habituation enable researchers to understand what a newborn can or cannot see?

2. What are the cephalocaudal and proximodistal rules?

3. What happens at each of Piaget's stages of cognitive development?

4. What does the false-belief task demonstrate?

5. Which factors determine how quickly and early a child will acquire a theory of mind?

6. What skills allow children to learn from other members of their cultures?

Infancy and Childhood: Bonding and Helping

Infants and children learn how to think about the world, about their minds, and about other minds. But they also learn to form relationships and establish emotional bonds with these other minds, as well as to reason about right and wrong and behave accordingly. Social development and moral development are among the most important projects of infancy and childhood, so let's explore each in turn.

Social Development

When Konrad Lorenz was a child, his neighbour gave him a day-old duckling that soon began to follow Lorenz wherever he went. A few decades later, Lorenz was awarded the Nobel Prize in Physiology for explaining how and why that had happened (Lorenz, 1952). Everyone who had ever raised a duckling already knew that it would follow its mother and assumed that this behaviour was some sort of hardwired instinct. But Lorenz realized that evolution had not designed ducklings to follow their mothers; rather, it had designed them to follow the first noisy moving object they saw upon hatching. In most cases, that object was indeed their mother, but if it just so happened to be a little boy, then the duckling would ignore its mother and follow the boy instead. Ducklings were not prepared to follow their mothers in particular; they were prepared to form a bond.

Becoming Attached

Like ducklings, human infants need adults to survive, and therefore they too come into the world prepared to form a bond. Because they cannot waddle after an adult, they instead do things to make adults waddle after them: They cry, gurgle, coo, and smile, and these signals cause adults to move towards them, pick them up, comfort them, change them, and feed them. At first, newborns will send these signals to any adult within range, but they seem to keep a "mental tally" of how different adults respond to their signals, and at about 6 months they begin to direct those signals towards the adult who responds first, best, fastest, and most often.

That person is known as the *primary caregiver,* and he or she quickly becomes the emotional centre of the infant's universe. Infants feel safe in the primary caregiver's presence and will happily crawl around and explore the environment. If their primary caregiver gets a little too far away, the infant will begin to feel unsafe and will take action to close the gap, either by moving towards the primary caregiver or by crying until the caregiver moves towards them. The *emotional bond with a primary caregiver* is called an **attachment** (Bowlby, 1969, 1973, 1980). This bond is so important that infants who, by unfortunate circumstances, are deprived of the opportunity to form one are at serious risk for a wide range of physical, mental, and emotional impairments (Gillespie & Nemeroff, 2007; O'Connor & Rutter, 2000; Rutter, O'Connor, & the English and Romanian Adoptees Study Team, 2004; Kessler et al., 2008).

Attachment Styles

Infants form attachments, but not all of these attachments are of the same quality (Ainsworth et al., 1978). A common method for measuring the quality of an attachment involves bringing an infant and his or her primary caregiver (usually the mother) to a laboratory room and then staging a series of episodes in which the primary caregiver briefly leaves the room and then returns. Infants tend to react to these episodes in one of four ways, which are known as **attachment styles**, or *characteristic patterns of reacting to the presence and absence of one's primary caregiver* (**FIGURE 11.9**).

Like hatchlings, human infants need to stay close to their mothers to survive. Unlike hatchlings, human infants know how to get their mothers to come to them rather than the other way around.

attachment The emotional bond with a primary caregiver.

attachment styles Characteristic patterns of reacting to the absence and presence of one's primary caregiver.

In a series of classic studies, psychologist Harry Harlow (1958) raised baby rhesus monkeys in isolation and then put them in a cage with two "artificial mothers." One was made of wire and dispensed food while the other was made of cloth and did not. The baby monkeys spent most of their time clinging to the cloth mother, leading Harlow to conclude that even monkeys are "born to bond."

- Infants with a *secure* attachment style may or may not be distressed when their caregiver leaves the room, but they respond positively to her when she returns—either by acknowledging her with a glance or a smile (if the infant was not distressed) or by going to her for calming (if the infant was distressed). The majority of infants in all cultures have a secure attachment style.

- Infants with an *ambivalent* attachment style are distressed when their caregiver leaves the room, but when she returns they respond negatively to her—either by rebuffing her, or by refusing her attempts at calming.

- Infants with an *avoidant* attachment style are not distressed when their caregiver leaves the room, and they don't respond positively or negatively when she returns—they mainly just ignore her.

- Infants with a *disorganized* attachment style show no consistent pattern of response to either their caregiver's absence or return.

What makes infants react in these different ways? A bit of nature and a bit of nurture. Infants are born with a **temperament**, or a *biologically based pattern of attentional and emotional reactivity* (Kagan, 1997; Rothbart & Bates, 2006; Thomas & Chess, 1977). About 40% of infants are *easy babies* who adjust easily to new situations, quickly establish routines, and are generally cheerful and easy to calm; about 10% are *difficult babies* who are slow to adjust to new experiences and are likely to react negatively and intensely to novel stimuli and events; about 15% are *slow-to-warm-up babies* who are somewhat difficult at first but then become easier over time; and the remaining 35% cannot be easily classified (Thomas & Chess, 1977; but see Gartstein et al., 2017). Not only are these differences present at birth, but they are quite stable over time (Baker et al., 2013). For example, difficult babies who react

temperament A biologically based pattern of attentional and emotional reactivity.

Figure 11.9

Attachment Styles How an infant responds when the primary caregiver leaves and returns allows researchers to identify the infant's attachment style. If the infant does not consistently show one of these three patterns, then the infant's attachment style is said to be disorganized.

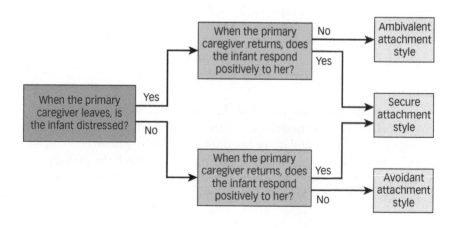

fearfully to novel stimuli—such as sudden movements, loud sounds, or unfamiliar people—tend to become quiet, cautious, and shy adults who avoid unfamiliar people and novel situations (Schwartz et al., 2003). Nature clearly plays a role in how infants react to situations, including the absence and return of their primary caregiver.

But nurture seems to play an even bigger role. How caregivers think, feel, and act has a strong influence on an infant's attachment style. For instance, mothers of securely attached infants tend to be especially sensitive to signs of their child's emotional state, especially good at detecting their infant's "requests" for reassurance, and especially responsive to those requests (Ainsworth et al., 1978; De Wolff & van IJzendoorn, 1997; van IJzendoorn & Sagi, 1999). Mothers of securely attached infants also tend to be "mind-minded," which is to say that they think of their infants as unique individuals with mental and emotional lives, not just as creatures with urgent physical needs (Meins, 2003; Meins et al., 2001; McMahon & Bernier, 2017).

A mother's behaviour is correlated with her infant's attachment style—but is it actually a cause of her infant's attachment style? It appears so. Researchers studied a group of young mothers whose infants were particularly irritable or difficult. When the infants were about 6 months old, half the mothers participated in a training program designed to sensitize them to their infants' emotional signals and to encourage them to be more responsive. A year later, infants whose mothers had received the training were more likely to be securely attached than were infants whose mothers did not (van den Boom, 1994, 1995). Clearly, it takes two to make a bond.

Some parents worry that placing their child in day care may impair the attachment process. But a massive long-term study by the U.S. National Institute for Child Health and Human Development showed that while attachment style is strongly influenced by maternal sensitivity and responsiveness, the amount, stability, or type of day care have little or no influence (Friedman & Boyle, 2008).

The Effects of Attachment Styles

As a result of interactions with their primary caregivers, infants develop *a set of beliefs about the way relationships work,* which psychologists call the infant's **internal working model** (Bretherton & Munholland, 1999). Infants with different attachment styles appear to have different internal working models (see **FIGURE 11.10**). Infants with a secure attachment style seem to be confident that their primary caregivers will respond when they feel insecure, whereas infants with an avoidant attachment style seem to be confident that they won't. Both sets of infants have clear expectations about what will happen when they feel insecure. On the other hand, infants with an ambivalent attachment style do not have a clear expectation: They seem to be uncertain about whether or not their primary caregiver will respond on any particular occasion. Finally, infants with a disorganized attachment style just seem to be confused about their relationships with their primary caregivers, which has led some psychologists to speculate that this style primarily characterizes children who have been abused (Carolson, 1998; Cicchetti & Toth, 1998).

An infant's attachment style, and the internal working model that goes with it, have a long-lasting influence (Waters et al., 2015). For example, adults who were securely attached as infants have greater academic success (Jacobson & Hoffman, 1997), superior cognitive functioning (Bernier et al., 2015), and higher psychological well-being (Madigan et al., 2013). They also have more successful social relationships (McElwain, Booth-LaForce, & Wu, 2011; Schneider, Atkinson, & Tardif, 2001; Simpson, Collins, & Salvatore, 2011; Sroufe, Egeland, & Kruetzer, 1990; Steele et al., 1999; Vondra et al., 2001). One study that tracked participants over two decades showed that 1-year-old infants who are securely attached are less likely to experience negative emotions when trying to resolve major relationship conflicts with their romantic partners at the age of 21 (Simpson et al., 2007). They are also more likely to rebound from conflicts with their romantic partners (Salvatore et al., 2011). The bond we form with that first noisy moving object—the one that most of us call Mom or Dad—is a powerful force that impacts our development for years to come. (See Other Voices: We Know How to Serve First Nations Youth Better—We Just Aren't Doing Better for an illustration of how social welfare policies in Canada are damaging the social development of First Nations youth, contributing to intergenerational trauma and insecure attachment.)

Figure 11.10

Internal Working Models Do infants really have internal working models? It appears they do. Infants stare longer when they see something they don't expect, and securely attached infants will stare longer at a cartoon of a mother ignoring rather than comforting her child. Infants who are not securely attached do just the opposite (Johnson, Dweck, & Chen, 2007).

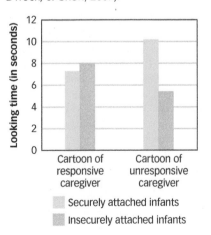

internal working model A set of beliefs about the way relationships work.

We Know How to Serve First Nations Youth Better—We Just Aren't Doing Better

This week, the story of a newborn baby removed from her family in Manitoba added to a litany of reports about the over-representation of First Nations children in child-welfare care. The number and persistence of these stories lead many to believe this is a problem without a solution. But real answers have been on the books for decades—governments just need to implement them.

In 1967, social worker George Caldwell observed that 80 percent of the children placed in residential schools in Saskatchewan were there as child-welfare placements. He called upon Indian Affairs to put more emphasis on services to support families and to ensure services were culturally appropriate.

In the succeeding decades, his recommendations were never properly implemented and a plethora of provincial and federal reports followed, finding the same problem and recommending the same solutions. These reports suffered the same fate as Mr. Caldwell's recommendations: piecemeal government implementation or being flat out ignored.

It has been a year since outgoing Indigenous Services Minister Jane Philpott called the over-representation of First Nations children in child welfare a "humanitarian crisis."

As the Truth and Reconciliation Commission noted in its 2015 report, First Nations children are placed in child-welfare care at 12 times the rate of other children, due largely to poverty, poor housing, parental addictions and mental-health issues. Yet, despite all of the discussion, the public knows very little about First Nations child welfare and what can be done to tackle the heartbreaking pace at which these children and youth are separated from their families. First Nations have always had ways to address child well-being in their communities; however, these systems were displaced and, in some cases, fractured by the imposition of the residential-school system in the late 1800s.

While residential schools slowly began to close in the 1940s, with the last one in Saskatchewan shuttering its doors in 1996, the ones that remained gradually morphed into child-welfare placements.

Meanwhile, the federal government amended the Indian Act in the 1950s to allow "laws of general application," including provincial child welfare laws, to apply on reserves. Services resulting from these laws are federally funded. The amendment created an overlap between residential schools operating as child-welfare placements and the provincial child-welfare system. As a result, social workers who knew little of the trauma of residential schools removed large numbers of First Nations children and placed them, often permanently, with non-Indigenous families in what is now known as the Sixties Scoop.

Beginning in the 1970s, First Nations urgently called on the federal government to create First Nations child-welfare agencies on reserves. And although Canada agreed, the implementation fell far short of perfect.

Provincial and territorial child-welfare laws would be enforced despite the fact they were not tailored to the needs of First Nations children and families, who by this point had suffered generations of colonial trauma. The agencies could only serve on reserve and although the federal government would fund them, it would be at a far lesser level than other children received off-reserve.

Today, there are more than 105 First Nations child-welfare agencies across Canada that serve clients both on- and off-reserve, but the legislative and funding constraints persist. On a positive note, despite the barriers, First Nations children served by these agencies are more likely to be able to stay safely at home than those served by provincial agencies off-reserve.

The on-reserve funding deficit for child welfare is being addressed thanks to the five orders issued by the Canadian Human Rights Tribunal that require the federal government to properly fund the agencies and family-support programs, paying due account to the unique cultures and contexts of First Nations children. While there are persistent concerns with the federal government's compliance with the tribunal's orders, the funding relief is already paying dividends for families who are now able to access basic support services available to other Canadian families.

COURTESY FIRST NATIONS CHILD & FAMILY CARING SOCIETY OF CANADA

Cindy Blackstock is the executive director of the First Nations Child and Family Caring Society of Canada. She is a professor at the School of Social Work at McGill University.

However, federal funding shortfalls on reserve for basics such as water, sanitation, early childhood and education programs continue, undermining the ability of First Nations families to care for their children.

Off-reserve, provincial legislation and funding apply, but few programs answer Mr. Caldwell's call—now more than 50 years old—for culturally based services that target the reasons why First Nations children end up in care at such high rates. The expansion of First Nations agency services off reserve would provide some much-needed assistance, as would bolstering culturally based family supports.

First Nations youth in care have repeatedly called for more programs to promote healthy connections to family and culture, improved supports to address issues stemming from childhood trauma, youth addictions and turnover in service providers, as well as supports so they are not just left on their own when they turn 18. These are basics a compassionate and rich country such as ours should provide without question, but doesn't.

The over-representation of First Nations children in care is a problem with a solution.

There have been numerous reports over the years calling for the same things: First, to ensure child-welfare programs are based on the unique cultures of First Nations with the affirmation of First Nations jurisdiction; secondly, that family supports are put in place to address the reasons why children are at risk; third, to end the shortfalls in child welfare and other services First Nations children need and to provide higher quality care for children and youth who cannot live at home; lastly, to institute culturally based alternative justice approaches to replace or augment the current role of the provincial courts and provide a check system when children are removed.

While we do all of this, we need to ensure child-welfare policy is driven by facts, instead of exceptional cases or social-media exposure of vulnerable children and youth.

More than a decade ago, I sat with children and youth—some of whom were in care—to talk about ethical engagement. They told me we need to be very careful with their stories. Videos and photos of their most tragic moments will endure a lifetime and should only be shared with those in a position to do something to ensure their safety, dignity and well-being—not the public. While public scrutiny of child welfare is needed, it can be done without violating the privacy of children, youth and families.

After more than 30 years of seeing the over-representation of First Nations children and youth in child welfare, I know one thing for sure: Unless the public puts pressure on provincial, territorial and federal governments, the good solutions on the books will not be implemented. We must tell our politicians: literally thousands of children need our help.

Excerpt from "For Indigenous kids' welfare, our government knows better; it just needs to do better," *The Globe and Mail*, January 2019.

Moral Development

Infants can make one distinction quickly and well, and that's the distinction between pleasure and pain. Before their bottoms hit their very first diaper, infants can tell when something feels good or bad and can demonstrate to anyone within earshot that they strongly prefer the former. But over the next few years, they begin to notice that their pleasures ("Throwing food is fun") can be someone else's pain ("Throwing food makes Mom mad"), which is a problem because infants need those other people to survive, and making them mad is not a winning strategy. Infants care what adults think about them (Botto & Rochat, 2018), so they learn to balance their needs with the needs of those around them, and they do this in part by developing a distinction between *right* and *wrong*. How does this happen?

Moral Reasoning

Piaget spent time playing games with children and quizzing them about how they came to know the rules of those games and what they thought should happen to children who broke those rules. By listening carefully to what children said, Piaget concluded that as they develop, children's thinking about right and wrong—that is, their moral reasoning—changes in three ways (Piaget, 1932/1965).

- First, Piaget noticed that children's moral reasoning tends to shift *from realism to relativism*. Very young children regard moral rules as real, inviolable truths about the world. For the young child, the rightness or wrongness of an action is like the height and weight of an object: They have an actual existence in the world and do not depend on what people think or say. That's why young children generally don't believe that a bad action such as hitting someone can ever be good, even if everyone agrees to allow it. But as they mature, children begin to realize that some moral rules are human inventions and that people can agree to adopt them, change them, or abandon them entirely.

- Second, Piaget noticed that children's moral reasoning tends to shift *from prescriptions to principles*. Young children think of moral rules as guidelines for specific actions in specific situations. ("Each child can play with the iPad for 5 minutes and must then pass it to the child sitting to their left.") As they mature, children come to see that these rules are expressions of more general principles, such as fairness and equity, which means that specific rules can be abandoned or modified when they fail to uphold the general principle ("If Jason missed his turn with the iPad, then he should get two turns now.")

According to Piaget, young children do not realize that moral rules can vary across persons and cultures. For example, Hindus consider it immoral to eat cows, but Canadians eat more than 31 million kilograms of beef each year at McDonald's alone!

During World War II, many Albanian Muslims shielded their Jewish neighbours from the Nazis. "There was no government conspiracy; no underground railroad; no organized resistance of any kind. Only individual Albanians, acting alone, to save the lives of people whose lives were in immediate danger," wrote Norman Gershman, who photographed Muslims such as Baba Haxhi Dede Reshat Bardhi (pictured) who saved so many Jewish lives.

- Third, Piaget noticed that children's moral reasoning tends to shift *from outcomes to intentions.* For the young child, an unintentional action that causes great harm ("Reiko accidentally broke the iPad") seems "more wrong" than an intentional action that causes slight harm ("Reiko got mad and broke the pencil") because young children tend to judge the morality of an action by its outcome rather than by the actor's intentions. As they mature, children begin to see that the morality of an action is critically dependent on the actor's state of mind (Cushman et al., 2013; Nobes, Panagiotaki, & Engelhardt, 2017).

The psychologist Lawrence Kohlberg used Piaget's insights as the basis of a detailed theory of the development of moral reasoning (Kohlberg, 1958, 1963, 1986). Kohlberg asked both children and adults how they would resolve a series of "moral dilemmas" (e.g., should a poor husband steal a drug from a pharmacy to save his dying wife?). On the basis of their responses, he concluded that there are three distinct stages of moral development. According to Kohlberg:

- Most children are at the **preconventional stage**, which is *a stage of moral development in which the morality of an action is primarily determined by its consequences for the actor.* A person at this stage might reason: "If the husband steals the drug he could end up in jail, so he shouldn't."
- Most adolescents are at the **conventional stage**, which is *a stage of moral development in which the morality of an action is primarily determined by the extent to which it conforms to social rules.* A person at this stage might reason: "Stealing is against the law, so the husband shouldn't steal the drug."
- Most adults are at the **postconventional stage**, which is *a stage of moral development in which the morality of an action is determined by a set of general principles that reflect core values.* A person at this stage might reason: "Human life is sacred, so the husband should steal the drug."

Beyond Moral Reasoning

Although Kohlberg got many things right, we now know that he also got a few things wrong. First, although the development of moral reasoning does seem to follow the basic trajectory described by his theory, the three stages are not as discrete as Kohlberg thought. For instance, a person might apply preconventional, conventional, and postconventional thinking in different circumstances, which suggests that the person did not "reach a stage" so much as "acquire a skill" that he or she may or may not use at a particular time. Second, Kohlberg's theory does a better job of describing the development of moral reasoning in Western societies than in non-Western societies (McNamara et al., 2019). For example, some non-Western societies value obedience and community more than liberty and individuality; thus, the moral reasoning of people in such societies may *appear* to reflect a conventional devotion to social norms when it actually reflects a postconventional consideration of deeply held ethical principles. Third, moral reasoning turns out to be just a piece of the story of moral development. What does that mean?

Research on moral reasoning portrays people as deliberating judges who use rational analysis—sometimes simple and sometimes sophisticated—to decide what's right and what's wrong. But recent studies show that long before children are capable of deliberation or rational analysis, they display a surprising amount of "moral sense" (Blake, McAuliffe, & Warneken, 2014; Zahn-Waxler et al., 1992). For instance, when 16-month-olds watch a puppet show in which one puppet helps others and another puppet hinders others, they are more likely to reach out and touch the puppet who helped (Hamlin, Wynn, & Bloom, 2007; Margoni & Surian, 2018). Even 3-month-old infants who can't yet reach out will tend to look at the helper longer than at the hinderer (Hamlin, Wynn, & Bloom, 2011; cf. Scarf et al., 2012; Hamlin, 2014). When 16-month-olds watch toys being distributed, they are surprised when one person gets

preconventional stage A stage of moral development in which the morality of an action is primarily determined by its consequences for the actor.

conventional stage A stage of moral development in which the morality of an action is primarily determined by the extent to which it conforms to social rules.

postconventional stage A stage of moral development in which the morality of an action is determined by a set of general principles that reflect core values.

more than another (Bian, Sloan, & Baillargeon, 2018; Sloan et al., 2012; Sommerville et al., 2013), and they prefer those who distribute the toys fairly to those who don't (Geraci & Surian, 2011). One-year-olds will helpfully point towards an object that they can see an adult searching for (Liszkowski et al., 2006), and 2-year-olds smile more after giving someone else a tasty treat than after receiving one themselves (Aknin, Hamlin, & Dunn, 2012). In short, infants and young children seem to have many of the moral sensibilities of adults.

They also seem to have many of the same moral limitations: They favour people who have been kind to them in the past (Paulus, 2016), they favour familiar people over strangers, they favour members of their own group over members of other groups, and so on (Wynn et al., 2018). Studies such as these suggest that morality is not simply the result of reasoning, but also of basic psychological tendencies—such as a sense of fairness or a desire to help and cooperate—whose roots may be part of our evolutionary heritage.

Most people are upset by the suffering of others, and research suggests that even young children have this response, which may be the basis of their emerging morality.

Build to the Outcomes

1. How is attachment assessed?
2. How do caregivers influence an infant's attachment style?
3. According to Piaget, what three shifts characterize moral development?
4. What are Kohlberg's three stages of moral development?
5. What kind of evidence suggests that infants and children have a "moral sense"?

Adolescence: Minding the Gap

Between childhood and adulthood is an extended developmental stage that may not qualify for a hood of its own, but that is clearly distinct from the stages that come before and after. **Adolescence** is *the period of development that begins with the onset of sexual maturity (about 11 to 14 years of age) and lasts until the beginning of adulthood (about 18 to 21 years of age)*. Unlike the transition from embryo to fetus or from infant to child, this transition is abrupt and well-marked. In just 3 or 4 years, the average adolescent gains about 18 kilograms and grows about 25 centimetres. For girls, all this growing starts at about the age of 10 and ends when they reach their full heights at about the age of 16; for boys, it starts and ends about 2 years later.

The beginning of this growth spurt signals the onset of **puberty**, which is *the onset of bodily changes associated with sexual maturity*. These changes involve the **primary sex characteristics**, which are *bodily structures that change at puberty and are directly involved in reproduction* (e.g., girls begin to menstruate and boys begin to ejaculate), as well as the **secondary sex characteristics**, which are *bodily structures that change at puberty but are not directly involved in reproduction* (e.g., girls develop breasts and boys develop facial hair). All of these changes are caused by the increased production of hormones—specifically, estrogen in girls and testosterone in boys.

Just as the body changes during adolescence, so too does the brain. For example, just before puberty there is a marked increase in the growth rate of the tissue that connects different regions of the brain (Thompson et al., 2000). Connections between neurons (synapses) also increase before and during puberty, and then begin to decrease (see **FIGURE 11.11**). The Czech-Canadian researcher Tomáš Paus and his colleagues have demonstrated that the connections between two regions essential for language function—Broca's area in the frontal lobe, and Wernicke's area in the parietal lobe—become stronger and denser between the ages of 4 and 17 (Paus et al., 2005). These connections presumably allow brain areas to share information faster and more efficiently. The most significant neural changes occur in the prefrontal cortex, the part

Learning Outcomes

- Explain why the protraction of adolescence matters.
- Describe the determinants of sexual orientation and behaviour.
- Explain how adolescents are influenced by their peers.

adolescence The period of development that begins with the onset of sexual maturity (about 11 to 14 years of age) and lasts until the beginning of adulthood (about 18 to 21 years of age).

puberty The onset of bodily changes associated with sexual maturity.

primary sex characteristics Bodily structures that change at puberty and are directly involved in reproduction.

secondary sex characteristics Bodily structures that change at puberty but are not directly involved in reproduction.

Adolescents are often described as gawky because different parts of their faces and bodies mature at different rates. But as the actress Rashida Jones can attest, the gawkiness generally clears up.

PAUL BRUINOOGE/PATRICK MCMULLAN VIA GETTY IMAGES

of the brain associated with the ability to regulate emotions and to control attention and behaviour. An infant's brain forms many more new synapses than it actually needs, and by the time children are 2 years old, they have about 15,000 synapses per neuron, which is roughly twice as many as the average adult (Huttenlocher, 1979). This early period of *synaptic proliferation* is followed by a period of *synaptic pruning,* in which the connections that are not frequently used are eliminated. Scientists used to think that proliferation-and-pruning happened only during infancy, but we now know that the prefrontal cortex undergoes a second wave of proliferation just before puberty, and a second wave of pruning during adolescence (Giedd et al., 1999). During this period, the prefrontal cortex also seems to be forming faster, more efficient connections with the rest of the brain (Paus et al., 2005). The adolescent brain seems to be a work in progress.

Figure 11.11

Your Brain on Puberty These graphs show changes in "synaptic density" (which is the number of synapses per unit area) in different regions of the brain. As you can see, density peaks in the frontal and parietal lobes at about age 12 (a, b); in the temporal lobe at about age 16 (c); and in the occipital lobe at different ages for males and females (d).

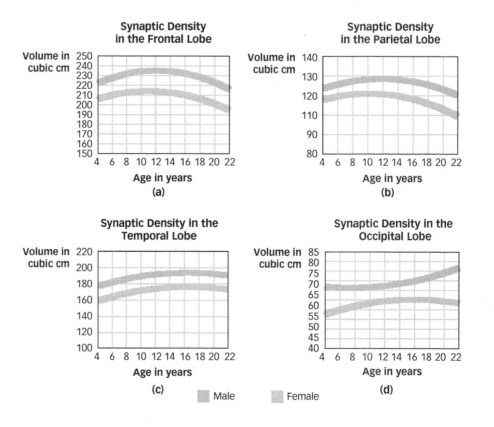

The Protraction of Adolescence

The age at which puberty begins varies across individuals (e.g., people tend to reach puberty at about the same age as their same-sexed parent did) and across ethnic groups (e.g., African American girls tend to reach puberty before European American girls do). It also varies across generations (Malina, Bouchard, & Beunen, 1988; Sawyer et al., 2018). For example, in the 19th century, girls in Scandinavia, the United Kingdom, and the United States tended to have their first menstrual periods when they were about 17 years old, but by 1960, that age had fallen to about 13 years (Patton & Viner, 2007). In newly industrialized countries like China, the age at which girls have their first menstrual period has decreased by almost 5 months every decade for the past 25 years (Song et al., 2014). Similarly, the average age at which American boys show the early signs of puberty has fallen to between 9 and 10 years old (Herman-Giddens et al., 2012).

Puberty is happening much earlier today than it did just a few decades ago. But why? For girls at least, the main reason appears to be diet (Ellis & Garber, 2000). Young women have more body fat today than ever before, and body fat secretes estrogen, which hastens puberty. Some evidence suggests that exposure to environmental toxins that mimic estrogen may also play a role (Buck Louis et al., 2008). Stress appears to be another cause of early puberty in girls (Belsky, 2012; Belsky et al., 2015). Studies show that girls reach puberty earlier if they grow up in unpredictable households with high levels of conflict, in households without a biological father, or if they are victims of early sexual abuse (Greenspan & Deardorff, 2014).

Whatever its causes, early puberty has important psychological consequences. Just two centuries ago, the gap between childhood and adulthood was relatively brief because people became physically mature at roughly the same time that they were ready to accept adult roles in society—that is, to marry and get a job. But today, people typically spend 3 to 10 more years in school, and they take jobs and get married much later than they once did (Fitch & Ruggles, 2000). So while the age at which people become physically adult has gone down, the age at which they take on adult roles and responsibilities has gone up, resulting in a *protracted* period of adolescence. Some researchers argue that in the Western world, adolescence now lasts for a full 15 years (Sawyer et al., 2018).

What are the consequences of protracted adolescence? Adolescence is often characterized as a time of internal turmoil and external recklessness, and some psychologists have speculated that the protraction of adolescence is partly to blame for its sorry reputation (Moffitt, 1993). According to these theorists, adolescents are adults who have temporarily been denied a place in adult society. American teenagers are subjected to 10 times as many restrictions as older adults, and twice as many restrictions as people who serve in the military or incarcerated felons (Epstein, 2007a). As such, they feel especially compelled to do things to protest these restrictions and demonstrate their adulthood, such as smoking, drinking, using drugs, having sex, and committing crimes. In a sense, adolescents are people who have been forced to live in a strange gap between two worlds, and the pathologies of adolescence are a result of this predicament. As one researcher noted, "Isolated from adults and wrongly treated like children, it is no wonder that some teens behave, by adult standards, recklessly or irresponsibly" (Epstein, 2007b).

With that said, the storm and stress of adolescence is not quite as prevalent as HBO might lead us to believe (Steinberg & Morris, 2001). Research suggests that the "moody adolescent" who is a victim of "raging hormones" is largely a myth. Adolescents are no moodier than children (Buchanan, Eccles, & Becker, 1992), and fluctuations in their hormone levels have a very small impact on their moods (Brooks-Gunn, Graber, & Paikoff, 1994). Although they can be more impulsive and susceptible to peer influence than adults (see **FIGURE 11.12**), they are just as capable of making wise decisions based on good information (Steinberg, 2007).

The famous Leipzig Boy's Choir is in trouble. Boys enter the choir at the age of 9 and sing soprano until their voices change. Back in 1723, when Johann Sebastian Bach was the choirmaster, that change happened at about the age of 17. Today, it happens at about the age of 12. As a result, by the time a soprano learns to sing he isn't a soprano anymore. As a result, the choir is struggling.

About 60% of preindustrial societies don't have a word for adolescence because there is no such stage. When a Krobo girl menstruates for the first time, older women take her into seclusion for two weeks and teach her about sex, birth control, and marriage. Afterwards, a public ceremony is held, and the young woman who was regarded as a child just days earlier is thereafter forever regarded as an adult.

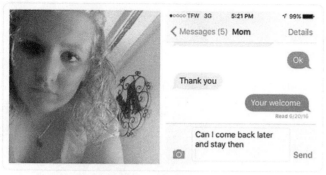

9:18 AM - 30 Jun 2016

Adolescents who experiment with reckless behaviour generally don't become reckless adults—if they live that long. This is the text that 17-year-old Maria Droesch was sending to her mother when she crashed the car she was driving and died. Her mother now hauls the wreckage of Maria's car from town to town to persuade people not to text while driving. In 2017, in a large survey of Ontario high school students, about 1 in 3 students with a driver's license admitted to texting while driving (Boak et al., 2018). Whether texting is to blame or not, about 1 in 12 high-school-aged drivers is involved in a car collision every year.

Canadian adolescents do some fairly questionable stuff—about 10% have tried vaping, about 19% have tried cannabis, and about 42% try alcohol—but few go farther than that (Boak et al., 2017). Those who try these substances generally don't develop problems that impair their academic success or personal relationships (Hughes, Power, & Francis, 1992; Johnston, Bachman, & O'Malley, 1997). Adolescents minor in misbehaviour but they don't major in it, and most of what they do ends up having no long-term consequences (Warren et al., 2016). The fact is that adolescence is not a terribly troubled time, and most adolescents "age out" of whatever troubles they manage to get themselves into (Epstein, 2007b; Martin et al., 2014; Sampson & Laub, 1995).

Emerging Sexuality

Puberty can be a difficult time, but it is especially difficult for girls who reach puberty before the majority of their peers. These early bloomers are at elevated risk for a wide range of negative consequences, from distress and depression to delinquency and disease (Mendle, Ryan, & McKone, 2018; Mendle, Turkheimer, & Emery, 2007). This happens for several reasons (Ge & Natsuaki, 2009). First, early bloomers don't have as much time as their peers do to develop the skills necessary to cope with adolescence (Petersen & Grockett, 1985). And yet, because they look so mature, people expect them to act like adults. In other words, early puberty creates unrealistic expectations that these adolescents may have trouble fulfilling. Second, older men may draw these girls into activities that they are not ready to engage in, from drinking to sex (Ge, Conger, & Elder, 1996). Some research suggests that for girls, the *timing* of puberty has a greater influence on emotional and behavioural problems than does the occurrence of puberty itself (Buchanan et al., 1992).

The timing of puberty does not have such a consistent effect on boys. Some studies suggest that early maturing boys do better than their peers, some suggest they do worse, and some suggest that it makes no difference at all (Ge, Conger, & Elder, 2001). Interestingly, recent research shows that for boys, the *tempo* or speed with which they make the transition from the first to the last stages of puberty may be a better predictor of negative outcomes than is the timing (Mendle et al., 2010; Mendle, 2014).

Sexual Orientation: A Matter of Biology

For some adolescents, puberty is further complicated by the fact that they are attracted to members of the same sex. Why does this make puberty complicated? Almost half of lesbian, gay, bisexual, or transgender (LGBT) youth surveyed in a

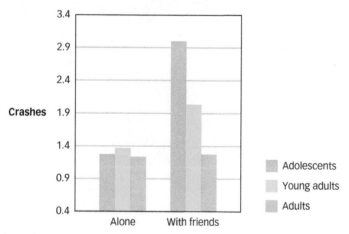

Figure 11.12

How Do Peers Affect Decision Making? Adolescents make better decisions when no one is around! Participants in one study played a video driving game with or without their peers in the room. The presence of peers greatly increased the number of risks taken and crashes experienced by adolescents but had little or no effect on adults (Gardner & Steinberg, 2005).

2011 Canadian research study indicated that they did not feel like they belonged to their school community, compared to only 3.5% of their non-LGBT youth counterparts (Taylor & Peter, 2011). A sense of belonging to a group or community is a key component of social inclusion and is important if the transition to adulthood is to be successful. These adolescents are different from the vast majority of their peers, and as you probably know, adolescents care a whole lot about "fitting in" with their peers (Somerville et al., 2013). Not only are these adolescents a minority, but they are a minority that is often subject to the disdain and disapproval of family, friends, and community. Engaging in sexual activity with members of the same sex is illegal in 75 nations and punishable by death in 11 (Bailey et al., 2016). A majority of Canadians (80%) believe that society should accept homosexuality (Pew Research Center for People & the Press, 2013), and Canada is much more accepting of homosexuality than are many other nations (see **FIGURE 11.13**), but some still disapprove.

The happiness and well-being of adolescents with non-normative sexual orientations are of great concern to mental health professionals. Several provincial legislatures have enacted laws to reduce gender-based violence and acts of homophobia in primary and secondary schools. For example, in Ontario, students at any school can set up clubs called "Gay Straight Alliances." The hope is that these groups will promote tolerance of all people, regardless of sexual orientation.

What determines whether a person's sexuality is primarily oriented towards the same or the opposite sex? For a long time, psychologists thought the answer was upbringing. For example, during the 1940s and 1950s, psychoanalytic theorists suggested that boys who grew up with domineering mothers and cold, distant fathers were less likely to identify with their fathers and therefore more likely to become gay. The only trouble with this theory is that scientific research has failed to identify *any* aspect of parenting that has a significant impact on a child's ultimate sexual orientation. Indeed, researchers have not even been able to find evidence that a parent's sexual orientation has any influence on the sexual orientation of his or her child (Patterson, 2013). Similarly, peers have a measurable influence on both the decision to engage in sexual activity and the desire for romantic relationships, but they have no influence on an adolescent's sexual orientation (Brakefield et al., 2014).

So what *does* determine a person's sexual orientation? Considerable evidence suggests that biology and genetics play major roles. First, same-sex sexual activity appears to predate civilization itself and is observed in almost all mammals (Nash, 2001). Second, sexual orientation varies in the same way that many other heritable traits do. For instance, the fraternal twin of a gay man (with whom he shares 50% of his genes) has a 15% chance of being gay, but the identical twin of a gay man (with whom he shares

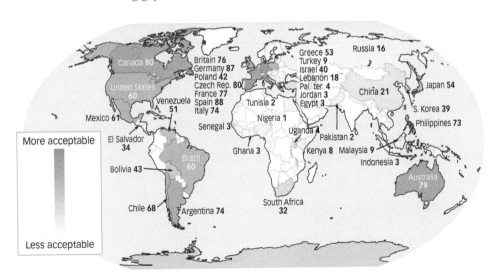

Figure 11.13
Attitudes Towards Homosexuality Diverge Sharply Around the World
A 2013 survey of attitudes of adults from 39 countries revealed huge variability from region to region in the percentage of people who said that homosexuality should be accepted by society (Pew Research Center for People & the Press, 2013).

100% of his genes) has about a 50% chance (Bailey & Pillard, 1991; Gladue, 1994). A similar pattern characterizes women (Bailey et al., 1993). Third, the brains of gay and lesbian people look in some ways like the brains of opposite-sex straight people (Savic & Lindström, 2008). For example, the cerebral hemispheres of straight men and gay women (both of whom are *gynephilic,* or attracted to women) tend to be of different sizes, whereas the hemispheres of straight women and gay men (both of whom are *androphilic,* or attracted to men) tend to be the same size. Some evidence suggests that high levels of androgens in the womb may predispose a fetus—whether male or female—to become an androphilic adult (Ellis & Ames, 1987; Meyer-Bahlberg et al., 1995), while other studies suggest that a mother's immune system may play a role in determining her male child's sexual orientation (Balthazart, 2018)

The fourth striking piece of evidence for the role of biology and genetics in determining sexual orientation is the fact that a child's behaviour is a surprisingly good predictor of his or her adult sexual orientation (Bailey & Zucker, 1995). Most children go through a period in which they adamantly refuse to do anything that is stereotypically associated with the opposite gender (Halim et al., 2014). But a few children are eager to engage in what researchers call "gender nonconforming behaviour," which for boys includes dressing like a girl and playing with dolls, and for girls includes dressing like a boy and engaging in rough play. These behaviours usually emerge by the time the child is 2 to 4 years old, despite the fact that parents typically discourage them (Cohen-Kettenis & Pfäfflin, 2003). As it turns out, children who engage in gender nonconforming behaviour are significantly more likely to become gay, lesbian, or bisexual adults (Li, Kung, & Hines, 2017). Experimental participants who are shown family videos or photos of children are able to predict the child's ultimate sexual orientation with relative accuracy (Rieger et al., 2010; Watts et al., 2018). This does not mean that every little boy who likes mermaid costumes will become a gay man or that every little girl who likes toy trucks will become a lesbian, but it does mean that some signs of adult sexual orientation are observable long before people begin to experience sexual attraction around the age of 10.

Although men and women both *have* a sexual orientation, they seem to *experience* them differently. For example, men's sexual orientations are good predictors of their physiological arousal to erotic stimuli: Straight men are aroused by erotic pictures of women but not of men, and gay men are aroused by erotic pictures of men but not of women. But women's sexual orientations are not such good predictors of their physiological arousal to erotic stimuli. For instance, Queen's University researcher Meredith Chivers has found that straight women are equally aroused by erotic pictures of women and men, and lesbians are only slightly more aroused by erotic pictures of women than of men (Chivers et al., 2004; Chivers, Seto, & Blanchard, 2007). Men's sexual orientations also appear to be more rigid and less fluid than women's. For example, men are more likely than women to report being either exclusively heterosexual or exclusively homosexual, whereas women are more likely than men to report being either "mostly heterosexual" or bisexual (Savin-Williams & Vrangalova, 2013). Women's sexual orientations are also more likely to depend on circumstances and to shift over time (Bailey et al., 2016; Baumeister, 2000). It is important to note that just because people's sexual orientations *can* change does not mean that they can *be* changed: There is no evidence to suggest that "conversion" or "reparative" therapies can transform gay, lesbian, or bisexual people into heterosexuals (American Psychological Association, 2009).

The science of sexual orientation is still young and fraught with conflicting findings, but at least two conclusions are noncontroversial. First, whatever the complete story of its determinants turns out to be, sexual orientation clearly has biological and genetic components. It is not a "lifestyle choice." Second, human sexual orientation is far more complex and diverse than one-word labels like "straight" and "gay" suggest. Physiological arousal, psychological attraction, sexual behaviour, biological sex, and gender identity are different things that combine in seemingly endless variations that defy the simple categorization that language

The Real World | Coming to Terms with Ourselves

		SEX			
		Male		Female	
		Gender		**Gender**	
		Man	Woman	Man	Woman
Sexual Orientation Towards...	Males	Cisgender gay man	Transgender straight woman	Transgender gay man	Cisgender straight woman
	Females	Cisgender straight man	Transgender lesbian	Transgender straight man	Cisgender lesbian
	Males & Females	Cisgender bisexual man	Transgender bisexual woman	Transgender bisexual man	Cisgender bisexual woman

Sexuality involves both the body and the mind. But people's bodies are hidden beneath their clothes, and people's minds are hidden behind their eyes, so the complexity and diversity of sexuality in the real world is all too easy to miss. Understanding it requires understanding three distinct but related concepts.

Sex refers to the bodies we are born with. Most (though not all) human bodies are either male (i.e., they have XY chromosomes and a penis) or female (i.e., they have XX chromosomes and a vagina). *Gender* refers to our identities—how we see ourselves, how we want others to see us, and how it feels to be inside our own skins. Most (though not all) adults identify themselves as men or women. Last, *sexual orientation* refers to the kinds of people to whom we find ourselves attracted. Most (though not all) adults are attracted to people of the opposite sex and gender. These three dimensions don't capture every important aspect of human sexuality, but they do allow us to build a classification scheme that helps us understand and talk to each other. The accompanying table shows the terms that are typically used to refer to people who differ on these dimensions. (For more on this topic, go to http://www.glaad.org /reference/transgender.)

In Latin, the prefix *trans* means "on the other side of," and the prefix *cis* means "on this side of." So the term *transgender* refers to anyone whose gender and sex do not match, and the term *cisgender* refers to anyone whose gender and sex do match. Notice also that the terms

male and *female* refer to a person's sex, whereas the terms *man* and *woman* refer to a person's gender. Most people prefer to be described in terms of their gender rather than their sex, so both transgender and cisgender women typically prefer to be called *she,* and both cisgender and transgender men typically prefer to be called *he.* There are some people who feel that none of these adjectives or pronouns properly describe them. In general, it makes sense to think about other people's sex, gender, and orientation the way they think about it themselves.

It also makes sense to talk about them that way. Over time, descriptors of marginalized groups often take on pejorative connotations. The word *homosexual,* for example, has traditionally been used as a neutral description of people with same-sex orientations, but in some circles it has become an unflattering way to refer to gay and lesbian people. Conversely, terms that were once pejorative are occasionally

reclaimed by the people whom they were initially meant to demean. For example, in some circles, *queer* is now a positive description of anyone who is not cisgender and straight.

The term "two-spirit" is used by some Indigenous people to describe their sexual, gender, and/or spiritual identity, and it refers to someone who identifies as having both a feminine and a masculine spirit.

The vast majority of humans are cisgender and straight, and all these other complicated terms and categories make some of them wistful for simpler times. But the truth is that there never were simpler times—just times in which the complexity of human sexuality was a secret, hidden from our view. In most of North America, those times have now passed, and the full range of our diversity is proudly on display. For those of us who are not in the most populated categories, and for those of us who hope to understand human behaviour scientifically, this is a welcome change.

imparts (see The Real World: Coming to Terms with Ourselves). Indeed, in a survey of American adults, the percentage who identified as gay or lesbian was only slightly larger than the percentage who identified as "something else" or who said they didn't know the answer (Ward et al., 2014). Human beings are sexual creatures who still have a great deal to learn about themselves.

Sexual Behaviour: A Matter of Choice

Sexual orientation may not be a choice, but sexual activity is—and many teenagers choose it. Although the percentage of Canadian high school students who are sexually active has been declining in recent years (see **FIGURE 11.14**), it is still close to a third among 15- to 17-year-olds. Sex is a positive and rewarding experience for many teenagers (Vasilenko, Maas, & Lefkowitz, 2015), but it is a problem for others—especially for those who start having it too early. Teenagers who begin having sex before

Figure 11.14

Teenagers Are Having Less Sex The number of American high school students who are sexually active (which is defined as having had intercourse in the last 3 months) has been dropping over the last decade. The same is probably true in Canada as well (Rotermann, 2012).

ADAPTED FROM THE CENTERS FOR DISEASE CONTROL AND PREVENTION'S "YOUTH RISK BEHAVIOR SURVEY 1991–2017," HTTPS://WWW.CDC.GOV/HEALTHYYOUTH /DATA/YRBS/PDF/TRENDSREPORT.PDF

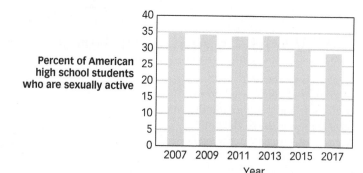

Percent of American high school students who are sexually active

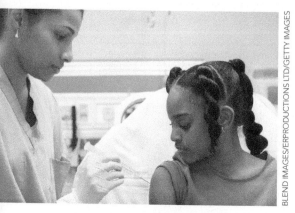

The human papilloma virus is a sexually transmitted infection that can lead to cervical cancer. Luckily, there is a vaccine that can prevent it. Studies show that young women who have been vaccinated do not have sex any earlier than those who have not been vaccinated.

the age of 15 have a lower sense of self-worth and higher rates of anxiety, depression, aggressiveness, and substance abuse (Golden, Furman, & Collibee, 2016).

Contraceptive use is fairly widespread among high school students in Canada. A Canadian survey revealed that 91% of 15- to 17-year-olds who have sex usually used a method of contraception during the year preceding the survey, with 69% of them reporting using condoms (Joubert & Du Mays, 2014). However, barely more than half of sexually active adolescents always use contraceptives when engaging in sexual relations (Amialchuk & Gerhardinger, 2015). Sexually transmitted infections such as chlamydia, gonorrhea, and syphilis are increasingly common in Canada, particularly among young people aged 15 to 29 (Government of Canada, 2019).

What can be done to help teenagers make wise choices about their sexual behaviour? Comprehensive sex education is a powerful tool. Research shows that it leads teens to delay having sex for the first time, decreases the number of partners they have, increases the likelihood they will use condoms and other forms of birth control when they do have sex, and lowers the likelihood that they will get pregnant or get a sexually transmitted infection (Chin et al., 2012; Mueller, Gavin, & Kulkarni, 2008; Satcher, 2001).

From Parents to Peers

Children's views of themselves and their world are tightly tied to the views of their parents, but puberty creates a new set of needs that snip away at those bonds by orienting adolescents towards peers rather than parents. The psychologist Erik Erikson (1959) characterized each stage of life by the major task confronting the individual at that stage. His *stages of psychosocial development* (shown in **TABLE 11.2**) suggest that the major task of adolescence is the development of an adult identity (Becht et al., 2017). Adolescents achieve their identities in different ways: Some explore a variety of identities before finally committing to one of them, while others do little personal exploration and instead adopt the identities prescribed for them by family, religion, or culture (Kroger, 2017; Marcia, 1966, 1993). Regardless of how and when they find them, adolescent identities all have one thing in common: An expanded focus on peers (Roisman et al., 2004).

This shift from parents to peers can be difficult for several reasons. First, children cannot choose their parents, but adolescents can choose their peers and therefore have the power to shape themselves by joining groups that will lead them to develop new values, attitudes, beliefs, and perspectives (Shin & Ryan, 2014). In a sense, adolescents have the opportunity to invent the adults they will soon become, and the responsibility this opportunity entails can be overwhelming (Tarantino et al., 2014). Second, as adolescents strive for greater autonomy, their parents naturally rebel. For instance, parents and adolescents tend to disagree about the age at which certain adult behaviours—such as staying out late or having sex—are permissible, and you don't need a psychologist to tell you which position each party in this conflict tends to hold (Deković, Noom, & Meeus, 1997; Holmbeck & O'Donnell, 1991).

"You're free-range when I say you're free-range."

TABLE 11.2

ERIKSON'S STAGES OF PSYCHOSOCIAL DEVELOPMENT
According to Erikson, at each "stage" of development a "key event" creates a challenge or "crisis" that a person can resolve positively or negatively.

Ages	Key Event	Crisis	Positive Resolution
1. Birth to 12–18 months	Feeding	Trust vs. mistrust	Child develops a belief that the environment can be counted on to meet his or her basic physiological and social needs.
2. 18 months to 3 years	Toilet training	Autonomy vs. shame/doubt	Child learns what he or she can control and develops a sense of free will and a corresponding sense of regret and sorrow for inappropriate use of self-control.
3. 3–6 years	Independence	Initiative vs. guilt	Child learns to begin action, to explore, to imagine, and to feel remorse for actions.
4. 6–12 years	School	Industry vs. inferiority	Child learns to do things well or correctly in comparison to a standard or to others.
5. 12–18 years	Peer relationships	Identity vs. role confusion	Adolescent develops a sense of self in relation to others and to own internal thoughts and desires.
6. 19–40 years	Love relationships	Intimacy vs. isolation	Person develops the ability to give and receive love; begins to make long-term commitment to relationships.
7. 40–65 years	Parenting	Generativity vs. stagnation	Person develops interest in guiding the development of the next generation.
8. 65 to death	Reflection on and acceptance of one's life	Ego integrity vs. despair	Person develops a sense of acceptance of life as it was lived and the importance of the people and relationships that the individual developed over the life span.

Because adolescents and parents often have different ideas about who should control the adolescents' behaviour, their relationships become more conflictive and less close, their interactions become briefer and less frequent (Larson & Richards, 1991), and their parents become less happy about it (Luthar & Ciciolla, 2016). Even so, most adolescents don't have a particularly large number of conflicts with their parents (Chung, Flook, & Fuligni, 2009), and when they do, they tend to be conflicts over relatively minor issues, such as dress and language (which may explain why teenagers argue more with their mothers, who are typically in charge of such issues, than with their fathers; Caspi et al, 1993).

When adolescents pull away from their parents, they move towards their peers. Across a wide range of cultures, historical epochs, and even species, these peer relations evolve in a similar way (Dunphy, 1963; Weisfeld, 1999). Most young adolescents

ADRIAN SHERRATT/ALAMY

Adolescents form same-sex cliques that meet opposite-sex cliques in public places. Eventually, most of them will form mixed-sex cliques, pair off into romantic relationships, get married, have children, and then worry about those kids when they do all the same things.

initially form groups or "cliques" with same-sex peers, many of whom were friends during childhood (Brown, Mory, & Kinney, 1994). Next, male cliques and female cliques begin to meet in public places, such as town squares or shopping malls, and they begin to interact—but only in groups and only in public. After a few years, the older members of these same-sex cliques peel off and form smaller, mixed-sex cliques, which may assemble in private as well as in public, but they usually assemble as a group (Molloy et al., 2014). Finally, couples (typically, but not always, a male and a female) peel off from the small, mixed-sex clique and begin romantic relationships.

Studies show that throughout adolescence, people spend increasing amounts of time with opposite-sex peers while maintaining the amount of time they spend with same-sex peers (Richards et al., 1998), and they accomplish this by spending less time with their parents (Larson & Richards, 1991). Although peers exert considerable influence on adolescents' beliefs and behaviours, this influence generally occurs because adolescents like their peers and want to impress them, and not because the peers exert pressure (Smith, Chein, & Steinberg, 2014; Susman et al., 1994). As they age, adolescents show an increasing tendency to resist whatever peer pressure they do experience (Steinberg & Monahan, 2007). Acceptance by peers is of tremendous importance to adolescents, and those who are rejected by their peers tend to be withdrawn, lonely, and depressed (Pope & Bierman, 1999), in part because adolescents take negative feedback from their peers much more seriously than adults do (Rodman, Powers, & Somerville, 2017). Fortunately for those of us who were seventh-grade nerds, people who are unpopular in early adolescence can become popular in later adolescence as their peers become less rigid and more tolerant (Kinney, 1993).

Build to the Outcomes

1. How does the brain change at puberty?
2. What are the consequences of early puberty?
3. What makes adolescence especially difficult?
4. What determines sexual orientation?

5. What unwise choices do some adolescents make about sex?
6. What are Erikson's stages of psychosocial development?
7. How do family and peer relationships change during adolescence?

Adulthood: Change We Can't Believe In

Learning Outcomes

- Specify the physical and socioemotional changes that occur in adulthood.

- Describe how marriage and children affect adults' happiness.

It takes fewer than 7,000 days for a single-celled zygote to reach **adulthood**, which is *the stage of development that begins around 18 to 21 years and lasts for the remainder of life*. Many of us think of adulthood as the destination to which the process of development finally delivers us, and that once we've arrived, our journey is pretty much complete: Middle-aged adults are just young adults with mortgages, and older adults are just middle-aged adults with wrinkles. But this conception of development is wrong. Although they are a bit more difficult to see, a whole host of physical, cognitive, and emotional changes take place between our first legal beer and our last legal breath.

Changing Abilities

adulthood The stage of development that begins around 18 to 21 years and lasts for the remainder of life.

The early 20s are the peak years for health, stamina, vigour, and prowess, and because our psychology is so closely tied to our biology, these are also the years during which many of our cognitive abilities are at their sharpest. If you are a typical university student, then at this very moment you see farther, hear better, remember more, and weigh less than you ever will again. Make sure to take pictures, because this glorious moment at your physical peak will be over in just a few dozen months. That's right: *months*. Somewhere between the ages of 26 and 30, your body will start the slow process of breaking down in every way. Your muscles will slowly be replaced by fat, your skin will slowly become less elastic, your hair will start to thin and your bones will start to weaken. Your sensory abilities will become less acute and your brain cells will die at an accelerated rate. Other than becoming more resistant to colds and less sensitive to pain, your aging body just won't work as well as your youthful body does.

These physical changes will have measurable psychological consequences (Hartshorne & Germine, 2015; Salthouse, 2006). For instance, as your brain ages, your prefrontal cortex and its associated subcortical connections will deteriorate more quickly than the other areas of your brain (Raz, 2000), and you will experience a noticeable decline in many cognitive tasks that require effort, initiative, or strategy. Your memory will get worse overall, and some kinds will get worse faster than others. For example, you will experience a greater decline in working memory (the ability to hold information "in mind") than in long-term memory (the ability to retrieve information), a greater decline in episodic memory (the ability to remember particular past events) than in semantic memory (the ability to remember general information such as the meanings of words), and a greater decline in retrieval accuracy than in recognition accuracy. Also, your memory will get worse overall, and some kinds will get worse faster than others. Sorry. Did we say that already? As **FIGURE 11.15** shows, performance on most (but not all) cognitive tasks peaks when people are young.

So the bad news is that older adults experience declines in memory and attention. The good news is that they compensate by doing things differently (Bäckman & Dixon, 1992; Park & McDonough, 2013; Salthouse, 1987). Older chess players *remember* chess positions more poorly than younger players do, but they *play* just as well because they learn to search the board more efficiently (Charness, 1981). Older

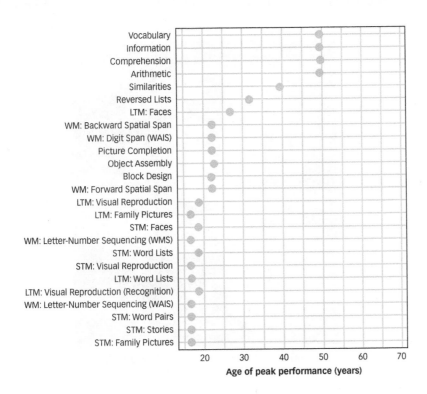

Figure 11.15
Age-Related Changes in Cognitive Performance This chart shows the age of peak performances on a wide variety of cognitive tests, some of which measure working memory (WM), short-term memory (STM), and long-term memory (LTM). DATA FROM HARTSHORNE & GERMINE (2015).

One week before his 58th birthday, US Airways pilot Chesley "Sully" Sullenberger made a perfect emergency landing in New York City's Hudson River and saved the lives of everyone on board. None of the passengers wished they'd had a younger pilot.

typists *react* more slowly than younger typists do, but they *type* just as quickly and accurately because they are better at anticipating the next word in spoken or written text (Salthouse, 1984). Older airline pilots are worse than younger pilots when it comes to remembering a list of nonsense words, but they are just as good at remembering the heading commands that pilots receive from the control tower every flight (Morrow et al., 1994).

The brain itself begins to compensate for the toll that time takes. As you know from the Neuroscience chapter, young brains are highly differentiated—that is, they have different parts that do different things. But as the brain ages, it becomes *de-differentiated* (Lindenberger & Baltes, 1994). For example, regions of the visual cortex that specialize in face and scene perception in younger people are much less specialized in older people (Grady et al., 1992; Park et al., 2004). The brain is like a bunch of specialists who work independently when they are young and able, but who pull together as a team when each specialist gets older and slower (Park & McDonough, 2013). For instance, when young adults try to keep verbal information in working memory, the left prefrontal cortex is more strongly activated than the right, and when they try to keep spatial information in working memory, the right prefrontal cortex is more strongly activated than the left (Smith & Jonides, 1997). But this *bilateral asymmetry* pretty much disappears in older adults, which suggests that the older brain is compensating for the declining abilities of each individual neural structure by calling on its other neural structures to help out (Cabeza, 2002) (see **FIGURE 11.16**).

Figure 11.16

Bilaterality in Older and Younger Brains Across a variety of tasks, young brains show more bilateral asymmetry in their patterns of activation than do older brains. One explanation is that older brains compensate for the declining abilities of one neural structure by calling on other neural structures for help.

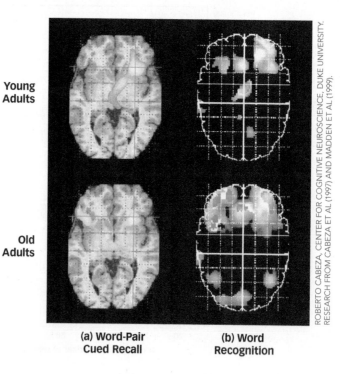

Young Adults

Old Adults

(a) Word-Pair Cued Recall

(b) Word Recognition

The physical machinery breaks down as time passes, and one of the ways in which the brain meets that challenge is by changing its division of labour.

Changing Goals

So one reason that Grandpa can't remember where he left his socks is that his prefrontal cortex doesn't work as well as it used to. But another reason is that the location of socks just isn't the sort of thing that grandpas work hard to remember (Haase, Heckhausen, & Wrosch, 2013). According to *socioemotional selectivity theory* (Carstensen & Turk-Charles, 1994), younger adults are largely oriented towards the acquisition of information that will be useful to them in the future (e.g., reading restaurant reviews), whereas older adults are generally oriented towards information that brings emotional satisfaction in the present (e.g., reading detective novels). Because young people have such long futures, they invest their time attending to, thinking about, and remembering potentially useful information that may fill their informational needs tomorrow. Because older people have much shorter futures, they spend their time attending to, thinking about, and remembering positive information that fills their emotional needs today.

Is There a Cognitive Decline With Age Regardless of Cognitive Stimulation? Go to launchpadworks.com.

For example, older people perform *much* more poorly than younger people when they are asked to remember a series of unpleasant faces, but only *slightly* more poorly when they are asked to remember a series of pleasant faces (Mather & Carstensen, 2003). Whereas younger adults show equal amounts of amygdala activation when they see very pleasant or very unpleasant pictures, older adults show much more activation when they see very pleasant than very unpleasant pictures, suggesting that older adults just aren't attending to information that doesn't make them happy (Mather et al., 2004; Mikels & Shuster, 2016). Indeed, compared with younger adults, older adults are generally better at sustaining positive emotions and curtailing negative ones (Isaacowitz, 2012; Isaacowitz & Blanchard-Fields, 2012; Mather & Carstensen, 2005; Ford et al., 2018). They experience fewer negative emotions in their daily lives (Carstensen et al., 2000; Charles, Reynolds, & Gatz, 2001; Mroczek & Spiro, 2005; Schilling, Wahl, & Wiegering, 2013; Stone et al., 2010), and are more accepting of them when they do (Shallcross et al., 2013). Even their daydreams seem to be more pleasant (Maillet et al, 2018)!

Because they are not concerned about "saving for tomorrow," older people are also more willing than younger people to forego personal financial gain and instead contribute to the public good (Freund & Blanchard-Fields, 2014) (see Hot Science: There's No Time Like the Present). And because they are oriented towards emotionally satisfying rather than profitable experiences, older adults become more selective about their interaction partners, choosing to communicate and spend time with family and a few close friends rather than with a large circle of acquaintances (Chui et al., 2014; David-Barrett et al., 2016). One study monitored a group of people from the 1930s to the 1990s and found that their rate of interaction with acquaintances declined from early to middle adulthood, but their rate of interaction with spouses, parents, and siblings remained stable or increased (Carstensen, 1992; Sander Schupp, & Richter, 2017) (see **FIGURE 11.17**). A study of older adults who ranged in age from 69 to 104 found that the oldest adults had fewer peripheral social partners than the younger adults did, but they had just as many emotionally close partners whom they identified as members of their "inner circle" (Lang & Carstensen, 1994; Zhaoyang et al., 2018). "Let's go meet some new people" isn't something that most 60-year-olds tend to say, but "Let's go hang out with some old friends" is. It is sad but instructive to note that many of these same cognitive and emotional changes can

Figure 11.17
Friends But Not Family Become Less Important As We Age The amount of time people spend with their families doesn't change much over the course of their lives, but the amount of time they spend with friends diminishes dramatically. ADAPTED FROM SANDER, SCHUPP, & RICHTER (2017).

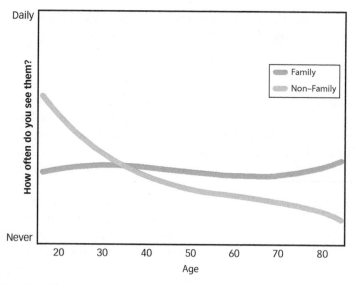

be observed among younger people who have discovered that their futures will be short because of a terminal illness (Carstensen & Fredrickson, 1998; Sullivan-Singh, Stanton, & Low, 2015).

Given all this, you shouldn't be surprised to learn that people find late adulthood to be one of the happiest and most satisfying periods of life. You *shouldn't*

Hot Science | There's No Time Like the Present

It is often said that children and their grandparents are so much alike because they share a common enemy. Kidding aside, there do seem to be ways in which younger and older people are more like each other than either group is like the folks in the middle, and recent research suggests that one of those ways is patience. We all know people who just "have to have it now" and others who are able to wait patiently until later. Researchers can measure these differences using an "intertemporal discounting task." The idea behind the task is simple: Give people a choice between receiving some amount of money today or receiving more money in the future, and then see how *much* more money it takes to get them to wait. The smallest amount required to convince a person to wait is a measure of their patience: The more money they require, the less patient they are.

Richter and Mata (2018) gave this task to more than 1,500 people ranging in age from 18 to 96. Would they rather receive $230 right now or wait and receive $235 in a year? How about $240? How about

$245? The researchers went all the way up to $360 and found something that you probably would have guessed yourself: Adolescents and young adults were less patient than their parents. What you might not have guessed is that elderly people were nearly as impatient as adolescents. Yes, young people were more likely than their parents to say, "Forget about tomorrow, I want it *now*." But so were their grandparents! When the

researchers controlled for variables such as cognitive ability, education, health, and financial security, the results did not change.

Exactly why this happened is anyone's guess, but one possibility is that younger people have not yet learned to think about the future, and older people don't have as much future to think about. Both of them care more about today than tomorrow, and so they eat dessert first.

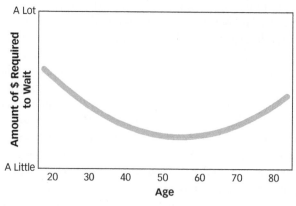

Adolescents and older adults have something in common: They don't like to wait for the things they want!

be surprised, but you probably are because young adults vastly overestimate the problems of aging (Pew Research Center for People & the Press, 2009; Sneed, 2005). Young adults predict that they will be happier at the age of 30 than at the age of 70, but 70-year-olds typically report greater happiness than 30-year-olds do (Lacey, Smith, & Ubel, 2006; but see Twenge, Sherman, & Lyubomirsky, 2016). Not only do older adults report feeling happier, they also report feeling hotter. Yes, you read that right. When people are asked whether they feel good about their physical appearance, they are more likely to say yes if they are over 65 than if they are under 34 (Gallup, 2014)!

Changing Roles

The psychological separation from parents that begins in adolescence usually becomes a physical separation in adulthood. In virtually all human societies, young adults leave home, pair off with another person, and have children of their own. Being in a committed, long-term relationship and parenthood are two of the most significant aspects of adult life. If you are right now a university-age Canadian, then you are likely to get married at around the age of 30 and have approximately 1.7 children because you believe that marriage and children will make you happy. But do they?

In fact, married people do report being somewhat happier than unmarried people—whether those unmarried people are single, widowed, divorced, or cohabiting (Dion, 2005; Johnson & Wu, 2002; Lucas & Dyrenforth, 2005). That's why some researchers consider marriage to be a good investment in one's happiness. But other researchers suggest that married people may be happier simply because happy people are more likely to get married and that marriage may be an effect—not a cause—of happiness (Lucas et al., 2003). The general consensus among scientists seems to be that both of these positions have some merit: Even before marriage, people who will end up married tend to be happier than those who will never marry, but marriage does seem to confer some further happiness benefit, particularly when the members of the couple regard each other as their "best friend" (Helliwell & Grover, 2014). It is worth noting that marriage has become less popular over the past few decades in most Western nations and that in Canada, about 20% of cohabiting couples are not married. In Quebec, where marriage rates have been falling for decades and cohabitation has all the rights and responsibilities of marriage, only 60% of couples who are living together are married. It seems reasonable to assume that the happiness benefit is generally realized by everyone living as though they were married and recognized by their society as such, regardless of whether or not there was a wedding.

Children are another story—not because the happiness boost is longer lasting, but because there isn't one. Research shows that children do not increase their parents' happiness; indeed, more often than not they decrease it (Stanca, 2016). Parents typically report lower marital satisfaction than do nonparents—and the more children they have, the less satisfaction they report (Twenge, Campbell, & Foster, 2003). Marital satisfaction decreases dramatically over the course of a marriage, and the presence of children appears to be responsible for some of that decline, which slows when the children grow up and leave home (Van Laningham, Johnson, & Amato, 2001).

Although the proportion of stay-at-home fathers has increased dramatically in the last 40 years (see **FIGURE 11.18**), mothers still generally do more child care than fathers. It is therefore not surprising that the negative impact of parenthood is stronger for women than for men. Mothers of young children experience role conflicts ("How am I supposed to manage being a full-time lawyer and a full-time mother?") and restrictions of freedom ("I never get to play tennis anymore")

JEFF KRAVITZ/GETTY IMAGES

Young adults overestimate the problems of aging. In the 1965 hit song "My Generation," Pete Townshend, the lead singer of The Who, sang, "Things they do look awfully cold, I hope I die before I get old." At the age of 74, Townshend is still touring and making records, so apparently he's reconsidered his position.

Figure 11.18
In Canada, the percentage of stay-at-home parents who are fathers has increased dramatically over the last 40 years. DATA FROM STATISTICS CANADA, 2018B.

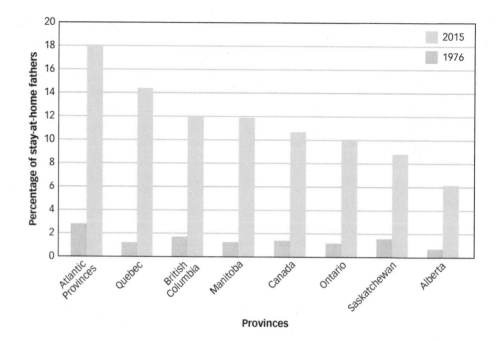

that fathers often side-step. A study that measured the moment-to-moment happiness of American women as they went about their daily activities found that women were less happy when taking care of their children than when eating, exercising, shopping, napping, or watching television—and only slightly happier than when they were doing housework (Kahneman et al., 2004). The relationship between children and happiness seems to change after children leave home: a survey of 200,000 older people in 86 countries has shown that, independent of sex, income, or partnership status, parents of adult children are happier the more children they have (Margolis & Myrskylä, 2011). Clearly, raising children is a challenging job that people find most rewarding when they're not in the middle of doing it.

On average, children lower their parents' happiness. But this effect is stronger in some countries than in others—and in about a third of all countries, children raise their parents' happiness. In 2015, parents in Macedonia (*left*) experienced the largest "happiness penalty" and parents in Montenegro (*right*) experienced the largest "happiness premium" (Stanca, 2016).

Build to the Outcomes

1. What cognitive changes are associated with adulthood?

2. How do adults compensate for their declining abilities?

3. How do people's goals change in adulthood?

4. Why is late adulthood such a happy time for most people?

5. What does research say about the effects of marriage and children on happiness?

Chapter Review

Prenatality: A Womb With a View

- Developmental psychology studies continuity and change across the life span.

- The prenatal stage of development begins when a sperm fertilizes an egg, producing a zygote. The zygote, which contains chromosomes from both the egg and the sperm, develops into an embryo at 2 weeks and then into a fetus at 8 weeks.

- Humans are born with underdeveloped brains, which is essential to the birth process and allows for adaptation to the social and physical environment after birth.

- The fetal environment has important physical and psychological effects. In addition to the food a pregnant woman eats, teratogens—agents that impair fetal development—can affect the fetus. The most common teratogens are tobacco and alcohol.

- The fetus can hear and becomes familiar with its mother's voice.

Infancy and Childhood: Perceiving, Doing, and Thinking

- Infants have a limited range of vision, but they can see and remember objects that appear within it. They learn to control their bodies from the top down and from the centre out.

- Infants slowly develop theories about how the world works. Piaget believed that these theories developed through four stages in which children learn basic facts about the world, such as the fact that objects continue to exist even when they are out of sight and the fact that objects have enduring properties that are not changed by superficial transformations. Children also learn that their minds represent objects; hence objects may not be as they appear, and others may not see them as the child does.

- Hearing language about thoughts and feelings helps children acquire a theory of mind.

- Cognitive development is also driven by social interactions, and infants have several abilities that allow them to learn from others.

Infancy and Childhood: Bonding and Helping

- At a very early age, human beings develop strong emotional ties to their primary caregivers. The quality of these ties—which are indexed by either secure, avoidant, ambivalent, or disorganized attachment styles—is determined both by the caregiver's behaviour and the child's temperament.

- Piaget concluded that children's reasoning about right and wrong develops in three ways. It is initially based on inviolable truths about the world, but expands to include concepts of fairness and equity. As they mature, children begin to consider the actor's intentions as well as the extent to which the action obeys abstract moral principles. Kohlberg outlined a theory of morality that progresses from evaluation of an action's consequences, to determination of whether it obeys social rules, and finally to how it aligns with core values.

- Infants seem to have some "moral sense," such as an affinity towards kind people and a concern with fairness.

Adolescence: Minding the Gap

- Adolescence begins with puberty, the onset of sexual maturity of the human body. Puberty now occurs earlier than ever before, and the entrance of young people into adult society occurs later.

- Adolescents are more likely to do things that are risky or illegal, but they rarely inflict serious or enduring harm on themselves or others.

- Although most people are attracted to members of the opposite sex, some are not, and research suggests that biology and genetics play key roles in determining a person's sexual orientation. Sex education has been shown to reduce risky sexual behaviour.

- As adolescents seek to develop their adult identities, they seek increasing autonomy from their parents and become more peer oriented, forming single-sex cliques, followed by mixed-sex cliques. Finally, they pair off as couples.

Adulthood: Change We Can't Believe In

- Performance on most cognitive tasks peaks when people are in their 20s, and older people develop a variety of strategies to compensate for their cognitive declines.

- Older adults are more oriented towards emotional satisfaction, which influences the way they attend to and remember information, the size and structure of their social networks, and their happiness.

- For most people, adulthood means leaving home, finding a partner, and having children. The responsibilities that parenthood entails present a significant challenge to people's happiness.

Key Concept Quiz

1. Learning begins
   a. in the womb.
   b. at birth.
   c. in the newborn stage.
   d. in infancy.

2. The proximodistal rule states that
   a. motor skills emerge in sequence from the centre to the periphery.
   b. motor skills emerge in sequence from the top to the bottom.
   c. motor skills such as rooting are hard-wired by nature.
   d. simple motor skills disappear as more sophisticated motor skills emerge.

3. According to Piaget, a child's theories about the way the world works is known as _____.
   a. assimilation
   b. accommodation
   c. a schema
   d. habituation

4. Once children understand that human behaviour is guided by mental representations, they are said to have acquired
   a. joint attention.
   b. a theory of mind.
   c. formal operational ability.
   d. egocentrism.

5. When infants in a new situation examine their mother's face for cues about what to do, they are demonstrating an ability known as
   a. joint attention.
   b. social referencing.
   c. imitation.
   d. all of the above.

6. The capacity for attachment may be innate, but the quality of attachment is influenced by
   a. the child's temperament.
   b. the primary caregiver's ability to read the child's emotional state.
   c. the interaction between the child and the primary caregiver.
   d. all of the above.

7. According to Kohlberg, each stage in the development of moral reasoning is characterized by a specific focus. What is the correct sequence of these stages?
   a. focus on consequences, focus on ethical principles, focus on social rules
   b. focus on ethical principles, focus on social rules, focus on consequences
   c. focus on consequences, focus on social rules, focus on ethical principles
   d. focus on social rules, focus on consequences, focus on ethical principles

8. Scientific evidence suggests that _____ play(s) a key role in determining a person's sexual orientation.
   a. personal choices
   b. parenting styles
   c. sibling relationships
   d. biology and genetics

9. Adolescents place the greatest emphasis on relationships with
   a. peers.
   b. parents.
   c. siblings.
   d. nonparental authority figures.

10. Data suggest that, for most people, the last decades of life are
    a. characterized by an increase in negative emotions.
    b. spent attending to the most useful information.
    c. extremely satisfying.
    d. a time during which they begin to interact with a much wider circle of people.

 **LearningCurve** macmillan learning

Don't stop now! Quizzing yourself is a powerful study tool. Go to LaunchPad to access the LearningCurve adaptive quizzing system and your own personalized learning plan. Visit launchpadworks.com.

Key Terms

developmental psychology (p. 426)

germinal stage (p. 427)

embryonic stage (p. 427)

fetal stage (p. 428)

myelination (p. 428)

teratogen (p. 428)

fetal alcohol syndrome (FAS) (p. 428)

infancy (p. 429)

motor development (p. 430)

motor reflexes (p. 430)

cephalocaudal rule (p. 430)

proximodistal rule (p. 431)

cognitive development (p. 432)

sensorimotor stage (p. 432)

schemas (p. 432)

assimilation (p. 432)

accommodation (p. 433)

object permanence (p. 433)

childhood (p. 434)

preoperational stage (p. 434)

concrete operational stage (p. 434)

conservation (p. 435)

formal operational stage (p. 435)

Changing Minds

1. One of your friends recently got married, and she and her husband are planning to have children. You mention to your friend that once this happens she'll have to stop drinking. She scoffs. "They make it sound as though a pregnant woman who drinks alcohol is murdering her baby. Look, my mom drank wine every weekend when she was pregnant with me, and I'm just fine." What is your friend failing to understand about the effects of alcohol on prenatal development? What other teratogens might you tell her about?

2. You are at the grocery store when you spot a crying child in a stroller. The mother picks up the child and cuddles it until it stops crying. A grocery clerk is standing next to you, stocking the shelves. He leans over and says, "Now, that's bad parenting. If you pick up and cuddle a child every time it cries, you're reinforcing the behaviour, and the result will be a very spoiled child." Do you agree? What do studies of attachment suggest about the effects of picking up and holding children when they cry?

3. You and your roommate are watching a movie in which a young man tells his parents that he's gay. The parents react badly and decide that they should send him to a "camp" where he can learn to change his sexual orientation. Your roommate turns to you: "Do you know anything about this? Can people really be changed from gay to straight?" What would you tell your friend about "conversion therapy" and about the factors that determine sexual orientation?

4. One of your cousins has just turned 30 and, to his horror, has discovered a grey hair. "This is the end," he says. "Soon I'll start losing my eyesight, growing new chins, and forgetting how to use a cell phone. Aging is just one long, slow, agonizing decline." What could you tell your cousin to cheer him up? Does everything in life get worse with age?

Answers to Key Concept Quiz

1. a; 2. a; 3. c; 4. b; 5. b; 6. d; 7. c; 8. d; 9. a; 10. c.

LaunchPad features the full e-book of *Psychology*, the LearningCurve adaptive quizzing system, videos, and a variety of activities to boost your learning. Visit LaunchPad at launchpadworks.com.

Personality

GROWING UP, STEFANI JOANNE ANGELINA GERMANOTTA seemed to have personality. As a child, she was said to have shown up at the occasional family gathering naked. As the pop star now known as Lady Gaga, she continues the tradition of being different. Her first albums, *The Fame* and *The Fame Monster,* as well as the fact that she calls her fans "Little Monsters" and herself the "Mother Monster," hinted she might have issues. But she, like most of us, is not one-dimensional. Yes, her style is eccentric (sometimes a dress made of meat, sometimes feathers), but she also is a serious supporter of humanitarian and personal causes, including equality for people who are gay, bisexual, lesbian, or transgender (as in her song "Born This Way"). Lady Gaga is one of a kind. She has personality in an important sense—she has qualities that make her psychologically different from other people.

The singer Lady Gaga in her meat dress at the MTV Video Music Awards (2010) and her feather dress at the premiere of *A Star Is Born* (2018).

THE FORCES THAT CREATE ANY ONE PERSONALITY ARE ALWAYS something of a mystery. Your personality is different from anyone else's and expresses itself pretty consistently across settings—at home, in the classroom, and elsewhere. But how and why do people differ psychologically? By studying many unique individuals, psychologists seek to gather enough information to answer these central questions of personality psychology scientifically.

Personality is *an individual's characteristic style of behaving, thinking, and feeling.* Whether Lady Gaga's quirks are real or merely for publicity, they certainly are identifiably hers and they show her distinct personality. In this chapter, we will explore personality, first by looking at what it is and how it is measured, and then by focusing on each of four main approaches to understanding personality: trait–biological, psychodynamic, humanistic–existential, and social–cognitive. Psychologists have personalities, too (well, *most* of them), so their different approaches, even to the topic of personality, shouldn't be that surprising. At the end of the chapter, we discuss the psychology of self to see how our views of what we are like can shape and define our personality.

Personality: What It Is and How It Is Measured

Learning Outcomes

- Explain how prior and anticipated events explain personality differences.

- Compare personality inventories and projective techniques.

If someone said, "You have no personality," how would you feel? Like a cookie-cutter person, a boring, greyish lump who should go out and get a personality as soon as possible? As a rule, people don't strive for a personality—one seems to develop naturally as we travel through life. As psychologists have tried to understand the process of personality development, they have pondered questions of description (*how* do people differ?), explanation (*why* do people differ?), and the more quantitative question of measurement (how can personality be *assessed*?).

Describing and Explaining Personality

As the first biologists earnestly attempted to classify all plants and animals (whether lichens or ants or fossilized lions), personality psychologists began by labelling and describing different personalities. And just as biology came of age with Darwin's theory of evolution, which *explained* how biological differences among species arose, the maturing study of personality also has developed explanations of the basis for psychological differences among people.

What leads Lady Gaga to all of her entertaining extremes? Many psychologists attempt to study and explain personality differences by thinking about them in terms of *prior events* that may have shaped an individual's personality or *anticipated events* that motivate the person to reveal particular personality characteristics. In a biological prior event, Stefani Germanotta inherited genes from her parents that may have led her to develop into the sort of person who loves putting on a display (not to mention putting on meat and feathers) and stirring up controversy. Researchers interested in events that happen prior to our behaviour study our genes, brains, and other aspects of our biological makeup; they also delve into our subconscious, as well as into our circumstances and interpersonal surroundings. The consideration of *anticipated events* emphasizes the person's own, subjective perspective and often seems intimate and personal in its reflection of the person's inner life (hopes, fears, and aspirations).

Of course, our understanding of how the baby named Stefani Germanotta grew into the adult Lady Gaga (or of the life of any woman or man) also depends on

Donald Trump   Justin Trudeau

Dwayne Johnson   Oprah Winfrey

How would you describe each of these personalities?

personality An individual's characteristic style of behaving, thinking, and feeling.

insights into the interaction between the prior and anticipated events: We need to know how her history may have shaped her motivations.

Measuring Personality

Of all the things psychologists have set out to measure, personality may be one of the toughest. How do you capture the uniqueness of a person? What aspects of people's personalities are important to know about? How should we quantify them? The general personality measures can be classified broadly into personality inventories and projective techniques.

Personality Inventories Rely on Self-Reporting

To learn about an individual's personality, you could follow the person around, clipboard in hand, and record every single thing the person does, says, thinks, and feels (including how long this goes on before the person calls the police). Some observations might involve your own impressions (Day 5: seems to be getting irritable); others would involve objectively observable events that anyone could verify (Day 7: grabbed my pencil and broke it in half, then bit my hand).

Psychologists have figured out ways to obtain objective data on personality without driving their subjects to violence. The most popular technique is **self-report**, *a method in which people provide subjective information about their own thoughts, feelings, or behaviours, typically via questionnaire or interview.* In most self-report measures, respondents are asked to circle a number on a scale indicating the degree to which they endorse that item as being self-descriptive (e.g., reporting on a scale of 0–5 to what extent they believe they are a "worrier") or to indicate whether an item is true or false in describing them. The researcher then combines the answers to get a general sense of the individual's personality with respect to a particular domain. **TABLE 12.1** shows the 10 items from a self-report test of different personality traits (Gosling, Rentfrow, & Swann, 2003). In this case, the respondent is asked to indicate whether each personality trait applies to him or her. To score the measure, simply add up the two items for each of the five traits listed at the bottom of the table.

How is a self-report scale created? The usual strategy is to collect sets of self-descriptive statements that indicate different degrees of a personality characteristic. To measure friendliness, for example, you could ask people to rate their agreement with statements ranging from "I am somewhat friendly" to "I am very outgoing," or even to "I love being around people." Adding up the number of statements the person endorses that indicate friendliness (and subtracting endorsements of those that indicate unfriendliness) yields a measure of the person's self-reported friendliness. Scales based on the content of self-reports have been devised to assess a whole range of personality characteristics, all the way from general tendencies such as overall happiness (Lyubomirsky, 2008) to specific ones such as responding rapidly to insults (Swann & Rentfrow, 2001) or complaining about poor service (Lerman, 2006).

One of the most commonly used personality tests is the **Minnesota Multiphasic Personality Inventory (MMPI)**, *a well-researched clinical questionnaire used to assess personality and psychological problems.* The MMPI was developed in 1939 and has been revised several times over the years, leading up to the current version, the MMPI–2–RF (restructured form) (Ben-Porath & Tellegen, 2008). The MMPI–2–RF consists of 338 self-descriptive statements to which the respondent answers "true," "false," or "cannot say." The MMPI–2–RF measures a wide range of psychological constructs: clinical problems (e.g., antisocial behaviour, thought dysfunction), somatic problems (e.g., head pain, cognitive complaints), internalizing problems (e.g., anxiety, self-doubt), externalizing problems

---

TABLE 12.1

TEN-ITEM PERSONALITY INVENTORY (TIPI)

Here are a number of personality traits that may or may not apply to you. Please write a number next to each statement to indicate the extent to which *you agree or disagree with that statement*. You should rate the extent to which the pair of traits applies to you, even if one characteristic applies more strongly than the other.

1 = Disagree strongly
2 = Disagree moderately
3 = Disagree a little
4 = Neither agree nor disagree
5 = Agree a little
6 = Agree moderately
7 = Agree strongly

I see myself as:

1. ____ Extraverted, enthusiastic
2. ____ Critical, quarrelsome
3. ____ Dependable, self-disciplined
4. ____ Anxious, easily upset
5. ____ Open to new experiences, complex
6. ____ Reserved, quiet
7. ____ Sympathetic, warm
8. ____ Disorganized, careless
9. ____ Calm, emotionally stable
10. ____ Conventional, uncreative

TIPI scale scoring (R = reverse-scored items): Extraversion (1, 6R); Agreeableness (2R, 7); Conscientiousness (3, 8R); Emotional Stability (4R, 9); Openness to Experience (5, 10R).

Information from Gosling, Rentfrow, & Swann, 2003.

Personality inventories ask people to report what traits they possess. Think about how you would rate yourself according to the items in Table 12.1. Can we rely on people to accurately report on their personality?

self-report A method in which people provide subjective information about their own thoughts, feelings, or behaviours, typically via questionnaire or interview.

Minnesota Multiphasic Personality Inventory (MMPI) A well-researched clinical questionnaire used to assess personality and psychological problems.

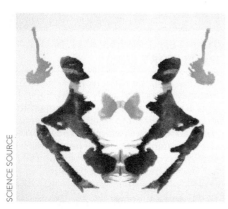

Figure 12.1

Sample Rorschach Inkblot Test takers are shown a card such as this sample and asked, "What might this be?" What they perceive, where they see it, and why they believe it looks that way are assumed to reflect unconscious aspects of their personality.

projective tests Tests designed to reveal inner aspects of individuals' personalities by analysis of their responses to a standard series of ambiguous stimuli.

Rorschach Inkblot Test A projective technique in which respondents' inner thoughts and feelings are believed to be revealed by analysis of their responses to a set of unstructured inkblots.

Thematic Apperception Test (TAT) A projective technique in which respondents' underlying motives, concerns, and the way they see the social world are believed to be revealed through analysis of the stories they make up about ambiguous pictures of people.

(e.g., aggression, substance abuse), and interpersonal problems (e.g., family problems, avoidance). The MMPI–2–RF also includes *validity scales* that assess a person's attitudes towards test taking and any tendency to try to distort the results by faking answers.

Personality inventories such as the MMPI–2–RF are easy to administer: All that is needed is the test and a pencil (or a computer-based version). The respondent's scores are then calculated and compared with the average ratings of thousands of other test takers. Because no human interpretation of the responses is needed (i.e., "true" means true, "false" means false, and so on), any potential biases of the person giving the test are minimized. Of course, an accurate measurement of personality will occur only if people provide accurate responses. Although self-report test results are easy to obtain, critics of this approach highlight several limitations. One problem is that many people have a tendency to respond in a socially desirable way, such that they underreport things that are unflattering or embarrassing. Perhaps even more problematic is that there are many things we don't know about ourselves and are thus unable to report them! Studies show that people often are inaccurate in their self-report about what they have experienced in the past, what factors motivate their behaviours in the present, or how they will feel or behave in the future (Wilson, 2009).

Projective Techniques Rely on Analysis of Ambiguous Information

A second, somewhat controversial, class of tools for evaluating personality, known as **projective tests**, are designed to circumvent the limitations of self-report just described. These tests are *designed to reveal inner aspects of individuals' personalities by analysis of their responses to a standard series of ambiguous stimuli.* The developers of projective tests assume that people will project personality factors that are below awareness—wishes, concerns, impulses, and ways of seeing the world—onto the ambiguous stimuli and will not censor these responses.

Probably the best known of these tests is the **Rorschach Inkblot Test**, *a projective technique in which respondents' inner thoughts and feelings are believed to be revealed by analysis of their responses to a set of unstructured inkblots.* An example inkblot is shown in **FIGURE 12.1**. Responses are scored according to complicated systems (derived in part from research involving people with psychological disorders) that classify what people see (Exner, 1993; Rapaport, 1946). For instance, most people who look at Figure 12.1 report seeing birds or people. Someone who reports seeing something very unusual (e.g., "I see two purple tigers eating a velvet cheeseburger") may be experiencing thoughts and feelings that are very different from those of most other people.

The **Thematic Apperception Test (TAT)** is *a projective technique in which respondents' underlying motives and concerns and the way they see the social world are believed to be revealed through analysis of the stories they make up about ambiguous pictures of people.* To get a sense of the test, look at **FIGURE 12.2**. The test administrator shows the respondent the card and asks him or her to tell a story about the picture, asking questions such as: Who is the woman shown on the card? What is happening? What led her to this moment? What will happen next? Many of the TAT drawings tend to elicit a consistent set of themes, such as successes and failures, competition and jealousy, conflict with parents and siblings, feelings about intimate relationships, aggression, and sexuality. Different people tell very different stories about the images. In creating the stories, the respondent is thought to identify with the main characters and to project his or her view of others and the world onto the other details in the drawing. Thus, any details that are not obviously drawn from the picture are believed to be projected onto the story from the respondent's own desires and internal conflicts.

The value of projective tests is debated by psychologists. Although they continue to be used by practicing clinicians, critics argue that tests such as the Rorschach and the TAT are open to the biases of the examiner. A TAT story may *seem* revealing; however, the examiner must always add an interpretation (was this about the respondent's actual father, about his own concerns about his academic failures, or about trying to be funny or provocative?), and that interpretation could well be the scorer's *own* projection into the mind of the test taker. Thus, despite the rich picture of a personality and the insights into an individual's motives that these tests may appear to offer, we should understand projective tests primarily as a way in which a psychologist can try to get to better know someone personally and intuitively (McClelland et al., 1953). When measured by rigorous scientific criteria, projective tests such as the TAT and the Rorschach have not been found to be reliable or valid in predicting behaviour (Lilienfeld, Lynn, & Lohr, 2003).

Methods Using Technology

Newer personality measurement methods are moving beyond both self-report inventories and projective tests (Robins, Fraley, & Krueger, 2007). High-tech methods such as wireless communication, real-time computer analysis, and automated behaviour identification open the door to personality measurements that are leaps beyond following the person around with a clipboard—and can lead to surprising findings. The stereotype that women are more talkative than men, for example, was challenged by research that involved 396 university students in the United States and Mexico who each spent several days wearing an EAR (electronically activated recorder) that captured random snippets of their talk (Mehl et al., 2007). The result? Women and men were *equally* talkative, each averaging about 16,000 words per day. The advanced measurement of how people differ (and how they do not) is a key step in understanding personality.

Psychologists are also using new forms of social media to better understand personality traits and how people express themselves in different ways. An important advantage of this approach, as with the EAR findings, is that it allows psychologists to study people as they actually behave out in the world while interacting with others (as opposed to in the lab under experimental conditions). For example, one study analyzed more than 700 million words and phrases that 75,000 people posted on their Facebook pages and compared them to the results from personality tests given to the same people (Schwartz et al., 2013). The results revealed significant differences in how males and females express themselves, as well as differences by age and personality. For instance, females use more words about emotions, whereas males use more words about objects and more swear words. People who posted about going out and partying scored high on extraversion; people who posted about being "sick of" things scored high on neuroticism; and people who posted about computers and Pokémon cards scored high on introversion. As the world creates newer forms of communicating, psychologists benefit by having newer ways of studying personality.

Figure 12.2

Sample Tat Card Test takers are shown cards that display ambiguous scenes such as the one shown in this sample and are asked to tell a story about what is happening in the picture. The main themes of the story, the thoughts and feelings of the characters, and how the story develops and resolves are considered useful indices of unconscious aspects of an individual's personality (Murray, 1943).

The EAR (electronically activated recorder) sampled conversations of hundreds of participants and found that women and men are equally talkative (Mehl et al., 2007).

Build to the Outcomes

1. What does it mean to say that personality is in the eye of the beholder?

2. Compare the reliability of personality inventories and projective tests.

3. What is the advantage of measurements taken with the EAR and other new technologies?

The Trait Approach: Identifying Patterns of Behaviour

Imagine writing a story about the people you know. To capture their special qualities, you might describe their traits: Keesha is *friendly, aggressive,* and *domineering;* Seth is *flaky, humorous,* and *superficial.* With a thesaurus and a free afternoon, you might even be able to describe Amir as *perspicacious, flagitious,* and *callipygian.* The trait approach to personality uses such trait terms to characterize differences among individuals. In attempting to create manageable and meaningful sets of descriptors, trait theorists face two significant challenges: narrowing down an almost infinite set of adjectives and answering the more basic question of why people have particular traits and whether those traits arise from biological or hereditary foundations.

Traits as Behavioural Dispositions and Motives

One way to think about personality is as a combination of traits. This was the approach of Gordon Allport (1937), one of the first trait theorists, who believed people could be described in terms of traits just as an object could be described in terms of its properties. He saw a **trait** as *a relatively stable disposition to behave in a particular and consistent way.* For example, a person who keeps his books organized alphabetically in bookshelves, hangs his clothing neatly in the closet, knows the schedule for the local bus, keeps a clear agenda in a smartphone or daily planner, and lists birthdays of friends and family in his calendar can be said to have the trait of *orderliness.* This trait consistently manifests itself in a variety of settings.

The orderliness trait *describes* a person but doesn't *explain* his or her behaviour. Why does the person behave in this way? A trait might provide an explanation for behaviour in two basic ways: The trait may be a preexisting disposition of the person that causes the person's behaviour, or it may be a motivation that guides the person's behaviour. Allport saw traits as preexisting dispositions, causes of behaviour that reliably trigger that behaviour. The person's orderliness, for example, is an inner property of the person that will cause the person to straighten things up and be tidy in a wide array of situations. Other personality theorists, such as Henry Murray (the creator of the TAT), suggested instead that traits reflect motives. Just as a hunger motive might explain someone's many trips to the snack bar, a need for orderliness might explain the neat closet, organized calendar, and familiarity with the bus schedule (Murray & Kluckhohn, 1953). Researchers examining traits as causes have used personality inventories to measure them, whereas those examining traits as motives have more often used projective tests.

Researchers have described and measured hundreds of different personality traits over the past several decades. Back in the late 1940s, in the wake of World War II, psychologists were very interested in right-wing *authoritarianism,* the tendency towards political conservatism, obedience to authority, and conformity. At that time, researchers were trying to understand what had made people support the rise of Nazi Germany and fascism (Adorno et al., 1950). Although research on the personality traits that lead to authoritarianism continues (Womick et al., 2019), the topic became less focal for researchers once World War II receded into history. Other traits that have come into vogue over the years include cognitive complexity, defensiveness, sensation seeking, and optimism. Like television shows and hairstyles, fashions in trait dimensions come and go over time.

SASHA MORDOVETS/GETTY IMAGES

By many accounts, Bashar al-Assad of Syria is a despotic ruler who imprisons, tortures, and kills those who oppose him. Why would anyone want to be a follower of such a dictator? The study of the authoritarian personality was inspired by the idea that some people might follow most anyone because their personalities make them adhere to hierarchies of authority, submitting to those above them and dominating those below them.

trait A relatively stable disposition to behave in a particular and consistent way.

The Search for Core Traits

Picking a fashionable trait and studying it in depth doesn't get us very far in the search for the core of human character: the basic set of traits that defines how humans differ from each other. People may differ strongly in their choice of Coke versus Pepsi, or dogs versus cats, but are these differences important? Researchers have used several different approaches in an effort to discover the core personality traits.

Early Research Focused on Adjectives That Describe Personality

The study of core traits began with an exploration of how personality is represented in the store of wisdom we call *language*. Generation after generation, people have described people with words, so early psychologists proposed that core traits could be discerned by finding the main themes in all the adjectives used to describe personality. In one such analysis, a painstaking count of relevant words in a dictionary of English resulted in a list of more than 18,000 potential traits (Allport & Odbert, 1936)! Attempts to narrow down the list to a more manageable set depend on the idea that traits might be related in a hierarchical pattern (see **FIGURE 12.3**), with more general or abstract traits at higher levels than more specific or concrete traits. Perhaps the more abstract traits represent the core of personality.

To identify this core, researchers have used the computational procedure called *factor analysis*, described in the Intelligence chapter, which sorts trait terms or self-descriptions into a small number of underlying dimensions, or *factors*, based on how people use the traits to rate themselves. In a typical study using factor analysis, hundreds of people rate themselves on hundreds of adjectives, indicating how accurately each one describes their personality. The researcher then performs calculations to determine similarities in the raters' usage, such as whether people who describe themselves as *ambitious* also describe themselves as *active* but not *laid-back* or *contented*. Factor analysis can also reveal

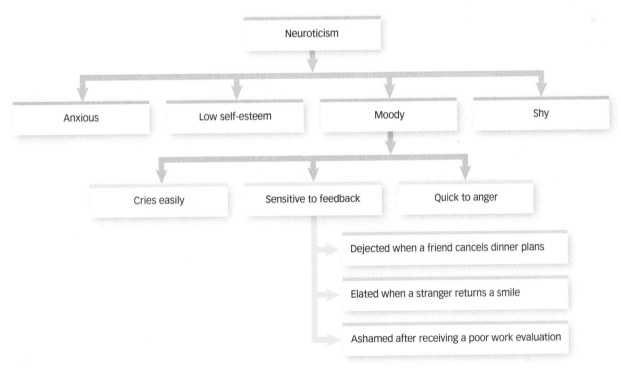

Figure 12.3

Hierarchical Structure of Traits Traits may be organized in a hierarchy in which many specific behavioural tendencies are associated with a higher-order trait (Eysenck, 1990).

which adjectives are unrelated. For example, if people who describe themselves as *ambitious* are neither more nor less likely to describe themselves as *creative* or *innovative,* the factor analysis would reveal that *ambitiousness* and *creativity/innovativeness* represent different factors. Each factor is typically presented as a continuum, ranging from one extreme trait (such as *ambitious*) to its opposite (in this case, *laid-back*).

Different factor analysis techniques have yielded different views of personality structure. Cattell (1950) proposed a 16-factor theory of personality (way down from 18,000, but still a lot), whereas others proposed theories with far fewer basic dimensions (John, Naumann, & Soto, 2008). Hans Eysenck (1967) simplified things nicely with a model of personality with only two major traits (although he later expanded it to three). Eysenck's two-factor analysis identified one dimension that distinguished people who are sociable and active (extraverts) from those who are quiet and introspective (introverts). His analysis also identified a second dimension ranging from the tendency to be very neurotic or emotionally unstable to the tendency to be more emotionally stable. He believed that many behavioural tendencies could be understood in terms of their relation to the core traits of extraversion and neuroticism. The third factor he proposed was psychoticism, which refers to the extent to which a person is impulsive or hostile. (Note that nowadays, the term *psychotic* refers to an abnormal mental state marked by detachment from reality. This is discussed further in the Disorders chapter.)

A Consensus Is Reached: The Big Five Dimensions of Personality

Today, most researchers agree that personality is best captured by 5 factors rather than 2, 3, 16, or 18,000 (Denissen et al., 2019; John & Srivastava, 1999). The **Big Five**, as they are affectionately called, are *the traits of the five-factor personality model: openness to experience, conscientiousness, extraversion, agreeableness, and neuroticism* (see **TABLE 12.2**) (remember them by the initials O.C.E.A.N.). The five-factor model, which overlaps with the pioneering work of Cattell and Eysenck, is now widely preferred for several reasons. First, modern factor analysis techniques confirm that this set of five factors strikes the right balance between accounting for as much variation in personality as possible while avoiding overlapping traits. Second, in a large number of studies using different kinds of data (people's descriptions of their own personalities, other people's descriptions of their personalities, interviewer checklists, and behavioural observation), the same five factors have emerged. Third, and perhaps most important, the basic five-factor structure seems to show up across a wide range of participants, including children, adults in other cultures, and even among those who use other languages, suggesting that the Big Five may be universal (Denissen et al., 2019).

The reality of these traits has been clearly established in research showing that self-reports on the Big Five are associated with predictable patterns of behaviour and social outcomes. People identified as high in extraversion, for example, tend to spend time with lots of other people and are more likely than introverts to look people in the eye. People high in conscientiousness generally perform well at work and tend to live longer. People low on conscientiousness and low in agreeableness are more likely than average to be juvenile delinquents (John & Srivastava, 1999). It turns out that the Big Five personality traits also predict people's online behaviour on social networking sites such as Instagram (see Hot Science: Personality on the Surface).

Big Five The traits of the five-factor model: openness to experience, conscientiousness, extraversion, agreeableness, and neuroticism.

TABLE 12.2		
THE BIG FIVE FACTOR MODEL		
	High on trait . . . Low on trait	
Openness to experience	imaginative	down-to-earth
	variety	routine
	independent	conforming
Conscientiousness	organized	disorganized
	careful	careless
	self-disciplined	weak-willed
Extraversion	social	retiring
	fun loving	sober
	affectionate	reserved
Agreeableness	softhearted	ruthless
	trusting	suspicious
	helpful	uncooperative
Neuroticism	worried	calm
	insecure	secure
	self-pitying	self-satisfied

Hot Science | **Personality on the Surface**

When you judge someone as friend or foe, interesting or boring, or as a potential life partner, how do you do it? It's nice to think that your impressions of personality are based on solid foundations—something deep. You wouldn't judge personality based on something as shallow as someone's looks, would you? You wouldn't form an impression of them from looking at what pops up on their Instagram or Twitter feed, would you? These criteria may seem to be flimsy bases for understanding personality, but it turns out that some valid personality judgements can be made from exactly such superficial cues. And in certain cases, such judgements are remarkably accurate.

It turns out that you *can* get some accurate information about a book by judging its cover. Researchers are increasingly using advances in computer science to study people's *digital footprints*—or the electronic information that they post online about themselves, including their written posts, photos, and videos—and examining the extent to which such information can tell us about people's personalities. It turns out that digital footprints can tell us quite a bit. One recent meta-analysis examined data from 14 different studies showing that the content of a person's social media posts (e.g., Instagram, Twitter, Facebook) correlate pretty well (.29 to .40) with self-reported ratings of Big Five personality traits (Azucar, Marengo, & Settanni, 2018). The signs of personality that appear on the surface may be more than skin deep.

Beyond social media use, studies of personality also have shown that digital and social behaviour correlates with personality in expected ways. For instance, analysis of smartphone data reveals that those who score high on extraversion and agreeableness spend more time with others (Wilt & Revelle, 2019). Extraverts also spend more time messaging friends via apps such as WhatsApp, whereas people high on conscientiousness spend much less time messaging (Montag et al., 2015). We can hope that those conscientious people are using the time they save to do other important things, such as their assigned Intro Psych reading.

They say you can't judge a book by its cover, but some new research suggests you can judge a person by his (or her) Instagram feed.

Research on the Big Five indicates the rather interesting finding that people's personalities tend to remain fairly stable through their lifetime: Scores at one time in life correlate strongly with scores at later dates, even decades later (Caspi, Roberts, & Shiner, 2005). William James offered the opinion that "in most of us, by the age of thirty, the character has set like plaster, and will never soften again" (James, 1890, p. 121), but this turns out to be too strong a view. Some variability is typical in childhood, and, though there is less in adolescence, some personality change can even occur in adulthood for some people (Srivastava et al., 2003).

In general, people become slightly more conscientious in their 20s (got to keep that job!) and a bit more agreeable in their 30s (got to keep those friends!). Neuroticism decreases with age, but only among women (Srivastava et al., 2003). So enjoy the personality you have now, because it may be changing soon.

DATA VISUALIZATION

Does Personality Remain Stable over Time? Go to launchpadworks.com.

Traits as Biological Building Blocks

Can we explain *why* a person has a stable set of personality traits? Many trait theorists have argued that unchangeable brain and biological processes produce the remarkable stability of traits over the life span. Allport viewed traits as characteristics of the brain that influence the way people respond to their environment. And, as you will see, Eysenck searched for a connection between his trait dimensions and specific individual differences in the workings of the brain.

Brain damage certainly can produce personality change, as the classic case of Phineas Gage so vividly demonstrates (see the Neuroscience and Behaviour chapter). You may recall that after the blasting accident that blew a steel rod through his frontal lobes, Gage showed a dramatic loss of social appropriateness and conscientiousness (Damasio, 1994). In fact, when someone experiences a profound change in personality, testing often reveals the presence of such brain pathologies as Alzheimer's disease, stroke, or brain tumour (Boyle, 2018). The administration of pharmaceutical treatments that change brain chemistry can also trigger personality changes, such as making people somewhat more extraverted and less neurotic (Bagby et al., 1999).

Genes, Traits, and Personality

Some of the most compelling evidence for the importance of biological factors in personality comes from the domain of behavioural genetics. Like researchers studying genetic influences on intelligence (see the Intelligence chapter), personality psychologists have looked at correlations between the traits in monozygotic (or identical) twins, who share the same genes, and dizygotic (or fraternal) twins, who on average share only half of their genes. Simply put, the more genes you have in common with someone, the more similar your personalities are likely to be. Genes seem to influence most personality traits, and current estimates, based on a recent study of more than 100,000 participants, place the average genetic component of personality at about .40 (Vukasović & Bratko, 2015). These heritability coefficients, as you learned in the Intelligence chapter, indicate that roughly 40% of the variability among individuals results from genetic factors, with the number appearing fairly stable across personality domains (see **TABLE 12.3**). Of course, genetic factors do not account for everything; the remaining 60% of the variability in personality remains to be explained by differences in life experiences and other factors.

Twin Studies Underscore the Importance of Genetics

Studies of twins suggest that the extent to which the Big Five traits derive from genetic differences ranges from .44 to .54 (Vukasović & Bratko, 2015). As in the study of intelligence, potential confounding factors must be ruled out to ensure that effects are truly due to genetics and not to environmental experiences. Are identical twins treated more similarly, and do they have a greater *shared environment,* than fraternal twins do? As children, were they dressed in the same snappy outfits and placed on the same competitive dance teams? Could this somehow have produced similarities in their personalities? Studies of identical twins reared far apart in adoptive families—an experience that pretty much eliminates the potential effect of shared environmental factors—suggest that shared environments have little impact: Reared-apart identical twins end up just as similar in personality as those who grow up together (McGue & Bouchard, 1998; Tellegen et al., 1988).

Indeed, one provocative related finding is that such shared environmental factors as parental divorce or parenting style may have little direct impact on personality (Plomin & Caspi, 1999). According to these researchers, simply growing up in the same family does not make people very similar. In fact, when two siblings are similar, this is thought to be due primarily to genetic similarities.

TABLE 12.3

HERITABILITY ESTIMATES FOR THE BIG FIVE PERSONALITY TRAITS

Trait Dimension	Heritability
Openness	.41
Conscientiousness	.31
Extraversion	.36
Agreeableness	.35
Neuroticism	.37

Information from Vukasović & Bratko, 2015.

Our genes influence our personality in various ways, such as affecting how rigidly versus flexibly we think about things. This causes family members to share such traits, but not enough to prevent all political and religious disagreements during Thanksgiving dinner.

SIMONKR/GETTY IMAGES

Researchers also have assessed specific behavioural and attitudinal similarities in twins, and the evidence for heritability in these studies is often striking. One such study examined the DNA of 13,000 people and measured the extent to which they reported conservative versus liberal attitudes. The researchers found associations between conservatism–liberalism and chromosomal regions linked to mental flexibility, or the extent to which people change their thinking in response to shifts in their environment, which could be one of the factors influencing our views on social and political issues (Hatemi et al., 2011). Current research by psychological scientists is aimed at better understanding how variations in our genetic code may contribute to the development of personality.

Gender Differences: Biology or Culture?

Do you think there is a typical female personality or a typical male personality? On a variety of personality characteristics, including helpfulness, men and women on average show no reliable differences. Overall, men and women seem to be far more similar in personality than they are different (Hyde, 2005). However, researchers have found some reliable differences between men and women with respect to their traits, attitudes, and behaviours. For example, males report having greater assertiveness, self-esteem, and sensation seeking, whereas women are higher on neuroticism, agreeableness, and conscientiousness (Costa, Terracciano, & McCrae, 2001; Schmitt et al., 2008).

Interestingly, many of the gender differences that do exist among adults seem to have developed over time. For instance, a recent review of more than 150 previous studies that included more than 20,000 participants found gender differences in the expression of emotion (with boys showing more externalizing emotions like anger and girls showing more internalizing emotions such as sadness and anxiety—consistent with the study noted in the last paragraph) (Chaplin & Aldao, 2013). However, these differences were much more pronounced as children aged into adolescence, suggesting that cultural factors play a role in how children learn to express their emotions. The finding that gender differences in personality do not begin to emerge until adolescence also has been reported in studies conducted across dozens of different cultures around the world, suggesting that this is a universal phenomenon (De Bolle et al., 2015) (see A World of Difference: Do Males and Females Have Different Personality Traits?).

Another factor that may contribute to the emergence of personality differences in adolescence is the simultaneous emergence of differences in sex hormones during puberty. As you know, a lot of things change during adolescence (e.g., more hormones, more interactions with friends, less time spent with parents), and it can be difficult to know what changes are causing what other changes. Interestingly, however, the effect of hormones on personality can be studied experimentally. One recent study followed a sample of transgender men over a 3-month period during which they were undergoing testosterone treatment (in an effort to make their bodies more masculine). Personality tests administered before and after testosterone treatment revealed that significant changes occurred, with the transgender men viewing themselves as being more masculine and their scores more closely matching those of nontransgender men (Keo-Meier et al., 2015).

Traits Are Wired in the Brain

What neurophysiological mechanisms might influence the development of personality traits? Much of the thinking on this topic has focused on the extraversion–introversion dimension. In his personality model, Eysenck (1967) speculated that extraversion and introversion might arise from individual differences in cortical arousal. Eysenck suggested that extraverts pursue stimulation because their *reticular*

Research has shown that there are small differences in the personalities of men versus women; however, these differences are largely absent during childhood and don't emerge until adolescence, suggesting that they may be learned based on cultural expectations. This brother and sister seem to have the same personality. Their dog looks happy though.

ERIC RAPTOSH PHOTOGRAPHY/GETTY IMAGES

ERIC RAPTOSH PHOTOGRAPHY/GETTY IMAGES

A World of Difference • Do Males and Females Have Different Personality Traits?

Although the gender differences in personality are quite small, they tend to get a lot of attention. The debate about the origins of gender differences in personality often involves contrasting an evolutionary biological perspective with a social–cognitive perspective known as *social role theory*. The evolutionary perspective holds that men and women have evolved different personality characteristics, in part because their reproductive success depends on different behaviours. For instance, aggressiveness in men may have an adaptive value in intimidating sexual rivals, whereas being agreeable and nurturing may have evolved more among women to protect and ensure the survival of their offspring (Campbell, 1999). In actuality, science has yet to reveal conclusive and replicable differences between the brains of men and women (Rippon, 2019).

According to social role theory, personality characteristics and behavioural differences between men and women result from cultural standards and expectations that assign them: socially permissible jobs, activities, and family positions (Eagly & Wood, 1999). Because of their physical size and their freedom from childbearing, men historically have taken roles of greater power—roles that in postindustrial society don't necessarily require physical strength. These differences then snowball, with men generally taking roles that require assertiveness and aggression (e.g., executive, school principal, surgeon) and women pursuing roles that emphasize greater supportiveness and nurturance (e.g., nurse, day-care worker, teacher). Regardless of the source of gender differences in personality, the degree to

ARDHANARISHVARA, UNIVERSITY OF CALIFORNIA, BERKELEY ART MUSEUM AND PACIFIC FILM ARCHIVE, GIFT OF JEAN AND FRANCIS MARSHALL, 1999.15.10. PHOTOGRAPHED BY BEN BLACKWELL

Cultures differ in their appreciation of male and female characteristics, but the Hindu deity Ardhanarishvara represents the value of combining both parts of human nature. Male on one side and female on the other, this god is symbolic of the dual nature of the sacred. The only real problem with such side-by-side androgyny comes in finding clothes that fit.

which people identify personally with masculine and feminine stereotypes may tell us about important personality differences between individuals. Sandra Bem (1974) designed a scale (the Bem Sex Role Inventory) that assesses the degree of identification with stereotypically masculine and feminine traits. Bem suggested that psychologically *androgynous* people (those who adopt the best of both worlds and identify with positive feminine traits such as kindness and positive masculine traits such as assertiveness) might be better adjusted than people who identify strongly with only one sex role or who don't identify much with either one. So far, the data seem to support this idea. For instance, those who endorse an androgynous sex role report fewer symptoms of depression than those with a masculine or feminine role, regardless of their biological sex (Vafaei et al., 2016). This is also good news for the Hindu deity pictured here.

Bem Sex Role Inventory Sample Items

Respondents taking the Bem Sex Role Inventory rate themselves on each of the items without seeing the gender categorization. Then the scale is scored for masculinity (use of stereotypically masculine items), femininity (use of stereotypically feminine items), and androgyny (the tendency to use both the stereotypically masculine and feminine adjectives to describe oneself) (Bem, 1974).

Masculine items	Feminine items
Self-reliant	Yielding
Defends own beliefs	Affectionate
Independent	Flatterable
Assertive	Sympathetic
Forceful	Sensitive to the needs of others

formation (the part of the brain that regulates arousal or alertness, as described in the Neuroscience and Behaviour chapter) is not easily stimulated. To achieve greater cortical arousal and feel fully alert, Eysenck argued, extraverts seek out social interaction, parties, and other activities to achieve mental stimulation. In contrast, introverts may prefer reading or quiet activities because their cortex is very easily stimulated to a point higher than optimal alertness.

Behavioural and physiological research generally supports Eysenck's view. When introverts and extraverts are presented with a range of intense stimuli, introverts respond more strongly, including salivating more when a drop of lemon juice is placed on their tongues and reacting more negatively to electric shocks or loud noises (Bartol & Costello, 1976; Stelmack, 1990). This reactivity has an impact on the ability to concentrate: Extraverts tend to perform well at tasks that are done in a noisy, arousing context (such as bartending or teaching), whereas introverts are better at tasks that require concentration in tranquil contexts (such as the work of a librarian or nighttime security guard) (Lieberman & Rosenthal, 2001; Matthews & Gilliland, 1999).

In a refined version of Eysenck's ideas about arousability, Jeffrey Gray (1970) proposed that the dimensions of extraversion–introversion and neuroticism reflect two basic brain systems. The *behavioural activation system (BAS)*, essentially a "go" system, activates approach behaviour in response to the anticipation of reward. The extravert has a highly reactive BAS and will actively engage the environment, seeking social reinforcement and being on the go. The *behavioural inhibition system (BIS)*, a "stop" system, inhibits behaviour in response to stimuli signalling punishment. The anxious or introverted person, in turn, has a highly reactive BIS and will focus on negative outcomes and be on the lookout for stop signs. Because these two systems operate independently, it is possible for someone to be both a go and a stop person (simultaneously activated and inhibited), caught in a constant conflict between these two traits. An introverted person might be low on BAS (less motivated to seek out potentially rewarding social situations) and high on BIS (more likely to steer clear of others for fear of some form of punishment, such as outside criticism).

Studies of brain electrical activity (EEG) and functional brain imaging (fMRI) suggest that individual differences in activation and inhibition arise through the operation of distinct brain systems underlying these tendencies (DeYoung & Gray, 2009). More recent studies have suggested that the core personality traits described earlier may arise from individual variations in the volume of the different brain regions associated with each trait. For instance, self-reported neuroticism is correlated with the volume of brain regions involved in sensitivity to threat; agreeableness with areas associated with processing information about the mental states of other people; conscientiousness with regions involved in self-regulation; and extraversion with areas associated with processing information about reward (DeYoung et al., 2010). Research aimed at understanding how the structure and activity of our brains can contribute to the formation of our personality traits is still in its early stages, but it is a growing area of the field that many believe holds great promise for helping us better understand how we each develop into the unique humans that we are.

Do Animals Have Personalities?

Another source of evidence for the biological basis of human personality comes from the study of nonhuman animals. Any dog owner, zookeeper, or cattle farmer can tell you that individual animals have characteristic patterns of behaviour. One woman who reportedly enjoyed raising chickens in her suburban home said that the "best part" was "knowing them as individuals" (Tucker, 2003). As far as we know, this pet owner did not give her feathered companions a personality test, though the researcher Sam Gosling (1998) used this approach in a study of a group of spotted hyenas. Well, not exactly. He recruited four human observers to use personality scales to rate the different hyenas in the group. When he examined ratings on the scales, he found five dimensions; three closely resembled the Big Five traits of neuroticism (i.e., fearfulness, emotional reactivity), openness to experience (i.e., curiosity), and agreeableness (i.e., absence of aggression).

In similar studies of guppies and octopi, individual differences in traits resembling extraversion and neuroticism were reliably observed (Gosling & John, 1999). In each

Extraverts pursue stimulation in the form of people, loud noise, and bright colours. Introverts tend to prefer softer, quieter settings. Pop quiz: Miley Cyrus—introvert or extravert?

KEVIN WINTER/GETTY IMAGES

How would you rate this honey badger? Is it antagonistic or agreeable? Neurotic or emotionally stable? Researchers have found that even animals appear to have personalities. Or should they be called "animalities"?

study, researchers identified particular behaviours that they felt reflected each trait, based on their observation of the animals' normal repertoire of activities. Because different observers seem to agree on where an animal falls on a given dimension, the findings do not simply reflect a particular observer's imagination or tendency to *anthropomorphize* (attribute human characteristics to nonhuman animals). Such findings of cross-species commonality in behavioural styles help support the idea that biological mechanisms underlie personality traits shared by many species.

From an evolutionary perspective, differences in personality reflect alternative adaptations that have evolved in species—human and nonhuman—to deal with the challenges of survival and reproduction. For example, if you were to hang around a bar for an evening or two, you would soon see that evolution has provided humans with more than one way to attract and keep a mate. People who are extraverted would probably show off to attract attention, whereas you'd be likely to see people high in agreeableness displaying affection and nurturance (Buss, 1996). Both approaches might work well for attracting mates and reproducing successfully—depending on the environment. Through this process of natural selection, those characteristics that have proved successful in our evolutionary struggle for survival have been passed on to future generations.

Not only do animals have personalities but they also show consistency in these traits over time. For instance, one recent study examined 31 prior studies that measured the consistency of personality traits in dogs over time. It turns out that personality characteristics present during puppyhood tend to persist into dogs' adult years (Fratkin et al., 2013). Consistency in dog personality is important for working dogs (e.g., bomb-sniffing dogs, service dogs, etc.), as well as for pet owners who sometimes select their pets for their apparent personality. Beyond that, studying personality in nonhuman animals offers several serious benefits: improved ability to measure physiology, more opportunities for naturalistic observation (e.g., observing aggression and social hierarchies), and an accelerated lifespan (e.g., making longitudinal and lifespan studies much more efficient) (Gosling, 2008).

Build to the Outcomes

1. How might traits explain behaviour?
2. How do psychologists identify the core personality traits?
3. What role has factor analysis played in identifying different traits?
4. What are the strengths of the five-factor model?
5. What do studies of twins tell us about personality?
6. Are there significant personality differences between the genders?
7. What neurological differences explain why extraverts pursue more stimulation than introverts?
8. Why study animal behavioural styles?

The Psychodynamic Approach: Forces That Lie Beneath Awareness

Learning Outcomes

- Differentiate the id, ego, and superego.
- Explain how defence mechanisms reduce anxiety.

Rather than trying to understand personality in terms of broad theories for describing individual differences, Freud looked for personality in the details: the meanings and insights revealed by careful analysis of the tiniest blemishes in a person's thought and behaviour. Working with patients who came to him with disorders that did not seem to have any physical basis, he began by interpreting the origins of their everyday mistakes and memory lapses, errors that have come to be called *Freudian slips*.

Freud used the term *psychoanalysis* to refer to both his theory of personality and his method of treating patients. Freud's ideas were the first of many theories building on his basic idea that personality is a mystery to the person who "owns" it because we can't know our own deepest motives. The theories of Freud and his followers (discussed in the Treatment chapter) are referred to as the **psychodynamic approach**, which *regards personality as formed by needs, strivings, and desires largely operating outside of awareness—motives that can produce emotional disorders.* The real engines of personality, in this view, are forces of which we are largely unaware.

The Structure of the Mind: Id, Ego, and Superego

To explain the emotional difficulties that beset his patients, Freud proposed that the mind consists of three independent, interacting, and often conflicting systems: the id, the superego, and the ego.

The most basic system, the **id**, is *the part of the mind containing the drives present at birth; it is the source of our bodily needs, wants, desires, and impulses, particularly our sexual and aggressive drives.* The id operates according to the *pleasure principle*, the psychic force that motivates the tendency to seek immediate gratification of any impulse. If governed by the id alone, you would never be able to tolerate the buildup of hunger while waiting to be served at a restaurant but would simply grab food from tables nearby.

Opposite the id is the **superego**, *the mental system that reflects the internalization of cultural rules, mainly learned as parents exercise their authority.* The superego consists of a set of guidelines, internal standards, and other codes of conduct that regulate and control our behaviours, thoughts, and fantasies. It acts as a kind of conscience, punishing us when it finds we are doing or thinking something wrong (by producing guilt or other painful feelings) and rewarding us (with feelings of pride or self-congratulation) for living up to ideal standards.

The final system of the mind, according to psychoanalytic theory, is the **ego**, *the component of personality, developed through contact with the external world, that enables us to deal with life's practical demands.* The ego operates according to the *reality principle*, the regulating mechanism that enables us to delay gratifying immediate needs and function effectively in the real world. It is the mediator between the id and the superego. The ego helps you resist the impulse to snatch others' food and also finds the restaurant and pays the cheque.

Freud believed that the relative strength of the interactions among the three systems of mind (i.e., which system is usually dominant) determines an individual's basic personality structure. Together, the id force of personal needs, the superego force of pressures to quell those needs, and the ego force of reality's demands are in constant internal conflict. Freud believed that the dynamics among the id, superego, and ego are largely governed by *anxiety*, an unpleasant feeling that arises when unwanted thoughts or feelings occur, such as when the id seeks a gratification that the ego thinks will lead to real-world dangers or that the superego sees as leading to punishment.

When the ego receives an "alert" signal in the form of anxiety, it launches into a defensive position in an attempt to ward off the anxiety. According to Freud, it does so using one of several different **defence mechanisms**, *unconscious coping mechanisms that reduce the anxiety generated by threats from unacceptable impulses* (see **TABLE 12.4**). Psychodynamically oriented psychologists believe that defence mechanisms help us overcome anxiety and engage effectively with the outside world and that our characteristic style of defence becomes our signature in dealing with the world—and an essential aspect of our personality.

THE PHOTO WORKS

Sigmund Freud was the first psychology theorist to be honoured with his own bobblehead doll. Let's hope he's not the last.

psychodynamic approach An approach that regards personality as formed by needs, strivings, and desires largely operating outside of awareness—motives that also can produce emotional disorders.

id The part of the mind containing the drives present at birth; it is the source of our bodily needs, wants, desires, and impulses, particularly our sexual and aggressive drives.

superego The mental system that reflects the internalization of cultural rules, mainly learned as parents exercise their authority.

ego The component of personality, developed through contact with the external world, that enables us to deal with life's practical demands.

defence mechanisms Unconscious coping mechanisms that reduce the anxiety generated by threats from unacceptable impulses.

TABLE 12.4

DEFENCE MECHANISMS

Defence Mechanism	Description	Example
Repression	Removing painful experiences and unacceptable impulses from the conscious mind: "motivated forgetting."	Not lashing out physically in anger; putting a bad experience out of your mind.
Rationalization	Supplying a reasonable-sounding explanation for unacceptable feelings and behaviour to conceal (mostly from oneself) one's underlying motives or feelings.	Dropping calculus, allegedly because of poor ventilation in the classroom.
Reaction formation	Unconsciously replacing threatening inner wishes and fantasies with an exaggerated version of their opposite.	Being rude to someone you're attracted to.
Projection	Attributing one's own threatening feelings, motives, or impulses to another person or group.	Judging others as being dishonest because you believe that you are dishonest.
Regression	Reverting to an immature behaviour or earlier stage of development, a time when things felt more secure, to deal with internal conflict and perceived threat.	Using baby talk, even though able to use appropriate speech, in response to distress.
Displacement	Shifting unacceptable wishes or drives to a neutral or less threatening alternative.	Slamming a door; yelling at someone other than the person you're mad at.
Identification	Dealing with feelings of threat and anxiety by unconsciously taking on the characteristics of another person who seems more powerful or better able to cope.	A bullied child becoming a bully.
Sublimation	Channelling unacceptable sexual or aggressive drives into socially acceptable and culturally enhancing activities.	Diverting anger to the football or rugby field, or other contact sport.

Freud also proposed that a person's basic personality is formed before 6 years of age during a series of sensitive periods, or life stages, when experiences influence all that will follow. Freud called these periods *psychosexual stages,* distinct early life stages through which personality is formed as children experience sexual pleasures from specific body areas and as caregivers redirect or interfere with those pleasures (see **TABLE 12.5**). He argued that, as a result of adult interference with pleasure-seeking energies, the child experiences conflict. At each stage, a different bodily region dominates the child's subjective experience. Problems and conflicts encountered at any psychosexual stage, Freud believed, will influence personality in adulthood.

What should we make of all this? Critics argue that psychodynamic explanations lack any real evidence and tend to focus on provocative after-the-fact interpretation rather than testable prediction. The psychosexual stage theory offers a compelling set of story lines for interpreting lives once they have unfolded, but it has not generated clear-cut predictions supported by research.

TABLE 12.5

FREUD'S PSYCHOSEXUAL STAGES

Stage	Description
Oral	The stage in which experience centres on the pleasures and frustrations associated with the mouth, sucking, and being fed.
Anal	The stage in which experience is dominated by the pleasures and frustrations associated with the anus, retention, and expulsion of feces and urine, and toilet training.
Phallic	The stage in which experience is dominated by the pleasure, conflict, and frustration associated with the phallic–genital region, as well as coping with powerful incestuous feelings of love, hate, jealousy, and conflict.
Latency	The stage in which the primary focus is on the further development of intellectual, creative, interpersonal, and athletic skills.
Genital	The time for the coming together of the mature adult personality with a capacity to love, work, and relate to others in a mutually satisfying and reciprocal manner.

The Humanistic–Existential Approach: Personality as Choice

During the 1950s and 1960s, psychologists began trying to understand personality from a viewpoint quite different from trait theory's biological determinism and Freud's focus on unconscious drives. These new humanistic and existential theorists turned attention to how humans make *healthy choices* that create their personalities. *Humanistic psychologists* emphasized a positive, optimistic view of human nature that highlights people's inherent goodness and their potential for personal growth. *Existentialist psychologists* focused on the individual as a responsible agent who is free to create and live his or her life while negotiating the issue of meaning and the reality of death. The *humanistic–existential approach* integrates these insights with a focus on how a personality can become optimal.

Human Needs and Self-Actualization

Humanists see the **self-actualizing tendency**, *the human motive towards realizing our inner potential,* as a major factor in personality. The pursuit of knowledge, the expression of one's creativity, the quest for spiritual enlightenment, and the desire to give to society are all examples of self-actualization. As you saw in the Emotion and Motivation chapter, the noted humanistic theorist Abraham Maslow (1943) proposed a *hierarchy of needs,* a model of essential human needs arranged according to their priority, in which basic physiological and safety needs must be satisfied before a person can afford to focus on higher-level psychological needs. Only when these basic needs are met can one pursue higher needs, culminating in *self-actualization*: the need to be good, to be fully alive, and to find meaning in life.

Humanist psychologists explain individual personality differences as arising from the various ways that the environment facilitates—or blocks—attempts to satisfy psychological needs. For example, someone with the inherent potential to be a great scientist, artist, parent, or teacher might never realize these talents if his or her energies and resources are instead directed towards meeting basic needs of security, belongingness, and the like. Research indicates that when people shape their lives around goals that do not match their true nature and capabilities, they are less likely to be happy than those whose lives and goals do match (Ryan & Deci, 2000).

It feels great to be doing exactly what you are capable of doing. Mihaly Csikszentmihalyi (pronounced "me-high CHEEK-sent-me-high"; 1990) found that engagement in tasks that exactly match one's abilities creates a mental state of energized focus that he called *flow* (see **FIGURE 12.4**). Tasks that are below our abilities cause boredom, those that are too challenging cause anxiety, and those that are "just right" lead to the experience of flow. If you know how to play the piano, for example, and are playing a Chopin prelude that you know well enough that it just matches

Learning Outcomes

- Describe the humanistic–existential approach to personality.

- Explain the role of self-actualization and angst in personality development.

IMAGE SOURCE/GETTY IMAGES

Decades of research have shown that growing up in a distressed neighbourhood is associated with worse educational, occupational, and health outcomes. Humanistic psychologists would suggest that people in such settings must struggle to meet their basic daily needs and so do not have opportunities for self-actualization.

self-actualizing tendency The human motive towards realizing our inner potential.

Figure 12.4

Flow Experience It feels good to do things that challenge your abilities but that don't challenge them too much. Mihaly Csikszentmihalyi (1990) described this feeling between boredom and anxiety as the "flow experience."

your abilities, you are likely to experience this optimal state. People report being happier at these times than at any other times. Humanists believe that such peak experiences, or states of flow, reflect the realization of one's human potential and represent the height of personality development.

Personality as Existence

Existentialists agree with humanists about many of the features of personality but focus on challenges to the human condition that are more profound than the lack of a nurturing environment. Rollo May (1983) and Victor Frankl (2000), for example, argued that specific aspects of the human condition, such as awareness of our own existence and the ability to make choices about how to behave, have a double-edged quality: They bring an extraordinary richness and dignity to human life, but they also force us to confront realities that are difficult to face, such as the prospect of our own death. The **existential approach** is *a school of thought that regards personality as governed by an individual's ongoing choices and decisions in the context of the realities of life and death.*

According to the existential perspective, the difficulties we face in finding meaning in life and in accepting the responsibility of making free choices provoke a type of anxiety that existentialists call *angst* (the anxiety of fully being). The human ability to consider limitless numbers of goals and actions is exhilarating, but it can also open the door to profound questions such as "Why am I here?" and "What is the meaning of my life?"

Thinking about the meaning of existence also can evoke an awareness of the inevitability of death. What, then, should we do with each moment? What is the purpose of living if life as we know it will end one day, perhaps even today? Alternatively, does life have *more* meaning, given that it is so temporary? Existential theorists do not suggest that people consider these profound existential issues on a day-to-day and moment-to-moment basis. Rather than ruminating about death and meaning, people typically pursue superficial answers that help them deal with the angst and dread they experience, and the defences they construct form the basis of their personalities (May, 1983). Some people organize their lives around obtaining material possessions; others may immerse themselves in drugs or addictive behaviours such as compulsive Web browsing, video gaming, or television watching in order to numb the mind to existential realities.

For existentialists, a healthier solution is to face the issues head on and learn to accept and tolerate the pain of existence. Indeed, being fully human means confronting existential realities rather than denying them or embracing comforting illusions. This requires the courage to accept the inherent anxiety and the dread of nonbeing that is part of being alive. Such courage may be bolstered by developing supportive relationships with others who can supply unconditional positive regard. Something about being loved helps relieve the angst.

existential approach A school of thought that regards personality as being governed by an individual's ongoing choices and decisions in the context of the realities of life and death.

Build to the Outcomes

1. How does the humanistic–existential approach differ from the trait and psychodynamic approaches?
2. What does it mean to be self-actualized?
3. How is "flow" created?
4. What is the existential approach to personality?
5. What is angst? How is it created?

The Social–Cognitive Approach: Personalities in Situations

What is it like to be a person? The **social–cognitive approach** *views personality in terms of how a person thinks about the situations encountered in daily life and behaves in response to them.* Bringing together insights from social psychology, cognitive psychology, and learning theory, this approach emphasizes how the person experiences and interprets situations (Bandura, 1986; Mischel & Shoda, 1999; Wegner & Gilbert, 2000).

Researchers in social cognition believe that both the current situation and learning history are key determinants of behaviour, and focus on how people *perceive* their environments. People think about their goals, the consequences of their behaviour, and how they might achieve certain objectives in different situations (Lewin, 1951). The social–cognitive approach looks at how personality and situation interact to cause behaviour, how personality contributes to the way people construct situations in their own minds, and how people's goals and expectancies influence their responses to situations.

Learning Outcomes

- Describe the social–cognitive approach to personality.

- Explain how personal constructs are key to personality differences.

- Identify how one's perception of control influences behaviour.

Consistency of Personality Across Situations

Although social–cognitive psychologists attribute behaviour both to the individual's personality and to his or her situation, situation can often trump personality. For example, a person would have to be pretty strange to act exactly the same way at a memorial service as at a keg party. In their belief that the strong push and pull of situations can influence almost everyone, social–cognitive psychologists are somewhat at odds with the basic assumptions of classic personality psychology; that is, that personality characteristics (e.g., traits, needs, unconscious drives) cause people to behave in the same way across situations and over time. At the core of the social–cognitive approach is a natural puzzle, the **person–situation controversy,** which focuses on *the question of whether behaviour is caused more by personality or by situational factors.*

This controversy began in earnest when Walter Mischel (1968) argued that measured personality traits often do a poor job of predicting individuals' behaviour. He reviewed decades of research that compared scores on standard personality tests with actual behaviour, looking at evidence from studies that asked questions such as "Does a person with a high score on a test of introversion actually spend more time alone than someone with a low score?" Mischel's disturbing conclusion: The average correlation between trait and behaviour is only about .30. This is certainly better than zero (i.e., no relation at all) but not very good when you remember that a perfect prediction is represented by a correlation of 1.0.

Mischel also noted that knowing how a person will behave in one situation is not particularly helpful in predicting that person's behaviour in another situation. For example, in classic studies, Hugh Hartshorne and M. A. May (1928) assessed children's honesty by examining their willingness to cheat on a test and found that such dishonesty was not consistent from one situation to another. The assessment of a child's trait of honesty in a cheating situation was of almost no use in predicting whether that child would act honestly in a different

"He's not very exciting in social situations but on the net he's a wildman."

social–cognitive approach An approach that views personality in terms of how the person thinks about the situations encountered in daily life and behaves in response to them.

person–situation controversy The question of whether behaviour is caused more by personality or by situational factors.

situation, such as when given the opportunity to steal money. Mischel proposed that measured traits do not predict behaviours very well because behaviours are determined more by situational factors than personality theorists were willing to acknowledge.

Is there no personality, then? Do we all just do what situations require? The person–situation controversy has inspired many studies in the years since Mischel's critique, and it turns out that information about both personality and situation are necessary to predict behaviour accurately (Fleeson, 2004; Mischel, 2004). Some situations are particularly powerful, leading most everyone to behave similarly regardless of personality (Cooper & Withey, 2009). At a funeral, almost everyone looks sombre, and during an earthquake, almost everyone shakes. But in more moderate situations, personality can come to the fore to influence behaviour (Funder, 2001). Among the children in Hartshorne and May's (1928) studies, cheating versus not cheating on a test was actually a fairly good predictor of cheating on a test later—as long as the situation was similar. Personality consistency, then, appears to be a matter of when and where a certain kind of behaviour tends to be shown (see the Real World: Does Your Personality Change Depending on Who You're With?). Social–cognitive theorists believe these patterns of personality consistency arise from the way different people interpret situations and from how different people pursue goals within situations.

Personal Constructs: The Key to the Perceiver's Personality

How can we understand differences in how situations are interpreted? Recall our notion that personality often exists in the eye of the beholder. Situations may exist in the eye of the beholder as well. One person's gold mine may be another person's useless hole in the ground. George Kelly (1955) long ago realized that these differences

Is a student who cheats on a test more likely than others to steal candy or lie to her grandmother? Social–cognitive research indicates that behaviour in one situation does not necessarily predict behaviour in a different situation.

GLOW IMAGES/GETTY IMAGES

The Real World | Does Your Personality Change Depending on Who You're With?

Social–cognitive psychologists suggest that how you behave is influenced by both your personality and the situations you are in. For instance, you act differently when sitting in a classroom than you do when dancing at a club (unless it's a really fun class). But do your personality and behaviour also change when you're talking to different people regardless of context? For instance, do things such as your language, tone of voice, and level of warmth change depending on whom you are talking to?

For most people, the answer is yes. For example, we speak and act differently when interacting with our parents ("*Hello mother, hello father*") than with our friends ("*Yo! Sup, punk?!*"). Many people change their language and personality when interacting

with people from their own race or cultural group as opposed to those from other groups (e.g., Coates, 2015). And there is evidence from studies of bilingual speakers that people's personality traits shift slightly when they are speaking in one language versus another (Ramirez-Esparza et al., 2004). These are notably subtle shifts rather than complete personality transplants.

Why would our personality characteristics change when we are interacting with one person versus another? One possibility is that we shift our personality and language to match the people with whom we are interacting to signal closeness or affiliation with them. Another possibility is that we do this to influence what other people think about us. For instance, one recent

study found that people in positions of power tend to downplay their competence when interacting with subordinates to appear warmer and more likeable, whereas subordinates tend to conceal their warmth to appear more competent (Swencionis & Fiske, 2016). The authors suggest that in both situations, the participants are attempting to increase the perceived similarity between them and the person with whom they are interacting. The fact that things such as personality, similarity, and perceived competence can influence decisions about hiring and promotions (Rivera, 2012; Tews, Stafford, & Tracey, 2011) means that personality actually has a huge impact on the experiences you have in the real world.

Are two of these people taller and one shorter? Are two bareheaded while one wears a hood? Or are two the daughters and one the mom? George Kelly held that the personal constructs we use to distinguish among people in our lives are basic elements of our own personalities.

in perspective could be used to understand the *perceiver's* personality. He suggested that people view the social world from differing perspectives and that these different views arise through the application of **personal constructs**, *dimensions people use in making sense of their experiences.* Consider, for example, different individuals' personal constructs of a clown: One person may see him as a source of fun, another as a tragic figure, and yet another as so frightening that McDonald's must be avoided at all costs.

Kelly assessed personal constructs about social relationships by asking people to (1) list the people in their life; (2) consider three of the people and state a way in which two of them are similar to each other and different from the third; and (3) repeat this for other triads of people in their lives to produce a list of the dimensions that respondents use to classify friends and family. One respondent might focus on the degree to which people (self included) are lazy or hardworking, for example; someone else might attend to the degree to which people are sociable or unfriendly.

Kelly proposed that different personal constructs (*construals*) are the key to personality differences; that is, different construals lead people to engage in different behaviours. Taking a long break from work for a leisurely lunch might seem lazy to you. To your friend, the break might seem an ideal opportunity for catching up with friends and for wondering why *you* always choose to eat at your desk. Social–cognitive theory explains different responses to situations with the idea that people experience and interpret the world in different ways.

Personal Goals and Expectancies Lead to a Characteristic Style of Behaviour

Social–cognitive theories also recognize that a person's unique perspective on situations is reflected in his or her personal goals, which are often conscious. In fact, people can usually tell you their goals, whether to find a date for this weekend, get a good grade in psych, establish a fulfilling career, or just get this darn bag of chips open. These goals often reflect the tasks that are appropriate to the person's situation and, in a larger sense, fit the person's role and stage of life (Cantor, 1990; Vallacher & Wegner, 1985). For instance, common goals for adolescents include being popular, achieving greater independence from parents and family, and getting into a good university.

personal constructs Dimensions people use in making sense of their experiences.

Some days you feel like a puppet on a string. If you have an external locus of control and believe you are at the mercy of other people, or of fate, you may feel that way most days.

Common goals for adults include developing a meaningful career, finding a mate, securing financial stability, and starting a family.

People translate goals into behaviour in part through **outcome expectancies**, *a person's assumptions about the likely consequences of a future behaviour.* Just as a laboratory rat learns that pressing a bar releases a food pellet, we learn that "if I am friendly towards people, they will be friendly in return," and "if I ask people to pull my finger, they will withdraw from me." So we learn to perform behaviours that we expect will have the outcome of moving us closer to our goals. We learn outcome expectancies through direct experience, both bitter and sweet, and through merely observing other people's actions and the resulting consequences.

People differ in their generalized expectancy for achieving goals. Some people seem to feel that they are fully in control of what happens to them in life, whereas others feel that the world doles out rewards and punishments to them irrespective of their actions. Julian Rotter (1966) developed a questionnaire (see **TABLE 12.6**) to measure *a person's tendency to perceive the control of rewards as internal to the self or external in the environment,* a disposition he called **locus of control**. People whose answers suggest that they believe they control their own destiny are said to have an *internal* locus of control, whereas those who believe that outcomes are random, determined by luck, or controlled by other people are described as having an *external* locus of control. These beliefs translate into individual differences in emotion and behaviour. For example, people with an internal locus of control tend to be less anxious, achieve more, and cope better with stress than do people with an external orientation (Lefcourt, 1982). To get a sense of your standing on this trait dimension, choose one of the options for each of the sample items from the locus-of-control scale in Table 12.6.

outcome expectancies A person's assumptions about the likely consequences of a future behaviour.

locus of control A person's tendency to perceive the control of rewards as internal to the self or external in the environment.

TABLE 12.6
ROTTER'S LOCUS-OF-CONTROL SCALE

For each pair of items, choose the option that most closely reflects your personal belief. Then check the answer key below to see if you have more of an internal or external locus of control.

1. a. Many of the unhappy things in people's lives are partly due to bad luck.
   b. People's misfortunes result from the mistakes they make.

2. a. I have often found that what is going to happen will happen.
   b. Trusting to fate has never turned out as well for me as making a decision to take a definite course of action.

3. a. Becoming a success is a matter of hard work; luck has little or nothing to do with it.
   b. Getting a good job depends mainly on being in the right place at the right time.

4. a. When I make plans, I am almost certain that I can make them work.
   b. It is not always wise to plan too far ahead because many things turn out to be a matter of good or bad fortune anyhow.

Information from Rotter, 1966.

Answers: A more internal locus of control would be reflected in choosing options 1b, 2b, 3a, and 4a.

Build to the Outcomes

1. Do researchers in social cognition think that personality arises from past experiences or from the current environment?

2. How well do measured personality traits predict behaviour, according to the social–cognitive approach?

3. Does personality or the current situation predict a person's behaviour?

4. What are personal constructs?

5. What is the advantage of an internal, over an external, locus of control?

The Self: Personality in the Mirror

Imagine that you wake up tomorrow morning, drag yourself to the bathroom, look in the mirror, and don't recognize the face looking back at you. This was the plight of a patient studied by the neurologist Todd Feinberg (2001). The woman, married for 30 years and the mother of two grown children, one day began to respond to her mirror image as if it were a different person. She talked to and challenged the person in the mirror. When she got no response, she tried to attack it as if it were an intruder. Her husband, shaken by this bizarre behaviour, brought her to the neurologist, who was gradually able to convince her that the image in the mirror was in fact herself.

Most of us are pretty familiar with the face that looks back at us from every mirror. We develop the ability to recognize ourselves in mirrors by 18 months of age (as discussed in the Consciousness chapter), and we share this skill with chimpanzees and other apes that have been raised in the presence of mirrors. Self-recognition in mirrors signals our amazing capacity for reflexive thinking, for directing attention to our own thoughts, feelings, and actions—an ability that enables us to construct ideas about our own personality. Unlike a cow, which will never know that it has a poor sense of humour, or a cat, which will never know that it is awfully friendly, humans have rich and detailed self-knowledge.

Admittedly, none of us knows all there is to know about our own personality. In fact, sometimes others may know us better than we know ourselves (Vazire & Mehl, 2008). But we do have enough self-knowledge to respond reliably to personality inventories and report on our traits and behaviours. These observations draw on what we think about ourselves (our *self-concept*) and on how we feel about ourselves (our *self-esteem*). Self-concept and self-esteem are critically important facets of personality, not just because they reveal how people see their own personalities but because they also guide how people think others will see them.

Learning Outcomes

- Describe the features that make up the self-concept.
- Identify how self-esteem develops.
- Identify the motivations for self-esteem.

What do these self-portraits of Vincent van Gogh, Pablo Picasso, Frida Kahlo, Wanda Wulz, Jean-Michel Basquiat, and Salvador Dalí reveal about each artist's self-concept?

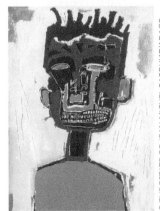

©DEAGOSTINI/SUPERSTOCK

© 2019 ESTATE OF PABLO PICASSO/ARS, NY. PHOTO: PAINTING/ALAMY

© 2019 BANCO DE MÉXICO DIEGO RIVERA FRIDA KAHLO MUSEUM TRUST, MEXICO, D.F./ARS, NY. PHOTO: ALBRIGHT-KNOX ART GALLERY/ART RESOURCE, NY.

ALINARI/ART RESOURCE, NY

© THE ESTATE OF JEAN-MICHEL BASQUIAT/ADAGP, PARIS/ARS, NEW YORK 2019. PHOTO: BANQUE D'IMAGES, ADAGP/ART RESOURCE, NY.

© 2019 SALVADOR DALÍ, FUNDACIÓ GALA-SALVADOR DALI, ARS, NY. PHOTO: ©PHILIPPE HALSMAN/ MAGNUM

Self-Concept

In his renowned psychology textbook, William James (1890) included a theory of self in which he pointed to the self's two facets, the *I* and the *Me*. The *I* is the self that thinks, experiences, and acts in the world; it is the self as a *knower*. The *Me* is the self that is an object in the world; it is the self that is *known*. The *I* is much like consciousness, then, a perspective on all of experience (see the Consciousness chapter), but the *Me* is less mysterious: It is just a concept of a person.

If asked to describe your *Me*, you might mention your physical characteristics (male or female, tall or short, dark-skinned or light); your activities (listening to hip-hop, alternative rock, jazz, or classical music); your personality traits (extraverted or introverted, agreeable or independent); or your social roles (student, son or daughter, member of a hiking club, krumper). These features make up the **self-concept**, *a person's explicit knowledge of his or her own behaviours, traits, and other personal characteristics*. A person's self-concept is an organized body of knowledge that develops from social experiences and has a profound effect on a person's behaviour throughout life.

Self-Concept Organization

Almost everyone has a place for memorabilia, a drawer or box somewhere that holds all those sentimental keepsakes—photos, yearbooks, cards and letters, maybe that scrap of the old security blanket—all memories of "life as *Me*." Perhaps you've wanted to organize these things sometime but have never gotten around to it. Fortunately, the knowledge of ourselves that we store in our *autobiographical memory* seems to be organized naturally in two ways: as narratives about episodes in our lives and in terms of traits (as would be suggested by the distinction between episodic memory and semantic memory discussed in the Memory chapter).

Self-Narratives Are Stories We Tell About Ourselves The aspect of the self-concept that is a *self-narrative* (a story that we tell about ourselves) can be brief or very lengthy. Your life story could start with your birth and upbringing, describe a series of defining moments, and end where you are today. You could select specific events and experiences, goals and life tasks, and memories of places and people that have influenced you. Self-narrative organizes the highlights (and low blows) of your life into a story in which you are the leading character and binds them together into your self-concept (McAdams, 1993; McLean, 2008). Psychodynamic and humanistic–existential psychologists suggest that people's self-narratives reflect their fantasies and thoughts about core motives and approaches to existence.

Self-Schemas are Sets of Traits We Use to Define Ourselves Self-concept is also organized in a more abstract way, in terms of personality traits. Just as you can judge an object on its attributes (is this apple green?), you can judge yourself on any number of traits—whether you are considerate or smart or lazy or active or, for that matter, green—and do so quite reliably, making the same rating on multiple occasions. Hazel Markus (1977) observed that each person finds certain unique personality traits particularly important for conceptualizing the self. One person might define herself as independent, for example, whereas another might not care much about her level of independence but instead emphasize her sense of style. Markus called the traits people use to define themselves *self-schemas*, emphasizing that they draw information about the self into a coherent scheme. She asked people to indicate whether they had a trait by pressing response buttons labelled *me* or *not me*. She found that participants' judgements reaction times were faster for self-schemas than for other traits. It's as though some facets of the self-concept have almost a knee-jerk quality—letting us tell quickly who we are and who we are not.

Research also shows that the traits people use to judge the self tend to stick in memory. When people make judgements of themselves on traits, they later recall the

Think about your own self-narrative (what you have done) and self-concept (how you view yourself). Are there areas that don't match up? Are there things that you've done, good or bad, that are not part of your self-concept? How might you explain that?

CAVAN IMAGES/GETTY IMAGES

self-concept A person's explicit knowledge of his or her own behaviours, traits, and other personal characteristics.

traits better than when they judge other people on the same traits (Rogers, Kuiper, & Kirker, 1977). For example, answering a question such as "Are you generous?"—no matter what your answer—is likely to enhance your memory for the trait generous. In studies of this effect of *self-relevance* on memory, researchers using brain-imaging technologies have found that the simple activity of making judgements about the trait self-concept is accompanied by activation of the medial prefrontal cortex (MPFC), a brain area involved in understanding people (Mitchell, Heatherton, & Macrae, 2002).

This activation is stronger, however, when people are judging their own standing on traits (see **FIGURE 12.5**) than when they are judging the standing of someone else (Kelley et al., 2002). Such stronger activation, then, is linked with better memory for the traits being judged (Macrae et al., 2004). Studies have not been entirely conclusive about which brain areas are most involved in the processing of self-information (Morin, 2002), but they do show that memory for traits is strengthened when the MPFC is activated during self-judgements.

Self-Narratives, Traits, and Behaviour Don't Always Match Up How do our behaviour self-narratives and trait self-concepts compare? These two methods of self-conceptualization don't always match up. You may think of yourself as an honest person, for example, but also recall that time you nabbed a handful of change from your parents' dresser and conveniently forgot to replace it. The traits we use to describe ourselves are generalizations, and not every episode in our life stories may fit them. In fact, research suggests that the stores of knowledge about our behaviours and traits are not very well integrated (Kihlstrom, Beer, & Klein, 2002). In people who develop amnesia, for example, memory for behaviours can be lost even though the trait self-concept remains stable (Klein, 2004). People can have a pretty strong sense of who they are even though they may not remember a single example of when they acted that way.

Causes and Effects of Self-Concept

How do self-concepts arise, and how do they affect us? In some sense, you learn something about yourself every day. Although we can gain self-knowledge in private moments of insight, we more often arrive at our self-concepts through interacting with others. Young children in particular receive plenty of feedback from their parents, teachers, siblings, and friends about their characteristics, which helps them form an idea of who they are. Even adults would find it difficult to hold a view of the self as "kind" or "smart" if no one else ever shared this impression. The sense of self, then, is largely developed and maintained in relationships with others.

Over the course of a lifetime, however, we become less and less impressed with what others have to say about us. The social theorist George Herbert Mead (1934) observed that all the things people have said about us accumulate after a while into what we see as a kind of consensus held by the "generalized other." We typically adopt this general view of ourselves and hold onto it stubbornly. As a result, the person who says you're a jerk may upset you momentarily, but you bounce back, secure in the knowledge that you actually are not a jerk. And just as we might argue vehemently with someone who tried to tell us a refrigerator is a pair of underpants, we are likely to defend our self-concept against anyone whose view of us departs from our own.

Because it is so stable, a major effect of the self-concept is to promote consistency in behaviour across situations (Lecky, 1945). We tend to engage in what William Swann (1983, 2012) called **self-verification**, *the tendency to seek evidence to confirm the self-concept,* and we find it disconcerting if someone sees us quite differently from the way we see ourselves. In one study, Swann (1983) gave people who considered themselves submissive feedback that they seemed very dominant and forceful. Rather than accepting this discrepant information, they went out of their way to act in an extremely submissive manner. As existential theorists emphasize, people derive a comforting sense of familiarity and stability from knowing who they are.

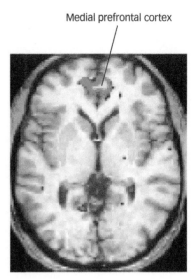

Medial prefrontal cortex

Figure 12.5
Self-Concept in the Brain fMRI scans reveal that the medial prefrontal cortex (MPFC) is activated (shown here in red and yellow) when people make judgements about whether they possess certain personality traits compared with when they are judging whether those traits apply to someone else (from Kelley et al., 2002). REPUBLISHED WITH PERMISSION. KELLEY, W. M., MACRAE, C. N., WYLAND, C. L., CAGLAR, S., INATI, S., & HEATHERTON, T. F. (2002). FINDING THE SELF? AN EVENT-RELATED FMRI STUDY. JOURNAL OF COGNITIVE NEUROSCIENCE, 14, 785-794. FIGURE 4. PERMISSION CONVEYED THROUGH COPYRIGHT CLEARANCE CENTER, INC.

self-verification The tendency to seek evidence to confirm the self-concept.

TABLE 12.7				
ROSENBERG SELF-ESTEEM SCALE				

Consider each statement and circle SA for strongly agree, A for agree, D for disagree, and SD for strongly disagree.

1. On the whole, I am satisfied with myself.	SA	A	D	SD
2. At times, I think I am no good at all.	SA	A	D	SD
3. I feel that I have a number of good qualities.	SA	A	D	SD
4. I am able to do things as well as most other people.	SA	A	D	SD
5. I feel I do not have much to be proud of.	SA	A	D	SD
6. I certainly feel useless at times.	SA	A	D	SD
7. I feel that I'm a person of worth, at least on an equal plane with others.	SA	A	D	SD
8. I wish I could have more respect for myself.	SA	A	D	SD
9. All in all, I am inclined to feel that I am a failure.	SA	A	D	SD
10. I take a positive attitude towards myself.	SA	A	D	SD

Information from Rosenberg, 1965.

Scoring: For items 1, 3, 4, 7, and 10, SA = 3, A = 2, D = 1, SD = 0; for items 2, 5, 6, 8, and 9, the scoring is reversed, with SA = 0, A = 1, D = 2, SD = 3. The higher the total score, the higher one's self-esteem.

Self-Esteem

When you think about yourself, do you feel good and worthy? Do you like yourself? Or do you feel bad and have negative, self-critical thoughts? **Self-esteem** is *the extent to which an individual likes, values, and accepts the self.* Thousands of studies have examined differences between people with high self-esteem (who generally like themselves) and those with relatively low self-esteem (who are less keen on, and may actively dislike, themselves). Researchers who study self-esteem typically ask participants to fill out a self-esteem questionnaire such as the one shown in **TABLE 12.7** (Rosenberg, 1965). This widely used measure of self-esteem asks people to evaluate themselves in terms of each statement. People who strongly agree with the positive statements about themselves and strongly disagree with the negative statements are considered to have high self-esteem.

Although some personality psychologists have argued that self-esteem determines virtually everything about a person's life (from a tendency to engage in criminal activity and violence to professional success), the accumulated evidence shows that the benefits of high self-esteem are less striking and all-encompassing but still significant. In general, compared with people with low self-esteem, those with high self-esteem tend to live happier and healthier lives, cope better with stress, and are more likely to persist at difficult tasks. In contrast, individuals with low self-esteem are more likely, for example, to perceive rejection in ambiguous feedback from others and to develop eating disorders than those with high self-esteem (Baumeister et al., 2003). How does this aspect of personality develop? And why does everyone—whether high or low in self-esteem—seem to *want* high self-esteem?

Sources of Self-Esteem

Some psychologists contend that high self-esteem arises primarily from being accepted and valued by significant others (Brown, 1993). Other psychologists focus on the influence of specific self-evaluations: judgements about one's value or competence in specific domains such as appearance, athletics, or scholastics.

An important factor is whom people choose for comparison. For example, James (1890) noted that an accomplished athlete who is the second best in the world should feel pretty proud, but this athlete might not feel that way if the standard of

"I don't want to be defined by who I am."

self-esteem The extent to which an individual likes, values, and accepts the self.

comparison involves being best in the world. In fact, athletes in the 1992 Olympics who had won silver medals looked less happy during the medal ceremony than those who had won bronze medals (Medvec, Madey, & Gilovich, 1995). If people see the actual self as falling short of the ideal self (the person that they would like to be), they tend to feel sad or dejected. When they become aware that the actual self is inconsistent with the self they have a duty to be, they are likely to feel anxious or agitated (Higgins, 1987).

The Desire for Self-Esteem

What's so great about self-esteem? Why do people want to see themselves in a positive light and avoid seeing themselves negatively?

Self-Esteem May Reflect High Social Status Does self-esteem feel good because it reflects our degree of social dominance or status? People with high self-esteem seem to carry themselves in a way that is similar to how high-status animals of other social species carry themselves. Dominant male gorillas, for example, appear confident and comfortable, not anxious or withdrawn. Perhaps high self-esteem in humans reflects high social status or suggests that the person is worthy of respect, and this perception triggers natural affective responses (Barkow, 1980; Maslow, 1937).

Self-Esteem May Have Played a Role in Evolution Could the desire for self-esteem come from a basic need to belong or to be related to others? Evolutionary theory holds that early humans who managed to survive and pass on their genes were those able to maintain good relations with others rather than being cast out to fend for themselves. Clearly, belonging to groups is adaptive, as is knowing whether you are accepted. Thus, self-esteem could be a kind of "sociometer," an inner gauge of how much a person feels included by others at any given moment (Leary & Baumeister, 2000). According to evolutionary theory, then, we seek higher self-esteem because we have evolved to seek out belongingness in our families, work groups, and culture, and higher self-esteem indicates that we are being accepted.

Self-Esteem Provides a Sense of Security Consistent with the existential and psychodynamic approaches to personality, self-esteem can be a matter of security. The studies of mortality salience discussed in the Emotion and Motivation chapter suggest that the source of distress underlying negative self-esteem is ultimately the fear of death (Solomon, Greenberg, & Pyszczynski, 1991). In this view, humans find it anxiety-provoking—in fact, terrifying—to contemplate their own mortality, so they try to defend against this awareness by immersing themselves in activities (e.g., earning money or dressing up to appear attractive) that their culture defines as meaningful and valuable. The desire for self-esteem may stem from a need to find value in ourselves as a way of escaping the anxiety associated with recognizing our mortality. The higher our self-esteem, the less anxious we feel with the knowledge that someday we will no longer exist.

But Can We All Be Above Average? Whatever the reason that low self-esteem feels so bad and high self-esteem feels so good, people are generally motivated to see themselves positively. In fact, we often process information in a biased manner in order to feel good about the self. Research on the **self-serving bias** shows that *people tend to take credit for their successes but downplay responsibility for their failures.* You may have noticed this tendency in yourself, particularly in terms of the attributions you make about exams when you get a good grade ("I studied really intensely, and I'm good at that subject") or a bad grade ("The test was ridiculously tricky, and the professor is unfair").

On the whole, most people satisfy the desire for high self-esteem and maintain a reasonably positive view of self by engaging in the self-serving bias (Miller & Ross, 1975; Shepperd, Malone, & Sweeny, 2008). In fact, if people are asked to rate themselves across a range of characteristics, they tend to see themselves as better than the average person in most domains (Alicke et al., 1995). For example, 90% of drivers

These are the figure skating ice dance free program medallists at the 2018 Winter Olympics. From left, Gabriella Papadakis and Guillaume Cizeron of France, silver; Tessa Virtue and Scott Moir of Canada, gold; Maia Shibutani and Alex Shibutani of USA, bronze. Notice the expressions on the faces of the silver medallists compared with those of the gold- and bronze-medal winners.

Survivor, The Bachelor, Big Brother. Why are shows in which everyone is fighting to remain a part of the group so popular today? Is it because these shows exploit the evolutionary desire to belong? (Or do people just like to see other people get kicked out of the club?)

self-serving bias People's tendency to take credit for their successes but downplay responsibility for their failures.

"I suffer from accurate self-esteem."

ARIEL MOLVIG/THE NEW YORKER COLLECTION/WWW
.CARTOONBANK.COM

Henry Head (1861–1940; *top*) and Walter Russell Brain (1895–1966; *bottom*) were British neurologists ("brain doctors"). Brain wrote a well-known textbook on neurology, *Brain's Diseases of the Nervous System*, and was, until his death, editor of the most influential neurology journal in the world, titled . . . *Brain*. For his contributions, he was dubbed the First Baron Brain in 1962. Henry Head was a previous editor of *Brain* (the journal). Head was much admired by Brain, who wrote an essay in *Brain* about Head. Dr. Brain doesn't look like he suffers from a lack of self-esteem, does he? Dr. Head probably didn't either.

narcissism A trait that reflects a grandiose view of the self, combined with a tendency to seek admiration from and exploit others.

describe their driving skills as better than average, and 86% of workers rate their performance on the job as above average. Even among university professors, 94% feel they are above average in teaching ability compared with other professors (Cross, 1977). These kinds of judgements simply cannot be accurate, statistically speaking, because the average of a group of people has to be the average, not better than average! This particular error may be adaptive, however. People who do not engage in this self-serving bias to boost their self-esteem tend to be more at risk for depression, anxiety, and related health problems (Taylor & Brown, 1988).

On the other hand, a few people take positive self-esteem to the extreme. Unfortunately, seeing yourself as way, way better than average—a trait called **narcissism**, *a grandiose view of the self, combined with a tendency to seek admiration from and exploit others*—brings some costs. In fact, at its extreme, narcissism is considered a personality disorder (see the Psychological Disorders chapter). Research has documented disadvantages of an overinflated view of self, most of which arise from the need to defend that grandiose view at all costs. For example, when highly narcissistic adolescents were given reason to be ashamed of their performance on a task, their aggressiveness increased in the form of willingness to deliver loud blasts of noise to punish their opponents in a laboratory game (Thomaes et al., 2008).

Implicit Egotism

What's your favourite letter of the alphabet? About 30% of people answer by picking what just happens to be the first letter of their first name. Could this choice indicate that some people think so highly of themselves that they base judgements of seemingly unrelated topics on how much those topics remind them of themselves?

This *name-letter effect* was discovered some years ago (Nuttin, 1985), but more recently researchers have gone on to discover how broad the egotistic bias in preferences can be. Brett Pelham and his colleagues have found subtle yet systematic biases towards this effect when people choose their home cities, streets, and even occupations (Pelham, Mirenberg, & Jones, 2002). People whose last name is Street seem biased towards addresses ending in *street,* whereas Lanes like to live on lanes. The name effect seems to work for occupations as well: Slightly more people named Dennis and Denise chose dentistry, and Lauras and Lawrences chose law, compared with other occupations. Although the biases are small, they are consistent across many tests of this hypothesis.

These biases have been called expressions of *implicit egotism* because people are not typically aware that they are influenced by the wonderful sound of their own names (Pelham, Carvallo, & Jones, 2005). When Otto moves to Ottawa, he is not likely to volunteer that he did so because it matched his name. Yet people who show this egotistic bias in one way also tend to show it in others: People who strongly prefer their own name letter also are likely to pick their birth date as their favourite number (Koole, Dijksterhuis, & van Knippenberg, 2001). And people who like their name letter were also found to evaluate themselves positively on self-ratings of personality traits. This was especially true when the self-ratings were made in response to instructions to work *quickly.* The people who preferred their name letter made snap judgements about themselves that leaned in a positive direction, suggesting that their special self-appreciation was an automatic response. At some level, a bit of egotism is probably good for us, yet implicit egotism is a curiously subtle error: a tendency to make biased judgements of what we will do and where we will go in life just because we happen to have a certain name.

The self is the part of personality that the person knows and can report about. Some of the personality measures we have seen in this chapter (such as personality inventories based on self-reports) are really no different from measures of self-concept. Both depend on the person's perceptions and memories of the self's behaviour and traits. But personality runs deeper than this as well. The unconscious forces identified in psychodynamic approaches provide themes for behaviour and sources of mental disorder that are not accessible for self-report. The humanistic and existential approaches remind us of the profound concerns we humans face and the difficulties we may have in understanding all the forces that shape our self-views. Finally, in emphasizing how personality shapes our perceptions of social life, the social–cognitive approach brings the self back to centre stage. The self, after all, is the hub of each person's social world.

Build to the Outcomes

1. What is the difference between *I* and *Me*?
2. What makes up our self-concept?
3. How does our self-narrative contribute to our self-concept?
4. What is a self-schema?
5. Why don't traits always reflect knowledge of behaviour?
6. How does self-concept influence behaviour?
7. What impact does self-verification have on our behaviours?
8. What is self-esteem? Why do we want to have a high level of it?
9. How do comparisons with others affect self-esteem?
10. How might self-esteem have played a role in evolution?
11. Why is it possible to have too much self-esteem?

Chapter Review

Personality: What It Is and How It Is Measured

- In psychology, *personality* refers to a person's characteristic style of behaving, thinking, and feeling. Personality differences can be studied from two points of view: *prior events*, such as biological makeup, life circumstances, and culture; and *anticipated events*, as reflected in a person's hopes, dreams, and fears.

- Personality inventories, such as the MMPI–2–RF, are easy to administer, but people are often inaccurate in their self-reporting. Projective techniques, such as the Rorschach Inkblot Test and the TAT, provide richer information for a one-to-one relationship but are subject to interpreter bias.

- Newer, high-tech methods are proving to be even more effective in measuring personality.

The Trait Approach: Identifying Patterns of Behaviour

- The trait approach tries to identify personality dimensions that can be used to characterize an individual's behaviour. Researchers have attempted to boil down the potentially huge array of things people do, think, and feel into some core personality dimensions.

- Researchers use factor analysis to study relationships between the adjectives that people use to self-report traits.

- Many personality psychologists currently focus on the Big Five personality factors: openness to experience, conscientiousness, extraversion, agreeableness, and neuroticism.

- These traits account for variations in personality and appear universal, on the basis of results from many different studies and cultures.

- Twin studies indicate that the more genes you have in common with someone else, the more similar your personalities will be. Studies with animals further support the idea that biological mechanisms underlie personality traits.

- Research indicates that the part of the brain that regulates arousal and alertness (the reticular formation) is more easily stimulated in introverts than in extraverts, who may need to seek out more interaction and activity to achieve mental stimulation.

The Psychodynamic Approach: Forces That Lie Beneath Awareness

- Freud believed that the personality results from forces that are largely unconscious, shaped by the interplay among id, superego, and ego.

- Defence mechanisms are techniques the mind may use to reduce anxiety generated by unacceptable impulses.

- Freud also believed that the developing person passes through a series of psychosexual stages and that failing to progress beyond one of the stages results in fixation, which is associated with corresponding personality traits.

- Critics argue that psychodynamic explanations lack real evidence and are after-the-fact interpretations.

The Humanistic–Existential Approach: Personality as Choice

- The humanistic–existential approach to personality grew out of philosophical traditions that are at odds with most of the assumptions of the trait and psychoanalytic approaches. It focuses on how people make healthy choices that form their personalities.

- Humanists see personality as directed by an inherent striving towards self-actualization and development of our unique human potentials.

- Existentialists focus on angst and the defensive response people often have to questions about the meaning of life and the inevitability of death.

The Social–Cognitive Approach: Personalities in Situations

- The social–cognitive approach focuses on personality as arising from individuals' behaviour in situations. According to social–cognitive personality theorists, the same person may behave differently in different situations but should behave consistently in similar situations.

- Personal constructs are dimensions people use to make sense of their experiences and that reveal the perceiver's personality.

- People translate their goals into behaviour through outcome expectancies. People differ in whether they believe they control their own destiny (internal locus of control) or are at the mercy of fate or of other people (external locus of control). Those with an internal locus of control tend to be better able to cope with stress and to achieve more.

The Self: Personality in the Mirror

- The self-concept is a person's knowledge of self, including both specific self-narratives and more abstract personality traits or self-schemas. People's self-concept develops through social feedback, and people often act to try to confirm these views through a process of self-verification.

- Self-esteem is a person's evaluation of self; it is derived from being accepted by others, as well as by how we evaluate ourselves in comparison to others. Theories of why we seek positive self-esteem suggest that we do so to achieve perceptions of status, or belonging, or of being symbolically protected against mortality.

- People strive for positive self-views through self-serving biases and implicit egotism.

Key Concept Quiz

1. From a psychological perspective, personality refers to
   a. a person's characteristic style of behaving, thinking, and feeling.
   b. physiological predispositions that manifest themselves psychologically.
   c. past events that have shaped a person's current behaviour.
   d. choices people make in response to cultural norms.

2. Projective techniques to assess personality involve
   a. personal inventories.
   b. self-reporting.
   c. responses to ambiguous stimuli.
   d. actuarial methodology.

3. A relatively stable disposition to behave in a particular and consistent way is a
   a. motive.
   b. goal.
   c. trait.
   d. reflex.

4. Compelling evidence for the importance of biological factors in personality is best seen in studies of
   a. parenting styles.
   b. identical twins reared apart.
   c. brain damage.
   d. factor analysis.

5. After performing poorly on an exam, you drop a class, saying that you and the professor are just a poor match. According to Freud, what defence mechanism are you employing?
   a. regression
   b. rationalization
   c. projection
   d. reaction formation

6. Humanists see personality as directed towards the goal of
   a. existentialism.
   b. self-actualization.
   c. ego control.
   d. sublimation.

7. According to the existential perspective, the difficulties we face in finding meaning in life and in accepting the responsibility for making free choices provoke a type of anxiety called
   a. angst.
   b. flow.
   c. the self-actualizing tendency.
   d. mortality salience.

8. According to social–cognitive theorists, _____ are the dimensions people use in making sense of their experiences.
   a. personal constructs
   b. outcome expectancies
   c. loci of control
   d. personal goals

9. What we think about ourselves is referred to as our _____, and how we feel about ourselves is referred to as our _____.
   a. self-narrative; self-verification
   b. self-concept; self-esteem
   c. self-concept; self-verification
   d. self-esteem; self-concept

10. When people take credit for their successes but downplay responsibility for their failures, they are exhibiting
    a. narcissism.
    b. implicit egotism.
    c. the self-serving bias.
    d. the name-letter effect.

Don't stop now! Quizzing yourself is a powerful study tool. Go to LaunchPad to access the LearningCurve adaptive quizzing system and your own personalized learning plan. Visit launchpadworks.com.

Key Terms

personality (p. 468)

self-report (p. 469)

Minnesota Multiphasic Personality Inventory (MMPI) (p. 469)

projective tests (p. 470)

Rorschach Inkblot Test (p. 470)

Thematic Apperception Test (TAT) (p. 470)

trait (p. 472)

Big Five (p. 474)

psychodynamic approach (p. 481)

id (p. 481)

superego (p. 481)

ego (p. 481)

defence mechanisms (p. 481)

self-actualizing tendency (p. 483)

existential approach (p. 484)

social–cognitive approach (p. 485)

person–situation controversy (p. 485)

personal constructs (p. 487)

outcome expectancies (p. 488)

locus of control (p. 488)

self-concept (p. 490)

self-verification (p. 491)

self-esteem (p. 492)

self-serving bias (p. 493)

narcissism (p. 494)

Changing Minds

1. A political candidate makes a Freudian slip on live TV, calling his mother "petty"; he corrects himself quickly and says he meant to say "pretty." The next day, the video has gone viral, and the morning talk shows discuss the possibility that the candidate has an unresolved Oedipal conflict. If so, he's stuck in the phallic stage and is likely a relatively unstable person preoccupied with issues of seduction, power, and authority (which may be why he wants to be president). Your roommate knows you're taking a psychology class and asks for your opinion: "Can we really tell that a person is sexually repressed, and maybe in love with his own mother, just because he stumbled over a single word?" How would you reply? How widely are Freud's ideas about personality accepted by modern psychologists?

2. While reading a magazine, you come across an article on the nature–nurture controversy in personality. The magazine describes several adoption studies in which adopted children (who share no genes with each other but grow up in the same household) are no more like each other than complete strangers. This suggests that family environment—and the influence of parental behaviour—on personality is very weak. You show the article to a friend, who has trouble believing the results: "I always thought parents who don't show affection produce kids who have trouble forming lasting relationships." How would you

explain to your friend the relationship between nature, nurture, and personality?

3. One of your friends has found an online site that offers personality testing. He takes the test and reports that the results prove he's an "intuitive" rather than a "sensing" personality, who likes to look at the big picture rather than focusing on tangible here-and-now experiences. "This explains a lot," he says, "like why I have trouble remembering details like other people's birthdays, and why it's hard for me to finish projects before the deadline." Aside from warning your friend about the dangers of self-diagnosis via Internet quizzes, what would you tell him about the relationship between personality types and behaviour? How well do scores on personality tests predict a person's actual behaviour?

4. One of your friends tells you that her boyfriend cheated on her, so she will never date him again or date anyone who has ever been unfaithful because "once a cheat, always a cheat." She goes on to explain that personality and character are stable over time, so people will always make the same decisions and repeat the same mistakes over time. What do we know about the interaction between personality and situations that might confirm or deny her statements?

Answers to Key Concept Quiz

1. a; 2. c; 3. c; 4. b; 5. b; 6. b; 7. a; 8. a; 9. b; 10. c.

LaunchPad features the full e-book of *Psychology*, the LearningCurve adaptive quizzing system, videos, and a variety of activities to boost your learning. Visit LaunchPad at launchpadworks.com.

Social Psychology

TERRY, NELSON, AND JOHN HAVE SOMETHING IN COMMON: They have all been tortured. Terry was a British hostage negotiator working in Lebanon when he was kidnapped by Hezbollah guerrillas; Nelson was a political activist whose protests against the apartheid regime in South Africa earned him 27 years in prison; and John was an American naval aviator when he was shot down and captured during the Vietnam War. All three men experienced a variety of tortures, and all agree on which was the worst.

> **Terry:** "I soon realized that if I was to survive, it was essential to maintain a strong inner life . . . because the threat of dissolving into madness was ever present."
>
> **Nelson:** "Nothing is more dehumanizing."
>
> **John:** "It is an awful thing. It crushes your spirit and weakens your resistance more effectively than any other form of mistreatment."

The cruel technique that these three men are describing has nothing to do with electric shock or waterboarding. It does not require wax, rope, or razor blades. It is a remarkably simple technique that has been used for millennia to break the body and destroy the mind. That technique is called solitary confinement. Terry Waite spent 4 years in a cell by himself, Nelson Mandela spent 6, and John McCain spent 2.

Terry Waite (*left*), Nelson Mandela (*middle*), and John McCain (*right*) each spent years in isolation and described it as the worst form of torture. Waite was a hostage negotiator in the 1980s; Mandela was President of South Africa from 1994–1999; McCain was a U.S. Senator from 1987–2018.

Torture involves depriving people of something they desperately need, such as oxygen, water, food, or sleep, and as torturers have known for ages, the need for social interaction is every bit as vital. "I found solitary confinement the most forbidding aspect of prison life," Mandela wrote. "I have known men who took half a dozen lashes in preference to being locked up alone." Studies of prisoners show that extensive periods of isolation can induce symptoms of psychosis (Grassian, 2006), and even in smaller doses, social isolation takes a toll. Ordinary people who are socially isolated are more likely to become depressed, to become ill, and to die prematurely. Indeed, being socially isolated is as dangerous to your health as is smoking or being obese (Cacioppo & Patrick, 2008; Holt-Lunstad, 2018). Human beings are the most social animal on our planet, and connecting to each other is nearly as important as breathing.

But why are we built that way? Snails and centipedes aren't social. Neither are skunks, moose, badgers, or aardvarks. In fact, the majority of the earth's animals are loners that rely on no one but themselves and lead a solitary existence. Why are we so different? **Social psychology** is *the study of the causes and consequences of sociality*, and it provides an answer to this question. Like all other animals, human beings must solve the twin problems of survival and reproduction, and, as you will see in the first two sections ("Interpersonal Behaviour" and "Interpersonal Attraction"), sociality is a brilliant solution to both of these problems.

But any species that uses sociality to solve these problems must be capable of two things. First, individuals must be able to *understand and predict each other* so that they know whom they can and cannot trust. In the third section of this chapter ("Interpersonal Perception"), you'll see how people do this by forming impressions of each other—impressions that sometimes are right, but that other times are tragically mistaken. The second thing that members of a social species must be able to do is *influence each other*—that is, get others to accept them as mates, like them as friends, do favours for them, obey them, and so on. In the final section ("Interpersonal Influence"), you'll see some of the ingenious techniques that human beings have developed to manipulate and control each other—sometimes for better, and sometimes for worse.

Interpersonal Behaviour

Learning Outcomes

- Identify biological and cultural influences on aggression.
- Explain why cooperation is risky.
- Describe the costs and benefits of groups.
- Distinguish between apparent and genuine altruism.

social psychology The study of the causes and consequences of sociality.

aggression Behaviour whose purpose is to harm another.

All animals need food and water, some need mates and shelter, and one appears to need the limited-edition iPhone on the day it is released. All these things are resources, and the problem with resources is that there's rarely enough of them to go around—so if somebody gets them, then somebody else doesn't. We'd all rather be the one who gets them, of course, and human beings have developed two tactics to make sure that happens: *Hurting* and *helping*. Although these words are antonyms, they turn out to be different solutions to the same problem.

Aggression

Whether the scarce resource is a carrot, a cave, or an iPhone, the simplest way to make sure you get one is simply to take it—and kick the stuffing out of anyone who tries to stop you. **Aggression** is *behaviour whose purpose is to harm another* (Anderson & Bushman, 2002; Bushman & Huesmann, 2010), and it is a strategy used by virtually all animals to achieve their goals. The **frustration–aggression hypothesis** suggests that *animals aggress when their goals are frustrated* (Berkowitz, 1989; Dollard et al., 1939). The word "frustration" here refers not to a feeling, but rather to the obstruction of a goal. A chimp who wants a banana (*goal*) that is in the hands of another chimp (*frustration*) may attack in order to get that banana (*aggression*), just as a person who wants money (*goal*) that is in the hands of another person (*frustration*) may attack (*aggression*) to get that money.

Strategic behaviour of this kind is known as **proactive aggression**, which is *aggression that is planned and purposeful* (Wrangham, 2017). The mafia hit man who executes a rival gangster in cold blood is engaging in proactive aggression. Because this kind of aggression is a means to an end, it tends to be specifically directed towards a relevant target (the hit man's task is to kill the gangster and not just anybody who happens to be eating in the restaurant that day), it tends to occur only when the aggressor believes that the benefits will outweigh the costs (the hit man won't pull the trigger if he thinks there's a good chance he'll be caught), and it is not associated with a heightened state of arousal (hey, it's just a job).

But not all aggression is proactive. **Reactive aggression** is *aggression that occurs spontaneously in response to a negative affective state.* The man who gets fired, gets angry, and yells at his wife when he gets home is engaging in reactive aggression. This kind of aggression is strongly associated with the experience of pain or anger and is not always directed towards a relevant target. When rats are given painful electric shocks, they will attack whatever happens to be in their cage, whether that's another rat or a tennis ball (Kruk et al., 2004), and when experimental participants are made to experience physical pain (which can safely be done by having people immerse their hands in ice water), they will hurt others who had nothing to do with their pain (Anderson, 1989; Anderson, Bushman, & Groom, 1997).

DATA VISUALIZATION

Do Humans Have a "Social Brain"?
Go to launchpadworks.com.

Unlike proactive aggression, reactive aggression occurs even when the costs outweigh the benefits: The angry man who screams at his wife has done nothing to get his job back, and he's probably just made his life worse instead of better. Reactive aggression is typically a response to the experience of negative affect (Berkowitz, 1990), which explains why so many acts of violence—from murders to brawls—are more likely to occur on hot days, when people are already feeling uncomfortable, irritated, and easily angered (Rinderu, Bushman, & Van Lange, 2018) (see **FIGURE 13.1**). Indeed, the relationship between temperature and violence is so reliable that scientists can predict precisely how much more violent

frustration–aggression hypothesis A principle stating that animals aggress when their goals are frustrated.

proactive aggression Aggression that is planned and purposeful.

reactive aggression Aggression that occurs spontaneously in response to a negative affective state.

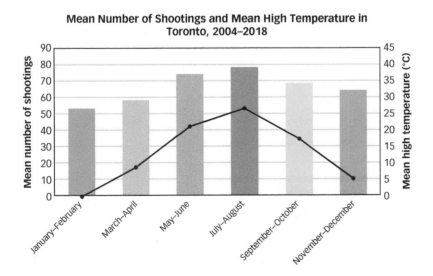

Mean Number of Shootings and Mean High Temperature in Toronto, 2004–2018

Figure 13.1

Heat and Aggression This graph shows the relationship between mean high temperature (in Celsius) and the mean number of shooting victims in Toronto, for 6 time points throughout the year, over a 14-year period. The number of victims is highest in the warmest months, and lowest in the coldest months. DATA FROM TORONTO POLICE SERVICE, 2019; CURRENT RESULTS, 2019.

crime and civil conflict that different parts of the world will experience over the next few decades due to climate change (Burke, Hsiang, & Miguel, 2015). Hint: It's a lot.

How Biology Influences Aggression

If you want to know whether someone is likely to engage in reactive aggression and you can ask them just one question, it should be this: "Are you a man?" Violence is one of the most gendered of all behaviours. Crimes such as assault, battery, and murder are almost exclusively perpetrated by men (and especially by young men), who are responsible for 78% of the violent crimes in Canada (Statistics Canada, 2019b). Although socialization practices all over the world encourage males to be more aggressive than females (more on that shortly), male aggressiveness is not merely the product of playing with toy soldiers or watching hockey. Studies show that aggression is associated with the presence of a hormone called *testosterone,* which is typically much higher in men than in women, and much higher in younger men than in older men (Carré & Archer, 2018).

How does testosterone promote aggression? Testosterone isn't "bad mood juice" so much as it is "bad ass juice." A man's testosterone levels wax and wane, and when those levels wax, men tend to feel more powerful and confident in their ability to prevail in interpersonal conflicts (Eisenegger, Haushofer, & Fehr, 2011; Eisenegger et al., 2010). Men with high levels of testosterone in their bloodstream tend to walk more purposefully, focus more directly on the people they are talking to, and speak in a more forwards and independent manner (Dabbs et al., 2001). What's more, testosterone makes men more sensitive to provocations (Ronay & Galinsky, 2011) and less sensitive to signs of retaliation. For example, participants in one experiment watched a face as its expression changed from neutral to threatening and were asked to respond as soon as the expression became threatening (see **FIGURE 13.2**). Participants who were given a small dose of testosterone were slower to recognize the threatening expression (van Honk & Schutter, 2007; see also Olsson et al., 2016). As you can imagine, feeling powerful while simultaneously failing to realize that the guy whose parking space you just stole looks really, really mad is a good way to end up in a fist fight.

One of the most reliable methods for raising a man's testosterone levels and provoking an aggressive response is to challenge his beliefs about his own status or dominance. Indeed, three-quarters of all murders can be classified as "status competitions" or "contests to save face" (Daly & Wilson, 1988). Contrary to popular wisdom, it isn't men with unusually low self-esteem who are most prone to this sort of aggression, but men with unusually *high* self-esteem, because those men are especially likely to perceive other people's actions as a challenge to their inflated sense of self-worth (Baumeister, Smart, & Boden, 1996). Men seem especially sensitive to such challenges when they are competing for the attention of women

Figure 13.2

I Spy Threat Subjects who were given testosterone needed to see a more threatening expression before they were able to recognize it as such. RESEARCH FROM VAN HONK, J., & SCHUTTER, D. J. (2007).

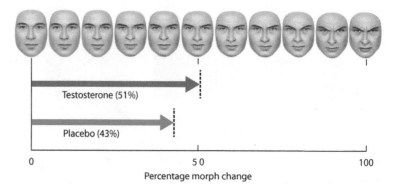

(Ainsworth & Maner, 2012), and losing those competitions can be deadly—especially for the women. The rate at which women in their reproductive years die at the hands of a current or former partner is about as high as the rate at which they die of cancer (Garcia-Moreno et al., 2006).

So that's men. Are women, by contrast, all sweetness and light? Hardly. Women can be just as aggressive as men, but their aggression tends to be proactive rather than reactive. Although women are considerably less likely than men to engage in physical aggression, they are just as likely to engage in verbal aggression (Denson et al., 2018) and cyber-bullying (Barlett & Coyne, 2014). Indeed, women may even be more likely than men to aggress by causing social harm—for example, by ostracizing others (Benenson et al., 2011) or by spreading malicious rumors about them (Bjorkqvist, 2018; Card et al., 2008; Richardson, 2014). Several studies suggest that women tend to use rumors to damage the reputations of other women whom they see as romantic rivals (Keys & Bhogal, 2018; Muggleton, Tarran, & Fincher, 2019); Reynolds, Baumeister, & Maner, 2018; Wyckoff, Asao, & Buss, 2019). Men and women both use aggression as a tool, but they use it in different ways.

How Culture Influences Aggression

"Our ancestors have bred pugnacity into our bone and marrow," wrote William James (1911, p. 272) "and thousands of years of peace won't breed it out of us." Is that true? If James was saying that aggression is part of our biological heritage and that humans will always be capable of it, then yes, he was surely right. But if he was saying that our biological heritage means that we are destined to rape, pillage, and plunder our way through the rest of history, then he was surely wrong. How do we know? Two reasons. First, human beings have become remarkably less aggressive in just the last century alone. As the psychologist Steven Pinker (2007) noted:

> We have been getting kinder and gentler. Cruelty as entertainment, human sacrifice to indulge superstition, slavery as a labor-saving device, conquest as the mission statement of government, genocide as a means of acquiring real estate, torture and mutilation as routine punishment, the death penalty for misdemeanors and differences of opinion, assassination as the mechanism of political succession, rape as the spoils of war, pogroms as outlets for frustration, homicide as the major form of conflict resolution—all were unexceptionable features of life for most of human history. But, today, they are rare to nonexistent in the West, far less common elsewhere than they used to be, concealed when they do occur, and widely condemned when they are brought to light.

Second, just as the prevalence of aggression changes over time, so too does it vary across locations. For example, violent crime in the United States is more prevalent in the South, where men are taught to react aggressively when they feel their status has been challenged, than in the North, where men are taught to resolve conflicts by appealing to authority (Brown, Osterman, & Barnes, 2009; Nisbett & Cohen, 1996). In one set of experiments (Cohen et al., 1996), researchers insulted American men from northern and southern states. As the participants were leaving the experiment via a narrow hallway, a large man (who was a trained actor) came walking towards them. What happened? The previously insulted southerners got right up in the man's face before letting him pass, whereas the previously insulted northerners simply stepped aside. Are northern men just nicer? Nope. Because in another condition of the study in which the participants were *not* insulted, southern men stepped aside *before* northern men did. Southern men, it seems, are more aggressive when insulted but more polite otherwise.

These variations over time and across locations suggest that the environment plays an important role in determining whether our innate capacity for aggression will result in aggressive behaviour (Leung & Cohen, 2011). For example, aggression is

Male aggression is often a response to a status threat. In 2017, the 17-year-old Mexican YouTube star Juan Luis Lagunas Rosales posted a video in which he insulted a local drug lord. Shortly thereafter, a group of armed men found Rosales at a bar and shot the teenager to death. Over. Some. Words.

Major League Baseball pitchers have extremely good aim, so when they hit a batter with a "bean ball" you can assume they meant it. Statistics show that pitchers born in southern U.S. states are 40% more likely to throw a bean ball than are pitchers born in northern U.S. states (Timmerman, 2007).

Depending on where you live, violence can be ordinary or unthinkable. In Iraq, where children are exposed to the brutality of extremist groups such as ISIS, mock executions can be part of daily play. In contrast, the Jains of India believe that every form of life is sacred, and children wear masks so that they do not accidentally harm insects or microbes by inhaling them.

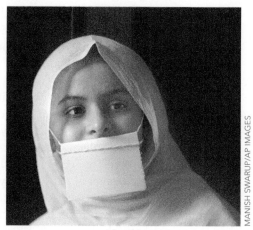

more likely in environments that make it easy. The U.S. murder rate is three times higher than the murder rate in Canada, and one reason is that while Americans are just 4% of the world's population, they own about half the world's guns. Aggression is more likely when it is easy to accomplish, but also when it is easy to imagine (Labella & Masten, 2017). Research suggests that watching violent movies and playing violent video makes people (and especially children) behave more aggressively (Anderson et al., 2010; Anderson et al., 2017; Bender, Plante, & Gentile, 2017; Calvert et al., 2017) and less cooperatively (cf. Ferguson, 2010; Sheese & Graziano, 2005). As one researcher noted, "Violence can be viewed as a contagious disease which can be caught simply through its observation" (Huesmann, 2017, p. 119). That's the bad news. The good news is that just as a culture can accidentally encourage aggression, so too can it purposefully discourage it (Fry, 2012). For example, the Inuit people of the Canadian Arctic do not resolve conflicts with guns or knives, but with song contests in which the person who delivers the most effective musical put-down of his opponent is declared the winner (Briggs, 2000). Replacing war with *American Idol* sounds like a remarkably sane idea.

Cooperation

Two wolves can fight over a dead rabbit, or they can work together to bring down a gazelle. Aggression may be the simplest way to solve the problem of scarce resources, but it is rarely the most effective way, because when individuals work together, each of them can often get more resources per capita than either could get alone. **Cooperation** is *behaviour by two or more individuals that leads to mutual benefit* (Rand & Nowak, 2016), and it is one of our species' greatest achievements—right up there with language, fire, and free two-day delivery (Axelrod, 1984; Henrich, 2018; Nowak, 2006; Rand, 2016). Every roadway and supermarket, every toothbrush and cell phone, every ballet and surgery is the result of cooperation, and it is hard to think of any important human accomplishment that could possibly have happened without it. But if the benefits of cooperation are clear, why don't we cooperate all the time?

Why Cooperation Is Risky

Cooperation is potentially beneficial, but it is also risky, as demonstrated by a game called the *prisoner's dilemma*. Imagine that you and your friend Tucker have been arrested for hacking into a bank's mainframe and directing a few million dollars to your personal accounts. The police have found some stolen bank codes on your laptops, but they don't know which of you actually did the hacking. You and Tucker are now being interrogated in separate rooms, and the detectives ask each of you to sign

cooperation Behaviour by two or more individuals that leads to mutual benefit.

	Tucker refuses to sign (i.e., he cooperates with you)	Tucker signs (i.e., he does not cooperate with you)
You refuse to sign (i.e., you cooperate with Tucker)	You both serve 1 year	You serve 3 years Tucker goes free
You sign (i.e., you do not cooperate with Tucker)	You go free Tucker serves 3 years	You both serve 2 years

Figure 13.3

The Prisoner's Dilemma Game The prisoner's dilemma game illustrates the risk of cooperation. Mutual cooperation leads to a moderate benefit to both players, but if one player cooperates and the other one doesn't, the cooperator gets no benefit and the noncooperator gets a large benefit. (And in case you were wondering, the game was devised in 1950 by the mathematician Albert Tucker.)

a statement saying that the other was the actual hacker. They explain that if you both sign, then you'll both get 2 years in prison for hacking, and if you both refuse to sign, then you'll both get 1 year in prison for possession of the stolen codes. However, if one of you signs and the other refuses, then the one who signs will go free, and the one who refuses will get 3 years in prison. What should you do (other than math)? As **FIGURE 13.3** shows, it would be best if you and Tucker cooperated and refused to implicate each other, because you'd both get off with a very light sentence. But if you agree to cooperate and then Tucker gets sneaky and decides to sign, you'll serve a long sentence while Tucker goes free. So should you cooperate with Tucker or not? Oh my. What a dilemma!

The prisoner's dilemma is not just a game (which is good, because compared with *Cards Against Humanity* it pretty much sucks). It is also a metaphor for the potential costs and benefits of cooperation in everyday life. For example, consider the dilemma taxpayers face at tax time. If everyone pays their taxes, then the government can afford to maintain the roads and bridges that everyone needs; and if no one pays their taxes, then the roads buckle and the bridges fall down. So there is benefit to everyone if everyone cooperates and pays their fair share; but there is a much *bigger* benefit to the sneaky cheater who avoids paying his own taxes because he gets to use all the roads and bridges for free. So should you pay your fair share and risk being taken advantage of by a sneaky cheater, or should you *be* a sneaky cheater and risk the possibility that everyone will do the same, which will cause the bridges to collapse? If you are like most citizens, you'd be more than happy to cooperate in this situation as long as you knew that everyone else would, but you aren't sure that everyone else will—and *that's* the dilemma that cooperation so often produces.

Because so much of social life is essentially a prisoner's dilemma game, it isn't surprising that people in every culture value and reward those who play the game honourably, and despise and sanction those who don't (Feinberg, Willer, & Shultz, 2014). When people are asked what single quality they most want those around them to have, the answer is *trustworthiness* (Cottrell, Neuberg, & Li, 2007), and when those around us fail to demonstrate that quality, we respond with disappointment, anger, and even retribution (unless they are on our side; see Hot Science: Partners in Crime).

For example, the *ultimatum game* requires one player (the divider) to divide a monetary prize into two parts and offer one of the parts to a second player (the decider) who can either accept or reject the offer. If the decider rejects the offer, then both players get nothing and the game is over. If deciders were economically rational, they would accept any offer: After all, something is always better than nothing. But human deciders are not economically rational and they typically reject offers that are much less than half the prize (Fehr & Gaechter, 2002; Thaler, 1988). People apparently dislike unfairness so much that they are willing to get nothing in order to make sure that someone who has treated them unfairly gets nothing too. The same goes for nonhumans, by the way. In one study, monkeys were willing to work for a slice

At roadside farm stands, customers select what they want, put money in a box, and leave. If a few people cheat, it won't matter much; but if a lot of people cheat, then the farmer will have to close the stand. "Honour systems" such as these are real-world versions of the prisoner's dilemma.

Hot Science | Partners in Crime

Odds are good that most of your friends think of you as a fair, trustworthy, and honest person, because if they didn't, they probably wouldn't be your friends. The upside of having a reputation for honesty is that others will befriend you, work with you, share with you, and cooperate with you; but the downside is that you miss all the illicit benefits that dishonesty provides, such as free movies from pirate websites and free sodas from machines with a "no refills" sign. Is there any way to have the best of both worlds—to reap the reputational rewards of honesty while also reaping the material benefits of dishonesty?

There is: Be honest, and then team up with dishonest people who will do your dirty work. For example, you can honestly report every penny of your income to your accountant, but you can choose an accountant who is known to bend the rules when tax time rolls around. That way, your hands are clean, but you still get a major tax rebate! Can anyone say win-win? This strategy is devilishly sneaky but it sounds too clever by half. Do honest people really do such things? That's what Gross and colleagues (2018) wanted to know when they brought pairs of participants into their laboratory to play a potentially lucrative game. Here's how it worked.

The two participants sat in separate rooms that were electronically interconnected so that they and the experimenter could hear each other speak. Each participant rolled a die in the privacy of her own room, and her job was simply to announce the outcome of that die roll aloud so that the experimenter and the other participant could hear her. One participant was assigned to announce her outcome first (let's call her the First Mover), and the other participant was assigned to announce her outcome second (let's call her the Second Mover). Participants were told that they would receive a cash payment that corresponded to the number shown on their die. So if the participant reported that the outcome of her die roll was 1, she received a small payment; but if she reported that the outcome was 6, she received a large payment. Furthermore, participants were told that whenever they reported the same outcome, their payments would be doubled.

Now, if you think about it for a moment, you'll realize that this game was designed so that it was easy for participants to cheat. The First Mover could cheat by claiming that her die showed a 6 even when it didn't (which gave her a large payment), and the Second Mover could cheat by claiming that her die also showed a 6 even when it didn't (which gave her a large payment *and* which then doubled both her payment and the First Mover's payment). Were participants honest? Some were and some weren't, of course, but the really interesting part of the study was what happened next.

After playing a few rounds of the game, participants were allowed to choose new partners or keep their old ones. The results showed that when dishonest First Movers were paired with dishonest Second Movers, they almost never chose to switch partners; but when they were paired with honest Second Movers, they chose to switch about 40% of the time. In other words, dishonest participants were more likely to dump an honest partner than a dishonest one. So, what about honest participants? What did they do when offered the chance to switch? When honest First Movers were paired with honest Second Movers, they chose to switch about 40% of the time; but when they were paired with dishonest Second Movers, they chose to switch only 15% of the time! In other words, just like the dishonest participants, *honest participants were more likely to dump an honest partner than a dishonest one.*

One way to protect our own reputations for honesty while still benefiting from dishonesty is to team up with people who will do the sketchy stuff that we won't do ourselves. This study suggests that you don't have to be a criminal to seek a partner in crime.

---

of cucumber until they saw the experimenter give another monkey a more delicious food for doing less work (Brosnan & DeWaal, 2003), at which point the first set of monkeys went on strike and refused to participate further.

How Groups Minimize the Risks of Cooperation

Cooperation requires that we take a risk by benefiting others and then *trusting* that they will do the same. So how do we know whom to trust? A **group** is *a collection of people who have something in common that distinguishes them from others.* Every one of us is a member of many groups—from families and teams to religions and nations. Although these groups are quite different, they all have one thing in common: the members can generally trust that other members will be nice to them. **Prejudice** is *an evaluation of another person based solely on his or her group membership* (Dovidio & Gaertner, 2010), and although most people use this word to denote negative evaluations, psychologists use it to denote both positive and negative evaluations (Allport, 1954). Research suggests that although people are not always negatively prejudiced against members of other groups, they are almost always positively

group A collection of people who have something in common that distinguishes them from others.

prejudice A positive or negative evaluation of another person based solely on his or her group membership.

prejudiced towards members of their own groups (Brewer, 1999; DiDonato, Ullrich, & Krueger, 2011).

This tendency—known as *in-group favouritism*—is evolutionarily ancient (Fu et al., 2012; Mahajan et al., 2011), arises early in development (Dunham, Chen, & Banaji, 2013), and is easily elicited (Efferson, Lalive, & Fehr, 2008). Even when people are randomly assigned to be members of meaningless groups such as "Group 1" or "Group 2," they still favour members of their own group (Hodson & Sorrentino, 2001; Locksley, Ortiz, & Hepburn, 1980). It appears that simply knowing that "I'm one of *us* and not one of *them*" is sufficient to create in-group favouritism (Tajfel et al., 1971). Because group members can be trusted to favour each other, group membership makes cooperation less risky, and that's one of the reasons why our species became the groupiest animal on earth.

When it comes to cooperation, groups have benefits; but when it comes to other outcomes, they often have costs. For example, you've probably heard that two heads are better than one, but research shows that when groups try to make decisions, they rarely do better than the best member would have done alone—and they often do much worse (Baumeister, Ainsworth, & Vohs, 2016; Minson & Mueller, 2012). When a school board meets to solve its budget crisis, there are several reasons why its members will probably end up approving a plan that is not nearly as good as the plan the most qualified member would have developed on their own:

- Groups usually don't capitalize fully on the expertise of their members (Hackman & Katz, 2010). For instance, groups (such as a school board) often give too little weight to the opinions of members who are experts (the financial advisor) and too much weight to the opinions of members who happen to be high in status (the mayor) or especially talkative (the mayor).

- The **common knowledge effect** is *the tendency for group discussions to focus on information that all members share* (Gigone & Hastie, 1993; Kerr & Tindale, 2004). What makes this a problem is that the information everyone shares (the cost of running the cafeteria) is often relatively unimportant, whereas the truly important information (how a school in Sweden solved a similar budget crisis) is known to just a few.

- A group whose members come to the table with moderate opinions ("We probably shouldn't renovate the gym this year") can end up making an extreme decision ("Let's shut down the gym and fire the entire athletic staff") simply because, in the course of discussion, each member was exposed to many different arguments in favour of a single position (Isenberg, 1986). **Group polarization** is *the tendency for groups to make decisions that are more extreme than any member would have made alone* (Myers & Lamm, 1975).

- Group members usually care about how other members feel and are sometimes reluctant to "rock the boat" even when it needs a good rocking. **Groupthink** is *the tendency for groups to reach consensus in order to facilitate interpersonal harmony* (Janis, 1982). Harmony is important (especially if the group is a choir), but studies show that groups often sacrifice the soundness of their decisions in order to achieve it (Turner & Pratkanis, 1998).

For all of these reasons, then, groups underperform individuals in a wide variety of tasks. But the costs of groups go beyond making some suboptimal decisions. People in groups sometimes do truly terrible things that none of their members would do alone (Yzerbyt & Demoulin, 2010). Lynching, rioting, gang-raping—why do human beings sometimes behave so badly when they assemble? One reason is that when assembled in groups, people's attention is drawn towards others and away from themselves, and they become momentarily less likely to consider their personal values before taking action (Wicklund, 1975). **Deindividuation** occurs *when immersion in*

common knowledge effect The tendency for group discussions to focus on information that all members share.

group polarization The tendency of groups to make decisions that are more extreme than any member would have made alone.

groupthink The tendency of groups to reach consensus in order to facilitate interpersonal harmony.

deindividuation A phenomenon in which immersion in a group causes people to become less concerned with their personal values.

When are people most and least likely to cheat? Researchers posted a picture above an office coffee pot and found that people were less likely to take coffee without paying when the picture showed eyes than when it showed flowers (Bateson, Nettle, & Roberts, 2006). Other researchers paid people to sit alone in a room and complete puzzles for cash and found that people were less likely to cheat when the lights were bright than when the lights were low (Zhong, Bohns, & Gino, 2010). People behave better when they think they are being observed, and both watchful eyes and bright lights give them the feeling of being observed.

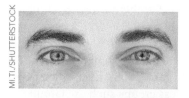

a group causes people to become less concerned with their personal values (Postmes & Spears, 1998) and this can lead people in groups to do things that they would not do on their own (Baumeister et al., 2016). You would never smash a store window and grab a Rolex on your own because looting conflicts with your personal values; but if you're pressed tightly into a big crowd and someone suddenly breaks a window, you may be so busy attending to what others are saying and doing (and stealing!) that you don't even stop to consider what you personally believe.

A second reason for the bad behaviour of people in groups is **diffusion of responsibility**, which refers to *the tendency of individuals to feel diminished responsibility for their actions when they are surrounded by others who are acting the same way*. Diffusion of responsibility is the main culprit behind something you've probably observed many times—a phenomenon that psychologists call **social loafing**, which is *the tendency of people to expend less effort when they are in a group than when they are alone* (Karau & Williams, 1993). For example, individuals in large groups are less likely than individuals in small groups to clap loudly after a performance (Latané, Williams, & Harkins, 1979), exert effort in a team sport (Williams et al., 1989), leave good tips at restaurants (Freeman et al., 1975), donate money to charity (Wiesenthal, Austrom, & Silverman, 1983), and even say hello to passersby (Jones & Foshay, 1984).

But social loafing is by no means the worst consequence of the diffusion of responsibility. Studies of **bystander intervention**—which is *the act of helping strangers in an emergency situation*—show that people are less likely to help an innocent person in distress when there are many other bystanders present, simply because they assume that the other bystanders are collectively more responsible than they are (Darley & Latané, 1968; Fischer et al., 2011). If you saw a fellow student fall off her bicycle in the middle of campus, you'd probably feel more responsible for stopping to help if you were the only person watching than if hundreds of other students were standing nearby because, in the former case, you'd own a greater share of the responsibility (see **FIGURE 13.4**).

So groups make bad decisions and foster bad behaviour. Might we be better off without them? Not bloody likely. Groups not only minimize the risks of cooperation (which makes human civilization possible), but they also contribute to our general health, happiness, and well-being (which makes human civilization worthwhile). Being excluded from groups is one of the most painful experiences people can have (Eisenberger, Lieberman, & Williams, 2003; Uskul & Over, 2014; Williams, 2007), so it isn't any wonder that people who are routinely excluded are anxious, lonely, depressed, and at increased risk for illness and premature death (Cacioppo & Patrick, 2008; Cohen, 1988; Leary, 1990). Belonging to groups is not just a source of psychological and physical well-being but also a source

diffusion of responsibility The tendency of individuals to feel diminished responsibility for their actions when surrounded by others who are acting the same way.

social loafing The tendency of people to expend less effort when they are in a group than when they are alone.

bystander intervention The act of helping strangers in an emergency situation.

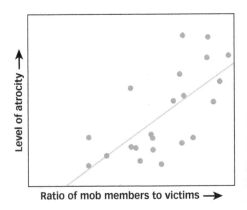

Figure 13.4
Mob Size and Level of Atrocity Mobs often do horrible things. These two men were rescued by police just as residents of their town prepared to lynch them for stealing a car. Because larger mobs provide more opportunity for diffusion of responsibility, they also commit more atrocious crimes. When researchers divide the number of mob victims by the number of mob members, they find that this ratio predicts the atrociousness of the mob's actions (Leader, Mullen, & Abrams, 2007; Ritchey & Ruback, 2018). Small mobs with many victims do bad things, and large mobs with few victims do even worse things.

of identity (Ellemers, 2012; Leary, 2010; Tajfel & Turner, 1986), which is why when you ask individuals to tell you about themselves, they typically describe the groups of which they are members ("I'm a female Canadian architect"). Groups sometimes cause us to misjudge and to misbehave, but they are essential to our cooperativeness, our health, and our happiness. Can't live with 'em, but can't live without 'em.

Altruism

Cooperation solves the problem of scarce resources: We can do better by cooperating than we can by competing. But is "doing better" the only reason we cooperate with others? Aren't we ever just . . . well, nice? **Altruism** is *intentional behaviour that benefits another at a potential cost to oneself,* and for centuries, scientists and philosophers have argued about whether people are ever truly altruistic. That may seem like an odd argument for a bunch of smart folks to be having. After all, people give their blood to the injured, their food to the homeless, and their time to the elderly. We volunteer, donate, contribute, and tithe. People do nice things all the time—so why is there any debate about whether people are altruistic?

Because behaviours that appear to be altruistic often have hidden benefits for those who do them. Consider some examples from the world of nonhuman animals. Squirrels emit alarm calls when they see a predator, which puts them at increased risk of being eaten but allows their fellow squirrels to escape. Honeybees spend their lives caring for the offspring of the queen rather than bearing offspring of their own. These behaviours appear to be thoroughly altruistic because the animals that engage in them clearly pay a large cost and appear to receive no benefits. But don't be fooled by appearances: There *are* benefits, because squirrels and honeybees are *genetically related* to the individuals they help. Squirrels emit alarm calls when they are closely related to the other squirrels in the den (Maynard-Smith, 1965), and, by an odd genetic quirk, honeybees are more closely related to the queen's offspring whom they are helping than they would be to their own offspring. When an animal promotes the survival of its relatives, it is actually benefitting itself by promoting the survival of its own genes (Hamilton, 1964). **Kin selection** is *the process by which evolution selects for individuals who cooperate with their relatives,* and although cooperating with relatives looks like altruism, many scientists consider it selfishness in disguise.

So what about cooperating with unrelated individuals? Well, that isn't necessarily altruistic either. Male baboons will sometimes risk injury to help an unrelated male baboon win a fight, and monkeys will spend time grooming unrelated monkeys when they could be doing something else, such as eating or resting. Are these examples of altruism? Not necessarily, because as it turns out, baboons and monkeys are pretty good at keeping score, and the ones that *do* favours today

In 2013, a customer at a Tim Horton's drive-through in Winnipeg, Canada, decided to perform a random act of kindness and pay for the order of the car behind him. This caused a chain reaction of altruism as 228 consecutive cars received free orders and, in turn, decided to pay for the order of the folks in the next car. The cascade ended when a customer who received four free coffees refused to pay for the three coffees ordered by the car behind him. There's always *that* guy.

altruism Intentional behaviour that benefits another at a potential cost to oneself.

kin selection The process by which evolution selects for individuals who cooperate with their relatives.

are the ones that *get* favours tomorrow. **Reciprocal altruism** is *behaviour that benefits another with the expectation that those benefits will be returned in the future,* and despite the second word in this term, many scientists think there is nothing altruistic about it (Trivers, 1972). In many ways, reciprocal altruism is merely cooperation extended over time—and cooperating is one of the most selfish things a smart animal can do!

The behaviour of nonhuman animals does not provide clear evidence of genuine altruism (cf. Bartal, Decety, & Mason, 2011). So what about us? Are we any different? Yes and no. Like squirrels and honeybees, we tend to help our kin more than strangers (Burnstein, Crandall, & Kitayama, 1994; Komter, 2010). Like baboons and monkeys, we tend to expect those we help to help us in return (Burger et al., 2009). But unlike these other animals, humans clearly *do* provide benefits to complete strangers who have no chance of repaying them (Batson, 2002; Warneken & Tomasello, 2009). We hold the door for people who share precisely none of our genes and tip waiters in restaurants to which we will never return. We give strangers directions, advice, free coffee, and sometimes even our parking spots (see A World of Difference: Do Me a Favour?). And we do much more than that (see **FIGURE 13.5**). When Wesley Autrey saw a student stumble and fall on the subway tracks just as a train was approaching, he didn't ask whether they shared his genes or how he would be repaid in the future. He just jumped onto the tracks and lay on top of the student, holding him down while the train passed over them—with less than an inch to spare. *That's* altruism.

Clearly, then, humans do help other humans, sometimes at a staggering cost to themselves. We are not only capable of genuine altruism, but we may be more capable than we realize (Gerbasi & Prentice, 2013; Miller & Ratner, 1998). Some scientists even argue that our altruistic orientation is the single essential characteristic that gave our species' dominion over all others (Hare, 2017). It is worth noting that although altruistic people do not help others in order to benefit themselves, they may benefit nonetheless. People who are oriented towards helping others have better psychological well-being, physical health, and social relationships (Crocker, Canevello, & Brown, 2017). And it might surprise Darwin to learn that they also have more children (Eriksson et al, 2019)!

Wesley Autrey jumped onto the subway tracks to save a stranger's life. "I had a split-second decision to make . . . I don't feel like I did something spectacular; I just saw someone who needed help. I did what I felt was right" (Buckley, 2007). Said no raccoon ever.

ROBERT KALFUS/SPLASH NEWS/NEWSCOM

reciprocal altruism Behaviour that benefits another with the expectation that those benefits will be returned in the future.

Figure 13.5

Organ Donation and Altruism
Canada's rate of organ donation by living donors in 2016 was 15.0 donors per million population (dpmp), slightly down from 15.7 dpmp the previous year. Every year, hundreds of living Canadians donate a liver or a kidney. Although many of these donations are for family and friends, fully 2 in 3 kidneys are donated anonymously by altruistic strangers (Canadian Blood Services, 2019). Another type of altruism in Canada is gestational surrogacy—the carrying of a child for people who cannot have a child on their own. In Canada, surrogates cannot be paid—only their expenses can be reimbursed, making this an altruistic act. In 2013, in Ontario alone, 145 babies were born to gestational surrogates (White, 2016).
DATA FROM CANADIAN BLOOD SERVICES, 2017.

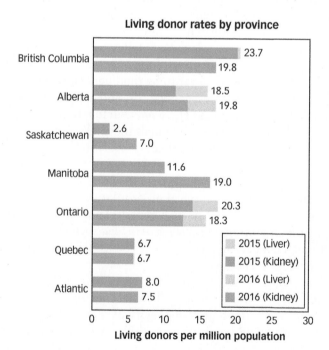

Living donor rates by province

Province	2015 (Liver)	2015 (Kidney)	2016 (Liver)	2016 (Kidney)
British Columbia			23.7	19.8
Alberta			18.5	19.8
Saskatchewan			2.6	7.0
Manitoba			11.6	19.0
Ontario			20.3	18.3
Quebec			6.7	6.7
Atlantic			8.0	7.5

Living donors per million population

A World of Difference · Do Me a Favour?

One of the many things that distinguish human beings from other animals is that we often do favours for strangers. Often, but not always. If a stranger walked up to you on the street and asked for the time, you'd probably tell him; but if he asked to borrow your credit card or move into your spare bedroom, you'd probably tell him to keep walking. Some requests are reasonable, and some are outrageous. So which are which?

The answer, it seems, depends on your cultural background. In one study (Jonas et al., 2009), researchers approached university students in a campus parking lot and asked them for one of two favours. Some students were asked to give up their parking privileges for a week ("Could I borrow your parking card this week so I can participate in a research project in a nearby building?") and others were asked to give up *everyone's* parking privileges for a week ("Would you mind if we closed the entire parking lot this week for a tennis tournament?"). Both of these requests required the students to relinquish their parking spots for a stranger, so both were a bit irritating. But which one was more irritating?

As the figure shows, European American students were more irritated when the researchers asked them—but *only* them—to give up their parking privileges. As members of families that came

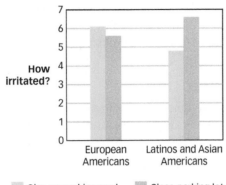

Give up parking card   Close parking lot

from individualistic cultures, in which every person is expected to look out for his own interests, these students were especially annoyed when the researcher singled them out and asked them to give up something that everyone else would be allowed to keep. European American students didn't mind suffering as long as they weren't the only ones to suffer. But Latino students and Asian American students had precisely the opposite reactions. As members of families that came from collectivist cultures, in which the needs of the many outweigh the needs of the few, these students were especially annoyed when the researcher suggested that many students should give up their parking privileges so that a few students could participate in a tennis tournament. Latino and Asian American

Social life involves favours—soliciting them, offering them, doing them, and denying them. When is a request too big to grant? It all depends on who you ask.

students didn't mind suffering as long as everyone didn't have to. Most people will do a reasonable favour for a stranger, but what counts as reasonable may depend on the culture in which one has been raised.

Build to the Outcomes

1. How does the frustration–aggression hypothesis explain aggressive behaviours?
2. How and why does gender influence aggression?
3. What evidence suggests that culture can influence aggression?
4. What are the potential costs and benefits of cooperation?
5. How do groups lower the risks of cooperation?
6. How and why do individuals behave differently when they are in groups?
7. How can we explain selfish behaviours that appear to be altruistic?

Interpersonal Attraction

Among sea horses, it is the male that carries the young, and, not coincidentally, males are more selective than are females.

Social behaviour is useful for survival, but it is essential for reproduction, which generally doesn't happen unless two people get extremely social with each other. The first step on the road to reproduction is finding someone who wants to travel that road with us, and psychologists know a lot about how people do that.

Selectivity

People don't mate randomly, at least not outside of Hollywood. Rather, they *select* their sexual partners, and, as anyone who has lived on earth for more than a few minutes knows, women tend to be more selective than men (Feingold, 1992a; Fiore et al., 2010). When researchers arranged for a trained actor to approach opposite-sex strangers on a university campus and ask, "Would you go out with me?" they found that roughly half of both the men and the women who were approached agreed to the request. On the other hand, when the actor asked the stranger, "Would you go to bed with me?" precisely *none* of the women said yes, but *three-quarters* of the men did (Clark & Hatfield, 1989). There are many reasons other than "being selective" that a woman might turn down a sexual offer from a strange man who approaches her in a public place (Conley, 2011), but research suggests that women tend to be choosier than men under most ordinary circumstances as well (Buss & Schmitt, 1993; Schmitt et al., 2012).

But why? Women are choosier than men, in part, because of differences in their biology. Women produce a small number of eggs in their lifetimes, conception eliminates their ability to conceive for at least 9 months, and pregnancy increases their nutritional requirements and puts them at risk of illness and maybe even death. When women have sex, they are taking a serious risk. Men, on the other hand, produce billions of sperm in their lifetimes, and their ability to conceive a child tomorrow is not inhibited by having conceived one today. When men have sex, they are risking a few minutes of their time and roughly a teaspoon of bodily fluid. Basic biology makes sex a much riskier proposition for women than for men, so it makes sense that women are much more selective about whom they mate with. If one person bet $1,000,000 on a horse race and another bet $1, we'd expect the first person to select their horse much more carefully.

Biology plays an important role in determining how selective a person will be, but other factors seem to play important roles as well (Finkel & Eastwick, 2009; Petersen & Hyde, 2010; Zentner & Mitura, 2012). For example, women are typically approached by men more often than men are approached by women (Conley et al., 2011), which means that women can afford to be more selective simply because they have a larger pool from which to select. A man at a club who turns down a willing partner may not find another, whereas a woman can pretty much just turn around and start dancing with someone else.

In addition, in most cultures, the reputational costs of promiscuity are higher for women than for men (Eagly & Wood, 1999; Kasser & Sharma, 1999). There is a long list of derogatory English terms for promiscuous women, but nearly none for promiscuous men—and the most common of these uncommon terms (e.g., Don Juan, Casanova, Lothario, Romeo) are the names of men who were generally admired. So biology makes sex a riskier proposition for women than for men, and culture typically exacerbates those risks. Interestingly, on those occasions when selecting a sexual partner presents a real risk for men (e.g., when selecting a wife instead of a date), they suddenly become every bit as choosy as women ordinarily are (Kenrick et al., 1990).

Attraction

For most of us, there is a very small number of people with whom we are willing to have sex, an even smaller number of people with whom we are willing to have children, and an astonishingly large number of people with whom we are unwilling to have either. So when we meet new people, how do we decide into which category we will place them? Many things go into choosing a date, a lover, or a life partner, but perhaps none is more important than the simple feeling we call *attraction* (Berscheid & Reis, 1998). Research suggests that this powerfully important feeling is the result of situational, physical, and psychological factors.

How Situational Factors Influence Attraction

We tend to think that we select our romantic partners on the basis of their personalities, appearances, and so on—and we do. But we can only select from the pool of people we've met, and the likelihood of meeting a potential partner naturally increases with proximity. Before you ever started ruling out potential romantic partners, geography had already ruled out more than 99.99% of the world's population for you (Festinger, Schachter, & Back, 1950). For most of human history, two people who were separated by geography had no chance of coming into contact, and although the Internet has changed that (Finkel et al., 2012; Okdie et al., 2014), online dating becomes offline mating only when the people live in relatively close proximity. Tinder is pretty much useless if you are "swiping right" on someone who lives an ocean away.

Proximity facilitates attraction in other ways too. The more proximal people are, the more likely we are to see them; and every time we see people, they become a bit more familiar to us. Research shows that humans and other animals generally prefer familiar to unfamiliar stimuli. For instance, in one experiment, faces were flashed on a computer screen at "subliminal speed," which means they appeared and disappeared so quickly that participants were unaware of having seen them. Next, participants were shown (at normal speed) some of the faces that had been flashed as well as some new faces. Although participants could not reliably distinguish between faces that had been flashed and faces that hadn't, they *liked* more the faces that had been flashed previously (Monahan, Murphy, & Zajonc, 2000). The **mere exposure effect** is *the tendency for liking of a stimulus to increase with the amount of exposure to that stimulus* (Bornstein, 1989; Van Dessel et al., 2019; Zajonc, 1968). Although there are some special circumstances under which mere exposure can decrease liking (Norton, Frost, & Ariely, 2007), for the most part it increases it (Reis et al., 2011). Familiarity, it seems, does not typically breed contempt. It breeds attraction.

Attraction can be the result of geographical accidents that put people in the same place at the same time, but some places and some times are better than others. For instance, researchers at the University of British Columbia observed men as they crossed the Capilano Bridge, a swaying suspension bridge in Vancouver. They arranged for an attractive female actor to approach the men—either when the men were in the middle of the bridge or after they had finished crossing it—and to ask them to complete a survey. After the men completed the survey, the woman gave them her phone number and offered to "explain her project in greater detail" if they called. Did they? Many did, but they were especially likely to call when they had met the woman in the middle of the swaying bridge than when they had met her at the end of it (Dutton & Aron, 1974). Why? As you learned in the Emotion and Motivation chapter, people sometimes misinterpret their physiological arousal as a sign of attraction (Byrne et al., 1975; Schachter & Singer, 1962). The men were presumably more aroused when they were in the middle of a swaying bridge, and some of those men mistook their arousal for attraction. (The fact that some of the men may have

When performer Tallia Storm looks at herself in the mirror, she probably likes what she sees, as do her fans. But she and her fans aren't seeing or liking the same thing. Tallia's fans usually see her face on a screen, so they probably prefer the image on the left; but Tallia usually sees her face in a mirror, so she probably prefers the "reversed image" on the right. Research on the mere exposure effect shows that people do indeed prefer mirror-reversed images of themselves, but not of others (Mita, Dermer, & Knight, 1977).

mere exposure effect the tendency for liking of a stimulus to increase with the amount of exposure to that stimulus.

In 2009, Ben Bostic and Laura Zych were strangers on a plane. After US Airways Flight 1549 crash-landed in the Hudson River in New York City, they fell in love. Research suggests that being in highly arousing situations together can lead to romantic attraction.

been gay, happily married, or otherwise uninterested in the woman may explain why they didn't call, but it can't explain why more men called in one condition than in the other.) The fact that arousing circumstances can promote attraction may help explain why roller coasters and horror movies are such popular locations for first dates.

How Physical Factors Influence Attraction

Once people are in the same place at the same time, they can begin to learn about each other's personal qualities, and the first personal quality they usually learn about is the other person's appearance. You probably can't tell whether the person who sits farthest from you in class likes sports, plays piano, or prefers dogs to cats, but you definitely know whether or not that person is hot. Does hotness matter?

It not only matters, it matters a lot. In one study (Walster et al., 1966), researchers hosted a dance for first-year university students who thought a computer algorithm would be matching them with an opposite-sex partner. But in fact, the nearly 800 students who bought tickets were *randomly* matched with an opposite-sex partner. Midway through the dance, the students confidentially reported how much they liked their partner and how much they would like to have another date with him or her. The researchers had already measured many of the students' other attributes—such as their academic performance, social skills, interests, extraversion, self-esteem, and more. When the researchers later crunched the data, they found that a person's physical appearance was the only factor correlated with their partner's feelings of attraction. In other words, appearance didn't just matter—it was the *only* thing that mattered! Other studies have confirmed the power of physical appearance. One experiment found that a man's height and a woman's weight are among the best predictors of how many responses a personal ad receives (Lynn & Shurgot, 1984), and one study found that physical attractiveness is the *only* factor that predicts the online dating choices of both women and men (Green, Buchanan, & Heuer, 1984).

Physical attractiveness gets us more than dates (Etcoff, 1999; Langlois et al., 2000). It may not be fair, but physically attractive people have more sex, more friends, and more fun than the rest of us do (Curran & Lippold, 1975). They even earn about 10% more money over the course of their lives (Hamermesh & Biddle, 1994). People expect physically attractive people to have superior personal qualities as well (Dion, Berscheid, & Walster, 1972; Eagly et al., 1991), and in some cases they do. For instance, because attractive people have more friends and more opportunities for social interaction, they tend to have better social skills than less attractive people do (Feingold, 1992b).

Size Matters. National Football League quarterback Tom Brady is 6′4″ (1.9 metres) tall, and his wife, supermodel Gisele Bündchen, is 5′10″ (1.7 metres) tall. Research shows that tall people earn about $800 more per inch per year (Mankiw & Weinzierl, 2010).

Standards of beauty can vary across cultures. Mauritanian women long to be heavy (*left*), and Ghanian men are grateful to be short (*right*).

Physical appearance is so powerful that it even influences non-romantic relationships: For example, mothers are more affectionate and playful when their children are cute than when they are not (Langlois et al., 1995). In fact, the only downside of being physically attractive is that other people sometimes feel threatened by beautiful people (Agthe, Spörrle, & Maner, 2010) and can be unsympathetic to a beautiful person's problems (Fisher & Ma, 2014). Research suggests that men and women are both powerfully and equally influenced by the physical appearance of their partners in the early stages of a relationship (Eastwick et al., 2011) but that this influence may fade more quickly for women than for men (Li et al., 2013; Meltzer et al., 2014).

So yes, it pays to be beautiful, but what exactly constitutes beauty? The answer to that question varies across cultures. For example, most American women want to be slender; but in Mauritania, young girls are encouraged to drink up to 5 gallons of high-fat milk every day so that someday they will be heavy enough to attract a husband. As one Mauritanian woman noted, "Men want women to be fat, and so they are fat" (LaFraniere, 2007). Similarly, most American men want to be tall; but in Ghana, men not only tend to be short, but they consider height a curse. "To be a tall person can be quite embarrassing," said one particularly altitudinous Ghanaian man. "When you are standing in a crowd, the short people start to jeer at you" (French, 1997). Tall and thin or short and fat, beauty is in the eye of the beholder.

But not entirely. Although different cultures do have different standards of beauty, it turns out that those standards have a surprising amount in common (Cunningham et al., 1995).

- *Body shape*. In most cultures, male bodies are considered attractive when they are shaped like a triangle (i.e., broad shoulders with a narrow waist and hips), and female bodies are considered attractive when they are shaped like an hourglass (i.e., broad shoulders and hips with a narrow waist; Deady & Law Smith, 2015; Singh, 1993). Culture may determine whether straight men prefer women who are slender or heavy, but in all cultures, straight men seem to prefer women whose waists are about 60% the size of their hips.

- *Symmetry*. People in all cultures seem to prefer faces and bodies that are *bilaterally symmetrical*—that is, faces and bodies whose left half is a mirror image of the right half (Perilloux, Webster, & Gaulin, 2010; Perrett et al., 1999).

© EMOTIONWISE GROUP/DR. LENNY KRISTAL

Straight women think men are sexier when they look proud rather than happy, but straight men think women are sexier when they look happy rather than proud (Tracy & Beall, 2011).

- *Age.* Characteristics such as large eyes, high eyebrows, and a small chin make people look immature or "baby faced" (Berry & McArthur, 1985). As a general rule, female faces are considered more attractive when they have immature features, whereas male faces are considered more attractive when they have mature features (Cunningham, Barbee, & Pike, 1990; Zebrowitz & Montepare, 1992). In every culture, straight women tend to prefer older men, and straight men tend to prefer younger women (Buss, 1989).

Is there any rhyme or reason to this list of scenic attractions? Some psychologists think so. They suggest that nature has designed us to be attracted to people who have good genes and who will be good parents (Gallup & Frederick, 2010; Neuberg, Kenrick, & Schaller, 2010). As it turns out, many of the features we all seem to find attractive are fairly reliable indicators of one or both of these things:

- *Body shape.* Testosterone causes male bodies to become "triangles," and men who are high in testosterone tend to be socially dominant and therefore have more resources to devote to their offspring (Hughes & Kumari, 2019). Estrogen causes female bodies to become "hourglasses," and women who are high in estrogen tend to be especially fertile and may have more offspring (Jasienska et al., 2004). In other words, body shape is an indicator of how many children a person can produce, and how well-fed those children will be.

- *Symmetry.* Asymmetry is often caused by disease or genetic mutation, which may explain why people are so good at detecting it (Jones et al., 2001; Thornhill & Gangestad, 1993). Indeed, women can distinguish between symmetrical and asymmetrical men by smell alone, and their preference for symmetrical men is especially pronounced when they are ovulating (Thornhill & Gangestad, 1999).

- *Age.* Younger women are generally more fertile than older women, whereas older men generally have more resources than younger men. As such, an immature appearance is an indicator of a woman's ability to bear children while a mature appearance is an indicator of a man's ability to provide for them.

All of this suggests that the feeling we call *attraction* is simply nature's way of telling us that we are in the presence of a fertile person who has healthy genes and the ability to provide for children. This may explain why straight people in different cultures appreciate so many of the same features in the opposite sex. And though research on this topic is sparse (Amos & McCabe, 2015), some studies suggest that gay and lesbian people appreciate these same features too (Legenbauer et al., 2009;

Swami & Tovée, 2008). For example, gay men find the same male faces attractive that straight women do (Valentová, Roberts, & Havlíček, 2013), and the tendency to find young faces more attractive than older ones is especially pronounced when straight men look at female faces and when gay men look at male faces (Teuscher & Teuscher, 2007).

It is important to note that attraction isn't action (Montoya, Kershaw, & Prosser, 2018). Studies show that although everyone may *desire* the most attractive person in the room, most people tend to approach, date, and marry someone who is about as attractive as they are (Berscheid et al., 1971; Lee et al., 2008). In one study (Kalick & Hamilton, 1986), researchers assigned robots different "attractiveness scores" and then programmed them to pair up by asking other robots on "dates." If both robots agreed to the date, they became a couple and left the dating game; if not, they both kept trying to pair up with other robots. In one version of the game, the robots were programmed to try pairing with the most attractive robot they could find, and in another version, the robots were programmed to try pairing with a robot that was about as attractive as they were. When the robots were programmed to find the most beautiful robot, the resulting couples were extremely similar in attractiveness ($r = .85$), and when the robots were programmed to seek a partner who was about as attractive as they were, the resulting couples were moderately similar in attractiveness ($r = .5$). What's interesting about this number is that $r = .5$ is the correlation commonly observed between the attractiveness ratings of real human couples, suggesting that most humans are seeking similar models rather than supermodels.

How Psychological Factors Influence Attraction

If attraction is all about big biceps and high cheekbones, then why don't we just skip the small talk and pick our life partners from photographs? Because for human beings, attraction is about much more than that. Physical appearance is assessed easily, early, and from across a crowded room (Lenton & Francesconi, 2010; Rogers & Hammerstein, 1949), and it definitely determines who first draws our attention and quickens our pulse. But once people begin interacting, they move beyond appearances (Cramer, Schaefer, & Reid, 1996; Regan, 1998), which is why physical attractiveness matters less when people have known each other for a long time (Hunt, Eastwick, & Finkel, 2015). People's *inner* qualities—their personalities, points of view, attitudes, beliefs, values, ambitions, and abilities—play an important role in determining their sustained interest in each other, and there isn't much mystery about the kinds of inner qualities that most people find attractive. For instance, intelligence, loyalty, trustworthiness, and kindness seem to be high on just about everybody's list (Daniel et al., 1985; Farrelly, Lazarus, & Roberts, 2007; Fletcher et al., 1999).

But exactly how much of those qualities do we want our mates to have? You might think the answer is "As much as possible!" but research suggests that people are actually most attracted to those who are similar to them on these and almost every other dimension (Byrne, Ervin, & Lamberth, 1970; Iyengar, Konitzer, & Tedin, 2018; Montoya & Horton, 2013). We marry people of a similar age, with similar levels of education, similar religious backgrounds, similar ethnicities, similar socioeconomic statuses, similar personalities, similar political beliefs, and so on (Botwin, Buss, & Shackelford, 1997; Buss, 1985; Caspi & Herbener, 1990). When researchers measured 88 distinct characteristics of 1,000 couples, they found that the couples were more similar than one would expect by chance on 66 of those characteristics, and less similar than one would expect by chance on precisely none (Burgess & Wallin, 1953). **Homophily** is *the tendency for people to like others who are similar to themselves,* and human beings turn out to be remarkably homophilous.

homophily The tendency for people to like others who are similar to themselves.

Indeed, of all the characteristics psychologists have measured, the only one for which the majority of people have a consistent preference for dissimilarity is gender.

Why is similarity so attractive? There are at least three reasons. First, it's easy to interact with people who are similar to us because we can easily agree on a wide range of issues, such as what to eat, where to live, how to raise children, and how to spend our money. Second, when someone shares our attitudes and beliefs, we feel validated, and we become more confident that our attitudes and beliefs are right (Byrne & Clore, 1970). Indeed, research shows that when a person's attitudes or beliefs are challenged, they become even more attracted to similar others (Greenberg et al., 1990; Hirschberger, Florian, & Mikulincer, 2002). Third, because we like people who share our attitudes and beliefs, we can reasonably expect them to like us for exactly the same reason, and *being liked* is a powerful source of attraction (Aronson & Worchel, 1966; Backman & Secord, 1959; Condon & Crano, 1988), especially when the people who like us don't seem to like everyone (Eastwick et al., 2007).

Our desire for similarity goes beyond attitudes and beliefs, extending to abilities as well. For example, we may admire extraordinary skill in quarterbacks and saxophone players, but when it comes to friends and lovers, extraordinary people can threaten our self-esteem and make us worry about our own competence (Tesser, 1991), and this is especially likely when the extraordinary person is a woman and the worried person is a man (Ratliff & Oishi, 2013). The fact that other people's competence can make us feel threatened may explain why people are attracted to those who display small pockets of incompetence, such as the brilliant scientist who can't seem to scramble an egg or the award-winning poet whose socks never match. A minor flaw can make a highly competent person seem a bit more human (Aronson, Willerman, & Floyd, 1966; Ein-Gar, Shiv, & Tormala, 2012). Maybe that explains why people even like robots more when the robots make small mistakes (Mirnig et al., 2017).

Similarity is a very strong source of attraction.

Relationships

Attraction is a feeling that can have important consequences, and one of those important consequences is called a relationship (Finkel, Simpson, & Eastwick, 2017). Most nonhuman animals have relationships that end approximately thirty seconds after sex is over, some have relationships that last through a breeding season, and just a few have relationships that endure for many years. Most human beings, on the other hand, have relationships that endure for a lifetime— or at least that they expected to endure for a lifetime when they first signed up (Clark & Lemay, 2010). Why are humans the leaders in the long-term relationships contest?

One slightly weird answer is that we're born half-baked. Because human beings have unusually large heads to house our unusually large brains, a fully developed human infant could not pass through its mother's birth canal. So, human mothers must give birth while their babies are relatively underdeveloped—and underdeveloped babies need a lot more care than one parent can provide. If human infants were more like tadpoles—ready at birth to swim, find food, and escape predators—then their parents might not need to form enduring relationships (Eastwick, 2009). But a human infant is just about the single most helpless creature on earth. Babies require years and years of nurturing and protection before they can even begin to fend for themselves, and that's one reason human adults tend to do their parenting in the context of committed, long-term relationships (see **FIGURE 13.6**).

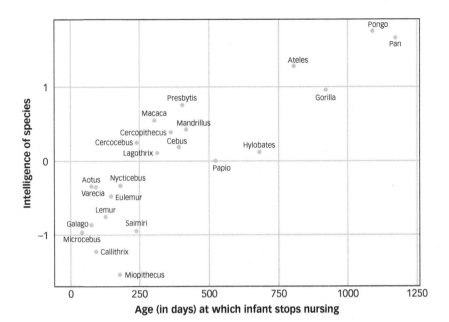

Figure 13.6

Big Brain Baby Smart animals tend to have helpless infants. This figure shows the relationship between the intelligence of different primate species and the age at which their offspring stop nursing. As you can see, the smarter a species is, the longer its infants remain reliant on their parents, which means their parents need to stick together and stick around.

DATA FROM PIANTADOSI & KIDD, 2016.

Love and Commitment

In most cultures, adults settle into committed long-term relationships in which they live together, and they often have children. (Although such relationships have traditionally been celebrated with marriage, rates of marriage are declining in Canada, whereas rates of enduring relationships are not.) Throughout history, marriage has traditionally served a variety of economic, practical, and decidedly unromantic functions, ranging from cementing agreements between clans to paying back debts. Even in North America, marriage was traditionally regarded as an alliance that helped people fulfill basic needs, such as growing food, building shelter, and protecting each other from violence; and although people have been falling in love for a very long time, it wasn't until the 20th century that they began to think of love as the reason to get married (Finkel, 2017). In 2017, almost 3 in 4 Canadians aged 25–64 lived with a partner, and nearly 4 in 5 of these couples were married, with the rest living under common law. The rate of common law unions has increased dramatically in Canada in the last few decades, from 6 in 100 couples in 1981, to 1 in 5 couples in 2017 (Statistics Canada, 2019e).

So what is this thing that modern people commit to each other for? Psychologists distinguish two basic kinds of love: **passionate love**, which is *an experience involving feelings of euphoria, intimacy, and intense sexual attraction*, and **companionate love**, which is *an experience involving affection, trust, and concern for a partner's well-being* (Acevedo & Aron, 2009; Hatfield, 1988; Rubin, 1973; Sternberg, 1986). The ideal romantic relationship gives rise to both types of love, but the speeds, trajectories, and durations of the two experiences are markedly different (see **FIGURE 13.7**). Passionate love is what brings people together: It has a rapid onset, reaches its peak quickly, and begins to diminish within just a few months (Aron et al., 2005). Companionate love is what keeps people together: It takes some time to get started, grows slowly, and need never stop growing (Gonzaga et al., 2001). Companionate love is more strongly associated with marital satisfaction than is passionate love (Sprecher & Regan, 1998), which may explain why the people who get the greatest happiness from marriage are those who say their best friend is their spouse (Grover & Helliwell, 2019). But passionate love matters too. Although it inevitably declines, if it declines too quickly or too much, marriages do suffer (Carswell & Finkel, 2018).

passionate love An experience involving feelings of euphoria, intimacy, and intense sexual attraction.

companionate love An experience involving affection, trust, and concern for a partner's well-being.

Figure 13.7
Passionate and Companionate Love
Passionate and companionate love have different time courses and trajectories. Passionate love begins to cool within just a few months, but companionate love can grow slowly yet steadily over years.

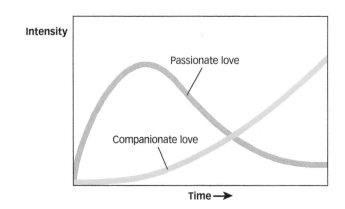

Divorce: Unmaking the Commitment

In 2017, 20 million Canadians were aged 25–64, and 2.9 million of them, or almost 3 in every 20, had experienced at least one termination of a marriage or common-law relationship (Statistics Canada, 2017). A committed relationship offers benefits (such as love, sex, and financial security), but it also imposes costs (such as additional responsibility, loss of personal freedom, and the potential for interpersonal conflict), and people tend to remain in relationships only as long as they perceive a favourable ratio of costs to benefits (Homans, 1961; Thibaut & Kelley, 1959). Whether a person considers a particular cost–benefit ratio to be favourable depends on at least two things (Le & Agnew, 2003; Lemay, 2016; Rusbult & Van Lange, 2003).

First, it depends on the person's **comparison level for alternatives**, which is *the cost–benefit ratio that a person believes he or she could attain in another relationship*. A cost–benefit ratio that seems favourable to two people stranded on a desert island may seem unfavourable to two people who live in a large city filled with other potential partners. And indeed, research shows that the better a person's imagined alternatives are, the more likely that person is to break up with his or her current partner (Simpson, 1987).

Second, the favourability of a cost–benefit ratio depends on how much the person has already invested in the relationship. A ratio that seems favourable to people who have been married for many years may seem unfavourable to people who have been married for just a few months, which is one of the reasons why new marriages are more likely to end than old ones are (Bramlett & Mosher, 2002; Cherlin, 1992). Indeed, people must be much less happy before they will take action to end an old marriage than a new one (White & Booth, 1991). It is also worth noting that people care about their partners' cost–benefit ratio as well as their own. **Equity** is *a state of affairs in which the cost–benefit ratios of two partners are roughly equally favourable* (Bolton & Ockenfels, 2000; Messick & Cook, 1983; Walster, Walster, & Berscheid, 1978), and research suggests that although people are naturally distressed when their ratio is less favourable than their partner's, they are also distressed when it is more favourable (Schafer & Keith, 1980).

comparison level for alternatives The cost–benefit ratio that a person believes he or she could attain in another relationship.

equity A state of affairs in which the cost–benefit ratios of two partners are roughly equally favourable.

Build to the Outcomes

1. Why are women generally more selective in choosing mates than men?
2. What situational factors play a role in attraction?
3. Why is physical appearance so important?
4. What kind of information does physical appearance convey?
5. Why is similarity such a powerful determinant of attraction?
6. What are the two basic kinds of love?
7. How do people weigh the costs and benefits of their relationships?

Interpersonal Perception

Kanye West is a creative genius—or at least that's what he tells anyone who will listen. Whether or not you agree with his self-assessment, just reading that sentence probably activated your medial prefrontal cortex, an area of your brain that becomes especially active when you think about other people but not when you think about inanimate objects such as houses or tools (Mitchell, Heatherton, & Macrae, 2002). Although most of your brain shows diminished activity when you are at rest, this area remains active all the time (Buckner, Andrews-Hanna, & Schacter, 2008; Spunt, Meyer, & Lieberman, 2015). Why does your brain have specific networks that seem specialized for processing information about just *one* of the millions of objects you might encounter—not just Kanye, but people in general? And why is this area constantly switched on?

Because of the millions of objects you might encounter, other human beings are the single most important. **Social cognition** is *the processes by which people come to understand others,* and your brain is doing it all day long. Whether you know it or not, your brain is constantly making inferences about other people's thoughts and feelings, beliefs and desires, abilities and aspirations, intentions, needs, and characters. These inferences are based on two kinds of information. **Category-based inferences** are *inferences based on information about the categories to which a person belongs,* and **target-based inferences** are *inferences based on information about an individual's behaviour.* As you are about to see, both kinds of information are essential, but both can be misused—and when they are, the results can be tragic.

Stereotyping: The Problem With Category-Based Inferences

One of the mind's best tricks is that it can put new things into old categories. As soon as you categorize a novel stimulus ("That's a textbook"), you can use your knowledge of the category to make educated guesses about the stimulus ("It's probably expensive") and then act accordingly towards it ("I think I'll borrow my friend's copy").

What the mind does with textbooks it also does with people. **Stereotyping** is *the process of drawing inferences about individuals based on their category membership.* The moment we categorize a person as a male baseball player from Japan, we can use our knowledge of those categories to make some educated guesses about him—for example, that he shaves his face but not his legs, that he understands the infield fly rule, and that he knows more about Tokyo than we do. When we give an elderly person our seat instead of our phone number, quiz our server about the fried zucchini instead of Fermat's Last Theorem, or comfort a lost child with candy instead of vodka, we are making inferences about people whom we have never met based solely on their category membership. As these examples suggest, stereotyping is not just useful—it is essential (Allport, 1954; Liberman, Woodward, & Kinzler, 2017). Without it, the world would be filled with perplexed seniors, irritated waiters, and children hoping to get lost more often.

And yet, ever since the journalist Walter Lippmann coined the word "stereotype" in 1936, it has had a distasteful connotation because stereotyping is a helpful process that often produces harmful results. Research suggests that this happens because stereotypes have four properties that make them subject to misuse. Let's examine each of those properties in turn.

Learning Outcomes

- Explain how stereotypes cause people to draw inaccurate conclusions about others.

- Explain why stereotypes are so difficult to overcome.

- Explain what an attribution is and what kinds of errors attributions entail.

GINO DOMENICO/AP IMAGES

Stereotypes can be inaccurate. Shlomo Koenig does not fit most people's stereotype of a police officer or a rabbi, but he is both.

social cognition The processes by which people come to understand others.

category-based inferences Inferences based on information about the categories to which a person belongs.

target-based inferences Inferences based on information about an individual's behaviour.

stereotyping The process of drawing inferences about individuals based on their category membership.

Figure 13.8

Stereotype Content Stereotypes tend to vary on the dimensions of warmth and competence. This figure shows how Canadians see Canadian groups in terms of these two dimensions. DATA FROM FISKE, 2012.

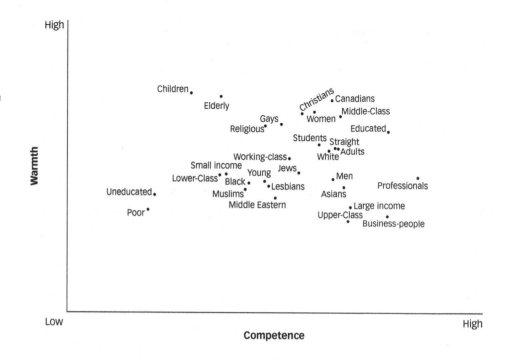

Stereotypes Can Be Inaccurate

Americans have a wide range of stereotypes that appear to vary on two important dimensions: warmth and competence (Cuddy, Fiske, & Glick, 2007; Fiske, 2018). When we say that someone is kind or unkind, honest or dishonest, we are talking about their warmth or about how much we like them; and when we say that someone is intelligent or unintelligent, powerful or powerless, we are talking about their competence or about their ability to accomplish their goals. As **FIGURE 13.8** shows, Canadians see some categories of people as warm and competent (women), others as warm but incompetent (children), others as cold and competent (business people), and others as cold and incompetent (uneducated people). Some of these stereotypes are probably accurate: It seems likely that, on average, educated professionals have advantages that allow them to accomplish their goals more easily than people with intellectual disabilities can. But others of these stereotypes are inaccurate: Not everyone in Vancouver spends the weekends hiking. So where do these inaccurate stereotypes come from?

Many of our inaccurate stereotypes are picked up from other people. We read tweets, watch TV, listen to song lyrics, overhear our parents talking, and all of these can be sources of inaccurate stereotypes. But inaccurate stereotypes also come from direct observation. For example, research participants in one study were shown a long series of positive and negative behaviours and were told that each behaviour had been performed by a member of one of two groups: Group A or Group B (see **FIGURE 13.9**). The behaviours were carefully arranged so that each group behaved negatively exactly one-third of the time. They were also carefully arranged so that there were more positive than negative behaviours in the series, and more members of Group A than of Group B. The result was that (1) negative behaviours were less common than positive behaviours, and (2) Group B members were less common than Group A members.

After seeing all the behaviours, participants correctly reported that Group A had behaved negatively one third of the time—but they incorrectly reported that Group B had behaved negatively more than *half* the time (Hamilton & Gifford, 1976). Why? Both *bad behaviour* and *Group B membership* were uncommon, and when two

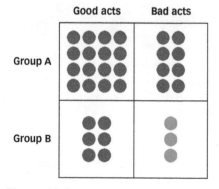

Figure 13.9

Seeing Correlations That Aren't Really There Both Group A and Group B engage in bad behaviour 1/3 of the time, so there is no real difference in the average "badness" of the two groups. However, bad behaviour and Group B membership are both uncommon, and when two uncommon things happen at the same time, we tend to notice and remember. This tendency can lead us to perceive a relationship between group membership and bad behaviour that isn't really there.

uncommon things happen at the same time, people pay special attention ("Look! There's one of those Group B'ers doing something terrible"). This is why members of majority groups tend to overestimate the number of violent crimes (which are relatively uncommon events) that are committed by members of minority groups (who are relatively uncommon people, hence the word *m-i-n-o-r-i-t-y*). The bottom line is that even when we directly observe people, we can still end up with inaccurate beliefs about the groups to which they belong.

Stereotypes Can Be Overused

Because all thumbtacks are pretty much alike, our stereotypes about thumbtacks (small, cheap, and painful when chewed) will rarely be mistaken if we generalize from one thumbtack to another. But human categories are so variable that our stereotypes may offer only the vaguest of clues about the individuals who populate those categories. You probably believe that men have greater upper body strength than women do, and this belief is right—*on average*. But the upper body strength of the individuals *within* each of these gender categories is so varied that knowing a person's gender doesn't give you *a lot* of insight into how much weight they can lift. If you randomly selected men and women and bet each time that the man could lift more weight, you'd be right more often than wrong—but not *a lot* more often.

So stereotypes are most useful when variability is low and least useful when it is high—and in human groups, variability is almost always high. So why do we use stereotypes anyway? One reason is that the mere act of categorizing a stimulus makes us believe that variability is lower than it actually is—and that stereotypes are therefore more useful than they actually are. Participants in one study were shown a series of lines of different lengths (see **FIGURE 13.10**; McGarty & Turner, 1992; Tajfel & Wilkes, 1963). For one group of participants, the longest lines were labelled *Group A* and the shortest lines were labelled *Group B*, as shown on the right side of Figure 13.10. For the second group of participants, the lines were shown without these category labels, as they are on the left side of Figure 13.10. Did placing the lines in categories change the way participants saw them? Indeed it did. When participants were later asked to remember the lengths of the lines, participants who had seen the category labels tended to underestimate the variability of the lines that shared a label. Simply placing lines of different lengths in the same category led participants to see them as more similar than they really were.

You probably experienced these effects yourself when you last saw a rainbow. Because we identify colours as members of categories such as *blue* or *green,* we tend to overestimate the similarity of colours that share a category label. That's why most of us see discrete *bands* of colour when we look at rainbows. But news alert: Rainbows do not have bands. The colours vary across a smooth chromatic continuum, and the apparently clear difference between the yellow and green bands is

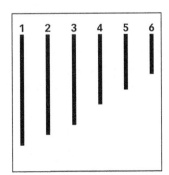
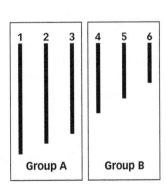

Figure 13.10

Categorization Reduces Perceived Variability People see less variability among lines 1–3 (and also among lines 4–6) if they see them labelled as they are on the right (Group A and Group B boxes), than if they see them unlabelled as they are in the left box.

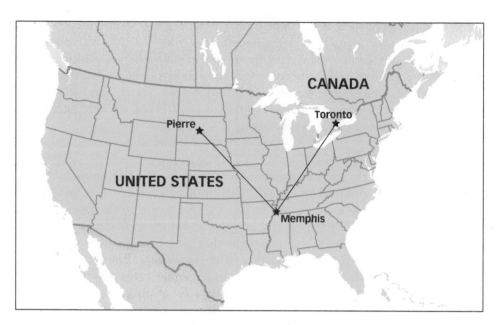

Figure 13.11
Perceiving Categories Categorization can influence how we see colours and estimate distances.

just an effect of your category label (see **FIGURE 13.11**). The same thing happens when we estimate distances. Memphis, Tennessee, is slightly closer to Toronto than to Pierre, South Dakota, but Americans think it is closer to Pierre than to Toronto. Why? Because Memphis and Pierre are both members of the category "American towns," but Toronto is not (Burris & Branscombe, 2005). Indeed, people are more likely to say that they will feel an earthquake whose epicentre is exactly 230 miles away when that epicentre is in the same American state rather than in a neighbouring state (Mishra & Mishra, 2010).

What's true of colours and cities is true of people as well. The mere act of categorizing people as Asian or Indigenous, as Jewish or Sikh, as artists or accountants, can cause us to underestimate the variability within those categories, which naturally leads us to overestimate how useful our stereotypes about those categories will be (Park & Hastie, 1987; Rubin & Badea, 2012).

Stereotypes Can Be Self-Perpetuating

When we meet a football player who likes ballet more than wrestling, or a Newfoundlander who prefers tacos to cod chowder, why don't we revise or even abandon our stereotypes of these groups? The answer is that stereotypes tend to be self-perpetuating. Like viruses and parasites, once they take up residence inside us, they resist even our most concerted efforts to eradicate them. When a person who holds a stereotype (the observer) interacts with a person about whom that stereotype is held (the target), three things can happen:

behavioural confirmation The tendency of targets to behave as observers expect them to behave.

stereotype threat The target's fear of confirming an observer's negative stereotypes.

- **Behavioural confirmation** (also known as "self-fulfilling prophecy") is *the tendency of targets to behave as observers expect them to behave.* For instance, when targets know that observers have a negative stereotype about them, they may experience **stereotype threat**, which is *the target's fear of confirming the observer's negative stereotypes* (Aronson & Steele, 2004; Schmader, Johns, & Forbes, 2008; Spencer, Logel, & Davies, 2016; Walton & Spencer, 2009). Ironically, this fear may cause targets to behave in ways that confirm the very stereotype that threatened them. In one study (Steele & Aronson, 1995), African American and White students took a test, and half the students in each group were asked to list their race at the top of the exam. When students were not asked to list their race, they performed at their academic level; but when students were asked to list their race, African American students became anxious about confirming a negative stereotype of their group, which caused them to perform well below their academic level. Stereotypes perpetuate themselves in part by causing targets to behave in precisely the ways that observers expect, thereby confirming the observers' stereotypes (Klein & Snyder, 2003).

- Even when targets do *not* confirm observers' stereotypes, observers may mistakenly think that they have. **Perceptual confirmation** is *the tendency of observers to see what they expect to see,* which can further perpetuate stereotypes. In one study, participants listened to a radio broadcast of a men's college basketball game in the United States (Stone, Perry, & Darley, 1997). Some participants were led to believe that a particular player was Black while others were led to believe that he was White. After listening to the game, participants evaluated the player's performance. When participants thought the player was Black, they reported that he had shown more athletic ability and played a better game; when they thought he was White, they reported that he had shown more basketball intelligence and hustle. Keep in mind that the participants who drew these disparate conclusions had all listened to *the same game!* Stereotypes perpetuate themselves in part by biasing our perception of individuals, leading us to believe that those individuals have confirmed our stereotypes even when they have not (Fiske, 1998).

- So what happens when targets clearly *dis*confirm an observer's stereotypes? **Subtyping** is *the tendency of observers to think of targets who disconfirm stereotypes as "exceptions to the rule"* (Weber & Crocker, 1983). For example, most of us think of people who work in public relations as sociable. In one study, participants learned about a PR agent who was *slightly* unsociable, and the results showed that their stereotypes about PR agents shifted a bit to accommodate this new information. So far, so good. But when participants learned about a PR agent who was *extremely* unsociable, their stereotypes did not change at all (Kunda & Oleson, 1997). Instead, they decided that the extremely unsociable PR agent was "an exception to the rule," which allowed them to keep their stereotypes intact. Subtyping is a powerful method of preserving our stereotypes in the face of contradictory evidence.

Stereotyping Can Be Unconscious and Automatic

Once we recognize that a stereotype is inaccurate and self-perpetuating, why don't we just make a firm resolution to stop using it? Because we often don't realize we were using it in the first place. Stereotyping often happens *unconsciously* (which means that we don't always know we are doing it) and *automatically* (which means that we often cannot avoid doing it even when we try) (Banaji & Heiphetz, 2010; Greenwald, McGhee, & Schwartz, 1998; Greenwald & Nosek, 2001).

Almost all of the research on this topic comes from psychology laboratories in the United States. In Canada, very few researchers work on unconscious and automatic stereotyping, although all the evidence suggests that Canadians harbour just as much unconscious and automatic bias as Americans. For example, in a recent poll of Canadian adults, almost half of all respondents admitted to having racist thoughts, and 1 in 4 respondents reported having been a victim of racism (Ipsos, 2019). For this reason, although the research reported below is American, do not think that it only applies in the United States.

In one American study, American participants played a video game in which photos of Black or White men holding either guns or cameras were flashed on the screen for less than 1 second each. Participants earned money by shooting men with guns and lost money by shooting men with cameras. The results showed that when participants made mistakes, they tended to be of two kinds: They shot Black men holding

COLORBLIND IMAGES/BLEND IMAGES/ALAMY

RADIUS IMAGES/ALAMY

The Implicit Association Test measures how easily people can learn to associate two things (Greenwald, McGhee, & Schwartz, 1998). Studies using the test show that 70 percent of White Americans find it easier to associate White faces with positive concepts, such as "peace," and Black faces with negative concepts, such as "bomb," than the other way around. Surprisingly, 40 percent of African Americans show this same pattern. You can take the IAT yourself at https://implicit.harvard.edu/implicit/

perceptual confirmation The tendency of observers to see what they expect to see.

subtyping The tendency of observers to think of targets who disconfirm stereotypes as "exceptions to the rule."

cameras and didn't shoot White men holding guns (Correll et al., 2002). The photos appeared on the screen so quickly that participants did not have enough time to consciously consider their stereotypes, but that didn't matter because their stereotypes worked unconsciously, causing them to mistake a camera for a gun when it was in the hands of a Black man and to mistake a gun for a camera when it was in the hands of a White man (Correll et al., 2015).

Were these White participants just a bunch of bigots? Probably not, because Black participants were just as likely to show this same pattern of errors! If bigotry wasn't the cause, then what was? Stereotypes comprise all the information about human categories that we have encountered and absorbed over the years—information from friends and uncles, books and blogs, jokes and movies and late-night television. When we see Black men holding guns in crime dramas and rap videos, our minds naturally associate these two things, and although we consciously recognize that we are seeing art and not news, our brains make and remember the association anyway because, as you saw in the Memory chapter and the Learning chapter, that's one of the things that brains do best. Once our brains have made these associations, we can't just *decide* not to be influenced by them any more than Pavlov's dogs could *decide* not to salivate when they heard the tone that they had come to associate with the appearance of food. In fact, some research suggests that consciously trying not to use a stereotype can cause people to use it even more (Macrae et al., 1994).

The effects of implicit bias can be devastating. In Canada, for example, race-based legislation has normalized serious inequities in health funding, resources, and services that systematically disadvantage indigenous groups (Allan & Smylie, 2015). Indigenous individuals also experience and anticipate racist treatment by health care providers: anticipation of racist treatment in Canada is a barrier to care and prevents some indigenous individuals from seeking treatment entirely (Browne et al., 2011). In the United States, it is well established that minorities receive fewer procedures and poorer quality medical care (Williams & Wyatt, 2015). Although systematic research has not been done, it seems reasonable to assume that this is the case in Canada as well. Unconscious bias can literally be a matter of life and death.

Are the Undesirable Consequences of Stereotyping Inevitable?

Although stereotyping is unconscious and automatic, that does not mean its undesirable consequences are inevitable (Blair, 2002; Kawakami et al., 2000; Milne & Grafman, 2001; Rudman, Ashmore, & Gary, 2001). For instance, American police

The reality show *The Voice* (*La Voix* in Quebec) features aspiring singers who, if they are good enough, get to be trained by some of the best artists in the recording business. Aspiring singers are selected by the coaches in blind auditions, where the coaches cannot see, but only hear the person auditioning. How do you think blind auditions change the way that coaches make their decisions?

officers who receive special training before playing the camera-or-gun video game described earlier do not show the same biases that ordinary people do (Correll et al., 2007; Johnson, Cesario, & Pleskac, 2018). Like the untrained participants, they take a few milliseconds longer to decide not to shoot a Black man than a White man, indicating that their stereotypes are still unconsciously and automatically influencing their perception. But unlike the untrained participants, they don't actually *shoot* Black men more often than White men, indicating that they have learned how to keep those stereotypes from influencing their behaviour (Phills et al., 2011; Todd et al., 2011). Other studies suggest that because stereotypes reflect all the information to which people are exposed through videos, advertisements, newscasts, and social media, changing that information can change the stereotypes. In laboratory experiments, for example, White American participants who are exposed to positive examples of African Americans (e.g., Michael Jordan and Denzel Washington) show a reduction in automatic anti-Black bias (Dasgupta, 2013).

So which techniques are most effective? In 2014, a team of American psychologists held a contest in which they invited researchers to submit techniques for reducing unconscious stereotyping of Blacks, and then tested each of the techniques against the other. As **FIGURE 13.12** shows, about half the techniques had some effect, and these tended to be techniques that exposed Whites to examples of Blacks who defied their stereotypes. For example, the most effective technique asked participants to imagine in gory detail that they were being assaulted by a White man and then to imagine being rescued by a Black man. The least effective techniques were those that simply encouraged people to feel compassion towards or to take the perspective of a Black person (see The Real World: Does Perspective-Taking Work?). And yet, even the best techniques were not very good: They tended to produce small and short-lived changes in unconscious bias, and those changes were not associated with any changes in people's conscious beliefs or actual behaviour (Forscher et al., 2019).

These findings are troubling for many reasons, not the least of which is that many of the failed techniques look a lot like the programs that are commonly used in schools, businesses, and other organizations to reduce unconscious stereotyping or "implicit bias". Virtually all Fortune 500 companies have some form of diversity training, as do the vast majority of universities, and yet "two-thirds of human resources specialists report that diversity training does not have positive effects, and several field studies have found no effect of diversity training on women's or minorities' careers or on managerial diversity" (Dobbin & Kalev, 2018, p. 48).

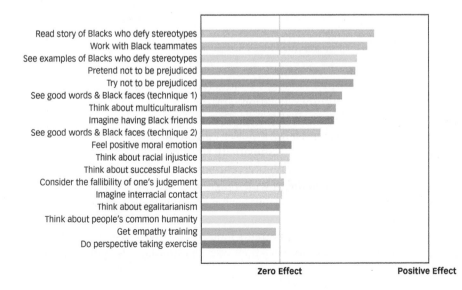

Figure 13.12

Stereotype Contest Results of a study that compared 18 techniques for reducing unconscious stereotyping of Blacks by Whites in the United States (Lai et al., 2014).

The Real World | Does Perspective-Taking Work?

In order to encourage diversity and inclusion, many organizations ask their members to participate in "perspective-taking exercises" that are meant to help them understand the world from other people's points of view. On the face of it, this seems like a promising idea. Maybe it works and maybe it doesn't, but what could possibly be the harm of taking some time to think about what it's like to live inside another person's skin?

That's what Silverman, Gwinn, and van Boven (2014) wondered when they gave sighted people the opportunity to experience blindness and then measured how well the participants understood what it's like to be a blind person. Participants reported to the laboratory, were blindfolded, and were then asked to perform a variety of ordinary tasks, ranging from filling a glass with water to finding the stairwell in a hallway. Participants in a control condition merely watched the first group perform these tasks. After either performing these tasks or watching others perform them, all participants reported their feelings towards blind people and then estimated how capable blind people are of working and living independently.

Wearing the blindfold did precisely what we might hope it would do: It made participants feel more compassionate—more empathetic, friendly, open, sympathetic, and warm towards blind people. So, was the exercise a success? Not exactly. Because compared with observers, participants who wore the blindfold also came to believe that blind people are much less competent and capable—less able to get around a city, to cook, to own their own business, to teach school or become an accountant, and so on. In other words, taking a blind person's perspective for a few minutes led participants to conclude that blind people were not capable of doing most of the tasks that daily life requires.

And that's not true. Most blind people are perfectly capable of performing ordinary tasks, such as pouring water and finding a stairwell, and perfectly capable of performing jobs from schoolteacher to accountant. Blindness is a disability to which people adapt extraordinarily well over time, and although there are a few things that blind people can't do as well as sighted people can (e.g., driving a car on the street), there are other things they can do even better (e.g., hearing a car on the street). Participants in this study had enough time to experience blindness but not enough time to adapt to it. Being blindfolded for a few minutes made them more compassionate towards blind people, but it also led them to mistakenly believe that they understood what a lifetime of blindness was like. Rather than becoming more accurate about what it is like to be disabled, they became less accurate.

All of us are forever trapped inside our own skins and can never really know what another person's experience of the world is like. Well-meaning exercises that are designed to expand our perspectives can sometimes do the opposite, suggesting that organizations would do well to consult with psychologists before implementing remedies that can make problems worse instead of better.

Paul Scruggs is blind, but that doesn't prevent him from working as a machine operator in a factory that makes military uniforms. You could probably run this machine with your eyes closed—but not in the first hour of trying.

Indeed, a team of psychologists conducted a thorough review of the scientific literature on "multicultural education, anti-bias instruction more generally, workplace diversity initiatives, dialogue groups, cooperative learning, moral and values education, intergroup contact, peace education, media interventions, reading interventions, intercultural and sensitivity training, cognitive training, and a host of miscellaneous techniques and interventions" and reluctantly concluded that "we currently do not know whether a wide range of programs and policies tend to work on average, and we are quite far from having an empirically grounded understanding of the conditions under which these programs work best" (Paluck & Green, 2009, p. 357). Although some new programs look promising (Forscher et al., 2017), the truth is that scientists do not yet know how to eliminate the pernicious effects of stereotyping.

Attribution: The Problem With Target-Based Inferences

In 1963, Dr. Martin Luther King Jr. gave a speech in which he described his vision for America: "I have a dream that my four children will one day live in a nation where they will not be judged by the color of their skin but by the content of their character." Research on stereotyping suggests that Dr. King's concern was well-justified. We do judge others by the colour of their skin—as well as by their gender, nationality, religion, age, and occupation—and in so doing, we sometimes make consequential mistakes. But are we any better at judging people by the content of their character? If we could somehow turn off our stereotypes and treat each person as a unique individual, would we judge them more accurately?

Dispositions Versus Situations

Not necessarily. Treating people as individuals means judging them by their own words and deeds. This is more difficult than it sounds because what a person says and does is not always a good indicator of what that person is actually like. Honest people sometimes lie to save a friend from embarrassment and dishonest people sometimes tell the truth to bolster their credibility. Happy people have weepy moments, polite people can be rude in traffic, and people who despise us can be flattering when they need a favour. In short, people's behaviour sometimes tells us about the kinds of people they are, but sometimes it simply tells us about the kinds of situations they happen to be in.

To understand people, we need to know not only *what* they say and do, but also *why* they say and do it. Is the politician who gave the pro-life speech really opposed to abortion, or was she just trying to win the conservative vote? Is the batter who hit the home run a talented slugger, or was the wind blowing in just the right direction at just the right time? When we answer questions such as these, we are making **attributions**, which are *inferences about the causes of people's behaviours* (Epley & Waytz, 2010; Gilbert, 1998). We make *situational attributions* when we decide that a person's behaviour was caused by some temporary aspect of the situation in which it happened ("He was lucky that the wind carried the ball into the stands"), and we make *dispositional attributions* when we decide that a person's behaviour was caused by a relatively enduring tendency to think, feel, or act in a particular way ("He's got a great eye and a powerful swing").

How can we know whether to make a dispositional or a situational attribution? We can ask three questions (Kelley, 1967). For example, why do you think the man in **FIGURE 13.13** is wearing a watermelon on his head? Is it because he has a goofy

attribution An inference about the cause of a person's behaviour.

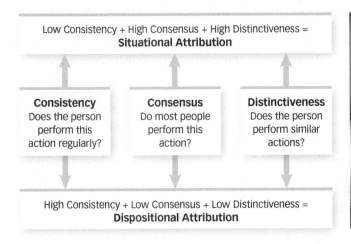

Low Consistency + High Consensus + High Distinctiveness =
Situational Attribution

Consistency
Does the person perform this action regularly?

Consensus
Do most people perform this action?

Distinctiveness
Does the person perform similar actions?

High Consistency + Low Consensus + Low Distinctiveness =
Dispositional Attribution

RYAN REMIORZ/THE CANADIAN PRESS

Figure 13.13
Three Attributional Questions To determine whether we should attribute a person's behaviour to the situation or to that person's dispositions, we simply need to ask whether the behaviour is consistent, consensual, and distinctive.

personality (a dispositional attribution) or because he's a perfectly normal guy who just happens to be on his way to a Saskatchewan football game (a situational attribution)? To answer that question, we should ask whether his behaviour is (1) *consistent* (does he usually wear a watermelon?); (2) *consensual* (are other people wearing watermelons on their heads?); and (3) *distinctive* (is this the only goofy thing the man does?). If he wears a watermelon every day, and if no one else wears a watermelon, and if he does lots of other goofy things too, then we should make a dispositional attribution ("He's an eccentric"). On the other hand, if he rarely wears a watermelon, if lots of other people are wearing watermelons, and if he doesn't tend to do other goofy things, then we should make a situational attribution ("He's a Roughriders fan on game day"). As Figure 13.13 shows, patterns of consistency, consensus, and distinctiveness provide the information we need to determine the true cause of the man's behaviour.

Attribution Errors

As sensible as this analysis may seem, research suggests that people don't always do it, and as a result, they often make the wrong attribution. The **correspondence bias** is *the tendency to make a dispositional attribution when we should instead make a situational attribution* (Gilbert & Malone, 1995; Jones & Harris, 1967; Ross, 1977). This bias is so common that it is often called the *fundamental attribution error*. For example, volunteers in one experiment (Ross, Amabile, & Steinmetz, 1977) played a trivia game in which one participant acted as the quizmaster and made up a list of unusual questions, a second participant acted as the contestant and tried to answer those questions, and a third participant acted as the observer and simply watched the game. The quizmasters were smart: They asked tricky questions based on their own idiosyncratic knowledge ("What store sells the shoes I am wearing?"), so it wasn't surprising that contestants were unable to answer most of them.

"I think success is all perspiration. You make your own luck," said Robert Herjavec, a successful businessman and a judge on *Shark Tank*. But research on the correspondence bias suggests that it is all too easy to credit success to intelligence and tenacity, and all too easy to blame failure on stupidity and laziness.

JOHN LAMPARSKI/WIREIMAGE/GETTY IMAGES

correspondence bias The tendency to make a dispositional attribution when we should instead make a situational attribution.

After watching the game, the observers were asked to decide how smart the quizmaster and the contestant were. Although the quizmasters had asked good questions and the contestants had given bad answers, it should have been clear to the observers that all this asking and answering was a product of the situation: Quizmasters had been given an easy job and contestants had been given a hard one. If their roles had been reversed, the contestants would have asked equally difficult questions and the quizmasters would have given equally bad answers. Instead, observers attributed the quizmasters' and contestants' performances to their dispositions, concluding that the quizmasters were actually *smarter* than the contestants. The fact is that even when we know that a successful athlete had a home-field advantage or that a successful entrepreneur had family connections, we tend to attribute their success to talent and tenacity.

What causes the correspondence bias? First, people often ignore the situational causes of behaviour because those causes are often invisible (Ichheiser, 1949). Professors tend to think that fawning students really do admire them in spite of the strong incentive for students to kiss up to those who control their grades because professors can *see* their students laughing at witless jokes and applauding after boring lectures, but they cannot *see* "control over grades." Situations are not as tangible or salient as behaviours, so it is all too easy to ignore them (Taylor & Fiske, 1975). Second, situational attributions are more difficult to make. When participants in one study (Gilbert, Pelham, & Krull, 1988) were asked to make attributions while simultaneously performing a mentally demanding task (i.e., keeping a seven-digit number in short-term memory), they had no difficulty making dispositional attributions; but they found it nearly impossible to make situational attributions. In short, information about situations is hard to get and hard to use, so we tend to believe that other peoples' actions are caused by their dispositions even when there is a perfectly reasonable situational explanation.

The correspondence bias is stronger in some cultures than in others (Choi, Nisbett, & Norenzayan, 1999) and among some people than others (D'Agostino & Fincher-Kiefer, 1992; Li et al., 2012). It is also stronger under some circumstances than others. For example, people are more prone towards correspondence bias when making attributions for other people's behaviour than when making attributions for their own. The **actor–observer effect** is *the tendency to make situational attributions for our own behaviours while making dispositional attributions for the identical behaviour of others* (Jones & Nisbett, 1972). When university students are asked to explain why they and their friends chose their majors, they tend to make situational attributions for their own choices ("I chose economics because my parents told me I have to support myself as soon as I'm done with college") and dispositional attributions for their friends' choices ("Leah chose economics because she's materialistic") (Nisbett et al., 1973).

The actor–observer effect occurs because people typically have more information about the situations that caused their own behaviour than about the situations that caused other people's behaviour. We will always remember getting the please-major-in-something-practical lecture from our parents, but we weren't at Leah's house to see her get the same lecture. As observers, our eyes are focused on another person's behaviour, but as actors, our eyes are quite literally focused on the situations in which our own behaviour occurs. That's why when people see themselves on video, and therefore see their own behaviour as observers had seen it, they suddenly make dispositional attributions about themselves (Storms, 1973; Taylor & Fiske, 1975).

What are we to make of these attribution errors? Are they just technical fouls, mistakes around the margin, or do they really matter? Gustav Ichheiser was the first psychologist to describe the correspondence bias, and he thought it mattered a lot. Ichheiser was Jewish and his entire family was murdered in the Nazi invasion of Austria. He fled to America, but things didn't go well for him there. He was poor, often unemployed, and ultimately took his own life; but his writings about social psychology were prescient. In 1949 Ichheiser wrote:

> We all have in everyday life the tendency to interpret and evaluate the behavior of other people in terms of specific personality characteristics rather than in terms of specific social situations in which those people are placed. . . . Many things which happened between the two world wars would not have happened if social blindness had not prevented the privileged from understanding the predicament of those who were living in an invisible jail. (p. 47)

Ichheiser argued that correspondence bias creates a kind of "social blindness" that keeps us from seeing the "invisible jails" that shape the behaviour of people who are marginalized, who are raised in poverty, who are the victims of pogroms, and more. Instead of recognizing that these people are profoundly affected by situations beyond their control, we mistakenly attribute their outcomes to their dispositions—to their choices and abilities and personalities and work ethic—and mistakenly conclude that they basically deserve what they've gotten (Lerner, 1980). The correspondence bias is not a mistake around the margin, but a significant source of human misunderstanding.

actor–observer effect The tendency to make situational attributions for our own behaviours while making dispositional attributions for the identical behaviour of others.

Build to the Outcomes

1. Where do stereotypes come from? What purpose do they serve?

2. When are stereotypes most and least likely to be useful?

3. Why do stereotypes sometimes seem more accurate than they really are?

4. Why is it difficult not to use stereotypes?

5. What are the three kinds of information that determine whether a dispositional or situational attribution is warranted?

6. Why do people tend to make dispositional attributions even when they should not?

Interpersonal Influence

Learning Outcomes

- Describe the hedonic motive and explain how appeals to it can backfire.

- Describe the approval motive and distinguish normative influence, conformity, and obedience.

- Describe the accuracy motive and distinguish informational influence, persuasion, and consistency.

If you grew up on X-Men and the Avengers, you've probably thought a bit about which of the standard superpowers you'd most like to have. Super strength and super speed have obvious benefits, invisibility and X-ray vision could be interesting as well as lucrative, and there's a lot to be said for flying. But when it comes down to it, the ability to control other people would probably be the most useful superpower of all. Why get in a death match with an alien overlord or rescue orphans from a burning building when you can convince someone else to do these jobs for you? The things we want from life—gourmet food, interesting jobs, big houses, fancy cars—can all be given to us by others, and the things we want most—loving families, loyal friends, admiring children, appreciative employers—cannot be acquired any other way.

Social influence is *the ability to change or direct another person's behaviour* (Cialdini & Goldstein, 2004). How does it work? If you want someone's time, money, allegiance, or affection, you'd be wise to consider first what it is *they* want. People have three basic motivations that turn out to be the levers of almost all attempts at social influence (Bargh, Gollwitzer, & Oettingen, 2010; Fiske, 2010). First, people are motivated to experience pleasure and to avoid experiencing pain (the *hedonic motive*). Second, people are motivated to be accepted and to avoid being rejected (the *approval motive*). Third, people are motivated to believe what is right and to avoid believing what is wrong (the *accuracy motive*). As you are about to see, most attempts at social influence appeal to one or more of these three motives.

The Hedonic Motive

Pleasure seeking is the most basic of all motives, and social influence often involves creating situations in which others can achieve more pleasure by doing what we want them to do than by doing something else. Parents, teachers, governments, and businesses influence our behaviour by offering rewards and threatening punishments (see **FIGURE 13.14**). There's nothing mysterious about how these influence attempts work, and they are often quite effective. When the Republic of Singapore warned its citizens that anyone caught chewing gum in public would face a year in prison and a $5,500 fine, gum chewing in Singapore fell to an all-time low. A jail term really gets your attention.

social influence The ability to change or direct another person's behaviour.

Huda Kattan is a social media influencer with more than 36 million followers on Instagram alone. That's roughly the population of Australia, Finland, and Costa Rica combined. Although her posts may change people's choices of skin care products, they probably have less impact on people's choices of careers, political candidates, and investments. Is Huda influential? That depends on whether you think influence should be defined more by its scope or by its depth.

hudabeauty ✓ Follow

14,126 posts 36.1m followers 543 following

Huda Kattan
Love my InstaFam
PROVING DREAMERS
CAN MAKE IT
Personal Page @hudakattan
MUA & Blogger, turned Business Woman
LOVE to support artists
youtu.be/ZxnfLeOiAFg

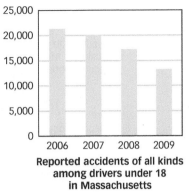

Reported accidents of all kinds among drivers under 18 in Massachusetts

JOURNAL-COURIER/CLAYTON STALTER/THE IMAGE WORKS

Figure 13.14

The Cost of Speeding The penalty for speeding in the American state of Massachusetts used to be a modest fine. Then the state legislature changed the law so that drivers under 18 who are caught speeding lose their licenses for 90 days—and to get them back, they have to pay $500, attend 8 hours of training classes, and retake the state's driving exam. Guess what? Deaths among drivers under 18 fell by 38% in just 3 years. In other words, more than 8,000 young lives were saved by appealing to the hedonic motive.

Rewards and punishments can be effective, but they can also backfire. The **overjustification effect** occurs *when a reward decreases a person's intrinsic motivation to perform a behaviour* (Deci, Koestner, & Ryan, 1999). For example, children in one study (Lepper, Greene, & Nisbett, 1973) were allowed to play with coloured markers, and then some children received a reward. When the children were given markers the next day, those who had received a reward the previous day were *less* likely to play with the markers than were those who had not received a reward. Why? Because children who had received a reward the first day came to think of drawing as something one does to receive rewards, not as something that was intrinsically rewarding; and if no one was going to give them a reward on the second day, then why the heck should they play with the markers?

Rewards and punishments can also backfire simply because people resent being bribed and threatened. **Reactance** is *an unpleasant feeling that arises when people feel they are being coerced,* and when people experience reactance, they often try to alleviate it by doing the very thing they were being coerced *not* to do—just to prove to themselves that they can. In one study (Pennebaker & Sanders, 1976), researchers placed signs in two restrooms on a university campus. One sign read "Please don't write on these walls" and the other read "Do not write on these walls under any circumstances." Two weeks later, the researchers returned to find that the walls in the second restroom had more graffiti than the walls in the first, presumably because students didn't appreciate the threatening tone of the second sign and wrote on the walls just to show that they could.

The Approval Motive

Other humans are the only thing standing between us and starvation, predation, loneliness, and all the other things that make getting shipwrecked such a bad idea. We depend on others for safety, sustenance, and solidarity, which is why being rejected or excluded by others is one of the most painful of all human experiences (Eisenberger et al., 2003; Uskul & Over, 2014; Williams, 2007). We are powerfully motivated to have others accept us, like us, and approve of us (Baumeister & Leary, 1995; Leary, 2010)—a noble motive to be sure, but one that leaves us vulnerable to social influence.

Normative Influence: We Do What We Think Is Appropriate

To see this vulnerability in action, just consider the rules of elevator etiquette. When you get on an elevator you are supposed to face forwards and not talk to the person next to you even if you were talking to that person before you got on the elevator unless you are the only two people on the elevator in which case it's okay to talk

overjustification effect An effect that occurs when a reward decreases a person's intrinsic motivation to perform a behaviour.

reactance An unpleasant feeling that arises when people feel they are being coerced.

Figure 13.15

The Perils of Connection Other people's behaviour defines what is normal, so we tend to do the things we see others doing. Overeating is one of those things. Research shows that if someone you know becomes obese, your chances of becoming obese can increase dramatically (Christakis & Fowler, 2007).

On average, your risk of becoming obese increases by ...

... **57%** if someone you consider a friend becomes obese.

... **171%** if a very close friend becomes obese.

... **100%** if you are a man and your male friend becomes obese.

... **38%** if you are a woman and your female friend becomes obese.

... **37%** if your spouse becomes obese.

... **40%** if one of your siblings becomes obese.

... **67%** if you are a woman and your sister becomes obese.

... **44%** if you are a man and your brother becomes obese.

FRANCIS DEAN/DEAN PICTURES/THE IMAGE WORKS

norms Customary standards for behaviour that are widely shared by members of a culture.

norm of reciprocity The unwritten rule that people should benefit those who have benefited them.

normative influence A phenomenon in which another person's behaviour provides information about what is appropriate.

door-in-the-face technique An influence strategy that involves getting someone to accept a small request by first getting them to refuse a large request.

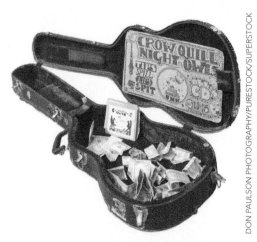

DON PAULSON PHOTOGRAPHY/PURESTOCK/SUPERSTOCK

Have you ever wondered which big spenders left bills for a tip? In fact, the bills are often put there by the very people you are tipping because they know that the presence of paper money will suggest to you that others are leaving big tips and that it would be socially appropriate for you to do the same.

and face sideways but still not backwards. Although no one ever taught you this long-winded rule, you probably picked it up somewhere along the way. The unwritten rules that govern social behaviour are called **norms**, which are *customary standards for behaviour that are widely shared by members of a culture* (Cialdini, 2013; Miller & Prentice, 1996; Hawkins, Goodman, & Goldstone, 2019). We learn norms with exceptional ease and we obey them with exceptional fidelity because we know that if we don't, others won't approve of us (Centola & Baronchelli, 2015). For example, every human culture has a **norm of reciprocity**, which is *the unwritten rule that people should benefit those who have benefited them* (Gouldner, 1960). When a friend buys you lunch, you return the favour, and if you don't, your friend gets miffed. The norm of reciprocity is so strong that when researchers randomly pulled the names of strangers from a telephone directory and sent them all Christmas cards, they received Christmas cards back from most (Kunz & Woolcott, 1976).

Norms are a powerful weapon in the game of social influence (Miller & Prentice, 2016). **Normative influence** occurs when *another person's behaviour provides information about what is appropriate* (see **FIGURE 13.15**). For example, restaurant servers often give customers a piece of candy along with the bill because they know about the norm of reciprocity. Studies show that customers who receive a candy feel obligated to do "a little extra" for the server who did "a little extra" for them (Strohmetz et al., 2002). Indeed, people will sometimes refuse small gifts precisely because they don't want to feel indebted to the gift giver (Shen, Wan, & Wyer, 2011).

The norm of reciprocity involves swapping, but the thing being swapped doesn't have to be a favour. The **door-in-the-face technique** is *an influence strategy that involves getting someone to accept a small request by first getting them to refuse a large request*. Here's how it works: You ask someone for something more valuable than you really want, you wait for that person to refuse (to "slam the door in your face"), and then you ask the person for what you really wanted in the first place. For example, in one study (Cialdini et al., 1975), researchers first asked some university students to volunteer to supervise adolescents who were going on a field trip. Only 17% of them accepted the request. Then the researchers asked a new group of students to commit to spending 2 hours per week for 2 years working at a youth detention centre (to which 100% of the students said no—or actually, no way!) and *then* asked them to supervise the field trip. Fifty percent of them said yes. Why? The researchers began by asking for a large favour that the students refused, so the researchers then "made a concession" by asking for a smaller favour. Because the researchers had made a

A perplexed participant (*centre*), flanked by trained actors, is on the verge of conforming in one of Solomon Asch's line-judging experiments.

concession, the norm of reciprocity demanded that the students make a concession too—by saying yes. And fully half of them did.

Conformity: We Do What We See Others Do

People can influence us by invoking familiar norms, such as the norm of reciprocity. But if you've ever found yourself at a fancy dinner, sneaking a peek at the person next to you in the hopes of discovering whether the little fork is supposed to be used for the shrimp or the salad, then you know that other people can also influence us by defining *new* norms in ambiguous, confusing, or novel situations. **Conformity** is *the tendency to do what others do,* and it results in part from normative influence.

In a classic study, the psychologist Solomon Asch (1951, 1956) had participants sit in a room with seven other people who appeared to be ordinary participants but who were actually trained actors. An experimenter explained that the participants would be shown cards with three printed lines, and their job was simply to say which of the three lines matched a "standard line" that was printed on another card (see **FIGURE 13.16**). The experimenter held up a card and then asked each person to answer in turn. The real participant was among the last to be called on. Everything went well on the first two trials, but then on the third trial, something weird happened: The actors all began giving the same wrong answer! What did the real participants do? Although most participants continued to give the right answer on most trials, 75% of them conformed and gave the patently wrong answer on at least one trial. Subsequent research has shown that these participants didn't actually misperceive the length of the lines but were instead succumbing to normative influence (Asch, 1955; Nemeth & Chiles, 1988). Giving the wrong answer was apparently the "right thing to do" in this confusing, novel, and ambiguous situation, so participants did it.

The behaviour of others can tell us what is proper, appropriate, expected, and accepted—in other words, it can define a norm—and once a norm is defined, we feel obliged to honour it. For instance, the managers of a Holiday Inn in Tempe, Arizona, USA, allowed researchers to leave a variety of different "message cards" in guests' bathrooms in the hopes of convincing those guests to reuse their towels

conformity The tendency to do what others do.

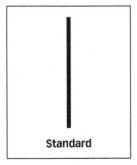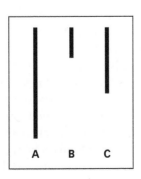

Standard   **A   B   C**

Figure 13.16

Asch's Conformity Study If you were asked which of the lines on the right (A, B, or C) matches the standard line on the left, what would you say? Research on conformity suggests that your answer would depend, in part, on how other people in the room answered the same question.

Normative Influence at Home In 2008, the Sacramento Municipal Utility District randomly selected 35,000 of its customers and sent them electric bills like the one to the right. The bill showed not only how much electricity the customer had used, but also how much electricity was used by neighbours (in U.S. state of California) who lived in similar-sized homes. When the utility crunched the numbers, they discovered that customers who had received this "compare with the neighbours" bill had reduced their electricity consumption by 2%, compared with customers who had received a traditional bill (Kaufman, 2009). Clearly, normative influence can be a force for good.

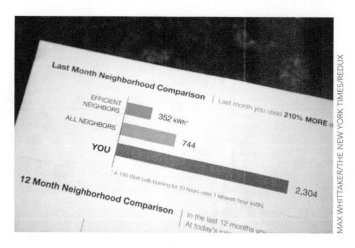

rather than having them laundered every day. The researchers discovered that the single most effective message was the one that defined a norm. It simply read: "Seventy-five percent of our guests use their towels more than once" (Cialdini, 2005). When the Sacramento Municipal Utility District randomly selected 35,000 customers and sent them electric bills showing how their energy consumption compared with that of their neighbours (in U.S. state of California), consumption fell by 2% (Kaufman, 2009; see also Jachimowicz et al., 2018). In another study (Yoeli et al., 2013), utility customers were much more likely to participate in an energy-conservation program when they could see that their neighbours (in U.S. state of California) had signed up, and this information was even more effective than a cash incentive of $25. Clearly, normative influence can be a force for good (see Other Voices: 91% of Students Love This Box).

Obedience: We Do What We're Told to Do

Other people's behaviour can provide information about existing norms or it can establish new ones. But in most situations, there are a few people whom we all recognize as having special authority both to define norms and to enforce them. The guy who works at the movie theatre may be some high-school fanboy with a 10:00 p.m. curfew, but in the context of the theatre, he is the authority. So when he asks you to stop texting in the middle of the movie, you do as you are told. **Obedience** is *the tendency to do what authorities tell us to do.*

Why do we obey authorities? Well, okay, yes, sometimes they have guns. But while authorities are often capable of rewarding and punishing us, research shows that much of their influence is *normative* (Tyler, 1990). The psychologist Stanley Milgram (1963) demonstrated this in one of psychology's most infamous experiments. The participants in this experiment reported to a laboratory at Yale University where they met a man who was introduced as another participant but who was actually a trained actor. An experimenter in a lab coat (the authority) explained that the participant would play the role of *teacher* and the actor would play the role of *learner*. The teacher and the learner would sit in different rooms, the teacher would read words to the learner over an intercom, and the learner would then repeat the words back to the teacher. If the learner made a mistake, the teacher would press a button on a machine that would deliver an electric shock to the learner (see **FIGURE 13.17**). The shock machine was fake, but its switches appeared to allow teachers to deliver 30 different levels of shock, ranging from 15 volts (labelled *slight shock*) to 450 volts (labelled *Danger: severe shock*).

After the learner was strapped into his chair, the experiment began. When the learner made his first mistake, the participant dutifully delivered a 15-volt shock. As the learner made more mistakes, he received more shocks, each stronger than the one before it. When the teacher delivered the 75-volt shock, the learner cried out in pain.

obedience The tendency to do what authorities tell us to do.

Other Voices ┆ 91% of Students Love This Box

Binge drinking is a problem on university campuses across the United States and Canada (Wechsler & Nelson, 2001). About half of all students report doing it, and those who do are much more likely to miss classes, fall behind in their school work, drive drunk, and have unprotected sex. So what to do?

Universities have tried a number of remedies—from education to abstinence—and none of them has worked particularly well. But lately, some schools have taken a new approach called "social norming." Although this approach is surprisingly effective, it is also controversial. Tina Rosenberg's most recent book is *Join the Club: How Peer Pressure Can Transform the World.* In the following essay, she describes both the technique and the controversy.

Like most universities, Northern Illinois University in DeKalb has a problem with heavy drinking. In the 1980s, the school was trying to cut down on student use of alcohol with the usual strategies. One campaign warned teenagers of the consequences of heavy drinking. "It was the 'don't run with a sharp stick you'll poke your eye out' theory of behavior change," said Michael Haines, who was the coordinator of the school's Health Enhancement Services. When that didn't work, Haines tried combining the scare approach with information on how to be well: "It's O.K. to drink if you don't drink too much—but if you do, bad things will happen to you."

That one failed, too. In 1989, 45 percent of students surveyed said they drank more than five drinks at parties. This percentage was slightly higher than when the campaigns began. And students thought heavy drinking was even more common; they believed that 69 percent of their peers drank that much at parties.

But by then Haines had something new to try. In 1987 he had attended a conference on alcohol in higher education sponsored by the United States Department of Education. There Wes Perkins, a professor of sociology at Hobart and William Smith Colleges, and Alan Berkowitz, a psychologist in the school's counseling center, presented a paper that they had just published on how student drinking is affected by peers. "There are decades of research on peer influence—that's nothing new," Perkins said at the meeting. What was new was their survey showing that when students were asked how much their peers drank, they grossly overestimated the amount. If the students were responding to peer pressure, the researchers said, it was coming from imaginary peers.

The "aha!" conclusion Perkins and Berkowitz drew was this: maybe students' drinking behavior could be changed by just telling them the truth.

Haines surveyed students at Northern Illinois University and found that they also had a distorted view of how much their peers drink. He decided to try a new campaign, with the theme "most students drink moderately." The centerpiece of the campaign was a series of ads in the *Northern Star,* the campus newspaper, with pictures of students and the caption "two thirds of Northern Illinois University students (72%) drink 5 or fewer drinks when they 'party.'" . . .

Haines's staff also made posters with campus drinking facts and told students that if they had those posters on the wall when an inspector came around, they would earn $5. (35 percent of the students did have them posted when inspected.) Later they made buttons for students in the fraternity and sorority system—these students drank more heavily—that said "Most of Us," and offered another $5 for being caught wearing one. The buttons were deliberately cryptic, to start a conversation.

Tina Rosenberg is a writer and winner of the Pulitzer Prize, the National Book Award, and the McArthur "Genius" Award. Her latest book is *Join the Club: How Peer Pressure Can Transform the World.*

After the first year of the social norming campaign, the perception of heavy drinking had fallen from 69 to 61 percent. Actual heavy drinking fell from 45 to 38 percent. The campaign went on for a decade, and at the end of it NIU students believed that 33 percent of their fellow students were episodic heavy drinkers, and only 25 percent really were—a decline in heavy drinking of 44 percent. . . .

Why isn't this idea more widely used? One reason is that it can be controversial. Telling college students "most of you drink moderately" is very different than saying "don't drink." (It's so different, in fact, that the National Social Norms Institute, with headquarters at the University of Virginia, gets its money from Anheuser Busch—a decision that has undercut support for the idea of social norming.) The approach angers people who lobby for a strong, unmuddied message of disapproval—even though, of course, disapproval doesn't reduce bad behavior, and social norming does.

Rosenberg's essay suggests that social norming is a powerful tool for changing behaviour, but its use raises important questions. When we tell students about drinking on campus, should we tell them what's true—even if the truth is a bit ugly? Or should we tell them what's best—even if they are unlikely to do it? There are no easy or obvious answers to this question, but as a society, we have no choice but to choose one.

Figure 13.17

Milgram's Obedience Studies The learner (*left*) is being hooked up to the shock generator (*right*) that was used in Stanley Milgram's obedience studies.

FROM THE FILM OBEDIENCE © 1968 BY STANLEY MILGRAM, © RENEWED 1993 BY ALEXANDRA MILGRAM; AND DISTRIBUTED BY ALEXANDER STREET PRESS. STANLEY MILGRAM, FROM THE FILM "OBEDIENCE." RIGHTS HELD BY ALEXANDRA MILGRAM.

At 150 volts, the learner screamed, "Get me out of here. I told you I have heart trouble. . . . I refuse to go on. Let me out!" With every shock, the learner's screams became more agonized as he pleaded pitifully for his freedom. Then, after receiving the 330-volt shock, the learner stopped responding altogether. Participants were naturally upset by all this and typically asked the experimenter to stop, but the experimenter simply replied, "You have no choice. You must go on." The experimenter never threatened the participant with punishment of any kind. Rather, he just stood there with his clipboard in hand, looking very authoritative, and calmly instructed the participant to continue.

So what did the participants do? Eighty percent of the participants continued to shock the learner even after he screamed, complained, pleaded, and then fell silent. And 62% of them went all the way, delivering the highest possible voltage. Although Milgram's study was conducted nearly half a century ago, more recent replications reveal about the same rate of obedience (Burger, 2009; Grzyb et al., 2017).

Were these participants psychopathic sadists? Would normal people electrocute a stranger just because some guy in a lab coat told them to? The answer, it seems, is *yes*—as long as *normal* means being sensitive to social norms (Zimbardo, 2007). The participants in this experiment knew that hurting others is *often* wrong but not *always* wrong: Doctors give painful injections, teachers give painful exams, and in these and many other situations, it is permissible for authorities to cause someone to suffer in the service of a higher goal. The experimenter's calm demeanor and persistent instruction suggested that he, and not the participants, knew what was appropriate in this particular situation, so the participants typically did as ordered. Subsequent research confirmed that participants' obedience was due to normative pressure. For instance, when the experimenter's authority to define the norm was undermined (e.g., when a second experimenter appeared to disagree with the first or when the instructions were given by a person who wasn't wearing a lab coat), the participants rarely obeyed the instructions (Milgram, 1974; Miller, 1986). Obedience, it seems, is not just for soldiers and Golden Retrievers.

The Accuracy Motive

When you are hungry, you open the refrigerator and grab an apple because you know that apples (a) taste good and (b) are in the refrigerator. This action, like most actions, relies on both an **attitude**, which is *an enduring positive or negative evaluation of a stimulus* ("Apples taste good") and a **belief**, which is *an enduring piece of knowledge about a stimulus* ("Apples are in the fridge"). In a sense, our attitudes tell us what to do (eat an apple) and our beliefs tell us how to do it (open the fridge). If our attitudes or beliefs are inaccurate—that is, if we can't tell good from bad or true from false—then our actions are likely to be fruitless. (A pun! Get it?) Because we rely so much on our attitudes and beliefs, it isn't surprising that we are motivated to have the right ones, and that motivation leaves us vulnerable to social influence. Here's how.

attitude An enduring positive or negative evaluation of a stimulus.

belief An enduring piece of knowledge about a stimulus.

Informational Influence: We Do What We Think Is Correct

If everyone in the mall suddenly ran screaming for the exit, you'd probably join them—not because you were afraid that they would disapprove of you if you didn't, but because their behaviour would suggest to you that there was something worth running from. **Informational influence** occurs when *another person's behaviour provides information about what is good or true.* You can observe the power of informational influence yourself just by standing in the middle of the sidewalk, tilting back your head, and staring at the top of a tall building. Research shows that within just a few minutes, other people will stop and stare too (Milgram, Bickman, & Berkowitz, 1969). Why? Because they will assume that if you are looking, then there must be something worth looking at.

You are the constant target of informational influence. When a salesperson tells you that "most people buy the laptop with extra memory," she is artfully suggesting that you should take other people's behaviour as information about which product is best. Advertisements that refer to soft drinks as "popular" or books as "best sellers" remind you that other people are buying these particular drinks and books, which suggests that they know something you don't and that you'd be wise to follow their example. Restaurants and clubs make people stand in line outside even when there is room to stand inside, because they know that passersby will see the line and assume there is something worth waiting for. In short, the world is full of stimuli about which we know little, and we can often cure our ignorance by paying attention to the way in which others are acting. Alas, the very thing that makes us open to information leaves us open to manipulation as well.

Persuasion: We Do What We Believe In

When the next provincial or federal election rolls around, two things will happen. First, the candidates will promise to earn your vote by making solid arguments that focus on the issues. Second, the candidates will then avoid arguments, ignore issues, and attempt to win your vote by dressing nicely and smiling a lot, attending pancake breakfasts and other homespun community events with lots of smiling children and honest-looking next-door-neighbour types, and so on. What the candidates promise to do and what they actually do reflect two basic forms of **persuasion**, which occurs when *a person's attitudes or beliefs are influenced by a communication from another person* (Albarracín & Shavitt, 2018; Berger, 2014; Petty & Wegener, 1998). The kind of persuasion the candidates will promise is known as **systematic persuasion**, which is *the process by which attitudes or beliefs are changed by appeals to reason*, but the kind they are most likely to deliver is known is as **heuristic persuasion**, which is *the process by which attitudes or beliefs are changed by appeals to habit or emotion* (Chaiken, 1980; Petty & Cacioppo, 1986).

How do these two forms of persuasion work? Systematic persuasion appeals to logic and reason and assumes that people will be more persuaded when evidence and arguments are strong rather than weak. Heuristic persuasion appeals to habit and emotion and assumes that rather than weighing evidence and analyzing arguments, people will often use *heuristics* (simple shortcuts or "rules of thumb") to help them decide whether to believe a communication. Which form of persuasion will be more effective depends on whether the person is willing and able to weigh evidence and analyze arguments.

In one study, students heard a speech that contained either strong or weak arguments in favour of instituting comprehensive exams at their university (Petty, Cacioppo, & Goldman, 1981). Some students were told that the speaker was a high-status university professor, and others were told that the speaker was a low-status high school student—a bit of information that the students could use as a heuristic or shortcut to decide whether to believe the speech (Hanel et al., 2018). In addition, some students were told that their university was considering implementing

Why do publishers and booksellers go out of their way to remind people that a book is a "best seller"? Because they know that people are more inclined to buy books when they think that others are buying them, too.

informational influence A phenomenon that occurs when another person's behaviour provides information about what is good or true.

persuasion A phenomenon that occurs when a person's attitudes or beliefs are influenced by a communication from another person.

systematic persuasion The process by which attitudes or beliefs are changed by appeals to reason.

heuristic persuasion The process by which attitudes or beliefs are changed by appeals to habit or emotion.

Heuristic persuasion can be powerful. Samsung hopes that pairing soccer star David Beckham with their newest phone (*left*) will cause you to prefer it—and it probably does. In fact, this effect is so basic that it even works with monkeys. When rhesus monkeys were shown various corporate logos paired with pictures of high-status monkeys (*middle*) and low-status monkeys (*right*), they came to prefer the former logos to the latter (Acikalin et al., 2018).

High Status Primate   High Status Primate   Low Status Primate

ACIKALIN MY, WATSON KK, FITZSIMONS GJ, PLATT ML (2018) RHESUS MACAQUES FORM PREFERENCES FOR BRAND LOGOS THROUGH SEX AND SOCIAL STATUS BASED ADVERTISING. PLOS ONE 13(3): E0193055. HTTPS://DOI.ORG/10.1371/JOURNAL. PONE.0194055

foot-in-the-door technique A technique that involves making a small request and then following it with a larger request.

these exams right away (which presumably made students feel motivated to analyze the evidence), whereas others were told that their university was considering implementing these exams in 10 years (which presumably made students feel unmotivated to analyze the evidence). As **FIGURE 13.18** shows, when students were motivated to analyze the evidence, they were systematically persuaded—that is, their attitudes and beliefs were influenced by the strength of the arguments but not by the status of the speaker. But when students were not motivated to analyze the evidence, they were heuristically persuaded—that is, their attitudes and beliefs were influenced by the status of the speaker but not by the strength of the arguments.

Consistency: We Believe in What We Do

If a friend told you that rabbits had just staged a coup in Antarctica and were halting all carrot exports, you probably wouldn't bother to check the CNN website. You'd know right away that your friend was either joking or high because the statement is logically inconsistent with other things that you know are true—for example, that rabbits do not foment revolution and that Antarctica does not export carrots. People evaluate the accuracy of new beliefs by assessing their *consistency* with old beliefs. Although this is not a foolproof method for determining whether something is true, it provides a pretty good approximation (Kruglanski et al., 2018). We are motivated to be accurate, and, because consistency is a rough indicator of accuracy, we are motivated to be consistent as well (Cialdini, Trost, & Newsom, 1995).

Like other motivations, this one leaves us vulnerable to social influence. For example, the **foot-in-the-door technique** involves *making a small request and then following it with a larger request* (Burger, 1999). In one study (Freedman & Fraser, 1966), experimenters went to a neighbourhood and knocked on doors to see if they

Figure 13.18

Two Types of Persuasion
Panel A shows systematic persuasion and Panel B shows heuristic persuasion (Petty, Cacioppo, & Goldman, 1981). Notice how, when motivation to analyze the evidence was high (at left), weak arguments were not persuasive, from either speaker. However, when motivation was low, students found weak arguments from the high (but not low) status speaker somewhat convincing.

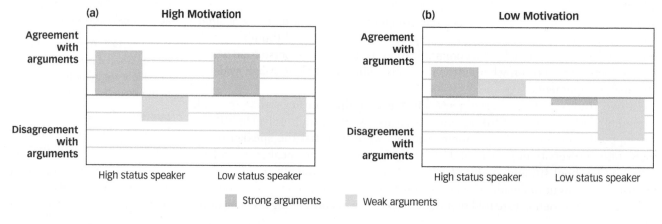

(a) **High Motivation**

Agreement with arguments

Disagreement with arguments

High status speaker   Low status speaker

(b) **Low Motivation**

Agreement with arguments

Disagreement with arguments

High status speaker   Low status speaker

Strong arguments   Weak arguments

could convince homeowners to install a big ugly "Drive Carefully" sign in their front yards. One group of homeowners was simply asked to install the sign, and only 17% said yes. A second group of homeowners was first asked to sign a petition urging the state legislature to promote safe driving (which almost all agreed to do) and was *then* asked to install the ugly sign. A full 55% said yes! Why would homeowners—or anyone else, for that matter—be more likely to grant two requests than one?

Well, just imagine how the homeowners in the second group felt. They had just said yes to signing a petition, but they didn't want to say yes to installing an ugly sign. But that's inconsistent! If you really care about safe driving, then you should do both of these things, and if you don't care, then you should do neither. As the homeowners wrestled with this inconsistency, they probably began to experience **cognitive dissonance**, which is *an unpleasant state that arises when a person recognizes the inconsistency of his or her actions, attitudes, or beliefs* (Festinger, 1957). When people experience cognitive dissonance, they naturally try to alleviate it. Although there are many ways to do this (Randles et al., 2015), one perfectly ordinary way is to put your money where your mouth is—that is, to be consistent (Aronson, 1969; Cooper & Fazio, 1984; Harmon-Jones, Harmon-Jones, & Levy, 2015). And so homeowners agreed to install the yard sign in order to be consistent with their signing of the petition. The lesson for any would-be social influencer is clear: You can often get people to take an action by first getting them to express an attitude with which that action is consistent. For instance, research shows that if hotel guests are subtly induced at check-in to say they are "Friends of the Earth," they are subsequently 25% more likely to reuse their towels during their stay (Baca-Motes et al., 2013).

Just as people take actions that are consistent with their expressed attitudes, so too do they adopt attitudes that are consistent with their actions. In a classic study (Aronson & Mills, 1958), female university students applied to join a weekly discussion on the "psychology of sex." Women in the control group were allowed to join the discussion, but women in the experimental group were allowed to join the discussion only after first passing an embarrassing test that involved reading pornographic fiction to a strange man. After either taking or not taking the embarrassing test, the women took part in a carefully scripted discussion that was deliberately extremely dull. Then the women were asked how much they enjoyed the discussion, and those who had taken the test said it was much more interesting than did those who hadn't. Why? Women who took the test knew that they had paid a steep price to join the group ("I read all that gross porn out loud to some creep!"), and that belief was inconsistent with the belief that the discussion was dull. This inconsistency caused the women to experience cognitive dissonance, which they alleviated by changing their beliefs about the value of the discussion.

We normally think that people pay for things because they value them, but as this study shows, people sometimes value things because they've paid for them—with money, time, attention, blood, sweat, tears, or embarrassment. It is little wonder that some university fraternities use hazing to instill loyalty, that some religions require their adherents to make large personal or monetary sacrifices to create commitment, that some gourmet restaurants charge outrageous amounts to keep their patrons coming back, or that some men and women play hard to get to stimulate their suitors' interest. Making people suffer for something is a powerful way to make them like it.

Although we are all motivated to behave in ways that are consistent with our beliefs, there are times when we simply can't. A friend's new hairstyle may resemble a wet skunk after an unfortunate encounter with a snow blower, but when he asks us, "What do you think of my new look?" we are likely to swallow hard and say that we like it. Yet we don't come to believe our own words. Why doesn't the inconsistency between our belief and our action in this case cause us to experience cognitive

University of Toronto engineering students engage in one of the many (probably unpleasant, certainly inconvenient) rituals associated with Frosh Week. Rituals like these foster group loyalty.

cognitive dissonance An unpleasant state that arises when a person recognizes the inconsistency of his or her actions, attitudes, or beliefs.

dissonance, which we might then alleviate by changing our belief? Because although complimenting our friend's hairstyle is inconsistent with our belief that it is actually quite hideous, our actions in this case seem *justified* by the strong incentive we have to maintain our friendship. When an inconsistency feels justified, it does not cause people to experience cognitive dissonance.

For example, participants in one study (Festinger & Carlsmith, 1959) were asked to perform a dull task that involved turning knobs one way, then the other way, and then back again. After the participants were sufficiently bored, the experimenter explained that he desperately needed a few more people to volunteer for the study, and he asked the participants to go into the hallway, find another person, and untruthfully tell that person that the knob-turning task was a load of fun and that they should participate. The experimenter offered some participants $1 to tell this lie, and he offered other participants $20. All participants succumbed to the social pressure to help the experimenter by telling a lie, and after they did so, they were asked to report their true enjoyment of the knob-turning task.

The results showed that participants liked the task *more* when they were paid $1 than $20 to lie about it. Why? Because $20 is a whole lot of money (and it was a whole lot more in 1959!), and getting that kind of money seemed to justify telling a little white lie. But $1 is not a lot of money—not nearly enough to justify lying to a fellow student—so participants in this condition experienced cognitive dissonance ("I said the task was fun, but I actually thought it was boring"), which they then alleviated by changing their beliefs about the task ("Now that I think about it, the task was kind of fun"). Getting people to behave in ways that they cannot justify is one of the most powerful ways to influence their beliefs.

Build to the Outcomes

1. What are the three basic motives that social influence involves?

2. Why do attempts to influence others with rewards and punishments sometimes backfire?

3. How can the norm of reciprocity be used to influence people?

4. Why do people sometimes do what they see others doing?

5. When and why do people obey authority?

6. What is the difference between normative and informational influence?

7. When is it more effective to engage in systematic persuasion rather than in heuristic persuasion?

8. Why does the accuracy motive lead to a desire for consistency?

9. What is cognitive dissonance? How do people alleviate it?

Chapter Review

Interpersonal Behaviour

- Both survival and reproduction require scarce resources, and aggression and cooperation are two ways to get them.

- Aggressions can be proactive or reactive. Proactive aggression is planned and purposeful. Reactive aggression typically results from negative affect, and the likelihood that people will engage in it is influenced both by biological and cultural factors.

- Cooperation is an excellent strategy for attaining resources, but it entails the risk that others will take advantage of us. One way to reduce that risk is to cooperate with members of one's own groups, who are likely to show in-group favouritism.

- Groups reduce the risk of cooperation, but they also have costs. They can promote unethical behaviour by causing people to lose sight of their personal values, and they often make decisions that are worse than the decisions their best members would have made on their own.

- Many behaviours that appear to be altruistic have hidden benefits for the person who performs them. Human beings, however, do appear to exhibit genuine altruism.

Interpersonal Attraction

- Both biology and culture make the costs of reproduction higher for women than for men, which is one reason that women tend to be choosier when selecting mates.
- Attraction is determined by situational, physical, and psychological factors.
- Most people participate in one or more long-term romantic relationships, which are often signified by marriage. People usually remain in these relationships as long as they believe the benefits outweigh the costs.

Interpersonal Perception

- We make inferences about people on the basis of the categories to which they belong, as well as on the basis of their individual behaviours.
- Category-based inferences can be mistaken because our stereotypes about categories are often inaccurate, overused, self-perpetuating, and unconscious and automatic.

- Target-based inferences can also be mistaken. People attribute behaviour to the actor's dispositions rather than to the situation in which the behaviour was performed.

Interpersonal Influence

- People are motivated to experience pleasure and avoid pain (the hedonic motive), and thus can be influenced by rewards and punishments. These influence attempts can sometimes backfire by changing how people think about their own behaviour or by making them feel as though they are being manipulated.
- People are motivated to attain the approval of others (the approval motive), and thus can be influenced by social norms, such as the norm of reciprocity. People often look to the behaviour of others to determine what kinds of behaviour are normative. People tend to obey authorities even when they should not.
- People are motivated to know what is true (the accuracy motive). People often look to the behaviour of others to determine what is true.
- People can be persuaded by appeals to reason or emotion. Each is effective under different circumstances.
- People feel bad when they notice inconsistency among their attitudes, beliefs, and actions, and they will often change one of these things in order to alleviate this feeling of "cognitive dissonance" and achieve consistency.

Key Concept Quiz

1. What best predicts whether a person will engage in reactive aggression?
   a. the outdoor temperature
   b. the person's gender
   c. the person's culture
   d. the availability of violent video games

2. When women aggress, they usually
   a. engage in reactive rather than proactive aggression.
   b. have high testosterone.
   c. cause social harm rather than physical harm.
   d. experience frustration.

3. The prisoner's dilemma game illustrates
   a. in-group favouritism.
   b. the diffusion of responsibility.
   c. group polarization.
   d. the benefits and costs of cooperation.

4. The apparently altruistic behaviour of non-human animals can often be explained by
   a. kin selection.
   b. obedience.
   c. informational influence.
   d. cognitive dissonance.

5. Which of the following is a situational factor that influences attraction?
   a. proximity
   b. similarity
   c. bilateral symmetry
   d. personality

6. The fact that people in relationships want their cost–benefit ratio to be about the same as their partner's is known as
   a. passionate love.
   b. bilateral symmetry.
   c. equity.
   d. comparison level for alternatives.

7. The fact that people prefer to experience pleasure rather than pain is known as
   a. group polarization.
   b. heuristic persuasion.
   c. social loafing.
   d. the hedonic motive.

8. The tendency to do what authorities tell us to do is known as
   a. persuasion.
   b. obedience.
   c. conformity.
   d. the self-fulfilling prophecy.

9. What is the process by which people come to understand others?
   a. social influence
   b. reciprocal altruism
   c. social cognition
   d. cognitive dissonance

10. The tendency to make a dispositional attribution even when a person's behaviour was caused by the situation is referred to as
    a. groupthink.
    b. the mere exposure effect.
    c. normative influence.
    d. correspondence bias.

Don't stop now! Quizzing yourself is a powerful study tool. Go to LaunchPad to access the LearningCurve adaptive quizzing system and your own personalized learning plan. Visit launchpadworks.com.

Key Terms

social psychology (p. 500)

aggression (p. 500)

frustration–aggression hypothesis (p. 500)

proactive aggression (p. 501)

reactive aggression (p. 501)

cooperation (p. 504)

group (p. 506)

prejudice (p. 506)

common knowledge effect (p. 507)

group polarization (p. 507)

groupthink (p. 507)

deindividuation (p. 507)

diffusion of responsibility (p. 508)

social loafing (p. 508)

bystander intervention (p. 508)

altruism (p. 509)

kin selection (p. 509)

reciprocal altruism (p. 510)

mere exposure effect (p. 513)

homophily (p. 517)

passionate love (p. 519)

companionate love (p. 519)

comparison level for alternatives (p. 520)

equity (p. 520)

social cognition (p. 521)

category-based inferences (p. 521)

target-based inferences (p. 521)

stereotyping (p. 521)

behavioural confirmation (p. 524)

stereotype threat (p. 524)

perceptual confirmation (p. 525)

subtyping (p. 525)

attributions (p. 529)

correspondence bias (p. 530)

actor-observer effect (p. 531)

social influence (p. 532)

overjustification effect (p. 533)

reactance (p. 533)

norms (p. 534)

norm of reciprocity (p. 534)

normative influence (p. 534)

door-in-the-face technique (p. 534)

conformity (p. 535)

obedience (p. 536)

attitude (p. 538)

belief (p. 538)

informational influence (p. 539)

persuasion (p. 539)

systematic persuasion (p. 539)

heuristic persuasion (p. 539)

foot-in-the-door technique (p. 540)

cognitive dissonance (p. 541)

Changing Minds

1. One of the MPPs from your province supports a bill that would impose heavy fines on aggressive drivers who run red lights. One of your classmates thinks this is a good idea. "The textbook taught us a lot about punishment and reward. It's simple. If we punish aggressive driving, its frequency will decline." Is your classmate right? Might the new law backfire? Might another policy be more effective in promoting safe driving?

2. One of your friends is outgoing, funny, and a star athlete on the men's varsity basketball team. He has started to date someone who is introverted and prefers playing computer games to attending parties. You tease him about the contrast in their personalities, and he replies, "Well, opposites attract." Is he right?

3. A large law firm is found guilty of discriminatory hiring practices. Your friend reads about the case and scoffs, "People are always so quick to claim racism. Sure, there are still a few racists out there, but if you do surveys and ask people what they think about people of other races, they generally say they feel fine about them." What would you tell your friend?

4. One of your friends wears a neon orange track suit and a battered fedora. Every. Single. Day. "Most people follow the crowd," your friend says. "But not me. I'm an individual, and I'm just not influenced by other people." Could your friend be right? What examples might you provide for or against your friend's claim?

5. A classmate learns about Stanley Milgram's 1963 study in which participants were willing to obey orders to administer painful electric shocks to a learner who begged them to stop. "Some people are such sheep!" she says. "I would never have done that." Is she right? What evidence would you give her to support or oppose her claim?

6. Your family gathers for a holiday dinner, and your cousin Wendy brings her fiancée, Amanda. It's the first time

Amanda has met the whole family, and she seems nervous. She talks too much, laughs too loud, and rubs everyone the wrong way. Later, one of your uncles says to you, "It's hard to imagine Wendy wanting to spend the rest of her life married to someone so annoying." Has your uncle fallen prey to the correspondence bias? How could you know?

Answers to Key Concept Quiz

1. b; 2. c; 3. d; 4. a; 5. a; 6. c; 7. d; 8. b; 9. c; 10. d

LaunchPad features the full e-Book of *Psychology*, the LearningCurve adaptive quizzing system, videos, and a variety of activities to boost your learning. Visit LaunchPad at launchpadworks.com.

Stress and Health

"I HAVE A KNIFE TO YOUR NECK. Don't make a sound. Get out of bed and come with me or I will kill you and your family." These are the words that awoke 14-year-old Elizabeth Smart in the middle of the night on June 5, 2002, while she was sleeping in her bedroom next to her 9-year-old sister Mary Katherine. Fearing for her life, and the lives of her family, she kept quiet and left with her abductor. Her little sister, terrified, hid in her bedroom for several hours before waking the girls' parents, who awoke to their daughter saying, "She's gone. Elizabeth is gone." Elizabeth was kidnapped by Brian David Mitchell, a man Elizabeth's parents had hired previously to do some roof work on their home. Mitchell broke into the family's home in Salt Lake City, Utah, through an open window and abducted Elizabeth. He and his wife, Wanda Ileen Barzee, held her in captivity for 9 months, during which time Mitchell repeatedly raped her and threatened to kill her and her entire family. Mitchell, Barzee, and Smart were spotted walking down the street by a couple who recognized them from a recent episode of the television show *America's Most Wanted* and called the police. Mitchell and Barzee were apprehended and Elizabeth was returned to her family.

Elizabeth suffered under unimaginable circumstances for a prolonged period of time in what can be thought of as one of the most stressful situations possible. So what became of Elizabeth? Fortunately, she is now safe

This smiling young face is that of Elizabeth Smart, who, between the times of these two photographs, was kidnapped, raped, and tortured for nearly a year. Stressful life events often affect us in ways that cannot be seen from the outside. Fortunately, there are things that we can do in response to even the most stressful of life events that can get us smiling again.

and sound, happily married, and working as an activist. She endured life-threatening stressors for months, and those experiences undoubtedly affected her in ways that will last her entire lifetime. At the same time, hers is a story of resilience. Despite the very difficult hand she was dealt, she appears to have bounced back and to be leading a happy, productive, and rewarding life. Hers is a story of both stress and health.

FORTUNATELY, FEW OF US WILL EVER HAVE TO ENDURE the type of stress that Elizabeth Smart lived through. But life can present a welter of frights, bothers, and looming disasters that can be difficult to manage. A reckless driver may nearly run you over; you may be discriminated against, threatened, or intimidated in some way; or a fire may leave you out on the street. Life has its **stressors**, *specific events or chronic pressures that place demands on a person or threaten the person's well-being.* Although such stressors rarely involve threats of death, they do have both immediate and cumulative effects that can influence health.

In this chapter, we'll look at what psychologists have learned about the kinds of life events that produce **stress**, *the physical and psychological response to internal or external stressors;* typical responses to such stressors; and ways to manage stress. Stress has such a profound influence on health that we consider stress and health together in this chapter. And because sickness and health are not merely features of the physical body, we then consider the more general topic of **health psychology**, *the subfield of psychology concerned with how psychological factors influence the causes and treatment of physical illness and the maintenance of health.* You will see how perceptions of illness can affect its course and how health-promoting behaviours can improve the quality of people's lives.

Sources of Stress: What Gets to You

What are the sources of stress in our lives? A natural catastrophe, such as a hurricane, earthquake, or volcanic eruption, is an obvious source. But for most of us, stressors are personal events that affect the comfortable pattern of our lives and the little annoyances that bug us day after day. Let's look at the life events that can cause stress, chronic sources of stress, and the relationship between lack of perceived control and the impact of stressors.

Stressful Events

People often seem to get sick after major life events. In pioneering work, Thomas Holmes and Richard Rahe (1967) followed up on this observation, proposing that major life changes cause stress and that increased stress causes illness. To test their idea, they asked people to rate the magnitude of readjustment required by each of many events found to be associated with the onset of illness (Rahe et al., 1964). The resulting list of life events is remarkably predictive: Simply adding up the stress ratings of each life change experienced is a significant indicator of a person's likelihood of future illness (Miller, 1996). Someone who gets divorced, loses a job, and has a friend die all in the same year, for example, is more likely to get sick than someone who escapes the year with only a divorce.

A version of this list adapted for the life events of university students (and sporting the snappy acronym CUSS, for College Undergraduate Stress Scale) is shown in **TABLE 14.1**. To assess your stressful events, check off any events that have happened

stressors Specific events or chronic pressures that place demands on a person or threaten the person's well-being.

stress The physical and psychological response to internal or external stressors.

health psychology The subfield of psychology concerned with how psychological factors influence the causes and treatment of physical illness and the maintenance of health.

TABLE 14.1

COLLEGE UNDERGRADUATE STRESS SCALE

Event	Stress Rating	Event	Stress Rating
Being raped	100	Lack of sleep	69
Finding out that you are HIV positive	100	Change in housing situation (hassles, moves)	69
Being accused of rape	98	Competing or performing in public	69
Death of a close friend	97	Getting in a physical fight	66
Death of a close family member	96	Difficulties with a roommate	66
Contracting a sexually transmitted disease (other than AIDS)	94	Job changes (applying, new job, work hassles)	65
Concerns about being pregnant	91	Declaring a major or concerns about future plans	65
Finals week	90	A class you hate	62
Concerns about your partner being pregnant	90	Drinking or use of drugs	61
Oversleeping for an exam	89	Confrontations with professors	60
Flunking a class	89	Starting a new semester	58
Having a boyfriend or girlfriend cheat on you	85	Going on a first date	57
Ending a steady dating relationship	85	Registration	55
Serious illness in a close friend or family member	85	Maintaining a steady dating relationship	55
Financial difficulties	84	Commuting to campus or work or both	54
Writing a major term paper	83	Peer pressures	53
Being caught cheating on a test	83	Being away from home for the first time	53
Drunk driving	82	Getting sick	52
Sense of overload in school or work	82	Concerns about your appearance	52
Two exams in one day	80	Getting straight A's	51
Cheating on your boyfriend or girlfriend	77	A difficult class that you love	48
Getting married	76	Making new friends; getting along with friends	47
Negative consequences of drinking or drug use	75	Fraternity or sorority rush	47
Depression or crisis in your best friend	73	Falling asleep in class	40
Difficulties with parents	73	Attending an athletic event	20
Talking in front of class	72		

Note: To compute your personal life change score, sum the stress ratings for all events that have happened to you in the last year. Information from Renner & Mackin (1998).

to you in the past year and sum your point total. In a large sample of students in an introductory psychology class, the average was 1,247 points, ranging from 182 to 2,571 (Renner & Mackin, 1998).

Looking at the list, you may wonder why positive events are included. Stressful life events are unpleasant, right? Why would getting married be stressful? Isn't a wedding supposed to be fun? Research has shown that, compared with negative events, positive events produce less psychological distress and fewer physical symptoms (McFarlane et al., 1980), and that happiness can sometimes even counteract the effects of negative events (Fredrickson, 2000). However, because positive events often require readjustment and preparedness that many people find extremely stressful (Brown & McGill, 1989), these events are included in computing life-change scores.

Chronic Stressors

Life would be simpler if an occasional stressful event such as a wedding or a lost job were the only pressures we faced. At least each event would be limited in scope, with a beginning, a middle, and, ideally, an end. But unfortunately, life brings

WARNER BROS/KOBAL/SHUTTERSTOCK

As the movie *Crazy Rich Asians* showcased perfectly, although weddings are positive events, they also can be stressful due to the often overwhelming amount of planning and decision making involved (and occasionally because of the difficulties in managing the interactions of friends and family).

City life can be fun, but the higher levels of noise, crowding, and violence can also be sources of chronic stress.

chronic stressors Sources of stress that occur continuously or repeatedly.

with it continued exposure to **chronic stressors**, *sources of stress that occur continuously or repeatedly.* Strained relationships, discrimination, bullying, overwork, money troubles—small stressors that may be easy to ignore if they happen only occasionally—can accumulate to produce distress and illness. People who report being affected by daily hassles also report more psychological symptoms (LaPierre et al., 2012) and physical symptoms (Piazza et al., 2013), and these effects often have a greater and longer-lasting impact than major life events.

Many chronic stressors are linked to social relationships. For instance, as described in the Social Psychology chapter, people often form different social groups based on race, culture, interests, popularity, and so on. Being outside the in-group can be stressful. Being actively targeted by members of the in-group can be even more stressful, especially if this happens repeatedly over time (see A World of Difference: Can Discrimination Cause Stress and Illness?). Chronic stressors also can be linked to particular environments. For example, features of city life—noise, traffic, crowding, pollution, and even the threat of violence—provide particularly insistent sources of chronic stress (Evans, 2006). More recent research has started to identify potential pathways through which this may occur. For instance, people who live in cities show significantly greater amygdala activity in response to stressors than do those who live in towns (slightly less activity) and in rural regions (much less activity)—a finding replicated across three different samples (Lederbogen et al., 2011). The realization that chronic stressors are linked to environments has spawned the subfield of *environmental psychology,* the scientific study of environmental effects on behaviour and health.

A World of Difference | Can Discrimination Cause Stress and Illness?

Have you ever been discriminated against because of your race, gender, sexual orientation, or some other characteristic? If so, then you know that this can be a pretty stressful experience. Discrimination that occurs repeatedly over time can be an especially powerful stressor for anyone. But what exactly does it *do* to people?

There are a number of ways in which discrimination can lead to elevated stress and negative health outcomes. People from socially disadvantaged groups who experience higher levels of stress as a result of discrimination engage more frequently in maladaptive behaviours (e.g., drinking, smoking, and overeating) in efforts to cope with stress. They also can experience difficulties in their interactions with health care professionals (e.g., clinician biases, patient suspiciousness about treatment) (Major, Mendes, & Dovidio, 2013). This may help explain why members of socially disadvantaged groups have significantly higher rates of health problems than do members of socially advantaged groups (Penner et al., 2010).

Research has begun to reveal how discrimination can literally "get under the skin"

to cause negative health outcomes. One American study by Wendy Mendes and colleagues (Jamieson et al., 2013) exposed Black and White participants to social rejection by a person of the same race or by a person of a different race to test whether there is something particularly harmful about discrimination, compared with social rejection in general. To test this hypothesis, research participants delivered a speech to two confederates in different rooms via a video chat program, after which the confederates provided negative feedback about the participant's speech. The confederates were not seen by the participant but were represented by computer avatars that either matched the participant's race or did not. In an interesting finding, although the nature of the rejection was the same in all cases, participants responded very differently if the people rejecting them were of a different race than if they were of the same race. Specifically, whereas being rejected by people of your own race was associated with greater displays of shame and physiological changes associated with an avoidance state (increased cortisol), being rejected by members of a different race was associated

with displays of anger, greater vigilance for danger, physiological changes associated with an approach state (i.e., higher cardiac output and lower vascular resistance), and higher risk taking. The results suggest that discrimination can lead to physiological, cognitive, and behavioural changes that in the short term prepare a person for action, but that in the long term could lead to negative health outcomes.

Studies such as this one help explain some of the health disparities that currently exist across different social groups. In a 2011–2014 survey (Statistics Canada, 2016), 60% of Canada's non-Indigenous population rated their health as good or excellent. In stark contrast, only 48.5%, 51.3%, and 44.9% of First Nations, Métis, and Inuit people respectively reported their health as such, and life expectancy is 5 to 10 years shorter for Indigenous people, compared to other Canadians (Statistics Canada, 2005). Although there are many reasons why Indigenous Peoples in this country suffer poorer health than others, chronic stress due to prejudice, discrimination, and systemic racism is probably one of them (Spence et al., 2016).

In a classic study of the influence of noise on children, environmental psychologists looked at the impact of attending schools under the flight path to Heathrow Airport in London, England. Did the noise of more than 1,250 jets flying overhead each day have an influence beyond making kids yell to be heard? Compared with children from matched control schools in low-noise areas, children who attended school under the flight path reported higher levels of noise annoyance and showed poorer reading comprehension (Haines et al., 2001). Next time you fly into an airport, please try to do so more quietly. For the children.

Perceived Control Over Stressful Events

What do catastrophes, stressful life changes, and daily hassles have in common? Right off the bat, of course, their threat to the person or the status quo is easy to see. Stressors challenge you to *do something*—to take some action to eliminate or overcome the stressors.

Paradoxically, events are most stressful when there is *nothing to do*—no way to deal with the challenge. Expecting that you will have control over what happens to you is associated with effectiveness in dealing with stress. The researchers David Glass and Jerome Singer (1972), in classic studies of *perceived control*, looked at the aftereffects of loud noise on people who could or could not control it. Participants were asked to solve puzzles and proofread in a quiet room or in a room filled with loud noise. Glass and Singer found that bursts of such noise hurt people's performance on the tasks after the noise was over. However, this dramatic decline in performance did not occur among participants who were told during the noise period that they could stop the noise just by pushing a button. They didn't actually take this option, but just having access to the "panic button" shielded them from the detrimental effects of the noise. In another classic study (Hanson, 1976), one group of monkeys was taught to press a lever to turn off a loud noise, whereas individuals in the "yoked group" were exposed to the identical amount of noise, but couldn't turn it off. These yoked monkeys had higher levels of cortisol (a stress hormone) and were more aggressive than monkeys who could control the noise. Interestingly, when control was removed from the first group, their cortisol and aggression levels were even higher than those in the yoked group! This tells us that history, and perceived control, are both very important for understanding how we respond to stress.

Subsequent studies have found that a lack of perceived control underlies the body's response to other stressors, too. The stressful effects of crowding, for example, appear to stem from the feeling that you can't control getting away from the crowded conditions (Evans & Stecker, 2004). Being jammed into a crowded dormitory room may be easier to handle, after all, the moment you realize you could take a walk and get away from it all.

Some stressful life events, such as those associated with drunk driving, are within our power to control. We gain control when we give the car keys to a designated driver.

KWAME ZIKOMO/PURESTOCK/ALAMY

Build to the Outcomes

1. Which of the events on the stress rating scale relate to you? Do any of the ratings surprise you?
2. How can positive events be stressful?
3. Give examples of chronic stressors.
4. What are some examples of environmental factors that cause chronic stress?
5. What makes events most stressful?

Stress Reactions: All Shook Up

It was a regular Tuesday morning in New York City. University students were sitting in their morning classes. People were arriving at work and the streets were beginning to fill with shoppers and tourists. Then, at 8:46 a.m., American Airlines Flight 11 crashed into the North Tower of the World Trade Center. People watched in horror. How could this have happened? This seemed like a terrible accident. Then at 9:03 a.m., United Airlines Flight 175 crashed into the South Tower of the World Trade Center. There

Learning Outcomes

- Explain physical responses to stress.
- Identify possible psychological responses to stress.

SPENCER PLATT/GETTY IMAGES

The threat of death or injury, such as many in New York City experienced at the time of the 9/11 attacks, can cause significant and lasting physical and psychological stress reactions.

were then reports of a plane crashing into the Pentagon, the headquarters of the United States Department of Defense. And another somewhere in the state of Pennsylvania.

The terrorist attacks on the World Trade Center on September 11, 2001, were an enormous stressor that had a lasting impact on many people, physically and psychologically. Research done several years after this event revealed that people who lived in close proximity to the World Trade Center (within 1.5 miles) on 9/11 now had less grey matter in the amygdala, hippocampus, insula, anterior cingulate, and medial prefrontal cortex than did those who lived more than 200 miles away during the attacks; this suggested that the stress associated with the attacks may have reduced the size of these parts of the brain that play an important role in emotion, memory, and decision making (Ganzel et al., 2008). The brain measurements were taken more than 3 years after 9/11: This tells us that the event had long-term consequences on brain structure. Children who watched more television coverage of 9/11 had higher symptoms of posttraumatic stress disorder than did children who watched less coverage (Otto et al., 2007). People around the United States who had a stronger acute stress response to the events of 9/11 had a 53% increased incidence of heart problems over the next 3 years (Holman et al., 2008). Stress can produce changes in every system of the body and mind, stimulating both physical reactions and psychological reactions. Let's consider each in turn.

Physical Reactions

You are at a party, and a guy jumps in front of you with his fists up ready to punch you in the face. What do you do?! Walter Cannon (1929) coined a phrase to describe the body's response to any threatening stimulus: the **fight-or-flight response**, *an emotional and physiological reaction to an emergency that increases readiness for action.* The mind asks, "Should I stay and fight this guy? Or should I flee this situation?" And the body prepares to react. Cannon recognized this common response across species and suspected that it might be the body's first mobilization to any threat.

Research conducted since Cannon's discovery has revealed what is happening in the brain and body during this reaction. Brain activation in response to threat occurs in the hypothalamus, stimulating the nearby pituitary gland, which in turn releases a hormone known as ACTH (short for adrenocorticotropic hormone). ACTH travels through the bloodstream and stimulates the adrenal glands atop the kidneys (see **FIGURE 14.1**). In this cascading response of the HPA (hypothalamic–pituitary–adrenocortical) axis, the adrenal glands are stimulated to release hormones, including the *catecholamines* (epinephrine and norepinephrine), which increase sympathetic nervous system activation (and therefore increase heart rate, blood pressure, and respiration rate) and decrease parasympathetic activation (see the Neuroscience and Behaviour chapter). The increased respiration and blood pressure make more oxygen available to the muscles to energize attack or to initiate escape. The adrenal glands also release *cortisol,* a hormone that increases the concentration of glucose in the blood to make fuel available to the muscles. Everything is prepared for a full-tilt response to the threat.

General Adaptation Syndrome

What might have happened if the terrorist attacks of 9/11 were spaced out over a period of days or weeks? Starting in the 1930s, Hans Selye, a Canadian physician in Montreal, undertook a variety of experiments that looked at the physiological consequences of severe threats to well-being. He subjected rats to heat, cold, infection, trauma, hemorrhage, and other prolonged stressors, making few friends among the rats or their sympathizers, but learning a lot about stress. His stressed-out rats developed physiological responses that included enlargement of the adrenal cortex, shrinking of the lymph glands, and ulceration of the stomach. Noting that many different kinds of stressors caused similar patterns of physiological change, he called the reaction the **general adaptation syndrome (GAS)**, which he defined as a *three-stage physiological stress response that appears regardless of the*

fight-or-flight response An emotional and physiological reaction to an emergency that increases readiness for action.

general adaptation syndrome (GAS) A three-stage physiological response that appears regardless of the stressor that is encountered.

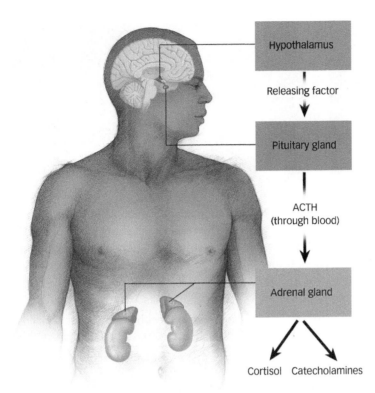

Figure 14.1

HPA Axis Just a few seconds after a fearful stimulus is perceived, the hypothalamus activates the pituitary gland to release adrenocorticotropic hormone (ACTH). The ACTH then travels through the bloodstream to activate the adrenal glands to release catecholamines and cortisol, which energize the fight-or-flight response.

stressor that is encountered. The GAS is *nonspecific*; that is, the response doesn't vary, no matter what the source of the repeated stress.

None of this is very good news. Although Friedrich Nietzsche once said, "What does not kill me makes me stronger," Selye found that severe stress takes a toll on the body. He saw the GAS as occurring in three phases (see **FIGURE 14.2**):

- First comes the *alarm phase,* in which the body rapidly mobilizes its resources to respond to the threat. Energy is required, and the body calls on its stored fat and muscle. The alarm phase is equivalent to Cannon's fight-or-flight response.

- Next, in the *resistance phase,* the body adapts to its high state of arousal as it tries to cope with the stressor. Continuing to draw on resources of fat and muscle, it shuts down unnecessary processes: Digestion, growth, and sex drive stall; menstruation stops; production of testosterone and sperm decreases. The body is being taxed to generate resistance, and all the fun stuff is put on hold.

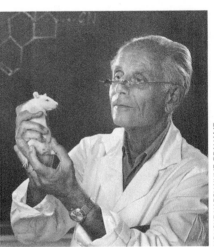

Hans Selye with rat. Given all the stress Selye put rats under, this one looks surprisingly calm.

YOUSUF KARSH/JULIE GRAHAME

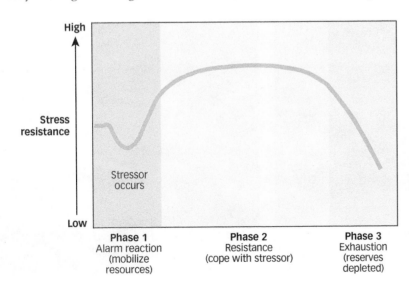

Figure 14.2

Selye's Three Phases of Stress Response In Selye's theory, resistance to stress builds over time, but then can only last so long before exhaustion sets in.

Chronic stress can actually speed the aging process. These pairs of pictures are from three world leaders, and the pictures are all taken 8 years apart. From left: Barack Obama, U.S. President, 2008–2016. Middle: Stephen Harper, Canadian Prime Minister, 2006–2015; and Angela Merkel, Chancellor of Germany, 2005 to present. University can be stressful, too, but hopefully not so much so that you have grey hair by graduation.

- If the GAS continues long enough, the *exhaustion phase* sets in. The body's resistance collapses. Many of the resistance-phase defences cause gradual damage as they operate, leading to costs for the body that can include susceptibility to infection, tumour growth, aging, irreversible organ damage, or death.

Stress Negatively Affects Health and Speeds Aging

Right now, you are (we hope!) enjoying years of healthy living. Unfortunately, as people age, the body slowly begins to break down. (Just ask any of the authors of this textbook.) Interestingly, recent research has revealed that stress significantly accelerates the aging process. Elizabeth Smart's parents noted that, on being reunited with her after 9 months of separation, they almost did not recognize her because she appeared to have aged so much (Smart, Smart, & Morton, 2003). Theirs is an extreme example; you can see examples of the effects of stress on aging around you in everyday life. People exposed to chronic stress, whether due to their relationships or jobs, or something else, experience actual wear and tear on their bodies and accelerated aging. Take a look at the pictures of these three political leaders before and after 8 years in office. As you can see, they appear to have aged much more than the 8 years that passed between their first and second photographs. How exactly can stressors in the environment speed up the aging process?

Understanding this process requires knowing a little bit about how aging occurs. The cells in our bodies are constantly dividing, and as part of this process, our chromosomes are repeatedly copied so that our genetic information is carried into the new cells. This process is facilitated by the presence of **telomeres**, *caps at the ends of the chromosomes that prevent the chromosomes from sticking to each other.* They are analogous to the metal or plastic sheaths at the end of your shoelaces that keep them from fraying and not working as efficiently. Each time a cell divides, the telomeres

telomeres Caps at the ends of the chromosomes that prevent the chromosomes from sticking to each other.

Dr. Elizabeth Blackburn was awarded a Nobel Prize in Physiology or Medicine in 2009 for her groundbreaking discoveries on the functions of telomeres (shown here in yellow) and telomerase.

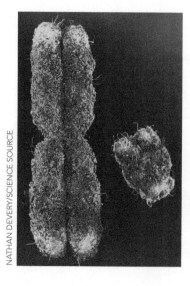

become slightly shorter. If they become too short, cells can no longer divide, which can lead to the development of tumours and a range of diseases.

Fortunately, our bodies fix this problem by producing a substance called **telomerase,** *an enzyme that rebuilds telomeres at the tips of chromosomes.* As cells repeatedly divide over the course of our lives, telomerase does its best to re-cap our chromosomes with telomeres. Ultimately, though, telomerase cannot keep up telomere repair at a sufficient pace, and over time cells lose their ability to divide, causing aging and, in the end, cell death. The recent discovery of the function of telomeres and telomerase and their relation to aging and disease by Elizabeth Blackburn and colleagues has been one of the most exciting advances in science in the past several decades (earning Dr. Blackburn a Nobel Prize in 2009).

Interestingly, social stressors can play an important role in this process. People exposed to chronic stress have shorter telomere length and lower telomerase activity (Epel et al., 2004). Laboratory studies suggest that cortisol can reduce the activity of telomerase, which in turn leads to shortened telomeres, with downstream negative effects in the form of accelerated aging and increased risk of a wide range of diseases including cancer, cardiovascular disease, diabetes, and depression (Blackburn, Epel, & Lin, 2015). This sounds dire, but there are things you can do to combat this process and potentially live a healthier and longer life! Activities such as exercise and meditation seem to prevent chronic stress from shortening telomere length, providing a potential explanation of how these activities may convey health benefits such as longer life and lower risk of disease (Epel et al., 2009; Puterman et al., 2010) (see Hot Science: Stress, Health, and Money).

telomerase An enzyme that rebuilds telomeres at the tips of chromosomes.

Hot Science Stress, Health, and Money

Many of us are motivated by money. But why? There has always been a general assumption that money will bring happiness. But does it? In a landmark study of 450,000 survey responses, Daniel Kahneman and Angus Deaton (2010), a pair of Nobel Prize winners, showed that as your income increases, your self-reported happiness goes up, and stress goes down. But this is true only up to a point—and that point is approximately $75,000 U.S. dollars (which is about the 66th percentile). Beyond that point, higher income is not associated with happiness *or* stress.

More recent research has shown more alarmingly that those with less money also are at risk for the most serious outcome: death. Using data from 1.4 billion U.S. tax and death records, researchers found that people with higher incomes live significantly longer than those with lower incomes (Chetty et al., 2016). How much longer? It turns out that the difference between the wealthiest 1% and the poorest 1% is approximately 15 years for men and 10 years for women, as shown in the accompanying figure. Even more concerning is that

the difference in life expectancy has been increasing over time, with life expectancy rising 2 to 3 years for the wealthiest, but only <.5 years for the poorest from 2001 to 2014.

But income is not destiny, and even among the poorest in society, behavioural and environmental factors can make a huge difference. For instance, Chetty and colleagues (2016) found that smoking and obesity are associated with a significantly higher death rate, whereas exercise is associated with a significantly lower rate of death. Moreover, if you are poor

but live in a place with higher population density, a higher percentage of immigrants and university graduates, higher government expenditures, and higher home values, you will live significantly longer. In follow-up research, Chetty and Hendren (2018) found that among children growing up in poor families, each year of life they spend living in a nicer neighbourhood (e.g., better schools, lower crime) is associated with a significant increase in the amount of money they will earn as an adult later in life.

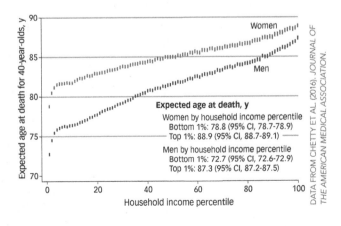

Expected age at death, y
Women by household income percentile
Bottom 1%: 78.8 (95% CI, 78.7-78.9)
Top 1%: 88.9 (95% CI, 88.7-89.1)
Men by household income percentile
Bottom 1%: 72.7 (95% CI, 72.6-72.9)
Top 1%: 87.3 (95% CI, 87.2-87.5)

DATA FROM CHETTY ET AL. (2016). JOURNAL OF THE AMERICAN MEDICAL ASSOCIATION.

Chris Rock's joke that "rich 50 is like poor 35!" matches up with data suggesting that wealthier people tend to be healthier and younger looking than poorer people.

Chronic Stress Affects the Immune Response

The **immune system** is *a complex response system that protects the body from bacteria, viruses, and other foreign substances.* The system includes white blood cells, such as **lymphocytes** (including T cells and B cells), *which produce antibodies that fight infection.* The immune system is remarkably responsive to psychological influences. *Psychoneuroimmunology* is the study of how the immune system responds to psychological variables, such as the presence of stressors. Stressors can cause hormones known as *glucocorticoids* (e.g., cortisol) to flood the brain (described in the Neuroscience and Behaviour chapter), wearing down the immune system and making it less able to fight invaders (Webster Marketon & Glaser, 2008).

For example, in one study, medical student volunteers agreed to receive small wounds to the roof of the mouth. Researchers observed that these wounds healed more slowly during exam periods than during summer vacation (Marucha, Kiecolt-Glaser, & Favagehi, 1998). In another series of studies, a set of selfless, healthy volunteers permitted researchers to swab the common cold virus in their noses (Cohen et al., 2012). You might think that a direct application of the virus would be like exposure to a massive full-facial sneeze and that all the participants would catch colds. The researchers observed, however, that some people got colds, but others didn't—and stress helped account for the difference. Volunteers who had experienced chronic stressors (lasting a month or longer) were especially likely to suffer from colds. In particular, participants who had lost a job or who were going through extended interpersonal problems with family or friends were most susceptible to the virus. Brief stressful life events (those lasting less than a month) had no impact. So if you're fighting with your friends or family, best to get it over with quickly; it's better for your health.

The effect of stress on immune response may help explain why social status is related to health. Studies of British civil servants beginning in the 1960s found that mortality varied precisely with civil service grade: the higher the classification, the lower the death rate, regardless of cause (Marmot et al., 1991). One explanation is that people in lower-status jobs more often engage in unhealthy behaviour such as smoking and drinking alcohol, and there is evidence of this. But there is also evidence that the stress of living life at the bottom levels of society increases the risk of infection by weakening the immune system. People who perceive themselves as low in social status and/or support are more likely to suffer from respiratory problems, for example, than those who do not bear this social burden (Lan et al., 2018).

Stress Affects Cardiovascular Health

The heart and circulatory system are also sensitive to stress. For example, one study of more than 60,000 U.S. military veterans found that among those who had been deployed during wartime, the ones who experienced combat had 93% higher odds of developing coronary heart disease (CHD) over the next few years than did those who did not experience combat (Crum-Cianflone et al., 2014). The association between major stressors and later heart disease also has been found in large (>1 million people) and rigorous studies of the general population (Song et al., 2019). The full story of how stress affects the cardiovascular system starts earlier than the actual occurrence of a heart attack: Chronic stress creates changes in the body that increase later vulnerability.

The main cause of CHD is *atherosclerosis,* a gradual narrowing of the arteries that occurs as fatty deposits, or plaque, build up on the inner walls of the arteries. Narrowed arteries reduce blood supply and, eventually, when an artery is blocked by a blood clot or detached plaque, result in a heart attack. Although smoking, a sedentary lifestyle, and a diet high in fat and cholesterol can cause CHD, chronic stress also is a major contributor (Silvani et al., 2016). As a result of stress-activated arousal of the sympathetic nervous system, blood pressure goes up and stays up, gradually

immune system A complex response system that protects the body from bacteria, viruses, and other foreign substances.

lymphocytes White blood cells that produce antibodies that fight infection, including T cells and B cells.

damaging the blood vessels. The damaged vessels accumulate plaque, and the more plaque, the greater the likelihood of CHD.

During the 1950s, the cardiologists Meyer Friedman and Ray Rosenman (1974) conducted a revolutionary study that demonstrated a link between work-related stress and CHD. They interviewed and tested 3,000 healthy middle-aged men and then tracked their subsequent cardiovascular health. From their research, Friedman and Rosenman developed the concept of the **Type A behaviour pattern**, which is characterized by *a tendency towards easily aroused hostility, impatience, a sense of time urgency, and competitive achievement strivings*. They compared Type A individuals with those who have a less-driven behaviour pattern (sometimes called *Type B*). The Type A men were identified not only by their answers to questions in the interview (agreeing that they walk and talk fast, work late, set goals for themselves, work hard to win, and easily get frustrated and angry at others) but also by the pushy and impatient way in which they answered the questions. They watched the clock, barked back answers, and interrupted the interviewer, at some points even slapping him with a fish. Okay, the part about the fish is wrong, but you get the idea: These people were intense. The researchers found that of the 258 men who had heart attacks in the 9 years following the interview, more than two-thirds had been classified as Type A, and only one-third had been classified as Type B.

A later study of stress and anger tracked medical students for up to 48 years to see how their behaviour during their youth related to their later susceptibility to coronary problems (Chang et al., 2002). Students who responded to stress with anger and hostility were found to be three times more likely to later develop premature heart disease and six times more likely to have an early heart attack than were students who did not respond with anger. Hostility, particularly in men, predicts heart disease better than any other major causal factor, such as smoking, high caloric intake, or even high levels of LDL cholesterol (Niaura et al., 2002; see also **FIGURE 14.3**). Stress affects the cardiovascular system to some degree in everyone, but it is particularly harmful in those people who respond to stressful events with hostility.

Psychological Reactions

The body's response to stress is intertwined with responses of the mind. Perhaps the first thing the mind does is try to sort things out—to interpret whether an event is threatening or not—and if it is, whether something can be done about it.

Type A behaviour pattern The tendency towards easily aroused hostility, impatience, a sense of time urgency, and competitive achievement strivings.

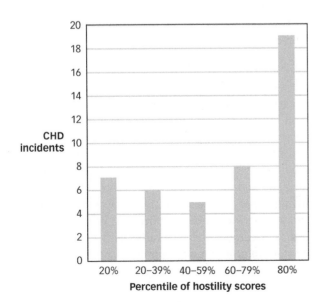

Figure 14.3

Hostility and Coronary Heart Disease Of 2,280 men studied over the course of 3 years, 45 suffered CHD incidents, such as heart attack. Many more of these incidents occurred in the men who had initially scored above the 80th percentile in hostility (Niaura et al., 2002).

Stress Interpretation Is a Two-step Process

The interpretation of a stimulus as being stressful or not is called *primary appraisal* (Lazarus & Folkman, 1984). Primary appraisal allows you to realize that a small, dark spot on your shirt is a stressor (spider!) or that a 120-kilometre-per-hour drop from a great height in a small car full of screaming people may not be (roller coaster!). In a demonstration of the importance of interpretation, researchers used a gruesome film of a subincision of the penis (a kind of genital surgery that is part of some tribal initiation rites) to severely stress volunteer participants (Speisman et al., 1964). Self-reports and participants' autonomic arousal (heart rate and skin conductance level) were used as measures of stress. Before viewing the film, one group heard an introduction that downplayed the pain and emphasized the coming-of-age aspect of the initiation. This interpretation markedly reduced the film viewers' stress compared with the stress of another group whose viewing was preceded by a lecture accentuating the pain and trauma.

The next step in interpretation is *secondary appraisal,* determining whether the stressor is something you can handle or not; that is, whether you have control over the event (Lazarus & Folkman, 1984). Interestingly, the body responds differently depending on whether the stressor is perceived as a *threat* (a stressor you believe you might *not* be able to overcome) or a *challenge* (a stressor you feel fairly confident you can control) (Blascovich & Tomaka, 1996). The same midterm exam is seen as a challenge if you are well prepared, but a threat if you didn't study.

Fortunately, interpretations of stressors can change threats into challenges. One study (Jamieson et al., 2010) showed that instructing students to reframe their anxiety about an upcoming exam as arousal that would help them on the test actually boosted their sympathetic arousal (signaling a challenge orientation) and improved test performance. Remember this technique next time you are feeling anxious about a test or presentation: Increased arousal can improve your performance!

Although both threats and challenges raise the heart rate, threats increase vascular reactivity (such as constriction of the blood vessels, which can lead to high blood pressure) (see A World of Difference: Can Discrimination Cause Stress and Illness?). In one study, researchers found that even interactions as innocuous as conversations can produce threat or challenge responses, depending on the race of the conversation partner. Asked to talk with another, unfamiliar student, White American students showed a challenge reaction when the unfamiliar student was White and a threat reaction when the student was African American (Mendes et al., 2002). Similar threat responses were found when White American students interacted with an unexpected partner, such as an Asian student with an accent characteristic of the American South (Mendes et al., 2007). It's as if social unfamiliarity creates the same kind of stress as lack of preparedness for an exam. Interestingly, previous interaction with members of an unfamiliar group tempers the threat reaction (Blascovich et al., 2001).

Chronic Stress Can Lead to Burnout

Did you ever take a class from an instructor who had lost interest in the job? The syndrome is easy to spot: The teacher looks distant and blank, almost robotic, giving predictable and humdrum lessons each day, as if it doesn't matter whether anyone is listening. Now imagine being this instructor. You decided to teach because you wanted to shape young minds. You worked hard, and for a while things were great. But one day, you looked up to see a room full of students who were bored and didn't care about anything you had to say. They scrolled through Instagram while you talked and started shuffling papers and putting things away long before the end of class. You're happy at work only when you're not in class. When people feel this way, especially about their jobs or careers, they are suffering from **burnout**, *a state of physical, emotional, and mental exhaustion resulting from long-term involvement in an emotionally demanding situation and accompanied by lowered performance and motivation.*

Burnout is a particular problem in the helping professions (Fernandez Nievas & Thaver, 2015). Teachers, nurses, clergy, doctors, dentists, psychologists, social

burnout A state of physical, emotional, and mental exhaustion resulting from long-term involvement in an emotionally demanding situation and accompanied by lowered performance and motivation.

Is there anything worse than taking a horribly boring class? How about being the teacher of that class? What techniques would prevent burnout from stress in people in helping professions (teachers, doctors, nurses, and so on)?

workers, police officers, and others who repeatedly encounter emotional turmoil on the job may be able to work productively only for a limited time. Eventually, many succumb to symptoms of burnout: overwhelming exhaustion, a deep cynicism and detachment from the job, and a sense of ineffectiveness and lack of accomplishment (Maslach, 2003). Their unhappiness can even spread to others; people with burn-out tend to become disgruntled employees who revel in their coworkers' failures and ignore their coworkers' successes (Brenninkmeijer, Vanyperen, & Buunk, 2001).

What causes burnout? One theory suggests that the culprit is using your job to give meaning to your life (Pines, 1993). If you define yourself only by your career and gauge your self-worth by success at work, you risk having nothing left when work fails. For example, a teacher in danger of burnout might do well to invest time in family, hobbies, or other self-expressions. Others argue that some emotionally stress-ful jobs lead to burnout no matter how they are approached and that active efforts to overcome the stress before burnout occurs are important. The stress management techniques discussed in the next section may be lifesavers for people in such jobs.

Build to the Outcomes

1. How does the body react to a fight-or-flight situation?
2. What are the three phases of GAS?
3. What is a telomere? What do telomeres do for us?
4. How does stress affect the immune system?
5. How does chronic stress increase the chance of a heart attack?
6. What causal factor most predicts heart attacks?
7. What is the difference between a threat and a challenge?
8. What contributes to burnout, especially in the helping professions?

Stress Management: Dealing With It

Most university students (92%) say they occasionally feel overwhelmed by the tasks they face, and over a third say they have dropped courses or received low grades in response to severe stress (Duenwald, 2002). No doubt you are among the lucky 8% who are entirely cool and report no stress. But just in case you're not, you may be interested in our exploration of stress management techniques: ways to counteract psychological and physical stress reactions directly by manag-ing your mind and body, as well as ways to sidestep stress altogether by managing your situation early on.

Learning Outcomes

- Explain techniques for coping with psychological stress.
- Identify physical activities that reduce stress.
- Define and give examples of situation management.

On April 23, 2018, a 25-year-old man intentionally drove his van into pedestrians on Yonge Street in Toronto, killing 10 and injuring 15 others. People deal with major stressful life events such as this in different ways. Repressive copers use avoidance; rational copers use acceptance, exposure, and understanding; and reframers try to think about the situation in more positive ways.

This young woman is praying during a vigil held for the victim of a gang rape in New Delhi. Extremely stressful events, such as rape, are not only acute stressors but often have lasting psychological consequences. Fortunately, there are effective techniques for learning to cope with such events that can lead to improved psychological health.

repressive coping Avoiding feelings, thoughts, or situations that are reminders of a stressor and maintaining an artificially positive viewpoint.

rational coping Facing a stressor and working to overcome it.

Mind Management

A significant part of stress management is control of the mind. Changing the way you think about potentially stressful events can change how you respond to them. Three ways of changing your thinking about stressors are the use of repression, rationalization, and reframing.

Repressive Coping: Holding an Artificially Positive Viewpoint

Controlling your thoughts is not easy, but some people do seem to be able to banish unpleasant thoughts from the mind. This style of dealing with stress, called **repressive coping**, is characterized by *avoiding feelings, thoughts, or situations that are reminders of a stressor and maintaining an artificially positive viewpoint*. Everyone has some problems, of course, but repressors are good at deliberately ignoring them (Barnier, Levin, & Maher, 2004). So, for example, when repressors suffer a heart attack, they are less likely than other people to report intrusive thoughts of their heart problems in the days and weeks that follow (Ginzburg, Solomon, & Bleich, 2002).

Like Elizabeth Smart, who for years after her rescue focused in interviews on what was happening in her life now, rather than repeatedly discussing her past in captivity, people often rearrange their lives to avoid stressful situations. Many victims of rape, for example, not only avoid the place where the rape occurred but may move away from their home or neighbourhood (Ellis, 1983). Anticipating and attempting to avoid reminders of the traumatic experience, they become wary of strangers, especially people who resemble the assailant, and they check doors, locks, and windows more frequently than before. It may make sense to try to avoid stressful thoughts and situations if you're the kind of person who is good at putting unpleasant thoughts and emotions out of mind (Coifman et al., 2007). For some people, however, the avoidance of unpleasant thoughts and situations is so difficult that it can turn into a grim preoccupation (Parker & McNally, 2008; Wegner & Zanakos, 1994). For those who can't avoid negative emotions effectively, it may be better to come to grips with them. This is the basic idea of rational coping.

Rational Coping: Working to Overcome

Rational coping involves *facing the stressor and working to overcome it*. This strategy is the opposite of repressive coping, so it may seem to be the most unpleasant and unnerving thing you could do when faced with stress. It requires approaching, rather than avoiding, a stressor in order to diminish its longer-term negative impact (Hayes, Strosahl, & Wilson, 1999). Rational coping is a three-step process: *acceptance,* coming to realize that the stressor exists and cannot be wished away; *exposure,* attending to the stressor, thinking about it, and even seeking it out; and *understanding,* working to find the meaning of the stressor in your life.

When the trauma is particularly intense, rational coping may be difficult to undertake. In rape trauma, for example, even accepting that the rape happened takes time and effort; the initial impulse is to deny the event and try to live as though it had never occurred. Psychological treatment may help during the exposure step by aiding victims in confronting and thinking about what happened. Using a technique called *prolonged exposure,* rape survivors relive the traumatic event in their imaginations by recording a verbal account of the event and then listening to the recording daily. In one study, rape survivors were instructed to seek out objectively safe situations that caused them anxiety or that they had avoided. This sounds like bitter medicine indeed, but it is remarkably effective, producing significant reductions in anxiety and symptoms of posttraumatic stress disorder compared with no therapy and compared with other therapies that promote more gradual and subtle forms of exposure (Foa & McLean, 2016).

The third element of rational coping involves coming to an understanding of the meaning of the stressful events. A trauma victim may wonder again and again: Why me?

Nervous about a class presentation or performance? Reframing that anxiety as arousal, which can help you perform better, can actually improve your performance. Get out there and reframe!

How did it happen? Why? Survivors of incest frequently voice the desire to make sense of their trauma (Weiss & Curcio Alexander, 2013), a process that is difficult, even impossible, during bouts of suppression and avoidance.

Reframing: Changing Your Thinking

Changing the way you think is another way to cope with stressful thoughts. **Reframing** involves *finding a new or creative way to think about a stressor that reduces its threat.* If you experience anxiety at the thought of public speaking, for example, you might reframe by shifting from thinking of an audience as evaluating you to thinking of yourself as evaluating them, which might make speech giving easier.

Reframing can be an effective way to prepare for a moderately stressful situation, but if something like public speaking is so stressful that you can't bear to think about it until you absolutely must, you may not be able to apply this technique. **Stress-inoculation training (SIT)** is *a reframing technique that helps people cope with stressful situations by developing positive ways to think about the situations.* For example, in one study, people who had difficulty controlling their anger were trained to rehearse and reframe their thoughts with phrases such as these: "You don't need to prove yourself"; "I'm not going to let him get to me"; and "I'll just let him make a fool of himself." Anger-prone people who practiced these thoughts were less likely to become physiologically aroused in response to laboratory-based provocations, both imaginary and real. Subsequent research on SIT has revealed that it can also be useful for people who have suffered prior traumatic events, helping them become more comfortable living with those events (Foa & Meadows, 1997).

Reframing can take place spontaneously if people are given the opportunity to spend time thinking and writing about stressful events. In an important series of studies, Jamie Pennebaker (1989) found that the physical health of university students improved after they spent a few hours writing about their deepest thoughts and feelings. Compared with students who had written about something else, members of the self-disclosure group were less likely in subsequent months to visit the student health centre; they also used less aspirin and achieved better grades (Pennebaker & Chung, 2007). In fact, engaging in such expressive writing was found to improve immune function as well (Pennebaker, Kiecolt-Glaser, & Glaser, 1988), whereas suppressing emotional topics weakened it (Petrie, Booth, & Pennebaker, 1998). The positive effect of self-disclosing writing may reflect its usefulness in reframing trauma and reducing stress.

reframing Finding a new or creative way to think about a stressor that reduces its threat.

stress-inoculation training (SIT) A reframing technique that helps people cope with stressful situations by developing positive ways to think about the situations.

Prince Harry, member of the British Royal Family, has been a prominent advocate for mental health and wellness. He recently shared that he is among the increasing number of people who engage in daily meditation, which has been shown to reduce stress and improve health.

ADRIAN DENNIS-WPA POOL/GETTY IMAGES

meditation The practice of intentional contemplation.

relaxation therapy A technique for reducing tension by consciously relaxing muscles of the body.

relaxation response A condition of reduced muscle tension, cortical activity, heart rate, breathing rate, and blood pressure.

Body Management

Stress can express itself as tension in your neck, back pain, a knot in your stomach, sweaty hands, or that distressed face you may glimpse in the mirror. Because stress often manifests itself through bodily symptoms, bodily techniques such as meditation, relaxation therapy, biofeedback, and aerobic exercise can be useful in managing it.

Meditation: Turning Inwards

Meditation is *the practice of intentional contemplation*. Techniques of meditation are associated with a variety of religious traditions and are increasingly being practiced outside religious contexts. The techniques vary widely. Some forms of meditation call for attempts to clear the mind of thought; others involve focusing on a single thought (e.g., thinking about a candle flame); still others involve concentration on breathing or on a *mantra* (a repetitive sound, such as *om*). At a minimum, these techniques have in common a period of quiet.

Time spent meditating can be restful and revitalizing. Beyond these immediate benefits, many people also meditate in an effort to experience deeper or transformed consciousness. Whatever the reason, meditation appears to have positive psychological effects (Hölzel et al., 2011). Many believe it does so, in part, by improving control over attention. The focus of many forms of meditation, such as mindfulness meditation, is on teaching ourselves how to remain focused on, and to accept, our immediate experience. Interestingly, experienced meditators show deactivation in the default mode network (which is associated with mind wandering; see Figure 5.6 in the Consciousness chapter) during meditation relative to nonmeditators (Brewer et al., 2011). Even short-term meditation training administered to university students has been shown to improve the connectivity between parts of the brain involved in conflict monitoring and cognitive and emotional control, and to do so via increased myelination (perhaps due to increased neuron firing) and other axonal changes (Tang et al., 2012).

Moreover, recent research suggests that those who engage in several weeks of intensive meditation show lengthening of their telomeres, which suggests a slight reversal of the effects of stress and aging as described earlier (Conklin et al., 2015). Taken together, these findings indicate that meditators may be better able to regulate their thoughts and emotions, which may translate to a better ability to manage interpersonal relations, anxiety, and a range of other activities that require conscious effort (Sedlmeier et al., 2012).

Relaxation: Picturing Peace

Imagine for a moment that you are scratching your chin. Don't actually do it; just think about it and notice that your body participates by moving ever so slightly, tensing and relaxing in the sequence of the imagined action. Edmund Jacobson (1932) discovered these effects with *electromyography* (EMG), a technique used to measure the subtle activity of muscles. A person asked to imagine rowing a boat or plucking a flower from a bush would produce slight levels of tension in the muscles involved in performing the act. Jacobson also found that thoughts of relaxing the muscles sometimes reduced EMG readings when people didn't even report feeling tense. Our bodies respond to all the things we think about doing every day. These thoughts create muscle tension even when we think we're doing nothing at all.

These observations led Jacobson to develop **relaxation therapy**, *a technique for reducing tension by consciously relaxing muscles of the body*. A person in relaxation therapy may be asked to relax specific muscle groups one at a time or to imagine warmth flowing through the body or to think about a relaxing situation. This activity draws on a **relaxation response**, *a condition of reduced muscle tension, cortical activity, heart rate, breathing rate, and blood pressure* (Benson, 1990). Basically, as soon as you get in a comfortable position, quiet down, and focus on something repetitive or soothing that holds your attention, you relax.

Setting aside time (e.g., 45 minutes) to relax on a regular basis can reduce symptoms of stress and even reduce blood levels of cortisol, the biochemical marker of the stress response (Cruess et al., 2000). How can you use this in your daily life? Quite simply: take a break. Go for a walk and take in nature. Experimental studies have shown that going for short walks in the park during workers' lunch breaks decreased their feelings of stress (de Bloom et al., 2017) and that 90-minute walks in nature (versus those in urban settings) decrease rumination and activity in parts of the brain associated with increased risk for mental disorders (Bratman et al., 2015).

Biofeedback: Enlisting the Help of an External Monitor

Wouldn't it be nice if, instead of having to learn to relax, you could just flip a switch and relax as fast as possible? **Biofeedback**, *the use of an external monitoring device to obtain information about a bodily function and then to possibly gain control over that function,* was developed with the goal of high-tech relaxation in mind. You might not be aware right now of whether your fingers are warm or cold, for example, but with an electronic thermometer displayed before you, the ability to sense your temperature might allow you (with a bit of practice) to make your hands warmer or cooler at will (e.g., Roberts & McGrady, 1996).

Biofeedback can help people control physiological functions they are not likely to become aware of in other ways. For instance, you probably have no idea what brain-wave patterns you are producing right now. In the late 1950s, Joe Kamiya (1969), a psychologist using the electroencephalograph (also called the EEG and discussed in the Neuroscience and Behaviour chapter), initiated a brain-wave biofeedback revolution when he found that people could change their brain waves from alert beta patterns to relaxed alpha patterns and back again when permitted to monitor their own EEG readings.

More recent studies suggest that EEG biofeedback (or neurofeedback) is moderately successful in treating brain-wave abnormalities in disorders such as epilepsy (Yucha & Gilbert, 2004) and in teaching people to down-regulate activity in regions of the brain that are involved in the strong emotional responses seen in some forms of psychopathology (Hamilton et al., 2010). Often, however, the use of biofeedback to produce relaxation in the brain turns out to be a bit of technological overkill and may not be much more effective than simply having the person stretch out in a hammock and hum a happy tune. Although biofeedback is not a magic bullet that gives people control over stress-induced health troubles, it has proven to be a useful technique for increasing relaxation and decreasing chronic pain (Palermo et al., 2011). People who do not benefit from relaxation therapy may find that biofeedback provides a useful alternative.

Aerobic Exercise: Boosting Mood

A jogger nicely decked out in a fresh new lululemon running suit bounces in place at the crosswalk and then springs away when the signal changes. It is tempting to assume that this jogger is the picture of psychological health: happy, unstressed, and even downright exuberant. As it turns out, this stereotype is true: Studies indicate that *aerobic exercise* (exercise that increases heart rate and oxygen intake for a sustained period) is associated with psychological well-being (Hassmen, Koivula, & Uutela, 2000). But does exercise *cause* psychological well-being, or does psychological well-being cause people to exercise? Perhaps general happiness is what inspires the jogger's bounce. Or could some unknown third factor (wearing lululemon?) cause both the need to exercise and the sense of well-being? As we've mentioned many times, correlation does not always imply causation.

To try to tease apart causal factors, researchers have randomly assigned people to aerobic exercise activities and no-exercise comparison groups and have found

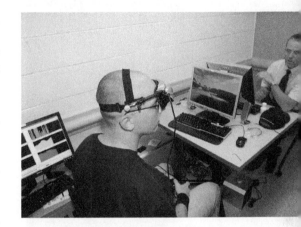

Biofeedback gives people access to visual or audio feedback showing levels of psychophysiological functions—such as heart rate, breathing, brain electrical activity, or skin temperature—that they would otherwise be unable to sense directly.
PHOTO BY CHARLES BALDWIN OF EAST CAROLINA UNIVERSITY/COURTESY DR. CARMEN RUSSONIELLO

biofeedback The use of an external monitoring device to obtain information about a bodily function and then to possibly gain control over that function.

MATT DUNHAM/AP IMAGES

Exercise helps reduce stress—unless, as for John Stibbard, your exercise involves carrying the Olympic torch on Vancouver's wobbly Capilano Suspension Bridge, 70 metres above the Capilano River.

that exercise actually does promote stress relief and happiness. One meta-analysis (a quantitative review of existing studies) compiled data from 90 studies that involved more than 10,000 people with chronic illness who were randomly assigned either to an exercise or a no-exercise condition. People assigned to the aerobic exercise condition experienced a significant reduction in depressive symptoms (Herring et al., 2012). Other meta-analyses have come to similar conclusions, showing, for instance, that exercise is as effective as the strongest psychological interventions for depression (Rimer et al., 2012) and that exercise even shows positive physical and mental health benefits for individuals with schizophrenia (Gorczynski & Faulkner, 2011). Pretty good effects for a simple, timeless intervention with no side effects!

The reasons for these positive effects are unclear. Researchers have suggested that the effects result from increases in the body's production of neurotransmitters such as serotonin, which can have a positive effect on mood (as discussed in the Neuroscience and Behaviour chapter) or from increases in the production of endorphins (the endogenous opioids discussed in the Neuroscience and Behaviour and Consciousness chapters).

Beyond boosting positive mood, exercise also stands to keep you healthy into the future. Recent research has shown that engaging in bouts of aerobic exercise helps you to recover more quickly from future stressors (Bernstein & McNally, 2017). Perhaps the simplest thing you can do to improve your happiness and health, then, is to participate regularly in an aerobic activity. Pick something you find fun: Sign up for a dance class, get into a regular basketball game, or start paddling a canoe—just not all at once.

Situation Management

After you have tried to manage stress by managing your mind and managing your body, what's left to manage? Look around and you'll notice a whole world out there. Perhaps that could be managed as well. Situation management involves changing your life situation as a way of reducing the impact of stress on your mind and body. Ways to manage your situation can include seeking out social support, religious or spiritual practice, and finding a place for humour in your life.

Social Support: "Swimming With a Buddy"

The wisdom of the U.S. National Safety Council's first rule—"Always swim with a buddy"—is obvious when you're in water over your head, but people often don't realize that the same principle applies whenever danger threatens. Other people can offer help in times of stress. **Social support** is *aid gained through interacting with others*. One of the more self-defeating things you can do in life is fail to connect to people in this way. Just failing to find a life partner, for example, is bad for your health. Single people have an elevated risk of mortality from cardiovascular disease, cancer, pneumonia and influenza, chronic obstructive pulmonary disease, and liver disease and cirrhosis (Johnson, Backlund et al., 2000). More generally, good ongoing relationships with friends and family and participation in social activities and religious groups can be as healthy for you as exercising and not smoking (Umberson et al., 2006). Social support is helpful on many levels:

- An intimate partner can help you remember to exercise and follow your doctor's orders, and together you'll probably follow a healthier diet than you would all alone with your snacks.

- Talking about problems with friends and family can offer many of the benefits of professional psychotherapy, usually without the hourly fees.

- Sharing tasks and helping each other when times get tough can reduce the amount of work and worry in each other's lives.

social support The aid gained through interacting with others.

Women are more likely than men to seek support when under stress.

Many first-year university students experience something of a crisis of social support. No matter how outgoing and popular they were in high school, newcomers typically find the task of developing satisfying new social relationships quite daunting. New friendships can seem shallow, connections with teachers may be perfunctory and even threatening, and social groups that are encountered can seem like islands of lost souls. ("Hey, we're forming a club to investigate the lack of clubs on campus—want to join?") It's not surprising that research shows that students who report the greatest feelings of isolation also show reduced immune responses to flu vaccinations (Pressman et al., 2005). Time spent getting to know people in new social situations can be an investment in your own health.

The value of social support in protecting against stress may be very different for women and men: Whereas women seek support under stress, men are less likely to do so. The fight-or-flight response to stress may be largely a male reaction, according to research on sex differences by Shelley Taylor (2002). Taylor suggested that the female response to stress is to *tend-and-befriend* by taking care of people and bringing them together. This is believed by some to be due at least in part to the release of *oxytocin,* a hormone secreted by the pituitary gland when women are pregnant or nursing, as well as in a range of other contexts. In the presence of estrogen, oxytocin triggers social responses: a tendency to seek out social contacts, nurture others, and create and maintain cooperative groups. After a hard day at work, a man may come home frustrated and worried about his job and end up drinking a beer and fuming alone. A woman under the same type of stress may be more likely to instead play with her kids or talk to friends on the phone. The tend-and-befriend response to stress may help explain why women are healthier and have a longer life span than men. The typical male response amplifies the unhealthy effects of stress, whereas the female response takes less of a toll on a woman's mind and body and provides social support for the people around her as well.

Religious Experiences: Reaping Earthly Rewards

Many people spend a significant amount of time in quiet prayer, reflection, and contemplation. National polls indicate that about 72% of Canadians believe in a God and that many people pray at least once per day. Although many who believe in a higher power believe that their faith will be rewarded in an afterlife, it turns out that there may be some benefits here on earth as well. An enormous body of research has examined the associations between *religiosity* (affiliation with or engagement in the practices of a particular religion) and *spirituality* (having a belief in and engagement with some higher power, not necessarily linked to any particular religion) and positive health outcomes. The helpful effects of religiosity and spirituality have been observed in a wide range of areas, including lower rates of heart disease, decreases in chronic pain, and improved psychological health (Seybold & Hill, 2001).

Why do people who endorse religiosity or spirituality have better mental and physical health? Is it divine intervention? Several testable ideas have been proposed. Engagement in religious or spiritual practices, such as attendance at

Figure 14.4

Pray For Me? To test whether praying for someone in his or her time of need actually helped, researchers randomly assigned 1,802 patients about to undergo cardiac bypass surgery to one of three conditions: those who were told they might be prayed for and were; those who were told they might be prayed for and weren't; and those who were told they definitely would be prayed for and were. Unfortunately, there were no differences in the presence of complications between those who were or were not prayed for. To make matters worse, those who knew they would be prayed for and who were prayed for experienced significantly more complications than the other two groups (Benson et al., 2006).

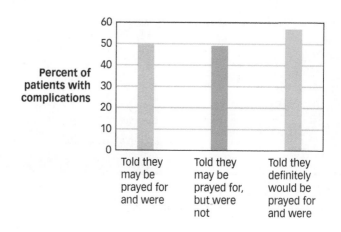

When Andrew Mason, CEO of the Internet company Groupon, left his position, his resignation letter read: "After four and a half intense and wonderful years as CEO of Groupon, I've decided that I'd like to spend more time with my family. Just kidding—I was fired today." He went on to add, "I am so lucky to have had the opportunity to take the company this far with all of you. I'll now take some time to decompress (FYI I'm looking for a good fat camp to lose my Groupon 40, if anyone has a suggestion), and then maybe I'll figure out how to channel this experience into something productive." This seems like a textbook case of using humour to mitigate stress, which is why we put it, um, you know where.

weekly religious services, may lead to the development of a stronger and more extensive social network, which has well-known health benefits. Those who are religious or spiritual also may fare better psychologically and physically as a result of following the healthy recommendations offered in many religious or spiritual teachings. That is, they may be more likely to observe dietary restrictions, abstain from the use of drugs or alcohol, or endorse a more hopeful and optimistic perspective of daily life events, all of which can lead to more positive health outcomes (Seeman, Dubin, & Seeman, 2003; Seybold & Hill, 2001). However, many claims made by some religious groups have not been supported, such as the beneficial effects of intercessory prayer (see **FIGURE 14.4**). Psychologists are actively testing the effectiveness of various religious and spiritual practices with the goal of better understanding how they might help explain, and improve, the human condition.

Humour: Laughing It Off

Wouldn't it be nice to laugh at your troubles and move on? Most of us recognize that humour can defuse unpleasant situations and bad feelings, and it makes sense that bringing some fun into your life could help reduce stress. The extreme point of view on this topic is staked out in self-help books with titles such as *Health, Healing, and the Amuse System* and *How Serious Is This? Seeing Humour in Daily Stress.* Is laughter truly the best medicine? Should we close down the hospitals and send in the clowns?

There is a kernel of truth to the theory that humour can help us cope with stress. For example, humour can reduce sensitivity to pain and distress, as researchers found when they subjected volunteers to an overinflated blood pressure cuff. Participants were more tolerant of the pain during a laughter-inducing comedy audiotape than during a neutral tape or guided relaxation (Cogan et al., 1987).

Humour can also reduce the time needed to calm down after a stressful event. For instance, men viewing a highly stressful film about industrial accidents were asked to narrate the film aloud, either by describing the events seriously or by making their commentary as funny as possible. Although men in both groups reported feeling tense while watching the film and showed increased levels of sympathetic nervous arousal (increased heart rate and skin conductance, decreased skin temperature), those looking for humour in the experience bounced back to normal arousal levels more quickly than did those in the serious story group (Newman & Stone, 1996).

If laughter and fun can alleviate stress quickly in the short term, do the effects accumulate to improve health and longevity? Sadly, the evidence suggests not (Provine, 2000). A study titled "Do Comics Have the Last Laugh?" tracked the longevity of comedians in comparison to other entertainers and non-entertainers

(Rotton, 1992). It was found that the comedians died younger—perhaps after too many nights on stage thinking, *I'm dying out here.*

Scheduling and Activating: Getting It Done

At one time or another, most of us have avoided carrying out a task or put it off to a later time. The task may be unpleasant, difficult, or just less entertaining than other things we could be doing at the moment. For university students, procrastination can affect a range of academic activities, such as writing a paper or preparing for an exam. Academic procrastination is not uncommon: University students report engaging in academic procrastination between 30% and 60% of the time (Rabin, Fogel, & Nutter-Upham, 2011). Although it's fun to hang out with your friends at night, it's not so much fun to worry for three days about your impending history exam or try to study at 4:00 a.m. the day of the test. Studying now, or at least a little bit each day, robs procrastination of its power over you.

Some procrastinators defend this practice by claiming that they tend to work best under pressure or by noting that as long as a task gets done, it doesn't matter all that much if it is completed just before the deadline. Is there any merit to such claims? Or are they just feeble excuses for counterproductive behaviour?

Among students, higher levels of procrastination are associated with poorer academic performance (Moon & Illingworth, 2005) and higher levels of psychological distress (Rice, Richardson, & Clark, 2012). In fact, recent evidence indicates that habitual procrastinators show higher levels of self-reported hypertension and cardiovascular disease, even when controlling for other personality traits associated with these health problems (Sirois, 2015). Although there is no proven method of eliminating procrastination, there is some evidence that procrastination in university students can be reduced by interventions that use training in time management or behavioural methods that target the processes that are believed to be responsible for procrastination (Glick & Orsillo, 2015). If you tend towards procrastination, we hope that the research discussed here can alert you to its pitfalls.

Are you a procrastinator?

MACMILLAN LEARNING

Build to the Outcomes

1. When is it useful to avoid stressful thoughts? When is avoidance a problem?
2. What are the three steps in rational coping?
3. What is the difference between repressive and rational coping?
4. How has writing about stressful events been shown to be helpful?
5. What are some positive outcomes of meditation?
6. How does biofeedback work?
7. What are the benefits of exercise?
8. What are the benefits of social support?
9. Why are religiosity and spirituality associated with health benefits?
10. How does humour mitigate stress?
11. How do good study habits support good health?

The Psychology of Illness: Mind Over Matter

One of the mind's most important influences on the body's health and illness is the mind's sensitivity to bodily symptoms. Noticing what is wrong with the body can be helpful when it motivates a search for treatment, but sensitivity can also lead to further problems when it snowballs into a preoccupation with illness that itself can cause harm.

Learning Outcome

- Describe the interrelationship between the mind and body relating to illness.

Psychological Effects of Illness

Why does it feel so bad to be sick? You notice scratchiness in your throat or the start of sniffles, and you think you might be coming down with something. And in just a few short hours, you're achy all over, energy gone, no appetite, feverish, feeling dull and listless. You're sick. The question is, why does it have to be like this? Why couldn't it feel good? As long as you're going to have to stay at home and miss out on things anyway, couldn't sickness be less of a pain?

Sickness makes you miserable for good reason. Misery is part of the *sickness response,* a coordinated, adaptive set of reactions to illness organized by the brain (Hart, 1988; Watkins & Maier, 2005). Feeling sick keeps you home, where you'll spread germs to fewer people. More important, the sickness response makes you withdraw from activity and lie still, conserving the energy for fighting illness that you'd normally expend on other behaviour. Appetite loss is similarly helpful: The energy spent on digestion is conserved. Thus, the behavioural changes that accompany illness are not random side effects; they help the body fight disease. These responses become prolonged and exaggerated with aging—subtle signs that we are losing the fight (Barrientos et al., 2009).

How does the brain know it should do this? The immune response to an infection begins with the activation of white blood cells that "eat" microbes and also release *cytokines,* proteins that circulate through the body and communicate with the other white blood cells and also communicate the sickness response to the brain (Maier & Watkins, 1998). Administering cytokines to an animal can artificially induce the sickness response, and administering drugs that oppose the action of cytokines can block the sickness response even during an ongoing infection. Cytokines do not enter the brain, but they activate the vagus nerve, which runs from the intestines, stomach, and chest to the brain and convey the "I am infected" message (Goehler et al., 2000; Klarer et al., 2014). Perhaps this is why we often feel sickness in the "gut," a gnawing discomfort in the very centre of the body.

Interestingly, the sickness response can be prompted without any infection at all, merely by the introduction of stress. The stressful presence of a predator's odour, for instance, can trigger the sickness response of lethargy in an animal, along with symptoms of infection such as fever and increased white blood cell count (Maier & Watkins, 2000). In humans, the connection among sickness response, immune reaction, and stress is illustrated in depression, a condition in which all the sickness machinery runs at full speed. So in addition to fatigue and malaise, depressed people show signs characteristic of infection, including high levels of cytokines circulating in the blood (Maes, 1995). Just as illness can make you feel a bit depressed, severe depression seems to recruit the brain's sickness response and make you feel ill (Watkins & Maier, 2005).

Recognizing Illness and Seeking Treatment

You probably weren't thinking about your breathing a minute ago, but now that you're reading this sentence, you notice it. Sometimes we are very attentive to our bodies. At other times, the body seems to be on "automatic," running along unnoticed until specific symptoms announce themselves or are pointed out by an annoying textbook writer.

People differ substantially in the degree to which they attend to and report bodily symptoms. People who report many physical symptoms tend to be negative in other ways as well, describing themselves as anxious, depressed, and under stress (Watson & Pennebaker, 1989). Do people with many symptom complaints truly have a lot of problems? Or are they just high-volume complainers? To answer this question, researchers used fMRI brain scans to compare the severity of reported sensation of

If you have been reading this very exciting textbook, there is no chance you have been yawning. However, seeing this guy yawning may cause your brain to initiate a yawn response as well.

STONE/GETTY IMAGES

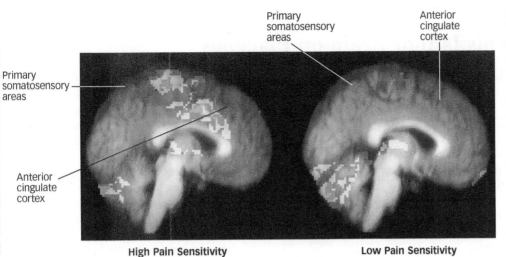

Primary somatosensory areas

Primary somatosensory areas

Anterior cingulate cortex

Anterior cingulate cortex

High Pain Sensitivity   **Low Pain Sensitivity**

Figure 14.5

The Brain in Pain These fMRI scans show brain activation in high- (*left*) and low-pain-sensitive (*right*) individuals during painful stimulation. The anterior cingulate cortex and primary somatosensory areas show greater activation in high-pain-sensitive individuals. Levels of activation are highest in yellow and red, then light blue and dark blue (Coghill, McHaffie, & Yen, 2003).

pain with the degree of activation in brain areas usually associated with pain experience. Volunteers underwent several applications of a thermal stimulus (43.3–48.9°C) to the leg; as you might expect, some of the participants found it more painful than did others. Scans during the painful events revealed that the anterior cingulate cortex, somatosensory cortex, and prefrontal cortex (brain areas known to respond to painful body stimulation) were particularly active in those participants who reported higher levels of pain experience (see **FIGURE 14.5**), suggesting that people can report accurately on the extent to which they experience pain (Coghill, McHaffie, & Yen, 2003) (see The Real World: This Is Your Brain on Placebos).

In contrast to complainers, other people underreport symptoms and pain or ignore or deny the possibility that they are sick. Insensitivity to symptoms comes with costs: It can delay the search for treatment, sometimes with serious repercussions. Of 2,404 patients in one study who had been treated for a heart attack, 40% had delayed going to the hospital for more than 6 hours from the time they first noticed suspicious symptoms (Gurwitz et al., 1997). Severe chest pain or a history of prior heart surgery did send people to the hospital in a hurry. Those with more subtle symptoms often waited around for hours, however, not calling an ambulance or their doctor, just hoping the problem would go away. This is not a good idea, because many of the treatments that can reduce the damage of a heart attack are most useful when provided early. When it comes to your own health, protecting your mind from distress through the denial of illness can result in exposing your body to great danger.

How much does it hurt? Pain is a psychological state that can be difficult to measure. One way to put a number on a pain is to have people judge with reference to the external expression of the internal state.

Wong-Baker FACES® Pain Rating Scale

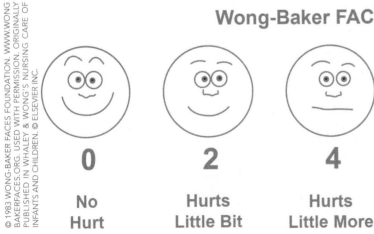

0 No Hurt   **2** Hurts Little Bit   **4** Hurts Little More   **6** Hurts Even More   **8** Hurts Whole Lot   **10** Hurts Worst

The Real World | This Is Your Brain on Placebos

There is something miraculous about Band-Aids. Your standard household toddler typically *requires* one for any injury at all, expecting and often achieving immediate relief. It is not unusual to find a child who reports that aches or pains are "cured" if a Band-Aid has been applied by a helpful adult. Of course, the Band-Aid is not *really* helping the pain—or is it?

Physicians and psychologists have long puzzled over the *placebo effect*, a clinically significant psychological or physiological response to a therapeutically inert substance or procedure. The classic placebo is the sugar pill, but Band-Aids, injections, heating pads, neck rubs, homeopathic remedies, and kind words can have placebo effects (Diederich & Goetz, 2008).

How do placebos operate? Do people being treated for pain really feel the pain but distort their report of the experience to make it fit their beliefs about treatment? Or does the placebo actually reduce the pain a patient experiences? Howard Fields and Jon Levine (1984) discovered that placebos trigger the release of endorphins (or *endogenous opioids*), painkilling chemicals similar to morphine that are produced by the brain (see the Consciousness chapter).

Placebos also have been found to lower the activation of specific brain areas associated with pain. One set of fMRI studies examined brain activation as volunteers were exposed to electric

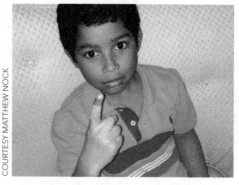

Can a Band-Aid cure all of your aches and pains? Many children, like this little guy, report immediate pain relief following application of a Band-Aid to whatever spot hurts. Although most adults know that Band-Aids don't treat pain, the placebo effect remains powerful throughout the life span.

COURTESY MATTHEW NOCK

shock or heat (Wager et al., 2004). In preparation for some exposures to these painful stimuli, a placebo cream was applied to the skin, and the participant was told it was an analgesic that would reduce the pain. Other participants merely experienced the pain. As you can see in the accompanying images, the fMRI scans showed decreased activation during placebo analgesia in the *thalamus, anterior cingulate cortex,* and *insula,* pain-sensitive brain regions that were activated during untreated pain. These findings suggest that placebos do not lead people to misreport their pain experience, but, rather, they reduce brain activity in areas that normally are active during pain experiences.

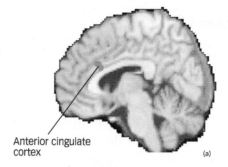
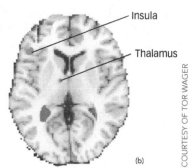

Insula

Thalamus

Anterior cingulate cortex

(a)   (b)

COURTESY OF TOR WAGER

The Brain's Response to Placebo These fMRI scans reveal that some brain regions that are normally activated when individuals report pain in response to shocks are deactivated when those individuals are given a placebo analgesic during the shock. These regions include (a) the anterior cingulate cortex and (b) the insula and thalamus (Wager et al., 2004).

Somatic Symptom Disorders

psychosomatic illness An interaction between mind and body that can produce illness.

somatic symptom disorders The set of psychological disorders in which people with at least one bodily symptom display significant health-related anxiety, express disproportionate concerns about their symptoms, and devote excessive time and energy to their symptoms or health concerns.

The flip side of denial is excessive sensitivity to illness, and it turns out that sensitivity also has its perils. Indeed, hypersensitivity to symptoms or to the possibility of illness underlies a variety of psychological problems and can also undermine physical health. Psychologists studying **psychosomatic illness**, *an interaction between mind and body that can produce illness,* explore ways in which mind (*psyche*) can influence body (*soma*) and vice versa. The study of mind–body interactions focuses on psychological disorders called **somatic symptom disorders**, in which *a person with at least one bodily symptom displays significant health-related anxiety, expresses disproportionate concerns about their symptoms, and devotes excessive time and energy to their symptoms or health concerns.* These are disorders such as those that will be discussed in the Psychological Disorders chapter, but their association with symptoms in the body makes them relevant to this chapter's concern with stress and health.

Disorders that focus on concerns about physical illness used to be called *somatoform disorders* and included categories such as hypochondriasis. Somatoform disorders were those in which people experienced unexplained medical symptoms believed to be generated by the mind. However, the focus on psychosomatic illness has shifted from concerns about mentally generated physical symptoms to excessive psychological concerns about explainable medical symptoms, with the idea that the latter are serious and could benefit from psychological intervention. Some believe this shift in focus is problematic and will lead psychologists and psychiatrists to label normal concern about one's health as a psychological disorder. The interesting and somewhat complicated question of what should be considered a psychological disorder and what should not is something we tackle more directly in the next chapter on Psychological Disorders.

On Being a Patient

Getting sick is more than a change in physical state; it can involve a transformation of identity. This change can be particularly profound with a serious illness: A kind of cloud settles over you, a feeling that you are now different, and this transformation can influence everything you feel and do in this new world of illness. You even take on a new role in life, a **sick role**, *a socially recognized set of rights and obligations linked with illness* (Parsons, 1975). The sick person is absolved of responsibility for many everyday obligations and enjoys exemption from normal activities. For example, in addition to skipping school and homework and staying on the couch all day, a sick child can watch TV and avoid eating anything unpleasant at dinner. At the extreme, the sick person can get away with being rude, lazy, demanding, and picky. In return for these exemptions, the sick role also incurs obligations. The properly "sick" individual cannot appear to enjoy the illness or reveal signs of wanting to be sick and must also take care to pursue treatment to end this "undesirable" condition. Parsons observed that illness has psychological, social, and even moral components. You may recall times when you have felt the conflict between sickness and health as though it were a moral decision: Should you drag yourself out of bed and try to make it to the chemistry exam or just slump back under the covers and wallow in your "pain"?

Some people feign medical or psychological symptoms to achieve something they want, a type of behaviour called *malingering*. Because many symptoms of illness cannot be faked (even facial expressions of pain are difficult to simulate) (Williams, 2002), malingering is possible only with a small number of illnesses. Faking illness is suspected when the secondary gains of illness—such as the ability to rest, to be freed from performing unpleasant tasks, or to be helped by others—outweigh the costs. Such gains can be very subtle, as when a child stays in bed because of the comfort provided by an otherwise distant parent, or they can be obvious, as when insurance benefits turn out to be a cash award for Best Actor. Some behaviours that may lead to illness may not be under the patient's control; for example, self-starvation may be part of an uncontrollable eating disorder (see the Emotion and Motivation chapter). For this reason, malingering can be difficult to diagnose and treat (Bass & Halligan, 2014).

Have you ever ridden on a crowded train next to a person with a hacking cough or aggressive sneeze? We are bombarded by advertisements for medicines designed to suppress symptoms of illness so we can keep going. Is staying home with a cold socially acceptable? Or is it considered malingering? How does this jibe with the concept of the *sick role*?

Patient–Practitioner Interaction

Medical care usually occurs through a strange interaction. On one side is a patient, often miserable, who expects to be questioned and examined and possibly prodded, pained, or given bad news. On the other side is a health care provider, who comes in knowing nothing about what brings the patient in but who hopes to quickly obtain information from the patient by asking lots of extremely personal questions (and examining extremely personal parts of the body); to identify the problem and a potential solution; to help in some way; and to achieve all of this as efficiently as possible because more patients are waiting. It seems less like a time for healing than an occasion for major awkwardness.

sick role A socially recognized set of rights and obligations linked with illness.

Figure 14.6

Antacid Intake A scatterplot of antacid intake measured by bottle count plotted against patient's stated intake for 116 patients. When the actual and stated intakes are the same, the point lies on the diagonal line; when stated intake is greater than actual, the point lies above the line. Most patients exaggerated their intake (Roth & Caron, 1978).

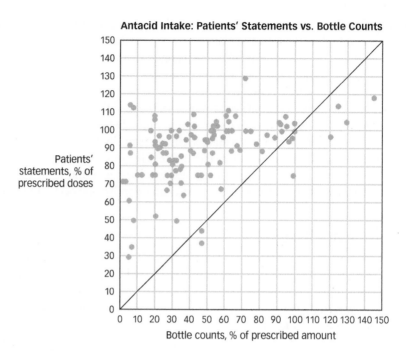

Antacid Intake: Patients' Statements vs. Bottle Counts

Patients' statements, % of prescribed doses

Bottle counts, % of prescribed amount

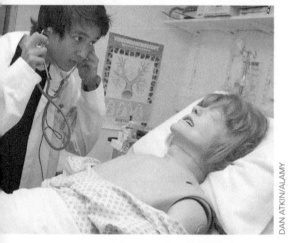

Doctor and patient have two modes of interaction, the technical and the interpersonal. Medical training with robot patients may help doctors learn the technical side of health care, but it is likely to do little to improve the interpersonal side.

One of the keys to an effective medical care interaction is physician empathy (Kelm et al., 2014). To offer successful treatment, the clinician must simultaneously understand the patient's physical state *and* psychological state. Physicians often err on the side of failing to acknowledge patients' emotions, focusing instead on technical issues of the case (Suchman et al., 1997). This is particularly unfortunate, because a substantial percentage of patients who seek medical care do so for treatment of psychological and emotional problems (Wiegner et al., 2015). As the Greek physician Hippocrates wrote in the 4th century BCE: "Some patients, though conscious that their condition is perilous, recover their health simply through their contentment with the goodness of the physician." The best physician treats the patient's mind as well as the patient's body.

Another important part of the medical care interaction is motivating the patient to follow the prescribed regimen of care (Miller & Rollnick, 2012). When researchers check compliance by counting the pills remaining in a patient's bottle after a prescription has been started, they find that patients often do an astonishingly poor job of following doctors' orders (see **FIGURE 14.6**). Compliance deteriorates when the treatment must be frequent, as when eye drops for glaucoma are required every few hours, or is inconvenient or painful, such as drawing blood or performing injections in managing diabetes. Finally, compliance decreases as the number of treatments increases. This is a worrisome problem, especially for older patients, who may have difficulty remembering when to take which pill. Failures in medical care may stem from the failure of health care providers to recognize the psychological challenges that are involved in self-care. Helping people follow doctors' orders involves psychology, not medicine, and is an essential part of promoting health.

Build to the Outcomes

1. What are the physical benefits of the sickness response?
2. What is the relationship between pain and activity in the brain?
3. How can hypersensitivity to symptoms undermine health?
4. What benefits might come from being ill?
5. Why is it important that a physician express empathy?

The Psychology of Health: Feeling Good

Two kinds of psychological factors influence personal health: health-relevant personality traits and health behaviour. Personality can influence health through relatively enduring traits that make some people particularly susceptible to health problems or stress while sparing or protecting others. The Type A behaviour pattern is an example. Because personality is not typically something we choose ("I'd like a bit of that sense of humour and extraversion over there, please, but hold the whininess"), this source of health can be beyond personal control. In contrast, engaging in positive health behaviours is something anyone can do, at least in principle.

Personality and Health

Different health problems seem to plague different social groups. For example, South Asian people in Canada have higher rates of heart disease and double the rate of diabetes, and they are more prone to becoming overweight compared to White people (Rana et al., 2014). Indigenous people in Canada also have much higher rates of heart disease (Reading, 2015), and First Nations people on reserves have 3 to 5 times the rate of diabetes (Public Health Agency of Canada, 2012).

Personality is a more subtle factor that turns out to matter for wellness, with individual differences in optimism and hardiness being important influences.

Optimism

Pollyanna is one of literature's most famous optimists. Eleanor H. Porter's 1913 novel *Pollyanna* portrayed her as a girl who greeted life with boundless good cheer, even when she was orphaned and sent to live with her cruel aunt. Her response to a sunny day was to remark on the good weather, of course, but her response to a gloomy day was to point out how lucky it is that not every day is gloomy! Her crotchety Aunt Polly had exactly the opposite attitude, somehow managing to turn every happy moment into an opportunity for strict correction. A person's level of optimism or pessimism tends to be fairly stable over time, and research comparing the personalities of twins reared together with those of twins reared apart suggests that this stability arises because these traits are moderately heritable (Plomin et al., 1992). Perhaps Pollyanna and Aunt Polly were each "born that way."

An optimist who believes that "in uncertain times, I usually expect the best" is likely to be healthier than a pessimist who believes that "if something can go wrong for me, it will." One recent review of dozens of studies including tens of thousands of participants concluded that of all the measures of psychological well-being examined, optimism is the one that most strongly predicted a positive outcome for cardiovascular health (Boehm & Kubzansky, 2012). It is important to note that the association between optimism and cardiovascular health remains even after statistically controlling for traditional risk factors for heart disease, including depression and anxiety, suggesting that it is not merely the absence of psychopathology but the presence of positive expectancies for the future that predicts positive health outcomes. Does just having positive thoughts about the future make it so? Unfortunately not.

Rather than improving physical health directly, optimism seems to aid in the maintenance of *psychological* health in the face of physical health problems. When sick, optimists are more likely than pessimists to maintain positive emotions, avoid negative emotions such as anxiety and depression, stick to the medical regimens their caregivers have prescribed, and keep up their relationships with others.

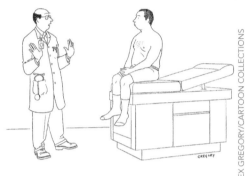

"Whoa—__way__ too much information."

ALEX GREGORY/CARTOON COLLECTIONS

BILL GREENE/THE BOSTON GLOBE VIA GETTY IMAGES

Adrianne Haslet was approximately 1.2 metres away from one of the bombs that exploded at the Boston Marathon in 2013. Although the explosion caused her to lose her left foot, Adrianne (*centre*) vowed that she would continue her career as a dancer—and she actually ran in the Boston Marathon in 2016. She is an optimist, and optimism can lead to positive health outcomes.

Among women who have surgery for breast cancer, for example, optimists are less likely to experience distress and fatigue after treatment than are pessimists, largely because they keep up social contacts and recreational activities during their treatment (Carver, Lehman, & Antoni, 2003).

Optimism also seems to aid in the maintenance of physical health. For instance, optimism appears to be associated with cardiovascular health because optimistic people tend to engage in healthier behaviours such as eating a balanced diet and exercising, which in turn leads to a healthier lipid profile, which decreases the risk of heart disease (Boehm et al., 2013). (Higher levels of high-density lipoprotein cholesterol help to prevent buildup in your arteries and lower triglycerides, which are the chemical form of fat storage in the body.) So being optimistic is a positive asset, but it takes more than just hope to obtain positive health benefits.

The benefits of optimism raise an important question: If the traits of optimism and pessimism are stable over time—even resistant to change—can pessimists ever hope to gain any of the advantages of optimism? Research has shown that even die-hard pessimists can be trained to become significantly more optimistic and that this training can improve their psychosocial health outcomes. For example, pessimistic breast cancer patients who received 10 weeks of training in stress management techniques became more optimistic and were less likely than those who received only relaxation exercises to suffer distress and fatigue during their cancer treatments (Antoni et al., 2001).

Hardiness

Some people seem to be thick-skinned, somehow able to take stress or abuse that could be devastating to others. Are there personality traits that contribute to such resilience and offer protection from stress-induced illness? To identify such traits, Suzanne Kobasa (1979) studied a group of stress-resistant business executives. These individuals reported high levels of stressful life events but had histories of relatively few illnesses compared with a similar group who succumbed to stress by getting sick. The stress-resistant group (Kobasa labeled them *hardy*) shared several traits, all conveniently beginning with the letter *C*. They showed a sense of *commitment,* an ability to become involved in life's tasks and encounters rather than just dabbling. They exhibited a belief in *control,* the expectation that their actions and words have a causal influence over their lives and environment. And they were willing to accept *challenge,* undertaking change and accepting opportunities for growth.

Can anyone develop hardiness? Researchers have attempted to teach hardiness and they have achieved some success. In one such attempt, participants attended 10 weekly hardiness-training sessions, in which they were encouraged to examine their stresses, develop action plans for dealing with them, explore their bodily reactions to stress, and find ways to compensate for unchangeable situations without falling into self-pity. Compared with control groups (who engaged in relaxation and meditation training or in group discussions about stress), the hardiness-training group reported greater reductions in their perceived personal stress, as well as fewer symptoms of illness (Maddi, Kahn, & Maddi, 1998). Hardiness training can have similar positive effects in university students, for some even boosting their marks (Maddi et al., 2009).

Health-Promoting Behaviours and Self-Regulation

Even without changing our personalities at all, we can do certain things to be healthy. The importance of healthy eating, safe sex, and giving up smoking are common knowledge. But we don't seem to be acting on the basis of this

Sometimes hardiness tips over the edge into foolhardiness. Here, participants in a polar bear dip in Charlottetown, Prince Edward Island, take the plunge into freezing cold water during the winter.

ANDREW VAUGHAN/THE CANADIAN PRESS VIA AP

knowledge. In 2018, 26.8% of Canadians aged 18 or older reported a BMI in the obese range (Statistics Canada, 2019a). The prevalence of unsafe sex is difficult to estimate, but out of every 50 sexually active 20- to 24-year-olds in Canada in 2016, 1 had a sexually transmitted infection (syphilis, chlamydia, gonorrhea, or hepatitis B), and these rates have continued to rise (Public Health Agency of Canada, November 2018). Another 63,000 people live with human immunodeficiency virus/acquired immune deficiency syndrome (HIV/AIDS). Of these, 1 in 7 is unaware of their infection, which is most often contracted through unprotected sex with an infected partner (Public Health Agency of Canada, 2018). And despite endless warnings, 15% of Canadians over 15 years of age smoke cigarettes (Statistics Canada, 2018c). What's going on?

Self-Regulation

Doing what is good for you is not necessarily easy. Mark Twain once remarked, "The only way to keep your health is to eat what you don't want, drink what you don't like, and do what you'd rather not." Engaging in health-promoting behaviours involves **self-regulation**, *the exercise of voluntary control over the self to bring the self into line with preferred standards.* When you decide on a salad rather than a cheeseburger, for instance, you control your impulse and behave in a way that will help make you the kind of person you would prefer to be—a healthy one. Self-regulation often involves putting off immediate gratification for longer-term gains.

Self-regulation requires a kind of inner strength or willpower. One theory suggests that self-control is a kind of strength that can be fatigued (Baumeister, Vohs, & Tice, 2007). In other words, trying to exercise control in one area may exhaust self-control, leaving behaviour in other areas unregulated. To test this theory, researchers seated hungry volunteers near a batch of fresh, hot, chocolate chip cookies. They asked some participants to leave the cookies alone but help themselves to a healthy snack of radishes, whereas others were allowed to indulge. When later challenged with an impossibly difficult figure-tracing task, the self-control group was more likely than the self-indulgent group to abandon the difficult task—behaviour interpreted as evidence that they had depleted their pool of self-control (Baumeister et al., 1998). The take-home message from this experiment is that to control behaviour successfully, we need to choose our battles, exercising self-control mainly on the personal weaknesses that are most harmful to health. Most important, however, the exact nature of this effect is still being debated; several research teams have failed to replicate this earlier work (e.g., Lurquin et al., 2016).

Sometimes self-regulation is less a matter of brute force than of strategy. Martial artists claim that anyone can easily overcome a large attacker with the right moves, and overcoming our own unhealthy impulses may also be a matter of finesse. Let's look carefully at healthy approaches to some key challenges for self-regulation—eating, safe sex, and smoking—to learn which "smart moves" can aid us in our struggles.

Eating Wisely

In many Western cultures, the weight of the average citizen is increasing alarmingly. One explanation is based on our evolutionary history: To ensure their survival, our ancestors found it useful to eat well in times of plenty to store calories for leaner times. In 21st-century postindustrial societies, however, there are no leaner times, and people can't burn all of the calories they consume (Pinel, Assanand, & Lehman, 2000). But why, then, isn't obesity endemic throughout the Western world? Why are people in France leaner on average than North Americans, even though their foods are high in fat? One reason has to do with the fact that

JEAN SANDER/FEATUREPICS

Nobody ever said self-control was easy. Probably the only reason you're able to keep yourself from eating this cookie is that it's just a picture of a cookie. Really. Don't eat it.

self-regulation The exercise of voluntary control over the self to bring the self into line with preferred standards.

JEFF GILBERT/ALAMY

One of the reasons that people in France are leaner than people in North America is that the average French diner spends 22 minutes to consume a fast-food meal, whereas the average North American diner spends only 15 minutes. How could the length of the average meal influence an individual's body weight?

activity level in France is higher. Research by Paul Rozin and his colleagues also finds that portion sizes in France are significantly smaller than in North America, but at the same time, people in France take longer to finish their smaller meals. At a McDonald's in France, diners take an average of 22 minutes to consume a meal, whereas in North America, people take less than 15 minutes (Rozin, Kabnick et al., 2003). The fact that people in France are eating less food more slowly may lead them to be more conscious of what they are eating. This, ironically, probably leads to lower French fry consumption.

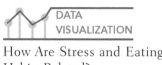

DATA VISUALIZATION

How Are Stress and Eating Habits Related?
Go to launchpadworks.com.

Short of moving to France, what can you do? Studies indicate that dieting doesn't always work because the process of conscious self-regulation can easily be undermined by stress, causing people who are trying to control themselves to lose control by overindulging in the very behaviour they had been trying to overcome. This may remind you of a general principle we discussed in the Consciousness chapter: Trying hard not to do something can often directly result in the unwanted behaviour (Wegner, 1994a, 1994b, 2009).

The restraint problem may be inherent in the very act of self-control. Rather than dieting, then, heading towards normal weight should involve a new emphasis on exercise and nutrition (Prochaska & Sallis, 2004). In emphasizing what is good to eat, a person can think freely about food rather than trying to suppress thoughts about it. A focus on increasing activity rather than reducing food intake, in turn, gives people another positive and active goal to pursue. Self-regulation is more effective when it focuses on what to do rather than on what *not* to do (Molden, Lee, & Higgins, 2009; Wegner & Wenzlaff, 1996).

Avoiding Sexual Risks

People put themselves at risk when they have unprotected vaginal, oral, or anal intercourse. Sexually active adolescents and adults are usually aware of such risks, not to mention the risk of unwanted pregnancy, yet many behave in risky ways nonetheless. Why doesn't awareness translate into avoidance? Risk takers harbour an *illusion of unique invulnerability,* a systematic bias towards believing that they are less likely to fall victim to the problem than are others (Perloff & Fetzer, 1986). For example, a classic study of female university students found that sexually active respondents judged their own likelihood of getting pregnant in the next year as less than 10%, but estimated the average for other women at the university to be 27% (Burger & Burns, 1988). Paradoxically, this illusion was even stronger among women in the sample who reported using inadequate or no contraceptive techniques. The tendency to think "It won't happen to me" may be most pronounced when it probably will.

Unprotected sex often is the impulsive result of last-minute emotions. When thought is further blurred by alcohol or recreational drugs, people often fail to use the latex condoms that can reduce their exposure to the risks of pregnancy, HIV, and many other STIs. Like other forms of self-regulation, the avoidance of sexual risk requires the kind of planning that can easily be undone by circumstances that hamper the ability to think ahead. One approach to reducing sexual risk taking, then, is simply finding ways to help people plan ahead. Sex education programs offer adolescents just such a chance by encouraging them, at a time when they have not had much sexual experience, to think about what they might do when they need to make decisions. Although sex education is sometimes criticized as increasing adolescents' awareness of and interest in sex, the research evidence is clear: Sex education reduces the likelihood that university students will engage in unprotected sexual activity and it benefits their health (Li et al., 2017).

ALEX GREGORY/CARTOON COLLECTIONS

"Boy, I'm going to pay for this tomorrow at yoga class."

Not Smoking

One in two smokers dies prematurely from smoking-related diseases such as lung cancer, heart disease, emphysema, and cancer of the mouth and throat. Lung cancer alone kills more people than any other form of cancer, and smoking causes 80% of lung cancers. Although the rate of cigarette smoking had been declining in Canada for years, the rate of 20- to 24-year-old smokers actually rose from 13% to 16% between 2015 and 2017, perhaps due to the rising popularity of vaping (Statistics Canada, 2018c). In the face of all the devastating health consequences, why don't people quit?

Nicotine, the active ingredient in cigarettes, is addictive, so smoking is difficult to stop once the habit is established (as discussed in the Consciousness chapter). As with other forms of self-regulation, the resolve to quit smoking is fragile and seems to break down under stress. And for some time after quitting, ex-smokers remain sensitive to cues in the environment: Eating or drinking, a bad mood, anxiety, or just seeing someone else smoking is enough to make them want a cigarette (Shiffman et al., 1996). The good news is that the urge diminishes, and people become less likely to relapse the longer they've been away from nicotine.

Psychological programs and techniques to help people kick the habit include nicotine replacement systems such as gum and skin patches, counselling programs, and hypnosis, but these programs are not always successful. Trying again and again in different ways is apparently the best approach (Schachter, 1982). After all, to quit smoking forever, you need to quit only one more time than you start up. But like the self-regulation of eating and sexuality, the self-regulation of smoking can require effort and thought. The ancient Greeks blamed self-control problems on *akrasia* (weakness of will). Modern psychology focuses less on blaming a person's character for poor self-regulation and points instead towards the difficulty of the task. Keeping healthy by behaving in healthy ways is one of the great challenges of life (see Other Voices: The Dangers of Overparenting).

Build to the Outcomes

1. Why do optimists tend to have better health?
2. What is hardiness?
3. Why is it difficult to achieve and maintain self-control?
4. Why is exercise a more effective weight-loss choice than dieting?
5. Why does planning ahead reduce sexual risk-taking?
6. To quit smoking forever, how many times do you need to quit?

Other Voices | The Dangers of Overparenting

Many parents want to protect their children from experiencing any stress or hardship. This is only natural; we want to protect the ones we love from being hurt, and we want to ensure that they have the best life possible. But is there a downside to doing so? Julie Lythcott-Haims, who for a decade served as Stanford University's Dean of Freshman, believes that "overparenting" can cause significant harm by depriving children of opportunities to learn creativity, competence, and confidence, and to develop a true sense of who they really are. In her book, *How to Raise an Adult,* Lythcott-Haims describes how overbearing "helicopter parenting" can backfire among university students.

I became a university dean because I'm interested in supporting humans in growing to become who they're meant to become, unfettered by circumstances or other people's expectations. I expected that the kids who would need my help would be first-generation college students or low-income kids, and these populations certainly benefited from the mentorship and support that a dean could provide. But it was my solidly middle- or upper-middle-class students who had the most bewildered looks on their faces, looks that turned to relief when Mom or Dad handled the situation, whatever it was. These parents seemed involved in their college students' lives in ways that held their kids back instead of propelling them forward.

In 2013 the news was filled with worrisome statistics about the mental health crisis on college campuses, particularly the number of students medicated for depression. Charlie Gofen, the retired chairman of the board at the Latin School of Chicago, a private school serving about 1,100 students, emailed the statistics off to a colleague at another school and asked, "Do you think parents at your school would rather their kid be depressed at Yale or happy at University of Arizona?" The colleague quickly replied, "My guess is 75 percent of the parents would rather see their kids depressed at Yale. They figure that the kid can straighten the emotional stuff out in his/her 20's, but no one can go back and get the Yale undergrad degree."

In 2013 the American College Health Association surveyed close to 100,000 college students from 153 different campuses about their health. When asked about their experiences, at some point over the past 12 months:

- 84.3 percent felt overwhelmed by all they had to do
- 60.5 percent felt very sad
- 57.0 percent felt very lonely
- 51.3 percent felt overwhelming anxiety
- 8.0 percent seriously considered suicide

You're right to be thinking *Yes, but do we know whether overparenting causes this rise in mental health problems?* The answer is that we don't have studies proving causation, but a number of recent studies show *correlation.*

Julie Lythcott-Haims is an author and advocate based in San Francisco, California.

In 2010, psychology professor Neil Montgomery of Keene State College in New Hampshire surveyed 300 college freshmen nationwide and found that students with helicopter parents were less open to new ideas and actions and more vulnerable, anxious, and self-conscious. "[In s]tudents who were given responsibility and not constantly monitored by their parents—so-called 'free rangers'—the effects were reversed," Montgomery's study found. A 2011 study by Terri LeMoyne and Tom Buchanan at the University of Tennessee at Chattanooga looking at more than 300 students found that students with "hovering" or "helicopter" parents are more likely to be medicated for anxiety and/or depression.

When parents have tended to do the stuff of life for kids—the waking up, the transporting, the reminding about deadlines and obligations, the bill-paying, the question-asking, the decision-making, the responsibility-taking, the talking to strangers, and the confronting of authorities, kids may be in for quite a shock when parents turn them loose in the world of college or work. They will experience setbacks, which will feel to them like failure. Lurking beneath the problem of whatever thing needs to be handled is the student's inability to differentiate the self from the parent.

Here's the point—and this is so much more important than I realized until rather recently when the data started coming in: The research shows that figuring out for themselves is a critical element to people's mental health. Your kids have to be there for *themselves.* That's a harder truth to swallow when your kid is in the midst of a problem or worse, a crisis, but taking the long view, it's the best medicine for them.

Is being exposed to stressful situations necessarily a bad thing? How else will we learn how to cope with difficult situations? If we never learn to do so, we may be more likely to experience some of the bad outcomes that Lythcott-Haims writes about. So get out there, get stressed, and manage it!

Chapter Review

Sources of Stress: What Gets to You

- Stressors are events and threats that place specific demands on a person or threaten well-being.
- Sources of stress include negative life events, but even happy ones require readjustment and preparedness. Chronic stress involves triggers that occur repeatedly, some that are social and some that can be traced to a particular environment.
- Events are most stressful when we perceive that there is no way to control or deal with the challenge.

Stress Reactions: All Shook Up

- The body responds to stress with an initial fight-or-flight reaction, which activates the hypothalamic–pituitary–adrenocortical (HPA) axis and prepares the body to face the threat or run away from it.
- The general adaptation syndrome (GAS) outlines three phases of stress response that occur regardless of the type of stressor: alarm, resistance, and exhaustion.
- Chronic stress can wear down the immune system, causing susceptibility to infection, aging, tumour growth, organ damage, and death. People who respond to stress with anger are most at risk of heart disease.
- The response to stress will vary depending on whether it's interpreted as something that can be overcome or not.
- If prolonged, the psychological response to stress can lead to burnout. It is a particular problem in professions in which emotional turmoil is part of the job.

Stress Management: Dealing With It

- The management of stress involves strategies for influencing the mind, the body, and the situation.
- People try to manage their minds by suppressing stressful thoughts or avoiding the situations that produce them, by rationally coping with the stressor, and by reframing.

- Body management strategies involve attempting to reduce stress symptoms through meditation, relaxation, biofeedback, and aerobic exercise.
- Overcoming stress by managing your situation can involve seeking out social support, engaging in religious experiences, or attempting to find humour in stressful events.
- The Learning chapter details reasons why it's important not to procrastinate when studying for a test, and there are health reasons as well.

The Psychology of Illness: Mind Over Matter

- The psychology of illness concerns how sensitivity to the body leads people to recognize illness and seek treatment.
- Somatic symptom disorders can stem from excessive sensitivity to physical problems.
- The sick role is a set of rights and obligations linked with illness; some people fake illness in order to accrue those rights.
- Successful health care providers interact with their patients to understand both the physical state and the psychological state.

The Psychology of Health: Feeling Good

- The connection between mind and body can be revealed through the influences of personality and self-regulation of behaviour on health.
- The personality traits of optimism and hardiness are associated with reduced risk for illnesses, perhaps because people with these traits can fend off stress.
- The self-regulation of behaviours such as eating, sexuality, and smoking is difficult for many people because self-regulation is easily disrupted by stress; strategies for maintaining self-control can pay off with significant improvements in health and quality of life.

Key Concept Quiz

1. What kinds of stressors are you likely to be exposed to if you live in a dense urban area with considerable traffic, noise, and pollution?
   a. cultural stressors
   b. intermittent stressors
   c. chronic stressors
   d. positive stressors

2. In an experiment, two groups are subjected to distractions while attempting to complete a task. Those in group A are told they can quiet the distractions by pushing a button. This information is withheld from group B. Why will group A's performance at the task likely be better than group B's?

   a. Group B is working in a different environment.
   b. Group A has perceived control over a source of performance-impeding stress.
   c. Group B is less distracted than group A.
   d. The distractions affecting group B are now chronic.

3. According to the general adaptation syndrome, during the _____ phase, the body adapts to its high state of arousal as it tries to cope with a stressor.
   a. exhaustion
   b. alarm
   c. resistance
   d. energy

4. Which statement most accurately describes the physiological response to stress?

   a. Type A behaviour patterns have psychological but not physiological ramifications.

   b. The link between work-related stress and coronary heart disease is unfounded.

   c. Stressors can cause hormones to flood the brain, strengthening the immune system.

   d. The immune system is remarkably responsive to psychological influences.

5. Engaging in aerobic exercise is a way of managing stress by managing the

   a. environment.

   b. body.

   c. situation.

   d. intake of air.

6. Finding a new or creative way to think about a stressor that reduces its threat is called

   a. stress inoculation.

   b. repressive coping.

   c. reframing.

   d. rational coping.

7. Faking an illness is a violation of

   a. malingering.

   b. somatoform disorder.

   c. the sick role.

   d. the Type B pattern of behaviour.

8. Which statement describes a successful health care provider?

   a. The provider displays empathy.

   b. The provider pays attention to both the physical and psychological states of the patient.

   c. The provider uses psychology to promote patient compliance.

   d. The provider uses all of the above.

9. When sick, optimists are more likely than pessimists to

   a. maintain positive emotions.

   b. become depressed.

   c. ignore their caregiver's advice.

   d. avoid contact with others.

10. Stress _____ the self-regulation of behaviours such as eating and smoking.

    a. strengthens

    b. has no effect on

    c. disrupts

    d. normalizes

 **LearningCurve** macmillan learning Don't stop now! Quizzing yourself is a powerful study tool. Go to LaunchPad to access the LearningCurve adaptive quizzing system and your own personalized learning plan. Visit launchpadworks.com.

Key Terms

stressors (p. 548)

stress (p. 548)

health psychology (p. 548)

chronic stressors (p. 550)

fight-or-flight response (p. 552)

general adaptation syndrome (GAS) (p. 552)

telomeres (p. 554)

telomerase (p. 555)

immune system (p. 556)

lymphocytes (p. 556)

Type A behaviour pattern (p. 557)

burnout (p. 558)

repressive coping (p. 560)

rational coping (p. 560)

reframing (p. 561)

stress-inoculation training (SIT) (p. 561)

meditation (p. 562)

relaxation therapy (p. 562)

relaxation response (p. 562)

biofeedback (p. 563)

social support (p. 564)

psychosomatic illness (p. 570)

somatic symptom disorders (p. 570)

sick role (p. 571)

self-regulation (p. 575)

Changing Minds

1. In 2002, researchers compared severe acne in university students during a relatively stress-free period with acne during a highly stressful exam period. After adjusting for other variables such as changes in sleep or diet, the researchers concluded that increased acne severity was strongly correlated with increased levels of stress. Learning about the study, your roommate is surprised. "Acne is a skin disease," your roommate says. "I don't see how it could have anything to do with your mental state." How would you weigh in on the role of stress in medical diseases? What other examples could you give of ways in which stress can affect health?

2. A friend of yours who is taking a heavy course load confides that he's feeling overwhelmed. "I can't take the stress," he says. "Sometimes I daydream of living on an island somewhere, where I can just lie in the sun and have no stress at all." What would you tell your friend about stress? Is all stress bad? What would a life with no stress really be like?

3. One of your classmates spent the summer interning in a neurologist's office. "One of the most fascinating things," she says, "was the patients with psychosomatic illness. Some had seizures or partial paralysis of an arm, and there were no neurological causes—so it was all psychosomatic.

The neurologist tried to refer these patients to psychiatrists, but a lot of the patients thought he was accusing them of faking their symptoms, and were very insulted." What would you tell your friend about psychosomatic illness?

Could a disease that's "all in the head" really produce symptoms such as seizures or partial paralysis, or are these patients definitely faking their symptoms?

Answers to Key Concept Quiz

1. c; 2. b; 3. c; 4. d; 5. b; 6. c; 7. c; 8. d; 9. a; 10. c

LaunchPad features the full e-book of *Psychology*, the LearningCurve adaptive quizzing system, videos, and a variety of activities to boost your learning. Visit LaunchPad at launchpadworks.com.

Psychological Disorders

ROBIN WILLIAMS WAS ONE OF THE FUNNIEST and most beloved comedians in history. Over the course of his nearly 40-year career, Williams was an amazingly successful stand-up comedian, television and movie star, and philanthropist. He was best known for his fun and zany improvisational style and his ability to consistently make others laugh. He appeared as an actor in over 100 films and television shows, including four major movies released in 2014. Then, on August 11, 2014, Williams locked himself in his bedroom and hanged himself with his belt, dying by suicide. Why would a person who appeared to be so happy, and who was so successful, active, and beloved purposely end his life?

Many people familiar with Robin Williams's professional career did not know that he had suffered from mental illness for years. Throughout his life, Williams struggled with drug- and alcohol-use disorders that impaired his ability to function and led to multiple hospitalizations. Williams also suffered from major depressive disorder, a condition characterized by long periods of depressed mood, diminished interest in pleasurable activities, feelings of worthlessness, and problems with eating and sleeping. Shortly before his death, he was also diagnosed with Parkinson's disease and dementia, conditions associated with a progressive decline of physical and mental abilities. Many people who are suicidal say that their motivation is not necessarily to be dead, but rather to escape from some seemingly intolerable situation, such as a long-term struggle with mental illness. That may have been the reason for Williams's suicide, although we will never know for sure.

The actor and comedian Robin Williams (1951–2014) was a brilliant performer who had audiences laughing for over 40 years. In his personal life, however, he suffered with bouts of addiction, depression, and dementia, ending with his suicide.

- **Defining Mental Disorders: What Is Abnormal?**

- **Anxiety Disorders: Excessive Fear, Anxiety, and Avoidance**

- **Obsessive-Compulsive Disorder: Persistent Thoughts and Repetitive Behaviours**

- **Posttraumatic Stress Disorder: Distress and Avoidance After a Trauma**

- **Depressive and Bipolar Disorders: Extreme Highs and Lows**

- **Schizophrenia and Other Psychotic Disorders: Losing the Grasp on Reality**

- **Disorders of Childhood and Adolescence**

- **Personality Disorders: Extreme Traits and Characteristics**

- **Self-Harm Behaviours: Intentionally Injuring Oneself**

Williams's case highlights several important facts about mental disorders. They can affect anyone, regardless of the amount of perceived happiness or success. They are characterized by extreme distress and impairment, often limiting a person's ability to carry out daily activities. At the same time, however, many people suffer silently, their suffering unknown to those around them, even to close friends and family. And finally, in extreme cases, mental disorders can be lethal, leading to severe self-injury or death by suicide. What are mental disorders, and what causes them?

IN THIS CHAPTER, WE FIRST CONSIDER THE QUESTION, "What is abnormal?" Robin Williams's bouts of addiction, depression, and dementia, along with his eventual suicide, certainly are abnormal in the sense that most people do not have these experiences. However, at times, he led a perfectly normal and happy life. The enormously complicated human mind can produce behaviours, thoughts, and emotions that change radically from moment to moment. How do psychologists decide when a person's thoughts, emotions, and behaviours are "disordered"? We will first examine the key factors that must be weighed in making such a decision. We'll then focus on several major forms of *mental disorder:* depressive and bipolar disorders; anxiety, obsessive-compulsive, and trauma-related disorders; schizophrenia; disorders that begin in childhood and adolescence; personality disorders; and self-harm behaviours. As we view each type of disorder, we will examine how they manifest and what is known about their prevalence and causes.

The disorders explored in this chapter represent a tragic loss of human potential. The contentment, peace, and productivity that people could be enjoying are crowded out by pain, suffering, and impairment. The current scientific approach to mental disorders considers the biological, psychological, and social factors that combine to cause disorders. Appropriately called the *biopsychosocial model,* this approach is beginning to sort out the symptoms and causes of mental disorders. As we will see in the next chapter, this approach already offers remarkably effective treatments for some disorders; for other disorders, it offers hope that pain and suffering can be alleviated in the future.

Defining Mental Disorders: What Is Abnormal?

Learning Outcomes

- Explain why the *DSM* has become a more credible diagnostic tool over the course of revisions to each edition.

- Identify the fundamental ideas behind the medical model, the biopsychosocial perspective, and the diathesis–stress model.

- Relate how the RDoC expands on the *DSM*.

- Explain why labelling someone with a disorder can be problematic.

The concept of a mental disorder seems simple at first glance, but it turns out to be very complex and quite tricky (similar to clearly defining "consciousness," "stress," or "personality"). Any extreme variation in your thoughts, feelings, or behaviours is not a mental disorder. For instance, severe anxiety before a test, sadness after the loss of a loved one, or a night of excessive alcohol consumption—although unpleasant—is not necessarily pathological. Similarly, a persistent pattern of deviating from the norm does not qualify as a mental disorder. If it did, we would diagnose mental disorders in the most creative and visionary people—anyone whose ideas deviate from those of people around them.

So what *is* a mental disorder? Perhaps surprisingly, there is no universal agreement on a precise definition of the term *mental disorder.* However, there is general agreement that a **mental disorder** can be broadly defined as *a persistent disturbance or dysfunction in behaviour, thoughts, or emotions that causes significant distress or impairment* (Stein et al., 2010; Wakefield, 2007). One way to think about mental disorders is as dysfunctions or deficits in the normal human psychological processes you have learned about throughout this textbook. People with mental disorders have problems with their perception, memory, learning, emotions, motivation, thinking, and social processes. Of course, this definition leaves many questions unanswered.

What kinds of disturbances count as mental disorders? How long must they last to be considered "persistent?" And how much distress or impairment is required? These are all still hotly debated questions in the field.

Conceptualizing Mental Disorders

Since ancient times, there have been reports of people acting strangely or reporting bizarre thoughts or emotions. Until fairly recently, such difficulties were conceptualized as the result of religious or supernatural forces. In some cultures, psychopathology is still interpreted as possession by spirits or demons, as enchantment by a witch or shaman, or as God's punishment for wrongdoing. In many societies, including our own, people with psychological disorders have been feared and ridiculed, and often treated as criminals: punished, imprisoned, or put to death for their "crime" of deviating from what is considered to be normal. However, focusing solely on deviating from the norm is problematic, as deviations from the norm can be extremely helpful to society – such as the case with creativity, athleticism, and entertainment.

Over the past 200 years, these ways of looking at psychological abnormalities have largely been replaced in most parts of the world by a **medical model**, an *approach that conceptualizes abnormal psychological experiences as illnesses that, like physical illnesses, have biological and environmental causes, defined symptoms, and possible cures*. Conceptualizing abnormal thoughts and behaviours as illness suggests that a first step is to determine the nature of the problem through *diagnosis*.

In diagnosis, clinicians seek to determine the nature of a person's mental disorder by assessing *signs* (objectively observed indicators of a disorder) and *symptoms* (subjectively reported behaviours, thoughts, and emotions) that suggest an underlying illness. So, for example, just as self-reported sniffles and a cough are symptoms of a cold, Robin Williams's depressed mood and struggles to control his use of mind-altering substances can be seen as symptoms of his depressive and substance-use disorders. Clinicians distinguish among three related general medical and classification terms:

- A *disorder* is a common set of signs and symptoms.
- A *disease* is a known pathological process affecting the body.
- A *diagnosis* is a determination as to whether a disorder or disease is present (Kraemer, Shrout, & Rubio-Stipec, 2007).

mental disorder A persistent disturbance or dysfunction in behaviour, thoughts, or emotions that causes significant distress or impairment.

medical model An approach that conceptualizes abnormal psychological experiences as illnesses that, like physical illnesses, have biological and environmental causes, defined symptoms, and possible cures.

Although mental disorders are deviations from normal behaviour, not all deviations from the norm are disordered. Indeed, people thinking differently about the world, and behaving in ways that deviated from the norm, have encouraged us all to think differently about ourselves and our place in the world. Pandemonia (*left*), an anonymous London-based conceptual artist characterized by an inflatable full-head mask, started their career by crashing fashion and social events. Juliana Huxtable (*middle*), a transgender artist, DJ, and poet, founded Shock Value, a New York-City-based nightlife collective aimed at elevating women performers. Tina Guo (*right*), a Chinese-American cellist, takes her cello performance outside of the classical realm and into the unexpected cinematic, video game, and metal music genres.

According to the theory of physiognomy, mental disorders could be diagnosed from facial features. This fanciful theory is now considered superstition, but it was popular from antiquity until the early 20th century.

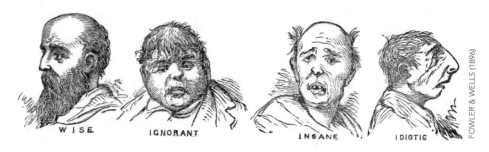

WISE   IGNORANT   INSANE   IDIOTIC

FOWLER & WELLS (1896)

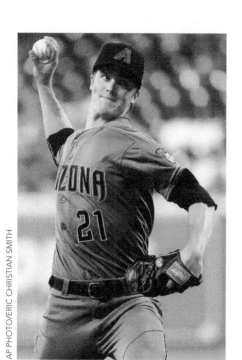

AP PHOTO/ERIC CHRISTIAN SMITH

Some critics of the medical model of mental disorders suggest that such an approach "pathologizes" normal human behaviour, such as calling shyness social phobia. However, proponents are quick to note that conditions such as social phobia are not merely normal shyness, but serious problems that can impair a person's functioning and ability to carry out a normal life. Here's just one example: The professional baseball player Zack Greinke was unable to play baseball in 2006, early in his professional career, due to social phobia. Fortunately, through effective treatment, he was able to return to the game and has gone on to have a very successful professional career.

Diagnostic and Statistical Manual of Mental Disorders (DSM)

A classification system that describes the features used to diagnose each recognized mental disorder and indicates how that disorder can be distinguished from other, similar problems.

Bear in mind that knowing that a disorder is present (i.e., diagnosed) does not necessarily mean that we know the underlying disease process in the body that gives rise to the signs and symptoms of the disorder.

Viewing mental disorders as medical problems reminds us that people who are suffering deserve care and treatment, not condemnation. Nevertheless, there are some criticisms of the medical model. Some psychologists argue that it is inappropriate to use clients' subjective self-reports, rather than physical tests of pathology (as in other areas of medical diagnostics), to determine underlying illness. Others argue that the model often "medicalizes" or "pathologizes" normal human behaviour. For instance, extreme sadness can be considered to be an illness called *major depressive disorder*; extreme shyness can be diagnosed as an illness called *social anxiety disorder*; and trouble concentrating in school is called *attention-deficit/hyperactivity disorder*. Although there are some valid concerns about the current method of defining and classifying mental disorders, it is a huge advance over older alternatives, such as viewing mental disorders as the product of witchcraft or as punishment for sin. Moreover, psychologists keep these concerns in mind as they work to improve the diagnostic procedures.

Classifying Disorders

So how is the medical model used to classify the wide range of abnormal behaviours that occur among humans? Psychologists, psychiatrists (physicians concerned with the study and treatment of mental disorders), and most other people working in the area of mental disorders use a standardized system for classifying mental disorders. In fact, there are currently two established systems for classifying mental disorders: The International Classification of Diseases (ICD-10) produced by the World Health Organization, and the **Diagnostic and Statistical Manual of Mental Disorders (DSM)** produced by the American Psychiatric Association (APA). Since the DSM tends to be the classification used most widely in North America, it is the one we shall focus on. The *DSM is a classification system that describes the symptoms used to diagnose each recognized mental disorder and indicates how the disorder can be distinguished from other, similar problems.* Each disorder is named and classified as a distinct illness. The initial version of the *DSM,* published in 1952, and its 1968 revision, *DSM–II,* provided a common language for talking about disorders. This was a major advance in the study of mental disorders; however, the diagnostic criteria listed in these early volumes were quite vague and based on thin theoretical assumptions. For instance, people who were extremely depressed or anxious for long periods of time might be given the general diagnosis of "neurosis reaction."

The next two editions of the *DSM (DSM–III,* published in 1980, and *DSM–IV,* published in 1994) moved from vague descriptions of disorders to very detailed lists of symptoms (or *diagnostic criteria*) that had to be present for a disorder to be diagnosed. For instance, in addition to being extremely sad or depressed (for at least 2 weeks), a person must have at least five of nine agreed-on symptoms of depression—for example, diminished interest in normally enjoyable activities, significant weight loss or gain, significantly increased or decreased sleep, loss of energy, feelings of worthlessness or guilt, trouble concentrating. The use of these detailed lists of symptoms for each of more than 200 disorders described in the *DSM* led to a dramatic increase in the reliability, or consistency, of diagnoses of mental disorders. Two clinicians interviewing the same individual were now much more likely to agree on what mental disorders were present, greatly increasing the credibility of the diagnostic process (and the fields of psychiatry and clinical psychology) and improving psychologists' ability to talk to each other, as well as to people suffering from these conditions, about the disorders being experienced.

In May 2013, the American Psychiatric Association released the current version of the manual, the *DSM–5*. The *DSM–5* describes 22 major categories containing more than 200 different mental disorders (see **TABLE 15.1**). Along with the disorders listed in these 22 categories, the *DSM–5* describes conditions that could be included as formal disorders but that, for now, require additional research. Furthermore, one section is devoted to cultural considerations in diagnosing mental disorders. Why the switch

---

TABLE 15.1

MAIN *DSM–5* CATEGORIES OF MENTAL DISORDERS

1. **Neurodevelopmental Disorders:** These conditions begin early in development and cause significant impairments in functioning, such as intellectual disability (formerly called "mental retardation"), autism spectrum disorder (ASD), and attention-deficit/hyperactivity disorder (ADHD).

2. **Schizophrenia Spectrum and Other Psychotic Disorders:** This group of disorders is characterized by major disturbances in perception, thought, language, emotion, and behaviour.

3. **Bipolar and Related Disorders:** These disorders include major fluctuations in mood—from mania to depression—and also can include psychotic experiences, which is why they are placed between the psychotic and depressive disorders in *DSM–5*.

4. **Depressive Disorders:** These conditions are characterized by extreme and persistent periods of depressed mood.

5. **Anxiety Disorders:** These disorders are characterized by excessive fear and anxiety that are extreme enough to impair a person's functioning, such as panic disorder, generalized anxiety disorder, and specific phobias.

6. **Obsessive-Compulsive and Related Disorders:** These conditions are characterized by the presence of obsessive thinking followed by compulsive behaviour in response to that thinking.

7. **Trauma- and Stressor-Related Disorders:** These disorders develop in response to a traumatic event, such as posttraumatic stress disorder.

8. **Dissociative Disorders:** These conditions are characterized by disruptions or discontinuity in consciousness, memory, or identity, such as dissociative identity disorder (formerly called "multiple personality disorder").

9. **Somatic Symptom and Related Disorders:** These are conditions in which a person experiences bodily symptoms (e.g., pain, fatigue) associated with significant distress or impairment.

10. **Feeding and Eating Disorders:** These are problems with eating that impair health or functioning, such as anorexia nervosa and bulimia nervosa.

11. **Elimination Disorders:** These involve inappropriate elimination of urine or feces (e.g., bedwetting).

12. **Sleep–Wake Disorders:** These are problems with the sleep–wake cycle, such as insomnia, narcolepsy, and sleep apnea.

13. **Sexual Dysfunctions:** These are problems related to unsatisfactory sexual activity, such as erectile disorder and premature ejaculation.

14. **Gender Dysphoria:** This is a single disorder characterized by incongruence between a person's experienced/expressed gender and assigned gender.

15. **Disruptive, Impulse-Control, and Conduct Disorders:** These conditions involve problems controlling emotions and behaviours, such as conduct disorder, intermittent explosive disorder, and kleptomania.

16. **Substance-Related and Addictive Disorders:** This collection of disorders involves persistent use of substances or some other behaviour (e.g., gambling) despite the fact that it leads to significant problems.

17. **Neurocognitive Disorders:** These are disorders of thinking caused by conditions such as Alzheimer's disease or traumatic brain injury.

18. **Personality Disorders:** These are enduring patterns of thinking, feeling, and behaving that lead to significant life problems.

19. **Paraphilic Disorders:** These conditions are characterized by inappropriate sexual activity, such as pedophilic disorder.

20. **Other Mental Disorders:** This is a residual category for conditions that do not fit into one of the above categories but are associated with significant distress or impairment, such as an unspecified mental disorder due to a medical condition.

21. **Medication-Induced Movement Disorders and Other Adverse Effects of Medication:** These are problems with physical movement (e.g., tremors, rigidity) that are caused by medication.

22. **Other Conditions That May Be the Focus of Clinical Attention:** These include disorders related to abuse, neglect, relationship, and other problems.

Information from *DSM–5* (American Psychiatric Association, 2013).

from Roman to Arabic numerals? The hope is that with more rapid advances in our understanding of mental disorders, rather than waiting another 20 years to update the *DSM,* we can make revisions as we learn more (*DSM–5.1, 5.2, 5.3,* and so on).

Each of the 22 chapters in the main body of the *DSM–5* lists the specific criteria that must be met in order for a person to be diagnosed with each disorder. According to the Canadian Mental Health Association (2019), by age 40, 1 in every 2 Canadians will have experienced a mental disorder. Many individuals with a mental disorder report **comorbidity,** *the co-occurrence of two or more disorders in a single individual* (Gadermann et al., 2012).

Disorders Appear in All Cultures

DATA VISUALIZATION

Comorbidity: How Often Do Multiple Disorders Occur? Go to launchpadworks.com.

Are mental disorders experienced by people around the world the same way? To better understand the *epidemiology* (the study of the distribution and causes of health and disease) of mental disorders, Ronald Kessler and colleagues launched the World Health Organization World Mental Health Survey Initiative, a large-scale study in which people from nearly two dozen countries around the world were assessed for the presence of mental disorders (Kessler & Üstün, 2008). The results of this 2007 study (see **FIGURE 15.1**) reveal that the major mental disorders seen in North America appear similarly in countries and cultures all around the world. For instance, depression, anxiety, attention-deficit/hyperactivity disorder, and substance use disorders occur all over the globe. They are reported at different rates in different countries, but depression and anxiety are always the most common, followed by impulse-control and substance use disorders (Kessler et al., 2007).

Although the common mental disorders described above are universal, it is clear that cultural context can influence how mental disorders are experienced, described, assessed, and treated (see A World of Difference: The Impact of Culture on Mental Disorders). To address this issue, the *DSM–5* includes a section containing a Cultural Formulation Interview (CFI). The CFI includes 16 questions that the clinician asks a client during a mental health assessment to help the clinician understand how the client's culture might influence the experience, expression, and explanation of his or her mental disorder.

The World Health Organization's *International Classification of Diseases (ICD)* is similar to the *DSM* in many ways. Hospitals and insurance companies generally use *ICD* codes (that is, each disorder is assigned a specific number) rather than

comorbidity The co-occurrence of two or more disorders in a single individual.

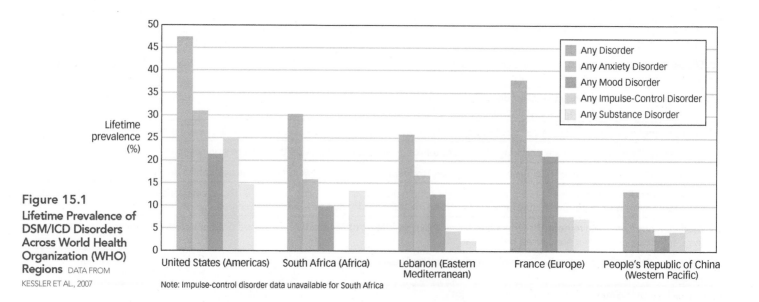

Figure 15.1

Lifetime Prevalence of DSM/ICD Disorders Across World Health Organization (WHO) Regions DATA FROM KESSLER ET AL., 2007

Note: Impulse-control disorder data unavailable for South Africa

A World of Difference | The Impact of Culture on Mental Disorders

Just as language, traditions, customs, and other factors differ across cultures, so does the manifestation of mental disorders. The disorders you learn about in this chapter (anxiety disorders, depressive disorders, psychotic disorders, and so on) appear in every culture, but cultural factors often influence the way these disorders are experienced, talked about, and explained. The *DSM–5* provides a framework for thinking about differences in cultural concepts of distress. It distinguishes among three important concepts:

- *Cultural syndromes* are groups of symptoms that tend to cluster together in specific cultures. For instance, *taijin kyofusho* is a cultural syndrome seen in Japan that is a combination of two *DSM*-5 conditions: social anxiety disorder (in which a person fears negative feedback from others) and body dysmorphic disorder (in which a person is preoccupied with perceived flaws in his or her own physical appearance).

- *Cultural idioms of distress* are ways of talking about or expressing distress that can differ across cultures. For instance, *kufungisisa*, or "thinking too much," is an idiom of distress in Zimbabwe (and many other countries/cultures, but by different names) that

ARIEF JUWONO/GETTY IMAGES

Taijin kyofusho is a Japanese syndrome in which a person fears and avoids contact with others due to the belief that they are inadequate or offensive in some way. This syndrome appears to be a combination of two *DSM–5* conditions: social anxiety disorder and body dysmorphic disorder.

is associated with a number of depressive and anxiety disorders.

- *Cultural explanations* are culturally recognized descriptions of what causes the symptoms, distress, or disorder. For example, in many South Asian cultures, mental disorder is believed to be caused by the loss of *dhat* or *dhatu,* a white substance believed to be in the body and essential for health that can exit the body in the form of semen or during urination or defecation.

So in addition to individual differences (across all people) in how we think, feel, and behave, the cultural context in which we are living can have an impact on how we experience, talk about, and explain mental disorders. This is important to keep in mind when trying to understand mental disorders within your own cultures, and also when trying to understand mental disorders in people from other cultures.

DSM codes in documenting which medical or psychological disorder a patient may be experiencing. The reason for this is that it allows all countries to work together to track the incidence and treatment of various conditions around the world.

Causation of Disorders

The medical model of mental disorder suggests that knowing a person's diagnosis is useful because any given category of mental illness is likely to have a distinctive cause. In other words, just as different viruses, bacteria, or genetic abnormalities cause different physical illnesses, a specifiable pattern of causes (or *etiology*) may exist for different psychological disorders. The medical model also suggests that each category of mental disorder is likely to have a common *prognosis*, a typical course over time and susceptibility to treatment and cure. Unfortunately, this basic medical model is usually an oversimplification; it is rarely useful to focus on a *single cause* that is *internal* to the person and that suggests a *single cure*.

To understand what factors might cause mental disorders, most psychologists take an integrated **biopsychosocial perspective** that *explains mental disorders as the result of interactions among biological, psychological, and social factors* (see **FIGURE 15.2a**). On the biological side, the focus is on genetic and epigenetic influences (see Figure 3.19),

biopsychosocial perspective
Explains mental disorders as the result of interactions among biological, psychological, and social factors.

Suppose that identical twins (with the same genetic profile) grow up in the same household (sharing the same parents, the same basic diet, the same access to television, and so on). When they are teenagers, one twin but not the other develops a mental disorder such as schizophrenia. How might this happen? Mental disorders can be caused by biological, psychological, and environmental factors. The diathesis–stress model suggests that a person may be predisposed for a psychological disorder that remains unexpressed until triggered by stress.

biochemical imbalances, and abnormalities in brain structure and function. The psychological perspective focuses on maladaptive learning and coping, cognitive biases, dysfunctional attitudes, and interpersonal problems. Social factors include poor socialization, stressful life experiences, and cultural and social inequities. The complexity of causation suggests that different individuals can experience a similar psychological disorder (e.g., depression) for different reasons. A person might fall into a depression as a result of biological causes (e.g., genetics, hormones), psychological causes (e.g., faulty beliefs, hopelessness, poor strategies for coping with loss), environmental causes (e.g., stress or loneliness), or more likely as a result of some combination of these factors. And, of course, multiple causes mean there may not be a single cure.

The observation that most disorders have both internal (biological/psychological) *and* external (environmental) causes has given rise to a theory known as the **diathesis–stress model**, which suggests that *a person may be predisposed to a psychological disorder that remains unexpressed until triggered by stress* (see Figure 15.2b). The diathesis is the internal predisposition, and the stress is the external trigger. For example, going away to university is a major change that can disrupt the equilibrium of a person's life. This is a stressor that may precipitate a psychological disorder in people who are susceptible (i.e., who have a diathesis). Although diatheses can be inherited, it's important to remember that heritability is not destiny. A person who inherits a diathesis may never encounter the precipitating stress, whereas someone with little genetic propensity to a disorder may come to suffer from it, given the right pattern of stress.

The issue of intergenerational trauma to Indigenous Peoples in Canada, resulting from Indian Residential School experiences, illustrates the complexity of tracing the cause of a psychological disorder. The Indian Residential School system was established in the 1880s, to assimilate Indigenous peoples based on the assumption that White European culture was inherently superior to others (Royal Commission on Aboriginal Peoples [RCAP], 1996). Approximately 150,000 Indigenous children attended residential schools over the 100 or so years that the schools were in existence. Children as young as 3 were forced by law to leave their families and communities to attend these schools, which systematically attempted to eliminate Indigenous languages, traditions, and beliefs. For many children, the trauma of losing family, culture, and community was compounded by woeful mistreatment, neglect, and abuse (RCAP, 1996) . This damage resulted in many of the children suffering from psychological disorders such as depressive and anxiety disorders, substance-related and addictive disorders, and trauma and stressor-related disorders (see Table 15.1; Elias et al, 2012; Wilk et al, 2017). These traumatized children

Figure 15.2

Proposed Models of How Disorders Develop (a) The biopsychosocial model suggests that biological, psychological, and social factors all interact to produce mental health or mental illness. (b) The diathesis–stress model suggests that mental illness develops when a person who has some predisposition or vulnerability to mental illness (the "diathesis") experiences a major life stressor (the "stress").

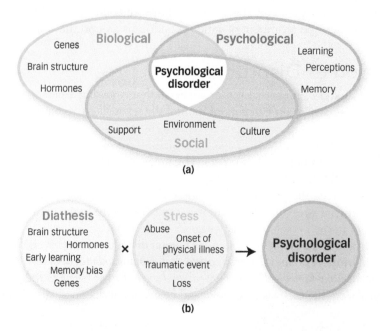

went on to become parents and grandparents of other children. As discussed later in this chapter, rates of suicide amongst Indigenous Peoples in Canada are at least three times as high as they are in the general population (Kumar & Tjepkema, 2019). If a First Nations adult living on-reserve has a parent or grandparent who attended an Indian Residential School, the chance of them thinking about suicide, and attempting suicide, is higher than it would otherwise be (McQuaid et al., 2017). If they have both a parent AND a grandparent who attended a residential school, the chance is higher still (McQuaid et al., 2017). This is an example of how severe stressors can be passed down through generations, affecting the mental health and quality of life of even those with potentially little genetic predisposition towards a disorder.

The example of intergenerational trauma in residential schools illustrates how incorrect it would be to oversimplify mental disorders by attributing them to single internal causes. Such oversimplification is nowhere more evident than in the interpretation of the role of the brain in psychological disorders. Brain scans of people with and without disorders can give rise to an unusually strong impression that psychological problems are internal and permanent, inevitable, and even untreatable. Brain influences and processes are fundamentally important for knowing the full story of psychological disorders, but they are not the only chapter in that story.

A New Approach to Understanding Mental Disorders: RDoC

Although the *DSM* and *ICD* provide a useful framework for classifying disorders, concern has been growing over the fact that the findings from scientific research on the biopsychosocial factors that appear to cause psychopathology do not map neatly onto individual *DSM/ICD* diagnoses. Succinctly characterizing the current state of affairs, one mental health leader has noted that although many people describe the *DSM* as a bible, it is more accurate to think of it as a dictionary that provides labels and current definitions: "People think that everything has to match *DSM* criteria, but you know what? Biology never read that book" (Thomas R. Insel, quoted in Belluck & Carey, 2013, p. A13).

To better understand what actually causes mental disorders, researchers have proposed a new framework for thinking about mental disorders, focused not on the currently defined *DSM/ICD* categories of disorders but on the more basic biological, cognitive, and behavioural constructs that are believed to be the building blocks of mental disorders. This new system is called the **Research Domain Criteria Project (RDoC)**, *a new initiative that aims to guide the classification and understanding of mental disorders by revealing the basic processes that give rise to them.* The RDoC is not intended to immediately replace the *DSM/ICD* but to inform future revisions to it in the coming years (see The Real World: How Are Mental Disorders Defined and Diagnosed?).

Using the RDoC, researchers study the causes of abnormal functioning by focusing on units (or levels) of analysis that include biological factors from genes to cells to brain circuits; psychological domains, such as learning, attention, memory; and various social processes and behaviour (see **TABLE 15.2** for a list of domains). The hope is that the RDoC approach will shift researchers away from studying currently defined *DSM/ICD* categories and towards the study of the dimensional biopsychosocial processes believed, at the extreme end of the continuum, to lead to mental disorders. These processes (e.g., fear, anxiety, attention, perception) are referred to as *constructs*, which are themselves grouped into broader categories referred to as *domains*. The six domains included in the RDoC are Negative Valence Systems, Positive Valence Systems, Cognitive Systems, Systems for Social Processes, Arousal/Regulatory Systems, and Sensorimotor Systems. The long-term goal is to better understand which abnormalities cause different disorders and to classify disorders on the basis of those underlying causes rather than on observed symptoms.

diathesis–stress model Suggests that a person may be predisposed to a psychological disorder that remains unexpressed until triggered by stress.

Research Domain Criteria Project (RDoC) A new initiative that aims to guide the classification and understanding of mental disorders by revealing the basic processes that give rise to them.

The Real World | How Are Mental Disorders Defined and Diagnosed?

Who decides what goes in the *DSM*? How are these decisions made? In psychology and psychiatry, as in the early days of most areas of the study of human health and behaviour, these decisions currently are made by consensus among leaders in the research field. These leaders meet repeatedly over several years to make decisions about which disorders should be included in the new revision of the *DSM* and how they should be defined. Over the years, these decisions have been based on descriptive research reporting in which clinical symptoms tend to cluster together.

Everyone agrees that we need a system for classifying and defining mental disorders; however, as the currently available body of knowledge about mental disorders grows, the field is moving beyond simple descriptive diagnostic categories towards others based on underlying biopsychosocial processes, such as the Research Domain Criteria Project. Future decisions about how mental disorders are defined will likely continue to be reached by consensus among leaders in the field but will be driven more directly by research on the underlying causes of these disorders.

Who decides whether someone actually has a diagnosable disorder? And how are these decisions made? Over the years, researchers have developed structured clinical interviews that convert the lists of symptoms included in the *DSM* into sets of interview questions through which the clinician (psychologist, psychiatrist, social worker) makes a determination about whether or not a given person meets the criteria for a given disorder (Nock et al., 2007). For instance, according to *DSM–5*, a person must have at least five of the nine symptoms of major depressive disorder in order to meet the criteria for this disorder. Structured clinical interviews typically include nine questions about depression (one per symptom), and if the person reports having at least five of these symptoms, the clinician may conclude that this person is suffering from major depression. Right now, diagnoses are determined primarily by client self-reporting of symptoms. With increasing attention to the underlying causes of mental disorders, many hope that in the future we will have biological and behavioural tests to help us make decisions about who has a mental illness and who does not.

This approach would bring the study of mental disorders in line with the study of other medical disorders. For example, if you are experiencing chest pain, severe headaches, fatigue, and difficulty breathing, it is unlikely that you are experiencing four separate disorders (*chest pain disorder, headache disorder,* and so on). Instead, we now know that these are all symptoms of an underlying disease process called hypertension. The RDoC approach similarly aims to shift the focus away from classifications based on surface symptoms and towards an understanding of the processes that give rise to disordered behaviour. For instance, rather than studying cocaine

TABLE 15.2

RESEARCH DOMAIN CRITERIA (RDoC)

Domains/Constructs					
Negative Valence Systems	**Positive Valence Systems**	**Cognitive Systems**	**Systems for Social Processes**	**Arousal/Regulatory Systems**	**Sensorimotor Systems**
acute threat ("fear")	approach motivation	attention	affiliation and attachment	arousal	motor actions
potential threat ("anxiety")	initial responsiveness to reward	perception	social communication	circadian rhythms	agency and ownership
sustained threat	sustained responsiveness to reward	working memory	perception and understanding of self	sleep and wakefulness	habit-sensorimotor
loss	reward learning	declarative memory	perception and understanding of others		innate motor patterns
frustrative nonreward		habit	language behaviour cognitive (effortful) control		
Units of Analysis					
genes molecules cells circuits physiology behaviour self-reports paradigms					

addiction as a distinct disorder, from the RDoC perspective researchers might try to understand what causes abnormalities in "responsiveness to reward," a factor seen in those with addiction to cocaine as well as in those with other addictive behaviours.

Indeed, recent research has shown that variations in a gene (*DRD2*) that codes for dopamine D2 receptors are associated with abnormal connections between two parts of the brain: the frontal lobe and the striatum (described in the Neuroscience and Behaviour chapter). This atypical connectivity is, in turn, related to the impulsiveness and responsiveness to rewards associated with a range of addictive behaviour disorders (Buckholtz & Meyer-Lindenberg, 2012), which may help explain why some people seem to have addictive personalities and have trouble inhibiting their reward-seeking behaviour. Importantly, understanding what processes cause problems such as addiction will help us to develop more effective treatments, a topic we address in more detail in the next chapter.

You might have noticed that the list of domains in Table 15.2 looks like a slightly more detailed version of the table of contents for this textbook! The RDoC approach has an overall emphasis on neuroscience (Chapter 3), and specific focuses on abnormalities in emotional and motivational systems (Chapter 8), cognitive systems such as memory (Chapter 6), learning (Chapter 7), language and cognition (Chapter 9), social processes (Chapter 13), and stress and arousal (Chapter 14). From the RDoC perspective, mental disorders can be thought of as the result of abnormalities or dysfunctions in normal psychological processes. By learning about many of these processes in this textbook, you will likely have a good understanding of new definitions of mental disorders as they are developed in the years ahead.

Dangers of Labelling

An important complication in the diagnosis and classification of psychological disorders is the effect of labelling. Psychiatric labels can have negative consequences because many carry the baggage of negative stereotypes and stigma, such as the idea that a mental disorder is a sign of personal weakness or the idea that all psychiatric patients are dangerous. The stigma associated with mental disorders may explain why most people with diagnosable psychological disorders (approximately 60%) do not seek treatment (Kessler et al., 2005c; Wang et al., 2005).

Unfortunately, educating people about mental disorders does not dispel the stigma borne by those with such conditions (Phelan et al., 1997). In fact, expectations created by psychiatric labels can sometimes even compromise the judgement of mental health professionals (Garb, 1998). In a classic demonstration of this phenomenon, the psychologist David Rosenhan and six associates reported to different mental hospitals complaining of "hearing voices," a symptom sometimes found in people with schizophrenia. Each was admitted to a hospital, and each promptly reported that the symptom had ceased. Even so, hospital staff were reluctant to identify these people as normal: It took an average of 19 days for these "patients" to secure their release, and even then they were released with the diagnosis of "schizophrenia in remission" (Rosenhan, 1973). Apparently, once hospital staff had labelled these patients as having a psychological disease, the label stuck.

These effects of labelling are particularly disturbing in light of evidence that hospitalizing people with mental disorders is seldom necessary. One set of studies followed the lives of patients who were thought to be too dangerous to release and therefore had been kept in the back wards of institutions for years. Their release resulted in no harm to the community (Harding et al., 1987), and further studies have shown that those with a mental disorder are no more likely to be violent than those without a disorder (Elbogen & Johnson, 2009).

Labelling may even affect how labelled individuals view themselves; persons given such a label may come to view themselves not just as mentally disordered but as hopeless or worthless. Such a view may cause them to develop an attitude of defeat and, as a result, to fail to work towards their own recovery. As one small step towards counteracting such consequences, clinicians have adopted the important practice

The new Research Domain Criteria (RDoC) are intended to help us better understand why some people seem to have addictive personalities and have trouble limiting their engagement in pleasurable experiences.

Although we label mental disorders, we should not apply those labels to people. For instance, rather than saying someone "is ADHD," we would say that the person currently meets diagnostic criteria for ADHD.

of applying labels to the disorder and not to the person with the disorder. For example, an individual might be described as "a person with schizophrenia," not as "a schizophrenic." You'll notice that we follow this convention in this text.

Build to the Outcomes

1. What is a mental disorder?
2. How does the medical model explain abnormal behaviour?
3. What is the first step in helping someone with a mental disorder?
4. What are the differences among disorder, disease, and diagnosis?
5. What is the *DSM*? How has it changed over time?
6. How do the biopsychosocial perspective and the diathesis–stress model explain disorders?
7. Why does assessment require looking at a number of factors?
8. What are the limitations of using brain scans for diagnosis?
9. What is the RDoC? How does it differ from the *DSM*?
10. Why might someone avoid seeking help for a disorder?
11. What are the dangers of labelling?

Anxiety Disorders: Excessive Fear, Anxiety, and Avoidance

Learning Outcomes

- Explain the major symptoms of anxiety disorders, including phobias, panic disorder, and GAD.

- Describe factors that contribute to phobias, panic disorder, and GAD.

"Okay, time for a pop quiz that will count for half your grade in this class." If your instructor had actually said that, you would probably have experienced a wave of anxiety. Your reaction would be appropriate and—no matter how intense the feeling—would not be a sign that you have a mental disorder. In fact, situation-related anxiety is normal and adaptive: in this case, perhaps by reminding you to keep up with your textbook assignments so you are prepared for pop quizzes. When anxiety arises that is out of proportion to real threats and challenges, however, it is maladaptive: It can take hold of people's lives, stealing their peace of mind and undermining their ability to function normally. Pathological anxiety is expressed as an **anxiety disorder**, *the class of mental disorders in which anxiety is the predominant feature*. People commonly experience more than one type of anxiety disorder at a given time, and there is significant comorbidity between anxiety and depression (Brown & Barlow, 2002; Jacobson & Newman, 2017). Among the anxiety disorders recognized in the *DSM–5* are phobic disorders, panic disorder, and generalized anxiety disorder.

Phobic Disorders

Consider Mary, a 47-year-old mother of three, who sought treatment for *claustrophobia*—an intense fear of enclosed spaces. She traced her fear to her childhood, when her older siblings would scare her by locking her in closets and confining her under blankets. Her own children grown, she wanted to find a job but could not because of a terror of elevators and other confined places that, she felt, shackled her to her home (Carson, Butcher, & Mineka, 2000). Many people feel a little anxious in enclosed spaces, but Mary's fears were abnormal and dysfunctional because they were disproportionate to any actual risk and impaired her ability to carry out a normal life. The *DSM–5* describes **phobic disorders** as characterized by *marked, persistent, and excessive fear and avoidance of specific objects, activities, or situations*. An individual with a phobic disorder recognizes that the fear is irrational but cannot prevent it from interfering with everyday functioning.

A **specific phobia** is *an irrational fear of a particular object or situation that markedly interferes with an individual's ability to function*. Specific phobias fall into five categories: (1) animals (e.g., dogs, cats, rats, snakes, spiders); (2) natural environments (e.g., heights,

anxiety disorder The class of mental disorders in which anxiety is the predominant feature.

phobic disorders Disorders characterized by marked, persistent, and excessive fear and avoidance of specific objects, activities, or situations.

specific phobia A disorder that involves an irrational fear of a particular object or situation that markedly interferes with an individual's ability to function.

darkness, water, storms); (3) situations (e.g., bridges, elevators, tunnels, enclosed places); (4) blood, injections, and injury; and (5) other phobias, including choking or vomiting; and in children, loud noises or costumed characters. Approximately 12% of people in the United States and Canada will develop a specific phobia during their lives (Kessler et al., 2005a; Anxiety Canada, 2019), with rates slightly higher among women than men (Kessler et al., 2012).

Social phobia involves *an irrational fear of being publicly humiliated or embarrassed.* Social phobia can be restricted to situations—such as public speaking, eating in public, or urinating in a public bathroom—or can be generalized to a variety of social situations that involve being observed or interacting with unfamiliar people. Individuals with social phobia try to avoid situations where unfamiliar people might evaluate them, and they experience intense anxiety and distress when public exposure is unavoidable. Social phobia can develop in childhood, but it typically emerges between early adolescence and early adulthood (Kessler et al., 2005a). Many people experience social phobia, with about 12% of men and 14% of women qualifying for a diagnosis at some time in their lives (Kessler et al., 2012).

Why are phobias so common? The high rates of both specific and social phobias suggest a predisposition to be fearful of certain objects and situations. Indeed, most of the situations and objects of people's phobias could pose a real threat, such as falling from a high place or being attacked by a vicious dog or a poisonous snake or spider. Social situations have their own dangers. A roomful of strangers may not attack or bite, but they could form impressions that affect your prospects for friends, jobs, or marriage. And of course, in some very rare cases, they could attack or bite.

Observations such as these are the basis for the **preparedness theory** of phobias, which maintains that *people are instinctively predisposed towards certain fears.* The preparedness theory, proposed by Martin E. P. Seligman (1971), is supported by research showing that both humans and monkeys can quickly be conditioned to have a fear response for stimuli such as snakes and spiders, but not for neutral stimuli such as flowers or toy rabbits (Cook & Mineka, 1989). Phobias are particularly likely to form for objects that evolution has predisposed us to avoid. This idea is also supported by studies of the heritability of phobias. Family studies of specific phobias indicate greater concordance rates for identical than for fraternal twins (Kendler, Myers, & Prescott, 2002; O'Laughlin & Malle, 2002).

Temperament may also play a role in vulnerability to phobias. Researchers have found that infants who display excessive shyness and inhibition are at an increased risk for developing a phobic behaviour later in life (Morris, 2001; Stein, Chavira, & Jang, 2001). Neurobiological factors may also play a role. Abnormalities in the neurotransmitters serotonin and dopamine are more common in individuals who report

social phobia A disorder that involves an irrational fear of being publicly humiliated or embarrassed.

preparedness theory The idea that people are instinctively predisposed towards certain fears.

COURTESY OF DANIEL WEGNER

The preparedness theory explains why most merry-go-rounds carry children on beautiful horses. This mom might have some trouble getting her daughter to ride on a big spider or snake.

MATHEW NOCK

Phobias are anxiety disorders that involve excessive and persistent fear of a specific object, activity, or situation. Some phobias may be learned through classical conditioning, in which a conditioned stimulus (CS) that is paired with an anxiety-evoking unconditioned stimulus (US) itself comes to elicit a conditioned fear response (CR). Suppose your friend has a phobia of dogs that is so intense that he is afraid to go outside in case one of his neighbours' dogs barks at him. Applying the principles of classical conditioning you studied in the Learning chapter, how might you help him overcome his fear?

phobias than among people who don't (Frick et al., 2015; Plavén-Sigray et al., 2017). In addition, individuals with phobias sometimes show abnormally high levels of activity in the amygdala, an area of the brain linked with the development of emotional associations (discussed in the chapter on Emotion and Motivation). Interestingly, although people with social phobia report feeling much more distressed than those without social phobia during tasks involving social evaluation (such as giving a speech), they are actually no more physiologically aroused than others (Jamieson, Nock, & Mendes, 2013). This suggests that social phobia may be due to a person's subjective experience of the situation, rather than an abnormal physiological stress response to such situations.

This evidence does not rule out the influence of environments and upbringing on the development of phobic overreactions. As the learning theorist John Watson (1924) demonstrated many years ago, phobias can be classically conditioned (see the discussion of Little Albert and the white rat in the Learning chapter). Similarly, the discomfort of a dog bite could create a conditioned association between dogs and pain, resulting in an irrational fear of all dogs. The idea that phobias are learned from emotional experiences with feared objects, however, is not a complete explanation for the occurrence of phobias. Most studies find that people with phobias are no more likely than people without phobias to recall personal experiences with the feared object that could have provided the basis for classical conditioning (Craske, 1999; McNally & Steketee, 1985). Moreover, many people are bitten by dogs, but few develop phobias. Despite its shortcomings, however, the idea that this is a matter of learning provides a useful model for therapy (see the Treatment chapter).

Panic Disorder and Agoraphobia

If you suddenly found yourself in danger of death (that lion is headed straight for us!), a wave of panic might wash over you. People who suffer panic attacks are frequently overwhelmed by such intense fears and by powerful physical symptoms of anxiety, even in the complete absence of actual danger. Wesley, a 20-year-old university student, began having panic attacks with increasing frequency, often two or three times a day, so he finally sought help at a clinic. The attacks would begin with a sudden wave of "intense, terrifying fear" that seemed to come out of nowhere, often accompanied by dizziness, a tightening of the chest, and the thought that he was going to pass out or possibly die. Wesley's attacks had started a few years earlier and had occurred intermittently ever since. He decided to seek treatment because he had begun to avoid buses, trains, and public places for fear that he would have an attack like this and not be able to escape.

Wesley's condition, called **panic disorder**, is characterized by *the sudden occurrence of multiple psychological and physiological symptoms that contribute to a feeling of stark terror.* The acute symptoms of a panic attack typically last only a few minutes and include shortness of breath, heart palpitations, sweating, dizziness, depersonalization (a feeling of being detached from one's body) or derealization (a feeling that the external world is strange or unreal), and a fear that one is going crazy or about to die. Not surprisingly, panic attacks often send people rushing to emergency rooms or to their physicians' offices for what they believe are heart attacks. Unfortunately, because many of the symptoms mimic various medical disorders, a correct diagnosis may take years in spite of costly medical tests that produce normal results (Meuret, Kroll, & Ritz, 2017). According to the *DSM–5* diagnostic criteria, a person has panic disorder only if he or she experiences recurrent unexpected attacks and reports significant anxiety about having another attack.

A disorder that sometimes co-occurs with panic disorder is **agoraphobia**, *a specific phobia involving a fear of public places.* Many people with agoraphobia, including Wesley, are not frightened of public places in themselves; instead, they are afraid that something terrible will happen (e.g., panic symptoms) while they are in a public

panic disorder A disorder characterized by the sudden occurrence of multiple psychological and physiological symptoms that contribute to a feeling of stark terror.

agoraphobia A specific phobia involving a fear of public places.

Agoraphobia is the fear of being in public because something bad is going to happen and escape will not be possible. It may prevent a person from going outside at all.

LOLOSTOCK/SHUTTERSTOCK

place and that they will not be able to escape or get help. In severe cases, people who have agoraphobia are unable to leave home, sometimes for years.

As many as 4 in 10 people have had or will have at least one panic attack at some point in their lives (eMentalHealth.ca, 2019), typically during a period of intense stress (Telch, Lucas, & Nelson, 1989). An occasional episode is not sufficient for a diagnosis of panic disorder: The individual also has to experience significant dread and anxiety about having another attack. When this criterion is applied, approximately 5% of people will have diagnosable panic disorder sometime in their lives (Kessler et al., 2005b). Panic disorder is more prevalent among women (7%) than men (3%) (Kessler et al., 2012). Family studies suggest some hereditary component to panic disorder, with 30 to 40% of the variance in liability for developing panic disorder attributed to genetic influence (Hettema, Neale, & Kendler, 2001).

In an effort to understand the role that physiological arousal plays in panic attacks, researchers have compared the responses of experimental participants with and without panic disorder to *sodium lactate,* a chemical that produces rapid, shallow breathing and heart palpitations. Those with panic disorder were found to be acutely sensitive to the chemical; within a few minutes after its being administered, 60 to 90% experienced a panic attack. Participants without the disorder rarely responded to this substance with a panic attack (Liebowitz et al., 1985).

The difference in responses to this chemical may be due to differing interpretations of physiological signs of anxiety; that is, people who experience panic attacks may be hypersensitive to physiological signs of anxiety, which they interpret as having disastrous consequences for their well-being. Supporting this cognitive explanation is research showing that people who are high in anxiety sensitivity (i.e., they believe that bodily arousal and other symptoms of anxiety can have dire consequences) have an elevated risk for experiencing panic attacks (Olatunji & Wolitzky-Taylor, 2009). Thus, panic attacks may be conceptualized as a "fear of fear" itself.

Generalized Anxiety Disorder

Gina, a 24-year-old woman, began to experience debilitating anxiety during her first year of graduate school for clinical psychology. At first, she worried about whether she was sufficiently completing all of her assignments, then she worried about whether her clients were improving or if she was actually making them worse. Soon her concerns spread to focus on her own health (did she have an undiagnosed medical problem?) as well as that of her boyfriend (he smokes cigarettes . . . perhaps he is currently giving himself cancer?). She worried incessantly for a year and ultimately took time off from school to get treatment for her worries, extreme agitation, fatigue, and feelings of sadness and depression.

Gina's symptoms are typical of **generalized anxiety disorder (GAD)**—called *generalized* because the unrelenting worries are not focused on any particular threat; they are, in fact, often exaggerated and irrational. GAD is *chronic excessive worry accompanied by three or more of the following symptoms: restlessness, fatigue, concentration problems, irritability, muscle tension, and sleep disturbance.* In people suffering from GAD, the uncontrollable worrying produces a sense of loss of control that can so erode self-confidence that simple decisions seem fraught with dire consequences. For example, Gina struggled to make everyday decisions as basic as which vegetables to buy at the market and how to prepare her dinner.

Approximately 1 in 16 people in the United States and Canada suffer from GAD at some time in their lives (Kessler et al., 2005a; Canadian Psychological Association, 2015), with women experiencing GAD at higher rates (1 in 12) than men (1 in 20) (Kessler et al., 2012). Research suggests that both biological and psychological factors contribute to the risk of GAD. Family studies indicate a mild to modest level of heritability (Norrholm & Ressler, 2009). Although identical twin studies of GAD are rare, some evidence suggests that, compared with fraternal twins, identical twins have modestly higher *concordance rates* (the percentage of pairs that share the characteristic) (Hettema et al., 2001). Moreover, teasing out environmental versus personality influences on concordance rates is quite difficult.

Biological explanations of GAD suggest that neurotransmitter imbalances may play a role in the disorder. The precise nature of this imbalance is not clear. *Benzodiazepines* (a class of sedative drugs such as Valium and Librium, discussed in the Treatment chapter) that appear to stimulate the neurotransmitter *gamma-aminobutyric acid (GABA)* can sometimes reduce the symptoms of GAD, suggesting a potential role for this neurotransmitter in the occurrence of GAD. However, other drugs that do not directly affect GABA levels (e.g., buspirone and antidepressants such as Prozac) can also be helpful in the treatment of GAD (Strawn et al., 2018). To complicate matters, these different prescription drugs do not help all individuals and, in some cases, can produce serious side effects and dependency.

Psychological explanations focus on anxiety-provoking situations in explaining high levels of GAD. The condition is especially prevalent among people who have low incomes, live in large cities, and/or face environments that are rendered unpredictable by political and economic strife. The relatively high rates of GAD among women may also be related to stress because women are more likely than men to live in poverty, experience discrimination, or be subjected to sexual or physical abuse (e.g., Dworkin et al., 2017). Research shows that unpredictable traumatic experiences in childhood increase the risk of developing GAD, and this evidence also

generalized anxiety disorder (GAD) A disorder characterized by chronic excessive worry accompanied by three or more of the following symptoms: restlessness, fatigue, concentration problems, irritability, muscle tension, and sleep disturbance.

The experience of major stressful life events, such as losing a job or a home, can lead to generalized anxiety disorder, a condition characterized by chronic, excessive worry.

JOHN HENLEY/GETTY IMAGES

supports the idea that stressful experiences play a role (Bandoli et al., 2017). Risk of GAD also increases following the experience of a loss or situation associated with future perceived danger (Kendler et al., 2003), such as loss of a home due to foreclosure (McLaughlin et al., 2012). Still, many people who might be expected to develop GAD don't, supporting the diathesis–stress notion that personal vulnerability must also be a key factor in this disorder.

Build to the Outcomes

1. What is an anxiety disorder?
2. When is anxiety helpful? When is it harmful?
3. What is a phobic disorder? What are the different types?
4. Why might we be predisposed to certain phobias?
5. What is a panic disorder?
6. What is it about public places that many people with agoraphobia fear?
7. What is generalized anxiety disorder (GAD)? What factors contribute to it?

Obsessive-Compulsive Disorder: Persistent Thoughts and Repetitive Behaviours

You may have had an irresistible urge to go back to check whether you actually locked the door or turned off the oven, even when you're pretty sure that you did. Or you may have been unable to resist engaging in some superstitious behaviour, such as not walking under a ladder or stepping on a crack. For some people, such thoughts and actions spiral out of control and become a serious problem.

Karen, a 34-year-old with four children, sought treatment after several months of experiencing intrusive, repetitive thoughts in which she imagined that one or more of her children was having a serious accident. In addition, an extensive series of protective counting rituals hampered her daily routine. For example, when grocery shopping, Karen had the feeling that if she selected the first item (say, a box of cereal) on a shelf, something terrible would happen to her oldest child. If she selected the second item, some unknown disaster would befall her second child, and so on for all four children. The children's ages were also important. The sixth item in a row, for example, was associated with her youngest child, who was 6 years old.

Karen's preoccupation with numbers extended to other activities, most notably, the pattern in which she smoked cigarettes and drank coffee. If she had one cigarette, she felt that she had to smoke at least four in a row or one of her children would be harmed in some way. If she drank one cup of coffee, she felt compelled to drink four more to protect her children from harm. She acknowledged that her counting rituals were irrational, but she became extremely anxious when she tried to stop (Oltmanns, Neale, & Davison, 1991).

Karen's symptoms are typical of **obsessive-compulsive disorder (OCD)**, in which *repetitive, intrusive thoughts (obsessions) and ritualistic behaviours (compulsions) designed to fend off those thoughts interfere significantly with an individual's functioning*. Anxiety plays a role in this disorder because the obsessive thoughts typically produce anxiety, and the compulsive behaviours are performed to reduce it. In OCD, these obsessions and compulsions are intense, frequent, and experienced as irrational and excessive. Attempts to cope with the obsessive thoughts by trying to suppress or ignore them are of little or no benefit. In fact (as discussed in the Consciousness chapter), thought suppression can backfire, increasing the frequency and intensity of

Learning Outcome

- Describe the symptoms and potential causes of OCD.

obsessive-compulsive disorder (OCD) A disorder in which repetitive, intrusive thoughts (obsessions) and ritualistic behaviours (compulsions) designed to fend off those thoughts interfere significantly with an individual's functioning.

CHARLES SYKES/AP IMAGES

Howie Mandel is a successful Canadian comedian, but his struggle with OCD is no laughing matter. Like approximately 2% of people in Canada and the United States, Mandel struggles with extreme fears of being contaminated by germs and engages in repeated checking and cleaning behaviours that often interfere with his daily life. He has spoken publicly about his struggles with OCD and about the importance of seeking effective treatment for this condition.

the obsessive thoughts (Wegner, 1989; Wenzlaff & Wegner, 2000). Despite anxiety's role, *DSM–5* classifies OCD separately from anxiety disorders, because researchers believe that this disorder has a distinct cause and is maintained via different neural circuitry in the brain than the anxiety disorders.

Although 2 in 7 adults in the United States and Canada report experiencing obsessions or compulsions at some point in their lives (Ruscio et al., 2010; Canadian Psychological Association, 2014), only 1 in 50 will develop actual OCD (Kessler et al., 2005a). Similar to anxiety disorders, rates of OCD are higher among women than men (Kessler et al., 2012). Among those with OCD, the most common obsessions and compulsions involve checking (79% of those with OCD), ordering (57%), moral concerns (43%), and contamination (26%) (Ruscio et al., 2010). Although compulsive behaviour is always excessive, it can vary considerably in intensity and frequency. For example, fear of contamination may lead to 15 minutes of hand washing in some individuals, whereas others may need to spend hours with disinfectants and extremely hot water, scrubbing their hands until they bleed.

The obsessions that plague individuals with OCD typically derive from concerns that could pose a real threat (such as contamination or disease), which supports preparedness theory. Thinking repeatedly about whether we've left a stove burner on when we leave the house makes sense, after all, if we want to return to a house that is not "well done." The concept of preparedness places OCD in the same evolutionary context as phobias (Szechtman & Woody, 2006). However, as with phobias, we need to consider other factors to explain why fears that may have served an evolutionary purpose can become so distorted and maladaptive.

OCD has been recognized by clinicians for more than 200 years, but the precise biological mechanisms driving this behaviour have eluded scientific understanding (Stone, 1997). Recent family and twin studies indicate a moderate to strong genetic heritability for OCD (~50%), which is even stronger for OCD traits (~70%) (Burston et al., 2018). But what exactly is passed on genetically that contributes to the behaviours observed in those with OCD? Brain-imaging research over the past few decades suggests that one key component of this disorder is abnormally high activity or connectedness between a specific brain circuit involved in habitual behaviour: the cortico-striato-thalamo-cortical loop (which connects parts of the cortex with the striatum and thalamus) (Dougherty et al., 2018; Milad & Rauch, 2012). Treatments for OCD that decrease the activity of this specific brain circuit using brain surgery or brain stimulation have shown some promise, but they are still being developed and tested (see the Treatment chapter for more on these approaches).

Build to the Outcomes

1. What is obsessive-compulsive disorder (OCD)?
2. How effective is willful effort in curing OCD?
3. What factors may contribute to OCD?

Posttraumatic Stress Disorder: Distress and Avoidance After a Trauma

Learning Outcome

• Describe the symptoms and potential causes of PTSD.

Psychological reactions to traumatic or stressful events can lead to stressor-related disorders. For example, a person who lives through a terrifying and uncontrollable experience may develop **posttraumatic stress disorder (PTSD)**, which is characterized by *chronic physiological arousal, recurrent unwanted thoughts or images of the trauma, and avoidance of things that call the traumatic event to mind.*

Psychological disorders following exposure to traumatic events are perhaps nowhere more apparent than in war. Many soldiers returning from combat experience symptoms of PTSD, including flashbacks of battle, exaggerated anxiety and startle reactions, and even medical conditions that do not arise from physical damage (e.g., paralysis or chronic fatigue). Most of these symptoms are normal, appropriate responses to horrifying events, and for most people, the symptoms subside with time. In PTSD, however, the symptoms can last much longer. For example, more than 40,000 Canadian Armed Forces members served in Afghanistan between 2001 and 2014, and approximately 1 in 6 of these members subsequently received support for PTSD (Global News, 2019). The effects of PTSD are now recognized not only among victims, witnesses, and perpetrators of war but also among ordinary people who are traumatized by terrible events in civilian life. A recent literature review involving 68,000 people in 24 different countries—including Canada and the United States—reveals that 7 in 10 people experience trauma during their lives (Kessler et al., 2017). A majority of these are unfortunately normal life events such as experiencing the unexpected death of a loved one or witnessing death. Four out of every 100 people who experience trauma will develop PTSD, with the rate depending on the type of trauma (Kessler et al., 2017). Intimate partner violence and sexual violence carry the highest risks (Kessler et al., 2017), which may be part of the reason why the incidence of PTSD is generally higher in women than in men (Kessler et al., 2017).

Research using brain-imaging techniques to examine brain structure and function has identified important neural correlates of PTSD. Specifically, those with PTSD show heightened activity in the amygdala (a region associated with the evaluation of threatening information and fear conditioning), decreased activity in the medial prefrontal cortex (a region important in the extinction of fear conditioning), and a smaller-size hippocampus (the part of the brain most linked with memory, as described in the Neuroscience and Behaviour and Memory chapters) (Shin, Rauch, & Pitman, 2006).

Of course, an important question is whether people whose brains have these characteristics are at greater risk for PTSD if traumatized, or if these characteristics are the consequences of trauma in some people. For instance, does reduced hippocampal volume reflect a preexisting condition that makes the brain sensitive to stress? Or does the traumatic stress itself somehow kill nerve cells? One important study suggests that although a group of combat veterans with PTSD showed reduced hippocampal volume, so did the identical (monozygotic) twins of those men (see **FIGURE 15.3**), even though the twins had never had any combat exposure or developed PTSD (Gilbertson et al., 2002). This suggests that the veterans' reduced hippocampal volumes weren't caused by the combat exposure; instead, both these veterans and their twin brothers might have had a smaller hippocampus to begin with, a preexisting condition that made them susceptible to developing PTSD when they were later exposed to trauma.

The South-West Asia Service Medal was introduced in 2002 to recognize Canadian military personnel who have served in Afghanistan. Many of these personnel have since experienced PTSD.

posttraumatic stress disorder (PTSD) A disorder characterized by chronic physiological arousal, recurrent unwanted thoughts or images of the trauma, and avoidance of things that call the traumatic event to mind.

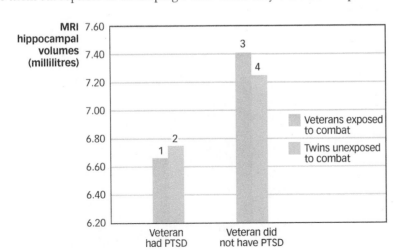

Figure 15.3

Hippocampal Volumes of War Veterans and Their Identical Twins Average hippocampal volumes for four groups of participants: (1) combat-exposed veterans who developed PTSD; (2) their combat-unexposed twins with no PTSD themselves; (3) combat-exposed veterans who never developed PTSD; and (4) their unexposed twins, also with no PTSD. Smaller hippocampal volumes were found for both the combat-exposed veterans with PTSD (Group 1) and their twins who had not been exposed to combat (Group 2), in contrast to veterans without PTSD (Group 3) and their twins (Group 4). This pattern of findings suggests that an inherited smaller hippocampus may make some people sensitive to conditions that cause PTSD (Gilbertson et al., 2002).

Build to the Outcomes

1. What is posttraumatic stress disorder (PTSD)?

2. How might brain structure and functioning be related to susceptibility to PTSD?

Depressive and Bipolar Disorders: Extreme Highs and Lows

Learning Outcomes

- Describe the symptoms of mood disorders, including depressive and bipolar disorders.

- Identify genetic and environmental factors that research indicates may be an influence in mood disorders.

You're probably in a mood right now. Maybe you're happy that it's almost time to get a snack or saddened by something you heard from a friend—or you may feel good or bad without having a clue why. As you learned in the Emotion and Motivation chapter, moods are relatively long-lasting, nonspecific emotional states—and *nonspecific* means we often may have no idea what has caused a mood. Changing moods lend variety to our experiences, like different-coloured lights shining on the stage as we play out our lives. However, for people like Robin Williams and others with mood disorders, moods can become so intense that they are pulled or pushed into life-threatening actions. **Mood disorders** are *mental disorders that have mood disturbance as their predominant feature* and take two main forms: *depression* (also called *unipolar depression*) and *bipolar disorder* (so named because people go from one end of the emotional pole [extreme depression] to the other [extreme mania]).

Depressive Disorders

Everyone feels sad, pessimistic, and unmotivated from time to time. For most people, these periods are relatively short lived and mild, but depression is much more than typical sadness. The experience of Mark, a 34-year-old man who visited his primary-care physician complaining of chronic fatigue, is fairly typical. During the visit, he mentioned difficulties falling asleep and staying asleep that left him chronically tired, so much so that he feared that maybe he had some kind of medical

mood disorders Mental disorders that have mood disturbance as their predominant feature.

The Blue Devils—!! George Cruikshank (1792–1878) portrayed a depressed man tormented by demons suggesting methods of suicide, harassing him as bill collectors, and forming a funeral procession.

'THE BLUE DEVILS!', PUBLISHED BY HANNAH HUMPHREY, 10TH JANUARY 1823 (COLOURED ENGRAVING)/CRUIKSHANK, GEORGE (1792–1878)/INDIVISION CHARMET/BIBLIOTHEQUE NATIONALE, PARIS, FRANCE/BRIDGEMAN IMAGES

problem. He complained that over the past 6 months, he no longer had the energy to exercise and had gained 10 pounds. He also lost all interest in going out with his friends or even talking to other people. Nothing he normally enjoyed, even sexual activity, gave him pleasure anymore; he had trouble concentrating and was forgetful, irritable, impatient, and frustrated. Mark's change in mood and behaviour, and the sense of hopelessness and weariness he felt, goes far beyond normal sadness. Instead, depressive disorders are dysfunctional and chronic, and they fall outside the range of socially or culturally expected responses.

Major depressive disorder (or **unipolar depression**), which we refer to here simply as "depression," is characterized by *a severely depressed mood and/or inability to experience pleasure that lasts 2 or more weeks and is accompanied by feelings of worthlessness, lethargy, and sleep and appetite disturbance.* In a related condition called **persistent depressive disorder**, *the same cognitive and bodily problems as in depression are present, but they are less severe and last longer, persisting for at least 2 years.* When both types co-occur, the resulting condition is called **double depression**, defined as *a moderately depressed mood that persists for at least 2 years and is punctuated by periods of major depression.*

Some people experience *recurrent depressive episodes in a seasonal pattern* that is commonly known as **seasonal affective disorder (SAD)**. In most cases, SAD episodes begin in fall or winter and remit in spring, in a pattern that is due to reduced levels of light over the colder seasons (Westrin & Lam, 2007). Nevertheless, recurrent summer depressive episodes have been reported. A winter-related pattern of depression appears to be more prevalent in higher latitudes.

Who Is at Risk?

Approximately 1 in 9 Canadians meets the criteria for depression at some point in their lives (Kessler et al., 2012; Pearson, Janz, & Ali, 2013). On average, major depression lasts about 12 weeks (Eaton et al., 2008). However, without treatment, approximately 80% of individuals will experience at least one recurrence of the disorder (Judd, 1997; Mueller et al., 1999). Compared with people who have a single episode, individuals with recurrent depression have more severe symptoms, higher rates of depression in their families, more suicide attempts, and higher rates of divorce (Merikangas, Wicki, & Angst, 1994).

Similar to that of anxiety disorders, the rate of depression is much higher in women (22%) than in men (14%) (Kessler et al., 2012). Socioeconomic standing has been

major depressive disorder (unipolar depression) A disorder characterized by a severely depressed mood and/or inability to experience pleasure that lasts 2 or more weeks and is accompanied by feelings of worthlessness, lethargy, and sleep and appetite disturbance.

persistent depressive disorder The same cognitive and bodily problems as in depression are present, but they are less severe and last longer, persisting for at least 2 years.

double depression A moderately depressed mood that persists for at least 2 years and is punctuated by periods of major depression.

seasonal affective disorder (SAD) Recurrent depressive episodes in a seasonal pattern.

Seasonal affective disorder is not merely having the blues because of the weather. It appears to be due to reduced exposure to light in the winter months.

Postpartum depression can strike women out of nowhere, often causing new mothers to feel extreme sadness, guilt, and disconnection, and even to experience serious thoughts of suicide. The actress Brooke Shields wrote about her experience with postpartum depression in a popular book on this condition.

invoked as an explanation for women's heightened risk: Their incomes are lower than those of men, and poverty could cause depression. Sex differences in hormones are another possibility: Estrogen, androgen, and progesterone influence depression; some women experience *postpartum depression* (depression following childbirth) due to changing hormone balances. It is also possible that the higher rate of depression in women reflects their greater willingness to face their depression and seek help, leading to higher rates of diagnosis (Nolen-Hoeksema, 2012). Women have a tendency to accept, disclose, and ruminate on their negative emotions, whereas men are more likely to deny negative emotions and engage in self-distractions such as work and drinking alcohol.

Neurotransmitters and Genes Play a Role, and So Does Stress

Beginning in the 1950s, researchers noticed that drugs that increased levels of the neurotransmitters norepinephrine and serotonin could sometimes reduce depression. This observation suggested that depression might be caused by an absolute or relative depletion of these neurotransmitters, which sparked a revolution in the pharmacological treatment of depression (Schildkraut, 1965) and led to the development and widespread use of popular prescription drugs such as Prozac and Zoloft, which increase the availability of serotonin in the brain. Further research has shown, however, that reduced levels of these neurotransmitters cannot be the whole story regarding the causes of depression. For example, some studies have found *increases* in norepinephrine activity among depressed individuals (Thase & Howland, 1995). Moreover, even though these antidepressant medications change neurochemical transmission in less than a day, they typically take at least 2 weeks to relieve depressive symptoms. In many cases, they are not effective in decreasing depressive symptoms. A biochemical model of depression has yet to be developed that accounts for all the evidence.

As with many other types of mental disorders, depression shows moderate heritability, with heritability estimates increasing as a function of severity. For instance, a relatively large study of nearly 500,000 people found that the heritability estimate for less severe depression was approximately 35%, whereas for severe depression it was close to 50% (Corfield et al., 2017).

Newer biological models of depression have tried to understand depression using a diathesis–stress framework. For example, Avshalom Caspi and his colleagues (2003) proposed, and reported, that a certain genetic diathesis related to the activity of the neurotransmitter serotonin is much more likely to lead to depression among those with major stressful life events. This appeared to be evidence that nature and nurture interact to influence brain structure, function, and chemistry in depression and was widely celebrated by the field. However, subsequent larger studies and meta-analyses combining such studies have failed to support such a finding (Culverhouse et al., 2017). Of course, this is how science works: initial discoveries must be consistently replicated in follow-up studies before they become accepted pieces of our scientific understanding.

Research also has begun to tell us what parts of the brain show abnormalities in depression. For instance, some important findings came out of a recent meta-analysis (which is a quantitative synthesis of the results of many individual studies) of 24 brain-imaging studies. Results showed that when viewing negative stimuli (words or images), people suffering from depression showed both increased activity in regions of the brain associated with processing emotional information and decreased activity in areas associated with cognitive control (see **FIGURE 15.4**) (Hamilton et al., 2012).

Of course, this is not the whole picture; these findings don't explain all of the symptoms seen in depression, why and when depression comes and goes, or how treatment works. Given that depression arises not from a single gene or brain region, but rather from the interactions of different biological systems that each give rise to the different psychological traits seen in depression, it will likely be many years before we fully understand the biological causes of this disorder (Young et al., 2016).

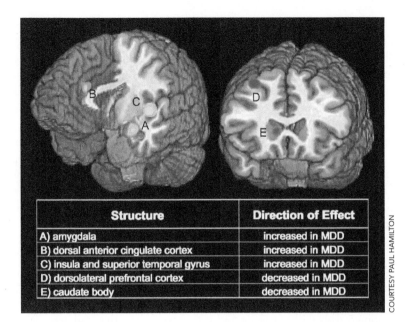

Structure	Direction of Effect
A) amygdala	increased in MDD
B) dorsal anterior cingulate cortex	increased in MDD
C) insula and superior temporal gyrus	increased in MDD
D) dorsolateral prefrontal cortex	decreased in MDD
E) caudate body	decreased in MDD

COURTESY PAUL HAMILTON

Figure 15.4

The Brain and Depression When presented with negative information, people with depression show increased activation in regions of the brain associated with emotional processing, such as the amygdala, insula, and dorsal anterior cingulate cortex (ACC), and decreased activity in regions associated with cognitive control, such as the dorsal striatum and dorsolateral prefrontal cortex (DLPFC) (Hamilton et al., 2012).

Negative Thoughts Contribute to Depression

If optimists see the world through rose-coloured glasses, people who suffer from depression tend to view the world through dark grey lenses. Their negative cognitive style is remarkably consistent and, some argue, begins in childhood with experiences that create a pattern of negative self-thoughts (Blatt & Homann, 1992; Gibb, Alloy, & Tierney, 2001). One of the first theorists to emphasize the role of thought in depression, Aaron T. Beck (1967), noted that his depressed patients distorted perceptions of their experiences and embraced dysfunctional attitudes that promoted and maintained negative mood states. His observations led him to develop a *cognitive model of depression,* which states that biases in how information is attended to, processed, and remembered lead to and maintain depression.

Elaborating on this initial idea, researchers proposed a theory of depression that emphasizes the role of people's negative inferences about the causes of their experiences (Abramson, Seligman, & Teasdale, 1978). **Helplessness theory**, which is a part of the cognitive model of depression, maintains that *individuals who are prone to depression automatically attribute negative experiences to causes that are internal (i.e., their own fault), stable (i.e., unlikely to change), and global (i.e., widespread).* For example, a student at risk for depression might view a bad grade on a math test as a sign of low intelligence (internal) that will never change (stable) and that will lead to failure in all his or her future endeavors (global). In contrast, a student without this tendency might have the opposite response, attributing the grade to something external (poor teaching), unstable (a missed study session), and/or specific (boring subject).

The relationship between one's perceptions and depression has been further developed and supported over the past several decades. The update to Beck's cognitive model suggests that due to a combination of a genetic vulnerability and negative early life events, people with depression have developed a negative *schema* (described in the Development chapter). This negative schema is characterized by biases in:

- interpretations of information (a tendency to interpret neutral information negatively—seeing the world through grey glasses)
- attention (trouble disengaging from negative information)
- memory (better recall of negative information) (Gotlib & Joormann, 2010)

MARY EVANS PICTURE LIBRARY/ALAMY

The cognitive model of depression is based on approaches to thinking developed by the Stoic philosophers of ancient Greece and Rome. Epictetus's famous quote, "Men are disturbed not by things, but by the principles and notions which they form concerning things," is commonly cited by cognitive theorists as a guiding principle of the cognitive model of depression.

helplessness theory The idea that individuals who are prone to depression automatically attribute negative experiences to causes that are internal (i.e., their own fault), stable (i.e., unlikely to change), and global (i.e., widespread).

For example, a student at risk for depression who gets a bad grade on a test might interpret a well-intentioned comment from the teacher ("Good job on the test") negatively ("She's being sarcastic!"); might have trouble forgetting about both the test score and the perceived negative comment; and might have better memory about this test in the future ("Sure, I did well on my English exam, but don't forget about that bad math test last month"). The presence of these biases may help to explain the internal, stable, and global attributions seen in depression. In addition, recent research suggests that some of the differences in brain structure and function seen in those with depression can help to explain some of these cognitive biases. For instance, people with depression show abnormalities in parts of the brain that are involved in attention and memory, especially when presented with negative information (Disner et al., 2011). Although we don't fully understand the causes of depression, pieces of the puzzle are being discovered and fit together even as you read this.

Bipolar Disorder

If depression is distressing and painful, would the opposite extreme be better? Not for Julie, a 20-year-old American university student. When first seen by a clinician, Julie had gone 5 days without sleep and was extremely active and expressing bizarre thoughts and ideas. She proclaimed to friends that she did not menstruate because she was "of a third sex, a gender above the two human sexes." She claimed to be a "superwoman," capable of avoiding human sexuality and yet still able to give birth. Preoccupied with the politics of global disarmament, she felt that she had switched souls with a prominent elected official from her state, had tapped into his thoughts and memories, and could save the world from nuclear destruction. She began to campaign for an elected position in the U.S. government (even though no elections were scheduled at that time). Worried that she would forget some of her thoughts, she had been leaving hundreds of notes about her ideas and activities everywhere, including on the walls and furniture of her bedroom (Vitkus, 1999).

In addition to her manic episodes, Julie had a history of depression. The diagnostic label for this constellation of symptoms is **bipolar disorder**, *a condition characterized by cycles of abnormal, persistent high mood (mania) and low mood (depression).* In about two-thirds of people with bipolar disorder, manic episodes immediately precede or immediately follow depressive episodes (Whybrow, 1997). The depressive phase of bipolar disorder is often clinically indistinguishable from major depression (Johnson, Cuellar, & Miller, 2009). In the manic phase, which must last at least 1 week to meet *DSM* requirements, mood can be elevated, expansive, or irritable. Other prominent symptoms include grandiosity, decreased need for sleep, talkativeness, racing thoughts, distractibility, and reckless behaviour (such as compulsive gambling, sexual indiscretions, and unrestrained spending sprees). Psychotic features such as hallucinations (erroneous perceptions) and delusions (erroneous beliefs) may be present, so the disorder can be misdiagnosed as schizophrenia (described in a later section of this chapter).

Here's how Kay Redfield Jamison (1993, p. 67), in *An Unquiet Mind: A Memoir of Madness,* described her own experience with bipolar disorder.

> There is a particular kind of pain, elation, loneliness, and terror involved in this kind of madness. When you're high it's tremendous. The ideas and feelings are fast and frequent like shooting stars, and you follow them until you find better and brighter ones. . . . But, somewhere, this changes. The fast ideas are far too fast, and there are far too many; overwhelming confusion replaces clarity. Memory goes. Humour and absorption on friends' faces are replaced by fear and concern. Everything previously moving with the grain is now against—you are irritable, angry, frightened, uncontrollable, and enmeshed totally in the blackest caves of the mind. You never knew those caves were there. It will never end, for madness carves its own reality.

The psychologist Kay Redfield Jamison has written several best-selling books about her own struggles with bipolar disorder.

LEONARDO CENDAMO/GETTY IMAGES

bipolar disorder A condition characterized by cycles of abnormal, persistent high mood (mania) and low mood (depression).

Who Is at Risk?

The lifetime risk for bipolar disorder is about 1 in 40 and does not differ between men and women (Kessler et al., 2012). Bipolar disorder is typically a recurrent condition, with approximately 90% of afflicted people suffering from several episodes over a lifetime (Coryell et al., 1995). About 10% of people with bipolar disorder have *rapid cycling bipolar disorder,* characterized by at least four mood episodes (either manic or depressive) every year. This form of the disorder is particularly difficult to treat (Post et al., 2008). Rapid cycling is more common in women than in men and is sometimes precipitated by taking certain kinds of antidepressant drugs (Liebenluft, 1996; Whybrow, 1997). Unfortunately, bipolar disorder tends to be persistent. In one study, 24% of the participants had relapsed within 6 months of recovery from an episode, and 77% had at least one new episode within 4 years of recovery (Coryell et al., 1995).

Some researchers have suggested that people with psychotic and mood (especially bipolar) disorders have higher creativity and intellectual ability (Andreasen, 2011). In bipolar disorder, this suggestion goes, before the mania becomes too pronounced, the energy, grandiosity, and ambition that it supplies may help people achieve great things. Notable individuals thought to have had the disorder include Isaac Newton, Vincent van Gogh, Abraham Lincoln, Ernest Hemingway, Virginia Woolf, Winston Churchill, and Florence Nightingale.

Genetics and Life Situation Play a Role

Among the various mental disorders, bipolar disorder has one of the highest rates of heritability, with concordance from 40 to 70% for identical twins and 10% for fraternal twins (Craddock & Jones, 1999). Like most other disorders, bipolar disorder is likely *polygenic,* arising from the interaction of multiple genes that combine to create the symptoms observed in those with this disorder; however, these genes have been difficult to identify. Adding to the complexity, there also is evidence of *pleiotropic effects,* in which one gene influences a person's susceptibility to multiple disorders. For instance, one recent study revealed a shared genetic vulnerability for bipolar disorder and schizophrenia. The genes linked to both disorders are associated with compromised abilities both in filtering unnecessary information and in recognition memory, as well as problems with dopamine and serotonin transmission—factors present in both types of disorders (Huang et al., 2010).

A follow-up study examining more than 60,000 people revealed that common genetic risk factors are associated with bipolar disorder and schizophrenia, as well as major depression, autism spectrum disorder, and attention-deficit/hyperactivity disorder. These disorders share overlapping symptoms such as problems with mood regulation, cognitive impairments, and social withdrawal (Cross-Disorder Group of the Psychiatric Genomics Consortium, 2013). Findings like these are exciting because they help us begin to understand why we see similar symptoms in people with what we previously thought were unrelated disorders. Although some genetic links have been made, we currently lack an understanding of how different biological factors work together to cause the symptoms observed in bipolar and other disorders.

There is growing evidence that the epigenetic changes you learned about in the Neuroscience and Behaviour chapter can help explain how genetic risk factors influence the development of bipolar and related disorders. Remember how rat pups whose moms spent less time licking and grooming them experienced epigenetic changes (decreased DNA methylation) that led to a poorer stress response? As you might expect, these same kinds of epigenetic effects seem to help explain who develops symptoms of mental disorders and who doesn't. For instance, studies examining monozygotic twin pairs (identical twins, who share 100% of their DNA) in which one develops bipolar disorder or schizophrenia and one doesn't, reveal significant epigenetic differences between the two, with decreased methylation at genetic locations known to be important in brain development and the occurrence of bipolar disorders and schizophrenia (Dempster et al., 2011; Labrie, Pai, & Petronis, 2012).

Stressful life experiences often precede manic and depressive episodes (S. L. Johnson et al., 2008). One study found that severely stressed individuals took an average of three times longer to recover from an episode than did individuals not affected by stress (Johnson & Miller, 1997). The stress–disorder relationship is not simple, however: High levels of stress have less impact on people with extraverted personalities than on those with more introverted personalities (Swendsen et al., 1995). Personality characteristics such as neuroticism and conscientiousness have also been found to predict increases in bipolar symptoms over time (Lozano & Johnson, 2001). Finally, people living with family members who are high in **expressed emotion**, which in this context is *a measure of how much hostility, criticism, and emotional over-involvement people communicate when speaking about a family member with a mental disorder*, are more likely to relapse than are people with supportive families (Miklowitz & Johnson, 2006). This is true not just of those with bipolar disorder: Expressed emotion is associated with higher rates of relapse across a wide range of mental disorders (Hooley, 2007).

expressed emotion A measure of how much hostility, criticism, and emotional overinvolvement people communicate when speaking about a family member with a mental disorder.

Build to the Outcomes

1. What is a mood disorder?
2. What is the difference between depression and sadness?
3. What are the types of depressive disorders?
4. What factors may explain why women experience higher rates of depression than men?
5. How does the diathesis–stress framework help explain depression?
6. What is the helplessness theory?
7. What elements of the negative schema characterize the outlook of some people with depression?
8. What is bipolar disorder?
9. Why is bipolar disorder sometimes misdiagnosed as schizophrenia?
10. How does our understanding of epigenetics further our understanding of genetic risk factors?
11. How does stress relate to manic–depressive episodes?
12. Define *expressed emotion* in the context of mood disorders.

Schizophrenia and Other Psychotic Disorders: Losing the Grasp on Reality

Learning Outcomes

- Compare the negative, positive, and cognitive symptoms of schizophrenia.
- Describe the biological factors contributing to schizophrenia.
- Explain the evidence for the influence of environmental factors.

Margaret, a 39-year-old mother, believed that God was punishing her for marrying a man she did not love and bringing two children into the world. As her punishment, God had made her and her children immortal so that they would have to suffer in their unhappy home life forever—a realization that came to her one evening when she was washing dishes and saw a fork lying across a knife in the shape of a cross. Margaret found further support for her belief in two pieces of evidence: First, a local television station was rerunning old episodes of *The Honeymooners*, a 1950s situation comedy in which the main characters often argue and shout at each other. She saw this as a sign from God that her own marital conflict would go on forever. Second, she believed (falsely) that the pupils of her children's eyes were fixed in size and would neither dilate nor constrict—a sign of their immortality.

At home, she would lock herself in her room for hours and sometimes days. The week before her diagnosis, she kept her 7-year-old son home from school so that he could join her and his 4-year-old sister in reading aloud from the Bible (Oltmanns et al., 1991). Margaret was suffering from the best-known, most widely studied psychotic disorder: schizophrenia, one of the most mystifying and devastating of all the mental disorders. Many people with this disorder experience a lifetime of suffering and impairment, but see Other Voices: Successful and Schizophrenic for a discussion of the fact that many with this disorder have very successful careers and fulfilling lives. A review of the symptoms of this disorder make clear why this condition can be so distressing and impairing.

Symptoms and Types of Schizophrenia

Schizophrenia is a psychotic disorder (*psychosis* is a break from reality) characterized by *the profound disruption of basic psychological processes; a distorted perception of reality; altered or blunted emotion; and disturbances in thought, motivation, and behaviour.* Traditionally, schizophrenia was regarded primarily as a disturbance of thought and perception, in which the sense of reality becomes severely distorted and confused. However, this condition is now understood to take different forms affecting a wide range of functions. According to the *DSM–5*, schizophrenia is diagnosed when two or more symptoms emerge during a continuous period of at least 1 month, with signs of the disorder persisting for at least 6 months. The symptoms of schizophrenia often are separated into *positive, negative,* and *cognitive symptoms.*

Positive symptoms of schizophrenia include *thoughts and behaviours, such as delusions and hallucinations, not seen in those without the disorder:*

- **Hallucinations** are *false perceptual experiences that have a compelling sense of being real despite the absence of external stimulation.* The perceptual disturbances associated with schizophrenia can include hearing, seeing, smelling, or having a tactile sensation of things that are not there. Schizophrenic hallucinations are often auditory (e.g., hearing voices that no one else can hear). Among people with schizophrenia, some 65% report hearing voices repeatedly (Frith & Fletcher, 1995). The British psychiatrist Henry Maudsley (1886) long ago proposed that these voices are in fact produced in the mind of the person with schizophrenia, and recent research substantiates his idea. In one PET imaging study (conducted, coincidentally, by researchers in the hospital named for Henry Maudsley in London, England), auditory hallucinations were accompanied by activation in Broca's area (McGuire, Shah, & Murray, 1993). As discussed in the Neuroscience and Behaviour chapter, Broca's area in the left frontal lobe is involved in speech production. Unfortunately, the voices heard in schizophrenia seldom sound like the self or like a kindly uncle offering advice. They command, scold, suggest bizarre actions, or offer snide comments. One individual reported a voice saying, "He's getting up now. He's going to wash. It's about time" (Frith & Fletcher, 1995).

- **Delusions** are *false beliefs, often bizarre and grandiose, that are maintained in spite of their irrationality.* For example, an individual with schizophrenia may believe that he or she is Jesus Christ, Napoleon, Joan of Arc, or some other well-known person. Such delusions of identity have helped foster the misconception that schizophrenia involves multiple personalities. However, adopted identities in schizophrenia do not alternate, exhibit amnesia for each other, or otherwise "split." Delusions of persecution are also common. Some individuals believe that the CIA, demons, extraterrestrials, or other malevolent forces are conspiring to harm them or control their minds, which may represent an attempt to make sense of the tormenting delusions (Roberts, 1991). People with schizophrenia have little or no insight into their disordered perceptual and thought processes (Karow et al., 2007). Without understanding that they have

Those suffering from schizophrenia often experience hallucinations and delusions, unable to determine what is real and what their own minds have created. The experience of John Nash, a Nobel Prize–winning economist with schizophrenia, was depicted in the book and movie *A Beautiful Mind.*

schizophrenia A disorder characterized by the profound disruption of basic psychological processes; a distorted perception of reality; altered or blunted emotion; and disturbances in thought, motivation, and behaviour.

positive symptoms Thoughts and behaviours, such as delusions and hallucinations, present in schizophrenia but not seen in those without the disorder.

hallucination A false perceptual experience that has a compelling sense of being real despite the absence of external stimulation.

delusion A false belief, often bizarre and grandiose, that is maintained in spite of its irrationality.

Other Voices | Successful and Schizophrenic

This chapter describes what we know about the characteristics and causes of mental disorders, and the next chapter describes how these disorders are commonly treated. For some of the more severe disorders, such as schizophrenia, the picture does not look good. People diagnosed with schizophrenia often are informed that it is a lifelong condition; and although current treatments show some effectiveness in decreasing the delusional thinking and hallucinations associated with schizophrenia, people with this disorder often are unable to hold down a full-time job, maintain healthy relationships, or achieve a high quality of life.

Elyn Saks is one such person. She received a diagnosis of schizophrenia and was informed of this prognosis. She described what happened next in a longer version of the following article, which appeared in the *New York Times*.

> Thirty years ago, I was given a diagnosis of schizophrenia. My prognosis was "grave": I would never live independently, hold a job, find a loving partner, get married. My home would be a board-and-care facility, my days spent watching TV in a day room with other people debilitated by mental illness. . . .
>
> Then I made a decision. I would write the narrative of my life. Today I am a chaired professor at the University of Southern California Gould School of Law. I have an adjunct appointment in the department of psychiatry at the medical school of the University of California, San Diego. The MacArthur Foundation gave me a genius grant.
>
> Although I fought my diagnosis for many years, I came to accept that I have schizophrenia and will be in treatment the rest of my life. . . . What I refused to accept was my prognosis.
>
> Conventional psychiatric thinking and its diagnostic categories say that people like me don't exist. Either I don't have schizophrenia (please tell that to the delusions crowding my mind), or I couldn't have accomplished what I have (please tell that to U.S.C.'s committee on faculty affairs). But I do, and I have. And I have undertaken research with colleagues at U.S.C. and U.C.L.A. to show that I am not alone. There are others with schizophrenia and such active symptoms as delusions and hallucinations who have significant academic and professional achievements.
>
> Over the last few years, my colleagues . . . and I have gathered 20 research subjects with high-functioning schizophrenia in Los Angeles. They suffered from symptoms like mild delusions or hallucinatory behavior. Their average age was 40. Half were male, half female, and more than half were minorities. All had high school diplomas, and a majority either had or were working toward college or graduate degrees. They were graduate students, managers, technicians and professionals, including a doctor, lawyer, psychologist and chief executive of a nonprofit group. At the same time, most were unmarried and childless, which is consistent with their diagnoses. . . . More than three-quarters had been hospitalized between two and five times because of their illness, while three had never been admitted.
>
> How had these people with schizophrenia managed to succeed in their studies and at such high-level jobs? We learned that, in addition to medication and therapy, all the participants had developed techniques to keep their schizophrenia at bay. For some, these techniques were cognitive. An educator with a master's degree said he had learned to face his hallucinations and ask, "What's the evidence for that? Or is it just a perception problem?" Another participant said, "I hear derogatory voices all the time. . . . You just gotta blow them off." . . .
>
> Other techniques that our participants cited included controlling sensory inputs. For some, this meant keeping their living space simple (bare walls, no TV, only quiet music), while for others, it meant distracting music. "I'll listen to loud music if I don't want to hear things," said a participant who is a certified nurse's assistant. Still others mentioned exercise, a healthy diet, avoiding alcohol and getting enough sleep. . . .
>
> One of the most frequently mentioned techniques that helped our research participants manage their symptoms was work. "Work has been an important part of who I am," said an educator in our group. "When you become useful to an organization and feel respected in that organization, there's a certain value in belonging there." This person works on the weekends too because of "the distraction factor." In other words, by engaging in work, the crazy stuff often recedes to the sidelines. . . .
>
> That is why it is so distressing when doctors tell their patients not to expect or pursue fulfilling careers. Far too often, the conventional psychiatric approach to mental illness is to see clusters of symptoms that characterize people. Accordingly, many psychiatrists hold the view that treating symptoms with medication is treating mental illness. But this fails to take into account individuals' strengths and capabilities, leading mental health professionals to underestimate what their patients can hope to achieve in the world. . . . A recent *New York Times Magazine* article described a new company that hires high-functioning adults with autism, taking advantage of their unusual memory skills and attention to detail. . . .
>
> An approach that looks for individual strengths, in addition to considering symptoms, could help dispel the pessimism surrounding mental illness. Finding "the wellness within the illness," as one person with schizophrenia said, should be a therapeutic goal. Doctors should urge their patients to develop relationships and engage in meaningful work. They should encourage patients to find their own repertory of techniques to manage their symptoms and aim for a quality of life as they define it. And they should provide patients with the resources—therapy, medication and support—to make these things happen.

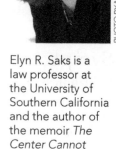

Elyn R. Saks is a law professor at the University of Southern California and the author of the memoir *The Center Cannot Hold: My Journey Through Madness.*

Elyn Saks's story is amazing and inspiring. It is also quite unusual. How should we incorporate stories like hers and the people in the research study she described? Are these people outliers—simply a carefully selected collection of people who had unusually favourable outcomes? (Given that Los Angeles is such a large city, it is reasonable to think one could amass a small sample of such cases.) Or has Professor Saks touched on an important limitation to the way in which the field currently conceptualizes, classifies, and treats mental disorders? Do we focus too much on what is wrong and on how professionalized health care can treat the pathology and not enough on what inherent strengths people have that can help them overcome their challenges, function at a high level, and achieve a high quality of life? These are all questions that are testable with the methods of psychological science, and the answers may help to improve the lives of many people.

lost control of their own minds, they may develop unusual beliefs and theories that attribute control to external agents.

- **Disorganized speech** is *a severe disruption of verbal communication in which ideas shift rapidly and incoherently among unrelated topics.* The abnormal speech patterns in schizophrenia reflect difficulties in organizing thoughts and focusing attention. Individuals often make irrelevant responses to questions, associate ideas loosely, and use words in peculiar ways. For example, asked by her doctor, "Can you tell me the name of this place?" one patient with schizophrenia responded, "I have not been a drinker for 16 years. I am taking a mental rest after a 'carter' assignment of 'quill.' You know, a 'penwrap.' I had contracts with Warner Brothers Studios and Eugene broke phonograph records but Mike protested. I have been with the police department for 35 years. I am made of flesh and blood—see, Doctor" [pulling up her dress] (Carson et al., 2000, p. 474).

- **Grossly disorganized behaviour** is *behaviour that is inappropriate for the situation or ineffective in attaining goals,* often with specific motor disturbances. An individual might exhibit constant childlike silliness, improper sexual behaviour (such as masturbating in public), dishevelled appearance, or loud shouting or swearing. Specific motor disturbances might include strange movements, rigid posturing, odd mannerisms, bizarre grimacing, or hyperactivity.

- **Catatonic behaviour** is *a marked decrease in all movement or an increase in muscular rigidity and overactivity.* Individuals with catatonia may actively resist movement (when someone is trying to move them) or become completely unresponsive and unaware of their surroundings, in a stupor. In addition, individuals receiving drug therapy may exhibit motor symptoms (such as rigidity or spasm) as a side effect of the medication. Indeed, the *DSM–5* includes a diagnostic category labelled "medication-induced movement disorders" that identifies motor disturbances arising from medications of the sort commonly used to treat schizophrenia.

Negative symptoms are *deficits in or disruptions of normal emotions and behaviours.* They include emotional and social withdrawal; apathy; poverty of speech; and other indications of the absence or insufficiency of normal behaviour, motivation, and emotion. These symptoms refer to things that are missing in people with schizophrenia. Negative symptoms may rob people of emotion, for example, leaving them with flat, deadpan responses; their interest in people or events may be undermined, or their capacity to focus attention may be impaired.

Cognitive symptoms are *deficits in cognitive abilities, specifically in executive functioning, attention, and working memory.* These are the least noticeable symptoms because they are much less bizarre and public than the positive and negative symptoms. However, these cognitive deficits often play a large role in preventing people with schizophrenia from achieving a high level of functioning, such as maintaining friendships and holding down a job (Green et al., 2000).

Schizophrenia occurs in about 0.5% of the population (Simeone et al., 2015) and is slightly more common in men than in women (McGrath et al., 2008). Early versions of the *DSM* suggested that schizophrenia might have a very early onset—in the form of infantile autism—but more recent studies suggest that these disorders are distinct and that schizophrenia rarely develops before early adolescence (Rapoport et al., 2009). The first episode typically occurs in late adolescence or early adulthood. Despite its relatively low frequency, people with schizophrenia are over-represented among psychiatric inpatients and have inpatient hospital stays that are significantly longer than those for other psychiatric patients (Chen et al., 2017). The disproportionate rate and length of hospitalization for schizophrenia is a testament to the devastation it causes in people's lives.

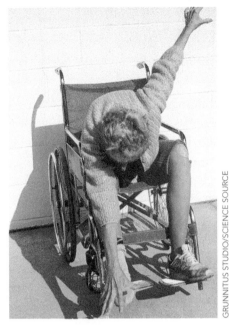

GRUNNITUS STUDIO/SCIENCE SOURCE

A person suffering from catatonic schizophrenia may assume an unusual posture and fail to move for hours.

disorganized speech A severe disruption of verbal communication in which ideas shift rapidly and incoherently among unrelated topics.

grossly disorganized behaviour Behaviour that is inappropriate for the situation or ineffective in attaining goals, often with specific motor disturbances.

catatonic behaviour A marked decrease in all movement or an increase in muscular rigidity and overactivity.

negative symptoms Deficits in or disruptions of normal emotions and behaviours (e.g., emotional and social withdrawal; apathy; poverty of speech; and other indications of the absence or insufficiency of normal behaviour, motivation, and emotion) that are present in those with schizophrenia.

cognitive symptoms Deficits in cognitive abilities, specifically executive functioning, attention, and working memory, present in those with schizophrenia.

Biological Factors

In 1899, when the German psychiatrist Emil Kraepelin first described the syndrome we now know as schizophrenia, he remarked that the disorder was so severe that it suggested "organic," or biological, origins. Over the years, accumulating evidence for the role of biology in schizophrenia has come from studies of genetic factors, biochemical factors, and neuroanatomy.

Genetic Factors and Environment Play a Role

Family studies indicate that the closer a person's genetic relatedness to someone with schizophrenia, the greater his or her likelihood of developing the disorder (Gottesman, 1991). As shown in **FIGURE 15.5,** concordance rates increase dramatically with biological relatedness. These rates are estimates and vary considerably from study to study, but almost every study over the years has found the average concordance rates to be much higher for monozygotic twins (33%) than for dizygotic twins (7%), which suggests a genetic component to the disorder (Hilker et al., 2018).

Although genetics clearly has a strong predisposing role in schizophrenia, considerable evidence suggests that environmental factors, such as prenatal and perinatal environments, also affect concordance rates (Jurewicz, Owen, & O'Donovan, 2001; Thaker, 2002). For example, because approximately 70% of identical twins share the same prenatal blood supply, toxins in the mother's blood could contribute to the high concordance rate. More recent studies (discussed in the earlier section on bipolar disorder) are contributing to a better understanding of how environmental stressors can trigger epigenetic changes that increase susceptibility to this disorder.

The Precise Role of Neurotransmitters Has Yet to Be Fully Understood

During the 1950s, researchers discovered major tranquilizers that could reduce the symptoms of schizophrenia by lowering levels of the neurotransmitter dopamine. The effectiveness of many drugs in alleviating schizophrenic symptoms is related to the drugs' capacity to reduce dopamine's role in neurotransmission in certain brain

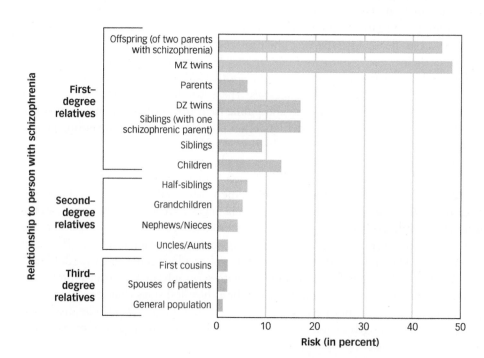

Figure 15.5
Average Risk of Developing Schizophrenia The risk of schizophrenia among biological relatives is greater for those with greater degrees of relatedness. An identical (MZ) twin of a person with schizophrenia has a 48% risk of developing schizophrenia, for example. Offspring of two parents with schizophrenia have a 46% risk of developing this disorder. DATA FROM GOTTESMAN, 1991.

tracts. This finding suggested the **dopamine hypothesis**, *the idea that schizophrenia involves an excess of dopamine activity.* The hypothesis has been invoked to explain why amphetamines, which increase dopamine levels, often exacerbate symptoms of schizophrenia (Harro, 2015).

If only things were so simple. Considerable evidence suggests that this hypothesis is inadequate (Moncrieff, 2009). For example, many individuals with schizophrenia do not respond favourably to dopamine-blocking drugs (e.g., major tranquilizers), and those who do respond seldom show a complete remission of symptoms. Moreover, the drugs block dopamine receptors very rapidly, yet individuals with schizophrenia typically do not show a beneficial response for weeks. Finally, research has implicated other neurotransmitters in schizophrenia, suggesting that the disorder may involve a complex interaction among a host of different biochemicals (Risman et al., 2008; Sawa & Snyder, 2002). In sum, the precise role of neurotransmitters in schizophrenia has yet to be determined.

Research Has Identified Structural Changes in the Brain

When neuroimaging techniques became available, researchers immediately started looking for distinctive anatomical features of the brain in individuals with schizophrenia. The earliest observations revealed enlargement of the *ventricles,* hollow areas filled with cerebrospinal fluid, lying deep within the core of the brain (see **FIGURE 15.6**) (Johnstone et al., 1976). In some individuals (primarily those with chronic, negative symptoms), the ventricles were abnormally enlarged, suggesting a loss of brain-tissue mass that could arise from an anomaly in prenatal development (Arnold et al., 1998).

Understanding the significance of this brain abnormality for schizophrenia is complicated by several factors, however. First, such enlarged ventricles are found in only a minority of individuals with schizophrenia. Second, some individuals who do not have schizophrenia also show evidence of enlarged ventricles. Finally, this type of brain abnormality can be caused by the long-term use of some types of antipsychotic medications commonly prescribed for schizophrenia (Jørgensen et al., 2016).

Neuroimaging studies provide evidence of a variety of brain abnormalities associated with schizophrenia. Paul Thompson and his colleagues (2001) examined changes in the brains of adolescents whose MRI scans could be traced sequentially from the onset of schizophrenia. By superimposing the scans onto an image of a standardized brain, the researchers were able to detect progressive tissue loss beginning in the parietal lobe and eventually encompassing much of the brain

dopamine hypothesis The idea that schizophrenia involves an excess of dopamine activity.

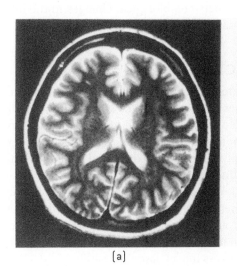 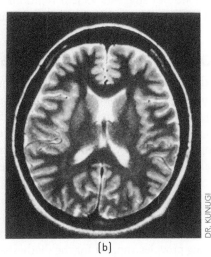

(a) (b)

DR. KUNUGI

Figure 15.6
Enlarged Ventricles in Schizophrenia These MRI scans of monozygotic twins reveal that (a) the twin affected by schizophrenia shows enlarged ventricles (all the central white space), compared with (b) the unaffected twin (Kunugi et al., 2003).

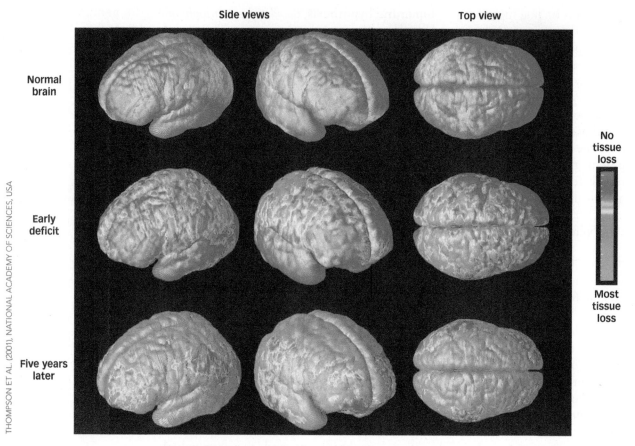

Side views   Top view

Normal brain

Early deficit

Five years later

No tissue loss

Most tissue loss

THOMPSON ET AL. (2001), NATIONAL ACADEMY OF SCIENCES, USA

Figure 15.7

Brain Tissue Loss in Adolescent Schizophrenia MRI scan composites reveal brain tissue loss in adolescents diagnosed with schizophrenia. Normal brains show minimal loss due to "pruning" (*top*). Early-deficit scans reveal loss in the parietal areas (*middle*); individuals at this stage may experience symptoms such as hallucinations or bizarre thoughts. Scans 5 years later reveal extensive tissue loss over much of the cortex (*bottom*); individuals at this stage are likely to suffer from delusions, disorganized speech and behaviour, and negative symptoms such as social withdrawal (Thompson et al., 2001).

(see **FIGURE 15.7**). All adolescents lose some grey matter over time in a kind of normal "pruning" of the brain, but in those developing schizophrenia, the loss was dramatic enough to seem pathological. A variety of specific brain changes found in other studies suggests a clear relationship between biological changes in the brain and the progression of schizophrenia (Cannon, 2015).

Social/Psychological Factors

With all these potential biological contributors to schizophrenia, you might think there would be few psychological or social causes of this disorder. However, several studies suggest that family environment plays a role in the development of and recovery from the condition. One large-scale study compared the risk of schizophrenia in children adopted into healthy families to those adopted into severely disturbed families (Tienari et al., 2004). (Disturbed families were defined as those with extreme conflict, lack of communication, or chaotic relationships.) Among children whose biological mothers had schizophrenia, the disturbed environment increased their likelihood of developing schizophrenia—an outcome that was not found among children who were also reared in disturbed families but whose biological mothers did *not* have schizophrenia. This finding provides support for the diathesis–stress model described earlier.

Build to the Outcomes

1. What is schizophrenia?
2. What are the positive, negative, and cognitive symptoms of schizophrenia?
3. What is the role of genetics in schizophrenia?

4. How do biochemical factors contribute to schizophrenia?
5. What changes appear in the brains of people with schizophrenia?
6. What environmental factors contribute to schizophrenia?

Disorders of Childhood and Adolescence

The disorders described thus far can have their onset during childhood, adolescence, or adulthood. In fact, half of all disorders begin by age 14 and three quarters by age 24 (Kessler et al, 2005a). Several of the disorders you have learned about, such as bipolar disorder and schizophrenia, tend not to begin until early adulthood. However, other disorders *always,* by definition, begin in childhood or adolescence—and if they don't, they will never manifest. These include autism spectrum disorder, attention-deficit/hyperactivity disorder, conduct disorder, intellectual disability (formerly called *mental retardation*), learning disorders, communication disorders, and motor skill disorders, in addition to many others. The first three are among the most common and best known, so we will review them briefly here.

Learning Outcomes

- Describe the characteristic indications of autism.
- Define the difference between normal problems with inattention and ADHD.
- Explain why it is difficult to pin down the causes of conduct disorder.

Autism Spectrum Disorder

Marco is a 4-year-old only child. His parents have become worried because, although his mother stays home with him all day and tries to talk with him and play with him, he still has not spoken a single word and he shows little interest in trying. He spends much of his time playing with his toy trains, which seem to be the thing he enjoys most in life. He often sits for hours staring at spinning train wheels or pushing a single train back and forth, seeming completely in his own world, uninterested in playing with anyone else. Marco's parents have become concerned about his apparent inability to speak, lack of interest in others, and development of some peculiar mannerisms, such as flapping his arms repeatedly for no apparent reason.

Autism spectrum disorder (ASD) is *a condition beginning in early childhood in which a person shows persistent communication deficits, as well as restricted and repetitive patterns of behaviours, interests, or activities.* In *DSM–5,* ASD now subsumes multiple disorders that were considered separate in *DSM–IV*: autistic disorder, Asperger's disorder, childhood disintegrative disorder, and pervasive developmental disorder not otherwise specified (i.e., these disorders are no longer recognized in the *DSM*).

The true rate of ASD is difficult to pinpoint, especially given the recent change in diagnostic definition. Estimates from the 1960s indicated that autism was a rare diagnosis, occurring in 4 per 10,000 children. Estimates have been creeping up over time and now stand at approximately 10 to 20 per 10,000 children. If one considers the full range of disorders that now fall under the ASD umbrella in the *DSM–5,* the rate is 60 per 10,000 children (Newschaffer et al., 2007). It is unclear whether this increased rate is due to increased awareness and recognition of ASD, better screening and diagnostic tools, or to some other factor. Boys have higher rates of ASD than girls by a ratio of about 4:1.

autism spectrum disorder (ASD) A condition beginning in early childhood in which a person shows persistent communication deficits as well as restricted and repetitive patterns of behaviours, interests, or activities.

Temple Grandin, a professor of animal sciences at Colorado State University, is living proof that people with autism spectrum disorder can have very successful professional careers.

Early theories of autism described it as "childhood schizophrenia," but it is now understood to be separate from schizophrenia, which is rarely diagnosed in children (emerging mainly in adolescence or young adulthood) (Kessler & Wang, 2008). ASD is currently viewed as a heterogeneous set of traits that cluster together in some families (heritability estimates for ASD are as high as 90%), leaving some children with just a few mild ASD traits and others with a more severe form of the disorder (Geschwind, 2009). Although the causes of ASD are not yet fully understood, one thing that is now clear is that despite a great deal of research examining the question, there is no evidence that ASD is caused by vaccinations (Mandy & Lai, 2016).

One current model suggested that ASD can be understood as an impaired capacity for *empathizing,* or knowing the mental states of others, combined with a superior ability for *systematizing,* or understanding the rules that organize the structure and function of objects (Baron-Cohen & Belmonte, 2005). Consistent with this model, brain-imaging studies show that people with autism have comparatively decreased activity in regions associated with understanding the minds of others and greater activation in regions related to basic object perception (Sigman, Spence, & Wang, 2006).

Although many people with ASD experience impairments throughout their lives that prevent them from having relationships and holding down a job, many go on to very successful careers. This is often due to the unique strengths that some people with ASD have, such as the abilities to perceive or remember details or to master symbol systems such as mathematics or music (Happé & Vital, 2009). The renowned behavioural scientist and author Temple Grandin has written of her personal experience with autism. She was diagnosed with autism at age 3, started learning to talk late, and then suffered teasing for odd habits and "nerdy" behaviour. Fortunately, she developed ways to cope and found a niche through her special talent—the ability to understand animal behaviour (Sacks, 1996).

She is now a Professor of Animal Sciences at Colorado State University; celebrated author of books such as *Animals in Translation*; designer of animal handling systems used widely in ranching, farming, and zoos; and the central character in a movie, starring American performer Claire Danes, based on her life. Temple Grandin's story lets us know that there are happy endings. Overall, those diagnosed with ASD as children have highly variable trajectories, with some achieving normal or better-than-normal functioning and others struggling with profound disorder. Autism is a childhood disorder that in adulthood can have many outcomes (see Hot Science: Optimal Outcome in Autism Spectrum Disorder).

Attention-Deficit/Hyperactivity Disorder

Chances are you have had the experience of being distracted during a lecture or while reading one of your *other* textbooks. We all have trouble focusing from time to time. Far beyond normal distraction, however, **attention deficit/hyperactivity disorder (ADHD)** is *a persistent pattern of severe problems with inattention and/or hyperactivity or impulsiveness that cause significant impairments in functioning.* This is quite different from occasional mind-wandering or bursts of activity. Meeting the criteria for ADHD requires having multiple symptoms of inattention (e.g., persistent problems with sustained attention, organization, memory, following instructions), hyperactivity–impulsiveness (e.g., persistent difficulties with remaining still, waiting for a turn, interrupting others), or both. Most children experience some of these behaviours at some point, but to meet the criteria for ADHD, a child has to have many of these behaviours for at least 6 months in at least two settings (e.g., home and school)—to the point where they impair the child's ability to perform at school or get along at home.

attention deficit/hyperactivity disorder (ADHD) A persistent pattern of severe problems with inattention and/or hyperactivity or impulsiveness that causes significant impairments in functioning.

Hot Science | Optimal Outcome in Autism Spectrum Disorder

What comes to mind when you think of the word *autism*? What kind of person do you imagine? If that person is an adult, what do you imagine that they do for a living? Can they hold a job? Can they care for themselves? Many people consider autism spectrum disorder (ASD) a lifelong condition and believe that those affected will forever experience significant difficulties and disabilities in their interpersonal, educational, and occupational functioning. However, recent studies are helping to change this outlook.

New research describes samples of people who had been diagnosed with autism as children, but who no longer meet the criteria for ASD (e.g., Shulman et al., 2019). How could this be? Researchers have begun to notice over the past few years that some portion of children diagnosed with autism later fail to meet diagnostic criteria. For instance, in one study, nearly 200 2- to 4-year-olds diagnosed with ASD were followed for two years; researchers found that approximately 10% no longer met diagnostic criteria at the end of the follow-up period (Olsson et al., 2015). There are several potential explanations for this change. The most obvious is that some portion of children diagnosed with ASD are misdiagnosed and don't really have this disorder. Perhaps they are overly shy or quiet, or develop speech later than other children, which in turn is misinterpreted as ASD. Another possibility is that children who lose their ASD diagnosis had a milder form of the disorder and/or were identified and treated earlier. There is some support for this idea, as one study found that 7 in every 40 children diagnosed with ASD at age 2 no longer met the criteria for this disorder at age 4. The strongest predictors of this optimal outcome were less severe symptoms, fewer repetitive behaviours, and stronger adaptive skills (Moulton et al., 2016).

The possibility of effectively treating ASD was first raised in an important study by Ivar Lovaas back in 1987. Lovaas assigned 19 children with autism to an intensive behavioural intervention, in which they received over 40 hours per week of one-on-one behaviour therapy for 2 years; another 40 children were assigned to control conditions, in which they received fewer than 10 hours per week of treatment. Amazingly, the follow-up of the treated children revealed that 9 of the 19 children in the intensive behaviour therapy condition obtained a normal level of intellectual and educational functioning—passing through a normal first-grade class—compared with only 1 of the 40 children in the control conditions.

Extending this earlier work, Geraldine Dawson and colleagues tested a program called the Early Start Denver Model (ESDM), an intensive behavioural intervention (20 hours per week for 2 years) similarly designed to improve outcomes among those with ASD. Using randomized, controlled trials, Dawson and her colleagues found that, compared with those receiving standard community treatment, toddlers with ASD who received ESDM showed significant improvements in IQ (a 17-point rise!), language, adaptive and social functioning, and ASD diagnosis (Dawson et al., 2010). Many of these gains persisted when the children were 6 years old, 2 years after the treatment ended (Estes et al., 2015). Interestingly, children in the ESDM showed normalized brain activity after treatment (i.e., greater brain activation when viewing faces), which was in turn associated with improved social behaviour; those in the control condition showed the opposite pattern (Dawson et al., 2012). A more recent multi-site randomized controlled trial of ESDM replicated some of the exciting findings from the 2010 study, such as those showing significantly improved language ability among those receiving the ESDM intervention (Rogers et al., 2019).

Given that early detection and treatment can lead to such positive outcomes for those with ASD, should we be screening all young children for ASD so we can catch it early and intervene? This is an area of intense debate. Dawson and others (e.g., Dawson & Sapiro, 2019) argue that because we have methods for accurately detecting and effectively treating ASD in young children, including new digital screening tools that can be widely and efficiently disseminated, we should screen all children for this disorder to maximize their chances of optimal outcomes. Researchers and policy makers will be working actively on this issue in the years ahead.

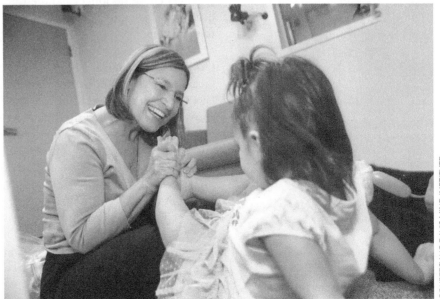

Autism was once viewed as a condition with lifelong impairments. New research suggests that early intervention, such as the Early Start Denver Model, can help many of those in whom ASD is diagnosed to achieve typical levels of functioning.

COURTESY UC DAVIS MIND INSTITUTE

Approximately 1 in 10 boys and 1 in 23 girls meet criteria for ADHD (Polanczyk et al., 2007). The *DSM–5* requires that symptoms of ADHD be present before the age of 12 to meet the criteria for this disorder. As you can imagine, children and adolescents with ADHD often struggle in the classroom. One recent study of 500 people with ADHD found that about half had a C average or lower, and about one-third were in special classes (Biederman et al., 2006). For a long time, ADHD was thought of as a disorder that affects only children and adolescents and that people "age out" of it. However, we now know that in many instances, this disorder persists into adulthood. The same symptoms are used to diagnose both children and adults. (For example, children with ADHD may struggle with attention and concentration in the classroom, whereas adults may experience the same problems in meetings.)

Approximately 1 in 23 adults meets the criteria for ADHD; they are more likely to be male, divorced, and unemployed—and most did not receive any treatment for their ADHD (Kessler et al., 2006). Unfortunately, most people still think of ADHD as a disorder of childhood and don't realize that adults can suffer from it as well. This could be why so few adults with ADHD receive treatment and why the disorder often wreaks havoc on job performance and relationships.

Because ADHD, like most disorders, is defined by the presence of a wide range of symptoms, it is unlikely that it emerges from one single cause or dysfunction. The exact cause of ADHD is not known, but there are some promising leads. Genetic studies suggest that there is a strong biological influence and they estimate that the heritability of ADHD is 76% (Faraone et al., 2005). Brain-imaging studies suggest that those with ADHD have smaller brain volumes (Castellanos et al., 2002) as well as structural and functional abnormalities in frontosubcortical networks associated with attention and behavioural inhibition (Makris et al., 2009). The good news is that current drug treatments for ADHD are effective and appear to decrease the risk of later psychological and academic problems (Biederman et al., 2009).

Conduct Disorder

Psychologists are attempting to identify the causes of conduct disorder in the hope of being able to decrease the harmful behaviours, such as bullying, that often accompany it.

conduct disorder A persistent pattern of deviant behaviour involving aggression towards people or animals, destruction of property, deceitfulness or theft, or serious rule violations.

Michael is an 8-year-old boy whose mother brought him into a local clinic because his behaviour had been getting progressively out of control, and his parents and teachers could no longer handle him. Although Michael's two older brothers and little sisters got along perfectly fine at home and at school, Michael had always gotten into trouble. At home, he routinely bullied his siblings, threw glasses and dishes at family members, and on numerous occasions punched and kicked his parents. Outside of the house, Michael had been getting into trouble for stealing from the local store, yelling at his teacher, and spitting at the principal of his school. The last straw came when Michael's parents found him trying to set fire to his bedspread one night. They tried punishing him by taking away his toys, restricting his privileges, and trying to encourage him with a sticker chart, but nothing seemed to change his behaviour.

Conduct disorder is a condition in which a child or adolescent engages in a *persistent pattern of deviant behaviour involving aggression to people or animals, destruction of property, deceitfulness or theft, or serious rule violations.* In Canada, a large study of 12- and 13-year-olds in the late 1990s (Lacourse et al., 2010) indicated that about 7 out of every 40 children exhibited symptoms of conduct disorder. This number may seem a bit high, but approximately 40% of those with conduct disorder have, on average, only three symptoms that cluster into one of three areas: rule breaking, theft/deceit, or aggression towards others. The other 60% have more symptoms, on average 6 to 8 of the 15 defined symptoms, with problems in many more areas and a much higher risk of having other mental disorders later in life (Nock et al., 2006).

Meeting the criteria for conduct disorder requires having any 3 of the 15 symptoms of conduct disorder. This means that approximately 32,000 different combinations of symptoms could lead to a diagnosis, which makes those with conduct disorder a pretty diverse group. This diversity makes it difficult to pin down the causes of conduct disorder. One thing that seems clear is that a wide range of genetic, biological, and environmental factors interact to produce this disorder. Indeed, risk factors for conduct disorder include maternal smoking during pregnancy, exposure to abuse and family violence during childhood, affiliation with deviant peer groups, and the presence of deficits in executive functioning (e.g., decision making, impulsiveness) (Boden, Fergusson, & Horwood, 2010; Burke, Loeber, & Birmaher, 2002).

Researchers are currently attempting to better understand the pathways through which inherited genetic factors interact with environmental stressors (e.g., childhood adversities) to create characteristics in brain structure and function (e.g., reduced activity in brain regions associated with planning and decision making) that interact with environmental factors (e.g., affiliation with deviant peers) to lead to the behaviours that are characteristic of conduct disorder. Not surprisingly, conduct disorder tends to co-occur with other disorders characterized by problems with decision making and impulsiveness, such as ADHD, substance use disorders, and antisocial personality disorder, which is described in more detail in the next section.

Build to the Outcomes

1. What is autism spectrum disorder (ASD)?
2. What is the relationship between ASD and empathy?
3. What is attention-deficit/hyperactivity disorder (ADHD)?
4. What are the criteria for an ADHD diagnosis?

5. What is conduct disorder?
6. How is it possible that there are 32,000 different combinations of symptoms that could lead to a diagnosis of conduct disorder? What does this say about the population of people who have been given this diagnosis?

Personality Disorders: Extreme Traits and Characteristics

As discussed in the chapter on Personalities, we all have one, and we all differ in the extent to which we have various ways of behaving, thinking, and feeling. Sometimes, personality traits can become so extreme that they can be considered mental disorders. **Personality disorders** are *enduring patterns of thinking, feeling, or relating to others or controlling impulses that deviate from cultural expectations and cause distress or impaired functioning.* Personality disorders begin in adolescence or early adulthood and are relatively stable over time. Let's look at the types of personality disorders and then more closely examine one that sometimes lands people in jail: antisocial personality disorder.

Learning Outcomes

- Identify the three types of personality disorders.
- Explain the diagnostic signs of APD.

Types of Personality Disorders

The *DSM–5* lists 10 specific personality disorders (see **TABLE 15.3**). They fall into three clusters: (1) *odd/eccentric,* (2) *dramatic/erratic,* and (3) *anxious/inhibited.* Personality disorders have been a bit controversial for several reasons. First, critics question whether having a problematic personality is really a disorder. Perhaps it might be better just to admit that a lot of people can be difficult to interact with and leave it at that.

personality disorders Enduring patterns of thinking, feeling, or relating to others or controlling impulses that deviate from cultural expectations and cause distress or impaired functioning.

TABLE 15.3

CLUSTERS OF PERSONALITY DISORDERS

Cluster	Personality Disorder	Characteristics
A. Odd/Eccentric	Paranoid	Distrust in others, suspicion that people have sinister motives; apt to challenge the loyalties of friends and read hostile intentions into others' actions; prone to anger and aggressive outbursts but otherwise emotionally cold; often jealous, guarded, secretive, overly serious.
	Schizoid	Extreme introversion and withdrawal from relationships; prefers to be alone, little interest in others; humourless, distant, often absorbed with own thoughts and feelings, a day-dreamer; fearful of closeness, with poor social skills, often seen as a "loner."
	Schizotypal	Peculiar or eccentric manners of speaking or dressing; strange beliefs; "magical thinking," such as belief in ESP or telepathy; difficulty forming relationships; may react oddly in conversation, not respond, or talk to self; speech elaborate or difficult to follow. (Possibly a mild form of schizophrenia.)
B. Dramatic/Erratic	Antisocial	Impoverished moral sense or "conscience"; history of deception, crime, legal problems, impulsive and aggressive or violent behaviour; little emotional empathy or remorse for hurting others; manipulative, careless, callous; at high risk for substance abuse and alcoholism.
	Borderline	Unstable moods and intense, stormy personal relationships; frequent mood changes and anger, unpredictable impulses; self-mutilation or suicidal threats or gestures to get attention or manipulate others; self-image fluctuation and a tendency to see others as "all good" or "all bad."
	Histrionic	Constant attention seeking; grandiose language, provocative dress, exaggerated illnesses, all to gain attention; believes that everyone loves them; emotional, lively, overly dramatic, enthusiastic, and excessively flirtatious; shallow and labile emotions; "onstage."
	Narcissistic	Inflated sense of self-importance, absorbed by fantasies of self and success; exaggerates own achievements, assumes others will recognize they are superior; good first impressions but poor longer-term relationships; exploitative of others.
C. Anxious/Inhibited	Avoidant	Socially anxious and uncomfortable unless they are confident of being liked; in contrast with schizoid person, yearns for social contact; fears criticism and worries about being embarrassed in front of others; avoids social situations due to fear of rejection.
	Dependent	Submissive, dependent, requiring excessive approval, reassurance, and advice; clings to people and fears losing them; lacking self-confidence; uncomfortable when alone; may be devastated by end of close relationship or suicidal if breakup is threatened.
	Obsessive-compulsive	Conscientious, orderly, perfectionist; excessive need to do everything "right"; inflexibly high standards and caution can interfere with their productivity; fear of errors can make them strict and controlling; poor expression of emotions. (Not the same as obsessive-compulsive disorder.)

Information from *DSM–5* (American Psychiatric Association, 2013).

Another question is whether personality problems correspond to "disorders" in that there are distinct *types*, or whether such problems might be better understood as extreme values on trait *dimensions* such as the Big Five traits discussed in the Personality chapter (Trull & Durrett, 2005). In *DSM–IV*, personality disorders appeared as a separate type of disorder from all other disorders described earlier. (Specifically, mood, anxiety, psychotic, substance, and other "major" disorders were all in a category called *Axis I*, and personality disorders were in *Axis II*.) However, in *DSM–5*, personality disorders earned equal footing as full-fledged disorders. One of the most thoroughly studied of all the personality disorders is antisocial personality disorder.

Antisocial Personality Disorder

Henri Desiré Landru began using personal ads to attract a woman "interested in matrimony" in Paris in 1914, and he succeeded in seducing 10 of them. He bilked them of their savings, poisoned them, and cremated them in his stove, also disposing of a boy and two dogs along the way. He recorded his murders in a notebook and maintained a marriage and a mistress all the while. The gruesome actions of serial killers such as Landru leave us frightened and wondering; however, bullies, compulsive liars, and even drivers who regularly speed through a school zone share the same shocking blindness to human pain. The *DSM–5* includes the category of **antisocial personality disorder (APD)**, defining it as *a pervasive pattern of disregard for and violation of the rights of others that begins in childhood or early adolescence and continues into adulthood.*

Adults with an APD diagnosis typically have a history of *conduct disorder* before the age of 15. In adulthood, a diagnosis of APD is given to individuals who show three or more of a set of seven diagnostic signs: illegal behaviour, deception, impulsivity, physical aggression, recklessness, irresponsibility, and a lack of remorse for wrongdoing. About 3.6% of the general population has APD, and the rate of occurrence in men is three times the rate in women (Grant et al., 2004).

The terms *sociopath* and *psychopath* describe people with APD who are especially coldhearted, manipulative, and ruthless—yet may appear friendly and charming (Cleckley, 1976; Hare, 1998). Many people with APD commit crimes, and many are caught because of the frequency and flagrancy of their infractions. Among 22,790 prisoners in one study, 47% of the men and 21% of the women were diagnosed with APD (Fazel & Danesh, 2002). Statistics such as these support the notion of a "criminal personality."

Both the early onset of conduct problems and the lack of success in treatment suggest that career criminality often has an internal cause (Lykken, 1995). Evidence of brain abnormalities in people with APD is also accumulating (Blair, Peschardt, & Mitchell, 2005). One line of investigation has looked at sensitivity to fear in psychopaths and individuals who show no such psychopathology. For example, criminal psychopaths who are shown negative emotional words such as *hate* or *corpse* exhibit less activity in the amygdala and hippocampus (two areas involved in fear conditioning) than do noncriminals (Kiehl et al., 2001). Research like this has suggested that psychopaths experience fear but appear to have decreased abilities for detecting and responding to threats in their environment (Hoppenbrouwers, Bulten, & Brazil, 2016).

Henri Desiré Landru (1869–1922) was a serial killer who met widows through ads he placed in newspapers' lonely-hearts columns. After obtaining enough information to embezzle money from them, he murdered 10 women and the son of one of the women. He was executed for serial murder in 1922.

antisocial personality disorder (APD) A pervasive pattern of disregard for and violation of the rights of others that begins in childhood or early adolescence and continues into adulthood.

Build to the Outcomes

1. What are personality disorders?
2. What are the different types of personality disorders?
3. What are the characteristics of a person with antisocial personality disorder (APD)?
4. Why do prison statistics support the idea of a "criminal personality"?

Self-Harm Behaviours: Intentionally Injuring Oneself

We all have an innate drive to keep ourselves alive. We eat when we are hungry, get out of the way of fast-moving vehicles, and go to school so we can earn a living to keep ourselves, and our families, alive (see the discussion of evolutionary psychology in The Evolution of Psychological Science chapter). One of the most extreme manifestations of abnormal human behaviour is revealed when a person acts in direct opposition to this drive for self-preservation and engages in intentionally self-destructive behaviour. Accounts of people intentionally harming themselves date back to the beginning of recorded history. However, it is only over the

Learning Outcomes

- Explain the factors that increase the risk of suicide.
- Explain what is currently known to be the motivation behind nonsuicidal self-injury.

We all have an innate desire to keep ourselves alive. So why do some people purposely do things to harm themselves?

past several decades that we have begun to gain an understanding of why people purposely do things to hurt themselves. *DSM–5* includes two self-destructive behaviours in its Section III (disorders in need of further study): suicidal behaviour disorder and nonsuicidal self-injury disorder.

Suicidal Behaviour

Tim, a 35-year-old accountant, had by all appearances been living a pretty happy, successful life. He was married to his high school sweetheart and had two young children. Over the past several years, though, his workload had increased, and he started to experience severe job-related stress. At around the same time, he and his wife began to experience some financial problems, and his alcohol consumption increased, all of which put significant strain on the family and began to affect his work. Tim's coworkers noted that he had become pretty angry and agitated lately—even yelling at coworkers on a few occasions. One evening Tim and his wife got into a heated argument about the family's finances and Tim's excessive alcohol use; Tim went into the bathroom and swallowed a bottle full of prescription medicine in an effort to end his life. He was taken to the hospital and kept there to be treated for suicidal behaviour.

Suicide, *intentional self-inflicted death,* is the second most common cause of death for people aged 15–34 in Canada, claiming the lives of 18 out of every 100,000 males and 5 out of every 100,000 females aged 10 and older (Statistics Canada, 2019g). There are large demographic differences in the suicide rate: For instance, in Canada, 75% of suicides occur among men, and immigrants are only about half as likely as those born in Canada to commit suicide (Statistics Canada, 2019h).

Rates of suicide in Indigenous populations are much higher. Between 2011 and 2016, the suicide rate amongst First Nations people was 3 times higher than in the non-Indigenous population. Among Métis, it was twice as high, and among Inuit, 9 times higher. Suicide rates were particularly high amongst adolescents and young adults aged 15 to 24. For Inuit in this age group, suicide rates are more than 30 times higher than in their non-Indigenous peers (Kumar & Tjepkema, 2019). The reasons for higher suicide rates in Indigenous groups are not fully understood, but probably include chronic life stressors such as poverty and unemployment, the effects of intergenerational trauma from forced resettlement and residential school attendance, the effects of historical and ongoing social inequities, and lack of access to health care (Kumar & Tjepkema, 2019).

Nonfatal **suicide attempts**, in which people engage in *potentially harmful behaviour with some intention of dying,* occur much more frequently than suicide deaths. Across a range of countries, approximately 9% of adults report that they have seriously considered suicide at some point in their lives, 3% have made a plan to kill themselves, and 3% have actually made a suicide attempt (Nock et al., 2008). As these numbers suggest, only one-third of those who think about suicide go on to make a suicide attempt.

Although many more men than women die by suicide, women experience suicidal thoughts and (nonfatal) suicide attempts at significantly higher rates than do men (Nock et al., 2008). Moreover, the rates of suicidal thoughts and attempts increase dramatically during adolescence and young adulthood. A recent study of a representative sample of approximately 10,000 American adolescents revealed that suicidal thoughts and behaviours are virtually nonexistent before age 10 but increase dramatically from ages 12 to 18 (see **FIGURE 15.8**) before leveling off during early adulthood (Nock et al., 2013).

So the numbers are staggering, but *why* do people try to kill themselves? The short answer is: We do not yet know, and it's complicated. When interviewed in the hospital following their suicide attempt, most people who have tried to kill themselves report that they did so to escape from an intolerable state of mind or impossible situation (Boergers, Spirito, & Donaldson, 1998). Consistent with this explanation,

suicide Intentional self-inflicted death.

suicide attempt Engagement in potentially harmful behaviour with some intention of dying.

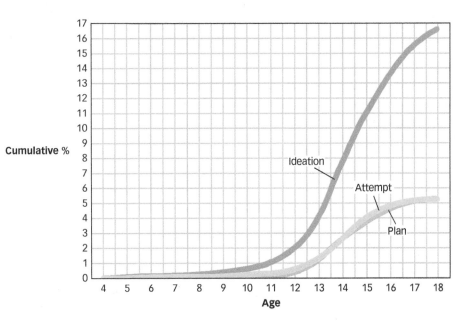

Figure 15.8
Age of Onset of Suicidal Behaviour During Adolescence A survey of American adolescents shows that although suicidal thoughts and behaviours are quite rare among children (the rate was 0.0 for ages 1–4), they increase dramatically starting at age 12 and continue to climb throughout adolescence. DATA FROM NOCK ET AL., 2013.

research has documented that the risk of suicidal behaviour is significantly increased if a person experiences factors that can create severely distressing states, such as the presence of multiple mental disorders (more than 90% of people who die by suicide have at least one mental disorder); the experience of significant negative life events during childhood and adulthood (e.g., physical or sexual assault); and the presence of severe medical problems (Nock, Borges, & Ono, 2012). The search is ongoing for a more comprehensive understanding of how and why some people respond to negative life events with suicidal thoughts and behaviours, as well as for methods of how to better predict and prevent these devastating outcomes.

Nonsuicidal Self-Injury

Louisa, an 18-year-old university student, secretly cuts her lower abdomen and upper thighs about once per week, typically when she is feeling intense anger and hatred, either towards herself or someone else. She has always had a bit of a "hot streak," as she calls it, but it wasn't until she turned 14 that she started to use self-injury as a way to calm herself down. Louisa says that she feels a little ashamed after each episode of cutting, but she doesn't know how else to calm down when she gets really upset, so she has no plans to stop this behaviour.

Louisa is engaging in a behaviour called **nonsuicidal self-injury (NSSI)**, the *direct, deliberate destruction of body tissue in the absence of any intent to die.* NSSI has been reported since the beginning of recorded history; however, it is a behaviour that appears to be on the rise over the past few decades. Recent studies suggest that as many as 15 to 20% of adolescents and 3 to 6% of adults report engaging in NSSI at some point in their lifetime (Muehlenkamp et al., 2012). The rates appear to be even between males and females, and for people of different races and ethnicities. Like suicidal behaviour, NSSI is virtually absent during childhood, increases dramatically during adolescence, and then appears to decrease across adulthood.

In some parts of the world, cutting or scarification of the skin is socially accepted, and in some cases encouraged as a rite of passage (Favazza, 2011). In parts of the world where self-cutting is not socially encouraged, why would a person purposely hurt him- or herself if not to die? Recent studies suggest that people who engage in self-injury have very strong emotional and physiological responses to negative events, that they perceive this response as intolerable, and that NSSI serves to diminish the intensity of this response (Nock, 2009). There also is some evidence that in many instances, people engage in self-injury as a means to communicate distress or elicit

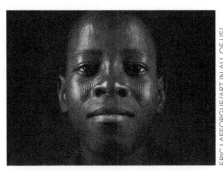

Although in Western cultures self-injury is considered pathological, in some parts of the world scarification of the skin is viewed as a rite of passage into adulthood and a symbol of one's tribe, as in the case of this young man from the Republic of Benin in West Africa.

nonsuicidal self-injury (NSSI)
Direct, deliberate destruction of body tissue in the absence of any intent to die.

help from others (Nock, 2010). Although we are beginning to get an understanding of why some people engage in NSSI, there are many aspects of this behaviour that we do not yet understand, and the study of NSSI is an increasingly active area of research.

Unfortunately, like suicidal behaviour, our understanding of the genetic and neurobiological influences on NSSI is limited, and there currently are no effective medications for these problems. There also is limited evidence for behavioural interventions or prevention programs (Mann et al., 2005). So, whereas suicidal behaviour and NSSI are some of the most disturbing and dangerous mental disorders, they also, unfortunately, are among the most perplexing. The field has made significant strides in our understanding of these behaviour problems in recent years, but there is a long way to go before we are able to predict and prevent them accurately and effectively.

Build to the Outcomes

1. What factors has research uncovered that create the distressing states that can lead to suicide?
2. What reasons have been given in hospital interviews for suicide attempts?
3. What is nonsuicidal self-injury (NSSI)?
4. How does culture play a role in the view of self-injury as pathological?
5. Why might people engage in self-injury?

Chapter Review

Defining Mental Disorders: What Is Abnormal?

- The *DSM–5* is a classification system that defines a mental disorder as occurring when a person experiences disturbances of thought, emotion, or behaviour that produce distress or impairment. The original volume provided a common language for talking about disorders, but diagnostic criteria were vague. The *DSM–5* includes detailed lists of criteria, including cultural considerations, designed to increase the validity of the process.

- The medical model conceptualizes abnormal thoughts and behaviours as illnesses with defined symptoms and possible cures.

- According to the biopsychosocial model, mental disorders arise from an interaction of biological, psychological, and social factors, often thought of as a combination of a diathesis (internal predisposition) and a stressor (environmental life event). The diathesis–stress model suggests that a person may be predisposed for a disorder that may or may not manifest, depending on whether it is triggered by stress.

- The RDoC is a new classification system that focuses on biological, cognitive, and behavioural aspects of mental disorders.

- Psychiatric labels may create negative stereotypes and may be one reason that many people do not seek help.

Anxiety Disorders: Excessive Fear, Anxiety, and Avoidance

- People with anxiety disorders have irrational worries and fears that undermine their ability to function normally.

- Phobic disorders are characterized by excessive fear and avoidance of specific objects, activities, or situations. The preparedness theory posits that people are instinctively predisposed towards certain fears, and heritability studies support this idea. Temperament and the influence of environment are additional factors.

- People who suffer from panic disorder experience a sudden, terrifying attack of intense anxiety. Agoraphobia can lead people to be housebound for fear of public humiliation. Panic disorder has a hereditary component, and people who experience panic attacks may be hypersensitive to physiological signs of anxiety.

- Generalized anxiety disorder (GAD) involves a chronic state of anxiety, whereas phobic disorders involve anxiety tied to a specific object or situation. Biological explanations of GAD suggest a role for neurotransmitters, but the evidence is unclear. Life situation and experience play a role as well, supporting the diathesis–stress notion.

Obsessive-Compulsive Disorder: Persistent Thoughts and Repetitive Behaviours

- People with obsessive-compulsive disorder experience recurring, anxiety-provoking thoughts that compel them to engage in ritualistic, irrational behaviour. Attempts to suppress this behaviour have little or no benefit.

- OCD derives from concerns that could be real, supporting the preparedness theory. Studies indicate a moderate genetic link; one hypothesis implicates heightened neural activity in a portion of the basal ganglia.

Posttraumatic Stress Disorder: Distress and Avoidance After a Trauma

- Terrifying, life-threatening events, such as combat experience or rape, can lead to the development of posttraumatic stress disorder (PTSD), in which a person experiences chronic physiological arousal, unwanted thoughts or images of the event, and avoidance of things or situations that remind the person of the event.
- Research has identified neural correlates of PTSD.

Depressive and Bipolar Disorders: Extreme Highs and Lows

- Mood disorders are mental disorders in which a disturbance in mood is the predominant feature.
- Major depression (or unipolar depression) is characterized by a severely depressed mood and/or inability to experience pleasure lasting at least 2 weeks; symptoms include excessive self-criticism, guilt, difficulty concentrating, suicidal thoughts, sleep and appetite disturbances, and lethargy. Persistent depressive disorder, a related disorder, involves less severe symptoms that persist for at least 2 years. Some people experience depression in a seasonal pattern.
- Bipolar disorder is an unstable emotional condition involving extreme mood swings of depression and mania. The manic phase is characterized by periods of abnormally and persistently elevated, expansive, or irritable mood, lasting at least 1 week.
- Depression has at its roots socioecomonic, hormonal, genetic, and neural factors. Helplessness theory indicates that biases in how information is processed can lead to depression.
- Bipolar disorder has one of the highest rates of heritability. Epigenetics helps explain some of the genetic risk factors, a link to the influence of environment.

Schizophrenia and Other Psychotic Disorders: Losing the Grasp on Reality

- Schizophrenia is a severe psychological disorder involving hallucinations, disorganized thoughts and behaviour, and emotional and social withdrawal.
- Positive symptoms are thoughts and behaviours *not* seen in those without the disorder; negative symptoms indicate an absence of normal behaviour; cognitive symptoms are impairments in executive functioning, attention, and working memory.
- Schizophrenia affects only 1% of the population, but it accounts for a disproportionate share of psychiatric hospitalizations. The likelihood of getting the disorder increases with biological relatedness.
- The first drugs that reduced the availability of dopamine sometimes reduced the symptoms of schizophrenia, suggesting that the disorder involved an excess of dopamine activity; but recent research suggests that

schizophrenia may involve a complex interaction among a variety of neurotransmitters.
- Brain changes are evident in people with schizophrenia, but evidence shows children whose biological mothers had schizophrenia are more likely to develop it if they are raised in an affected family.

Disorders of Childhood and Adolescence

- Some mental disorders always begin during childhood or adolescence, and in some cases (ASD, ADHD) persist into adulthood.
- Autism spectrum disorder (ASD) emerges in early childhood and is a condition in which a person has persistent communication deficits, including difficulty empathizing with others, as well as restricted and repetitive patterns of behaviour, interests, or activities.
- Attention-deficit/hyperactivity disorder (ADHD) begins by age 12 and involves a persistent pattern of severe problems with inattention and/or hyperactivity or impulsiveness that causes significant impairments in functioning.
- Conduct disorder begins in childhood or adolescence and involves a persistent pattern of deviant behaviour involving aggression towards people or animals, destruction of property, deceitfulness or theft, or serious rule violations. Because the diagnosis requires having any 3 of 15 symptoms, there are 32,000 different combinations. This suggests a wide diversity within the group of people who share this diagnosis.

Personality Disorders: Extreme Traits and Characteristics

- Personality disorders are enduring patterns of thinking, feeling, relating to others, or controlling impulses that cause distress or impaired functioning.
- They include three clusters: odd/eccentric, dramatic/erratic, and anxious/inhibited.
- Antisocial personality disorder (APD) is associated with a lack of moral emotions and behaviour. People with antisocial personality disorder can be manipulative, dangerous, and reckless, often hurting others and sometimes hurting themselves.

Self-Harm Behaviours: Intentionally Injuring Oneself

- Most people who die by suicide have a mental disorder. Suicide attempts most often are motivated by an attempt to escape intolerable mental states or situations.
- Nonsuicidal self-injury (NSSI), like suicidal behaviour, increases dramatically during adolescence, but for many it is a persistent problem throughout adulthood. Although NSSI is performed without suicidal intent, like suicidal behaviour, it is most often motivated by an attempt to escape from painful mental states.
- Indigenous people in Canada die from suicide at a rate that is 3 times higher than in non-Indigenous groups.

Key Concept Quiz

1. The conception of psychological disorders as diseases that have symptoms and possible cures is referred to as
   a. the medical model.
   b. physiognomy.
   c. the root syndrome framework.
   d. a diagnostic system.

2. The *DSM–5* is best described as a
   a. medical model.
   b. classification system.
   c. set of theoretical assumptions.
   d. collection of physiological definitions.

3. *Comorbidity of disorders* refers to
   a. symptoms stemming from internal dysfunction.
   b. the relative risk of death arising from a disorder.
   c. the co-occurrence of two or more disorders in a single individual.
   d. the existence of disorders on a continuum from normal to abnormal.

4. Irrational worries and fears that undermine one's ability to function normally are an indication of
   a. a genetic abnormality.
   b. dysthymia.
   c. diathesis.
   d. an anxiety disorder.

5. A(n) _____ disorder involves anxiety tied to a specific object or situation.
   a. generalized anxiety
   b. environmental
   c. panic
   d. phobic

6. Kelly's fear of germs leads her to wash her hands repeatedly throughout the day, often for a half hour or more, under extremely hot water. From which disorder does Kelly suffer?
   a. panic attacks
   b. obsessive-compulsive disorder
   c. phobia
   d. generalized anxiety disorder

7. Extreme moods swings between _____ characterize bipolar disorder.
   a. depression and mania
   b. stress and lethargy
   c. anxiety and arousal
   d. obsessions and compulsions

8. Schizophrenia is characterized by which of the following?
   a. hallucinations
   b. disorganized thoughts and behaviour
   c. emotional and social withdrawal
   d. all of the above

9. Autism spectrum disorder is characterized most often by which of the following?
   a. communication deficits and restricted, repetitive behaviour
   b. hallucinations and delusions
   c. suicidal thoughts
   d. schizophrenia

10. In Canada, some groups have higher risk of suicide than others. These higher-risk groups include
    a. men.
    b. Indigenous peoples.
    c. those with a mental disorder.
    d. all of the above

LearningCurve macmillan learning

Don't stop now! Quizzing yourself is a powerful study tool. Go to LaunchPad to access the LearningCurve adaptive quizzing system and your own personalized learning plan. Visit launchpadworks.com.

Key Terms

mental disorder (p. 584)

medical model (p. 585)

Diagnostic and Statistical Manual of Mental Disorders (DSM) (p. 586)

comorbidity (p. 588)

biopsychosocial perspective (p. 589)

diathesis–stress model (p. 590)

Research Domain Criteria Project (RDoC) (p. 591)

anxiety disorder (p. 594)

phobic disorders (p. 594)

specific phobia (p. 594)

social phobia (p. 595)

preparedness theory (p. 595)

panic disorder (p. 596)

agoraphobia (p. 596)

generalized anxiety disorder (GAD) (p. 598)

obsessive-compulsive disorder (OCD) (p. 599)

posttraumatic stress disorder (PTSD) (p. 600)

mood disorders (p. 602)

major depressive disorder (or unipolar depression) (p. 603)

persistent depressive disorder (p. 603)

double depression (p. 603)

seasonal affective disorder (SAD) (p. 603)

helplessness theory (p. 605)

bipolar disorder (p. 606)

expressed emotion (p. 608)

schizophrenia (p. 609)

positive symptoms (p. 609)

hallucination (p. 609)

delusion (p. 609)

disorganized speech (p. 611)

grossly disorganized behaviour (p. 611)

catatonic behaviour (p. 611)

negative symptoms (p. 611)

cognitive symptoms (p. 611)

dopamine hypothesis (p. 613)

autism spectrum disorder (ASD) (p. 615)

attention-deficit/hyperactivity disorder (ADHD) (p. 616)

conduct disorder (p. 618)

personality disorders (p. 619)

antisocial personality disorder (APD) (p. 621)

suicide (p. 622)

suicide attempt (p. 622)

nonsuicidal self-injury (NSSI) (p. 623)

Changing Minds

1. You catch a TV interview with a celebrity who describes his difficult childhood, living with a mother who suffered from major depression. "Sometimes my mother stayed in her bed for days, not even getting up to eat," he says. "At the time, the family hushed it up. My parents were immigrants, and they came from a culture where it was considered shameful to have mental problems. You are supposed to have enough strength of will to overcome your problems, without help from anyone else. So my mother never got treatment." How might the idea of a medical model of psychiatric disorders have helped this woman and her family in the decision whether to seek treatment?

2. You're studying for your upcoming psychology exam when your roommate breezes in, saying: "I was just at the gym and I ran into Sue. She's totally schizophrenic: nice one minute, mean the next." You can't resist the opportunity to set the record straight. What psychiatric disorder is your roommate (incorrectly) attributing to Sue? How is the behaviour your roommate is describing different from schizophrenia?

3. A friend of yours has a family member who is experiencing severe mental problems, including delusions and loss of motivation. "We went to one psychiatrist," she says, "and got a diagnosis of schizophrenia. We went for a second opinion, and the other doctor said it was probably bipolar disorder. They're both good doctors, and they're both using the same *DSM*—how can they come up with different diagnoses?"

4. After reading the chapter, one of your classmates turns to you with a sigh of relief. "I finally figured it out. I have a deadbeat brother who always gets himself into trouble and then blames other people for his problems. Even when he gets a ticket for speeding, he never thinks it's his fault—the police were picking on him, or his passengers were urging him to go too fast. I always thought he was just a loser, but now I realize he has a personality disorder!" Do you agree with your classmate's diagnosis of his brother? How would you caution your classmate about the dangers of self-diagnosis, or diagnosis of friends and family?

Answers to Key Concept Quiz

1. a; 2. b; 3. c; 4. d; 5. d; 6. b; 7. a; 8. d; 9. a; 10. c.

LaunchPad features the full e-book of Psychology, the LearningCurve adaptive quizzing system, videos, and a variety of activities to boost your learning. Visit LaunchPad at launchpadworks.com.

Treatment of Psychological Disorders

TODAY WE'RE GOING TO BE TOUCHING A DEAD MOUSE I found in the parking lot outside my office building this morning," Dr. Jenkins said. "Okay, let's do it, I'm ready," Christine responded. The pair walked down to the parking lot and spent the next 50 minutes touching, then stroking, the dead mouse. They then went back upstairs to plan out what other disgusting things Christine was going to touch over the next 7 days before coming back for her next therapy session. This is all part of the psychological treatment of Christine's obsessive-compulsive disorder (OCD). It is an approach called *exposure and response prevention* (ERP), in which people are gradually exposed to the content of their obsessions and prevented from engaging in their compulsions. Christine's obsessions include the fear that she is going to be contaminated by germs and die of cancer; her compulsive behaviour involves several hours per day of washing her body and scrubbing everything around her with alcohol wipes in order to decrease the possibility of her developing cancer. After dozens and dozens of exposures to the focus of their obsessions, without performing the compulsive behaviours that they believe have been keeping them safe, people undergoing ERP eventually learn that their obsessive thoughts are not accurate and that they don't have to act out their compulsions. ERP can be scary, but it has proven amazingly effective at decreasing obsessions and compulsions and helping people with OCD return to a high level of daily functioning. The condition was widely considered untreatable until the development of ERP, which is now considered to be the most effective way to treat it (Foa & McLean, 2016). Exposure and response prevention is just one of many approaches currently being used to help people overcome the mental disorders you learned about in the last chapter.

- **Treatment: Getting Help to Those Who Need It**
- **Psychological Treatments: Healing the Mind Through Interaction**
- **Biological Treatments: Healing the Mind by Physically Altering the Brain**
- **Treatment Effectiveness: For Better or for Worse**

Exposure-based treatments, in which a person learns to face the source of their fear and anxiety, have proven to be an effective way to treat anxiety disorders.

▲ LÍVIA FERNANDES-BRAZIL/MOMENT SELECT/GETTY IMAGES

KEITH BINNS/GETTY IMAGES

THERE ARE MANY DIFFERENT WAYS TO TREAT PSYCHOLOGICAL DISORDERS and to change the thoughts, behaviours, and emotions associated with them. In this chapter, we will explore the most common, and most effective, approaches to psychological treatment. We will examine why people seek psychological help in the first place, and then explore how psychological treatments are built on the major theories of the causes and cures of disorders, including psychoanalytic, humanistic, existential, behavioural, and cognitive theories. We will also consider biological treatment approaches that focus on directly modifying brain structure and function. We'll discuss which treatments are most effective and how we come to that conclusion. We'll also look to the future by exploring some exciting new directions in the assessment and treatment of disorders using innovative technologies.

Treatment: Getting Help to Those Who Need It

Learning Outcomes

- Describe reasons people with mental disorders may fail to get treatment.

- Outline different approaches to treatment.

In any given year, 1 in 5 Canadians suffers from a mental disorder (including addiction problems; Smetanin et al., 2011). The personal costs of these disorders include the anguish of the sufferers as well as interference in their ability to carry on the activities of daily life. Think about Christine from the example above. If she did not (or could not) seek treatment, she would continue to be crippled by her OCD, which was causing major problems in her life. She had had to quit her job at the local coffee shop because she was no longer able to touch money or anything else that had been touched by other people without washing her hands immediately afterward. Her relationship with her boyfriend was in trouble because he was growing tired of her constantly seeking reassurance regarding cleanliness (hers and his). All of these problems in turn increased her anxiety and depression, making her obsessions even stronger. She desperately wanted and needed some way to break out of this vicious cycle. She needed an effective treatment.

The personal and social burdens of mental disorders are enormous. Such disorders typically have earlier ages of onset than physical disorders and are associated with significant impairments in the person's ability to carry out daily activities, such as causing days out of school or work or problems in family and personal relationships. Impairments associated with mental disorders are as severe, and in many cases more severe, than those associated with physical disorders such as cancer, chronic pain, and heart disease (Ormel et al., 2008). For instance, a person with severe depression may be unable to hold down a job or even get organized enough to collect a disability pension; many disorders cause people to stop getting along with family, caring for their children, or trying to help others.

There are financial costs too. In any given week, at least half a million employed people in Canada are unable to work due to mental health problems, and the economic burden for all mental illness in Canada is estimated to be $14.4 billion (CAD) per year (Dewa et al., 2010; Lim et al., 2008; Smetanin et al., 2011). Depression is the second leading cause of all disability worldwide (Ferrari et al., 2013). People with severe depression often are unable to make it in to work due to their disorder, and even when they do make it to work they often perform poorly. In addition to the personal benefits of treatment, then, society also stands to benefit from the effective treatment of psychological disorders.

Do all people with a mental disorder receive treatment? Not by a long shot. In Canada, only about half of those requiring treatment for major depression received potentially adequate care. Of those people aged 15 or older who reported a mental health need in the past year, 1 in 3 stated that their needs were not fully met (Patten et al., 2016; Sunderland & Findlay, 2013). Three-quarters of children in Canada with mental disorders do not have access to specialized care (Waddell et al., 2005), and wait times for mental-health services for children can be up to a year or more in some parts of the country (Children's Mental Health Ontario, 2016). Treatment rates are even lower elsewhere around the world, especially in low-income or developing countries (Wang et al., 2007). Treatment rates are higher for those with more severe mental disorders.

Why Many People Fail to Seek Treatment

A physical symptom such as a toothache would send most people to the dentist—a trip that usually results in a successful treatment. The clear source of pain and the obvious solution make for a quick and effective response. In contrast, the path from a mental disorder to a successful treatment is often far less clear, and many people are less familiar with when they should seek treatment for a mental disorder or where they should go for it. Here are three of the most often reported reasons people fail to get treatment:

1. *People may not realize that they have a mental disorder that can be effectively treated.* Approximately 45% of those with a mental disorder who do not seek treatment report that they did not do so because they didn't think they needed to be treated (Mojtabai et al., 2011). Mental disorders often are not taken nearly as seriously as physical illness, perhaps because the origin of mental illness is "hidden" and usually cannot be diagnosed by a blood test or X-ray.

2. *Barriers to treatment such as beliefs and circumstances may keep people from getting help.* Individuals may believe that they should be able to handle things themselves. In fact, this is the primary reason that people with a mental disorder give for not seeking treatment (72.6%) and for dropping out of treatment prematurely (42.2%) (Mojtabai et al., 2011). Other attitudinal barriers for not seeking treatment include the belief that the problem was not that severe (16.9% of people not seeking treatment), the belief that treatment would be ineffective (16.4%), and a perceived stigma from others (9.1%).

3. *Structural barriers prevent people from physically getting to treatment.* Like finding a good lawyer or plumber, finding the right psychologist can be more difficult than simply flipping through the yellow pages or searching online. This confusion is understandable given the plethora of different types of treatments available (see The Real World: Types of Psychotherapists). Once you find the therapist for you, you may encounter structural barriers related to not being able to afford treatment (15.3% of non-treatment seekers), lack of clinician availability (12.8%), the inconvenience of attending treatment (9.8%), and trouble finding transportation to the clinic (5.7%) (Mojtabai et al., 2011).

In Canada, evidence-based psychological services, delivered by psychologists and other professionals, are not typically publicly funded, and private coverage is generally only available to those with good employment. People in Canada who are poor, unemployed, or underemployed are not included. Low-income communities experience higher rates of mental disorders, but the provision of psychological and

When your tooth hurts, you go to a dentist. But how do you know when to see a psychologist?

ALLISON LEACH/THE IMAGE BANK/GETTY IMAGES

The Real World | Types of Psychotherapists

What should you do if you're ready to seek the help of a mental health professional? To whom do you turn? Therapists have widely varying backgrounds and training, which affects the kinds of services they offer. Before you choose a therapist, it is useful to have a general understanding of a therapist's background, training, and areas of expertise. There are several major "flavours" of therapists.

- *Psychologist* A psychologist who practices psychotherapy holds a doctorate (a PhD or PsyD), with a specialization in clinical psychology. This degree takes about 6 years to complete after a bachelor's degree, and includes extensive training in therapy, the assessment of psychological disorders, and research. In a few provinces (e.g., Alberta and Saskatchewan), individuals can become chartered psychologists with a master's degree, which takes 2 years after the BA/BSc. The psychologist will sometimes have a specialty, such as working with adolescents or helping people overcome sleep disorders, and he or she will usually conduct therapy that involves talking. Psychologists must be licensed by the province, and most provinces require candidates to complete about 2 years of supervised practical training and a competency exam. If you look for a *psychologist* on the Internet or through a clinic, you will usually find someone with this background.

- *Psychiatrist* A psychiatrist is a medical doctor who has completed an M.D. with specialized training in assessing and treating mental disorders. Psychiatrists can prescribe medications, and some also practice psychotherapy. General-practice physicians can also prescribe medications for mental disorders, and they are often the first to see people with such disorders because people consult them for a wide range of health problems. However, general-practice physicians do not typically receive much training in the diagnosis or treatment of mental disorders, and they do not practice psychotherapy.

- *Clinical/psychiatric social worker* Social workers have a master's degree in social work and have training in working with

people in dire life situations such as poverty, homelessness, or family conflict. Clinical or psychiatric social workers also receive special training to help people in these situations who have mental disorders. Social workers often work in government or private social service agencies and may also work in hospitals or have a private practice.

- *Counsellor* Counsellors have a wide range of training. To be a counselling psychologist, for example, requires a doctorate and practical training—the title uses that key term *psychologist* and is regulated by provincial and territorial laws. But jurisdictions vary in how they define *counsellor*. In some cases, a counsellor must have a master's degree and extensive training in therapy, whereas in others, a counsellor may have minimal training or relevant education. Counsellors who work in schools usually have a master's degree and specific training in counselling in educational settings.

Some people offer therapy under made-up terms that sound professional—"mind/body healing therapist," for example, or "marital adjustment adviser." Often these are simply invented terms to mislead clients and avoid provincial and territorial regulatory bodies, such as the College of Psychologists of British Columbia—the "therapist" may have no training or expertise at all. And, of course, there are a few people who claim to be licensed practitioners who are not: Louise Wightman was convicted of fraud in 2007 after conducting psychotherapy as a psychologist with dozens of clients. She claimed she didn't know the PhD degree she had purchased over the Internet was bogus (Associated Press, 2007). People who offer therapy may be well meaning and even helpful, but they might do harm, too. To be safe, it is important to shop wisely for a therapist whose training and credentials reflect expertise and inspire confidence.

How should you shop? One way is to start talking with people you know: your general-practice physician, a school counsellor, or a trusted friend or family member who might know of a good therapist. Or you can visit your university clinic or hospital or contact the Web

site of a provincial or territorial regulatory body (such as the Ontario College of Psychologists), or the Canadian Register of Health Service Providers in Psychology (CRHSPP); these organizations provide contact details for licensed mental health care providers. When you do contact someone, he or she will often be able to provide you with further advice about who would be just the right kind of therapist to consult.

Before you agree to see a therapist for treatment, you should ask questions (such as those below) to evaluate whether the therapist's style or background is a good match for your problem:

- What type of treatment do you provide?
- How effective is this type of therapy for the type of problem I'm having?
- How will you know if my problem is improving? What kind of measures do you use to test this?

Not only will the therapist's answers to these questions tell you about his or her background and experience, but they will also tell you about his or her approach to treating clients. You can then make an informed decision about the type of service you need.

psychiatric services in such communities tends to be more limited than in large, affluent, urban centres. Canada's universal health care coverage tends to support "treatment for individuals with high socioeconomic status and comparatively milder [mental] disorders [more] than it supports care for disadvantaged groups or those with severe and persistent mental illness" (Steele et al., 2006).

Clearly, Canada has work to do to ensure that people who seek help can find it and get the most effective treatment. But this raises the question of what treatments are available, and which treatments are best for particular disorders.

Approaches to Treatment

DATA VISUALIZATION

How Has the Rate of ADHD Diagnosis Changed Over Time?
Go to launchpadworks.com.

Treatments can be divided broadly into two kinds: (1) psychological treatment, in which people interact with a clinician in order to use the environment to change their brain and behaviour; and (2) biological treatment, in which drugs, surgery, or some other direct intervention directly treat the brain. In some cases, however, patients receive both psychological *and* biological treatments. Christine's OCD, for example, might be treated not only with the ERP but also with medication that mitigates her obsessive thoughts and compulsive urges. For many years, psychological treatment was the main form of intervention for psychological disorders because few biological options were available. Folk remedies purporting to have a biological basis—such as hydrotherapy (pouring cold water on those with mental disorders), trephination (drilling holes in the skull to let the evil spirits escape), and bloodletting (the removal of blood from the body)—were once tried in efforts to cure psychological disorders (*Note:* Do not try these at home. It turns out they don't work.) As we learn more about the biology and chemistry of the brain, approaches to mental health that begin with the brain are becoming increasingly widespread.

Build to the Outcomes

1. What are some of the personal, social, and financial costs of mental illness?

2. What are the obstacles to treatment for the mentally ill?

3. What are the two broad types of treatment?

Psychological Treatments: Healing the Mind Through Interaction

Psychological treatment, or **psychotherapy**, *is an interaction between a socially sanctioned clinician and someone suffering from a psychological problem, with the goal of providing support or relief from the problem.* Over 500 different forms of psychotherapy exist. Although there are similarities among all the forms, each approach is unique in its goals, aims, and methods. A survey of 538 psychologists registered with provincial regulatory bodies asked them to describe their theoretical orientation (Hunsley, Ronson, & Cohen, 2013) (see **FIGURE 16.1**). Many reported using **eclectic psychotherapy**, *a form of psychotherapy that involves drawing on techniques from different forms of therapy, depending on the client and the problem.* This approach allows therapists to apply an appropriate theoretical perspective suited

Learning Outcomes

- Outline the aspects of each approach to psychotherapy.

- Describe the pros and cons of group treatment.

Figure 16.1

Approaches to Psychotherapy in the 21st Century Shown here are the dominant therapy orientations of Canadian clinical psychologists from 2009–2010. This chart shows the percentage of practitioners (out of the 538 who returned survey information) who chose each theoretical orientation as one to which they subscribed (Hunsley et al., 2013). The results of a large number of studies conducted over the last 30 years demonstrate the efficacy of cognitive behavioural therapy over other forms of therapy for a wide range of mood, anxiety, substance abuse, personality, and psychotic disorders, and there is a strong emphasis on evidence-based treatment in Canadian clinical psychology training programs (Hunsley et al., 2013; Section on Clinical Psychology of the Canadian Psychological Association, 2016). It is not surprising therefore that a cognitive behavioural orientation is the most popular one.

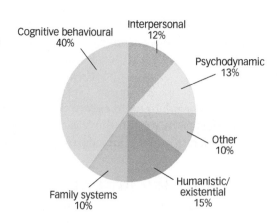

The stereotypic image you might have of psychological therapy—a person lying on a couch talking to a person sitting in a chair—springs from the psychoanalytic approach.

psychotherapy An interaction between a socially sanctioned clinician and someone suffering from a psychological problem, with the goal of providing support or relief from the problem.

eclectic psychotherapy A form of psychotherapy that involves drawing on techniques from different forms of therapy, depending on the client and the problem.

psychodynamic psychotherapies Therapies that explore childhood events and encourage individuals to use this understanding to develop insight into their psychological problems.

to the problem at hand, rather than adhering to a single theoretical perspective for all clients and all types of problems. Nevertheless, as Figure 16.1 shows, the majority of psychotherapy practitioners relied on one of five orientations in their work. Cognitive behavioural was the most popular, reflecting the wealth of research demonstrating the efficacy of this approach for a wide range of disorders (Hunsley et al., 2013; Section on Clinical Psychology of the Canadian Psychological Association, 2016). Interpersonal therapy is a proven treatment for depression (Markowitz, 1999). It draws on both the cognitive behavioural orientation and psychodynamic orientation, and is discussed in the psychodynamic theory section. Family systems therapy is a form of group therapy, used to treat issues involving both children and their parents (such as behavioural disorders that may be exacerbated by ineffective parenting). In the coming sections, we will examine psychodynamic therapy, humanistic and existential therapy, cognitive behavioural therapy, and group therapy in turn.

Psychodynamic Therapy

Psychodynamic psychotherapy has its roots in Freud's psychoanalytically oriented theory of personality. **Psychodynamic psychotherapies** *explore childhood events and encourage individuals to use the understanding gained from the exploration to develop insight into their psychological problems.* Psychoanalysis was the first psychodynamic therapy to be developed, but it has largely been replaced by modern psychodynamic therapies, such as interpersonal psychotherapy.

Psychoanalysis

As we saw in the Personality chapter, *psychoanalysis* assumes that people are born with aggressive and sexual urges that are repressed during childhood development through the use of defence mechanisms. Psychoanalysts encourage their clients to bring these repressed conflicts into consciousness so that the clients can understand them and reduce their unwanted influences. Psychoanalysts focus a great deal on early childhood events because they believe that urges and conflicts were likely to be repressed during this time.

Traditional psychoanalysis involves four or five sessions per week over an average of 3 to 6 years (Ursano & Silberman, 2003). During a session, the client reclines on a couch, facing away from the analyst, who asks the client to make *free associations*, in which the client expresses whatever thoughts and feelings come to mind. Occasionally, the therapist may comment on some information the client presents but does not express his or her values and judgements. The goal of psychoanalysis is for the client to understand the unconscious through a process Freud called *developing insight*.

Psychodynamic Therapy

Freud's original version of psychoanalysis is practiced by very few clinicians today (see Figure 16.1). However, many of his insights and techniques remain influential in a broader range of psychodynamic treatments that are used more frequently; the new treatments differ from classic psychoanalysis in both their content and their procedures. One of the most common psychodynamic treatments is **interpersonal psychotherapy (IPT)**, *a form of psychotherapy that focuses on helping clients improve current relationships* (Weissman, Markowitz, & Klerman, 2000). In terms of content, therapists using therapies such as IPT talk to clients about their interpersonal behaviours and feelings, rather than have them use free association. They pay particular attention to the client's grief (an exaggerated reaction to the loss of a loved one), role disputes (conflicts with a significant other), role transitions (changes in life status, such as starting a new job, getting married, or retiring), or interpersonal deficits (lack of the skills needed to start or maintain a relationship). The treatment focuses on interpersonal functioning, with the assumption that, as interpersonal relations improve, symptoms will subside.

Modern psychodynamic psychotherapies such as IPT also differ from classical psychoanalysis in what procedures are used. For starters, in modern psychodynamic therapy the therapist and client typically sit face to face. In addition, therapy is less intensive, with meetings often occurring only once a week and therapy lasting months rather than years. In contrast to classical psychoanalysis, modern psychodynamic therapists are more likely to see relief from symptoms as a reasonable goal for therapy (in addition to the goal of facilitating insight), and they are more likely to offer support or advice in addition to interpretation (Barber et al., 2013). Therapists are also now less likely to interpret a client's statements as a sign of unconscious sexual or aggressive impulses, as was commonly the case in psychoanalysis. However, other concepts, such as fostering insight into unconscious processes, remain features of most psychodynamic therapies. Freud's couch casts a long shadow.

In the classic movie *Good Will Hunting*, the lead character, played by Matt Damon, forms a strong bond with his therapist, played by Robin Williams. As in psychodynamic therapy, the therapist uses the doctor/patient relationship to help break down the patient's defence mechanisms and resolve an inner conflict. The amazing bond that was formed between therapist and patient and the life-changing treatment delivered are the stuff of therapists' dreams (and Hollywood scripts).

What Is the Evidence?

Although psychodynamic therapy has been around for a long time and continues to be widely practiced, there is limited evidence for its effectiveness. Although some researchers suggest that there is evidence that psychodynamic therapies are effective (Shedler, 2010), randomized trials and meta-analyses report that IPT (just discussed) and cognitive behaviour therapy (described below) are more effective than psychodynamic and other treatments, especially in the treatment of depressive and anxiety disorders (Tolin, 2010; Watzke et al., 2012; Zhou et al., 2015).

Humanistic and Existential Therapies

Humanistic and existential therapies emerged in the middle of the 20th century, in part as a reaction to the negative views that psychoanalysis holds about human nature (for instance, that we are focused primarily on sex and death). Humanistic and existential therapies assume that human nature is generally positive, and they emphasize the natural tendency of each individual to strive for personal improvement. Humanistic and existential therapies share the assumption that psychological problems stem from feelings of alienation and loneliness, and that those feelings can be traced to failure to reach one's potential (in the humanistic approach) or from failure to find meaning in life (in the existential approach). Although interest in these approaches peaked in the 1960s and 1970s, some therapists continue to practice these approaches today. Two well-known types are person-centred therapy (a humanistic approach) and gestalt therapy (an existential approach).

Person-Centred Therapy

Person-centred therapy (or client-centred therapy) *assumes that all individuals have a tendency towards growth and that this growth can be facilitated by acceptance by*

interpersonal psychotherapy (IPT) A form of psychotherapy that focuses on helping clients improve current relationships.

person-centred therapy (or client-centred therapy) A form of psychotherapy that assumes that all individuals have a tendency towards growth and that this growth can be facilitated by acceptance and genuine reactions from the therapist.

and genuine reactions from the therapist. The American psychologist Carl Rogers (1902–1987) developed person-centred therapy in the 1940s and 1950s (Rogers, 1951). This approach assumes that each person is qualified to determine his or her own goals for therapy, such as becoming more confident or making a career decision, and even the frequency and length of therapy. In this type of nondirective treatment, the therapist tends not to provide advice or suggestions about what the client should be doing, but instead paraphrases the client's words, mirroring the client's thoughts and sentiments (e.g., "I think I hear you saying . . ."). Person-centred therapists believe that with adequate support, the client will recognize the right things to do.

Rogers encouraged person-centred therapists to demonstrate three basic qualities: congruence, empathy, and unconditional positive regard. Congruence means openness and honesty in the therapeutic relationship and ensuring that the therapist communicates the same message at all levels. For example, the therapist must communicate the same message in words, in facial expressions, and in body language. Saying "I think your concerns are valid" while smirking simply will not do. Empathy is the continuous process of trying to understand the client by getting inside his or her way of thinking, feeling, and understanding the world. Interestingly, research has shown that the more empathic a client says the clinician is, the more similarity there is between the client's and therapist's levels of physiological arousal in that moment (Marci et al., 2007). This suggests that therapists who are being empathic may really be feeling some of what their clients are feeling. Seeing the world from the client's perspective enables the therapist to better appreciate the client's apprehensions, worries, or fears. Finally, the therapist must treat the client with unconditional positive regard by providing a nonjudgemental, warm, and accepting environment in which the client can feel safe expressing his or her thoughts and feelings.

The goal is not to uncover repressed conflicts, as in psychodynamic therapy, but instead to try to understand the client's experience and reflect that experience back to the client in a supportive way, encouraging the client's natural tendency towards growth. This style of therapy, however, is reminiscent of psychoanalysis in the way it encourages the client towards the free expression of thoughts and feelings.

Gestalt Therapy

Gestalt therapy was developed by Frederick "Fritz" Perls (1893–1970) and colleagues in the 1940s and 1950s (Perls, Hefferkine, & Goodman, 1951). **Gestalt therapy** *has the goal of helping the client become aware of his or her thoughts, behaviours, experiences, and feelings and to "own" or take responsibility for them.* Gestalt therapists are encouraged to be enthusiastic and warm towards their clients, an approach they share with person-centred therapists. To help facilitate the client's awareness, gestalt therapists also reflect back to the client their impressions of the client.

Gestalt therapy emphasizes the experiences and behaviours that are occurring at that particular moment in the therapy session. For example, if a client is talking about something stressful that occurred during the previous week, the therapist might shift the attention to the client's current experience by asking, "How do you feel as you describe what happened to you?" This technique is known as focusing. Clients are also encouraged to put their feelings into action. One way to do this is the empty chair technique, in which the client imagines that a person in their life (e.g., a spouse, a parent, a coworker) is in an empty chair sitting directly across from the client. The client then moves from chair to chair, alternating from role-playing what he or she would say to the other person and then role-playing how he or she imagines the other person would respond.

As part of gestalt therapy, clients may be encouraged to imagine that another person is sitting across from them in a chair. The client then moves from chair to chair, role-playing what he or she would say to the imagined person and how that person would answer.

gestalt therapy A form of psychotherapy whose goal is helping the client become aware of his or her thoughts, behaviours, experiences, and feelings and to "own" or take responsibility for them.

Behavioural and Cognitive Therapies

Unlike the older, more traditional talk therapies described above, behavioural and cognitive treatments emphasize actively changing a person's current thoughts and behaviours as a way to mitigate or eliminate their psychopathology. In the evolution of psychological treatments, clients started out lying down in psychoanalysis and then sitting in psychodynamic and related approaches, but in behavioural and cognitive therapies, they often stand and engage in behaviour-change homework assignments in their everyday life.

Behaviour Therapy: Changing Maladaptive Behaviour Patterns

Whereas Freud developed psychoanalysis as an offshoot of hypnosis and other clinical techniques that clinicians used before him, behaviour therapy was developed based on laboratory findings of behavioural psychologists. As you read in The Evolution of Psychological Science chapter, behaviourists rejected theories based on "invisible" mental properties that were difficult to test and impossible to observe directly. Behaviourists found psychoanalytic ideas particularly hard to test: How do you know whether a person has an unconscious conflict or whether insight has occurred? Behavioural principles, in contrast, focused solely on behaviours that could be observed (e.g., avoidance of a feared object, such as refusing to get on an airplane). **Behaviour therapy** assumes that *disordered behaviour is learned and that symptom relief is achieved through changing overt, maladaptive behaviours into more constructive behaviours.* A variety of behaviour therapy techniques have been developed for many disorders, based on the learning principles you encountered in the Learning chapter, including operant conditioning procedures (which focus on reinforcement and punishment) and classical conditioning procedures (which focus on extinction). Here are three examples of behaviour therapy techniques in action:

A behavioural psychologist might treat a temper tantrum using time-out for reinforcement, a method that is based on the behavioural principle of operant conditioning and one that ensures that a child will not be rewarded for her undesired behaviour.

Eliminating Unwanted Behaviours How would you change a 3-year-old's habit of throwing tantrums at the grocery store? A behaviour therapist might investigate what happens immediately before and after the tantrum: Did the child get candy to "shut him up"? The study of operant conditioning shows that behaviour can be influenced by its *consequences* (the reinforcing or punishing events that follow). Adjusting these might help change the behaviour. Making the consequences less reinforcing (giving candy will only reinforce the tantrum!) and more punishing (a period of time-out facing the wall in the grocery store while the parent watches from nearby rather than providing a rush of attention) could eliminate the problem behaviour over time.

Promoting Desired Behaviours Candy and time-outs can have a strong influence on child behaviour, but they work less well with adults. How might you get an individual with schizophrenia to engage in activities of daily living? How would you get a cocaine addict to stop using drugs? A behaviour therapy technique that has proven to be quite effective in such cases is the **token economy**, which *involves giving clients "tokens" for desired behaviours that they can later trade for rewards.* In the case of cocaine dependence, for instance, the desired behaviour is not using cocaine. Programs that reward non-use (verified by clean urine samples) with vouchers that can be exchanged for rewards such as money, bus passes, clothes, and so on, have been shown to significantly reduce cocaine use and associated psychological problems (Petry, Alessi, & Rash, 2013). Similar systems are used to promote desired behaviours in classrooms, the workplace, and commercial advertising (e.g., airline and credit card rewards programs).

Reducing Unwanted Emotional Responses One of the most powerful ways to reduce anxious behaviour is by gradual exposure to the feared object or situation. **Exposure therapy** is an *approach to treatment of the client that involves confronting an emotion-arousing stimulus directly and repeatedly, ultimately leading to a decrease in the emotional response.* This technique depends on the processes of habituation and response extinction. For example, in Christine's case her clinician gradually exposed her to the content of her obsessions (dirt and germs), which became less and less

behaviour therapy A type of therapy that assumes that disordered behaviour is learned and that symptom relief is achieved through changing overt maladaptive behaviours into more constructive behaviours.

token economy A form of behaviour therapy in which clients are given "tokens" for desired behaviours, which they can later trade for rewards.

exposure therapy An approach to treatment that involves confronting an emotion-arousing stimulus directly and repeatedly, ultimately leading to a decrease in the emotional response.

BENKRUT/ISTOCK/GETTY IMAGES

An exposure therapy client with obsessive-compulsive disorder who fears contamination in public restrooms might be given the "homework" of visiting three such restrooms in a week, touching the toilets, and then not washing up.

cognitive therapy Focuses on helping a client identify and correct any distorted thinking about self, others, or the world.

distressing with repeated exposure (as she learned that she would not actually be harmed by coming into contact with the previously feared stimulus). Similarly, for clients who are afraid of social interaction and unable to function at school or work, a behavioural treatment might involve exposure first to imagined situations in which they talk briefly with one person, then talk a bit longer to a medium-sized group, and finally, give a speech to a large group. It's now known that *in vivo* (live) exposure is more effective than imaginary exposure (Choy, Fyer, & Lipsitz, 2007). In other words, if a person fears social situations, it is better for that person to practice social interaction than merely to imagine it. Behavioural therapists use an exposure hierarchy to accustom the client gradually to the feared object or situation. Easier situations are practiced first, and as fear decreases, the client progresses to more difficult or frightening situations (see **TABLE 16.1**). It is vitally important that the person continue to be exposed to the feared stimulus until their anxiety decreases. If they leave the situation before that happens, their anxiety will be reinforced, because they fail to learn that the feared stimulus is not harmful and they also learn that avoiding it decreases their anxiety. So, if you have a fear of, say, public speaking, best to speak to increasingly large groups of people and to not leave each situation until your anxiety decreases!

Exposure therapy can also help people overcome unwanted emotional and behavioural responses through *exposure and response prevention*. Persons with OCD, for example, might have recurrent thoughts that their hands are dirty and need washing. Washing stops the uncomfortable feelings of contamination only briefly, though, and they wash again and again in search of relief. In exposure with response prevention, they might be asked in therapy to get their hands dirty on purpose (first by touching a coin picked up from the ground, then by touching a public toilet, and later by touching a dead mouse) and leave them dirty for hours. They may need to do this only a few times to break the cycle and be freed from the obsessive ritual (Foa et al., 2007).

Cognitive Therapy: Changing Distorted Thoughts

Whereas behaviour therapy focuses primarily on changing a person's behaviour, **cognitive therapy**, as the name suggests, *focuses on helping a client identify and correct any distorted thinking about self, others, or the world* (Beck, 2019). For example,

TABLE 16.1	
EXPOSURE HIERARCHY FOR SOCIAL PHOBIA	
Item	**Fear (0–100)**
1. Have a party and invite everyone from work	99
2. Go to a holiday party for 1 hour without drinking	90
3. Invite Cindy to have dinner and see a movie	85
4. Go for a job interview	80
5. Ask boss for a day off work	65
6. Ask questions in a meeting at work	65
7. Eat lunch with coworkers	60
8. Talk to a stranger on the bus	50
9. Talk to cousin on the telephone for 10 minutes	40
10. Ask for directions at the gas station	35

Information from Ellis (1991).

behaviourists might explain a phobia as the outcome of a classical conditioning experience such as being bitten by a dog; the dog bite leads to the development of a dog phobia through the association of the dog with the experience of pain. Cognitive theorists might instead emphasize the *interpretation* of the event. It might not be the event itself that caused the fear, but rather the individual's beliefs and assumptions about the event and the feared stimulus. In the case of a dog bite, to explain the fear, cognitive theorists might focus on a person's new or strengthened belief that dogs are dangerous.

A principal technique of cognitive therapies is called **cognitive restructuring**, which *teaches clients to question the automatic beliefs, assumptions, and predictions that often lead to negative emotions and to replace negative thinking with more realistic and positive beliefs*. Specifically, clients are taught to examine the evidence for and against a particular belief or to be more accepting of outcomes that may be undesirable yet still manageable. For example, a depressed client may believe that she is stupid and will never pass her university courses—all on the basis of one poor grade. In this situation, the therapist would work with the client to examine the validity of this belief. The therapist would consider relevant evidence such as grades on previous exams, performance on other coursework, and examples of her intelligence outside school. It may be that the client has never failed a course before and has achieved good grades in this particular course in the past. In this case, the therapist would encourage the client to consider all this information in determining whether she is truly "stupid." **TABLE 16.2** shows a variety of common, potentially irrational ideas that can unleash unwanted emotions such as anger, depression, or anxiety. Any of these irrational beliefs might bedevil a person with serious emotional problems if left unchallenged; for that reason such beliefs are potential targets for cognitive restructuring. In therapy sessions, the cognitive therapist will help the client to identify evidence that either supports or fails to support each negative thought, in order to help the client generate more balanced thoughts that more accurately reflect the true state of affairs. In other words, the clinician tries to remove the dark lens through which the client views the world, not with the goal of replacing it with rose-coloured glasses, but instead with replacing it

The approach to psychotherapy developed by cognitive therapist Aaron Beck employs a direct and rational approach to help people change maladaptive thinking patterns.

cognitive restructuring A therapeutic approach that teaches clients to question the automatic beliefs, assumptions, and predictions that often lead to negative emotions and to replace negative thinking with more realistic and positive beliefs.

TABLE 16.2

COMMON IRRATIONAL BELIEFS AND THE EMOTIONAL RESPONSES THEY CAN CAUSE

Belief	Emotional Response
I have to get this done immediately.	Anxiety, stress
I must be perfect.	
Something terrible will happen.	
Everyone is watching me.	Embarrassment, social anxiety
I won't be able to make friends.	
People know something is wrong with me.	
I'm a loser and will always be a loser.	Sadness, depression
Nobody will ever love me.	
She did that to me on purpose.	Anger, irritability
He is evil and should be punished.	
Things ought to be different.	

Information from Ellis (1991).

with clear glasses. Here is a brief sample transcript of what part of a cognitive therapy session might sound like.

Clinician: Last week I asked you to keep a thought record of situations that made you feel very depressed, at least one per day, and the automatic thoughts that popped into your mind. Were you able to do that?

Client: Yes.

Clinician: Great. Did you bring it in with you today?

Client: Yes, here it is.

Clinician: Wonderful, I'm glad you were able to complete this assignment. Let's take a look at this together. What's the first situation that you recorded?

Client: Well . . . I went out on Friday night with my friends, which I thought would be fun and help me to feel better. But I was feeling kind of down about things and I ended up not really talking to anyone, which led me to just sit in the corner and drink all night, which caused me to get so drunk that I passed out at the party. I woke up the next day feeling embarrassed and more depressed than ever.

Clinician: Okay, sounds like a tough situation. So the situation is you had too much to drink and passed out. The resulting emotion you had was depression. How intense was your feeling of depression on a scale of 0 to 100?

Client: Ninety.

Clinician: Okay, and what thoughts automatically popped into your head?

Client: I can't control myself. I'll never be able to control myself. My friends think I'm a loser and will never want to hang out with me again.

Clinician: Okay, and which of these thoughts led you to feel most depressed?

Client: That my friends think I'm a loser and won't want to hang out with me anymore.

Clinician: All right, so let's focus on that one for a minute. What evidence can you think of that supports this thought?

Client: Well . . . um . . . I got really drunk and so they *have* to think I'm a loser. I mean, who does that?

Clinician: Okay, write that down on your thought record in this column here. Anything else? Is there any other evidence you can think of that supports those thoughts?

Client: No.

Clinician: All right. Now let's take a moment to think about whether there is any evidence that doesn't support those thoughts. Did anything happen that suggests that your friends don't think you are a loser or that they do want to keep hanging out with you?

Client: Well . . . apparently some kids were making fun of me when I was passed out and my friends stopped them. And they also brought me home safely and then called the next day and joked about what happened and my one friend Tommy said something like "we've all been there" and that he wants to hang out again this weekend.

Clinician: Okay, great, write that down in this next column. This is very interesting. So on one hand, you feel depressed and have thoughts that you are a loser and your friends don't like you. But on the other hand, you have some pretty real-world evidence that even though you drank too much, they were still there for you and they do in fact want to hang out with you again, yes?

Client: Yeah, I guess you're right if you put it that way. I didn't think about it like that.

Clinician: So now if we were going to replace your first thoughts, which don't seem to have a lot of real-world evidence, with a more balanced thought based on the evidence, what would that new thought be?

Client: Probably something like, my friends probably weren't happy about the fact that I got so drunk because then they had to take care of me, but they are my friends and were there for me and want to keep hanging out with me.

Clinician: Excellent job. I think that sounds just right based on the evidence. Write that down in the next column. And how much do you believe in this new thought on a scale of 0 to 100?

Client: I think it's actually pretty accurate, so I would say 95.

Clinician: And thinking about this new more balanced thought rather than your first one, how would you rate your depression?

Client: Much lower than before. Probably a 40. I'm still not happy that I got so drunk, but I'm less depressed about my friends.

In addition to cognitive restructuring techniques, which try to change a person's thoughts to be more balanced or accurate, some forms of cognitive therapy also include techniques for coping with unwanted thoughts and feelings, techniques that resemble meditation (see the Consciousness chapter). Clients may be encouraged to attend to their troubling thoughts or emotions or be given meditative techniques that allow them to gain a new focus (Hofmann & Asmundson, 2008). One such technique, called **mindfulness meditation**, *teaches an individual to be fully present in each moment; to be aware of his or her thoughts, feelings, and sensations; and to detect symptoms before they become a problem.* Researchers found mindfulness meditation to be helpful for preventing relapse in patients who have recovered from depression. In one study, people recovering from depression were about half as likely to relapse during a 60-week assessment period if they received mindfulness meditation-based cognitive therapy than if they received treatment as usual (Teasdale et al., 2000). Cognitive and cognitive behavioural therapies (covered below) do well in preventing relapse because once a person learns the skills taught in these therapies, they can continue to use them in future situations all on their own, without guidance from a clinician (DeRubeis, Siegle, & Hollon, 2008). This is in contrast to medications, which only work as long as they are present in the body.

Whereas traditional forms of cognitive therapy focused largely on changing maladaptive thoughts, some newer forms incorporate meditation practices to help people become more aware of such thoughts and to simply let them pass on by—like clouds in the sky.

Cognitive Behavioural Therapy: Blending Approaches

Historically, cognitive and behavioural therapies were considered distinct systems of therapy, and some people continue to follow this distinction, using solely behavioural *or* solely cognitive techniques. Today, the extent to which therapists use cognitive versus behavioural techniques depends on the individual therapist as well as the type of problem being treated. Most therapists working with anxiety and depression use **cognitive behavioural therapy (CBT)**, *a blend of cognitive and behavioural therapeutic strategies.* This technique acknowledges that there may be behaviours that people cannot control through rational thought, but also that there are ways of helping people think more rationally when thought does play a role. In contrast to traditional behaviour therapy and cognitive therapy, CBT is *problem-focused*, meaning that it is undertaken for specific problems (e.g., reducing the frequency of panic attacks or returning to work after a bout of depression), and *action-oriented*, meaning that the therapist tries to assist the client in selecting specific strategies that could help address those problems. The client is expected to *do* things, such as engage in exposure exercises, practice behaviour-change skills, or use a diary to monitor relevant symptoms (e.g., the severity of depressed mood, panic attack symptoms). This is in contrast to psychodynamic or other therapies in which goals may not be explicitly discussed or agreed on and the client's only necessary action is to attend the therapy session.

CBT also contrasts with psychodynamic approaches in its assumptions about what the client can know. CBT is *transparent* in that nothing is withheld from the client. By the end of the course of therapy, most clients have a very good understanding of the treatment they have received as well as the specific techniques that are used

mindfulness meditation Teaches an individual to be fully present in each moment; to be aware of his or her thoughts, feelings, and sensations; and to detect symptoms before they become a problem.

cognitive behavioural therapy (CBT) A blend of cognitive and behavioural therapeutic strategies.

to make the desired changes. For example, clients with OCD who fear contamination would feel confident in knowing how to confront feared situations such as public washrooms and why confronting these situations is helpful.

Cognitive behavioural therapies have been found to be effective for a number of disorders (Butler et al., 2006) (see Hot Science: "Rebooting" Psychological Treatment).

Hot Science | "Rebooting" Psychological Treatment

Modern psychological treatments have advanced far beyond the days of Freud and his free-associating patients. We now have more sophisticated treatments that are based on recent advances in psychological science and supported by experimental studies that show that the new treatments actually do decrease peoples' psychological suffering. However, psychological treatment is still pretty primitive in many ways. It usually involves a patient meeting once per week with a clinician who attempts to talk them out of their psychological disorder—just as it did in the earliest days of psychological treatment. One of the world's leading researchers of traditional psychological treatments, Alan Kazdin, has called for a "rebooting" of psychotherapy research and practice (Kazdin, 2018; Kazdin & Blase, 2011). What is needed, he argues, is a portfolio of treatment delivery approaches that take advantage of recent advances in technology.

Although most psychologists providing treatment to those with psychological disorders still employ traditional psychotherapy, researchers are developing and testing new methods of treatment that make creative use of new technologies. For instance, using apps that monitor people's symptoms by having them answer daily surveys sent to their smartphones, psychologists have learned that among people experiencing suicidal thoughts, those thoughts tend to come and go repeatedly throughout the week (Kleiman et al., 2018). Since traditional therapists see patients once per week, what should suicidal patients do when their thoughts come and go in between sessions? Researchers have begun to create computer- and phone-based apps that can identify people at risk and beam interventions to their computers and phones at any time. For instance, one platform uses

artificial intelligence and automated chat-bots to scan the content of people's text messages to identify periods of psychological distress and then encourage them to reach out to others for help (e.g., Jaroszewski, Morris, & Nock, 2019).

Another smartphone-based app called Therapeutic Evaluative Conditioning (TEC) presents the user with several different images (see figure) and has him or her repeatedly pair suicidal or self-injury-related images with aversive images such as snakes or spiders. The idea is that, as with classical conditioning, by repeatedly pairing these images, over time people will come to associate the suicidal or self-injury-related images with the aversive feeling evoked by the pictures of snakes and spiders. Researchers found in

three different randomized controlled trials that people who played this matching game for a few minutes each day for one month showed significant reductions in self-injury and suicidal behaviour (Franklin et al., 2016).

The development of computer- or smartphone-based interventions has been extremely exciting; however, although there are an increasing number of apps, very few can show data supporting their effectiveness (Wisniewski et al., 2019). So, although the development of computerized approaches has opened up lots of new opportunities for intervention, it is important that psychologists carefully evaluate which ones can help improve health outcomes and which are simply fancier ways of providing ineffective treatment.

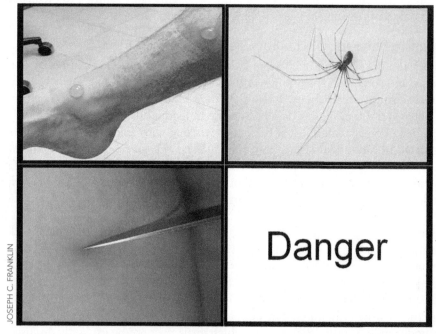

In Therapeutic Evaluative Conditioning (TEC), patients are trained to repeatedly pair suicidal or self-injury-related images (*bottom left*) with aversive images (*top right*). Over time, people making such pairings develop an aversion to suicide/self-injury and show a decrease in these self-harm behaviours.

Substantial positive effects of CBT have been found for clients with unipolar depression, generalized anxiety disorder, panic disorder, social phobia, posttraumatic stress disorder, and childhood depressive and anxiety disorders. CBT has moderate but less substantial positive effects for marital distress, anger, somatic disorders, and chronic pain.

Group Treatments: Healing Multiple Minds at the Same Time

It is natural to think of psychopathology as an illness that affects only one individual. A particular person "is depressed," for example, or "has anxiety." Yet each person lives in a world of other people, and interactions with others may intensify and even cause disorders. A depressed person may be lonely after moving away from friends and loved ones, or an anxious person could be worried about pressure from parents. These ideas suggest that people might be able to recover from disorders in the same way they got into them—not just as an individual effort, but through social processes.

Couple and Family Therapy

When a couple is "having problems," it may be that neither individual suffers from any psychopathology. Rather, it may be the relationship itself that is disordered. In *couple therapy*, a married, co-habiting, or dating couple is seen together in therapy to work on problems usually arising within the relationship. A traditional situation for couple therapy might involve a couple seeking help because they are unhappy with their relationship. In this scenario, both members of the couple are expected to attend therapy sessions because the problem is seen as arising from their interaction rather than from the problem(s) of one half of the couple. Treatment strategies would target changes in *both* parties, focusing on ways to break their repetitive dysfunctional pattern.

In some cases, therapy with even larger groups is warranted. An individual may be having a problem—say, an adolescent is abusing alcohol—but the source of the problem is the individual's relationships with family members; perhaps the mother is herself an alcoholic who subtly encourages the adolescent to drink, and the father travels and neglects the family. In this case, it could be useful for the therapist to work with the whole group at once in *family therapy*—psychotherapy involving members of a family. Family therapy can be particularly effective when adolescent children are having problems (Masten, 2004).

In family therapy, the "client" is the entire family. Family therapists believe that problem behaviours exhibited by a particular family member are the result of a dysfunctional family dynamic. For example, an adolescent girl suffering from bulimia might be treated in therapy with her mother, father, and older brother. The therapist would work to understand how the family members relate to one another, how the family is organized, and how it changes over time. In the discussions, the therapist might discover that the parents' excessive enthusiasm about her brother's athletic career led the daughter to try to gain their approval by controlling her weight to become "beautiful." Both couple and family therapy involve more than one person attending therapy together, since the problems and solutions are seen as arising from the *interactions* of these individuals rather than simply from any one individual.

Group Therapy

Taking these ideas one step further, if individuals (or families) can benefit from talking with a psychotherapist, perhaps they can also benefit from talking with other clients who are talking with the therapist. This is **group therapy**, *a type of therapy in which multiple participants (who often do not know one another at the outset) work on their individual*

Families enter therapy for many reasons, sometimes to help particular members and other times because there are problems in one or more of the relationships in the family.

group therapy A type of therapy in which multiple participants (who often do not know each other at the outset) work on their individual problems in a group atmosphere.

problems in a group atmosphere. The therapist in group therapy serves more as a group facilitator than as a personal therapist, conducting the sessions both by talking with individuals and by encouraging them to talk with each other. Group therapy is often useful for people who have a common problem, such as substance abuse, but it can also be beneficial for those with differing problems. It is important to note that group therapy is not an approach in itself but a mode of delivering treatment. That is, group therapy can be psychodynamic, cognitive, cognitive behavioural, and so on, in its approach.

Why do people choose group therapy? One advantage is that attending a group with others who have similar problems shows clients that they are not alone in their suffering. In addition, group members model appropriate behaviours for each other and share their insights about how to deal with their problems. Group therapy is often just as effective as individual therapy (e.g., Jonsson & Hougaard, 2009). From a societal perspective, then, group therapy is much more efficient.

Group therapy also has disadvantages. It may be difficult to assemble a group of individuals who have similar needs. This is particularly an issue with CBT, which tends to focus on specific problems such as depression or panic disorder. Group therapy may also become a problem if one or more members undermine the treatment of other group members. This can occur if some group members dominate the discussions, threaten other group members, or make others in the group uncomfortable (e.g., attempting to date other members). Finally, clients in group therapy get less attention than each might receive in individual psychotherapy.

Self-Help and Support Groups

Some important types of group therapy are *self-help groups* and *support groups,* which are discussion groups that focus on a particular disorder or difficult life experience; they are often run by peers (rather than a clinician) who have themselves struggled with the same issues. The most famous self-help and support groups are Alcoholics Anonymous (AA), Gamblers Anonymous, and Al-Anon (a program for families and friends of those with alcohol problems). Other self-help groups offer support to cancer survivors or to parents of children with autism or to people with mood disorders, eating disorders, and substance abuse problems. In fact, self-help and support groups exist for just about every psychological disorder. In addition to being cost effective, self-help and support groups allow people to realize that they are not the only ones with a particular problem, and the groups give them the opportunity to offer guidance and support to each other that has arisen from their own personal experiences of success.

In some cases, though, self-help and support groups can do more harm than good. Some members may be disruptive or aggressive or encourage each other to engage in behaviours that are countertherapeutic (e.g., continuing to avoid feared situations or using alcohol to cope). People with moderate problems who may be exposed to others with severe problems may become over-sensitized to symptoms they might not otherwise have found disturbing. Because self-help and support groups are usually not led by trained therapists, mechanisms to evaluate these groups or to ensure their quality are rarely in place.

AA has more than 2 million members in Canada, the United States, and around the world, with an estimated 4,956 groups in Canada alone (Alcoholics Anonymous, 2018). Members are encouraged to follow *12 steps* to reach the goal of lifelong abstinence from all drinking; the steps include believing in a higher power, practicing prayer and meditation, and making amends for harm to others. Most members attend group meetings several times per week, and between meetings they receive additional support from their "sponsor." A few studies have examined the effectiveness of AA, and it appears that 12-step programs like AA can be as effective as cognitive and behavioural interventions at helping people to stop using addictive substances (Kelly et al., 2017).

Considered together, the many social approaches to psychotherapy reveal how important interpersonal relationships are for each of us. It may not always be clear how psychotherapy works, whether one approach is better than another, or what

Self-help groups are a cost-effective, time-effective, and treatment-effective solution for dealing with some types of psychological problems. Many people like self-help groups, but are they effective? How could you test this?

STURTI/GETTY IMAGES

particular theory best explains how problems have developed. What *is* clear, however, is that social interactions among people—both in individual therapy and in all the different forms of group therapy—can be useful in treating psychological disorders.

Build to the Outcomes

1. What is the basis for psychoanalysis and what are its key techniques?

2. In what common ways do modern psychodynamic theories differ from Freudian analysis?

3. How does a humanistic view of human nature differ from a psychodynamic view?

4. What are the characteristics of person-centred and gestalt therapies?

5. How do behavioural therapies compensate for what behaviourists saw as problems with psychoanalytic ideas?

6. What is the idea behind the concept of cognitive restructuring?

7. How is CBT both *problem-focused* and *action-oriented*?

8. When is group therapy the best option?

9. How do self-help and support groups differ from traditional psychotherapy?

Biological Treatments: Healing the Mind by Physically Altering the Brain

People have ingested foreign substances in an attempt to change or improve their mental state since the beginning of recorded history. Humans have been fermenting fruits and other natural substances to create alcohol since about 7000 BCE (McGovern et al., 2004). Over a period of more than 1,500 years, Greek physicians prescribed a substance called *theriac* to treat a wide range of ailments, including anxiety and depression. Theriac was composed of dozens of different ingredients (including red roses, carrots, and viper's flesh), although we now know that one ingredient in particular (opium) likely was responsible for its positive effects. In the more recent past, physicians found that another substance also worked wonders as a cure for depression, headaches, indigestion, and a range of other problems. That substance was cocaine, and it turns out that it has many negative side effects, which led to it falling out of favour as a sanctioned medicine (Markel, 2011). Since then, drug treatments have been developed that don't lead users to feel euphoric (as is the case with opium and cocaine). Instead they target specific neurotransmitters in the brain that researchers believe are involved in different mental disorders. These treatments have grown in variety, effectiveness, and popularity; they are now the most common medical approach in treating psychological disorders (see **FIGURE 16.2**).

Antipsychotic Medications

The story of drug treatments for severe psychological disorders starts in the 1950s, with chlorpromazine (brand-name Thorazine); it was originally developed as a sedative, but when it was administered to agitated patients with schizophrenia they often became euphoric and docile (Barondes, 2003). The first in a series of **antipsychotic drugs**, which *treat schizophrenia and related psychotic disorders,* chlorpromazine completely changed the way schizophrenia was managed. Related medications, such as thioridazine (Mellaril) and haloperidol (Haldol), followed. Before antipsychotic drugs were introduced, people with schizophrenia often exhibited bizarre symptoms and were sometimes so disruptive and difficult to manage that the only way to protect them (and other people) was to keep them in hospitals for people with mental disorders; initially called *asylums,*

Learning Outcomes

- Explain how antipsychotic medications affect the brain.

- Identify the risks of antianxiety medications.

- Explain how modern antidepressants affect the brain.

- Identify which herbal supplements have been proven to be effective.

- Debate pros and cons of combining psychological therapy with drug therapy.

- Identify the more extreme treatment options when psychotherapy and medications are unsuccessful.

antipsychotic drugs Medications that are used to treat schizophrenia and related psychotic disorders.

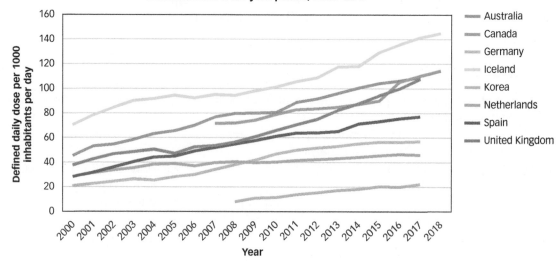

Figure 16.2

Antidepressant Use The popularity of psychiatric medications has skyrocketed in recent years. A recent report from the Organisation for Economic Cooperation and Development (OECD) reveals that antidepressant use among Canadians is among the highest in the world. The OECD survey revealed that antidepressant consumption has been increasing across a range of OECD member countries, including Canada and the other seven shown here. The "defined daily dose" is the drug-specific standard maintenance dose for an adult—so, a value of 100 on the y-axis means that, for every 1,000 people every day, the equivalent of 100 maintenance doses of antidepressant are taken (OECD, 2019).

these hospitals are now referred to as *psychiatric hospitals*. After the antipsychotic drugs were introduced, the number of people in psychiatric hospitals decreased by more than two-thirds. The drugs led to the deinstitutionalization of hundreds of thousands of people and gave a major boost to the field of **psychopharmacology**, *the study of drug effects on psychological states and symptoms.*

Researchers believe that antipsychotic medications exert their effect by blocking dopamine receptors in certain parts of the brain, such as the mesolimbic pathway: a pathway paved with dopamine neurons extending from the ventral tegmental area (VTA) to the nucleus accumbens in the basal ganglia. (see the Neuroscience and Behaviour chapter). The effectiveness of these medications for schizophrenia led to the dopamine hypothesis (described in the Psychological Disorders chapter), which suggests that schizophrenia may be caused by excess dopamine in the synapse. Research has indeed found that dopamine overactivity in the mesolimbic pathway of the brain is related to the more bizarre positive symptoms of schizophrenia, such as hallucinations and delusions (Marangell et al., 2003).

Although antipsychotic drugs work well for positive symptoms, it turns out that the negative symptoms of schizophrenia, such as emotional numbing and social withdrawal, may be related to dopamine *under*activity in the mesocortical pathways of the brain (connections between parts of the VTA and the cerebral cortex), which may help explain why antipsychotic medications do not relieve negative symptoms well. Instead of a drug that blocks dopamine receptors, negative symptoms require one that *increases* the amount of dopamine available at the synapse. This is a good example of how medical treatments can have broad psychological effects but do not target specific psychological symptoms.

Over the past few decades, a new class of antipsychotic drugs has been introduced that includes clozapine (Clozaril), risperidone (Risperdal), and olanzepine (Zyprexa). These newer drugs are often referred to as *atypical* antipsychotics. (The older drugs are now often referred to as *conventional* or *typical* antipsychotics.) Unlike the older

psychopharmacology The study of drug effects on psychological states and symptoms.

antipsychotic medications, these newer drugs appear to affect both the dopamine and serotonin systems, blocking both types of receptors. The ability to block serotonin receptors appears to be a useful addition, because enhanced serotonin activity in the brain has been implicated in some of the core difficulties in schizophrenia, such as cognitive and perceptual disruptions, as well as mood disturbances. This may explain why atypical antipsychotics work at least as well as older drugs for the positive symptoms of schizophrenia but also work fairly well for the negative symptoms, especially when the antipsychotic medication prescribed is augmented with a second antipsychotic (Galling et al., 2017).

Like most medications, antipsychotic drugs have side effects, which can be sufficiently unpleasant that some people "go off their meds," preferring their symptoms to the drug effects. A side effect that often occurs with long-term use of these drugs is *tardive dyskinesia,* a condition of involuntary movements of the face, mouth, and extremities. In fact, people often need to take another medication to treat the unwanted side effects of the conventional antipsychotic drugs. Side effects of the newer medications tend to be different from and are sometimes milder than those of the older ones. For that reason, the atypical antipsychotics are now usually the front-line treatments for schizophrenia (Meltzer, 2013).

"The drug has, however, proved more effective than traditional psychoanalysis."

Antianxiety Medications

Antianxiety medications are *drugs that help reduce a person's experience of fear or anxiety.* The most commonly used antianxiety medications are the benzodiazepines, a type of tranquilizer that works by facilitating the action of the neurotransmitter gamma-aminobutyric acid (GABA). As you learned in the Neuroscience and Behaviour chapter, GABA inhibits certain neurons in the brain. This inhibitory action can produce a calming effect for the person. Commonly prescribed benzodiazepines include diazepam (Valium), lorazepam (Ativan), and alprazolam (Xanax). The benzodiazepines typically take effect in a matter of minutes and are extremely effective for reducing symptoms of anxiety disorders.

Nonetheless, doctors are relatively cautious when prescribing benzodiazepines since they have the potential for abuse (Bandelow et al., 2017). They are also often associated with the development of *drug tolerance,* which is the need for higher dosages over long-term use to achieve the same effects (see the Consciousness chapter). Furthermore, after people have become tolerant of the drug, they risk significant withdrawal symptoms when it's discontinued. Some withdrawal symptoms include increased heart rate, shakiness, insomnia, agitation, and anxiety—the very symptoms the drug was taken to eliminate! Therefore, people who take benzodiazepines for extended periods may have difficulty coming off these drugs; they should discontinue

antianxiety medications Drugs that help reduce a person's experience of fear or anxiety.

If you watch American television you have seen advertisements for specific prescription drugs. Does this direct-to-consumer advertising really work? Sure does! One recent study sent people posing as patients to physicians' offices asking for specific drugs and found that patient requests had a huge impact on doctors' behaviour: Those asking about specific drugs were much more likely to receive a prescription than those who did not make a request (Kravitz et al., 2005).

MONKEY BUSINESS/GETTY IMAGES

them gradually to minimize withdrawal symptoms (Bandelow et al., 2017). Another consideration when prescribing benzodiazepines is their side effects. The most common side effect is drowsiness, although they can also have negative effects on coordination and memory. And benzodiazapines combined with alcohol can depress respiration, potentially causing accidental death.

When anxiety leads to insomnia, drugs known as hypnotics may be useful as sleep aids. One such drug, zolpidem (Ambien), is widely used and is often effective, but there are some reports of sleepwalking, sleep-eating, and even sleep-driving (Hughes, 2007). Another alternative for anxiety is buspirone (Buspar), which has been shown to reduce anxiety among individuals who suffer from generalized anxiety disorder.

Antidepressants and Mood Stabilizers

Antidepressants are *a class of drugs that help lift people's moods.* They were first introduced in the 1950s, when iproniazid, a drug used to treat tuberculosis, was found to elevate mood (Selikoff, Robitzek, & Ornstein, 1952). Iproniazid is a *monoamine oxidase inhibitor (MAOI),* a medication that prevents the enzyme monoamine oxidase from breaking down neurotransmitters such as norepinephrine, serotonin, and dopamine. A second category of antidepressants that was introduced in the 1950s are the tricyclic antidepressants, including drugs such as imipramine (Tofranil) and amitriptyline (Elavil), which block the reuptake of norepinephrine and serotonin, thereby increasing the amount of neurotransmitter in the synaptic space between neurons. The two classes of antidepressants are used sparingly due to their side effects, which include potentially dangerous increases in blood pressure, constipation, difficulty urinating, blurred vision, and a racing heart (Marangell et al., 2003).

Among the most commonly used antidepressants today are the *selective serotonin reuptake inhibitors,* or SSRIs, which include drugs such as fluoxetine (Prozac), citalopram (Celexa), and paroxetine (Paxil). The SSRIs work by blocking the reuptake of serotonin in the brain, which makes more serotonin available in the synaptic space between neurons. The greater availability of serotonin in the synapse gives the neuron a better chance of "recognizing" and using this neurotransmitter in sending the desired signal. The SSRIs were developed on the basis of the hypothesis that low levels of serotonin are a causal factor in depression. Supporting this hypothesis, SSRIs are effective for depression, as well as for a wide range of other problems. SSRIs are called *selective* because, unlike the tricyclic antidepressants, which work on the serotonin and norepinephrine systems, SSRIs work more specifically on the serotonin system (see **FIGURE 16.3**).

antidepressants A class of drugs that help lift people's moods.

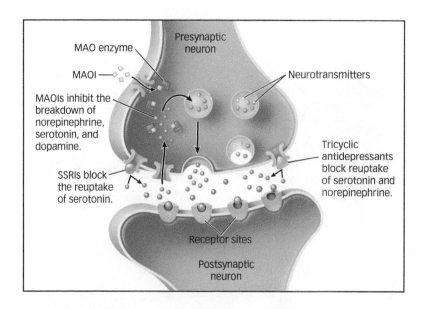

Figure 16.3
Antidepressant Drug Actions
Antidepressant drugs, such as MAOIs, SSRIs, and tricyclic antidepressants, act on neurotransmitters such as serotonin, dopamine, and norepinephrine by inhibiting their breakdown and blocking reuptake. These actions make more of the neurotransmitter available for release and leave more of the neurotransmitter in the synaptic gap to activate the receptor sites on the postsynaptic neuron. These drugs relieve depression and often alleviate anxiety and other disorders.

Finally, antidepressants such as venlafaxine (Effexor) and ibupropion (Wellbutrin) offer other alternatives. Effexor is an example of a serotonin and norepinephrine reuptake inhibitor (SNRI). Whereas SSRIs act only on serotonin, SNRIs act on both serotonin and norepinephrine. Wellbutrin, in contrast, is a norepinephrine and dopamine reuptake inhibitor. These and other newly developed antidepressants appear to have fewer (or at least different) side effects than the tricyclic antidepressants and MAOIs.

Antidepressants and Anxiety Disorders

Most antidepressants can take up to a month before they start to have an effect on mood. Besides relieving symptoms of depression, almost all of the antidepressants effectively treat anxiety disorders, and many of them can resolve other problems, such as eating disorders. In fact, several companies that manufacture SSRIs have marketed their drugs as treatments for anxiety disorders rather than for their anti-depressant effects.

How well do antidepressants work in treating these conditions? Although many studies supported by drug companies show positive results, there is evidence that drug companies are more likely to publish results of studies that suggest their drugs are effective and less likely to publish results that suggest their drugs don't work. In one meta-analysis, researchers found that 97% of studies of antidepressants that found positive results (that is, results favouring the effectiveness of the drug) were published, compared with only 12% of studies that found negative results (Turner et al., 2008). Researchers who obtained relevant unpublished data found that when combining *all* available data, antidepressants are only slightly more effective than a placebo (i.e., a sugar pill containing no active medicine) (Kirsch et al., 2008). These authors also found that antidepressants had stronger effects for some types of patients. (Check out A World of Difference: Differences in People's Responses to Treatment to learn more.)

Mood Stabilizers Are Used for Bipolar Disorder

Although antidepressants are commonly used to treat major depression, they are not recommended for treating bipolar disorder, which is characterized by manic or hypo-manic episodes (see the Psychological Disorders chapter). In this case, antidepres-sants are not prescribed because, in the process of lifting the person's mood, they might actually trigger a manic episode in a person with bipolar disorder. Instead, bipolar disorder is treated with *mood stabilizers,* which are medications used to sup-press swings between mania and depression. Lithium and valproate are commonly used mood stabilizers. Even in unipolar depression, lithium is sometimes effective when combined with traditional antidepressants in people who do not respond to anti-depressants alone.

Lithium has proven to be the most effective mood stabilizer currently available (Kessing et al., 2018); however, because it also has been associated with possible long-term kidney and thyroid problems, people taking lithium must monitor their blood levels of lithium on a regular basis. In sum, although antidepressants are effec-tive for a wide variety of problems, mood stabilizers may be required when a person's symptoms include extreme swings between highs and lows, such as those experi-enced by people with bipolar disorder.

Herbal and Natural Products

In a survey of 18,000 Canadians 45 years old and older, approximately 15% reported using alternative "medications" such as herbal medicines, megavitamins, homeo-pathic remedies, or naturopathic remedies to treat anxiety and depression (Crabb & Hunsley, 2011). Major reasons people use these products are that they are available over the counter, are less expensive, and are perceived as "natural" alternatives to

A World of Difference | **Differences in People's Responses to Treatment**

We are all different. We like different foods, different music, different books, and so on. It turns out that we also differ in how we respond to treatments for psychological disorders. For instance, one study compared the decrease in symptoms of depression seen in 718 patients randomly assigned to receive either antidepressant medication or placebo pill (Fournier et al., 2010). Participants receiving the real medication showed a dramatic decrease in symptoms over the course of treatment. However, so did those taking a placebo. Closer examination of the data revealed that for those with mild or moderate depression, a placebo is just as effective as antidepressant medication at decreasing a person's

symptoms; it is only for people with severe depression that antidepressants seem to work better than a placebo (see figure).

More recent research is examining further what predicts which kind of people will respond best to which kind of treatment. For instance, a recent study by Robert DeRubeis and colleagues (2014) found that data collected before people are randomized to a given treatment (e.g., cognitive behavioural therapy versus medication) could be used to predict accurately which treatment would benefit them most. A follow-up study by DeRubeis and colleagues found a similar result when they compared two other kinds of treatment (i.e., cognitive

therapy and interpersonal psychotherapy; Huibers et al., 2015). In this study, patients who were randomly assigned to the treatment that was predicted to be more effective for them improved significantly more than those assigned to their nonoptimal treatment. Such findings suggest that in the future, psychologists will be able to collect information from new patients that will help them determine which of the many available treatments will benefit the patients the most. This personalized, or tailored, approach to treatment is likely to lead to much better outcomes for users of psychological services in the future, and in this way is expected to make a world of difference!

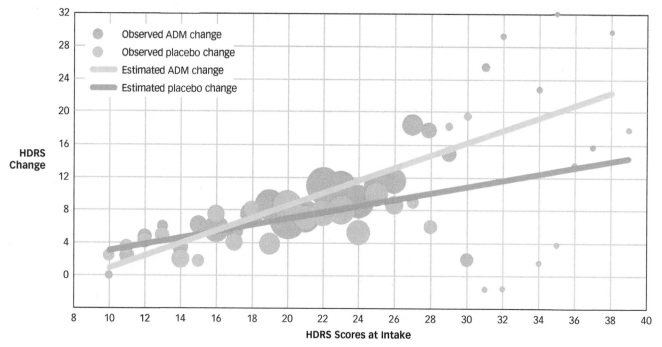

In six different studies, a total of 713 depressed individuals were given pills to treat their depression. Half were randomly assigned to receive an antidepressant medication (ADM) and half to receive a pill placebo. Importantly, the participants did not know if they were taking an antidepressant or simply a placebo. For those with mild or moderate depression, as measured by the Hamilton Depression Rating Scale (HDRS), antidepressants did not work any better than the placebo. However, those with severe depression showed much greater improvement on antidepressants than on the placebo. The circle size represents the number of people with data at each point. DATA FROM FOURNIER ET AL., 2010.

synthetic or man-made "drugs." Are herbal and natural products effective in treating mental health problems? Or are they just "snake oil"?

The answer to this question isn't simple. Health Canada does not consider herbal and natural products to be drugs, but does consider them their own category ("Natural Health Products") and does impose some regulations to ensure quality and to document side effects. Nevertheless, there is little scientific information about

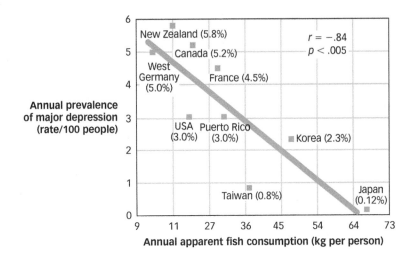

Figure 16.4
Omega-3 Fatty Acids and Depression
Recent studies have shown that consumption of omega-3 fatty acids is associated with a wide range of positive mental health outcomes. For instance, Joe Hibbeln (1998) showed that countries that consume more fish (a main dietary source of omega-3s) have significantly lower rates of depression. But remember, correlation does not mean causation! It could be that some other factor explains this association. For instance, it could be that living closer to the ocean or a greater focus on health overall predicts both greater omega-3 consumption and lower rates of depression.

herbal products, including possible interactions with other medications, possible tolerance and withdrawal symptoms, appropriate dosages, how they work, or even *whether* they work.

There is research support for the effectiveness of some herbal and natural products, but the evidence is not overwhelming (Lake, 2009). Products such as inositol (a sugar alcohol), kava (an herb related to black pepper), omega-3 fatty acid (a fish oil), and SAM-e (an amino acid derivative) are sold as health foods and are described as having positive psychological effects of various kinds, but the evidence is mixed. For example, in the case of St. John's wort (a wort, it turns out, is an herb), some studies have shown it has an advantage over a placebo condition (Lecrubier et al., 2002) for the treatment of depression, whereas others show no advantage (Hypericum Depression Trial Study Group, 2002). Omega-3 fatty acids have been linked with lower rates of depression and suicide (see **FIGURE 16.4**), and several treatment studies have shown that omega-3s are superior to placebo at decreasing depression (Lewis et al., 2011; Parker et al., 2006). Overall, although herbal medications and treatments are worthy of continued research, these products should be closely monitored and used judiciously until more is known about their safety and effectiveness.

Phototherapy, *a therapy that involves repeated exposure to bright light,* is another natural treatment that may be helpful to people who have a seasonal pattern to their depression. This could include people suffering with seasonal affective disorder (SAD) (see the Psychological Disorders chapter), or those who experience depression only in the winter months due to the lack of sunlight. Typically, people are exposed to bright light in the morning using a lamp designed for this purpose. Phototherapy has not been as well researched as psychological treatment or medication, but available studies suggest that it is about as effective as antidepressant medication in the treatment of SAD (Thaler et al., 2011); it also has shown positive effects (and no side effects) in the treatment of non-seasonal depression as well (Perera et al., 2018).

Combining Medication and Psychotherapy

Given that psychological treatments and medications both have shown an ability to treat mental disorders effectively, some natural next questions are: Which is more effective? Is the combination of psychological and medicinal treatments better than either by itself?

Many studies have compared psychological treatments, medications, and combinations of these approaches for addressing psychological disorders. The studies' results often depend on the particular problem being considered. For example, in the cases of schizophrenia and bipolar disorder, researchers have found that medication

phototherapy A therapy that involves repeated exposure to bright light.

Figure 16.5

The Effectiveness of Medication and Psychotherapy for Panic Disorder
One study of CBT and medication (imipramine) for panic disorder found that the effects of CBT, medication, and treatment that combined CBT and medication were not significantly different over the short term, although all three were superior to the placebo condition (Barlow et al., 2000).

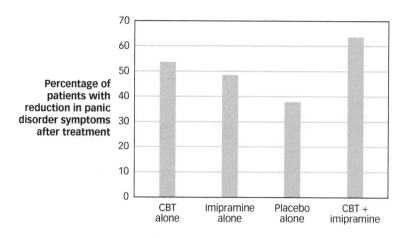

is more effective than psychological treatment and so is considered a necessary part of treatment; recent studies, however, have tended to examine whether adding psychotherapeutic treatments such as social skills training or cognitive behavioural treatment can be helpful. (They can.) In the case of mood and anxiety disorders, medication and psychological treatments are equally effective. One landmark study compared cognitive behavioural therapy (CBT), imipramine (the antidepressant also known as Tofranil), and the combination of these treatments (CBT plus imipramine) with a placebo (administration of an inert medication) for the treatment of panic disorder (Barlow et al., 2000). After 12 weeks of treatment, either CBT alone or imipramine alone was found to be superior to a placebo. For the CBT-plus-imipramine condition, the response rate also exceeded the rate for the placebo but was not significantly better than the rate for either CBT or imipramine alone. In other words, either treatment was better than nothing, but the combination of treatments was not significantly more effective than one or the other (see **FIGURE 16.5**). More is not always better (see Other Voices: Diagnosis: Human).

Given that both therapy and medications are effective, one question is whether they work through similar mechanisms. A study of people with social phobia examined patterns of cerebral blood flow following treatment in which either citalopram (an SSRI) or CBT were used (Furmark et al., 2002). Participants in both groups were alerted to the possibility that they would soon have to speak in public. In both groups, those who responded to treatment showed decreased activation in the amygdala, hippocampus, and neighbouring cortical areas during the public speaking challenge (see **FIGURE 16.6**); the amygdala, located next to the hippocampus (see Figure 6.20) plays a significant role in memory for emotional information. These findings suggest that both therapy and medication affect the brain in regions associated with a reaction to threat. Although we might expect that events that influence the brain

Figure 16.6

The Effects of Medication and Therapy in the Brain   PET scans of individuals with social phobia showed similar reductions in activation of the amygdala–hippocampus region after they received treatment with CBT (*left*) and with citalopram (*right*), an SSRI.

RESEARCH FROM FURMARK ET AL., 2002.

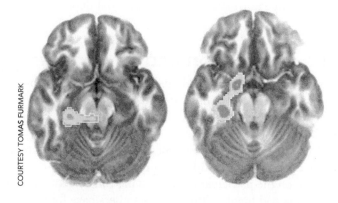

COURTESY TOMAS FURMARK

Other Voices ⦁ **Diagnosis: Human**

COURTESY TED GUP

Ted Gup is an author and a Visiting Lecturer in English at Brown University.

Should more people receive psychological treatment or medications? Or should fewer? On one hand, data indicate that most people with a mental disorder do not receive treatment and that untreated mental disorders are an enormous source of pain and suffering. On the other hand, some argue that we have become too quick to label normal human behaviour as "disordered" and too willing to medicate any behaviour, thought, or feeling that makes us uncomfortable. Ted Gup is one of these people. The following is a version of his op-ed piece that appeared in the *New York Times* on April 3, 2013, under the headline "Diagnosis: Human."

The news that 11 percent of school-age children now receive a diagnosis of attention deficit hyperactivity disorder—some 6.4 million—gave me a chill. My son David was one of those who received that diagnosis.

In his case, he was in the first grade. Indeed, there were psychiatrists who prescribed medication for him even before they met him. One psychiatrist said he would not even see him until he was medicated. For a year I refused to fill the prescription at the pharmacy. Finally, I relented. And so David went on Ritalin, then Adderall, and other drugs that were said to be helpful in combating the condition.

In another age, David might have been called "rambunctious." His battery was a little too large for his body. And so he would leap over the couch, spring to reach the ceiling and show an exuberance for life that came in brilliant microbursts.

As a 21-year-old college senior, he was found on the floor of his room, dead from a fatal mix of alcohol and drugs. The date was Oct. 18, 2011. No one made him take the heroin and alcohol, and yet I cannot help but hold myself and others to account. I had unknowingly colluded with a system that devalues talking therapy and rushes to medicate, inadvertently sending a message that self-medication, too, is perfectly acceptable.

My son was no angel (though he was to us) and he was known to trade in Adderall, to create a submarket in the drug among his classmates who were themselves all too eager to get their hands on it. What he did cannot be excused, but it should be understood. What he did was to create a market that perfectly mirrored the society in which he grew up, a culture where Big Pharma itself prospers from the off-label uses of drugs, often not tested in children and not approved for the many uses to which they are put.

And so a generation of students, raised in an environment that encourages medication, are emulating the professionals by using drugs in the classroom as performance enhancers.

And we wonder why it is that they use drugs with such abandon. As all parents learn—at times to their chagrin—our children go to school not only in the classroom but also at home, and the culture they construct for themselves as teenagers and young adults is but a tiny village imitating that to which they were introduced as children. . . .

Ours is an age in which the airwaves and media are one large drug emporium that claims to fix everything from sleep to sex. I fear that being human is itself fast becoming a condition. It's as if we are trying to contain grief, and the absolute pain of a loss like mine. We have become increasingly disassociated and estranged from the patterns of life and death, uncomfortable with the messiness of our own humanity, aging and, ultimately, mortality.

Challenge and hardship have become pathologized and monetized. Instead of enhancing our coping skills, we undermine them and seek shortcuts where there are none, eroding the resilience upon which each of us, at some point in our lives, must rely.

Have we gone too far in the labelling and treatment of mental disorders? Or have we not gone far enough? On one hand, we shouldn't rush to diagnose and medicate normal behaviour, but on the other hand, we must provide help to those who are suffering with a true mental disorder. One possible way forwards is to ensure that people are diagnosed and treated only after a thorough evaluation by a well-trained professional. This way, we will know that a mental health professional has carefully considered whether the problems a person is having are truly disordered and in need of intervention, or just part of being human.

should be physical—after all, the brain is a physical object—it is important to keep in mind that environmental learning experiences, such as psychological treatment, produce similar influences on the brain.

One problem in combining medication and psychotherapy is that the two treatments are often provided by different people. Psychiatrists are MDs trained in the administration of medication (although they may also provide psychological treatment), whereas psychologists provide psychological treatment but

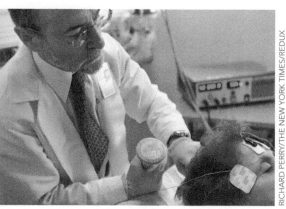

Electroconvulsive therapy (ECT) can be an effective treatment for severe depression. To reduce side effects, it is administered under general anaesthesia.

electroconvulsive therapy (ECT) A treatment that involves inducing a brief seizure by delivering an electrical shock to the brain.

transcranial magnetic stimulation (TMS) A treatment that involves placing a powerful pulsed magnet over a person's scalp to alter neuronal activity in the brain.

cannot prescribe medication. Thus, the coordination of treatment often requires cooperation between psychologists and psychiatrists.

The question of whether psychologists should be licensed to prescribe medications has long been a source of debate among psychologists and physicians. Opponents of prescription privileges argue that psychologists do not have the medical training to understand how medications interact with other drugs. Proponents argue that patient safety would not be compromised as long as rigorous training procedures were established. This issue remains a focus of debate, and at present, the coordination of medication and psychological treatment usually involves a team effort of psychiatry and psychology.

Biological Treatments Beyond Medication

Medication can be an effective biological treatment, but for some people medications do not work, or their side effects are intolerable. If these people don't respond to psychotherapy either, what other options do they have for symptom relief? There are additional avenues of help available but some are risky or poorly understood.

One biological treatment sometimes used to treat severe mental disorders that do not respond to psychological treatment or medication is **electroconvulsive therapy (ECT)**, *a treatment that involves inducing a brief seizure by delivering an electrical shock to the brain;* it is also sometimes referred to as *shock therapy.* The shock is applied to the person's scalp for less than a second. ECT is used primarily to treat severe depression that has not responded to antidepressant medications, although it may also be useful for treating bipolar disorder (Khalid et al., 2008; Poon et al., 2012). Patients are pretreated with muscle relaxants and are under general anaesthetic during treatment, so they are not conscious of the procedure. The main side effect of ECT is impaired short-term memory, which usually improves over the first month or two after the end of treatment. In addition, patients sometimes report headaches and muscle aches afterward. Despite these side effects, the treatment can be helpful: it is more effective than simulated ECT, a placebo, and antidepressant drugs such as tricyclics and MAOIs (Pagnin et al., 2008).

Another biological approach that does not involve medication is **transcranial magnetic stimulation (TMS)**, *a treatment that involves placing a powerful pulsed magnet over a person's scalp to alter neuronal activity in the brain.* When TMS is used as a treatment for depression, the magnet is placed just above

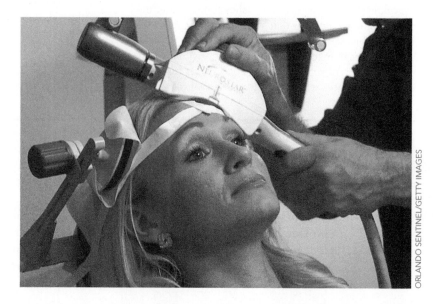

Transcranial magnetic stimulation (TMS) is an exciting new technique that allows researchers and clinicians to change brain activity using a magnetic wand—no surgery is required.

the right or left eyebrow in an effort to stimulate the right or left prefrontal cortex (areas of the brain implicated in depression). TMS is an exciting development because it is noninvasive and has fewer side effects than ECT (see the Neuroscience and Behaviour chapter). Side effects are minimal; they include mild headache and a small risk of seizure, but TMS has no impact on memory or concentration. TMS applied daily to the left prefrontal cortex for 4 to 6 weeks has been found to be effective in treating depression in patients who have not responded to medication (Perera et al., 2016). In fact, a study comparing TMS with ECT found that both procedures were effective, with no significant differences between them (Janicak et al., 2002). Other studies have found that TMS can also be used to treat auditory hallucinations in patients with schizophrenia (Aleman, Sommer, & Kahn, 2007).

In very rare cases, **psychosurgery**, *the surgical destruction of specific brain areas,* may be used to treat severe and unresponsive psychological disorders. Psychosurgery has a controversial history, beginning in the 1930s with the invention of the lobotomy by the Portuguese physician Antonio Egas Moniz (1874–1955). After discovering that certain surgical procedures on animal brains calmed behaviour, Moniz began to use similar techniques on violent or agitated human patients. Lobotomies involved inserting an instrument into the brain through the patient's eye socket or through holes drilled in the side of the head. The objective was to sever connections between the frontal lobes and inner brain structures, such as the thalamus, known to be involved in emotion.

Although some lobotomies produced highly successful results and Moniz received the 1949 Nobel Prize for his work, significant side effects, such as extreme lethargy or childlike impulsiveness, detracted from these benefits. Lobotomy was used widely for years despite this, leaving many people devastated by these permanent side effects; because of this, for many years there was a movement challenging the awarding of the Nobel Prize to Moniz. (It was never revoked.) The development of antipsychotic drugs during the 1950s provided a safer way to treat violent individuals, and the practice of lobotomy was brought to an end (Swayze, 1995).

Psychosurgery is rarely used these days and is reserved for extremely severe cases for which no other interventions have been effective, and the symptoms of the disorder are intolerable to the patient. For instance, psychosurgery is sometimes used in severe cases of obsessive compulsive disorder (OCD) in which the person is completely unable to function in daily life, and psychological treatment and medication are not effective. In contrast to the earlier days of lobotomy, when broad regions of brain tissue were destroyed, modern psychosurgery involves a very precise destruction of brain tissue in order to disrupt the brain circuits known to be involved in generating obsessions and compulsions. This increased precision has produced better results. For example, people suffering from OCD who fail to respond to treatment (including several trials of medication and cognitive behavioural treatment) may benefit from specific surgical procedures called *cingulotomy* and *anterior capsulotomy*. Cingulotomy involves destroying part of the corpus callosum (see Figure 3.18) and the cingulate gyrus (the ridge just above the corpus collosum). Anterior capsulotomy involves creating small lesions to disrupt the pathway between the caudate nucleus and the putamen. Because of the relatively small number of cases of psychosurgery, there are not as many studies of these techniques as there are for other treatments. However, available studies have shown that psychosurgery typically leads to substantial improvements in both the short and long term for people with severe OCD (Csigó et al., 2010; van Vliet et al., 2013).

A final approach, called *deep brain stimulation* (DBS), combines the use of psychosurgery with electrical currents (as in ECT and TMS). In DBS, a treatment pioneered only recently, a small, battery-powered device is implanted in the patient's body to deliver electrical stimulation to specific areas of the brain known to be involved in the disorder being targeted (**FIGURE 16.7**). This technique has been successful for OCD treatment (Abelson et al., 2009) and can also provide benefits for people with a variety of neurologic conditions. The tremor that accompanies Parkinson's disease has proven to be treatable in this way (Perlmutter & Mink, 2006), as have some cases of severe

psychosurgery Surgical destruction of specific brain areas.

Figure 16.7

DBS Deep brain stimulation involves the insertion of battery-powered electrodes that deliver electrical pulses to specific areas of the brain believed to be causing a person's mental disorder.

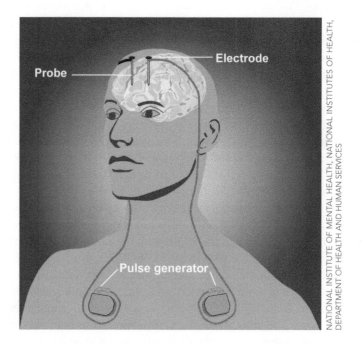

depression that were otherwise untreatable (Mayberg et al., 2005). The early view of psychosurgery as a treatment of last resort is being replaced by a cautious hope that newer, focused treatments that target brain circuits known to be functioning abnormally in those with certain mental disorders can have beneficial effects (Ressler & Mayberg, 2007).

Build to the Outcomes

1. What do antipsychotic drugs do?
2. What are the advantages of the newer, atypical antipsychotic medications?
3. What are some reasons for caution when prescribing antianxiety medications?
4. How do antidepressant drugs affect neurotransmitters?
5. Why are antidepressants not prescribed for bipolar disorder?
6. Why aren't herbal and natural products given the same scrutiny as pharmacological drugs are given?
7. Which herbal remedies have been proven to be effective?
8. Do therapy and medications work similarly in treating mental illness?
9. What are the benefits of ECT? The risks?
10. What is the procedure for TMS?
11. When would psychosurgery be appropriate?

Treatment Effectiveness: For Better or For Worse

Learning Outcomes

- Describe treatment illusions.
- Explain research methods used in treatment studies.
- Explain the criteria used to determine a treatment's effectiveness.

Think back to Christine and the dead mouse at the beginning of this chapter. What if, instead of exposure and response prevention, Christine had been treated with psychoanalysis or psychosurgery? Would those alternatives have been just as effective for treating her OCD? Throughout this chapter, we have explored various psychological and biological treatments that might help people with psychological disorders. But do these treatments actually work? Which ones work better than the others?

As you learned in the Methods in Psychology chapter, pinning down a specific cause for an effect can be a difficult detective exercise. Detection is made even more difficult because clients and doctors may approach treatment evaluation very unscientifically, often by simply noticing an improvement (or no improvement, or even a worsening of symptoms) and reaching a conclusion based on that sole observation. Determining a treatment's effectiveness can be misdirected by illusions that can only be overcome by careful, scientific evaluation.

Treatment Illusions

Imagine you're sick and the doctor says, "Take this pill." You follow the doctor's orders and you get better. To what do you attribute your improvement? One possibility is that the pill cured you, but there are at least three other explanations: Maybe you would have gotten better naturally; maybe it was your expectation that the pill would be helpful is what led to you feeling better; or maybe you weren't really feeling that bad and after taking the pill you mistakenly remember being more ill than you really were. These possibilities point to three potential illusions of treatment: that improvements were produced by natural improvement, by placebo effects, and by reconstructive memory.

Natural Improvement

Natural improvement is the tendency of symptoms to return to their mean or average level. The illusion in this case happens when you conclude, mistakenly, that a treatment has made you better when you would have gotten better anyway. People typically turn to therapy or medication when their symptoms are at their worst. When this is the case, the client's symptoms will often improve regardless of whether there was any treatment at all; when you're at rock bottom, there's nowhere to move but up. In most cases, for example, depression that becomes severe enough to make individuals candidates for treatment will tend to lift in several months *no matter what they do*. A person who enters therapy for depression may develop the illusion that the therapy works because the therapy coincides with the typical course of the illness and the person's natural return to health. How can we know a treatment is effective, or if the change we observe following that treatment is caused by natural improvement? As discussed in the Methods in Psychology chapter, we could do an experiment in which we assign half of the people who are depressed to receive treatment and the other half to receive no treatment, and then monitor them over time to see if the ones who got treatment actually show greater improvement. This is precisely how researchers test out different interventions, as described in more detail below.

Placebo Effects

Recovery also could be the result of *nonspecific treatment effects* that are not related to the proposed active ingredient of the treatment. For example, the doctor prescribing the medication might simply be a pleasant and hopeful individual who gives the

"If this doesn't help you don't worry, it's a placebo."

client a sense of hope or optimism that things will improve. Client and doctor alike might attribute the client's improvement to the effects of medication on the brain, whereas the true active ingredient was the warm relationship with the doctor or an improved outlook on life.

Simply knowing that you are getting a treatment can be a nonspecific treatment effect. These instances include the positive influences that can be produced by a **placebo**, *an inert substance or procedure that has been applied with the expectation that it will produce a healing response.* For example, if you have a headache and take a sugar pill that does not contain any painkiller, thinking it is Tylenol or aspirin, the pill is a placebo if the headache goes away. Placebos can have profound effects in the case of psychological treatments. Research shows that a large percentage of individuals with anxiety, depression, and other emotional and medical problems experience significant improvement after a placebo treatment (see A World of Difference: Differences in People's Responses to Treatment).

Reconstructive Memory

A third treatment illusion can come about when the client's motivation to get well causes errors in *reconstructive memory* for the original symptoms. You might think that you've improved because of a treatment when in fact you're simply misremembering, mistakenly believing that your symptoms before treatment were worse than they actually were. This tendency was first observed in research that examined the effectiveness of a study skills class (Conway & Ross, 1984). Some students who wanted to take the class were enrolled, while others were randomly assigned to a waiting list until the class could be offered again. When their study abilities were measured afterward, those students who took the class were no better at studying than their wait-listed counterparts. However, those who took the class *said* that they had improved. How could this be? Those participants recalled their study skills before the class as being worse than they had actually been. Conway and Ross (1984) dubbed this motivated reconstruction of the past "Getting What You Want by Revising What You Had." Applying that kind of reconstructive memory to psychology, a client who forms a strong expectation of therapy success might later conclude that even a useless treatment had worked wonders by recalling past symptoms and troubles as worse than they had been, which would make the treatment seem effective.

Treatment Studies: Seeking Evidence

How can we make sure that we use treatments that actually work and not waste time with procedures that may be useless or even harmful? Research psychologists use approaches covered in the Methods in Psychology chapter to run experiments that test which treatments are effective for the different mental disorders described in the Psychological Disorders chapter.

Treatment outcome studies are designed to evaluate whether a particular treatment works to decrease a person's symptoms. For example, let's say that you have a new treatment for depression. How can you know if it works? One possibility is to recruit a sample of people with depression and administer your treatment. If after, say, 6 weeks, the people in your study report being less depressed, you might want to conclude that it was your treatment that caused changes in the patients' depression. However, how can you know that it was your treatment and not one of the treatment illusions described above, such as natural improvement or reconstructive memory, that were responsible? Indeed, we do know that people tend to come in for treatment when their symptoms are most severe, and that after some period of time symptoms of depression will often decrease naturally without any treatment.

Researchers use different types of control conditions to test the extent to which we can conclude that the observed changes in patient symptoms were due to the

placebo An inert substance or procedure that has been applied with the expectation that it will produce a healing response.

treatment rather than some alternative explanation. For example, we can rule out that the observed changes were due simply to the passage of time by randomly assigning half of our depressed patients to 6 weeks of our preferred treatment and the other half to a 6-week no-treatment control condition. Comparing the change in the depressive symptoms of both groups, we can learn how much more of a change in depressive symptoms was caused by the treatment compared to the control condition.

On the other hand, we also know that receiving any treatment can cause a change in symptoms via the placebo effect. To rule out that the observed changes are due to such an effect, we can randomly assign half of our patients to our preferred treatment, and the other half to another condition that *appears* to be an effective treatment. Ideally, a treatment should be assessed in a *double-blind experiment*, a study in which neither the participant nor the researcher/therapist know which treatment the participant is receiving. In drug studies, this isn't hard to arrange because active drugs and placebos can be made to look the same to both the participants and the researchers during the study. Keeping all involved "in the dark" is much harder in the study of psychological treatments. Nevertheless, by comparing treatments either with no treatment or with other active interventions (such as other psychological treatments or medications), researchers can determine which treatments work and which are most effective for different disorders.

Which Treatments Work According to the Evidence?

The German-born British psychologist Hans Eysenck (1916–1997) reviewed the relatively few studies of psychotherapy's effectiveness available in 1957 and raised a furor among therapists by concluding that psychotherapy—particularly psychoanalysis—was not only was ineffective but seemed to *impede* recovery (Eysenck, 1957). Much larger numbers of studies that have been examined statistically since then support a more optimistic conclusion: The typical psychotherapy client is better off than three-quarters of untreated individuals (Seligman, 1995; Smith, Glass, & Miller, 1980). Although critiques of psychotherapy continue to point out weaknesses in how clients are tested, diagnosed, and treated (Baker, McFall, & Shoham, 2009; Dawes, 1994), strong evidence generally supports the effectiveness of many different treatments (Nathan & Gorman, 2007), including psychodynamic therapy (Shedler, 2010). The key question then becomes: Which treatments are effective for which problems (Hunsley & Di Giulio, 2002)?

One of the most enduring debates in clinical psychology concerns how the various psychotherapies compare with each other. Some psychologists have argued for years that evidence supports the conclusion that most psychotherapies work about equally well. In this view, common factors shared by all forms of psychotherapy, such as contact with and empathy from a professional, contribute to change (Luborsky et al., 2002). In contrast, others have argued that there are important differences among therapies and that certain treatments are more effective than others, especially for treating particular types of problems. For instance, studies of children, adolescents, and adults have revealed that for depression and anxiety, for example, cognitive behavioural therapy (CBT) and interpersonal psychotherapy (IPT) lead to significantly better outcomes than do other approaches (Tolin, 2010; Zhou et al., 2015). How can we make sense of these differing perspectives?

In 1995, the American Psychological Association (APA) published one of the first attempts to define criteria for determining whether a particular type of psychotherapy is effective for a particular problem (Task Force on Promotion and Dissemination of Psychological Procedures, 1995). The Canadian Psychological Association (CPA) followed, generally endorsing the APA guidelines, and elaborating upon them in a Canadian context ("Empirically Supported Treatments: Recommendations for Canadian Professional Psychology") in 1998. The official criteria for empirically validated treatments in the APA report defined two levels of empirical support: *well-established treatments,* those with a high level of support (e.g., evidence from several randomized controlled trials); and *probably efficacious treatments,* those with preliminary support. After these criteria were established, the APA published a list of empirically supported treatments (Chambless et al., 1998; Woody & Sanderson, 1998). More recent reviews have highlighted several specific psychological treatments that have been shown to work as well as, or even better than, other available treatments, including medication (Barlow et al., 2013). **TABLE 16.3** lists several of these treatments.

Some researchers and clinicians have questioned whether treatments shown to work in well-controlled studies conducted at university clinics will work in the real world. For instance, some psychologists have noted that most treatment studies reported in the literature do not have large numbers of ethnic minority participants, and so it is unclear if these treatments will work with ethnically and culturally diverse groups. A review of available data suggests that despite gaps in the literature, current evidence-based psychological treatments work as well with ethnic minority clients as with White clients (Miranda et al., 2005).

Even trickier than the question of establishing whether a treatment works is whether a form of psychotherapy or a medication might actually do harm. The dangers of drug treatment should be clear to anyone who has read a magazine ad for a drug and studied the fine print, with its list of side effects, potential drug interactions, and complications. Some drugs used in psychological treatment can be addictive, creating long-term dependency and serious withdrawal symptoms. The strongest critics of drug treatment claim that drugs do no more than trade one unwanted symptom for another: trading depression for lack of sexual interest, trading anxiety for intoxication, or trading agitation for lethargy and dulled emotion (Breggin, 2000).

The dangers of psychotherapy are more subtle, but one is clear enough in some cases that there is actually a name for it. **Iatrogenic illness** is *a disorder or symptom that occurs as a result of a medical or psychotherapeutic treatment itself* (Boisvert & Faust, 2002). Such an illness might arise, for instance, when a psychotherapist becomes convinced that a client has a disorder that in fact the client does not have. As a result, the therapist works to help the client accept that diagnosis and participate in psychotherapy to treat the disorder. Being treated for a disorder can, under certain conditions, make a person show signs of that very disorder—and so an iatrogenic illness is born.

iatrogenic illness A disorder or symptom that occurs as a result of a medical or psychotherapeutic treatment itself.

TABLE 16.3

SELECTED LIST OF SPECIFIC PSYCHOLOGICAL TREATMENTS COMPARED WITH MEDICATION OR OTHER TREATMENTS

Disorder	Treatment	Results
Depression	CBT	PT = meds; PT + meds > either alone
Panic disorder	CBT	PT > meds at follow-up; PT = meds at end of treatment; both > placebo
Posttraumatic stress disorder	CBT	PT > present-centred therapy
Insomnia	CBT	PT > medication or placebo
Depression and physical health in Alzheimer's patients	Exercise and behavioural management	PT > routine medical care
Gulf War veterans' illnesses	CBT and exercise	PT > Usual care or alternative treatments

Note: CBT = cognitive behavioural therapy; PT = psychological treatment; Meds = medication.
Information from Barlow et al. (2013).

Treatments shown to be effective in research studies (which often include only a small percentage of ethnic minority patients) have been found to work equally well with people from different backgrounds and cultures (Miranda et al., 2005).

In some cases, clients who have been influenced through hypnosis and/or repeated suggestions in therapy come to believe that they have dissociative identity disorder (even coming to express multiple personalities) or to believe that they were subjected to traumatic events as a child and then "recover" memories of such events when an investigation reveals no evidence for these problems prior to therapy (McNally, 2003). Some people enter therapy with a vague sense that something odd has happened to them; after hypnosis or other imagination-enhancing techniques they emerge with the conviction that their therapist's theory was right: They *were* abducted by space aliens (Clancy, 2005). Needless to say, a therapy that leads clients to develop such bizarre beliefs does more harm than good.

Just as psychologists have created lists of treatments that work, they have also begun to establish lists of treatments that *harm*. The purpose of doing so is to inform other researchers, clinicians, and the public which treatments they should avoid. Many people are under the impression that although every psychological treatment may not be effective, some treatment is better than no treatment. However, it turns out that a number of interventions intended to help alleviate people's symptoms actually make them worse! Did your elementary or high school have a D.A.R.E. (Drug Abuse and Resistance Education) program? Have you heard of critical-incident stress debriefing (CISD), Scared Straight, and boot-camp programs? They all sound as if they might work, but careful scientific experiments have determined that people who participate in these interventions are actually worse off afterward (see **TABLE 16.4**) (Lilienfeld, 2007)!

To regulate the potentially powerful influence of different therapies, psychologists hold themselves to a set of ethical standards for the treatment of people with mental disorders (American Psychological Association, 2002; Canadian Psychological Association, 2000). Adherence to these standards is required for membership in the American Psychological Association, and the Canadian Psychological Association and provincial and territorial regulatory bodies also monitor adherence to ethical principles in therapy. The ethical standards in Canada are based on four principles: (1) respect for the dignity of persons, which includes protecting the welfare of vulnerable people and seeking fairness in treatment and avoiding biases; (2) responsible caring, which includes striving to benefit clients and taking care to do no harm; (3) integrity in relationships (promoting accuracy, honesty, and truthfulness); and (4) responsibility to society, which means that when psychological knowledge is used in the development of social policies, it will only be used for beneficial purposes (i.e., those that reflect the first three principles). When people suffering from mental disorders come to psychologists for help, adhering to these guidelines is the least that psychologists can do. Ideally, in the hope of relieving suffering, they can do much more.

TABLE 16.4

SOME PSYCHOLOGICAL TREATMENTS THAT CAUSE HARM

Type of Treatment	Potential Harm	Source of Evidence
CISD	Increased risk of PTSD	RCTs
Scared Straight	Worsening of conduct problems	RCTs
Boot-camp interventions for conduct problems	Worsening of conduct problems	Meta-analysis (review of studies)
DARE programs	Increased use of alcohol and drugs	RCTs

Note: CISD = critical-incident stress debriefing; PTSD = posttraumatic stress disorder; RCTs = randomized controlled trials.

Information from Lilienfeld (2007).

Build to the Outcomes

1. What are the three kinds of treatment illusions?
2. What is the placebo effect?
3. What methods are used in treatment outcome studies?
4. Why is a double-blind experiment so important in assessing treatment effectiveness?
5. How do psychologists know which treatments work and which might be harmful?
6. How might psychotherapy cause harm?

Chapter Review

Treatment: Getting Help to Those Who Need It

- Mental illness is often misunderstood, and because of this, it too often goes untreated.

- Untreated mental illness can be extremely costly, not only affecting an individual's ability to function but also causing social and financial burdens.

- Many people who suffer from mental illness do not get the help they need: They may be unaware that they have a problem, they may be uninterested in getting help for their problem, or they may face structural barriers to getting treatment.

- Treatments include psychotherapy, which focuses on the mind; medical and biological methods, which focus on the brain and body; and the combination of the two approaches.

Psychological Treatments: Healing the Mind Through Interaction

- Psychodynamic therapies, including psychoanalysis, emphasize helping clients gain insight into their unconscious conflicts. Traditional psychoanalysis involves four to five treatment sessions per week, with the client lying on a couch and free-associating; modern psychodynamic therapies involve one session per week with face-to-face interactions in which therapists help clients solve interpersonal problems.

- Humanistic approaches (e.g., person-centred therapy) and existential approaches (e.g., gestalt therapy) focus on helping people develop a sense of personal worth.

- Behaviour therapy applies learning principles to specific behaviour problems.

- Cognitive therapy is focused on helping people change the way they think about events in their lives, and teaching them to challenge irrational thoughts.

- Cognitive behavioural therapy (CBT), which merges cognitive and behavioural approaches, has been shown to be effective for treating a wide range of psychological disorders.

- Group therapies target couples, families, or groups of clients brought together for the purpose of working together to solve their problems.

- Self-help and support groups, such as AA, are common around the world but are not well studied.

Biological Treatments: Healing the Mind by Physically Altering the Brain

- Antipsychotic medications block dopamine receptors in parts of the brain, thus reducing dopamine activity. They are used to treat the positive symptoms of schizophrenia.

- Antianxiety medications are used to treat anxiety disorders but have the potential for abuse, especially because of the development of drug tolerance.
- Antidepressants affect the level of serotonin in the brain and are used to treat depression and related disorders.
- Herbal and natural products are not considered medications by regulatory agencies and so are not subject to strict scrutiny. Although there is little scientific information on their effectiveness, some do seem to have mild positive effects.
- Medications are often combined with psychotherapy in treatment. Evidence from a study on social phobia suggests that both affect the brain in regions associated with threat.
- Other biomedical treatments include electroconvulsive therapy (ECT), transcranial magnetic stimulation (TMS), deep brain stimulation (DBS), and psychosurgery—this last used in extreme cases, when other methods of treatment have been exhausted.

Treatment Effectiveness: For Better or for Worse

- Observing improvement during treatment does not necessarily mean that the treatment was effective; it might instead reflect natural improvement, nonspecific treatment effects (e.g., the placebo effect), and reconstructive memory processes.
- Treatment studies focus on both treatment outcomes and processes, applying scientific research methods such as placebo controls and double-blind techniques.
- Treatments for psychological disorders are generally more effective than no treatment at all, but some (e.g., cognitive behavioural therapy and interpersonal psychotherapy) are more effective than others for certain disorders; both medication and psychotherapy have dangers that ethical practitioners must consider carefully.

Key Concept Quiz

1. Which statement is NOT a reason that people fail to get treatment for mental illness?
   a. People may not realize that their disorder needs to be treated.
   b. Levels of impairment for people with mental illness are comparable to or higher than those of people with chronic medical illnesses.
   c. There may be barriers to treatment, such as beliefs and circumstances that keep people from getting help.
   d. Even people who acknowledge they have a problem may not know where to look for services.

2. Eclectic psychotherapy
   a. concentrates on the interpretation of dreams.
   b. introduces clients to strange situations.
   c. draws on techniques from different forms of therapy.
   d. focuses on the analysis of resistance.

3. The different psychodynamic therapies all share an emphasis on
   a. the influence of the collective unconscious.
   b. the importance of taking responsibility for psychological problems.
   c. combining behavioural and cognitive approaches.
   d. developing insight into the unconscious sources of psychological disorders.

4. Which type of therapy would likely work best for someone with an irrational fear of heights?
   a. psychodynamic therapy
   b. gestalt therapy
   c. behavioural therapy
   d. humanistic therapy

5. Mindfulness meditation is part of which kind of therapy?
   a. interpersonal therapy
   b. humanistic therapy
   c. psychodynamic therapy
   d. cognitive therapy

6. Which type of therapy emphasizes action on the part of the client, as well as complete transparency from the therapist as to the specifics of the treatment?
   a. cognitive behavioural therapy
   b. humanistic therapy
   c. existential therapy
   d. group therapy

7. Examining the failure to reach one's potential reflects the _____ approach, whereas examining one's failure to find meaning in life reflects the _____ approach.
   a. cognitive; behavioural
   b. humanistic; existential
   c. psychodynamic; cognitive behavioural
   d. existential; humanistic

8. Antipsychotic drugs were developed to treat
   a. depression.
   b. schizophrenia.
   c. anxiety.
   d. mood disorders.

9. Atypical antipsychotic drugs
   a. act on different neurotransmitters depending on the individual.
   b. affect only the dopamine system.
   c. affect only the serotonin system.
   d. act on both the dopamine and serotonin systems.

10. Antidepressant medications have the strongest effects for people with _____ depression.
    a. no
    b. mild
    c. moderate
    d. severe

 **LearningCurve** Don't stop now! Quizzing yourself is a powerful study tool. Go to LaunchPad to access
the LearningCurve adaptive quizzing system and your own personalized learning plan.
Visit launchpadworks.com.

Key Terms

psychotherapy (p. 633)

eclectic psychotherapy
(p. 633)

psychodynamic
psychotherapies (p. 634)

interpersonal psychotherapy
(IPT) (p. 635)

person-centred therapy (or
client-centred therapy)
(p. 635)

gestalt therapy (p. 636)

behaviour therapy (p. 637)

token economy (p. 637)

exposure therapy (p. 637)

cognitive therapy (p. 638)

cognitive restructuring
(p. 639)

mindfulness meditation
(p. 641)

cognitive behavioural
therapy (CBT) (p. 641)

group therapy (p. 643)

antipsychotic drugs (p. 645)

psychopharmacology
(p. 646)

antianxiety medications
(p. 647)

antidepressants (p. 648)

phototherapy (p. 651)

electroconvulsive therapy
(ECT) (p. 654)

transcranial magnetic
stimulation (TMS) (p. 654)

psychosurgery (p. 655)

placebo (p. 658)

iatrogenic illness (p. 660)

Changing Minds

1. One of your friends recently lost a close family member in
a tragic car accident, and he's devastated. He hasn't been
attending classes, and when you check up on him you learn
that he's not sleeping well or eating regularly. You want to
help him but feel out of your depth. You suggest he visit
the campus counselling centre and talk to a therapist. "Only
crazy people go to therapy," he says. What could you tell
your friend to dispel this wrong assumption?

2. While you're talking to your bereaved friend, his roommate
comes in. The roommate agrees with your suggestion about
therapy but takes it further. "I'll give you the name of my
therapist. He helped me quit smoking—he'll be able to cure
your depression in no time." Why is it dangerous to assume
that a good therapist can cure anyone and anything?

3. In the Methods in Psychology chapter you read about
Louise Hay, whose best-selling book, *You Can Heal Your
Life*, promotes a kind of psychotherapy: teaching readers
how to change their thoughts and thereby improve not
only their inner lives but also their physical health. The
chapter quotes Hay as saying that scientific evidence is
unnecessary to validate her claims. Is her view correct? Is

there a scientific basis for the major types of psychotherapy
described in this chapter? How is scientific experimentation
used to assess their effectiveness?

4. In June 2009, the pop icon Michael Jackson died from a
fatal dose of the anaesthetic propofol, which is sometimes
used off-label as an antianxiety drug. An autopsy confirmed
that his body contained a cocktail of prescription drugs,
including the benzodiazepines lorazepam and diazepam.
(Jackson's cardiologist, Dr. Conrad Murray, was later convicted of involuntary manslaughter for administering the
fatal propofol dose.) Other celebrities whose deaths have
been attributed to medications commonly prescribed for
anxiety and depression include Prince in 2016, Heath Led-
ger in 2008, and Anna Nicole Smith in 2007. "These drugs
are dangerous," your roommate notes. "People who have
psychological problems should seek out talk therapy for
their problems and stay away from the medications, even if
they're prescribed by a responsible doctor." You agree that
medications can be dangerous if misused, but how would
you justify the use of drug treatment for serious mental
disorders?

Answers to Key Concept Quiz

1. b; 2. c; 3. d; 4. c; 5. d; 6. a; 7. b; 8. b; 9. d; 10. d.

 **LaunchPad** LaunchPad features the full e-Book of *Psychology*, the LearningCurve adaptive
quizzing system, videos, and a variety of activities to boost your learning. Visit
LaunchPad at launchpadworks.com.

GLOSSARY

absentmindedness A lapse in attention that results in memory failure.

absolute threshold The minimal intensity needed to just barely detect a stimulus in 50% of trials.

accommodation The process by which infants revise their schemas in light of new information; the process whereby the eye maintains a clear image on the retina.

acetylcholine (ACh) A neurotransmitter involved in a number of functions, including voluntary motor control.

acquisition The phase of classical conditioning when the CS and the US are presented together.

action potential An electric signal that is conducted along a neuron's axon to a synapse.

action tendencies A readiness to engage in a specific set of emotion-related behaviours.

activation–synthesis model The theory that dreams are produced when the brain attempts to make sense of random neural activity that occurs during sleep.

actor–observer effect The tendency to make situational attributions for our own behaviours while making dispositional attributions for the identical behaviour of others.

acuity How well we can distinguish two very similar stimuli.

adolescence The period of development that begins with the onset of sexual maturity (about 11 to 14 years of age) and lasts until the beginning of adulthood (about 18 to 21 years of age).

adulthood The stage of development that begins around 18 to 21 years and lasts for the remainder of life.

aggression Behaviour whose purpose is to harm another.

agonists Drugs that increase the action of a neurotransmitter.

agoraphobia A specific phobia involving a fear of public places.

alcohol myopia A condition that results when alcohol hampers attention, leading people to respond in simple ways to complex situations.

algorithm A well-defined sequence of procedures or rules that guarantees a solution to a problem.

altered state of consciousness A form of experience that departs significantly from the normal subjective experience of the world and the mind.

altruism Intentional behaviour that benefits another at a potential cost to oneself.

amygdala A part of the limbic system, located at the tip of each horn of the hippocampus, that plays a central role in many emotional processes, particularly the formation of emotional memories.

analogical problem solving The process of solving a problem by finding a similar problem with a known solution and applying that solution to the current problem.

anorexia nervosa An eating disorder characterized by an intense fear of being overweight and a severe restriction of food intake.

antagonists Drugs that block the function of a neurotransmitter.

anterograde amnesia The inability to transfer new information from the short-term store into the long-term store.

antianxiety medications Drugs that help reduce a person's experience of fear or anxiety.

antidepressants A class of drugs that help lift people's moods.

antipsychotic drugs Medications that are used to treat schizophrenia and related psychotic disorders.

antisocial personality disorder (APD) A pervasive pattern of disregard for and violation of the rights of others that begins in childhood or early adolescence and continues into adulthood.

anxiety disorder The class of mental disorders in which anxiety is the predominant feature.

aphasia Difficulty in producing or comprehending language.

apparent motion The perception of movement as a result of signals appearing in rapid succession in different locations.

appraisal Conscious or unconscious evaluations and interpretations of the emotion-relevant aspects of a stimulus or event.

approach motivation The motivation to experience positive outcomes.

area A1 The primary auditory cortex in the temporal lobe.

area V1 The part of the occipital lobe that contains the primary visual cortex.

assimilation The process by which infants apply their schemas in novel situations.

association areas Areas in the cerebral cortex composed of neurons that help provide sense and meaning to information registered in the cortex.

attachment The emotional bond with a primary caregiver.

attachment styles Characteristic patterns of reacting to the absence and presence of one's primary caregiver.

attention The active and conscious processing of particular information.

attention-deficit/hyperactivity disorder (ADHD) A persistent pattern of severe problems with inattention and/or hyperactivity or impulsiveness that causes significant impairments in functioning.

attitude An enduring positive or negative evaluation of a stimulus.

attributions An inference about the cause of a person's behaviour.

autism spectrum disorder (ASD) A condition beginning in early childhood in which a person shows persistent communication deficits as well as restricted and repetitive patterns of behaviours, interests, or activities.

autonomic nervous system (ANS) A set of nerves that carries involuntary and automatic commands that control blood vessels, body organs, and glands.

availability bias The concept that items that are more readily available in memory are judged as having occurred more frequently.

avoidance motivation The motivation to avoid experiencing negative outcomes.

axon The part of a neuron that carries information to other neurons, muscles, or glands.

balanced placebo design A study design in which behaviour is observed following the presence or absence of an actual stimulus and also following the presence or absence of a placebo stimulus.

basal ganglia A set of subcortical structures that directs intentional movements.

basilar membrane A structure in the inner ear that moves up and down in time with vibrations relayed from the ossicles, transmitted through the oval window.

behaviour therapy A type of therapy that assumes that disordered behaviour is learned and that symptom relief is achieved through changing overt maladaptive behaviours into more constructive behaviours.

behavioural confirmation The tendency of targets to behave as observers expect them to behave.

behavioural neuroscience The study of the relationship between the brain and behaviour (especially in non-human animals).

behaviourism An approach to psychology that restricts scientific inquiry to observable behaviour.

belief An enduring piece of knowledge about a stimulus.

belief bias The idea that people's judgements about whether to accept conclusions depend more on how believable the conclusions are than on whether the arguments are logically valid.

bias The distorting influences of present knowledge, beliefs, and feelings on recollection of previous experiences.

Big Five The traits of the five-factor model: openness to experience, conscientiousness, extraversion, agreeableness, and neuroticism.

binding problem How the brain links features together so that we see unified objects in our visual world rather than free-floating or miscombined features.

binge eating disorder (BED) An eating disorder characterized by recurrent and uncontrolled episodes of eating a large number of calories in a short time.

binocular disparity The difference in the retinal images of the two eyes that provides information about depth.

biofeedback The use of an external monitoring device to obtain information about a bodily function and then to possibly gain control over that function.

biological preparedness A propensity for learning particular kinds of associations over other kinds.

biopsychosocial perspective Explains mental disorders as the result of interactions among biological, psychological, and social factors.

bipolar disorder A condition characterized by cycles of abnormal, persistent high mood (mania) and low mood (depression).

blind spot A location in the visual field that produces no sensation on the retina.

blocking A failure to retrieve information that is available in memory even though you are trying to produce it.

bulimia nervosa An eating disorder characterized by binge eating followed by compensatory behaviour.

burnout A state of physical, emotional, and mental exhaustion resulting from long-term involvement in an emotionally demanding situation and accompanied by lowered performance and motivation.

bystander intervention The act of helping strangers in an emergency situation.

case method A procedure for gathering scientific information by studying a single individual.

catatonic behaviour A marked decrease in all movement or an increase in muscular rigidity and overactivity.

category-based inferences Inferences based on information about the categories to which a person belongs.

category-specific deficit A neurological syndrome characterized by an inability to recognize objects that belong to a particular category, although the ability to recognize objects outside the category is undisturbed.

cell body (soma) The part of a neuron that coordinates information-processing tasks and keeps the cell alive.

central nervous system (CNS) The part of the nervous system that is composed of the brain and spinal cord.

cephalocaudal rule The "top-to-bottom" rule that describes the tendency for motor skills to emerge in sequence from the head to the feet.

cerebellum A large structure of the hindbrain that controls fine motor skills.

cerebral cortex The outermost layer of the brain, visible to the naked eye and divided into two hemispheres.

change blindness Failure to detect changes to the visual details of a scene.

childhood The stage of development that begins at about 18 to 24 months and lasts until about 11 to 14 years.

chromosomes Strands of DNA wound around each other in a double-helix configuration.

chronic stressors Sources of stress that occur continuously or repeatedly.

chunking Combining small pieces of information into larger clusters or chunks that are more easily held in short-term memory.

circadian rhythm A naturally occurring 24-hour cycle.

classical conditioning A type of learning that occurs when a neutral stimulus produces a response after being paired with a stimulus that naturally produces a response.

cochlea A fluid-filled tube that contains cells that transduce sound vibrations into neural impulses.

cocktail-party phenomenon A phenomenon in which people tune into one message even while they filter out others nearby.

cognitive behavioural therapy (CBT) A blend of cognitive and behavioural therapeutic strategies.

cognitive development The process by which infants and children gain the ability to think and understand.

cognitive dissonance An unpleasant state that arises when a person recognizes the inconsistency of his or her actions, attitudes, or beliefs.

cognitive enhancers Drugs that improve the psychological processes that underlie intelligent performance.

cognitive map A mental representation of the physical features of the environment.

cognitive neuroscience The study of the relationship between the brain and the mind (especially in humans).

cognitive psychology The study of human information-processing.

cognitive restructuring A therapeutic approach that teaches clients to question the automatic beliefs, assumptions, and predictions that often lead to negative emotions and to replace negative thinking with more realistic and positive beliefs.

cognitive symptoms Deficits in cognitive abilities, specifically executive functioning, attention, and working memory, present in those with schizophrenia.

cognitive therapy Focuses on helping a client identify and correct any distorted thinking about self, others, or the world.

cognitive unconscious All the mental processes that give rise to a person's thoughts, choices, emotions, and behaviour even though they are not experienced by the person.

colour-opponent system Theory stating that pairs of cone types (channels) work in opposition.

common knowledge effect The tendency for group discussions to focus on information that all members share.

comorbidity The co-occurrence of two or more disorders in a single individual.

companionate love An experience involving affection, trust, and concern for a partner's well-being.

comparison level for alternatives The cost–benefit ratio that a person believes he or she could attain in another relationship.

concept A mental representation that groups or categorizes shared features of related objects, events, or other stimuli.

concrete operational stage The stage of cognitive development that begins at about 6 years and ends at about 11 years, during which children learn how various actions, or *operations*, can transform the concrete objects of the physical world.

conditioned response (CR) A reaction that resembles an unconditioned response but is produced by a conditioned stimulus.

conditioned stimulus (CS) A previously neutral stimulus that produces a reliable response in an organism after being paired with an unconditioned stimulus.

conduct disorder A persistent pattern of deviant behaviour involving aggression towards people or animals, destruction of property, deceitfulness or theft, or serious rule violations.

cones Photoreceptors that detect colour, operate under normal daylight conditions, and allow us to focus on fine detail.

conformity The tendency to do what others do.

conjunction fallacy Thinking that two events are more likely to occur together than either individual event is alone.

conscious motivations Motivations of which people are aware.

consciousness A person's subjective experience of the world and the mind.

conservation The understanding that the quantitative properties of an object are invariant despite changes in the object's appearance.

consolidation The process by which memories become stable in the brain.

construct validity The extent to which the thing being measured adequately characterizes the property.

conventional stage A stage of moral development in which the morality of an action is primarily determined by the extent to which it conforms to social rules.

cooperation Behaviour by two or more individuals that leads to mutual benefit.

corpus callosum A thick band of nerve fibres that connects large areas of the cerebral cortex on each side of the brain and supports communication of information across the hemispheres.

correlation The relationship that results when variations in the value of one variable are synchronized with variations in the value of the other.

correlation coefficient (*r*) A mathematical measure of both the direction and strength of a correlation, which is symbolized by the letter *r*.

correspondence bias The tendency to make a dispositional attribution when we should instead make a situational attribution.

crystallized intelligence The ability to apply knowledge that was acquired through experience.

cultural psychology The study of how culture influences mental life.

debriefing A verbal description of the true nature and purpose of a study.

defence mechanisms Unconscious coping mechanisms that reduce the anxiety generated by threats from unacceptable impulses.

deindividuation A phenomenon in which immersion in a group causes people to become less concerned with their personal values.

delusion A false belief, often bizarre and grandiose, that is maintained in spite of its irrationality.

demand characteristics Those aspects of an observational setting that cause people to behave as they think someone else wants or expects them to.

dendrite The part of a neuron that receives information from other neurons and relays it to the cell body.

dependent variable The variable that is measured in an experiment.

depressants Substances that reduce the activity of the central nervous system.

developmental psychology The study of continuity and change across the life span.

developmental psychology The study of the ways in which psychological phenomena change over the life span.

deviation IQ A statistic obtained by dividing a person's test score by the average test score for people of that age and then multiplying the quotient by 100.

Diagnostic and Statistical Manual of Mental Disorders (DSM) A classification system that describes the features used to diagnose each recognized mental disorder and indicates how that disorder can be distinguished from other, similar problems.

diathesis–stress model Suggests that a person may be predisposed to a psychological disorder that remains unexpressed until triggered by stress.

dichotic listening A task in which people wearing headphones hear different messages in each ear.

diffusion chain A process whereby individuals initially learn a behaviour by observing another individual perform that behaviour, and then become models from which other individuals learn the behaviour.

diffusion of responsibility The tendency of individuals to feel diminished responsibility for their actions when surrounded by others who are acting the same way.

discrimination The capacity to distinguish between similar but distinct stimuli.

disorganized speech A severe disruption of verbal communication in which ideas shift rapidly and incoherently among unrelated topics.

display rule A norm for the appropriate expression of emotion.

DNA methylation Adding a methyl group to DNA.

door-in-the-face technique An influence strategy that involves getting someone to accept a small request by first getting them to refuse a large request.

dopamine A neurotransmitter that regulates motor behaviour, motivation, pleasure, and emotional arousal.

dopamine hypothesis The idea that schizophrenia involves an excess of dopamine activity.

double depression A moderately depressed mood that persists for at least 2 years and is punctuated by periods of major depression.

double-blind study A study in which neither the researcher nor the participant knows how the participants are expected to behave.

drive-reduction theory A theory suggesting that the primary motivation of all organisms is to reduce their drives.

drug tolerance The tendency for larger doses of a drug to be required over time to achieve the same effect.

dual process theories Theories that suggest that we have two different systems in our brains for processing information: one dedicated to fast, automatic, and unconscious processing, and the other dedicated to slow, effortful, and conscious processing.

dynamic unconscious An active system encompassing a lifetime of hidden memories, the person's deepest instincts and desires, and the person's inner struggle to control these forces.

echoic memory A fast-decaying store of auditory information.

eclectic psychotherapy A form of psychotherapy that involves drawing on techniques from different forms of therapy, depending on the client and the problem.

ego The component of personality, developed through contact with the external world, that enables us to deal with life's practical demands.

egocentrism The failure to understand that the world appears different to different people.

electroconvulsive therapy (ECT) A treatment that involves inducing a brief seizure by delivering an electrical shock to the brain.

electroencephalograph (EEG) A device used to record electrical activity in the brain.

electrooculograph (EOG) An instrument that measures eye movements.

embryonic stage The period of prenatal development that lasts from the 2nd week until about the 8th week.

emotion A temporary state that includes unique subjective experiences and physiological activity, and that prepares people for action.

emotion regulation The strategies people use to influence their own emotional experiences.

emotional expression An observable sign of an emotional state.

emotional intelligence The ability to reason about emotions and to use emotions to enhance reasoning.

empirical method A set of rules and techniques for observation.

empiricism The belief that accurate knowledge can be acquired through observation.

encoding The process of transforming what we perceive, think, or feel into an enduring memory.

encoding specificity principle The idea that a retrieval cue can be an effective reminder when it helps re-create the specific way in which information was initially encoded.

endocrine system A network of glands that produce and secrete into the bloodstream chemical messages known as hormones, which influence a wide variety of basic functions, including metabolism, growth, and sexual development.

endorphins Chemicals that act within the pain pathways and emotion centres of the brain.

epigenetic marks Chemical modifications to DNA that can turn genes on or off.

epigenetics The study of environmental influences that determine whether or not genes are expressed, or the degree to which they are expressed, without altering the basic DNA sequences that constitute the genes themselves.

episodic memory The collection of past personal experiences that occurred at a particular time and place.

equity A state of affairs in which the cost–benefit ratios of two partners are roughly equally favourable.

evolutionary mismatch The idea that traits that were adaptive in an ancestral environment may be maladaptive in a modern environment.

evolutionary psychology The study of the ways in which the human mind has been shaped by natural selection.

exemplar theory The concept that we make category judgements by comparing a new instance with stored memories of other instances of the category.

existential approach A school of thought that regards personality as being governed by an individual's ongoing choices and decisions in the context of the realities of life and death.

expectancy theory The idea that alcohol effects can be produced by people's expectations of how alcohol will influence them in particular.

experimentation A technique for establishing the causal relationship between variables.

explicit memory The act of consciously or intentionally retrieving past experiences.

exposure therapy An approach to treatment that involves confronting an emotion-arousing stimulus directly and repeatedly, ultimately leading to a decrease in the emotional response.

expressed emotion A measure of how much hostility, criticism, and emotional overinvolvement people communicate when speaking about a family member with a mental disorder.

external validity An attribute of an experiment in which variables have been defined in a normal, typical, or realistic way.

extinction The gradual elimination of a learned response that occurs when the CS is repeatedly presented without the US.

extrinsic motivation A motivation to take actions that lead to reward.

facial feedback hypothesis The theory that emotional expressions can cause the emotional experiences they typically signify.

false recognition A feeling of familiarity about something that hasn't been encountered before.

fast mapping The process whereby children map a word onto an underlying concept after only a single exposure.

feature-integration theory The idea that focused attention is not required to detect the individual features that make up a stimulus (e.g., the colour, shape, size, and location of letters), but it is required to bind those individual features together.

fetal alcohol syndrome (FAS) A developmental disorder that stems from heavy alcohol use by the mother during pregnancy.

fetal stage The period of prenatal development that lasts from about the 9th week until birth.

fight-or-flight response An emotional and physiological reaction to an emergency that increases readiness for action.

fixed-interval (FI) schedule An operant conditioning principle whereby reinforcers are presented at fixed time periods, provided that the appropriate response is made.

fixed-ratio (FR) schedule An operant conditioning principle whereby reinforcement is delivered after a specific number of responses have been made.

flashbulb memories Detailed recollections of when and where we heard about shocking events.

fluid intelligence The ability to solve and reason about novel problems.

foot-in-the-door technique A technique that involves making a small request and then following it with a larger request.

formal operational stage The final stage of cognitive development that begins around the age of 11, during which children learn to reason about abstract concepts.

fovea An area of the retina where vision is clearest and there are no rods at all.

framing effects A bias whereby people give different answers to the same problem depending on how the problem is phrased (or framed).

fraternal (dizygotic) twins Siblings who develop from two different eggs that were fertilized by two different sperm.

frequency distribution A graphic representation showing the number of times that the measurement of a property takes on each of its possible values.

frontal lobe The region of the cerebral cortex that has specialized areas for movement, abstract thinking, planning, memory, and judgement.

frustration–aggression hypothesis A principle stating that animals aggress when their goals are frustrated.

full consciousness A level of consciousness in which you know and are able to report your mental state.

functional fixedness The tendency to perceive the functions of objects as unchanging.

functionalism An approach to psychology that emphasized the adaptive significance of mental processes.

GABA (gamma-aminobutyric acid) The primary inhibitory neurotransmitter in the brain.

gate-control theory A theory of pain perception based on the idea that signals arriving from pain receptors in the body can be stopped, or *gated*, by interneurons in the spinal cord via feedback from the skin or from the brain.

gateway drug A drug whose use increases the risk of the subsequent use of more harmful drugs.

gene The major unit of hereditary transmission.

general adaptation syndrome (GAS) A three-stage physiological response that appears regardless of the stressor that is encountered.

generalization The conditioned response is observed even though the conditioned stimulus (CS) is slightly different from the CS used during acquisition.

generalized anxiety disorder (GAD) A disorder characterized by chronic excessive worry accompanied by three or more of the following symptoms: restlessness, fatigue, concentration problems, irritability, muscle tension, and sleep disturbance.

genetic dysphasia A syndrome characterized by an inability to learn the grammatical structure of language despite having otherwise normal intelligence.

germinal stage The 2-week period of prenatal development that begins at conception.

gestalt psychology An approach to psychology that emphasized the way in which the mind creates perceptual experience.

gestalt therapy A form of psychotherapy whose goal is helping the client become aware of his or her thoughts, behaviours, experiences, and feelings and to "own" or take responsibility for them.

glial cells Support cells found in the nervous system.

glutamate The major excitatory neurotransmitter in the brain.

grammar A set of rules that specify how the units of language can be combined to produce meaningful messages.

grossly disorganized behaviour Behaviour that is inappropriate for the situation or ineffective in attaining goals, often with specific motor disturbances.

group A collection of people who have something in common that distinguishes them from others.

group polarization The tendency of groups to make decisions that are more extreme than any member would have made alone.

group therapy A type of therapy in which multiple participants (who often do not know each other at the outset) work on their individual problems in a group atmosphere.

groupthink The tendency of groups to reach consensus in order to facilitate interpersonal harmony.

habituation A general process in which repeated or prolonged exposure to a stimulus results in a gradual reduction in responding.

hallucination A false perceptual experience that has a compelling sense of being real despite the absence of external stimulation.

hallucinogens Drugs that alter sensation and perception and often cause visual and auditory hallucinations.

haptic perception The active exploration of the environment by touching and grasping objects with our hands.

health psychology The subfield of psychology concerned with how psychological factors influence the causes and treatment of physical illness and the maintenance of health.

hedonic principle The claim that people are motivated to experience pleasure and avoid pain.

helplessness theory The idea that individuals who are prone to depression automatically attribute negative experiences to causes that are internal (i.e., their own fault), stable (i.e., unlikely to change), and global (i.e., widespread).

heritability A measure of the variability of behavioural traits among individuals that can be accounted for by genetic factors.

heritability coefficient A statistic (commonly denoted as $h2$) that describes the proportion of the difference between people's IQ scores that can be explained by differences in their genes.

heuristic A fast and efficient strategy that may facilitate decision making but does not guarantee that a solution will be reached.

heuristic persuasion The process by which attitudes or beliefs are changed by appeals to habit or emotion.

hindbrain The area of the brain that coordinates information coming into and out of the spinal cord.

hippocampus A structure critical for creating new memories and integrating them into a network of knowledge so that they can be stored indefinitely in other parts of the cerebral cortex.

histone modification Adding chemical modifications to proteins called histones that are involved in packaging DNA.

homeostasis The tendency for a system to take action to keep itself in equilibrium.

homophily The tendency for people to like others who are similar to themselves.

human sexual response cycle The stages of physiological arousal during sexual activity.

hypnosis A social interaction in which one person (the hypnotist) makes suggestions that lead to a change in another person's (the participant's) subjective experience of the world.

hypnotic analgesia The reduction of pain through hypnosis in people who are susceptible to hypnosis.

hypothalamus A subcortical structure that regulates body temperature, hunger, thirst, and sexual behaviour.

hypothesis A falsifiable prediction made by a theory.

hysteria A loss of function that has no obvious physical origin.

iatrogenic illness A disorder or symptom that occurs as a result of a medical or psychotherapeutic treatment itself.

iconic memory A fast-decaying store of visual information.

id The part of the mind containing the drives present at birth; it is the source of our bodily needs, wants, desires, and impulses, particularly our sexual and aggressive drives.

identical (monozygotic) twins Siblings who develop from the splitting of a single egg that was fertilized by a single sperm.

illusory conjunction A perceptual mistake whereby the brain incorrectly combines features from multiple objects.

illusory truth effect An error in reasoning that occurs when repeated exposure to a statement increases the likelihood that people will judge that statement to be true.

immune system A complex response system that protects the body from bacteria, viruses, and other foreign substances.

implicit learning Learning that takes place largely independent of awareness of both the process and the products of information acquisition.

implicit memory The influence of past experiences on later behaviour and performance, even without an effort to remember them or an awareness of the recollection.

inattentional blindness A failure to perceive objects that are not the focus of attention.

independent variable The variable that is manipulated in an experiment.

infancy The stage of development that begins at birth and lasts between 18 and 24 months.

informational influence A phenomenon that occurs when another person's behaviour provides information about what is good or true.

informed consent A verbal agreement to participate in a study made by an adult who has been informed of all the risks that participation may entail.

inner hair cells Specialized auditory receptor neurons embedded in the basilar membrane.

insomnia Difficulty in falling asleep or staying asleep.

intelligence The ability to use one's mind to solve novel problems and learn from experience.

intermittent reinforcement An operant conditioning principle whereby only some of the responses made are followed by reinforcement.

intermittent reinforcement effect The fact that operant behaviours that are maintained under intermittent reinforcement schedules resist extinction better than those maintained under continuous reinforcement.

internal validity An attribute of an experiment that allows it to establish causal relationships.

internal working model A set of beliefs about the way relationships work.

interneurons Neurons that connect sensory neurons, motor neurons, or other interneurons.

interpersonal psychotherapy (IPT) A form of psychotherapy that focuses on helping clients improve current relationships.

intrinsic motivation A motivation to take actions that are themselves rewarding.

introspection The analysis of subjective experience by trained observers.

ironic processes of mental control A mental process that can produce ironic errors because monitoring for errors can itself produce them.

James–Lange theory The theory that feelings are simply the perception of one's own physiological responses to a stimulus.

just noticeable difference (JND) The minimal change in a stimulus (e.g., its loudness or brightness) that can just barely be detected.

kin selection The process by which evolution selects for individuals who cooperate with their relatives.

language A system for communicating with others using signals that are combined according to rules of grammar and that convey meaning.

latent content A dream's true underlying meaning.

latent learning A process in which something is learned, but it is not manifested as a behavioural change until sometime in the future.

law of effect The principle that behaviours that are followed by a "satisfying state of affairs" tend to be repeated, whereas those that produce an "unpleasant state of affairs" are less likely to be repeated.

learning The acquisition, from experience, of new knowledge, skills, or responses that results in a relatively permanent change in the state of the learner.

linguistic relativity hypothesis The idea that language shapes the nature of thought.

locus of control A person's tendency to perceive the control of rewards as internal to the self or external in the environment.

long-term memory A type of storage that holds information for hours, days, weeks, or years.

long-term potentiation (LTP) A process whereby repeated communication across the synapse between neurons strengthens the connection, making further communication easier.

loss aversion The tendency to care more about avoiding losses than about achieving equal-size gains.

loudness A sound's intensity.

lymphocytes White blood cells that produce antibodies that fight infection, including T cells and B cells.

major depressive disorder (or unipolar depression) A disorder characterized by a severely depressed mood and/or inability to experience pleasure that lasts 2 or more weeks and is accompanied by feelings of worthlessness, lethargy, and sleep and appetite disturbance.

manifest content A dream's apparent topic or superficial meaning.

manipulation A technique for determining the causal power of a variable by actively changing its value.

marijuana (cannabis) The leaves and buds of the hemp plant, which contain a psychoactive drug called tetrahydrocannabinol (THC).

mean The average value of all the measurements.

means–ends analysis A process of searching for the means or steps to reduce differences between the current situation and the desired goal.

median The value that is greater than or equal to half the measurements and less than or equal to half the measurements.

medical model An approach that conceptualizes abnormal psychological experiences as illnesses that, like physical illnesses, have biological and environmental causes, defined symptoms, and possible cures.

meditation The practice of intentional contemplation.

medulla An extension of the spinal cord into the skull that coordinates heart rate, circulation, and respiration.

memory The ability to store and retrieve information over time.

memory misattribution Assigning a recollection or an idea to the wrong source.

mental control The attempt to change conscious states of mind.

mental disorder A persistent disturbance or dysfunction in behaviour, thoughts, or emotions that causes significant distress or impairment.

mere exposure effect the tendency for liking of a stimulus to increase with the amount of exposure to that stimulus.

metabolism The rate at which the body uses energy.

mind–body problem The issue of how the mind is related to the brain and body.

mindfulness meditation Teaches an individual to be fully present in each moment; to be aware of his or her thoughts, feelings, and sensations; and to detect symptoms before they become a problem.

minimal consciousness A low-level kind of sensory awareness and responsiveness that occurs when the mind inputs sensations and may output behaviour.

Minnesota Multiphasic Personality Inventory (MMPI) A well-researched clinical questionnaire used to assess personality and psychological problems.

mirror neurons Neurons that are active when an animal performs a behaviour (e.g., reaching for or manipulating an object), as well as when another animal observes that animal performing the same behaviour.

mode The value of the most frequently observed measurement.

monocular depth cues Aspects of a scene that yield information about depth when viewed with only one eye.

mood disorders Mental disorders that have mood disturbance as their predominant feature.

morphemes The smallest meaningful units of language.

morphological rules A set of rules that indicate how morphemes can be combined to form words.

motivation The internal causes of purposeful behaviour.

motor development The emergence of the ability to execute physical actions.

motor neurons Neurons that carry signals from the spinal cord to the muscles to produce movement.

motor reflexes Motor responses that are triggered by specific patterns of sensory stimulation.

multisensory Events that stimulate multiple senses at the same time.

myelin sheath An insulating layer of fatty material.

myelination The formation of a fatty sheath around the axons of a neuron.

narcissism A trait that reflects a grandiose view of the self, combined with a tendency to seek admiration from and exploit others.

narcolepsy A disorder in which sudden sleep attacks occur in the middle of waking activities.

narcotics (opiates) Highly addictive drugs derived from opium that relieve pain.

nativist theory The view that language development is best explained as an innate, biological capacity.

natural correlation A correlation observed in the world around us.

natural selection The process by which the specific attributes that promote an organism's survival and reproduction become more prevalent in the population over time.

naturalistic observation A technique for gathering scientific information by unobtrusively observing people in their natural environments.

need for achievement The motivation to solve worthwhile problems.

negative symptoms Deficits in or disruptions of normal emotions and behaviours (e.g., emotional and social withdrawal; apathy; poverty of speech; and other indications of the absence or insufficiency of normal behaviour, motivation, and emotion) that are present in those with schizophrenia.

nervous system An interacting network of neurons that conveys electrochemical information throughout the body.

neurons Cells in the nervous system that communicate with one another to perform information-processing tasks.

neurotransmitters Chemicals that transmit information across the synapse to a receiving neuron's dendrites.

night terrors (sleep terrors) Abrupt awakenings with panic and intense emotional arousal.

nonshared environment Features of the environment that are not experienced by all relevant members of a household.

nonsuicidal self-injury (NSSI) Direct, deliberate destruction of body tissue in the absence of any intent to die.

norepinephrine A neurotransmitter that is particularly involved in states of vigilance or heightened awareness of dangers in the environment.

norm of reciprocity The unwritten rule that people should benefit those who have benefited them.

normal distribution A mathematically defined distribution in which the frequency of measurements is highest in the middle and decreases symmetrically in both directions.

normative influence A phenomenon in which another person's behaviour provides information about what is appropriate.

norms Customary standards for behaviour that are widely shared by members of a culture.

obedience The tendency to do what authorities tell us to do.

object permanence The fact that objects continue to exist even when they are not visible.

observational learning A process in which an organism learns by watching the actions of others.

observer bias The tendency for observers' expectations to influence both what they believe they observed and what they actually observed.

obsessive-compulsive disorder (OCD) A disorder in which repetitive, intrusive thoughts (obsessions) and ritualistic behaviours (compulsions) designed to fend off those thoughts interfere significantly with an individual's functioning.

occipital lobe A region of the cerebral cortex that processes visual information.

olfactory bulb A brain structure located above the nasal cavity beneath the frontal lobes.

olfactory receptor neurons (ORNs) Receptor cells that transduce odourant molecules into neural impulses.

operant behaviour Behaviour that an organism performs that has some impact on the environment.

operant conditioning A type of learning in which the consequences of an organism's behaviour determine whether it will repeat that behaviour in the future.

operational definition A description of a property in measurable terms.

optimism bias A bias whereby people believe that, compared with other individuals, they are more likely to experience positive events and less likely to experience negative events in the future.

organizational encoding The process of categorizing information according to the relationships among a series of items.

outcome expectancies A person's assumptions about the likely consequences of a future behaviour.

overjustification effect An effect that occurs when a reward decreases a person's intrinsic motivation to perform a behaviour.

panic disorder A disorder characterized by the sudden occurrence of multiple psychological and physiological symptoms that contribute to a feeling of stark terror.

parallel processing The brain's capacity to perform multiple activities at the same time.

parasympathetic nervous system A set of nerves that helps the body return to a normal resting state.

parietal lobe A region of the cerebral cortex whose functions include processing information about touch.

passionate love An experience involving feelings of euphoria, intimacy, and intense sexual attraction.

perception The organization, identification, and interpretation of a sensation in order to form a mental representation.

perceptual confirmation The tendency of observers to see what they expect to see.

perceptual constancy A perceptual principle stating that even as aspects of sensory signals change, perception remains consistent.

perceptual contrast The phenomenon that occurs when the sensory information from two things may be very similar but we perceive the objects as different.

perceptual organization The process of grouping and segregating features to create whole objects organized in meaningful ways.

peripheral nervous system (PNS) The part of the nervous system that connects the central nervous system to the body's organs and muscles.

persistence The intrusive recollection of events that we wish we could forget.

persistent depressive disorder The same cognitive and bodily problems as in depression are present, but they are less severe and last longer, persisting for at least 2 years.

personal constructs Dimensions people use in making sense of their experiences.

personality An individual's characteristic style of behaving, thinking, and feeling.

personality disorders Enduring patterns of thinking, feeling, or relating to others or controlling impulses that deviate from cultural expectations and cause distress or impaired functioning.

person-centred therapy (or client-centred therapy) A form of psychotherapy that assumes that all individuals have a tendency towards growth and that this growth can be facilitated by acceptance and genuine reactions from the therapist.

person–situation controversy The question of whether behaviour is caused more by personality or by situational factors.

persuasion A phenomenon that occurs when a person's attitudes or beliefs are influenced by a communication from another person.

phenomenology The study of how things seem to the conscious person.

pheromones Biochemical odourants emitted by other members of an animal's species that can affect its behaviour or physiology.

philosophical dualism The view that mind and body are fundamentally different things.

philosophical empiricism The view that all knowledge is acquired through experience.

philosophical idealism The view that perceptions of the physical world are the brain's interpretation of information from the sensory organs

philosophical materialism The view that all mental phenomena are reducible to physical phenomena.

philosophical nativism The view that some knowledge is innate rather than acquired.

philosophical realism The view that perceptions of the physical world are produced entirely by information from the sensory organs.

phobic disorders Disorders characterized by marked, persistent, and excessive fear and avoidance of specific objects, activities, or situations.

phoneme The smallest unit of sound that is recognizable as speech rather than as random noise.

phonological rules A set of rules that indicate how phonemes can be combined to produce speech sounds.

phototherapy A therapy that involves repeated exposure to bright light.

pitch How high or low a sound is.

pituitary gland The "master gland" of the body's hormone-producing system, which releases hormones that direct the functions of many other glands in the body.

place code The process by which the brain uses information about the relative activity of hair cells (e.g., which ones are more active and which are less active) across the whole basilar membrane to help determine the pitch you hear.

placebo An inert substance or procedure that has been applied with the expectation that it will produce a healing response.

pons A brain structure that relays information from the cerebellum to the rest of the brain.

population A complete collection of people.

positive symptoms Thoughts and behaviours, such as delusions and hallucinations, present in schizophrenia but not seen in those without the disorder.

postconventional stage A stage of moral development in which the morality of an action is determined by a set of general principles that reflect core values.

posthypnotic amnesia The failure to retrieve memories following hypnotic suggestions to forget.

posttraumatic stress disorder (PTSD) A disorder characterized by chronic physiological arousal, recurrent unwanted thoughts or images of the trauma, and avoidance of things that call the traumatic event to mind.

power A detector's ability to detect the presence of differences or changes in the magnitude of a property.

preconventional stage A stage of moral development in which the morality of an action is primarily determined by its consequences for the actor.

prejudice A positive or negative evaluation of another person based solely on his or her group membership.

preoperational stage The stage of cognitive development that begins at about 2 years and ends at about 6 years, during which children develop a preliminary understanding of the physical world.

preparedness theory The idea that people are instinctively predisposed towards certain fears.

primary sex characteristics Bodily structures that change at puberty and are directly involved in reproduction.

priming An enhanced ability to think of a stimulus, such as a word or object, as a result of a recent exposure to that stimulus during an earlier study task.

principle of reinforcement A principle stating that any behaviour that is rewarded will be repeated and any behaviour that isn't rewarded won't be repeated.

proactive aggression Aggression that is planned and purposeful.

proactive interference Situations in which information learned earlier impairs memory for information acquired later.

problem of other minds The fundamental difficulty we have in perceiving the consciousness of others.

procedural memory The gradual acquisition of skills as a result of practice, or "knowing how" to do things.

projective tests Tests designed to reveal inner aspects of individuals' personalities by analysis of their responses to a standard series of ambiguous stimuli.

proprioception Your sense of bodily position.

prospect theory The theory that people choose to take on risk when evaluating potential losses and avoid risks when evaluating potential risks.

prospective memory Remembering to do things in the future.

prototype theory The concept that we classify new objects by comparing them to the "best" or "most typical" member (the *prototype*) of a category.

proximodistal rule The "inside-to-outside" rule that describes the tendency for motor skills to emerge in sequence from the centre to the periphery.

psychoactive drugs Chemicals that influence consciousness or behaviour by altering the brain's chemical message system.

psychoanalysis A therapy that aims to give people insight into the contents of their unconscious minds.

psychoanalytic theory A general theory that emphasizes the influence of the unconscious on feelings, thoughts, and behaviours.

psychodynamic approach An approach that regards personality as formed by needs, strivings, and desires largely operating outside of awareness—motives that also can produce emotional disorders.

psychodynamic psychotherapies Therapies that explore childhood events and encourage individuals to use this understanding to develop insight into their psychological problems.

psychology The scientific study of mind and behaviour.

psychopharmacology The study of drug effects on psychological states and symptoms.

psychophysics Methods that systematically relate the physical characteristics of a stimulus to an observer's perception.

psychosomatic illness An interaction between mind and body that can produce illness.

psychosurgery Surgical destruction of specific brain areas.

psychotherapy An interaction between a socially sanctioned clinician and someone suffering from a psychological problem, with the goal of providing support or relief from the problem.

puberty The onset of bodily changes associated with sexual maturity.

punisher Any stimulus or event that decreases the likelihood of the behaviour that led to it.

random assignment A procedure that assigns participants to a condition by chance.

random sampling A technique for choosing participants that ensures that every member of a population has an equal chance of being included in the sample.

range The value of the largest measurement in a frequency distribution minus the value of the smallest measurement.

ratio IQ A statistic obtained by dividing a person's mental age by the person's physical age and then multiplying the quotient by 100.

rational choice theory The classical view that we make decisions by determining how likely something is to happen, judging the value of the outcome, and then multiplying the two.

rational coping Facing a stressor and working to overcome it.

reactance An unpleasant feeling that arises when people feel they are being coerced.

reaction time The amount of time between the onset of a stimulus and a person's response to that stimulus.

reactive aggression Aggression that occurs spontaneously in response to a negative affective state.

reappraisal The process of changing one's emotional experience by changing the way one thinks about the emotion-eliciting stimulus.

reasoning A mental activity that consists of organizing information or beliefs into a series of steps in order to reach conclusions.

rebound effect of thought suppression The tendency of a thought to return to consciousness with greater frequency following suppression.

receptors Parts of the cell membrane that receive the neurotransmitter and initiate or prevent a new electric signal.

reciprocal altruism Behaviour that benefits another with the expectation that those benefits will be returned in the future.

reconsolidation The process whereby memories can become vulnerable to disruption when they are recalled, thus requiring them to be consolidated again.

referred pain Feeling of pain on the surface of the body, but due to internal damage; occurs because sensory information from internal and external areas converges on the same nerve cells in the spinal cord.

reflex arc A neural pathway that controls reflex actions.

refractory period The time following an action potential during which a new action potential cannot be initiated.

reframing Finding a new or creative way to think about a stressor that reduces its threat.

rehearsal The process of keeping information in short-term memory by mentally repeating it.

reinforcer Any stimulus or event that increases the likelihood of the behaviour that led to it.

relaxation response A condition of reduced muscle tension, cortical activity, heart rate, breathing rate, and blood pressure.

relaxation therapy A technique for reducing tension by consciously relaxing muscles of the body.

reliability A detector's ability to detect the absence of differences or changes in the magnitude of a property

REM sleep A stage of sleep characterized by rapid eye movements and a high level of brain activity.

replication An experiment that uses the same procedures as a previous experiment but with a new sample from the same population.

representativeness heuristic A mental shortcut that involves making a probability judgement by comparing an object or event with a prototype of the object or event.

repression A mental process that removes unacceptable thoughts and memories from consciousness and keeps them in the unconscious.

repressive coping Avoiding feelings, thoughts, or situations that are reminders of a stressor and maintaining an artificially positive viewpoint

Research Domain Criteria Project (RDoC) A new initiative that aims to guide the classification and understanding of mental disorders by revealing the basic processes that give rise to them.

resting potential The difference in electric charge between the inside and outside of a neuron's cell membrane.

reticular formation A brain structure that regulates sleep, wakefulness, and levels of arousal.

retina A layer of light-sensitive tissue lining the back of the eyeball.

retrieval The process of bringing to mind information that has been previously encoded and stored.

retrieval cue External information that is associated with stored information and helps bring it to mind.

retrieval-induced forgetting A process by which retrieving an item from long-term memory impairs subsequent recall of related items.

retroactive interference Situations in which information learned later impairs memory for information acquired earlier.

retrograde amnesia The inability to retrieve information that was acquired before a particular date, usually the date of an injury or surgery.

rods Photoreceptors that become active under low-light conditions for night vision.

Rorschach Inkblot Test A projective technique in which respondents' inner thoughts and feelings are believed to be revealed by analysis of their responses to a set of unstructured inkblots.

sample A partial collection of people or animals or things drawn from a population.

schemas Theories about the way the world works.

schizophrenia A disorder characterized by the profound disruption of basic psychological processes; a distorted perception of reality; altered or blunted emotion; and disturbances in thought, motivation, and behaviour.

scientific method A procedure for using empirical evidence to establish facts.

seasonal affective disorder (SAD) Recurrent depressive episodes in a seasonal pattern.

secondary sex characteristics Bodily structures that change at puberty but are not directly involved in reproduction.

second-order conditioning A type of learning whereby a CS is paired with a stimulus that became associated with the US in an earlier procedure.

self-actualizing tendency The human motive towards realizing our inner potential.

self-concept A person's explicit knowledge of his or her own behaviours, traits, and other personal characteristics.

self-consciousness A distinct level of consciousness in which the person's attention is drawn to the self as an object.

self-esteem The extent to which an individual likes, values, and accepts the self.

self-regulation The exercise of voluntary control over the self to bring the self into line with preferred standards.

self-report A method in which people provide subjective information about their own thoughts, feelings, or behaviours, typically via questionnaire or interview.

self-selection A problem that occurs when anything about a participant determines the participant's condition.

self-serving bias People's tendency to take credit for their successes but downplay responsibility for their failures.

self-verification The tendency to seek evidence to confirm the self-concept.

semantic encoding The process of relating new information in a meaningful way to knowledge that is already stored in memory.

semantic memory A network of associated facts and concepts that make up our general knowledge of the world.

sensation Simple stimulation of a sense organ.

sensitivity How responsive we are to faint stimuli.

sensitization A simple form of learning that occurs when presentation of a stimulus leads to an increased response to a later stimulus.

sensorimotor stage A stage of cognitive development that begins at birth and lasts through infancy, during which infants acquire information about the world by sensing it and moving around within it.

sensory adaptation The process whereby sensitivity to prolonged stimulation tends to decline over time as an organism adapts to current (unchanging) conditions.

sensory memory A type of storage that holds sensory information for a few seconds or less.

sensory neurons Neurons that receive information from the external world and convey this information to the brain via the spinal cord.

serial position effect The observation that the first few and last few items in a series are more likely to be recalled than the items in the middle.

serotonin A neurotransmitter that is involved in the regulation of sleep and wakefulness, eating, and aggressive behaviour.

shaping Learning that results from the reinforcement of successive steps to a final desired behaviour.

shared environment Features of the environment that are experienced by all relevant members of a household.

short-term memory A type of storage that holds nonsensory information for more than a few seconds but less than a minute.

sick role A socially recognized set of rights and obligations linked with illness.

signal detection theory A way of analyzing data from psychophysics experiments that measures an individual's perceptual sensitivity while also taking noise, expectations, motivations, and goals into account.

sleep apnea A disorder in which the person stops breathing for brief periods while asleep.

sleep paralysis The experience of waking up unable to move.

social cognition The processes by which people come to understand others.

social influence The ability to change or direct another person's behaviour.

social loafing The tendency of people to expend less effort when they are in a group than when they are alone.

social phobia A disorder that involves an irrational fear of being publicly humiliated or embarrassed.

social psychology The study of the causes and consequences of sociality.

social support The aid gained through interacting with others.

social–cognitive approach An approach that views personality in terms of how the person thinks about the situations encountered in daily life and behaves in response to them.

somatic nervous system A set of nerves that conveys information between voluntary muscles and the central nervous system.

somatic symptom disorders The set of psychological disorders in which people with at least one bodily symptom display significant health-related anxiety, express disproportionate concerns about their symptoms, and devote excessive time and energy to their symptoms or health concerns.

somnambulism (sleepwalking) Occurs when a person arises and walks around while asleep.

source memory Recall of when, where, and how information was acquired.

spatial acuity The ability to distinguish two features that are very close together in space.

specific phobia A disorder that involves an irrational fear of a particular object or situation that markedly interferes with an individual's ability to function.

spinal reflexes Simple pathways in the nervous system that rapidly generate muscle contractions.

spontaneous recovery The tendency of a learned behaviour to recover from extinction after a rest period.

standard deviation A statistic that describes how each of the measurements in a frequency distribution differs from the mean.

state-dependent retrieval The process whereby information tends to be better recalled when the person is in the same state during encoding *and* retrieval.

stereotype threat The fear of confirming the negative beliefs that others may hold.

stereotype threat The target's fear of confirming an observer's negative stereotypes.

stereotyping The process of drawing inferences about individuals based on their category membership.

stimulants Substances that excite the central nervous system, heightening arousal and activity levels.

storage The process of maintaining information in memory over time.

stress The physical and psychological response to internal or external stressors.

stress-inoculation training (SIT) A reframing technique that helps people cope with stressful situations by developing positive ways to think about the situations.

stressors Specific events or chronic pressures that place demands on a person or threaten the person's well-being.

structuralism An approach to psychology that attempted to isolate and analyze the mind's basic elements.

subcortical structures Areas of the forebrain housed under the cerebral cortex near the very centre of the brain.

subtyping The tendency of observers to think of targets who disconfirm stereotypes as "exceptions to the rule."

suggestibility The tendency to incorporate misleading information from external sources into personal recollections.

suicide Intentional self-inflicted death.

suicide attempt Engagement in potentially harmful behaviour with some intention of dying.

sunk-cost fallacy A framing effect in which people make decisions about a current situation on the basis of what they have previously invested in the situation.

superego The mental system that reflects the internalization of cultural rules, mainly learned as parents exercise their authority.

syllogistic reasoning Determining whether a conclusion follows from two statements that are assumed to be true.

sympathetic nervous system A set of nerves that prepares the body for action in challenging or threatening situations.

synapse The junction or region between the axon of one neuron and the dendrites or cell body of another.

syntactic rules A set of rules that indicate how words can be combined to form phrases and sentences.

systematic persuasion The process by which attitudes or beliefs are changed by appeals to reason.

tactile receptive field A small patch of skin that relates information about pain, pressure, texture, pattern, or vibration to a receptor.

target-based inferences Inferences based on information about an individual's behaviour.

taste buds The organ of taste transduction.

tectum A part of the midbrain that orients an organism in the environment.

tegmentum A part of the midbrain that is involved in movement and arousal.

telegraphic speech Speech that is devoid of function morphemes and consists mostly of content words.

telomerase An enzyme that rebuilds telomeres at the tips of chromosomes.

telomeres Caps at the ends of the chromosomes that prevent the chromosomes from sticking to each other.

temperament A biologically based pattern of attentional and emotional reactivity.

temporal acuity The ability to distinguish two features that are very close together in time.

temporal code The process whereby the brain uses the timing of the action potentials on the auditory nerve to help determine the pitch you hear.

temporal lobe A region of the cerebral cortex responsible for hearing and language.

teratogen Any substance that passes from mother to unborn child and impairs development.

terminal buttons Knoblike structures that branch out from an axon.

terror management theory The theory that people respond to the knowledge of their own mortality by developing a cultural worldview.

thalamus A subcortical structure that relays and filters information from the senses and transmits the information to the cerebral cortex.

Thematic Apperception Test (TAT) A projective technique in which respondents' underlying motives, concerns, and the way they see the social world are believed to be revealed through analysis of the stories they make up about ambiguous pictures of people.

theories A hypothetical explanation of a natural phenomenon.

theory of mind The understanding that the mind produces representations of the world and that these representations guide behaviour.

third-variable problem The fact that the natural correlation between two variables cannot be taken as evidence of a causal relationship between them because a third variable might be causing them both.

thought suppression The conscious avoidance of a thought.

timbre The quality of sound that allows you to distinguish two sources with the same pitch and loudness.

token economy A form of behaviour therapy in which clients are given "tokens" for desired behaviours, which they can later trade for rewards.

trait A relatively stable disposition to behave in a particular and consistent way.

transcranial magnetic stimulation (TMS) A treatment that involves placing a powerful pulsed magnet over a person's scalp to alter neuronal activity in the brain.

transduction The process whereby sense receptors convert physical signals from the environment into neural signals that are sent to the central nervous system.

transfer-appropriate processing The idea that memory is likely to transfer from one situation to another when the encoding and retrieval contexts of the situations match.

transience Forgetting what occurs with the passage of time.

travelling wave The up-and-down movement that sound causes in the basilar membrane.

two-factor theory of emotion The theory that stimuli trigger a general state of physiological arousal which is then interpreted as a specific emotion.

two-factor theory of intelligence Spearman's theory suggesting that a person's performance on a test is due to a combination of general ability and skills that are specific to the test.

Type A behaviour pattern The tendency towards easily aroused hostility, impatience, a sense of time urgency, and competitive achievement strivings.

Type I error An error that occurs when researchers conclude that there is a causal relationship between two variables when in fact there is not.

Type II error An error that occurs when researchers conclude that there is not a causal relationship between two variables when in fact there is.

unconditioned response (UR) A reflexive reaction that is reliably produced by an unconditioned stimulus.

unconditioned stimulus (US) Something that reliably produces a naturally occurring reaction in an organism.

unconscious The part of the mind that contains information of which people are not aware.

unconscious motivations Motivations of which people are not aware.

universal grammar A collection of processes that facilitate language learning.

universality hypothesis The theory that all emotional expressions mean the same thing to all people in all places at all times.

variable A property that can take on different values.

variable-interval (VI) schedule An operant conditioning principle whereby a behaviour is reinforced on the basis of an average time that has expired since the last reinforcement.

variable-ratio (VR) schedule An operant conditioning principle whereby the delivery of reinforcement is based on a particular average number of responses.

ventriloquist illusion The fact that you depend on your visual system for reliable information about spatial location.

vestibular system The three fluid-filled semicircular canals and adjacent organs located next to the cochlea in the inner ear.

visual acuity The ability to see fine detail.

visual imagery encoding The process of storing new information by converting it into mental pictures.

visual receptive field The region of the visual field to which each neuron responds.

Weber's law For every sense domain, the change in a stimulus that is just noticeable is a constant ratio of the standard stimulus, over a range of standard intensities.

working memory Active maintenance of information in short-term storage.

REFERENCES

Aarts, H., Custers, R., & Marien, H. (2008). Preparing and motivating behavior outside of awareness. *Science, 319,* 1639.

Abel, T., Alberini, C., Ghirardi, M., Huang, Y.-Y., Nguyen, P., & Kandel, E. R. (1995). Steps toward a molecular definition of memory consolidation. In D. L. Schacter (Ed.), *Memory distortion: How minds, brains and societies reconstruct the past* (pp. 298–328). Cambridge, MA: Harvard University Press.

Abelson, J., Curtis, G., Sagher, O., Albucher, R., Harrigan, M., Taylor, S. F., . . . Giordani, B. (2009). Deep brain stimulation for refractory obsessive-compulsive disorder. *Biological Psychiatry, 57,* 510–516.

Abrams, M., & Reber, A. S. (1988). Implicit learning: Robustness in the face of psychiatric disorders. *Journal of Psycholinguistic Research, 17,* 425–439.

Abramson, L. Y., Seligman, M. E. P., & Teasdale, J. D. (1978). Learned helplessness in humans: Critique and reformulation. *Journal of Abnormal Psychology, 87,* 49–74.

Acevedo, B. P., & Aron, A. (2009). Does a long-term relationship kill romantic love? *Review of General Psychology, 13,* 59–65.

Acevedo-Garcia, D., McArdle, N., Osypuk, T. L., Lefkowitz, B., & Krimgold, B. K. (2007). *Children left behind: How metropolitan areas are failing America's children.* Boston: Harvard School of Public Health.

Achter, J. A., Lubinski, D., & Benbow, C. P. (1996). Multipotentiality among the intellectually gifted: "It was never there and already it's vanishing." *Journal of Counseling Psychology, 43,* 65–76.

Acikalin, M. Y., Watson, K. K., Fitzsimons, G. J., & Platt, M. L. (2018). Rhesus macaques form preferences for brand logos through sex and social status-based advertising. *PLoS ONE, 13*(3), e0193055. doi:org/10.1371/journal.pone.0194055

Ackerman, P. L. (2014). Adolescent and adult intellectual development. *Current Directions in Psychological Science, 23*(4), 246–251.

Ackerman, P. L. (2017). Adult intelligence: The construct and the criterion problem. *Perspectives on Psychological Science, 12*(6), 987–998.

Addis, D. R., Wong, A. T., & Schacter, D. L. (2007). Remembering the past and imagining the future: Common and distinct neural substrates during event construction and elaboration. *Neuropsychologia, 45,* 1363–1377.

Addis, D. R., Wong, A. T., & Schacter, D. L. (2008). Age-related changes in the episodic simulation of future events. *Psychological Science, 19,* 33–41.

Adelmann, P. K., & Zajonc, R. B. (1989). Facial efference and the experience of emotion. *Annual Review of Psychology, 40,* 249–280.

Adolph, K. E., Cole, W. G., Komati, M., Garciaguirre, J. S., Badaly, D., Lingeman, J. M., . . . Sotsky, R. B. (2012). How do you learn to walk? Thousands of steps and dozens of falls per day. *Psychological Science, 23*(11), 1387–1394.

Adolphs, R., Russell, J. A., & Tranel, D. (1999). A role for the human amygdala in recognizing emotional arousal from unpleasant stimuli. *Psychological Science, 10,* 167–171.

Adolphs, R., Tranel, D., Damasio, H., & Damasio, A. R. (1995). Fear and the human amygdala. *Journal of Neuroscience, 15,* 5879–5891.

Adorno, T. W., Frenkel-Brunswik, E., Levinson, D. J., & Sanford, R. N. (1950). *The authoritarian personality.* New York: Harper & Row.

Aggleton, J. (Ed.). (1992). *The amygdala: Neurobiological aspects of emotion, memory and mental dysfunction.* New York: Wiley-Liss.

Agin, D. (2007). *Junk science: An overdue indictment of government, industry, and faith groups that twist science for their own gain.* New York: Macmillan.

Agren, T., Engman, J., Frick, A., Björkstrand, J., Larsson, E. M., Furmark, T., & Fredrikson, M. (2012). Disruption of reconsolidation erases a fear memory trace in the human amygdala. *Science, 337,* 1550–1552.

Agthe, M., Spörrle, M., & Maner, J. K. (2010). Don't hate me because I'm beautiful: Anti-attractiveness bias in organizational evaluation and decision making. *Journal of Experimental Psychology, 46*(6), 1151–1154. doi:10.1016/j.jesp.2010.05.007

Aharon, I., Etcoff, N., Ariely, D., Chabris, C. F., O'Conner, E., & Breiter, H. C. (2001). Beautiful faces have variable reward value: fMRI and behavioral evidence. *Neuron, 32,* 537–551.

Ahlskog, J. E. (2011). Pathological behaviors provoked by dopamine agonist therapy of Parkinson's disease. *Physiology & Behavior, 104,* 168–172.

Ainsworth, M. D. S., Blehar, M. C., Waters, E., & Wall, S. (1978). *Patterns of attachment: A psychological study of the strange situation.* Hillsdale, NJ: Erlbaum.

Ainsworth, S. E., & Maner, J. K. (2012). Sex begets violence: Mating motives, social dominance, and physical aggression in men. *Journal of Personality and Social Psychology, 103*(5), 819–829. doi:10.1037/a0029428

Aknin, L. B., Hamlin, J. K., & Dunn, E. W. (2012). Giving leads to happiness in young children. *PLoS ONE, 7*(6), e39211. doi:10.1371/journal.pone.0039211

Alasaari, J. S., Lagus, M., Ollila, H. M., Toivola, A., Kivimaki, M., Vahterra, J., . . . Paunio, T. (2012). Environmental stress affects DNA methylation of a CpG rich promoter region of serotonin transporter gene in a nurse cohort. *PLoS One, 7,* e45813. doi:10.1371/journal.pone.0045813

Albarracín, D., & Shavitt, S. (2018). Attitudes and attitude change. *Annual Review of Psychology, 69*(1), 299–327.

Alcoholics Anonymous. (2018). *A. A. Fact File.* New York: General Service Office of Alcoholics Anonymous.

Aleman, A., Sommer, I. E., & Kahn, R. S. (2007). Efficacy of slow repetitive transcranial magnetic stimulation in the treatment of resistant auditory hallucinations in schizophrenia: A meta-analysis. *Journal of Clinical Psychiatry, 68,* 416–421.

Alicke, M. D., Klotz, M. L., Breitenbecher, D. L., Yurak, T. J., & Vredenburg, D. S. (1995). Personal contact, individuation, and the better-than-average effect. *Journal of Personality and Social Psychology, 68,* 804–824.

Allan, B., & Smylie, J. (2015). First Peoples, second-class treatment: The role of racism in the health and well-being of Indigenous peoples in Canada. Toronto, ON: The Wellesley Institute.

Allen, J. G., Flanigan, S. S., LeBlanc, M., Vallarino, J., MacNaughton, P., Stewart, J. H., & Christiani, D. C. (2016). Flavoring chemicals in e-cigarettes: Diacetyl, 2,3-pentanedione, and acetoin in a sample of 51 products, including fruit-, candy-, and cocktail-flavored e-cigarettes. *Environmental Health Perspectives, 124*(6), 733–739.

Allen, P., Laroi, F., McGuire, P. K., & Aleman, A. (2008). The hallucinating brain: A review of structural and functional neuroimaging studies of hallucinations. *Neuroscience and Biobehavioral Reviews, 32,* 175–191.

Allison, D. B., Kaprio, J., Korkeila, M., Koskenvuo, M., Neale, M. C., & Hayakawa, K. (1996). The heritability of body mass index among an international sample of monozygotic twins reared apart. *International Journal of Obesity, 20*(6), 501–506.

Alloway, T. P. (Ed.). (2018). *Working memory and clinical developmental disorders.* London and New York: Routledge.

Alloway, T. P., Gathercole, S. E., Kirkwood, H., & Elliott, J. (2009). The cognitive and behavioral characteristics of children with low working memory. *Child Development, 80,* 606–621.

Allport, G. W. (1937). *Personality: A psychological interpretation.* New York: Holt.

Allport, G. W. (1954). *The nature of prejudice.* Cambridge, MA: Addison-Wesley.

Allport, G. W., & Odbert, H. S. (1936). Trait-names: A psycholexical study. *Psychological Monographs, 47,* 592.

Al-Sahab, B., Saqib, M., Hauser, G., & Tamim, H. (2010). Prevalence of smoking during pregnancy and associated risk factors among Canadian women: A national survey. *BMC Pregnancy and Childbirth, 10*(1), 24.

Alvarez, L. W. (1965). A pseudo experience in parapsychology. *Science, 148,* 1541.

American Psychiatric Association. (2013). *Diagnostic and Statistical Manual of Mental Disorders (DSM-5)* (5th ed.). Washington, DC: American Psychiatric Publishing.

American Psychological Association. (2002). *Ethical principles of psychologists and code of conduct.* Washington, DC: Author. Retrieved from apa.org/code/ethics/index.aspx [includes 2010 amendments]

American Psychological Association. (2009). *Report of the American Psychological Association task force on appropriate therapeutic responses to sexual orientation.* Washington, DC: Author.

Amialchuk, A., & Gerhardinger, L. (2015). Contraceptive use and pregnancies in adolescents' romantic relationships: Role of relationship activities and parental attitudes and communication. *Journal of Developmental & Behavioral Pediatrics, 36*(2), 86–97.

Amos, N., & McCabe, M. P. (2015). Conceptualizing and measuring perceptions of sexual attractiveness: Are there differences across gender and sexual orientation? *Personality and Individual Differences, 76,* 111–122. doi:10.1016/j.paid.2014.11.057

Anand, S., & Hotson, J. (2002). Transcranial magnetic stimulation: Neurophysiological applications and safety. *Brain and Cognition, 50,* 366–386.

Anderson, C. A. (1989). Temperature and aggression: Ubiquitous effects of heat on occurrence of human violence. *Psychological Bulletin, 106,* 74–96.

Anderson, C. A., & Bushman, B. J. (2002). Human aggression. *Annual Review of Psychology, 53,* 27–51.

Anderson, C. A., Berkowitz, L., Donnerstein, E., Huesmann, L. R., Johnson, J. D., Linz, D., . . . Wartella, E. (2003). The influence of media violence on youth. *Psychological Science in the Public Interest, 4,* 81–110.

Anderson, C. A., Bushman, B. J., & Groom, R. W. (1997). Hot years and serious and deadly assault: Empirical tests of the heat hypothesis. *Journal of Personality and Social Psychology, 73,* 1213–1223.

Anderson, C. A., Shibuya, A., Ihori, N., Swing, E. L., Bushman, B. J., Sakamoto, A., . . . Saleem, M. (2010). Violent video game effects on aggression, empathy, and prosocial behavior in Eastern and Western countries: A meta-analytic review. *Psychological Bulletin, 136*(2), 151–173.

Anderson, C. A., Suzuki, K., Swing, E. L., Groves, C. L., Gentile, D. A., Prot, S., . . . Petrescu, P. (2017). Media violence and other aggression risk factors in seven nations. *Personality and Social Psychology Bulletin, 43*(7), 986–998.

Anderson, J. R., & Schooler, L. J. (1991). Reflections of the environment in memory. *Psychological Science, 2,* 396–408.

Anderson, J. R., & Schooler, L. J. (2000). The adaptive nature of memory. In E. Tulving & F. I. M. Craik (Eds.), *Handbook of memory* (pp. 557–570). New York: Oxford University Press.

Anderson, M. C. (2003). Rethinking interference theory: Executive control and the mechanisms of forgetting. *Journal of Memory and Language, 49,* 415–445.

Anderson, M. C., Bjork, R. A., & Bjork, E. L. (1994). Remembering can cause forgetting: Retrieval dynamics in long-term memory. *Journal of Experimental Psychology: Learning, Memory, and Cognition, 20,* 1063–1087.

Anderson, M. C., Ochsner, K. N., Kuhl, B., Cooper, J., Robertson, E., Gabrieli, S. W., . . . Gabrieli, J. D. E. (2004). Neural systems underlying the suppression of unwanted memories. *Science, 303,* 232–235.

Anderson, M. L. (2008). Multiple inference and gender differences in the effects of early intervention: A reevaluation of the Abecedarian, Perry Preschool, and Early Training Projects. *Journal of the American Statistical Association, 103*(484), 1481–1495.

Anderson, R. C., Pichert, J. W., Goetz, E. T., Schallert, D. L., Stevens, K. V., & Trollip, S. R. (1976). Instantiation of general terms. *Journal of Verbal Learning and Verbal Behavior, 15,* 667–679.

Andreasen, N. C. (2011). A journey into chaos: Creativity and the unconscious. *Mens Sana Monographs, 9,* 42–53.

Andrewes, D. (2001). *Neuropsychology: From theory to practice.* Hove, England: Psychology Press.

Andrews, I. (1982). Bilinguals out of focus: A critical discussion. *International Review of Applied Linguistics in Language Teaching, 20,* 297–305.

Andrews-Hanna, J. R. (2012). The brain's default network and its adaptive role in internal mentation. *Neuroscientist, 18,* 251–270.

Andrieux, M., & Proteau, L. (2014). Mixed observation favors motor learning through better estimation of the model's performance. *Experimental Brain Research, 232,* 3121–3132.

Annis, L. F., & Annis, D. B. (1982). A normative study of students' reported preferred study techniques. *Literacy Research and Instruction, 21,* 201–207.

Ansfield, M., Wegner, D. M., & Bowser, R. (1996). Ironic effects of sleep urgency. *Behavior Research and Therapy, 34,* 523–531.

Anstis, S. (2010). Visual filling in. *Current Biology, 20*(16), R664–R666. doi:10.1016/j.cub.2010.06.029

Antoni, M. H., Lehman, J. M., Klibourn, K. M., Boyers, A. E., Culver, J. L., Alferi, S. M., . . . Carver, C. S. (2001). Cognitive-behavioral stress management intervention decreases the prevalence of depression and enhances benefit finding among women under treatment for early-stage breast cancer. *Health Psychology, 20,* 20–32.

Anxiety Canada. (2019). Specific phobia. Retrieved from https://anxietycanada.com/disorders/specific-phobia/

Apperly, I. A., & Butterfill, S. A. (2009). Do humans have two systems to track beliefs and belief-like states? *Psychological Review, 116,* 953–970.

Ardekani, B. A., Convit, A., & Bachman, A. H. (2016). Analysis of the MIRIAD data shows sex differences in hippocampal atrophy progression. *Journal of Alzheimer's Disease, 50,* 847–857.

Arden, R., & Adams, M. J. (2016). A general intelligence factor in dogs. *Intelligence, 55,* 79–85.

Ariel, R., & Karpicke, J. D. (2018). Improving self-regulated learning with a retrieval practice intervention. *Journal of Experimental Psychology: Applied, 24,* 43–56.

Armstrong, D. M. (1980). *The nature of mind.* Ithaca, NY: Cornell University Press.

Arnold, M. B. (Ed.). (1960). *Emotion and personality: Psychological aspects* (Vol. 1). New York: Columbia University Press.

Arnold, S. E., Trojanowski, J. Q., Gur, R. E., Blackwell, P., Han, L., & Choi, C. (1998). Absence of neurodegeneration and neural injury in the cerebral cortex in a sample of elderly patients with schizophrenia. *Archives of General Psychiatry, 55,* 225–232.

Aron, A., Fisher, H., Mashek, D., Strong, G., Li, H., & Brown, L. (2005). Reward, motivation, and emotion systems associated with early-stage intense romantic love. *Journal of Neurophysiology, 93,* 327–337.

Aronson, E. (1963). Effect of the severity of threat on the devaluation of forbidden behavior. *Journal of Abnormal and Social Psychology, 66,* 584–588.

Aronson, E. (1969). The theory of cognitive dissonance: A current perspective. In L. Berkowitz (Ed.), *Advances in experimental social psychology* (Vol. 4, pp. 1–34): Academic Press.

Aronson, E., & Mills, J. (1958). The effect of severity of initiation on liking for a group. *Journal of Abnormal and Social Psychology, 59,* 177–181.

Aronson, E., & Worchel, P. (1966). Similarity versus liking as determinants of interpersonal attractiveness. *Psychonomic Science, 5,* 157–158.

Aronson, E., Willerman, B., & Floyd, J. (1966). The effect of a pratfall on increasing interpersonal attractiveness. *Psychonomic Science, 4,* 227–228.

Aronson, J., & Steele, C. M. (2004). Stereotypes and the fragility of academic competence, motivation, and self-concept. In A. J. Elliot & C. S. Dweck (Eds.), *Handbook of competence and motivation* (pp. 436–456). New York: Guilford Press.

Asch, S. E. (1951). Effects of group pressure on the modification and distortion of judgments. In H. Guetzkow (Ed.), *Groups, leadership, and men* (pp. 177–190). Pittsburgh, PA: Carnegie Press.

Asch, S. E. (1955). Opinions and social pressure. *Scientific American, 193,* 31–35.

Asch, S. E. (1956). Studies of independence and conformity: 1. A minority of one against a unanimous majority. *Psychological Monographs: General and Applied, 70,* 1–70.

Aschoff, J. (1965). Circadian rhythms in man. *Science, 148,* 1427–1432.

Aserinsky, E., & Kleitman, N. (1953). Regularly occurring periods of eye motility, and concomitant phenomena, during sleep. *Science, 118,* 273–274.

Ash, M., & Boyce, J. K. (2018). Racial disparities in pollution exposure and employment at U.S. industrial facilities. *Proceedings of the National Academy of Sciences, USA, 115,* 10636–10641.

Ashby, F. G., & Ell, S. W. (2001). The neurobiology of human category learning. *Trends in Cognitive Sciences, 5,* 204–210.

Ashby, F. G., & O'Brien, J. B. (2005). Category learning and multiple memory systems. *Trends in Cognitive Sciences, 9,* 83–89.

Ashby, F. G., & Rosedahl, L. (2017). A neural interpretation of exemplar theory. *Psychological Review, 124,* 472–482.

Associated Press. (2007). Former stripper guilty of posing as psychologist. *Boston Herald.* Retrieved from http://www.bostonherald.com

Astington, J. W., & Baird, J. (2005). *Why language matters for theory of mind.* Oxford, England: Oxford University Press.

Atance, C. M., Bélanger, M., & Meltzoff, A. N. (2010). Preschoolers' understanding of others' desires: Fulfilling mine enhances my understanding of yours. *Developmental Psychology, 46*(6), 1505–1513. doi:10.1037/a0020374

Atkinson, R. C., & Shiffrin, R. M. (1968). Human memory: A proposed system and its control processes. In K. W. Spence & J. T. Spence (Eds.), *The psychology of learning and motivation* (Volume 2, pp. 89–195). New York: Academic Press.

Au, J., Sheehan, E., Tsai, N., Duncan, G. J., Buschkuehl, M., & Jaeggi, S. (2015). Improving fluid intelligence with training on working memory: A meta-analysis. *Psychonomic Bulletin & Review, 22,* 366–377.

Avena-Koenigsberger, A., Misic, B., & Sporns, O. (2018). Communication dynamics in complex brain networks. *Nature Reviews Neuroscience, 19,* 17–33.

Aviezer, H., Hassin, R. R., Ryan, J., Grady, C., Susskind, J., Anderson, A., . . . Bentin, S. (2008). Angry, disgusted, or afraid? Studies on the malleability of emotion perception. *Psychological Science, 19,* 724–732.

Avolio, B. J., & Waldman, D. A. (1994). Variations in cognitive, perceptual, and psychomotor abilities across the working life span: Examining the effects of race, sex, experience, education, and occupational type. *Psychology and Aging, 9,* 430–442.

Axelrod, R. (1984). *The evolution of cooperation.* New York: Basic Books.

Ayduk, O., Shoda, Y., Cervone, D., & Downey, G. (2007). Delay of gratification in children: Contributions to social-personality psychology. In G. Downey, Y. Shoda, & C. Cervone (Eds.), *Persons in context: Building a science of the individual* (pp. 97–109). New York: Guilford Press.

Ayres, C. E. (1921). Instinct and capacity. 1. The instinct of belief-in-instincts. *Journal of Philosophy, 18,* 561–565.

Azucar, D., Marengo, D., & Settanni, M. (2018). Predicting the Big 5 personality traits from digital footprints on social media: A meta-analysis. *Personality and Individual Differences, 124,* 150–159.

Azuma, H., & Kashiwagi, K. (1987). Descriptors for an intelligent person: A Japanese study. *Japanese Psychological Research, 29,* 17–26.

Baars, B. J. (1986). *The cognitive revolution in psychology.* New York: Guilford Press.

Baca-Motes, K., Brown, A., Gneezy, A., Keenan, E. A., & Nelson, L. D. (2013). Commitment and behavior change: Evidence from the field. *Journal of Consumer Research, 39*(5), 1070–1084. doi:10.1086/667226

Backman, C. W., & Secord, P. F. (1959). The effect of perceived liking on interpersonal attraction. *Human Relations, 12,* 379–384.

Bäckman, L., & Dixon, R. A. (1992). Psychological compensation: A theoretical framework. *Psychological Bulletin, 112,* 259–283.

Baddeley, A. D. (2001). Is working memory still working? *American Psychologist, 56,* 851–864.

Baddeley, A. D. (2012). Working memory: Theories, models, and controversies. *Annual Review of Psychology, 63,* 1–29.

Baddeley, A. D., & Hitch, G. J. (1974). Working memory. In S. Dornic (Ed.), *Attention and performance* (Vol. 6, pp. 647–667). Hillsdale, NJ: Erlbaum.

Baddeley, A. D., & Hitch, G. J. (2019). The phonological loop as a buffer store: An update. *Cortex, 112,* 91–106.

Baddeley, A. D., Allen, R. J., & Hitch, G. J. (2011). Binding in visual working memory: The role of the episodic buffer. *Neuropsychologia, 49,* 1393–1400.

Badets, A., Boutin, A., & Michelet, T. (2018). A safety mechanism for observational learning. *Psychonomic Bulletin & Review, 25,* 643–650.

Bagby, R. M., Levitan, R. D., Kennedy, S. H., Levitt, A. J., & Joffe, R. T. (1999). Selective alteration of personality in response to noradrenergic and serotonergic antidepressant medication in depressed sample: Evidence of non-specificity. *Psychiatry Research, 86,* 211–216.

Bahrick, H. P. (1984). Semantic memory content in permastore: 50 years of memory for Spanish learned in school. *Journal of Experimental Psychology: General, 113,* 1–29.

Bahrick, H. P. (2000). Long-term maintenance of knowledge. In E. Tulving & F. I. M. Craik (Eds.), *The Oxford handbook of memory* (pp. 347–362). New York: Oxford University Press.

Bahrick, H. P., Hall, L. K., & Berger, S. A. (1996). Accuracy and distortion in memory for high school grades. *Psychological Science, 7,* 265–271.

Bahrick, H. P., Hall, L. K., & DaCosta, L. A. (2008). Fifty years of college grades: Accuracy and distortions. *Emotion, 8,* 13–22.

Bailey, J. M., & Pillard, R. C. (1991). A genetic study of male sexual orientation. *Archives of General Psychiatry, 48,* 1089–1096.

Bailey, J. M., & Zucker, K. J. (1995). Childhood sex-typed behavior and sexual orientation: A conceptual analysis and quantitative review. *Developmental Psychology, 31,* 43–55.

Bailey, J. M., Pillard, R. C., Neale, M. C., & Agyes, Y. (1993). Heritable factors influence sexual orientation in women. *Archives of General Psychiatry, 50,* 217–223.

Bailey, J. M., Vasey, P. L., Diamond, L. M., Breedlove, S. M., Vilain, E., & Epprecht, M. (2016). Sexual orientation, controversy, and science. *Psychological Science in the Public Interest, 17*(2), 45–101.

Baillargeon, R., Scott, R. M., & He, Z. (2010). False-belief understanding in infants. *Trends in Cognitive Sciences, 14*(3), 110–118.

Baillargeon, R., Spelke, E. S., & Wasserman, S. (1985). Object permanence in 5-month-old infants. *Cognition, 20,* 191–208.

Baird, B., Castelnovo, A., Gosseries, O., & Tononi, G. (2018). Frequent lucid dreaming associated with increased functional connectivity between frontopolar cortex and temporoparietal association areas. *Scientific Reports, 8,* 17798.

Baker, D. P., Eslinger, P. J., Benavides, M., Peters, E., Dieckmann, N. F., & Leon, J. (2015). The cognitive impact of the education revolution: A possible cause of the Flynn Effect on population IQ. *Intelligence, 49,* 144–158.

Baker, E., Shelton, K. H., Baibazarova, E., Hay, D. F., & van Goozen, S. H. M. (2013). Low skin conductance activity in infancy predicts aggression in toddlers 2 years later. *Psychological Science, 24*(6), 1051–1056. doi:10.1177/0956797612465198

Baker, M., Strickland, A., & Fox, N. D. (2019). Choosing a meal to increase your appeal: How relationship status, sexual orientation, dining partner sex, and attractiveness impact nutritional choices in social dining scenarios. *Appetite, 133,* 262–269.

Baker, T. B., Brandon, T. H., & Chassin, L. (2004). Motivational influences on cigarette smoking. *Annual Review of Psychology, 55,* 463–491.

Baker, T. B., McFall, R. M., & Shoham, V. (2009). Current status and future prospects of clinical psychology: Toward a scientifically principled approach to mental and behavioral health care. *Psychological Science in the Public Interest, 9*(2), 67–103.

Baldwin, V. N., & Powell, T. (2015). Google Calendar: A single case experimental design study of a man with severe memory problems. *Neuropsychological Rehabilitation, 25,* 617–636.

Baler, R. D., & Volkow, N. D. (2006). Drug addiction: The neurobiology of disrupted self-control. *Trends in Molecular Medicine, 12,* 559–566.

Balthazart, J. (2018). Fraternal birth order effect on sexual orientation explained. *Proceedings of the National Academy of Sciences, USA, 115,* 234–236.

Banaji, M. R., & Heiphetz, L. (2010). Attitudes. In S. T. Fiske, D. T. Gilbert, & G. Lindzey (Eds.), *The handbook of social psychology* (5th ed., Vol. 1, pp. 348–388). New York: Wiley.

Bandelow, B., Michaelis, S., & Wedekind, D. (2017). Treatment of anxiety disorders. *Dialogues in Clinical Neuroscience, 19*(2), 93–107.

Bandoli, G., Campbell-Sills, L., Kessler, R. C., Heeringa, S. G., Nock, M. K., . . . Stein, M. B. (2017). Childhood adversity, adult stress, and the risk of major depression or generalized anxiety disorder in U.S. soldiers: A test of the stress sensitization hypothesis. *Psychological Medicine, 47,* 2379–2392.

Bandura, A. (1965). Influence of models' reinforcement contingencies on the acquisition of imitative responses. *Journal of Social and Personality Psychology, 1,* 589–595.

Bandura, A. (1977). *Social learning theory.* Englewood Cliffs, NJ: Prentice Hall.

Bandura, A. (1986). *Social foundations of thought and action: A social cognitive theory.* Englewood Cliffs, NJ: Prentice Hall.

Bandura, A. (1994). Social cognitive theory of mass communication. In J. Bryant & D. Zillmann (Eds.), *Media effects: Advances in theory and research* (pp. 61–90). Hillsdale, NJ: Erlbaum.

Bandura, A., Ross, D., & Ross, S. (1961). Transmission of aggression through imitation of adult models. *Journal of Abnormal and Social Psychology, 63,* 575–582.

Bandura, A., Ross, D., & Ross, S. (1963). Vicarious reinforcement and imitative learning. *Journal of Abnormal and Social Psychology, 67,* 601–607.

Banks, M. S., & Salapatek, P. (1983). Infant visual perception. In M. Haith & J. Campos (Eds.), *Handbook of child psychology: Biology and infancy* (pp. 435–572). New York: Wiley.

Banse, R., & Scherer, K. R. (1996). Acoustic profiles in vocal emotion expression. *Journal of Personality and Social Psychology, 70,* 614–636.

Barber, J. P., Muran, J. C., McCarthy, K. S., & Keefe, J. R. (2013). Research on dynamic therapies. In M. Lambert (Ed.), *Bergin and Garfield's handbook of psychotherapy and behavior change* (6th ed., pp. 443–494). Hoboken, NJ: Wiley.

Barber, S. J., Harris, C. B., & Rajaram, S. (2015). Why two heads apart are better than two heads together: Multiple mechanisms underlie the collaborative inhibition effect in memory. *Journal of Experimental Psychology: Learning, Memory, and Cognition, 41,* 559–566.

Barber, S. J., Rajaram, S., & Fox, E. B. (2012). Learning and remembering with others: The key role of retrieval in shaping group recall and collective memory. *Social Cognition, 30,* 121–132.

Barbey, A. K. (2018). Network neuroscience theory of human intelligence. *Trends in Cognitive Sciences, 22*(1), 8–20.

Bareš, M., Apps, R., Avanzino, L., Breska, A., D'Angelo, E., Filip, P., . . . Lusk, N. A. (2019). Consensus paper: Decoding the contributions of the cerebellum as a time machine. From neurons to clinical applications. *The Cerebellum, 18*(2), 266–286.

Bargh, J. A., Gollwitzer, P. M., & Oettingen, G. (2010). Motivation. In S. T. Fiske, D. T. Gilbert, & G. Lindzey (Eds.), *The handbook of social psychology* (5th ed., Vol. 1, pp. 263–311). New York: Wiley.

Bargh, J. A., Gollwitzer, P. M., Lee-Chai, A., Barndollar, K., & Trötschel, R. (2001). The automated will: Nonconscious activation and pursuit of behavioral goals. *Journal of Personality and Social Psychology, 81,* 1014–1027.

Barker, A. T., Jalinous, R., & Freeston, I. L. (1985). Noninvasive magnetic stimulation of the human motor cortex. *Lancet, 2,* 1106–1107.

Barkow, J. (1980). Prestige and self-esteem: A biosocial interpretation. In D. R. Omark, F. F. Stayer, & D. G. Freedman (Eds.), *Dominance relations* (pp. 319–322). New York: Garland.

Barlett, C., & Coyne, S. M. (2014). A meta-analysis of sex differences in cyber-bullying behavior: The moderating role of age. *Aggressive Behavior, 40,* 474–488.

Barlow, D. H., Bullis, J. R., Comer, J. S., & Ametaj, A. A. (2013). Evidence-based psychological treatments: An update and a way forward. *Annual Review of Clinical Psychology, 9,* 1–27.

Barlow, D. H., Gorman, J. M., Shear, M. K., & Woods, S. W. (2000). Cognitive-behavioral therapy, imipramine, or their combination for panic disorder: A randomized controlled trial. *Journal of the American Medical Association, 283*(19), 2529–2536.

Barnier, A. J., Levin, K., & Maher, A. (2004). Suppressing thoughts of past events: Are repressive copers good suppressors? *Cognition and Emotion, 18,* 457–477.

Baron-Cohen, S. (1991). Do people with autism understand what causes emotion? *Child Development, 62,* 385–395.

Baron-Cohen, S., & Belmonte, M. K. (2005). Autism: A window onto the development of the social and analytic brain. *Annual Review of Neuroscience, 28,* 109–126.

Baron-Cohen, S., Leslie, A., & Frith, U. (1985). Does the autistic child have a "theory of mind"? *Cognition, 21,* 37–46.

Barondes, S. H. (2003). *Better than Prozac: Creating the next generation of psychiatric drugs.* New York: Oxford University Press.

Barr, W. B., & Karantzoulis, S. (2019). Chronic traumatic encephalopathy. In L. D. Ravdin &,H. L. Katzen (Eds.), *Handbook on the neuropsychology of aging and dementia (Clinical handbooks in neuropsychology)* (pp. 727–745). Cham, Switzerland: Springer Nature Switzerland.

Barragán, R., Coltell, O., Portolés, O., Asensio, E. M., Sorlí, J. V., . . . Corella, D. (2018). Bitter, sweet, salty, sour and umami taste perception decreases with age: Sex-specific analysis, modulation by genetic variants and taste-preference associations in 18- to 80-year-old subjects. *Nutrients, 10*(10), E1539. doi:10.3390/nu10101539

Barrett, L. F., Mesquita, B., & Gendron, M. (2011). Context in emotion perception. *Current Directions in Psychological Science, 20*(5), 286–290. doi:10.1177/0963721411422522

Barrientos, R. M., Watkins, L. R., Rudy, J. W., & Maier, S. F. (2009). Characterization of the sickness response in young and aging rats following *E. coli* infection. *Brain, Behavior, and Immunity, 23,* 450–454.

Bartal, I. B.-A., Decety, J., & Mason, P. (2011). Empathy and prosocial behavior in rats. *Science, 334*(6061), 1427–1430.

Bartlett, F. C. (1932). *Remembering: A study in experimental and social psychology.* Cambridge, England: Cambridge University Press.

Bartol, C. R., & Costello, N. (1976). Extraversion as a function of temporal duration of electric shock: An exploratory study. *Perceptual and Motor Skills, 42,* 1174.

Bartoshuk, L. M. (2000). Comparing sensory experiences across individuals: Recent psychophysical advances illuminate genetic variation in taste perception. *Chemical Senses, 25,* 447–460.

Bartoshuk, L. M., & Beauchamp, G. K. (1994). Chemical senses. *Annual Review of Psychology, 45,* 419–445.

Basden, B. H., Basden, D. R., Bryner, S., & Thomas, R. L. (1997). A comparison of group and individual remembering: Does collaboration disrupt retrieval strategies? *Journal of Experimental Psychology: Learning, Memory, and Cognition, 23,* 1176–1191.

Bass, C. & Halligan, P. (2014) Factitious disorders and malingering: Challenges for clinical assessment and management. *Lancet, 383,* 1422–1432.

Bates, E., & Goodman, J. C. (1997). On the inseparability of grammar and the lexicon: Evidence from acquisition, aphasia, and real-time processing. *Language and Cognitive Processes, 12,* 507–584.

Bates, T. C., Hansell, N. K., Martin, N. G., & Wright, M. J. (2016). When does socioeconomic status (SES) moderate the heritability of IQ? No evidence for g × SES interaction for IQ in a representative sample of 1176 Australian adolescent twin pairs. *Intelligence, 56,* 10–15.

Bateson, M., Nettle, D., & Roberts, G. (2006). Cues of being watched enhance cooperation in a real-world setting. *Biology Letters, 2*(3), 412–414.

Batson, C. D. (2002). Addressing the altruism question experimentally. In S. G. Post & L. G. Underwood (Eds.), *Altruism & altruistic love: Science, philosophy, & religion in dialogue* (pp. 89–105). London: Oxford University Press.

Batterink, L. J., Westerberg, C. E., & Paller, K. A. (2017). Vocabulary learning benefits from REM after slow-wave sleep. *Neurobiology of Learning & Memory, 144,* 102–113.

Batty, G. D., Deary, I. J., Schoon, I., & Gale, C. R. (2007). Mental ability across childhood in relation to risk factors for premature mortality in adult life: The 1970 British Cohort Study. *Journal of Epidemiology & Community Health, 61*(11), 997–1003.

Baumeister, R. F. (2000). Gender differences in erotic plasticity: The female sex drive as socially flexible and responsive. *Psychological Bulletin, 126,* 347–374.

Baumeister, R., Ainsworth, S., & Vohs, K. (2016). Are groups more or less than the sum of their members? The moderating role of individual identification. *Behavioral and Brain Sciences, 39,* e137. doi:10.1017/S0140525X15000618

Baumeister, R. F., & Leary, M. R. (1995). The need to belong: Desire for interpersonal attachments as a fundamental human motivation. *Psychological Bulletin, 117,* 497–529.

Baumeister, R. F., Bratslavsky, E., Muraven, M., & Tice, D. M. (1998). Ego depletion: Is the active self a limited resource? *Journal of Personality and Social Psychology, 74,* 1252–1265.

Baumeister, R. F., Campbell, J. D., Krueger, J. I., & Vohs, K. D. (2003). Does high self-esteem cause better performance, interpersonal success, happiness, or healthier lifestyles? *Psychological Science in the Public Interest, 4,* 1–44.

Baumeister, R. F., Cantanese, K. R., & Vohs, K. D. (2001). Is there a gender difference in strength of sex drive? Theoretical views, conceptual distinctions, and a review of relevant evidence. *Personality and Social Psychology Review, 5,* 242–273.

Baumeister, R. F., Smart, L., & Boden, J. M. (1996). Relation of threatened egotism to violence and aggression: The dark side of high self-esteem. *Psychological Review, 103,* 5–33.

Baumeister, R. F., Vohs, K. D., & Tice, D. M. (2007). The strength model of self-control. *Current Directions in Psychological Science, 16,* 351–355.

Bayley, P. J., Frascino, J. C., & Squire, L. R. (2005). Robust habit learning in the absence of awareness and independent of the medial temporal lobe. *Nature, 436,* 550–553.

Bayley, P. J., Gold, J. J., Hopkins, R. O., & Squire, L. R. (2005). The neuroanatomy of remote memory. *Neuron, 46,* 799–810.

Beaty, R. E., Benedek, M., Silvia, P. J., & Schacter, D. L. (2016). Creative cognition and brain network dynamics. *Trends in Cognitive Sciences, 20,* 87–95.

Beaty, R. E., Thakral, P. P., Madore, K. P., Benedek, M., & Schacter, D. L. (2018). Core network contributions to remembering the past, imagining the future, and thinking creatively. *Journal of Cognitive Neuroscience, 30*(12), 1939–1951.

Bechara, A., Damasio, A. R., Damasio, H., & Anderson, S. W. (1994). Insensitivity to future consequences following damage to human prefrontal cortex. *Cognition, 50,* 7–15.

Bechara, A., Damasio, H., Tranel, D., & Damasio, A. R. (1997). Deciding advantageously before knowing the advantageous strategy. *Science, 275,* 1293–1295.

Bechara, A., Dolan, S., Denburg, N., Hindes, A., & Anderson, S. W. (2001). Decision-making deficits, linked to a dysfunctional ventromedial prefrontal cortex, revealed in alcohol and stimulant abusers. *Neuropsychologia, 39,* 376–389.

Bechara, A., Tranel, D., & Damasio, H. (2000). Characterization of the decision-making deficit of patients with ventromedial prefrontal cortex lesions. *Brain, 123,* 2189–2202.

Becht, A. I., Nelemans, S. A., Branje, S. T., Vollebergh, W. M., Koot, H. M., & Meeus, W. J. (2017). Identity uncertainty and commitment making across adolescence: Five-year within-person associations using daily identity reports. *Developmental Psychology, 53*(11), 2103–2112. doi:10.1037/dev0000374

Beck, A. T. (1967). *Depression: Causes and treatment.* Philadelphia: University of Pennsylvania Press.

Beck, A. T. (2019). A 60-year evolution of cognitive theory and therapy. *Perspectives on Psychological Science, 14*(1), 16–20.

Bédard, A.-C., Nichols, S., Barbosa, J. A., Schachar, R., Logan, G. D., & Tannock, R. (2002). The development of selective inhibitory control across the life span. *Developmental Neuropsychology, 21,* 93–111.

Bedny, M., & Saxe, R. (2012). Insights into the origins of knowledge from the cognitive neuroscience of blindness. *Cognitive Neuropsychology, 29,* 56–84.

Beek, M. R., Levin, D. T., & Angelone, B. (2007). Change blindness: Beliefs about the roles of intention and scene complexity in change detection. *Consciousness and Cognition, 16,* 31–51.

Begg, I. M., Anas, A., & Farinacci, S. (1992). Dissociation of processes in belief: Source recollection, statement familiarity, and the illusion of truth. *Journal of Experimental Psychology: General, 121,* 446–458.

Békésy, G. von. (1960). *Experiments in hearing.* New York: McGraw-Hill.

Bell, R., Roer, J. P., & Buchner, A. (2015). Adaptive memory: Thinking about function. *Journal of Experimental Psychology: Learning, Memory, & Cognition, 41,* 1038–1048.

Belluck, P., & Carey, B. (2013, May 7). Psychiatry's guide is out of touch with science, experts say. *New York Times.* Retrieved from http://www.nytimes.com/2013/05/07/psychiatrys-new-guide-falls-short-experts-say.html

Belsky, J. (2012). The development of human reproductive strategies: Progress and prospects. *Current Directions in Psychological Science, 21*(5), 310–316. doi:10.1177/0963721412453588

Belsky, J., Ruttle, P. L., Boyce, W. T., Armstrong, J. M., & Essex, M. J. (2015). Early adversity, elevated stress physiology, accelerated sexual maturation, and poor health in females. *Developmental Psychology, 51*(6), 816–822. doi:10.1037/dev0000017

Belzak, L., & Halverson, J. (2018). Evidence synthesis: The opioid crisis in Canada: A national perspective. *Health Promotion and Chronic Disease Prevention in Canada: Research, Policy and Practice, 38*(6), 224.

Bem, S. L. (1974). The measure of psychological androgyny. *Journal of Consulting and Clinical Psychology, 42,* 155–162.

Benartzi, S., & Thaler, R. (2013) Behavioral economics and the retirement savings crisis. *Science, 339,* 1152–1153.

Bender, P. K., Plante, C., & Gentile, D. A. (2017). The effects of violent media content on aggression. *Current Opinion in Psychology, 19,* 104–108.

Benedek, M., Jauk, E., Fink, A., Koschutnig, K., Reishofer, G., Ebner, F., & Neubauer, A. C. (2014). To create or to recall? Neural mechanisms underlying the generation of creative new ideas. *NeuroImage, 88,* 125–133.

Benenson, J. F., Markovits, H., Thompson, M. E., & Wrangham, R. W. (2011). Under threat of social exclusion, females exclude more than males. *Psychological Science, 22*(4), 538–544. doi:10.1177/0956797611402511

Bennett, I. J., Romano, J. C., Howard, J. H., & Howard, D. V. (2008). Two forms of implicit learning in young adults with dyslexia. *Annals of the New York Academy of Sciences, 1145,* 184–198.

Benoit, R. G., & Anderson, M. C. (2012). Opposing mechanisms support the voluntary forgetting of unwanted memories. *Neuron, 76,* 450–460.

Benoit, R. G., & Schacter, D. L. (2015). Specifying the core network supporting episodic simulation and episodic memory by activation likelihood estimation. *Neuropsychologia, 75,* 450–457.

Benoit, S. C., Kemp, C. J., Elias, C. F., Abplanalp, W., Herman, J. P., Migrenne, S., . . . Clegg, D. J. (2009). Palmitic acid mediates hypothalamic insulin resistance by altering PKC-theta subcellular localization in rodents. *Journal of Clinical Investigation, 119*(9), 2577–2589.

Ben-Porath, Y. S., & Tellegen, A. (2008). *Minnesota Multiphasic Personality Inventory–2–Restructured Form: Manual for administration, scoring, and interpretation.* Minneapolis: University of Minnesota Press.

Benson, H. (Ed.). (1990). *The relaxation response.* New York: Harper Torch.

Benson, H., Dusek, J. A., Sherwood, J. B., Lam, P., Bethea, C. F., Carpenter, W., . . . Hibberd, P. L. (2006). Study of the therapeutic effects of intercessory prayer (STEP) in cardiac bypass patients: A multicenter randomized trial of uncertainty and certainty of receiving intercessory prayer. *American Heart Journal, 151,* 934–942.

Bentz, D., & Schiller, D. (2015). Threat processing: Models and mechanisms. *WIREs Cognitive Science, 6,* 427–439.

Berger, H. (1929). Über das Elektrenkephalogramm des Menschen [Electroencephalogram of man]. *Archiv für Psychiatrie und Nervenkrankheiten, 87,* 527–570.

Berger, J. (2014). Word of mouth and interpersonal communication: A review and directions for future research. *Journal of Consumer Psychology, 24*(4), 586–607.

Bering, J. (2004). A critical review of the "enculturation hypothesis": The effects of human rearing on great ape social cognition. *Animal Cognition, 7,* 201–212.

Berkowitz, L. (1989). Frustration-aggression hypothesis: Examination and reformulation. *Psychological Bulletin, 106*(1): 59–73.

Berkowitz, L. (1990). On the formation and regulation of anger and aggression: A cognitive-neoassociationistic analysis. *American Psychologist, 45,* 494–503.

Bernard, L. L. (1924). *Instinct: A study in social psychology.* New York: Holt.

Bernier, A., Beauchamp, M. H., Carlson, S. M., & Lalonde, G. (2015). A secure base from which to regulate: Attachment security in toddlerhood as a predictor of executive functioning at school entry. *Developmental Psychology, 51*(9), 1177–1189. doi:10.1037/dev0000032

Bernstein, E. E., & McNally, R. J. (2017). Acute aerobic exercise hastens emotional recovery from a subsequent stressor. *Health Psychology, 36,* 560–567.

Berntsen, D. (2010). The unbidden past: Involuntary autobiographical memories as a basic mode of remembering. *Current Directions in Psychological Science, 19,* 138–142.

Berridge, K. C. (2007). The debate over dopamine's role in reward: The case for incentive salience. *Psychopharmacology, 191,* 391–431.

Berry, D. S., & McArthur, L. Z. (1985). Some components and consequences of a babyface. *Journal of Personality and Social Psychology, 48,* 312–323.

Berscheid, E., & Reis, H. T. (1998). Interpersonal attraction and close relationships. In D. T. Gilbert, S. T. Fiske, & G. Lindzey (Eds.), *The handbook of social psychology* (4th ed., Vol. 2, pp. 193–281). New York: McGraw-Hill.

Berscheid, E., Dion, K., Walster, E., & Walster, G. W. (1971). Physical attractiveness and dating choice: A test of the matching hypothesis. *Journal of Experimental Social Psychology, 7*(2), 173–189.

Bertenthal, B. I., Rose, J. L., & Bai, D. L. (1997). Perception–action coupling in the development of visual control of posture.

Journal of Experimental Psychology: Human Perception & Performance, 23, 1631–1643.

Berthoud, H.-R., & Morrison, C. (2008). The brain, appetite, and obesity. *Annual Review of Psychology, 59,* 55–92.

Bhargava, S. (2011). Diagnosis and management of common sleep problems in children. *Pediatrics in Review, 32,* 91.

Bialystok, E. (1999). Cognitive complexity and attentional control in the bilingual mind. *Child Development, 70,* 636–644.

Bialystok, E. (2009). Bilingualism: The good, the bad, and the indifference. *Bilingualism: Language and Cognitive Processes, 12,* 3–11.

Bialystok, E. (2017). The bilingual adaptation: How minds accommodate experience. *Psychological Bulletin, 143,* 233–262.

Bialystok, E., Craik, F. I. M., & Luk, G. (2012). Bilingualism: Consequences for mind and brain. *Trends in Cognitive Sciences, 16,* 240–250.

Bian, L., Sloane, S., & Baillargeon, R. (2018). Infants expect ingroup support to override fairness when resources are limited. *Proceedings of the National Academy of Sciences, USA, 115*(11), 2705–2710.

Bickerton, D. (1990). *Language and species.* Chicago: University of Chicago Press.

Biederman, J., Faraone, S. V., Spencer, T. J., Mick, E., Monuteaux, M. C., & Aleardi, M. (2006). Functional impairments in adults with self-reports of diagnosed ADHD: A controlled study of 1001 adults in the community. *Journal of Clinical Psychiatry, 67,* 524–540.

Biederman, J., Monuteaux, M. C., Spencer, T., Wilens, T. E., & Faraone, S. V. (2009). Do stimulants protect against psychiatric disorders in youth with ADHD? A 10-year follow-up study. *Pediatrics, 124,* 71–78.

Binet, A. (1905). New methods for the diagnosis of the intellectual level of subnormals. *L'Année psychologique, 12,* 191–244. Reprinted in A. Binet & T. Simon (1916). *The development of intelligence in children* (E. S. Kite, Trans.). Vineland, NJ: Publications of the Training School at Vineland.

Binet, A. (1909). *Les idées modernes sur les enfants* [Modern ideas about children]. Paris: Flammarion.

Biro, S., Alink, L. R., van IJzendoorn, M. H., & Bakermans-Kranenburg, M. J. (2014). Infants' monitoring of social interactions: The effect of emotional cues. *Emotion, 14*(2), 263–271. doi:10.1037/a0035589

Bjork, E. L., & Bjork, R. A. (2011). Making things hard on yourself, but in a good way: Creating desirable difficulties to enhance learning. In M. A. Gernsbacher, R. W. Pewe, L. M. Hough, & J. R. Pomerantz (Eds.), *Psychology and the real world: Essays illustrating fundamental contributions to society* (pp. 56–64). New York: Worth Publishers.

Bjork, R. A. (1975). Retrieval as a memory modifier. In R. Solso (Ed.), Information processing and cognition: The Loyola Symposium (pp. 123–144). Hillsdale, NJ: Erlbaum.

Bjork, R. A. (2011). On the symbiosis of remembering, forgetting, and learning. In A. S. Benjamin (Ed.), *Successful remembering and successful forgetting: A festschrift in honor of Robert A. Bjork* (pp. 1–22). London: Psychology Press.

Bjork, R. A., & Bjork, E. L. (1988). On the adaptive aspects of retrieval failure in autobiographical memory. In M. M. Gruneberg,

P. E. Morris, & R. N. Sykes (Eds.), *Practical aspects of memory: Current research and issues* (pp. 283–288). Chichester, UK: Wiley.

Bjork, R. A., Dunlosky, J., & Kornell, N. (2013). Self-regulated learning: Beliefs, techniques, and illusions. *Annual Review of Psychology, 64,* 417–444.

Bjorkqvist, K. (2018). Gender differences in aggression. *Current Opinion in Psychology, 19,* 39–42.

Blackburn, E. H., Epel, E. S., & Lin, J. (2015). Human telomere biology: A contributory and interactive factor in aging, disease risks, and protection. *Science, 350,* 1193–1198.

Blackstock, C. (2019, January 16). For Indigenous kids' welfare, our government knows better; it just needs to do better. *The Globe and Mail.* Retrieved from https://www.theglobeandmail.com/opinion/article-for-indigenous-kids-welfare-our-government-knows-better-they-just/

Blair, C. (2006). How similar are fluid cognition and general intelligence? A developmental neuroscience perspective on fluid cognition as an aspect of human cognitive ability. *Behavioral and Brain Sciences, 29*(2), 109–125 (article),125–160 (discussion).

Blair, I. V. (2002). The malleability of automatic stereotypes and prejudice. *Personality and Social Psychology Review, 6,* 242–261.

Blair, J., Peschardt, K., & Mitchell, D. R. (2005). *Psychopath: Emotion and the brain.* Oxford: Blackwell.

Blake, M. J., Trinder, J. A., & Allen, N. B. (2018). Mechanisms underlying the association between insomnia, anxiety, and depression in adolescence: Implications for behavioral sleep interventions. *Clinical Psychology Review, 63,* 25–40.

Blake, P. R., McAuliffe, K., & Warneken, F. (2014). The developmental origins of fairness: The knowledge-behavior gap. *Trends in Cognitive Sciences, 18*(11), 559–561.

Blascovich, J., & Mendes, W. B. (2000). Challenge and threat appraisals: The role of affective cues. In J. P. Forgas (Ed.), *Studies in emotion and social interaction, second series. Feeling and thinking: The role of affect in social cognition* (pp. 59–82). New York: Cambridge University Press.

Blascovich, J., & Tomaka, J. (1996). The biopsychosocial model of arousal regulation. In M. P. Zanna (Ed.), *Advances in experimental social psychology* (Vol. 28, pp. 1–51). San Diego, CA: Academic Press.

Blascovich, J., Mendes, W. B., Hunter, S. B., Lickel, B., & Kowai-Bell, N. (2001). Perceiver threat in social interactions with stigmatized others. *Journal of Personality and Social Psychology, 80,* 253–267.

Blatt, S. J., & Homann, E. (1992). Parent–child interaction in the etiology of dependent and self-critical depression. *Clinical Psychology Review, 12,* 47–91.

Blesch, A., & Tuszynski, M. H. (2009). Spinal cord injury: Plasticity, regeneration and the challenge of translational drug development. *Trends in Neurosciences, 32,* 41–47.

Bliss, T. V. P. (1999). Young receptors make smart mice. *Nature, 401,* 25–27.

Bliss, T. V. P., & Lømo, W. T. (1973). Long-lasting potentiation of synaptic transmission in the dentate area of the anesthetized rabbit following stimulation of the perforant path. *Journal of Physiology, 232,* 331–356.

Bloch, C., Kaiser, A., Kuenzli, E., Zappatore, D., Haller, S., Franceschini, R., . . . Nitsch, C. (2009). The age of second language acquisition determines the variability in activation elicited by narration in three languages in Broca's and Wernicke's area. *Neuropsychologia, 47,* 625–633.

Bloch, L., Haase, C. M., & Levenson, R. W. (2014). Emotion regulation predicts marital satisfaction: More than a wives' tale. *Emotion, 14*(1), 130–144. doi:10.1037/a0034272

Bloom, C. M., Venard, J., Harden, M., & Seetharaman, S. (2007). Non-contingent positive and negative reinforcement schedules of superstitious behaviors. *Behavioural Process, 75,* 8–13.

Blumen, H. M., & Rajaram, S. (2008). Influence of re-exposure and retrieval disruption during group collaboration on later individual recall. *Memory, 16,* 231–244.

Boak, A., Hamilton, H. A., & Adlaf, E. M. (2018). The mental health and well-being of Ontario students, 1991–2017: Detailed findings from the Ontario Student Drug Use and Health Survey (OSDUHS). Toronto, ON: Centre for Addiction and Mental Health.

Boak, A., Hamilton, H. A., Adlaf, E. M., & Mann, R. E. (2017). Drug use among Ontario students, 1977–2017: Detailed findings from the Ontario Student Drug Use and Health Survey (OSDUHS)(CAMH Research Document Series No. 46). *Toronto: Centre for Addiction and Mental Health.*

Boden, J. M., Fergusson, D. M., & Horwood, L. J. (2010). Risk factors for conduct disorder and oppositional/defiant disorder: Evidence from a New Zealand birth cohort. *Journal of the American Academy of Child and Adolescent Psychiatry, 49,* 1125–1133.

Boecker, H., Sprenger, T., Spilker, M. E., Henriksen, G., Koppenhoefer, M., Wagner, K. J., . . . Tolle, T. R. (2008). The runner's high: Opioidergic mechanisms in the human brain. *Cerebral Cortex, 18,* 2523–2531.

Boehm, J. K., & Kubzansky, L. D. (2012). The heart's content: The association between positive psychological well-being and cardiovascular health. *Psychological Bulletin, 138,* 655–691.

Boehm, J. K., Williams, D. R., Rimm, E. B., Ryff, C., & Kubzansky, L. D. (2013). Relation between optimism and lipids in midlife. *American Journal of Cardiology, 111,* 1425–1431.

Boergers, J., Spirito, A., & Donaldson, D. (1998). Reasons for adolescent suicide attempts: Associations with psychological functioning. *Journal of the American Academy of Child and Adolescent Psychiatry, 37,* 1287–1293.

Boinski, S., Quatrone, R. P., & Swartz, H. (2000). Substrate and tool use by brown capuchins in Suriname: Ecological contexts and cognitive bases. *American Anthropologist, 102,* 741–761.

Boisvert, C. M., & Faust, D. (2002). Iatrogenic symptoms in psychotherapy: A theoretical exploration of the potential impact of labels, language, and belief systems. *American Journal of Psychotherapy, 56*(2), 244–259.

Bolton, G. E., & Ockenfels, A. (2000). ERC: A theory of equity, reciprocity, and competition. *American Economic Review, 90,* 166–193.

Bond, C. F., & DePaulo, B. M. (2006). Accuracy of deception judgments. *Personality and Social Psychology Review, 10,* 214–234.

Bonnici, H. M., Cheke, L. G., Green, D. A. E., FitzGerald, T. H. M. B., & Simons, J. S. (2018). Specifying a causal role for angular gyrus in episodic memory. *Journal of Neuroscience, 38,* 10438–10443.

Boomsma, D., Busjahn, A., & Peltonen, L. (2002). Classical twin studies and beyond. *Nature Reviews Genetics, 3,* 872–882.

Bootzin, R. R., & Epstein, D. R. (2011). Understanding and treating insomnia. *Annual Review of Clinical Psychology, 7,* 435–458.

Bordone, V., Scherbov, S., & Steiber, N. (2015). Smarter every day: The deceleration of population ageing in terms of cognition. *Intelligence, 52,* 90–96.

Borghans, L., Golsteyn, B. H. H., Heckman, J. J., & Humphries, J. E. (2016). What grades and achievement tests measure. *Proceedings of the National Academy of Sciences, USA, 113*(47), 13354–13359.

Boring, E. G. (1929). A history of experimental psychology. New York: The Century Company, p. 624.

Born, R. T., & Bradley, D. C. (2005). Structure and function of visual area MT. *Annual Review of Neuroscience, 28,* 157–189.

Bornstein, R. F. (1989). Exposure and affect: Overview and meta-analysis of research, 1968–1987. *Psychological Bulletin, 106,* 265–289.

Botto, S. V., & Rochat, P. (2018). Sensitivity to the evaluation of others emerges by 24 months. *Developmental Psychology, 54,* 1723–1734.

Botwin, M. D., Buss, D. M., & Shackelford, T. K. (1997). Personality and mate preferences: Five factors in mate selection and marital satisfaction. *Journal of Personality, 65,* 107–136.

Bouchard, S. M., Brown, T. G., & Nadeau, L. (2012). Decision making capacities and affective reward anticipation in DWI recidivists compared to non-offenders: A preliminary study. *Accident Analysis and Prevention, 45,* 580–587.

Bouchard, T. J., & McGue, M. (2003). Genetic and environmental influences on human psychological differences. *Journal of Neurobiology, 54,* 4–45.

Bouton, M. E. (1988). Context and ambiguity in the extinction of emotional learning: Implications for exposure therapy. *Behaviour Research and Therapy, 26,* 137–149.

Boutwell, B. B., Young, J. T. N., & Meldrum, R. C. (2018). On the positive relationship between breastfeeding & intelligence. *Developmental Psychology, 54*(8), 1426–1433.

Bower, G. H. (1981). Mood and memory. *American Psychologist, 36,* 129–148.

Bower, G. H., Clark, M. C., Lesgold, A. M., & Winzenz, D. (1969). Hierarchical retrieval schemes in recall of categorical word lists. *Journal of Verbal Learning and Verbal Behavior, 8,* 323–343.

Bowers, K. S., Regehr, G., Balthazard, C., & Parker, D. (1990). Intuition in the context of discovery. *Cognitive Psychology, 22,* 72–110.

Bowlby, J. (1969). *Attachment and loss: Vol. 1. Attachment.* New York: Basic Books.

Bowlby, J. (1973). *Attachment and loss: Vol. 2. Separation.* New York: Basic Books.

Bowlby, J. (1980). *Attachment and loss: Vol. 3. Loss: Sadness and depression.* New York: Basic Books.

Boyd, R. (2008, February 7). Do people use only 10 percent of their brains? *Scientific American.* Retrieved from http://www.scientificamerican.com/article.cfm?id=people-only-use-10-percent-of-brain&page=2

Boyle, L. L. (2018). Psychological and neuropsychological testing. In R. R. Tampi, D. J. Tampi, & L. L. Boyle (Eds.), *Psychiatric disorders late in life: A comprehensive review* (pp. 81–90). Switzerland: Springer International Publishing.

Bozarth, M. A. (Ed.). (1987). *Methods of assessing the reinforcing properties of abused drugs.* New York: Springer-Verlag.

Bozarth, M. A., & Wise, R. A. (1985). Toxicity associated with long-term intravenous heroin and cocaine self-administration in the rat. *Journal of the American Medical Association, 254,* 81–83.

Brackett, M. A., & Mayer, J. D. (2003). Convergent, discriminant, and incremental validity of competing measures of emotional intelligence. *Personality and Social Psychology Bulletin, 29,* 1147.

Brackett, M. A., Rivers, S. E., Shiffman, S., Lerner, N., & Salovey, P. (2006). Relating emotional abilities to social functioning: A comparison of self-report and performance measures of emotional intelligence. *Journal of Personality and Social Psychology, 91,* 780.

Brackett, M. A., Warner, R. M., & Bosco, J. (2005). Emotional intelligence and relationship quality among couples. *Personal Relationships, 12*(2), 197–212.

Bradmetz, J., & Schneider, R. (2004). The role of the counterfactually satisfied desire in the lag between false-belief and false-emotion attributions in children aged 4–7. *British Journal of Developmental Psychology, 22,* 185–196.

Braitenberg, V. (1961). Functional interpretation of cerebellar histology. *Nature, 190*(4775), 539.

Brakefield, T. A., Mednick, S. C., Wilson, H. W., De Neve, J. E., Christakis, N. A., & Fowler, J. H. (2014). Same-sex sexual attraction does not spread in adolescent social networks. *Archives of Sexual Behavior, 43*(2), 335–344.

Bramlett, M. D., & Mosher, W. D. (2002). *Cohabitation, marriage, divorce, and remarriage in the United States* (Vital and Health Statistics Series 23, No. 22). Hyattsville, MD: National Center for Health Statistics.

Brandt, K. R., Gardiner, J. M., Vargha-Khadem, F., Baddeley, A. D., & Mishkin, M. (2009). Impairment of recollection but not familiarity in a case of developmental amnesia. *Neurocase, 15,* 60–65.

Brant, A. M., Munakata, Y., Boomsma, D. I., Defries, J. C., Haworth, C. M. A., Keller, M. C., . . . Hewitt, J. K. (2013). The nature and nurture of high IQ: An extended sensitive period for intellectual development. *Psychological Science, 24*(8), 1487–1495.

Bratman, G. N., Hamilton, J. P., Hahn, K. S., Daily, G. C., & Gross, J. J. (2015). Nature experience reduces rumination and subgenual prefrontal cortex activation. *Proceedings of the National Academy of Sciences, USA, 112,* 8567–8572.

Bratsberg, B., & Rogeberg, O. (2018). Flynn effect and its reversal are both environmentally caused. *Proceedings of the National Academy of Sciences, USA, 115*(26), 6674–6678.

Braun, A. R., Balkin, T. J., Wesensten, N. J., Gwadry, F., Carson, R. E., Varga, M., . . . Herskovitch, P. (1998). Dissociated pattern of activity in visual cortices and their projections during rapid eye movement sleep. *Science, 279,* 91–95.

Breckler, S. J. (1994). Memory for the experiment of donating blood: Just how bad was it? *Basic and Applied Social Psychology, 15,* 467–488.

Brédart, S., & Valentine, T. (1998). Descriptiveness and proper name retrieval. *Memory, 6,* 199–206.

Bredy, T. W., Wu, H., Crego, C., Zellhoefer, J., Sun, Y. E., & Barad, M. (2007). Histone modifications around individual BDNF gene promoters in prefrontal cortex are associated with extinction of conditioned fear. *Learning and Memory, 14,* 268–276.

Breggin, P. R. (2000). *Reclaiming our children: A healing plan for a nation in crisis.* Cambridge, MA: Perseus Books.

Breland, K., & Breland, M. (1961). The misbehavior of organisms. *American Psychologist, 16,* 681–684.

Brennan, P. A., & Zufall, F. (2006). Pheromonal communication in vertebrates. *Nature, 444,* 308–315.

Brenninkmeijer, V., Vanyperen, N. W., & Buunk, B. P. (2001). I am not a better teacher, but others are doing worse: Burnout and perceptions of superiority among teachers. *Social Psychology of Education, 4*(3–4), 259–274.

Breslow, L., Pritchard, D. E., DeBoer, J., Stump, G. S., Ho, A. D., & Seaton, D. T. (2013). Studying learning in the worldwide classroom: Research into edX's first MOOC. *Research & Practice in Assessment, 8,* 13–25.

Bretherton, I., & Munholland, K. A. (1999). Internal working models in attachment relationships: A construct revisited. In J. Cassidy & P. R. Shaver (Eds.), *Handbook of attachment: Theory, research and clinical applications* (pp. 89–114). New York: Guilford Press.

Brewer, J. A., Worhunsky, P. D., Gray, J. R., Tang, Y.-Y., Weber, J., & Kober, H. (2011). Meditation experience is associated with differences in default mode network activity and connectivity. *Proceedings of the National Academy of Sciences, USA, 108,* 20254–20259.

Brewer, M. B. (1999). The psychology of prejudice: Ingroup love or outgroup hate? *Journal of Social Issues, 55*(3), 429–444. doi:10.1111/0022-4537.00126

Brewer, W. F. (1996). What is recollective memory? In D. C. Rubin (Ed.), *Remembering our past: Studies in autobiographical memory* (pp. 19–66). New York: Cambridge University Press.

Briggs, J. (2000). Conflict management in a modern Inuit community. In P. P. Schweitzer, M. Biesele, & R. K. Hitchcock (Eds.), *Hunters and gatherers in the modern world: Conflict, resistance, and self-determination* (pp. 110–124). New York: Berghahn Books.

Broberg, D. J., & Bernstein, I. L. (1987). Candy as a scapegoat in the prevention of food aversions in children receiving chemotherapy. *Cancer, 60,* 2344–2347.

Broca, P. (1861). Remarques sur le siège de la faculté du langage articulé; suivies d'une observation d'aphémie (perte de la parole) [Remarks on the seat of the faculty of articulated language, following an observation of aphemia (loss of speech)]. *Bulletin de la Société Anatomique de Paris, 36,* 330–357.

Broca, P. (1863). Localisation des fonctions cérébrales: Siège du langage articulé [Localization of brain functions: Seat of the faculty of articulated language]. *Bulletin de la Société d'Anthropologie de Paris, 4,* 200–202.

Brody, N. (2003). Construct validation of the Sternberg Triarchic Abilities Test: Comment and reanalysis. *Intelligence, 31*(4), 319–329.

Brooks, D. (2012, May 3). The campus tsunami. The *New York Times.* Retrieved from http://www.nytimes.com/2012/05/04/opinion/brooks-the-campus-tsunami.html

Brooks, R., & Meltzoff, A. N. (2002). The importance of eyes: How infants interpret adult looking behavior. *Developmental Psychology, 38,* 958–966.

Brooks-Gunn, J., Graber, J. A., & Paikoff, R. L. (1994). Studying links between hormones and negative affect: Models and measures. *Journal of Research on Adolescence, 4,* 469–486.

Brosnan, S. F., & DeWaal, F. B. M. (2003). Monkeys reject unequal pay. *Nature, 425,* 297–299.

Brown, A. S. (2004). *The déjà vu experience.* New York: Psychology Press.

Brown, B. B., Mory, M., & Kinney, D. (1994). Casting crowds in a relational perspective: Caricature, channel, and context. In G. A. R. Montemayor & T. Gullotta (Eds.), *Advances in adolescent development: Personal relationships during adolescence* (Vol. 5, pp. 123–167). Newbury Park, CA: Sage.

Brown, J. D. (1993). Self-esteem and self-evaluation: Feeling is believing. In J. M. Suls (Ed.), *The self in social perspective: Psychological perspectives on the self* (Vol. 4, pp. 27–58). Hillsdale, NJ: Erlbaum.

Brown, J. D., & McGill, K. L. (1989). The cost of good fortune: When positive life events produce negative health consequences. *Journal of Personality and Social Psychology, 57,* 1103–1110.

Brown, L. E., Wilson, E. T., & Gribble, P. L. (2009). Repetitive transcranial magnetic stimulation to the primary cortex interferes with motor learning by observing. *Journal of Cognitive Neuroscience, 21,* 1013–1022.

Brown, M. (2017, October 30). Ranking Canadian universities in 2018 on how they work—and party. *Maclean's.* https://www.macleans.ca/education/ranking-canadian-universities-in-2018-on-how-they-work-and-party/

Brown, R. (1958). *Words and things.* New York: Free Press.

Brown, R. P., Osterman, L. L., & Barnes, C. D. (2009). School violence and the culture of honor. *Psychological Science, 20*(11), 1400–1405.

Brown, R., & Kulik, J. (1977). Flashbulb memories. *Cognition, 5,* 73–99.

Brown, R., & McNeill, D. (1966). The "tip-of-the-tongue" phenomenon. *Journal of Verbal Learning and Verbal Behavior, 5,* 325–337.

Brown, S. C., & Craik, F. I. M. (2000). Encoding and retrieval of information. In E. Tulving & F. I. M. Craik (Eds.), *The Oxford handbook of memory* (pp. 93–107). New York: Oxford University Press.

Brown, T. A., & Barlow, D. H. (2002). Classification of anxiety and mood disorders. In D. H. Barlow (Ed.), *Anxiety and its disorders: The nature and treatment of anxiety and panic* (2nd ed.). New York: Guilford Press.

Browne, A. J., Smye, V., Rodney, P., Tang, S., Mussell, B., & O'Neil, J. (2011). Access to primary care from the perspective of Aboriginal patients at an urban emergency department. *Qualitative Health Research, 21*(3), 333–348.

Brownell, K. D., Greenwood, M. R. C., Stellar, E., & Shrager, E. E. (1986). The effects of repeated cycles of weight loss and regain in rats. *Physiology and Behavior, 38,* 459–464.

Bruneau, E. G, Jacoby, N., & Saxe, R. (2015). Empathic control through coordinated interaction of amygdala, theory of mind and extended pain matrix brain regions. *Neuroimage, 114,* 105–119. doi:10.1016/j.neuroimage.2015.04.034.

Bruner, J. S. (1983). Education as social invention. *Journal of Social Issues, 39,* 129–141.

Brunet, A., Orr, S. P., Tremblay, J., Robertson, K., Nader, K., & Pitman, R. K. (2008). Effects of post-retrieval propranolol on psychophysiologic responding during subsequent script-driven traumatic imagery in posttraumatic stress disorder. *Journal of Psychiatric Research, 42,* 503–506.

Brunet, A., Saumier, D., Liu, A., Streiner, D. L., Tremblay, J., & Pitman, R. K. (2018). Reduction of PTSD symptoms with pre-reactivation propranolol therapy: A randomized controlled trial. *American Journal of Psychiatry, 175*(4), 427–433.

Brunner, D. P., Dijk, D. J., Tobler, I., & Borbely, A. A. (1990). Effect of partial sleep deprivation on sleep stages and EEG power spectra. *Electroencephalography and Clinical Neurophysiology, 75,* 492–499.

Bryck, R. L., & Fisher, P. A. (2012). Training the brain: Practical applications of neural plasticity from the intersection of cognitive neuroscience, developmental psychology, and prevention science. *American Psychologist, 67,* 87–100.

Bschaden, A., Pietrynik, K., Schulenberg, I., Dieze, A., Rack, I., & Stroebele-Benschop, N. (2019). Preparation sequence of two snack components influences snack composition and calorie intake. *Appetite, 133,* 199–203.

Buchanan, C. M., Eccles, J. S., & Becker, J. B. (1992). Are adolescents the victims of raging hormones? Evidence for activational effects of hormones on moods and behavior at adolescence. *Psychological Bulletin, 111,* 62–107.

Buchanan, T. W. (2007). Retrieval of emotional memories. *Psychological Bulletin, 133,* 761–779.

Buck Louis, G. M., Gray, L. E., Marcus, M., Ojeda, S. R., Pescovitz, O. H., Witchel, S. F., . . . Euling, S. Y. (2008). Environmental factors and puberty timing: Expert panel research. *Pediatrics, 121*(Suppl. 3), S192–S207. doi:10.1542/peds1813E

Buckholtz, J. W., & Meyer-Lindenberg, A. (2012). Psychopathology and the human connectome: Toward a transdiagnostic model of risk for mental illness. *Neuron, 74,* 990–1003.

Buckley, C. (2007, January 3). Man is rescued by stranger on subway tracks. The *New York Times.* http://www.nytimes.com/2007/01/03/nyregion/03life.html

Buckner, R. L., Andrews-Hanna, J. R., & Schacter, D. L. (2008). The brain's default network: Anatomy, function, and relevance to disease. *Annals of the New York Academy of Sciences, 1124,* 1–38.

Buckner, R. L., Petersen, S. E., Ojemann, J. G., Miezin, F. M., Squire, L. R., & Raichle, M. E. (1995). Functional anatomical studies of explicit and implicit memory retrieval tasks. *The Journal of Neuroscience, 15,* 12–29.

Bulteau, C., Grosmaitre, C., Save-Pédebos, J., Leunen, D., Delalande, O., Dorfmüller, G., . . . Jambaqué, I. (2015). Language recovery after left hemispherotomy for Rasmussen encephalitis. *Epilepsy & Behavior, 53,* 51–57.

Bunce, D. M., Flens, E. A., & Neiles, K. Y. (2011). How long can students pay attention in class? A study of student attention decline using clickers. *Journal of Chemical Education, 87,* 1438–1443.

Burger, J. M. (1999). The foot-in-the-door compliance procedure: A multiple-process analysis and review. *Personality and Social Psychology Review, 3,* 303–325.

Burger, J. M. (2009). Replicating Milgram: Would people still obey today? *American Psychologist, 64,* 1–11.

Burger, J. M., & Burns, L. (1988). The illusion of unique invulnerability and the use of effective contraception. *Personality and Social Psychology Bulletin, 14,* 264–270.

Burger, J. M., Sanchez, J., Imberi, J. E., & Grande, L. R. (2009). The norm of reciprocity as an internalized social norm: Returning favors even when no one finds out. *Social Influence, 4*(1), 11–17.

Burgess E. W., & Wallin, P. (1953). *Engagement and marriage.* Philadelphia: J. B. Lippincott.

Burke, D., MacKay, D. G., Worthley, J. S., & Wade, E. (1991). On the tip of the tongue: What causes word failure in young and older adults? *Journal of Memory and Language, 30,* 237–246.

Burke, J. D., Loeber, R., & Birmaher, B. (2002). Oppositional defiant disorder and conduct disorder: Part II. A review of the past 10 years. *Journal of the American Academy of Child and Adolescent Psychiatry, 41,* 1275–1293.

Burke, M., Hsiang, S. M., & Miguel, E. (2015). Climate and conflict. *Annual Review of Economics, 7*(1), 577–617.

Burke, S. L., Hu, T., Fava, N. M, Li, T., Rodriguez, M., Schuldiner, K. L., . . . Laird, A. (2019). Sex differences in the development of mild cognitive impairment and probable Alzheimer disease as predicted by hippocampal volume or white matter hyperintensities. *Journal of Women and Aging, 31,* 140–164.

Burkham, D. T., Ready, D. D., Lee, V. E., & LoGerfo, L. F. (2004). Social-class differences in summer learning between kindergarten and first grade: Model specification and estimation. *Sociology of Education, 77,* 1–31.

Burks, S. V., Carpenter, J. P., Goette, L., & Rustichini, A. (2009). Cognitive skills affect economic preferences, strategic behavior, and job attachment. *Proceedings of the National Academy of Sciences USA, 106*(19), 7745–7750. doi:10.1073/pnas. 0812360106

Burns, D. J., Hwang, A. J., & Burns, S. A. (2011). Adaptive memory: Determining the proximate mechanisms responsible for the memorial advantages of survival processing. *Journal of Experimental Psychology: Learning, Memory, and Cognition, 37,* 206–218.

Burnstein, E., Crandall, C., & Kitayama, S. (1994). Some neo-Darwinian decision rules for altruism: Weighing cues for inclusive fitness as a function of the biological importance of the decision. *Journal of Personality and Social Psychology, 67,* 773–789.

Burris, C. T., & Branscombe, N. R. (2005). Distorted distance estimation induced by a self-relevant national boundary. *Journal of Experimental Social Psychology, 41,* 305–312.

Burton, C. L., Park, L. S., Corfield, E. C., Forget-Dubois, N., Dupuis, A., Sinopoli, V. M., . . . Arnold, P. D. (2018). Heritability of obsessive-compulsive trait dimensions in youth from the general population. *Translational Psychiatry, 8,* 191.

Bushdid, C., Magnasco, M. O., Vosshall, L. B., & Keller, A. (2014). Humans can discriminate more than one trillion olfactory stimuli. *Science, 343*(6177), 1370–1372. doi:10.1126/ science.1249168

Bushman, B. J., & Huesmann, L. R. (2010). Aggression. In S. T. Fiske, D. T. Gilbert, & G. Lindzey (Eds.), *The handbook of social psychology* (5th ed., Vol. 2, pp. 833–863). New York: Wiley.

Buss, D. M. (1985). Human mate selection. *American Scientist, 73,* 47–51.

Buss, D. M. (1989). Sex differences in human mate preferences: Evolutionary hypotheses tested in 37 cultures. *Behavioral and Brain Sciences, 12,* 1–49.

Buss, D. M. (1996). Social adaptation and five major factors of personality. In J. S. Wiggins (Ed.), *The five-factor model of personality: Theoretical perspectives* (pp. 180–208). New York: Guilford Press.

Buss, D. M., & Schmitt, D. P. (1993). Sexual strategies theory: An evolutionary perspective on human mating. *Psychological Review, 100,* 204–232.

Butler, A. C., Chapman, J. E., Forman, E. M., & Beck, A. T. (2006). The empirical status of cognitive-behavioral therapy: A review of meta-analyses. *Clinical Psychology Review, 26*(1), 17–31.

Butler, M. A., Corboy, J. R., & Filley, C. M. (2009). How the conflict between American psychiatry and neurology delayed the appreciation of cognitive dysfunction in multiple sclerosis. *Neuropsychology Review, 19,* 399–410.

Byers-Heinlein, K., Burns, T. C., & Werker, J. F. (2010). The roots of bilingualism in newborns. *Psychological Science, 21*(3), 343–348. doi:10.1177/0956797609360758

Byrne, D., & Clore, G. L. (1970). A reinforcement model of evaluative responses. *Personality: An International Journal, 1,* 103–128.

Byrne, D., Allgeier, A. R., Winslow, L., & Buckman, J. (1975). The situational facilitation of interpersonal attraction: A three-factor hypothesis. *Journal of Applied Social Psychology, 5,* 1–15.

Byrne, D., Ervin, C. R., & Lamberth, J. (1970). Continuity between the experimental study of attraction and real-life computer dating. *Journal of Personality and Social Psychology, 16,* 157–165.

Cabeza, R. (2002). Hemispheric asymmetry reduction in older adults: The HAROLD model. *Psychology and Aging, 17,* 85–100.

Cabeza, R., Rao, S., Wagner, A. D., Mayer, A., & Schacter, D. L. (2001). Can medial temporal lobe regions distinguish true from false? An event-related fMRI study of veridical and illusory recognition memory. *Proceedings of the National Academy of Sciences, USA, 98,* 4805–4810.

Cacioppo, J. T., & Patrick, B. (2008). *Loneliness: Human nature and the need for social connection.* New York: Norton.

Cadario, R., & Chandon, P. (2019). Which healthy eating nudges work best? A meta-analysis of field experiments. *Marketing Science* (in press). Available at SSRN: https://ssrn.com/abstract=3090829 or doi:10.2139/ssrn.3090829

Cahill, L., & McGaugh, J. L. (1998). Mechanisms of emotional arousal and lasting declarative memory. *Trends in Neurosciences, 21,* 294–299.

Cahill, L., Haier, R. J., Fallon, J., Alkire, M. T., Tang, C., Keator, D., . . . McGaugh, J. L. (1996). Amygdala activity at encoding correlated with long-term, free recall of emotional information. *Proceedings of the National Academy of Sciences, USA, 93,* 8016–8021.

Callaghan, T., Rochat, P., Lillard, A., Claux, M. L., Odden, H., Itakura, S., . . . Singh, S. (2005). Synchrony in the onset of mental-state reasoning: Evidence from five cultures. *Psychological Science, 16,* 378–384.

Calvert, S. L., Appelbaum, M., Dodge, K. A., Graham, S., Nagayama Hall, G. C., Hamby, S., . . . Hedges, L. V. (2017, Feb–Mar). The American Psychological Association Task Force assessment of violent video games: Science in the service of public interest. *American Psychologist, 72*(2), 126–143.

Calvin, C. M., Deary, I. J., Fenton, C., Roberts, B. A., Der, G., Leckenby, N., & Batty, G. D. (2011). Intelligence in youth and all-cause-mortality: Systematic review with meta-analysis. *International Journal of Epidemiology, 40*(3), 626–644.

Cameron, C. D., & Payne, B. K. (2011). Escaping affect: How motivated emotion regulation creates insensitivity to mass suffering. *Journal of Personality and Social Psychology, 100*(1), 1–15.

Campbell, A. (1999). Staying alive: Evolution, culture, and women's intra-sexual aggression. *Behavioral & Brain Sciences, 22,* 203–252.

Campbell, F. A., Ramey, C. T., Pungello, E., Sparling, J., & Miller-Johnson, S. (2002). Early childhood education: Young adult outcomes from the Abecedarian Project. *Applied Developmental Science, 6*(1), 42–57.

Campos, B., Shiota, M. N., Keltner, D., Gonzaga, G. C., & Goetz, J. L. (2013). What is shared, what is different? Core relational themes and expressive displays of eight positive emotions. *Cognition & Emotion, 27*(1), 37–52.

Canadian Blood Services. (2017). Organ donation and transplantation in Canada: 2016 System progress report update. Retrieved from https://professionaleducation.blood.ca/sites/msi/files/odt _report-2017-final.pdf

Canadian Blood Services. (2019). Backgrounder: Kidney paired donation program. Retrieved from https://blood.ca/en /news-and-events/media-resources/kidney-paired-donation /backgrounder-kidney-paired-donation-program

Canadian Mental Health Association. (2019). Fast facts about mental illness. Retrieved from https://cmha.ca /fast-facts-about-mental-illness

Canadian Psychological Association. (2000). Canadian Code of Ethics for Psychologists (3rd ed.). Retrieved from http://www.cpa .ca/docs/File/Ethics/cpa_code_2000_eng_jp_jan2014.pdf

Canadian Psychological Association. (2014). "Psychology works" fact sheet: Obsessive compulsive disorder. Retrieved from http://www .cpa.ca/docs/File/Publications/FactSheets/PsychologyWorksFactSheet _ObsessiveCompulsiveDisorder.pdf

Canadian Psychological Association. (2015). "Psychology works" fact sheet: Generalized anxiety disorder. Retrieved from http:// www.cpa.ca/docs/File/Publications/FactSheets/Psychology WorksFactSheet_GeneralizedAnxietyDisorder.pdf

Cannon, T. D. (2015). How schizophrenia develops: Cognitive and brain mechanisms underlying onset of psychosis. *Trends in Cognitive Science, 19,* 744–756.

Cannon, W. B. (1929). *Bodily changes in pain, hunger, fear, and rage: An account of recent research into the function of emotional excitement* (2nd ed.). New York: Appleton-Century-Crofts.

Cantor, J. R., Zillmann, D., & Bryant, J. (1975). Enhancement of experienced sexual arousal in response to erotic stimuli through misattribution of unrelated residual excitation. *Journal of Personality and Social Psychology, 32*(1), 69–75.

Cantor, N. (1990). From thought to behavior: "Having" and "doing" in the study of personality and cognition. *American Psychologist, 45,* 735–750.

Card, N. A., Stucky, B. D., Sawalani, G. M., & Little, T. D. (2008). Direct and indirect aggression during childhood and adolescence: A meta-analytic review of gender differences, intercorrelations, and relations to maladjustment. *Child Development, 79,* 1185–1229. http://dx.doi.org/10.1111/j.1467-8624.2008.01184.x

Carey, N. (2012). *The epigenetics revolution: How modern biology is rewriting our understanding of genetics, disease, and inheritance.* New York: Columbia University Press.

Carmena, J. M., Lebedev, M. A., Crist, R. E., O'Doherty, J. E., Santucci, D. M., Dimitrov, D. F., . . . Nicolelis, M. A. (2003). Learning to control a brain–machine interface for reaching and grasping by primates. *Public Library of Science Biology, 1,* 193–208.

Carmichael Olson, H., Streissguth, A. P., Sampson, P. D., Barr, H. M., Bookstein, F. L., & Thiede, K. (1997). Association of prenatal alcohol exposure with behavioral and learning problems in early adolescence. *Journal of the American Academy of Child & Adolescent Psychiatry, 36*(9), 1187–1194.

Carney, D. R., Cuddy, A. J. C., & Yap, A. J. (2010). Power posing: Brief nonverbal displays affect neuroendocrine levels and risk tolerance. *Psychological Science, 21*(10), 1363–1368. doi:10.1177/0956797610383437

Carolson, E. A. (1998). A prospective longitudinal study of attachment disorganization/disorientation. *Child Development, 69,* 1107–1128.

Caron, M.-J., Mottron, L., Berthiaume, C., & Dawson, M. (2006). Cognitive mechanisms, specificity and neural underpinnings of visuospatial peaks in autism. *Brain, 129,* 1789–1802.

Carpenter, A. C., & Schacter, D. L. (2017). Flexible retrieval: When true inferences produce false memories. *Journal of Experimental Psychology: Learning, Memory, and Cognition, 43,* 335–349.

Carpenter, S. K. (2012). Testing enhances the transfer of learning. *Current Directions in Psychological Science, 21,* 279–283.

Carré, J. M., & Archer, J. (2018). Testosterone and human behavior: The role of individual and contextual variables. *Current Opinion in Psychology, 19,* 149–153.

Carroll, J. B. (1993). *Human cognitive abilities.* Cambridge: Cambridge University Press.

Carson, R. C., Butcher, J. N., & Mineka, S. (2000). *Abnormal psychology and modern life* (11th ed.). Boston: Allyn & Bacon.

Carstensen, L. L. (1992). Social and emotional patterns in adulthood: Support for socioemotional selectivity theory. *Psychology and Aging, 7,* 331–338.

Carstensen, L. L., & Fredrickson, B. L. (1998). Influence of HIV status and age on cognitive representations of others. *Health Psychology, 17,* 1–10.

Carstensen, L. L., & Turk-Charles, S. (1994). The salience of emotion across the adult life span. *Psychology and Aging, 9,* 259–264.

Carstensen, L. L., Pasupathi, M., Mayr, U., & Nesselroade, J. R. (2000). Emotional experience in everyday life across the adult life span. *Journal of Personality and Social Psychology, 79,* 644–655.

Carswell, K. L., & Finkel, E. J. (2018). Can you get the magic back? The moderating effect of passion decay beliefs on relationship commitment. *Journal of Personality and Social Psychology, 115*(6), 1002–1033.

Carver, C. S. (2006). Approach, avoidance, and the self-regulation of affect and action. *Motivation and Emotion, 30,* 105–110.

Carver, C. S., & Harmon-Jones, E. (2009). Anger is an approach-related affect: Evidence and implications. Psychological Bulletin, 135(2), 183–204.

Carver, C. S., & White, T. L. (1994). Behavioral inhibition, behavioral activation, and affective responses to impending reward and punishment: The bis/bas scales. *Journal of Personality and Social Psychology, 67*(2), 319–333.

Carver, C. S., Lehman, J. M., & Antoni, M. H. (2003). Dispositional pessimism predicts illness-related disruption of social and recreational activities among breast cancer patients. *Journal of Personality and Social Psychology, 84,* 813–821.

Casazza, K., Fontaine, K. R., Astrup, A., Birch, L. L., Brown, A. W., Bohan Brown, M. M., . . . Allison, D. B. (2013). Myths, presumptions, and facts about obesity. *New England Journal of Medicine, 368*(5), 446–454.

Caspi, A., & Herbener, E. S. (1990). Continuity and change: Assortative marriage and the consistency of personality in adulthood. *Journal of Personality and Social Psychology, 58,* 250–258.

Caspi, A., Lynam, D., Moffitt, T. E., & Silva, P. A. (1993). Unraveling girls' delinquency: Biological, dispositional, and contextual contributions to adolescent misbehavior. *Developmental Psychology, 29,* 19–30.

Caspi, A., Roberts, B. W., & Shiner, R. L. (2005). Personality development: Stability and change. *Annual Review of Psychology, 56,* 453–484.

Caspi, A., Sugden, K., Moffitt, T. E., Taylor, A., Craig, I. W., Harrington, H., . . . Poulton, R. (2003). Influence of life stress on depression: Moderation by a polymorphism in the 5-HTT gene. *Science, 301,* 386–389.

Castel, A. D., McCabe, D. P., & Roediger, H. L., III. (2007). Illusions of competence and overestimation of associate memory for identical items: Evidence from judgments of learning. *Psychonomic Bulletin & Review, 14,* 197–111.

Castellani, R. J., Perry, G., & Iverson, G. L. (2015). Chronic effects of mild neurotrauma: Putting the cart before the horse? *Journal of Neuropathology & Experimental Neurology, 74,* 493–499.

Castellanos, F. X., Patti, P. L., Sharp, W., Jeffries, N. O., Greenstein, D. K., Clasen, L. S., . . . Rapoport, J. L. (2002). Developmental trajectories of brain volume abnormalities in children and adolescents with attention-deficit/hyperactivity disorder. *Journal of the American Medical Association, 288,* 1740–1748. doi:10.1001/jama.288.14.1740

Catrambone, R. (2002). The effects of surface and structural feature matches on the access of story analogs. *Journal of Experimental Psychology: Learning, Memory, & Cognition, 28,* 318–334.

Cattell, R. B. (1950). *Personality: A systematic, theoretical, and factual study.* New York: McGraw-Hill.

Ceci, S. J. (1991). How much does schooling influence general intelligence and its cognitive components? A reassessment of the evidence. *Developmental Psychology, 27,* 703–722.

Ceci, S. J., & Williams, W. M. (1997). Schooling, intelligence, and income. *American Psychologist, 52,* 1051–1058.

Ceci, S. J., DeSimone, M., & Johnson, S. (1992). Memory in context: A case study of "Bubbles P.," a gifted but uneven memorizer. In D. J. Herrmann, H. Weingartner, A. Searleman, & C. McEvoy (Eds.), *Memory improvement: Implications for memory theory* (pp. 169–186). New York: Springer-Verlag.

Ceci, S. J., Ginther, D. K., Kahn, S., & Williams, W. M. (2014). Women in academic science: A changing landscape. *Psychological Science in the Public Interest, 15*(3), 75–141. doi:10.1177/1529100614541236

Ceci, S. J., Williams, W. M., & Barnett, S. M. (2009). Women's underrepresentation in science: Sociocultural and biological considerations. *Psychological Bulletin, 135*(2), 218–261.

Cellini, N., & Capuozzo, A. (2018). Shaping memory consolidation via targeted memory reactivation during sleep. *Annals of the New York Academy of Sciences, 1426,* 52–71.

Centola, D., & Baronchelli, A. (2015). The spontaneous emergence of conventions: An experimental study of cultural evolution. *Proceedings of the National Academy of Sciences, USA, 112*(7), 1989–1994.

Centre for Addiction and Mental Health. (2014). *Cannabis policy framework.* Retrieved from http://www.camh.ca/en/hospital /about_camh/influencing_public_policy/documents/camhcanna-bispolicyframework.pdf

Cepeda, N. J., Pashler, H., Vul, E., Wixted, J. T., & Rohrer, D. (2006). Distributed practice in verbal recall tests: A review and quantitative synthesis. *Psychological Bulletin, 132,* 354–380.

Cerf-Ducastel, B., & Murphy, C. (2001). fMRI activation in response to odorants orally delivered in aqueous solutions. *Chemical Senses, 26*(6), 625–637.

Chabris, C. F., Hebert, B. M., Benjamin, D. J., Beauchamp, J., Cesarini, D., van der Loos, M., & Laibson, D. (2012). Most reported genetic associations with general intelligence are probably false positives. *Psychological Science, 23*(11), 1314–1323.

Chabris, C., & Simons, D. (2012, November 16). Using just 10% of your brains? Think again. *Wall Street Journal Online.* Retrieved from https://www.wsj.com/articles/SB1000142412788732455630 45 78119351875421218

Chaiken, S. (1980). Heuristic versus systematic information processing and the use of source versus message cues in persuasion. *Journal of Personality and Social Psychology, 39,* 752–766.

Chalmers, D. (1996). *The conscious mind: In search of a fundamental theory.* New York: Oxford University Press.

Chambless, D. L., Baker, M. J., Baucom, D. H., Beutler, L. E., Calhoun, K. S., Crits-Christoph, P., . . . Woody, S. R. (1998). Update on empirically validated therapies, II. *Clinical Psychologist, 51*(1), 3–14.

Chandler, J., & Schwarz, N. (2009). How extending your middle finger affects your perception of others: Learned movements influence concept accessibility. *Journal of Experimental Social Psychology, 45,* 123–128.

Chang, P. P., Ford, D. E., Meoni, L. A., Wang, N., & Klag, M. J. (2002). Anger in young men and subsequent premature cardiovascular disease. *Archives of Internal Medicine, 162,* 901–906.

Chaplin, T. M., & Aldao, A. (2013). Gender differences in emotion expression in children: A meta-analytic review. *Psychological Bulletin, 139,* 735–765.

Chapman, H. A., Kim, D. A., Susskind, J. M., & Anderson, A. K. (2009). In bad taste: Evidence for the oral origins of moral disgust. *Science, 27,* 1222–1226.

Charles, S. T., Reynolds, C. A., & Gatz, M. (2001). Age-related differences and change in positive and negative affect over 23 years. *Journal of Personality and Social Psychology, 80,* 136–151.

Charness, N. (1981). Aging and skilled problem solving. *Journal of Experimental Psychology: General, 110,* 21–38.

Charpak, G., & Broch, H. (2004). *Debunked! ESP, telekinesis, and other pseudoscience* (B. K. Holland, Trans.). Baltimore: Johns Hopkins University Press.

Chartrand, T. L., & Bargh, J. A. (1999). The chameleon effect: The perception-behavior link and social interaction. *Journal of Personality and Social Psychology, 76,* 893–910.

Chartrand, T. L., & Kay, A. (2006). *Mystery moods and perplexing performance: Consequences of succeeding and failing at a nonconscious goal.* Unpublished manuscript.

Chen, C., Crivelli, C., Garrod, O. G. B., Schyns, P. G., Fernández-Dols, J.-M., & Jack, R. E. (2018). Distinct facial expressions represent pain and pleasure across cultures. *Proceedings of the National Academy of Sciences, USA, 115*(43), e10013–e10021. doi.org/10.1073/pnas.1807862115

Chen, E., Cohen, S., & Miller, G. E. (2010). How low socioeconomic status affects 2-year hormonal trajectories in children. *Psychological Science, 21*(1), 31–37.

Chen, Q., & Yan, Z. (2015). Does multitasking with mobile phones affect learning? A review. *Computers in Human Behavior, 54,* 34–42.

Chen, S., Collins, A., Anderson, K., McKenzie, K., & Kidd, S. (2017). Patient characteristics, length of stay, and functional improvement for schizophrenia spectrum disorders: A population study of inpatient care in Ontario 2005 to 2015. *Canadian Journal of Psychiatry, 62,* 854–863.

Cheney, D. L., & Seyfarth, R. M. (1990). *How monkeys see the world.* Chicago: University of Chicago Press.

Cheng, D. T., Disterhoft, J. F., Power, J. M., Ellis, D. A., & Desmond, J. E. (2008). Neural substrates underlying human delay and trace eyeblink conditioning. *Proceedings of the National Academy of Sciences, USA, 105,* 8108–8113.

Cherlin, A. J. (Ed.). (1992). *Marriage, divorce, remarriage* (2nd ed.). Cambridge, MA: Harvard University Press.

Cherry, C. (1953). Some experiments on the recognition of speech with one and two ears. *Journal of the Acoustical Society of America, 25,* 275–279.

Chetty, R., & Hendren, N. (2018). The impacts of neighborhoods on intergenerational mobility. II: County-level estimates. *Quarterly Journal of Economics, 133*(3), 1163–1228.

Chetty, R., Stepner, M., Abraham, S., Lin, S., Scuderi, B., Turner, N., . . . Cutler, D. (2016). The association between income and life expectancy in the United States, 2001–2014. *Journal of the American Medical Association, 315*(16), 1750–1766.

Children's Mental Health Ontario. (2016). Ontario's children waiting up to 1.5 years for urgently needed mental healthcare. Retrieved from https://cmho.org/blog/article2/6519717-ontario -s-children-waiting-up-to-1-5-years-for-urgently-needed-mental -healthcare-3

Chin, A., Markey, A., Bhargava, S., Kassam, K. S., & Loewenstein, G. (2017). Bored in the USA: Experience sampling and boredom in everyday life. *Emotion, 17,* 359–368.

Chin, H. B., Sipe, T. A., Elder, R., Mercer, S. L., Chattopadhyay, S. K., Jacob, V., . . . Santelli, J. (2012). The effectiveness of group-based comprehensive risk-reduction and abstinence education interventions to prevent or reduce the risk of adolescent pregnancy, human immunodeficiency virus, and sexually transmitted infections: Two systematic reviews for the Guide to Community Preventive Services. *American Journal of Preventive Medicine, 42,* 272–294.

Chivers, M. L., Rieger, G., Latty, E., & Bailey, J. M. (2004). A sex difference in the specificity of sexual arousal. *Psychological Science, 15,* 736–744.

Chivers, M. L., Seto, M. C., & Blanchard, R. (2007). Gender and sexual orientation differences in sexual response to sexual activities versus gender of actors in sexual films. *Journal of Personality and Social Psychology, 93,* 1108–1121.

Choi, I., Nisbett, R. E., & Norenzayan, A. (1999). Causal attribution across cultures: Variation and universality. *Psychological Bulletin, 125,* 47–63.

Chomsky, N. (1957). *Syntactic structures.* The Hague: Mouton.

Chomsky, N. (1959). A review of *Verbal Behavior* by B. F. Skinner. *Language, 35,* 26–58.

Chomsky, N. (1986). *Knowledge of language: Its nature, origin, and use.* New York: Praeger.

Chorover, S. L. (1980). *From Genesis to genocide: The meaning of human nature and the power of behavior control.* Cambridge, MA: MIT Press.

Choy, Y., Fyer, A. J., & Lipsitz, J. D. (2007). Treatment of specific phobia in adults. *Clinical Psychology Review, 27*(3), 266–286.

Christ, S. E., White, D. A., Mandernach, T., & Keys, B. A. (2001). Inhibitory control across the life span. *Developmental Neuropsychology, 20*(3), 653–669.

Christakis, N. A., & Fowler, J. H. (2007). The spread of obesity in a large social network over 32 years. *New England Journal of Medicine, 357*(4), 370–379.

Christianson, S.-A., & Loftus, E. F. (1987). Memory for traumatic events. *Applied Cognitive Psychology, 1,* 225–239.

Christie, I. C., & Friedman, B. H. (2004). Autonomic specificity of discrete emotion and dimensions of affective space: A multivariate approach. *International Journal of Psychophysiology, 51,* 143–153. doi.org/10.1016/j.ijpsycho.2003.08.002

Chui, H., Hoppmann, C. A., Gerstorf, D., Walker, R., & Luszcz, M. A. (2014). Social partners and momentary affect in the oldest-old: The presence of others benefits affect depending on who we are and who we are with. *Developmental Psychology, 50*(3), 728–740.

Chung, G. H., Flook, L., & Fuligni, A. J. (2009). Daily family conflict and emotional distress among adolescents from Latin American, Asian, and European backgrounds. *Developmental Psychology, 45,* 1406–1415.

Cialdini, R. B. (2005). Don't throw in the towel: Use social influence research. *American Psychological Society, 18,* 33–34.

Cialdini, R. B. (2013). The focus theory of normative conduct. In P. A. M. van Lange, A. W. Kruglanski, & E. T. Higgins (Eds.), *Handbook of theories of social psychology* (Vol. 3, pp. 295–312). New York: Sage.

Cialdini, R. B., & Goldstein, N. J. (2004). Social influence: Compliance and conformity. *Annual Review of Psychology, 55*(1), 591–621. doi:10.1146/annurev.psych.55.090902.142015

Cialdini, R. B., Trost, M. R., & Newsom, J. T. (1995). Preference for consistency: The development of a valid measure and the discovery of surprising behavioral implications. *Journal of Personality and Social Psychology, 69,* 318–328.

Cialdini, R. B., Vincent, J. E., Lewis, S. K., Catalan, J., Wheeler, D., & Darby, B. L. (1975). Reciprocal concessions procedure for inducing compliance: The door-in-the-face technique. *Journal of Personality and Social Psychology, 31,* 206–215.

Ciarrochi, J. V., Chan, A. Y., & Caputi, P. (2000). A critical evaluation of the emotional intelligence concept. *Personality & Individual Differences, 28,* 539.

Ciarrochi, J., Heaven, P. C. L., & Skinner, T. (2012). Cognitive ability and health-related behaviors during adolescence: A prospective study across five years. *Intelligence, 40*(4), 317–324.

Cicchetti, D., & Toth, S. L. (1998). Perspectives on research and practice in developmental psychopathology. In I. E. Sigel & K. A. Renninger (Eds.), *Handbook of child psychology: Vol. 4. Child psychology in practice* (5th ed., pp. 479–583). New York: Wiley.

Clancy, S. A. (2005). *Abducted: How people come to believe they were kidnapped by aliens.* Cambridge, MA: Harvard University Press.

Clark, C. A., & Dagher, A. (2014). The role of dopamine in risk taking: A specific look at Parkinson's disease and gambling. *Frontiers in Behavioral Neuroscience, 8,* 196. doi: 10.3389 /fnbeh.2014.00196

Clark, I. A., & Maguire, E. A. (2016). Remembering preservation in hippocampal amnesia. *Annual Review of Psychology, 67,* 51–82.

Clark, M. S., & Lemay, E. P. (2010). Close relationships. In S. T. Fiske, D. T. Gilbert, & G. Lindzey (Eds.), *The handbook of social psychology* (5th ed., Vol. 2). New York: Wiley.

Clark, R. D., & Hatfield, E. (1989). Gender differences in receptivity to sexual offers. *Journal of Psychology and Human Sexuality, 2,* 39–55.

Clarke, A., & Tyler, L. K. (2015). Understanding what we see: How we derive meaning from vision. *Trends in Cognitive Sciences, 19*(11), 677–687.

Clark-Polner, E., Johnson, T., & Barrett, L. F. (2017). Multivoxel pattern analysis does not provide evidence to support the existence of basic emotions. *Cerebral Cortex, 27,* 1944–1948.

Cleary, A. M., & Claxton, A. B. (2018). Déjà vu: An illusion of prediction. *Psychological Science, 29,* 635–644.

Cleary, A. M., Brown, A. S., Sawyer, B. D., Nomi, J. S., Ajoku, A. C., & Ryals, A. J. (2012). Familiarity from the configuration of objects in 3-dimensional space and its relation to déjà vu: A virtual reality investigation. *Consciousness and Cognition, 21,* 969–975.

Cleckley, H. M. (1976). *The mask of sanity* (5th ed.). St. Louis: Mosby.

Coates, T. (2015). *Between the world and me.* New York: Spiegel & Grau.

Coe, C. L., & Lubach, G. R. (2008). Fetal programming prenatal origins of health and illness. *Current Directions in Psychological Science, 17,* 36–41.

Cogan, R., Cogan, D., Waltz, W., & McCue, M. (1987). Effects of laughter and relaxation on discomfort thresholds. *Journal of Behavioral Medicine, 10,* 139–144.

Coghill, R. C., McHaffie, J. G., & Yen, Y. (2003). Neural correlates of individual differences in the subjective experience of pain. *Proceedings of the National Academy of Sciences, USA, 100,* 8538–8542.

Cohen, A. O., Breiner, K., Steinberg, L., Bonnie, R. J., Scott, E. S., Taylor-Thompson, K. A., . . . Casey, B. J. (2016). When is an adolescent an adult? Assessing cognitive control in emotional and nonemotional contexts. *Psychological Science, 27*(4), 549–562.

Cohen, D., Nisbett, R. E., Bowdle, B. F., & Schwarz, N. (1996). Insult, aggression, and the southern culture of honor: An "experimental ethnography." *Journal of Personality and Social Psychology, 70,* 945–960.

Cohen, G. (1990). Why is it difficult to put names to faces? *British Journal of Psychology, 81,* 287–297.

Cohen, S. (1988). Psychosocial models of the role of social support in the etiology of physical disease. *Health Psychology, 7,* 269–297.

Cohen, S., Janicki-Deverts, D., Doyle, W. J., Miller, G. E., Frank, E., Rabin, B. S., & Turner, R. B. (2012). Chronic stress, glucocorticoid receptor resistance, inflammation, and disease risk. *Proceedings of the National Academy of Sciences, USA, 109,* 5995–5999.

Cohen-Kettenis, P. T., & Pfäfflin, F. (2003). *Transgenderism and intersexuality in childhood and adolescence: Making choices.* Thousand Oaks, CA: SAGE.

Coifman, K. G., Bonanno, G. A., Ray, R. D., & Gross, J. J. (2007). Does repressive coping promote resilience? Affective-autonomic response discrepancy during bereavement. *Journal of Personality and Social Psychology, 92,* 745–758.

Colcombe, S. J., Erickson, K. I., Scalf, P. E., Kim, J. S., Prakesh, R., McAuley, E., . . . Kramer, A. F. (2006). Aerobic exercise training increases brain volume in aging humans. *Journals of Gerontology Series A: Biological Sciences and Medical Sciences, 61,* 1166–1170.

Colcombe, S. J., Kramer, A. F., Erickson, K. I., Scalf, P., McAuley, E., Cohen, N. J., . . . Elavsky, S. (2004). Cardiovascular fitness, cortical plasticity, and aging. *Proceedings of the National Academy of Sciences, USA, 101,* 3316–3321.

Coman, A., Manier, D., & Hirst, W. (2009). Forgetting the unforgettable through conversation: Social shared retrieval-induced forgetting of September 11 memories. *Psychological Science, 20,* 627–633.

Condon, J. W., & Crano, W. D. (1988). Inferred evaluation and the relation between attitude similarity and interpersonal attraction. *Journal of Personality and Social Psychology, 54,* 789–797.

Conklin, Q., King, B., Zanesco, A., Pokorny, J., Hamidi, A., Lin, J., . . . Saron, C. (2015). Telomere lengthening after three weeks of an intensive insight meditation retreat. *Psychoneuroendocrinology, 61,* 26–27.

Conley, T. D. (2011). Perceived proposer personality characteristics and gender differences in acceptance of casual sex offers. *Journal of Personality and Social Psychology, 100*(2), 309–329.

Conley, T. D., Moors, A. C., Matsick, J. L., Ziegler, A., & Valentine, B. A. (2011). Women, men, and the bedroom: Methodological and conceptual insights that narrow, reframe, and eliminate gender differences in sexuality. *Current Directions in Psychological Science, 20*(5), 296–300.

Conway, M., & Ross, M. (1984). Getting what you want by revising what you had. *Journal of Personality and Social Psychology, 47*(4), 738–748.

Cook, M., & Mineka, S. (1989). Observational conditioning of fear to fear-relevant versus fear-irrelevant stimuli in rhesus monkeys. *Journal of Abnormal Psychology, 98*(4), 448–459.

Cook, M., & Mineka, S. (1990). Selective associations in the observational conditioning of fear in rhesus monkeys. *Journal of Experimental Psychology: Animal Behavior Process, 16*, 372–389.

Cooke, J. E., Kochendorfer, L. B., Stuart-Parrigon, K. L., Koehn, A. J., & Kerns, K. A. (2018). Parent–child attachment and children's experience and regulation of emotion: A meta-analytic review. *Emotion.* doi.org/10.1037/emo0000504

Cooper, H., Nye, B., Charlton, K., Lindsay, J., & Greathouse, S. (1996). The effects of summer vacation on achievement test scores: A narrative and meta-analytic review. *Review of Educational Research, 66*(3), 227–268.

Cooper, J. C., Hollon, N. G., Wimmer, G. E., & Knutson, B. (2009). Available alternative incentives modulate anticipatory nucleus accumbens activation. *Social Cognitive and Affective Neuroscience, 4*, 409–416.

Cooper, J. M., & Strayer, D. L. (2008). Effects of simulator practice and real-world experience on cell-phone-related driver distraction. *Human Factors, 50*, 893–902.

Cooper, J. R., Bloom, F. E., & Roth, R. H. (2003). *Biochemical basis of neuropharmacology.* New York: Oxford University Press.

Cooper, J., & Fazio, R. H. (1984). A new look at dissonance theory. In L. Berkowitz (Ed.), *Advances in experimental social psychology* (Vol. 17, pp. 229–266). New York: Academic Press.

Cooper, M. L. (2006). Does drinking promote risky sexual behavior? A complex answer to a simple question. *Current Directions in Psychological Science, 15*, 19–23.

Cooper, W. H., & Withey, W. J. (2009). The strong situation hypothesis. *Personality and Social Psychology Review, 13*, 62–72.

Cordaro, D. T., Keltner, D., Tshering, S., Wangchuk, D., & Flynn, L. M. (2016). The voice conveys emotion in ten globalized cultures and one remote village in Bhutan. *Emotion, 16*(1), 117–128.

Cordaro, D. T., Sun, R., Keltner, D., Kamble, S., Huddar, N., & McNeil, G. (2018). Universals and cultural variations in 22 emotional expressions across five cultures. *Emotion, 18*(1), 75–93.

Cordovani, L., & Cordovani, D. (2016). A literature review on observational learning for medical motor skills and anesthesia teaching. *Advances in Health Sciences Education: Theory and Practice, 21*, 1113–1121.

Coren, S. (1997). *Sleep thieves.* New York: Free Press.

Corfield, E. C., Yang, Y., Martin, N. G., & Nyholt, D. R. (2017). A continuum of genetic liability for minor and major depression. *Translational Psychiatry, 7*, e1131.

Corkin, S. (2002). What's new with the amnesic patient HM? *Nature Reviews Neuroscience, 3*, 153–160.

Corkin, S. (2013). *Permanent present tense: The unforgettable life of the amnesic patient, H.M.* New York: Basic Books.

Correll, J., Park, B., Judd, C. M., & Wittenbrink, B. (2002). The police officer's dilemma: Using ethnicity to disambiguate potentially threatening individuals. *Journal of Personality and Social Psychology, 83*, 1314–1329.

Correll, J., Park, B., Judd, C. M., Wittenbrink, B., Sadler, M. S., & Keesee, T. (2007). Across the thin blue line: Police officers and racial bias in the decision to shoot. *Journal of Personality and Social Psychology, 92*, 1006–1023.

Correll, J., Wittenbrink, B., Crawford, M. T., & Sadler, M. S. (2015). Stereotypic vision: How stereotypes disambiguate visual stimuli. *Journal of Personality and Social Psychology, 108*(2), 219–233. doi:10.1037/pspa0000015

Corsi, P. (Ed.). (1991). *The enchanted loom: Chapters in the history of neuroscience.* New York: Oxford University Press.

Corti, E. (1931). *A history of smoking* (P. England, Trans.). London: Harrap.

Coryell, W., Endicott, J., Maser, J. D., Mueller, T., Lavori, P., & Keller, M. (1995). The likelihood of recurrence in bipolar affective disorder: The importance of episode recency. *Journal of Affective Disorders, 33*, 201–206.

Cosmides, L., & Tooby, J. (2000). The evolutionary psychology of the emotions and their relationship to internal regulatory variables. In M. Lewis, J. M. Haviland-Jones, & L. Feldman Barrett (Eds.), *Handbook of emotions,* (3rd ed.). New York: Guilford.

Costa, P. T., Terracciano, A., & McCrae, R. R. (2001). Gender differences in personality traits across cultures: Robust and surprising findings. *Journal of Personality and Social Psychology, 81*, 322–331.

Costanza, A., Weber, K., Gandy, S., Bouras, C., Hof, P. R., Giannakopoulos, G., & Canuto, A. (2011). Contact sport–related chronic traumatic encephalopathy in the elderly: Clinical expression and structural substrates. *Neuropathology and Applied Neurobiology, 37*, 570–584.

Cotton, J. L. (1981). A review of research on Schachter's theory of emotion and the misattribution of arousal. *European Journal of Social Psychology, 11*(4), 365–397.

Cottrell, C. A., Neuberg, S. L., & Li, N. P. (2007). What do people desire in others? A sociofunctional perspective on the importance of different valued characteristics. *Journal of Personality and Social Psychology, 92*, 208–231.

Cowen, A. S., & Keltner, D. (2017). Self-report captures 27 distinct categories of emotion bridged by continuous gradients. *Proceedings of the National Academy of Sciences, USA, 114*(38), E7900 LP-E7909. doi:10.1073/pnas.1702247114

Crabb, R., & Hunsley, J. (2011). Age-related patterns in mental health–related complementary and alternative medicine utilization in Canada. *International Psychogeriatrics, 23*(3), 459–471.

Craddock, N., & Jones, I. (1999). Genetics of bipolar disorder. *Journal of Medical Genetics, 36*, 585–594.

Craik, F. I. M., & Tulving, E. (1975). Depth of processing and the retention of words in episodic memory. *Journal of Experimental Psychology: General, 104*, 268–294.

Craik, F. I. M., Barense, M. D., Rathbone, C. J., Grusec, J. E., Stuss, D. T., Gao, F., . . . Black, S. E. (2014). VL: A further case of erroneous recollection. *Neuropsychologia, 56,* 367–380.

Craik, F. I. M., Govoni, R., Naveh-Benjamin, M., & Anderson, N. D. (1996). The effects of divided attention on encoding and retrieval processes in human memory. *Journal of Experimental Psychology: General, 125,* 159–180.

Cramer, R. E., Schaefer, J. T., & Reid, S. (1996). Identifying the ideal mate: More evidence for male–female convergence. *Current Psychology, 15,* 157–166.

Crane, C. A., Godleski, S. A., Przybyla, S. M., Schlauch, R. C., & Testa, M. (2015). The proximal effects of acute alcohol consumption on male-to-female aggression: A meta-analytic review of the experimental literature. *Trauma, Violence, & Abuse.* doi:10.1177/1524838015584374

Crane, J. M. G., Keough, M., Murphy, P., Burrage, L., & Hutchens, D. (2011). Effects of environmental tobacco smoke on perinatal outcomes: a retrospective cohort study. *BJOG: An International Journal of Obstetrics & Gynaecology, 118*(7), 865–871.

Craske, M. G. (1999). *Anxiety disorders: Psychological approaches to theory and treatment.* Boulder, CO: Westview Press.

Creery, J. D., Oudiette, D., Antony, J. W., & Paller, K. A. (2015). Targeted memory reactivation during sleep depends on prior learning. *Sleep, 38,* 755–763.

Crivelli, C., Carrera, P., & Fernández-Dols, J.-M. (2015). Are smiles a sign of happiness? Spontaneous expressions of judo winners. *Evolution and Human Behavior, 36*(1), 52–58.

Crocker, J., Canevello, A., & Brown, A. A. (2017). Social motivation: Costs and benefits of selfishness and otherishness. *Annual Review of Psychology, 68,* 299–325.

Crocq, M.-A. (2007). Historical and cultural aspects of man's relationship with addictive drugs. *Dialogues in Clinical Neuroscience, 9,* 355–361.

Crombag, H. F. M., Wagenaar, W. A., & Van Koppen, P. J. (1996). Crashing memories and the problem of "source monitoring." *Applied Cognitive Psychology, 10,* 95–104.

Cross, E. S., Kraemer, D. J. M., Hamilton, A. F. de C., Kelley, W. M., & Grafton, S. T. (2009). Sensitivity of the action observation network to physical and observational learning. *Cerebral Cortex, 19,* 315–326.

Cross, K. P. (1977). Not can, but will college teachers be improved? *New Directions for Higher Education, 17,* 1–15.

Cross-Disorder Group of the Psychiatric Genomics Consortium. (2013). Identification of risk loci with shared effects on five major psychiatric disorders: A genome-wide analysis. *Lancet, 381,* 1371–1379.

Cruess, D. G., Antoni, M. H., Kumar, M., & Schneiderman, N. (2000). Reductions in salivary cortisol are associated with mood improvement during relaxation training among HIV-seropositive men. *Journal of Behavioral Medicine, 23,* 107–122.

Crum-Cianflone, N. F., Bagnell, M. E., Schaller, E., Boyko, E. J., Smith, B., . . . Smith, T. C. (2014). Impact of combat deployment and posttraumatic stress disorder on newly reported coronary heart disease among U.S. active duty and reserve forces. *Circulation, 129,* 1813–1820.

Cruse, D., Chennu, S., Chatelle, C., Fernández-Espejo, D., Bekinschtein, T. A., Pickard, J. D., . . . Owen A. M. (2012). Relationship between etiology and covert cognition in the minimally conscious state. *Neurology, 78*(11), 816–822. doi:10.1212/WNL.0b013e318249f764

Csigó, K., Harsányi, A., Demeter, G., Rajkai, C., Németh, A., & Racsmány, M. (2010). Long-term follow-up of patients with obsessive-compulsive disorder treated by anterior capsulotomy: A neuropsychological study. *Journal of Affective Disorders, 126*(1–2), 198–205.

Csikszentmihalyi, M. (1990). *Flow: The psychology of optimal experience.* New York: Harper & Row.

Cuc, A., Koppel, J., & Hirst, W. (2007). Silence is not golden: A case of socially shared retrieval-induced forgetting. *Psychological Science, 18,* 727–733.

Cuddy, A. J. C., Fiske, S. T., & Glick, P. (2007). The BIAS map: Behaviors from intergroup affect and stereotypes. *Journal of Personality and Social Psychology, 92*(4), 631–648.

Culverhouse, R. C., Saccone, N. L., Horton, A. C., Ma, Y., Antsey, K. J., . . . Bierut, L. J. (2017). Collaborative meta-analysis finds no evidence of a strong interaction between stress and 5-HTTLPR genotype contributing to the development of depression. *Molecular Psychiatry, 23,* 133–142.

Cummins, D. D. (2012). *Good thinking: Seven powerful ideas that influence the way we think.* New York: Cambridge University Press.

Cunningham, M. R., Barbee, A. P., & Pike, C. L. (1990). What do women want? Facial metric assessment of multiple motives in the perception of male facial physical attractiveness. *Journal of Personality and Social Psychology, 59,* 61–72.

Cunningham, M. R., Roberts, A. R., Barbee, A. P., Druen, P. B., & Wu, C.-H. (1995). "Their ideas of beauty are, on the whole, the same as ours": Consistency and variability in the cross-cultural perception of female physical attractiveness. *Journal of Personality and Social Psychology, 68,* 261–279.

Cunningham, W. A., & Brosch, T. (2012). Motivational salience: Amygdala tuning from traits, needs, values, and goals. *Current Directions in Psychological Science, 21*(1), 54–59.

Curran, J. P., & Lippold, S. (1975). The effects of physical attraction and attitude similarity on attraction in dating dyads. *Journal of Personality, 43,* 528–539.

Current Results. (2019). Toronto temperatures: Averages by month. Retrieved from https://www.currentresults.com/Weather/Canada/Ontario/Places/toronto-temperatures-by-month-average.php

Curtiss, S. (1977). *Genie: A psycholinguistic study of a modern-day "wildchild."* New York: Academic Press.

Cushman, F., Sheketoff, R., Wharton, S., & Carey, S. (2013). The development of intend-based moral judgment. *Cognition, 127,* 6–21.

D'Agostino, P. R., & Fincher-Kiefer, R. (1992). Need for cognition and correspondence bias. *Social Cognition, 10,* 151–163.

D'Esposito, M. & Postle, B. R. (2015). The cognitive neuroscience of working memory. *Annual Review of Psychology, 66,* 115–142.

Dabbs, J. M., Bernieri, F. J., Strong, R. K., Campo, R., & Milun, R. (2001). Going on stage: Testosterone in greetings and meetings. *Journal of Research in Personality, 35,* 27–40.

Dael, N., Mortillaro, M., & Scherer, K. R. (2012). Emotion expression in body action and posture. *Emotion, 12,* 1085–1101.

Dagher, A., & Robbins, T. W. (2009). Personality, addiction, dopamine: Insights from Parkinson's disease. *Neuron, 61,* 502–510.

Dalton, P. (2003). Olfaction. In H. Pashler & S. Yantis (Eds.), *Stevens' handbook of experimental psychology: Vol. 1. Sensation and perception* (3rd ed., pp. 691–746). New York: Wiley.

Daly, M., & Wilson, M. (1988). Evolutionary social psychology and family homicide. *Science, 242,* 519–524.

Damasio, A. R. (1989). Time-locked multiregional retroactivation: A systems-level proposal for the neural substrates of recall and recognition. *Cognition, 33,* 25–62.

Damasio, A. R. (1994). *Descartes' error: Emotion, reason, and the human brain.* New York: Putnam.

Damasio, A. R. (2005). *Descartes' error: Emotion, reason, and the human brain.* New York: Penguin.

Damasio, A. R., Grabowski, T. J., Bechara, A., Damasio, H., Ponto, L. L. B., Parvisi, J., & Hichwa, R. D. (2000). Subcortical and cortical brain activity during the feeling of self-generated emotions. *Nature Neuroscience, 3,* 1049–1056.

Damasio, H., Grabowski, T. J., Tranel, D., Hichwa, R. D., & Damasio, A. R. (1996). A neural basis for lexical retrieval. *Nature, 380,* 499–505.

Damerius, L. A., Forss, S. I. F., Kosonen, Z. K., Willems, E. P., Burkhart, J. M., Call, J., . . ., van Schaik, C. P. (2017). Orientation toward humans predicts cognitive performance in orang-utans. *Scientific Reports, 7,* Art. No.: 40052.

Damsma, G., Pfaus, J. G., Wenkstern, D., Phillips, A. G., & Fibiger, H. C. (1992). Sexual behavior increases dopamine transmission in the nucleus accumbens and striatum of male rats: Comparison with novelty and locomotion. *Behavioral Neurosciences, 106,* 181–191.

Daneshvar, D. H., Nowinski, C. J., McKee, A. C., & Cantu, R. C. (2011). The epidemiology of sport-related concussion. *Clinical Sports Medicine, 30,* 1–17.

Daniel, H. J., O'Brien, K. F., McCabe, R. B., & Quinter, V. E. (1985). Values in mate selection: A 1984 campus survey. *College Student Journal, 19,* 44–50.

Danner, U. N., Ouwehand, C., van Haastert, N. L., Homsveld, H., & de Ridder, D. T. (2012). Decision-making impairments in women with binge eating disorder in comparison with obese and normal weight women. *European Eating Disorders Review, 20,* e56–e62.

Darley, J. M., & Gross, P. H. (1983). A hypothesis-confirming bias in labeling effects. *Journal of Personality and Social Psychology, 44,* 20–33.

Darley, J. M., & Latané, B. (1968). Bystander intervention in emergencies: Diffusion of responsibility. *Journal of Personality and Social Psychology, 8,* 377–383.

Dar-Nimrod, I., & Heine, S. J. (2006). Exposure to scientific theories affects women's math performance. *Science, 314,* 435.

Darwin, C. (2007). *The expression of the emotions in man and animals.* New York: Bibliobazaar. (Original work published 1899.)

Darwin, C. J., Turvey, M. T., & Crowder, R. G. (1972). An auditory analogue of the Sperling partial report procedure: Evidence for brief auditory storage. *Cognitive Psychology, 3,* 255–267.

Dasgupta, N. (2013). Implicit attitudes and beliefs adapt to situations: A decade of research on the malleability of implicit prejudice, stereotypes, and the self-concept. *Advances in Experimental Social Psychology, 47,* 233–279.

Dauer, W., & Przedborski, S. (2003). Parkinson's disease: Mechanisms and models. *Neuron, 39,* 889–909.

Daum, I., Schugens, M. M., Ackermann, H., Lutzenberger, W., Dichgans, J., & Birbaumer, N. (1993). Classical conditioning after cerebellar lesions in humans. *Behavioral Neuroscience, 107,* 748–756.

David-Barrett, T., Kertesz, J., Rotkirch, A., Ghosh, A., Bhattacharya, K., Monsivais, D., & Kaski, K. (2016). Communication with family and friends across the life course. *PLoS ONE, 11*(11), 1–15. https://doi.org/10.1371/journal.pone.0165687

Davidson, R. J., Ekman, P., Saron, C., Senulis, J., & Friesen, W. V. (1990). Emotional expression and brain physiology I: Approach/withdrawal and cerebral asymmetry. *Journal of Personality and Social Psychology, 58,* 330–341.

Davidson, R. J., Putnam, K. M., & Larson, C. L. (2000). Dysfunction in the neural circuitry of emotion regulation—a possible prelude to violence. *Science, 289,* 591–594.

Davies, G, Tenesa, A., Payton, A., Yang, J., Harris, S. E., Liewald, D., . . . Deary, I. J. (2011). Genome-wide association studies establish that human intelligence is highly heritable and polygenic. *Molecular Psychiatry, 16*(10), 996–1005.

Davies, G. (1988). Faces and places: Laboratory research on context and face recognition. In G. M. Davies & D. M. Thomson (Eds.), *Memory in context: Context in memory* (pp. 35–53). New York: Wiley.

Davila Ross, M., Menzler, S., & Zimmermann, E. (2008). Rapid facial mimicry in orangutan play. *Biology Letters, 4*(1), 27–30.

Davis, S., & Wahlin-Jacobsen, S. (2015). Testosterone in women—the clinical significance. *Lancet Diabetes & Endocrinology, 3,* 980–992.

Dawes, R. M. (1994). *House of cards: Psychology and psychotherapy built on myth.* New York: Free Press.

Dawood, K., Kirk, K. M., Bailey, J. M., Andrews, P. W., & Martin, N. G. (2005). Genetic and environmental influences on the frequency of orgasm in women. *Twin Research, 8,* 27–33.

Dawson, G., & Sapiro, G. (2019). Potential for digital behavioral measurement tools to transform the detection and diagnosis of autism spectrum disorder. *Journal of the American Medical Association Pediatrics, 173,* 305–306.

Dawson, G., Jones, E. J. H., Merkle, K., Venema, K., Lowry, R., Faja, S., . . . Webb, S. J. (2012). Early behavioral intervention is associated with normalized brain activity in young children with autism. *Journal of the American Academy of Child and Adolescent Psychiatry, 51,* 1150–1159.

Dawson, G., Rogers, S., Munson, J., Smith, M., Winter, J., Greenson, J., . . . Varley, J. (2010). Randomized, controlled trial of an intervention for toddlers with autism: The Early Start Denver Model. *Pediatrics, 125,* e17–e23.

Dawson, M., Soulieres, I., Gernsbacher, M. A., & Mottron, L. (2007). The level and nature of autistic intelligence. *Psychological Science, 18,* 657–662.

Day, J. J., & Sweatt, J. D. (2011). Epigenetic mechanisms in cognition. *Neuron, 70,* 813–829.

Dayan, E., & Bar-Hillel, M. (2011). Nudge to nobesity II: Menu positions influence food orders. *Judgment and Decision Making, 6*(4), 333–342.

Dayan, P., & Huys, Q. J. M. (2009). Serotonin in affective control. *Annual Review of Neuroscience, 32,* 95–126.

de Araujo, I. E., Rolls, E. T., Velazco, M. I., Margot, C., & Cayeux, I. (2005). Cognitive modulation of olfactory processing. *Neuron, 46,* 671–679.

de Bloom, J., Sianoja, M., Korpela, K., Tuomisto, M., Lilja, A., Geurts, S., & Kinnunen, U. (2017). Effects of park walks and relaxation exercises during lunch breaks on recovery from job stress: Two randomized controlled trials. *Journal of Environmental Psychology, 51,* 14–30.

De Bolle, M., De Fryut, F., McCrae, R. R., Löckenhoff, C. E., Costa, P. T. Jr., Aguilar-Valfae, M. E., . . . Terracciano, A. (2015). The emergence of sex differences in personality traits in early adolescence: A cross-sectional, cross-cultural study. *Journal of Personality and Social Psychology, 108,* 171–185.

De Neys, W., & Van Gelder, E. (2009). Logic and belief across the lifespan: The rise and fall of belief inhibition during syllogistic reasoning. *Developmental Science, 12,* 123–130.

de Rosnay, M., Pons, F., Harris, P. L., & Morrell, J. M. B. (2004). A lag between understanding false belief and emotion attribution in young children: Relationships with linguistic ability and mothers' mental-state language. *British Journal of Developmental Psychology, 24*(1), 197–218.

De Simoni, C., & von Bastian, C. C. (2018). Working memory updating and binding training: Bayesian evidence supporting the absence of transfer. *Journal of Experimental Psychology: General, 147,* 829–858.

De Vries, M. H., Barth, A. C. R., Maiworm, S., Knecht, S., Zwitserlood, P., & Flöel, A. (2010). Electrical stimulation of Broca's area enhances implicit learning of an artificial grammar. *Journal of Cognitive Neuroscience, 22,* 2427–2436.

De Wolff, M., & van IJzendoorn, M. H. (1997). Sensitivity and attachment: A meta-analysis on parental antecedents of infant attachment. *Child Development, 68,* 571–591.

Deady, D. K., & Law Smith, M. J. (2015) Changing male preferences for female body type in the U.S.: An adaptive response to a changing socioeconomic climate. *Journal of Behavioral and Brain Science, 5,* 570–577. http://dx.doi.org/10.4236/jbbs.2015.513054

Deák, G. O. (2006). Do children really confuse appearance and reality? *Trends in Cognitive Sciences, 10*(12), 546–550.

Deary, I. J. (2000). *Looking down on human intelligence: From psychometrics to the brain.* New York: Oxford University Press.

Deary, I. J. (2012). Intelligence. *Annual Review of Psychology, 63*(1), 453–482.

Deary, I. J., Batty, G. D., & Gale, C. R. (2008). Bright children become enlightened adults. *Psychological Science, 19*(1), 1–6.

Deary, I. J., Batty, G. D., Pattie, A., & Gale, C. R. (2008). More intelligent, more dependable children live longer: A 55-year longitudinal study of a representative sample of the Scottish nation. *Psychological Science, 19,* 874.

Deary, I. J., Taylor, M. D., Hart, C. L., Wilson, V., Smith, G. D., Blane, D., & Starr, J. M. (2005). Intergenerational social mobility and mid-life status attainment: Influences of childhood intelligence, childhood social factors, and education. *Intelligence, 33*(5), 455–472.

Deary, I. J., Weiss, A., & Batty, G. D. (2011). Intelligence and personality as predictors of illness and death: How researchers in differential psychology and chronic disease epidemiology are collaborating to understand and address health inequalities. *Psychological Science in the Public Interest, 11*(2), 53–79.

Deci, E. L. (1971). Effects of externally mediated rewards on intrinsic motivation. *Journal of Personality and Social Psychology, 18,* 105–115.

Deci, E. L., Koestner, R., & Ryan, R. M. (1999). A meta-analytic review of experiments examining the effects of extrinsic rewards on intrinsic motivation. *Psychological Bulletin, 125,* 627–668.

Deese, J. (1959). On the prediction of occurrence of particular verbal intrusions in immediate recall. *Journal of Experimental Psychology, 58,* 17–22.

DeFelipe, J., & Jones, E. G. (1988). *Cajal on the cerebral cortex: An annotated translation of the complete writings.* New York: Oxford University Press.

Degenhardt, L., Chiu, W. T., Sampson, N., Kessler, R. C., Anthony, J. C., Angermeyer, M., . . . Wells, J. E. (2008). Toward a global view of alcohol, tobacco, cannabis, and cocaine use: Findings from the WHO World Mental Health surveys. *PLoS Medicine, 5,* e141.

Dekker, M. C., & Koot, H. M. (2003). DSM–IV disorders in children with borderline to moderate intellectual disability: I. Prevalence and impact. *Journal of the American Academy of Child and Adolescent Psychiatry, 42*(8), 915–922.

Dekker, S., Lee, N. C., Howard-Jones, P., & Jolles, J. (2012). Neuromyths in education: Prevalence and predictors of misconceptions among teachers. *Frontiers in Psychology, 3,* 429. doi:10.3389/fpsyg.2012.00429

Deković, M., Noom, M. J., & Meeus, W. (1997). Expectations regarding development during adolescence: Parental and adolescent perceptions. *Journal of Youth and Adolescence, 26,* 253–272.

Del Vicario, M., Bessi, A., Zollo, F., Petroni, F., Scalaa, A., Caldarelli, G., . . . Quattrociocchi, W. (2016). The spreading of misinformation online. *Proceedings of the National Academy of Sciences USA, 113*(3), 554–559. doi:10.1073/pnas.1517441113

Delgado, M. R., Frank, R. H., & Phelps, E. A. (2005). Perceptions of moral character modulate the neural systems of reward during the trust game. *Nature Neuroscience, 8,* 1611–1618.

DeLoache, J. S., Uttal, D. H., & Rosengren, K. S. (2004). Scale errors offer evidence for a perception–action dissociation early in life. *Science, 304*(5673), 1027–1029.

Demb, J. B., Desmond, J. E., Wagner, A. D., Vaidya, C. J., Glover, G. H., & Gabrieli, J. D. E. (1995). Semantic encoding and retrieval in the left inferior prefrontal cortex: A functional MRI study of task difficulty and process specificity. *Journal of Neuroscience, 15,* 5870–5878.

Dement, W. C. (1959, November 30). Dreams. *Newsweek.*

Dement, W. C. (1978). *Some must watch while some must sleep.* New York: Norton.

Dement, W. C. (1999). *The promise of sleep.* New York: Delacorte Press.

Dement, W. C., & Kleitman, N. (1957). The relation of eye movements during sleep to dream activity: An objective method for the study of dreaming. *Journal of Experimental Psychology, 53,* 339–346.

Dement, W. C., & Wolpert, E. (1958). Relation of eye movements, body motility, and external stimuli to dream content. *Journal of Experimental Psychology, 55,* 543–553.

Dempster, E. L., Pidsley, R., Schalkwyk, L. C., Owens, S., Georgiades, A., Kane, F., . . . Mill, J. (2011). Disease-associated epigenetic changes in monozygotic twins discordant for schizophrenia and bipolar disorder. *Human Molecular Genetics, 20,* 4786–4796.

Denissen, J. J., Geenen, R., Soto, C. J., John, O. P., & van Aken, M. A. G. (2019). The Big Five Inventory-2: Replication of psychometric properties in a Dutch adaptation and first evidence for the discriminant predictive validity of the facet scales. *Journal of Personality Assessment.* doi:10.1080/00233891.2018.1539004

Dennett, D. (1991). *Consciousness explained.* New York: Basic Books.

Denny, B. T., & Ochsner, K. N. (2014). Behavioral effects of longitudinal training in cognitive reappraisal. *Emotion, 14*(2), 425–433. doi:10.1037/a0035276

Denson, T. F., O'Dean, S. M., Blake, K. R., & Beames, K. R. (2018). Aggression in women: Behavior, brain and hormones. *Frontiers in Behavioral Neuroscience, 12.* doi-org.ezp-prod1.hul.harvard.edu/10.3389/fnbeh.2018.00081

DePaulo, B. M., Charlton, K., Cooper, H., Lindsay, J. J., & Muhlenbruck, L. (1997). The accuracy–confidence correlation in the detection of deception. *Personality and Social Psychology Review, 1,* 346–357.

DePaulo, B. M., Lindsay, J. J., Malone, B. E., Muhlenbruck, L., Charlton, K., & Cooper, H. (2003). Cues to deception. *Psychological Bulletin, 129,* 74–118.

Der, G., Batty, G. D., & Deary, I. J. (2009). The association between IQ in adolescence and a range of health outcomes at 40 in the 1979 U.S. national longitudinal study of youth. *Intelligence, 37*(6), 573–580.

DeRubeis, R. J., Cohen, Z. D., Forand, N. R., Fournier, J. C., Gelfand, L. A., & Lorenzo-Luaces, L. (2014). The personalized advantage index: Translating research on prediction into individualized treatment recommendations: A demonstration. *PLoS ONE, 9,* e83875.

DeRubeis, R. J., Siegle, G. J., & Hollon, S. D. (2008). Cognitive therapy vs. medication for depression: Treatment outcomes and neural mechanisms. *Nature Reviews Neuroscience, 9*(10), 788–796.

DeVilliers, P. (2005). The role of language in theory-of-mind development: What deaf children tell us. In J. W. Astington & J. A. Baird (Eds.), *Why language matters for theory of mind* (pp. 266–297). Oxford: Oxford University Press.

Dewa, C. S., Chau, N., & Dermer, S. (2010). Examining the comparative incidence and costs of physical and mental health–related disabilities in an employed population. *Journal of Occupational and Environmental Medicine, 52*(7), 758–762.

Dewhurst, S. A., Anderson, R. J., Grace, L., & van Esch, L. (2016). Adaptive false memories: Imagining future scenarios increases false memories in the DRM paradigm. *Memory & Cognition, 44,* 1076–1084.

DeYoung, C. G., & Gray, J. R. (2009). Personality neuroscience: Explaining individual differences in affect, behavior, and cognition. In P. J. Corr & G. Matthews (Eds.), *The Cambridge handbook of personality psychology* (pp. 323–346). New York: Cambridge University Press.

DeYoung, C. G., Hirsh, J. B., Shane, M. S., Papademetris, X., Rajeevan, N., & Gray, J. R. (2010). Testing predictions from personality neuroscience: Brain structure and the Big Five. *Psychological Science, 21,* 820–828.

Diaconis, P., & Mosteller, F. (1989). Methods for studying coincidences. *Journal of the American Statistical Association, 84,* 853–861.

Diano, S., Farr, S. A., Benoit, S. C., McNay, E. C., da Silva, I., Horvath, B., . . . Horvath, T. L. (2006). Ghrelin controls hippocampal spine synapse density and memory performance. *Nature Neuroscience, 9*(3), 381–388.

Dickens, W. T., & Flynn, J. R. (2001). Heritability estimates versus large environmental effects: The IQ paradox resolved. *Psychological Review, 108,* 346–369.

Dickinson, A., Watt, A., & Griffiths, J. H. (1992). Free-operant acquisition with delayed reinforcement. *Quarterly Journal of Experimental Psychology Section B: Comparative and Physiological Psychology, 45,* 241–258.

Didden, R., Sigafoos, J., Lang, R., O'Reilly, M., Drieschner, K., & Lancioni, G. E. (2012). Intellectual disabilities. In P. Sturmey & M. Hersen (Eds.), *Handbook of evidence-based practice in clinical psychology.* Hoboken, NJ: Wiley.

DiDonato, T. E., Ullrich, J., & Krueger, J. I. (2011). Social perception as induction and inference: An integrative model of intergroup differentiation, ingroup favoritism, and differential accuracy. *Journal of Personality and Social Psychology, 100*(1), 66–83. doi:10.1037/a0021051

Diederich, N. J., & Goetz, C. G. (2008). The placebo treatments in neurosciences: New insights from clinical and neuroimaging studies. *Neurology, 71,* 677–684.

Diedrichsen, J., King, M., Hernandez-Castillo, C., Sereno, M., & Ivry, R. B. (2019). Universal transform or multiple functionality? Understanding the contribution of the human cerebellum across task domains. *Neuron, 102*(5), 918–928.

Diekelmann, S., & Born, J. (2010). The memory function of sleep. *Nature Reviews Neuroscience, 11,* 114–126

Dijksterhuis, A. (2004). Think different: The merits of unconscious thought in preference development and decision making. *Journal of Personality and Social Psychology, 87,* 586–598.

Dimberg, U. (1982). Facial reactions to facial expressions. *Psychophysiology, 19,* 643–647.

Dion, K. L. (2005). Marital status as stimulus variable and subject variable. *Psychological Inquiry, 16,* 104–110.

Dion, K., Berscheid, E., & Walster, E. (1972). What is beautiful is good. *Journal of Personality and Social Psychology, 24,* 285–290.

Dismukes, R. K. (2012). Prospective memory in workplace and everyday situations. *Current Directions in Psychological Science, 21,* 215–220.

Disner, S. G., Beevers, C. G., Haigh, E. A., & Beck, A. T. (2011). Neural mechanisms of the cognitive model of depression. *Nature Reviews Neuroscience, 12,* 467–477.

Dittrich, W. H., Troscianko, T., Lea, S., & Morgan, D. (1996). Perception of emotion from dynamic point-light displays represented in dance. *Perception, 25,* 727–738. doi:10.3389/fpsyg.2011.00337

Dobbin, F., & Kalev, A. (2018). Why doesn't diversity training work? The challenge for industry and academia. *Anthropology Now, 10*(2), 48–55.

Dollard, J., Doob, L. W., Miller, N. E., Mowrer, O. H., & Sears, R. R. (1939). *Frustration and aggression.* Oxford: Yale University Press.

Domjan, M. (2005). Pavlovian conditioning: A functional perspective. *Annual Review of Psychology, 56,* 179–206.

Dostoyevsky, F. (1863/1988). *Winter notes on summer impressions* (D. Patterson, Trans.). Evanston, IL: Northwestern University Press.

Doucet, S., Soussignan, R., Sagot, P., & Schaal, B. (2009). The secretion of areolar (Montgomery's) glands from lactating women elicits selective, unconditional responses in neonates. *PLoS ONE, 4,* e7579. doi:10.1371/journal.pone.0007579

Doucet, S., Soussignan, R., Sagot, P., & Schaal, B. (2012). An overlooked aspect of the human breast: Areolar glands in relation with breastfeeding pattern, neonatal weight gain, and the dynamics of lactation. *Early Human Development, 88,* 119–128.

Dougherty, D. D., Brennan, B. P., Stewart, S. E., Wilhelm, S., Widge, A. S., & Rauch, S. L. (2018). Neuroscientifically informed formulation and treatment planning for patients with obsessive-compulsive disorder: A review. *Journal of the American Medical Association Psychiatry, 75,* 1081–1087.

Dovidio, J. F., & Gaertner, S. L. (2010). Intergroup bias. In S. T. Fiske, D. T. Gilbert, & G. Lindzey (Eds.), *The handbook of social psychology* (5th ed., Vol. 2, pp. 1085–1121). New York: Wiley.

Downer, J. D. C. (1961). Changes in visual gnostic function and emotional behavior following unilateral temporal damage in the "split-brain" monkey. *Nature, 191,* 50–51.

Dresler, M., Shirer, W. R., Konrad, B. N., Müller, N. C. J., Wagner, I. C., Fernández, G., . . . Greicius, M.D. (2017). Mnemonic training reshapes brain networks to support superior memory. *Neuron, 93*(5), 1227–1235.

Duckworth, A. L., & Seligman, M. E. P. (2005). Self-discipline outdoes IQ in predicting academic performance of adolescents. *Psychological Science, 16,* 939–944.

Dudai, Y. (2012). The restless engram: Consolidations never end. *Annual Review of Neuroscience, 35,* 227–247.

Dudycha, G. J., & Dudycha, M. M. (1933). Some factors and characteristics of childhood memories. *Child Development, 4,* 265–278.

Duenwald, M. (2002, September 12). Students find another staple of campus life: Stress. *New York Times.* Retrieved from http://www.nytimes.com/2002/09/17/health/students-find-another-staple-of-campus-life-stress.html?pagewanted=all&src=pm

Duff, M. C., Kurczek, J., Rubin, R., Cohen, N. J., & Tranel, D. (2013). Hippocampal amnesia disrupts creative thinking. *Hippocampus, 23,* 1143–1149.

Duñabeitia, J. A., Hernández, J. A., Antón, E., Macizo, P., Estévez, A., Fuentes, L. J., & Carreiras, M. (2014). The inhibitory advantage in bilingual children revisited: Myth or reality? *Experimental Psychology, 61,* 234–251.

Duncan, G. J., Yeung, W. J., Brooks-Gunn, J., & Smith, J. R. (1998). How much does childhood poverty affect the life chances of children? *American Sociological Review, 63,* 406–423.

Duncker, K. (1945). On problem-solving. (L. S. Lees, Trans.). *Psychological Monographs, 58*(5), i–113.

Dunham, Y., Chen, E. E., & Banaji, M. R. (2013). Two signatures of implicit intergroup attitudes: Developmental invariance and early enculturation. *Psychological Science, 6,* 860–868. doi:10.1177/0956797612463081

Dunlap, K. (1919). Are there any instincts? *Journal of Abnormal Psychology, 14,* 307–311.

Dunlop, S. A. (2008). Activity-dependent plasticity: Implications for recovery after spinal cord injury. *Trends in Neurosciences, 31,* 410–418.

Dunlosky, J., & Rawson, K. A. (2012). Overconfidence produces underachievement: Inaccurate self-evaluations undermine students' learning and retention. *Learning and Instruction, 22,* 271–280.

Dunlosky, J., & Thiede, K. W. (2013). Four cornerstones of calibration research: Why understanding students' judgments can improve their achievement. *Learning and Instruction, 24,* 58–61.

Dunlosky, J., Rawson, K. A., Marsh, E. J., Nathan, M. J., & Willingham, D. T. (2013). Improving students' learning with effective learning techniques: Promising directions from cognitive and educational psychology. *Psychological Science in the Public Interest, 14*(1), 4–58.

Dunn, J. C., & Kirsner, K. (2011). The search for HMAS Sydney II: Analysis and integration of survivor reports. *Journal of Applied Cognitive Psychology, 25,* 513–527.

Dunphy, D. C. (1963). The social structure of urban adolescent peer groups. *Sociometry, 26,* 230–246.

Dutton, D. G., & Aron, A. P. (1974). Some evidence for heightened sexual attraction under conditions of high anxiety. *Journal of Personality and Social Psychology, 30,* 510–517.

Dutton, E., van der Linden, D., Lynn, R. (2016). The negative Flynn effect: A systematic literature review. *Intelligence, 59,* 163–169.

Duval, S., & Wicklund, R. A. (1972). *A theory of objective self-awareness.* New York: Academic Press.

Dworkin, E. R., Menon, S. V., Bystrynski, J., & Allen, N. E. (2017). Sexual assault victimization and psychopathology: A review and meta-analysis. *Clinical Psychology Review, 56,* 65–81.

Eagly, A. H., & Wood, W. (1999). The origins of sex differences in human behavior: Evolved dispositions versus social roles. *American Psychologist, 54,* 408–423.

Eagly, A. H., Ashmore, R. D., Makhijani, M. G., & Longo, L. C. (1991). What is beautiful is good, but . . . : A meta-analytic review of research on the physical attractiveness stereotype. *Psychological Bulletin, 110,* 109–128.

Eastwick, P. W. (2009). Beyond the Pleistocene: Using phylogeny and constraint to inform the evolutionary psychology of human mating. *Psychological Bulletin, 135,* 794–821.

Eastwick, P. W., Eagly, A. H., Finkel, E. J., & Johnson, S. E. (2011). Implicit and explicit preferences for physical attractiveness in a romantic partner: A double dissociation in predictive validity.

Journal of Personality and Social Psychology, 101(5), 993–1011. doi:10.1037/a0024061

Eastwick, P. W., Finkel, E. J., Mochon, D., & Ariely, D. (2007). Selective versus unselective romantic desire: Not all reciprocity is created equal. *Psychological Science, 18,* 317–319.

Eaton, W. W., Shao, H., Nestadt, G., Lee, B. H., Bienvenu, O. J., & Zandi, P. (2008). Population-based study of first onset and chronicity of major depressive disorder. *Archives of General Psychiatry, 65,* 513–520.

Ebbinghaus, H. (1908). *Psychology: An elementary textbook.* Boston: Heath.

Ebbinghaus, H. (1964). *Memory: A contribution to experimental psychology.* New York: Dover. (Original work published 1885)

Ecklund, E. H., Scheitle, C. P., & Pennsylvania, T. (2007). Religion among academic scientists: Distinctions, disciplines, and demographics. *Social Problems, 54*(2), 289–307.

Eddy, D. M. (1982). Probabilistic reasoning in clinical medicine: Problems and opportunities. In D. Kahneman, P. Slovic, & A. Tversky (Eds.), *Judgments under uncertainty: Heuristics and biases* (pp. 249– 267). New York: Cambridge University Press.

Edgerton, V. R., Tillakaratne, J. K. T., Bigbee, A. J., deLeon, R. D., & Roy, R. R. (2004). Plasticity of the spinal neural circuitry after injury. *Annual Review of Neuroscience, 27,* 145–167.

Edwards, W. (1955). The theory of decision making. *Psychological Bulletin, 51,* 201–214.

Efferson, C., Lalive, R., & Fehr, E. (2008). The coevolution of cultural groups and ingroup favoritism. *Science, 321,* 1844–1849.

Eguchi, A., Isbister, J. B., Ahmad, N., & Stringer, S. (2018). The emergence of polychronization and feature binding in a spiking neural network model of the primate ventral visual system. *Psychological Review, 125,* 545–571.

Eich, J. E. (1995). Searching for mood dependent memory. *Psychological Science, 6,* 67–75.

Eichenbaum, H. (2008). *Learning & memory.* New York: Norton.

Eichenbaum, H., & Cohen, N. J. (2001). *From conditioning to conscious recollection: Memory systems of the brain.* New York: Oxford University Press.

Eimas, P. D., Siqueland, E. R., Jusczyk, P., & Vigorito, J. (1971). Speech perception in infants. *Science, 171,* 303–306.

Ein-Gar, D., Shiv, B., & Tormala, Z. L. (2012). When blemishing leads to blossoming: The positive effect of negative information. *Journal of Consumer Research, 38,* 846–859.

Einstein, G. O., & McDaniel, M. A. (1990). Normal aging and prospective memory. *Journal of Experimental Psychology: Learning, Memory, and Cognition, 16,* 717–726.

Einstein, G. O., & McDaniel, M. A. (2005). Prospective memory: Multiple retrieval processes. *Current Direction in Psychological Science, 14,* 286–290.

Eisenberg, M. J., Atallah, R., Grandi, S. M., Windle, S. B., & Berry, E. M. (2011). Legislative approaches to tackling the obesity epidemic. *CMAJ, 183*(13), 1496–1500. doi:10.1503/cmaj.101522

Eisenberg, N., Fabes, R. A., Guthrie, I. K., & Reiser, M. (2000). Dispositional emotionality and regulation: Their role in predicting quality of social functioning. *Journal of Personality and Social Psychology, 78,* 136.

Eisenberger, N. I., Lieberman, M. D., & Williams, K. D. (2003). Does rejection hurt? An fMRI study of social exclusion. *Science, 302,* 290–292. doi:10.1126/science.1089134

Eisenegger, C., Haushofer, J., & Fehr, E. (2011). The role of testosterone in social interaction. *Trends in Cognitive Sciences, 15*(6), 263–271. doi:10.1016/j.tics.2011.04.008

Eisenegger, C., Naef, M., Snozzi, R., Heinrichs, M., & Fehr, E. (2010). Prejudice and truth about the effect of testosterone on human bargaining behaviour. *Nature, 463,* 356–359.

Ekman, P. (1965). Differential communication of affect by head and body cues. *Journal of Personality and Social Psychology, 2,* 726–735.

Ekman, P. (1972). Universals and cultural differences in facial expressions of emotion. In J. K. Cole (Ed.), *Nebraska Symposium on Motivation, 1971* (pp. 207–283). Lincoln: University of Nebraska Press.

Ekman, P. (2003). Darwin, deception, and facial expression. *Annals of the New York Academy of Sciences, 1000,* 205–221.

Ekman, P. (2016). What scientists who study emotion agree about. *Perspectives on Psychological Science, 11*(1), 31–34.

Ekman, P., & Friesen, W. V. (1968). Nonverbal behavior in psychotherapy research. In J. M. Shlien (Ed.), *Research in psychotherapy* (Vol. 3, pp. 179–216). Washington, DC: American Psychological Association.

Ekman, P., & Friesen, W. V. (1971). Constants across cultures in the face and emotion. *Journal of Personality and Social Psychology, 17,* 124–129.

Ekman, P., & Friesen, W. V. (1982). Felt, false, and miserable smiles. *Journal of Nonverbal Behavior, 6,* 238–252.

Ekman, P., Levenson, R. W., & Friesen, W. V. (1983). Autonomic nervous system activity distinguishes among emotions. *Science, 221,* 1208–1210.

El Haj, M., Gallouj, K., & Antoine, P. (2017). Google Calendar enhances prospective memory in Alzheimer's disease: A case report. *Journal of Alzheimer's Disease, 57,* 285–291.

Elbogen, E. B., & Johnson, S. C. (2009). The intricate link between violence and mental disorder. *Archives of General Psychiatry, 66*(2), 152–161.

Eldridge, L. L., Knowlton, B. J., Furmanski, C. S., Bookheimer, S. Y., & Engel, S. A. (2000). Remembering episodes: A selective role for the hippocampus during retrieval. *Nature Neuroscience, 3,* 1149–1152.

Eldridge, M. A., Barnard, P. J., & Bekerian, D. A. (1994). Autobiographical memory and daily schemas at work. *Memory, 2,* 51–74.

Elfenbein, H. A., & Ambady, N. (2002). On the universality and cultural specificity of emotion recognition: A meta-analysis. *Psychological Bulletin, 128,* 203–235.

Elfenbein, H. A., Beaupré, M., Lévesque, M., & Hess, U. (2007). Toward a dialect theory: Cultural differences in the expression and recognition of posed facial expressions. *Emotion, 7*(1), 131–146.

Elias, B., Mignone, J., Hall, M., Hong, S. P., Hart, L., & Sareen, J. (2012). Trauma and suicide behaviour histories among a Canadian indigenous population: An empirical exploration of the potential role of Canada's residential school system. *Social Science & Medicine, 74*(10), 1560–1569.

Ellemers, N. (2012). The group self. *Science, 336*(6083), 848–852. doi:10.10.1126/science.1220987

Ellenbogen, J. M., Payne, J. D., & Stickgold, R. (2006). The role of sleep in declarative memory consolidation: Passive, permissive, or none? *Current Opinion in Neurobiology, 16,* 716–722.

Elliott, R., Sahakian, B. J., Matthews, K., Bannerjea, A., Rimmer, J., & Robbins, T. W. (1997). Effects of methylphenidate on spatial working memory and planning in healthy young adults. *Psychopharmacology, 131,* 196–206.

Ellis, A. (1991). *Reason and emotion in psychotherapy.* New York: Carol.

Ellis, B. J., & Garber, J. (2000). Psychosocial antecedents of variation in girls' pubertal timing: Maternal depression, stepfather presence, and marital and family stress. *Child Development, 71,* 485–501.

Ellis, E. M. (1983). A review of empirical rape research: Victim reactions and response to treatment. *Clinical Psychology Review, 3,* 473–490.

Ellis, L., & Ames, M. A. (1987). Neurohormonal functioning in sexual orientation: A theory of homosexuality–heterosexuality. *Psychological Bulletin, 101,* 233–258.

Ellman, S. J., Spielman, A. J., Luck, D., Steiner, S. S., & Halperin, R. (1991). REM deprivation: A review. In S. J. Ellman & J. S. Antrobus (Eds.), *The mind in sleep: Psychology and psychophysiology* (2nd ed., pp. 329–376). New York: Wiley.

Ellsworth, P. C., & Scherer, K. R. (2003). Appraisal processes in emotion. In R. J. Davidson, K. R. Scherer, & H. H. Goldsmith (Eds.), *The handbook of affective science* (pp. 572–595). New York: Oxford University Press.

Elsey, J. W. B., Van Ast, V. A., & Kindt, M. (2018). Human memory reconsolidation: A guiding framework and critical review of the evidence. *Psychological Bulletin, 144,* 797–848.

eMentalHealth.ca. (2019, June 9). Panic attacks in adults. Retrieved from http://www.ementalhealth.ca/Ottawa-Carleton /Panic-Attacks-Adults/index.php?m=article&ID=8899

Emerson, R. C., Bergen, J. R., & Adelson, E. H. (1992). Directionally selective complex cells and the computation of motion energy in cat visual cortex. *Vision Research, 32,* 203–218.

Epel, E. S., Blackburn, E. H., Lin, J., Dhabhar, F. S., Adler, N. E., Morrow, J. D., & Cawthorn, R. M. (2004). Accelerated telomere shortening in response to life stress. *Proceedings of the National Academy of Sciences, USA, 101,* 17312–17315.

Epel, E. S., Daubenmier, J., Moskowitz, J. T., Foldman, S., & Blackburn, E. H. (2009). Can meditation slow rate of cellular aging? Cognitive stress, mindfulness, and telomerase. *Annals of the New York Academy of Sciences, 1172,* 34–53.

Epley, N., & Waytz, A. (2010). Mind perception. In S. T. Fiske, D. T. Gilbert, & G. Lindzey (Eds.), *The handbook of social psychology* (5th ed., Vol. 1, pp. 498–541). New York: Wiley.

Epstein, R. (2007a). *The case against adolescence: Rediscovering the adult in every teen.* New York: Quill Driver.

Epstein, R. (2007b). The myth of the teen brain. *Scientific American Mind, 18,* 27–31.

Erffmeyer, E. S. (1984). Rule-violating behavior on the golf course. *Perceptual and Motor Skills, 59,* 591–596.

Ericsson, K. A., & Charness, N. (1999). Expert performance: Its structure and acquisition. In S. J. Ceci & W. M. Williams (Eds.), *The nature–nurture debate: The essential readings* (pp. 200–256). Oxford, England: Blackwell.

Erikson, E. H. (1959). *Identity and the life cycle.* New York: International Universities Press.

Eriksson, K., Vartanova, I., Strimling, P., & Simpson, B. (2019). Generosity pays: Selfish people have fewer children and earn less money. *Journal of Personality and Social Psychology.* http://dx.doi.org/10.1037/pspp0000213

Estes, A., Munson, J., Rogers, S. J., Greenson, J., Winter, J., & Dawson, G. (2015). Long-term outcomes of early intervention in 6-year-old children with Autism Spectrum Disorder. *Journal of the American Academy of Child and Adolescent Psychiatry, 54,* 580–587.

Etcoff, N. (1999). *Survival of the prettiest: The science of beauty.* New York: Doubleday.

Evans, G. W. (2006). Child development and the physical environment. *Annual Review of Psychology, 57,* 423–451.

Evans, G. W., & Stecker, R. (2004). Motivational consequences of environmental stress. *Journal of Environmental Psychology, 24,* 143–165.

Evans, J. St. B., Barston, J. L., & Pollard, P. (1983), On the conflict between logic and belief in syllogistic reasoning. *Memory & Cognition, 11,* 295–306.

Evans, S. W., & Kim, P. (2012). Childhood poverty and young adults' allostatic load: The mediating role of childhood cumulative risk exposure. *Psychological Science, 23*(9), 979–983.

Exner, J. E. (1993). *The Rorschach: A comprehensive system.* Vol. 1. *Basic Foundations.* New York: Wiley.

Eysenck, H. J. (1957). The effects of psychotherapy: An evaluation. *Journal of Consulting Psychology, 16*(5), 319–324.

Eysenck, H. J. (1967). *The biological basis of personality.* Springfield, IL: Charles C. Thomas.

Eysenck, H. J. (1990). Biological dimensions of personality. In L. A. Pervin (Ed.), *Handbook of personality: Theory and research* (pp. 244–276). New York: Guilford Press.

Falk, R., & McGregor, D. (1983). The surprisingness of coincidences. In P. Humphreys, O. Svenson, & A. Vari (Eds.), *Analysing and aiding decision processes* (pp. 489–502). New York: North Holland.

Fan, R., Varol, O., Varamesh, A., Barron, A., van de Leemput, I. A., Scheffer, M., & Bollen, J. (2019). The minute-scale dynamics of online emotions reveal the effects of affect labeling. *Nature Human Behaviour, 3*(1), 92–100. doi:10.1038/s41562-018-0490-5

Fancher, R. E. (1979). *Pioneers in psychology.* New York: W. W. Norton.

Fantz, R. L. (1964). Visual experience in infants: Decreased attention to familiar patterns relative to novel ones. *Science, 164,* 668–670.

Farah, M. J., & Rabinowitz, C. (2003). Genetic and environmental influences on the organization of semantic memory in the brain: Is "living things" an innate category? *Cognitive Neuropsychology, 20,* 401–408.

Farah, M. J., Hutchinson, J. B., Phelps, E. A., & Wagner, A. D. (2014). Functional MRI-based lie detection: Scientific and societal challenges. *Nature Reviews Neuroscience, 15*(2), 123–131.

Farah, M. J., Illes, J., Cook-Deegan, R., Gardner, H., Kandel, E., King, P., . . . Wolpe, P. R. (2004) Neurocognitive enhancement: What can we do and what should we do? *Nature Reviews Neuroscience, 5,* 421–426.

Faraone, S. V., Perlis, R. H., Doyle, A. E., Smoller, J. W., Goralnick, J. J., Holmgren, M. A., & Sklar, P. (2005). Molecular genetics of attention-deficit/hyperactivity disorder. *Biological Psychiatry, 57,* 1313–1323.

Farooqi, I. S., Bullmore, E., Keogh, J., Gillard, J., O'Rahilly, S., & Fletcher, P. C. (2007). Leptin regulates striatal regions and human eating behavior. *Science, 317,* 1355.

Farooqi, I. S., Matarese, G., Lord, G. M., Keogh, J. M., Lawrence, E., Agwu, C., & O'Rahilly, S. (2002). Beneficial effects of leptin on obesity, T cell hyporesponsiveness, and neuroendocrine/metabolic dysfunction of human congenital leptin deficiency. *Journal of Clinical Investigation, 110*(8), 1093–1103.

Farrar, M. J. (1990). Discourse and the acquisition of grammatical morphemes. *Journal of Child Language, 17,* 607–624.

Farrelly, D., Lazarus, J., & Roberts, G. (2007). Altruists attract. *Evolutionary Psychology, 5,* 313–329.

Favazza, A. (2011). *Bodies under siege: Self-mutilation, nonsuicidal self-injury, and body modification in culture and psychiatry.* Baltimore: Johns Hopkins University Press.

Fazel, S., & Danesh, J. (2002). Serious mental disorder in 23,000 prisoners: A review of 62 surveys. *Lancet, 359,* 545–550.

Fazio, L. K., Brashier, N. M., Payne, B. K., & Marsh, E. J. (2015). Knowledge does not protect against illusory truth. *Journal of Experimental Psychology: General, 144,* 993–1002.

Fechner, G. T. (1966). *Elements of psychophysics* (H. E. Alder, Trans.). New York: Holt, Rinehart and Winston. (Original work published 1860).

Feczer, D., & Bjorklund, P. (2009). Forever changed: Posttraumatic stress disorder in female military veterans, a case report. *Perspectives in Psychiatric Care, 45,* 278–291.

Fehr, E., & Gaechter, S. (2002). Altruistic punishment in humans. *Nature, 415,* 137–140.

Feinberg, M., Willer, R., & Schultz, M. (2014). Gossip and ostracism promote cooperation in groups. *Psychological Science, 25*(3), 656–664. doi:10.1177/0956797613510184

Feinberg, T. E. (2001). *Altered egos: How the brain creates the self.* New York: Oxford University Press.

Feingold, A. (1992a). Gender differences in mate selection preferences: A test of the parental investment model. *Psychological Bulletin, 112,* 125–139.

Feingold, A. (1992b). Good-looking people are not what we think. *Psychological Bulletin, 111,* 304–341.

Feinstein, J. S., Buzza, C., Hurlemann, R., Follmer, R. L., Dahdaleh, N. S., Coryell, W. H., . . . Wemmie, J. A. (2013). Fear and panic in humans with bilateral amygdala damage. *Nature Neuroscience, 16*(3), 270–272.

Feldman, D. E. (2009). Synaptic mechanisms for plasticity in neocortex. *Annual Review of Neuroscience, 32,* 33–55.

Felleman, D. J., & Van Essen, D. C. (1991). Distributed hierarchical processing in the primate cerebral cortex. *Cerebral Cortex, 1,* 1–47.

Ferguson, C. J. (2010). Blazing angels or resident evil? Can violent video games be a force for good? *Review of General Psychology, 14*(2), 68–81.

Fernald, A., Marchman, V. A., & Weisleder, A. (2013). SES differences in language processing skill and vocabulary are evident at 18 months. *Developmental Science, 16,* 234–248.

Fernandez Nievas, I. F., & Thaver, D. (2015) Work-life balance: A different scale for doctors. *Frontiers in Pediatrics, 3,* 115.

Ferrari, A. J., Charlson, F. J., Norman, R. E., Patten, S. B., Freedman, G., Murray, C. J., . . . Whiteford, H. A. (2013). Burden of depressive disorders by country, sex, age, and year: Findings from the Global Burden of Disease Study 2010. *PLoS Medicine, 10*(11), e1001547.

Ferretti, M. T., Iulita, M. F., Cavedo, E., Chiesa, P. A., Dimech, A. S., Chadha, A. S., . . . Hampel, H. (2018). Sex differences in Alzheimer's disease—the gateway to precision medicine. *Nature Reviews Neuroscience, 14,* 457–469.

Ferster, C. B., & Skinner, B. F. (1957). *Schedules of reinforcement.* New York: Appleton-Century-Crofts.

Festinger, L. (1957). *A theory of cognitive dissonance.* Stanford, CA: Stanford University Press.

Festinger, L., & Carlsmith, J. M. (1959). Cognitive consequences of forced compliance. *Journal of Abnormal and Social Psychology, 58,* 203–210.

Festinger, L., Schachter, S., & Back, K. (1950). *Social pressures in informal groups: A study of human factors in housing.* Oxford, UK: Harper & Row.

Field, G. C. (1921). Faculty psychology and instinct psychology. *Mind, 30,* 257–270.

Fields, H. L., & Levine, J. D. (1984). Placebo analgesia: A role for endorphins? *Trends in Neurosciences, 7,* 271–273.

Figlio, D. N., Freese, J., Karbownik, K., & Roth, J. (2017). Socioeconomic status and genetic influences on cognitive development. *Proceedings of the National Academy of Sciences, USA, 114*(51), 13441–13446.

Finkel, E. J. (2017). *The all-or-nothing marriage: How the best marriages work.* NY: Dutton.

Finkel, E. J., & Eastwick, P. W. (2009). Arbitrary social norms influence sex differences in romantic selectivity. *Psychological Science, 20,* 1290–1295.

Finkel, E. J., Eastwick, P. W., & Reis, H. T. (2017). Replicability and other features of a high-quality science: Toward a balanced and empirical approach. *Journal of Personality and Social Psychology.* https://doi.org/10.1037/pspi0000075

Finkel, E. J., Eastwick, P. W., Karney, B. R., Reis, H. T., & Sprecher, S. (2012). Online dating: A critical analysis from the perspective of psychological science. *Psychological Science in the Public Interest, 13*(1), 3–66.

Finkel, E. J., Simpson, J. A., & Eastwick, P. W. (2017). The psychology of close relationships: Fourteen core principles. *Annual Review of Psychology, 68*(1), 383–411.

Finkelstein, K. E. (1999, October 17). In concert, searchers retrieve Yo-Yo Ma's lost Stradivarius. *New York Times.*

http://www.nytimes.com/1999/10/17/nyregion/in-concert-searchers-retrieve-yo-yo-ma-slost-stradivarius.html

Finn, R. (1991). Different minds. *Discover, 12,* 54–59.

Fiore, A. T., Taylor, L. S., Zhong, X., Mendelsohn, G. A., & Cheshire, C. (2010). Who's right and who writes: People, profiles, contacts, and replies in online dating. *Proceedings of the 43rd Hawaii International Conferences on System Sciences,* 1–10. CA, USA: IEEE Computer Society. doi.10.1109/HICSS.2010.444

Fiorillo, C. D., Newsome, W. T., & Schultz, W. (2008). The temporal precision of reward prediction in dopamine neurons. *Nature Neuroscience, 11,* 966–973.

Fischer, P., Krueger, J. I., Greitemeyer, T., Vogrincic, C., Kastenmüller, A., Frey, D., . . . Kainbacher, M. (2011). The bystander-effect: A meta-analytic review on bystander intervention in dangerous and non-dangerous emergencies. *Psychological Bulletin, 137*(4), 517–537. doi: 10.1037/a0023304

Fisher, D. W., Bennett, D. A., & Dong, H. (2018). Sexual dimorphism in predisposition to Alzheimer's disease. *Neurobiology of Aging, 70,* 308–324.

Fisher, R. J., & Ma, Y. (2014). The price of being beautiful: Negative effects of attractiveness on empathy for children in need. *Journal of Consumer Research, 41*(2), 436–450. doi:10.1086/676967

Fisher, R. P., & Craik, F. I. M. (1977). The interaction between encoding and retrieval operations in cued recall. *Journal of Experimental Psychology: Human Learning and Perception, 3,* 153–171.

Fiske, S. T. (1998). Stereotyping, prejudice, and discrimination. In D. T. Gilbert, S. T. Fiske, & G. Lindzey (Eds.), *The handbook of social psychology* (4th ed., Vol. 2, pp. 357–411). New York: McGraw-Hill.

Fiske, S. T. (2010). *Social beings: A core motives approach to social psychology.* Hoboken, NJ: Wiley.

Fiske, S. T. (2012). Warmth and competence: Stereotype content issues for clinicians and researchers. *Canadian Psychology /Psychologie canadienne, 53*(1), 14–20. doi:10.1037/a0026054

Fiske, S. T. (2018). Stereotype content: Warmth and competence endure. *Current Directions in Psychological Science, 27*(2), 67–73.

Fitch, C. A., & Ruggles, S. (2000). Historical trends in marriage formation, United States 1850–1990. In L. J. Waite (Ed.), *The ties that bind: Perspectives on marriage and cohabitation* (pp. 59–88). Piscataway, NJ: Transaction Publishers.

Fleeson, W. (2004). Moving personality beyond the person-situation debate: The challenge and opportunity of within-person variability. *Current Directions in Psychological Science, 13,* 83–87.

Flegal, K. M., & Troiano, R. P. (2000). Changes in the distribution of body mass index of adults and children in the U.S. population. *International Journal of Obesity, 24,* 807–818.

Flensborg-Madsen, T., & Mortensen, E. L. (2018). Developmental milestones during the first three years as precursors of adult intelligence. *Developmental Psychology, 54,* 1434–1444.

Fletcher, G. J. O., Simpson, J. A., Thomas, G., & Giles, L. (1999). Ideals in intimate relationships. *Journal of Personality and Social Psychology, 76,* 72–89. doi:10.1037/0022-3514.76.1.72

Fletcher, P. C., Shallice, T., & Dolan, R. J. (1998). The functional roles of prefrontal cortex in episodic memory. I. Encoding. *Brain, 121,* 1239–1248.

Flores, S., Bailey, H. R., Eisenberg, M. L., & Zacks, J. M. (2017). Event segmentation improves memory up to one month later. *Journal of Experimental Psychology: Learning, Memory, & Cognition, 43,* 1183–1202.

Flynn, E. (2008). Investigating children as cultural magnets: Do young children transmit redundant information along diffusion chains? *Philosophical Transactions of the Royal Society of London Series B, 363,* 3541–3551.

Flynn, E., & Whiten, A. (2008). Cultural transmission of tool-use in young children: A diffusion chain study. *Social Development, 17,* 699–718.

Flynn, J. R. (2012). *Are we getting smarter? Rising IQ in the twenty-first century.* New York: Cambridge University Press.

Foa, E. B., & McLean, C. P. (2016) The efficacy of exposure therapy for anxiety-related disorders and its underlying mechanisms: The case of OCD and PTSD. *Annual Review of Clinical Psychology, 12,* 1–28.

Foa, E. B., & Meadows, E. A. (1997). Psychosocial treatments for posttraumatic stress disorder: A critical review. *Annual Review of Psychology, 48,* 449–480.

Foa, E. B., Liebowitz, M. R., Kozak, M. J., Davies, S., Campeas, R., Franklin, M. E., . . . Tu, X. (2007). Randomized, placebo-controlled trial of exposure and ritual prevention, clomipramine, and their combination in the treatment of obsessive-compulsive disorder. *Focus, 5*(3), 368–380.

Fogassi, L., Ferrari, P. F., Gesierich, B., Rozzi, S., Chersi, F., & Rizzolatti, G. (2005). Parietal lobe: From action organization to intention understanding. *Science, 308,* 662–667.

Ford, J. H., DiBiase, H. D., Ryu, E., & Kensinger, E. A. (2018). It gets better with time: Enhancement of age-related positivity effect in the six months following a highly negative public event. *Psychology and Aging, 33*(3), 419–424. doi:10.1037/pag0000250

Forkstam, C., Hagoort, P., Fernández, G., Ingvar, M., & Petersson, K. M. (2006). Neural correlates of artificial syntactic structure classification. *NeuroImage, 32,* 956–967.

Fornito, A., Zalesky, A., & Breakspear, M. (2015). The connectomics of brain disorders. *Nature Reviews Neuroscience, 16,* 159–172.

Foroni, F., & Semin, G. R. (2009). Language that puts you in touch with your bodily feelings: The multimodal responsiveness of affective expressions. *Psychological Science, 20*(8), 974–980.

Forscher, P. S., Lai, C. K., Axt, J., Ebersole, C. R., Herman, M., Devine, P. G., & Nosek, B. A. (2019). A meta-analysis of procedures to change implicit measures. *Journal of Personality and Social Psychology, 117*(3), 522–559.

Forscher, P. S., Mitamura, C., Dix, E. L., Cox, W. T. L., & Devine, P. G. (2017). Breaking the prejudice habit: Mechanisms, time-course, and longevity. *Journal of Experimental Social Psychology, 72,* 133–146.

Fournier, J. C., DeRubeis, R., Hollon, S. D., Dimidjian, S., Amsterdam, J. D., Shelton, R. C., & Fawcett, J. (2010). Antidepressant drug effects and depression severity: A patient-level meta-analysis. *Journal of the American Medical Association, 303,* 47–53.

Fouts, R. S., & Bodamer, M. (1987). Preliminary report to the National Geographic Society on "Chimpanzee intrapersonal signing." *Friends of Washoe, 7,* 4–12.

Fox, M. J. (2009). *Always looking up.* New York: Hyperion.

Fragaszy, D. M., Izar, P., Visalberghi, E., Ottoni, E. B., & de Oliveria, M. G. (2004). Wild capuchin monkeys (*Cebus libidinosus*) use anvils and stone pounding tools. *American Journal of Primatology, 64,* 359–366.

Franchow, E. I., & Suchy, Y. (2015). Naturally-occurring expressive suppression in daily life depletes executive functioning. *Emotion, 15*(1), 78–89. doi:10.1037/emo0000013

Francis, D., Diorio, J., Liu, D., & Meaney, M. J. (1999). Nongenomic transmission across generations of maternal behavior and stress responses in the rat. *Science, 286,* 1155–1158.

Frank, M. G., & Stennet, J. (2001). The forced-choice paradigm and the perception of facial expressions of emotion. *Journal of Personality and Social Psychology, 80,* 75–85.

Frankl, V. (2000). *Man's search for meaning.* New York: Beacon Press.

Franklin, J. C., Fox, K. R., Franklin, C. R., Kleiman, E. M., Ribeiro, J. D., Jaroszewski, A. C., . . . Nock, M. K. (2016). A brief mobile app reduces nonsuicidal and suicidal self-injury: Evidence from three randomized controlled trials. *Journal of Consulting and Clinical Psychology, 84*(6), 544–557.

Frati, A., Pesce, A., Palmieri, M., Iasanzaniro, M., Familiari, P., . . . Raco, A. (2019). Hypnosis-aided awake surgery for the management of intrinsic brain tumors versus standard awake-asleep-awake protocol: A preliminary, promising experience. *World Neurosurgery, 121,* e882–891.

Fratkin, J. L., Sinn, D. L., Patall, E. A., & Gosling, S. D. (2013). Personality consistency in dogs: A meta-analysis. *PLoS ONE, 8,* e54907.

Fredman, T., & Whiten, A. (2008). Observational learning from tool using models by human-reared and mother-reared capuchin monkeys (*Cebus apella*). *Animal Cognition, 11,* 295–309.

Fredrickson, B. L. (2000). Cultivating positive emotions to optimize health and well-being. *Prevention and Treatment, 3,* Article 0001a. doi:10.1037/1522-3736.3.1.31a

Freedman, J. L., & Fraser, S. C. (1966). Compliance without pressure: The foot-in-the-door technique. *Journal of Personality and Social Psychology, 4,* 195–202.

Freeman, S., Walker, M. R., Borden, R., & Latané, B. (1975). Diffusion of responsibility and restaurant tipping: Cheaper by the bunch. *Personality and Social Psychology Bulletin, 1,* 584–587.

French, H. W. (1997, February 26). In the land of the small it isn't easy being tall. *New York Times.* Retrieved from www.nytimes.com/1997/02/26/world/in-the-land-of-the-small-it-isn-t-easy-beingtall.html

Freud, S. (1965). *The interpretation of dreams* (J. Strachey, Trans.). New York: Avon. (Original work published 1900)

Freund, A. M., & Blanchard-Fields, F. (2014). Age-related differences in altruism across adulthood: Making personal financial gain versus contributing to the public good. *Developmental Psychology, 50*(4), 1125–1136.

Frick, A., Ahs, F., Engman, J., Jonasson, M., Alaie, I., Björkstrand, J., . . . Furmark, T. (2015). Serotonin synthesis and reuptake in social anxiety disorder: A positron emission tomography study. *Journal of the American Medical Association Psychiatry, 72,* 794–802.

Frick, R. W. (1985). Communicating emotion: The role of prosodic features. *Psychological Bulletin, 97,* 412–429.

Friedman, J. M. (2003). A war on obesity, not the obese. *Science, 299*(5608), 856–858.

Friedman, J. M., & Halaas, J. L. (1998). Leptin and the regulation of body weight in mammals. *Nature, 395*(6704), 763–770.

Friedman, M., & Rosenman, R. H. (1974). *Type A behavior and your heart.* New York: Knopf.

Friedman, S. L., & Boyle, D. E. (2008). Attachment in U.S. children experiencing nonmaternal care in the early 1990s. *Attachment & Human Development, 10*(3), 225–261.

Friesen, W. V. (1972). *Cultural differences in facial expressions in a social situation: An experimental test of the concept of display rules* (Doctoral dissertation, University of California, San Francisco).

Frijda, N. H., Kuipers, P., & ter Schure, E. (1989). Relations among emotion, appraisal, and emotional action readiness. *Journal of Personality and Social Psychology, 57*(2), 212–228.

Frith, C. D., & Fletcher, P. (1995). Voices from nowhere. *Critical Quarterly, 37,* 71–83.

Frith, U. (2003). *Autism: Explaining the enigma.* Oxford: Blackwell.

Fry, D. P. (2012). Life without war. *Science, 336*(6083), 879–884. doi:10.1126/science.1217987

Fu, F., Tarnita, C. E., Christakis, N. A., Wang, L., Rand, D. G., & Novak, M. A. (2012). Evolution of in-group favoritism. *Scientific Reports, 2,* Article 460. doi:10.1038/srep00460

Fukui, H., Murai, T., Fukuyama, H., Hayashi, T., & Hanakawa, T. (2005). Functional activity related to risk anticipation during performance of the Iowa gambling task. *NeuroImage, 24,* 253–259.

Funder, D. C. (2001). Personality. *Annual Review of Psychology, 52,* 197–221.

Furmark, T., Tillfors, M., Marteinsdottir, I., Fischer, H., Pissiota, A., Långström, B., & Fredrikson, M. (2002). Common changes in cerebral blood flow in patients with social phobia treated with citalopram or cognitive-behavioral therapy. *Archives of General Psychiatry, 59*(5), 425–433.

Furnham, A. (2001). Self-estimates of intelligence: Culture and gender difference in self and other estimates of both general (g) and multiple intelligences. *Personality and Individual Differences, 31*(8), 1381–1405.

Fuss, J., Steinle, J., Bindila, L., Auer, M. K., Kirchherr, H., Lutz, B., & Gass, P. (2015). A runner's high depends on cannabinoid receptors in mice. *Proceedings of the National Academy of Sciences, USA, 112,* 13105–13108.

Fuster, J. M. (2003). *Cortex and mind.* New York: Oxford University Press.

Gadermann, A. M., Alonso, J., Vilagut, G., Zaslavsky, A. M., & Kessler, R. C. (2012). Comorbidity and disease burden in the National Comorbidity Survey Replication (NCS-R). *Depression and Anxiety, 29,* 797–806.

Gagnepain, P., Hulbert, J. C., & Anderson, M. C. (2017). Parallel regulation of memory and emotion supports the suppression of intrusive memories. *Journal of Neuroscience, 37,* 6423–6441.

Gais, S., & Born, J. (2004). Low acetylcholine during slow-wave sleep is critical for declarative memory consolidation. *Proceedings of the National Academy of Sciences, USA, 101,* 2140–2144.

Galanter, E. (1962). Contemporary psychophysics. In R. Brown, E. Galanter, E. H. Hess, & G. Mandler (Eds.), *New directions in psychology.* New York: Holt, Rinehart, & Winston.

Galati, D., Scherer, K. R., & Ricci-Bitt, P. E. (1997). Voluntary facial expression of emotion: Comparing congenitally blind with normally sighted encoders. *Journal of Personality and Social Psychology, 73,* 1363–1379.

Gale, C. R., Batty, G. D., McIntosh, A. M., Porteous, D. J., Deary, I. J., & Rasmussen, F. (2012). Is bipolar disorder more common in highly intelligent people? A cohort study of a million men. *Molecular Psychiatry, 18*(2), 190–194.

Gale, C. R., Batty, G. D., Tynelius, P., Deary, I. J., & Rasmussen, F. (2010). Intelligence in early adulthood and subsequent hospitalization for mental disorders. *Epidemiology, 21*(1), 70–77.

Galef, B. (1998). Edward Thorndike: Revolutionary psychologist, ambiguous biologist. *American Psychologist, 53,* 1128–1134.

Galling, B., Roldán, A., Hagi, K., Rietschel, L., Walyzada, F., & Correll, C. U. (2017). Antipsychotic augmentation vs. monotherapy in schizophrenia: Systematic review, meta-analysis and meta-regression analysis. *World Psychiatry, 16*(1), 77–89.

Gallistel, C. R. (2000). The replacement of general-purpose learning models with adaptively specialized learning modules. In M. S. Gazzaniga (Ed.), *The new cognitive neurosciences* (pp. 1179–1191). Cambridge, MA: MIT Press.

Gallo, D. A. (2006). *Associative illusions of memory.* New York: Psychology Press.

Gallo, D. A. (2010). False memories and fantastic beliefs: 15 years of the DRM illusion. *Memory & Cognition, 38,* 833–848.

Gallup (2014a, July 9). Obesity linked to lower social well-being. Retrieved from http://www.gallup.com/poll/172253/obesity-linked-lower-social.aspx.

Gallup (2014b, July 10). Older Americans feel best about their physical appearance. Retrieved from http://www.gallup.com/poll/172361/older-americans-feel-best-physical-appearance.aspx

Gallup, G. G. (1977). Self-recognition in primates: A comparative approach to the bidirectional properties of consciousness. *American Psychologist, 32,* 329–338.

Gallup, G. G. (1997). On the rise and fall of self-conception in primates. *Annals of the New York Academy of Sciences, 818,* 73–84.

Gallup, G. G., & Frederick, D. A. (2010). The science of sex appeal: An evolutionary perspective. *Review of General Psychology, 14*(3), 240–250. doi: 10.1037/a0020451

Galton, F. (1869). *Hereditary genius: An inquiry into its laws and consequences.* London: Macmillan/Fontana.

Gangestad, S. W., & Haselton, M. G. (2015). Human estrus: Implications for relationship science. *Current Opinion in Psychology, 1,* 45–51.

Ganzel, B. L., Kim, P., Glover, G. H., & Temple, E. (2008). Resilience after 9/11: Multimodal neuroimaging evidence for stress-related change in the healthy adult brain. *NeuroImage, 40,* 788–795.

Garb, H. N. (1998). *Studying the clinician: Judgment research and psychological assessment.* Washington, DC: American Psychological Association.

Garcia, J., & Koelling, R. A. (1966). Relation of cue to consequence in avoidance learning. *Psychonomic Science, 4,* 123–124.

García-García, I., Zeighami, Y., & Dagher, A. (2017). Reward prediction errors in addiction and Parkinson's disease: From neurophysiology to neuroimaging. *Current Neurology and Neuroscience Reports, 17,* 46. doi.10.1007/s11910-017-0755-9

Garcia-Moreno, C., Jansen, H. A. F. M., Ellsberg, M., Heise, L., & Watts, C. H. (2006). Prevalence of intimate partner violence: Findings from the WHO multi-country study on women's health and domestic violence. *Lancet, 368*(9543), 1260–1269.

Gardner, M., & Steinberg, L. (2005). Peer influence on risk taking, risk preference, and risky decision making in adolescence and adulthood: An experimental study. *Developmental Psychology, 41*(4), 625–635.

Gardner, R. A., & Gardner, B. T. (1969). Teaching sign language to a chimpanzee. *Science, 165,* 664–672.

Garrett, B. L. (2011). *Convicting the innocent: Where criminal prosecutions go wrong.* Cambridge, MA: Harvard University Press.

Gartstein, M. A., Prokasky, A., Bell, M. A., Calkins, S., Bridgett, D. J., Braungart-Rieker, J., . . . Seamon, E. (2017). Latent profile and cluster analysis of infant temperament: Comparisons across person-centered approaches. *Developmental Psychology, 53*(10), 1811–1825. doi:10.1037/dev0000382

Gathercole, S. E. (2008). Nonword repetition and word learning: The nature of the relationship. *Applied Psycholinguistics, 27,* 513–543.

Gazzaniga, M. S. (2006). Forty-five years of split brain research and still going strong. *Nature Reviews Neuroscience, 6,* 653–659.

Ge, D., Fellay, J., Thompson, A. J., Simon, J. S., Shianna, K. V., Urban, T. J., . . . Goldstein, D. B. (2009). Genetic variation in il28b predicts hepatitis C treatment-induced viral clearance. *Nature, 461,* 399–401.

Ge, X. J., & Natsuaki, M. N. (2009). In search of explanations for early pubertal timing effects on developmental psychopathology. *Current Directions in Psychological Science, 18,* 327–331.

Ge, X. J., Conger, R. D., & Elder, G. H. (1996). Coming of age too early: Pubertal influences on girls' vulnerability to psychological distress. *Child Development, 67,* 3386–3400.

Ge, X. J., Conger, R. D., & Elder, G. H., Jr. (2001). Pubertal transition, stressful life events, and the emergence of gender differences in adolescent depressive symptoms. *Developmental Psychology, 37*(3), 404–417.

Gegenfurtner, K. R., Bloj, M., & Toscani, M. (2015). The many colours of 'the dress.' *Current Biology, 25,* R543–R544.

Gendron, M., Crivelli, C., & Barrett, L. F. (2018). Universality reconsidered: Diversity in making meaning of facial expressions. *Current Directions in Psychological Science, 27*(4), 211–219. doi:10.1177/0963721417746794

Gendron, M., Roberson, D., van der Vyver, J. M., & Barrett, L. F. (2014). Perceptions of emotion from facial expressions are not culturally universal: Evidence from a remote culture. *Emotion, 14,* 251–262. doi:10.1037/a0036052

George, O., & Koob, G. F. (2017). Individual differences in the neuropsychopathology of addiction. *Dialogues in Clinical Neuroscience, 19*(3), 217–229.

Geraci, A., & Surian, L. (2011). The developmental roots of fairness: Infants' reactions to equal and unequal distributions of resources. *Developmental Science, 14,* 1012–1020. doi: 10.1111/j.1467-7687.2011.01048.x

Gerbasi, M. E., & Prentice, D. A. (2013). The self- and other-interest inventory. *Journal of Personality and Social Psychology, 105*(3), 495–514.

Gershoff, E. T. (2002). Corporal punishment by parents and associated child behaviors and experiences: A meta-analytic and theoretical review. *Psychological Bulletin, 128,* 539–579.

Geschwind, D. H. (2009). Advances in autism. *Annual Review of Medicine, 60,* 67–80.

Gibb, B. E., Alloy, L. B., & Tierney, S. (2001). History of childhood maltreatment, negative cognitive styles, and episodes of depression in adulthood. *Cognitive Therapy and Research, 25,* 425–446.

Gibbons, F. X. (1990). Self-attention and behavior: A review and theoretical update. In M. P. Zanna (Ed.), *Advances in experimental social psychology* (Vol. 23, pp. 249–303). San Diego, CA: Academic Press.

Gibson, C. E., Losee, J., & Vitiello, C. (2014). A replication attempt of stereotype susceptibility (Shih, Pittinsky, & Ambady, 1999): Identity salience and shifts in quantitative performance. *Social Psychology, 45*(3), 194–198.

Gick, M. L., & Holyoak, K. J. (1980). Analogical problem solving. *Cognitive Psychology, 12,* 306–355. [FIG. 9.12]

Giedd, J. N., Blumenthal, J., Jeffries, N. O., Castellanos, F. X., Liu, H., Zijdenbos, A., . . . Rapoport, J. L. (1999). Brain development during childhood and adolescence: A longitudinal MRI study. *Nature Neuroscience, 2,* 861–863.

Gierlach, E., Blesher, B. E., & Beutler, L. E. (2010). Cross-cultural differences in risk perceptions of disasters. *Risk Analysis, 30,* 1539–1549.

Gignac, G. E., & Bates, T. C. (2017). Brain volume and intelligence: The moderating role of intelligence measurement quality. *Intelligence, 64,* 18–29.

Gigone, D., & Hastie, R. (1993). The common knowledge effect: Information sharing and group judgment. *Journal of Personality and Social Psychology, 54,* 959–974.

Gilbert, D. T. (1991). How mental systems believe. *American Psychologist, 46,* 107–119.

Gilbert, D. T. (1998). Ordinary personology. In D. T. Gilbert, S. T. Fiske, & G. Lindzey (Eds.), *The handbook of social psychology* (4th ed., Vol. 2, pp. 89–150). New York: McGraw-Hill.

Gilbert, D. T. (2006). *Stumbling on happiness.* New York: Knopf.

Gilbert, D. T., & Malone, P. S. (1995). The correspondence bias. *Psychological Bulletin, 117,* 21–38.

Gilbert, D. T., Brown, R. P., Pinel, E. C., & Wilson, T. D. (2000). The illusion of external agency. *Journal of Personality and Social Psychology, 79,* 690–700.

Gilbert, D. T., King, G., Pettigrew, S., & Wilson, T. D. (2016). Comment on "Estimating the reproducibility of psychological science." *Science, 351* (6277). doi:10.1126/science.aad7243

Gilbert, D. T., Pelham, B. W., & Krull, D. S. (1988). On cognitive busyness: When persons perceivers meet persons perceived. *Journal of Personality and Social Psychology, 54,* 733–740.

Gilbert, S. J. (2015). Strategic offloading of delayed intentions into the environment. *The Quarterly Journal of Experimental Psychology, 68,* 971–992.

Gilbertson, M. W., Shenton, M. E., Ciszewski, A., Kasai, K., Lasko, N. B., Orr, S. P., & Pitman, R. K. (2002). Smaller hippocampal volume predicts pathological vulnerability to psychological trauma. *Nature Neuroscience, 5,* 1242–1247.

Gillespie, C. F., & Nemeroff, C. B. (2007). Corticotropin-releasing factor and the psychobiology of early-life stress. *Current Directions in Psychological Science, 16,* 85–89.

Gillette, J., Gleitman, H., Gleitman, L., & Lederer, A. (1999). Human simulation of vocabulary learning. *Cognition, 73,* 135–176.

Gilovich, T. (1991). *How we know what isn't so: The fallibility of human reason in everyday life.* New York: Free Press.

Gino, F., & Pierce, L. (2009). The abundance effect: Unethical behavior in the presence of wealth. *Organizational Behavior and Human Decision Processes, 109*(2), 142–155. doi: 10.1016/j.obhdp.2009.03.003

Ginzburg, K., Solomon, Z., & Bleich, A. (2002). Repressive coping style, acute stress disorder, and posttraumatic stress disorder after myocardial infarction. *Psychosomatic Medicine, 64,* 748–757.

Giovanello, K. S., Schnyer, D. M., & Verfaellie, M. (2004). A critical role for the anterior hippocampus in relational memory: Evidence from an fMRI study comparing associative and item recognition. *Hippocampus, 14,* 5–8.

Gladue, B. A. (1994). The biopsychology of sexual orientation. *Current Directions in Psychological Science, 3,* 150–154.

Glanzer, M. & Cunitz, A. R. (1966). Two storage mechanisms in free recall. *Journal of Verbal Learning and Verbal Behavior, 5,* 351–360.

Glass, D. C., & Singer, J. E. (1972). *Urban stress.* New York: Academic Press.

Glenwick, D. S., Jason, L. A., & Elman, D. (1978). Physical attractiveness and social contact in the singles bar. *Journal of Social Psychology, 105,* 311–312.

Glick, D. M., & Orsillo, S. M. (2015). An investigation of the efficacy of acceptance-based behavioral therapy for academic procrastination. *Journal of Experimental Psychology: General, 144,* 400–409.

Global News. (2019, April 22). 6,700 Canadian veterans who fought in Afghan war receiving federal support for PTSD. Retrieved from https://globalnews.ca/news/5191803/canadian-veterans-afghan-war-ptsd/

Glynn, L. M., & Sandman, C. A. (2011). Prenatal origins of neurological development: A critical period for fetus and mother. *Current Directions in Psychological Science, 20*(6), 384–389. doi:10.1177/0963721411422056

Gneezy, U., & Rustichini, A. (2000). A fine is a price. *Journal of Legal Studies, 29,* 1–17.

Goddard, H. H. (1913). *The Kallikak family: A study in the heredity of feeble-mindedness.* New York: Macmillan.

Godden, D. R., & Baddeley, A. D. (1975). Context-dependent memory in two natural environments: On land and underwater. *British Journal of Psychology, 66,* 325–331.

Goehler, L. E., Gaykema, R. P. A., Hansen, M. K., Anderson, K., Maier, S. F., & Watkins, L. R. (2000). Vagal immune-to-brain communication: A visceral chemosensory pathway. *Autonomic Neuroscience: Basic and Clinical, 85,* 49–59.

Goel, V. (2007). Anatomy of deductive reasoning. *Trends in Cognitive Sciences, 11,* 435–441.

Goel, V., & Dolan, R. J. (2003). Explaining modulation of reasoning by belief. *Cognition, 87,* 11–22.

Goff, L. M., & Roediger, H. L., III. (1998). Imagination inflation for action events—repeated imaginings lead to illusory recollections. *Memory & Cognition, 26,* 20–33.

Golden, R. L., Furman, W., & Collibee, C. (2016). The risks and rewards of sexual debut. *Developmental Psychology, 52*(11), 1913–1925. doi:10.1037/dev0000206

Goldman, M. S., Brown, S. A., & Christiansen, B. A. (1987). Expectancy theory: Thinking about drinking. In H. T. Blane & K. E. Leonard (Eds.), *Psychological theories of drinking and alcoholism* (pp. 181–266). New York: Guilford Press.

Goldstein, D. G., Hershfield, H. E., & Benartzi, S. (2016). The illusion of wealth and its reversal. *Journal of Marketing Research, 53,* 804–813.

Goldstein, M. H., Schwade, J. A., Briesch, J., & Syal, S. (2010). Learning while babbling: Prelinguistic object-directed vocalizations signal a readiness to learn. *Infancy, 15,* 362–391.

Gontier, N. (2008). Genes, brains, and language: An epistemological examination of how genes can underlie human cognitive behavior. *Review of General Psychology, 12,* 170–180.

Gonzaga, G. C., Keltner, D., Londahl, E. A., & Smith, M. D. (2001). Love and the commitment problem in romantic relations and friendship. *Journal of Personality and Social Psychology, 81,* 247–262.

Goodale, M. A., Milner, A. D., Jakobson, L. S., & Carey, D. P. (1991). A neurological dissociation between perceiving objects and grasping them. *Nature, 349,* 154–156.

Goodfellow, I., Bengio, Y., & Courville, A. (2016). *Deep learning* (pp. 1–26). Cambridge, MA: MIT Press.

Gootman, E. (2003, March 3). Separated at birth in Mexico, united at campuses on Long Island. *New York Times.* Retrieved from http://www.nytimes.com/2003/03/03/nyregion/separated-at-birth-in-mexico-reunited-at-campuses-on-li.html?_r=0

Gopnik, A. (2012). Scientific thinking in young children: Theoretical advances, empirical research, and policy implications. *Science, 337*(6102), 1623–1627. doi:10.1126/science.1223416

Gopnik, M. (1990a). Feature-blind grammar and dysphasia. *Nature, 344,* 715.

Gopnik, M. (1990b). Feature blindness: A case study. *Language Acquisition: A Journal of Developmental Linguistics, 1,* 139–164.

Gorczynski, P., & Faulkner, G. (2011). Exercise therapy for schizophrenia. *Cochrane Database of Systematic Reviews, 5,* CD004412.

Gordon, P. (2004). Numerical cognition without words: Evidence from Amazonia. *Science, 306,* 496–499.

Gorno-Tempini, M. L., Price, C. J., Josephs, O., Vandenberghe, R., Cappa, S. F., Kapur, N., & Frackowiak, R. S. (1998). The neural systems sustaining face and proper-name processing. *Brain, 121,* 2103–2118.

Gosling, S. D. (1998). Personality dimensions in spotted hyenas (*Crocuta crocuta*). *Journal of Comparative Psychology, 112,* 107–118.

Gosling, S. D. (2008). Personality in non-human animals. *Social and Personality Psychology Compass, 2,* 985–1001.

Gosling, S. D., & John, O. P. (1999). Personality dimensions in nonhuman animals: A cross-species review. *Current Directions in Psychological Science, 8,* 69–75.

Gosling, S. D., Rentfrow, P. J., & Swann, W. B., Jr. (2003). A very brief measure of the Big-Five personality domains. *Journal of Research in Personality, 37,* 504–528.

Gotlib, I. H., & Joormann, J. (2010). Cognition and depression: Current status and future directions. *Annual Review of Clinical Psychology, 6,* 285–312.

Gottesman, I. I. (1991). *Schizophrenia genesis: The origins of madness.* New York: Freeman.

Gottesman, I. I., & Hanson, D. R. (2005). Human development: Biological and genetic processes. *Annual Review of Psychology, 56,* 263–286.

Gottfredson, L. S. (1997). Mainstream science on intelligence: An editorial with 52 signatories, history, and bibliography. *Intelligence, 24,* 13–23.

Gottfredson, L. S. (2003). Dissecting practical intelligence theory: Its claims and evidence. *Intelligence, 31*(4), 343–397.

Gottfried, J. A. (2008). Perceptual and neural plasticity of odor quality coding in the human brain. *Chemosensory Perception, 1,* 127–135.

Gouldner, A. W. (1960). The norm of reciprocity. *American Sociological Review, 25,* 161–178.

Government of Canada. (2019, April). National report: Apparent opioid-related deaths in Canada. Retrieved from https://health-infobase.canada.ca/datalab/national-surveillance-opioid-mortality.html

Government of Canada. (2019, May 7). Canadian Guidelines on Sexually Transmitted Infections: Summary of Recommendations for Chlamydia trachomatis (CT), Neisseria gonorrhoeae (NG) and Syphilis. Retrieved from www.canada.ca/en/services/health/publications/diseases-conditions/guidelines-sti-recommendations-chlamydia-trachomatis-neisseria-gonorrhoeae-syphilis-2019.html

Grady, C. L., Haxby, J. V., Horwitz, B., Schapiro, M. B., Rapoport, S. I., Ungerleider, L. G., . . . Herscovitch, P. (1992). Dissociation of object and spatial vision in human extrastriate cortex: Age-related changes in activation of regional cerebral blood flow measured with [15O] water and positron emission tomography. *Journal of Cognitive Neuroscience, 4*(1), 23–34.

Graf, P., & Schacter, D. L. (1985). Implicit and explicit memory for new associations in normal subjects and amnesic patients. *Journal of Experimental Psychology: Learning, Memory, and Cognition, 11,* 501–518.

Grant, B. F., Hasin, D. S., Stinson, F. S., Dawson, D. A., Chou, S. P., & Ruan, W. J. (2004). Prevalence, correlates, and disability of personality disorders in the U.S.: Results from the National Epidemiologic Survey on Alcohol and Related Conditions. *Journal of Clinical Psychiatry, 65,* 948–958.

Grassian, S. (2006). Psychiatric effects of solitary confinement. *Washington University Journal of Law and Policy, 22,* 1–24.

Gray, H. M., Gray, K., & Wegner, D. M. (2007). Dimensions of mind perception. *Science, 315,* 619.

Gray, J. A. (1970). The psychophysiological basis of introversion–extraversion. *Behavior Research and Therapy, 8,* 249–266.

Gray, J. A. (1990). Brain systems that mediate both emotion and cognition. *Cognition and Emotion, 4,* 269–288.

Greely, H., Sahakian, B., Harris, J., Kessler, R. C., Gazzaniga, M., Campbell, P., & Farah, M. J. (2008). Towards responsible use of cognitive enhancing drugs by the healthy. *Nature, 456*(7223), 702–705.

Green, D. A., & Swets, J. A. (1966). *Signal detection theory and psychophysics.* New York: Wiley.

Green, M. F., Kern, R. S., Braff, D. L., & Mintz, J. (2000). Neurocognitive deficits and functional outcome in schizophrenia: Are we measuring the "right stuff"? *Schizophrenia Bulletin, 26,* 119–136.

Green, S. K., Buchanan, D. R., & Heuer, S. K. (1984). Winners, losers, and choosers: A field investigation of dating initiation. *Personality and Social Psychology Bulletin, 10,* 502–511.

Greenberg, J., Pyszczynski, T., Solomon, S., Rosenblatt, A., Veeder, M., Kirkland, S., & Lyon, D. (1990). Evidence for terror management theory: II. The effects of mortality salience on reactions to those who threaten or bolster the cultural worldview. *Journal of Personality and Social Psychology, 58,* 308–318.

Greenberg, J., Solomon, S., & Arndt, J. (2008). A basic but uniquely human motivation: Terror management. In J. Y. Shah & W. L. Gardner (Eds.), *Handbook of motivation science* (pp. 114–134). New York: Guilford Press.

Greenspan, L., & Deardorff, J. (2014). *The new puberty: How to navigate early development in today's girls.* Emmaus, PA: Rodale Books.

Greenwald, A. G. (1992). New look 3: Unconscious cognition reclaimed. *American Psychologist, 47,* 766–779.

Greenwald, A. G., & Nosek, B. A. (2001). Health of the Implicit Association Test at age 3. *Zeitschrift für Experimentelle Psychologie, 48,* 85–93.

Greenwald, A. G., McGhee, D. E., & Schwartz, J. L. K. (1998). Measuring individual differences in implicit cognition: The implicit association test. *Journal of Personality and Social Psychology, 74,* 1464–1480.

Gropp, E., Shanabrough, M., Borok, E., Xu, A. W., Janoschek, R., Buch, T., . . . Brüning, J. C. (2005). Agouti-related peptide-expressing neurons are mandatory for feeding. *Nature Neuroscience, 8,* 1289–1291.

Gross, J. J. (1998). Antecedent-and-response-focused emotion regulation: Divergent consequences for experience, expression, and physiology. *Journal of Personality and Psychology, 74*(1), 224–237.

Gross, J. J. (2002). Emotion regulation: Affective, cognitive, and social consequences. *Psychophysiology, 39,* 281–291.

Gross, J. J., & Munoz, R. F. (1995). Emotion regulation and mental health. *Clinical Psychology: Science and Practice, 2,* 151–164.

Gross, J., Leib, M., Offerman, T., & Shalvi, S. (2018). Ethical free riding: When honest people find dishonest partners. *Psychological Science, 29*(12), 1956–1968.

Grover, S., & Helliwell, J. F. (2019). How's life at home? New evidence on marriage and the set point for happiness. *Journal of Happiness Studies, 20,* 373.

Groves, B. (2004, August 2). Unwelcome awareness. *San Diego Union-Tribune,* p. 24.

Grün, F., & Blumberg, B. (2006). Environmental obesogens: Organotins and endocrine disruption via nuclear receptor signaling. *Endocrinology, 147,* s50–s55.

Grzyb, T., Trojanowski, J., Grzybała, P., Doliński, D., Folwarczny, M., Krzyszycha, K., & Martynowska, K. (2017). Would you

deliver an electric shock in 2015? Obedience in the experimental paradigm developed by Stanley Milgram in the 50 years following the original studies. *Social Psychological and Personality Science, 8*(8), 927–933.

Guerin, S. A., Robbins, C. A., Gilmore, A. W., & Schacter, D. L. (2012a). Interactions between visual attention and episodic retrieval: Dissociable contributions of parietal regions during gist-based false recognition. *Neuron, 75,* 1122–1134.

Guerin, S. A., Robbins, C. A., Gilmore, A. W., & Schacter, D. L. (2012b). Retrieval failure contributes to gist-based false recognition. *Journal of Memory and Language, 66,* 68–78.

Guilford, J. P. (1967). *The nature of human intelligence.* New York: McGraw-Hill.

Guillery, R. W., & Sherman, S. M. (2002). Thalamic relay functions and their role in corticocortical communication: Generalizations from the visual system. *Neuron, 33,* 163–175.

Gunnery, S. D., Hall, J. A., & Ruben, M. A. (2013). The deliberate Duchenne smile: Individual differences in expressive control. *Journal of Nonverbal Behavior, 37,* 29–41.

Gurwitz, J. H., McLaughlin, T. J., Willison, D. J., Guadagnoli, E., Hauptman, P. J., Gao, X., & Soumerai, S. B. (1997). Delayed hospital presentation in patients who have had acute myocardial infarction. *Annals of Internal Medicine, 126,* 593–599.

Gusnard, D. A., & Raichle, M. E. (2001). Searching for a baseline: Functional imaging and the resting human brain. *Nature Reviews Neuroscience, 2,* 685–694.

Gustafsson, J.-E. (1984). A unifying model for the structure of intellectual abilities. *Intelligence, 8,* 179–203.

Gutchess, A. H., & Schacter, D. L. (2012). The neural correlates of gist-based true and false recognition. *NeuroImage, 59,* 3418–3426.

Guzmán-Vélez, E., & Tranel, D. (2015). Does bilingualism contribute to cognitive reserve? Cognitive and neural perspectives. *Neuropsychology, 29,* 129–150.

Haase, C. M., Heckhausen, J., & Wrosch, C. (2013). Developmental regulation across the life span: Toward a new synthesis. *Developmental Psychology, 49*(5), 964–972.

Hackman, D. A., & Farah, M. J. (2008). Socioeconomic status and the developing brain. *Trends in Cognitive Sciences, 13,* 65–73.

Hackman, J. R., & Katz, N. (2010). Group behavior and performance. In S. T. Fiske, D. T. Gilbert, & G. Lindzey (Eds.), *The handbook of social psychology* (5th ed., Vol. 2, pp. 1208–1251). New York: Wiley.

Haedt-Matt, A. A., & Keel, P. K. (2011). Revisiting the affect regulation model of binge eating: A meta-analysis of studies using ecological momentary assessment. *Psychological Bulletin, 137*(4), 660–681.

Hagen, L., Krishna, A., & McFerran, B. (2016). Rejecting responsibility: Low physical involvement in obtaining food promotes unhealthy eating. *Journal of Marketing Research, 54*(4), 589–604.

Haggard, P., & Tsakiris, M. (2009). The experience of agency: Feelings, judgments, and responsibility. *Current Directions in Psychological Science, 18,* 242–246.

Haidt, J., & Keltner, D. (1999). Culture and facial expression: Open-ended methods find more expressions and a gradient of recognition. *Cognition and Emotion, 13*(3), 225–266.

Haines, M. M., Stansfeld, S. A., Job, R. F., Berglund, B., & Head, J. (2001). Chronic aircraft noise exposure, stress responses, mental health and cognitive performance in school children. *Psychological Medicine, 31,* 265–277.

Halim, M. L., Ruble, D. N., Tamis-LeMonda, C. S., Zosuls, K. M., Lurye, L. E., & Greulich, F. K. (2014). Pink frilly dresses and the avoidance of all things "girly": Children's appearance rigidity and cognitive theories of gender development. *Developmental Psychology, 50*(4), 1091–1101.

Hallett, M. (2000). Transcranial magnetic stimulation and the human brain. *Nature, 406,* 147–150.

Halliday, R., Naylor, H., Brandeis, D., Callaway, E., Yano, L., & Herzig, K. (1994). The effect of D-amphetamine, clonidine, and yohimbine on human information processing. *Psychophysiology, 31,* 331–337.

Halpern, B. (2002). Taste. In H. Pashler & S. Yantis (Eds.), *Stevens' handbook of experimental psychology: Vol. 1. Sensation and perception* (3rd ed., pp. 653–690). New York: Wiley.

Halpern, D. F., Benbow, C. P., Geary, D. C., Gur, R. C., Hyde, J. S., & Gernsbacher, M. A. (2007). The science of sex differences in science and mathematics. *Psychological Science in the Public Interest, 8*(1), 1–51.

Hambrick, D. Z., Oswald, F. L., Altmann, E. M., Meinz, E. J., Gobet, F., & Campitelli, G. (2013). Deliberate practice: Is that all it takes to become an expert? *Intelligence, 45,* 34–45.

Hamermesh, D. S., & Biddle, J. E. (1994). Beauty and the labor market. *American Economic Review, 84,* 1174–1195.

Hamilton, A. F. C. (2013). Reflecting on the mirror neuron system in autism: A systematic review of current theories. *Developmental Cognitive Neuroscience, 3,* 91–105.

Hamilton, A. F., & Grafton, S. T. (2006). Goal representation in human anterior intraparietal sulcus. *Journal of Neuroscience, 26,* 1133–1137.

Hamilton, A. F., & Grafton, S. T. (2008). Action outcomes are represented in human inferior frontoparietal cortex. *Cerebral Cortex, 18,* 1160–1168.

Hamilton, D. L., & Gifford, R. K. (1976). Illusory correlation in interpersonal perception: A cognitive basis of stereotypic judgements. *Journal of Experimental Social Psychology, 12,* 392–407.

Hamilton, J. P., Etkin, A., Furman, D. J., Lemus, M. G., Johnson, R. F., & Gotlib, I. H. (2012). Functional neuroimaging of major depressive disorder: A meta-analysis and new integration of baseline activation and neural response data. *American Journal of Psychiatry, 169,* 693–703.

Hamilton, J. P., Glover, G. H., Hsu, J. J., Johnson, R. F., & Gotlib, I. H. (2010). Modulation of subgenual anterior cingulated cortex activity with real-time neurofeedback. *Human Brain Mapping, 32,* 22–31.

Hamilton, W. D. (1964). The genetical evolution of social behaviour. *Journal of Theoretical Biology, 7,* 1–16.

Hamlin, J. K. (2014). The case for social evaluation in preverbal infants: Gazing toward one's goal drives infants' preferences for Helpers over Hinderers in the hill paradigm. *Frontiers in Psychology,* 5(Oct.), 1–9. doi.org/10.3389/fpsyg.2014.01563

Hamlin, J. K., Wynn, K., & Bloom, P. (2007). Social evaluation by preverbal infants. *Nature, 450,* 557–559.

Hamlin, J. K., Wynn, K., & Bloom, P. (2011). 3-month-olds show a negativity bias in their social evaluation. *Developmental Science, 13*(6), 923–929. doi.org/10.1111/j.1467-7687.2010.00951.x.3-month-olds

Hanel, P. H. P., Wolfradt, U., Maio, G. R., & Manstead, A. S. R. (2018). The source attribution effect: Demonstrating pernicious disagreement between ideological groups on non-divisive aphorisms. *Journal of Experimental Social Psychology, 79,* 51–63.

Hanson, J. D., Larson, M. E., & Snowdon, C. T. (1976). The effects of control over high intensity noise on plasma cortisol levels in rhesus monkeys. *Behavioral Biology, 16*(3), 333–340.

Happé, F. G. E. (1995). The role of age and verbal ability in the theory of mind performance of subjects with autism. *Child Development, 66,* 843–855.

Happé, F. G. E., & Vital, P. (2009). What aspects of autism predispose to talent? *Philosophical Transactions of the Royal Society B: Biological Science, 364,* 1369–1375.

Happé, F., & Frith, U. (2006). The weak coherence account: Detail-focused cognitive style in autism spectrum disorders. *Journal of Autism and Developmental Disorders, 36,* 5–25.

Harand, C., Bertran, F., La Joie, R., Landeau, B., Mézenge, F., Desgranges, B., . . . Rauchs, G. (2012). The hippocampus remains activated over the long term for the retrieval of truly episodic memories. *PLoS ONE, 7,* e43495. doi:10.1371/journal.pone.0043495

Harding, C. M., Brooks, G. W., Ashikaga, T., Strauss, J. S., & Brier, A. (1987). The Vermont longitudinal study of persons with severe mental illness, II: Long-term outcome of subjects who retrospectively met DSM-III criteria for schizophrenia. *American Journal of Psychiatry, 144,* 727–735.

Hare, B. (2017). Survival of the friendliest: *Homo sapiens* evolved via selection for prosociality. *Annual Review of Psychology, 68*(1), 155–186.

Hare, R. D. (1998). *Without conscience: The disturbing world of the psychopaths among us.* New York: Guilford Press.

Harlow, H. F. (1958). The nature of love. *American Psychologist, 13,* 573–685.

Harlow, J. M. (1848). Passage of an iron rod through the head. *Boston Medical and Surgical Journal, 39,* 389–393.

Harlow, J. M. (1868). Recovery from the passage of an iron bar through the head. *Publications of the Massachusetts Medical Society, 2,* 327–347.

Harmon-Jones, E., Harmon-Jones, C., & Levy, N. (2015). An action-based model of cognitive-dissonance processes. *Current Directions in Psychological Science, 24*(3), 184–189.

Harris, B. (1979). Whatever happened to Little Albert? *American Psychologist, 34,* 151–160.

Harris, D. J., Vine, S. J., Wilson, M. R., McGrath, J. S., LeBel, M.-E., & Buckingham, G. (2018). Action observation for sensorimotor learning in surgery. *British Journal of Surgery, 105,* 1713–1720.

Harris, P. L., de Rosnay, M., & Pons, F. (2005). Language and children's understanding of mental states. *Current Directions in Psychological Science, 14,* 69–73.

Harris, P. L., Johnson, C. N., Hutton, D., Andrews, G., & Cooke, T. (1989). Young children's theory of mind and emotion. *Cognition and Emotion, 3,* 379–400.

Harro, J. (2015). Neuropsychiatric adverse effects of amphetamine and methamphetamine. *International Review of Neurobiology, 120,* 179–204.

Hart, B. L. (1988). Biological basis of the behavior of sick animals. *Neuroscience and Biobehavioral Reviews, 12,* 123–137.

Hart, B., & Risley, T. R. (1995). *Meaningful differences in the everyday experience of young American children.* Baltimore, MD: Brookes.

Hart, W., Albarracin, D., Eagly, A. H., Lindberg, M. J., Merrill, L., & Brechan, I. (2009). Feeling validated versus being correct: A meta-analysis of selective exposure to information. *Psychological Bulletin, 135,* 555–588.

Hartshorne, H., & May, M. (1928). *Studies in deceit.* New York: Macmillan.

Hartshorne, J. K., & Germine, L. T. (2015). When does cognitive functioning peak? The asynchronous rise and fall of different cognitive abilities across the life span. *Psychological Science, 26* (4), 433–443.

Hasher, L., Goldstein, D., & Toppino, T. (1977). Frequency and the conference of referential validity. *Journal of Verbal Learning and Verbal Behavior, 16,* 107–112.

Haslam, C., Wills, A. J., Haslam, S. A., Kay, J., Baron, R., & McNab, F. (2007). Does maintenance of colour categories rely on language? Evidence to the contrary from a case of semantic dementia. *Brain and Language, 103,* 251–263.

Hassabis, D., Kumaran, D., Summerfield, C., & Botvinick, M. (2017). Neuroscience-inspired artificial intelligence. *Neuron, 95,* 245–258.

Hassabis, D., Kumaran, D., Vann, S. D., & Maguire, E. A. (2007). Patients with hippocampal amnesia cannot imagine new experiences. *Proceedings of the National Academy of Sciences, USA, 104,* 1726–1731.

Hasselmo, M. E. (2006). The role of acetylcholine in learning and memory. *Current Opinion in Neurobiology, 16,* 710–715.

Hassin, R. R., Bargh, J. A., & Zimerman, S. (2009). Automatic and flexible: The case of non-conscious goal pursuit. *Social Cognition, 27,* 20–36.

Hassmen, P., Koivula, N., & Uutela, A. (2000). Physical exercise and psychological well-being: A population study in Finland. *Preventive Medicine, 30,* 17–25.

Hasson, U., Hendler, T., Bashat, D. B., & Malach, R. (2001). Vase or face? A neural correlate of shape-selective grouping processes in the human brain. *Journal of Cognitive Neuroscience, 13,* 744–753.

Hatemi, P. K., Gillespie, N. A., Eaves, L. J., Maher, B. S., Webb, B. T., Heath, A. C., . . . Martin, N. G. (2011). A genome-wide analysis of liberal and conservative political attitudes. *Journal of Politics, 73,* 271–285.

Hatfield, E. (1988). Passionate and companionate love. In R. J. Sternberg & M. L. Barnes (Eds.), *The psychology of love* (pp. 191–217). New Haven, CT: Yale University Press.

Häusser, M. (2000). The Hodgkin–Huxley theory of the action potential. *Nature Neuroscience, 3,* 1165.

Hawkins, R. X. D., Goodman, N. D., & Goldstone, R. L. (2019). The emergence of social norms and conventions. *Trends in Cognitive Sciences, 23*(2), 158–169.

Haworth, C. M. A., Wright, M. J., Luciano, M., Martin, N. G., de Geus, E. J. C., van Beijsterveldt, C. E. M., . . . Plomin, R. (2010). The heritability of general cognitive ability increases linearly from childhood to young adulthood. *Molecular Psychiatry, 15*(11), 1112–1120.

Hayes, J. E., Bartoshuk, L. M., Kidd, J. R., & Duffy, V. B. (2008). Supertasting and PROP bitterness depends on more than the TAS2R38 gene. *Chemical Senses, 23,* 255–265.

Hayes, K., & Hayes, C. (1951). The intellectual development of a home-raised chimpanzee. *Proceedings of the American Philosophical Society, 95,* 105–109.

Hayes, S. C., Strosahl, K., & Wilson, K. G. (1999). *Acceptance and commitment therapy: An experiential approach to behavior change.* New York: Guilford Press.

Heath, S. B. (1983). *Way with words: Language, life and work in communities and classrooms.* Cambridge, UK: Cambridge University Press.

Heavey, C. L., Hurlburt, R. T., & Lefforge, N. L. (2012). Toward a phenomenology of feelings. *Emotion, 12*(4), 763–777.

Hebb, D. O. (1949). *The organization of behavior.* New York: Wiley.

Hebl, M. R., & Heatherton, T. F. (1997). The stigma of obesity in women: The difference is Black and White. *Personality and Social Psychology Bulletin, 24,* 417–426.

Hebl, M. R., & Mannix, L. M. (2003). The weight of obesity in evaluating others: A mere proximity effect. *Personality and Social Psychology Bulletin, 29,* 28–38.

Hedges, L. V., & Nowell, A. (1995). Sex differences in mental test scores, variability, and numbers of high-scoring individuals. *Science, 269*(5220), 41–45.

Heerey, E. A., Keltner, D., & Capps, L. M. (2003). Making sense of self-conscious emotion: Linking theory of mind and emotion in children with autism. *Emotion, 3,* 394–400.

Heine, S. J., & Lehman, D. R. (1995). Cultural variation in unrealistic optimism: Does the West feel more invulnerable than the East? *Journal of Personality and Social Psychology, 68,* 595–607.

Heiy, J. E., & Cheavens, J. S. (2014). Back to basics: A naturalistic assessment of the experience and regulation of emotion. *Emotion, 14*(5), 878–891. doi:10.1037/a0037231

Helliwell, J., & Grover, S. (2014, December). How's life at home? New evidence on marriage and the set point for happiness. NBER Working Paper No. 20794.

Henderlong, J., & Lepper, M. R. (2002). The effects of praise on children's intrinsic motivation: A review and synthesis. *Psychological Bulletin, 128,* 774–795.

Henrich, J. (2018). Human cooperation: The hunter-gatherer puzzle. *Current Biology, 28*(19), R1143–R1145.

Henrich, J., Heine, S. J., & Norenzayan, A. (2010). Most people are not WEIRD. *Nature, 466,* 29.

Herman, C. P., Roth, D. A., & Polivy, J. (2003). Effects of the presence of others on food intake: A normative interpretation. *Psychological Bulletin, 129,* 873–886.

Herman-Giddens, M. E., Steffes, J., Harris, D., Slora, E., Hussey, M., Dowshen, S. A., & Reiter, E. O. (2012). Secondary sexual characteristics in boys: Data from the pediatric research in office settings network. *Pediatrics, 130*(5), e1058–e1068. doi:10.1542/peds.2011-3291

Herring, M. P., Puetz, T. W., O'Connor, P. J., & Dishman, R. K. (2012). Effect of exercise training on depressive symptoms among patients with chronic illness: A systematic review and meta-analysis of randomized controlled trials. *Archives of Internal Medicine, 172*(2), 101–111.

Hershfield, H. E., Shu, S., & Benartzi, S. (2019, February 2). Temporal reframing and savings: A field experiment. *Marketing Science.* Available at http://dx.doi.org/10.2139/ssrn.3097468

Hertenstein, M. J., Holmes, R., McCullough, M., & Keltner, D. (2009). The communication of emotion via touch. *Emotion, 9,* 566–573.

Hertig, M. M., & Nagel, B. J. (2012). Aerobic fitness relates to learning on a virtual Morris water maze task and hippocampal volume in adolescents. *Behavioral Brain Research, 233,* 517–525.

Herz, R. S., & von Clef, J. (2001). The influence of verbal labeling on the perception of odors. *Perception, 30,* 381–391.

Hettema, J. M., Neale, M. C., & Kendler, K. S. (2001). A review and meta-analysis of the genetic epidemiology of anxiety disorders. *American Journal of Psychiatry, 158,* 1568–1578.

Heyes, C. (2016). Born pupils? Natural pedagogy and cultural pedagogy. *Perspectives on Psychological Science, 11*(2), 280–295. doi:10.1177/1745691615621276

Heyes, C. M., & Foster, C. L. (2002). Motor learning by observation: Evidence from a serial reaction time task. *Quarterly Journal of Experimental Psychology (A), 55,* 593–607.

Heyman, G. M. (2009). *Addiction: A disorder of choice.* Cambridge, MA: Harvard University Press.

Heymsfield, S. B., Greenberg, A. S., Fujioka, K., Dixon, R. M., Kushner, R., Hunt, T., . . . McCarnish, M. (1999). Recombinant leptin for weight loss in obese and lean adults: A randomized, controlled, dose-escalation trial. *Journal of the American Medical Association, 282*(16), 1568–1575.

Hibbeln, J. R. (1998). Fish consumption and major depression. *Lancet, 351,* 1213.

Hickok, G. (2009). Eight problems for the mirror neuron theory of action understanding in monkeys and humans. *Journal of Cognitive Neuroscience, 21,* 1229–1243.

Hickok, G. (2014). The myth of mirror neurons: The real neuroscience of communication and cognition. New York: Norton.

Higgins, E. T. (1987). Self-discrepancy theory: A theory relating self and affect. *Psychological Review, 94,* 319–340.

Higgins, E. T. (1997). Beyond pleasure and pain. *American Psychologist, 52,* 1280–1300.

Hilgard, E. R. (1965). *Hypnotic susceptibility.* New York: Harcourt, Brace and World.

Hilgard, E. R. (1986). *Divided consciousness: Multiple controls in human thought and action.* New York: Wiley-Interscience.

Hilker, R., Helenius, D., Fagerlund, B., Skytthe, A., Christensen, K., Werge, T. M., . . . Glenthøj, B. (2018). Heritability of schizophrenia and schizophrenia spectrum based on the nationwide Danish twin register. *Biological Psychiatry, 83,* 492–498.

Hill, S. E., Prokosch, M. L., DelPriore, D. J., Griskevicius, V., & Kramer, A. (2016). Low childhood socioeconomic status promotes eating in the absence of energy need. *Psychological Science, 27,* 354–364. doi:10.1177/0956797615621901

Hillman, C. H., Erickson, K. I., & Kramer, A. F. (2008). Be smart, exercise your heart: Exercise effects on brain and cognition. *Nature Reviews Neuroscience, 9,* 58–65.

Hilts, P. (1995). *Memory's ghost: The strange tale of Mr. M and the nature of memory.* New York: Simon & Schuster.

Hintzman, D. L., Asher, S. J., & Stern, L. D. (1978). Incidental retrieval and memory for coincidences. In M. M. Gruneberg, P. E. Morris, & R. N. Sykes (Eds.), *Practical aspects of memory* (pp. 61–68). New York: Academic Press.

Hirschberger, G., Florian, V., & Mikulincer, M. (2002). The anxiety buffering function of close relationships: Mortality salience effects on the readiness to compromise mate selection standards. *European Journal of Social Psychology, 32,* 609–625.

Hirsh-Pasek, K., Adamson, L. B., Bakeman, R., Owen, M. T., Golinkoff., R. M., Pace, A., . . . & Suma, K. (2015). The contribution of early communication quality to low-income children's language success. *Psychological Science, 26,* 1071–1083.

Hirst, W., & Echterhoff, G. (2012). Remembering in conversations: The social sharing and reshaping of memory. *Annual Review of Psychology, 63,* 55–79.

Hirst, W., Phelps, E. A., Buckner, R. L., Budson, A. E., Cuc, A., Gabrieli, J. D. E., . . . Vaidya, C. J. (2009). Long-term memory for the terrorist attack of September 11: Flashbulb memories, event memories, and the factors that influence their retention. *Journal of Experimental Psychology: General, 138,* 161–176.

Hirst, W., Phelps, E. A., Meksin, R., Vaidya, C. J., Johnson, M. K., Mitchell, K. J., . . . Olsson, A. (2015). A ten-year follow-up of a study of memory for the attack of September 11, 2001: Flashbulb memories and memories for flashbulb events. *Journal of Experimental Psychology: General, 144,* 604–623.

Hirst, W., Phelps, E. A., Meksin, R., Vaidya, C. J., Johnson, M. K., Mitchell, K. J., . . . Olsson, A. (2015). A ten-year follow-up of a study of memory for the attack of September 11, 2001: Flashbulb memories and memories for flashbulb events. *Journal of Experimental Psychology: General, 144,* 604–623.

Hobson, J. A. (1988). *The dreaming brain.* New York: Basic Books.

Hobson, J. A., & McCarley, R. W. (1977). The brain as a dream-state generator: An activation–synthesis hypothesis of the dream process. *American Journal of Psychiatry, 134,* 1335–1368.

Hochberg, L. R., Bacher, D., Jarosiewicz, B., Masse, N. Y., Simeral, J. D., Vogel, J., . . . Donoghue, J. P. (2012). Reach and grasp by people with tetraplegia using a neurally controlled robotic arm. *Nature, 485,* 372–377.

Hockley, W. E. (2008). The effects of environmental context on recognition memory and claims of remembering. *Journal of Experimental Psychology: Learning, Memory, and Cognition, 34,* 1412–1429.

Hodgkin, A. L., & Huxley, A. F. (1939). Action potential recorded from inside a nerve fibre. *Nature, 144,* 710–712.

Hodson, G., & Sorrentino, R. M. (2001). Just who favors the ingroup? Personality differences in reactions to uncertainty in the minimal group paradigm. *Group Dynamics, 5,* 92–101.

Hoek, H. W., & van Hoeken, D. (2003). Review of the prevalence and incidence of eating disorders. *International Journal of Eating Disorders, 34,* 383–396.

Hoffrage, U., & Gigerenzer, G. (1996). The impact of information representation on Bayesian reasoning. In G. Cottrell (Ed.),

Proceedings of the Eighteenth Annual Conference of the Cognitive Science Society (pp. 126–130). Mahwah, NJ: Erlbaum.

Hoffrage, U., & Gigerenzer, G. (1998). Using natural frequencies to improve diagnostic inferences. *Academic Medicine, 73,* 538–540.

Hofmann, S. G., & Asmundson, G. J. G. (2008). Acceptance and mindfulness-based therapy: New wave or old hat? *Clinical Psychology Review, 28*(1), 1–16.

Hofmann, W., Vohs, K. D., & Baumeister, R. F. (2012). What people desire, feel conflicted about, and try to resist in everyday life. *Psychological Science, 23,* 582–588.

Hogan, M. J., & Strasburger, V. C. (2008). Body image, eating disorders, and the media. *Adolescent Medicine: State of the Art Reviews, 19*(3), 521–46, x–xi.

Hoge, M. (2018). *Brainwashed: The bad science behind CTE and the plot to destroy football.* Herndon, VA: Mascot Books.

Hollins, M. (2010). Somesthetic senses. *Annual Review of Psychology, 61,* 243–271.

Holman, E. A., Silver, R. C., Poulin, M., Andersen, J., Gil-Rivas, V., & McIntosh, D. N. (2008). Terrorism, acute stress, and cardiovascular health. *Archives of General Psychiatry, 65,* 73–80.

Holmbeck, G. N., & O'Donnell, K. (1991). Discrepancies between perceptions of decision making and behavioral autonomy. In R. L. Paikoff (Ed.), *New directions for child development: Shared views in the family during adolescence* (no. 51, pp. 51–69). San Francisco: Jossey-Bass.

Holmes, J., Gathercole, S. E., & Dunning, D. L. (2009). Adaptive training leads to sustained enhancement of poor working memory in children. *Developmental Science, 12,* F9–F15.

Holmes, T. H., & Rahe, R. H. (1967). The social readjustment rating scale. *Journal of Psychosomatic Research, 11,* 213–318.

Holt-Lunstad, J. (2018). Why social relationships are important for physical health: A systems approach to understanding and modifying risk and protection. *Annual Review of Psychology, 69*(1), 437–458.

Hölzel, B. K., Carmody, J., Vangel, M., Congleton, C., Yerramsetti, S. M., Gard, T., & Lazar, S. W. (2011). Mindfulness practice leads to increases in regained gray matter density. *Psychiatry Research: Neuroimaging, 191,* 36–43.

Homans, G. C. (1961). *Social behavior.* New York: Harcourt, Brace and World.

Homonoff, T. (2013, March 27). Can small incentives have large effects? The impact of taxes versus bonuses on disposable bag use. Working Papers (Princeton University. Industrial Relations Section). Retrieved from http://arks.princeton.edu/ark:/88435/dsp014q77fr47j.

Hooley, J. M. (2007). Expressed emotion and relapse of psychopathology. *Annual Review of Clinical Psychology, 3,* 329–352.

Hoppenbrouwers, S. S., Bulten, B. H., & Brazil, I. A. (2016). Parsing fear: A reassessment of the evidence for fear deficits in psychopathy. *Psychological Bulletin, 142,* 573–600.

Hopper, L. M., Flynn, E. G., Wood, L. A. N., & Whiten, A. (2010). Observational learning of tool use in children: Investigating cultural spread through diffusion chains and learning mechanisms through ghost displays. *Journal of Experimental Child Psychology, 106,* 82–97.

Horn, J. L., & Cattell, R. B. (1966). Refinement and test of the theory of fluid and crystallized general intelligences. *Journal of Educational Psychology, 5,* 253–270.

Horner, A. J., Bisby, J. A., Bush, D., Lin, W.-J., & Burgess, N. (2015). Evidence for holistic episodic recollection via hippocampal pattern completion. *Nature Communications, 6,* 7462. doi:10.1038/ncomms8462

Horner, V., Whiten, A., Flynn, E., & de Waal, F. B. M. (2006). Faithful replication of foraging techniques along cultural transmission chains by chimpanzees and children. *Proceedings of the National Academy of Sciences, USA, 103,* 13878–13883.

Horrey, W. J., & Wickens, C. D. (2006). Examining the impact of cell phone conversation on driving using meta-analytic techniques. *Human Factors, 48,* 196–205.

Horta, B. L., Victora, C. G., Menezes, A. M., Halpern, R., & Barros, F. C. (1997). Low birthweight, preterm births and intrauterine growth retardation in relation to maternal smoking. *Paediatric and Perinatal Epidemiology, 11*(2), 140–151.

Hosking, S. G., Young, K. L., & Regan, M. A. (2009). The effects of text messaging on young drivers. *Human Factors, 51,* 582–592.

Howard, J. D., & Kahnt, T. (2018). Identity prediction errors in the human midbrain update reward–identity expectations in the orbitofrontal cortex. *Nature Communication, 9,* Art. No.: 1611.

Howard, J. H., Jr., & Howard, D. V. (1997). Age differences in implicit learning of higher order dependencies in serial patterns. *Psychology and Aging, 12,* 634–656.

Howard, M. O., Brown, S. E., Garland, E. L., Perron, B. E., & Vaughn, M. G. (2011). Inhalant use and inhalant use disorders in the United States. *Addiction Science & Clinical Practice, 6,* 18–31.

Howes, D. (2005) *Empire of the senses.* Oxford: Berg.

Howes, M., Siegel, M., & Brown, F. (1993). Early childhood memories—accuracy and affect. *Cognition, 47,* 95–119.

Hua, X., Hibar, D. P., Lee, S., Toga, A. W., Jack, C. R., Jr., Weiner, M. W., . . . Alzheimer's Disease Neuroimaging Initiative. (2010). Sex and age differences in atrophic rates: An ADNI study with n = 1368 MRI scans. *Neurobiology of Aging, 31,* 1463–1480.

Huang, J., Perlis, R. H., Lee, P. H., Rush, A. J., Fava, M., Sachs, G. S., . . . Smoller, J. W. (2010). Cross-disorder genome-wide analysis of schizophrenia, bipolar disorder, and depression. *American Journal of Psychiatry, 167,* 1254–1263.

Hubel, D. H. (1988). *Eye, brain, and vision.* New York: W. H. Freeman.

Hubel, D. H., & Wiesel, T. N. (1962). Receptive fields, binocular interaction and functional architecture in the cat's visual cortex. *Journal of Physiology, 160,* 106–154.

Hubel, D. H., & Wiesel, T. N. (1998). Early exploration of the visual cortex. *Neuron, 20,* 401–412.

Hudson, J. I., Hiripi, E., Pope, H. G., & Kessler, R. C. (2006). The prevalence and correlates of eating disorders in the National Comorbidity Survey Replication. *Biological Psychiatry, 61*(3), 348–358.

Huesmann, L. R. (2017). An integrative theoretical understanding of aggression: A brief exposition. *Current Opinion in Psychology, 19,* 119–124.

Huesmann, L. R., Moise-Titus, J., Podolski, C.-L., & Eron, L. D. (2003). Longitudinal relations between children's exposure to TV violence and their aggressive and violent behavior in young adulthood: 1977–1992. *Developmental Psychology, 39,* 201–221.

Hughes, A., & Kumari, M. (2019). Testosterone, risk, and socioeconomic position in British men: Exploring causal directionality. *Social Science and Medicine, 220,* 129–140.

Hughes, J. R. (2007). A review of sleepwalking (somnambulism): The enigma of neurophysiology and polysomnography with differential diagnosis of complex partial seizures. *Epilepsy & Behavior, 11*(4), 483–491.

Hughes, S., Power, T., & Francis, D. (1992). Defining patterns of drinking in adolescence: A cluster analytic approach. *Journal of Studies on Alcohol, 53,* 40–47.

Huibers, M. J., Cohen, Z. D., Lemmens, L. H., Arntz, A., Peeters, F. P., Cuijpers, P., & DeRubeis, R. J. (2015). Predicting optimal outcomes in cognitive therapy or interpersonal psychotherapy for depressed individuals using the personalized advantage index approach. *PLoS One, 10,* e0140771.

Hull, C. L. (1943). *Principles of behavior.* New York: Appleton-Century-Crofts.

Hunsley, J., & Di Giulio, G. (2002). Dodo bird, phoenix, or urban legend? The question of psychotherapy equivalence. *Scientific Review of Mental Health Practice, 1*(1), 13–24.

Hunsley, J., Ronson, A., & Cohen, K. R. (2013). Professional psychology in Canada: A survey of demographic and practice characteristics. *Professional Psychology: Research and Practice, 44*(2), 118–126.

Hunt, E. B. (2011). *Human intelligence.* New York: Cambridge University Press.

Hunt, L. L., Eastwick, P. W., & Finkel, E. J. (2015). Leveling the playing field: Longer acquaintance predicts reduced assortative mating on attractiveness. *Psychological Science, 26*(7), 1046–1053.

Hunt, M. (2007). *The story of psychology* (Exp. & Rev. Ed.). New York: Anchor Books.

Hurst, N. (2017). How does human echolocation work? Smithsonian.com. Retrieved from https://www.smithsonianmag.com /innovation/how-does-human-echolocation-work-180965063/

Hurvich, L. M., & Jameson, D. (1957). An opponent process theory of color vision. *Psychological Review, 64,* 384–404.

Hussey, E., & Safford, A. (2009). Perception of facial expression in somatosensory cortex supports simulationist models. *Journal of Neuroscience, 29*(2), 301–302.

Hutchison, R. M., Culham, J. C., Everling, S., Flanagan, J. R., & Gallivan, J. P. (2014). Distinct and distributed functional connectivity patterns across cortex reflect the domain-specific constraints of object, face, scene, body, and tool category-selective modules in the ventral visual pathway. *Neuroimage, 96,* 216–236. doi:10.1016/j.neuroimage.2014.03.068.

Huttenlocher, P. R. (1979). Synaptic density in human frontal cortex—developmental changes and effects of aging. *Brain Research, 163,* 195–205.

Huxley, A. (1954). *The doors of perception.* New York: Harper & Row.

Hyde, J. S. (2005) The gender similarities hypothesis. *American Psychologist, 60,* 581–592.

Hyman, I. E., Jr., & Pentland, J. (1996). The role of mental imagery in the creation of false childhood memories. *Journal of Memory and Language, 35,* 101–117.

Hyman, I. E., Jr., Boss, S. M., Wise, B. M., McKenzie, K. E., & Caggiano, J. M. (2010). Did you see the unicycling clown? Inattentional blindness while walking and talking on a cell phone. *Applied Cognitive Psychology, 24*(5), 597–607.

Hyman, I. E., Sarb, B. A., & Wise-Swanson, B. M. (2014). Failure to see money on a tree: Inattentional blindness for objects that guided behavior. *Frontiers in Psychology, 5,* 336. doi: 10.3389/fpsyg.2014.00356

Hypericum Depression Trial Study Group. (2002). Effect of Hypericum perforatum (St. John's wort) in major depressive disorder: A randomized controlled trial. *Journal of the American Medical Association, 287*(14), 1807–1814.

Iacoboni, M. (2009). Imitation, empathy, and mirror neurons. *Annual Review of Psychology, 60,* 653–670.

Iacoboni, M., Molnar-Szakacs, I., Gallese, V., Buccino, G., Mazziotta, J. C., & Rizzolatti, G. (2005). Grasping the intentions of others with one's own mirror neuron system. *PLoS Biology, 3,* 529–535.

Ichheiser, G. (1949). Misunderstandings in human relations: A study in false social perceptions. *American Journal of Sociology, 55* (Pt. 2):1–70.

Imbo, I., & LeFevre, J.-A. (2009). Cultural differences in complex addition: Efficient Chinese versus adaptive Belgians and Canadians. *Journal of Experimental Psychology: Learning, Memory, and Cognition, 35,* 1465–1476.

Inciardi, J. A. (2001). *The war on drugs III.* New York: Allyn & Bacon.

Ingvar, M., Ambros-Ingerson, J., Davis, M., Granger, R., Kessler, M., Rogers, G. A., . . . Lynch, G. (1997). Enhancement by an ampakine of memory encoding in humans. *Experimental Neurology, 146,* 553–559.

Inniss, D., Steiger, H., & Bruce, K. (2011). Threshold and subthreshold post-traumatic stress disorder in bulimic patients: Prevalences and clinical correlates. *Eating and Weight Disorders, 16*(1), e30–36. doi:10.1007/BF03327518

Inui, A. (2001). Ghrelin: An orexigenic and somatotrophic signal from the stomach. *Nature Reviews Neuroscience, 2,* 551–560.

Ipsos. (2019, May 21). Nearly half (47%) of Canadians think racism is a serious problem in Canada today, down 22 points since 1992 (69%). Retrieved from https://www.ipsos.com/en-ca /news-polls/Half-of-Canadians-think-racism-is-a-serious-problem

Irvine, J. T. (1978). Wolof magical thinking: Culture and conservation revisited. *Journal of Cross-Cultural Psychology, 9,* 300–310.

Isaacowitz, D. M. (2012). Mood regulation in real time: Age differences in the role of looking. *Current Directions in Psychological Science, 21*(4), 237–242.

Isaacowitz, D. M., & Blanchard-Fields, F. (2012). Linking process and outcome in the study of emotion and aging. *Perspectives on Psychological Science, 7*(1), 3–17.

Isenberg, D. J. (1986). Group polarization: A critical review and meta-analysis. *Journal of Personality and Social Psychology, 50*(6), 1141–1151.

Ittelson, W. H. (1952). *The Ames demonstrations in perception.* Princeton, NJ: Princeton University Press.

Iturrate, I., Chavarriaga, R., Montesano, L., Minguez, J., & del R. Millán, J. (2015). Teaching brain–machine interfaces as an alternative paradigm to neuroprosthetics control. *Scientific Reports, 5,* Article number: 13893. doi:10.1038/srep13893

Iverson, G. L. (2015). Suicide and chronic traumatic encephalopathy. *Journal of Neuropsychiatry & Clinical Neurosciences, 28,* 9–16. doi:10.1176/appi.neuropsych.15070172

Iyengar, S., Konitzer, T., & Tedin, K. (2018). The home as a political fortress: Family agreement in an era of polarization. *The Journal of Politics, 80*(4), 1326–1338.

Izard, C. E. (1971). *The face of emotion.* New York: Appleton-Century-Crofts.

Jachimowicz, J. M., Hauser, O. P., O'Brien, J. D., Sherman, E., & Galinsky, A. D. (2018). The critical role of second-order normative beliefs in predicting energy conservation. *Nature Human Behaviour, 2*(10), 757–764.

Jack, R. E., & Schyns, P. G. (2017). Toward a social psychophysics of face communication. *Annual Review of Psychology, 68,* 269–297. doi:10.1146/annurev-psych-010416-044242

Jacobson, E. (1932). The electrophysiology of mental activities. *American Journal of Psychology, 44,* 677–694.

Jacobson, N. C., & Newman, M. G. (2017). Anxiety and depression as bidirectional risk factors for one another: A meta-analysis of longitudinal studies. *Psychological Bulletin, 143,* 1155–1200.

Jacobson, T., & Hoffman, V. (1997). Children's attachment representations: Longitudinal relations to school behavior and academic competency in middle childhood and adolescence. *Developmental Psychology, 33,* 703–710.

Jaeger, A., Eisenkraemer, R. E., & Stein, L. M. (2015). Test-enhanced learning in third-grade children. *Educational Psychology, 35,* 513–521.

James, T. W., Culham, J., Humphrey, G. K., Milner, A. D., & Goodale, M. A. (2003). Ventral occipital lesions impair object recognition but not object-directed grasping: An fMRI study. *Brain, 126,* 2463–2475.

James, W. (1890). *The principles of psychology.* Cambridge, MA: Harvard University Press.

James, W. (1911). *Memories and studies.* New York: Longman

James, W. (1920). In H. James, Ed., *The letters of William James.* Boston: Atlantic Monthly Press.

Jamieson, J. P., Koslov, K., Nock, M. K., & Mendes, W. B. (2013). Experiencing discrimination increases risk-taking. *Psychological Science, 24,* 131–139.

Jamieson, J. P., Mendes, W. B., Blackstock, E., & Schmader, T. (2010). Turning the knots in your stomach into bows: Reappraising arousal improves performance on the GRE. *Journal of Experimental Social Psychology, 46,* 208–212.

Jamieson, J. P., Nock, M. K., & Mendes, W. B. (2013). Changing the conceptualization of stress in social anxiety disorder: Affective and physiological consequences. *Clinical Psychological Science, 1*(4), 363–374.

Jamison, K. R. (1993). *Touched with fire: Manic-depressive illness and the artistic temperament.* New York: Free Press.

Janicak, P. G., Dowd, S. M., Martis, B., Alam, D., Beedle, D., Krasuski, J., . . . Viana, M. (2002). Repetitive transcranial magnetic stimulation versus electroconvulsive therapy for major depression: Preliminary results of a randomized trial. *Biological Psychiatry, 51*(8), 659–667.

Janis, I. L. (1982). *Groupthink: Scientific studies of policy decisions and fiascoes.* Boston: Houghton-Mifflin.

Jaroszewski, A. C., Morris, R., & Nock, M. K. (2019). Randomized controlled trial of an online machine learning-driven risk assessment and intervention platform for increasing the use of crisis services. *Journal of Consulting and Clinical Psychology, 87*(4), 370–379.

Jasieńska, G., Ziomkiewicz, A., Ellison, P. T., Lipson, S. F., & Thune, I. (2004). Large breasts and narrow waists indicate high reproductive potential in women. *Proceedings of the Royal Society: Biological Sciences, 271,* 1213–1217.

Jausovec, N., & Jausovec, K. (2005). Differences in induced gamma and upper alpha oscillations in the human brain related to verbal performance and emotional intelligence. *International Journal of Psychophysiology, 56,* 223.

Jausovec, N., Jausovec, K., & Gerlic, I. (2001). Differences in even-trelated and induced electroencephalography patterns in the theta and alpha frequency bands related to human emotional intelligence. *Neuroscience Letters, 311,* 93.

Jaynes, J. (1976). *The origin of consciousness in the breakdown of the bicameral mind.* London, UK: Allen Lane.

Jenkins, H. M., Barrera, F. J., Ireland, C., & Woodside, B. (1978). Signal-centered action patterns of dogs in appetitive classical conditioning. *Learning and Motivation, 9,* 272–296.

Jenkins, J. G., & Dallenbach, K. M. (1924). Obliviscence during sleep and waking. *American Journal of Psychology, 35,* 605–612.

Jing, H. G., Madore, K. P., & Schacter, D. L. (2017). Preparing for what might happen: An episodic specificity induction impacts the generation of alternative future events. *Cognition, 169,* 118–128.

Jing, H. G., Szpunar, K. K., & Schacter, D. L. (2016). Interpolated testing influences focused attention and improves integration of information during a video-recorded lecture. *Journal of Experimental Psychology: Applied, 22,* 305–318.

John, O. P., & Srivastava, S. (1999). The Big Five trait taxonomy: History, measurement, and theoretical perspectives. In L. A. Pervin & O. P. John (Eds.), *Handbook of personality: Theory and research* (2nd ed., pp. 102–138). New York: Guilford Press.

John, O. P., Naumann, L. P., & Soto, C. J. (2008). Paradigm shift to the integrative Big-Five trait taxonomy: History, measurement, and conceptual issues. In O. P. John, R. W. Robins, & L. A. Pervin (Eds.), *Handbook of personality: Theory and research* (3rd ed., pp. 114–158). New York: Guilford Press.

Johnson, C. A., Xiao, L., Palmer, P., Sun, P., Wang, Q., Wei, Y. L., . . . Bechara, A. (2008). Affective decision-making deficits, linked to dysfunctional ventromedial prefrontal cortex, revealed in 10th-grade Chinese adolescent binge drinkers. *Neuropsychologia, 46,* 714–726.

Johnson, D. J., Cesario, J., & Pleskac, T. J. (2018). How prior information and police experience impact decisions to shoot. *Journal of Personality and Social Psychology, 115*(4), 601–623.

Johnson, D. R., & Wu, J. (2002). An empirical test of crisis, social selection, and role explanations of the relationship between marital disruption and psychological distress: A pooled time-series analysis of four-wave panel data. *Journal of Marriage and the Family, 64,* 211–224.

Johnson, J. D., Noel, N. E., & Sutter-Hernandez, J. (2000). Alcohol and male sexual aggression: A cognitive disruption analysis. *Journal of Applied Social Psychology, 30,* 1186–1200.

Johnson, J. S., & Newport, E. L. (1989). Critical period effects in second language learning: The influence of maturational state on the acquisition of English as a second language. *Cognitive Psychology, 21,* 60–99.

Johnson, K. (2002). Neural basis of haptic perception. In H. Pashler & S. Yantis (Eds.), *Stevens' handbook of experimental psychology: Vol. 1. Sensation and perception* (3rd ed., pp. 537–583). New York: Wiley.

Johnson, M. H., Dziurawiec, S., Ellis, H. D., & Morton, J. (1991). Newborns' preferential tracking of face-like stimuli and its subsequent decline. *Cognition, 40,* 1–19.

Johnson, M. K., Hashtroudi, S., & Lindsay, D. S. (1993). Source monitoring. *Psychological Bulletin, 114,* 3–28.

Johnson, N. J., Backlund, E., Sorlie, P. D., & Loveless, C. A. (2000). Marital status and mortality: The National Longitudinal Mortality Study. *Annual Review of Epidemiology, 10,* 224–238.

Johnson, S. C., Dweck, C. S., & Chen, F. S. (2007). Evidence for infants' internal working models of attachment. *Psychological Science, 18,* 501–2.

Johnson, S. L., & Miller, I. (1997). Negative life events and time to recover from episodes of bipolar disorder. *Journal of Abnormal Psychology, 106,* 449–457.

Johnson, S. L., Cuellar, A. K., & Miller, C. (2009). Unipolar and bipolar depression: A comparison of clinical phenomenology, biological vulnerability, and psychosocial predictors. In I. H. Gottlib & C. L. Hammen (Eds.), *Handbook of depression* (2nd ed., pp. 142–162). New York: Guilford Press.

Johnson, S. L., Cuellar, A. K., Ruggiero, C., Winnett-Perman, C., Goodnick, P., White, R., & Miller, I. (2008). Life events as predictors of mania and depression in bipolar 1 disorder. *Journal of Abnormal Psychology, 117,* 268–277.

Johnston, L., Bachman, J., & O'Malley, P. (1997). *Monitoring the future.* Ann Arbor, MI: Institute for Social Research.

Johnstone, E. C., Crow, T. J., Frith, C., Husband, J., & Kreel, L. (1976). Cerebral ventricular size and cognitive impairment in chronic schizophrenia. *Lancet, 2,* 924–926.

Jokela, M., Elovainio, M., Singh-Manoux, A., & Kivimaki, M. (2009). IQ, socioeconomic status, and early death: The US National Longitudinal Survey of Youth. *Psychosomatic Medicine, 71*(3), 322–328.

Jonas, E., Graupmann, V., Kayser, D. N., Zanna, M., Traut-Mattausch, E., & Frey, D. (2009). Culture, self, and the emergence of reactance: Is there a "universal" freedom? *Journal of Experimental Social Psychology, 45,* 1068–1080.

Jones, B. C., Little, A. C., Penton-Voak, I. S., Tiddeman, B. P., Burt, D. M., & Perrett, D. I. (2001). Facial symmetry and judgements of apparent health: Support for a "good genes" explanation of the attractiveness–symmetry relationship. *Evolution and Human Behavior, 22,* 417–429.

Jones, E. E., & Harris, V. A. (1967). The attribution of attitudes. *Journal of Experimental Social Psychology, 3,* 1–24.

Jones, E. E., & Nisbett, R. E. (1972). The actor and the observer: Divergent perceptions of the causes of behavior. In E. E. Jones, D. E. Kanouse, H. H. Kelley, R. E. Nisbett, S. Valins, & B. Weiner (Eds.), *Attribution: Perceiving the causes of behavior* (pp. 79–94). Morristown, NJ: General Learning Press.

Jones, J. H. (1993). *Bad blood: The Tuskegee Syphilis Experiment* (Exp. Ed., p. 10). New York: Free Press.

Jones, L. M., & Foshay, N. N. (1984). Diffusion of responsibility in a nonemergency situation: Response to a greeting from a stranger. *Journal of Social Psychology, 123,* 155–158.

Jones, M. J., Moore, S. R., & Kobor, M. S. (2018). Principles and challenges of applying epigenetic epidemiology to psychology. *Annual Review of Psychology, 69,* 459–485.

Jones, S. S. (2007). Imitation in infancy. *Psychological Science, 18*(7), 593–599.

Jonsson, H., & Hougaard, E. (2009). Group cognitive behavioural therapy for obsessive-compulsive disorder: A systematic review and meta-analysis. *Acta Psychiatrica Scandinavica, 119*(2), 98–106.

Jørgensen, K. N., Nesvåg, R., Gunleiksrud, S., Raballo, A., Jönsson, E. G., & Agartz, I. (2016). First- and second-generation antipsychotic drug treatment and subcortical brain morphology in schizophrenia. *European Archives of Psychiatry and Clinical Neuroscience, 266,* 451–460.

Joubert, K., & Du Mays, D. (2014). Relations sexuelles et contraception: Un portrait des jeunes au cours des années 2000. Bulletin *Zoom Santé, 45,* Gouvernement du Québec. Institut de la statistique du Québec.

Judd, L. L. (1997). The clinical course of unipolar major depressive disorders. *Archives of General Psychiatry, 54,* 989–991.

Judd, T. (2014). Making sense of multitasking: The role of Facebook. *Computers & Education, 70,* 194–202.

Julian, J. B., Ryan, J., & Epstein, R. A. (2017). Coding of object size and object category in human visual cortex. *Cerebral Cortex, 27*(6), 3095–3109. doi:10.1093/cercor/bhw150

Jung-Beeman, M. (2005). Bilateral brain processes for comprehending natural language. *Trends in Cognitive Sciences, 9,* 512–518.

Jung-Beeman, M., Bowden, E. M., Haberman, J., Frymiare, J. L., Arambel-Liu, S., Greenblatt, R., . . . Kounios, J. (2004). Neural activity when people solve verbal problems with insight. *PLoS Biology, 2,* 500–510.

Jurewicz, I., Owen, R. J., & O'Donovan, M. C. (2001). Searching for susceptibility genes in schizophrenia. *European Neuropsychopharmacology, 11,* 395–398.

Kaas, J. H. (1991). Plasticity of sensory and motor maps in adult mammals. *Annual Review of Neuroscience, 14,* 137–167.

Kagan, J. (1997). Temperament and the reactions to unfamiliarity. *Child Development, 68,* 139–143.

Kahneman, D. (2011). *Thinking fast and slow.* New York: Farrar, Straus and Giroux.

Kahneman, D., & Deaton, A. (2010). High income improves evaluation of life but not emotional well-being. *Proceedings of the National Academy of Sciences, USA, 107,* 16489–16493.

Kahneman, D., & Tversky, A. (1973). On the psychology of prediction. *Psychological Review, 80,* 237–251.

Kahneman, D., & Tversky, A. (1979). Prospect theory: An analysis of decision under risk. *Econometrica, 47,* 263–291.

Kahneman, D., & Tversky, A. (1984). Choices, values, and frames. *American Psychologist, 39,* 341–350.

Kahneman, D., Krueger, A. B., Schkade, D. A., Schwarz, N., & Stone, A. A. (2004). A survey method for characterizing daily life experience: The day reconstruction method. *Science, 306,* 1776–1780.

Kalb. J. (2015, January 12). Give me a smile. *New Yorker.*

Kalick, S. M., & Hamilton, T. E. (1986). The matching hypothesis reexamined. *Journal of Personality and Social Psychology, 51,* 673–682.

Kalokerinos, E. K., Greenaway, K. H., & Denson, T. F. (2015). Reappraisal but not suppression downregulates the experience of positive and negative emotion. *Emotion, 15*(3), 271–275. doi:10.1037/emo0000025

Kamin, L. J. (1959). The delay-of-punishment gradient. *Journal of Comparative and Physiological Psychology, 52,* 434–437.

Kamiya, J. (1969). Operant control of the EEG alpha rhythm and some of its reported effects on consciousness. In C. S. Tart (Ed.), *Altered states of consciousness* (pp. 519–529). Garden City, NY: Anchor Books.

Kan, P. F., & Kohnert, K. (2008). Fast mapping by bilingual preschool children. *Journal of Child Language, 35,* 495–514.

Kandel, E. R. (2000). Nerve cells and behavior. In E. R. Kandel, G. H. Schwartz, & T. M. Jessell (Eds.), *Principles of neural science* (pp. 19–35). New York: McGraw-Hill.

Kandel, E. R. (2006). *In search of memory: The emergence of a new science of mind.* New York: Norton.

Kang, S. H. K., McDermott, K. B., & Roediger, H. L., III. (2007). Test format and corrective feedback modify the effect of testing on long-term retention. *European Journal of Cognitive Psychology, 19,* 528–558.

Kanwisher, N. (2000). Domain specificity in face perception. *Nature Neuroscience, 3,* 759–763.

Kanwisher, N. (2010). Functional specificity in the human brain: A window into the functional architecture of the mind. *Proceedings of the National Academy of Sciences, USA, 107,* 11163–11170.

Kanwisher, N., McDermott, J., & Chun, M. M. (1997). The fusiform face area: A module in human extrastriate cortex specialized for face perception. *Journal of Neuroscience, 17,* 4302–4311.

Kapur, S., Craik, F. I. M., Tulving, E., Wilson, A. A., Houle, S., & Brown, G. M. (1994). Neuroanatomical correlates of encoding in episodic memory: Levels of processing effects. *Proceedings of the National Academy of Sciences, USA, 91,* 2008–2011.

Karau, S. J., & Williams, K. D. (1993) Social loafing: A meta-analytic review and theoretical integration. *Journal of Personality and Social Psychology, 65*(4), 681–706.

Karazsia, B. T., Murnen, S. K., & Tylka, T. L. (2017). Is body dissatisfaction changing across time? A cross-temporal meta-analysis. *Psychological Bulletin, 143*(3), 293–320. doi.org/10.1037/bul0000081

Kardes, F. R., & Sanbonmatsu, D. M. (2003). Omission neglect: The importance of missing information. *Skeptical Inquirer, 27,* 42–16.

Karlson, K. (2016). We tested over 100 different Facebook ads in one month – here's what we learned. Retrieved from https://adespresso.com/blog/test-100-facebook-ads-one-month-what-we-learned/

Karow, A., Pajonk, F. G., Reimer, J., Hirdes, F., Osterwald, C., Naber, D., & Moritz, S. (2007). The dilemma of insight into illness in schizophrenia: Self- and expert-rated insight and quality of life. *European Archives of Psychiatry and Clinical Neuroscience, 258,* 152–159.

Karpicke, J. D. (2012). Retrieval-based learning: Active retrieval promotes meaningful learning. *Current Directions in Psychological Science, 21,* 157–163.

Karpicke, J. D., & Aue, W. R. (2015). The testing effect is alive and well with complex materials. *Educational Psychology Review, 27,* 317–326.

Karpicke, J. D., & Blunt, J. R. (2011). Retrieval practice produces more learning than elaborative studying with concept mapping. *Science, 331,* 772–775.

Karpicke, J. D., & Roediger, H. L., III. (2008). The critical importance of retrieval for learning. *Science, 319,* 966–968.

Kashdan, T. B., Goodman, F. R., Stiksma, M., Milius, C. R., & McKnight, P. E. (2018). Sexuality leads to boosts in mood and meaning in life with no evidence for the reverse direction: A daily diary investigation. *Emotion, 18*(4), 563–576. doi.org/10.1037/emo0000324

Kasser, T., & Sharma, Y. S. (1999). Reproductive freedom, educational equality, and females' preference for resource-acquisition characteristics in mates. *Psychological Science, 10,* 374–377.

Kassin, S. M. (2007). Internalized false confessions. In M. Toglia, J. Read, D. Ross, & R. Lindsay (Eds.), *Handbook of eyewitness psychology: Volume 1, Memory for events* (pp. 175–192). Mahwah, NJ: Erlbaum.

Kassin, S. M. (2015). The social psychology of false confessions. *Social Issues and Policy Review, 9,* 25–51.

Kaufman, A. S. (2001). WAIS-III IQs, Horn's theory, and generational changes from young adulthood to old age. *Intelligence, 29,* 131–167.

Kaufman, L. (2009, January 30). Utilities turn their customers green, with envy. The *New York Times.* Retrieved from http://www.nytimes.com/2009/01/31/science/earth/31compete.html

Kawakami, K., Dovidio, J. F., Moll, J., Hermsen, S., & Russin, A. (2000). Just say no (to stereotyping): Effects of training in the negation of stereotypic associations on stereotype activation. *Journal of Personality and Social Psychology, 78,* 871–888.

Kayyal, M., Widen, S., & Russell, J. A. (2015). Context is more powerful than we think: Contextual cues override facial cues even for valence. *Emotion, 15*(3), 287–291. doi:10.1037/emo0000032

Kazdin, A. E. (2018). *Innovations in psychological interventions and their delivery: Leveraging cutting-edge science to improve the world's mental health.* New York: Oxford University Press.

Kazdin, A. E., & Blase, S. L. (2011). Rebooting psychotherapy research and practice to reduce the burden of mental illness. *Perspectives on Psychological Science, 6,* 21–37.

Keefe, F. J., Abernathy, A. P., & Campbell, L. C. (2005). Psychological approaches to understanding and treating disease-related pain. *Annual Review of Psychology, 56,* 601–630.

Keefe, F. J., Lumley, M., Anderson, T., Lynch, T., & Carson, K. L. (2001). Pain and emotion: New research directions. *Journal of Clinical Psychology, 57,* 587–607.

Kelley, H. H. (1967). Attribution theory in social psychology. In D. Levine (Ed.), *Nebraska Symposium on Motivation* (Vol. 15, pp. 192–238). Lincoln: University of Nebraska Press.

Kelley, M. R., Neath, I., & Surprenant, A. M. (2013). Three more semantic serial position functions and a SIMPLE explanation. *Memory & Cognition, 41,* 600–610.

Kelley, W. M., Macrae, C. N., Wyland, C. L., Caglar, S., Inati, S., & Heatherton, T. F. (2002). Finding the self? An event-related fMRI study. *Journal of Cognitive Neuroscience, 14,* 785–794.

Kelly, G. (1955). *The psychology of personal constructs.* New York: Norton.

Kelly, J. F., Karminer, Y., Kahler, C. W., Hoeppner, B., Yeterian, J., Cristello, J. V., & Timko, C. (2017). A pilot randomized clinical trial testing integrated 12-step facilitation (iTSF) treatment for adolescent substance use disorder. *Addiction, 112*(12), 2155–2166.

Kelm, Z., Womer, J., Walter, J. K., & Feudtner, C. (2014) Interventions to cultivate physician empathy: A systematic review. *BMC Medical Education, 14,* 219.

Keltner, D. (1995). Signs of appeasement: Evidence for the distinct displays of embarrassment, amusement, and shame. *Journal of Personality and Social Psychology, 68,* 441–454.

Keltner, D., & Buswell, B. N. (1996). Evidence for the distinctness of embarrassment, shame, and guilt: A study of recalled antecedents and facial expressions of emotion. *Cognition and Emotion, 10,* 155–171.

Keltner, D., & Haidt, J. (1999). Social functions of emotions at four levels of analysis. *Cognition and Emotion, 13,* 505–521.

Keltner, D., & Harker, L. A. (1998). The forms and functions of the nonverbal signal of shame. In P. Gilbert & B. Andrews (Eds.), *Shame: Interpersonal behavior, psychopathology, and culture* (pp. 78–98). New York: Oxford University Press.

Kendler, K. S., Hettema, J. M., Butera, F., Gardner, C. O., & Prescott, C. A. (2003). Life event dimensions of loss, humiliation, entrapment, and danger in the prediction of onsets of major depression and generalized anxiety. *Archives of General Psychiatry, 60,* 789–796.

Kendler, K. S., Myers, J., & Prescott, C. A. (2002). The etiology of phobias: An evaluation of the stress–diathesis model. *Archives of General Psychiatry, 59,* 242–248.

Kenrick, D. T., Griskevicius, V., Neuberg, S. L., & Schaller, M. (2010). Renovating the pyramid of needs: Contemporary extensions built upon ancient foundations. *Perspectives on Psychological Science, 5*(3), 292–314. doi:10.1177/1745691610369469

Kenrick, D. T., Sadalla, E. K., Groth, G., & Trost, M. R. (1990). Evolution, traits, and the stages of human courtship: Qualifying the parental investment model. *Journal of Personality, 58,* 97–116.

Kensinger, E. A., & Schacter, D. L. (2005). Emotional content and reality monitoring ability: fMRI evidence for the influence of encoding processes. *Neuropsychologia, 43,* 1429–1443.

Kensinger, E. A., & Schacter, D. L. (2006). Amygdala activity is associated with the successful encoding of item, but not source, information for positive and negative stimuli. *The Journal of Neuroscience, 26,* 2564–2570.

Kensinger, E. A., Clarke, R. J., & Corkin, S. (2003). What neural correlates underlie successful encoding and retrieval? A functional magnetic resonance imaging study using a divided attention paradigm. *Journal of Neuroscience, 23,* 2407–2415.

Keo-Meier, C. L., Herman, L. I., Reisner, S. L., Pardo, S. T., Sharp, C., & Babcock, J. C. (2015). Testosterone treatment and MMPI–2 improvement in transgender men: A prospective controlled study. *Journal of Consulting and Clinical Psychology, 83,* 143–156.

Kerr, N. L., & Tindale, R. S. (2004). Group performance and decision making. *Annual Review of Psychology, 55,* 623–655.

Kershaw, T. C., & Ohlsson, S. (2004). Multiple causes of difficulty in insight: The case of the nine-dot problem. *Journal of Experimental Psychology: Learning, Memory, and Cognition, 30,* 3–13.

Kertai, M. D., Pal, N., Palanca, B. J., Lin, N., Searleman, S. A., Zhang, L., . . . B-Unaware Study Group. (2010). Association of perioperative risk factors and cumulative duration of low bispectral index with intermediate-term mortality after cardiac surgery in the B-Unaware trial. *Anesthesiology, 112*(5), 1116–1127.

Kessing, L. V., Bauer, M., Nolen, W. A., Severus, E., Goodwin, G. M., & Geddes, J. (2018). Effectiveness of maintenance therapy of lithium vs. other mood stabilizers in monotherapy and in combinations: A systematic review of evidence from observational studies. *Bipolar Disorders, 20,* 419–431.

Kessler, R. C., & Üstün, T. B. (Eds.). (2008). *The WHO Mental Health surveys: Global perspectives on the epidemiology of mental health.* Cambridge: Cambridge University Press.

Kessler, R. C., & Wang, P. S. (2008). The descriptive epidemiology of commonly occurring mental disorders in the United States. *Annual Reviews of Public Health, 29,* 115–129.

Kessler, R. C., Adler, L., Barkley, R., Biederman, J., Connors, C. K., Demler, O., . . . Zaslavsky, A. M. (2006). The prevalence and correlates of adult ADHD in the United States: Results from the National Comorbidity Study Replication. *American Journal of Psychiatry, 163,* 716–723.

Kessler, R. C., Aguilar-Gaxiola, S., Alonso, J., Benjet, C., Bromet, E. J., Cardoso, G., . . . Koenen, K. C. (2017). Trauma and PTSD in the WHO world mental health surveys. *European Journal of Psychotraumatology, 8*(suppl 5), 1353383.

Kessler, R. C., Angermeyer, M., Anthony, J. C., deGraaf, R., Demyittenaere, K., Gasquet, I., . . . Üstün, T. B. (2007). Lifetime prevalence and age-of-onset distributions of mental disorders in the World Health Organization World Mental Health Survey Initiative. *World Psychiatry, 6,* 168–176.

Kessler, R. C., Berglund, P., Demler, M. A., Jin, R., Merikangas, K. R., & Walters, E. E. (2005a). Lifetime prevalence and age of onset distributions of *DSM-IV* disorders in the National Comorbidity Survey replication. *Archives of General Psychiatry, 62,* 593–602.

Kessler, R. C., Chiu, W. T., Dernier, O., & Walters, E. E. (2005b). Prevalence, severity, and comorbidity of 12-month *DSM–IV* disorders in the National Comorbidity Survey replication. *Archives of General Psychiatry, 62,* 617–627.

Kessler, R. C., Demler, O., Frank, R. G., Olfson, M., Pincus, H. A., Walters, E. E., . . . Zaslavsky, A. M. (2005c). Prevalence and treatment of mental disorders, 1990 to 2003. *New England Journal of Medicine, 352*(24), 2515–2523.

Kessler, R. C., Pecora, P. J., Williams, J., Hiripi, E., O'Brien, K., English, D., . . . Sampson, N. A. (2008). Effects of enhanced foster care on the long-term physical and mental health of foster care alumni. *Archives of General Psychiatry, 65*, 625–633.

Kessler, R. C., Petukhova, M., Sampson, N. A., Zaslavsky, A. M., & Wittchen, H. U. (2012). Twelve-month and lifetime prevalence and lifetime morbid risk of anxiety and mood disorders in the United States. *International Journal of Methods in Psychiatric Research, 21*(3), 169–184.

Keuler, D. J., & Safer, M. A. (1998). Memory bias in the assessment and recall of pre-exam anxiety: How anxious was I? *Applied Cognitive Psychology, 12*, S127–S137.

Keys, E., & Bhogal, M. S. (2018). Mean girls: Provocative clothing leads to intra-sexual competition between females. *Current Psychology, 37*(3), 543–551.

Khalid, N., Atkins, M., Tredget, J., Giles, M., Champney-Smith, K., & Kirov, G. (2008). The effectiveness of electroconvulsive therapy in treatment-resistant depression: A naturalistic study. *Journal of ECT, 24*(2), 141–145.

Khalid, R. (1991). Personality and academic achievement: A thematic apperception perspective. *British Journal of Projective Psychology, 36*, 25–34.

Kiefer, M., Schuch, S., Schenk, W., & Fiedler, K. (2007). Mood states modulate activity in semantic brain areas during emotional word encoding. *Cerebral Cortex, 17*, 1516–1530.

Kiehl, K. A., Smith, A. M., Hare, R. D., Mendrek, A., Forster, B. B., Brink, J., & Liddle, P. F. (2001). Limbic abnormalities in affective processing by criminal psychopaths as revealed by functional magnetic resonance imaging. *Biological Psychiatry, 50*, 677–684.

Kihlstrom, J. F., Beer, J. S., & Klein, S. B. (2002). Self and identity as memory. In M. R. Leary & J. P. Tangney (Eds.), *Handbook of self and identity* (pp. 68–90). New York: Guilford Press.

Kim, G., Walden, T. A., & Knieps, L. J. (2010). Impact and characteristics of positive and fearful emotional messages during infant social referencing. *Infant Behavior and Development, 33*, 189–195.

Kim, U. K., Jorgenson, E., Coon, H., Leppert, M., Risch, N., & Drayna, D. (2003). Positional cloning of the human quantitative trait locus underlying taste sensitivity to phenylthiocarbamide. *Science, 299*, 1221–1225.

Kinney, D. A. (1993). From nerds to normals—the recovery of identity among adolescents from middle school to high school. *Sociology of Education, 66*, 21–40.

Kirchner, W. H., & Towne, W. F. (1994). The sensory basis of the honeybee's dance language. *Scientific American, 270*(6), 74–80.

Kirk, N. W., Fiala, L., Scott-Brown, K. C., & Kempe, V. (2014). No evidence for reduced Simon cost in elderly bilingual and bidialecticals. *Journal of Cognitive Psychology (Hove), 26*(6), 640–648.

Kirsch, I., Cardena, E., Derbyshire, S., Dienes, Z., Heap, M., Kallio, S., . . . Whalley, M. (2011). Definitions of hypnosis and hypnotizability and their relation to suggestion and suggestibility: A consensus statement. *Contemporary Hypnosis and Integrative Therapy, 28*, 107–115.

Kirsch, I., Deacon, B. J., Huedo-Medine, T. B., Scoboria, A., Moore, T. J., & Johnson, B. T. (2008). Initial severity and antidepressant benefits: A meta-analysis of data submitted to the Food and Drug Administration. *PLoS Medicine, 5*, e45.

Kirwan, C. B., Bayley, P. J., Galvan, V. V., & Squire, L. R. (2008). Detailed recollection of remote autobiographical memory after damage to the medial temporal lobe. *Proceedings of the National Academy of Sciences, USA, 105*, 2676–2680.

Kish, S. J., Lerch, J., Furukawa, Y., Tong, J., McCluskey, T., Wilkins, D., . . . Bioleau, I. (2010). Decreased cerebral cortical serotonin transporter binding in ecstasy users: A positron emission tomography [11c] DASB and structural brain imaging study. *Brain, 133*, 1779–1797.

Klarer, M., Arnold, M., Günther, L., Winter, C., Langhans, W., & Meyer, U. (2014) Gut vagal afferents differentially modulate innate anxiety and learned fear. *Journal of Neuroscience, 34*, 7067–7076.

Kleiman, E. M., Turner, B. J., Fedor, S., Beale, E. E., Picard, R. W., Huffman, J. C., & Nock, M. K. (2018). Digital phenotyping of suicidal thoughts. *Depression and Anxiety, 35*(7), 601–608.

Klein, C. T. F., & Helweg-Larsen, M. (2002). Perceived control and the optimistic bias: A meta-analytic review. *Psychology and Health, 17*, 437–446.

Klein, O., & Snyder, M. (2003). Stereotypes and behavioral confirmation: From interpersonal to intergroup perspectives. In M. P. Zanna (Ed.), *Advances in experimental social psychology* (Vol. 35, pp. 153–234). San Diego, CA: Elsevier Academic Press.

Klein, R. A., Ratliff, K. A., Vianello, M., Adams, R. B., Jr., Bahník, Š., Bernstein, M. J., . . . Nosek, B. A. (2014). Investigating variation in replicability: A "many labs" replication project. *Social Psychology, 45*(3), 142–152. http://dx.doi.org/10.1027/1864-9335/a000178

Klein, R. M., Christie, J., & Parkvail, M. (2016). Does multilingualism affect the incidence of Alzheimer's disease? A worldwise analysis by country. *SSM – Population Health, 2*, 463–467.

Klein, S. B. (2004). The cognitive neuroscience of knowing one's self. In M. Gazzaniga (Ed.), *The cognitive neurosciences* (3rd ed., pp. 1077–1089). Cambridge, MA: MIT Press.

Klein, S. B., Robertson, T. E., & Delton, A. W. (2011). The future-orientation of memory: Planning as a key component mediating the high levels of recall found with survival processing. *Memory, 19*, 121–139.

Klingberg, T. (2010). Training and plasticity of working memory. *Trends in Cognitive Sciences, 14*, 317–324.

Klump, K. L., Strober, M., Bulik, C. M., Thornton, L., Johnson, C., Devlin, B., . . . Kaye, W. H. (2004). Personality characteristics of women before and after recovery from an eating disorder. *Psychological Medicine, 34*(8), 1407–1418. doi:10.1017/S0033291704002442

Klüver, H., & Bucy, P. C. (1937). "Psychic blindness" and other symptoms following bilateral temporary lobectomy in rhesus monkeys. *American Journal of Physiology, 119*, 352–353.

Klüver, H., & Bucy, P. C. (1939). Preliminary analysis of the temporal lobes in monkeys. *Archives of Neurology and Psychiatry, 42*, 979–1000.

Knowlton, B. J., Ramus, S. J., & Squire, L. R. (1992). Intact artificial grammar learning in amnesia: Dissociation of classification learning and explicit memory for specific instances. *Psychological Science, 3,* 173–179.

Knutson, B., Adams, C. M., Fong, G. W., & Hommer, D. (2001). Anticipation of increasing monetary reward selectively recruits nucleus accumbens. *Journal of Neuroscience, 21,* 159.

Kobasa, S. (1979). Stressful life events, personality, and health: An inquiry into hardiness. *Journal of Personality and Social Psychology, 37,* 1–11.

Koehler, J. J. (1993). The influence of prior beliefs on scientific judgments of evidence quality. *Organizational Behavior and Human Decision Processes, 56,* 28–55.

Koffka, K. (1935). *Principles of Gestalt psychology.* New York: Harcourt, Brace and World.

Kohlberg, L. (1958). *The development of modes of thinking and choices in years 10 to 16* (Unpublished doctoral dissertation, University of Chicago).

Kohlberg, L. (1963). Development of children's orientation towards a moral order: 1. Sequencing in the development of moral thought. *Vita Humana, 6,* 11–36.

Kohlberg, L. (1986). A current statement on some theoretical issues. In S. Modgil & C. Modgil (Eds.), *Lawrence Kohlberg: Concensus and controversy* (pp. 485–546). Philadelphia: Falmer.

Kolb, B., & Whishaw, I. Q. (2015). *Fundamentals of human neuropsychology* (7th ed.). New York: Worth Publishers.

Koller, D. (2011, December 5). Death knell for the lecture: Technology as a passport to personalized education. Retrieved from http://www.nytimes.com/2011/12/06/science/daphne-koller-technology-as-a-passport-to-personalized-education.html?pageswanted=all

Kolotkin, R. L., Meter, K., & Williams, G. R. (2001). Quality of life and obesity. *Obesity Reviews, 2,* 219–229.

Komter, A. (2010). The evolutionary origins of human generosity. *International Sociology, 25*(3), 443–464.

Koob, G. F., & Volkow, N. D. (2016). Neurobiology of addiction: A neurocircuitry analysis. *The Lancet Psychiatry, 3,* 760–773.

Koole, S. L., Dijksterhuis, A., & van Knippenberg, A. (2001). What's in a name: Implicit self-esteem and the automatic self. *Journal of Personality and Social Psychology, 80,* 669–685.

Kornblith, S., & Tsao, D. Y. (2017). How thoughts arise from sights: Inferotemporal and prefrontal contributions to vision. *Current Opinion in Neurobiology, 46,* 208–218.

Kosslyn, S. M., Alpert, N. M., Thompson, W. L., Chabris, C. F., Rauch, S. L., & Anderson, A. K. (1993). Visual mental imagery activates topographically organized visual cortex: PET investigations. *Journal of Cognitive Neuroscience, 5,* 263–287.

Kounios, J., & Beeman, M. (2009). The Aha! moment. *Current Directions in Psychological Science, 18,* 210–216.

Kounios, J., & Beeman, M. (2015). *The eureka factor: Aha moments, creative insight, and the brain.* New York: Random House.

Kounios, J., Frymiare, J. L., Bowden, E. M., Fleck, J. I., Subramaniam, K., Parrish, T. B., & Jung-Beeman, M. (2006). The prepared mind: Neural activity prior to problem presentation predicts subsequent solution by sudden insight. *Psychological Science, 17,* 882–890.

Kraemer, H. C., Shrout, P. E., & Rubio-Stipec, M. (2007). Developing the *Diagnostic and Statistical Manual–V:* What will "statistical" mean in *DSM–V? Social Psychiatry and Psychiatric Epidemiology, 42,* 259–267.

Kraus, M. W., Piff, P. K., & Keltner, D. (2011). Social class as culture: The convergence of resources and rank in the social realm. *Current Directions in Psychological Science, 20*(4), 246–250. doi:10.1177/0963721411414654

Kravitz, D. J., Saleem, K. S., Baker, C. I., & Mishkin, M. (2011). A new neural framework for visuospatial processing. *Nature Reviews Neuroscience, 12,* 217–230.

Kravitz, D. J., Saleem, K. S., Baker, C. I., Ungerleider, L. G., & Mishkin, M. (2013). The ventral visual pathway: An expanded neural framework for the processing of object quality. *Trends in Cognitive Sciences, 17,* 26–49.

Kravitz, R. L., Epstein, R. M., Feldman, M. D., Franz, C. E., Azari, R., Wilkes, M. S., . . . Franks, P. (2005). Influence of patients' requests for direct-to-consumer advertised antidepressants: A randomized controlled trial. *Journal of the American Medical Association, 293*(16), 1995–2002.

Kredlow, M. A., & Otto, M. W. (2015). Interference with the reconsolidation of trauma-related memories in adults. *Depression and Anxiety, 32,* 32–37.

Kreibig, S. D. (2010). Autonomic nervous system activity in emotion: A review. *Biological Psychology, 84*(3), 394–421. doi:10.1016/j.biopsycho.2010.03.010

Kristensen, P., & Bjerkedal, T. (2007). Explaining the relation between birth order and intelligence. *Science, 316,* 1717.

Kroeze, W. K., & Roth, B. L. (1998). The molecular biology of serotonin receptors: Therapeutic implications for the interface of mood and psychosis. *Biological Psychiatry, 44,* 1128–1142.

Kroger, J. (2017, February). Identity development in adolescence and adulthood. *Oxford Research Encyclopedia of Psychology.* Retrieved 13 Sep. 2018, from psychology.oxfordre.com/view/10.1093/acrefore/9780190236557.001.0001/acrefore-9780190236557-e-54.

Kruglanski, A. W., Jasko, K., Milyavsky, M., Chernikova, M., Webber, D., Pierro, A., & di Santo, D. (2018). Cognitive consistency theory in social psychology: A paradigm reconsidered. *Psychological Inquiry 29*(2), 45–59.

Kruk, M. R., Halasz, J., Meelis, W., & Haller, J. (2004). Fast positive feedback between the adrenocortical stress response and a brain mechanism involved in aggressive behavior. *Behavioral Neuroscience, 118,* 1062–1070.

Krupenye, C., Kano, F., Hirata, S., Call, J., & Tomasello, M. (2016). Great apes anticipate that other individuals will act according to false beliefs. *Science, 354*(6308), 110–114.

Kucyi, A., & Davis, K. D. (2015). The dynamic pain connectome. *Trends in Neurosciences, 38,* 86–95.

Kuffler, D. P. (2018). Origins of phantom limb pain. *Molecular Neurobiology, 55,* 60–69.

Kuhl, B. A., Dudukovic, N. M., Kahn, I., & Wagner, A. D. (2007). Decreased demands on cognitive control reveal the neural processing benefits of forgetting. *Nature Neuroscience, 10,* 908–917.

Kuhl, P. K. (2010). Brain mechanisms in early language acquisition. *Neuron, 67,* 713–727.

Kuhl, P., & Rivera-Gaxiola, M. (2008). Neural substrates of language acquisition. *Annual Review of Neuroscience, 31,* 511–534.

Kulke, L., von Duhn, B., Schneider, D., & Rakoczy, H. (2018). Is implicit theory of mind a real and robust phenomenon? Results from a systematic replication study. *Psychological Science, 29,* 888–900.

Kumar, M. B., & Tjepkema, M. (2019, June 28). Suicide among First Nations people, Métis and Inuit (2011–2016): Findings from the 2011 Canadian Census Health and Environment Cohort (CanCHEC). Retrieved from https://www150.statcan.gc.ca/n1/pub/99-011-x/99-011-x2019001-eng.htm

Kunda, Z. (1990). The case for motivated reasoning. *Psychological Bulletin, 108,* 480–498.

Kunda, Z., & Oleson, K. C. (1997). When exceptions prove the rule: How extremity of deviance determines the impact of deviant examples on stereotypes. *Journal of Personality and Social Psychology, 72,* 965–979.

Kundakovic, M., Gudsnuk, K, Herbstman, J. B., Tang, D. L., Perera, F. P., & Champagne, F. A. (2015). DNA methylation of BDNF as a biomarker of early-life adversity. *Proceedings of the National Academy of Sciences, USA, 112,* 6807–6813.

Kunugi, H., Urushibara, T., Murray, R. M., Nanko, S., & Hirose, T. (2003). Prenatal underdevelopment and schizophrenia: A case report of monozygotic twins. *Psychiatry and Clinical Neurosciences, 57,* 271–274.

Kunz, P. R., & Woolcott, M. (1976). Season's greetings: From my status to yours. *Social Science Research, 5,* 269–278.

Kurby, C. A., & Zacks, J. M. (2008). Segmentation in the perception and memory of events. *Trends in Cognitive Sciences, 12,* 72–79.

Kvavilashvili, L., Mirani, J., Schlagman, S., Foley, K., & Kornbrot, D. E. (2009). Consistency of flashbulb memories of September 11 over long delays: Implications for consolidation and wrong time slice hypotheses. *Journal of Memory and Language, 61,* 556–572.

Kwon, M.-K., Setoodehnia, M., Baek, J., Luck, S. J., & Oakes, L. M. (2016). The development of visual search in infancy: Attention to faces versus salience. *Developmental Psychology, 52*(4), 537–555.

LaBar, K. S., & Phelps, E. A. (1998). Arousal-mediated memory consolidation: Role of the medial temporal lobe in humans. *Psychological Science, 9,* 490–493.

Labella, M. H., & Masten, A. S. (2017). Family influences on the development of aggression and violence. *Current Opinion in Psychology, 19,* 11–13.

Labrie, V., Pai, S., & Petronis, A. (2012). Epigenetics of major psychosis: Progress, problems, and perspectives. *Trends in Genetics, 28,* 427–435.

Lacey, H. P., Smith, D. M., & Ubel, P. A. (2006). Hope I die before I get old: Mispredicting happiness across the adult lifespan. *Journal of Happiness Studies, 7*(2), 167–182.

Lackner, J. R., & DiZio, P. (2005). Vestibular, proprioceptive, and haptic contributions to spatial orientation. *Annual Review of Psychology, 56,* 115–147.

Lacourse, E., Baillargeon, R., Dupéré, V., Vitaro, F., Romano, E., & Tremblay, R. (2010). Two-year predictive validity of conduct disorder subtypes in early adolescence: A latent class analysis of a Canadian longitudinal sample. *Journal of Child Psychology and Psychiatry, 51*(12), 1386–1394.

Lafer-Sousa, R., & Conway, B. R. (2017). #TheDress: Categorical perception of an ambiguous color image. *Journal of Vision, 17*(12), 25. doi:10.1167/17.12.25

Lafer-Sousa, R., Hermann, K. L., & Conway, B. R. (2015). Striking individual differences in color perception uncovered by "the dress" photograph. *Current Biology, 25,* R1–R2.

LaFraniere, S. (2007, July 4). In Mauritania, seeking to end an overfed ideal. The *New York Times.* Retrieved from www.nytimes.com/2007/07/04/world/africa/04mauritania.html?pagewanted=all

Lai, C. K., Lehr, S. A., Cerruti, C., Joy-Gaba, J. A., Teachman, B. A., Koleva, S. P., . . . Hawkins, C. B. (2014). Reducing implicit racial preferences: I. A comparative investigation of 17 interventions. *Journal of Experimental Psychology, General, 143*(4), 1765–1785.

Lai, Y., & Siegal, J. (1999). Muscle atonia in REM sleep. In B. Mallick & S. Inoue (Eds.), *Rapid eye movement sleep* (pp. 69–90). New Delhi, India: Narosa Publishing House.

Lake, J. (2009). Natural products used to treat depressed mood as monotherapies and adjuvants to antidepressants: A review of the evidence. *Psychiatric Times, 26*(10), 1–6.

Lakhan, S. E., & Kirchgessner, A. (2012, March 12). Chronic traumatic encephalopathy: The dangers of getting "dinged." *Springer Plus,* 1:2. doi:10.1186/2193-1801-1-2

Lakin, J. M. (2013). Sex differences in reasoning abilities: Surprising evidence that male–female ratios in the tails of the quantitative reasoning distribution have increased. *Intelligence, 41*(4), 263–274.

Lakshminarayanan, V. R., Chen, M. K., & Santos, L. R. (2011). The evolution of decision-making under risk: Framing effects in monkey risk preferences. *Journal of Experimental Social Psychology, 47*(3), 689–693. doi:10.1016/j.jesp.2010.12.011

Lam, L. L., Emberly, E., Fraser, H. B., Neumann, S. M., Chen, E., Miller, G. E., . . . Kobor, M. S. (2012). Factors underlying variable DNA methylation in a human community cohort. *Proceedings of the National Academy of Sciences, USA, 109*(Suppl. 2), 17253–17260.

Lamm, C., Decety, J., & Singer, T. (2011). Meta-analytic evidence for common and distinct neural networks associated with directly experienced pain and empathy for pain. *Neuroimage, 54*(3), 2492–2502.

Lan, P. H., Miller, G. E., Chiang, J. J., Levine, C. S., Le, V., . . . Chen, E. (2018). One size does not fit all: Links between shift-and-persist and asthma in youth are moderated by perceived social status and experience of unfair treatment. *Development and Psychopathology, 30,* 1699–1714.

Landry, M., Lifshitz, M., & Raz, A. (2017). Brain correlates of hypnosis: A systematic review and meta-analytic exploration. *Neuroscience & Biobehavioral Reviews, 81,* 75–98.

Lane, J. D., Harris, P. L., Gelman, S. A., & Wellman, H. M. (2014). More than meets the eye: Young children's trust in claims that defy their perceptions. *Developmental Psychology, 50*(3), 865–871. doi:10.1037/a0034291

Lang, F. R., & Carstensen, L. L. (1994). Close emotional relationships in late life: Further support for proactive aging in the social domain. *Psychology and Aging, 9,* 315–324.

Langlois, J. H., Kalakanis, L., Rubenstein, A. J., Larson, A., Hallam, M., & Smoot, M. (2000). Maxims or myths of beauty? A meta-analytic and theoretical review. *Psychological Bulletin, 126,* 390–423.

Langlois, J. H., Ritter, J. M., Casey, R. J., & Sawin, D. B. (1995). Infant attractiveness predicts maternal behaviors and attitudes. *Developmental Psychology, 31,* 464–472.

Lanphear, B. P. (2015). The impact of toxins on the developing brain. *Annual Review of Public Health, 36*(1), 211–230.

LaPierre, S., Boyer, R., Desjardins, S., Dubé, M., Lorrain, D., Préville, M., & Brassard, J. (2012). Daily hassles, physical illness, and sleep problems in older adults with wishes to die. *International Psychogeriatrics, 24,* 243–252.

Lareau, A. (2003). *Unequal childhoods: Class, race, and family life.* Berkeley: University of California Press.

Larsen, S. F. (1992). Potential flashbulbs: Memories of ordinary news as baseline. In E. Winograd & U. Neisser (Eds.), *Affect and accuracy in recall: Studies of "flashbulb memories"* (pp. 32–64). New York: Cambridge University Press.

Larson, R., & Richards, M. H. (1991). Daily companionship in late childhood and early adolescence—changing developmental contexts. *Child Development, 62,* 284–300.

Latané, B., Williams, K., & Harkins, S. (1979). Many hands make light the work: The causes and consequences of social loafing. *Journal of Personality and Social Psychology, 37,* 822–832.

Lattal, K. A. (2010). Delayed reinforcement of operant behavior. *Journal of the Experimental Analysis of Behavior, 93,* 129–139.

Lavie, P. (2001). Sleep–wake as a biological rhythm. *Annual Review of Psychology, 52,* 277–303.

Lawrence, N. S., Jollant, F., O'Daly, O., Zelaya, F., & Phillips, M. L. (2009). Distinct roles of prefrontal cortical subregions in the Iowa Gambling Task. *Cerebral Cortex, 19,* 1134–1143.

Lazarus, R. S. (1984). On the primacy of cognition. *American Psychologist, 39,* 124–129.

Lazarus, R. S., & Alfert, E. (1964). Short-circuiting of threat by experimentally altering cognitive appraisal. *Journal of Abnormal and Social Psychology, 69,* 195–205.

Lazarus, R. S., & Folkman, S. (1984). *Stress, appraisal, and coping.* New York: Springer.

Le, B., & Agnew, C. R. (2003). Commitment and its theorized determinants: A meta–analysis of the Investment Model. *Personal Relationships, 10*(1), 37–57.

Leader, T., Mullen, B., & Abrams, D. (2007). Without mercy: The immediate impact of group size on lynch mob atrocity. *Personality and Social Psychology Bulletin, 33*(10), 1340–1352.

Leary, M. R. (1990). Responses to social exclusion: Social anxiety, jealousy, loneliness, depression, and low self-esteem. *Journal of Social and Clinical Psychology, 9,* 221–229.

Leary, M. R. (2010). Affiliation, acceptance, and belonging: The pursuit of interpersonal connection. In S. T. Fiske, D. T. Gilbert, & G. Lindzey (Eds.), *The handbook of social psychology* (5th ed., Vol. 2, pp. 864–897). New York: Wiley.

Leary, M. R., & Baumeister, R. F. (2000). The nature and function of self-esteem: Sociometer theory. In M. P. Zanna (Ed.), *Advances in experimental social psychology* (Vol. 32, pp. 1–62). San Diego: Academic Press.

Lecky, P. (1945). *Self-consistency: A theory of personality.* New York: Island Press.

Lecrubier, Y., Clerc, G., Didi, R., & Kieser, M. (2002). Efficacy of St. John's wort extract WS 5570 in major depression: A double-blind, placebo-controlled trial. *American Journal of Psychiatry, 159,* 1361–1366.

Lederbogen, F., Kirsch, P., Haddad, L., Streit, F., Tost, H. . . . Meyer-Lindenberg, A. (2011). City living and urban upbringing affect neural social stress processing in humans. *Nature, 474,* 498–501.

Lederman, S. J., & Klatzky, R. L. (2009). Haptic perception: A tutorial. *Attention, Perception, & Psychophysics, 71,* 1439–1459.

LeDoux, J. E. (1992). Brain mechanisms of emotion and emotional learning. *Current Opinion in Neurobiology, 2,* 191–197.

LeDoux, J. E., Iwata, J., Cicchetti, P., & Reis, D. J. (1988). Different projections of the central amygdaloid nucleus mediate autonomic and behavioral correlates of conditioned fear. *Journal of Neuroscience, 8,* 2517–2529.

Lee, D. N., & Aronson, E. (1974). Visual proprioceptive control of standing in human infants. *Perception & Psychophysics, 15,* 529–532.

Lee, L., Loewenstein, G., Ariely, D., Hong, J., & Young, J. (2008). If I'm not hot, are you hot or not? Physical-attractiveness evaluations and dating preferences as a function of one's own attractiveness. *Psychological Science, 19,* 669–677.

Lee, M. H., Smyser, C. D., & Shimony, J. S. (2013). Resting-state fMRI: A review of methods and clinical applications. *American Journal of Neuroradiology, 34,* 1866–1872. doi: 10.3174/ajnr.A3263

Lefcourt, H. M. (1982). *Locus of control: Current trends in theory and research* (2nd ed.). Hillsdale, NJ: Erlbaum.

Legare, C. H., & Nielsen, M. (2015). Imitation and innovation: The dual engines of cultural learning. *Trends in Cognitive Sciences, 19,* 688–699.

Legenbauer, T., Vocks, S., Schäfer, C., Schütt-Strömel, S., Hiller, W., Wagner, C., & Vögele, C. (2009). Preference for attractiveness and thinness in a partner: Influence of internalization of the thin ideal and shape/weight dissatisfaction in heterosexual women, heterosexual men, lesbians, and gay men. *Body Image, 6*(3), 228–234.

Lehtonen, M., Soveri, A., Laine, A., Järvenpää, J., de Bruin, A., & Antfolk, J. (2018). Is bilingualism associated with enhanced executive functioning in adults? A meta-analytic review. *Psychological Bulletin, 144,* 394–425.

Lemann, N. (1999, March 29). The IQ meritocracy: Our test-obsessed society has Binet and Terman to thank—or to blame. *Time,* 115–116.

Lemay, E. P. (2016). The forecast model of relationship commitment. *Journal of Personality and Social Psychology, 111*(1), 34–52.

Lempert, D. (2007). *Women's increasing wage penalties from being overweight and obese.* Washington, DC: U.S. Bureau of Labor Statistics.

Lenton, A. P., & Francesconi, M. (2010). How humans cognitively manage an abundance of mate options. *Psychological Science, 21*(4), 528–533.

Lentz, M. J., Landis, C. A., Rothermel, J., & Shaver, J. L. (1999). Effects of selective slow wave sleep disruption on musculoskeletal pain and fatigue in middle-aged women. *Journal of Rheumatology, 26,* 1586–1592.

Leon, D. A., Lawlor, D. A., Clark, H., Batty, G. D., & Macintyre, S. (2009). The association of childhood intelligence with mortality risk from adolescence to middle age: Findings from the Aberdeen children of the 1950s cohort study. *Intelligence, 37*(6), 520–528.

Lepage, M., Ghaffar, O., Nyberg, L., & Tulving, E. (2000). Prefrontal cortex and episodic memory retrieval mode. *Proceedings of the National Academy of Sciences, USA, 97,* 506–511.

LePort, A. K. R., Mattfield, A. T., Dickinson-Anson, H., Fallon, J. H., Stark, C. E. L., Kruggel, F., . . . McGaugh, J. L. (2012). Behavioral and neuroanatomical investigation of highly superior autobiographical memory (HSAM). *Neurobiology of Learning and Memory, 98,* 78–92.

Lepper, M. R., Greene, D., & Nisbett, R. E. (1973). Undermining children's intrinsic interest with extrinsic rewards: A test of the "overjustification" hypothesis. *Journal of Personality and Social Psychology, 28,* 129–137.

Lerman, D. (2006). Consumer politeness and complaining behavior. *Journal of Services Marketing, 20,* 92–100.

Lerman, D. C., & Vorndran, C. M. (2002). On the status of knowledge for using punishment: Implications for treating behavior disorders. *Journal of Applied Behavior Analysis, 35,* 4312–4464.

Lerner, M. J. (1980). *The belief in a just world: A fundamental delusion.* New York: Plenum.

Leung, A. K.-Y., & Cohen, D. (2011). Within- and between-culture variation: Individual differences and the cultural logics of honor, face, and dignity cultures. *Journal of Personality and Social Psychology, 100*(3), 507–526.

Levelt Committee, Noort Committee, Drenth Committee. (2012, November 28). *Flawed science: The fraudulent research practices of social psychologist Diederik Stapel.* Retrieved from http://www .tilburguniversity.edu/nl/nieuws-en-agenda/finalreportLevelt.pdf

Levenson, J. M., & Sweatt, J. D. (2005). Epigenetic mechanisms in memory formation. *Nature Reviews Neuroscience, 6,* 108–118.

Levenson, R. W., Cartensen, L. L., Friesen, W. V., & Ekman, P. (1991). Emotion, physiology, and expression in old age. *Psychology and Aging, 6,* 28–35.

Levenson, R. W., Ekman, P., & Friesen, W. V. (1990). Voluntary facial action generates emotion-specific autonomic nervous system activity. *Psychophysiology, 27,* 363–384.

Levenson, R. W., Ekman, P., Heider, K., & Friesen, W. V. (1992). Emotion and automatic nervous system activity in the Minangkabau of West Sumatra. *Journal of Personality and Social Psychology, 62,* 972–988.

Levin, R., & Nielsen, T. (2009). Nightmares, bad dreams, and emotion dysregulation: A review and new neurocognitive model of dreaming. *Current Directions in Psychological Science, 18,* 84–88.

Levine, L. J., Lench, H. C., Karnaze, M. M., & Carlson, S. J. (2018). Bias in predicted and remembered emotion. *Current Opinion in Behavioral Sciences, 19,* 73–77.

Levine, R. V., & Norenzayan, A. (1999). The pace of life in 31 countries. *Journal of Cross-Cultural Psychology, 30*(2), 178–205.

Levy, J., Trevarthen, C., & Sperry, R. W. (1972). Perception of bilateral chimeric figures following hemispheric disconnection. *Brain, 95,* 61–78.

Lewandowsky, S., Oberauer, K., & Gignac, G. E. (2013). NASA faked the moon landing—therefore, (climate) science is a hoax: An anatomy of the motivated rejection of science. *Psychological Science, 24,* 622–633.

Lewin, K. (1948). Resolving social conflicts; selected papers on group dynamics. (G. W. Lewin (Ed.) New York: Harper & Row.

Lewin, K. (1951). Behavior and development as a function of the total situation. In K. Lewin (Ed.), *Field theory in social science: Selected theoretical papers* (pp. 791–843). New York: Harper & Row.

Lewin, K., Lippitt, R., & White, R. K. (1939). Patterns of aggressive behavior in experimentally created social climates. *Journal of Social Psychology, 10,* 271–299.

Lewis, M. B. (2012). Exploring the positive and negative implications of facial feedback. *Emotion, 12*(4), 852–859.

Lewis, M. D., Hibbeln, J. R., Johnson, J. E., Lin, Y. H., Hyun, D. Y., & Loewke, J. D. (2011). Suicide deaths of active-duty US military and omega-3 fatty acid status: A case-control comparison. *Journal of Clinical Psychiatry, 72*(12), 1585–1590.

Lewis, M., & Brooks-Gunn, J. (1979). *Social cognition and the acquisition of self.* New York: Plenum Press.

Lewontin, R., Rose, S., & Kamin, L. J. (1984). *Not in our genes.* New York: Pantheon.

Li, C., Cheng, Z., Wu, T., Liang, X., Gaoshan, J., Li, L., . . ., Tang, K. (2017). The relationships of school-based sexuality education, sexual knowledge, and sexual behaviors—A study of 18,000 Chinese college students. *Reproductive Health, 14,* 103.

Li, G., Kung, K. F., & Hines, M. (2017). Childhood gender-typed behavior and adolescent sexual orientation: A longitudinal population-based study. *Developmental Psychology, 53*(4), 764–777.

Li, N. P., van Vugt, M., & Colarelli, S. M. (2018). The evolutionary mismatch hypothesis: Implications for psychological science. *Current Directions in Psychological Science, 27*(1), 38–44.

Li, N. P., Yong, J. C., Tov, W., Sng, O., Fletcher, G. J. O., Valentine, K. A., . . . Balliet, D. (2013). Mate preferences do predict attraction and choices in the early stages of mate selection. *Journal of Personality and Social Psychology, 105*(5), 757–776.

Li, Y. J., Johnson, K. A., Cohen, A. B., Williams, M. J., Knowles, E. D., & Chen, Z. (2012). Fundamental(ist) attribution error: Protestants are dispositionally focused. *Journal of Personality and Social Psychology, 102*(2), 281–290.

Liberman, Z., Woodward, A. L., & Kinzler, K. D. (2017). The origins of social categorization. *Trends in Cognitive Sciences, 21*(7), 556–568.

Libet, B. (1985). Unconscious cerebral initiative and the role of conscious will in voluntary action. *Behavioral and Brain Sciences, 8,* 529–566.

Liebenluft, E. (1996). Women with bipolar illness: Clinical and research issues. *American Journal of Psychiatry, 153,* 163–173.

Lieberman, M. D., & Rosenthal, R. (2001). Why introverts can't always tell who likes them: Multitasking and nonverbal decoding. *Journal of Personality and Social Psychology, 80,* 294–310.

Lieberman, M. D., Inagaki, T. K., Tabibnia, G., & Crockett, M. J. (2011). Subjective responses to emotional stimuli during labeling, reappraisal, and distraction. *Emotion, 11,* 468–480.

Liebowitz, M. R., Gorman, J. M., Fyer, A. J., Levitt, M., Dillon, D., Levy, G., . . . Davies, S. O. (1985). Lactate provocation of panic attacks: II. Biochemical and physiological findings. *Archives of General Psychiatry, 42,* 709–719.

Lilienfeld, S. O. (2007). Psychological treatments that cause harm. *Perspectives on Psychological Science, 2*(1), 53–70.

Lilienfeld, S. O., Lynn, S. J., & Lohr, J. M. (Eds.). (2003). *Science and pseudoscience in clinical psychology.* New York: Guilford Press.

Lilienfeld, S. O., Wood, J. M., & Garb, H. N. (2000). The scientific status of projective techniques. *Psychological Science in the Public Interest, 1,* 27–66.

Lim, K. L., Jacobs, P., Ohinmaa, A., Schopflocher, D., & Dewa, C. S. (2008). A new population-based measure of the economic burden of mental illness in Canada. *Chronic Diseases in Canada, 28*(3), 92–98.

Lindenberger, U., & Baltes, P. B. (1997). Intellectual functioning in old and very old age: Cross-sectional results from the Berlin aging study. *Psychology and Aging, 12,* 410–432.

Lindquist, K. A., Wager, T. D., Kober, H., Bliss-Moreau, E., & Barrett, L. F. (2012). The brain basis of emotion: A meta-analytic review. *Behavioral and Brain Sciences, 35*(3), 121–143. doi:10.1017/S0140525X11000446

Lindquist, K., & Barrett, L. F. (2008). Constructing emotion: The experience of fear as a conceptual act. *Psychological Science, 19,* 898–903.

Lindquist, S. I., & McLean, J. P. (2011). Daydreaming and its correlates in an educational environment. *Learning and Individual Differences, 21,* 158–167.

Liou, A. P., Paziuk, M., Luevano, J.-M., Machineni, S., Turnbaugh, P. J., & Kaplan, L. M. (2013). Conserved shifts in the gut microbiota due to gastric bypass reduce host weight and adiposity. *Science Translational Medicine, 5*(178), 178ra41.

Liszkowski, U., Carpenter, M., Striano, T., & Tomasello, M. (2006). 12- and 18-month-olds point to provide information for others. *Journal of Cognition and Development, 7*(2), 173–187.

Liu, D., Diorio, J., Tannenbaum, B., Caldji, C., Francis, D., Freedman, A., . . . Meaney, M. J. (1997). Maternal care, hippocampal glucocorticoid receptors, and hypothalamic–pituitary–adrenal responses to stress. *Science, 277,* 1659–1662.

Liu, D., Wellman, H. M., Tardif, T., & Sabbagh, M. A. (2008). Theory of mind development in Chinese children: A meta-analysis of false belief understanding across cultures and languages. *Developmental Psychology, 44,* 523–531.

Liu, S., Ullman, T. D., Tenenbaum, J. B., & Spelke, E. S. (2017). Ten-month-old infants infer the value of goals from the costs of actions. *Science, 358*(6366), 1038–1041.

Livingstone, M., & Hubel, D. (1988). Segregation of form, color, movement, and depth: Anatomy, physiology, and perception. *Science, 240,* 740–749.

Locke, J. (1690). *Essay on human understanding.* Pennsylvania State University, *Electronic Classics Series.* Hazleton, PA: Pennsylvania State University.

Locksley, A., Ortiz, V., & Hepburn, C. (1980). Social categorization and discriminatory behavior: Extinguishing the minimal intergroup discrimination effect. *Journal of Personality and Social Psychology, 39,* 773–783.

Loehlin, J. C. (1973). Blood group genes and Negro–White ability differences. *Behavior Genetics, 3*(3), 263–270.

Loftus, E. F. (1993). The reality of repressed memories. *American Psychologist, 48,* 518–537.

Loftus, E. F. (2003). Make-believe memories. *American Psychologist, 58,* 867–873.

Loftus, E. F., & Ketchum, K. (1994). *The myth of repressed memory.* New York: St. Martin's Press.

Loftus, E. F., & Klinger, M. R. (1992). Is the unconscious smart or dumb? *American Psychologist, 47,* 761–765.

Loftus, E. F., & Pickrell, J. E. (1995). The formation of false memories. *Psychiatric Annals, 25,* 720–725.

Lonegran, M. H., Olivera-Figueroa, L. A., Pitman, R. K., & Brunet, A. (2013). Propranolol's effects on the consolidation and reconsolidation of long-term emotional memory in healthy participants: A meta-analyis. *Journal of Psychiatry & Neuroscience, 38,* 222–231.

Long, P. (2017, May 30). My déjà vu is so extreme I can't tell what's real any more. https://mosaicscience.com/story/my-deja-vu-so-extreme-i-cant-tell-whats-real-any-more/

Lopes, P. N., Grewal, D., Kadis, J., Gall, M., & Salovey, P. (2006). Emotional intelligence and positive work outcomes. *Psicothema, 18,* 132.

Lord, C. G., Ross, L., & Lepper, M. R. (1979). Biased assimilation and attitude polarization: The effects of prior theories on subsequently considered evidence. *Journal of Personality and Social Psychology, 37,* 2098–2109.

Lorenz, K. (1952). *King Solomon's ring.* New York: Crowell.

Lovaas, O. I. (1987). Behavioral treatment and normal educational and intellectual functioning in young autistic children. *Journal of Consulting and Clinical Psychology, 55,* 3–9.

Low, J., & Watts, J. (2013). Attributing false beliefs about object identity reveals a signature blind spot in humans' efficient mind-reading system. *Psychological Science, 24*(3), 305–311. doi:10.1177/0956797612451469

Lozano, B. E., & Johnson, S. L. (2001). Can personality traits predict increases in manic and depressive symptoms? *Journal of Affective Disorders, 63,* 103–111.

Lubinski, D. (2016). From Terman to today: A century of findings on intellectual precocity. *Review of Educational Research, 86*(4), 900–944.

Luborsky, L., Rosenthal, R., Diguer, L., Andrusyna, T. P., Berman, J. S., Levitt, J. T., . . . Krause, E. D. (2002). The dodo bird verdict is alive and well—mostly. *Clinical Psychology: Science and Practice, 9,* 2–12.

Lucas, R. E., & Dyrenforth, P. S. (2005). The myth of marital bliss? *Psychological Inquiry, 16*(2/3), 111–115.

Lucas, R. E., Clark, A. E., Georgellis, Y., & Diener, E. (2003). Reexamining adaptation and the set point model of happiness: Reactions to changes in marital status. *Journal of Personality and Social Psychology, 84,* 527–539.

Ludwig, A. M. (1966). Altered states of consciousness. *Archives of General Psychiatry, 15,* 225–234.

Lurquin, J. H., Michaelson, L. E., Barker, J. E, Gustavson, D. E., von Bastian, C. C., Carruth, N. P., & Miyake, A. (2016). No evidence of the ego-depletion effect across task characteristics and individual differences: A pre-registered study. *PLoS ONE, 11*(2), e0147770.

Luthar, S. S., & Ciciolla, L. (2016). What it feels like to be a mother: Variations by children's developmental stages. *Developmental Psychology, 52*(1), 143–154.

Lyden, J., & Binswanger, I. A. (2019). The United States opioid epidemic. *Seminars in Perinatology.* doi.10.1053/j.semperi.2019.01.001

Lykken, D. T. (1995). *The antisocial personalities.* Hillsdale, NJ: Erlbaum.

Lynn, M., & Shurgot, B. A. (1984). Responses to lonely hearts advertisements: Effects of reported physical attractiveness, physique, and coloration. *Personality and Social Psychology Bulletin, 10,* 349–357.

Lynn, R. (2009). What has caused the Flynn effect? Secular increases in the development quotients of infants. *Intelligence, 37*(1), 16–24.

Lynn, R. (2013). Who discovered the Flynn effect? A review of early studies of the secular increase of intelligence. *Intelligence, 41*(6), 765–769.

Lyons, D. E., Young, A. G., & Keil, F. C. (2007). The hidden structure of overimitation. *Proceedings of the National Academy of Sciences, 104*(50), 19751–19756.

Lyubomirsky, S. (2008). *The how of happiness: A scientific approach to getting the life you want.* New York: Penguin.

MacCann, C., Joseph, D. L., Newman, D. A., & Roberts, R. D. (2014). Emotional intelligence is a second-stratum factor of intelligence: Evidence from hierarchical and bifactor models. *Emotion, 14*(2), 358–374.

MacDonald, S., Uesiliana, K., & Hayne, H. (2000). Cross-cultural and gender differences in childhood amnesia. *Memory, 8,* 365–376.

MacGregor, J. N., Ormerod, T. C., & Chronicle, E. P. (2001). Information processing and insight: A process model of performance on the nine-dot and related problems. *Journal of Experimental Psychology: Learning, Memory, and Cognition, 27,* 176–201.

Maclean, P. D. (1970). The triune brain, emotion, and scientific bias. In F. O. Schmitt (Ed.), *The neurosciences: A second study program* (pp. 336–349). New York: Rockefeller University Press.

MacLeod, M. D. (2002). Retrieval-induced forgetting in eyewitness memory: Forgetting as a consequence of remembering. *Applied Cognitive Psychology, 16,* 135–149.

MacLeod, M. D., & Saunders, J. (2008). Retrieval inhibition and memory distortion: Negative consequences of an adaptive process. *Current Directions in Psychological Science, 17,* 26–30.

Macmillan, M. (2000). *An odd kind of fame: Stories of Phineas Gage.* Cambridge, MA: MIT Press.

Macmillan, N. A., & Creelman, C. D. (2005). *Detection theory.* Mahwah, NJ: Erlbaum.

Macrae, C. N., Bodenhausen, G. V., Milne, A. B., & Jetten, J. (1994). Out of mind but back in sight: Stereotypes on the rebound. *Journal of Personality and Social Psychology, 67,* 808–817.

Macrae, C. N., Moran, J. M., Heatherton, T. F., Banfield, J. F., & Kelley, W. M. (2004). Medial prefrontal activity predicts memory for self. *Cerebral Cortex, 14,* 647–654.

Maddi, S. R., Harvey, R. H., Khoshaba, D. M., Fazel, M., & Resurreccion, N. (2009). Hardiness training facilitates performance in college. *Journal of Positive Psychology, 4,* 566–577.

Maddi, S. R., Kahn, S., & Maddi, K. L. (1998). The effectiveness of hardiness training. *Consulting Psychology Journal: Practice and Research, 50,* 78–86.

Maddux, W. W., Mullen, E., & Galinsky, A. D. (2008). Chameleons bake bigger pies and take bigger pieces: Strategic behavioral mimicry facilitates negotiation outcomes. *Journal of Experimental Social Psychology, 44,* 461–468.

Madigan, S., Atkinson, L., Laurin, K., & Benoit, D. (2013). Attachment and internalizing behavior in early childhood: A meta-analysis. *Developmental Psychology, 49*(4), 672–689. doi:10.1037/a0028793

Madore, K. P., Addis, D., & Schacter, D. L. (2015). Creativity and memory: Effects of an episodic specificity induction on divergent thinking. *Psychological Science, 26,* 1461–1468.

Madore, K. P., Thakral, P. P., Beaty, R. E., Addis, D. R., & Schacter, D. L. (2019). Neural mechanisms of episodic retrieval support divergent creative thinking. *Cerebral Cortex, 29*(1), 150–166.

Maes, M. (1995). Evidence for an immune response in major depression: A review and hypothesis. *Progress in Neuro-Psychopharmacology and Biological Psychiatry, 19,* 11–38.

Maguire, E. A., Gadian, D. G., Johnsrude, I. S., Good, C. D., Ashburner, J., Frackowiak, R. S. J., and Frith, C. D. (2000). Navigation-related structural change in the hippocampi of taxi drivers. *Proceedings of the National Academy of Sciences USA, 97,* 4398–4403.

Mahajan, N., Martinez, M. A., Gutierrez, N. L., Diesendruck, G., Banaji, M. R., & Santos, L. R. (2011). The evolution of intergroup bias: Perceptions and attitudes in rhesus macaques. *Journal of Personality and Social Psychology, 100*(3), 387–405.

Mahon, B. Z., & Caramazza, A. (2009). Concepts and categories: A cognitive neuropsychological perspective. *Cognitive Neuropsychology, 60,* 27–51.

Mahon, B. Z., Anzellotti, S., Schwarzbach, J., Zampini, M., & Caramazza, A. (2009). Category-specific organization in the human brain does not require visual experience. *Neuron, 63,* 397–405.

Mahowald, M., & Schenck, C. (2000). REM sleep parasomnias. In M. Kryger, T. Roth, & W. Dement (Eds.), *Principles and practices of sleep medicine* (3rd ed., pp. 724–741). Philadelphia: Saunders.

Maier, S. F., & Watkins, L. R. (1998). Cytokines for psychologists: Implications of bidirectional immune-to-brain communication for understanding behavior, mood, and cognition. *Psychological Review, 105,* 83–107.

Maier, S. F., & Watkins, L. R. (2000). The immune system as a sensory system: Implications for psychology. *Current Directions in Psychological Science, 9,* 98–102.

Maillet, D., Beaty, R. E., Jordano, M. L., Touron, D. R., Adnan, A. Silvia, P. J., . . . Kane, M. J. (2018). Age-related differences in mind-wandering in daily life. *Psychology and Aging, 33*(4), 643–653. doi:10.1037/pag0000260

Majid, A., Roberts, S. G., Cilissen, L., Emmorey, K., Nicodemus, B., O'Grady, L., . . . Levinson, S. C. (2018).

Differential coding of perception in the world's languages. *Proceedings of the National Academy of Sciences, USA, 115,* 11369–11375.

Major, B., Mendes, W. B., & Dovidio, J. F. (2013). Intergroup relations and health disparities: A social psychological perspective. *Health Psychology, 32,* 514–524.

Makel, M. C., Kell, H. J., Lubinski, D., Putallaz, M., & Benbow, C. P. (2016). When lightning strikes twice: Profoundly gifted, profoundly accomplished. *Psychological Science, 27*(7), 1004–1018.

Makris, N., Biederman, J., Monuteaux, M. C., & Seidman, L. J. (2009). Towards conceptualizing a neural systems-based anatomy of attention-deficit/hyperactivity disorder. *Developmental Neuroscience, 31,* 36–49.

Malina, R. M., Bouchard, C., & Beunen, G. (1988). Human growth: Selected aspects of current research on well-nourished children. *Annual Review of Anthropology, 17,* 187–219.

Malooly, A. M., Genet, J. J., & Siemer, M. (2013). Individual differences in reappraisal effectiveness: The role of affective flexibility. *Emotion, 13*(2), 302–313. doi:10.1037/a0029980

Mampe, B., Friederici, A. D., Christophe, A., & Wermke, K. (2009). Newborns' cry melody is shaped by their native language. *Current Biology, 19,* 1–4.

Mandler, G. (1967). Organization and memory. In K. W. Spence & J. T. Spence (Eds.), *The psychology of learning and motivation* (Vol. 1, pp. 327–372). New York: Academic Press.

Mandy, W., & Lai, M. C. (2016). The role of the environment in the developmental psychopathology of autism spectrum condition. *Journal of Child Psychology and Psychiatry, 57,* 271–292.

Mankiw, N. G., & Weinzierl, M. (2010). The optimal taxation of height: A case study of utilitarian income redistribution. *American Economic Journal: Economic Policy, 2,* 155–176.

Mann, J. J. (2005). The medical management of depression. *New England Journal of Medicine, 353,* 1819–1834.

Mann, J. J., Apter, A., Bertolote, J., Beautrais, A., Currier, D., Haas, A., . . . Hendin, H. (2005). Suicide prevention strategies: A systematic review. *Journal of the American Medical Association, 294*(16), 2064–2074.

Marangell, L. B., Silver, J. M., Goff, D. M., & Yudofsky, S. C. (2003). Psychopharmacology and electroconvulsive therapy. In R. E. Hales & S. C. Yudofsky (Eds.), *The American Psychiatric Publishing textbook of clinical psychiatry* (4th ed., pp. 1047–1149). Washington, DC: American Psychiatric Publishing.

Marci, C. D., Ham, J., Moran, E., & Orr, S. P. (2007). Physiologic correlates of perceived therapist empathy and social-emotional process during psychotherapy. *Journal of Nervous and Mental Disease, 195*(2), 103–111.

Marcia J. E. (1993) The ego identity status approach to ego identity. In James E. Marcia, Alan S. Waterman, David R. Matteson, Sally L. Archer, & Jacob L. Orlofsky (Eds.), *Ego identity: A handbook for psychosocial research* (pp. 3–21). New York: Springer.

Marcia, J. E. (1966). Development and validation of ego-identity status. *Journal of Personality and Social Psychology, 3,* 551–558.

Marcus, G. (2012, December 3). Neuroscience fiction. *New Yorker.* http://www.newyorker.com/news/news-desk /neuroscience-fiction

Marcus, G. B. (1986). Stability and change in political attitudes: Observe, recall, and "explain." *Political Behavior, 8,* 21–44.

Margolis, R., & Myrskylä, M. (2011). A global perspective on happiness and fertility. *Population and Development Review, 37*(1), 29–56.

Margoni, F., & Surian, L. (2018). Infants' evaluation of prosocial and antisocial agents: A meta-analysis. *Developmental Psychology, 54,* 1445–1455.

Markel, H. (2011). *An anatomy of addiction: Sigmund Freud, William Halsted, and the miracle drug cocaine.* New York: Pantheon.

Markowitz, J. C. (1999). Developments in interpersonal psychotherapy. *The Canadian Journal of Psychiatry, 44*(6), 556–561.

Markus, H. (1977). Self-schemata and processing information about the self. *Journal of Personality and Social Psychology, 35,* 63–78.

Marlatt, G. A., & Rohsenow, D. (1980). Cognitive processes in alcohol use: Expectancy and the balanced placebo design. In N. K. Mello (Ed.), *Advances in substance abuse: Behavioral and biological research* (pp. 159–199). Greenwich, CT: JAI Press.

Marmot, M. G., Stansfeld, S., Patel, C., North, F., Head, J., White, L., . . . Feeney, A. (1991). Health inequalities among British civil servants: The Whitehall II study. *Lancet, 337,* 1387–1393.

Marsh, A. A., Rhoads, S. A., & Ryan, R. M. (2018). A multi-semester classroom demonstration yields evidence in support of the facial feedback effect. *Emotion.* doi:10.1037/emo0000532

Marsolek, C. J. (1995). Abstract visual-form representations in the left cerebral hemispheres. *Journal of Experimental Psychology: Human Perception and Performance, 21,* 375–386.

Martin, A. (2007). The representation of object concepts in the brain. *Annual Review of Psychology, 58,* 25–45.

Martin, A., & Caramazza, A. (2003). Neuropsychological and neuroimaging perspectives on conceptual knowledge: An introduction. *Cognitive Neuropsychology, 20,* 195–212.

Martin, A., & Chao, L. L. (2001). Semantic memory and the brain: Structure and processes. *Current Opinion in Neurobiology, 11,* 194–201.

Martin, D. (2018). Use the behavioral tips to "science" your clients on savings. *Journal of Financial Planning, 31,* 20–21.

Martin, J., Rychlowska, M., Wood, A., & Niedenthal, P. (2017). Smiles as multipurpose social signals. *Trends in Cognitive Sciences, 21*(11), 864–877.

Martin, M. J., Blozis, S. A., Boeninger, D. K., Masarik, A. S., & Conger, R. D. (2014). The timing of entry into adult roles and changes in trajectories of problem behaviors during the transition to adulthood. *Developmental Psychology, 50*(11), 2473–2484.

Martins, D., Mehta, M. A., & Prata, D. (2017). The "highs and lows" of the human brain on dopaminergics: Evidence from neuropharmacology. *Neuroscience and Biobehavioral Reviews, 80,* 351–371.

Martins, S. S., Sampson, L., Cerda, M., & Galea, S. (2015). Worldwide prevalence and trends in unintentional drug overdose: A systematic review of the literature. *American Journal of Public Health, 105,* E29–E49.

Marucha, P. T., Kiecolt-Glaser, J. K., & Favagehi, M. (1998). Mucosal wound healing is impaired by examination stress. *Psychosomatic Medicine, 60,* 362–365.

Marufu, T. C., Ahankari, A., Coleman, T., & Lewis, S. (2015). Maternal smoking and the risk of stillbirth: Systematic review and meta-analysis. *BMC Public Health, 15*(1), 239. doi:10.1186 /s12889-015-1552-5.

Marzuk, P. M., Tardiff, K., Leon, A. C., Hirsch, C., Portera, L., Iqbal, M. I., . . . Hartwell, N. (1998). Ambient temperature and mortality from unintentional cocaine overdose. *Journal of the American Medical Association, 279,* 1795–1800.

Maslach, C. (2003). Job burnout: New directions in research and intervention. *Current Directions in Psychological Science, 12,* 189–192.

Maslow, A. H. (1937). Dominance-feeling, behavior, and status. In R. J. Lowry (Ed.), *Dominance, self-esteem, self-actualization: Germinal papers by A. H. Maslow* (pp. 49–70). Monterey, CA: Brooks-Cole.

Maslow, A. H. (1943). A theory of human motivation. *Psychological Review, 50,* 370–396.

Maslow, A. H. (1954). *Motivation and personality.* New York: Harper & Row.

Mason, M. F., Norton, M. I., Van Horn, J. D., Wegner, D. M., Grafton, S. T., & Macrae, C. N. (2007). Wandering minds: The default network and stimulus-independent thought. *Science, 315,* 393–395.

Masten, A. S. (2004). Family therapy as a treatment for children: A critical review of outcome research. *Family Process, 18*(3), 323–335.

Masters, W. H., & Johnson, V. E. (1966). *Human sexual response.* Boston: Little, Brown.

Masuda, T., & Nisbett, R. E. (2001). Attending holistically vs. analytically: Comparing the context sensitivity of Japanese and Americans. *Journal of Personality and Social Psychology, 81,* 922–934.

Mather, M., & Carstensen, L. L. (2003). Aging and attentional biases for emotional faces. *Psychological Science, 14,* 409–415.

Mather, M., & Carstensen, L. L. (2005). Aging and motivated cognition: The positivity effect in attention and memory. *Trends in Cognitive Sciences, 9*(10), 496–502.

Mather, M., Canli, T., English, T., Whitfield, S., Wais, P., Ochsner, K., . . . Cartensen, L. L. (2004). Amygdala responses to emotionally valenced stimuli in older and younger adults. *Psychological Science, 15,* 259–263.

Matsumoto, D., & Willingham, B. (2009). Spontaneous facial expressions of emotion of congenitally and noncongenitally blind individuals. *Journal of Personality and Social Psychology, 96,* 1–10.

Mattar, A. A. G., & Gribble, P. L. (2005). Motor learning by observing. *Neuron, 46,* 153–160.

Matthews, G., & Gilliland, K. (1999). The personality theories of H. J. Eysenck and J. A. Gray: A comparative review. *Personality and Individual Differences, 26,* 583–626.

Matzel, L. D., Han, Y. R., Grossman, H., Karnik, M. S., Patel, D., Scott, N., . . . Gandhi, C. C. (2003). Individual differences in the expression of a general learning ability in mice. *Journal of Neuroscience, 23*(16), 6423–6433.

Maudsley, H. (1886). *Natural causes and supernatural seemings.* London: Kegan Paul, Trench.

Mauss, I. B., & Robinson, M. D. (2009). Measures of emotion: A review. *Cognition and Emotion, 23,* 209–237.

Mauss, I. B., Levenson, R. W., McCarter, L., Wilhelm, F. H., & Gross, J. J. (2005). The tie that binds? Coherence among emotion experience, behavior, and physiology. *Emotion, 5*(2), 175–190. doi:10.1037/1528-3542.5.2.175

Max, A. (2006, September 16). Dutch reach new heights. *USA Today.* Retrieved from http://usatoday30.usatoday.com/news /offbeat/2006-09-16-dutch-tall_x.htm

May, R. (1983). *The discovery of being: Writings in existential psychology.* New York: Norton.

Mayberg, H., Lozano, A., Voon, V., McNeely, H. E., Seminowicz, D., Hamani, C., . . . Kennedy, S. H. (2005). Deep brain stimulation for treatment-resistant depression. *Neuron, 45*(5), 651–660.

Mayer, J. D., Caruso, D. R., & Salovey, P. (1999). Emotional intelligence meets traditional standards for an intelligence. *Intelligence, 27,* 267.

Mayer, J. D., Caruso, D. R., Zigler, E., & Dreyden, J. I. (1989). Intelligence and intelligence-related personality traits. *Intelligence, 13*(2), 119–133.

Mayer, J. D., Roberts, R. D., & Barsade, S. G. (2008). Human abilities: Emotional intelligence. *Annual Review of Psychology, 59,* 507–536.

Maynard-Smith, J. (1965). The evolution of alarm calls. *American Naturalist, 100,* 637–650.

Mayr, E. (1942). *Systematics and the origin of species, from the viewpoint of a zoologist.* New York: Columbia University Press.

Mazure, C. M. & Swendsen, J. (2016). Sex differences in Alzheimer's disease and other dementias. *The Lancet Neurology, 15,* 451–452.

McAdams, D. (1993). *The stories we live by: Personal myths and the making of the self.* New York: Morrow.

McClelland, D. C., Atkinson, J. W., Clark, R. A., & Lowell, E. L. (1953). *The achievement motive.* New York: Appleton-Century-Crofts.

McDaniel, M. A., Thomas, R. C., Agarwal, P. K., McDermott, K. B., & Roediger, H. L. (2013). Quizzing in middle-school science: Successful transfer performance on classroom exams. *Applied Cognitive Psychology, 27,* 360–372.

McDermott, K. B., Agarwal, P. K., D'Antonio, L., Roediger, H. L., & McDaniel, M. A. (2014). Both multiple-choice and short-answer quizzes enhance later exam performance in middle and high school classes. *Journal of Experimental Psychology: Applied, 20,* 3–21.

McDonald, A., Haslam, C., Yates, P., Gurr, B., Leeder, G., & Sayers, A. (2011). Google Calendar: A new memory aid to compensate for prospective memory deficits following acquired brain injury. *Neuropsychological Rehabilitation, 21,* 784–807.

McElwain, N. L., Booth-LaForce, C., & Wu, X. (2011). Infant–mother attachment and children's friendship quality: Maternal mental state talk as an intervening mechanism. *Developmental Psychology, 47*(5), 1295–1311. doi:10.1037/a0024094

McEvoy, S. P., Stevenson, M. R., McCartt, A. T., Woodward, M., Haworth, C., Palamara, P., & Circarelli, R. (2005). Role of mobile phones in motor vehicle crashes resulting in hospital attendance: A case-crossover study. *British Medical Journal, 331,* 428–430.

McFarlane, A. H., Norman, G. R., Streiner, D. L., Roy, R., & Scott, D. J. (1980). A longitudinal study of the influence of the psychosocial environment on health status: A preliminary report. *Journal of Health and Social Behavior, 21,* 124–133.

McGarty, C., & Turner, J. C. (1992). The effects of categorization on social judgement. *British Journal of Social Psychology, 31,* 253–268.

McGaugh, J. L. (2000). Memory: A century of consolidation. *Science, 287,* 248–251.

McGaugh, J. L. (2006). Make mild moments memorable: Add a little arousal. *Trends in Cognitive Sciences, 10,* 345–347.

McGaugh, J. L. (2015). Consolidating memories. *Annual Review of Psychology, 66,* 1–24.

McGovern, P. E., Zhang, J., Tang, J., Zhang, Z., Hall, G. R., Moreau, R. A., . . . Wang, C. (2004). Fermented beverages of pre- and proto-historic China. *Proceedings of the National Academy of Sciences, USA, 101*(51), 17593–17598.

McGowan, P. O., Sasaki, A., D'Alessio, A. D., Dymov, S., Labonté, B., Szyf, M., . . . Meaney, M. J. (2009). Epigenetic regulation of the glucocorticoid receptor in human brain associates with childhood abuse. *Nature Neuroscience, 12,* 342–348.

McGowan, P. O., Suderman, M., Sasaki, A., Huang, T. C. T., Hallett, M., Meaney, J. J., & Szyf, M. (2011). Broad epigenetic signature of maternal care in the brain of adult rats. *PLoS One, 6*(2), e14739. doi:10.1371/journal.pone.0014739

McGrath, J., Saha, S., Chant, D., & Welham, J. (2008). Schizophrenia: A concise overview of incidence, prevalence, and mortality. *Epidemiologic Reviews, 30,* 67–76.

McGue, M., & Bouchard, T. J. (1998). Genetic and environmental influences on human behavioral differences. *Annual Review of Neuroscience, 21,* 1–24.

McGuire, P. K., Shah, G. M., & Murray, R. M. (1993). Increased blood flow in Broca's area during auditory hallucinations in schizophrenia. *Lancet, 342,* 703–706.

McIntyre, S. H., & Munson, J. M. (2008). Exploring cramming: Student behaviors, beliefs, and learning retention in the Principles of Marketing course. *Journal of Marketing Education, 30,* 226–243.

McKee, A. C., Cantu, R. C., Nowinski, C. J., Hedley-Whyte, E. T., Gavett, B. E., Budson, A. E., . . . Stern, R. A. (2009). Chronic traumatic encephalopathy in athletes: Progressive tauopathy after repetitive head injury. *Journal of Neuropathology and Experimental Neurology, 68,* 709–735.

McKetin, R., Ward, P. B., Catts, S. V., Mattick, R. P., & Bell, J. R. (1999). Changes in auditory selective attention and event-related potentials following oral administration of D-amphetamine in humans. *Neuropsychopharmacology, 21,* 380–390.

McLaughlin, K. A., Nandi, A., Keyes, K. M., Uddin, M., Aiello, A. E., Galea, S., & Koenen, K. C. (2012). Home foreclosure and risk of psychiatric morbidity during the recent financial crisis. *Psychological Medicine, 42,* 1441–1448.

McLean, K. C. (2008). The emergence of narrative identity. *Social and Personality Psychology Compass, 2*(4), 1685–1702.

McMahon, C. A., & Bernier, A. (2017). Twenty years of research on parental mind-mindedness: Empirical findings, theoretical and methodological challenges, and new directions. *Developmental Review, 46,* 54–80.

McNally, R. J. (2003). *Remembering trauma.* Cambridge, MA: Belknap Press of Harvard University Press.

McNally, R. J., & Clancy, S. A. (2005). Sleep paralysis, sexual abuse, and space alien abduction. *Transcultural Psychiatry, 42,* 113–122.

McNally, R. J., & Geraerts, E. (2009). A new solution to the recovered memory debate. *Perspective on Psychological Science, 4,* 126–134.

McNally, R. J., & Steketee, G. S. (1985). Etiology and maintenance of severe animal phobias. *Behavioral Research and Therapy, 23,* 431–435.

McNamara, R. A., Willard, A. K., Norenzayan, A., & Henrich, J. (2019). Weighing outcome vs. intent across societies: How cultural models of mind shape moral reasoning. *Cognition, 182,* 95–108.

McNeilly, A. S., Robinson, I. C., Houston, M. J., & Howie, P. W. (1983). Release of oxytocin and prolactin in response to suckling. *British Medical Journal, 286,* 257–259.

McPhetres, J., & Zuckerman, M. (2017). Religious people endorse different standards of evidence when evaluating religious versus scientific claims. *Social Psychological and Personality Science, 8,* 836–842.

McQuaid, R. J., Bombay, A., McInnis, O. A., Humeny, C., Matheson, K., & Anisman, H. (2017). Suicide ideation and attempts among First Nations peoples living on-reserve in Canada: The intergenerational and cumulative effects of Indian residential schools. *The Canadian Journal of Psychiatry, 62*(6), 422–430.

Mead, G. H. (1934). *Mind, self, and society.* Chicago: University of Chicago Press.

Meade, M. L., Harris, C. B., Van Bergen, P., Sutton, J., & Barnier, A. J. (Eds.). (2018). *Collaborative remembering: Theories, research and applications.* Oxford: Oxford University Press.

Meaidi, A., Jennum, P., Ptito, M., & Kupers, R. (2014). The sensory construction of dreams and nightmare frequency in congenitally blind and late blind individuals. *Sleep Medicine, 15,* 586–595.

Means, B., Toyama, Y., Murphy, R., Bakia, M., & Jones, K. (2010). *Evaluation of evidence-based practices in online learning: Meta-analysis and review of online learning studies.* Washington, DC: U.S. Department of Education. Retrieved from https://www2.ed.gov/rschstat/eval/tech/evidence-based-practices/finalreport.pdf

Mechelli, A., Crinion, J. T., Noppeney, U., O'Doherty, J., Ashburner, J., Frackowiak, R. S., & Price, C. J. (2004). Neurolinguistics: Structural plasticity in the bilingual brain. *Nature, 431,* 757.

Meder, D., Herz, D. M., Rowe, J. B., Lehéricy, S., & Siebner, H. R. (2018). The role of dopamine in the brain—lessons learned from Parkinson's disease. *NeuroImage.* https://doi.org/10.1016/j.neuroimage.2018.11.021

Medin, D. L., & Schaffer, M. M. (1978). Context theory of classification learning. *Psychological Review, 85,* 207–238.

Medvec, V. H., Madey, S. F., & Gilovich, T. (1995). When less is more: Counterfactual thinking and satisfaction among Olympic medalists. *Journal of Personality and Social Psychology, 69,* 603–610.

Mehl, M. R., Vazire, S., Ramirez-Esparza, N., Slatcher, R. B., & Pennebaker, J. W. (2007). Are women really more talkative than men? *Science, 317,* 82.

Mehu, M., & Scherer, K. R. (2015). Emotion categories and dimensions in the facial communication of affect: An integrated approach. *Emotion, 15*(6), 798–811. doi:10.1037/a0039416

Meindl, J. N., & Casey, L. B. (2012). Increasing the suppressive effect of delayed punishers: A review of basic and applied literature. *Behavioral Interventions, 27,* 129–150.

Meins, E. (2003). Emotional development and attachment relationships. In A. Slater & G. Bremner (Eds.), *An introduction to developmental psychology* (pp. 141–164). Malden, MA: Blackwell.

Meins, E., Fernyhough, C., Fradley, E., & Tuckey, M. (2001). Rethinking maternal sensitivity: Mothers' comments on infants' mental processes predict security of attachment at 12 months. *Journal of Child Psychology & Psychiatry & Allied Disciplines, 42,* 637–648.

Mellon, R. C. (2009). Superstitious perception: Response-independent reinforcement and punishment as determinants of recurring eccentric interpretations. *Behaviour Research and Therapy, 47,* 868–875.

Meltzer, A. L., McNulty, J. K., Jackson, G. L., & Karney, B. R. (2014). Sex differences in the implications of partner physical attractiveness for the trajectory of marital satisfaction. *Journal of Personality and Social Psychology, 106*(3), 418–428.

Meltzer, H. Y. (2013). Update on typical and atypical antipsychotic drugs. *Annual Review of Medicine, 64,* 393–406.

Meltzoff, A. N. (1995). Understanding the intentions of others: Reenactment of intended acts by 18-month-old children. *Developmental Psychology, 31,* 838–850.

Meltzoff, A. N. (2007). "Like me": A foundation for social cognition. *Developmental Science, 10*(1), 126–134. doi:10.1111/j.1467-7687.2007.00574x

Meltzoff, A. N., & Moore, M. K. (1977). Imitation of facial and manual gestures by human neonates. *Science, 198,* 75–78.

Meltzoff, A. N., Kuhl, P. K., Movellan, J., & Sejnowski, T. J. (2009). Foundations for a new science of learning. *Science, 325,* 284–288.

Meltzoff, A. N., Murray, L., Simpson, E., Heimann, M., Nagy, E., Nadel, J., . . . Ferrari, P. F. (2018). Re-examination of Oostenbroek et al. (2016): Evidence for neonatal imitation of tongue protrusion. *Developmental Science, 21,* 1–8.

Melzack, R., & Wall, P. D. (1965). Pain mechanisms: A new theory. *Science, 150,* 971–979.

Mendes, W. B., Blascovich, J., Hunter, S. B., Lickel, B., & Jost, J. T. (2007). Threatened by the unexpected: Physiological responses during social interactions with expectancy-violating partners. *Journal of Personality and Social Psychology, 92,* 698–716.

Mendes, W. B., Blascovich, J., Lickel, B., & Hunter, S. (2002). Challenge and threat during social interaction with White and Black men. *Personality & Social Psychology Bulletin, 28,* 939–952.

Mendle, J. (2014). Beyond pubertal timing: New directions for studying individual differences in development. *Current Directions in Psychological Science, 23*(3), 215–219.

Mendle, J., Harden, K. P., Brooks-Gunn, J., & Graber, J. A. (2010). Development's tortoise and hare: Pubertal timing, pubertal tempo, and depressive symptoms in boys and girls. *Developmental Psychology, 46*(5), 1341–1353. doi:10.1037/a0020205

Mendle, J., Ryan, R. M., & McKone, K. M. P. (2018). Age at menarche, depression, and antisocial behavior in adulthood. *Pediatrics, 141*(1), e20171703.

Mendle, J., Turkheimer, E., & Emery, R. E. (2007). Detrimental psychological outcomes associated with early pubertal timing in adolescent girls. *Developmental Review, 27,* 151–171.

Merikangas, K. R., Wicki, W., & Angst, J. (1994). Heterogeneity of depression: Classification of depressive subtype by longitudinal course. *British Journal of Psychiatry, 164,* 342–348.

Mervis, C. B., & Bertrand, J. (1994). Acquisition of the Novel Name–Nameless Category (N3C) principle. *Child Development, 65,* 1646–1662. doi:10.2307/1131285

Merzenich, M. M., Recanzone, G. H., Jenkins, W. M., & Grajski, K. A. (1990). Adaptive mechanisms in cortical networks underlying cortical contributions to learning and nondeclarative memory. *Cold Spring Harbor Symposia on Quantitative Biology, 55,* 873–887.

Mesoudi, A., Chang, L., Dall, S. R. X., & Thornton, A. (2015). The evolution of individual and cultural variation in social learning. *Trends in Ecology & Evolution, 31,* 215–225.

Messick, D. M., & Cook, K. S. (1983). *Equity theory: Psychological and sociological perspectives.* New York: Praeger.

Meston, C. M., & Buss, D. M. (2007). Why humans have sex. *Archives of Sexual Behavior, 36,* 477–507.

Mestre, J. M., Guil, R., Lopes, P. N., Salovey, P., & Gil-Olarte, P. (2006). Emotional intelligence and social and academic adaptation to school. *Psicothema, 18,* 112.

Metcalfe, J. (2009). Metacognitive judgments and control of study. *Current Directions in Psychological Science, 18,* 159–163.

Metcalfe, J., & Finn, B. (2008). Evidence that judgments of learning are causally related to study choice. *Psychonomic Bulletin & Review, 15,* 174–179.

Metcalfe, J., & Wiebe, D. (1987). Intuition in insight and noninsight problem solving. *Memory & Cognition, 15,* 238–246.

Methven, L., Allen, V. J., Withers, G. A., & Gosney, M. A. (2012). Ageing and taste. *Proceedings of the Nutrition Society, 71,* 556–565.

Meuret, A. E., Kroll, J., & Ritz, T. (2017). Panic disorder comorbidity with medical conditions and treatment implications. *Annual Review of Clinical Psychology, 13,* 209–240.

Meyer-Bahlberg, H. F. L., Ehrhardt, A. A., Rosen, L. R., & Gruen, R. S. (1995). Prenatal estrogens and the development of homosexual orientation. *Developmental Psychology, 31,* 12–21.

Michaela, R., Florian, S., Gert, G. W., & Ulman, L. (2009). Seeking pleasure and seeking pain: Differences in prohedonic and contrahedonic motivation from adolescence to old age. *Psychological Science, 20*(12), 1529–1535.

Mikels, J. A., & Shuster, M. M. (2016). The interpretative lenses of older adults are not rose-colored—just less dark: Aging and the interpretation of ambiguous scenarios. *Emotion, 16*(1), 94–100.

Miklowitz, D. J., & Johnson, S. L. (2006). The psychopathology and treatment of bipolar disorder. *Annual Review of Clinical Psychology, 2,* 199–235.

Mikolajczak, M., Avalosse, H., Vancorenland, S., Verniest, R., Callens, M., van Broeck, N., . . . Mierop, A. (2015). A nationally representative study of emotional competence and health. *Emotion, 15*(5), 653–667.

Milad, M. R., & Rauch, S. L. (2012). Obsessive-compulsive disorder: Beyond segregated cortico-striatal pathways. *Trends in Cognitive Sciences, 16*, 43–51.

Milgram, S. (1963). Behavioral study of obedience. *Journal of Abnormal and Social Psychology, 67*, 371–378.

Milgram, S. (1974). *Obedience to authority.* New York: Harper & Row.

Milgram, S., Bickman, L., & Berkowitz, O. (1969). Note on the drawing power of crowds of different size. *Journal of Personality and Social Psychology, 13*, 79–82.

Miller, A. J. (1986). *The obedience experiments: A case study of controversy in social science.* New York: Praeger.

Miller, D. T., & Prentice, D. A. (1996). The construction of social norms and standards. In E. T. Higgins & A. W. Kruglanski (Ed.), *Social psychology: Handbook of basic principles* (pp. 799–829). New York: Guilford Press.

Miller, D. T., & Prentice, D. A. (2016). Changing norms to change behavior. *Annual Review of Psychology, 67*(1), 339–361.

Miller, D. T., & Ratner, R. K. (1998). The disparity between the actual and assumed power of self-interest. *Journal of Personality and Social Psychology, 74*, 53–62.

Miller, D. T., & Ross, M. (1975). Self-serving biases in the attribution of causality: Fact or fiction? *Psychological Bulletin, 82*, 213–225.

Miller, G. A. (1956). The magical number seven, plus or minus two: Some limits on our capacity for processing information. *Psychological Review, 63*, 81–96.

Miller, G. A. (2003). The cognitive revolution: A historical perspective. *Trends in Cognitive Sciences, 7*(3), 141–144.

Miller, K. L., Alfaro-Almagro, F., Bangerter, N. K., Thomas, D. L., Yacoub, E., Xu, J., . . . Smith, S. M. (2016). Multimodal population brain imaging in the UK Biobank prospective epidemiological study. *Nature Neuroscience, 19*, 1523–1536.

Miller, N. E. (1960). Motivational effects of brain stimulation and drugs. *Federation Proceedings, 19*, 846–854.

Miller, T. W. (Ed.). (1996). *Theory and assessment of stressful life events.* Madison, CT: International Universities Press.

Miller, W. R., & Rollnick, S. (2012). *Motivational interviewing: Helping people change* (3rd ed.). New York: Guilford Press.

Mills, P. J., & Dimsdale, J. E. (1991). Cardiovascular reactivity to psychosocial stressors. A review of the effects of beta-blockade. *Psychosomatics, 32*, 209–220.

Milne, E., & Grafman, J. (2001). Ventromedial prefrontal cortex lesions in humans eliminate implicit gender stereotyping. *Journal of Neuroscience, 21*, 1–6.

Milner, A. D., & Goodale, M. A. (1995). *The visual brain in action.* Oxford: Oxford University Press.

Milner, B. (1962). Laterality effects in audition. In V. B. Mountcastle (Ed.), *Interhemispheric relations and cerebral dominance* (pp. 177–195). Baltimore: Johns Hopkins University Press.

Milner, B. (1970). Memory and the medial temporal regions of the brain. In K. Pribram (Ed.), *Biology of memory* (pp. 29–50). New York: Elsevier.

Milyavsky, M., Webber, D., Fernandez, J. R., Kruglanski, A. W., Goldenberg, A., Suri, G., & Gross, J. J. (2019). To reappraise or not to reappraise? Emotion regulation choice and cognitive energetics. *Emotion. 19*(6), 964–981.

Min, B. K., Chavarriaga, R., & Millán, J. D. R. (2017). Harnessing prefrontal cognitive signals for brain-machine interfaces. *Trends in Biotechnology, 35*, 585–597.

Mineka, S., & Cook, M. (1988). Social learning and the acquisition of snake fear in monkeys. In T. Zentall & B. G. Galef, Jr. (Eds.), *Social learning* (pp. 51–73). Hillsdale, NJ: Erlbaum.

Mineka, S., & Ohman, A. (2002). Born to fear: Non-associative vs. associative factors in the etiology of phobia. *Behaviour Research and Therapy, 40*, 173–184.

Mingroni, M. A. (2007). Resolving the IQ paradox: Heterosis as a cause of the Flynn effect and other trends. *Psychological Review, 114*, 806–829.

Minsky, M. (1986). *The society of mind.* New York: Simon & Schuster.

Minson, J. A., & Mueller, J. S. (2012). The cost of collaboration: Why joint decision making exacerbates rejection of outside information. *Psychological Science, 23*(3), 219–224. doi:10.1177/0956797611429132

Miranda, J., Bernal, G., Lau, A., Kohn, L., Hwang, W. C., & LaFromboise, T. (2005). State of the science on psychological interventions for ethnic minorities. *Annual Review of Clinical Psychology, 1*, 113–142.

Mirnig, N., Stollnberger, G., Miksch, M., Stadler, S., Giuliani, M., & Tscheligi, M. (2017). To err is robot: How humans assess and act toward an erroneous social robot. *Frontiers in Robotics and AI.* Retrieved from www.frontiersin.org/article/10.3389/frobt.2017.00021

Mischel, W. (1968). *Personality and assessment.* New York: Wiley.

Mischel, W. (2004). Toward an integrative science of the person. *Annual Review of Psychology, 55*, 1–22.

Mischel, W., & Shoda, Y. (1999). Integrating dispositions and processing dynamics within a unified theory of personality: The cognitive–affective personality system. In L. A. Pervin & O. P. John (Eds.), *Handbook of personality: Theory and research* (pp. 197–218). New York: Guilford Press.

Mischel, W., Ayduk, O., Baumeister, R. F., & Vohs, K. D. (2004). Willpower in a cognitive-affective processing system: The dynamics of delay of gratification. In *Handbook of self-regulation: Research, theory, and applications* (pp. 99–129). New York: Guilford Press.

Mischel, W., Shoda, Y., & Rodriguez, M. L. (1989). Delay of gratification in children. *Science, 244*, 933–938.

Mishra, A., & Mishra, H. (2010). Border bias: The belief that state borders can protect against disasters. *Psychological Science, 21*(11), 1582–1586. doi: 10.1177/0956797610385950

Mishra, A., Mishra, H., & Masters, T. M. (2012). The influence of bite size on quantity of food consumed: A field study. *Journal of Consumer Research, 38*(5), 791–795. doi:10.1086/660838

Mita, T. H., Dermer, M., & Knight, J. (1977). Reversed facial images and the mere-exposure hypothesis. *Journal of Personality and Social Psychology, 35*, 597–601.

Mitchell, J. P. (2006). Mentalizing and Marr: An information processing approach to the study of social cognition. *Brain Research, 1079*(1), 66–75.

Mitchell, J. P., Heatherton, T. F., & Macrae, C. N. (2002). Distinct neural systems subserve person and object knowledge. *Proceedings of the National Academy of Sciences, USA, 99,* 15238–15243.

Mitchell, K. J., & Johnson, M. K. (2009). Source monitoring 15 years later: What have we learned from fMRI about the neural mechanisms of source memory? *Psychological Bulletin, 135,* 638–677.

Miura, I. T., Okamoto, Y., Kim, C. C., & Chang, C. M. (1994). Comparisons of children's cognitive representation of number: China, France, Japan, Korea, Sweden and the United States. *International Journal of Behavioral Development, 17,* 401–411.

Miyamoto, Y., Ma, X., & Petermann, A. G. (2014). Cultural differences in hedonic emotion regulation after a negative event. *Emotion, 14*(4), 804–815. doi:10.1037/a0036257

Moffitt, T. E. (1993). Adolescence-limited and life-course-persistent antisocial behavior: A developmental taxonomy. *Psychological Review, 100,* 674–701.

Moffitt, T. E. (2005). Genetic and environmental influences on antisocial behaviors: Evidence from behavioral-genetic research. *Advances in Genetics, 55,* 41–104.

Moghaddam, B., & Bunney, B. S. (1989). Differential effect of cocaine on extracellular dopamine levels in rat medial prefrontal cortex and nucleus accumbens: Comparison to amphetamine. *Synapse, 4,* 156–161.

Mojtabai, R., Olfson, M., Sampson, N. A., Jin, R., Druss, B., Wang, P. S., . . . Kessler, R. C. (2011). Barriers to mental health treatment: Results from the National Comorbidity Survey Replication. *Psychological Medicine, 41*(8), 1751–1761.

Mokdad, A. H., Ford, E. S., Bowman, B. A., Dietz, W. H., Vinicor, F., Bales, V. S., & Marks, J. S. (2003). Prevalence of obesity, diabetes, and obesity-related health risk factors, 2001. *Journal of the American Medical Association, 289*(1), 76–79. doi:10.1001/jama.289.1.76

Molden, D., Lee, A. Y., & Higgins, E. T. (2009). Motivations for promotion and prevention. In J. Shah & W. Gardner (Eds.), *Handbook of motivation science* (pp. 169–187). New York: Guilford Press.

Molloy, L. E., Gest, S. D., Feinberg, M. E., & Osgood, D. W. (2014). Emergence of mixed-sex friendship groups during adolescence: Developmental associations with substance use and delinquency. *Developmental Psychology, 50*(11), 2449–2461.

Monahan, J. L., Murphy, S. T., & Zajonc, R. B. (2000). Subliminal mere exposure: Specific, general, and diffuse effects. *Psychological Science, 11,* 462–466.

Moncrieff, J. (2009). A critique of the dopamine hypothesis of schizophrenia and psychosis. *Harvard Review of Psychiatry, 17,* 214–225.

Montag, C., Błaszkiewicz, K., Sariyska, R., Lachman, B., Andone, I., Trendafilov, B., . . . Markowetz, A. (2015). Smartphone usage in the 21st century: Who is active on WhatsApp? *BMC Research Notes, 81*(1), 331.

Montague, C. T., Farooqi, I. S., Whitehead, J. P., Soos, M. A., Rau, H., Wareham, N. J., . . . O'Rahilly, S. (1997). Congenital leptin deficiency is associated with severe early-onset obesity in humans. *Nature, 387*(6636), 903–908.

Montenigro, P. H., Corp, D. T., Stein, T. D., Cantu, R. C., & Stern, R. A. (2015). Chronic traumatic encephalopathy: Historical origins and current perspective. *Annual Review of Clinical Psychology, 11,* 309–330.

Monti, M. M., Vanhaudenhuyse, A., Coleman, M. R., Boly, M., Pickard, J. D., Tshibanda, L., . . . Laureys, S. (2010). Willful modulation of brain activity in disorders of consciousness. *New England Journal of Medicine, 362,* 579–589.

Montoya, R. M., & Horton, R. S. (2013). A meta-analytic investigation of the processes underlying the similarity-attraction effect. *Journal of Social and Personal Relationships, 30*(1), 64–94.

Montoya, R. M., Kershaw, C., & Prosser, J. L. (2018). A meta-analytic investigation of the relation between interpersonal attraction and enacted behavior. *Psychological Bulletin, 144*(7), 673–709.

Mook, D. G. (1983). In defense of external invalidity. *American Psychologist, 38,* 379–387.

Moon, S. M., & Illingworth, A. J. (2005). Exploring the dynamic nature of procrastination: A latent growth curve analysis of academic procrastination. *Personality and Individual Differences, 38,* 297–309.

Moore, E. G. J. (1986). Family socialization and the IQ test performance of traditionally and transracially adopted Black children. *Developmental Psychology, 22,* 317–326.

Moran, P., Klinteberg, B. A., Batty, G. D., & Vågerö, D. (2009). Brief report: Childhood intelligence predicts hospitalization with personality disorder in adulthood: Evidence from a population-based study in Sweden. *Journal of Personality Disorders, 23*(5), 535–540.

Moray, N. (1959). Attention in dichotic listening: Affective cues and the influence of instructions. *Quarterly Journal of Experimental Psychology, 11,* 56–60.

Morin, A. (2002). Right hemisphere self-awareness: A critical assessment. *Consciousness & Cognition, 11,* 396–401.

Morin, A. (2006). Levels of consciousness and self-awareness: A comparison of various neurocognitive views. *Consciousness & Cognition, 15,* 358–371.

Morin, C. M., Bélanger, L., LeBlanc, M., Ivers, H., Savard, J., Espie, C. A., . . . Grégoire, J. P. (2009). The natural history of insomnia: A population-based 3-year longitudinal study. *Archives of Internal Medicine, 169,* 447–453.

Morris, C. D., Bransford, J. D., & Franks, J. J. (1977). Levels of processing versus transfer-appropriate processing. *Journal of Verbal Learning and Verbal Behavior, 16,* 519–533.

Morris, R. G., Anderson, E., Lynch, G. S., & Baudry, M. (1986). Selective impairment of learning and blockade of long-term potentiation by an N-methyl-D-aspartate receptor antagonist, AP5. *Nature, 319,* 774–776.

Morris, T. L. (2001). Social phobia. In M. W. Vasey & M. R. Dadds (Eds.), *The developmental psychopathology of anxiety* (pp. 435–458). New York: Oxford University Press.

Morrow, D., Leirer, V., Altiteri, P., & Fitzsimmons, C. (1994). When expertise reduces age differences in performance. *Psychology and Aging, 9,* 134–148.

Moruzzi, G., & Magoun, H. W. (1949). Brain stem reticular formation and activation of the EEG. *Electroencephalography and Clinical Neurophysiology, 1,* 455–473.

Moscovitch, M. (1994). Memory and working-with-memory: Evaluation of a component process model and comparisons with other models. In D. L. Schacter & E. Tulving (Eds.), *Memory systems 1994* (pp. 269–310). Cambridge, MA: MIT Press.

Moscovitch, M., Cabeza, R., Winocur, G., & Nadel, L. (2016). Episodic memory and beyond: The hippocampus and cortex in transformation. *Annual Review of Psychology, 67,* 105–134.

Moscovitch, M., Nadel, L., Winocur, G., Gilboa, A., & Rosenbaum, R. S. (2006). The cognitive neuroscience of remote episodic, semantic and spatial memory. *Current Opinion in Neurobiology, 16,* 179–190.

Moulin, C. J. A. (2013). Disordered recognition memory: Recollective confabulation. *Cortex, 49,* 1541–1552.

Moulin, C. J. A., Conway, M. A., Thompson, R. G., James, N., & Jones, R. W. (2005). Disordered memory awareness: Recollective confabulation in two cases of persistent déja vecu. *Neuropsychologia, 43,* 1362–1378.

Moulton, E., Barton, M., Robins, D. L., Abrams, D. N., & Fein, D. (2016) Early characteristics of children with ASD who demonstrate optimal progress between age two and four. *Journal of Autism and Developmental Disorders, 46,* 2160–2173.

Moura, A. C. A. de, & Lee, P. C. (2004). Capuchin stone tool use in Caatinga dry forest. *Science, 306,* 1909.

Mroczek, D. K., & Spiro, A. (2005). Change in life satisfaction during adulthood: Findings from the Veterans Affairs Normative Aging Study. *Journal of Personality and Social Psychology, 88,* 189.

Muehlenkamp, J. J., Claes, L., Havertape, L., & Plener, P. L. (2012). International prevalence of adolescent non-suicidal self-injury and deliberate self-harm. *Child and Adolescent Psychiatry and Mental Health, 6*(10). doi:10.1156/1753-2000-6-10

Mueller, T. E., Gavin, L. E., & Kulkarni, A. (2008). The association between sex education and youth's engagement in sexual intercourse, age at first intercourse, and birth control use at first sex. *Journal of Adolescent Health, 42*(1), 89–96.

Mueller, T. I., Leon, A. C., Keller, M. B., Solomon, D. A., Endicott, J., Coryell, W., . . . Maser, J. D. (1999). Recurrence after recovery from major depressive disorder during 15 years of observational follow-up. *American Journal of Psychiatry, 156,* 1000–1006.

Muenter, M. D., & Tyce, G. M. (1971). L-dopa therapy of Parkinson's disease: Plasma L-dopa concentration, therapeutic response, and side effects. *Mayo Clinic Proceedings, 46,* 231–239.

Muggleton, N. K., Tarran, S. R., & Fincher, C. L. (2019). Who punishes promiscuous women? Both women and men are prejudiced towards sexually-accessible women, but only women inflict costly punishment. *Evolution and Human Behavior. 40*(3), 259–268.

Mullen, M. K. (1994). Earliest recollections of childhood: A demographic analysis. *Cognition, 52,* 55–79.

Müller, K., & Schwarz, C. (2018, November 30). Fanning the flames of hate: Social media and hate crime. Available at doi.org/10.2139/ssrn.3082972

Murayama, K., Miyatsu, T., Buchli, D., & Storm, B. C. (2014). Forgetting as a consequence of retrieval: A meta-analytic review of retrieval-induced forgetting. *Psychological Bulletin, 140,* 1383–1409.

Murray, C. (2002). *IQ and income inequality in a sample of sibling pairs from advantaged family backgrounds.* Paper presented at the 114th Annual Meeting of the American Economic Association.

Murray, H. A. (1943). *Thematic Apperception Test manual.* Cambridge, MA: Harvard University Press.

Murray, H. A., & Kluckhohn, C. (1953). Outline of a conception of personality. In C. Kluckhohn, H. A. Murray, & D. M. Schneider (Eds.), *Personality in nature, society, and culture* (2nd ed., pp. 3–52). New York: Knopf.

Myers, D. G., & Lamm, H. (1975). The polarizing effect of group discussion. *American Scientist, 63*(3), 297–303.

Myles, P. S., Leslie, K., McNell, J., Forbes, A., & Chan, M. T. V. (2004). Bispectral index monitoring to prevent awareness during anaesthesia: The B-Aware randomized controlled trial. *Lancet, 363,* 1757–1763.

Nadasdy, A. (1995). Phonetics, phonology, and applied linguistics. *Annual Review of Applied Linguistics, 15,* 68–77.

Nader, K., & Hardt, O. (2009). A single standard for memory: The case of reconsolidation. *Nature Reviews Neuroscience, 10,* 224–234.

Nader, K., Shafe, G., & LeDoux, J. E. (2000). Fear memories require protein synthesis in the amygdala for reconsolidation after retrieval. *Nature, 406,* 722–726.

Nagasako, E. M., Oaklander, A. L., & Dworkin, R. H. (2003). Congenital insensitivity to pain: An update. *Pain, 101,* 213–219.

Nagell, K., Olguin, R. S., & Tomasello, M. (1993). Processes of social learning in the tool use of chimpanzees (*Pan troglodytes*) and human children (*Homo sapiens*). *Journal of Comparative Psychology, 107,* 174–186.

Nairne, J. S., Pandeirada, J. N. S., & Thompson, S. R. (2008). Adaptive memory: The comparative value of survival processing. *Psychological Science, 19,* 176–180.

Nairne, J. S., Thompson, S. R., & Pandeirada, J. N. S. (2007). Adaptive memory: Survival processing enhances retention. *Journal of Experimental Psychology: Learning, Memory, and Cognition, 33,* 263–273.

Nakazato, M., Murakami, N., Date, Y., Kojima, M., Matsuo, H., Kangawa, K., & Matsukura, S. (2001). A role for ghrelin in the central regulation of feeding. *Nature, 409,* 194–198.

Nanos Research. (2013). Animal Welfare. Retrieved from http://www.ccac.ca/Documents/2013_National_Survey.pdf

Naqvi, N., Shiv, B., & Bechara, A. (2006). The role of emotion in decision making: A cognitive neuroscience perspective. *Current Directions in Psychological Science, 15,* 260–264.

Nash, G. (2001). The subversive male: Homosexual and bestial images on European Mesolithic rock art. In L. Bevan (Ed.), *Indecent exposure: Sexuality, society and the archaeological record* (pp. 43–55). Glasgow: Cruithne Press.

Nassi, J. J., & Callaway, E. M. (2009). Parallel processing strategies of the primate visual system. *Nature Reviews Neuroscience, 10,* 360–372.

Nathan, P. E. & Gorman, J. M. (2007). *A guide to treatments that work* (3rd ed.). New York: Oxford University Press.

National Center for Health Statistics. (2016a). Health of Black or African American non-Hispanic population. Atlanta: Centers for Disease Control and Prevention. Retrieved from http://www.cdc.gov/nchs/fastats/black-health.htm

National Center for Health Statistics. (2016b). Child health. Atlanta: Centers for Disease Control and Prevention. Retrieved from http://www.cdc.gov/nchs/fastats/child-health.htm

National Research Council. (2003). *The polygraph and lie detection.* Washington, DC: National Academies Press.

National Science Foundation, National Center for Science and Engineering Statistics. (2018). Doctorate recipients from U.S. universities: 2017. *Special Report NSF 19-301.* Alexandria, VA. Available at https://ncses.nsf.gov/pubs/nsf19301/.

Nave, G., Jung, W. H., Linnér, R. K., Kable, J. W., & Koellinger, P. D. (2019). Are bigger brains smarter? Evidence from a large-scale pre-registered study. *Psychological Science, 30,* 43–54.

NCD Risk Factor Collaboration. (2016). A century of trends in adult human height. *eLife, 5,* e13410.

Neimark, J. (2004, July/August). The power of coincidence. *Psychology Today,* pp. 47–52.

Neisser, U. (Ed.). (1998). *The rising curve: Long-term gains in IQ and related measures.* Washington, DC: American Psychological Association.

Neisser, U., & Harsch, N. (1992). Phantom flashbulbs: False recollections of hearing the news about *Challenger.* In E. Winograd & U. Neisser (Eds.), *Affect and accuracy in recall: Studies of "flashbulb memories"* (pp. 9–31). Cambridge: Cambridge University Press.

Neisser, U., Boodoo, G., Bouchard, T. J., Jr., Boykin, A. W., Brody, N., Ceci, S. J., . . . Loehlin, J. C. (1996). Intelligence: Knowns and unknowns. *American Psychologist, 51,* 77–101.

Nelson, A. B., & Kreitzer, A. C. (2015). Reassessing models of basal ganglia function and dysfunction. *Annual Review of Neuroscience, 37,* 117–135.

Nelson, C. A., Zeanah, C. H., Fox, N. A., Marshall, P. J., Smyke, A. T., & Guthrie, D. (2007). Cognitive recovery in socially deprived young children: The Bucharest early intervention project. *Science, 318,* 1937–1940.

Nemeth, C., & Chiles, C. (1988). Modelling courage: The role of dissent in fostering independence. *European Journal of Social Psychology, 18,* 275–280.

Nes, L. S., & Sergerstrom, S. C. (2006). Dispositional optimism and coping: A meta-analytic review. *Personality and Social Psychology Review, 10,* 235–251.

Neuberg, S. L., Kenrick, D. T., & Schaller, M. (2010). Evolutionary social psychology. In S. T. Fiske, D. T. Gilbert, & G. Lindzey (Eds.), *The handbook of social psychology* (5th ed., Vol. 2, pp. 761–796). New York: Wiley.

Neugebauer, R., Hoek, H. W., & Susser, E. (1999). Prenatal exposure to wartime famine and development of antisocial personality in early adulthood. *Journal of the American Medical Association, 282,* 455–462.

Newbold, R. R., Padilla-Banks, E., Snyder, R. J., & Jefferson, W. N. (2005). Developmental exposure to estrogenic compounds and obesity. *Birth Defects Research Part A: Clinical and Molecular Teratology, 73,* 478–480.

Newman, A. J., Bavelier, D., Corina, D., Jezzard, P., & Neville, H. J. (2002). A critical period for right hemisphere recruitment in American Sign Language processing. *Nature Neuroscience, 5,* 76–80.

Newman, J. P., Wolff, W. T., & Hearst, E. (1980). The feature-positive effect in adult human subjects. *Journal of Experimental Psychology: Human Learning and Memory, 6,* 630–650.

Newman, M. G., & Stone, A. A. (1996). Does humor moderate the effects of experimentally induced stress? *Annals of Behavioral Medicine, 18,* 101–109.

Newschaffer, C. J., Croen, L. A., Daniels, J., Giarelli, E., Grether, J. K., Levy, S. E., . . . Windham, G. C. (2007). The epidemiology of autism spectrum disorders. *Annual Review of Public Health, 28,* 235–258.

Newsome, W. T., & Paré, E. B. (1988). A selective impairment of motion perception following lesions of the middle temporal visual area (MT). *Journal of Neuroscience, 8,* 2201–2211.

Neylan, T. C., Metzler, T. J., Best, S. R., Weiss, D. S., Fagan, J. A., Libermans, A., . . . Marmar, C. R. (2002). Critical incident exposure and sleep quality in police officers. *Psychosomatic Medicine, 64,* 345–352.

Ng, M., Fleming, T., Robinson, M., Thomson, B., Graetz, N., Margono, C., . . . Gakidou, E. (2016). Global, regional, and national prevalence of overweight and obesity in children and adults during 1980–2013: A systematic analysis for the Global Burden of Disease Study 2013. *Lancet, 384,* 766–781. doi:10.1016 /S0140-6736(14)60460-8

Niaura, R., Todaro, J. F., Stroud, L., Spiro, A. III, Ward, K. D., & Weiss, S. (2002). Hostility, the metabolic syndrome, and incident coronary heart disease. *Health Psychology, 21,* 588–593.

Nicoladis, E., & Genesee, F. (1997). Language development in preschool bilingual children. *Journal of Speech-Language Pathology & Audiology, 21,* 258–270.

Nicolas, S., Andrieu, B., Croizet, J.-C., Sanitioso, R. B., & Burman, J. T. (2013). Sick? Or slow? On the origins of intelligence as a psychological object. *Intelligence, 41*(5), 699–711.

Niedenthal, P. M., Barsalou, L. W., Winkielman, P., Krauth-Gruber, S., & Ric, F. (2005). Embodiment in attitudes, social perception, and emotion. *Personality and Social Psychology Review, 9*(3), 184–211.

Nikles, C. D., II, Brecht, D. L., Klinger, E., & Bursell, A. L. (1998). The effects of current concern- and nonconcern-related waking suggestions on nocturnal dream content. *Journal of Personality and Social Psychology, 75,* 242–255.

Nikolaev, B., & Salahodjaev, R. (2016). The role of intelligence in the distribution of national happiness. *Intelligence, 56,* 38–45.

Nir, Y., & Tononi, G. (2010). Dreaming and the brain: From phenomenology to neurophysiology. *Trends in Cognitive Sciences, 14*(2), 88–100.

Nisbett, R. E. (2009). *Intelligence and how to get it.* New York: Norton.

Nisbett, R. E., & Cohen, D. (1996). *Culture of honor: The psychology of violence in the South.* Boulder, CO: Westview Press.

Nisbett, R. E., Aronson, J., Blair, C., Dickens, W., Flynn, J., Halpern, D. F., & Turkheimer, E. (2012). Intelligence: New findings and theoretical developments. *American Psychologist, 67*(2), 130–159.

Nisbett, R. E., Caputo, C., Legant, P., & Maracek, J. (1973). Behavior as seen by the actor and as seen by the observer. *Journal of Personality and Social Psychology, 27,* 154–164.

Nissen, M. J., & Bullemer, P. (1987). Attentional requirements of learning: Evidence from performance measures. *Cognitive Psychology, 19,* 1–32.

Noah, T., Schul, Y., & Mayo, R. (2018). When both the original study and its failed replication are correct: Feeling observed eliminates the facial-feedback effect. *Journal of Personality and Social Psychology, 114*(5), 657–664. doi.org/10.1037/pspa0000121

Nobes, G., Panagiotaki, G., & Engelhardt, P. E. (2017). The development of intention-based morality: The influence of intention salience and recency, negligence, and outcome on children's and adults' judgments. *Developmental Psychology, 53*(10), 1895–1911. doi:10.1037/dev0000380

Nock, M. K. (2009). Why do people hurt themselves? New insights into the nature and functions of self-injury. *Current Directions in Psychological Science, 18,* 78–83. doi:10.1111/j.1467-8721.2009.01613.x

Nock, M. K. (2010). Self-injury. *Annual Review of Clinical Psychology, 6,* 339–363. doi:10.1146/annurev.clinpsy.121208.131258

Nock, M. K., Borges, G., & Ono, Y. (Eds.). (2012). *Suicide: Global perspectives from the WHO World Mental Health Surveys.* New York: Cambridge University Press.

Nock, M. K., Borges, G., Bromet, E. J., Alonso, J., Angermeyer, M., Beautrais, A., . . . Williams, D. (2008). Cross-national prevalence and risk factors for suicidal ideation, plans, and attempts. *British Journal of Psychiatry, 192,* 98–105.

Nock, M. K., Green, J. G., Hwang, I., McLaughlin, K. A., Sampson, N. A., Zaslavsky, A. M., & Kessler, R. C. (2013). Prevalence, correlates and treatment of lifetime suicidal behavior among adolescents: Results from the National Comorbidity Survey Replication–Adolescent Supplement (NCSA–A). *Journal of the American Medical Association Psychiatry, 70*(3), 300–310.

Nock, M. K., Holmberg, E. G., Photos, V. I., & Michel, B. D. (2007). Structured and semi-structured interviews. In M. Hersen & J. C. Thomas (Eds.), *Handbook of clinical interviewing with children* (pp. 30–49). Thousand Oaks, CA: Sage.

Nock, M. K., Kazdin, A. E., Hiripi, E., & Kessler, R. C. (2006). Prevalence, subtypes, and correlates of *DSM–IV* conduct disorder in the National Comorbidity Survey Replication. *Psychological Medicine, 36,* 699–710.

Nolen-Hoeksema, S. (2012). Emotion regulation and psychopathology: The role of gender. *Annual Review of Clinical Psychology, 8,* 161–187.

Norby, S. (2015). Why forget? On the adaptive value of memory loss. *Perspectives on Psychological Science, 10,* 551–578.

Norrholm, S. D., & Ressler, K. J. (2009). Genetics of anxiety and trauma-related disorders. *Neuroscience, 164,* 272–287.

Norton, M. I., Frost, J. H., & Ariely, D. (2007). Less is more: The lure of ambiguity, or why familiarity breeds contempt. *Journal of Personality and Social Psychology, 92*(1), 97–105.

Nosofsky, R. M., Sanders, C., & McDaniel, M. (2018). A formal psychological model of classification applied to natural-science category learning. *Current Directions in Psychological Science, 27,* 129–135.

Nowak, M. A. (2006). Five rules for the evolution of cooperation. *Science, 314,* 1560–1563.

Nuttin, J. M. (1985). Narcissism beyond Gestalt and awareness: The name-letter effect. *European Journal of Social Psychology, 15,* 353–361.

Nyborg, H., & Jensen, A. R. (2001). Occupation and income related to psychometric g. *Intelligence, 29,* 45–55.

O'Connor, T. G., & Rutter, M. (2000). Attachment disorder following early severe deprivation: Extension and longitudinal follow-up. *Journal of the American Academy of Child and Adolescent Psychiatry, 39,* 703–712.

O'Laughlin, M. J., & Malle, B. F. (2002). How people explain actions performed by groups and individuals. *Journal of Personality and Social Psychology, 82,* 33–48.

O'Sullivan, L. F., & Allgeier, E. R. (1998). Feigning sexual desire: Consenting to unwanted sexual activity in heterosexual dating relationships. *Journal of Sex Research, 35*(3), 234–243.

Ochsner, K. N. (2000). Are affective events richly recollected or simply familiar? The experience and process of recognizing feelings past. *Journal of Experimental Psychology: General, 129,* 242–261.

Ochsner, K. N., Bunge, S. A., Gross, J. J., & Gabrieli, J. D. E. (2002). Rethinking feelings: An fMRI study of the cognitive regulation of emotion. *Journal of Cognitive Neuroscience, 14,* 1215–1229.

Ofshe, R. J. (1992). Inadvertent hypnosis during interrogation: False confession due to dissociative state, misidentified multiple personality, and the satanic cult hypothesis. *International Journal of Clinical and Experimental Hypnosis, 40,* 125–126.

Ohayon, M. M. (2002). Epidemiology of insomnia: What we know and what we still need to learn. *Sleep Medicine, 6,* 97–111.

Ohayon, M. M., Guilleminault, C., & Priest, R. G. (1999). Night terrors, sleepwalking, and confusional arousals in the general population: Their frequency and relationship to other sleep and mental disorders. *Journal of Clinical Psychiatry, 60,* 268–276.

Okdie, B. M., Ewoldsen, D. R., Muscanell, N. L., Guadagno, R. E., Eno, C. A., Velez, J. A., . . . Smith, L. R. (2014). Missed programs (you can't TiVo this one): Why psychologists should study media. *Perspectives on Psychological Science, 9*(2), 180–195.

Okuda, J., Fujii, T., Ohtake, H., Tsukiura, T., Tanji, K., Suzuki, K., . . . Yamadori, A. (2003). Thinking of the future and the past: The roles of the frontal pole and the medial temporal lobes. *NeuroImage, 19,* 1369–1380.

Olatunji, B. O., & Wolitzky-Taylor, K. B. (2009). Anxiety sensitivity and the anxiety disorders: A meta-analytic review and synthesis. *Psychological Bulletin, 135,* 974–999.

Olds, J. (1956, October). Pleasure center in the brain. *Scientific American, 195,* 105–116.

Olds, J., & Fobes, J. I. (1981). The central basis of motivation: Intracranial self-stimulation studies. *Annual Review of Psychology, 32,* 523–574.

Olds, J., & Milner, P. (1954). Positive reinforcement produced by electrical stimulation of septal areas and other regions of rat brains. *Journal of Comparative and Physiological Psychology, 47,* 419–427.

Ollers, D. K., & Eilers, R. E. (1988). The role of audition in infant babbling. *Child Development, 59,* 441–449.

Olsson, A., & Phelps, E. A. (2007). Social learning of fear. *Nature Neuroscience, 10,* 1095–1102.

Olsson, A., Kopsida, E., Sorjonen, K., & Savic, I. (2016). Testosterone and estrogen impact social evaluations and vicarious emotions: A double-blind placebo-controlled study. *Emotion, 16,* 515–523.

Olsson, M. B., Westerlund, J., Lundström, S., Giacobini, M., Fernell, E., & Gillberg, C. (2015). Recovery from the diagnosis of autism—and then? *Neuropsychiatric Disease and Treatment, 11,* 999–1005.

Oltmanns, T. F., Neale, J. M., & Davison, G. C. (1991). *Case studies in abnormal psychology* (3rd ed.). New York: Wiley.

Olton, D. S., & Samuelson, R. J. (1976). Remembrance of places passed: Spatial memory in rats. *Journal of Experimental Psychology: Animal Behavior Processes, 2,* 97–116.

Onishi, K. H., & Baillargeon, R. (2005). Do 15-month-old infants understand false beliefs? *Science, 308,* 255–258.

Ono, K. (1987). Superstitious behavior in humans. *Journal of the Experimental Analysis of Behavior, 47,* 261–271.

Oostenbroek, J., Suddendorf, T., Nielsen, M., Redshaw, J., Kennedy-Costantini, S., Davis, J., . . . Slaughter, V. (2016). Comprehensive longitudinal study challenges the existence of neonatal imitation in humans. *Current Biology, 26,* 1334–1338.

Open Science Collaboration, Nosek, B. A., Aarts, A. A., Anderson, C. J., Anderson, J. E., . . . & Kappes, H. B. (2015). Estimating the reproducibility of psychological science. *Science, 349* (6251), aac4716–aac4716. ISSN 0036-8075 DOI:10.1126 /science.aac4716

Ophir, E., Nass, C., & Wagner, A. D. (2009). Cognitive control in media multitaskers. *Proceedings of the National Academy of Sciences, USA, 106,* 15583–15587.

Orban, P., Lungu, O., & Doyon, J. (2008). Motor sequence learning and developmental dyslexia. *Annals of the New York Academy of Sciences, 1145,* 151–172.

Organisation for Economic Cooperation and Development. (2019). *OECD Health Statistics 2019* [database]. Retrieved from http://stats.oecd.org/

Ormel, J., Petukhova, M., Chatterji, S., Aguilar-Gaxiola, S., Alonso, J., Angermeyer, M. C., . . . Kessler, R. C. (2008). Disability and treatment of specific mental and physical disorders across the world: Results from the WHO World Mental Health Surveys. *British Journal of Psychiatry, 192*(5), 368–375.

Osgood, C. E., Suci, G. J., & Tannenbaum, P. (1967). *The Measurement of Meaning,* Champaign, IL: University of Illinois Press.

Oswald, L., Taylor, A. M., & Triesman, M. (1960). Discriminative responses to stimulation during human sleep. *Brain, 83,* 440–453.

Otto, M. W., Henin, A., Hirshfeld-Becker, D. R., Pollack, M. H., Biederman, J., & Rosenbaum, J. F. (2007). Posttraumatic stress disorder symptoms following media exposure to tragic events: Impact of 9/11 on children at risk for anxiety disorders. *Journal of Anxiety Disorders, 21,* 888–902.

Oudiette, D. & Paller, K. A. (2013). Upgrading the sleeping brain with targeted memory reactivation. *Trends in Cognitive Sciences, 17,* 142–149.

Owen, A. M., Coleman, M. R., Boly, M., Davis, M. H., Laureys, S., & Pickard, J. D. (2006). Detecting awareness in the vegetative state. *Science, 313*(5792), 1402.

Owens, W. A. (1966). Age and mental abilities: A second adult followup. *Journal of Educational Psychology, 57,* 311–325.

Oztekin, I., Curtis, C. E., & McElree, B. (2009). The medial temporal lobe and left inferior prefrontal cortex jointly support interference resolution in verbal working memory. *Journal of Cognitive Neuroscience, 21,* 1967–1979.

Paap, K. R., & Sawi, O. (2014). Bilingual advantages in executive functioning: Problems in convergent validity, discriminant validity, and the identification of the theoretical constructs. *Frontiers in Psychology, 5,* 962. http://dx.doi.org/10.3389/fpsyg.2014.00962

Paap, K. R., Johnson, H. A., & Sawi, O. (2015). Bilingual advantages in executive functioning either do not exist or are restricted to very specific and undetermined circumstances. *Cortex, 69,* 265–278.

Pagnin, D., de Queiroz, V., Pini, S., & Cassano, G. B. (2008). Efficacy of ECT in depression: A meta-analytic review. *Focus, 6,* 155–162.

Paivio, A. (1971). *Imagery and verbal processes.* New York: Holt, Rinehart and Winston.

Paivio, A. (1986). *Mental representations: A dual coding approach.* New York: Oxford University Press.

Palermo, T. M., Eccleston, C., Lewandowski, A. S., Williams, A. C., & Morley, S. (2011). Randomized controlled trials of psychological therapies for management of chronic pain in children and adolescents: An updated meta-analytic review. *Pain, 148,* 387–397.

Palombo, D. J., Alain, C., Soderlund, H., Khuu, W., & Levine, B. (2015). Severely deficient autobiographical memory (SDAM) in healthy adults: A new mnemonic syndrome. *Neuropsychologia, 72,* 105–118.

Palombo, D. J., Bacopulos, A., Amaral, R. S. C., Olsen, R. K., Todd, R. M., Anderson, A. K., & Levine, B. (2018). Episodic autobiographical memory is associated with variation in the size of hippocampal subregions. *Hippocampus, 28,* 69–75.

Paluck, B. L., & Green, D. P. (2009). Prejudice reduction: What works? A review and assessment of research and practice. *Annual Review of Psychology, 60,* 339–367.

Pan, S. C., & Rickard, T. C. (2018). Transfer of test-enhanced learning: Meta-analytic review and synthesis. *Psychological Bulletin, 144,* 710–756.

Pandit, J. J., Andrade, J., Bogod, D. G., Hitchman, J. M., Jonker, W. R., . . . Cook, T. M. (2014). The 5th National Audit Project (NAP5) on accidental awareness during general anaesthesia: Summary of main findings and risk factors. *Anaesthesia, 69,* 1089–1101.

Pang, W., Esping, A., & Plucker, J. A. (2017). Confucian conceptions of human intelligence. *Review of General Psychology, 21*(2), 161–169.

Papez, J. W. (1937). A proposed mechanism of emotion. *Archives of Neurology and Pathology, 38,* 725–743.

Park, B., & Hastie, R. (1987). Perception of variability in category development: Instance- versus abstraction-based stereotypes. *Journal of Personality and Social Psychology, 53*(4), 621–635.

Park, D. C., & McDonough, I. M. (2013). The dynamic aging mind: Revelations from functional neuroimaging research. *Perspectives on Psychological Science, 8*(1), 62–67.

Park, D. C., Polk, T. A., Park, R., Minear, M., Savage, A., & Smith, M. R. (2004). Aging reduces neural specialization in ventral visual cortex. *Proceedings of the National Academy of Sciences, USA, 101*(35), 13091–13095.

Parker, E. S., Cahill, L. S., & McGaugh, J. L. (2006). A case of unusual autobiographical remembering. *Neurocase, 12,* 35–49.

Parker, G., Gibson, N. A., Brotchie, H., Heruc, G., Rees, A. M., & Hadzi-Pavlovic, D. (2006). Omega-3 fatty acids and mood disorders. *American Journal of Psychiatry, 163*(10), 969–978.

Parker, H. A., & McNally, R. J. (2008). Repressive coping, emotional adjustment, and cognition in people who have lost loved ones to suicide. *Suicide and Life-Threatening Behavior, 38,* 676–687.

Parkin, B. L., Ekhtiari, H., & Walsh, V. F. (2015). Non-invasive brain stimulation in cognitive neuroscience: A primer. *Neuron, 87,* 932–945.

Parkinson, B., & Totterdell, P. (1999). Classifying affect-regulation strategies. *Cognition and Emotion, 13,* 277–303.

Parkinson, C., Walker, T. T., Memmi, S., & Wheatley, T. (2017). Emotions are understood from biological motion across remote cultures. *Emotion, 17*(3), 459–477. doi.org/10.1037/emo0000194

Parrott, A. C. (2001). Human psychopharmacology of Ecstasy (MDMA): A review of 15 years of empirical research. *Human Psychopharmacology, 16,* 557–577.

Parrott, A. C., Morinan, A., Moss, M., & Scholey, A. (2005). *Understanding drugs and behavior.* Chichester, UK: Wiley.

Parsons, T. (1975). The sick role and the role of the physician reconsidered. *Milbank Memorial Fund Quarterly, Health and Society, 53*(3), 257–278.

Pascual-Ferrá, P., Liu, Y., & Beatty, M. J. (2012). A meta-analytic comparison of the effects of text messaging to substance-induced impairment on driving performance. *Communication Research Reports, 29,* 229–238.

Pascual-Leone, A., Amedi, A., Fregni, F., & Merabet, L. B. (2005). The plastic human brain cortex. *Annual Review of Neuroscience, 28,* 377–401.

Pascual-Leone, A., Houser, C. M., Reese, K., Shotland, L. I., Grafman, J., Sato, S., . . . Cohen, L. G. (1993). Safety of rapid-rate transcranial magnetic stimulation in normal volunteers. *Electroencephalography and Clinical Neurophysiology, 89,* 120–130.

Pasupathi, M., McLean, K. C., & Weeks, T. (2009). To tell or not to tell: Disclosure and the narrative self. *Journal of Personality, 77,* 1–35.

Patall, E. A., Cooper, H., & Robinson, J. C. (2008). The effects of choice on intrinsic motivation and related outcomes: A meta-analysis of research findings. *Psychological Bulletin, 134*(2), 270–300.

Patihis, L., Frenda, S. J., LePort, A. K. R., Petersen, N., Nichols, R. M., Stark, C. E. L., . . . Loftus, E. F. (2013). False memories in highly superior autobiographical memory individuals. *Proceedings of the National Academy of Sciences USA, 110,* 20947–20952.

Patten, S. B., Williams, J. V., Lavorato, D. H., Wang, J. L., McDonald, K., & Bulloch, A. G. (2016). Major depression in Canada: What has changed over the past 10 years? *The Canadian Journal of Psychiatry, 61*(2), 80–85.

Patterson, C. J. (2013). Sexual orientation and family lives. In G. W. Peterson & K. R. Bush (Eds.), *The handbook of marriage and the family.* New York: Springer.

Patton, G. C., & Viner, R. (2007). Pubertal transitions in health. *Lancet, 369,* 1130–1139.

Paulus, M. (2016). It's payback time: Preschoolers selectively request resources from someone they had benefitted. *Developmental Psychology, 52*(8), 1299–1306.

Paus, T. (2005). Mapping brain maturation and cognitive development during adolescence. *Trends in Cognitive Sciences, 9*(2), 60–68.

Pavlidou, E. V., Williams, J. M., & Kelly, L. M. (2009). Artificial grammar learning in primary school children with and without developmental dyslexia. *Annals of Dyslexia, 59,* 55–77.

Pavlov, I. P. (1923a). New researches on conditioned reflexes. *Science, 58,* 359–361.

Pavlov, I. P. (1923b, July 23). Pavloff. *Time, 1*(21), 20–21.

Pavlov, I. P. (1927). *Conditioned reflexes.* Oxford, UK: Oxford University Press.

Payne, J. D., & Kensinger, E. A. (2018). Stress, sleep, and the selective consolidation of emotional memories. *Current Opinion in Behavioral Sciences, 19,* 36–43.

Payne, J. D., Kensinger, E. A., Wamsley, E., Spreng, R. N., Alger, S., Gibler, K., . . . & Stickgold, R. (2015). Napping and the selective consolidation of negative aspects of scenes. *Emotion, 15,* 176–186.

Payne, J. D., Schacter, D. L., Propper, R., Huang, L., Wamsley, E., Tucker, M. A., . . . Stickgold, R. (2009). The role of sleep in false memory formation. *Neurobiology of Learning and Memory, 92,* 327–334.

Payne, J. D., Stickgold, R., Swanberg, K., & Kensinger, E. A. (2008). Sleep preferentially enhances memory for emotional components of scenes. *Psychological Science, 19,* 781–788.

Pearce, J. M. (1987). A model of stimulus generalization for Pavlovian conditioning. *Psychological Review, 84,* 61–73.

Pearson, C., Janz, T., & Ali, J. (2013, September). Health at a glance: Mental and substance use disorders in Canada. Retrieved from https://www150.statcan.gc.ca/n1/en/pub/82-624-x/2013001/article/11855-eng.pdf?st=KuZBOmSe

Pearson, J., & Kosslyn, S. M. (2015). The heterogeneity of mental representation: Ending the imagery debate. *Proceedings of the National Academy of Sciences USA, 112,* 10089–10092.

Peelen, M. V., & Kastner, S. (2009). A nonvisual look at the functional organization of visual cortex. *Neuron, 63,* 284–286.

Peeters, A., Barendregt, J. J., Willekens, F., Mackenbach, J. P., Al Mamun, A., Bonneux, L., & Netherlands Epidemiology and Demography Compression of Morbidity Research Group. (2003). Obesity in adulthood and its consequences for life expectancy: A lifetable analysis. *Annals of Internal Medicine, 138*(1), 24–32.

Pelham, B. W., Carvallo, M., & Jones, J. T. (2005). Implicit egotism. *Current Directions in Psychological Science, 14,* 106–110.

Pelham, B. W., Mirenberg, M. C., & Jones, J. T. (2002). Why Susie sells seashells by the seashore: Implicit egotism and major life decisions. *Journal of Personality and Social Psychology, 82,* 469–487.

Penfield, W., & Perot, P. (1963). The brain's record of auditory and visual experience. *Brain, 86,* 596–696.

Penfield, W., & Rasmussen, T. (1950). *The cerebral cortex of man: A clinical study of localization of function.* New York: Macmillan.

Pennebaker, J. W. (1989). Confession, inhibition, and disease. *Advances in Experimental Social Psychology, 22,* 211–244.

Pennebaker, J. W., & Chung, C. K. (2007). Expressive writing, emotional upheavals, and health. In H. Friedman & R. Silver (Eds.), *Handbook of health psychology* (pp. 263–284). New York: Oxford University Press.

Pennebaker, J. W., & Sanders, D. Y. (1976). American graffiti: Effects of authority and reactance arousal. *Personality and Social Psychology Bulletin, 2,* 264–267.

Pennebaker, J. W., Kiecolt-Glaser, J. K., & Glaser, R. (1988). Disclosure of traumas and immune function: Health implications for psychotherapy. *Journal of Consulting and Clinical Psychology, 56,* 239–245.

Penner, L. A., Albrecht, T. L., Orom, H., Coleman, D. K., & Underwood, W. (2010). Health and health care disparities. In J. F. Dovidio, M. Hewstone, P. Glick, & V. M. Esses (Eds.), *The Sage handbook of prejudice, stereotyping and discrimination* (pp. 472–489). Thousand Oaks, CA: Sage.

Pennycook, G., Cannon, T. D., & Rand, D. G. (2018). Prior exposure increases perceived accuracy of fake news. *Journal of Experimental Psychology: General.* http://dx.doi.org/10.1037/xge0000465

Perenin, M.-T., & Vighetto, A. (1988). Optic ataxia: A specific disruption in visuomotor mechanisms. I. Different aspects of the deficit in reaching for objects. *Brain, 111,* 643–674.

Perera, S., Eisen, R., Bhatt, M., Bhatnagar, N., de Souza, R., & Thabane, L. (2018). Light therapy for non-seasonal depression: Systematic review and meta-analysis. *British Journal of Psychiatry, 2*(2), 116–126.

Perera, T., George, M. S., Grammer, G., Janicak, P. G., Pascual-Leone, A., & Wirecki, T. S. (2016). The Clinical TMS Society consensus review and treatment recommendations for TMS therapy for major depressive disorder. *Brain Stimulation, 9*(3), 336–346.

Perilloux, H. K., Webster, G. D., & Gaulin, S. J. C. (2010). Signals of genetic quality and maternal investment capacity: The dynamic effects of fluctuating asymmetry and waist-to-hip ratio on men's ratings of women's attractiveness. *Social Psychological and Personality Science, 1*(1), 34–42.

Perlmutter, J. S., & Mink, J. W. (2006). Deep brain stimulation. *Annual Review of Neuroscience, 29,* 229–257.

Perloff, L. S., & Fetzer, B. K. (1986). Self-other judgments and perceived vulnerability to victimization. *Journal of Personality and Social Psychology, 50,* 502–510.

Perls, F. S., Hefferkine, R., & Goodman, P. (1951). *Gestalt therapy: Excitement and growth in the human personality.* New York: Julian Press.

Perrett, D. I., Burt, D. M., Penton-Voak, I. S., Lee, K. J., Rowland, D. A., & Edwards, R. (1999). Symmetry and human facial attractiveness. *Evolution and Human Behavior, 20,* 295–307.

Perrett, D. I., Rolls, E. T., & Caan, W. (1982). Visual neurons responsive to faces in the monkey temporal cortex. *Experimental Brain Research, 47,* 329–342.

Pessiglione, M., Seymour, B., Flandin, G., Dolan, R. J., & Frith, C. D. (2006). Dopamine-dependent prediction errors underpin reward-seeking behavior in humans. *Nature, 442,* 1042–1045.

Petersen, A. C., & Grockett, L. (1985). Pubertal timing and grade effects on adjustment. *Journal of Youth and Adolescence, 14,* 191–206.

Petersen, J. L., & Hyde, J. S. (2010). A meta-analytic review of research on gender differences in sexuality, 1993–2007. *Psychological Bulletin, 136*(1), 21–38.

Peterson, C., & Siegal, M. (1999). Representing inner worlds: Theory of mind in autistic, deaf and normal hearing children. *Psychological Science, 10,* 126–129.

Peterson, C., Slaughter, V., Moore, C., & Wellman, H. M. (2016). Peer social skills and theory of mind in children with autism, deafness, or typical development. *Developmental Psychology, 52*(1), 46–57. doi:10.1037/a0039833

Peterson, C., Wang, Q., & Hou, Y. (2009). "When I was little": Childhood recollections in Chinese and European Canadian grade school children. *Child Development, 80,* 506–518.

Peterson, G. B. (2004). A day of great illumination: B. F. Skinner's discovery of shaping. *Journal of the Experimental Analysis of Behavior, 82,* 317–328.

Peterson, L. R., & Peterson, M. J. (1959). Short-term retention of individual verbal items. *Journal of Experimental Psychology, 58,* 193–198.

Petersson, K. M., Forkstam, C., & Ingvar, M. (2004). Artificial syntactic violations activate Broca's region. *Cognitive Science, 28,* 383–407.

Petitto, L. A., & Marentette, P. F. (1991). Babbling in the manual mode: Evidence for the ontogeny of language. *Science, 251,* 1493–1496.

Petrie, K. P., Booth, R. J., & Pennebaker, J. W. (1998). The immunological effects of thought suppression. *Journal of Personality and Social Psychology, 75,* 1264–1272.

Petry, N. M., Alessi, S. M., & Rash, C. J. (2013). Contingency management treatments decrease psychiatric symptoms. *Journal of Consulting and Clinical Psychology, 81*(5), 926–931.

Petty, R. E., & Cacioppo, J. T. (1986). The elaboration likelihood model of persuasion. In L. Berkowitz (Ed.), *Advances in experimental social psychology* (Vol. 19, pp. 123–205). New York: Academic Press.

Petty, R. E., & Wegener, D. T. (1998). Attitude change: Multiple roles for persuasion variables. In D. T. Gilbert, S. T. Fiske, & G. Lindzey (Eds.), *The handbook of social psychology* (4th ed., Vol. 1, pp. 323–390). Boston: McGraw-Hill.

Petty, R. E., Cacioppo, J. T., & Goldman, R. (1981). Personal involvement as a determinant of argument-based persuasion. *Journal of Personality and Social Psychology, 41,* 847–855.

Pew Research Center for People & the Press. (2009). *Growing old in America: Expectations vs. reality.* Retrieved from http://pewsocialtrends.org/pubs/736/getting-old-in-america

Pew Research Center for People & the Press. (2013, June 13). A survey of LGBT American attitudes, experiences and values in changing times. http://www.pewsocialtrends.org/wp-content/uploads/sites/3/2013/06/SDT_LGBT-Americans_06-2013.pdf

Phelan, J., Link, B., Stueve, A., & Pescosolido, B. (1997, August). *Public conceptions of mental illness in 1950 in 1996: Has*

sophistication increased? Has stigma declined? Paper presented at the American Sociological Association, Toronto, Ontario.

Phelps, E. A. (2006). Emotion and cognition: Insights from studies of the human amygdala. *Annual Review of Psychology, 57*(1), 27–53.

Phelps, E. A., & LeDoux, J. E. (2005). Contributions of the amygdala to emotion processing: From animal models to human behavior. *Neuron, 48*(2), 175–187.

Phills, C. E., Kawakami, K., Tabi, E., Nadolny, D., & Inzlicht, M. (2011). Mind the gap: Increasing associations between the self and Blacks with approach behaviors. *Journal of Personality and Social Psychology, 100*(2), 197–210.

Piaget, J. (1954). *The child's conception of number.* New York: Norton.

Piaget, J. (1965). *The moral judgment of the child.* New York: Free Press. (Original work published 1932)

Piaget, J. (1977). The first year of life of the child. In H. E. Gruber & J. J. Voneche (Eds.), *The essential Piaget: An interpretative reference and guide* (pp. 198–214). New York: Basic Books. (Original work published 1927)

Piaget, J., & Inhelder, B. (1974). *The child's construction of quantities.* London: Routledge and Kegan Paul Ltd.

Piantadosi, S. T., & Kidd, C. (2016). Extraordinary intelligence and the care of infants. *Proceedings of the National Academy of Sciences, USA, 113* (2016), 1–6.

Piazza, J. R., Charles, S. T., Sliwinski, M. J., Mogle, J., & Almeida, D. M. (2013). Affective reactivity to daily stressors and long-term risk of reporting a chronic physical health condition. *Annals of Behavioral Medicine, 45,* 110–120.

Pierce, L. J., Klein, D., Chen, J. K., Delcenserie, A., & Genesee, F. (2014). Mapping the unconscious maintenance of a lost first language. *Proceedings of the National Academy of Sciences, USA, 111*(48), 17314–17319.

Pietschnig, J., & Voracek, M. (2015). One century of global IQ gains: A formal meta-analysis of the Flynn effect (1909–2013). *Perspectives on Psychological Science, 10*(3), 282–306.

Pietschnig, J., Penke, L., Wicherts, J. M., Zeiler, M., & Voracek, M. (2015). Meta-analysis of associations between human brain volume and intelligence differences: How strong are they and what do they mean? *Neuroscience & Behavioral Reviews, 57,* 411–432.

Piff, P. K., Kraus, M. W., Côté, S., Cheng, B. H., & Keltner, D. (2010). Having less, giving more: The influence of social class on prosocial behavior. *Journal of Personality and Social Psychology, 99*(5), 771–784. doi:10.1037/a0020092

Piff, P. K., Stancato, D. M., Côté, S., Mendoza-Denton, R., & Keltner, D. (2012). Higher social class predicts increased unethical behavior. *Proceedings of the National Academy of Sciences of the United States of America, USA, 109*(11), 4086–4091. doi:10.1073/pnas.1118373109

Pinel, J. P. J., Assanand, S., & Lehman, D. R. (2000). Hunger, eating, and ill health. *American Psychologist, 55,* 1105–1116.

Pines, A. M. (1993). Burnout: An existential perspective. In W. B. Schaufeli, C. Maslach, & T. Marek (Eds.), *Professional burnout: Recent developments in theory and research* (pp. 33–51). Washington, DC: Taylor & Francis.

Pinker, S. (1994). *The language instinct.* New York: Morrow.

Pinker, S. (2003). *The blank slate: The modern denial of human nature.* New York: Viking.

Pinker, S. (2007, March 19). A history of violence: We're getting nicer every day. *The New Republic Online.* Retrieved from https://newrepublic.com/article/64340/history-violence-were-getting-nicer-every-day

Pinker, S., & Bloom, P. (1990). Natural language and natural selection. *Behavioral and Brain Sciences, 13,* 707–727.

Pitcher, D., Garrido, L., Walsh, V., & Duchaine, B. C. (2008). Transcranial magnetic stimulation disrupts the perception and embodiment of facial expressions. *Journal of Neuroscience, 28*(36), 8929–8933.

Plack, C. J. (2018a). Pitch and periodicity coding. In *The sense of hearing* (3rd ed., pp. 128–148). New York: Routledge.

Plack, C. J. (2018b). Spatial hearing. In *The sense of hearing* (3rd ed., pp. 171–191). New York: Routledge.

Platek, S. M., Critton, S. R., Myers, T. E., & Gallup, G. G. Jr. (2003). Contagious yawning: The role of self-awareness and mental state attribution. *Cognitive Brain Research, 17,* 223–227.

Plavén-Sigray, P., Hedman, E., Victorsson, P., Matheson, G. J., Forsberg, A., Djurfeldt, D. R., . . . Cervenka, S. (2017). Extrastriatal dopamine D2-receptor availability in social anxiety disorder. *European Neuropsychopharmacology, 27,* 462–469.

Plomin, R., & Caspi, A. (1999). Behavioral genetics and personality. In L. A. Pervin & O. P. John (Eds.), *Handbook of personality: Theory and research* (Vol. 2, pp. 251–276). New York: Guilford Press.

Plomin, R., & Spinath, F. M. (2004). Intelligence: Genetics, genes, and genomics. *Journal of Personality and Social Psychology, 86,* 112–129.

Plomin, R., DeFries, J. C., McClearn, G. E., & McGuffin, P. (2001). *Behavioral genetics* (4th ed.). New York: W. H. Freeman.

Plomin, R., Haworth, C. M. A., Meaburn, E. L., Price, T. S., Wellcome Trust Case Control Consortium 2, & Davis, O. S. P. (2013). Common DNA markers can account for more than half of the genetic influence on cognitive abilities. *Psychological Science, 24*(4), 562–568.

Plomin, R., Scheier, M. F., Bergeman, C. S., Pedersen, N. L., Nesselroade, J. R., & McClearn, G. E. (1992). Optimism, pessimism, and mental health: A twin/adoption analysis. *Personality and Individual Differences, 13,* 921–930.

Plotnik, J. M., de Waal, F. B. M., & Reiss, D. (2006). Self-recognition in an Asian elephant. *Proceedings of the National Academy of Sciences, USA, 103,* 17053–17057.

Polanczyk, G., de Lima, M. S., Horta, B. L., Biederman, J., & Rohde, L. A. (2007). The worldwide prevalence of ADHD: A systemic review and metaregression analysis. *American Journal of Psychiatry, 164,* 942–948.

Polderman, T. J. C., Benyamin, B., de Leeuw, C. A., Sullivan, P. F., van Bochoven, A., Visscher, P. M., & Posthuma, D. (2015). Meta-analysis of the heritability of human traits based on fifty years of twin studies. *Nature Genetics, 47*(7), 702–709.

Poldrack, R. A. (2018). *The new mind readers: What neuroimaging can and cannot reveal about our thoughts.* Princeton, NJ: Princeton University Press.

Poliak, S., & Peles, E. (2003). The local differentiation of myelinated axons at nodes of Ranvier. *Nature Reviews Neuroscience, 4,* 968–980.

Poole, D. A., Lindsay, S. D., Memon, A., & Bull, R. (1995). Psychotherapy and the recovery of memories of childhood sexual abuse: U.S. and British practitioners' opinions, practices, and experiences. *Journal of Consulting and Clinical Psychology, 63,* 426–487.

Poon, S. H., Sim, K., Sum, M. Y., Kuswanto, C. N., & Baldessarini, R. J. (2012). Evidence-based options for treatment-resistant adult bipolar disorder patients. *Bipolar Disorders, 14*(6), 573–584.

Pope, A. W., & Bierman, K. L. (1999). Predicting adolescent peer problems and antisocial activities: The relative roles of aggression and dysregulation. *Developmental Psychology, 35,* 335–346.

Posner, M. I., & Raichle, M. E. (1994). *Images of mind.* New York: W. H. Freeman.

Post, R. M., Frye, M. A., Denicoff, G. S., Leverich, G. S., Dunn, R. T., Osuch, E. A., . . . Jajodia, K. (2008). Emerging trends in the treatment of rapid cycling bipolar disorder: A selected review. *Bipolar Disorders, 2,* 305–315.

Postman, L., & Underwood, B. J. (1973). Critical issues in interference theory. *Memory & Cognition, 1,* 19–40.

Postmes, T., & Spears, R. (1998). Deindividuation and antinormative behavior: A meta-analysis. *Psychological Bulletin, 123,* 238–259.

Powell, R. A., Symbaluk, D. G., MacDonald, S. E., & Honey, P. L. (2009). *Introduction to learning and behavior* (3rd ed.). Belmont, CA: Wadsworth Cengage Learning.

Power, M. L., & Schulkin, J. (2009). *The evolution of obesity.* Baltimore: Johns Hopkins University Press.

Prakash, R. S., Voss, M. W., Erickson, K. I., & Kramer, A. F. (2015). Moving towards a healthier brain and mind. *Annual Review of Psychology, 66,* 769–797.

Prasada, S., & Pinker, S. (1993). Generalizations of regular and irregular morphology. *Language and Cognitive Processes, 8,* 1–56.

Pressman, S. D., Cohen, S., Miller, G. E., Barkin, A., Rabin, B. S., & Treanor, J. J. (2005). Loneliness, social network size, and immune response to influenza vaccination in college freshmen. *Health Psychology, 24,* 297–306.

Price, J. L., & Davis, B. (2008). *The woman who can't forget: The extraordinary story of living with the most remarkable memory known to science.* New York: Free Press.

Prince, M., Wimo, A., Guerchet, M., Ali, G.-C., Wu, Y-T, Prina, M., & Alzheimer's Disease International. (2015). World Alzheimer Report 2015: The global impact of dementia: An analysis of prevalence, incidence, cost and trends. London, UK: Alzheimer's Disease International.

Prior, H., Schwartz, A., & Güntürkün, O. (2008). Mirror-induced behavior in the magpie (*Pica pica*): Evidence of self-recognition. *PLoS Biology, 6,* e202.

Prochaska, J. J., & Sallis, J. F. (2004). A randomized controlled trial of single versus multiple health behavior change: Promoting physical activity and nutrition among adolescents. *Health Psychology, 23,* 314–318.

Procopio, M., & Marriott, P. (2007). Intrauterine hormonal environment and risk of developing anorexia nervosa. *Archives of General Psychiatry, 64*(12), 1402–1407.

Protzko, J. (2015). The environment in raising early intelligence: A meta-analysis of the fadeout effect. *Intelligence, 53,* 202–210.

Protzko, J. (2016). Does the raising IQ-raising *g* distinction explain the fadeout effect? *Intelligence, 56,* 65–71.

Protzko, J. (2017). Raising IQ among school-aged children: Five meta-analyses and a review of randomized controlled trials. *Developmental Review, 46,* 81–101.

Protzko, J., Aronson, J., & Blair, C. (2013). How to make a young child smarter: Evidence from the database of raising intelligence. *Perspectives on Psychological Science, 8*(1), 25–40.

Provencal, N., & Binder, E. B. (2015). The neurobiological effects of stress as contributors to psychiatric disorders: Focus on epigenetics. *Current Opinion in Neurobiology, 30,* 31–37.

Provine, R. R. (2000). *Laughter: A scientific investigation.* New York: Viking.

Public Health Agency of Canada and Canadian Institute for Health Information. (2009). *Obesity in Canada.* Retrieved from http://www.phac-aspc.gc.ca/hp-ps/hl-mvs/oic-oac/index-eng.php.

Public Health Agency of Canada. (2012, July 4). Diabetes in Canada: Facts and figures from a public health perspective. Retrieved from https://www.canada.ca/en/public-health/services/chronic-diseases/reports-publications/diabetes/diabetes-canada-facts-figures-a-public-health-perspective.html

Public Health Agency of Canada. (2016, January). The Chief Public Health Officer's Report on the State of Public Health in Canada, 2015: Alcohol Consumption in Canada. Retrieved from https://www.canada.ca/en/public-health/services/publications/chief-public-health-officer-reports-state-public-health-canada/2015-alcohol-consumption-canada.html

Public Health Agency of Canada. (2017). Dementia in Canada, including Alzheimer's disease: Highlights from the Canadian chronic disease surveillance system. Retrieved from http://publications.gc.ca/collections/collection_2018/aspc-phac/HP35-84-2017-eng.pdf

Public Health Agency of Canada. (2018, July). Summary: Estimates of HIV incidence, prevalence and Canada's progress on meeting the 90-90-90 HIV targets, 2016. Retrieved from https://www.canada.ca/en/public-health/services/publications/diseases-conditions/summary-estimates-hiv-incidence-prevalence-canadas-progress-90-90-90.html

Public Health Agency of Canada. (2018, November 25). Reported cases from 1991 to 2016 in Canada—Notifiable diseases on-line. Retrieved from https://diseases.canada.ca/notifiable/charts?c=yl

Punjabi, N. M. (2008). The epidemiology of adult obstructive sleep apnea. *Proceedings of the American Thoracic Society, 5,* 136–143.

Puterman, E., Lin, J., Blackburn, E. H., O'Donovan, A., Adler, N., & Epel, E. (2010). The power of exercise: Buffering the effect of chronic stress on telomere length. *PLoS ONE, 5,* e10837.

Pyc, M. A., & Rawson, K. A. (2009). Testing the retrieval effort hypothesis: Does greater difficulty correctly recalling information lead to higher levels of memory? *Journal of Memory and Language, 60,* 437–447.

Pyers, J. E., & Senghas, A. (2009). Language promotes false-belief understanding: Evidence from learners of a new sign language. *Psychological Science, 20*(7), 805–812.

Pyers, J. E., Shusterman, A., Senghas, A., Spelke, E. S., & Emmorey, K. (2010). Evidence from an emerging sign language reveals that language supports spatial cognition. *Proceedings of the National Academy of Sciences, USA,107,* 12116–12120.

Pyszczynski, T., Holt, J., & Greenberg, J. (1987). Depression, self-focused attention, and expectancies for positive and negative future life events for self and others. *Journal of Personality and Social Psychology, 52,* 994–1001.

Querleu, D., Lefebvre, C., Titran, M., Renard, X., Morillon, M., & Crepin, G. (1984). Réactivité de nouveau-né de moins de deux heures de vie à la voix maternelle [Reactivity of a newborn at less than two hours of life to the mother's voice]. *Journal de Gynécologie Obstétrique et de Biologie de la Reproduction, 13,* 125–134.

Quiroga, R. (2016). Neuronal codes for visual perception and memory. *Neuropsychologia, 83,* 227–241.

Quiroga, R. Q., Reddy, L., Kreiman, G., Koch, C., & Fried, I. (2005). Invariant visual representation by single neurons in the human brain. *Nature, 435,* 1102–1107.

Qureshi, A., & Lee-Chiong, T. (2004). Medications and their effects on sleep. *Medical Clinics of North America, 88,* 751–766.

Rabbitt, P., Diggle, P., Holland, F., & McInnes, L. (2004). Practice and drop-out effects during a 17-year longitudinal study of cognitive aging. *Journal of Gerontology: Psychological Sciences and Social Sciences, 59*(2), 84–97.

Rabin, L. A., Fogel, J., & Nutter-Upham, K. E. (2011). Academic procrastination in college students: The role of self-reported executive function. *Journal of Clinical and Experimental Neuropsychology, 33,* 344–357.

Race, E., Keane, M. M., & Verfaellie, M. (2011). Medial temporal lobe damage causes deficits in episodic memory and episodic future thinking not attributable to deficits in narrative construction. *Journal of Neuroscience, 31,* 10262–10269.

Radford, E., & Radford, M. A. (1949). *Encyclopedia of superstitions.* New York: Philosophical Library.

Rahe, R. H., Meyer, M., Smith, M., Klaer, G., & Holmes, T. H. (1964). Social stress and illness onset. *Journal of Psychosomatic Research, 8,* 35–44.

Raichle, M. E. (2015). The brain's default mode network. *Annual Review of Neuroscience, 38,* 433–447.

Raichle, M. E., & Mintun, M. A. (2006). Brain work and brain imaging. *Annual Review of Neuroscience, 29,* 449–476.

Rajaram, S. (2011). Collaboration both hurts and helps memory: A cognitive perspective. *Current Directions in Psychological Science, 20,* 76–81.

Rajaram, S., & Pereira-Pasarin, L. P. (2010). Collaborative memory: Cognitive research and theory. *Perspectives on Psychological Science, 6,* 649–663.

Ramachandran, V. S., & Blakeslee, S. (1998). *Phantoms in the brain: Probing the mysteries of the human mind.* New York: Morrow.

Ramachandran, V. S., & Brang, D. (2015). Phantom touch. In T. J. Prescott, E. Ahissar, & E. Izhikevich (Eds.), *Scholarpedia of Touch* (pp. 377–386). Amsterdam, Netherlands: Atlantis Press.

Ramachandran, V. S., Brang, D., & McGeoch, P. D. (2010). Dynamic reorganization of referred sensations by movements of phantom limbs. *NeuroReport, 21,* 727–730.

Ramachandran, V. S., Rodgers-Ramachandran, D., & Stewart, M. (1992). Perceptual correlates of massive cortical reorganization. *Science, 258,* 1159–1160.

Ramirez-Esparza, N., Gosling, S. D., Benet-Martinez, V., & Potter, J. P. (2004). Do bilinguals have two personalities? A special case of cultural frame-switching. *Journal of Research in Personality, 40,* 99–120.

Ramsden, S., Richardson, F. M., Josse, G., Thomas, M. S., Ellis, C., Shakeshaft, C., . . . & Price, C. J. (2011). Verbal and non-verbal intelligence changes in the teenage brain. *Nature, 479*(7371), 113. Addendum in 2012. *Nature, 485*(7400), 666.

Rana, A., de Souza, R. J., Kandasamy, S., Lear, S. A., & Anand, S. S. (2014). Cardiovascular risk among South Asians living in Canada: A systematic review and meta-analysis. *CMAJ Open, 2*(3), E183–E191.

Rand, D. G. (2016). Cooperation, fast and slow: Meta-analytic evidence for a theory of social heuristics and self-interested deliberation. *Psychological Science, 27*(9), 1192–1206.

Rand, D. G., & Nowak, M. A. (2016). Human cooperation. *Trends in Cognitive Sciences, 17*(8), 413–425.

Randles, D., Inzlicht, M., Proulx, T., Tullett, A. M., & Heine, S. J. (2015). Is dissonance reduction a special case of fluid compensation? Evidence that dissonant cognitions cause compensatory affirmation and abstraction. *Journal of Personality and Social Psychology, 108*(5), 697–710.

Rapaport, D. (1946). *Diagnostic psychological testing: The theory, statistical evaluation, and diagnostic application of a battery of tests.* Chicago: Year Book Publishers.

Rapoport, J., Chavez, A., Greenstein, D., Addington, A., & Gogtay, N. (2009). Autism-spectrum disorders and childhood onset schizophrenia: Clinical and biological contributions to a relationship revisited. *Journal of the American Academy of Child and Adolescent Psychiatry, 48,* 10–18.

Rasmussen, A. S., & Berntsen, D. (2011). The unpredictable past: Spontaneous autobiographical memories outnumber autobiographical memories retrieved strategically. *Consciousness and Cognition, 20,* 1843–1846.

Ratliff, K. A., & Oishi, S. (2013). Gender differences in implicit self-esteem following a romantic partner's success or failure. *Journal of Personality and Social Psychology, 105*(4), 688–702.

Raven, J., Raven, J. C., & Court, J. H. (2004). *Manual for Raven's Progressive Matrices and Vocabulary Scales.* San Antonio: Harcourt Assessment.

Raz, N. (2000). Aging of the brain and its impact on cognitive performance: Integration of structural and functional findings. In F. I. M. Craik & T. A. Salthouse (Eds.), *The handbook of aging and cognition* (pp. 1–90). Mahwah, NJ: Erlbaum.

Reading, J. (2015). Confronting the growing crisis of cardiovascular disease and heart health among aboriginal peoples in Canada. *Canadian Journal of Cardiology, 31*(9), 1077–1080.

Reber, A. S. (1967). Implicit learning of artificial grammars. *Journal of Verbal Learning and Verbal Behavior, 6,* 855–863.

Reber, A. S. (1996). *Implicit learning and tacit knowledge: An essay on the cognitive unconscious.* New York: Oxford University Press.

Reber, A. S., & Allen, R. (2000). Individual differences in implicit learning. In R. G. Kunzendorf & B. Wallace (Eds.), *Individual differences in conscious experience* (pp. 227–247). Philadelphia: John Benjamins.

Reber, A. S., Walkenfeld, F. F., & Hernstadt, R. (1991). Implicit learning: Individual differences and IQ. *Journal of Experimental Psychology: Learning, Memory, and Cognition, 17,* 888–896.

Reber, P. J. (2013). The neural basis of implicit learning and memory: A review of neuropsychological and neuroimaging research. *Neuropsychologia, 51,* 2026–2042.

Reber, P. J., Gitelman, D. R., Parrish, T. B., & Mesulam, M. M. (2003). Dissociating explicit and implicit category knowledge with fMRI. *Journal of Cognitive Neuroscience, 15,* 574–583.

Rechsthaffen, A., Gilliland, M. A., Bergmann, B. M., & Winter, J. B. (1983). Physiological correlates of prolonged sleep deprivation in rats. *Science, 221,* 182–184.

Redick, T. S. (2015). Working memory training and interpreting interactions in intelligence interventions. *Intelligence, 50,* 14–20.

Redick, T. S., Shipstead, Z., Harrison, T. L., Hicks, K. L., Fried, D. E., Hambrick, D. Z., . . . Engle, R. W. (2013). No evidence of intelligence improvement after working memory training: A randomized, placebo-controlled study. *Journal of Experimental Psychology: General, 142,* 359–379. doi:10.1037/a002908

Reed, D. R. (2008). Birth of a new breed of supertaster. *Chemical Senses, 33,* 489–491.

Reed, G. (1988). *The psychology of anomalous experience* (rev. ed.). Buffalo, NY: Prometheus Books.

Reeve, C. L., Heggestad, E. D., & Lievens, F. (2009). Modeling the impact of test anxiety and test familiarity on the criterion-related validity of cognitive ability tests. *Intelligence, 37*(1), 34–41.

Regan, P. C. (1998). What if you can't get what you want? Willingness to compromise ideal mate selection standards as a function of sex, mate value, and relationship context. *Personality and Social Psychology Bulletin, 24,* 1294–1303.

Regier, T., & Kay, P. (2009). Language, thought, and color: Whorf was half right. *Trends in Cognitive Sciences, 13,* 439–446.

Reid, V. M., Dunn, K., Young, R. J., Amu, J., Donovan, T., & Reissland, N. (2017). The human fetus preferentially engages with face-like visual stimuli. *Current Biology, 27,* 1825–1828.e3.

Reis, H. T., Maniaci, M. R., Caprariello, P. S., Eastwick, P. W., & Finkel, E. J. (2011). Familiarity does indeed promote attraction in live interaction. *Journal of Personality and Social Psychology, 101*(3), 557–570.

Reiss, D., & Marino, L. (2001). Mirror self-recognition in the bottlenose dolphin: A case of cognitive convergence. *Proceedings of the National Academy of Sciences, USA, 98,* 5937–5942.

Reissland, N. (1988). Neonatal imitation in the first hour of life: Observations in rural Nepal. *Developmental Psychology, 24,* 464–469.

Renner, K. E. (1964). Delay of reinforcement: A historical review. *Psychological Review, 61,* 341–361.

Renner, M. J., & Mackin, R. (1998). A life stress instrument for classroom use. *Teaching of Psychology, 25,* 46–48.

Rensink, R. A. (2002). Change detection. *Annual Review of Psychology, 53,* 245–277.

Rensink, R. A., O'Regan, J. K., & Clark, J. J. (1997). To see or not to see: The need for attention to perceive changes in scenes. *Psychological Science, 8,* 368–373.

Repacholi, B. M., & Gopnik, A. (1997). Early reasoning about desires: Evidence from 14- and 18-month-olds. *Developmental Psychology, 33,* 12–21.

Reschke, P. J., Walle, E. A., Knothe, J. M., & Lopez, L. D. (2019). The influence of context on distinct facial expressions of disgust. *Emotion. 19*(2), 365–370.

Rescorla, R. A. (2006). Stimulus generalization of excitation and inhibition. *Quarterly Journal of Experimental Psychology, 59,* 53–67.

Rescorla, R. A., & Wagner, A. R. (1972). A theory of Pavlovian conditioning: Variations in the effectiveness of reinforcement and nonreinforcement. In A. H. Black & W. F. Prokasy (Eds.), *Classical conditioning II: Current research and theory* (pp. 64–99). New York: Appleton-Century-Crofts.

Ressler, K. J., & Mayberg, H. S. (2007). Targeting abnormal neural circuits in mood and anxiety disorders: From the laboratory to the clinic. *Nature Neuroscience, 10*(9), 1116–1124.

Ressler, K. J., & Nemeroff, C. B. (1999). Role of norepinephrine in the pathophysiology and treatment of mood disorders. *Biological Psychiatry, 46,* 1219–1233.

Reynolds, T., Baumeister, R. F., & Maner, J. K. (2018). Competitive reputation manipulation: Women strategically transmit social information about romantic rivals. *Journal of Experimental Social Psychology, 78,* 195–209.

Rice, K. G., Richardson, C. M. E., & Clark, D. (2012). Perfectionism, procrastination, and psychological distress. *Journal of Counseling Psychology, 39,* 288–302.

Richards, B. A., & Frankland, P. W. (2017). The persistence and transience of memory. *Neuron, 94,* 1071–1084.

Richards, M. H., Crowe, P. A., Larson, R., & Swarr, A. (1998). Developmental patterns and gender differences in the experience of peer companionship during adolescence. *Child Development, 69,* 154–163.

Richards, M., Black, S., Mishra, G., Gale, C. R., Deary, I. J., & Batty, D. G. (2009). IQ in childhood and the metabolic syndrome in middle age: Extended follow-up of the 1946 British birth cohort study. *Intelligence, 37*(6), 567–572.

Richardson, D. S. (2014). Everyday aggression takes many forms. *Current Directions in Psychological Science, 23*(3), 220–224.

Richter, D., & Mata, R. (2018). Age differences in intertemporal choice: U-shaped associations in a probability sample of German households. *Psychology and Aging, 33*(5), 782–788. doi:10.1037/pag0000266

Richters, J., de Visser, R., Rissel, C., & Smith, A. (2006). Sexual practices at last heterosexual encounter and occurrence of orgasm in a national survey. *Journal of Sex Research, 43,* 217–226.

Ridenour, T. A., & Howard, M. O. (2012). Inhalants abuse: Status of etiology and intervention. In J. C. Verster, K. Brady, M. Galanter, & P. Conrod (Eds.), *Drug abuse and addiction in medical illness: Causes, consequences, and treatment* (pp. 189–199). New York: Springer.

Rieger, G., Linsenmeier, J. A., Gygax, L., Garcia, S., & Bailey, J. M. (2010). Dissecting "gaydar": Accuracy and the role of masculinity–femininity. *Archives of Sexual Behavior, 39,* 124–140.

Riggs, J. E. (1993). Stone-age genes and modern lifestyle: Evolutionary mismatch or differential survival bias. *Journal of Clinical Epidemiology, 46*(11), 1289–1291. doi:10.1016/0895-4356(93)90093-g (via Elsevier Science Direct).

Rigoli, F., Rutledge, R. B., Chew, B., Ousdal, O. T., Dayan, P., & Dolan, R. J. (2016). Dopamine increases a value-independent gambling propensity. *Neuropsychopharmacology, 41,* 2658–2667.

Rimer, J., Dwan, K., Lawlor, D. A., Greig, C. A., McMurdo, M., Morley, W., & Mead, G. E. (2012). Exercise for depression. *Cochrane Database of Systematic Reviews, 7,* CD004366.

Rinderu, M. I., Bushman, B. J., & Van Lange, P. A. M. (2018). Climate, aggression, and violence (CLASH): A cultural-evolutionary approach. *Current Opinion in Psychology, 19,* 113–118.

Ringach, D. L., & Jentsch, J. D. (2009). We must face the threats. *Journal of Neuroscience, 29,* 11417–11418.

Rippon, G. (2019). *The gendered brain: The new neuroscience that shatters the myth of the female brain.* New York: Penguin Books.

Risko, E. F., & Gilbert, S. J. (2016). Cognitive offloading. *Trends in Cognitive Sciences, 20,* 676–688.

Risko, E. F., Anderson, N., Sarwal, A., Engelhardt, M., & Kingstone, A. (2012). Every attention: Variation in mind wandering and memory in a lecture. *Applied Cognitive Psychology, 26,* 234–242.

Risman, J. E., Coyle, J. T., Green, R. W., Javitt, D. C., Benes, F. M., Heckers, S., & Grace, A. A. (2008). Circuit-based framework for understanding neurotransmitter and risk gene interactions in schizophrenia. *Trends in Neurosciences, 31,* 234–242.

Ritchey, A. J., & Ruback, R. B. (2018). Predicting lynching atrocity: The situational norms of lynchings in Georgia. *Personality and Social Psychology Bulletin, 44*(5), 619–637.

Ritchie, S. J., & Tucker-Drob, E. M. (2018). How much does education improve intelligence? A meta-analysis. *Psychological Science, 29*(8), 1358–1369.

Rivera, L. A. (2012) Hiring as cultural matching: The case of elite professional service firms. *American Sociological Review, 77,* 999–1022.

Rizzolatti, G. (2004). The mirror-neuron system and imitation. In S. Hurley & N. Chater (Eds.), *Perspectives on imitation: From mirror neurons to memes* (pp. 55–76). Cambridge, MA: MIT Press.

Rizzolatti, G., & Craighero, L. (2004). The mirror-neuron system. *Annual Review of Neuroscience, 27,* 169–192.

Rizzolatti, G., & Rozzi, S. (2018). The mirror mechanism in the parietal lobe. *Handbook of Clinical Neurology, 151,* 555–573.

Rizzolatti, G., & Sinigaglia, C. (2010). The functional role of the parieto-frontal mirror circuit. *Nature Reviews Neuroscience, 11,* 264–274.

Roberson, D., Davidoff, J., Davies, I. R. L., & Shapiro, L. R. (2004). The development of color categories in two languages: A longitudinal study. *Journal of Experimental Psychology: General, 133,* 554–571.

Roberts, G. A. (1991). Delusional belief and meaning in life: A preferred reality? *British Journal of Psychiatry, 159,* 20–29.

Roberts, G. A., & McGrady, A. (1996). Racial and gender effects on the relaxation response: Implications for the development of hypertension. *Biofeedback and Self-Regulation, 21,* 51–62.

Robertson, L. C. (2003). Binding, spatial attention and perceptual awareness. *Nature Reviews Neuroscience, 4,* 93–102.

Robins, L. N., Helzer, J. E., Hesselbrock, M., & Wish, E. (1980). Vietnam veterans three years after Vietnam. In L. Brill & C. Winick (Eds.), *The yearbook of substance use and abuse* (Vol. 11). New York: Human Sciences Press.

Robins, R. W., Fraley, R. C., & Krueger, R. F. (Eds.). (2007). *Handbook of research methods in personality psychology.* New York: Guilford Press.

Rodieck, R. W. (1998). *The first steps in seeing.* Sunderland, MA: Sinauer.

Rodman, A. M., Powers, K. E., & Somerville, L. H. (2017). Development of self-protective biases in response to social evaluative feedback. *Proceedings of the National Academy of Sciences, USA, 114*(50), 13158–13163.

Roediger, H. L. III. (2000). Why retrieval is the key process to understanding human memory. In E. Tulving (Ed.), *Memory, consciousness, and the brain: The Tallinn conference* (pp. 52–75). Philadelphia: Psychology Press.

Roediger, H. L. III, & Karpicke, J. D. (2006). Test-enhanced learning: Taking memory tests improves long-term retention. *Psychological Science, 17,* 249–255.

Roediger, H. L., III, & Karpicke, J. D. (2018). Reflections on the resurgence of interest in the testing effect. *Perspectives on Psychological Science, 13,* 236–241.

Roediger, H. L. III, & McDermott, K. B. (1995). Creating false memories: Remembering words not presented in lists. *Journal of Experimental Psychology: Learning, Memory, and Cognition, 21,* 803–814.

Roediger, H. L. III, & McDermott, K. B. (2000). Tricks of memory. *Current Directions in Psychological Science, 9,* 123–127.

Roediger, H. L. III, Weldon, M. S., & Challis, B. H. (1989). Explaining dissociations between implicit and explicit measures of retention: A processing account. In H. L. Roediger & F. I. M. Craik (Eds.), *Varieties of memory and consciousness: Essays in honour of Endel Tulving* (pp. 3–39). Hillsdale, NJ: Erlbaum.

Roelofs K. (2017). Freeze for action: Neurobiological mechanisms in animal and human freezing. *Philosophical Transactions of the Royal Society of London. Series B, Biological Sciences, 372*(1718), 20160206. doi:1098/rstb.2016.0206

Rogers, C. R. (1951). *Client-centered therapy: Its current practice, implications, and theory.* Boston: Houghton Mifflin.

Rogers, R., & Hammerstein II, O. (1949). *Some enchanted evening.* Concord Music Publishing LLC, New York, NY.

Rogers, S. J., Estes, A., Lord, C., Munson, J., Rocha, M., Winter, J., . . . Talbott, M. (2019). A multisite randomized controlled two-phase trial of the Early Start Denver Model compared to treatment as usual. *Journal of the American Academy of Child and Adolescent Psychiatry.* doi:10.1016/j.jaac.2019.01.004

Rogers, T. B., Kuiper, N. A., & Kirker, W. S. (1977). Self-reference and the encoding of personal information. *Journal of Personality and Social Psychology, 35,* 677–688.

Rohrer, D. (2015). Student instruction should be distributed over long time periods. *Educational Psychology Review, 27,* 635–643.

Rohrer, D., Dedrick, R. F., & Sterschic, S. (2015). Interleaved practice improves mathematics learning. *Journal of Educational Psychology, 107,* 900–908.

Roig, M., Skriver, K., Lundbye-Jensen, J., Kiens, B., & Nielsen, J. B. (2012). A single bout of exercise improves motor memory. *PLoS One, 7,* e44594.

Roisman, G. I., Masten, A. S., Coatsworth, J. D., & Tellegen, A. (2004). Salient and emerging developmental tasks in the transition to adulthood. *Child Development, 75,* 123–133.

Rolls, E. T. (2015). Taste, olfactory, and food reward value processing in the human brain. *Progress in Neurobiology, 127–128,* 64–90.

Romero-Corral, A., Montori, V. M., Somers, V. K., Korinek, J., Thomas, R. J., Allison, T. G., . . . Lopez-Jiminez, F. (2006). Association of body weight with total mortality and with cardiovascular events in coronary artery disease: A systematic review of cohort studies. *Lancet, 368*(9536), 666–678.

Ronay, R., & Galinsky, A. D. (2011). Lex talionis: Testosterone and the law of retaliation. *Journal of Experimental Social Psychology, 47*(3), 702–705.

Rondan, C., & Deruelle, C. (2004). Face processing in high-functioning autistic adults: A look into spatial frequencies and the inversion effect. *Journal of Cognitive and Behavioral Psychotherapies, 4,* 149–164.

Roney, J. R., & Simmons, Z. L. (2013). Hormonal predictors of women's sexual desire in normal menstrual cycles. *Hormones and Behavior, 63,* 636–645.

Rosch, E. H. (1973). Natural categories. *Cognitive Psychology, 4,* 328–350.

Rosch, E. H. (1975). Cognitive representations of semantic categories. *Journal of Experimental Psychology: General, 104,* 192–233.

Rosch, E. H., & Mervis, C. B. (1975). Family resemblances: Studies in the internal structure of categories. *Cognitive Psychology, 7,* 573–605.

Rose, S. P. R. (2002). Smart drugs: Do they work? Are they ethical? Will they be legal? *Nature Reviews Neuroscience, 3,* 975–979.

Roseman, I. J. (1984). Cognitive determinants of emotion: A structural theory. *Review of Personality and Social Psychology, 5,* 11–36.

Roseman, I. J., & Smith, C. A. (2001). Appraisal theory: Overview, assumptions, varieties and controversies. In K. R. Scherer, A. Schorr, & T. Johnstone (Eds.), *Appraisal processes in emotion: Theory, methods, research* (pp. 3–19). New York: Oxford University Press.

Rosenbaum, S. (2016, June 9). Models keep getting skinnier and skinnier. *New York Post,* retrieved from https://nypost.com/2016/06/09/models-keep-getting-skinnier-and-skinnier/.

Rosenberg, M. (1965). *Society and the adolescent self-image.* Princeton, NJ: Princeton University Press.

Rosenhan, D. (1973). On being sane in insane places. *Science, 179,* 250–258.

Rosenkranz, K., Williamon, A., & Rothwell, J. C. (2007). Motorcortical excitability and synaptic plasticity is enhanced in professional musicians. *Journal of Neuroscience, 27,* 5200–5206.

Rosenthal, R., & Fode, K. L. (1963). The effect of experimenter bias on the performance of the albino rat. *Behavioral Science, 8,* 183–189.

Roser, M. E., Aslin, R. N., McKenzie, R., Zahra, D., & Fiser, J. (2015). Enhanced visual statistical learning in adults with autism. *Neuropsychology, 29,* 163–172.

Ross, L. (1977). The intuitive psychologist and his shortcomings: Distortions in the attribution process. *Advances in Experimental Social Psychology, 10,* 173–220.

Ross, L., Amabile, T. M., & Steinmetz, J. L. (1977). Social roles, social control, and biases in social-perception processes. *Journal of Personality and Social Psychology, 35,* 485–494.

Ross, M., Blatz, C. W., & Schryer, E. (2008). Social memory processes. In H. L. Roediger III (Ed.), *Learning and memory: A comprehensive reference* (Vol. 2, pp. 911–926). Oxford: Elsevier.

Rossano, F., Carpenter, M., & Tomasello, M. (2012). One-year-old infants follow others' voice direction. *Psychological Science, 23*(11), 1298–1302. doi:10.1177/0956797612450032

Rotermann, M. (2012). Sexual behaviour and condom use of 15- to 24-year-olds in 2003 and 2009/2010. *Health Reports, 23*(1), 41–45.

Roth, B., Becker, N., Romeyke, S., Schäfer, S., Domnick, F., & Spinath, F. M. (2015). Intelligence and school grades: A meta-analysis. *Intelligence, 53,* 118–137.

Roth, H. P., & Caron, H. S. (1978). Accuracy of doctors' estimates and patients' statements on adherence to a drug regimen. *Clinical Pharmacology and Therapeutics, 23,* 361–370.

Rothbart, M. K., & Bates, J. E. (2006). Temperament. In W. Damon, R. Lerner, & N. Eisenberg (Eds.), *Handbook of child psychology.* Vol. 3. *Social, emotional, and personality development* (6th ed., pp. 99–166). New York: Wiley.

Rothbaum, B. O., & Schwartz, A. C. (2002). Exposure therapy for posttraumatic stress disorder. *American Journal of Psychotherapy, 56,* 59–75.

Rotter, J. B. (1966). Generalized expectancies for internal versus external locus of control of reinforcement. *Psychological Monographs: General and Applied, 80,* 1–28.

Rotton, L. (1992). Trait humor and longevity: Do comics have the last laugh? *Health Psychology, 11,* 262–266.

Royal Commission on Aboriginal Peoples. (1996). Looking forward, looking back: Report of the Royal Commission on Aboriginal Peoples (Vol. 1). Ottawa, Canada: Communication Group.

Rozin, P. (1968). Are carbohydrate and protein intakes separately regulated? *Journal of Comparative and Physiological Psychology, 65,* 23–29.

Rozin, P., & Kalat, J. W. (1971). Specific hungers and poison avoidance as adaptive specializations of learning. *Psychological Review, 78,* 459–486.

Rozin, P., Bauer, R., & Catanese, D. (2003). Food and life, pleasure and worry, among American college students: Gender differences and regional similarities. *Journal of Personality and Social Psychology, 85,* 132–141.

Rozin, P., Dow, S., Moscovitch, M., & Rajaram, S. (1998). What causes humans to begin and end a meal? A role for memory for what has been eaten, as evidenced by a study of multiple meal eating in amnesic patients. *Psychological Science, 9,* 392–396.

Rozin, P., Kabnick, K., Pete, E., Fischler, C., & Shields, C. (2003). The ecology of eating: Smaller portion size in France than in the United States helps to explain the French paradox. *Psychological Science, 14,* 450–454.

Rozin, P., Scott, S., Dingley, M., Urbanek, J. K., Jiang, H., & Kaltenbach, M. (2011). Nudge to nobesity: I. Minor changes in accessibility decrease food intake. *Judgment and Decision Making, 6,* 323–332.

Rozin, P., Trachtenberg, S., & Cohen, A. B. (2001). Stability of body image and body image dissatisfaction in American college students over about the last 15 years. *Appetite, 37,* 245–248.

Rubin, M., & Badea, C. (2012). They're all the same! . . . but for several different reasons: A review of the multicausal nature of perceived group variability. *Current Directions in Psychological Science, 21*(6), 367–372.

Rubin, Z. (1973). *Liking and loving.* New York: Holt, Rinehart & Winston.

Rubin-Fernandez, P., & Geurts, B. (2012). How to pass the false-belief task before your fourth birthday. *Psychological Science, 24*(1), 27–33. doi:10.1177/0956797612447819

Rudman, L. A., Ashmore, R. D., & Gary, M. L. (2001). "Unlearning" automatic biases: The malleability of implicit prejudice and stereotypes. *Journal of Personality and Social Psychology, 81,* 856–868.

Ruffman, T., Puri, A., Galloway, O., Su, J., & Taumoepeau, M. (2018). Variety in parental use of "want" relates to subsequent growth in children's theory of mind. *Developmental Psychology, 54,* 677–688.

Running, C. A., Craig, B. A., & Mattes, R. D. (2015). Oleogustus: The unique taste of fat. *Chemical Senses, 40,* 507–516.

Rusbult, C. E., & Van Lange, P. A. M. (2003). Interdependence, interaction and relationships. *Annual Review of Psychology, 54,* 351–375.

Ruscio, A. M., Stein, D. J., Chiu, W. T., & Kessler, R. C. (2010). The epidemiology of obsessive-compulsive disorder in the National Comorbidity Survey Replication. *Molecular Psychiatry, 15,* 53–63.

Rushton, J. P., & Templer, D. I. (2009). National differences in intelligence, crime, income, and skin color. *Intelligence, 37*(4), 341–346.

Russell, B. (1945). *A history of Western philosophy.* New York: Simon & Schuster.

Russell, J. A. (1980). A circumplex model of affect. *Journal of Personality and Social Psychology, 39,* 1161–1178.

Russell, J., Gee, B., & Bullard, C. (2012). Why do young children hide by closing their eyes? Self-visibility and the developing concept of self. *Journal of Cognition and Development, 13*(4), 550–576.

Rutledge, R. B., Lazzaro, S. C., Lau, B., Myers, C. E., Gluck, M. A., & Glimcher, P. W. (2009). Dopaminergic drugs modulate learning rates and perseveration in Parkinson's patients in a dynamic foraging task. *Journal of Neuroscience, 29,* 15104–15114.

Rutter, M., & Silberg, J. (2002). Gene–environment interplay in relation to emotional and behavioral disturbance. *Annual Review of Psychology, 53,* 463–490.

Rutter, M., O'Connor, T. G., & the English and Romanian Adoptees Study Team. (2004). Are there biological programming effects for psychological development? Findings from a study of Romanian adoptees. *Developmental Psychology, 40,* 81–94.

Ryan, R. M., & Deci, E. L. (2000). Self-determination theory and the facilitation of intrinsic motivation, social development, and well-being. *American Psychologist, 55,* 68–78.

Ryle, G. (1949). *The concept of mind.* Lyndhurst, NJ: Barnes & Noble.

Sacks, O. (1995). *An anthropologist on Mars.* New York: Knopf.

Saffran, J. R., Aslin, R. N., & Newport, E. I. (1996). Statistical learning by 8-month-old infants. *Science, 274,* 1926–1928.

Sager, M. (2007). Ray Charles: What I've learned. *Esquire* magazine interview. Retrieved from https://www.esquire.com/entertainment/interviews/a763/esq0803-aug-wil/

Sahakian, B., & Morein-Zamir, S. (2007). Professor's little helper. *Nature, 450*(7173), 1157–1159.

Sala, G., & Gobet, F. (2018, September 8). Elvis has left the building: Correlational but not causal relationship between music skill and cognitive ability. Retrieved from https://doi.org/10.31234/osf.io/auzry

Salmon, D. P., & Bondi, M. W. (2009). Neuropsychological assessment of dementia. *Annual Review of Psychology, 60,* 257–282.

Salovey, P., & Grewal, D. (2005). The science of emotional intelligence. *Current Directions in Psychological Science, 14*(6), 281–285.

Salthouse, T. A. (1984). Effects of age and skill in typing. *Journal of Experimental Psychology: General, 113,* 345–371.

Salthouse, T. A. (1987). Age, experience, and compensation. In C. Schooler & K. W. Schaie (Eds.), *Cognitive functioning and social structure over the life course* (pp. 142–150). Norwood, NJ: Ablex.

Salthouse, T. A. (1996a). General and specific mediation of adult age differences in memory. *Journal of Gerontology: Series B: Psychological Sciences and Social Sciences, 51B,* P30–P42.

Salthouse, T. A. (1996b). The processing-speed theory of adult age differences in cognition. *Psychological Review, 103,* 403–428.

Salthouse, T. A. (2000). Pressing issues in cognitive aging. In D. Park & N. Schwartz (Eds.), *Cognitive aging: A primer* (pp. 43–54). Philadelphia: Psychology Press.

Salthouse, T. A. (2001). Structural models of the relations between age and measures of cognitive functioning. *Intelligence, 29,* 93–115.

Salthouse, T. A. (2006). Mental exercise and mental aging. *Perspectives on Psychological Science, 1*(1), 68–87.

Salvatore, J. E., Kuo, S. I.-C., Steele, R. D., Simpson, J. A., & Collins, W. A. (2011). Recovering from conflict in romantic relationships: A developmental perspective. *Psychological Science, 22*(3), 376–383. doi:10.1177/0956797610397055

Sampson, R. J., & Laub, J. H. (1995). Understanding variability in lives through time: Contributions of life-course criminology. *Studies of Crime Prevention, 4,* 143–158.

San Roque, L., Kendrick, K. H., Norcliffe, E., Brown, P., Defina, R., Dingemanse, M., . . . Majid, A. (2015). Vision verbs dominate in conversation across cultures, but the ranking of non-visual verbs varies. *Cognitive Linguistics, 26*(1), 31–60.

Sander, J., Schupp, J., & Richter, D. (2017). Getting together: Social contact frequency across the life span. *Developmental Psychology, 53*(8), 1571–1588. doi:10.1037/dev0000349

Santangelo, V., Cavallina, C., Colucci, C., Santori, A., Macri, S., McGaugh, J. L., & Campolongo, P. (2018). Enhanced brain activity associated with memory access in highly superior autobiographical memory. *Proceedings of the National Academy of Sciences, USA, 115*(30), 7795–7800.

Sara, S. J. (2000). Retrieval and reconsolidation: Toward a neurobiology of remembering. *Learning & Memory, 7,* 73–84.

Sarris, V. (1989). Max Wertheimer on seen motion: Theory and evidence. *Psychological Research, 51,* 58–68.

Sarter, M. (2006). Preclinical research into cognition enhancers. *Trends in Pharmacological Sciences, 27,* 602–608.

Sasanuma, S. (1975). Kana and kanji processing in Japanese aphasics. *Brain and Language, 2,* 369–383.

Satcher, D. (2001). *The Surgeon General's call to action to promote sexual health and responsible sexual behavior.* Washington, DC: U.S. Government Printing Office.

Sauter, D. A., Eisner, F., Calder, A. J., & Scott, S. K. (2010). Perceptual cues in non-verbal vocal expressions of emotion. *Quarterly Journal of Experimental Psychology, 63*(11), 2251–2272. doi:10.1080/17470211003721642

Savage, C. R., Deckersbach, T., Heckers, S., Wagner, A. D., Schacter, D. L., Alpert, N. M., . . . Rauch, S. L. (2001). Prefrontal regions supporting spontaneous and directed application of verbal learning strategies: Evidence from PET. *Brain, 124,* 219–231.

Savage-Rumbaugh, S., & Lewin, R. (1996). *Kanzi: The ape on the brink of the human mind.* New York: Wiley.

Savage-Rumbaugh, S., Shanker, G., & Taylor, T. J. (1998). *Apes, language, and the human mind.* Oxford, UK: Oxford University Press.

Savic, I., & Lindstrom, P. (2008). PET and MRI show differences in cerebral asymmetry and functional connectivity between homo- and heterosexual subjects. *Proceedings of the National Academy of Sciences, USA, 105*(27), 9403–9408.

Savin-Williams, R. C., & Vrangalova, Z. (2013). Mostly heterosexual as a distinct sexual orientation group: A systematic review of the empirical evidence. *Developmental Review, 33,* 58–88.

Sawa, A., & Snyder, S. H. (2002). Schizophrenia: Diverse approaches to a complex disease. *Science, 295,* 692–695.

Sawyer, S. M., Azzopardi, P. S., Wickremarathne, D., & Patton, G. C. (2018). The age of adolescence. *The Lancet: Child and Adolescent Health, 2,* 223–228.

Scarf, D., Imuta, K., Colombo, M., & Hayne, H. (2012). Golden rule or valence matching? Methodological problems in Hamlin et al. *Proceedings of the National Academy of Sciences, USA, 109*(22), E1426.

Scarr, S., Pakstis, A. J., Katz, S. H., & Barker, W. B. (1977). Absence of a relationship between degree of White ancestry and intellectual skills within a Black population. *Human Genetics, 39*(1), 69–86.

Schaal, B., & Al Aïn, S. (2014). Chemical signals 'selected for' newborns in mammals. *Animal Behaviour, 97,* 289–299. doi:10.1016/j.anbehav.2014.08.022

Schachter, S. (1982). Recidivism and self-cure of smoking and obesity. *American Psychologist, 37,* 436–444.

Schachter, S., & Singer, J. E. (1962). Cognitive, social, and psychological determinants of emotional state. *Physiological Review, 69,* 379–399.

Schacter, D. L., & Szpunar, K. K. (2015). Enhancing attention and memory during video-recorded lectures. *Scholarship of Teaching and Learning in Psychology, 1,* 60–71.

Schacter, D. L. (1987). Implicit memory: History and current status. *Journal of Experimental Psychology: Learning, Memory, and Cognition, 13,* 501–518.

Schacter, D. L. (1996). *Searching for memory: The brain, the mind, and the past.* New York: Basic Books.

Schacter, D. L. (1999). The seven sins of memory: Insights from psychology and cognitive neuroscience. *American Psychologist, 54*(3), 182–203.

Schacter, D. L. (2001a). *Forgotten ideas, neglected pioneers: Richard Semon and the story of memory.* Philadelphia: Psychology Press.

Schacter, D. L. (2001b). *The seven sins of memory: How the mind forgets and remembers.* Boston: Houghton Mifflin.

Schacter, D. L. (2012). Adaptive constructive processes and the future of memory. *American Psychologist, 67,* 603–613.

Schacter, D. L., & Addis, D. R. (2007). The cognitive neuroscience of constructive memory: Remembering the past and imagining the future. *Philosophical Transactions of the Royal Society of London, B, 362,* 773–786.

Schacter, D. L., & Curran, T. (2000). Memory without remembering and remembering without memory: Implicit and false memories. In M. S. Gazzaniga (Ed.), *The new cognitive neurosciences* (2nd ed., pp. 829–840). Cambridge, MA: MIT Press.

Schacter, D. L., & Loftus, E. F. (2013). Memory and law: What can cognitive neuroscience contribute? *Nature Neuroscience, 16,* 119–123.

Schacter, D. L., & Madore, K. P. (2016). Remembering the past and imagining the future: Identifying and enhancing the contribution of episodic memory. *Memory Studies, 9,* 245–255.

Schacter, D. L., & Tulving, E. (1994). *Memory systems 1994.* Cambridge, MA: MIT Press.

Schacter, D. L., Addis, D. R., & Buckner, R. L. (2008). Episodic simulation of future events: Concepts, data, and applications. *Annals of the New York Academy of Sciences, 1124,* 39–60.

Schacter, D. L., Addis, D. R., Hassabis, D., Martin, V. C., Spreng, R. N., & Szpunar, K. K. (2012). The future of memory: Remembering, imagining, and the brain. *Neuron, 16,* 582–583.

Schacter, D. L., Alpert, N. M., Savage, C. R., Rauch, S. L., & Albert, M. S. (1996a). Conscious recollection and the human hippocampal formation: Evidence from positron emission tomography. *Proceedings of the National Academy of Sciences, USA, 93,* 321–325.

Schacter, D. L., Dobbins, I. G., & Schnyer, D. M. (2004). Specificity of priming: A cognitive neuroscience perspective. *Nature Reviews Neuroscience, 5,* 853–862.

Schacter, D. L., Gaesser, B., & Addis, D. R. (2013). Remembering the past and imagining the future in the elderly. *Gerontologist, 59*(2), 143–151. doi:10.1159/000342198

Schacter, D. L., Guerin, S. A., & St. Jacques, P. L. (2011). Memory distortion: An adaptive perspective. *Trends in Cognitive Sciences, 15,* 467–474.

Schacter, D. L., Harbluk, J. L., & McLachlan, D. R. (1984). Retrieval without recollection: An experimental analysis of source amnesia. *Journal of Verbal Learning and Verbal Behavior, 23,* 593–611.

Schacter, D. L., Israel, L., & Racine, C. A. (1999). Suppressing false recognition in younger and older adults: The distinctiveness heuristic. *Journal of Memory and Language, 40,* 1–24.

Schacter, D. L., Reiman, E., Curran, T., Yun, L. S., Bandy, D., McDermott, K. B., & Roediger, H. L., III. (1996b). Neuroanatomical correlates of veridical and illusory recognition memory: Evidence from positron emission tomography. *Neuron, 17,* 267–274.

Schacter, D. L., Wagner, A. D., & Buckner, R. L. (2000). Memory systems of 1999. In E. Tulving & F. I. M. Craik (Eds.), *The Oxford handbook of memory* (pp. 627–643). New York: Oxford University Press.

Schacter, D. L., Wig, G. S., & Stevens, W. D. (2007). Reductions in cortical activity during priming. *Current Opinion in Neurobiology, 17,* 171–176.

Schafer, R. B., & Keith, P. M. (1980). Equity and depression among married couples. *Social Psychology Quarterly, 43,* 430–435.

Schaie, K. W. (1996). *Intellectual development in adulthood: The Seattle Longitudinal Study.* New York: Cambridge University Press.

Schaie, K. W. (2005). *Developmental influences on adult intelligence: The Seattle Longitudinal Study.* New York: Oxford University Press.

Schapira, A. H. V., Emre, M., Jenner, P., & Poewe, W. (2009). Levodopa in the treatment of Parkinson's disease. *European Journal of Neurology, 16,* 982–989.

Scheibe, S., Sheppes, G., & Staudinger, U. M. (2015). Distract or reappraise? Age-related differences in emotion-regulation choice. *Emotion, 15,* 677–681. doi:10.1037/a0039246

Scherer, K. R. (1999). Appraisal theory. In T. Dalgleish & M. Power (Eds.), *Handbook of cognition and emotion* (pp. 637–663). New York: Wiley.

Scherer, K. R. (2001). The nature and study of appraisal: A review of the issues. In K. R. Scherer, A. Schorr, & T. Johnstone (Eds.), *Appraisal processes in emotion: Theory, methods, research* (pp. 369–391). New York: Oxford University Press.

Schiff, M., Duyme, M., Stewart, J., Tomkiewicz, S., & Feingold, J. (1978). Intellectual status of working-class children adopted early in upper-middle-class families. *Science, 200,* 1503–1504.

Schildkraut, J. J. (1965). The catecholamine hypothesis of affective disorders: A review of supporting evidence. *American Journal of Psychiatry, 122,* 509–522.

Schiller, D., Monfils, M. H., Raio, C. M., Johnson, D. C., LeDoux, J. E., & Phelps, E. A. (2010). Preventing the return of fear in humans using reconsolidation update mechanisms. *Nature, 463,* 49–54.

Schilling, O. K., Wahl, H.-W., & Wiegering, S. (2013). Affective development in advanced old age: Analyses of terminal change in positive and negative affect. *Developmental Psychology, 49*(5), 1011–1020.

Schlesinger, J. (2012). *The insanity hoax: Exposing the myth of the mad genius.* Ardsley-on-Hudson, NY: Shrinktunes Media.

Schmader, T., Johns, M., & Forbes, C. (2008). An integrated process model of stereotype threat effects on performance. *Psychological Review, 115,* 336–356.

Schmidt, F. L., & Hunter, J. E. (1998). The validity and utility of selection methods in personnel psychology: Practical and theoretical implications of 85 years of research findings. *Psychological Bulletin, 124,* 262–274.

Schmitt, D. P., Jonason, P. K., Byerley, G. J., Flores, S. D., Illbeck, B. E., O'Leary, K. N., & Qudrat, A. (2012). A reexamination of sex differences in sexuality: New studies reveal old truths. *Current Directions in Psychological Science, 21*(2), 135–139.

Schmitt, D. P., Realo, A., Voracek, M., & Allik, J. (2008). Why can't a man be more like a woman? Sex differences in personality traits across 55 cultures. *Journal of Personality and Social Psychology, 94,* 168–182.

Schneider, B. H., Atkinson, L., & Tardif, C. (2001). Child–parent attachment and children's peer relations: A quantitative review. *Developmental Psychology, 37,* 86–100.

Schnorr, J. A., & Atkinson, R. C. (1969). Repetition versus imagery instructions in the short- and long-term retention of paired associates. *Psychonomic Science, 15,* 183–184.

Schoenemann, P. T., Sheenan, M. J., & Glotzer, L. D. (2005). Prefrontal white matter volume is disproportionately larger in humans than in other primates. *Nature Neuroscience, 8,* 242–252.

Schonberg, T., O'Doherty, J. P., Joel, D., Inzelberg, R., Segev, Y., & Daw, N. D. (2009). Selective impairment of prediction error signaling in human dorsolateral but not ventral striatum in Parkinson's disease patients: Evidence from a model-based fMRI study. *NeuroImage, 49,* 772–781.

Schott, B. J., Henson, R. N., Richardson-Klavehn, A., Becker, C., Thoma, V., Heinze, H. J., & Duzel, E. (2005). Redefining implicit and explicit memory: The functional neuroanatomy of priming, remembering, and control of retrieval. *Proceedings of the National Academy of Sciences, USA, 102,* 1257–1262.

Schreiner, T., & Rasch, B. (2015). Boosting vocabulary learning by verbal cueing during sleep. *Cerebral Cortex, 25,* 4169–4179.

Schubert, T. W., & Koole, S. L. (2009). The embodied self: Making a fist enhances men's power-related self-conceptions. *Journal of Experimental Social Psychology, 45,* 828–834.

Schulreich, S., Gerhardt, H., & Heekeren, H. R. (2016). Incidental fear cues increase monetary loss aversion. *Emotion, 16*(3), 402–412. doi:10.1037/emo0000124

Schultz, D., Izard, C. E., & Bear, G. (2004). Children's emotion processing: Relations to emotionality and aggression. *Development and Psychopathology, 16*(2), 371–387.

Schultz, W. (2016). Dopamine reward prediction error coding. *Dialogues in Clinical Neuroscience, 18,* 23–32.

Schultz, W., Dayan, P., & Montague, P. R. (1997). A neural substrate of prediction and reward. *Science, 275,* 1593–1599.

Schwartz, B. L. (2002). *Tip-of-the-tongue states: Phenomenology, mechanisms, and lexical retrieval.* Mahwah, NJ: Erlbaum.

Schwartz, C. E., Wright, C. I., Shin, L. M., Kagan, J., & Rauch, S. L. (2003). Inhibited and uninhibited infants "grown up": Adult amygdalar response to novelty. *Science, 300,* 1952–1953.

Schwartz, H. A., Eichstaedt, J. C., Kern, M. L., Dziurzynski, L., Ramones, S. M., Agrawal, M., . . . Ungar, L. H. (2013). Personality, gender, and age in the language of social media: The open-vocabulary approach. *PLoS ONE, 8,* e73791.

Schwartz, J. H., & Westbrook, G. L. (2000). The cytology of neurons. In E. R. Kandel, G. H. Schwartz, & T. M. Jessell (Eds.), *Principles of neural science* (pp. 67–104). New York: McGraw-Hill.

Schwartz, L., & Yovel, G. (2016). The roles of perceptual and conceptual information in face recognition. *Journal of Experimental Psychology: General, 145*(11), 1493–1511. http://dx.doi.org/10.1037/xge0000220

Schwartz, S., & Maquet, P. (2002). Sleep imaging and the neuropsychological assessment of dreams. *Trends in Cognitive Sciences, 6*, 23–30.

Schwartzman, A. E., Gold, D., & Andres, D. (1987). Stability of intelligence: A 40-year follow-up. *Canadian Journal of Psychology, 41*, 244–256.

Schweizer, T. A., Ware, J., Fischer, C. E., Craik, F. I. M., & Bialystok, E. (2012). Bilingualism as a contributor to cognitive reserve: Evidence from brain atrophy in Alzheimer's disease. *Cortex, 48*, 991–996.

Scott, R. M., & Baillargeon, R. (2017). Early false-belief understanding. *Trends in Cognitive Sciences, 21*, 237–249.

Scoville, W. B., & Milner, B. (1957). Loss of recent memory after bilateral hippocampal lesions. *Journal of Neurology, Neurosurgery, and Psychiatry, 20*, 11–21.

Scribner, S. (1984). Studying working intelligence. In B. Rogoff & J. Lave (Eds.), *Everyday cognition: Its development in social context* (pp. 9–40). Cambridge, MA: Harvard University Press.

Section on Clinical Psychology of the Canadian Psychological Association. (2016). Empirically Supported Treatments in Psychology: Recommendations for Canadian Professional Psychology. Retrieved from http://www.cpa.ca/documents/empiric_p5.html

Sedlmeier, P., Eberth, J., Schwarz, M., Zimmermann, D., Haarig, F., Jaeger, S., & Kunze, S. (2012). The psychological effects of meditation: A meta-analysis. *Psychological Bulletin, 138*, 1139–1171.

Seeman, T. E., Dubin, L. F., & Seeman, M. (2003). Religiosity/spirituality and health: A critical review of the evidence for biological pathways. *American Psychologist, 58*, 53–63.

Sehulster, J. R. (1989). Content and temporal structure of autobiographical knowledge: Remembering twenty-five seasons at the Metropolitan Opera. *Memory & Cognition, 17*, 590–596.

Seligman, M. E. P. (1971). Phobias and preparedness. *Behavior Therapy, 2*, 307–320.

Seligman, M. E. P. (1995). The effectiveness of psychotherapy: The *Consumer Reports* study. *American Psychologist, 50*(12), 965–974.

Selikoff, I. J., Robitzek, E. H., & Ornstein, G. G. (1952). Toxicity of hydrazine derivatives of isonicotinic acid in the chemotherapy of human tuberculosis: A preliminary report. *Quarterly Bulletin of Sea View Hospital, 13*(1), 17–26.

Selye, H., & Fortier, C. (1950). Adaptive reaction to stress. *Psychosomatic Medicine, 12*, 149–157.

Semenza, C. (2009). The neuropsychology of proper names. *Mind & Language, 24*, 347–369.

Semenza, C., & Zettin, M. (1989). Evidence from aphasia for the role of proper names as pure referring expressions. *Nature, 342*, 678–679.

Senghas, A., Kita, S., & Ozyurek, A. (2004). Children create core properties of language: Evidence from an emerging sign language in Nicaragua. *Science, 305*, 1782.

Senju, A., Maeda, M., Kikuchi, Y., Hasegawa, T., Tojo, Y., & Osanai, H. (2007). Absence of contagious yawning in children with autism spectrum disorder. *Biology Letters, 3*(6), 706–708.

Senju, A., Southgate, V., Snape, C., Leonard, M., & Csibra, G. (2011). Do 18-month-olds really attribute mental states to others? A critical test. *Psychological Science, 22*(7), 878–880. doi:10.1177/0956797611411584

Senju, A., Southgate, V., White, S., & Frith, U. (2009). Mindblind eyes: An absence of spontaneous theory of mind in Asperger syndrome. *Science, 325*, 883–885.

Serpell, R. (1974). Aspects of intelligence in a developing country. *African Social Research, 17*, 578–596.

Seybold, K. S., & Hill, P. C. (2001). The role of religion and spirituality in mental and physical health. *Current Directions in Psychological Science, 10*, 21–23.

Shah, J. Y., Higgins, E. T., & Friedman, R. S. (1998). Performance incentives and means: How regulatory focus influences goal attainment. *Journal of Personality and Social Psychology, 74*, 285–293.

Shahaeian, A., Peterson, C. C., Slaughter, V., & Wellman, H. M. (2011). Culture and the sequence of steps in theory of mind development. *Developmental Psychology, 47*(5), 1239–1247.

Shallcross, A. J., Ford, B. Q, Floerke, V. A., & Mauss, I. B. (2013). Getting better with age: The relationship between age, acceptance, and negative affect. *Journal of Personality and Social Psychology, 104*(4), 734–749.

Shallice, T., Fletcher, P., Frith, C. D., Grasby, P., Frackowiak, R. S. J., & Dolan, R. J. (1994). Brain regions associated with acquisition and retrieval of verbal episodic memory. *Nature, 368*, 633–635.

Shariff, A. F., & Tracy, J. L. (2011). What are emotion expressions for? *Current Directions in Psychological Science, 20*(6), 395–399.

Sharot, T. (2011). *The optimism bias: A tour of the irrationally positive brain*. New York: Pantheon Books.

Shaw, J. & Porter, S. (2015). Constructing rich false memories of committing crime. *Psychological Science, 26*, 291–301.

Shaw, J. S., Bjork, R. A., & Handal, A. (1995). Retrieval-induced forgetting in an eyewitness paradigm. *Psychonomic Bulletin & Review, 13*, 1023–1027.

Shedler, J. (2010). The efficacy of psychodynamic psychotherapy. *American Psychologist, 65*(2), 98–109.

Sheese, B. E., & Graziano, W. G. (2005). Deciding to defect: The effects of video-game violence on cooperative behavior. *Psychological Science, 16*, 354–357.

Shen, H., Wan, F., & Wyer, R. S. (2011). Cross-cultural differences in the refusal to accept a small gift: The differential influence of reciprocity norms on Asians and North Americans. *Journal of Personality and Social Psychology, 100*(2), 271–281.

Shepherd, G. M. (1988). *Neurobiology*. New York: Oxford University Press.

Shepperd, J., Malone, W., & Sweeny, K. (2008). Exploring the causes of the self-serving bias. *Social and Personality Psychology Compass, 2*(2), 895–908.

Sherry, S. B., & Hall, P. A. (2009). The perfectionism model of binge eating: Tests of an integrative model. *Journal of Personality and Social Psychology, 96*(3), 690–709.

Shichuan Du, Y.-T., & Martinez, A. M. (2014, April 15). Compound facial expressions of emotion. *Proceedings of the National Academy of Sciences, USA, 111*(15), e1454–e1462. doi:10.1073/pnas.1322355111

Shiffman, S., Gnys, M., Richards, T. J., Paty, J. A., & Hickcox, M. (1996). Temptations to smoke after quitting: A comparison of lapsers and maintainers. *Health Psychology, 15,* 455–461.

Shih, M., Pittinsky, T. L., & Ambady, N. (1999). Stereotype susceptibility: Identity salience and shifts in quantitative performance. *Psychological Science, 10,* 80–83.

Shimamura, A. P., & Squire, L. R. (1987). A neuropsychological study of fact memory and source amnesia. *Journal of Experimental Psychology: Learning, Memory, and Cognition, 13,* 464–473.

Shin, H., & Ryan, A. M. (2014). Early adolescent friendships and academic adjustment: Examining selection and influence processes with longitudinal social network analysis. *Developmental Psychology, 50*(11), 2462–2472.

Shin, L. M., Rauch, S. L., & Pitman, R. K. (2006). Amygdala, medial prefrontal cortex, and hippocampal function in PTSD. *Annals of the New York Academy of Science, 1071,* 67–79.

Shinskey, J. L., & Munakata, Y. (2005). Familiarity breeds searching. *Psychological Science, 16*(8), 596–600.

Shiota, M. N., Neufeld, S. L., Yeung, W. H., Moser, S. E., & Perea, E. F. (2011). Feeling good: Autonomic nervous system responding in five positive emotions. *Emotion, 11*(6), 1368–1378. doi.org/10.1037/a0024278

Shipstead, Z., Redick, T. S., & Engle, R. W. (2012). Is working memory training effective? *Psychological Bulletin, 138,* 628–654.

Shomstein, S., & Yantis, S. (2004). Control of attention shifts between vision and audition in human cortex. *Journal of Neuroscience, 24,* 10702–10706.

Shore, C. (1986). Combinatorial play: Conceptual development and early multiword speech. *Developmental Psychology, 22,* 184–190.

Shulman, L., D'Agostino, E., Lee, S., Valicenti-McDermott, M., Seijo, R., Tulloch, E., . . . Tarshis, N. (2019). When an early diagnosis of autism spectrum disorder resolves, what remains? *Journal of Child Neurology, 34*(7), 382–386.

Siebert, A. (2018, November). Canada's grand cannabis experiment has set scientists free. The *New York Times.* Retrieved from www.nytimes.com/2018/11/20/opinion/cannabis-science-legal-marijauna-canada.html

Siegel, A., Roeling, T. A. P., Gregg, T. R., & Kruk, M. R. (1999). Neuropharmacology of brain-stimulation-evoked aggression. *Neuroscience and Biobehavioral Reviews, 23,* 359–389.

Siegel, E. H., Sands, M. K., Van den Noortgate, W., Condon, P., Chang, Y., Dy, J., . . ., Barrett, L. F. (2018). Emotion fingerprints or emotion populations? A meta-analytic investigation of autonomic features of emotion categories. *Psychological Bulletin, 144*(4), 343–393.

Siegel, S. (1976). Morphine analgesia tolerance: Its situational specificity supports a Pavlovian conditioning model. *Science, 193,* 323–325.

Siegel, S. (1984). Pavlovian conditioning and heroin overdose: Reports by overdose victims. *Bulletin of the Psychonomic Society, 22,* 428–430.

Siegel, S. (2005). Drug tolerance, drug addiction, and drug anticipation. *Current Directions in Psychological Science, 14,* 296–300.

Siegel, S. (2016). The heroin overdose mystery. *Current Directions in Psychological Science, 25,* 375–379.

Siegel, S., Baptista, M. A. S., Kim, J. A., McDonald, R. V., & Weise-Kelly, L. (2000). Pavlovian psychopharmacology: The associative basis of tolerance. *Experimental and Clinical Psychopharmacology, 8,* 276–293.

Siegrist, M., & Cousin, M. E. (2009). Expectations influence sensory experience in a wine tasting. *Appetite, 52*(3), 762–765. https://doi.org/10.1016/j.appet.2009.02.002

Siemer, M., Mauss, I., & Gross, J. J. (2007). Same situation—Different emotions: How appraisals shape our emotions. *Emotion, 7*(3), 592–600. doi:10.1037/1528-3542.7.3.592

Sigman, M., Spence, S. J., & Wang, T. (2006). Autism from developmental and neuropsychological perspectives. *Annual Review of Clinical Psychology, 2,* 327–355.

Sigurdsson, T., Doyere, V., Cain, C. K., & LeDoux, J. E. (2007). Long-term potentiation in the amygdala: A cellular mechanism of fear learning and memory. *Neuropharmacology, 52,* 215–227.

Silvani, A., Calandra-Buonaura, G., Dampney, R. A., & Cortelli, P. (2016). Brain–heart interactions: Physiology and clinical implications. *Philosophical Transactions of the Royal Society, A, 347.* doi:10.1098/rsta.2015.0181

Silverman, A. M., Gwinn, J. D., & Van Boven, L. (2014). Stumbling in their shoes: Disability simulations reduce judged capabilities of disabled people. *Social Psychological and Personality Science, 6*(4), 464–471.

Silverman, C., Strapagiel, L., Shaban, H., Hall, E., & Singer-Vine, J. (2016). Hyperpartisan Facebook pages are publishing false and misleading information at an alarming rate. *Buzzfeed News.* Retrieved from https://www.buzzfeed.com/craigsilverman/partisan-fb-pages-analysis

Simeone, J. C., Ward, A. J., Rotella, P., Collins, J., & Windisch, R. (2015). An evaluation of variation in published estimates of schizophrenia prevalence from 1990–2013: A systematic literature review. *BMC Psychiatry, 15,* 193.

Simons, D. J., & Chabris, C. F. (1999). Gorillas in our midst: Sustained inattentional blindness for dynamic events. *Perception, 28,* 1059–1074.

Simons, D. J., & Levin, D. T. (1998). Failure to detect changes to people during a real-world interaction. *Psychonomic Bulletin & Review, 5,* 644–649.

Simons, D. J., & Rensink, R. A. (2005). Change blindness: Past, present, and future. *Trends in Cognitive Sciences, 9,* 16–20.

Simons, D., Lleras, A., Martinez-Conde, S., Slichter, D., Caddigan, E., & Nevarez, G. (2006). Induced visual fading of complex images. *Journal of Vision, 6,* 1093–1101. doi:10.1167/6.10.9

Simonton, D. K. (2014). The mad-genius paradox: Can creative people be more mentally healthy but highly creative people more mentally ill? *Perspectives on Psychological Science, 9*(5), 470–480.

Simpson, A., & Riggs, K. J. (2011). Three- and 4-year-olds encode modeled actions in two ways leading to immediate imitation and delayed emulation. *Developmental Psychology, 47*(3), 834–840. doi:10.1037/a0023270

Simpson, J. A. (1987). The dissolution of romantic relationships: Factors involved in relationship stability and emotional distress. *Journal of Personality and Social Psychology, 53*(4), 683–692.

Simpson, J. A., Collins, W. A., & Salvatore, J. E. (2011). The impact of early interpersonal experience on adult romantic relationship functioning: Recent findings from the Minnesota Longitudinal Study of Risk and Adaptation. *Current Directions in Psychological Science, 20*(6), 355–359.

Simpson, J. A., Collins, W. A., Tran, S., & Haydon, K. C. (2007). Attachment and the experience and expression of emotions in romantic relationships: A developmental perspective. *Journal of Personality and Social Psychology, 92*(2), 355–367. doi:10.1037/0022-3514.92.2.355

Simpson, S. J., & Raubenheimer, D. (2014). Perspective: Tricks of the trade. *Nature, 508*, S66. doi:10.1038/508S66a

Sinclair, R. C., Hoffman, C., Mark, M. M., Martin, L. L., & Pickering, T. L. (1994). Construct accessibility and the misattribution of arousal: Schachter and Singer revisited. *Psychological Science, 5*(1), 15–19. doi:10.1111/j.1467-9280.1994.tb00607.x

Singer, P. (1975). *Animal liberation: A new ethics for our treatment of animals.* New York: Random House.

Singh, D. (1993). Adaptive significance of female physical attractiveness: Role of waist-to-hip ratio. *Journal of Personality and Social Psychology, 65*, 293–307.

Sirois, F. M. (2015). Is procrastination a vulnerability factor for hypertension and cardiovascular disease? Testing an extension of the procrastination–health model. *Journal of Behavioral Medicine, 38*, 578–589.

Skinner, B. F. (1938). *The behavior of organisms: An experimental analysis.* New York: Appleton-Century-Crofts.

Skinner, B. F. (1948). "Superstition" in the pigeon. *Journal of Experimental Psychology, 38*, 168–172.

Skinner, B. F. (1950). Are theories of learning necessary? *Psychological Review, 57*, 193–216.

Skinner, B. F. (1953). *Science and human behavior.* New York: Macmillan.

Skinner, B. F. (1957). *Verbal behavior.* New York: Appleton-Century-Crofts.

Skinner, B. F. (1958). Teaching machines. *Science, 129*, 969–977.

Skinner, B. F. (1972). The operational analysis of psychological terms. In B. F. Skinner, *Cumulative record* (3rd ed., pp. 370–384). New York: Appleton-Century-Crofts. (Original work published 1945)

Skinner, B. F. (1974). *About behaviorism.* New York: Alfred A. Knopf.

Skinner, B. F. (1977). Why I am not a cognitive psychologist. *Behaviorism, 5*, 1–10.

Skinner, B. F. (1979). *The shaping of a behaviorist: Part two of an autobiography.* New York: Knopf.

Skotko, B. G., Levine, S. P., & Goldstein, R. (2011a). Having a brother or sister with Down syndrome: Perspectives from siblings. *American Journal of Medical Genetics Part A, 155*(10), 2348–2359.

Skotko, B. G., Levine, S. P., & Goldstein, R. (2011b). Self-perceptions from people with Down syndrome. *American Journal of Medical Genetics Part A, 155*(10), 2360–2369.

Skvortsova, V., Degos, B., Welter, M.-L., Vidailhet, M., & Pessiglione, M. (2017). A selective role for dopamine in learning to maximize reward but not to minimize effort: Evidence from patients with Parkinson's disease. *Journal of Neuroscience, 37*, 6087–6097.

Slagter, H. A. (2012). Conventional working memory training may not improve intelligence. *Trends in Cognitive Sciences, 16*, 582–583.

Slater, A., Morison, V., & Somers, M. (1988). Orientation discrimination and cortical function in the human newborn. *Perception, 17*, 597–602.

Sloane, S., Baillargeon, R., & Premack, D. (2012). Do infants have a sense of fairness? *Psychological Science, 23*(2), 196–204.

Slotnick, S. D., & Schacter, D. L. (2004). A sensory signature that distinguished true from false memories. *Nature Neuroscience, 7*, 664–672.

Small, D. M., Gerber, J. C., Mak, Y. E., & Hummel, T. (2005). Differential neural responses evoked by orthonasal versus retronasal odorant perception in humans. *Neuron, 47*(4), 593–605.

Smart, E., Smart, L., & Morton, L. (2003). *Bringing Elizabeth home: A journey of faith and hope.* New York: Doubleday.

Smetacek, V. (2002). Balance: Mind-grasping gravity. *Nature, 415*, 481.

Smetanin, P., Stiff, D., Briante, C., Adair, C.E., Ahmad, S., & Khan, M. (2011, December). The life and economic impact of major mental illnesses in Canada. Retrieved from https://www.mentalhealthcommission.ca/sites/default/files/MHCC_Report_Base_Case_FINAL_ENG_0_0.pdf

Smith, A. R., Chein, J., & Steinberg, L. (2014). Peers increase adolescent risk taking even when the probabilities of negative outcomes are known. *Developmental Psychology, 50*(5), 1564–1568.

Smith, C. N., Frascino, J. C., Hopkins, R. O., & Squire, L. R. (2013). The nature of anterograde and retrograde impairment after damage to the medial temporal lobe. *Neuropsychologia, 51*, 2709–2714.

Smith, E. E., & Jonides, J. (1997). Working memory: A view from neuroimaging. *Cognitive Psychology, 33*, 5–42.

Smith, E. N., Romero, C., Donovan, B., Herter, R., Paunesku, D., Cohen, G. L., . . . Gross, J. J. (2018). Emotion theories and adolescent well-being: Results of an online intervention. *Emotion, 18*(6), 781–788. doi:10.1037/emo0000379

Smith, M. L., Glass, G. V., & Miller, T. I. (1980). *The benefits of psychotherapy.* Baltimore: Johns Hopkins University Press.

Smith, N., & Tsimpli, I.-M. (1995). *The mind of a savant.* Oxford, UK: Oxford University Press.

Snedeker, J., Geren, J., & Shafto, C. (2007). Starting over: International adoption as a natural experiment in language development. *Psychological Science, 18*, 79–87.

Snedeker, J., Geren, J., & Shafto, C. (2012). Disentangling the effects of cognitive development and linguistic expertise: A longitudinal study of the acquisition of English in internationally adopted children. *Cognitive Psychology, 65*, 39–76.

Sneed, J. R. (2005). Models of the aging self. *Journal of Social Issues, 61*(2), 375–388.

Sniekers, S., Stringer, S., Watanabe, K., Jansen, P. R., Coleman, J. R. I., Krapohl, E., . . . Posthuma, D. (2017).

Genome-wide association meta-analysis of 78,308 individuals identifies new loci and genes influencing human intelligence. *Nature Genetics, 49,* 1107. Retrieved from doi.org/10.1038/ng.3869

Snowdon, R., Thompson, P., & Troscianko, T. (2012). *Basic vision: An introduction to visual perception* (2nd ed.). New York: Oxford University Press.

Soderstrom, N. C., & Bjork, R. A. (2014). Testing facilitates the regulation of subsequent study time. *Journal of Memory and Language, 73,* 99–115.

Sodian, B., & Kristen-Antonow, S. (2015). Declarative joint attention as a foundation of theory of mind. *Developmental Psychology, 51*(9), 1190–1200.

Sokol-Hessner, P., Lackovic, S. F., Tobe, R. H., Camerer, C. F., Leventhal, B. L., & Phelps, E. A. (2015). Determinants of propanolol's selective effect on loss aversion. *Psychological Science, 26,* 1123–1130.

Solomon, S., Greenberg, J., & Pyszczynski, T. (1991). A terror management theory of social behavior: The psychological functions of self-esteem and cultural worldviews. In M. P. Zanna (Ed.), *Advances in experimental social psychology* (Vol. 24, pp. 93–159). New York: Academic Press.

Solomon, S., Greenberg, J., & Pyszczynski, T. (2004). The cultural animal: Twenty years of terror management theory and research. In J. Greenberg, S. L. Koole, & T. Pyszczynski (Eds.), *Handbook of experimental existential psychology* (pp. 13–34). New York: Guilford Press.

Sommerville, J. A., Schmidt, M. F. H., Yun, J., & Burns, M. (2013). The development of fairness expectations and prosocial development in the second year of life. *Infancy, 18*(1), 40–66.

Son, L. K., & Metcalfe, J. (2000). Metacognitive and control strategies in study-time allocation. *Journal of Experimental Psychology: Learning, Memory, and Cognition, 26,* 204–221.

Song, H., Fang, F., Arnberg, F. K., Mataix-Cols, D., de la Cruz, L. F., Almqvist, C., . . ., Valdimarsdóttir, U. A. (2019). Stress-related disorders and risk of cardiovascular disease: Population based, sibling controlled cohort study. *British Medical Journal, 365,* 1255.

Song, Y., Ma, J., Wang, H. J., Wang, Z., Hu, P., Zhang, B., & Agardh, A. (2014). Trends of age at menarche and association with body mass index in Chinese school-aged girls, 1985–2010. *Journal of Pediatrics, 165,* 1172–1177.

Sonnby-Borgstrom, M., Jonsson, P., & Svensson, O. (2003). Emotional empathy as related to mimicry reactions at different levels of information processing. *Journal of Nonverbal Behavior, 27,* 3–23.

Southgate, V., Senju, A., & Csibra, G. (2007). Action anticipation through attribution of false belief by two-year-olds. *Psychological Science, 18,* 587–592.

Soveri, A., Antfolk, J., Karlsson, L., Salo, B., & Laine, M. (2017). Working memory training revisited: A multi-level meta-analysis of n-back training studies. *Psychonomic Bulletin & Review, 24,* 1077–1096.

Sparrow, B., Liu, J., & Wegner, D. M. (2011). Google effects on memory: Cognitive consequence of having information at our fingertips. *Science, 333,* 776–778.

Spearman, C. (1904). "General intelligence," objectively determined and measured. *American Journal of Psychology, 15,* 201–293.

Speisman, J. C., Lazarus, R. S., Moddkoff, A., & Davison, L. (1964). Experimental reduction of stress based on ego-defense theory. *Journal of Abnormal and Social Psychology, 68,* 367–380.

Spelke, E. S. (2005). Sex differences in intrinsic aptitude for mathematics and science: A critical review. *The American Psychologist, 60*(9), 950–958.

Spence, N. D., Wells, S., Graham, K., & George, J. (2016). Racial discrimination, cultural resilience, and stress. *The Canadian Journal of Psychiatry, 61*(5), 298–307.

Spencer, S. J., Logel, C., & Davies, P. G. (2016). Stereotype threat. *Annual Review of Psychology, 67*(1), 415–437.

Sperling, G. (1960). The information available in brief visual presentations. *Psychological Monographs, 74*(11), 1–29.

Sperry, R. W. (1964). The great cerebral commissure. *Scientific American, 210,* 42–52.

Spiegel, A. (2011). How psychology solved a WWII shipwreck mystery. NPR. https://www.npr.org/templates/transcript/transcript.php?storyId=140816037

Sporns, O., & Betzel, R. F. (2016). Modular brain networks. *Annual Review of Psychology, 67,* 613–640.

Sprecher, S. (1999). "I love you more today than yesterday": Romantic partners' perceptions of changes in love and related affect over time. *Journal of Personality and Social Psychology, 76,* 46–53.

Sprecher, S., & Regan, P. C. (1998). Passionate and companionate love in courting and young married couples. *Sociological Inquiry, 68,* 163–185.

Spunt, R. P., Meyer, M. L., & Lieberman, M. D. (2015). The default mode of human brain function primes the intentional stance. *Journal of Cognitive Neuroscience, 27*(6), 1116–1124.

Squire, L. R. (1992). Memory and the hippocampus: A synthesis from findings with rats, monkeys, and humans. *Psychological Review, 99,* 195–231.

Squire, L. R. (2009). The legacy of patient HM for neuroscience. *Neuron, 61,* 6–9.

Squire, L. R., & Kandel, E. R. (1999). *Memory: From mind to molecules.* New York: Scientific American Library.

Squire, L. R., & Wixted, J. T. (2011). The cognitive neuroscience of memory since HM. *Annual Review of Neuroscience, 34,* 259–288.

Squire, L. R., Knowlton, B., & Musen, G. (1993). The structure and organization of memory. *Annual Review of Psychology, 44,* 453–495.

Srivastava, S., John, O. P., Gosling, S. D., & Potter, J. (2003). Development of personality in early and middle adulthood: Set like plaster or persistent change? *Journal of Personality and Social Psychology, 84,* 1041–1053.

Sroufe, L. A., Egeland, B., & Kruetzer, T. (1990). The fate of early experience following developmental change: Longitudinal approaches to individual adaptation in childhood. *Child Development, 61,* 1363–1373.

St. Jacques, P. L., & Schacter, D. L. (2013). Modifying memory: Selectively enhancing and updating personal memories for a museum tour by reactivating them. *Psychological Science, 24,* 537–543.

Staddon, J. E. R., & Simmelhag, V. L. (1971). The "superstition" experiment: A reexamination of its implications for the principles of adaptive behavior. *Psychological Review, 78,* 3–43.

Stahl, A. E., & Feigenson, L. (2015). Observing the unexpected enhances infants' learning and exploration. *Science, 348*(6230), 91–94.

Stanca, L. (2016). The geography of parenthood and well-being: Do children make us happy, where and why? In J. Helliwell, R. Layard, & J. Sachs (Eds.), *World Happiness Report 2016, Special Rome Edition* (Vol. II, pp. 89–103). New York: Sustainable Development Solutions Network. Retrieved from http://worldhappiness.report/#happiness2016

Stanovich, K. E. (2009). *What intelligence tests miss: The psychology of rational thought.* New Haven, CT: Yale University Press.

Stanovich, K. E., & West, R. F. (2000). Individual differences in reasoning: Implications for the rationality debate? *Behavioral and Brain Sciences, 23,* 645–726.

Statistics Canada. (2005, June 28). Projections of the Aboriginal Populations, Canada, Provinces and Territories, 2001 to 2017. Retrieved from https://www150.statcan.gc.ca/n1/pub/91-547-x/2005001/4072106-eng.htm

Statistics Canada. (2015, July 17). Table 1: Mean height, weight, body mass index (BMI) and prevalence of obesity, by collection method and sex, household population aged 18 to 79. Canada 2008, 2007 to 2009, and 2005. Retrieved from https://150statcan.gc.ca/n1/pub/82-003-x2011003/article/11533/tb1-eng.htm

Statistics Canada. (2016, December 9). Health indicators by Aboriginal identity, 2011 to 2014. Retrieved from https://www150.statcan.gc.ca/n1/daily-quotidien/161209/dq161209e-eng.htm

Statistics Canada. (2017). Family matters: Being separated or divorced in Canada [Infographic]. Retrieved from https://www150.statcan.gc.ca/n1/pub/11-627-m/11-627-m2019033-eng.pdf)

Statistics Canada. (2018a). Obesity in Canadian Adults, 2016 and 2017. Retrieved from https://www150.statcan.gc.ca/n1/pub/11-627-m/11-627-m2018033-eng.htm.

Statistics Canada. (2018b, May 17). Changing profile of stay-at-home parents. Retrieved from https://www150.statcan.gc.ca/n1/pub/11-630-x/11-630-x2016007-eng.htm

Statistics Canada. (2018c, October 30). Canadian Tobacco, Alcohol and Drugs Survey, 2017. Retrieved from https://www150.statcan.gc.ca/n1/daily-quotidien/181030/dq181030b-eng.htm?HPA=1

Statistics Canada. (2019a). Measured adult body mass index (BMI) (World Health Organization classification), by age group and sex, Canada and provinces, Canadian Community Health Survey - Nutrition. Retrieved from https://www150.statcan.gc.ca/t1/tbl1/en/tv.action?pid=1310079401.

Statistics Canada. (2019b, July 22). Uniform Crime Reporting Survey (UCR). Retrieved from http://www23.statcan.gc.ca/imdb/p2SV.pl?Function=getSurvey&SDDS=3302

Statistics Canada. (2019c, June 25). Heavy drinking, 2018. Retrieved from https://www150.statcan.gc.ca/n1/en/pub/82-625-x/2019001/article/00007-eng.pdf?st=szFhaXCt

Statistics Canada. (2019d, June 25). Overweight and obese adults, 2018. Retrieved from https://www150.statcan.gc.ca/n1/pub/82-625-x/2019001/article/00005-eng.htm

Statistics Canada. (2019e, May 1). Family matters: Being common-law, married, separated or divorced in Canada. Retrieved from https://www150.statcan.gc.ca/n1/daily-quotidien/190501/dq190501b-eng.htm

Statistics Canada. (2019f, October 25). Mental health indicators. Retrieved from https://www150.statcan.gc.ca/t1/tbl1/en/tv.action?pid=1310046501

Statistics Canada. (2019g, October 14). Deaths and age-specific mortality rates, by selected grouped causes. Retrieved from https://www150.statcan.gc.ca/t1/tbl1/en/tv.action?pid=1310039201

Statistics Canada. (2019h, October 14). Suicide in Canada's immigrant population. Retrieved from https://www150.statcan.gc.ca/n1/en/catalogue/82-003-X20030026807

Statton, M. A., Encarnacion, M., Celnik, P., & Bastian, A. J. (2015). A single bout of moderate aerobic exercise improves motor skill acquisition. *PLoS One, 10*(10), e0141393.

Staw, B. M., & Hoang, H. (1995). Sunk costs in the NBA: Why draft order affects playing time and survival in professional basketball. *Administrative Science Quarterly, 40,* 474–494.

Steele, C. M., & Aronson, J. (1995). Stereotype threat and the intellectual test performance of African Americans. *Journal of Personality and Social Psychology, 69,* 797–811.

Steele, C. M., & Josephs, R. A. (1990). Alcohol myopia: Its prized and dangerous effects. *American Psychologist, 45,* 921–933.

Steele, H., Steele, M., Croft, C., & Fonagy, P. (1999). Infant-mother attachment at one year predicts children's understanding of mixed emotions at six years. *Social Development, 8,* 161–178.

Steele, L. S., Glazier, R. H., & Lin, E. (2006). Inequity in mental health care under Canadian universal health coverage. *Psychiatric Services, 57*(3), 317–324.

Stein, D. J., Phillips, K. A., Bolton, D., Fulford, K. W. M., Sadler, J. Z., & Kendler, K. S. (2010). What is a mental/psychiatric disorder? From *DSM–IV* to *DSM–V. Psychological Medicine, 40*(11), 1759–1765. doi:10.1017/S0033291709992261

Stein, M. B., Chavira, D. A., & Jang, K. L. (2001). Bringing up bashful baby: Developmental pathways to social phobia. *Psychiatric Clinics of North America, 24,* 661–675.

Stein, M., Federspiel, A., Koenig, T., Wirth, M., Lehmann, C., Wiest, R., . . . Dierks, T. (2009). Reduced frontal activation with increasing second language proficiency. *Neuropsychologia, 47,* 2712–2720.

Steinbaum, E. A., & Miller, N. E. (1965). Obesity from eating elicited by daily stimulation of hypothalamus. *American Journal of Physiology, 208,* 1–5.

Steinberg, L. (2007). Risk taking in adolescence: New perspectives from brain and behavioral science. *Current Directions in Psychological Science, 16*(2), 55–59. doi:10.1111/j.1467-8721.2007.00475x

Steinberg, L., & Monahan, K. C. (2007). Age differences in resistance to peer influence. *Developmental Psychology, 43,* 1531–1543.

Steinberg, L., & Morris, A. S. (2001). Adolescent development. *Annual Review of Psychology, 52,* 83–110.

Steiner, J. E. (1973). The gustofacial response: Observation on normal and anencephalic newborn infants. In J. F. Bosma (Ed.), *Fourth symposium on oral sensation and perception: Development in the fetus and infant* (DHEW 73–546; pp. 254–278). Bethesda, MD: U.S. Department of Health, Education, and Welfare.

Steiner, J. E. (1979). Human facial expressions in response to taste and smell stimulation. *Advances in Child Development and Behavior, 13,* 257–295.

Stellar, J. R., & Stellar, E. (1985). *The neurobiology of motivation and reward.* New York: Springer-Verlag.

Stellar, J. R., Kelley, A. E., & Corbett, D. (1983). Effects of peripheral and central dopamine blockade on lateral hypothalamic self-stimulation: Evidence for both reward and motor deficits. *Pharmacology, Biochemistry, and Behavior, 18,* 433–442.

Stelmack, R. M. (1990). Biological bases of extraversion: Psychophysiological evidence. *Journal of Personality, 58,* 293–311.

Stemmler, G., Aue, T., & Wacker, J. (2007). Anger and fear: Separable effects of emotion and motivational direction on somatovisceral responses. *International Journal of Psychophysiology, 66*(2), 141–153. doi.org/10.1016/j.ijpsycho.2007.03.019

Stephens, R. S. (1999). Cannabis and hallucinogens. In B. S. McCrady & E. E. Epstein (Eds.), *Addictions: A comprehensive guidebook* (pp. 121–140). New York: Oxford University Press.

Stern, J. A., Brown, M., Ulett, A., & Sletten, I. (1977). A comparison of hypnosis, acupuncture, morphine, Valium, aspirin, and placebo in the management of experimentally induced pain. In W. E. Edmonston (Ed.), *Conceptual and investigative approaches to hypnosis and hypnotic phenomena* (Vol. 296, pp. 175–193). New York: New York Academy of Sciences.

Stern, W. (1914). *The psychological methods of testing intelligence* (G. M. Whipple, Trans.). Baltimore, MD: Warwick & York.

Sternberg, R. J. (1986). A triangular theory of love. *Psychological Review, 93,* 119–135.

Sternberg, R. J. (1999). The theory of successful intelligence. *Review of General Psychology, 3*(4), 292–316.

Sternberg, R. J. (2006). The Rainbow Project: Enhancing the SAT through assessments of analytical, practical, and creative skills. *Intelligence, 34*(4), 321–350.

Sternberg, R. J., & Grigorenko, E. L. (2004). Intelligence and culture: How culture shapes what intelligence means, and the implications for a science of well-being. *Philosophical Transaction of the Royal Society B, 359*(1449), 1427–1434.

Stevens, J. (1988). An activity approach to practical memory. In M. M. Gruneberg, P. E. Morris, & R. N. Sykes (Eds.), *Practical aspects of memory: Current research and issues* (Vol. 1, pp. 335–341). New York: Wiley.

Stevens, L. A. (1971). *Explorers of the brain.* New York: Knopf.

Stevenson, R. J. (2017). Psychological correlates of habitual diet in healthy adults. *Psychological Bulletin, 143*(1), 53–90. doi.org/10.1037/bul0000065

Stevenson, R. J., & Francis, H. M. (2017). The hippocampus and the regulation of human food intake. *Psychological Bulletin, 143*(10), 1011–1032. doi.org/10.1037/bul0000109

Stice, E., & Yokum, S. (2016). Neural vulnerability factors that increase risk for future weight gain. *Psychological Bulletin, 142*(5), 447–471. doi.org/10.1037/bul0000044

Stickgold, R., Hobson, J. A., Fosse, R., & Fosse, M. (2001). Sleep, learning, and dreams: Off-line memory reprocessing. *Science, 294,* 1052–1057.

Stickgold, R., Malia, A., Maguire, D., Roddenberry, D., & O'Connor, M. (2000). Replaying the game: Hypnagogic images in normals and amnesics. *Science, 290,* 350–353.

Stillman, C. M., Howard, J. H., Jr., & Howard, D. V. (2016). The effects of structural complexity on age-related deficits in implicit probabilistic sequence learning. *Journals of Gerontology Series B, Psychological Sciences and Social Sciences, 71,* 212–219.

Stockman, A., & Sharpe, L. T. (2000). Spectral sensitivities of the middle- and long-wavelength sensitive cones derived from measurements in observers of known genotype. *Vision Research, 40,* 1711–1737. See "cone fundamentals" at http://www.cvrl.org/

Stoet, G., & Geary, D. C. (2018). The gender equality paradox in STEM education. *Psychological Science.* Advanced online http://journals.sagepub.com/doi/full/10.1177/0956797617741719

Stone, A. A. (2018). Ecological momentary assessment in survey research. In D. L. Vannette & J. A. Krosnick (Eds.), *The Palgrave handbook of survey Research* (pp. 221–226). Cham, Switzerland: Palgrave Macmillan.

Stone, A. A., Schwartz, J. E., Broderick, J. E., & Deaton, A. (2010). A snapshot of the age distribution of psychological well-being in the United States. *Proceedings of the National Academy of Sciences, USA, 107*(22), 9985–9990.

Stone, J., Perry, W., & Darley, J. M. (1997). "White men can't jump": Evidence for the perceptual confirmation of racial stereotypes following a basketball game. *Basic and Applied Social Psychology, 19*(3), 291–306.

Stone, M. H. (1997). Introduction: The history of obsessive-compulsive disorder from the early period to the turn of the twentieth century. In D. J. Stein & M. H. Stone (Eds.), *Essential Papers on Obsessive-Compulsive Disorder* (pp. 19–33). New York: New York University Press.

Stoodley, C. J., Ray, N. J., Jack, A., & Stein, J. F. (2008). Implicit learning in control, dyslexic, and garden-variety poor readers. *Annals of the New York Academy of Sciences, 1145,* 173–183.

Storm, B. C., & Stone, S. M. (2015). Saving-enhanced memory: The benefits of saving on the learning and remembering of new information. *Psychological Science, 26,* 182–188.

Storm, B. C., Bjork, E. L., Bjork, R. A., & Nestojko, J. F. (2006). Is retrieval success a necessary condition for retrieval-induced forgetting? *Psychonomic Bulletin & Review, 2,* 249–253.

Storm, B. C., Stone, S. M., & Benjamin, A. S. (2017). Using the Internet to access information inflates future use of the Internet to access other information. *Memory, 25,* 717–723.

Storms, M. D. (1973). Videotape and the attribution process: Reversing actors' and observers' points of view. *Journal of Personality and Social Psychology, 27,* 165–175.

Stott, D. H. (1983). Brain size and "intelligence." *British Journal of Developmental Psychology, 1,* 279–287.

Strack, F. (2016). Reflections on the smiling registered replication report. *Perspectives on Psychological Science, 11,* 929–930. doi:10.1177/1745691616674460

Strack, F., Martin, L. L., & Stepper, S. (1988). Inhibiting and facilitating conditions of the human smile: A nonobtrusive test of the facial feedback hypothesis. *Journal of Personality and Social Psychology, 54,* 768–777.

Strawn, J. R., Geracioti, L., Rajdev, N., Clemenza, K., & Levine, A., (2018). Pharmacotherapy for generalized anxiety disorder in adult and pediatric patients: An evidence-based treatment review. *Expert Opinion on Pharmacotherapy, 19,* 1057–1070.

Strayer, D. L., Drews, F. A., & Johnston, W. A. (2003). Cell phone–induced failures of visual attention during simulated driving. *Journal of Experimental Psychology: Applied, 9,* 23–32.

Streissguth, A. (2007). Offspring effects of prenatal alcohol exposure from birth to 25 years: The Seattle Prospective Longitudinal Study. *Journal of Clinical Psychology in Medical Settings, 14*(2), 81–101. doi:10.1007/s10880-007-9067-6

Streissguth, A. P., Barr, H. M., Bookstein, F. L., Sampson, P. D., & Carmichael Olson, H. (1999). The long-term neurocognitive consequences of prenatal alcohol exposure: A 14-year study. *Psychological Science, 10,* 186–190.

Striano, T., & Reid, V. M. (2006). Social cognition in the first year. *Trends in Cognitive Sciences, 10*(10), 471–476.

Striegel-Moore, R. H., & Bulik, C. M. (2007). Risk factors for eating disorders. *American Psychologist, 62,* 181–198.

Strohmetz, D. B., Rind, B., Fisher, R., & Lynn, M. (2002). Sweetening the till: The use of candy to increase restaurant tipping. *Journal of Applied Social Psychology, 32,* 300–309.

Stuss, D. T., & Benson, D. F. (1986). *The frontal lobes.* New York: Raven Press.

Suchman, A. L., Markakis, K., Beckman, H. B., & Frankel, R. (1997). A model of empathic communication in the medical interview. *Journal of the American Medical Association, 277,* 678–682.

Suddendorf, T., & Corballis, M. C. (2007). The evolution of foresight: What is mental time travel and is it unique to humans? *Behavioral and Brain Sciences, 30,* 299–313.

Suderman, M., McGowan, P. O., Sasaki, A., Huang, T. C. T., Hallett, M. T., Meaney, M. J., . . . Szyf, M. (2012). Conserved epigenetic sensitivity to early life experiences in the rat and human hippocampus. *Proceedings of the National Academy of Sciences, USA, 109*(Suppl. 2), 17266–17272.

Sullivan-Singh, S. J., Stanton, A. L., & Low, C. A. (2015). Living with limited time: Socioemotional selectivity theory in the context of health adversity. *Journal of Personality and Social Psychology, 108,* 900–916.

Sunderland, A., & Findlay, L. C. (2013). Perceived need for mental health care in Canada: Results from the 2012 Canadian community health survey-mental health (pp. 3–9). Ottawa: Statistics Canada.

Sundet, J. M., Eriksen, W., & Tambs, K. (2008). Intelligence correlations between brothers decrease with increasing age difference: Evidence for shared environmental effects in young adults. *Psychological Science, 19,* 843–847.

Susman, S., Dent, C., McAdams, L., Stacy, A., Burton, D., & Flay, B. (1994). Group self-identification and adolescent cigarette smoking: A 1-year prospective study. *Journal of Abnormal Psychology, 103,* 576–580.

Susser, E. B., Brown, A., & Matte, T. D. (1999). Prenatal factors and adult mental and physical health. *Canadian Journal of Psychiatry, 44*(4), 326–334.

Suthana, N., & Fried, I. (2012). Percepts to recollections: Insights from single neuron recordings in the human brain. *Trends in Cognitive Sciences, 16,* 427–436.

Sutin, A. R., Stephan, Y., & Terracciano, A. (2015). Weight discrimination and risk of mortality. *Psychological Science, 26*(11), 1803–1811. doi:10.1177/0956797615601103

Suzuki, L. A., & Valencia, R. R. (1997). Race–ethnicity and measured intelligence: Educational implications. *American Psychologist, 52,* 1103–1114.

Swami, V., & Tovée, M. J. (2008). The muscular male: A comparison of the physical attractiveness preferences of gay and heterosexual men. *International Journal of Men's Health, 7*(1), 59–71.

Swann, W. B., Jr. (1983). Self-verification: Bringing social reality into harmony with the self. In J. M. Suls & A. G. Greenwald (Eds.), *Psychological perspectives on the self* (Vol. 2, pp. 33–66). Hillsdale, NJ: Erlbaum.

Swann, W. B., Jr. (2012). Self-verification theory. In P. Van Lang, A. Kruglanski, & E. T. Higgins (Eds.), *Handbook of theories of social psychology* (Vol. 2, pp. 23–42). London: Sage.

Swann, W. B., Jr., & Rentfrow, P. J. (2001). Blirtatiousness: Cognitive, behavioral, and physiological consequences of rapid responding. *Journal of Personality and Social Psychology, 81*(6), 1160–1175.

Swayze, V. W., II. (1995). Frontal leukotomy and related psychosurgical procedures before antipsychotics (1935–1954): A historical overview. *American Journal of Psychiatry, 152*(4), 505–515.

Sweatt, J. D. (2019). The epigenetic basis of individuality. *Current Opinion in Behavioral Sciences, 25,* 51–56.

Sweeny, K., Carroll, P. J., & Shepperd, J. A. (2006). Is optimism always best? Future outlooks and preparedness. *Current Directions in Psychological Science, 15,* 302–306.

Swencionis, J. K., & Fiske, S. T. (2016) Promote up, ingratiate down: Status comparisons drive warmth-competence tradeoffs in impression management. *Journal of Experimental Social Psychology, 64,* 27–34.

Swendsen, J., Hammen, C., Heller, T., & Gitlin, M. (1995). Correlates of stress reactivity in patients with bipolar disorder. *American Journal of Psychiatry, 152,* 795–797.

Swinkels, A. (2003). An effective exercise for teaching cognitive heuristics. *Teaching of Psychology, 30,* 120–122.

Szechtman, H., & Woody, E. Z. (2006). Obsessive-compulsive disorder as a disturbance of security motivation: Constraints on comorbidity. *Neurotoxicity Research, 10,* 103–112.

Szpunar, K. K. (2010). Episodic future thought: An emerging concept. *Perspectives on Psychological Science, 5,* 142–162.

Szpunar, K. K., Khan, N. Y., & Schacter, D. L. (2013). Interpolated memory tests reduce mind wandering and improve learning of online lectures. *Proceedings of the National Academy of Sciences, USA, 110,* 6313–6317.

Szpunar, K. K., Watson, J. M., & McDermott, K. B. (2007). Neural substrates of envisioning the future. *Proceedings of the National Academy of Sciences, USA, 104,* 642–647.

Tajfel, H., & Turner, J. C. (1986). The social identity theory of intergroup behavior. In S. Worchel & W. G. Austin (Eds.), *Psychology of intergroup relations* (pp. 7–24). Chicago: Nelson.

Tajfel, H., & Wilkes, A. L. (1963). Classification and quantitative judgement. *British Journal of Psychology, 54,* 101–114.

Tajfel, H., Billig, M. G., Bundy, R. P., & Flament, C. (1971). Social categorization and intergroup behaviour. *European Journal of Social Psychology, 1,* 149–178.

Talamas, S. N., Mavor, K. I., Axelsson, J., Sundelin, T., & Perrett, D. I. (2016). Eyelid-openness and mouth curvature influence perceived intelligence beyond attractiveness. *Journal of Experimental Psychology: General, 145*(5), 603–620.

Talhelm, T., Oishi, S., & Zhang, X. (2018). Who smiles while alone? Rates of smiling lower in China than U.S. *Emotion.* doi.org/10.1037/emo0000459

Tamir, M., Bigman, Y. E., Rhodes, E., Salerno, J., & Schreier, J. (2015). An expectancy-value model of emotion regulation: Implications for motivation, emotional experience, and decision making. *Emotion, 15*(1), 90–103.

Tamir, M., & Ford, B. Q. (2012). Should people pursue feelings that feel good or feelings that do good? Emotional preferences and well-being. *Emotion, 12,* 1061–1070.

Tamminga, C. A., Nemeroff, C. B., Blakely, R. D., Brady, L., Carter, C. S., Davis, K. L., . . . Suppes, T. (2002). Developing novel treatments for mood disorders: Accelerating discovery. *Biological Psychiatry, 52,* 589–609.

Tanaka, K. Z., He, H., Tomar, A., Niisato, K., Huang, A. J. Y., & McHugh, T. J. (2018). The hippocampal engram maps experience but not place. *Science, 361,* 392–397.

Tang, D. W., Fellows, L. K., & Dagher, A. (2014). Behavioral and neural valuation of foods is driven by implicit knowledge of caloric content. *Psychological Science, 25*(12), 2168–2176. doi:10.1177/0956797614552081

Tang, Y. Y., Lu, Q., Fan, M., Yang, Y., & Posner, M. I. (2012). Mechanisms of white matter changes induced by meditation. *Proceedings of the National Academy of Sciences, USA, 109,* 10570–10574.

Tang, Y.-P., Shimizu, E., Dube, G. R., Rampon, C., Kerchner, G. A., Zhuo, M., . . . Tsien, J. Z. (1999). Genetic enhancement of learning and memory in mice. *Nature, 401,* 63–69.

Tarantino, N., Tully, E. C., Garcia, S. E., South, S., Iacono, W. G., & McGue, M. (2014). Genetic and environmental influences on affiliation with deviant peers during adolescence and early adulthood. *Developmental Psychology, 50*(3), 663–673.

Task Force on Promotion and Dissemination of Psychological Procedures. (1995). Training in and dissemination of empirically validated psychological treatments: Report and recommendations. *Clinical Psychologist, 48,* 3–23.

Taylor, C., & Peter, T., with McMinn, T. L., Elliott, T., Beldom, S., Ferry, A., Gross, Z., Paquin, S., & Schacter, K. (2011). Every class in every school: The first national climate survey on homophobia, biphobia, and transphobia in Canadian schools. Retrieved from https://egale.ca/wp-content/uploads/2011/05/EgaleFinalReport-web.pdf

Taylor, S. E. (1989). *Positive illusions.* New York: Basic Books.

Taylor, S. E. (2002). *The tending instinct: How nurturing is essential to who we are and how we live.* New York: Times Books.

Taylor, S. E., & Brown, J. D. (1988). Illusion and well-being: A social psychological perspective on mental health. *Psychological Bulletin, 103,* 193–210.

Taylor, S. E., & Fiske, S. T. (1975). Point-of-view and perceptions of causality. *Journal of Personality and Social Psychology, 32,* 439–445.

Teasdale, J. D., Segal, Z. V., & Williams, J. M., Ridgeway, V. A., Soulsby, J. M., & Lau, M. (2000). Prevention of relapse/recurrence in major depression by mindfulness-based cognitive therapy. *Journal of Consulting and Clinical Psychology, 68*(4), 615–623.

Telch, M. J., Lucas, J. A., & Nelson, P. (1989). Non-clinical panic in college students: An investigation of prevalence and symptomology. *Journal of Abnormal Psychology, 98,* 300–306.

Tellegen, A., Lykken, D. T., Bouchard, T. J., Wilcox, K., Segal, N., & Rich, A. (1988). Personality similarity in twins reared together and apart. *Journal of Personality and Social Psychology, 54,* 1031–1039.

ten Brinke, L., Vohs, K. D., & Carney, D. R. (2016). Can ordinary people detect deception after all? *Trends in Cognitive Sciences, 20*(8), 579–588.

Tepper, T. (2018). Americans say this is their biggest financial regret. www.bankrate.com/banking/savings/financial-security-may-2018/

Terman, L. M. (1916). *The measurement of intelligence.* Boston: Houghton Mifflin.

Tesser, A. (1991). Emotion in social comparison and reflection processes. In J. Suls & T. A. Wills (Ed.), *Social comparison: Contemporary theory and research* (pp. 117–148). Hillsdale, NJ: Erlbaum.

Teuscher, U., & Teuscher, C. (2007). Reconsidering the double standard of aging: Effects of gender and sexual orientation on facial attractiveness ratings. *Personality and Individual Differences, 42*(4), 631–639.

Tews, M. J., Stafford, K., & Tracey, J. B. (2011) What matters most? The perceived importance of ability and personality for hiring decisions. *Cornell Hospitality Quarterly, 52,* 94–101.

Teyler, T. J., & DiScenna, P. (1986). The hippocampal memory indexing theory. *Behavioral Neuroscience, 100,* 147–154.

Thaker, G. K. (2002). Current progress in schizophrenia research. Search for genes of schizophrenia: Back to defining valid phenes. *Journal of Nervous and Mental Disease, 190,* 411–412.

Thakral, P., Madore, K. P., & Schacter, D. L. (2017). A role for the left angular gyrus in episodic simulation and memory. *Journal of Neuroscience, 37,* 8142–8149.

Thaler, K., Delivuk, M., Chapman, A., Gaynes, B. N., Kaminski, A., & Gartlehner, G. (2011). Second-generation antidepressants for seasonal affective disorder. *Cochrane Database of Systematic Reviews,* CD008591.

Thaler, L., Arnott, S. R., & Goodale, M. A. (2011). Neural correlates of natural human echolocation in early and late blind echolocation experts. *PLoS ONE 6*(5): e20162. https://doi.org/10.1371/journal.pone.0020162

Thaler, R. H. (1988). The ultimatum game. *Journal of Economic Perspectives, 2,* 195–206.

Thaler, R. H., & Sunstein, C. R. (2008). Nudge: Improving decisions about health, wealth, and happiness. New York: Penguin Books.

Thase, M. E., & Howland, R. H. (1995). Biological processes in depression: An updated review and integration. In E. E. Beckham & W. R. Leber (Eds.), *Handbook of depression* (2nd ed., pp. 213–279). New York: Guilford Press.

Thibaut, J. W., & Kelley, H. H. (1959). *The social psychology of groups.* New York: Wiley.

Thomaes, S., Bushman, B. J., Stegge, H., & Olthof, T. (2008). Trumping shame by blasts of noise: Narcissism, self-esteem, shame, and aggression in young adolescents. *Child Development, 79*(6), 1792–1801.

Thomas, A., & Chess, S. (1977). *Temperament and development.* New York: Brunner/Mazel.

Thomason, M., & Thompson, P. M. (2011). Diffusion imaging, white matter, and psychopathology. *Annual Review of Clinical Psychology, 7,* 63–85.

Thompson, C. P., Skowronski, J., Larsen, S. F., & Betz, A. (1996). *Autobiographical memory: Remembering what and remembering when.* Mahwah, NJ: Erlbaum.

Thompson, P. M., Giedd, J. N., Woods, R. P., MacDonald, D., Evans, A. C., & Toga, A. W. (2000). Growth patterns in the developing brain detected by using continuum mechanical tensor maps. *Nature, 404,* 190–193.

Thompson, P. M., Vidal, C., Giedd, J. N., Gochman, P., Blumenthal, J., Nicolson, R., . . . Rapoport, J. L. (2001). Accelerated gray matter loss in very early-onset schizophrenia. *Proceedings of the National Academy of Sciences, USA, 98,* 11650–11655.

Thompson, R. F. (2005). In search of memory traces. *Annual Review of Psychology, 56,* 1–23.

Thomson, D. M. (1988). Context and false recognition. In G. M. Davies & D. M. Thomson (Eds.), *Memory in context: Context in memory* (pp. 285–304). Chichester, UK: Wiley.

Thorndike, E. L. (1898). Animal intelligence: An experimental study of associative processes in animals. *Psychological Review Monograph Supplements, 2,* i–109.

Thornhill, R., & Gangestad, S. W. (1993). Human facial beauty: Averageness, symmetry, and parasite resistance. *Human Nature, 4,* 237–269.

Thornhill, R., & Gangestad, S. W. (1999). The scent of symmetry: A human sex pheromone that signals fitness? *Evolution and Human Behavior, 20,* 175–201.

Thurber, J. (1956). *Further fables of our time.* New York: Simon & Schuster.

Thurstone, L. L. (1938). *Primary mental abilities.* Chicago: University of Chicago Press.

Tienari, P., Wynne, L. C., Sorri, A., Lahti, I., Läksy, K., Moring, J., . . . Wahlberg, K. E. (2004). Genotype–environment interaction in schizophrenia-spectrum disorder: Long-term follow-up study of Finnish adoptees. *British Journal of Psychiatry, 184,* 216–222.

Timmerman, T. A. (2007). "It was a thought pitch": Personal, situational, and target influences on hit-by-pitch events across time. *Journal of Applied Psychology, 92,* 876–884.

Tobey, E. A., Thal, D., Niparko, J. K., Eisenberg, L. S., Quittner, A. L., Wang, N. Y., & CDaCI Investigative Team. (2013). Influence of implantation age on school-age language performance in pediatric cochlear implant users. *International Journal of Audiology, 52*(4), 219–229. doi:10.3109/14992027.2012.759666

Todd, A. R., Bodenhausen, G. V., Richeson, J. A., & Galinsky, A. D. (2011). Perspective taking combats automatic expressions of racial bias. *Journal of Personality and Social Psychology, 100*(6), 1027–1042.

Todes, D. P. (2014). *Ivan Pavlov: A Russian life in science.* New York: Oxford University Press.

Toga, A. W., Clark, K. A., Thompson, P. M., Shattuck, D. W., & Van Horn, J. D. (2012). Mapping the human connectome. *Neurosurgery, 71,* 1–5.

Tolin, D. F. (2010). Is cognitive-behavioral therapy more effective than other therapies? A meta-analytic review. *Clinical Psychology Review, 30*(6), 710–720.

Tolman, E. C., & Honzik, C. H. (1930a). "Insight" in rats. *University of California Publications in Psychology, 4,* 215–232.

Tolman, E. C., & Honzik, C. H. (1930b). Introduction and removal of reward and maze performance in rats. *University of California Publications in Psychology, 4,* 257–275.

Tolman, E. C., Ritchie, B. F., & Kalish, D. (1946). Studies in spatial learning. I: Orientation and short cut. *Journal of Experimental Psychology, 36,* 13–24.

Tomasello, M., & Call, J. (2004). The role of humans in the cognitive development of apes revisited. *Animal Cognition, 7,* 213–215.

Tomasello, M., Davis-Dasilva, M., Camak, L., & Bard, K. (1987). Observational learning of tool use by young chimpanzees. *Human Evolution, 2,* 175–183.

Tomasello, M., Savage-Rumbaugh, S., & Kruger, A. C. (1993). Imitative learning of actions on objects by children, chimpanzees, and enculturated chimpanzees. *Child Development, 64,* 1688–1705.

Tomkins, S. S. (1981). The role of facial response in the experience of emotion. *Journal of Personality and Social Psychology, 40,* 351–357.

Tootell, R. B. H., Reppas, J. B., Dale, A. M., Look, R. B., Sereno, M. I., Malach, R., . . . Rosen, B. R. (1995). Visual-motion aftereffect in human cortical area MT revealed by functional magnetic resonance imaging. *Nature, 375,* 139–141.

Toronto Police Service. (2019). TPS Crime Statistics—Shootings. Retrieved from https://data.torontopolice.on.ca/pages/shootings

Torre, J. B. & Lieberman, M. D. (2018). Putting feelings into words: Affect labeling as implicit emotion regulation. *Emotion Review, 10,* 116–124.

Tracy, J. L., & Beall, A. T. (2011). Happy guys finish last: The impact of emotion expressions on sexual attraction. *Emotion, 11*(6), 1379–1387.

Tracy, J. L., Randles, D., & Steckler, C. M. (2015). The nonverbal communication of emotions. *Current Opinion in Behavioral Sciences, 3,* 25–30.

Tracy, J. L., Shariff, A. F., Zhao, W., & Henrich, J. (2013). Cross-cultural evidence that the nonverbal expression of pride is an automatic status signal. *Journal of Experimental Psychology: General, 142*(1), 163–180.

Treede, R. D., Kenshalo, D. R., Gracely, R. H., & Jones, A. K. (1999). The cortical representation of pain. *Pain, 79,* 105–111.

Treisman, A. (1998). Feature binding, attention and object perception. *Philosophical Transactions of the Royal Society B, 353,* 1295–1306.

Treisman, A. (2006). How the deployment of attention determines what we see. *Visual Cognition, 14,* 411–443.

Treisman, A., & Gelade, G. (1980). A feature integration theory of attention. *Cognitive Psychology, 12,* 97–136.

Treisman, A., & Schmidt, H. (1982). Illusory conjunctions in the perception of objects. *Cognitive Psychology, 14,* 107–141.

Trivers, R. L. (1972). Parental investment and sexual selection. In B. Campbell (Ed.), *Sexual selection and the descent of man, 1871–1971* (pp. 139–179). Chicago: Aldine.

Troy, A. S., Saquib, S., Thal, J., & Ciuk, D. J. (2018). The regulation of negative and positive affect in response to daily stressors. *Emotion, 19*(5), 751–763. doi.org/10.1037/emo0000486

Trull, T. J., & Durrett, C. A. (2005). Categorical and dimensional models of personality disorder. *Annual Review of Clinical Psychology, 1,* 355–380.

Tucker, E. (2003, June 25). Move over, Fido! Chickens are becoming hip suburban pets. *USA Today*. Retrieved from http://usatoday30.usatoday.com/money/2003-06-25-pet-chickens_x.htm.

Tucker-Drob, E. M., & Bates, T. C. (2016). Large cross-national differences in Gene × Socioeconomic Status interaction on intelligence. *Psychological Science, 27*(2), 138–149.

Tucker-Drob, E. M., Briley, D. A., & Harden, K. P. (2013). Genetic and environmental influences on cognition across development and context. *Current Directions in Psychological Science, 22*(5), 349–355.

Tucker-Drob, E. M., Rhemtulla, M., Harden, K. P., Turkheimer, E., & Fask, D. (2010). Emergence of a Gene × Socioeconomic Status interaction on infant mental ability between 10 months and 2 years. *Psychological Science, 22*(1), 125–133.

Tuerlinckx, F., De Boeck, P., & Lens, W. (2002). Measuring needs with the Thematic Apperception Test: A psychometric study. *Journal of Personality and Social Psychology, 82,* 448–461.

Tulving, E. (1972). Episodic and semantic memory. In E. Tulving & W. Donaldson (Eds.), *Organization of memory* (pp. 381–403). New York: Academic Press.

Tulving, E. (1983). *Elements of episodic memory.* Oxford: Clarendon Press.

Tulving, E. (1985). Memory and consciousness. *Canadian Psychologist, 25,* 1–12.

Tulving, E. (1998). Neurocognitive processes of human memory. In C. von Euler, I. Lundberg, & R. Llins (Eds.), *Basic mechanisms in cognition and language* (pp. 261–281). Amsterdam: Elsevier.

Tulving, E., & Pearlstone, Z. (1966). Availability versus accessibility of information in memory for words. *Journal of Verbal Learning and Verbal Behavior, 5,* 381–391.

Tulving, E., & Schacter, D. L. (1990). Priming and human memory systems. *Science, 247,* 301–306.

Tulving, E., & Thompson, D. M. (1973). Encoding specificity and retrieval processes in episodic memory. *Psychological Review, 80,* 352–373.

Tulving, E., Kapur, S., Craik, F. I. M., Moscovitch, M., & Houle, S. (1994). Hemispheric encoding/retrieval asymmetry in episodic memory: Positron emission tomography findings. *Proceedings of the National Academy of Sciences, USA, 91,* 2016–2020.

Tulving, E., Schacter, D. L., & Stark, H. (1982). Priming effects in word-fragment completion are independent of recognition memory. *Journal of Experimental Psychology: Learning, Memory, and Cognition, 8,* 336–342.

Turkheimer, E., Haley, A., Waldron, M., D'Onofrio, B., & Gottesman, I. I. (2003). Socioeconomic status modifies heritability of IQ in young children. *Psychological Science, 14,* 623–628.

Turner, D. C., & Sahakian, B. J. (2006). Neuroethics of cognitive enhancement. *BioSocieties, 1,* 113–123.

Turner, D. C., Robbins, T. W., Clark, L., Aron, A. R., Dowson, J., & Sahakian, B. J. (2003). Cognitive enhancing effects of modafinil in healthy volunteers. *Psychopharmacology, 165,* 260–269.

Turner, E. H., Matthews, A. M., Linardatos, E., Tell, R. A., & Rosenthal, R. (2008). Selective publication of antidepressant trials and its influence on apparent efficacy. *New England Journal of Medicine, 358*(3), 252–260.

Turner, M. E., & Pratkanis, A. R. (1998). Twenty-five years of groupthink theory and research: Lessons from the evaluation of a theory. *Organizational Behavior and Human Decision Processes, 73*(2–3), 105–115.

Tversky, A., & Kahneman, D. (1973). Availability: A heuristic for judging frequency and probability. *Cognitive Psychology, 5,* 207–232.

Tversky, A., & Kahneman, D. (1974). Judgment under uncertainty: Heuristics and biases. *Science, 185,* 1124–1131.

Tversky, A., & Kahneman, D. (1981). The framing of decisions and the psychology of choice. *Science, 211,* 453–458.

Tversky, A., & Kahneman, D. (1983). Extensional versus intuitive reasoning: The conjunction fallacy in probability judgment. *Psychological Review, 90,* 293–315.

Tversky, A., & Kahneman, D. (1992). Advances in prospect theory: Cumulative representation of uncertainty. *Journal of Risk and Uncertainty, 5,* 297–323.

Twenge, J. M., Campbell, W. K., & Foster, C. A. (2003). Parenthood and marital satisfaction: A meta-analytic review. *Journal of Marriage and Family, 65,* 574–583.

Twenge, J. M., Sherman, R. A., & Lyubomirsky, S. (2016). More happiness for young people and less for mature adults: Time period differences in subjective well-being in the United States, 1972–2014. *Social Psychological and Personality Science, 7,* 131–141.

Tyler, T. R. (1990). *Why people obey the law.* New Haven, CT: Yale University Press.

Uchikawa, K., Morimoto, T., & Matsumoto, T. (2017). Understanding individual differences in color appearance of "#TheDress" based on the optimal color hypothesis. *Journal of Vision, 17*(8), 10. doi:10.1167/17.8.10

Umberson, D., Williams, K., Powers, D. A., Liu, H., & Needham, B. (2006). You make me sick: Marital quality and health over the life course. *Journal of Health and Social Behavior, 47,* 1–16.

Uncapher, M. R., & Rugg, M. D. (2008). Fractionation of the component processes underlying successful episodic encoding: A combined fMRI and divided-attention study. *Journal of Cognitive Neuroscience, 20,* 240–254.

Ungerleider, L. G., & Mishkin, M. (1982). Two cortical visual systems. In D. J. Ingle, M. A. Goodale, & R. J. W. Mansfield (Eds.), *Analysis of visual behavior* (pp. 549–586). Cambridge, MA: MIT Press.

Urban, N. B. L., Girgis, R. R., Talbot, P. S., Kegeles, L. S., Xu, X., Frankie, W. G., . . . Laruelle, M. (2012). Sustained recreational use of ecstasy is associated with altered pre- and postsynaptic markers of serotonin transmission in neocortical areas: A PET study with [11c] DASB and [11c] MDL 100907. *Neuropsychopharmacology, 37,* 1465–1473.

Ursano, R. J., & Silberman, E. K. (2003). Psychoanalysis, psychoanalytic psychotherapy, and supportive psychotherapy. In R. E. Hales & S. C. Yudofsky (Eds.), *The American Psychiatric Publishing textbook of clinical psychiatry* (4th ed., pp. 1177–1203). Washington, DC: American Psychiatric Publishing.

Uskul, A. K., & Over, H. (2014). Responses to social exclusion in cultural context: Evidence from farming and herding communities. *Journal of Personality and Social Psychology, 106*(5), 752–771.

Vacha, E., & McBride, M. (1993). Cramming: A barrier to student success, a way to beat the system, or an effective strategy? *College Student Journal, 27*, 2–11.

Vafaei, A., Ahmed, T., Falcao Freire A., Zunzunegui, M. V., & Guerra, R. O. (2016). Depression, sex and gender roles in older adult populations: The international mobility in aging studies (IMIAS). *PLoS ONE, 11*, e0146867.

Valentine, T., Brennen, T., & Brédart, S. (1996). *The cognitive psychology of proper names: On the importance of being Ernest.* London: Routledge.

Valentová, J., Roberts, S. C., & Havlíček, J. (2013). Preferences for facial and vocal masculinity in homosexual men: The role of relationship status, sexual restrictiveness, and self-perceived masculinity. *Perception, 42*(2), 187–197.

Valian, V. (2015). Bilingualism and cognition. *Bilingualism: Language and Cognition, 18*, 3–24.

Vallacher, R. R., & Wegner, D. M. (1985). *A theory of action identification.* Hillsdale, NJ: Erlbaum.

Vallacher, R. R., & Wegner, D. M. (1987). What do people think they're doing? Action identification and human behavior. *Psychological Review, 94*, 3–15.

van Anders, S. M. (2012). Testosterone and sexual desire in healthy women and men. *Archives of Sexual Behavior, 41*, 1471–1484.

van den Boom, D. C. (1994). The influence of temperament and mothering on attachment and exploration: An experimental manipulation of sensitive responsiveness among lower-class mothers with irritable infants. *Child Development, 65*, 1457–1477.

van den Boom, D. C. (1995). Do first year intervention effects endure? Follow-up during toddlerhood of a sample of Dutch irritable infants. *Child Development, 66*, 1798–1816.

Van Dessel, P., Mertens, G., Smith, C. T., & De Houwer, J. (2019). Mere exposure effects on implicit stimulus evaluation: The moderating role of evaluation task, number of stimulus presentations, and memory for presentation frequency. *Personality and Social Psychology Bulletin, 45*(3), 447–460.

van Dis, I., Kromhout, D., Geleijnse, J. M., Boer, J. M. A., & Verschuren, W. M. M. (2009). Body mass index and waist circumference predict both 10-year nonfatal and fatal cardiovascular disease risk: Study conducted in 20,000 Dutch men and women aged 20–65 years. *European Journal of Cardiovascular Prevention & Rehabilitation, 16*(6), 729–734.

Van Gog, T., Kester, L., Dirkx, K., Hoogerheide, V., Boerboom, J., & Verkoeijen, P. P. J. L. (2015). Testing after worked example study does not enhance delayed problem-solving performance compared to restudy. *Educational Psychology Review, 27*, 265–289.

van Honk, J., & Schutter, D. J. L. G. (2007). Testosterone reduces conscious detection of signals serving social correction: Implications for antisocial behavior. *Psychological Science, 18*, 663–667.

van IJzendoorn, M. H., & Sagi, A. (1999). Cross-cultural patterns of attachment: Universal and contextual dimensions. In J. Cassidy & P. R. Shaver (Eds.), *Handbook of attachment: Theory, research and clinical applications* (pp. 713–734). New York: Guilford Press.

van IJzendoorn, M. H., Juffer, F., & Klein Poelhuis, C. W. (2005). Adoption and cognitive development: A meta-analytic comparison of adopted and nonadopted children's IQ and school performance. *Psychological Bulletin, 131*, 301–316.

Van Laningham, J., Johnson, D. R., & Amato, P. (2001). Marital happiness, marital duration, and the U-shaped curve: Evidence from a five-wave panel study. *Social Forces, 79*, pp. 1313–1341.

van Praag, H. (2009). Exercise and the brain: Something to chew on. *Trends in Neuroscience, 32*, 283–290.

van Stegeren, A. H., Everaerd, W., Cahill, L., McGaugh, J. L., & Gooren, L. J. G. (1998). Memory for emotional events: Differential effects of centrally versus peripherally acting blocking agents. *Psychopharmacology, 138*, 305–310.

Van Vliet, I. M., van Well, E. P., Bruggeman, R., Campo, J. A., Hijman, R., Van Megen, H. J., . . . Van Rijen, P. C. (2013). An evaluation of irreversible psychosurgical treatment of patients with obsessive-compulsive disorder in the Netherlands, 2001–2008. *Journal of Nervous and Mental Disease, 201*(3), 226–228.

Vargha-Khadem, F., Gadian, D. G., Copp, A., & Mishkin, M. (2005). FOXP2 and the neuroanatomy of speech and language. *Nature Reviews Neuroscience, 6*, 131–138.

Vargha-Khadem, F., Gadian, D. G., Watkins, K. E., Connelly, A., Van Paesschen, W., & Mishkin, M. (1997). Differential effects of early hippocampal pathology on episodic and semantic memory. *Science, 277*, 376–380.

Vasilenko, S. A., Maas, M. K., & Lefkowitz, E. S. (2015). "It felt good but weird at the same time": Emerging adults' first experiences of six different sexual behaviors. *Journal of Adolescent Research, 30*, 586–606. http://dx.doi.org/10.1177/0743558414561298

Vazire, S., & Mehl, M. R. (2008). Knowing me, knowing you: The relative accuracy and unique predictive validity of self-ratings and other ratings of daily behavior. *Journal of Personality and Social Psychology, 95*, 1202–1216.

Vinter, A., & Perruchet, P. (2002). Implicit motor learning through observational training in adults and children. *Memory & Cognition, 30*, 256–261.

Vitkus, J. (1999). *Casebook in abnormal psychology* (4th ed.). New York: McGraw-Hill.

Volkow, N. D., & Boyle, M. (2018). Neuroscience of addiction: Relevance to prevention and treatment. *American Journal of Psychiatry, 175*, 729–740.

Volkow, N. D., Jones, E. B., Einstein, E. B., & Wargo, E. M. (2019). Prevention and treatment of opioid misuse and addiction: A review. *Journal of the American Medical Association Psychiatry* (epub online Dec 5).

Volkow, N. D., Koob, G. F., & McLellan, A. T. (2016). Neurobiologic advances from the brain disease model of addiction. *New England Journal of Medicine, 374*, 363–371.

von Bartheld, C. S., Bahney, J., & Herculano-Houzel, S. (2016) The search for true numbers of neurons and glial cells in the human brain: A review of 150 years of cell counting. *Journal of Comparative Neurology, 524*, 3865–3895.

Von Frisch, K. (1974). Decoding the language of the bee. *Science, 185*, 663–668.

von Stumm, S., & Plomin, R. (2015). Socioeconomic status and the growth of intelligence from infancy through adolescence. *Intelligence, 48*, 30–36.

Vondra, J. I., Shaw, D. S., Swearingen, L., Cohen, M., & Owens, E. B. (2001). Attachment stability and emotional and behavioral regulation from infancy to preschool age. *Development and Psychopathology, 13,* 13–33.

Vorster, A. P. & Born, J. (2015). Sleep and memory in mammals, birds and invertebrates. *Neuroscience and Biobehavioral Reviews, 50,* 103–119.

Vortac, O. U., Edwards, M. B., & Manning, C. A. (1995). Functions of external cues in prospective memory. *Memory, 3,* 201–219.

Vrij, A., Granhag, P. A., Mann, S., & Leal, S. (2011). Outsmarting the liars: Toward a cognitive lie detection approach. *Current Directions in Psychological Science, 20*(1), 28–32.

Vukasović, T., & Bratko, D. (2015) Heritability of personality: A meta-analysis of behavior genetic studies. *Psychological Bulletin, 141,* 769–785.

von Bastian, C. C., Souza, A. S., & Gasde, M. (2016). No evidence for bilingual cognitive advantages: A test of four hypotheses. *Journal of Experimental Psychology: General, 145,* 246–258.

Vygotsky, L. S. (1978). *Mind in society: The development of higher psychological processes.* Cambridge, MA: Harvard University Press.

Waddell, C., McEwan, K., Shepherd, C. A., Offord, D. R., & Hua, J. M. (2005). A public health strategy to improve the mental health of Canadian children. *The Canadian Journal of Psychiatry, 50*(4), 226–233.

Wade, K. A., Garry, M., & Pezdek, K. (2018). Deconstructing rich false memories of committing crime: Commentary on Shaw and Porter (2015). *Psychological Science, 29,* 471–476.

Wade, S. E., Trathen, W., & Schraw, G. (1990). An analysis of spontaneous study strategies. *Reading Research Quarterly, 25,* 147–166.

Wadhwa, P. D., Sandman, C. A., & Garite, T. J. (2001). The neurobiology of stress in human pregnancy: Implications for prematurity and development of the fetal central nervous system. *Progress in Brain Research, 133,* 131–142.

Wager, T. D., Rilling, J., K., Smith, E. E., Sokolik, A., Casey, K. L., Davidson, R. J., . . . Cohen, J. D. (2004). Placebo-induced changes in fMRI in the anticipation and experience of pain. *Science, 303,* 1162–1167.

Wager, T., & Atlas, L. Y. (2013). How is pain influenced by cognition? Neuroimaging weighs in. *Perspectives on Psychological Science, 8,* 91–97.

Wagner, A. D., Schacter, D. L., Rotte, M., Koutstaal, W., Maril, A., Dale, A. M., . . . Buckner, R. L. (1998). Remembering and forgetting of verbal experiences as predicted by brain activity. *Science, 281,* 1188–1190.

Wagner, G., & Morris, E. (1987). Superstitious behavior in children. *Psychological Record, 37,* 471–488.

Wai, J., Putallaz, M., & Makel, M. C. (2012). Studying intellectual outliers: Are there sex differences, and are the smart getting smarter? *Current Directions in Psychological Science, 21*(6), 382–390.

Wainer, H., & Zwerling, H. L. (2006). Evidence that smaller schools do not improve student achievement. *Phi Delta Kappan, 88*(4), 300–303.

Wakefield, J. C. (2007). The concept of mental disorder: Diagnostic implications of the harmful dysfunction analysis. *World Psychiatry, 6,* 149–156.

Walden, T. A., & Ogan, T. A. (1988). The development of social referencing. *Child Development, 59,* 1230–1240.

Waldfogel, S. (1948). The frequency and affective character of childhood memories. *Psychological Monographs: General and Applied, 62*(4), i–39. doi:10.1037/h0093581

Walker, N. P., McConville, P. M., Hunter, D., Deary, I. J., & Whalley, L. J. (2002). Childhood mental ability and lifetime psychiatric contact. *Intelligence, 30*(3), 233–245.

Wallbott, H. G. (1998). Bodily expression of emotion. *European Journal of Social Psychology, 28,* 879–896.

Walster, E., Aronson, V., Abrahams, D., & Rottmann, L. (1966). Importance of physical attractiveness in dating behavior. *Journal of Personality and Social Psychology, 4,* 508–516.

Walster, E., Walster, G. W., & Berscheid, E. (1978). *Equity: Theory and research.* Boston: Allyn & Bacon.

Walton, G. M., & Spencer, S. J. (2009). Latent ability: Grades and test scores systematically underestimate the intellectual ability of negatively stereotyped students. *Psychological Science, 20,* 1132–1139.

Waltzman, S. B. (2006). Cochlear implants: Current status. *Expert Review of Medical Devices, 3,* 647–655.

Wammes, J. D., Seli, P., Cheyne, J. A., Boucher, P. O., & Smilek, D. (2016). Mind wandering during lectures. II: Relation to academic performance. *Scholarship of Teaching and Learning in Psychology, 2,* 33–48.

Wamsley, E. J., & Stickgold, R. (2011). Memory, sleep, and dreaming: Experiencing consolidation. *Sleep Medicine Clinics, 6,* 97–108.

Wang, P. S., Aguilar-Gaxiola, S., Alonso, J., Angermeyer, M. C., Borges, G., Bromet, E. J., . . . Wells, J. E. (2007). Use of mental health services for anxiety, mood, and substance disorders in 17 countries in the WHO World Mental Health Surveys. *Lancet, 370*(9590), 841–850.

Wang, P. S., Berglund, P., Olfson, M., Pincus, H. A., Wells, K. B., & Kessler, R. C. (2005). Failure and delay in initial treatment contact after first onset of mental disorders in the National Comorbidity Survey Replication. *Archives of General Psychiatry, 62*(6), 629–640.

Wang, S. M., Allen, R. J., Lee, J. R., & Hsieh, C. E. (2015). Evaluating the developmental trajectory of the episodic buffer component of working memory and its relation to word recognition in children. *Journal of Experimental Child Psychology, 133,* 16–28.

Wang, S., & Allen, R. J. (2018). Cross-modal working memory binding and word recognition skills: How specific is the link? *Memory, 26,* 514–523.

Wang, S.-H., & Baillargeon, R. (2008). Detecting impossible changes in infancy: A three-system account. *Trends in Cognitive Sciences, 12*(1), 17–23.

Wansink, B., & Wansink, C. S. (2010). The largest last supper: Depictions of food portions and plate size increased over the millennium. *International Journal of Obesity, 34,* 943–944.

Ward, B. W., Dahlhamer, J. M., Galinsky, A. M., & Joestl, S. S. (2014). Sexual orientation and health among US adults: National Health Interview Survey, 2013. *National Health Statistics Reports, 15,* 1–10.

Ward, J., Parkin, A. J., Powell, G., Squires, E. J., Townshend, J., & Bradley, V. (1999). False recognition of unfamiliar people:

"Seeing film stars everywhere." *Cognitive Neuropsychology, 16,* 293–315.

Warneken, F., & Tomasello, M. (2009). Varieties of altruism in children and chimpanzees. *Trends in Cognitive Sciences, 13,* 397–402.

Warner, L. A., Kessler, R. C., Hughes, M., Anthony, J. C., & Nelson, C. B. (1995). Prevalence and correlates of drug use and dependence in the United States: Results from the National Comorbidity Survey. *Archives of General Psychiatry, 52,* 219–229.

Warren, K. R., & Hewitt, B. G. (2009). Fetal alcohol spectrum disorders: When science, medicine, public policy, and laws collide. *Developmental Disabilities Research Reviews, 15,* 170–175.

Warren, M. T., Wray-Lake, L., Rote, W. M., & Shubert, J. (2016). Thriving while engaging in risk? Examining trajectories of adaptive functioning, delinquency, and substance use in a nationally representative sample of adolescents. *Developmental Psychology, 52*(2), 296–310.

Warrington, E. K., & McCarthy, R. A. (1983). Category specific access dysphasia. *Brain, 106,* 859–878.

Warrington, E. K., & Shallice, T. (1984). Category specific semantic impairments. *Brain, 107,* 829–854.

Warrington, E. K., & Weiskrantz, L. (1968). New method of testing long-term retention with special reference to amnesic patients. *Nature, 217,* 972–974.

Watanabe, S., Sakamoto, J., & Wakita, M. (1995). Pigeons' discrimination of painting by Monet and Picasso. *Journal of the Experimental Analysis of Behavior, 63,* 165–174.

Waters, T. E. A., Fraley, R. C., Groh, A. M., Steele, R. D., Vaughn, B. E., Bost, K. K., . . . Roisman, G. I. (2015). The latent structure of secure base script knowledge. *Developmental Psychology, 51*(6), 823–830. doi:10.1037/dev0000012

Watkins, L. R., & Maier, S. F. (2005). Immune regulation of central nervous system functions: From sickness responses to pathological pain. *Journal of Internal Medicine, 257,* 139–155.

Watson, D., & Pennebaker, J. W. (1989). Health complaints, stress, and distress: Exploring the central role of negative affectivity. *Psychological Review, 96,* 234–254.

Watson, D., & Tellegen, A. (1985). Toward a consensual structure of mood. *Psychological Bulletin, 98,* 219–235.

Watson, J. (1924). *Behaviorism.* New York: The People's Institute Publishing.

Watson, J. B. (1913). Psychology as the behaviorist views it. *Psychological Review, 20,* 158–177.

Watson, J. B. (1919). *Psychology from the standpoint of a behaviorist.* Philadelphia, PA: J. B. Lippincott.

Watson, J. B. (1930). *Behaviorism.* Chicago: University of Chicago Press.

Watson, J. B., & Rayner, R. (1920). Conditioned emotional reactions. *Journal of Experimental Psychology, 3,* 1–14.

Watson, R. I. (1978). *The great psychologists.* New York: Lippincott.

Watt, H. J. (1905). Experimentelle beitraege zu einer theorie des denkens [Experimental contributions to a theory of thinking]. *Archiv fuer die gesamte Psychologie, 4,* 289–436.

Watts, T. M., Holmes, L., Raines, J., Orbell, S., & Rieger, G. (2018). Gender nonconformity of identical twins with discordant sexual orientations: Evidence from childhood photographs. *Developmental Psychology, 54,* 788–801.

Watzke, B., Rüddel, H., Jürgensen, R., Koch, U., Kriston, L., Grothgar, B., & Schulz, H. (2012). Longer term outcome of cognitive-behavioural and psychodynamic psychotherapy in routine mental health care: Randomised controlled trial. *Behaviour Research and Therapy, 50*(9), 580–587.

Weaver, I. C. G., Cervoni, N., Champagne, F. A., D'Alessio, A. C., Sharma, S., Seckl, J. R., . . . Meaney, M. J. (2004). Epigenetic programming by maternal behavior. *Nature Neuroscience, 7,* 847–854.

Webb, T. L., Miles, E., & Sheeran, P. (2012). Dealing with feeling: A meta-analysis of the effectiveness of strategies derived from the process model of emotional regulation. *Psychological Bulletin, 138*(4), 775–808.

Weber, R., & Crocker, J. (1983). Cognitive processes in the revision of stereotypic beliefs. *Journal of Personality and Social Psychology, 45,* 961–977.

Webster Marketon, J. I., & Glaser, R. (2008). Stress hormones and immune function. *Cellular Immunology, 252,* 16–26.

Wechsler, H., & Nelson, T. F. (2001). Binge drinking and the American college student: What's five drinks? *Psychology of Addictive Behaviors, 15*(4), 287–291.

Wegner, D. M. (1989). *White bears and other unwanted thoughts.* New York: Viking.

Wegner, D. M. (1994a). Ironic processes of mental control. *Psychological Review, 101,* 34–52.

Wegner, D. M. (1994b). *White bears and other unwanted thoughts: Suppression, obsession, and the psychology of mental control.* New York: Guilford Press.

Wegner, D. M. (1997). Why the mind wanders. In J. D. Cohen & J. W. Schooler (Eds.), *Scientific approaches to consciousness* (pp. 295–315). Mahwah, NJ: Erlbaum.

Wegner, D. M. (2002). *The illusion of conscious will.* Cambridge, MA: MIT Press.

Wegner, D. M. (2009). How to think, say, or do precisely the worst thing for any occasion. *Science, 325,* 48–51.

Wegner, D. M., & Gilbert, D. T. (2000). Social psychology: The science of human experience. In H. Bless & J. Forgas (Eds.), *The message within: Subjective experience in social cognition and behavior* (pp. 1–9). Philadelphia: Psychology Press.

Wegner, D. M., & Wenzlaff, R. M. (1996). Mental control. In E. T. Higgins & A. Kruglanski (Eds.), *Social psychology: Handbook of basic mechanisms and processes* (pp. 466–492). New York: Guilford Press.

Wegner, D. M., & Zanakos, S. (1994). Chronic thought suppression. *Journal of Personality, 62,* 615–640.

Wegner, D. M., Ansfield, M., & Pilloff, D. (1998). The putt and the pendulum: Ironic effects of the mental control of action. *Psychological Science, 9,* 196–199.

Wegner, D. M., Broome, A., & Blumberg, S. J. (1997). Ironic effects of trying to relax under stress. *Behavior Research and Therapy, 35,* 11–21.

Wegner, D. M., Erber, R. E., & Zanakos, S. (1993). Ironic processes in the mental control of mood and mood-related thought. *Journal of Personality and Social Psychology, 65,* 1093–1104.

Wegner, D. M., Erber, R., & Raymond, P. (1991). Transactive memory in close relationships. *Journal of Personality and Social Psychology, 61,* 923–929.

Wegner, D. M., Schneider, D. J., Carter, S. R., & White, T. L. (1987). Paradoxical effects of thought suppression. *Journal of Personality and Social Psychology, 53,* 5–13.

Wegner, D. M., Vallacher, R. R., Macomber, G., Wood, R., & Arps, K. (1984). The emergence of action. *Journal of Personality and Social Psychology, 46,* 269–279.

Wegner, D. M., Wenzlaff, R. M., & Kozak, M. (2004). Dream rebound: The return of suppressed thoughts in dreams. *Psychological Science, 15,* 232–236.

Weiner, W. J., Shulman, L. M., & Lang, A. E. (2013). *Parkinson's disease* (3rd ed.). Baltimore, MD: Johns Hopkins University Press.

Weinstein, N. D. (1980). Unrealistic optimism about future life events. *Journal of Personality and Social Psychology, 39,* 806–820.

Weintraub, D., Papay, K., & Siderowf, A. (2013). Screening for impulse control symptoms in patients with de novo Parkinson disease: A case-control study. *Neurology, 80,* 176–180.

Weir, C., Toland, C., King, R. A., & Martin, L. M. (2005). Infant contingency/extinction performance after observing partial reinforcement. *Infancy, 8,* 63–80.

Weiser, M., Zarka, S., Werbeloff, N., Kravitz, E., & Lubin, G. (2010). Cognitive test scores in male adolescent cigarette smokers compared to non-smokers: A population-based study. *Addiction, 105*(2), 358–363.

Weisfeld, G. (1999). *Evolutionary principles of human adolescence.* New York: Basic Books.

Weiss, K. J., & Curcio Alexander, J. (2013). Sex, lies, and statistics: Inferences from the child sexual abuse accommodation syndrome. *Journal of the American Academy of Psychiatry and the Law, 41,* 412–420.

Weissman, M. M., Markowitz, J. C., & Klerman, G. L. (2000). *Comprehensive guide to interpersonal psychotherapy.* New York: Basic Books.

Weldon, M. S. (2001). Remembering as a social process. In D. L. Medin (Ed.), *The psychology of learning and motivation: Advances in research and theory* (Vol. 40, pp. 67–120). San Diego, CA: Academic Press.

Wellman, H. M., Fang, F., Liu, D., Zhu, L., & Liu, L. (2006). Scaling theory-of-mind understandings in Chinese children. *Psychological Science, 17,* 1075–1081.

Wenzlaff, R. M., & Wegner, D. M. (2000). Thought suppression. In S. T. Fiske (Ed.), *Annual review of psychology* (Vol. 51, pp. 51–91). Palo Alto, CA: Annual Reviews.

Wernicke, K. (1874). *Der Aphasische Symptomenkomplex* [The aphasic symptom complex]. Breslau: Cohn and Weigart.

Wertheimer, M. (1982). *Productive thinking.* Chicago: University of Chicago Press. (Originally published 1945)

Wesch, N. N., Law, B., & Hall, C. R. (2007). The use of observational learning by athletes. *Journal of Sport Behavior, 30,* 219–231.

Westbrook, A., & Frank, M. (2018). Dopamine and proximity in motivation and cognitive control. *Current Opinion in Behavioral Science, 22,* 28–34.

Westrin, A., & Lam, R. W. (2007). Seasonal affective disorder: A clinical update. *Journal of Clinical Psychiatry, 19,* 239–246.

Wexler, K. (1999). Maturation and growth of grammar. In W. C. Ritchie & T. K. Bhatia (Eds.), *Handbook of child language acquisition* (pp. 55–110). San Diego: Academic Press.

Wheeler, M. A., Petersen, S. E., & Buckner, R. L. (2000). Memory's echo: Vivid recollection activates modality-specific cortex.

Proceedings of the National Academy of Sciences, USA, 97, 11125–11129.

White, F. J. (1996). Synaptic regulation of mesocorticolimbic dopamine neurons. *Annual Review of Neuroscience, 19,* 405–436.

White, G. L., & Kight, T. D. (1984). Misattribution of arousal and attraction: Effects of salience of explanations for arousal. *Journal of Experimental Social Psychology, 20*(1), 55–64.

White, G. L., Fishbein, S., & Rutsein, J. (1981). Passionate love and the misattribution of arousal. *Journal of Personality and Social Psychology, 41*(1), 56–62. doi:10.1037/0022-3514.41.1.56

White, G. M., & Kirkpatrick, J. (Eds.). (1985). *Person, self, and experience: Exploring pacific ethnopsychologies.* Berkeley: University of California Press.

White, L. K., & Booth, A. (1991). Divorce over the life course: The role of marital happiness. *Journal of Family Issues, 12,* 5–21.

White, N. M., & Milner, P. M. (1992). The psychobiology of reinforcers. *Annual Review of Psychology, 41,* 443–471.

White, P. M. (2016, September 28). Hidden from view: Canadian surrogacy. Retrieved from https://impactethics.ca/2016/09/28/hidden-from-view-canadian-surrogacy/

Whiten, A. (2017). Social learning and culture in child and chimpanzee. *Annual Review of Psychology, 68,* 129–154.

Whiten, A., & van de Waal, E. (2018). The pervasive role of social learning in primate lifetime development. *Behavioral Ecology and Sociobiology, 72,* 80.doi.10.1007/s00265-018-2489-3

Whorf, B. (1956). *Language, thought, and reality.* Cambridge, MA: MIT Press.

Whybrow, P. C. (1997). *A mood apart.* New York: Basic Books.

Wibowo, E., & Wassersug, R. (2014). Estrogen in men. *American Scientist, 102,* 452–459.

Wicklund, R. (1975). Objective self-awareness. In L. Berkowitz (Ed.), Advances in experimental social psychology (Vol. 8, pp. 233–275). New York: Academic Press.

Wiederman, M. W. (1997). Pretending orgasm during sexual intercourse: Correlates in a sample of young adult women. *Journal of Sex & Marital Therapy, 23,* 131–139.

Wiegner, L., Hange, D., Björkelund, C., & Ahlbirg, G. Jr. (2015). Prevalence of perceived stress and associations to symptoms of exhaustion, depression, and anxiety in a working age population seeking primary care: An observational study. *BMC Family Practice, 16,* 38.

Wiesenthal, D. L., Austrom, D., & Silverman, I. (1983). Diffusion of responsibility in charitable donations. *Basic and Applied Social Psychology, 4,* 17–27.

Wig, G. S., Buckner, R. L., & Schacter, D. L. (2009). Repetition priming influences distinct brain systems: Evidence from task-evoked data and resting-state correlations. *Journal of Neurophysiology, 101,* 2632–2648.

Wiggs, C. L., & Martin, A. (1998). Properties and mechanisms of perceptual priming. *Current Opinion in Neurobiology, 8,* 227–233.

Wilcoxon, H. C., Dragoin, W. B., & Kral, P. A. (1971). Illness-induced aversions in rats and quail: Relative salience of visual and gustatory cues. *Science, 171,* 826–828.

Wiley, J. L. (1999). Cannabis: Discrimination of "internal bliss"? *Pharmacology, Biochemistry, & Behavior, 64,* 257–260.

Wilk, P., Maltby, A., & Cooke, M. (2017). Residential schools and the effects on Indigenous health and well-being in Canada—a scoping review. *Public Health Reviews, 38*(1), 8.

Wilkinson, L., Teo, J. T., Obeso, I., Rothwell, J. C., & Jahanshahi, M. (2010). The contribution of primary motor cortex is essential for probabilistic implicit sequence learning: Evidence from theta burst magnetic stimulation. *Journal of Cognitive Neuroscience, 22,* 427–436.

Williams, A. C. (2002). Facial expression of pain: An evolutionary account. *Behavioral and Brain Sciences, 25,* 439–488.

Williams, C. M., & Kirkham, T. C. (1999). Anandamide induces overeating: Mediation by central cannabinoid (CB1) receptors. *Psychopharmacology, 143,* 315–317.

Williams, D. R., & Wyatt, R. (2015). Racial bias in health care and health: Challenges and opportunities. *Journal of the American Medical Association, 314*(6), 555–556.

Williams, K. D. (2007). Ostracism. *Annual Review of Psychology, 58,* 425–452.

Williams, K. D., Nida, S. A., Baca, L. D., & Latané, B. (1989). Social loafing and swimming: Effects of identifiability on individual and relay performance of intercollegiate swimmers. *Basic and Applied Social Psychology, 10,* 73–81.

Willingham, D. T. (2007). Critical thinking: Why is it so hard to teach? *American Educator, 31*(2), 8–19.

Wilson, B. M., & Wixted, J. T. (2018). The prior odds of testing a true effect in cognitive and social psychology. *Advances in Methods and Practices in Psychological Science, 1*(2), 186–197. https://doi.org/10.1177/2515245918767122

Wilson, K., & Korn, J. H. (2007). Attention during lectures: Beyond ten minutes. *Teaching of Psychology, 34,* 85–89.

Wilson, T. D. (2009). Know thyself. *Perspectives on Psychological Science, 4,* 384–389.

Wilson, T. D., & Lassiter, G. D. (1982). Increasing intrinsic interest with superfluous extrinsic constraints. *Journal of Personality and Social Psychology, 42,* 811–819.

Wilson, T. D., Meyers, J., & Gilbert, D. T. (2003). "How happy was I, anyway?" A retrospective impact bias. *Social Cognition, 21,* 421–446.

Wilt, J., & Revelle, W. (2019). The Big Five, everyday contexts and activities, and affective experience. *Personality and Individual Differences, 136,* 140–147.

Wimber, M., Alink, A., Charest, I., Kriegeskorte, N., & Anderson, M.C. (2015). Retrieval induces adaptive forgetting of competing memories via cortical pattern suppression. *Nature Neuroscience, 18,* 582–589.

Wimber, M., Rutschmann, R. N., Greenlee, M. W., & Bauml, K.-H. (2009). Retrieval from episodic memory: Neural mechanisms of interference resolution. *Journal of Cognitive Neuroscience, 21,* 538–549.

Wimmer, H., & Perner, J. (1983). Beliefs about beliefs: Representations and constraining function of wrong beliefs in young children's understanding of deception. *Cognition, 13,* 103–128.

Winawer, J., Witthoft, N., Frank, M. C., Wu, L., Wade, A. R., & Boroditsky, L. (2007). Russian blues reveal effects of language on color discrimination. *Proceedings of the National Academy of Sciences, USA, 104,* 7780–7785.

Winblad, B., Amouyel, P., Andrieu, S., Ballard, C., Brayne, C., Brodaty, H., . . . Zetterberg, H. (2016). Defeating Alzheimer's disease and other dementias: A priority for European science and society. *The Lancet Neurology, 15,* 455–532.

Windeler, J., & Kobberling, J. (1986). Empirische Untersuchung zur Einschatzung diagnostischer Verfahren am Beispiel des Haemoccult-Tests [An empirical study of the value of diagnostic procedures using the example of the hemoccult test]. *Klinische Wochenshrift, 64,* 1106–1112.

Winkler, A. D., Spillmann, L., Werner, J. S., & Webster, M. A. (2015). Asymmetries in blue–yellow color perception and in the color of 'the dress.' *Current Biology, 25,* R547–R548.

Winner, E. (2000). The origins and ends of giftedness. *American Psychologist, 55,* 159–169.

Winocur, G., Moscovitch, M., & Bontempi, B. (2010). Memory formation and long-term retention in humans and animals: Convergence towards a transformation account of hippocampal–neocortical interactions. *Neuropsychologia, 48,* 2339–2356.

Winterer, G., & Weinberger, D. R. (2004). Genes, dopamine and cortical signal-to-noise ratio in schizophrenia. *Trends in Neuroscience, 27,* 683–690.

Wise, R. A. (1989). Brain dopamine and reward. *Annual Review of Psychology, 40,* 191–225.

Wise, R. A. (2005). Forebrain substrates of reward and motivation. *Journal of Comparative Neurology, 493,* 115–121.

Wisniewski, H., Liu, G., Henson, P., Vaidyam, A., Hajratalli, N. K., Onnela, J. P., & Torous, J. (2019). Understanding the quality, effectiveness and attributes of top-rated smartphone health apps. *Evidence-Based Mental Health, 22*(1), 4–9.

Wixted, J. T., & Ebbensen, E. (1991). On the form of forgetting. *Psychological Science, 2,* 409–415.

Wolff, P., & Holmes, K. J. (2011). Linguistic relativity. WIRES *Cognitive Science, 2,* 253–265.

Womick, J., Ward, S. J., Heintzelman, S. J., Woody, B., & King, L. A. (2019). The existential function of right-wing authoritarianism. *Journal of Personality.* doi:10.1111/jopy.12457

Wong, D. T., Bymaster, F. P., & Engleman, E. A. (1995). Prozac (fluoxetine, Lilly 110140), the first selective serotonin uptake inhibitor and an antidepressant drug: Twenty years since its first publication. *Life Sciences, 57,* 411–441.

Wood, A., Rychlowska, M., & Niedenthal, P. M. (2016). Heterogeneity of long-history migration predicts emotion recognition accuracy. *Emotion, 16*(4), 413–420. doi:1037/emo0000137

Wood, J. M., & Bootzin, R. R. (1990). Prevalence of nightmares and their independence from anxiety. *Journal of Abnormal Psychology, 99,* 64–68.

Wood, J. M., Bootzin, R. R., Rosenhan, D., Nolen-Hoeksema, S., & Jourden, F. (1992). Effects of the 1989 San Francisco earthquake on frequency and content of nightmares. *Journal of Abnormal Psychology, 101,* 219–224.

Woods, S. C., Seeley, R. J., Porte, D., Jr., & Schwartz, M. W. (1998). Signals that regulate food intake and energy homeostasis. *Science, 280,* 1378–1383.

Woody, S. R., & Sanderson, W. C. (1998). Manuals for empirically supported treatments: 1998 update. *Clinical Psychologist, 51,* 17–21.

Woumans, E., Santens, P., Sieben, A., Versijpt, J., Stevens, M., & Duyck, W. (2015). Bilingualism delays clinical manifestation of Alzheimer's disease. *Bilingualism: Language and Cognition, 18,* 568–574.

Wrangham, R. W. (2017). Two types of aggression in human evolution. *Proceedings of the National Academy of Sciences, USA, 115*(2), 245–253.

Wraw, C., Deary, I. J., Gale, C. R., & Der, G. (2015). Intelligence in youth and health at age 50. *Intelligence, 53* (2015), 23–32.

Wren, A. M., Seal, L. J., Cohen, M. A., Brynes, A. E., Frost, G. S., Murphy, K. G., . . . Bloom, S. R. (2001). Ghrelin enhances appetite and increases food intake in humans. *Journal of Clinical Endocrinology and Metabolism, 86*, 5992–5995.

Wrenn, C. C., Turchi, J. N., Schlosser, S., Dreiling, J. L., Stephenson, D. A., & Crawley, J. N. (2006). Performance of galanin transgenic mice in the 5-choice serial reaction time attentional task. *Pharmacology Biochemistry and Behavior, 83*, 428–440.

Wundt, W. (1912/1973). *An introduction to psychology.* New York: Arno Press.

Wyatt, T. D. (2015). The search for human pheromones: The lost decades and the necessity of returning to first principles. *Proceedings Royal Society. B, 282*(1804), 20142994. doi: 10.1098/rspb.2014.2994

Wyckoff, J. P., Asao, K., & Buss, D. M. (2019). Gossip as an intrasexual competition strategy: Predicting information sharing from potential mate versus competitor mating strategies. *Evolution and Human Behavior, 40*(1), 96–104.

Wynn, K., Bloom, P., Jordan, A., Marshall, J., & Sheskin, M. (2018). Not noble savages after all: Limits to early altruism. *Current Directions in Psychological Science, 27*, 3–8.

Yamaguchi, S. (1998). Basic properties of umami and its effects in humans. *Physiology and Behavior, 49*, 833–841.

Yang, S., & Sternberg, R. J. (1997). Conceptions of intelligence in ancient Chinese philosophy. *Journal of Theoretical and Philosophical Psychology, 17*, 101–119.

Yeo, B. T. T., Krienen, F. M., Sepulcre, J., Sabuncu, M. R., Lashkari, D., Hollinshead, M., . . . Buckner, R. L. (2011). The organization of the human cerebral cortex estimated by intrinsic functional connectivity. *Journal of Neurophysiology, 106*, 1125–1165.

Yik, M., Russell, J. A., & Steiger, J. H. (2011). A 12-point circumplex structure of core affect. *Emotion, 11*(4), 705–731.

Yoeli, E., Hoffman, M., Rand, D. G., & Nowak, M. A. (2013, June). Powering up with indirect reciprocity. *Proceedings of the National Academy of Sciences USA, 110*(Suppl. 2), 10424–10429. doi:10.1073/pnas.1301210110

Young, J. J., Silber, T., Bruno, D., Galatzer-Levy, I. R., Pomara, N., & Marmar, C. R. (2016). Is there progress? An overview of selecting biomarker candidates for major depressive disorder. *Frontiers in Psychiatry, 7*, 72.

Young, R. M. (1990). *Mind, brain, and adaptation in the nineteenth century: Cerebral localization and its biological context from Gall to Ferrier.* New York: Oxford University Press.

Yu, Y., & Kushnir, T. (2014). Social context effects in 2- and 4-year-olds' selective versus faithful imitation. *Developmental Psychology, 50*(3), 922–933. doi:10.1037/a0034242

Yucha, C., & Gilbert, C. D. (2004). *Evidence-based practice in biofeedback and neurofeedback.* Colorado Springs: Association for Applied Psychophysiology and Biofeedback.

Yzerbyt, V., & Demoulin, S. (2010). Intergroup relations. In S. T. Fiske, D. T. Gilbert, & G. Lindzey (Eds.), *The handbook of social psychology* (5th ed., Vol. 2, pp. 1024–1083). New York: Wiley.

Zahn-Waxler, C., Radke-Yarrow, M., Wagner, E., & Chapman, M. (1992). Development of concern for others. *Developmental Psychology, 28*, 126–136.

Zajonc, R. B. (1968). Attitudinal effects of mere exposure. *Journal of Personality and Social Psychology, 9*, 1–27.

Zaki, J., Wager, T. D., Singer, T., Keysers, C., & Gazzola, V. (2016). The anatomy of suffering: Understanding the relationship between nociceptive and empathic pain. *Trends in Cognitive Sciences, 20*(4), 249–259.

Zebrowitz, L. A., & Montepare, J. M. (1992). Impressions of babyfaced individuals across the life span. *Developmental Psychology, 28*, 1143–1152.

Zeki, S. (1993). *A vision of the brain.* London: Blackwell Scientific.

Zeki, S. (2001). Localization and globalization in conscious vision. *Annual Review of Neuroscience, 24*, 57–86.

Zentall, T. R., Sutton, J. E., & Sherburne, L. M. (1996). True imitative learning in pigeons. *Psychological Science, 7*, 343–346.

Zentner, M., & Mitura, K. (2012). Stepping out of the caveman's shadow: Nations' gender gap predicts degree of sex differentiation in mate preferences. *Psychological Science, 23*(10), 1176–1185.

Zerwas, S., & Bulik, C. M. (2011). Genetics and epigenetics of eating disorders. *Psychiatric Annals, 41*(11), 532–538. doi:10.3928/00485713-20111017-06

Zhang, T. Y., & Meaney, M. J. (2010). Epigenetics and the environmental regulation of the genome and its function. *Annual Review of Psychology, 61*, 439–466.

Zhaoyang, R., Sliwinski, M. J., Martire, L. M., & Smyth, J. M. (2018). Age differences in adults' daily social interactions: An ecological momentary assessment study. *Psychology and Aging, 33*(4), 607–618. doi:10.1037/pag0000242

Zhong, C.-B., Bohns, V. K., & Gino, F. (2010). Good lamps are the best police: Darkness increases dishonesty and self-interested behavior. *Psychological Science, 21*(3), 311–314.

Zhou, X., Hetrick, S. E., Cuijpers, P., Qin, B., Barth, J., Whittington, C. J., . . . Xie, P. (2015). Comparative efficacy and acceptability of psychotherapies for depression in children and adolescents: A systematic review and network analysis. *World Psychiatry, 14*(2), 207–222.

Zickfeld, J. H., Schubert, T. W., Seibt, B., Blomster, J. K., Arriaga, P., Basabe, N., . . . Fiske, A. P. (2019). Kama muta: Conceptualizing and measuring the experience often labelled being moved across 19 nations and 15 languages. *Emotion. 19*(3), 402–424. doi:10.1037/emo0000450

Zihl, J., von Cramon, D., & Mai, N. (1983). Selective disturbance of movement vision after bilateral brain damage. *Brain, 106*, 313–340.

Zillmann, D., & Bryant, J. (1974). Effect of residual excitation on the emotional response to provocation and delayed aggressive behavior. *Journal of Personality and Social Psychology, 30*(6), 782–791. doi:10.1037/h0037541

Zimbardo, P. (2007). *The Lucifer effect: Understanding how good people turn evil.* New York: Random House.

Zimprich, D., & Martin, M. (2002). Can longitudinal changes in processing speed explain longitudinal age changes in fluid intelligence? *Psychology and Aging, 17*, 690–695.

Zwart, F. S., Vissers, C. T. W. M., Kessels, R. P. C., & Maes, J. H. R. (2018). Implicit learning seems to come naturally for children with autism, but not for children with specific language impairment: Evidence from behavioral and ERP data. *Autism Research, 11*, 1050–1061.

NAME INDEX

SUBJECT INDEX

Note: Page numbers followed by f indicate figures; those followed by t indicate tables.